Communications for Cooperating Systems

OSI, SNA, and TCP/IP

Communications for Cooperating Systems

OSI, SNA, and TCP/IP

R. J. Cypser

ADDISON-WESLEY PUBLISHING COMPANY
Reading, Massachusetts • Menlo Park, California • New York
Don Mills, Ontario • Wokingham, England • Amsterdam • Bonn • Sydney
Singapore • Tokyo • Madrid • San Juan • Milan • Paris

This book is in the
Addison-Wesley Systems Programming Series

Consulting Editors: IBM Editorial Board

Library of Congress Cataloging-in-Publication Data
Cypser, R. J.
    Communications for cooperating systems : OSI, SNA, and TCP/IP / by R. J. Cypser.
      p. cm.
    Includes bibliographical references and index.
    ISBN 0-201-50775-7
    1. Computer networks. 2. Computer network architectures.
    I. Title.
    TK5105.5.C964 1991
    621.39'81—dc20   91-14191
                                                    CIP

ISBN 0-201-50775-7

1 2 3 4 5 6 7 8 9 10–DO–9594939291

To Betty

Foreword

The field of systems programming primarily grew out of the efforts of many programmers and managers whose creative energy went into producing practical, utilitarian systems programs needed by the rapidly growing computer industry. Programming was practiced as an art where each programmer invented his own solutions to problems, with little guidance beyond that provided by his immediate associates. In 1968, the late Ascher Opler, then at IBM, recognized that it was necessary to bring programming knowledge together in a form that would be accessible to all systems programmers. Surveying the state of the art, he decided that enough useful material existed to justify a significant codification effort. On his recommendation, IBM decide to sponsor The Systems Programming Series as a long term project to collect, organize, and publish those principles and techniques that would have lasting value throughout the industry. Since 1968, eighteen titles have been published in the Series, of which six are currently in print.

The Series consists of an open-ended collection of text-reference books. The contents of each book represent the individual author's view of the subject area and do not necessarily reflect the views of the IBM Corporation. Each is organized for course use but is detailed enough for reference.

Representative topic areas already published, or that are contemplated to be covered by the Series, include: database systems, communication systems, graphics systems, expert systems, and programming process management. Other topic areas will be included as the systems programming discipline evolves and develops.

The Editorial Board

Preface

The past two years, during which this book was written, seem to have had a more rapid evolution of communication technology than I have ever witnessed, in the thirty-five years of my participation in it. Happily, the theme has been the development of very practical commonality in the midst of exploding diversity. My hope is that this work will further that commonality.

System Design Objectives

The system designer of communications networks is pressed to achieve three objectives:

1. To *obtain a return on the investments* already made in networks
2. To evolve the network based on *today's* technical possibilities and economic *realities*
3. To have a sharp eye on the *future trends* and possibilities, so as to maximize the future life and value of today's decisions

The wise designer carefully balances among these three sometimes conflicting objectives.

Book Objectives

This book adds to the in-depth technical understanding needed for such network planning and design. The intended audience is experienced systems engineers and other practitioners who are already familiar with basic telecommunications principles. Another intended audience is the senior or graduate student in telecommunications, who has had earlier courses in basic communications.

The book describes the current network technologies and the future trends in *cooperating systems*. This term is used in a broad sense, encompassing what also has been called distributed processing in distributed systems or client–server computing. In general, we refer to all such systems as cooperating systems.

The book brings into focus the rapid evolutions and consolidations that are occurring in a multivendor environment. It describes the needs for and approaches to a macroarchitecture that incorporates multiple communication architectures. This particularly includes the strategic integration of **OSI** and **SNA** (with its extension, APPN), and interoperation with **TCP/IP**, **NetBIOS**, and other protocol systems. Major underlying questions are: How do SNA, OSI, TCP, NetBIOS, SAA, and AIX relate? How do they or can they all fit together? How do they relate to the industry-standard Distributing Computing Environment of the Open Software Foundation (OSF)? How do they use the coming broadband facilities? The resulting view is that of a macroarchitecture for heterogeneous systems with an evolutionary thrust toward multiprotocol interoperability and standards.

Any technical base for a network plan must try to integrate both current and future requirements. This book is therefore based on a vision as to where the industry requirements and technologies will take networks in the coming years. This vision is largely a view of the multivendor world, as seen through the eyes of many IBM professionals, since I have crystallized this view from conversations with over two hundred technical professionals in the various IBM laboratories, as well as the general literature. My goal is to provide an objective, factual report by an observer of a large-scale, evolutionary, communications-development process. The interpretations are, of course, my own, and are not necessarily those of the IBM Corporation.

The aim of this book is to *educate*, not to *train*. Specific architectures and products are frequently referred to, to provide concrete examples. Details needed for actual use, however, are often omitted to prevent overload and to conserve space. Some detail, useful for understanding, is put in the end-of-chapter Technical Reference sections. Important concepts and terms are included in the Glossary.

Organization of the Book

Contrary to most prior treatments of communications architecture, the book is organized from the top down—that is, starting with the upper layers and working down, rather than starting at the link level and working up. This top–down approach is taken in the sequence of chapters and within each chapter.

The book is divided into six parts, beginning with a general overview and progressing to a discussion of the four macro-layers of the architecture and a closing chapter.

1. *An overview* of the evolving architecture, its reasons for existence, the trends that motivate it, and its major stuctures

2. *Common application-services*, such as network management and distributed data services

3. *End-to-end data-exchange facilities*, such as conversation services and remote procedure calls

4. *End-to-end transport-service-providers,* including end-to-end recovery, flow control, and inter-subnetwork services of OSI, SNA, and TCP/IP

5. *Common link and subnetwork-access facilities*, such as X.25, LANs, and high-speed subnetworks
6. *Current multiple protocol systems illustrations,* involving elements such as NetBIOS, SNA, Novell/IPX, X.25, and TCP/IP

At the end are an extensive glossary, general references, cited references, a list of the standards on which the book is based, and a comprehensive index. There also are the answers to the end-of-chapter exercises. These exercises seek to highlight the key points covered in each chapter.

Some typographic standards have been used. Commands and calls appear in Courier, as in `Allocate`. Parameters appear in lowercase italics, as in *serial_number*. Values of parameters and return codes appear as small capitals, as in NONE.

Some readers will benefit from only the overview chapters and the beginnings of some chapters. Others, in need of more information, will benefit from a more complete reading.

Relation to Products

The emphasis is on architecture, rather than products. An architecture incorporates the results of research and standards efforts, so as to provide a consistent, up-to-date structure for products to draw from. Products, in fact, usually implement only a subset of a broader architecture. Products are frequently mentioned in this book, however, to add realism to the architecture and to illustrate the diversity of interconnections that are feasible. Where specific product information is needed, the reader is strongly urged to seek up-to-date and more detailed information from the appropriate product manuals.

International Standards

A major part of today's evolution of networks is guided by international standards. These are heavily referenced in the text. Again, however, the treatment of standards is educational and is not presumed to be complete or definitive. For actual implementations, the reader must refer to the current standards documentation.

ACKNOWLEDGMENTS

The view of communications systems design that is reflected in this book is a composite of many complementary views, which have been gathered over several years. Prominent among these sources have been the technical staffs at the IBM development laboratories at Raleigh, North Carolina. Significant input has also been obtained from other IBM locations, particularly from IBM laboratories at Austin, Texas; Dallas, Texas; Fujisawa, Japan; Heidelburg, Germany; Hursley, England; La Gaude, France; Palo Alto, California; Rochester, New York; Santa Clara, California; Toronto, Canada; Yorktown, New York; and Zurich, Switzerland. The open literature contributed the rest.

Reluctantly, it is not possible to give adequate credits to the many hundreds of IBM people who have made significant contributions here. It would fill a book in itself. Major insights for this book were, however, contributed by Eric Broockman, George Deaton, Jim Gray, V. Hoberecht, Phillipe Janson, Ellis Miller, and Jerry Mouton, with whom I consulted regularly. The following overall reviewers made valuable suggestions in many chapters: M. Pozefsky, N. Ellis, J. Pickens, and R. Ahlgren. Specific acknowledgments are given in the chapters to the sixty-four persons who provided primary input or reviews for certain chapters. My sincere thanks go to them and to the m•ny other persons who graciously contributed to my understanding.

In general, this text would not have been possible without the initial encouragement of Ellen Hancock, vice-president and general manager of communications systems, and the steady support and cooperation of John Hunter, director of communications systems architecture and technology, and Rick McGee, manager of communications systems architecture at IBM.

Finally, many thanks are due to Betty Cypser who produced the initial artwork for all of the diagrams in this book, using PageMaker. The extensive reviews would not have been possible without that.

Any errors remaining in the text are, of course, my own responsibility.

R. J. Cypser
Katonah, New York

Contents

PART 1
THE NETWORK: A SERVANT WITH STRUCTURE   **1**

CHAPTER 1
THE ENTERPRISE NEEDS   **3**

1.1   Introduction   3
1.2   General Communicability   4
1.3   The Network as the Enterprise Server   7
1.4   Diversity and Change   8
1.5   Operating Environments   10
1.6   Three Main Ingredients   11
1.7   Toward Interoperability   16
1.8   The Prospect of OSNA   19
       Conclusion   20
       Acknowledgments   21
       Exercises   21

CHAPTER 2
COOPERATING SYSTEMS   **23**

2.1   Introduction   23
2.2   Distributed System Structures   25
2.3   Cooperative Processing Features   28
2.4   Types of Cooperation   30
2.5   Distributed Application-Services   33
2.6   OSF Distributed Computing Environment   39
2.7   Network Synthesis   40

Conclusion   43
Acknowledgments   44
Exercises   44

CHAPTER 3
ARCHITECTURAL STRUCTURES   **45**

3.1   Introduction   45
3.2   OSI/SNA Structure Overview   45
3.3   Function Subsets   59
3.4   Multiarchitecture Boundaries   62
3.5   Layer Terminology   67
3.6   Logical Connections   72
3.7   Formats and Protocols   75
3.8   Connection-Oriented and Connectionless   79
3.9   Relating to TCP/IP   84
3.10 Common Communications Support   85
      Conclusion   86
      Acknowledgments   86
      Exercises   86

PART 2
DISTRIBUTED APPLICATION-SERVICES   **87**

CHAPTER 4
SYSTEMS MANAGEMENT   **89**

4.1   Introduction   89
4.2   System Management Process   90
4.3   System Management Structures   95
4.4   Management Applications   101
4.5   Inter-Node System Management Communication   115
4.6   Multiple Protocol Management   118
4.7   Management Databases   126
4.8   System Management Illustrations   127
      Conclusion   137
      Acknowledgments   137
      Technical Reference   138
      Exercises   138

CHAPTER 5
DISTRIBUTED RESOURCE MANAGERS   **141**

5.1   Introduction   141
5.2   Distributed Data   142
5.3   Resource-Recovery   159
5.4   Application Managers   168
5.5   LAN Requester/Server   170

5.6	Mainframe Servers	172
5.7	TCP/IP Client–Servers	174
5.8	Virtual Terminal Client–Server	177
5.9	DECnet–SNA Client–Servers	178
	Conclusion	180
	Acknowledgments	181
	Exercises	181

CHAPTER 6
INFORMATION INTERCHANGE   **183**

6.1	Introduction	183
6.2	Data Streams	187
6.3	Message Handling Systems Overview	199
6.4	OSI MHS Design (X.400)	202
6.5	SNA MHS Design (SNADS)	206
6.6	Mail System Interoperability	207
6.7	Electronic Data Interchange (EDI)	215
6.8	Voice/Data Combinations	216
	Conclusion	223
	Acknowledgments	223
	Technical Reference	223
	Exercises	224

PART 3
END-TO-END DATA-EXCHANGE FACILITIES   **225**

CHAPTER 7
COMMUNICATION APIs   **227**

7.1	Introduction	227
7.2	SAA Common Programming Interface	227
7.3	Conversation, Message, or Remote Procedure Call (RPC)	231
7.4	Conversations	232
7.5	Remote Procedure Call	241
7.6	Transaction Message Queueing	244
	Conclusion	245
	Acknowledgments	245
	Technical Reference	246
	Exercises	246

CHAPTER 8
DIRECTORIES AND LOGICAL CONNECTIONS   **249**

8.1	Introduction	249
8.2	Naming	249
8.3	Name to Address Resolution	254
8.4	X.500 Directory Services	256

8.5	Common OSI/SNA Directory	260
8.6	Control-Point Distribution	265
8.7	OSI Connection Services	270
8.8	SNA Connection Services	276
	Conclusion	278
	Acknowledgments	278
	Technical Reference	278
	Exercises	280

CHAPTER 9
PRESENTATION AND SESSION SERVICES   281

9.1	Introduction	281
9.2	Presentation Services	282
9.3	SNA Sessions	288
9.4	OSI Session Layer	291
9.5	OSI Primitives and PDUs	294
9.6	OSI/SNA Comparable Functions	294
	Conclusion	297
	Acknowledgments	297
	Technical References	297
	Exercises	307

CHAPTER 10
SNA LOGICAL UNITS   309

10.1	Introduction	309
10.2	SNA Logical Units	309
10.3	SNA/LU 6.2	311
10.4	APPC/MVS—An Illustration	321
	Conclusion	322
	Acknowledgments	322
	Technical References	322
	Exercises	324

CHAPTER 11
OSI/COMMUNICATIONS SUBSYSTEM   325

11.1	Introduction	325
11.2	Functional Overview	325
11.3	Subsystem Structure	328
11.4	Subsystem Programming Interface	329
11.5	Defining the Subsystem Resources	332
11.6	OSI-SNA Shared Resources	332
	Conclusion	334
	Acknowledgments	334
	Technical References	334
	Exercises	336

PART 4
TRANSPORT-SERVICE-PROVIDERS:
TRANSPORT INTER-SUBNETWORK FACILITIES   337

CHAPTER 12
TRANSPORT-SERVICE-PROVIDERS   339

12.1	Introduction	339
12.2	The Transport-Service-Provider Layers	340
12.3	Address Spaces	342
12.4	Routing Function	350
12.5	Bridges, Layer-3 Routers, Gateways	359
12.6	Protocol Encapsulation versus Protocol Conversion	361
12.7	Subnetwork Combinations	366
12.8	Inter-Subnetworking	369
12.9	The Multiprotocol Backbone	384
	Conclusion	393
	Acknowledgments	394
	Technical Reference	394
	Exercises	395

CHAPTER 13
TRANSPORT-SERVICE-PROVIDERS: OSI, TCP, NETBIOS   397

13.1	Introduction	397
13.2	OSI Transport Layer	398
13.3	OSI Inter-Subnetworking	403
13.4	OSI Connectionless (Internet) Layer	403
13.5	OSI X.25 Packet-Level Interface	407
13.6	Express Transfer Protocol (XTP)	417
13.7	X/Open Transport Interface (XTI)	419
13.8	TCP/IP	421
13.9	NetBIOS	426
13.10	Protocol Stack Selection	428
	Conclusion	430
	Acknowledgments	430
	Technical References	431
	Exercises	437

CHAPTER 14
TRANSPORT-SERVICE-PROVIDER: SNA/APPN   441

14.1	Introduction	441
14.2	SNA Transmission Control	442
14.3	APPN Overview	443
14.4	APPN Network-Directory Services	454
14.5	APPN EN-NN Protocols	456
14.6	APPN Topology and Route Services	459

14.7   Adaptive Pacing   469
14.8   APPN-OSI Integrated Nodes   471
14.9   APPN Interoperation Examples   474
        Conclusion   475
        Acknowledgments   476
        Technical References   476
        Exercises   478

CHAPTER 15
TRANSPORT-SERVICE-PROVIDER: SNA/SUBAREA AND APPN   481

15.1   Introduction   481
15.2   Subarea-Nodes, Types 5 and 4   482
15.3   Cross-Domain LU-LU Sessions   484
15.4   Cross-Network LU-LU Sessions   486
15.5   Dynamic APPN-Subarea LU-LU Sessions   490
15.6   Other Dynamic Subarea Definition   497
15.7   Subarea Path Control   499
        Conclusion   502
        Acknowledgments   504
        Exercises   504

PART 5
LINK AND SUBNETWORK ACCESS   507

CHAPTER 16
LINK/SUBNETWORK STRUCTURES
AND ADDRESS RESOLUTION   509

16.1   Introduction   509
16.2   Transmission Options   509
16.3   Logical-Links and Access-Links   511
16.4   Subnetwork Trends   511
16.5   Link/Subnetwork Terminology   512
16.6   Architectural Relationships   514
16.7   Lower-Layer Shared Facilities   515
16.8   The LSA Switching Boundary   517
16.9   Link/Subnetwork Directory Protocols   517
        Conclusion   525
        Acknowledgments   526
        Technical References   526
        Exercises   529

CHAPTER 17
LOCAL AREA NETWORKS   531

17.1   Introduction   531
17.2   LAN Standards   532

17.3	LAN Feature Overview	536
17.4	LAN Bridges and Routers	546
17.5	LAN Systems	555
	Conclusion	570
	Acknowledgments	570
	Technical References	570
	Exercises	574

CHAPTER 18
HIGH-SPEED SERVICES   575

18.1	Introduction	575
18.2	The Bandwidth Explosion	575
18.3	High-Speed Options	577
18.4	FDDI	579
18.5	High-Performance Routing (Switching)	586
18.6	Metropolitan Area Network (802.6)	593
18.7	ISDN	602
18.8	Frame Relay (I.122)	613
18.9	Broadband ISDN	615
18.10	Enterprise System Connection (ESCON)	618
18.11	NSFNet	620
18.12	Gigabit Networks	622
	Conclusion	624
	Acknowledgments	625
	Technical References	625
	Exercises	634

PART 6
WORKING TOGETHER   635

CHAPTER 19
MULTIPROTOCOL INTERCONNECTIONS   637

19.1	Introduction	637
19.2	LAN/WAN/LAN Connectivity	639
19.3	Multivendor Connectivity	644
19.4	SNA/X.25 Connectivity Overview	649
19.5	The SNA-X.25 DTE Interface	652
19.6	SNA-WAN As Passthru for X.25	654
19.7	SNA/TCP/IP Connectivity	659
19.8	Attachment of Diverse Devices	662
19.9	Multiprotocol End-Systems	672
19.10	Value-Added Networks	674
	Conclusion	675
	Acknowledgments	676
	Technical References	676
	Exercises	679

ANSWERS TO EXERCISES   681

GLOSSARY   691

CITED REFERENCES   713

GENERAL REFERENCES   725

COMMUNICATIONS STANDARDS   731

INDEX   735

Part 1
The Network: A Servant with Structure

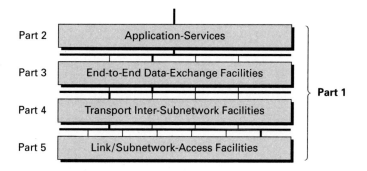

Part 2	Application-Services
Part 3	End-to-End Data-Exchange Facilities
Part 4	Transport Inter-Subnetwork Facilities
Part 5	Link/Subnetwork-Access Facilities

Part 1 describes the problem and maps the solution.

    Chapter 1, The Enterprise Needs, examines the needs of the enterprise for general communicability in a multifunction, heterogeneous, multivendor environment. The role of the network is described in terms of the support it gives to applications throughout the enterprise. The balance between the search for standards and the need to accommodate diversity and change is discussed. An approach to heterogeneous systems is outlined involving:

1. Common communications-oriented application-services and application programming interfaces

2. A communications macroarchitecture that integrates multiple subarchitectures, including full use of OSI, TCP/IP, SNA, and NetBIOS

    Chapter 2, Cooperating Systems, focuses on the strategy for network synthesis in support of cooperating heterogeneous systems. It describes the nature of cooperative processing, and examines its different categories.

    Chapter 3, Architected Structures, presents a top-down view of the architectural structure of networks. The approach to heterogeneity, involving a potential growth of commonality among OSI, SNA, TCP, and NetBIOS, is further outlined. It offers a basic understanding of all communication architectures, particularly relating OSI and SNA, and often using the OSI reference model for comparison. The basic layer functions common to the OSI and SNA architectures are summarized. The SAA Common Communications Support (CCS) for this joint environment is introduced.

1
The Enterprise Needs

1.1 INTRODUCTION

The world is steadily becoming more interconnected, more interdependent, more aware, and (we hope) more cooperative. Almost every part of each enterprise benefits from the assistance of computers. Preserving a degree of autonomy, parts of an enterprise can become directly or indirectly linked to the other parts via networks of computers. We are witnessing a gradual networking of humankind's thought resources. An ambitious vision of the future has been simply stated:

> It is the vision of a world on-line, any to any, with instant responsiveness, not limited by bandwidth or proprietary considerations—a world in which the network conforms to our work habits rather than the other way around, with people manipulating images as easily as they manipulate words and data today—and all with continuous availability, high reliability, tight security, and automatic network management.[1]

The architecture for such an evolution to near-universal networking must strive for commonality through international standards. It must also accommodate heterogeneity and multiple subarchitectures. There is simultaneous extension and convergence. The architecture therefore is a living entity, large in scope, but integrating all the vital components in meaningful ways.

The underlying thesis of this book is that the evolution of cooperating systems is proceeding in diverse but complementary ways. The result is not homogeneity. It is a mixture of proprietary advances and convergence to standards. It is technology driven. It is an evolving architecture for effective cooperation of heterogeneous elements. We

---

1. Presented as IBM's telecommunications vision by Ellen Hancock, vice president and general manager of IBM Communications Systems, at COMNET '89, in Washington, D.C., February 8, 1989.

observe key features of this process as:

1. Expanding importance of application-services, such as distributed directories, distributed databases, and multimedia information interchange, designed to promote interoperability among diverse environments

2. Extensions to and increasing effectiveness of system management of integrated systems, involving local area, metropolitan area, and wide area networks

3. Growing commonality in Application Programming Interfaces (API), providing independence from communication protocols

4. Multiple protocol stacks, such as Open Systems Interconnection (OSI), Transmission Control Protocol/Internet Protocol (TCP/IP), Systems Network Architecture (SNA), and Network Basic Input/Output System (NetBIOS), for end-to-end data exchange[2]

5. Creation of a common, multiprotocol addressing structure, within international standards

6. Growing commonality in transport facilities like local area networks (LANs), subnetworks having X.25, frame relay, and ISDN interfaces for the higher-level protocols of OSI, SNA, and TCP/IP

7. Strong emphasis on the use of high-speed transmission facilities, occasioned by the widespread use of optical fiber

8. Promotion of heterogeneous interoperability through umbrella organizations such as the Open Software Foundation (OSF), OSI/Network Management Forum, X/Open, and Corporation for Open Systems (COS)

1.2   GENERAL COMMUNICABILITY

1.2.1   Basic User Requirements

The Enterprise Information System is the aggregate of the enterprise information processing resources interconnected by a variety of communications subnetworks.[3] In the past, these facilities only supported the enterprise, today they are becoming more and more essential to the very conduct of the enterprise.

The Enterprise Information System must offer the ability to control, share, and communicate all types of information. Both the range of services and the reach to users are growing. This involves combinations of text, graphics, image, voice, and sometimes video forms. Broader populations must have easy access to this growing span of information,

---

2. The term *end-to-end data-exchange facilities* in this book refers to the upper-layer programming support at each end-system that helps to manage the conversation or dialog between two end users.

3. The word *subnetwork* (defined in the ISO 8648 standard) means any collection of equipment and physical media that forms an autonomous whole, and that can be used to interconnect other real systems for purposes of communication. LANs and X.25 packet switching data networks are examples of subnetworks.

based on easy-to-use systems and applications. The system must serve the productivity of technical and business professionals, data professionals, secretarial, clerical, and production personnel, all of whom are to a degree knowledge workers. The solution must support the interaction of such users within their specialized work group areas, and furthermore integrate them as appropriate into an enterprise-wide system with common resources. The communications system must reach throughout departments, across departments and divisions, to customers, to suppliers, and to vendors. For all these users, the network provides a base for the intake, creation, processing, and distribution of information.

1.2.2 Multivendor Systems

The system, moreover, must facilitate cooperation among departments and enterprises that have grown up separately. It must also allow *external* contractors, suppliers, and perhaps customers (which have diverse terminal and computer equipments) to tie directly into the Enterprise Information System. New internal relationships must regularly be established. Moreover, reorganizations, mergers, acquisitions, partnerships, and alliances all can require integration of business processes and can change the network greatly. In general, therefore, the growing network involves communication among systems from different vendors having different operating systems and different communication protocols. Private and public subnetworks must interoperate, within security constraints. It is a heterogeneous, multivendor, multisubnetwork system, with an evolutionary thrust to multiprotocol-interoperability, and industry and international standards. The goal is that network users, operators, and programmers will be able to use, run, and access heterogeneous networks in a homogeneous way. While this involves many factors, primary ones include:

- Comprehensive (end-to-end) *system management*
- *Multiple application-services*, which are software packages, such as file transfer and store and forward messaging, intended to support many applications
- *Multiple communication architectures*, like the OSI standard, the IBM SNA, the earlier TCP/IP,[4] and the LAN protocols, such as NetBIOS[5]
- Diverse *subnetworks*, like the X.25 packet switched data networks, frame relay packet switched data networks, Synchronous Data Link Control (SDLC) wide area networks (WANs), local area networks (LANs such as Ethernet and token rings), the Fiber Distributed Data Interface (FDDI), Integrated Services Digital Network (ISDN), and

---

4. Though originally encouraged by the U.S. Department of Defense, TCP/IP development has been a cooperative effort among universities, industry, and government.

5. NetBIOS was defined as an interface, rather than as a set of communication protocols. It is fundamentally different from the three primary protocols, OSI, SNA, and TCP/IP. Nevertheless, the NetBIOS related services, though minimal, do make an effective transport-service-provider when used in concert with LAN facilities. Thus, though not of the same completeness or "industrial strength" as SNA or OSI, or TCP/IP, we include NetBIOS as one of the key protocol systems because it represents a class of protocols that are primarily of importance on the LANs.

Broadband ISDN, and proprietary networks like DECnet, all interconnected by bridges, routers, and gateways.

While accommodating heterogeneity is necessary in this complex, diverse, and changing world, homogeneity is attractive where it can be found. Hence, at the same time, *a primary strategy has to be the integration of international standards (particularly OSI) for basic multivendor communications.* This must be done with the continued support and enhancement of earlier protocols so that enterprises can use OSI on a self-determined timeframe relative to their needs and skills.

Multivendor configurations can involve diverse types of components, subsystems, and interconnections. Of major importance is the continued growth of LANs, their interconnection, the movement to higher-speed LANs, and the linking of the LAN and WAN worlds.

1.2.3   Network Operations Requirements

There is no doubt that user satisfaction, particularly regarding response time and dependability are uppermost in the minds of operations personnel. However, the needs are much deeper. Networks must be readily *operable.* Among the operational functions of great concern, to managers of enterprise networks, are the following:

- *Ease of installation and operation*, to reduce personnel and time requirements. Major advantages result from:
    - Minimal coordinated system definitions
    - Automatic awareness of total topology
    - Automatic location of named destinations
    - Automatic and optimized route selection.
- *Continuous system availability* with planned maintenance and unplanned outages. This requires nondisruptive, dynamic reconfiguration.
- Flexibility in *centralized and/or distributed and partitioned system management*, to accommodate organizational jurisdictions and delegation of responsibility.
- *Transparency of transport-service-providers*, from the user's viewpoint, to simplify programming and allow the use of diverse end-systems.
- *Function granularity* to match options to needs.
- *Smooth growth and evolution* from existing networks.

1.2.4   Cost Optimization

Cost, of course, is the pacing element. Cost must be balanced with many factors, such as performance, security, and growth potential. As network costs grow, the total cost optimization of the network becomes crucial. Short-term advantage must be balanced with long-term costs and effectiveness. Corporations consider the financial aspects of telecommunications in two ways:

- As a function whose continued operation is increasingly vital to the real-time, hour-by-hour business operations

- As a significant competitive advantage

The network is usually a major investment that must provide adequate returns. This encompasses not only the physical plant (lines, Private Branch Exchanges (PBXs), multiplexors, processors, etc.), but also the data, image, and voice services that make up the system. Despite the potential complexity of such a system, costs must be controlled and contained, performance must be predictable, and the system must be fully manageable. Major cost savings are sought in five ways:

1. *By developing new applications* that improve efficiency of old or new processes. These must serve the distributed operations of the organization and adapt to the changing needs of the organization.

2. *By reducing costs of application development.* Productivity of application development continues to be a prime pacer of system evolution and hence enterprise effectiveness. A key factor in programmer productivity, in turn, is the portability of applications among systems of different sizes, among systems of different vendors, and among systems having multiple communications protocols. Hence the evolution of common programming interfaces across these systems becomes important.

3. *By reducing costs of transmission facilities.* Efficient operation and high utilization of transmission facilities has always been a prime consideration. Despite the availability of increased bandwidths, these will continue to be important factors. Sharing of high-bandwidth facilities for multimedia and *diverse protocols* is key.

4. *By reducing system down time.* For critical applications, the system must, in effect, never be down. This requires that networks must be dynamically reconfigurable, adding or deleting nodes without disruption of service.

5. *By improving and reducing costs of system management.* Shortages and costs of skilled personnel to efficiently manage multiple unrelated networks are limiting factors. Lacking adequate management systems and skilled personnel results in system unavailability that the enterprise cannot tolerate. Hence integrated system management facilities, with higher degrees of automation, which can be effectively and efficiently used by relatively small skilled staffs are mandatory elements of a successful network.

1.3   THE NETWORK AS THE ENTERPRISE SERVER

Autonomy, and the ability to rapidly exploit new applications independently has often been valuable in getting production started quickly. As systems mature, sharing and interaction within groups and among groups becomes important. Increasingly, an entire network, including server nodes at many locations, is considered as a single entity. The eventual need is for general communicability among these servers and common programming interfaces to these servers, so that users at any node can benefit from the services of any server. The system aspects become crucial. Data integrity, security considerations, and general systems management are added to general accessibility as vital requirements.

1.3.1 Application-Services

In each operating environment, a set of services supports the executing applications. These are often referred to as "application-services" or "application enablers." Included in this set are database services, file transfer services, job submission services, print services, document distribution services, asynchronous (office-systems) message services, and overall system management. These application enablers have often been significantly different for each different operating environment, being tailored to the capabilities of each environment and the needs of the customer sets for which each environment was designed. Today, there is an increasing need for many, diverse, remote systems to function cooperatively. Application-to-application communication, distributed database services, and front-end services to back-end processing are examples. Such cooperative processing requires that the application-services be designed with this internode cooperation in mind.

Technology has advanced to the point where very significant and compatible application enabling services can be provided across a wide range of systems. Though the system capabilities cover a broad range (e.g., from mainframe systems—such as MVS[6]— to PC workstations), it is now feasible to have many consistent application-services to facilitate cooperative processing across that range. Moreover, the design of application-services can promote application portability across this range of systems. With a full-function and consistent operating environment in the programmable workstation, as well as in mainframes, the end user can have effective cooperation among systems that provides the advantages of personal computing, local computing, and remote host-based computing.

The effect of the growing array of application-services is to create a network operating system (across local area and wide area networks). The functions are distributed and are available to all users of the network. The user should be increasingly unaware of the network components that underlie these application-services, the protocols among these components, and the locations of data or application-services within the network.

1.4 DIVERSITY AND CHANGE

The world's enterprises, however, are characterized by change and diversity. Technology seems to have an ever-increasing rate of change. In every area, we can expect the technical possibilities five years from now to eclipse today's possibilities. At the same time, the needs of enterprises are likewise evolving. Their markets, processes, economies, and internal organizations are in a constant state of flux.

Despite the reality of this diversity and rapid change, the industry faces a growing need for more universal communication in all its possible forms. There is a crying need for compatibility among the systems used by different groups throughout the world. All users would like to face a single-system view of an enterprise's data-processing resources. That single view should apply to a wide range of communications elements, involving

---

6.   MVS stands for Multiple Virtual Systems. It is the S/390 operating system with comprehensive batch, interactive, database, and communications capabilities.

programmable workstations, interconnected terminals, midrange departmental processors, and the largest central processors, wherever they might be. We need systems and applications that are easier to learn and to use. We seek the ultimate ability to communicate "any-to-any" user, with any user having access to multiple hosts, and with an integrated, easy to use, system management facility. We need the appearance of a single shareable and manageable network that functions as one computing system. Hence the search for standards to which all might comply.

1.4.1 The Search for Standards

The international standards draw from the experience of major corporations, carriers, and government agencies. Ideally, each feature should be honed by years of experience with large numbers of customers. Great diversity within each architecture, to meet ever-new needs, leads to a kind of survival of the fittest, and so the architecture evolves. A great many of the functions of proprietary protocols have thus been incorporated into standards. This amalgam, in turn, influences the further evolution of architectures like SNA, whose later advances can also be fed back into standards.

The fundamental difficulty, of course, is that standards must be agreed to by some consensus process that (a) takes a considerable number of years to accomplish (about three to six years), (b) has to address the needs of many different interests, and (c) has to address the multiplicity of needs by a multiplicity of options. International standards must be worked on by a vast network of committees and must undergo a very lengthy process of proposal, review, modification, and stages of approval. Occasionally, technically superior approaches are sacrificed to the need for compromise or political expediency. For these reasons the inevitable result is standards that lag the technological possibilities and also the evolving needs. Therefore, some standards will be somewhat obsolete by the time they are finally approved.

Today's standard will inevitably be just another option in the not too distant future, as technology moves on. Some nonstandard approaches will be sufficiently superior to displace a standard. *Nevertheless, standards are extremely valuable.* They help to maintain a drift to convergence, against the tide of divergence that is also constantly at work. The name of the game is to pursue international standards and to strive to keep them evolving as rapidly as is practical and feasible.

Other, less official standards can, in the meantime, be set more readily, and can evolve more rapidly. In particular, we have multivendor associations, like the Open Software Foundation (OSF), which seeks the adoption of common technologies by participating corporations, using standards plus other agreements that are well ahead of formal standardization. OSF is sponsored by DEC, Groupe Bull, Hewlett-Packard, Hitachi, IBM, Nixdorf, Phillips, and Siemens. Since OSF's founding, over 150 members have been added. We now see iterative cycles of vendor experience, negotiation among vendors in these organizations, vendor adoption of de facto standards, international standards, vendor extensions to standards, etc. And so the cycles continue.

The real world, therefore, within any large enterprise, has the challenge of achieving the best possible communicability, using the best technologies available, and keeping up with the latest requirements. This must be done through a balanced use of both the best that the international standards community has achieved and the best that the industry leaders' de facto standards can offer in advanced function. By a combination, the diversity of implementations can be reduced while the evolving needs can be better satisfied. The trick is to exploit these dual approaches, to get the best of both worlds, without significantly complicating either the use of the systems or the management of the systems. The industry has learned that to make this practical, systems have to be designed for orderly diversity and evolution.

In this real world, therefore, a major information services provider has the obligation to perform three complementary services:

1. To *meet the advanced needs* of enterprises in a timely fashion, using the best that advanced technology can offer

2. To help *evolve international standards* and to incorporate those as components of its offerings when they adequately meet the need

3. To *provide continuity of system evolution*, with adequate protection of prior enterprise investments in yesterday's leading developments

The networks of a company like IBM, accordingly, must inherently be hybrids, incorporating elements of all three services. The SNA architecture is necessarily incorporated in a higher-level architecture that includes multiple architectures like OSI, TCP/IP, SNA, and NetBIOS. This "macroarchitecture" seeks to generalize management and control services, like fault management and security management, that can be common to all options. It seeks common application-services, like distributed data services and distributed print services. It seeks to share facilities among protocol sets. It must be predominantly an "open architecture" to further the multivendor evolution of systems. This book attempts to provide a bird's-eye view of such a balance as it exists today and a look at where it is headed in the future. Because this convergence to a macroarchitecture, which is still in process, has become a major new paradigm, we choose to give it a name: *Open Systems Network Architecture* (*OSNA*).

1.5   OPERATING ENVIRONMENTS

Operating environments are much more than communications. They include the *operating systems* and the structures imposed on software in systems. They affect the way in which applications and application-services can communicate in a distributed system.

Operating environments differ for good reasons. The fact is that a degree of specialization is often needed to do a job well. Having a single system in a single operating environment sounds desirable, but this approach has its limits. With the broad spectrum of application requirements and technologies up ahead, we still have to face the tasks of making more specialized systems and groups of systems perform and cooperate. The vision is that these heterogeneous systems nevertheless increasingly become logically transparent (i.e., transparent except for some performance or propagation delay effects),[7] wherever that is appropriate. From the user's and the application programmer's point of

---

7. The term *transparent* will often be used to mean that a specific distinction can be ignored, but may be detected if required.

view, the assemblage of different operating environments should appear to be an integrated computing environment.

The following illustrates how an establishment in an IBM context may first need to consider selections from three sets of operating-system environments:

1. System Application Architecture (SAA) Environments[8]
    - MVS
    - VM
    - OS/400
    - OS/2
2. Non-SAA, widely used environments
    - UNIX (e.g., AIX/OSF,[9] IBM's implementation of UNIX, incorporating the functions of the OSF operating system)
    - DOS/Windows
3. Selected other-vendor environments

For each set of these operating-system environments, one needs to provide communications facilities that make interoperation feasible.

1.6   THREE MAIN INGREDIENTS

The purpose of this book is to address the communications needs in this mix of environments. While focusing on ever-evolving standards, the paradigm for design must be multivendor and multiprotocol systems. Toward this end, we address three main ingredients, from an IBM perspective:

1. The growing importance of the international standards for Open Systems Interconnection (OSI)
2. *SAA* and *AIX/OSF*, two strategic sets of systems that promote interoperability, and thereby provide the tools for interoperability with still other environments
3. *Open-Systems Network Architecture (OSNA)*, an evolving macroarchitecture for heterogeneous systems, embracing multiple communication protocols, providing both the communications foundation of SAA and AIX/OSF systems, and *also facilitating communication with still other systems*

1.6.1   Open Systems Interconnection (OSI)

Prodigious efforts, by people from a host of countries, have produced almost two hundred OSI international standards, concerning various aspects of the OSI seven-layer communications architecture. Each of these standards has been a set of agreements hammered out

---

8. SAA is IBM's Systems Application Architecture for programmers to create a similar look and feel for applications on workstations and mainframes.

9. AIX stands for Advanced Interactive Executive. The term AIX/OSF is used here to indicate the incorporation of OSF/1 into AIX, as indicated by IBM. The term is not, however, an official IBM term.

over a period of about four years. The overall OSI effort spans more than twelve years. Key parts of the OSI international standards for data communications become integral parts, and available options, of the evolving OSNA. The OSI architectures embodied in OSNA include a wide range of communications facilities:

- Application-services (such as messaging and file transfer)

- End-to-end data-exchange facilities (such as support for transaction-program dialogs)

- End-to-end transport services (for recovery and flow control)

- Intersubnetwork connectivity and routing

- A wide variety of transport subnetworks (such as LANs, ISDN, and those using the X.25 packet-switching interface)

Also included as requirements in OSNA, are facilities for TCP/IP and interoperation with LAN-oriented protocols like NetBIOS. These are very important today, and will be for years to come, even though many of these systems will experience a gradual transition to OSI and mixed OSI/SNA systems. That transition can be expected to accelerate only when equivalents with high performance and superior function appear in the strategic communication systems. Even then, investment in existing technologies will keep part of the network in slow transition for a long time.

1.6.2   Systems Application Architecture (SAA) and AIX/OSF

SAA is an IBM-identified set of architectures, the purpose of which is to increase consistency, ease of use, and productivity for a very broad range of intelligent workstations and small-, intermediate-, and large-scale data-processing systems [GC26-4341]. It emphasizes interoperation among its members and *with non-SAA systems*. The direction of SAA is to support industry standards and to increase the use of published architecture and open interfaces. We will discuss the *Common Communications Support*, on all SAA systems, for communications among a wide range of multivendor systems.

The intent of SAA is not merely to provide basic communications among its participating systems. Beyond that, the family of application-services (enablers) and Common Communication Services provide full interoperability among cooperating systems. To be effective, these diverse functions must have consistency across the product sets and have the benefit of full testing for compliance.

The AIX/OSF operating system is IBM's implementation of an advanced UNIX [GC23-2002]. This system evolution stems from the earlier work of AT&T's UNIX V, Berkeley's BSD.4 UNIX, and Microsoft's XENIX. The stated IBM strategy is to adhere, in the AIX environment, to the specifications of the Open Software Foundation (OSF), including its Distributed Computing Environment (DCE).[10]

SAA is a thus a *heterogeneous-system solution*, which aims to enable consistent, integrated access, by application programs, to resources across four different operating

---

10.   IBM has stated its intention to incorporate OSF/X, the OSF version of UNIX, into its AIX offerings. Moreover, elements of the DCE, such as Remote Procedure Call and an X.500 directory, will be common to AIX/OSF and SAA.

environments (MVS, VM, OS/400, and OS.2 EE). The objective is distributed services, with each of these types of operating systems optimized for a somewhat different set of application roles. The corresponding hardware includes: mainframes (S/390s), midrange systems (AS/400s), and workstations (PS/2s). AIX/OSF, on the other hand, implements *one operating environment* across different hardware architectures, from the PS/2 and RISC/6000 to the S/390.

SAA and AIX/OSF environments will be linked together to foster interoperability through common languages, common directories, common databases, user interface consistency, common communications protocols, and a single administrative scope encompassing network and data topologies.[11,12] Gateways or more direct integration will also enable mail interchange and overall system management. Thus, the SAA and AIX/OSF systems will share a common interoperability capability.

1.6.3 Open Systems Network Architecture (OSNA)

In the past seventeen years, SNA has gone through several major growth stages, evolving from a single host environment, to multiple host, mesh networking, and Advanced Peer-to-Peer Networking. Originally, SNA was only SDLC and routing, less than two of the OSI seven-layer protocol stack. Today, SNA includes all seven layers of the OSI structure, particularly many link and subnetwork facilities, such as LANs, X.25, and ISDN. These are common to SNA and OSI. The evolutionary strategy continues to be the extension of SNA and its simultaneous convergence with OSI. The developing next stage, which we call OSNA (a name coined for the purpose of this book), amounts to an architecture of architectures with a higher level of organization. Like all living architectures, it must support three stages of product development:

1. *Known requirements*, which are acknowledged industry requirements under current study

2. *Statements of direction*, which are definite statements of intent to incorporate features in products

3. *Product implementation*, with the gradual growth of products employing the architecture

To understand the orientation of OSNA, we should examine the architecture in all three stages. Where appropriate, this is done in the following chapters.

Basically, OSNA is a systematic approach, combining tools and techniques, for heterogeneous systems. While OSNA fully uses standards to the extent possible, the architecture broadly addresses the heterogeneous world. It integrates today's dominant subarchitectures, provides a transition from them to standards, and provides further transitions to leading edge facilities beyond standards.

---

11.   Speech by T.R. Lautenbach to UNIFORUM, San Francisco, February 28, 1989.

12.   IBM has stated its intent to support OSI, SNA, and TCP/IP across all the SAA and AIX/OSF operating platforms, and to include X.25, token ring LAN (802.5), and Ethernet (802.3) under each of these.

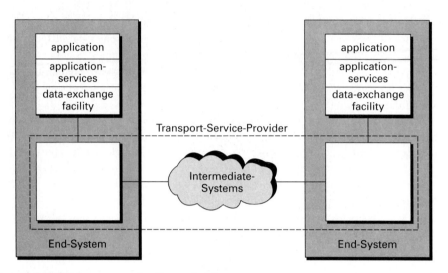

Figure 1.1 Basic communications structure.

OSNA particularly offers the communications support for the SAA and AIX/OSF operating environments, and the Distributed Computing Environment of the Open Software Foundation (OSF).

A basic communications structure is shown in Figure 1.1. End-systems attach to and use the services of intermediate-systems. The transport-service-provider has its parts within each end-system, as well as in the intermediate-systems. The primary OSNA building blocks within this structure are shown in Figure 1.2. Five protocol systems within the transport-service-provider are illustrated. The leading edge communication direction emphasizes the APPN and OSI integration. The OSNA design must, moreover, also include subarea networks, TCP/IP, and NetBIOS,[13] and the continued use and enrichment of all of these protocols.

Primary subnetworks potentially include SDLC/HDLC links, the local and metropolitan area networks complying with the IEEE 802.2 standards (802.3/4/5/6), FDDI, ISDN, Frame Relay, X.25, and the mainframe-oriented Enterprise System Connection (ESCON), a serial optical channel. The direction of IBM's architecture is for a growing degree of sharing of these subnetworks among sets of the aforementioned higher-level protocol systems.[14]

---

13.   There are many different NetBIOS implementations. In general, we will be referring to the IBM implementation of NetBIOS.

14.   While the architecture must anticipate the need for many combinations of upper- and lower-layer facilities, the market probably will not justify all possibilities.

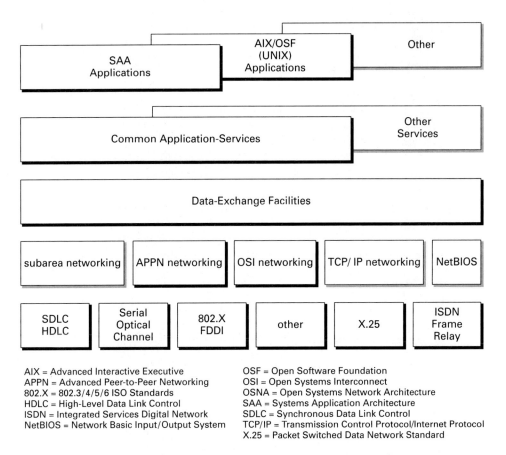

AIX = Advanced Interactive Executive
APPN = Advanced Peer-to-Peer Networking
802.X = 802.3/4/5/6 ISO Standards
HDLC = High-Level Data Link Control
ISDN = Integrated Services Digital Network
NetBIOS = Network Basic Input/Output System

OSF = Open Software Foundation
OSI = Open Systems Interconnect
OSNA = Open Systems Network Architecture
SAA = Systems Application Architecture
SDLC = Synchronous Data Link Control
TCP/IP = Transmission Control Protocol/Internet Protocol
X.25 = Packet Switched Data Network Standard

Figure 1.2 The primary data-oriented building blocks of the OSNA concept.

Within this architecture, an enterprise (or portions thereof) may use all OSI protocols, all TCP/IP protocols, all SNA subarea/APPN protocols, all NetBIOS protocols, or a combination of these. The OSNA architecture, then, seeks commonality, particularly in management and control functions, shared use of common subnetworks, and common programming interfaces. The design directions of OSNA include (but are not limited to):

- Peer-to-peer networking
- Dynamic directory, topology, and routing services
- Integration of OSI and SNA
- High-speed networking

- Total system management
- TCP/IP as a long-term transition vehicle
- Voice/image/video/data integration

Concerning the last point, the coming decade will see increased use of multimedia communications. Data traffic already includes components for FAX and digitized image. Group 3 FAX has revolutionized the way much business is done around the world. The inclusion of video is not far behind. The entire data network is then seen as a companion to the digitized voice network and its services (see Section 6.8). The sharing of broadband transport facilities among voice, image, and ordinary data, using bandwidth management, offers further economies (see Section 18.5.3).

1.7 TOWARD INTEROPERABILITY

There are various kinds of interoperability. We note here some of the strongest requirements and possibilities.

1.7.1 Subsystem Incorporation

The effective cooperation between dissimilar communication environments is furthered as multiple services have been implemented to work together within larger concepts. Some possible combinations include:

- ISDN, LANs, and X.25 subnetworks within a TCP/IP-based transport-service-provider
- ISDN, LANs, and X.25 within SNA and OSI
- SNA subarea with APPN peer-to-peer
- TCP migrating to OSI
- OSI with SNA
- SNA and OSI within SAA
- SAA with AIX/OSF

This list is not meant to be exhaustive, or to indicate priority, but it does illustrate the trend.

1.7.2 Interoperation

Interoperation is the working together of two unlike environments, involving some form of protocol conversion, or encapsulation at the boundaries of the two environments. This interoperability can involve things like subnetworks, distributed file systems, and distributed databases. Basic types of interoperation would include the following:

- *End-systems capable of using multiple types of transport-service-providers* (see Figure 1.3(a)): For example, applications designed to use an SNA end-to-end communications environment can traverse multiple subnetworks, such as an intervening SNA subnetwork, an X.25 subnetwork, or multiple types of LANs.

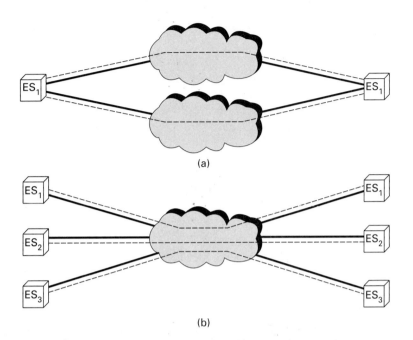

Figure 1.3 Interoperation examples. Part **(a)** shows multiple subnetworks per end-system; part **(b)** shows multiple end-to-end protocols per subnetwork.

- *Transport-service-providers capable of handling multiple types of end-systems* (see Figure 1.3(b)): For example, a pair of end-systems[15] designed to work with X.25 packet switching networks can use an SNA transport subnetwork if the latter contains appropriate protocol-mapping services.

- *Application-services that can function with multiple operating systems*: For example, a common distributed file system can use different operating systems in different nodes.

Communication architecture independence is a particular form of interoperability that provides transparency for the programmer of the underlying communication protocols. This transparency is at the application programming interface (API), with independence from a number of different communication subsystems (e.g., SNA or OSI end-to-end (higher-level) data-exchange protocols and a variety of transport facilities like X.25, LANs, and ISDN).

The mechanism for this transparency, at the API, for the application programmer, is the SAA Common Programming Interface (CPI), with appropriate mapping functions (when necessary) to translate the CPI calls into the verbs for each of the chosen protocol sets.

---

15.   An end-system usually is a node that contains the interface to an end user and the end-to-end services for a communication. Thus, networks are said to have two parts, the end-systems and the intermediate-systems that convey information between end-systems.

The essential goal of API-level independence of communication architecture is that application-processes (or supporting application-services) should be unchanged whether the end-to-end data-exchange protocol stack is SNA-based or OSI-based. Other communication protocols might also be made to participate in the CPI. Moreover, with API-level network independence, the distributed application-processes should be transparently connectable via a variety of transport-service-providers, including SNA subarea, APPN, X.25, ISDN, or one of the multiple LANs, such as Ethernet (the 802.3 standard or the older version 2) or token ring or FDDI.

The distinction between network-independence and other interoperability is shown further in Figure 1.4. There, the nodes X and Y both use the Common Programming Interface (CPI) for some of their applications. Applications A and A' are built on the CPI and have network independence, using either OSI or SNA. Those applications A and A' enjoy API-level network independence. Other applications in those same nodes have their private means of connection, without network independence (the addition of TCP/IP under the CPI is also technically feasible, and hopefully will follow). Nodes X and Y, in that figure, might use different SAA operating systems (e.g., MVS and VM). Either node could also be an AIX/OSF node, or a non-IBM (Other Equipment Manufacturer, or OEM) node, if they support the same CPI and associated mappings as the SAA node.

Common transport-service-providers.   Network independence also needs to be pushed down lower in the system structure than the CPI. More of the system should be implemented only once, and be independent of the variability beneath it. Lower layers must be shared by the upper layers. In particular, end-systems often contain upper-level protocol stacks for data

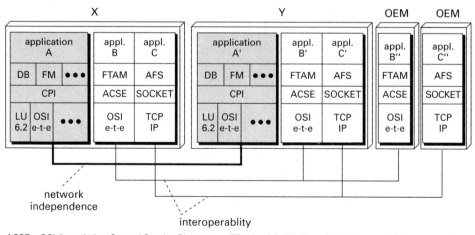

ACSE = OSI Association Control Service Element   FTAM = OSI File Transfer, Access, and Management
AFS = Andrew File System   OEM = Other Equipment Manufacturers
DB = SAA QL Database Management   OSI e-t-e = OSI End-to-End Data-Exchange Facilities
FM = SAA File Management

Figure 1.4 Network independence and interoperability among SAA and non-SAA nodes.

exchange that were designed to work with certain transport-service-providers, such as OSI, TCP/IP, or SNA. With suitable protocol-mapping or encapsulation, all subnetworks, including LANs, MANs, and WANs, should be able to transport any of the common upper-level protocol stacks (i.e., the end-to-end data-exchange facilities that are originally designed to work with SNA, OSI, TCP, or NetBIOS subnetworks). This is a case of multiple types of end-systems using one transport-service-provider.

Adaptability of the end-system. When the common transport-service-provider is absent, we sometimes have the need for one end-system to use multiple types of transport-service-providers. For example, a mainframe host may need to communicate with other end-nodes on a LAN that only understand NetBIOS. Or, the host using OSI or SNA end-to-end data-exchange facilities may need to use transport-service-providers that had been built to handle TCP/IP.

1.8 THE PROSPECT OF OSNA

In summary, then, OSNA is a term used here to describe and project a full-function, multiprotocol communications network solution, that is evolving today. It reflects the trends evident in today's products. The primary components of a projected OSNA are:

- *Common application-services*—system management, naming system, directories, and security services that apply to multiple communication protocol systems
- *Common Programming Interfaces* that shield the programmer from the underlying communications protocols
- *End-to-end data-exchange facilities* for OSI-, SNA-, TCP/IP-, and NetBIOS-based applications
- *Transport-service-providers*, emphasizing minimum systems definition, dynamic topology update, nondisruptive reconfiguration, and capability for carrying traffic from end-systems that were designed for many other transport architectures
- *Common subnetwork and link services* with interconnections among many different combinations of local, metropolitan, and wide area subnetworks
- *High performance options* appropriate for the expanding bandwidths available from optical fiber
- *Voice, data, and video*, application-service and transport-capabilities
- *End-systems* capable of using multiple types of transport-service-providers, such as those based on OSI, SNA, TCP/IP, and NetBIOS

1.8.1 SNA/OSI Convergence

Within the broader objectives cited above, a primary thrust of OSNA is the steady convergence of OSI and SNA facilities. The SAA Common Programming Interface (CPI), for example, applies to a growing number of application-services, such as system management, distributed database and resource-recovery, as well as communications.

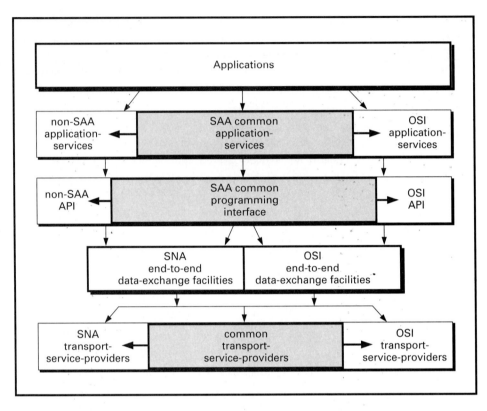

Figure 1.5 Evolution of the Common Programming Interface, common application-services, and common transport-service-providers.

Using the CPI, both applications and such application-services should be independent of the underlying OSI or SNA communications protocols. Figure 1.5 illustrates the goal, in an SAA environment, of extending the OSI/SNA commonality in three areas: the Common Programming Interface, the common application-services, and common transport-service-providers (which share many transport facilities like LANs, X.25 packet-switched data networks, Integrated Service Digital Networks, etc.). To some extent, these same convergence and sharing concepts apply to the TCP/IP communication protocols.

Conclusion

The networking of the entire enterprise and its interconnection with other enterprises is well underway. The need for general communicability drives us toward the use of common communication interfaces and common protocols, even while technical advancement and application growth drive us to diversity and change. Hence, in the foreseeable future, there will be a need for combinations of coexistence, interoperation, and incorporation of different protocol systems. For the application programmers, independence from the underlying communications protocols is especially needed. Beyond that, a certain ecumenism and commonality of transport-service-providers are necessary. To meet these real needs, a multiprotocol architecture (referred to here as OSNA) is discussed in the following chapters.

Acknowledgments

Discussions with many persons have aided the formulation of this chapter, which sets the framework for the book, but special thanks are due to J. P. Gray, Philippe Janson, and E. L. Miller for sharing their insight. I am also indebted to the following for valuable comments: Stefano Zatti, Jerry Mouton, O. K. Baek, V. Hoberecht, J. R. Pickens, M. C. Schein, J. A. Rego, and G. D. Schultz.

EXERCISES

1.1 Give six key features of the evolving multiprotocol architecture.

1.2 Name the four parts of a basic communications structure for an end-system.

1.3 What is meant by network independence?

1.4 Identify three prime targets for commonality between OSI and SNA.

1.5 What are three basic types of interoperation?

1.6 Identify eight building blocks of the transport-service-provider in the OSNA concept.

2
Cooperating Systems

2.1 INTRODUCTION

Any taxonomy of cooperating systems has many dimensions. In the current stages of their development, there still are many challenges. This chapter first provides an overview of what constitutes a network of cooperating systems.[1] An abstract model of a generalized node structure is presented. The concepts of the distributed operating system,[2] the features of cooperating systems, the types of cooperation in use today, and the distribution of application-services are outlined further. Within this context, the strategy for network synthesis in a multiprotocol, multivendor environment are outlined.

2.1.1 Defining Cooperating Systems

We use the term *cooperating systems* in a very broad sense. It includes cooperation of all kinds among mixtures of workstations and mainframes. In general, it refers to applications running on two or more computer systems working together to accomplish a single work scope. The systems may be of different architectures and capabilities. It includes parceling out pieces of an application, its data, and/or its user interface, among these systems, so that each part runs on the system that suits the needs of the enterprise best.

In general, there are three places where it may be feasible to split a system. As shown in Figure 2.1, these splits can produce (a) distributed dialog and presentation management, (b) distributed application programs and (c) distributed data systems. All three splits have been found to be advantageous in different situations.

---

1. A *system*, in this context, is any programmable unit that is connectable via communication lines to other programmable units.

2. An *operating system* is a control program providing services that manage the resources of a programmable unit, and allow those resources to be shared among multiple users or application programs.

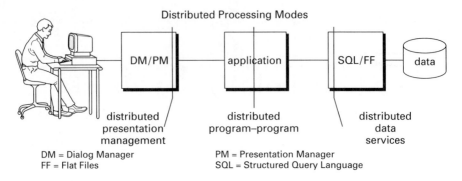

Figure 2.1 Three primary distribution points.

Cooperating processes often join the traditional information-systems (IS) world of "data processing" on the host with the user-oriented world on the workstation. The word *host*, however, has to be understood to now include powerful multitasking PCs, such as the PS/2 and RISC/6000, whose capabilities continue to grow, as well as the mainframes, such as the AS/400 and S/390. In this terminology, "data processing" on a host is usually oriented toward the efficient storage and retrieval of data, printing services, and/or the ability to perform complex or high-volume operations on the data. The workstations are heavily oriented toward the end user, emphasizing improvements in human productivity, achieved through meaningful presentation and effective interaction with a person.

2.1.2   The Rationale for Distribution

Central processing, using mainframes, has traditionally been favored because of the economies of scale (in systems and personnel), a single point of control, and the sharing of data among multiple applications. The central processors have often been "data rich," with very large amounts of data immediately available to diverse applications. This has facilitated data management, data integrity, and data security, using a single, highly trained staff. Central "help desk" operations with a trained network management staff similarly have been advantageous. Sharing of high-cost peripherals, particularly printers, has been routine. Functions very suitable to the mainframe hosts include things like data applications that involve larger amounts of storage, sharing of applications and data among numbers of users, resource access control, higher-performance applications, and management control of the system.

With the advent of low-cost distributed processors, including PCs, it has been more feasible to put some of the computing power, and sometimes the data, where it is most used, rather than in a central location. The data-processing configuration could therefore conform to the company organization, provide local control by the using department, and perhaps also improve accessibility for those department users. Applications can also be placed where it runs best, exploiting the characteristics of different hardware or software systems.

Functions very suitable to the programmable workstation (PWS) include things like sophisticated user interfaces, editing, and private data. The PWS designer can assume that the PWS is working for only one person; this considerably simplifies the system software, customized for the user, making it more efficient and responsive.

The distribution of function may be dictated by intangibles, such as the desire of line management at each location to control its vital data-processing operations. It may be driven by performance needs of the user interface, as the trend is toward higher interaction rates and more powerful programmable workstations. It may be driven by the desire to reduce communication costs. (With volume sensitive tariffs, particularly, as with many packet switching data networks, increased distributed processing may reduce communication costs.)

The search for higher overall availability and disaster protection also leads to consideration of distributed systems. Adequate back-up facilities that are designed for distributed systems and the planning that makes that feasible are essential. Then the scope of a given failure or other disruption at one node is limited to that node of the network. Other nodes can be planned to assume some level of the workload of the disabled components.

The end result is a new balance between the central mainframe systems, departmental processors, and programmable workstations.

2.2 DISTRIBUTED SYSTEM STRUCTURES

As expressed above, the network acquires the capability of a distributed operating system, as its distributed application-services grow. These components are linked by a diversity of communications services. Figure 2.2 illustrates a possible structure in one node of the projected OSNA network. This is an abstract model, against which distributed systems might be tested. The distributed systems structure could support three sets of application-services:

1. A *core* of application-services that defines the general purpose and essential network operating system

2. A *basic* set, which includes other very commonly used application-services

3. More specialized, *advanced* application-services

The selection of services that are appropriate in a particular installation is, of course, variable with each enterprise. However, many networks would thrive with a set consisting of the following distributed-services:

- Core system support
  - Program instantiation
  - Security (see Section 4.4.7)
  - Resource recovery (see Section 5.3)
  - Directory (see Chapter 8)
  - Data conversion

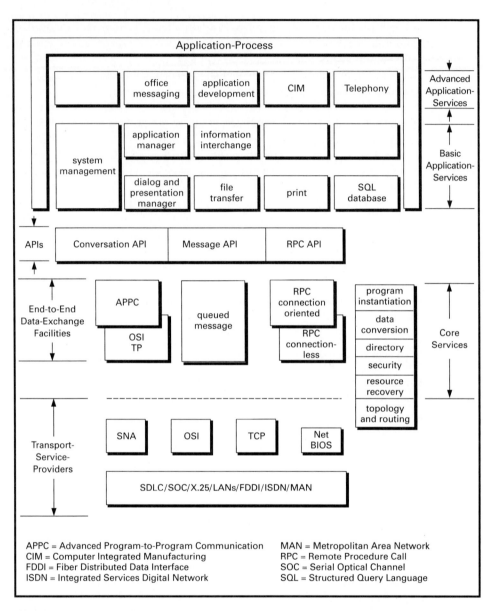

Figure 2.2 Distributed system structure, indicating the major components of an Open System Network Architecture (OSNA).

- Basic application support
    - System management (see Chapter 4)
    - File transfer (see Section 5.2.3)

- SQL database and query (see Section 5.2.4)
- Application manager (see Section 5.4)
- Multimedia information interchange (see Section 6.2)
- Print (see Section 5.5)
- Dialog/presentation manager

In addition, advanced or specialized application-services might, for example, include services for:

- Store and forward messaging (see Section 6.3)
- Telephony application-services (see Section 6.8)
- Application development environment
- Computer integrated manufacturing applications

The end-to-end data-exchange facilities (upper part of the protocol stack in Figure 2.2; see also Chapter 7) will likely be one or more of the following:

- Conversational communications, involving a common API to either the SNA Advanced Program-to-Program Communications (APPC) or the OSI Transaction Processing support
- Remote Procedure Call (RPC), using either connection-oriented or connectionless versions
- Transaction message services

The transport-service-providers (lower part of the protocol stack in Figure 2.2) are in three parts:

- Transport layer end-to-end functions, for SNA, OSI, TCP, and NetBIOS (see Chapters 13 and 14)
- Multisubnetwork or internet routing (see Chapters 12 to 15)
- Link and subnetwork access facilities, including HDLC/SDLC, Serial Optical Channels, X.25 PSDNs, LANs, FDDI, ISDN, Frame Relay, and MAN (see Chapters 16 to 18)

One trend is to make application-services and end-to-end data-exchange facilities common across the distributed network, applicable to a wide range of systems (e.g., the entire range of SAA and AIX/OSF systems). A parallel longer-range trend also is to make these independent of the underlying transport-service-providers, whether they be SNA, TCP, OSI, or NetBIOS, or any of the associated links and subnetworks.

This commonality, of course, is a big challenge. Today, we find that applications, application-services, and end-to-end data-exchange facilities are not always separate. More often, two or three of these are so integrated into individual products that broader sharing is not feasible. Many of these products will be with us for a long time. Hence, the commonality and sharing will be evolutionary. Nevertheless, dramatic steps can be taken.

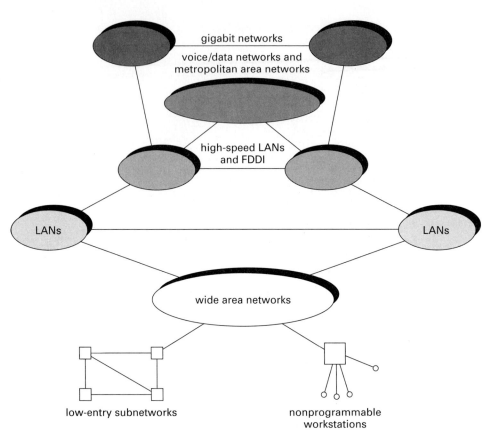

Figure 2.3 Enterprise connectivity directions.

2.3 COOPERATIVE PROCESSING FEATURES

2.3.1 Speed Planes

The type of distribution and the degree of transparency that is feasible depends, obviously, on the end-to-end speed of the communications that links the participants. Figure 2.3 illustrates the range of transmission facilities available, from the lower-speed WANs (kilobit to low megabit per second) to LANs (4 to 16 Mbps), FDDI (100 Mbps) and MANs (1 to 100 Mbps), high-speed, SONET-based[3] wide-area voice-data networks (51 to 1000 Mbps), and still higher-speed, SONET-based, computer-computer links (1 to 2.5 gigabits per second). Within each of the shaded areas there may be multiple subnetworks (connected by bridges and routers). For discussion purposes, we can characterize these in

---

3. SONET is a set of standards being put in place for high-speed transmissions in the range of 51 to 2488 Mbps (see Section 18.2).

three major speed planes:

- The *multi-gigabit* plane
- The *multi-megabit* plane
- The *multi-kilobit* plane

End-system attachments are made at all planes; communication is both within a plane and between planes. Each plane can feed higher speed planes. The higher speed planes facilitate mixtures of data, voice, graphics, image, and possibly video. In general, the cost per unit distance traveled is greatest in the upper planes and least in the lower planes, but the cost per packet is least in the upper planes. However, the actual costs change dramatically with time. Advancing optical fiber technology is greatly increasing the distances that are feasible in the upper planes, as well. Thus, Figure 2.3 portrays speed ranges, but it is less and less correlated with geographical coverage.

2.3.2   Clusters and Domains

In cooperating systems, we find multiple speed planes of communication, corresponding types (or degrees) of cooperation, and a wide spread in system capabilities and architectures. Some services and their transparency may be global, while other services and their transparency may be only regional, and limited to a speed plane. Management may be required (and able) to enforce transparency rules, in different degrees, for different subsystems.

This "regionalization of service" has been given many names. One way to describe it is given in the "Distributed Computing Environment"[4] of the Open Software Foundation. It, for example, uses the concept of *clusters* and *cells* that have different types and degrees of transparency. (Some writers use the term *region*, *realm*, or *domain* instead of cell; I prefer *domain*.)

The cluster has the highest degree of transparent services. It enforces a high level of single image by a uniformity of the name space for all resources within the cluster, including processes and data. Within a cluster, each machine, each user, and each process sees the same resources, with the same names. In some cases, processing power then may be available wherever it exists in the cluster, and processes might be moved to balance the network and individual machine loads. The cluster can benefit from the highest communication speeds (multi-megabit or multi-gigabit.)

The domain is a larger collection of networked computers that still permits location-transparent access to some data within the domain. Each domain usually is also a domain for administration and security. Certain functions, such as directory accesses, may also be performed with higher speed when it is known that all queries come from within a well-defined domain.

---

4. The "Distributed Computing Environment" of the OSF is based on a proposal by Hewlett-Packard Co., IBM, Locus Computing, and Transarc Corporations, jointly with DEC and Microsoft Corp., to Open Software Foundation, October 6, 1989.

Some sharing among domains is also supported. However, interdomain communication typically would involve longer distances and delays, unknown and probably heterogeneous machines, or different administration policies.

Thus, transparency would start with nationwide, if not worldwide interdomain naming, increase within the domain, and peak with the cluster.

One can, of course, have various definitions of cluster and domain characteristics. Generalizing the cluster/domain concept somewhat, one can project clusters and domains in the three speed planes mentioned previously:

- In the upper (gigabit) plane we have the clusters of larger processors and databases, with the greatest transparency, using, for example, the gigabit abilities of inter-CPU optical fiber communication, usually over modest distances of tens of kilometers.

- In the mid (megabit) plane we have clusters with less transparency, using, for example, the 100 megabit FDDI and comparable speed MANs.

- Also in the mid plane we have domains that interconnect clusters, providing a degree of distributed functional transparency over greater physical or organizational distances. These domains might, for example, use 4–16 megabit LANs and MANs spanning 50 kilometers.

- In the lower (kilobit) plane we have domains with the smallest amounts of functional transparency, using the national or even global WANs.

Of course, some enterprises may have only one or two of these three speed planes. Some, however, already have the ingredients of all three.

Ascending planes have greater communications speeds and correspondingly greater processing and data handling capabilities. Each plane connects to, and may feed upper planes. Note therefore, that a high-transparency cluster may require higher-speed communications (multi-megabit or multi-gigabit planes), to achieve adequate distributed performance. Nevertheless, the use of the cluster's single image facilities may be opened to workstations at all speed planes.

Some application-services may be achievable at one plane, and all higher planes, but not at lower planes. For example, task management may best be done only at the highest (e.g., optical channel) plane. Distributed SQL database functions may be applicable to both mid (LAN) and higher (optical channel) planes, but with different performance at the two planes. Store and forward messaging services would be applicable across all planes.

2.4 TYPES OF COOPERATION

There are many variations on how systems will cooperate with each other. The host or server function may be provided by workstations (such as the PC or PS/2) or by mainframes (such as the AS/400 or S/390). Application-to-application interaction can take place among workstations, among mainframes, and between workstations and mainframes.

The cooperating systems might be solely workstations on interconnected LANs, with some (more powerful) workstations performing as hosts (or servers) for others. Or, the hosts (servers) on the LAN might be mainframes, or a combination of PS/2s and mainframes. Or, these might be connected via a WAN, or connected by both LANs and WANs. LANs may also have LAN servers that cache data, which they in turn obtain from more remote mainframes.

A given workstation might work with multiple workstations and with hosts (servers) on LANs, WANs, or both. An Open Systems Network Architecture (OSNA) must allow all these combinations, and must allow flexible changes from one configuration to another.

Thus, the variations are many, and can be classified in many ways. A few of the different types of cooperation follow.

Loose workgroups

One of the very popular types is where much of the work is done in isolation, on a single workstation, and a server on a LAN facilitates occasional sharing of files, printing services, and message distribution among members of a department or other workgroup. Spreadsheets, data entry, word processing, and desktop publishing are examples in this category.

Front-end processing.   Front-end processing is a related technique where the primary or coordinating workload is done in a remote host, but work set-up is performed in the workstation. Some examples of the types of applications that can benefit from front-end processing are: editing of large documents with many participants, applications that benefit from graphics and/or image presentation techniques, complex queries involving customization of the query, and applications based on expert-system techniques.

Distributed processing.   The central bank with its bank branches is a clear example of another kind of cooperation. There, the applications on different systems are clearly distinct, and may be physically remote from each other, but there is a strong cooperation between the central bank and a branch when the occasion demands it. A major banking system, for example, may have only several central locations, with say, from two to ten large mainframes at each. However, the branches may aggregate several tens of thousands of PC-class computers. The aggregate MIPS (millions of instructions per second) in the branches may be lightly utilized, and may far exceed those in the central locations. On the other hand, the databases in the centrals may far exceed the aggregate storage in the branches.

Another major example of distributed processing is computer integrated manufacturing, with its separation of orders, production-control, inventory, and manufacturing components. Again, this becomes a network of processes, which may be in farflung locations, but they can be part of a coordinated system design that facilitates close and automated cooperation among these components.

Interactive.   The interactive model is a further technique that creates a sequential, personalized application-environment for each user in a remote host. The usual assumption is that the application will access and update data that is private to the user. This is distinct from the transactional model which uses prestructured applications, and assumes concurrency of users with common data, but no continuity of the user-environment between transactions.[5]

---

5.   VM/CMS and MVS/TSO are two existing interactive subsystems that run on S/390 hosts.

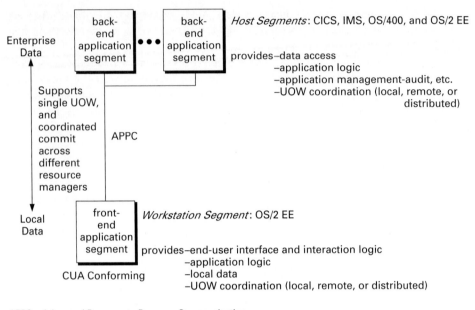

APPC = Advanced Program-to-Program Communication
CUA = Common User Access
UOW = Unit of Work

Figure 2.4 The transaction processing model.

Transaction processing. Interprogram cooperation is sometimes referred to as *transaction processing*, when the emphasis is on access to and update of shared resources, a granular level of sharing (e.g., record level locking), high data integrity, high transaction rates, and low cost per transaction. Multiple parallel sessions from programmable workstations is a corollary of this. An illustration of all this is the transaction processing model shown in Figure 2.4. A front-end workstation works cooperatively with multiple back-end segments, which range from PS/2s to large mainframes.

The inclusion of the word *transaction* emphasizes the *atomic*[6] nature of the interaction. Provisions in the network must insure that either all its operations complete satisfactorily, or the partial results must be eliminated, leaving the system as if the transaction had never been started. It always involves two or more programs, cooperating to carry out some processing function. This requires program-program communication to share each other's many local resources, such as processor cycles, databases, work queues, or human interfaces such as keyboards and displays.

This allows an optimization of the control structures in the PWS and the host. The host is designed to drive up the transaction rates, assuming the inquiry is defined, and with

---

6. *Atomic* here pertains to the discrete, independent, and self-contained nature of a transaction, without dependence on other transactions.

no waits for further human intervention. Transactions can therefore be handled efficiently in atomic fashion. The PWS, on the other hand, is designed to wait on each transaction, as each user slowly constructs the entire request. The PWS provides the user-assists, with prompting and editing, for interactive query formulation.

Data and application logic are located on both a front-end processor and one or more back-end processors; however, in most instances the bulk of the data is on the back-end processors. The atomic Unit of Work (UOW) involves all concerned processors and must be coordinated by all. The UOW comes in different flavors of complexity, depending on the complexity of the inquiry and the number of back-end processors (see Section 5.3).

2.5 DISTRIBUTED APPLICATION-SERVICES

2.5.1 Network Utility

The obvious purpose of the network is to serve the enterprise. It can only really do this through the applications that use the network. The enterprise-view of the network, therefore, is that shown in Figure 2.5, an assembly of distributed application-services connected so that they and the applications can cooperate via the network. A growing array

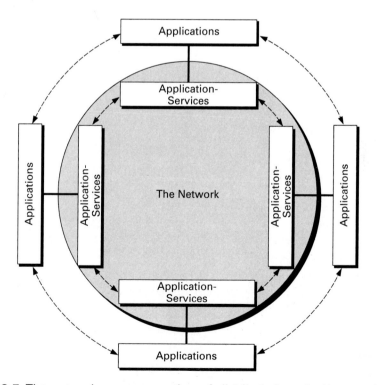

Figure 2.5 The network as a connection of distributed applications and related application-services.

of network-oriented application-services includes such things as:

- Print services and spooling
- Program-to-program services
- Directory services
- Distributed file services
- Distributed database services
- Distributed application management
- Message distribution
- Remote job scheduling/distribution
- Authentication and access control for security
- System management
- Distributed time services
- Data conversion and mapping

The distributed application-services have a peer-peer communication between like services, although they can be formed into hierarchies, also. The distributed application-services have resource managers that constitute a *distributed operating system*. With gradually improving transparency to location, the distributed operating system maps user requests for named resources to specific system resources. The network, with these application-services, thus become the servers for many applications and the enablers for new applications.

2.5.2   Single System Image

The goal of the network should be that, though widely distributed, perhaps over diverse transport-service-providers, the user should perceive a single system image. This entails painstaking design to move toward the following:

- *Location transparency*: the user should be able to access distributed resources (applications, application-services, data, printers, etc.) by specifying the resource name, without needing to know on exactly which remote system the resource is located (there are cases, however, where this transparency is not wanted).

- *Incremental growth*: additions or deletions of resources anywhere in the network should not affect the concurrent operations of the network. The user's single image should not be subject to any abnormal interruption or termination because of these changes.

- *Performance*: distribution of function should be geared to the performance requirements of each application and the bandwidth available in different segments of the network. The bandwidth may vary from that within the "glass house" computing center to that of high-speed LANs within the building or a building complex and to lower speeds over greater distances. Where necessary, the performance should be a known trade-off with benefits of distribution.

- *Availability*: redundancy of the communication facilities, the distributed processing facilities, and the applications themselves must be planned. Fault-tolerance and quick restart or takeover capability must also be built into the distributed system. Failures of any component must not interrupt the service beyond some predefined limit.

- *Centralized or regionalized system management*, including problem determination, security, accounting, and other system management applications (see Chapter 4).

2.5.3   Clients and Servers

The client–server model is certainly not the only model for cooperating systems; it is, however, one of the foremost models for distributing resources. Specialized functions are said to be provided by *servers*. Servers provide a resource-management service, and, on the client side, an application program interface (API) through which a service can be requested. Typical servers include: file, print, high-function-graphics, and directory servers. Those local functions that facilitate use of the remote server, often by means of an easy-to-use interface, are called *clients*. An illustrative cooperative system involving distributed servers is shown in Figure 2.6. The hosts 1 through 4, for example, might be remote mainframes. Note that the print server on the LAN is not necessarily restricted to serve only workstations on the LAN. If, for example, an application in one of the hosts (say, Host 3) uses the print server, then Host 3 needs to contain both client and server functions.

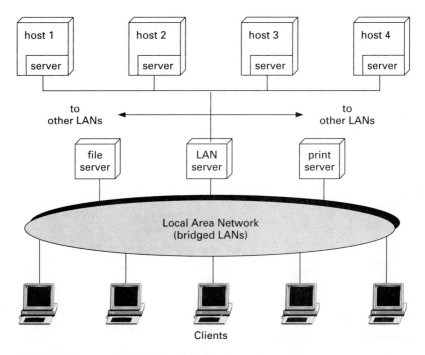

Figure 2.6 LAN-host connectivity with distributed servers.

In very simple systems, a workstation may work with only one server. The concept, however, has many other potentials. We can have one or more clients communicating with one or more servers. Each host may contain multiple servers; and each LAN may have dedicated or nondedicated servers on either workstations or mainframes. In a fully distributed environment, workstations and mainframes may have both private and public data; each such workstation or mainframe could, in effect, provide a limited server function.

Resource managers.   For each application-service, there are resources to be managed, and often these are distributed resources. Hence, we have the concept of distributed *resource managers*, such as a distributed file manager, distributed resource recovery manager, and so forth. A resource manager is a set of related service programs that (1) maintain state information relative to some set of resources, and (2) provide a set of formal interfaces through which operations may be performed on those resources. In OSI these resource managers are often referred to as *application-service–elements* (*ASEs*).

In principle, each resource manager may be distributed, having client and server components, as shown in Figure 2.7. The resource manager function thus exists partly in both the client and the server, and is distributed over several nodes. Client–server relations may, however, be very intricate and interactive, or they may be very simple and involve only a single exchange. Some clients are intimately dependent on the design of a particular server, while other clients are relatively independent of any particular server design.

Each application-service–element (or resource manager) may interact with the "outside world" via three types of interface:

- *Functional Application Programming Interfaces (APIs)* provide (or request) the services offered by this or other resource managers.

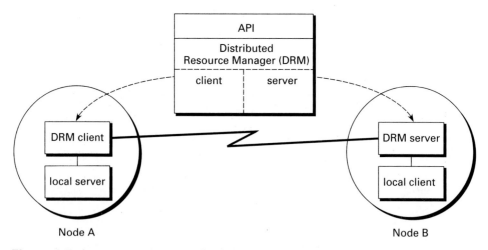

Figure 2.7 A resource manager distributed as client and server.

- *Administrative/Control APIs* initiate and terminate the resource manager. They may also define and query the resource manager.

- *Problem-Determination/Service APIs* respond to requests for traces or dumps, provide alerts, and otherwise support system management.

Portions of a distributed application-service may be located in any size node, from programmable workstations to intermediate processors to large mainframes. Some, like flat file and print services, have been housed in PCs and tailored for service on a LAN. (These are variously known as LAN servers and LAN managers.) Those same functions, however, have also been ported to departmental and mainframe processors.[7] With that porting, support for virtual disks on the host can be almost unlimited in size and number, and the data security facilities of the host are available. Other services, like SQL database servers, have initially been structured to operate over both LANs and WANs, and in all sizes of processors. We find, then, many gradations, such as:

1. *Single servers*, usually on LANs, serving a small group

2. *Multiple servers* on interconnected LANs, serving multiple groups

3. *Multiple servers* distributed over LANs and interconnected mainframes using broadband WANs

4. *Complete distribution*, where every node qualifies as a potential server, though only partially devoted to that function

These gradations emphasize the fundamental nature of cooperative processing with distributed resource managers. As bandwidths improve, so too does the applicability spread, from items 1 to 4 above. In Chapters 4 through 8, a selection of key resource managers is made in order to illustrate their distributed nature, and their communications facilities.

Tiered systems.   Multiple tiers of function can appear, but the relation between tiers can be more peer-to-peer than hierarchical. Most people, for example, consider it a peer-to-peer relationship between a workstation and a server, even though the server has unique capabilities for multiple workstations. In a three tier system, there may be:

1. The workstation that supports a single end user.

2. The set of local servers that serve a local group of users—usually for frequent, casual sharing of work in process. This may also involve multiple servers for related work groups.

3. A part that supports the first two parts with common services such as larger shared databases, archiving, and software-release updates.

A server may act as a client of another server, in order to complete a part of the service it was asked to perform. We thus have both a *two-tier relationship*: client/workgroup-

---

7.   Microsoft reportedly has licensed the source code for the Microsoft LAN Manager local area network operating system to Micro Tempus for porting to IBM MVS, VM, and DOS/VSE mainframe operating environments.

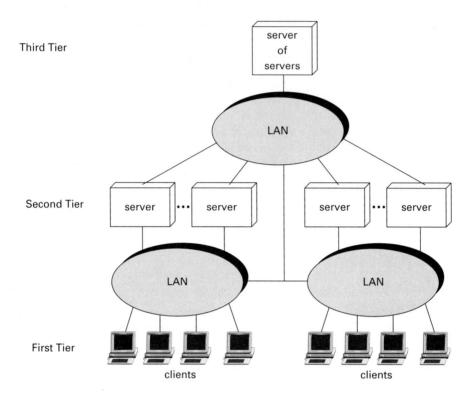

Figure 2.8 Two- and three-tier client–server configurations.

server, and a *three-tier relationship*: client/workgroup-server/server of the workgroup-server. The latter, server of the workgroup-server, may support multiple workgroup-servers. Each second-tier server interfaces to a workgroup. All three tiers may be on the same LAN, on different LANs, as illustrated in Figure 2.8, or on a mixture of LANs and WANs. In these cases, the second tier performs as a server to the first tier, and as a client to the third tier (a functioning three-tier data server is described in Section 5.2.3).

The functions of servers in these three tiers may involve:

- Common flat files, messaging, and printer services
- Transaction processing
- Common relational databases
- Data repository for other servers
- Common applications and subroutine repository
- Allocation of application-process to other servers
- Allocation of job tasks to other servers
- Back-up and recovery to other servers

- Administrative services, including access control for multiple clients to multiple servers

Client–server issues.   Systems providing client–server facilities need to address complex issues, including: client–server communications-interfaces and protocols, naming rules, name-to-address resolution, transformation of different data streams used by different systems, access control, and authentication of both clients and servers. Servers, moreover, need to address special problems of distributed processing, such as concurrency of requests from clients, work prioritization among clients, distributed problem determination, coordinated resource recovery, and accounting. All systems wishing to participate in distributed services, therefore, must have some kernel of such facilities that are designed for distribution.

These issues are undoubtedly simpler if the clients and servers are drawn from one set of homogeneous systems with homogeneous operating environments. The world is not, however, that simple. It appears that SAA distributed resource manager servers will need to function in many operating environments, including, for example, PC-DOS, OS/2, OS/400, MVS, VM S/390, and AIX/OSF (UNIX) operating environments. Beyond that, the resource managers will have to cooperate with their counterparts in multivendor systems. The corresponding communications protocols must include (a) OSI, (b) NetBIOS, which is widely used on LANs, (c) TCP/IP for interoperability with AIX/OSF/UNIX, and (d) both APPN, and SNA Subarea.

2.6   OSF DISTRIBUTED COMPUTING ENVIRONMENT

While no one set of technologies will meet all requirements for long, serious efforts have been made to find multivendor commonalities. A prime example is the Open Software Foundation (OSF), which has selected a family of technologies for common use by its member companies. The companies that are members of OSF will integrate the technologies of the Distributed Computing Environment (DCE) into their respective operating systems.

The aim is to provide a degree of transparent computing in heterogeneous operating environments.[8] OSF provides portable source code (written in C language) and specifications to facilitate portage. The OSF distributed environment thus promises to encompass many operating systems, including UNIX (and its associates like AIX/OSF), MS-DOS, VMS, CRAY, the SAA environments, and others. Common communication protocols, common system management, and common data services are among the goals. In particular, OSF/DCE is intended to offer commonality and to help integrate the following key components:

- *Remote Procedure Call* (RPC) that hides the complexities of the distributed environment (see Section 7.5)

---

8.   IBM executives have stated IBM's intention to implement DCE technologies on AIX products and to extend SAA to incorporate elements of DCE.

- *Naming* (directory), to use information independent of location, system or local naming conventions (see Section 8.4)
- *Distributed file system*, for transparent use of files at remote locations (see Section 5.2.3)
- *Security*, to prevent unauthorized access to distributed resources (see Section 4.4.7)
- *PC integration*, to help provide MS-DOS PCs access to DCE services
- *System management* facilities (see Chapter 4)

2.7   NETWORK SYNTHESIS

The taxonomy of cooperating systems thus has many dimensions. We have discussed multiple operating environments, sets of application-services, different speed planes, different types of cooperating systems, and organizations of clusters and domains. It is no wonder that cooperating systems have grown up in isolated groups. The current stage is to expand the clusters and domains, link the domains, and to extend the cooperation across multiple domains.

2.7.1   SNA/OSI Integration

Protocol systems like TCP/IP and NetBIOS will be with us for a long time, and must be included as starting points of a network synthesis. Much of the following could apply to TCP/IP as well. However, the first requirement of our synthesis is to take full advantage of the basic services provided by the international standards underway, particularly OSI. The integration of OSI within OSNA thus becomes the keystone of the synthesis. Other integrations, then, are add-ons. The technical direction of the evolution of SNA/OSI integration can take advantage of five factors:

1. The transport facilities, such as X.25 packet switching data networks, LANs, FDDI, MAN, ISDN, Frame Relay, and wide area data-link networks, are *independent of the upper layers*, and so can be *fully integrated*, *to be shared* by SNA and OSI applications equally well.

2. The SNA and OSI end-to-end data-exchange facilities can be treated as options, which can be made available to applications and application-services that are equipped to use them. Hence, the OSI- and SNA-based applications can readily *coexist* in the same node, and in the future may be designed to attach to either SNA or OSI transport-service-providers.

3. Much of the differences in the communications subsystems can be made transparent to the application programmers through the use of a *common programming interface*. Communication architecture independence can be achieved at this level.

4. *Common support functions* ultimately can be provided efficiently for both SNA and OSI services, including:

    - Application-services such as system management, security services, and directory services

- ▪ Shared node services (e.g., node operations, buffer management, process creation)
- ▪ Shared line resources

5. Lowering costs of high performance *bridges, routers, and gateways*, make them more feasible, where necessary.

Taking full advantage of all these factors can result in the progressive integration of SNA and OSI as key aspects of OSNA within SAA. The end result sought is a major enlargement and enrichment of evolving services, including key OSI facilities, the new network usability provided by SAA, and growth in new function.

2.7.2   Steps to Communicability

To enable communication in the multivendor world, therefore, OSNA needs to evolve to include:

1. *Common program interfaces* that shield the application from the differences in the several (SNA and OSI) end-to-end protocol stacks (see Section 7.2).

2. *Multiple subnetworks.* Communication should be feasible, across (for example) any of the six subnetworks shown in Figure 2.9 (i.e., SDLC WAN, X.25, LANs, MANs, ISDN, Frame Relay, and voice/data bandwidth managers), for pairs of applications (in end-systems) having the same end-to-end data exchange facilities. For example:

   a) Applications on SNA data-exchange facility at both ends
   b) Applications on OSI data-exchange facilities at both ends

   Figure 2.9 conveys that any of these subnetworks (including the one featuring voice/ data bandwidth management), may be used by the end-systems shown.

3. *Concatenation* of various combinations of the subnetworks shown in Figure 2.9. Bridges or routers may connect pairs of such subnetworks, so that an end-system on one subnetwork can communicate with an end-system on another subnetwork. (This is discussed in Chapters 12, 17, and 19.)

4. *A backbone network*, through which traffic using other protocols (SNA Subarea, APPN, OSI, TCP/IP, NetBIOS) may pass. In this case, many different types of end-systems can use a common multiprotocol transport.

5. *Gateways* to transform some widely used application-services and end-to-end protocols, like electronic mail and file transfer. These gateways will be mostly at layer 7 (see Section 6.6).

6. *Common services* for multiple protocol stacks. Prime candidates (for some combinations of stacks) include:

   - ▪ System management
   - ▪ Network-wide directory services
   - ▪ Routing based on dynamic topology data
   - ▪ Nondisruptive dynamic reconfiguration
   - ▪ Recovery by synch point and backout facilities

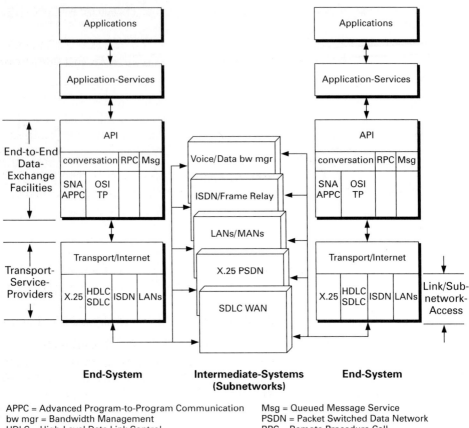

Figure 2.9 Target capability of general interoperability.

- Software download and automated change management
- Overall control of congestion
- Bandwidth management
- Performance optimization

One illustration of a combination of the above objectives, highlighting items 3 and 4, is shown in Figure 2.10. Each of the LANs shown may in fact be clusters of connected LANs. The multiprotocol backbone could be high-speed versions of one the types shown: voice/data bandwidth managers, ISDN, Frame Relay, LANs, MANs, X.25 Packet Switched Data Network, or SDLC WANs. Where needed, the backbone could be parallel combinations of these alternatives. The linkage between the peripheral LANs and the

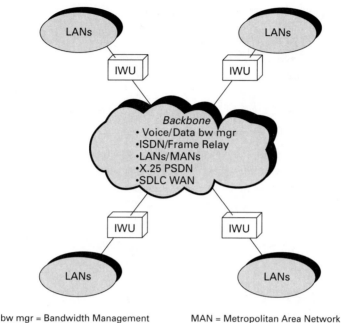

bw mgr = Bandwidth Management   MAN = Metropolitan Area Network
ISDN = Integrated Services Digital Network PSDN = Packet Switched Data Network
IWU = Inter Working Unit   SDLC = Synchronous Data Link Control
LAN = Local Area Network   WAN = Wide Area Network

Figure 2.10 Concatenated subnetworks via a backbone.

high-speed backbones (Inter Working Units) would be by bridge and/or router functions. Structures such as these are discussed in Chapter 12.

Conclusion

Chapter 1 described the needs of the enterprise for general communicability in a multiprotocol, multivendor, networking system. Chapter 2 takes an introductory step toward examining the structures and other requirements to meet these needs.

The broad distributed system structure, in macrolayers, is introduced, featuring the major segments: application-services, end-to-end data-exchange facilities, and the transport-service-providers.

A wide range of speed planes, types of cooperation, and domains of cooperation are acknowledged. Nevertheless, a single system image to the network as a utility is sought. The important concept of clients and servers is introduced.

Finally, the objectives of network synthesis are outlined, with attention to the integration of the SNA and OSI protocols, the expanding use of high-speed backbone facilities, and the ability of the backbone to pass multiple types of communication protocols.

Acknowledgments

I am indebted to P. Janson, M. D. Ayres, M. R. Jones, Jr., and M. C. Schein for valuable inputs and reviews of this chapter.

EXERCISES

2.1 Give a definition of cooperating systems.

2.2 Identify eight examples of application-services.

2.3 What are the three major types of application program interfaces for communications?

2.4 What are the three major speed planes for digital communication?

2.5 Give a definition of a domain for cooperative processing.

2.6 Name four types of cooperation among computing systems.

2.7 Give a definition of a client in a client–server relationship.

2.8 Identify five key functions that potentially can be shared by OSI- and SNA-based applications.

3
Architectural Structures

3.1 INTRODUCTION

This chapter is devoted to the communications architecture layers. They provide an orderly structure for communication in the multivendor environment. Though the layer definitions and the functions vary from one communications architecture to the next, the concept of layering helps us understand each of them; and we find a large amount of commonality.

A common, OSNA model incorporating multiple protocols is described, including OSI, SNA, TCP/IP, and NetBIOS. Four macrolayers, with the potential of three multiprotocol boundaries are involved. The potential of switch points at these boundaries offers the possibility of multiple combinations and permutations of mixed stacks in a multiprotocol system.

Where possible, the OSI model is used as a common reference. The concepts of logical connections and using formats and protocols are discussed. The layered functions of OSI, SNA, and TCP/IP are outlined and related.

3.2 OSI/SNA STRUCTURE OVERVIEW

3.2.1 Layering Structure

Layer design objectives

In all layered architectures, the designers seek layer definitions that will (a) insure *independence* among layers, so that future changes are limited to one layer, (b) allow *simple interlayer boundaries*, and (c) allow for multiple future *options* within a layer. Each layer makes use of the services of the layer below, and provides services to the layer above. Lower layers should be transparent to data sent from an upper layer.

Different design teams will follow these same criteria somewhat differently. A simplified overview of the OSI model (some parts are still under development) is shown

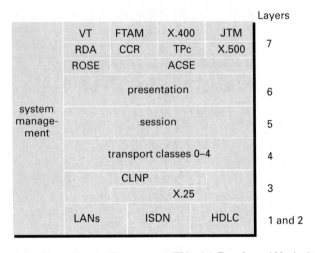

ACSE = Association Control Service Element   JTM = Job Transfer and Manipulate
CCR = Commit, Concurrency, and Recovery   RDA = Remote Data Access
CLNP = Connectionless Network Protocol   ROSE = Remote Operations Service Element
FTAM = File Transfer, Access, and Management TPc = Transaction Processing
HDLC = High-Level Data Link Control   VT = Virtual Terminal
ISDN = Integrated Services Digital Network   X.500 = Directories
                                             X.400 = Messaging

Figure 3.1 Overview of the OSI model and its component standards.

in Figure 3.1. At the top are application-services. Then come the three end-to-end services layers, in the presentation, session, and transport layers. Next are the connectionless and X.25 connection-oriented network protocols. Finally, at the bottom, are the various link-layer protocols, including multiple types of Local Area Networks (LANs) and their media attachments. Both OSI and SNA structures follow a seven-layer pattern. For comparison, the names and the approximate relationships of the SNA and OSI layers are shown in Figure 3.2. (Note that the layers do not line up exactly. A few functions that are in OSI layer n are in SNA layer $n+1$.)

The logical independence of layers is a condition that is difficult to achieve and can never be complete. Parameters for one layer are naturally generated in or passed from other layers. Nevertheless, a valuable degree of separation and independence has been achieved.

Layer liberties

The layers have proven to be somewhat large, leading to the designation of sublayers within layers, especially within layers 2 and 3. The distinction between layers and sublayers then becomes blurred and somewhat arbitrary. The location of functions within layers has also not proven to be sacred. Routing that is normally in layer 3 must sometimes be performed in layer 2 if performance in high-speed wide area networks (WANs) is to be obtained.

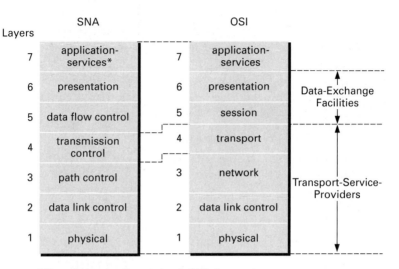

*Also called transaction services in SNA documents

Figure 3.2 SNA and OSI layers.

Also, although each layer assumes the existence of its lower layer, that lower layer may in fact be null. That is sometimes the case, for example, when the connection is only over a local area network, whose routing services exist within the data link control layer, and layer 3 may be null. Another type of situation is where performance demands a consolidation and simplification of upper layers. An example of this is the XTP protocols (see Section 13.6), where layers 4 and 5 have been combined.

Thus, the architecture can be expected to evolve continuously. Some liberties with the structure may be necessary to meet changing needs. Nevertheless, the layer structures provide the essential reference model for coordinated efforts.

Two macro layers

The seven layers of SNA and OSI are not identical. However, they are very similar. They both fit the general description shown in Figure 3.3, which first divides the structure into upper and lower layers as follows:

Lower layers (transport-service-providers). The lower layers consist of diverse subnetworks, and an end-to-end transport facilitator in layer 4. These transport-service-providers in layers 1 through 4 are then available for any of the upper-layer protocol stacks.

▪   *Layers 1–3.* The lower three layers include transmission subnetworks, like X.25 packet switching data networks, LANs, ISDN, and wide area, multihop networks using data link controls such as HDLC, SDLC, or newer frame relays at the lowest layers. These may be highly complex, involving many intermediate nodes in the transmission of messages from end to end. The services provided in layers 1, 2, and 3, may pass messages

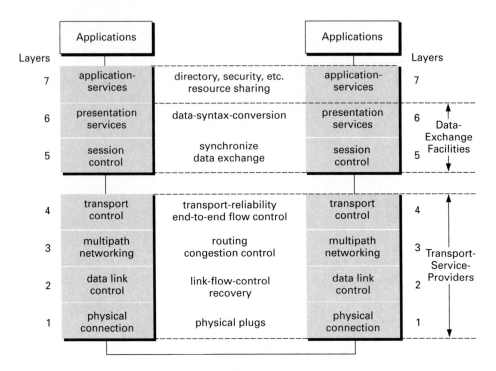

Figure 3.3 Functions within two macro layers.

along a complex route from origin to destination. LANs, leased lines, and switched services may act as links within a larger network.

- *Layer 4.* This layer oversees communication across multiple underlying transport facilities. It may be concerned with end-to-end transport reliability and end-to-end flow control.

Layers 2, 3, or 4 may contain *error recovery* and *flow control* functions. The optimum distribution of these functions among the three layers can depend on the technology available. In particular, the use of high-speed links and switches, with low error rates, encourage a trend toward lighter and faster protocols, and more dependence on end-box to end-box recovery and flow control at layer 4, rather than intermediate box-to-box facilities at layer 2. The NetBIOS protocol is not a networking protocol, but is designed for point-to-point operations on a LAN. Its occupation of layers 3 and 4 is therefore minimal to nonexistent.

Upper layers (end-to-end facilities).   The upper layers are formed into multiple stacks, such as stacks for SNA or OSI protocols. Different application programming interfaces, such as conversation, remote procedure call, and transaction messaging, may require somewhat different upper-layer stacks. These upper layers have two primary purposes:

- *End-to-End Data-Exchange*. Layer 5 provides a set of common signals that may be used by partner applications for their own purposes of synchronizing and regulating the dialog between them. Layer 6 may include data conversion to suit the needs of the end users.

- *Application-Services*. Layer 7 includes common application-services like file transfer, store-and-forward messaging services, and system management.

The term **end-to-end logical connection** is variously defined, but is understood generally to designate all the services in layers 5 through 7 that are established to further a communication between two application-processes. End-to-end services for the logical connection are distributed as a matched pair, with function in the origin node and the destination node. The functional interaction is between processes in the origin and destination nodes, regardless of the number of intermediate nodes in between. The distribution of function in these two end-nodes need not be equal.

Network control services, for directory and connection assistance, are also in layer 7; they are distributed among control points in the network. In APPN and OSI, these control points can be in every node. In SNA subarea networks, the corresponding services are distributed among the regional System Service Control Points (SSCPs). Nevertheless, in both APPN and subarea networks, there is a bilevel of network control for the end-nodes. In subarea networks, the bilevel is between the end-nodes and a SSCP. In APPN, that bilevel is between the end-node and its adjacent serving network-node.

The end-user's view of the network (that of the application-process) tends to focus attention on the elements of layers 7 through 5. This view sees the end-to-end logical connection as the important users of the "cloud" that is the common transport-service-provider, layers 4 through 1.

The "cloud (or transport-service-provider) people," on the other hand, concentrate on the many variations in the transmission process in layers 1 through 4. Fortunately, the complexities of the transmission subsystems can be immaterial to the layers above that cloud.

OSI/SNA layer functions

The basic functions of each of the seven layers are further outlined in Figure 3.3. The functions provided are very similar in the SNA and the OSI specifications, even though the details of the functions differ, and the distribution of functions among the layers is somewhat different in the two systems. These key functions are:

- *Layer 7:* This layer, application-services (called transaction services in SNA), controls such functions as the establishment of facilities for program-to-program communication, configuration activation services, directory services, distributed data services, messaging services, and document interchange. These are architected services.

- *Layer 6:* This layer, presentation services, is concerned with the interpretation of verbs received from APIs. It also does the conversion of data between the possibly different syntax and formats of the communicating end users (program, device, or person).

- *Layers 5 and 4:* These layers are both end-to-end control facilities. In OSI and SNA, the functions are distributed somewhat differently between layers 5 and 4. In both architectures, their layer-5 purpose is to synchronize the data exchange in an orderly interchange; and to regulate the user's send/receive flows. Layer 4 seeks to exercise end-to-end flow control, so that the two ends are able to handle the flow; to insure the reliability of the underlying transmission subsystems, including sequence numbering; and to encipher data if security is needed. Layer 5 primarily is under the control of the application. Layer 4 has flows, signals, and operations with the transport facilities beneath.

- *Layer 3:* This layer may have two distinct functions: (1) *a subnetwork,* involving *multipath routing* from source to destination end-nodes, among multiple intermediate-nodes. These nodes may be connected by links using protocols such as SDLC or HDLC. Also involved are *flow controls* within this subnetwork of intermediate-nodes. Multiplexing, segmenting, and blocking may be involved. (2) *Internetworking* for concatenated subnetworks, such as LANs, X.25 subnetworks, and ISDNs.

- *Layer 2:* Two sets of functions are found in the data link control layer: (1) *Fixed-path configurations* may include point-to-point connections, multipoint, or party-line connections, and local area networks. Fixed-path data link control may (or may not) provide link-layer flow controls and link-layer recovery from error, in flows between adjacent nodes. (2) *Multipath routing* can exist at layer 2 among intermediate-nodes of a wide area subnetwork. The purpose (but not the technique) of such routing is comparable to that in layer 3, but it is sometimes done at this lower layer for simplicity and performance.

- *Layer 1:* This layer, physical connections to adjacent nodes, involves the physical plugs and associated electrical signals, to provide a transparent transmission of any bit stream.

All of the layers need to be part of a composite connection and routing process. For these purposes, many of the layers may also have one or both of the following functions:

- *Logical connection establishment* with its peer, to prepare for message exchange and arrange for needed resources at that layer

- *Address handling*, which may involve interpretation or translation of the address for use within that layer

In addition, the following functions may need to be done within the layers of subnetworks and/or the end-to-end controls:

- *Message size manipulation*, possibly involving blocking, deblocking, segmenting, and re-assembly of messages

- *Error detection and recovery,* when the performance of the lower layers requires surveillance and correction

- *Flow control*

Error detection and flow control, as well as the maintenance of orderly flows, all can be aided by numbering or counting the successive message units, at one or more layers. Missing, duplicated, or out-of-sequence message units can be detected. Since the message units are numbered, the sender can expect orderly acknowledgments. If, after a set time interval, no acknowledgment is received, the sender will know that a particular numbered message needs to be resent. In addition, the sender can agree to avoid over-running the receiver, by sending a limited number of messages, and then waiting until the receiver acknowledges receipt of a numbered message.

The link level (layer 2), the network level, (layer 3), and layers 4 and 5, dealing with end-to-end controls, each have different flow-control and error-control problems. Hence, separate sequence numbering is sometimes used at one or more of these layers, particularly layers 2 and/or 4.

In summary, an overall sketch of the primary functions in all seven layers is shown in the "wineglass" of Figure 3.4. This illustrates the fact that the upper cup and the base contain a wide variety of facilities. Both of these can be expected to grow further.

3.2.2 Networks and Subnetworks

The term *network* deserves some further discussion. A difficulty is that every network can be viewed as part of some larger network concept. As discussed in Chapter 2, and illustrated in Figure 2.5, the network includes not only data-delivery functions but also a

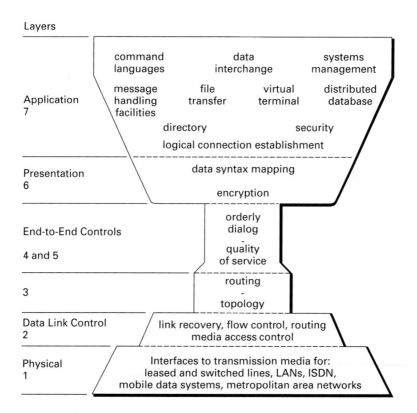

Figure 3.4 The wineglass of layered functions.

growing variety of application-services, such as file transfer, distributed data, messaging, directory, and remote job managing services. It is all relative. Hence different persons will refer to something as a network or a subnetwork, depending on their viewpoint.

An increasingly useful term is the *transport-service-provider*, or transport network, referring to the aggregate of everything in layer 4 and below. Occasionally, one also refers to the network, such as a LAN, that exists at the data link control layer. They are each part of the broader network. Within a Data Link Control (DLC) network, one can, moreover, have switched facilities managed by the carrier, using its own internal set of protocols. Alternatively, there may be a high-performance T1[1] mesh network within the DLC network.

SNA has used the term **subnetwork** to mean "administratively autonomous among others, all of which can be joined to form an integrated, composite, logical network."

OSI defines a **subnetwork** as "*a collection of equipment and physical media that forms an autonomous whole, and that can be used to interconnect other real systems for purposes of communications.*" Examples of such subnetworks would be commonly recognized carrier-supplied public networks (like X.25 packet switching networks), the data-delivery portions of private-supplied networks, and local area networks.

Adopting the OSI terminology, each of the networks described above, as being within another network, can be termed a *subnetwork*. In OSI terminology (ISO 8648),[2] the data transmission systems, which have commonly been called "networks," can be considered to be *subnetworks* within the larger concept of network that includes application-services, end-to-end data-exchange facilities, and transport-service-providers.

3.2.3   Primary Transmission Subnetworks

Another categorization deals with *end-systems* and *intermediate-systems*. As shown in Figure 3.5, the end-systems and (one or more) intermediate-systems together make the network (or subnetwork).[3] Intermediate-systems perform only functions allocated to the lowest three layers of the OSI reference model, having to do with data delivery. Functions within the end-systems may also provide these same intermediate functions, but end-systems must additionally provide the functions above these three lowest layers. The point at which the *subnetwork services* are offered is usually within the end-systems, as shown in Figure 3.5. In APPN architecture, the end-system is called an *end-node*, and the intermediate-systems are called *network-nodes*. These terms describe the primary mission of the nodes.[4]

---

1.   T1 lines are generally available at speeds of 1.54 Mbps.

2.   International Standard ISO 8648: 1988 (E), Information processing systems—Open Systems Interconnection—Internal organization of the Network Layer.

3.   The term "intermediate-system" is sometimes used for an entire data delivery subnetwork, and sometimes for the individual intermediate-nodes of which the subnetwork is composed.

4.   Despite these primary missions, the network-node may at times also contain applications, and the end-node does have a small routing capability to an adjacent network-node.

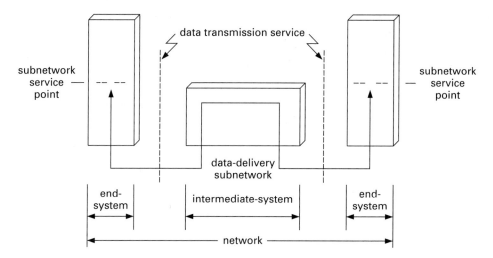

Figure 3.5 Subnetwork services offered at points within the end-systems.

Internode protocols often use the abbreviations for these node types, as shown in Figure 3.6. Hence we have ES-IS protocols, EN-NN protocols, IS-IS protocols, and NN-NN protocols. The user is primarily interested in the ES-IS and EN-NN protocols, while the transport-service-provider is more concerned with the other two.

A simplified overview of the target enterprise network is illustrated in Figure 3.7. There are five types of data-delivery *subnetworks* that will have large numbers of users:

1. Local area networks, including bridged combinations of the five LANs already accepted or proposed as standards: collision detection or Ethernet (version 2 and the 802.3 standard), token ring, token bus, fiber FDDI, and metropolitan area networks

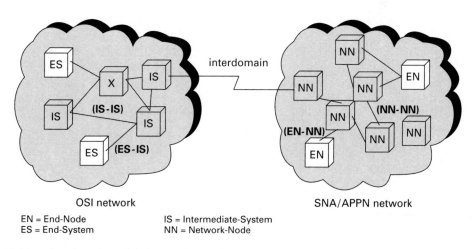

EN = End-Node   IS = Intermediate-System
ES = End-System   NN = Network-Node

Figure 3.6 (IS-IS), (ES-IS), (NN-NN), (EN-NN), and interdomain protocols.

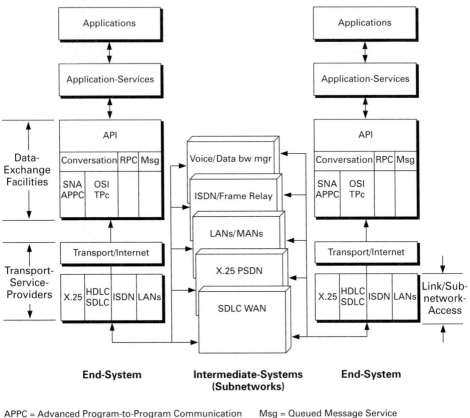

Figure 3.7 Target capability of general interoperability.

2. X.25 packet switched data networks (PSDNs)

3. SDLC wide area networks (including both subarea and advanced peer-to-peer networks)

4. ISDN (including narrowband and broadband) and Frame Relay

5. Bandwidth-managed networks (IDNX-like)[5] for voice, video, and data transmissions

The SDLC system is a wide area network, providing routing among mesh-connected intermediate-nodes. So too is the X.25 packet switching data network. LANs provide

5. IDNX is a series of products for voice/data bandwidth management, produced by Network Equipment Technologies, Inc.

higher-speed transmission over smaller distances. ISDN promises the ability to handle digitized image, voice, and data on access lines as well as in long-haul transmission. Private bandwidth-managed subnetworks mix voice and data. These are layer-2 facilities, which in theory could match any of the end-system transport facilities shown.

Each of these can be considered as a network, whose function is the delivery of data from one end-system to another end-system. Moreover, each may be used as a subnetwork within another network. Not every enterprise will have need of all five of these types of subnetworks. However, many enterprises are faced with two or more of these. In particular, local area networks, X.25 PSDN, and some proprietary networks (like SDLC WAN) are found in many. All of these subnetworks are largely independent of the higher-layer protocols and standards (layers 5 through 7) used for end-to-end communication. All of these subnetworks are currently part of SNA. It is feasible, therefore, for all of them to be further integrated into an overall, multiprotocol network architecture.

3.2.4   End-to-End Data-Exchange Facilities

Controlling the data flows and synchronizing the flows over these subnetworks will be the control functions at the two ends of each communication. For generality, we refer to these as *end-to-end data-exchange facilities*. These concern things like data flow control, queueing, and data conversion. The strategic direction, for many applications, will be to focus on a common *conversational interface* and only two sets of such *end-to-end control stacks*: one will be those of OSI; the other will be an industry standard, such as SNA's LU 6.2. Another very popular API is the *Remote Procedure Call (RPC)*; as explained in Section 7.5, industry standards for RPC are underway. Finally, some applications use a *messaging* (or message queue) type of API.

3.2.5   Transport-Service-Providers

The lower layers of the end-system contains transport-service-providers. The lower part of these transport-service-providers includes the means to access leased and switched lines, and subnetworks like X.25, LANs, MANs, and ISDN. The upper part of the transport-service-providers houses the network layer and the transport layer. The latter is an end-to-end service to insure the performance of the lower-layer transmission functions. The network layer includes the interworking of cascaded links and/or multiple subnetworks, in those cases where it is needed. This interworking may be based on network protocols of SNA, OSI, or TCP/IP.

3.2.6   Backbones and Boundary-Nodes

The end-nodes, in Figure 3.7, may have multiple interfaces for multiple types of subnetworks. More than one, of course, will not always be feasible, particularly in the smaller nodes. The other desirable feature, therefore, is to have one subnetwork, a *backbone subnetwork*, capable of serving multiple types of end-nodes. Such a backbone is said to be a *multiprotocol transport network*. *Boundary-nodes* are those nodes of the backbone subnetwork that have this capability to serve multiple types of end-nodes. The boundary nodes have *network-access* units, with *interface converters*, and transfer capa-

Layers

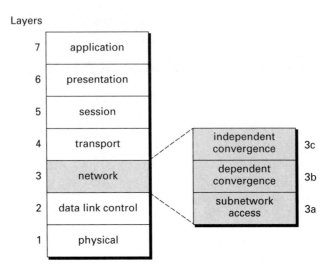

Figure 3.8 Partitioning the OSI network layer into three sublayers.

bilities (these network-access units, however, are not necessarily packaged within the boundary-nodes; see Section 12.9.4). Then, any of the popular end-nodes (each with any *one* of the popular end-node interfaces) can, with the help of network-access units, have efficient passage through the backbone network. In that case, the protocols used within the backbone are probably less important than the ease of connection of diverse end-nodes, and the efficiency of transport.

Lower-cost and special-purpose end-nodes may also have limited capabilities to participate in networking. Their interfaces to the network may be simplified to the point where the boundary-node to which the end-node is attached must absorb some of the end-node's inadequacies. Hence, a number of special end-node attachments and procedures may be necessary.

3.2.7 OSI Network Sublayers

The OSI layer 3 has been subdivided into three sublayers, as shown in Figure 3.8, for three roles [Burg89]:

- *Subnetwork Independent Convergence Protocol (SNICP)* at layer 3c
- *Subnetwork Dependent Convergence Protocol (SNDCP)* at layer 3b
- *Subnetwork Access Protocol (SNAcP)* at layer 3a

These are possible roles. Sometimes only one of these roles will be needed. Also, it is not necessary for the three roles to be fulfilled by three distinct protocols. A single protocol may fulfill one, two, or three roles. Consider Figure 3.9 where two end-systems wish to communicate across two subnetworks (a LAN and an X.25 PSDN). The two subnetworks

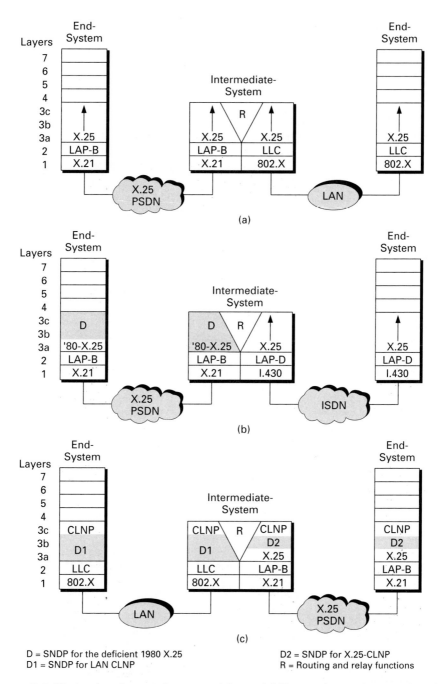

D = SNDP for the deficient 1980 X.25   D2 = SNDP for X.25-CLNP
D1 = SNDP for LAN CLNP   R = Routing and relay functions

Figure 3.9 Three situations at the network layer: **(a)** Harmonious subnetworks using 1984 X.25 Packet Level Protocols. No 3b or 3c sublayers are involved. **(b)** Hop-by-hop harmonization. **(c)** Internetwork protocol [Burg89].

are joined by an intermediate-system that contains an appropriate protocol relay. This network layer substructure is designed to handle three situations.

- *Case 1*. The 3a protocol in both of the subnetworks being interconnected is sufficient to support all the elements of the OSI Network Service (NS). No further protocols in 3b or 3c are needed. This is true, for example, when both subnetworks fully support the *1984 X.25 Packet Level Protocol (PLP)*, as in Figure 3.9(a).

- *Case 2*. One or both of the subnetwork 3a protocols is somewhat deficient and needs to be augmented so as to support all the elements of the OSI NS. This has been called the "hop-by-hop harmonization method." The *1980 version of X.25 PLP* would be one example of a deficient protocol (because it does not include features specified in the later 1984 version). That augmentation is the role of the SNDCP (3b) sublayer. No 3c sublayer is needed. (See Figure 3.9(b).)

- *Case 3*. This case is the use of an internet protocol as the SNICP (3c) across all the subnetworks. The 3b layer then provides the "glue" to make the 3a and 3c work together, as shown in Figure 3.9(c).

In each case, a relay function connecting subnetworks insures that the semantics of the data is maintained across the interworking unit. This includes, for example, the passing of OSI addresses, the boundaries of the transport layer's data, and perhaps the quality-of-service characteristics associated with that communication.

The *Subnetwork Independent Functions* supply full-duplex Network Protocol Data Unit (NPDU) transmission between any pair of neighbor systems. They are independent of the specific subnetwork or data link service operating below them, except for recognizing two generic types of subnetworks [ISO10589].

- *General topology subnetworks*, which include HDLC point-to-point, HDLC multipoint, and dynamically established data links (such as X.25, X.21, and Public Switched Telephone Network (PSTN) links)

- *Broadcast subnetworks*, which include ISO 8.802 LANs

The CLNP is usually referred to as the *internet protocol*. Unfortunately, this can be confused with a particular internet protocol developed as part of the TCP/IP system.[6] The OSI internet is the successor to the TCP Internet. In principle, layer 3c accepts any subnetwork protocol (e.g., X.25 or SNA Path Control) at the subnetwork-access 3a layer. As described in Chapter 12, this same sublayer concept can be applied in the SNA realm, where the SNA path control performs a layer-3c function, and the X.25 PLP again functions as a layer 3a.

The *subnetwork dependent functions* mask the characteristics of the subnetwork or data link services from the subnetwork independent functions. These include:

- Determining Subnetwork Point of Attachment (SNPA) addresses

---

6.   The TCP/IP Internet protocol was originally initiated by the U.S. Department of Defense.

- Initializing data links
- Segmentation
- Call establishment and clearing on dynamically established data links

3.3 FUNCTION SUBSETS

Function subsets are prescribed families of options that exist within each layer. For example, the data flow control for one end-to-end logical connection need not be the same as the data flow control for another logical connection. Even within a given node, one application-process in one logical connection may employ one function subset of a given layer; a different application-process using another logical connection may employ a different function subset in the same layer.

3.3.1 Option Profiles

Both the SNA and OSI layers contain a growing number of options, to meet the diverse needs of widely differing applications. This finer structure is illustrated in Figure 3.10. OSI, for example has defined twelve functional units at the session layer and five classes at the transport layer.

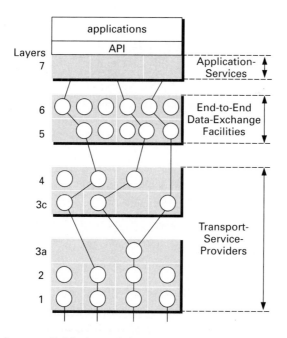

Figure 3.10 Options available in each layer.

A vertical set of options is required by each application. Looking at the seven functional layers and the variety of functions that can be offered in each layer, we see that the total number of possible function combinations is very large. The architecture needs to provide a unifying structure for all these situations; it must also specify a limited set of common functions, so as to permit a more general communicability among programs and devices in the combined network.

OSI profiles

Because of the relatively large number of options, the selection of preferred option sets, called **profiles**, has been the preoccupation of many groups. For OSI, this has included the following:

- EWOS—European Workshop for Open Systems
- CCTA—(U.K.) Central Computer and Telecommunications Agency
- AOWS—OSI Asia-Oceania Workshop
- CEN—Comite European de Normalisation
- CENELEC—Comite European Electricite de Normalisation
- SPAG—Standards Promotion and Application Group
- NIST/OWI—National Institute of Standards and Technology OSI Implementation Workshop
- INTAP—Interoperability Technology Association for Information Processing

A gradual consensus among these groups, on key sets of OSI options, at each layer, encourages manufacturers to concentrate on their selections. In this process of consensus on option sets, focal points include the development of key sets of profiles and specifications:

- EN/ENV—European profiles developed by CEN/CENELEC
- INTAP profiles
- U.S. GOSIP—U.S. Government OSI Profile
- U.K. GOSIP—U.K. Government OSI Profile
- COSAC—Canadian Open Systems Application Criteria
- CALS—Computer Aided Logistics Support

The regional profiles may eventually reference a set of International Standard Profiles (ISPs) being developed by ISO. These, however, are not very far along in many areas.

SNA profiles

Profiles (i.e., commonly used sets of options) are also defined in SNA for its upper layers, including presentation services, data flow control, and transmission control layers— referred to as Presentation Services (PS), Function Management (FM), and Transmission Service (TS) profiles, respectively. These profiles continue to evolve as common usage dictates.

Only a particular combination of these profiles is supported by products. In SNA, this grouping is called an *LU type. A given LU type will only support sessions that draw from its allowable mix of PS, FM, and TS profiles.* A distinguishing feature of a product is the LU types it supports. All sessions should subscribe to one of the common LU types if general communicability is to be promoted.[7] For a given session, these LU types and the selected profiles are specified in fields (of the Bind commands) called profile and usage fields. This Bind process is discussed more fully in Section 8.7.2.

In SNA, some profiles, such as those for path control and data link control, are usually built into the products at design time. (Products that have common subsets of transmission facilities are identified as SNA node types. These are defined in Section 8.6.4.) Other subsets, namely, those pertaining to the session-oriented functions (layers 4 through 7), may be selected at the time of session establishment. (That selection is done via parameters in the SNA Bind command and OSI Connect Protocol Data Units.)

The combination of layering, the availability of options for function subsets within each layer, and the grouping of commonly used functions into LU types are all steps toward the goal of permitting systems to be tailored, but also promoting broad communicability.

3.3.2   U.S. GOSIP/MAP/TOP OSI Options

We illustrate the selection of OSI options with three sets, those specified by U.S. GOSIP and those supported currently by MAP and TOP.

- *MAP* (Manufacturing Automation Protocol) was initially undertaken in the early 1980s by General Motors to facilitate plant automation that involved communication among diverse vendor computers and other programmed automation equipments. The successive versions of MAP (a profile) have been largely reached in appropriate NIST workshops. The result has been a seven-layer specification, using appropriate OSI standards. It includes the broadband 802.4 token bus for plant floor distribution.

- *TOP* (Technical and Office Protocol) was originally initiated by the Boeing Company to facilitate communication among its large and small computer systems. It, too, is based largely on OSI standards. It favors the 802.3 LAN for local area communications, but also includes 802.4 and 802.5. TOP 3.0 currently is a superset of MAP 3.0, containing all the MAP 3.0 functions except manufacturing messaging.

- *GOSIP* is the U.S. government–sponsored effort to arrive at profiles to be used in all government procurements.

A comparison of these three (GOSIP version 1, MAP, TOP) sets of profiles is given in Figure 3.11. The core of the OSI standards are common to all three. MAP does not however, use X.25; and MAP and TOP both have selected a few standards that the other has not selected. Later versions of GOSIP add other facilities. Version 2, for example, adds the Virtual Terminal and Narrowband ISDN.[8]

---

7.   LU type 6.2 is the one recommended for future development (see Chapter 10).
8.   SAA supports the GOSIP and MAP 3.0 profiles.

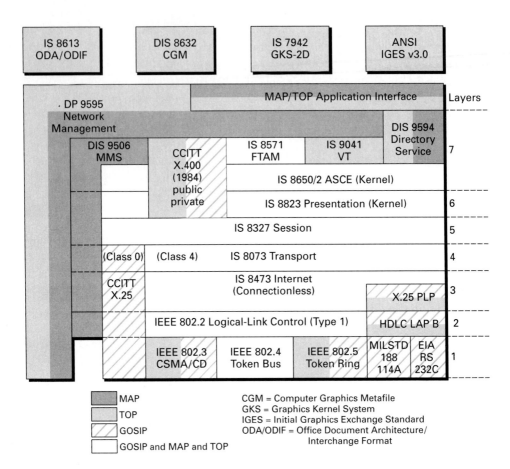

Figure 3.11 GOSIP, MAP, and TOP profiles.

3.4 MULTIARCHITECTURE BOUNDARIES

Experience has shown the need for flexibility in the use of multiple options and the interoperability of facilities in various combinations. Having examined the layering structures of communications architectures, in the above, we now review the ways in which these layers could be grouped and packaged, so as to mix and match capabilities of different architectures in complex network configurations.

We generally assume that two communicating end-systems have the same upper-level (layers 5 through 7) protocols (see Figure 3.3). A given upper-layer stack may then use one of several lower-layer (layers 1 through 4) transport stacks. Within the latter, the layers have a large and varied set of links and subnetworks that are commonly available to all of the transport-layer services (and hence to all upper-layer services as well).

3.4.1 The Transport Boundary

In the preceding chapter, it was noted that the seven layers of network structures can be advantageously grouped into two macro layers: the upper layers dealing with end-to-end data-exchange facilities, and the lower layers dealing with transport-service-providers. The boundary between these groups is one possible switching point, to provide flexible combinations of upper and lower options.

The significance of this boundary is reflected in the proposal by part of the UNIX community to provide a *transport API* at the top of the transport layer. This particularly includes advocates of the Transport Layer Interface (TLI) as a stable programming interface.[9] Similarly, X/Open Company Limited, a worldwide association of vendors, provides a portability guide, XPG3, that includes an XTI (X-Open Transport Interface) *for OSI and TCP/IP* networks. The XTI allows a user to employ either protocol stack, in a streaming data mode, after providing an identifier for the transport desired (see Section 13.7). Another indication of the utility of a boundary at this level was the proposal of the TOP user's group to produce a specification that allows NetBIOS based applications to run over the OSI Transport Layer Class 4 [LANTech89].

Perhaps the most significant insights, however, are in the proposals for multiprotocol gateways using the transport boundary [Simpson90]. Both Rose [Rose90] and Svobodova et al [Svobodova90] have published proposals for OSI T-4 to OSI T-0 gateways that in essence swap primitives at the transport layer.[10] Rose further proposes a similar transport bridge between OSI T-4 and TCP/IP. This would allow OSI end-systems to use a TCP/IP transport service. Rose also suggests a transport bridge between LU 6.2 and an OSI transport, allowing LU 6.2 end-systems to use an OSI transport service.

The proposed use of a boundary at this level (either a semantic boundary or an interface with defined syntax) has opened possibilities of having mixed stacks. For example, upper and lower groups could be related as *many to one*, as in Figure 3.12. The objective would be to provide a *common transport network that would be largely independent of upper-layer protocols* (even if some boundary-node intelligence were needed for each). Assuming that each pair of end-systems used the same upper-layer protocols, such a common transport could carry a variety of upper-layer protocols across the transport network. (This concept is further discussed in Section 12.9.)

The upper and lower groups could also be related as *one to many*, as shown in Figure 3.13. This objective would be that a given end-system could have the ability to select and use one of a number of alternative transport-service-providers.

---

9. The term *interface* is usually interpreted to mean a place where both the semantics and the syntax are architected. The term *protocol boundary*, on the other hand, is used for a place where the semantics are defined, but the syntax is not defined. Different systems will use different hardware or software syntax, such as program calls, interrupts, or supervisor calls.

10. This "primitive swapping" at the service boundary is different from a gateway that directly converts from one transport protocol to the other.

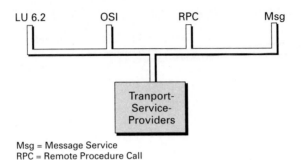

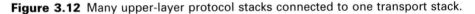

Msg = Message Service
RPC = Remote Procedure Call

Figure 3.12 Many upper-layer protocol stacks connected to one transport stack.

3.4.2   Three Protocol Boundaries

We now observe that there are two other switching points, at which mixed stacks are potentially feasible. These can exist within the upper and lower macro layers, as shown in Figure 3.14. The three potential switch boundaries then are at the:

- *Application Programming Interfaces (APIs)*, at the presentation services boundary, which serve both the application-processes and the common application-services.[11] One ultimate purpose of this boundary is to make the application program independent of all the underlying communication protocols. Today, this is the SAA Common Programming Interface (CPI).

---

11.   Figure 3.14 uses a simplification of the position of the API; in reality, elements of the API are not all at one level. The SAA Common Programming Interface, for example, has multiple elements, some of which are application programming interfaces to the application-services shown above the API in Figure 3.14. Examples of the elements of the SAA CPI include those for communications, resource/recovery, distributed database, and presentation manager.

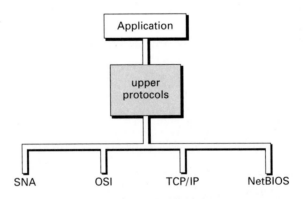

Figure 3.13 One upper-layer protocol stack connectable to any one of many transport stacks.

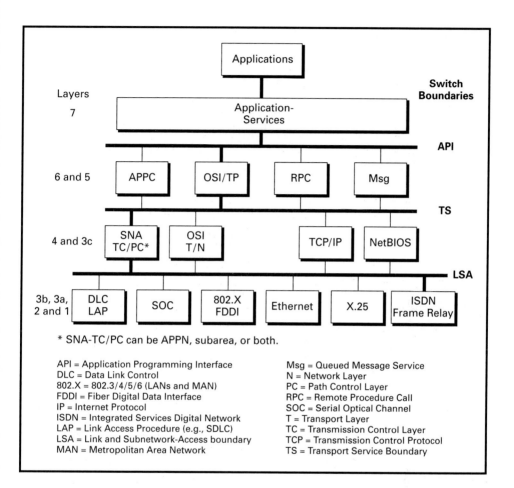

Figure 3.14 Potential service-switch-points at the API, transport, and link services boundaries (one of many possible paths indicated).

- *Transport Service (TS) boundary*, in the neighborhood below the application-oriented layers (layers 7, 6, and 5), and above the networking-oriented layers (layers 4 and 3c). As discussed above, the ultimate purpose of this boundary is to give the application, with its end-to-end data-exchange facilities, the opportunity to use alternative transport-service-providers.

- *Link/Subnetwork-Access (LSA) boundary*, below the networking-oriented layers (layers 4 and 3c), and above the link-access and subnetwork-access layers (layers 3a, 2, and 1). The ultimate purpose of this boundary is to make all the lower-layer link and subnetwork services commonly available to the protocol stacks, layer 3c and above. This is becoming an architected SNA open interface.

As shown in Figure 3.14, at each of the three boundaries, it is potentially feasible for any one of the elements above each boundary to connect to any one of the elements below the boundary. This is the one-to-multiple case. One application could use any one of multiple end-to-end data-exchange facilities. Also one end-to-end data-exchange facility could use one of multiple transports (layer 4). Also one network (layer 3c) could use one of multiple link/subnetwork access facilities (layers 2 to 3a). At the two lower boundaries, there also is the multiple-to-one case. That is, multiple kinds of end-to-end data-exchange facilities (e.g., SNA/OSI conversation, RPC, or message) could be carried over one transport (layer 4). Also multiple kinds of network (layer 3c) protocols could be carried over one link/subnetwork. Only one of these possible paths is highlighted in Figure 3.14; it shows the combination of OSI at layers 6 and 5, SNA at layers 4 and 3c, and ISDN at the lowest layers.

The concept of option profiles in Figure 3.10 is thus broadened. In addition to options at each layer within an architecture, there is the possibility of option groups drawn from multiple architectures. To achieve mixed stacks, the syntax at each boundary of Figure 3.14 need not be the same for each protocol stack. What is needed is that there be sufficient common semantics among the participants of a boundary that economical mappings are feasible.

Of course, not every possible path and mixed-stack combination is equally desirable or feasible. Larger end-systems might offer different combinations of such options, but many end-systems could economically offer only one combination. The efficiency of the architecture and design then determines how far in this direction it is economically feasible to go. SAA has published the CPI-C [SC26-4399]. IBM has published an initial version of the link/subnetwork-access boundary [HLMa]. X/Open has published the X/Open Transport Interface (XTI) [X/Open]. Of the three potential switch boundaries (the API at the presentation layer, the transport-services boundary, and the link/subnetwork-access boundary), the TS boundary is the most controversial. In particular, it has been argued that mixed stacks at this level are less desirable because they can delay migration to full OSI stacks. Time will tell which boundaries achieve greater utility.

Four layer groups

A summary of the four layer groups (layers 1 through 3a, layers 3c through 4, layers 5 through 6, and layer 7), involving multiple architectures and separated by the preceding three switching points, follows. Starting from the top:

1.   At *layer 7*, the *application layer*, there are groups of application-services, such as security, recovery, distributed data, remote job entry, and store and forward messaging. This layer also contains parts of key application subsystems, such as IBM's TSO, IMS and CICS. These application-services can have many components, and the preferred set evolves as applications evolve. Some of these application-services need to be shared so as to serve more than one of the underlying upper-layer protocol stacks. The SAA Common Programming Interface is the start of a trend for network independence at this API level. This independence, in effect, allows both applications and application-services to switch at the API between multiple upper-layer protocol stacks. A single API, for example, will be mapped to both OSI and SNA LU 6.2 stacks.

2.   At *layers 6 and 5*, there are a small number of parallel *end-to-end stacks* of protocol machines for the end-to-end services just beneath the APIs. Key examples are the OSI

protocols for presentation and session layers, and the corresponding SNA stacks (contained in LU 6.2) to provide APPC services. Remote procedure call services and messaging services also are located there. The corresponding layer-5 connection-oriented services for TCP and NetBIOS are usually incorporated in applications.

3.   *Layer 4 and the upper part of layer 3 (3c)* provide the upper, end-to-end layers with a multisubnetwork *transport service*. In OSI this layer 3c is the internetworking layer, and can contain either Connectionless Network Service (CLNS) or X.25 Connection-Oriented Service. In TCP, the corresponding sublayer is the Internet Protocol (IP) sublayer, that connects multiple subnetworks. In SNA, many of the same functions are provided by the APPN or Subarea path control layer. Except in the case of NetBIOS, a key element at this layer is the *network-entity* that is concerned with multipath routing. NetBIOS has no internet protocol or intermediate-system routing capability.

4.   *Layers 1, 2, and the lower part of layer 3 (sublayer 3a)* can be common to all of the above. This lowest region includes a set of links and subnetworks (called *link-services* in SNA). This set includes the subnetwork access X.25 packet switching protocols, multiple LANs (802.3, 4, 5, 6), FDDI, ISDN, Frame Relay, Serial Optical Channels, and SDLC data links. (A middle 3b sublayer may also be present to compensate for deficiencies in the 3a subnetwork access protocol.) These link/subnetwork services, therefore, can occupy positions corresponding to OSI layers 1, 2, 3a, and 3b. The services can exist as alternative, parallel options for the network sublayer 3c above. The link/subnetwork-access services can also be nested and cascaded to form composite subsystems (see Section 12.7).

3.5   LAYER TERMINOLOGY

A further understanding of the layering concepts and their architecture can be obtained by reviewing some layer-related definitions and terminology. While these are drawn from a combination of the OSI and SNA architectures, the concepts can help to illuminate any layered architecture.

3.5.1   Application-Process

We reserve the term **application-process** for that source or destination of information that is external to the network. The end user may be a program, an operator at an input/output device, or a storage medium such as cards, disks, or tapes. *However, any of these can be represented by code or logic that then appears to be the application-process.* Any application-process should be able to establish communication with another application-process via the network if the originating process knows (or can be told) only the nickname (the **symbolic_destination_name**) of the destination process.

An important unit within an application-process, which handles self-contained transactions, with definite beginnings and endings, is called in SNA a **transaction program (TP)** (see Figure 3.15). There may be multiple transaction programs in a given application-process. In OSI terminology, these are called **transaction program service units (TPSUs).**

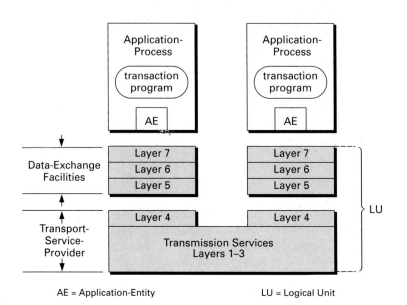

Figure 3.15 Positions of application-process, transaction program, and application-entity.

Also shown in Figure 3.15 is the SNA term **Logical Unit (LU)**. It was defined to include all end-to-end services, thus including the facilities in layers 4 through 6 and some connection services in layer 7 (but not including application-services like file transfer or network management).

3.5.2 Entities

An **entity**, in general, is a collection of services that is capable of sending or receiving information. It is composed of a group of **service elements**, each of which implements a set of communications services within a layer. An entity associates with a particular layer, so we refer to an n-entity, where n is the number of the layer in which the entity resides. Thus we have application-layer entities, like File Transfer, and network-layer entities, like internetworking.

Peer entities are entities in the same layer, which exchange messages according to a protocol, in order to achieve a common objective. The relationships between peer entities are illustrated in Figure 3.16. The peer protocol is a formal language, with defined message formats, syntax, and semantics. A simple "primitive" command given to a layer may generate a complex series of exchanges between the peer entities. These protocol exchanges are not usually visible to the user who issued the primitive service request.

Only a small part of an application-process is responsible for communication functions. That part is called an **application-entity** (see Figure 3.15). An application-process may use more than one application-entity. However, each application-entity represents only one application-process.

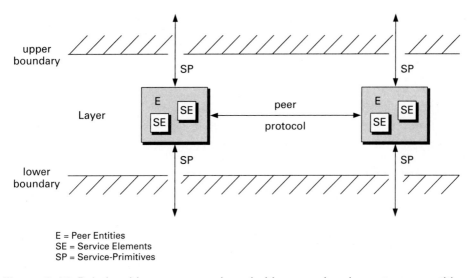

E = Peer Entities
SE = Service Elements
SP = Service-Primitives

Figure 3.16 Relationships among service primitives, service elements, peer entities, and peer protocols.

SNA does not talk about the application-entity, as OSI does, but there must be roughly comparable functions in every application-process that uses communications. Hence, even in the SNA world, we can refer to an *SNA application-entity*, understanding that while the basic purposes are similar, the protocols used are different, and the internal structures are variable in both the OSI and SNA cases.

3.5.3   Service-Access-Points

Service-Access-Point (SAP) is a term that denotes the means by which a user entity in layer *n+1* accesses a service of a provider entity in layer *n*. At a given time *a SAP connects only one pair of entities* in the two adjacent layers. However, an entity may have multiple SAPs associated with it at any time, as illustrated in Figure 3.17. A chain of SAPs connects each application-entity to its Network-layer Service-Access-Point (NSAP), as shown in Figure 3.18.[12] SAPs at a given layer are assigned a number to identify each one. These are called the **selectors** for that layer.

A given service-access-point may be the conduit for messages from different end-to-end logical connections. Within a service-access-point, therefore, there can be multiple **Connection-End-Points (CEPs)** in each SAP, as shown in Figure 3.19. A chain of SAPs (and CEPs within the SAPs) connects the entities in the presentation, session, and transport layers for a given association.

---

12.   In IBM's OSI/Communication Subsystem, this chain is assigned at the time the application-entity is registered at its node.

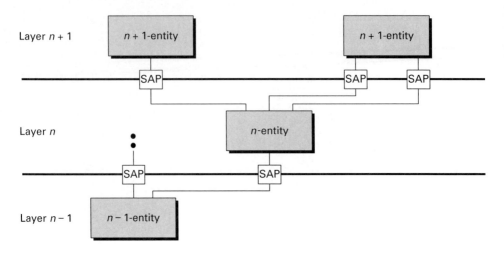

Layer $n + 1$

Layer n

Layer $n - 1$

SAP = Service-Access-Point

Figure 3.17 Service-access-points serving larger entities.

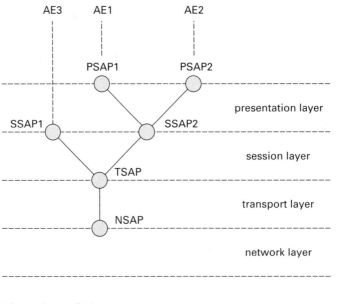

AE = Application-Entity
SAP = Service-Access-Point
XSAP = SAP for Layer X

Figure 3.18 String of service-access-points for each application-entity.

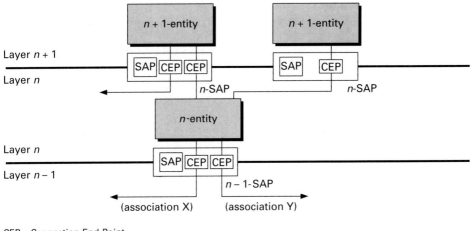

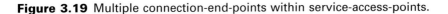

CEP = Connection-End-Point
SAP = Service-Access-Point

Figure 3.19 Multiple connection-end-points within service-access-points.

Each application-entity is unambiguously identified by a Presentation Service-Access-Point (PSAP) to which it is connected. Each PSAP, in turn, is connected, one-to-one to a Session layer SAP (SSAP).

Each service-access-point connects to only one entity in the layer above. A **connection** is the link between the service-access-points below two communicating *peer entities*. Logically, the connection behaves as if the two peers were directly connected. The support of the underlying layers is invisible to the entities engaged.

Multiplexing and splitting

Multiplexing and splitting (demultiplexing) are illustrated in Figure 3.20. As shown, multiplexing involves the connection of two or more CEPs at one layer (via a layer entity) to one CEP of the lower layer. This can, therefore, multiplex multiple logical connections on a given physical connection. The data thus multiplexed must carry sufficient ids to permit later separation of the multiple data streams. Splitting, on the other hand, involves the connection of one CEP at one layer (via a layer entity) to more than one CEP at the lower layer. A single circuit can thus be divided among multiple circuits. In this case, the data thus split must carry sufficient segmentation ids to permit later reconstruction of the split data stream.

A comparison with SNA shows a significant difference. First, we can say that the upper interface of LU 6.2 corresponds to the PSAP, and the lower LU boundary provides the LU with access to path control, much as an NSAP offers OSI transport entities access to the OSI network service. However, the multiplexing and splitting we saw in OSI is not present in SNA. In SNA, each equivalent PSAP is tied one-to-one to its own equivalent NSAP.

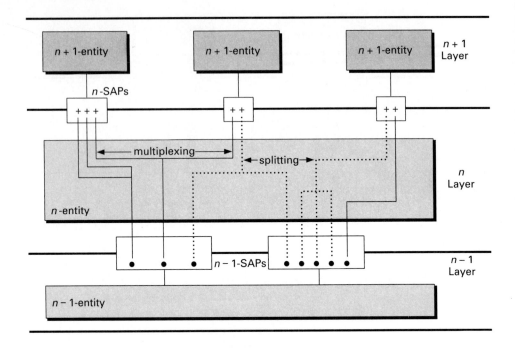

+ = (n) CEP
● = (n − 1) CEP

CEP = Connection-End-Point
SAP = Service-Access-Point

Figure 3.20 Multiplexing and splitting (demultiplexing) via connection-end-points in service-access-points.

Thus, in SNA both PSAPs and NSAPs are associated with individual applications, and they are tied together by a common address. In OSI, on the other hand, while the PSAPs are associated with applications, the NSAPs are not necessarily so tied. The OSI NSAP is more associated with a system (usually a node). Instead of the SNA PSAPs one-to-one correspondence with the NSAP, the OSI PSAP addresses, of applications located at the same NSAP, are hierarchically structured and include the address of that common NSAP (see Section 12.3.3).

3.6 LOGICAL CONNECTIONS

In both SNA and OSI, facilities can be established at both ends so that the upper layers of the partners can be connected and communicate effectively. In SNA, these sets of facilities at the two partners, the logical connection between them, and the consequent flows between them is called a **session**. In OSI, the roughly corresponding term is the **association** (plus a P-connection, S-connection, and T-connection). (See Section 9.6.)

3.6.1   SNA Sessions

A basic SNA concept is that of a session. *The session is a temporary logical connection for an exchange of messages in accordance with ground rules that have been agreed to for that exchange.* These ground rules are reflected in the set of SNA functions that are assigned to that session. The ground rules pertain to such functions as pacing the flows (to prevent exceeding session buffer capacities), recovery facilities at the session layer, waiting for responses, groupings of requests and responses, and data formatting.

Sessions connect logical units (LUs; see Figure 3.15). The LUs, in turn represent a pair of application-entities, which are the real object of the session. Each LU can support multiple sessions, each session being associated with an LU of a different destination. Some LUs can also support parallel sessions—that is, multiple sessions between the same pair of LUs. Thus, the LUs provide multiple ports for access to the inner layers of the SNA network. The objective is to achieve general communicability among application-processes via the LUs.

Sessions are established with a specific **mode**. The mode identifies session parameters, such as the maximum RU (Request Unit) size, and whether encryption is to be used. The *class of service* requested of the route to the destination currently can be derived from the mode name.

3.6.2   OSI Associations

The OSI **association** is a cooperative relationship between entities in the application layer, to which a specific context, or set of ground rules, has been applied. Associations can exist without underlying transport connectivity. The OSI association can be said to roughly correspond to the SNA session, in that, in both cases, their establishment leads to the further establishment of a set of peer entities in the end-system's layers 4 through 7. It is more precise, therefore, to say that the session is roughly analogous to the association plus a P-connection, S-connection, and T-connection.

Each association connects a pair of application-entities, as illustrated in Figure 3.15. In each layer (4 through 7), then, there are layer entities that serve a given association. These layer entities, for a given association, are connected by a string of service-access-points, as was shown in Figure 3.19.

An application-process may have multiple application-entities. Each application-entity may have multiple associations. However, each application-entity normally connects to only one PSAP. Thus, multiple associations of one application-entity can share one PSAP. In that PSAP each association has a unique CEP. The CEP at each layer is built only as the connection for an association is completed at that layer.

The **PSAP address** is, in effect, a unique application-entity address. An application-entity's PSAP address consists of one or more NSAP addresses and the SAP selectors in each of the upper layers. That address thus defines the route through SAPs and entities in layers 4 through 7. Multiple PSAPs generally converge to fewer SAPs in the lower layers. In fact, all PSAPs may converge to a single NSAP for the node, although this is not necessary (see Figure 3.18).

To reiterate, at any instant in time, each application_entity_title is bound to a single presentation address. Each application-entity can support multiple associations at the same time. These associations may be to different partners. Parallel associations to the same partner are also allowed. Each association is supported by connections at a PSAP, SSAP, and TSAP that define the presentation address of the application-entity. Each association uses separate connection-end-points in each of the SAPs, except when there is multiplexing in the transport layer, for then multiple associations may share a connection-end-point in an NSAP.

An association can be initiated in several ways. It may be in response to a Call at the API. (APIs can be implemented at several points in the OSI stack. A common point for the API is the services of the presentation layer.) In response to such a Call, the OSI **Association Control Service Element (ACSE)** (which is responsible for the establishment, maintenance, and termination of associations) issues an A-Associate command. That command contains two application_entity_titles and two PSAP addresses, which are needed to establish an association. At the API, the association is given an **association-id**. At the transport layer, a corresponding **reference number** is kept and applied to every PDU for that association.

OSI session and presentation layers do not include multiplexing. Hence, there is a one-to-one correspondence between a transport connection, a session connection, and a presentation connection. Therefore, knowing the transport connection (from the *reference number*) determines the remainder of the incoming path to an application-entity.

3.6.3 Logical-Links

At the lower layers, also, we have many ways of providing physical connections. These include many types of physical links and physical subnetworks, such as CPU-CPU channels, point-to-point connections, LANs, MANs, ISDN, Frame Relay, and X.25 PSDNs. We need a way of talking about these in general. A very useful concept, therefore, is that of the **logical-link** *between a pair of network-layer entities*. This concept, in the lower half of the seven-layer structure, complements the concept of the *end-to-end logical-connection* in the upper half. Logical-links may exist between two end-systems, but logical-links may also be concatenated to form a chain of logical-links. The physical links (of many varieties) between a succession of intermediate-nodes carry such a chain of logical-links. The logical-link concept is very general, and applies to the wide variety of technologies used in the lower layers.

A logical-link exists at layers 1, 2, and 3a. The latter is involved when a layer-3a subnetwork, like X.25, provides the connection between two layer-3c entities (e.g., the CLNP internet entities). In the case where layer 3c is null, the logical-link connects a pair of transport-layer entities.

Logical-links ordinarily link a pair of network-entities in end-systems on the same subnetwork. A single logical-link may also extend across multiple subnetworks, as in LANs connected by bridges. However, since logical-links are limited to links or subnetworks, they may need to be cascaded when an information path extends between end-systems on very different subnetworks. In that case, the layer-3c inter-subnetwork routers (see Section 12.8.3) may be used as intermediate terminating points. That is, the origin and destination end-systems may have logical-links to their nearest inter-subnetwork router; and an intervening series of logical-links may be established between such routers, forming a chain of logical-links along the path.

3.7 FORMATS AND PROTOCOLS

In our usage, formats and protocols mean a set of agreements involving three things:

1. The syntax (or format) of commands and headers to be exchanged
2. The semantics (or meaning) of these commands and headers in terms of what shall be done upon the receipt of each
3. The state machines distributed between two machines, often pictured as sequences of commands between the state machines

In general, the formats are the structure of the data and the protocols determine the action to be taken. The SNA and OSI networks, and the layers of these networks, are defined by the services they provide, and the formats and protocols used to achieve those services.

As shown in Figure 3.21, communication takes place between components of the same layer that possibly are in different nodes. To achieve this peer communication, data is sent via inner layers that provide a transparent transportation service for the outer layers. At the same time, an outer layer will pass parameters (that are needed for inner-layer operations) to an inner layer. Each layer defines the parameters that outer layers must provide to obtain its services. These parameters, and the data that will be passed transparently, constitute the boundary between layers.

3.7.1 Interlayer Communication

A subsystem complies with the OSI (or SNA) standards if the Protocol Data Units (PDUs) that flow between subsystems obey the OSI (or SNA) standards. All this, however, is distinct from *interlayer communication* (e.g., between the presentation, session, transport, and network layers). SNA and OSI do define functional relationships between adjacent layers, and do specify the semantics of information that must be passed between layers. However, performance could be adversely affected by too great a formalization of the boundaries between layers. In some implementations, several layers may best be built with no visible boundary between them. The communication architectures, therefore, do not uniquely define all the formats for every interlayer communication within a node.

OSI interlayer primitives

The information passed between a service user, in one layer, and a service provider, in an adjacent lower layer, is called a **service primitive**. These OSI interlayer communications are defined semantically by the standard, but not syntactically. Remember that an n-layer service exists across multiple nodes; two n-service users, in layer $n+1$, may be physically located in different physical nodes. They communicate with each other, using n-service primitives, via their respective n-SAPs. Each service user gains access to the service provider at one SAP.

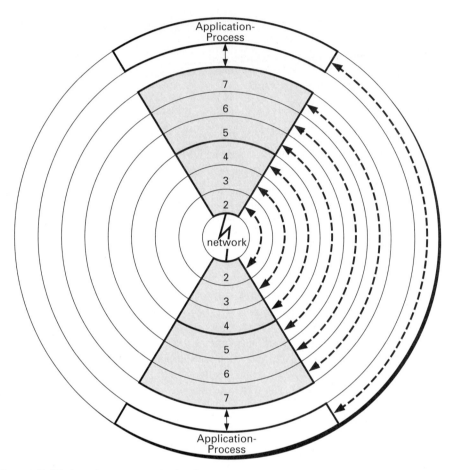

Figure 3.21 Intralayer communication.

There are four types of service primitives: **request, indication, response**, and **confirm**. All these primitives take part in a confirmed service, functioning in sequence, as illustrated in Figure 3.22. One user issues a *request*; the provider (in the lower layer) performs a service and sends a notification to the other user via an *indication*; the second user replies with a *response*; the provider sends this back to the first user by a *confirm*. This is the appearance given to the service users in layer $n+1$. In reality, the messages flow from layer n down through layer 1 in one node, and back up from layer 1 through layer n in the other node.

There are three other cases, also: (1) with a nonconfirmed service, only the request and indication are used; (2) sometimes it is the provider who generates the confirm,

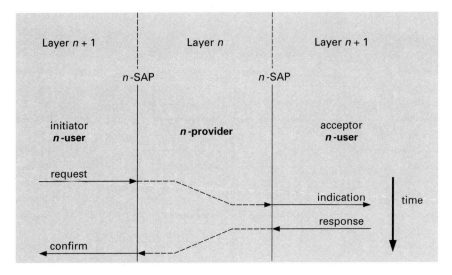

n-SAP = Service-Access-Point for Layer n

Figure 3.22 Time sequence diagram for the four types of service primitives.

without any response from the user; and (3) at other times, the only primitives are indications given by the provider to both users.

3.7.2 Intralayer Communications

We refer to functional units *in the same layer*, though possibly in different nodes, as **peer entities**. Thus, there can be peer entities, in different nodes, in each of the layers shown in Figure 3.21. The coded commands or control headers of that protocol are understood within a layer and need not be understood by other layers.

A **peer protocol** is a language used by peer entities to exchange instructions and data. The peer protocols serve to coordinate the operations throughout the layer even though the components are distributed among multiple nodes.

In OSI, a data unit that flows between peer entities is called a **Protocol Data Unit (PDU)**. OSI layer entities may respond to service primitives by building PDUs and using lower-layer services to send them to their peer layer entities. A PDU has two parts: a header, which controls the joint operation of the peer entities, called the Protocol Control Information (PCI), and the User Data (UD). A one-letter prefix identifies the layer involved (e.g., PPDU for presentation PDU). Though intended for the peer, each PDU is handed to the next lower layer for transmission. *As each layer receives a PDU from the layer above, it treats it as data, and adds its own enveloping header, so as to piggy-back*

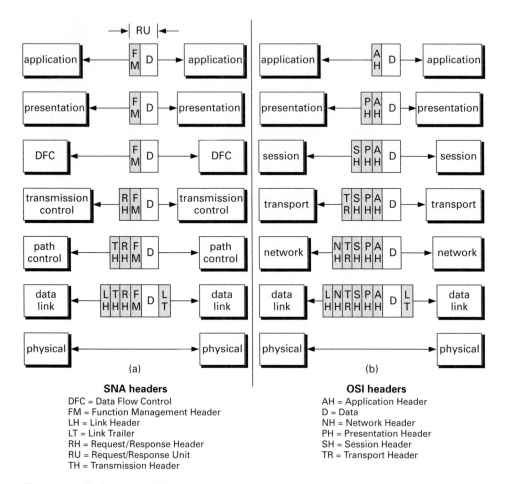

Figure 3.23 SNA and OSI headers.

its own control communications with its peer. The successive additions of each layer's header is shown in Figure 3.23(b).

The corresponding additions of SNA headers is shown in Figure 3.23(a). In SNA, the application message is called a **Request/Response Unit (RU)**. The first part of the RU may include an FM header provided by the application layer. Note also that, in SNA, two headers (the RH and the FM) combine the control information for the four layers 4, 5, 6, and 7. Note, too, that the data link control layer (in both OSI and SNA) may add both a header and a trailer that are for error control. Each heading is understood only by peer components in each layer.

A typical message will pass from an application-process, via the end-to-end data-exchange facilities, to the SNA path control or OSI network services, then to data link control, and then back through these same layers to another application-process.

At the receiving node, each layer, in turn, strips off its control headers (if any) and processes the remaining data in accordance with the information found within its own header.

3.8 CONNECTION-ORIENTED AND CONNECTIONLESS

At any layer, two kinds of services are theoretically possible: connection-oriented and connectionless. From a practical standpoint, connection-oriented and/or connectionless operations can exist at layers 2, 3, or 4. Connection-oriented operations are well suited to pairs of applications or pairs of terminals and terminal-oriented applications that involve a continuing stream of exchanges of data. Its reliability and recovery advantages are persuasive. There are instances, however, where the overhead of connection establishment may be unjustified. Examples include occasional sensor inputs, highly redundant, real-time inputs, such as radar data, and most postal services. SNA, to date, has used only connection-oriented operations at layer 3; and supports both connection-oriented and connectionless operations at layer 2.

3.8.1 Connection-Oriented

The term **connection-oriented** is reserved to forms of communication for which a pre-established set of resources and protocols is used for flow control and recovery operations between the connected entities. In this mode, a *logical connection* is agreed upon and set up, between the communicating partners, before the exchange of data takes place. Sequence numbering is allowed, to provide orderly flows, flow control, and error recovery. Routes can be established for a conversation or a sequence of messages.

Because the connection is set up prior to data transmission, each subsequent data packet needs to carry very little protocol overhead. All options for the connection are agreed to during the call establishment. The full addresses of the calling and called parties is carried only during the set-up. Subsequent packets need carry only a short id that identifies the connection. Connection-oriented service is therefore well suited when many data units are exchanged during a typical connection.

Connections are made between entities in the transport layer and above, for end-to-end communications. Connections are made between entities in the network layer and below for transmission purposes. Say, for example, that two entities at layer n wish to establish a connection with each other. One of these entities will call on the services of the lower layer, n-1, which will establish a connection between two n-1 SAPs. The two n entities will then use these SAPs to communicate with each other.

More than one connection may exist between any two SAPs. Each end point of the n-1 connection is called an n-1 *connection end point*, within the n-1 SAP.

Phases

All connection-oriented subnetworks have three phases for communications across them. These are the *connection establishment phase,* the *data phase,* and the *termination phase.*

The connection establishment phase establishes logical connections between two end-systems. Examples of this are the session establishment in SNA and the transport-layer connection for association establishment in OSI. Both of these establish end-to-end data-exchange facilities. With an SNA-based stack, the commands during the first phase include the `Bind` command, and the preceding requests to directory services to locate a particular symbolic_destination_name or named destination LU. With an OSI stack, the first phase includes the `Connect` commands and the preceding request to directory services to locate an application_entity_title.

A *logical-link* is the logical connection (or circuit) between a pair of network-entities in two systems. To establish a connection-oriented logical-link between a pair of network-entities requires the preliminary exchange of commands, between those two network-entities, according to some protocol. The form of a connection request and its protocol depend on the nature of the network at layers 1, 2, and possibly 3a to which the network-entity at layer 3c is attached. Two forms are:

- Call Request packets from X.25 DTEs for an X.25 virtual circuit[13]
- Q.931 requests from ISDN attached devices

If a physical line is not yet in place, as in switched lines rather than leased lines, then a prior connection-establishment phase is needed for the establishment of the physical connection.

3.8.2 Connectionless

A logical-link is said to exist between network-entities for both connection-oriented and connectionless operations. However, in the case of connectionless, there is no explicit activation process to establish the logical-link. In this mode, each data unit is independent of all others, and no formal network-layer connection between communicating partners is set up prior to data flows. Each data unit contains all the information needed for delivery, including a destination address and priority. These addresses, included as a part of each data packet, are used by the network to route the packet through the network to the addressed entity. Negotiations are absent, but options used may be prearranged, or identified in the protocol. Ordered delivery, flow control, acknowledgments, and error control are not provided at the layer that is connectionless.

With connectionless communication at layer n, the upper layer entity at layer $n+1$ can send and receive data, but the lower connectionless layer entity does not guarantee that any of the data sent arrived safely at the remote destination.

Connectionless approach does not spend time and resources to set up and take down connections. It therefore is best for short, self-contained transactions. It also is well suited to multicast and broadcast operations, which do not involve a series of return messages or acknowledgments.

---

13.   The Date Terminal Equipment (DTE) is the carrier term for an end-system. A virtual circuit appears to be a point-to-point connection between two DTEs, but actually is a series of shared lines between a mesh of data switching centers.

In a connectionless subnetwork, routes may be calculated anew for each data unit. Accordingly, there are no pre-established resources, for a particular connection, along a route. While many connectionless subnetworks use destination routing, calculating the next hop "on the fly" at each intermediary node, this is not always the case. Source routing can also be used in a connectionless subnetwork. In that case, information on the entire route must be carried with each packet being transmitted.

Gateway congestion can be more of a problem with connectionless than with the connection-oriented approach. With ISO internet protocol, there is no direct flow control between the gateway and the sender [McGurrin88]. If the gateway buffers fill up, the gateway simply discards additional packets received and may indicate congestion to the sender. When the sender does not receive a transport-layer acknowledgment of the data it has sent, it will retransmit the data, which can magnify the gateway congestion problem.

A curious circumstance is where a **datagram** (a single packet, originated as a connectionless transmission) must traverse a WAN that has connection-oriented capabilities. That datagram may be carried on a connection that is constantly active between datagram servers on the WAN. In this case, a connection is not started for each datagram, but a WAN connection is used as a link in the path of the datagram.

Layer-3 route information may not be sufficient for delivery of a datagram if the destination end-system is a device on a subnetwork such as a LAN. In that case, a LAN-attached intermediate-node, with layer-3 addressing capability, must have the ability to search the LAN for the corresponding LAN station address and link SAP address. This is the functional equivalent of the TCP/IP Address Resolution Protocols. For example, one could have connectionless operation at layer 3, and then every packet must carry the layer 3 address of the destination. The last node to handle the information packet must then be capable of associating the layer-3 address with the layer-2 address of the destination.

In a similar way, if an end-system is directly attached, by a point-to-point or multidrop line, to an intermediate-node, the latter is responsible for the translation of the layer-3 address to the layer-2 station address.

3.8.3   Some Examples

At layer 4, the transport layer has both connection-oriented and connectionless options. The OSI standard assumes that the two communicating entities in layer 4 (at two end-systems) will be of the same transport class, calling for either connection-oriented or connectionless transmission services. However, regardless of that choice, the standard allows that layers 2 and/or 3 may be connection-oriented or connectionless. In fact, even sublayers of layer 3 may have different modes. Some examples are:

- At the link layer, there are connection-oriented (type-2) and connectionless (type-1) versions of 802.2 LANs. SDLC and HDLC also have both versions, the connectionless being called "unnumbered."
- At layer 3a (or 3c), the X.25 packet level protocol is only connection-oriented.
- At layer 3c, the IP of TCP/IP is connectionless and the corresponding OSI layer 3c (CLNP) is connectionless also.

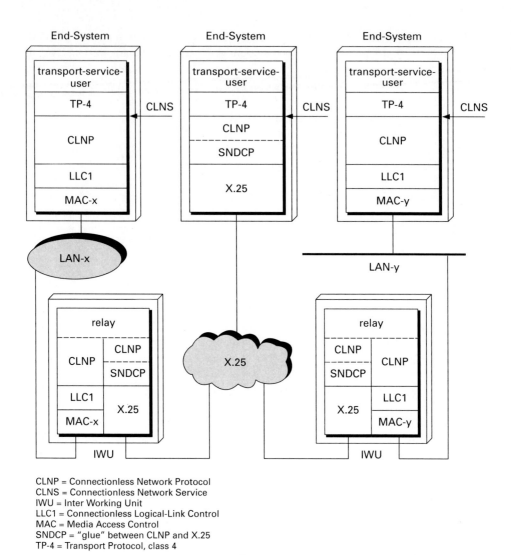

CLNP = Connectionless Network Protocol
CLNS = Connectionless Network Service
IWU = Inter Working Unit
LLC1 = Connectionless Logical-Link Control
MAC = Media Access Control
SNDCP = "glue" between CLNP and X.25
TP-4 = Transport Protocol, class 4

Figure 3.24 Consistent use of TP4/CLNS [Svobodova90].

Two different combinations of OSI protocols are popular [Svobodova90].

1.   The transport class 4 and CLNP protocols *(T-4/CLNP)* were chosen for the MAP/TOP functional specifications. They also have been endorsed by the NIST[14] Workshop for implementation of OSI in private domains. Since T4/CLNP is very similar to the Internet

14.   NIST (National Institute of Standards and Technology) was formerly called National Bureau of Standards (NBS).

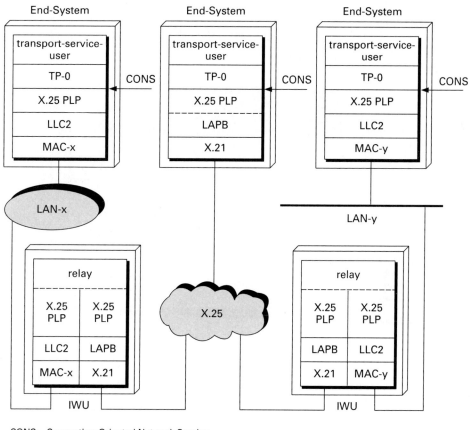

CONS = Connection-Oriented Network Service
IWU = Inter Working Unit
LAPB = Link Access Procedure, type B
LLC2 = Connection-Oriented Logical-Link Control
MAC = Media Access Control
PLP = Packet Layer Protocol
TP-0 = Transport Protocol, class 0

Figure 3.25 Consistent use of TPO/CONS [Svobodova90].

TCP/IP protocols, this combination was chosen to replace TCP/IP in the transition to OSI. The consistent use of T-4/CLNP across both LANs and WANs is illustrated in Figure 3.24 (the SNDP shown there is essentially a facility for managing virtual X.25 circuits).

2. NIST functional standards also define a second combination, T-0 over connection-oriented service *(T-0/CONS)*, for public message handling systems supporting X.400. This is illustrated in Figure 3.25. T-0 or 2 over connection-oriented *(T-0,2/CONS)*, is typical in Europe, where X.25 networks are prevalent.

Japan adopted the T-0,2/CONS combination as the functional profile for WANs, and the T-4/CLNP combination as the functional profile for LANs.

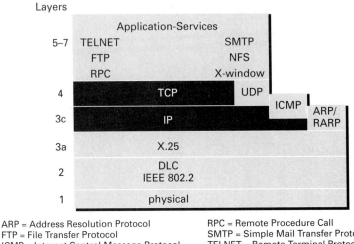

Layers

ARP = Address Resolution Protocol
FTP = File Transfer Protocol
ICMP = Internet Control Message Protocol
IP = Internet Protocol
NFS = Network File System
RARP = Reverse Address Resolution Protocol

RPC = Remote Procedure Call
SMTP = Simple Mail Transfer Protocol
TELNET = Remote Terminal Protocol
TCP = Transmission Control Protocol
UDP = User Datagram Protocol
X-window = Window Manager

Figure 3.26 The TCP/IP layers and functions.

Transport classes at two communicating end-systems must be the same. Hence, end-systems using T-4/CLNP cannot communicate with end-systems using T-0,2/CONS, without an intervening gateway.

3.9   RELATING TO TCP/IP

Our purpose here is only to position the main TCP/IP elements relative to the layered structures we have been discussing. Further treatments of these elements are in later chapters. The TCP/IP architecture is often portrayed as only four layers: an application layer, the transmission-control layer, the Internet layer, and a subnetwork-access layer, including subnetworks such as X.25, or a LAN [Reinhold]. The latter may, for example, be Ethernet (802.3) or token ring (802.5), or some other LAN. The relation of these TCP/IP layers to the seven-layer model is shown in Figure 3.26. The X.25 packet level protocol *corresponds to layer 3a* (subnetwork access protocol) of the OSI reference model. (The X.25 is not the only subnetwork that can be used at layer 3a beneath the IP. For example, the SNA path control subnetwork could be used, if a proper connection were made. The other TCP/IP layers are independent of this.) The LANs correspond to layer 2 (link layer) in OSI.

The next layer is the **Internet Protocol (IP)**, *corresponding to layer 3c* (independent convergence layer) of the OSI reference model [RFC791]. This IP provides for the routing of messages, across multiple subnetworks, in connectionless (best-effort) fashion. It adds its own header to each segment received from upper layers such as TCP (see Section 13.8.3).

IP uses the services of each subnetwork it routes through, to actually move data from node to node. If necessary, at any IP gateway,[15] IP can further segment the message to meet the needs of the next subnetwork (see also Section 12.8).

Supporting protocols are the **Address Resolution Protocol (ARP)** and the **Reverse Address Resolution Protocol (RARP)**. These convergence protocols (*corresponding to layer 3b*) are used to broadcast a search for the local address that corresponds to an Internet address, or vice versa (see Section 16.9).

The next layer is the **Transmission Control Protocol (TCP)**, roughly *corresponding to layer 4* of the OSI reference model [RFC793]. This provides for reliable transmission of the data, in order, without error, using error checking. It also assembles and disassembles packets to and from logical messages, and recovers from lost or errored segments. It is stream-oriented (rather than structured records) and handles full-duplex flows.

TCP is connection-oriented. Its functions are further described in Section 13.8.2. In the case of socket types of TCP/IP implementations, a TCP connection is completely identified by the two **sockets** (a socket is the TCP equivalent of an OSI TSAP). That pair of sockets involves four parameters: originating port and IP_address, and destination port and IP_address (see also Section 12.3.5).

There also are two connectionless protocol alternatives to TCP, called the *User Datagram Protocol (UDP)* [RFC768], and a special datagram service for error and status messages, called the *Internet Control Message Protocol (ICMP)* [RFC792].

The upper layer of the TCP/IP layer structure consists of a family of application-service packages *that span layers 5 through 7*. These are discussed in Section 5.7.

3.10   COMMON COMMUNICATIONS SUPPORT

Given the possibility of so many options, both within an architecture like OSI, and among the multiple architectures discussed above, there is a product-management challenge. The development of families of products must be managed to insure that common facilities are, in fact, accurately and consistently provided. That is the goal of *SAA Common Communications Support (CCS)*. It is an IBM maintained set of profiles and a catalog of support for architecture profiles. It provides the consistent implementation of both SNA and OSI communication architectures and protocols in each of the SAA operating-system environments. This includes, the IBM 390/MVS, 390/VM, OS/400, and OS/2 environments. The SAA Common Communications Support (CCS) includes selected OSI architectures that then also facilitate communications among multivendor systems that support these architectures. For example, CCS provides communications for: program-to-program, program-to-terminal, and programmable workstation, distributed data, document distribution, and network management. Though not always a part of CCS (not necessarily supporting all environments), a similar product coordination is provided (for TCP/IP, SNA, NetBIOS, and OSI facilities) in both AIX/OSF and SAA systems.[16]

---

15. The term *IP gateway* is common; however, the function performed is really that of a router (see Section 12.5).

16. "I think that before the dust settles, you'll see [TCP/IP as part of SAA] happen. I could say the same thing about Ethernet," quote from Earl Wheeler, IBM vice president and general manager of programming systems, according to interview in *Communications Week*, July 2, 1990.

Conclusion

This chapter provides the basic architectural structures that the remaining chapters use. The concepts and terminology of layering, peer protocols, sublayering within the network layer, subnetworks, and backbone subnetworks were described. The possibility of switch points for mixed stacks at three boundaries in a multiprotocol system were considered. This structure holds promise for the integration of OSI, SNA, TCP, and NetBIOS protocol options in a flexible and practical way, for maximum sharing of function and independence of lower-layer protocols.

Acknowledgments

I am particularly indebted to E. L. Miller, J. Mouton, and E. C. Broockman, for their valuable input and reviews of this chapter.

EXERCISES

3.1 What are the layers and general content of the upper and lower macro layers?

3.2 What is the OSI definition of a subnetwork?

3.3 Name five types of subnetworks with limited areas of coverage. Name five types of wide area networks.

3.4 What are three types of data-exchange facilities?

3.5 What are the three sublayers into which OSI layer 3 has been subdivided?

3.6 Name three interfaces or boundaries where protocol stack selection can take place.

3.7 What is an OSI entity?

3.8 What is a service-access-point?

3.9 Which SNA layers are included in the SNA logical unit?

3.10 In what way are the SNA *Bind* and the OSI *A-Associate* commands similar?

3.11 What is meant by a peer protocol?

3.12 What are the characteristics of connectionless operation?

Part 2
Distributed Application-Services

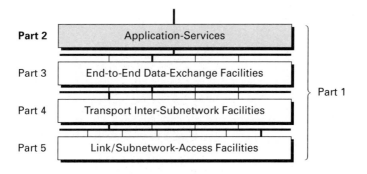

Part 2	Application-Services	
Part 3	End-to-End Data-Exchange Facilities	Part 1
Part 4	Transport Inter-Subnetwork Facilities	
Part 5	Link/Subnetwork-Access Facilities	

Part 2 describes some of the key distributed application-services that support the cooperating systems. Operating in the top layer (layer 7 of the OSI model, this growing set of services provides assistance to the end-users and network operations in many ways.

Chapter 4, Systems Management, explains the requirements and approaches to effective management. Emphasis is on the ability to manage multiple subnetworks with different architectures and multiple vendors, including local area networks and wide area networks, data and voice systems. Fault, configuration, operations, change, performance, accounting, and security all need a coordinated management structure and architected facilities, which are moving to an OSI standards base.

Chapter 5, Distributed Resource Managers, gives particular attention to distributed data, including the powerful relational databases, as well as byte files and record-oriented files. An integrated structure for workstations and mainframes is described. The operation of the resource-recovery facility, to guarantee the integrity of a distributed unit of work is included. The key roles of LAN servers (including mainframes) for sharing resources on LANs and other client–server facilities are discussed. DECnet/SNA client–server operations are included.

Chapter 6, Information Interchange, looks ahead to the architected interchange of information, including text, graphics, image, voice, and even video. The Office Document

Architecture (ODA) international standards, which provide the starting base for this, and the corresponding IBM implementations of ODA are reviewed.

The OSI X.400 and SNA architectures for message-handling systems are then compared. Their interoperability and the inclusion of office systems are described.

The complementary architecture for interaction between data-processing systems and voice PBX/CBXs is described.

4
Systems Management

4.1 INTRODUCTION

Every network resource must be "governed" by different services:

1. *Network management*, involving fault, configuration, operations, security, performance, accounting, asset, and change management.

2. *System management*, includes network management, and adds coordination of system installations, coordination of data resources, optimizing the usage of all resources, planning, inventory control, and financial management. System management is the broader and the preferred OSI term, and it often replaces the term network management, except where historical contexts make that awkward.

3. *Directory and logical-connection services*:

   a) Application-layer-directory and associated naming
   b) Logical-connection services, and associated control-points

4. *Layer 2 to 3 services*: directories, topology updates, route selection, and bandwidth management.

All four of these categories are evolving in three ways. First, they are being extended in function; second, they are being structured so as to apply to multiple vendors and multiple underlying communications protocols; and third, they are being integrated to provide mutually supporting functions, with a unified, consistent view.

This chapter addresses system management, but primarily its application to the communications functions. Application-layer-directory and logical-connection services are addressed in Chapter 8. Layer 2 to 3 services are addressed in Chapters 14 and 18.

4.2   SYSTEM MANAGEMENT PROCESS

4.2.1   Perspectives

The management perspective.   Those concerned with the management of large, distributed systems see a number of growing problem areas. Personnel for systems management require more and more skills; training is expensive, in time and dollars; and the turnover rate is higher than normal because of the demand for those skills. Systems become ever more complex, and involve multiple vendors, with multiple technologies, terminologies, and practices. At the same time, the 100 percent availability of the systems is increasingly essential to the operation of the business. Clearly, the techniques for management of the distributed system are crucial. Improved management at lower cost is the objective.

The operations perspective.   Those charged with the operation of distributed systems likewise find a growing set of challenges. Data, voice, image, and sometimes, video systems are increasingly intermixed. Wide area, metropolitan area, local area, and optical channel subnetworks are interconnected. Multiple protocol systems, such as SNA, OSI, TCP/IP, DECnet, and NetBIOS operate concurrently.[1] The system involves multiple operating systems and application-services. The messages, commands, and needed responses vary with each of these. Problems affect multiple subsystems and subnetworks; and messages from many sources may converge after an incident. These reports provide information from different perspectives and contain information on different aspects of the problem.

The growing complexity requires a higher degree of automation with built-in intelligence that is capable of prompt action and some learning from experience. Portions of the network must be unattended, with remote monitoring. Stored knowledge about the relationships of events must enable the system to sort through voluminous inputs and focus on the kernel of the problem. Mundane operations must be removed from the operator. Actions must be automatically taken, or at least guides must be given to the operator for remaining decisions.

The properties of reliability, availability, data-integrity, recoverability, serviceability, and security cannot be obtained by only adding a layer of management. Those subsystems and components of the information system that are vital to the enterprise must be designed to support these properties at the levels that the enterprise requires.

4.2.2   Functional Objectives

In the light of the above, the effective management of a complex system, if not its very survival, demands progress along the following lines:

- *Usability*: System-management processes must be task-oriented, rather than product-oriented; the interfaces must, accordingly, be independent of products and be user-friendly.

----

1.   For example, IBM's statement of direction is to support full OSI system management over OSI, TCP/IP, and SNA networks.

- *Consistent data*: The definition of system elements must be accomplished once and stored in a common repository with an enterprisewide view. Operational data for a subsystem or subnetwork must be at that subunit but also readily available to the enterprise system personnel.

- *Enterprise-wide management applications*: The management applications must address all vital subsystems and subnetworks, include multivendor components, and span the entire range of large central, departmental midrange, and small workstation components.

- *Product design for management*: Built-in product features should facilitate management, such as health-state indicators, failure detection/prediction, dynamic, nondisruptive reconfiguration, consistent logging and tracing facilities, and time-event synchronization features.

- *Automation*: User-developed and supplier-developed automation programs must have easy-to-use, published, programming interfaces, with some assistance from knowledge-based expert-systems tools.

4.2.3   SystemView Model

To meet the above objectives, a fresh approach and a new discipline is needed that will effectively integrate system-management processes. **SystemView** is the IBM strategy for achieving this goal. SystemView defines an architecturelike structure for the IBM systems-management process. The four dimensions of this structure, illustrated in Figure 4.1, are:

- *End-use dimension*—to provide consistent, task-oriented interfaces, using advanced dialog and graphics techniques, based on programmable workstation capabilities. Pointing to an object and picking from a set of alternatives offered will give an intuitive perception of control.

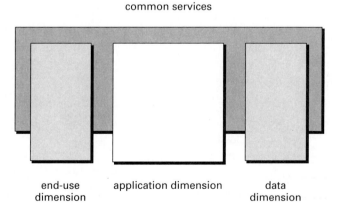

common services

end-use   application dimension   data
dimension   dimension

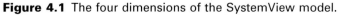

Figure 4.1 The four dimensions of the SystemView model.

- *Data dimension*—to provide a common repository for enterprisewide system elements, which need to be defined only once, and which conform to an enterprisewide object/attribute model. This will also facilitate the handling of changes, through the definition and use of relationships among data. The data descriptions will be extendable by IBM, vendors, and customers.

- *Application dimension*—in support of user- and supplier-provided distributed applications for the programmed reaction to events and the automation of tasks. This involves the creation of tasks that cross operating system and network boundaries.

- *Common services*—in support of the above, such as communication, automation, graphic presentation, and data services.

The goal is an integrated set of products, from multiple vendors, meeting these structural guidelines. The product set must have a similar "look and feel," to improve productivity and reduce learning and training effort. They must use common modeled data.

4.2.4   System Management Approach

The core of systems management is a multiprotocol, open architecture.

System management basics.   The management of networks (especially large and complex networks) involves six simple steps:

1. *Collecting* information about the status/well-being of network and systems components (hardware and software):
   - *Defined resource information*—These include events, object attributes, and operational actions. Many of these definitions should be standardized.
   - *Instrumentation*—the components in the entire network must be thoroughly instrumented to provide the necessary events, alarms, statistics, and responses to operational commands.[2]

2. *Transforming* that information into architected formats:
   - *SM protocols*—the rules and procedures to coordinate the system manager and agent processes
   - *SM syntax*—the rules for encoding and decoding the resource information and protocols

3. *Transporting* it to one or more points for:

4–6.*Storing, analyzing, and acting* by a human or an automation routine
   - Providing a *dynamic view* of the network—logical and physical
   - *Correlating* and coordinating events
   - *Automating action* wherever possible

---

2.   Such instrumentation actually has evolved through a decade of experimentation in diverse systems.

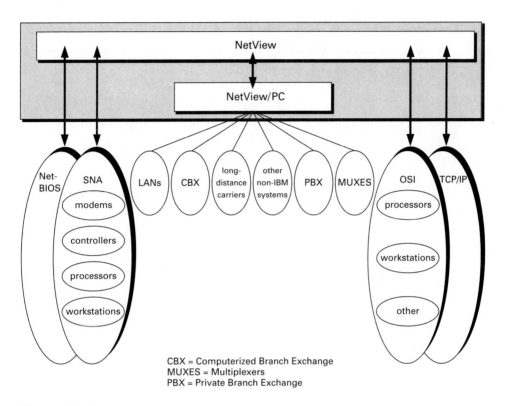

Figure 4.2 System management scope.

The analyzing and acting are the key ingredients that makes this process management, rather than merely data collection.

Scope. The communications system increasingly involves a broad diversity of subsystems and functions. These all need to be managed with a comprehensive overview of all components and their inevitable interactions. The growth of LANs, in particular, requires their early inclusion in overall operational services, in ways that preserve workgroup autonomy but add the synergy of mainframe and LAN tools. The design direction, to achieve this overall integration, is illustrated by the scope of NetView and NetView/PC,[3] shown in Figure 4.2. The movement in this direction is shown in the current integrations, in NetView, of diverse subsytems and managers that are produced by diverse vendors. These include:

- Token ring and PC Network LANs, with data from LAN Network Managers (see Section 4.8.1)

---

3. NetView is the IBM product, running on S/370s, for central system management. NetView/PC is a supporting product to perform an agent or service-point function, often for non-IBM products. LAN Network Manager is the associated LAN subsystem manager.

- Ethernets via NetView/PC applications (such as LattisNet[4])
- LAN servers such as the IBM LAN Server and Novell's NetWare (see Section 4.8.1)
- OSI networks, with data fed from the OSI/Communications Subsystem[5] and OSI agents
- Voice networks, with data from Private Branch Exchanges (PBXs) and Computerized Branch Exchanges (CBXs) (see Sections 4.8.3 and 6.7)
- Voice/data integration, with data from T1 resource managers (such as IDNXs;[6] see Section 18.5.2)
- X.25 PSDNs, with data from the X.25 Network Supervisory Facility (see Section 4.8.2)
- TCP/IP SNMP and TCP/IP agents
- A wide range of non-SNA network components, via a RISC S/6000 workstation running AIX, of the ITM Multivendor Automated eXpert Management (MAXM) system[7]

Multiple architectures. The *SNA* system management facilities have evolved "from the ground up," over the past decade, based on the needs of thousands of installations. *OSI* international standards, in the system management area, are now being completed "from the top down," taking full advantage of broad industry experience. These standards provide a further base for multivendor management systems. These standards include:

- ISO 7498-1 Concept of Systems Management
- ISO 7498-4 OSI Management Framework
- ISO/IEC 9595 Common Management Information Services (CMIS)
- ISO/IEC 9596 Common Management Information Protocol (CMIP)
- ISO 9072-1 Remote Operations Service Definition
- ISO 9072-2 Remote Operations Protocol Specification
- ISO/IEC 10040-System Management Overview
- ISO/IEC 10164 System Management Functions
- ISO/IEC 10165 System Management Information

The IBM system SystemView, in turn, incorporates these standards and provides extensions beyond them, so that they become a viable subset within the Open Systems

---

4. LattisNet is a NetView/PC application from Synoptics, Inc.

5. OSI/Communications Subsystem is the IBM implementation of the OSI protocol stack for SAA environments.

6. IDNX is a product of Network Equipment Technologies, Inc., which mixes voice and data traffic.

7. The ITM Multivendor Automated eXpert Management (MAXM) system is produced by International TeleManagement Corp.

Network Architecture (OSNA). The system management applications and the end-user interface for system management then must bring together a cohesive and comprehensive view of all components in the network. This integration involves resolving the different semantics and syntax of data from many computer systems of all sizes, multiple computer vendors, multiple communication product vendors, and multiple carriers.

An open system management architecture.   An *open system management* means, first of all, providing management support for all of the major networking protocols, such as SNA subarea, APPN, OSI, TCP/IP, DECnet, and NetBIOS protocols.[8] It means integrating submanagers for segments of the system, such as LANs, other parts of the physical network, and specialized segments like voice subsystems. An open system management, therefore, must include:

- *Published SM (system management) data formats and architectures*
- *Published programming interfaces*, so that customers and vendors can have easy access to the management data and the commands that communicate with system resources
- *Network management applications* that facilitate effective management of multi-vendor product components in the network

Beyond that, an open system management must be highly customizable by customers and vendors. It should, for example, allow:

- User-defined alerts and messages
- User-defined responses and actions to messages
- User-designed filtering of messages before they are sent or received by a higher-level system manager
- User-written applications, to receive messages from and send alerts and/or messages to user-written command processors in central managers
- User alteration of Help and Alert displays

4.3 SYSTEM MANAGEMENT STRUCTURES

Several basic principles of a structure for a multiprotocol, open system management are:

1. A managed object is *independent of communication protocols.*
2. A common agent is required in each node to serve *all* objects in that node.
3. *Each* communication subsystem should support transmission of management information between distributed management services.

---

8. IBM introduced its Open Network Management concept in 1986 to begin to address the management of heterogeneous networks. Since then products supporting TCP/IP and OSI have rolled out, and IBM has stated its intention to embrace the OSI Systems Management Standards as part of its overall systems management strategy.

4.3.1 System Management Terminology

At least three sets of system management terms have evolved and are in common use.

1. At the *lowest level*, we have:
   - For OSI: *objects*
   - For earlier SNA: *devices*
   - Other industry usage: *network elements*

2. At the *node level*, we have:
   - For OSI: *agents*
   - For earlier SNA: *entry points* and *service points*
   - Other industry usage: *network element managers*

3. At the *regional management level*, we have:
   - For OSI: *system managers*
   - For earlier SNA: *focal points*
   - Other industry usage: *domain managers*

Wherever feasible, we will use the OSI terminology, which is becoming more universally used.

4.3.2 The Multidomain Structure

Our system management model allows hierarchical system managers, which may be determined by company organization. For example, one could have five management entities, in four tiers, as illustrated in Figure 4.3. The *enterprise system manager*, together with its operators (human or programmed), represent the level at which multidomain decisions are made. It is the point for any centralized control and overall administration. A *domain system manager* is very similar, but has responsibility for only its portion of the network. Responsibilities for functions such as fault management, security, and so on, can be partitioned into these domains. Communication among domain system managers may also be required. Domain system managers can exist for data subsystems, voice subsystems, and transmission elements. Tier two is sometimes needed for a nested system manager or *collection points* for the purpose of collecting inputs from the lower structures. At the lowest management level, an *agent* manages basic network elements like the components in an end-node, or combinations of modems and multiplexors. The *service point* is a somewhat specialized agent. Referring again to Figure 4.3, we now further define the management components.

A **system manager** is a set of programs located at a regional or central place, to which messages requiring action are directed. System managers may be nested. A manager may, for example, be an *enterprise system manager* or the manager of a *domain* within an enterprise (examples of system managers are the S/390 NetView and the OS/400 Alert manager). The system manager includes management applications for the consolidation and correlation of data from all the resources (i.e., objects) managed by that system manager. The system-manager application programs support operator surveillance and decisions, and also provide an increasing degree of automatic systems operation. From the

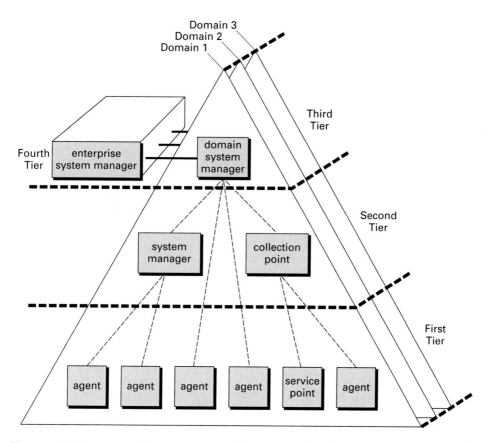

Figure 4.3 One possible management structure, showing four tiers of system management.

system manager, commands are sent to the portion of the network under the manager's control. The number and placement of system managers is determined by the customer's requirements for central versus distributed management of the network.

System managers may be nested, hierarchically. For example, we can have multiple levels of domain system managers, and domain system managers can be coordinated by an enterprise system manager. Peer system managers may also act as agents for each other. However, at any one time, one of these peer system managers will have the responsibility for a set of decisions affecting both system managers.

An **agent** is the set of programs which collects system management information in a *node* or a *network element*, performs the degree of management appropriate to that level, and forwards information to a remote system manager. Philosophically, automation of management should begin here, putting the automatic facilities as close to the problem as is feasible. Data sent to the higher-level system manager might include problem awareness, diagnostic data, product id, or product characteristics. Problem information may be in the form of a structured Alert or a message to the operator. Such a message might be determined by the outcome of local attempts to recover. Every SNA and OSI node is an agent. Agents may also filter malfunction messages from distributed application-services (examples of the latter include remote job entry services, messaging services, and communications-oriented, interactive, database subsystems).

A **collection point** is another name for a nested system manager. It acts as an agent with respect to a higher-level system manager, but an agent that also *has responsibility for other agents. As an intermediary, it serves as the system manager to an inferior and an agent to a superior.* Note that the difference between a domain system manager and a collection point pertains to the extent of management applications present. Hence, a NetView, OS/400 Alert Manager, LAN Network Manager, or an OSI/Communications Subsystem Manager could be seen as either a domain system manager or a collection point, depending on the extent of its management applications.

A **service point** is another name for a somewhat specialized agent. It is a set of programs that perform the agent function for another node, often a non-IBM node *that does not use the architected protocols.* For example, a PC might provide this function for a PBX, an Ethernet, or a T1 network manager. Examples are NetView/PC, LAN Network Managers, and the Transmission Network Manager for Integrated Digital Network Exchanges (IDNX). The service point is addressable and can translate system management data and requests between the system manager and nonstandard devices.

The NetView/PC, for example, provides an API that can be used by customers and vendors to write applications that can communicate with multivendor products using these products' proprietary interfaces. With this capability, these applications can transform proprietary management information into architected system-management data, and forward that information to a system manager. System manager (e.g., NetView) commands that apply to the NetView/PC service points are given in this chapter's Technical Reference section. Other APIs are planned for the LAN Network Manager.

A self-managed system would run both manager applications and agent functions.

TCP/IP management points. TCP/IP domain management is called **Simple Network Management Protocols (SNMP)**. Consistent with Figure 4.3, certain asynchronous events (TRAPS) received by the SNMP domain network manager from a TCP/IP agent may also be forwarded to the controlling enterprise system manager.

Alert filtering. Effective system management must allow for a balance between centralized and distributed control [Taber89]. This requires a design that specifies which situations will be called to the attention of the domain or enterprise system manager, and which will not. Only in predetermined cases need the central facility be concerned about distributed systems. Some of these central alerts will be those cases where a distributed system normally would correct the problem locally, but is unable to do so. The *alert filter* may use criteria such as resource name and type, alert type, and even the specific failure condition. The corresponding alert displays at the enterprise system manager would include a *domain name* to indicate the originating distributed system.

Historical event data and statistical data should be kept by each distributed domain. This, however, must also be made available to the enterprise system manager, on occasion. When an operator is viewing data about a given alert, he or she may ask to see the most recent events or statistics for that resource. In that case, NetView, for example, will automatically retrieve the desired data from the domain that has it. To make the query, the operator need not be concerned with where the data is located.

Of course, system managers can fail, too. Hence it is necessary for the system to provide for system manager backup, which will be automatically used when it is impossible to forward alerts to the primary system manager.

4.3.3 Node SM Structures

The **OSI system management node structure** is shown in Figure 4.4. A **Layer Management Entity (LME)** may (optionally) be associated with each OSI layer. The LMEs are not addressable and are purely conceptual models for an internal system's functions. The LME functions include:

- Collection of management information
- Asynchronous event reporting
- Change of operational parameters
- Change of state of layer operation

LMEs interface to the individual layers. They obtain information about those layers, and effect changes to those layers. Each LME, then, communicates with a node **Management Information Base (MIB)**. The MIB is a collection of objects and attributes in a system. This may include, for example, state information, counters, thresholds, and operational parameters.

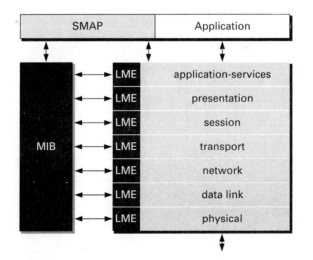

LME = Layer Management Entity
MIB = Management Information Base
SMAP = System Management Application-Process

Figure 4.4 OSI node system management functions.

In each node, there is a **System Management Application-Process (SMAP)**, which is the interface of the MIB to the outside world. The SMAP functions as an application and communicates with other SMAPs in other nodes. The SMAP, moreover, supports a program or human interface. The LME detects errors within its layer, takes corrective actions, and notifies the SMAP when the number of errors exceeds a threshold.

SMAP uses a **Systems Management Application-Entity (SMAE)** in the application-services layer to provide protocol facilities for OSI management. SMAE uses the **Common Management Information Protocols (CMIP)** for exchanges of data between nodes (see Figure 4.5). That data may be in response to predefined commands, such as: Get management information, Set a value in management information, request an Action, and generate an Event_Report.

SMAE is the combination of all **System Management Application-Service–Elements (SMASEs)** relevant to management. Each of these application-services specifies the structure of the messages to be exchanged over CMIP. For example, alarm reporting specifies the structure of reporting faults using the CMIP service M-Event_Report. Nonfault events use a different application-service and use a different message structure.

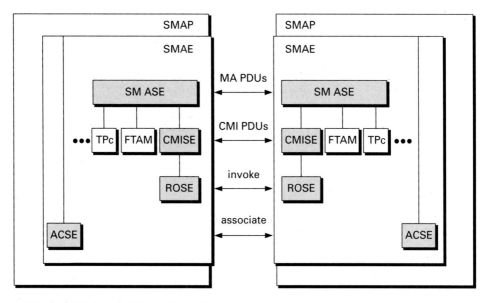

ACSE = Association Control Service Element
CMISE - Common Management Information Service Element
MA = Management Applications
PDU = Protocol Data Unit
ROSE = Remote Operation Service Element
SMAE = System Management Application-Entity
SMAP = System Management Application-Process
SMASE = System Management Application-Service Element
TPc = Transaction Processing

Figure 4.5 The major components of the System Management Application-Entity.

The SNA/APPN system management node structure is very similar to the OSI structure shown in Figure 4.4. Again, a layer function, now called Layer Management Services (LMS), interfaces to each layer, and communicates with the node's Control Point Management Services (CPMS). The control point, in turn, communicates with a higher-level system manager (see Section 8.6).

Note that in APPN, the communication between two CPMS is via a session of type LU 6.2. In contrast, in a subarea network, the node SM function (there called the PUMS rather than CPMS) communicates with a system manager via an SSCP-PU session.

4.4 MANAGEMENT APPLICATIONS

The heart of system management is its management applications. These span a very wide and growing spectrum of disciplines, including fault, configuration, change, operations, performance, security, accounting, and administrative (inventory and asset) management. The categories are somewhat arbitrary, but serve to provide a framework.

OSI refers to such disciplines as *functional areas*. There is a high degree of commonality between the OSI functional areas and the IBM SystemView disciplines. The following is a current snapshot of the IBM view, as one expects the SystemView disciplines to become a much expanded superset of the OSI functional areas.

4.4.1 Fault Management

The earlier approaches to fault management were content to monitor the network, gather large quantities of data, and present the data in graphical form for human consideration. Later approaches delegate the collection and consideration of data to lower-level agents. These instrumented agents now have the responsibility of declaring an event only when a real problem has been discerned. The reporting of the event then has the purpose of initiating diagnostic and recovery mechanisms.

Fault management in a distributed network can be very challenging. Hardware and software faults, and physical and logical relationships all are involved. Statistics must be kept and analyzed in order to recognize components that have intermittent failures. *Often, to locate the problem, the path taken must be known.* Supposed fixes have to be monitored to be sure that the basic problem (and not merely some consequent problem) has been corrected.

Graphic monitors, using color and icons have helped to speed the understanding of complex assortments of fault information. Figure 4.6 shows two types of images: the geographic image of resource clusters in (a) and the logical image of a backbone network in (b).[9] In (a), for example, one cluster might be colored yellow to indicate that certain of the backbone resources at that city are in a degraded state. In (b), the specific hosts (squares) and communication controllers (circles) in the backbone network are shown. One or more of those entities might be colored red, indicating a severely degraded status for all the resources associated with that node. A further "zoom" could be made to obtain specific information on one particular node.

---

9.   These images were taken from the NetView Graphic Monitor Facility.

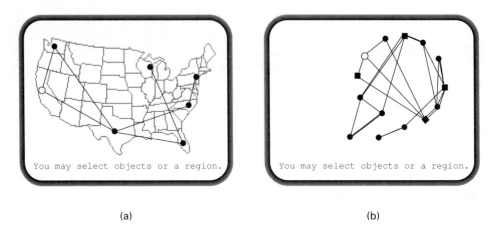

(a)   (b)

Figure 4.6 Displays of geographic and logical backbone views: **(a)** U.S.A. view; **(b)** Backbone view.

Problem phases.   Fault management handles error conditions in all network components, in five time phases:

- *Fault detection*—the detection of loss or impending loss of availability of a system resource, the isolation of the problem to a failing hardware, software, or microcode component, and the determination of the organization responsible for problem diagnosis.

- *Problem diagnosis*—to gather and analyze information so as to determine the cause of a problem and the precise action required to resolve it.

- *Bypass and recovery*—rapid execution of a procedure, automatically where feasible, but often temporary, so as to circumvent the problem.

- *Resolution*—the restoration of the network, undoing bypass actions, once appropriate corrective actions have been completed.

- *Tracking and control*—the tracking and correlation of many concurrent problems until their final resolution. Subsequent performance and trend analysis aids in problem prevention.

Physical and logical problems.   Three steps are involved: (1) the relationships between physical and logical constructs must be understood; (2) adequate instrumentation and measurements need to be put in place; and (3) information about both logical and physical activities must be correlated and placed in single graphical views, so as to allow for ease of navigation among related elements.

The two most common types of *physical problems* are malfunctioning devices or links, and hardware-use errors such as incorrect hardware setup. Hardware monitors provide regular notification of certain events, alerts on malfunctions, and statistics on operations. The system manager analyzes the alerts from malfunctioning resources and provides a set of probable causes and recommended actions.

In SNA's connection-oriented service, fault management is aided by the fact that the path of each session is known, and an outage along that path can be correlated with session failures. Also, that same path is used for outage notification. Then, when a link fails, an outage report is sent in the direction opposite to the failure, by the nodes using that link. That notification reaches both ends of the path. There, all LUs using that path are notified. If an end-node fails, that will similarly be detected as a link outage, and the same report-process applies.

Logical fault management typically addresses software problems, which have been difficult to resolve in the past. The two most common types of logical problems are errors in the software program itself and incorrect resource definitions. If only a logical part of one end-node malfunctions, a component in that end-node will generate a message to the other partner. *Session-information-retrieval* assists an operator to diagnose SNA session problems, such as hung or slow-responding sessions. The operator can view and analyze previously captured setup-data-parameters, and some trace data from the session end points. By thus recording operations prior to a failure, it is easier to identify and isolate failing software in the network. The operator can also obtain flow control data from each node in the session path (e.g., the route the session is taking).

The monitors can also capture and display information about logical problems through the use of generic alerts, which can be programmed to trigger when certain software problems occur. Other aids by the session monitor, for logical-problem-determination, include periodic measurements of session response times and session trace data.

Autonomy. Today, each SNA node is at least partially responsible for its own error analysis, to determine if a problem exists, and whether local recovery action can be performed to resolve the problem. Only if the local resources are inadequate is recovery assistance from a higher level requested. OSI nodes will follow that same pattern. Continuing this evolution throughout the industry will involve the gradual incorporation of facilities in each of the data/image/voice subnetworks to support proactive fault management. The objective includes continuous monitoring of self-healing subnetworks. The subnetwork discovers its problems, and may have automatic recovery, automated problem tracking, and automated service-order entries.

Automated recovery, in either subnetworks or higher-level system managers, is highly practical. Based upon current NetView experience, it is not unreasonable to strive for guided procedures to handle 99 percent of the alerts received. It has been estimated that fully 80 percent of the messages received in normal operations can be filtered out as being of no immediate significance. Of the 20 percent remaining, fully 80 percent can be handled with relatively simple procedures. Of the 4 percent remaining, fully 80 percent can be handled by predetermined but complex procedures. The remaining 1 percent, then, probably require unplanned accommodation.

Remote operations include automatic startup and shutdown procedures and remote console operations. Managers like NetView include capabilities for: powering on resources, loading initial programs, initializing major subsystems, and activating network resources.

Beyond that, a Distributed Console Access Facility allows one PC to control and monitor the display and keyboard input of another. This is used for remote alert management and fault management, such as monitoring end-user displays by help-desk personnel, executing applications on the user workstation, and remote trace or dump analysis. That facility is also used for remote control of a LAN Network Manager. The two workstations communicate via an LU 6.2 connection across an SNA WAN, or LU 6.2 via an OS/2 gateway to a NetBIOS workstation on a LAN, or via a switched asynchronous link. The target workstation receives keystrokes from the controlling workstation, with the resulting screen images displayed on both the controlling and target workstations.

Software serviceability.   The strategic direction toward automated software problem detection and automated support hinges on software technology using *proactive data capture*. This involves easy-to-learn functions that programmers in multiple vendors will use in their everyday coding. It enables *customized dumps with standardized keywords* for unique problem identification. With this, then, it is feasible to provide immediate notification to a system manager to enable automated software support.

Given the above, a current IBM system known as *Failure Analysis and Support Technology Service (FASTService)* automatically, upon notification, searches the local problem database for known problems, updates records on known problems, and assigns each new problem to the responsible customer support for resolution. New and upgraded products from multiple vendors will produce such customized dumps with a symptom string. This will facilitate recognition of known problems and issue a generic alert for immediate problem notification. The generic alert in conjunction with FASTService enables the automated software support at the customer location.

4.4.2   Configuration and Operations Management

Operations are concerned with establishing and modifying the network configuration, monitoring the continued operation of all elements, providing backup/archive services, and helping to control workflows throughout the network. The latter may include the scheduling of jobs and tasks throughout the distributed I/S operations.

Operations must sometimes be managed from a centralized location, from decentralized locations, or from a combination of the two. A degree of centralization not only permits analysis in the wider context it also concentrates the expertise of the operations staff. The degree chosen depends on the organizational structures of the enterprise and on the levels of skills available at each organizational entity. The roles may even shift, depending on the time of day.

An example of complete centralization is the Communications Management Center (CMC) where, in an SNA subarea network, all the network resources are managed from a single SSCP (Systems Service Control Point), even though there may be many SSCPs in the network. This, in effect, creates an enterprise system manager that owns all of the communications resources of the network. In those configurations, a backup CMC with take-over facilities is usually provided.

Configuration control.   Network configuration operations include bring-up, take-down, and reconfiguration. For example, an operator using a single console can activate multiple processors, set clocks, power devices on and off, initialize operating systems (without knowledge of each system's unique operations language), and initialize major subsystems. As another example, a system manager can send commands to a LAN Network Manager on a token ring LAN in order to control the stations attached to the ring. The LAN Network Manager is responsible for forwarding the command to the appropriate LAN station.

APPN networks enjoy dynamic reconfiguration, in which each node entering the network advises the rest of the network of its arrival (see Section 14.6). In support of this, at each node, power must be turned on and initialization must be performed for operating systems, network control programs, and peripheral node software. This may be done locally or be controlled remotely.

Subarea networks, on the other hand, are activated by a hierarchy of activation commands from one or more SSCPs. The sequence often is:

1. Physical units and logical units in mainframe hosts
2. Links to "adjacent" nodes
3. Link stations in adjacent nodes
4. Physical units in adjacent nodes
5. Logical units in adjacent nodes

Link stations, of course, can be on point-to-point, multipoint, or LAN configurations. They may also be across packet switched data networks (PSDNs). For switched SDLC links, the adjacent link stations dial and send `Exchange_Identification` (XID) commands and responses to each other. That determines which station will take on the primary role and send the `Set_Normal_Response_Mode` (SNRM) activation command to the other. Setting up virtual circuits has another command sequence (see Section 13.5). In subarea networks, these sets of activation commands for PUs, LUs, and link stations cascade through the network, as one after the other subarea becomes activated. The sequence of activation commands for a large network can be automated. A single operator command can activate an entire subarea or an entire network. Similarly, all or parts of a network can be deactivated.

Back-up and archiving. Large, decentralized LANs, multiple LAN servers, and distributed data on widely scattered hosts, all add to the possibilities of data loss. A well-organized and strictly enforced back-up procedure is increasingly vital. This involves both end-user initiated and timer-initiated services. Proper archiving with ready access for recovery purposes complements the service.[10,11]

Persistent sessions. This Virtual Telecommunications Access Method (VTAM) function enables users to more quickly reestablish contact with applications after a failure. When a

---

10.   For example, the Sytos Plus/IBM OS/2 File Backup Utilities allows an administrator to define the files to be backed up (possibly only files that have been changed since the last back-up), and the day and time for the utility to be executed.

11.   Backing up, archiving, and restoring disk or diskette data files, by allowing a S/390 VM system to act as a server for workstations and personal computers, is the objective of Datakeep/VM.

VTAM application fails, the VTAM maintains the LU-LU session information. When the VTAM application recovers, the sessions are immediately available. In-bound data that was in transit, having been saved, is presented to the VTAM application. Thus, upon a failure, the session is *retained*, instead of being terminated. Recovery with *resumption* of the interrupted session is facilitated, instead of *reestablishing* a failed session. Application restart requires no recovery-oriented network traffic, thus significantly reducing restart time.

The **Extended Recovery Facility (XRF)** *establishes a back-up session* for an active session that requests it. The back-up and backed-up sessions are identified by a common *Session-Correlation-Identifier (SC-id)*, which is included in the `Bind` commands for both sessions. The XRF back-up session extends from the primary LU to an XRF switchpoint located in the boundary function for the secondary LU. The back-up session becomes active only if the normal session fails. In that case, the XRF uses the `Switch` request to terminate the failed session and activate the back-up session. This prearrangement reduces the time ordinarily needed to establish a back-up session.

4.4.3 Change Management

Change management refers to the expansion, upgrade, and replacement of software, microcode, and hardware features [Ballard89]. These may be due to planned changes or to new releases of software or microcode modules, fixes resulting from fault management actions, engineering changes, feature changes, or other unforeseen events.

A change request, for example, may require coordination of operations and communications personnel, security people, and systems programmers at local and remote sites. Systems and subsystems tables may have to be regenerated. Software, hardware, and/or microcode may have to be installed. Cabling and devices may have to be installed. Testing of the configuration both before and after the change may have to be planned and evaluated.

The control of PC software used in far-flung workstations is another distinct problem. In SAA, for example, the management of PC software inventory and contracts are combined with the functions of software distribution and control (see Section 5.4).

Change management phases.   The major components of change management are:

■ *Planning*. The change planning process begins with a comprehensive body of information on the current levels of hardware, software, and microcode in the network. The plan for change then needs to be readily executable. This often requires the ability to automatically distribute, remotely install, and track the installation of many changes.

■ *Distributing*. Done electronically [Autru89], distributing includes the planning, scheduling, and tracking of the distribution of data, software, and microcode. Upgrades and fixes can be involved. The delivery systems used are those that the involved nodes are capable of handling. For SNA nodes, this involves using the SNA Distribution Services (SNADS). SNADS provides both fan-out and store-and-forward functions, that are valuable for change distribution.

■ *Installing*. This may involve unattended installation of changes at a remote location. For example, microcode can be distributed and installed at multiple 3174 (cluster controller[12]) sites, without the need for an installation person at each of many 3174 locations. Because such changes may not be wholly successful, a rapid back-out capability is needed to restore the resource to its prior condition. Changes may also be installed on a trial basis, or be scheduled for installation and activation at a particular date and time.

- *Tracking.* As each installation is completed, the central configuration database must be updated.

NetView Distribution Manager.   The NetView Distribution Manger (NV/DM) supports the change management function. It allows the NetView application to send requests to other systems that will:

- Retrieve, send, or delete database file members, save files, and other objects
- Retrieve or submit batch job streams
- Send messages to the system operator message queues

It can keep track of what is installed at each of the systems in the network. Administrators of LANs can use NetView DM/2, installed on an OS/2 workstation, to distribute and install programs and upgrades to both DOS and OS/2 workstations on the LAN.

4.4.4   Performance Management

Performance management strives to insure optimum performance of the network, or at least to provide the level of performance that was committed to users. Performance is, from the user's perspective, throughput, responsiveness, and availability. Examples of functions in this area are:

- *Response time measurements* (from the time an LU receives a request from its end user to the time that a response is received from the partner LU). These may be solicited by the network operator, or sent unsolicited, based on exceeding a predefined threshold. Graphic displays compare response times with objectives, by terminal and by session. Volume and response time data, for lines, routes, and applications, can be viewed.
- *Availability monitoring* and the provision of such data for later transmission to management.
- *Utilization monitoring* and the initiation of fault management if service levels are exceeded.
- *Component delay monitoring,* identifying network traffic bottlenecks, and the starting of fault management if service levels are exceeded.

For example, alerts in communication control units may concern line utilization and percentage of buffers used. Thus, as buffers fill up, operators or applications can take action in a timely manner to prevent unnecessary degradation. Conditions detected by the

---

12.   The cluster (or establishment) controller is a serving unit for a wide variety of attaching devices, particularly displays, printers, and workstations.

NetView Performance Monitor can be sent to an operator or to NetView applications for automatic resolution.

4.4.5 Financial Services

The diverse services, distributed throughout the network, are increasingly viewed as a utility by users anywhere in the network. It therefore becomes necessary to provide good accounting of network assets and service usage.

The *accounting application* provides, for example, data regarding usage charges, and accounting exits, so that customers can create billing applications using the network activity data. Sufficient information on both data and voice traffic is needed to provide departmental billings according to user-id and phone extension. As an example, some of the useful accounting-type information includes:

- Time connection started and ended
- Reason connection ended
- Number of text messages sent and received
- Number of text bytes sent and received
- Product name
- Reporting node name
- Event identifier
- Names of service-access-points
- Service-access-point selectors
- Connection-end-point id

Accounting applications may set limits on the use of managed objects and may monitor these thresholds. Costs of the use of multiple objects may be combined and periodic reports to users may be prepared.

4.4.6 Inventory Control

Keeping track of the new components, moves, and other changes in a widely distributed network can be time consuming. Determining whether ports are empty or relatively unused is another regular operation when new demands are to be met. These labor-intensive jobs have led to the creation of automatic signaling from the network elements themselves [Leet89].

Increasingly, units like cluster (establishment) controllers can respond to a request to identify themselves and their location, and supply other information for an up-to-date central asset report. **Vital-product-data (VPD)** is forwarded upstream. The cluster controller, in addition, can report on whether a device has been turned on since the last request for vital-product-data. Additional information, useful in configuration management, may include resource names, addresses, location, contacts and phone numbers, vendor or other organizations responsible for service, and other items.[13] The VPD available from OS/2 and DOS workstations will be increased by the LAN Network Manager and the LAN Station Manager [G01F-0281]. A request initiated at a NetView console goes to all remote LANs that have the LAN Network Manager installed. The latter then gathers the data from any attached workstations that have the LAN Station Manager installed, and returns it to the central requester. The data includes the PS/2 processor serial numbers, installed adapter serial numbers, and the installed operating system version level. The installed status of all LAN-attached OS/2 and DOS workstations can thus be obtained in minutes.

A different kind of asset management is needed for the **voice** area. There, network administration means the control and management of parts inventory, the paths of installed cable/wiring, and moves or changes in equipments. Tools[14] also provide for the management of work activities.

4.4.7 Security

Introduction

The life of the enterprise can often be challenged by violations of security. Increasing attention is accordingly being given to means for protecting against data loss, such as data interception, data deletion, data alteration, change of message sequence, substitution of messages, and unauthorized connection.

In general, a network-wide security management structure[15,16] must provide appropriate mechanisms for the following:

- *User identification and authentication*: recognizing and verifying the claimed identity of a user (or server)

- *Resource access controls*: allowing resource usage only by those suitably authorized

- *Confidentiality:* including secure communication and the management of keys for encryption

- *Data integrity:* the preservation of data from unauthorized changes

- *Security management*

Identity and authentication.   Most existing computer systems provide one-way authentication: a user proves his or her identity to a server. Generally, the user does not challenge

---

13.   Tools and applications to manage hardware and software assets are the object of the *System View Asset Manager*. The Integrated Solution Facility for Information/Management enables functions in the Asset Manager to update information in Information/Management.

14.   The *NetView Voice Facilities Management* package addresses this area.

15.   OSI Reference Model—Part 2: Security Architecture, ISO/DIS 7498-2.

16.   Another key component of the standards work is the evolving IEEE 802.10 standard for LAN security. This will specify: layer 2 functions for confidentiality, data integrity, access control services, and data origin authentication; and layer 7 functions for peer entity authentication, access control services, key management, and audit services.

the server to prove its identity. As distributed systems grow, this trust of the server may diminish, and hence two-way authentication may become more frequently necessary.

Another consequence of widely distributed systems is the requirement that users do not have to prove their identity to each and every server they use. A single sign-on is desired to an *authentication service*, which then can facilitate the certification of the user to any and all servers.

Access authorization.   The distribution of databases and the ease of access to a broad range of information and facilities are prime objectives of many enterprises. These very advantages however, also tend to increase the security exposure.

Responsibility for each file is preferably at one place. Sending copies of files to be duplicated at multiple nodes is undesirable because it distributes responsibility for the authorization checks. Using distributed data facilities, with easy access to remote files and databases, instead, keeps control of the data in one place, with the owner of the data. Then each node that is responsible for data must provide (or obtain) an adequate authorization check for the use of its data in the way that is requested.

Within these guidelines, a number of different approaches to access control can be used. Most systems employ an access control system where the owner of a resource can specify who can access that resource, and what types of access are allowed. Another type, used by the U.S. Department of Defense, is based on levels of clearance. In it, all data is placed in a specified access class. Each user is given authority to access only data with specified access classes. In this model, users whose privilege is equal to or greater than the access class of the data are permitted to read that data.

Data encryption

The transmission media and data storage also need to be secured. For this purpose, applications have an increasing need for data encryption. Simple link-level encryption is not possible in the X.25 environment, because the network headers have to be read and understood by the network. Higher-level support is needed to encrypt only the data portion. Encryption of this kind brings an added benefit in that, in case of error, the decryption process will fail and an error will be detected[17] if even a single bit of the message is corrupted, or if a packet that is only part of a message is lost or duplicated.

Private and public encryption.   Two types of encryption have appeared in the standards: private key, or symmetric encryption, and public key, or asymmetric encryption. These two processes are sketched in Figure 4.7.

Private-key cryptography transforms the sender's data by means of a public encryption algorithm and a single binary number key that is private, known only to the sender and the receiver. That private key, therefore, must be protected. The most popular technique for such encryption in use today is the Data Encryption Standard (DES) algorithm. The DES algorithm (created by IBM) was adopted by the NIST in 1977.

Public-key cryptography, on the other hand, uses *two keys*—one must be kept private by the key owner and the other can be public, perhaps even published in a directory.

---

17.   Failure of the decryption process results in the appearance of garbage. Some higher level (human or program) must recognize this and take appropriate action.

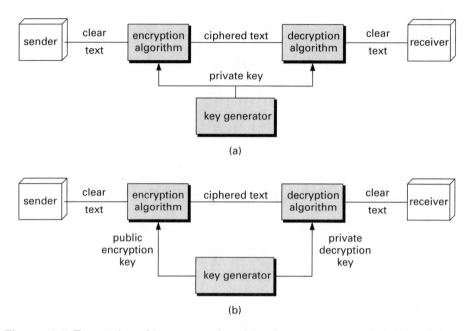

Figure 4.7 Two styles of key encryption: **(a)** private-key encryption; **(b)** public-key encryption.

Both are generated together, and the public key cannot be used to derive the private key. The well-known algorithm for public-key encryption is the RSA algorithm, developed by Rivest, Shamir, and Adleman. Using public-key methods, the sender and receiver do not have to share a common secret key. Only the private key must be protected; if it (and the public key) are generated by the receiver, the private key need not be transmitted. Two different facilities are possible:

- *Secret message.* In order to send a secret message to a receiver, the sender encrypts the message under the *public key*. This message can only be decrypted under the receiver's matching private key. It cannot be decrypted with the public key.

- *Guaranteed signature.* In order to simply identify the sender, with no secrecy of the message, the sender encrypts the message under the *private key*. That message can then be decrypted by anyone who has the public key. The recipient can be certain that the sender possessed the corresponding private key. This technique amounts to a secure *digital signature*.

The drawback of public-key systems is that they rely on hard-to-invert mathematical functions, for which low-cost implementations are hard to achieve. This is less of a drawback for digital signature than for secrecy in data transmissions, because the former is infrequent relative to the latter.

One conclusion from the above is that (a) the secret-key systems are more practical for data secrecy and integrity between communicating partners and (b) the public-key systems are attractive for digital signatures and sender authentication.

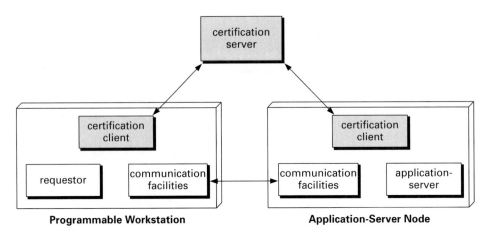

Figure 4.8 Certification in an untrusted network.

Distributing keys in large networks.   With the distribution of function among many parties in large networks, being authenticated at each and every node destination becomes intolerable. *The user should need to be authenticated only upon initial access to the distributed system* (i.e., a single logon), even though multiple remote servers may be used. Then, however, the user-id of an authenticated user needs to be propagated to servers throughout the distributed system with the requests for distributed service. The system is thus responsible for insuring that only authenticated user-ids are passed around.

Certification servers.   To address the security requirements in large networks, and an "untrusted network" environment, special procedures have been proposed. One of these, a mutual suspicion/**trusted-third-party** scheme was developed through work done at MIT.[18] The Kerberos approach, based on the Needham and Schroeder model [Needham78], uses **certificates** provided by a third party, as a way to distribute DES keys in a secret way. Certificates in this system are never transmitted in the clear (without encryption).

To implement the Kerberos type of security over untrusted networks, a local user-authentication service, the **certification client (CC)**, must work in conjunction with a remote, trusted third party, the **certification server (CS)**. There are many variations on third-party protocols. However, an understanding of the basic idea can be gotten from a consideration of a hypothetical system, as follows [Steiner88] (see Figure 4.8):

1.   Each certification server knows the passwords for all users and application-servers in its domain. The certificate server also knows two keys: one that is known to the client, and one that is known to the application-server. That information is stored in a secure way in its *certification server (CS) database*. The management of passwords is simplified because

---

18.   OSF selected the Kerberos version 5 (private key) protocol specification, with enhancements to ensure that applications are portable to public key authentication, as specified in X.509.

all passwords for users and application-servers within a control domain are managed at this one place in the domain. During logon, the user is authenticated to the certification server once. Then, as required, the CS certifies the user's identity to appropriate target application-servers.

2.   When a client program wishes to make an authenticated request to an application-server, it first applies to the certificate server for a certificate for that server. The certificate server creates the certificate, encrypted in the application-server's key. *The certificate contains the client's identity, along with a temporary key, or session-key.* The certificate server encrypts both the certificate and another copy of the *session-key* in the client's key, and returns them to the client.

The client decrypts the returned message with its client-key, stores the certificate and the *session-key* away for future use, and passes the certificate on to the application-server. The application-server decrypts the certificate with its application-server key and retrieves the *session-key* and the identity of the client.

At this point, the application-server is certain of the identity of the client, and both the client and the server share the same *session-key*. They thus can use the common session-key for communication purposes.

All of the communications with the certification server should be hidden from the user. The process might be initiated by the user's layer 5 to 7 data-exchange facility, on the occasion of its request for communication with the application-server. That, for example, could be occasioned by the *RPC Call*, in the case of Remote Procedure Call, or an `Allocate`, when using conversation mode.

Multiple security domains.   There may be multiple certification servers in a network, each responsible for a domain in that network. The location of the correct certification server for a given programmable workstation (PWS) may be previously defined or it might be determined by interrogating an application-level directory during logon.

If a cross-domain communication is desired, when the PWS and the application-server are in different administrative domains, cooperation between two certification servers is needed. The PWS and the application-server should, however, see no difference in their security procedures. The dialog between the two certification servers can be such as to make them appear to be a single server, as far as the certification clients are concerned. (This is analogous to the cooperation between two SSCPs for cross-domain session establishment in subarea networks.)

When the user and the application-server are in different enterprises, the third party must be some trusted middle entity. This might, for example, be a value-added network, that spans the several enterprises, such as TELENET or the IBM Information Network (IIN).

SNA security services

End-user authentication.   User verification is called by the LOGON program, and possibly others, to determine that the user is who he says he is. Passwords and user-ids have been commonly used. Other techniques, including smart-cards, and biometric measurements continue to be explored and can supplement the normal procedures in some cases.

SNA LU 6.2s use passwords and user-ids to verify the identity of remote end users prior to allowing them access to a transaction program or other resources. A request unit carries a password and user-id in an `Attach` FM header. For access control, the requesting program may be required to supply an access profile. The receiving LU can use this to check the access rights of the end user by referring to a predefined authorization list. How passwords and user-ids are verified and enforced is implementation-defined.

Partner LU authentication.   At the session level, the LUs verify the identity of each other. This occurs by an exchange between the two LUs at session activation time. Passwords are defined for each pair of LUs at system definition time or later. For added security, the passwords themselves are never transmitted. Instead, they are used as keys for enciphering random data sent between the two LUs. (The encryption used is the Data Encryption Standard algorithm.)

The method is simply to see if both LUs can encrypt random data in exactly the same way, since they have identical keys. The `Bind` command, which establishes the session, contains a field of random data. The secondary LU enciphers this and returns it in the `Bind` response, along with its own choice of random data. The primary LU then compares the returned enciphered data with its own enciphered copy. If this step is successful, the primary has verified the identity of the secondary. Then, the primary enciphers the secondary's random data and returns it to the secondary. This permits the secondary to verify the identity of the primary.

Session cryptography.   To preserve confidentiality, SNA depends primarily on cryptographic facilities. These are currently DES based. In *mandatory cryptographic* sessions, LUs encipher all RUs (i.e., all message units). In *selective cryptographic* sessions, LUs encipher only data RUs that have the enciphered data indicator (EDI) set in the request header. Today, type 6.2 LUs can provide either mandatory data encryption, selective data encryption, or no data encryption.[19]

Cryptographic interfaces.   As one illustration of a current security service, the IBM Transaction Security system provides a *cryptographic interface* for a large number of cryptographic functions. This API accepts cryptographic requests from applications written for S/390s, PS/2s, and PCs, in a range of higher-level languages. The security server translates the security API requests via its command processors into commands for cryptographic hardware.

To further simplify the user involvement, a *Personal Security Card* can securely hold cryptographic keys and perform Personal Identification Number (PIN) verification functions. It is a standard-size chip-card package, containing a single-chip microprocessor. The card contains the Data Encryption Algorithm (DEA/DES), secure data areas and related support routines in order to start an end-to-end security system with cryptographic capabilities right at the starting point of a transaction. The card is used with a unit[20]

---

19.   As of this writing, this can be implemented only on SSCP-dependent LUs, and not in APPN independent LUs.

20.   The IBM Personal Security Card is inserted into the 4754 Security Interface Unit, which, in turn, is connected to the workstation.

connected to a workstation. A user profile for each user includes:

- *User-id*—comparable to that used for logon
- *PIN*—a secret Personal Identification Number
- *Authority level*—relative to other users
- *PIN failure count and limit*—control the number of invalid attempts to access the card
- *User expiration date*

An alternative to the PIN verification process is a signature verification pen. This measures the acceleration and pressure of the user's hand during the signature. The system requires five signatures stored in the Personal Security Card as reference.

4.4.8   Command Lists

In a given situation, a whole series of predetermined steps may need to be taken quickly. This is the purpose of **command lists**. It is simply a set of commands and special instructions, grouped together under one name like a computer program. Command lists can be executed, for example, in response to an operator's request, by a timer, or by message processors. They facilitate the system management, and provide rapid, and even automatic reaction to given situations. Command lists evolve as the network grows, and procedures improve. Hence, it is important that they be readily upgradable. Both network operators and local programmers need to be fluent in this development. For that reason, NetView has adopted the easy-to-use Procedure Language/REXX of SAA for its command list generations. The possible sophistication is further enhanced by allowing REXX to invoke high-level language command processors written in PL/1 or C language.

4.5   INTER-NODE SYSTEM MANAGEMENT COMMUNICATION

The *objects* that are controlled, their parameters, and the way in which information about them is formatted and communicated, all need to be defined. Here, too, a multiprotocol approach, with a gradual creation and transition toward standard is underway.

4.5.1   SNA System Management Formats

SNA management services vectors.   SNA Management Services (MS) has used a three-tiered coding scheme for system management information. Called the **major vector format**, it is illustrated in Figure 4.9. The id identifies the general type of MS data the major vector contains (fault management data, for example). The major vector is the envelope for one or more **subvectors**. Each subvector has a length field and an I field which further identifies what kind of data will follow. Any number of subvectors can be defined. Some subvectors are further divided into **subfields**. Note that here only three levels of nesting are defined. Formats and screen designs are contained in the references [GA27-3136], [SC30-3346]. The published structure enables vendors and customers to write their own application programs and to generate data for non-SNA products.

SNA Generic Alerts.   A good example of the use of vectors is the SNA Generic Alert. These are architected messages that are independent of particular products, and hence

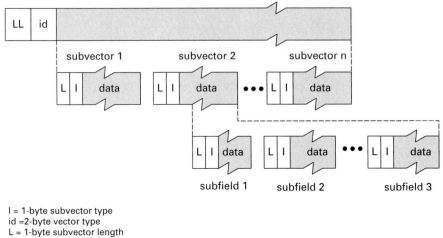

I = 1-byte subvector type
id =2-byte vector type
L = 1-byte subvector length
LL = 2-byte vector length

Figure 4.9 SNA Management Services (MS) major vector format.

facilitate uniform reporting of events from a very wide variety of products. The generic alerts provide **code points** for descriptions and displays of alerts, and also the following supporting information [Moore88]:

- A ranked listing of the *probable causes* of the problem
- A set of *recommended actions* to be taken
- In some cases, *time* at which the error was detected, unique product information, or unique protocol information
- The *product identity* and the *network identity* of the Alert sender
- The identity of the *network resource* most closely related to the problem
- An indication of whether the problem is a *temporary* or a *permanent* failure

The 1- or 2-byte code point values index into *short strings of text* stored in tables in the NetView. The text strings, retrieved as the result of table lookups, are combined to form the display for the Alert (the text strings can be in any language, and are customer changeable). Generic alerts similarly facilitate automation of fault management. Alerts from similar devices, describing the same type of problem, can evoke a standardized automated response. The message table support allows for a variable number of criteria to be specified and compared against an incoming message. The resulting actions may include executing a command processor, displaying, or logging the message. A basic set of vectors makes it feasible to incorporate non-SNA products into a comprehensive system management support system. In addition, customers can enter new code points and text strings. Generic alert architecture is published, so that any vendor can use them.

Application communication. System management applications in one system manager need to communicate in a general way with related applications in other system managers and agents. NetView, for example, supports communication via LU 6.2 for application-to-application conversation. This increases the potential for remote automation and further reduces the need for personnel at remote sites.

4.5.2 OSI Managed Objects

OSI has specified a general model of **managed objects**, which offers formats for collecting comparable information on a wide variety of object types. Examples of managed objects include logical objects like layer entities, and connections, or pieces of physical equipment like a modem. Objects then have attributes, that can be manipulated, such as counters and states. As far as the management system is concerned, the object is an abstraction of the resource itself. The object then is the knowledge about the element in question, including the data and the operations that are defined on that data. Management can invoke functions in a manner similar to the calling of a subroutine, with the parameters of the call. The resulting actions are those that had been formally defined in the definition of the object. This is a broad framework for future development in all system management.

Each managed object is an instance of a class of objects. Each managed object class is a named set of managed objects that all share the same general definition and have the same set of attributes. OSI objects, moreover, can be related in hierarchies of two types. One type is by containment of subordinates within a superior (e.g., media access control (MAC) within the link layer). The other type is by subclass within a class (e.g., modems as one subclass within the class of signal converters). A subclass inherits all of the properties of the superclass, from which it is descended.

Thus, each managed object is a member (an instance) of a managed object class, and managed object classes are organized according to common features with the inheritance relationship. A managed object may contain other managed objects, and a variety of other relationships between managed objects may be defined [NMF 90]. Included as parts of the definition of a managed object are:

- The *management operations* that can be performed on the object
- The *effect* of these operations on the object and its attributes
- The *notifications* that the object can emit
- The *conditions* that caused the notification

OSI SM communications.   Referring again to Figure 4.5, the SMAP coordinates the management services for the node. The SMAP communicates with other SMAPs by using a cluster of functions known as the System Management Application-Entity (SMAE). (As noted in Section 3.3.2, the term application-entity is a general OSI term for clusters of application-service–elements.) The structure of the SMAE is shown in Figure 4.5.

The key communications component in the SMAE is the Common Management Information Service Elements (CMISE). It responds to its users by generating appropriate management information protocols. These are the Common Management Information

Protocols (CMIP).[21] Other service elements may also be part of the SMAE, only some of which are shown in Figure 4.5. CMISE commands are in two categories: notification and operations. The latter includes both information transfer and control.

- *Event notifications* are unsolicited. They are used by an agent in one node to report events to a system manager. These services are invoked by a single service primitive `M-Event_Report`, to report an event to a peer CMISE service user.
- The *information transfer* service is a solicited transfer of management information. The `M-Get` service primitive is sent from a manager to an agent, to retrieve management information. There is also a `Cancel_Get` command.
- *Control services* are used to change values of parameters or to perform an operation. These control services set parameters (`M-Set`), create a managed object (`M-Create`), delete a managed object (`M-Delete`), or perform an action on a managed object (`M-Action`).

A CMIP PDU cannot be sent without *an envelope of some kind to provide request-reply correlation*. The CMIP operations of event, information transfer, and control, along with their parameters, are carried as data by the **Remote Operations Service Element (ROSE)** (refer again to Figure 4.5, and Section 8.7.4). Data carried in OSI system management commands use the Abstract Syntax Notation (ASN.1), which is described in Section 9.2.2.

The management PDU therefore includes three sets of control headers for: *SMASE* (DIS 10164/1 and 10164/11), *CMIP* (IS 9595/9596), and *ROSE* (IS 9072) protocols. That aggregate then is enclosed in the usual five headers for the presentation, session, transport, network, and DLC layers.

4.6 MULTIPLE PROTOCOL MANAGEMENT

Practical approaches are developed (and described below), which work toward the integration of SNA, OSI, and TCP/IP system management, and yet (at least for a time) allow them to be distinct and semi-autonomous.

4.6.1 SNA/OSI System Management Comparisons

The feasibility of converging the SNA and OSI system management facilities, and making the latter a subset of the OSNA facilities is encouraged by the similarities of the SNA and OSI system management architectures. Both are designed with the management functions at the application layer, drawing information from each of the other layers. Both have specified very similar functions; most of what is in the standard bears a close resemblance to what has been in SNA/MS; and even the definition of terms is usually close.

The format of the data, however, has been markedly different in the two cases. OSI uses the Abstract Syntax Notation (ASN.1) and the Basic Encoding Rules (BER), in order

---

21. IBM's statement is that, over time, it will base its Open System Management internodal communications on these OSI System Management standards.

to make the data structure independent of any product or system. SNA has used the General Data Stream (GDS) to tag the data (see Section 10.3.3), and uses vector encoding techniques to describe the formats. This, too, provides for nested data streams. A combination of SNA and OSI formats and data streams is, however, feasible, with a transition to the OSI systems.

The command structures have also been different. OSI uses a generic protocol, the Common Management Information Protocol (CMIP), between management-application-entities. SNA instead has used unique major vectors for different classes of function. For example, SNA uses the Alert major vector to notify the system manager of problems, and uses a different major vector, the PD Statistics major vector, for fault management statistics. OSI, on the other hand, uses the generic CMIP-EVENT primitive for all asynchronous reports, and uses the CMIP-GET to retrieve fault management statistics or any other management data. *The IBM strategy is for the CMIP protocols to become the dominant future usage.*

The two formats and command structures can coexist in a single management system, with each used for separate products, and with a common analysis and presentation service. Convergence would be expected, with a gradual shift to include the more generic standards of OSI, for new functions. As time progresses, more and more products will speak the OSI system management language, as a subset of a broader capability.

4.6.2 SNA/OSI System Manager

To bring together the management information from both SNA and OSI units, the OSI domain system manager must be connected to a combined enterprise system manager (e.g., an enterprise system manager that coordinates SNA and OSI domain system managers and/or collection points). Figure 4.10 shows the basic architecture for an enterprise system manager, in an integrated SNA/OSI node. This node has both SNA and OSI communication subsystems, which receive the SNA and OSI management protocols, respectively. The common control point for management systems assembles a common Management Information Base (MIB), containing both SNA and OSI models. The management applications—accounting, performance, change-control, fault determination, and security—all can use this common MIB. A common user interface for these management applications can be increasingly transparent to these underlying protocols.

OSI/Communications Subsystem Manager [Jerves89].   In the IBM OSI/Communications Subsystem design, the OSI System Manager of Figure 4.11 serves two functions: (1) as the local System Management Application-Process (SMAP) for the local OSI/Communications Subsystem, and (2) as the System Management Application-Entity (SMAE) to handle all exchanges of management data with OSI agents and the enterprise system manager. In support of these combined roles, there are three distinct functions within the OSI System Manager:

- *The command handler* processes requests from either a local or a remote management function. These requests may be for some management action, to get management data, or to set parameter values. Requests to remote nodes are sent to the SMAE for delivery.

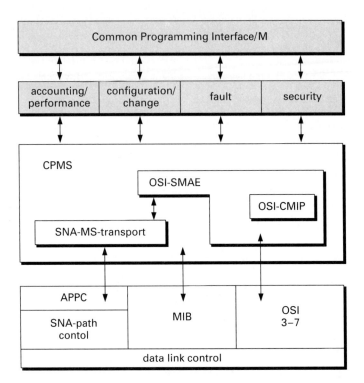

APPC = Advanced Program-to-Program Communication
CMIP = Common Management Information Protocol
CPMS = Control Point Management Service
MIB = Management Information Base
MS = Management Service
SMAE = System Management Application-Entity

Figure 4.10 Joint SNA-OSI system management support.

- *The event handler* receives reports of problems where immediate corrective action has failed. Certain types of reports, specified by the customer, are filtered out, and the remainder are sent on to a management application. (If the management application is in NetView, then Netview may do additional filtering.)

- *The resource manager* monitors the OSI/Communications Subsystem for resource depletion and congestion. This manager takes immediate corrective action on situations like buffer shortages. Problems that cannot be immediately corrected are reported.

As an interim procedure, OSI events are converted to generic SNA-format alerts, with a proper identification of the OSI event. These converted alerts are then sent to NetView via the SNA Communications Network Management Interface (CNMI), as shown in Figure 4.11. The Command Facility is used for the operator to communicate in the reverse direction, back to the OSI System Manager. Here, these operator commands are interpreted and forwarded to the OSI agent.

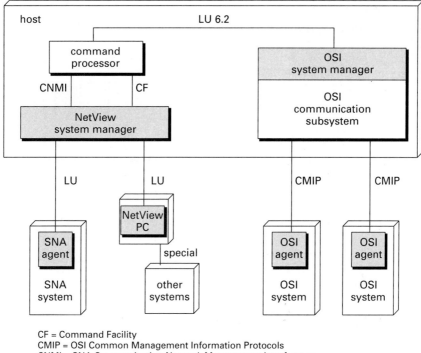

CF = Command Facility
CMIP = OSI Common Management Information Protocols
CNMI = SNA Communication Network Management Interference

Figure 4.11 Protocol flows for OSI and SNA system management.

Pending the completion of the full OSI system management standards, OSI/Communications Subsystem supports those objects defined by MAP 3.0. Additional parts of the OSI object-oriented network architecture will be implemented as it is approved. As that occurs, one can also expect the transporting of CMIP directly over SNA flows to system managers, without prior conversion to SNA CNMI format.

OSI-SM via SNA. In those cases where the node containing the enterprise system manager does not have an OSI communications subsystem, the OSI protocols can be enveloped, at some intermediate node, within SNA protocols, as shown in Figure 4.12. The OSI protocols are delivered via SNA to an OSI System Management Application-Entity (SMAE) in the system manager node. The protocols seen on the connecting lines are shown in Figure 4.13. This approach avoids unnecessary transformations. These SMAE's employ the OSI protocols to send commands, responses, and event reports to and from OSI systems. The OSI resources are thus managed through the SNA backbone, and the full OSI protocol stack is not necessary at every system manager's node.

NetView's OSI role. It is expected that NetView will ultimately accept the OSI CMIP information directly from any source, and integrate that data into its overall resource manager

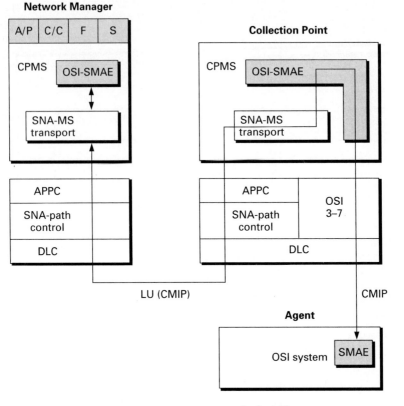

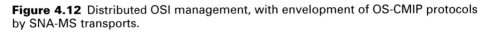

A/P = Accounting/Performance Management
APPC = Advanced Program-to-Program Communication
C/C = Configuration/Change Management
CMIP = Common Management Information Protocol
CPMS = Control Point Management Service

F = Fault Management
MS = Management Service
S = Security Management
SMAE = System Management Application-Entity

Figure 4.12 Distributed OSI management, with envelopment of OS-CMIP protocols by SNA-MS transports.

databases. NetView then may add broader functions (beyond those of the standards) to the management of both OSI and non-OSI systems. These could, for example, include things like:

- Automated command lists, or command processor execution

- Expert system aids to automation

- Unattended operation facilities

- System manager alert filtering

- User exits for user-tailored functions

- Logging and tracking services

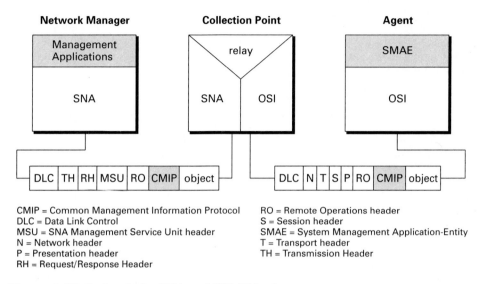

CMIP = Common Management Information Protocol
DLC = Data Link Control
MSU = SNA Management Service Unit header
N = Network header
P = Presentation header
RH = Request/Response Header

RO = Remote Operations header
S = Session header
SMAE = System Management Application-Entity
T = Transport header
TH = Transmission Header

Figure 4.13 Protocols for SNA and OSI NM relay.

NetView must continue to evolve, to handle complex data management and data correlation tasks. It must collect, transform, and correlate the data so as to present the composite results while shielding the complexity from the user. Information overload can defeat the purpose, so automated screening, significance selection, reduction of redundancy, and correlation of seemingly unrelated reports are all essential. Effective process control then will depend on sophisticated automation. Automation must progress from analysis and guidance toward system-directed and completely automatic action in a significant percentage of the frequently occurring situations.

4.6.3   TCP's SNMP

The **Simple Network Management Protocol (SNMP)** of TCP/IP is defined in a series of documents called RFCs.[22] A Network Management Station (NMS) gives an administrator an overview of network status and direct control over devices. Agents may be located, for example, in routers, bridges, servers, and workstations. Strictly speaking, SNMP (specified in RFC 1157) is the protocol that carries information back and forth between the manager (NMS) and the various agents.

The Management Information Base (MIB) specifications (contained in RFC 1155 and 1156) describes objects that can be managed using SNMP. Managed information objects at each node are organized in the MIB as a global tree (comparable to the naming conventions used in the X.500 directory). Objects—the leaves of the tree—are uniquely named by object identifiers. Each object identifier consists of a sequence of integers that

---

22.   RFC 1028, 1052, 1065, 1089, 1098, 1109, and 1157. The associated Management Information Base (MIB) is defined in RFC 1066, 1155, and 1156.

denotes the path of traversal through the tree to the root [Case90]. Objects are generally statistics: counters for packets sent, connections attempted or made, number of error packets transmitted, and number of collisions on a given (Ethernet) LAN segment.

A few commands relate the manager to the agent, as follows:

- `Get`—manager to agent: Return current value of MIB variable
- `Get_Response`—agent to manager: Response with requested data-value
- `Get_Next`—manager to agent: Get the next logical object in the MIB
- `Set`—manager to agent: Change the values of MIB variables to...
- `Trap`—agent to manager: Sending an asynchronous event, in response to a status change or event

Typically, the manager periodically polls each agent, collects statistics, and stores them in the database. Management applications then can use thresholds to anticipate problems and direct corrective actions. `Trap` messages may be initiated on link failure, link restart, agent initialization, agent restart, and authentication failure (the latter is when a user attempts to gain access to the agent software without proper authorization).

NetView's TCP/IP role. In a manner similar to that described earlier for OSI, the SNMP manager in a S/390[23] allows NetView to act as the enterprise system management user interface for its TCP/IP network. This SNMP manager thus enables the communication between the NetView operator and supported TCP/IP machines in the network. Asynchronous events (`Traps`), from any SNMP agent, are forwarded, for example, from the VM SNMP manager to NetView. `Traps` from designated sources may optionally be filtered by the VM SNMP manager before they are passed to NetView. NetView applications can be written to automate the gathering of statistical data with presentation of the status of the TCP/IP network. An illustrative `Trap` scenario follows:

1. An SNMP agent issues a `Trap` message in ASN.1 syntax.
2. UDP (User Datagram Protocol) delivers the `Trap` message to a port at the manager's host.
3. The message may be authenticated and is transformed from ASN.1 syntax to local data structure (e.g., "C" data structure).
4. NetView's `Trap` command processor maps the `Trap` information into a generic alert, and enqueues the alert to either the automation facility or the hardware monitor.
5. Automation may invoke a process that can do further analysis, or issue `Get` commands for more data, or `Set` commands to change the operational environment of the `Trap`-issuing agent.
6. The NetView hardware monitor logs and/or displays the alert information.

---

23. IBM has stated that fault management using the OSI CMIS/CMIP and the TCP/IP SNMP will be supported in all SAA and AIX environments. Network management capability originally provided for S/390 OSI networks will support SAA and AIX systems that implement OSI/ Communications Subsystem or the equivalent management services.

The NetView operator can solicit management data, such as message counts or transmission error statistics, that are accumulated by the TCP/IP agents. In addition, the operator can set certain values such as gateway routing tables entries, if the target agent supports this function.

On the other hand, NetView is not a prerequisite for SNMP in networks consisting of TCP/IP systems. For example, the RISC S/6000 series provides support for both manager and agent functions. It works in conjunction with SNMP agents or managers in other systems.

4.6.4   SNA/OSI/TCP INTEGRATION

To function in a multivendor environment, NetView must be able to oversee the operations of networks with multiple protocols. In particular, this includes the three protocols of primary usage: SNA, OSI, and TCP/IP. The integration of system management for this variety requires convergence or accommodation in three areas:

1.   Event data formats

2.   Formats and protocols that communicate management functions

3.   The programming interface for managemnt applications

Each of these three protocols provides a somewhat different set of management information. SNA `Alerts`, TCP/IP `Traps`, and OSI `Events` must all be "caught" and processed, as illustrated in Figure 4.14. Even with the gradual transition to CMIP protocols, an interim accommodation of existing protocols is needed.

In the proposed scenario of Figure 4.14, management applications would be written to an API that could make use of all the CMIS commands (`Set`, `Get`, and so on), plus a few others to handle nonstandard situations. A subset of these commands would be translatable into those understood by older SNA and TCP/IP nodes. Of course, the application-processes would be sensitive to the different objects in different nodes. Therefore only the commands understood by different nodes would be applied to them. With that caveat,

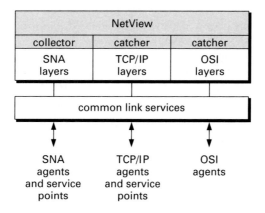

Figure 4.14 Use of management data from three primary protocol systems.

however, the application would be independent of whether the node was OSI or SNA or TCP/IP based.

Another variation may be used in large TCP/IP networks during a transition to OSI. CMOT stands for CMIP-Over-TCP/IP. CMOT has essentially the same structure as CMIP—only the transport layer has been made TCP/IP, instead of the OSI transport protocol.

4.7 MANAGEMENT DATABASES

Almost all system management applications involve the collection and use of databases. The problem of managing this data becomes ever more crucial. Fault, configuration, operations, accounting, change, and asset management, all have interrelated data. For example, one of the primary problems in voice/data management is the constantly changing inventory of customer-premises facilities, persons associated with each facility, and users. Everything from cable management and phone locations to trouble calls, change requests and work orders are involved. Changes affect assets and cause network problems. New users affect accounting, equipment changes, and asset inventory. Each change can cause malfunctions.

As applications grow, they tend to create their own, isolated databases. A basic need exists to replace these disparate databases with an object-oriented repository of information, which can have data entered only once per item. That database would be accessed by all system management applications and others who need that information.

A step in this direction is the current provision of a bridge between NetView and other databases. With this facility, one can automate transactions between non-NetView databases and NetView. Current examples of databases that can be accessed by the NetView bridge are the Information Management database and databases containing configuration information and service definitions. An example of the use of this linkage would be the automatic creation of problem records from NetView, and their subsequent tracking. The trouble ticket is routed to the assigned problem solver, and an escalation timer is invoked. If the problem is closed within the designated time frame, the escalation timer and notice will be canceled. Otherwise, an escalation notice is sent to a designated person. Problem records placed into the Information Management database are updated from NetView to reflect the latest status information.

Now, system management tools are progressively being built around distributed relational databases (see Section 5.2.4). The longer-range goal is that these separate databases will be merged into a commonly accessible, distributed relational (or object-oriented) database for system management. These databases then can be managed as part of an enterprise data management operation. The SystemView direction is to develop integrated multivendor solutions that will provide for:

- Integration of multiple vendor-supplied tools, and common services to be used by all tools

- A single point of control, at one workstation, for database management on multiple SAA systems

- A database object navigator that will enable users to browse database catalogs to find objects upon which systems management tasks are to be performed

4.8   SYSTEM MANAGEMENT ILLUSTRATIONS

The "manager of managers" concept is still evolving, as more and more semi-independent subsystems and subnetworks are integrated into an overall system management capability. The following will, however, indicate the direction that this evolution is taking.

4.8.1   LAN Network Management

LANs are themselves very large networks. Each token-ring segment can handle up to 260 stations. Then, by using bridges or routers to interconnect LANs (token rings, token bus, Ethernets, PC Networks, and FDDIs), thousands of stations can form one vast local area network. Moreover, by using routers and remote bridges, LANs that are spread across the entire country can be interconnected into one larger network. This poses a growing challenge for system management, and adequate management tools are needed.

The keys to this are the LAN Network Managers, performing local LAN management functions, working in concert with the Station Managers that provide information at individual nodes, and the NetView for central coordination at enterprise system managers. These facilities are adaptable to all types of LANs. Potentially, most of the network applications described in Section 4.4 have applicability to LAN management.

The **IBM LAN Manager** [Vig89],[Willett88] was initially designed to help diagnose and manage problems on bridged IBM LANs—the Token-Ring Network and the PC Network. It also applies to the bridge (8209) between token rings and Ethernets, and to LANs extended by optical fiber converters. It works alone, with a local display or a remote dial-up console; or it works in concert with the central NetView manager.[24] The concepts, however, are equally applicable to other LANs, such as Ethernet and FDDI, as well.

The **LAN Network Manager** (the later evolution of the IBM LAN Manager) addresses more of the LAN management problem, and works with the LAN Station Manager. The LAN Network Manager basically analyzes and isolates faults, filters the alerts, and sends selected alerts or alarms to the user locally, and to NetView in the larger network's enterprise system manager.[25] The LAN can be managed locally, using the operator interface of the LAN Network Manager, or centrally from an enterprise NetView. Commands also can be sent from that NetView system manager to the LAN Network Manager to query for status, test LAN operations, or remove faulty devices from the network. The LAN Network Manager also provides notification of problem recovery.

Alerts from the LAN Network Manager identify a fault location, the probable causes, and the recommended actions. In addition to reporting hard errors, a count is also kept of

---

24.   The LAN Manager was provided as software in a PS/2. Largely equivalent function was also provided as software integrated in the OS/400 support in the AS/400.

25.   IBM plans APIs for its LAN Network Manager, according to IBM's Bill Warner (*Communications Week*, March 25, 1991).

soft errors, which do not bring down the network, but could affect performance now or later. Token-ring adapters can periodically send their soft-error counts to servers containing the *Ring Error Monitor*. When thresholds are exceeded, they can be sent to the LAN Network Manager. The LAN Network Manger, in turn, may send an alert to a higher-level system manager.

Alerts also are generated when excessive traffic flows through a bridge. Bridge performance is monitored by logging bridge traffic statistics at the LAN Network Manager. The bridgelike 3172, which connects multiple LANs to the S/390 channel, likewise sends alerts to NetView via the LAN Network Manager. To further monitor key elements, the LAN Network Manager will periodically poll critical resources, such as file servers, gateways, and communication servers, to see if they are still functioning. If no response is received, an alert is sent to NetView.

Finally, a facility is provided for the customer to report their own unique alerts. A station may construct these alerts, send them in the standard system management formats, send them to the LAN Network Manager via the LAN, and have them forwarded to NetView at the enterprise system manager.

Through a user interface, the LAN Network Manager responds to a set of special operator commands. The operator, for example, can see the LAN configuration in three levels: the entire LAN, individual LAN segments, and displays of the Token Ring Controlled Access Units (described below) and the lobes attached to them. The operator can also see a log of the alerts, a description of the problem, and recommended actions.

LAN Station Manager.   For more effective LAN management, the LAN Network Manager should be able to communicate with a cooperating manager at each LAN-attached station, called a *LAN Station Manager*.[26] The purpose of the LAN Station Manager is to enable network management across mixed media LANs. While the base Station Manager provides a certain amount of management function in itself, it also is an enabler for attaching functions. The Station Manager provides the functions of an OSI system management *agent*, in communication with the LAN Network Manager. The LAN Network Manager then may be the manager for a workgroup and, in turn, then may communicate with a higher-level system manager, like NetView.

Because an installation may have diverse LANs and systems using the LANs, the LAN Station Manager architecture has to be independent of media, operating system, hardware platform, and user applications. The approach is to base the architecture on the OSI CMIP/RO specifications. To reduce overhead, these operate directly over logical-link control (LLC) type 1, rather than over the full seven-layer OSI stack.

Resource management is the individual station participation in the overall system management function. The Station Manager functions are primarily within the LLC sublayer of the data link control layer. Reports can be sent to both the local LAN Network Manager and to a higher-level system manager.

---

26.   As of this writing, LAN Station Managers exist for programmable workstations running either DOS or OS/2, attached to IBM Token Ring or PC Network LANs. However, the concept is extendable to other LANs.

The Resource Management part of the Station Manager can receive all of the CMIP commands: `Get`, `Set`, `Action`, `Create`, `Delete`, and `Cancel_Get`. The `Get` command can retrieve either product/location identifiers or performance information. The `Set` can establish various parameters at the station. Thresholds can be created or deleted. The Station Manager also sends the all-important `Event` and `Alarm` messages.

The intent is to provide several interfaces to promote wide applicability. A Managing Process (MP) interface is essentially an RO (Remote Operations) CMIP interface. This allows applications to issue RO/CMIP invocations to the Station Manager and to collect unsolicited CMIP notifications. The layer management entities (LMEs), associated with each layer, are also made visible via a Managed Entity (ME) interface. This, too, is essentially a CMIP interface. That is, the information that flows across it is the CMIP PDU. The ME interface allows the LAN Station Manager to perform operations on objects owned by local LMEs.

Architecturally, the Station Manager is an OSI System Management Application-Entity (SMAE) within the OSI System Management Application-Process (SMAP) of a particular node (see Section 4.3.3). Its data is encoded using the OSI ASN.1 format (see Section 9.2.2). It uses the OSI Common Management Information Protocol (CMIP) for communications between the LAN Station Manager and the LAN Network Manager.

Heterogeneous LAN Management, for multiple distinct LAN technologies in a single network, is being implemented using the LAN Station Manager and the OSI CMIP/RO architecture over link LLC type 1 [HLMa], [HLMb]. This standard is well defined and is gaining wide acceptance. The standard object definitions, on the other hand, are not yet so well defined. Therefore it is currently necessary to use proprietary object definitions that appear to be closest to the direction of future standards.

Controlled Access Unit. How does the system manager really know what the LAN attachments are? How can a malfunctioning unit or link be quickly removed to avoid system degradation? These are the important issues addressed by the Controlled Access Unit (CAU). The CAU is a means for physically connecting a node to a token-ring LAN. It can report station-insertion on the LAN to the LAN Network Manager.[27] When a device attached to a CAU inserts into the ring, the CAU reports its identifier, attachment module identifier, and the lobe identifier, automatically, to the LAN Network Manager. This information is verified with the information in the database. Any deviation may be configured to generate an alert. When necessary, the LAN Network Manager can issue a `Force_Remove` command to a station adapter. It can also issue a `Disable_Lobe` command to the CAU. Thus, unauthorized workstations may be kept from using the token-ring LAN. The CAU reports access attempts to the LAN Network Manager, including information regarding location of the port through which the security violation is being attempted. As part of the security system, an audit trail of stations and bridges entering and leaving the network can be created and queried.

The CAU also provides a reconfiguration function. When there is a physical problem with one section of the ring, the CAUs on the ring can send an `Alarm` to notify the LAN

---

27.   The Controlled Access Unit is modular. It supports up to 80 workstations in increments of 20 attachments per module, with up to 4 modules attached to one base unit.

Network Manager. The LAN Network Manager can query the configuration state and can initiate a "wrap." The ring can be wrapped into two separate rings—one that has the error and one that is operational.

Bridge Manager.   The Bridge Manager also assists in fault management, using a set of tracing and data collection facilities.[28] Four management servers support the LAN Management function. These servers include:

1. *Ring Error Monitor (REM)*: Collects and analyzes beacon frames (used for hard errors) and Soft Error Reports. REM will display the status of the ring and tabulate the reported errors according to location and type of error.

2. *Configuration Report Server (CRS)*: Collects reports of changes in the configuration of the ring. This includes physical additions, physical deletions, and function assignments (such as active monitor).

3. *Ring Parameter Server (RPS)*: Maintains consistent sets of operational parameters for the ring. During a station insertion, the incoming station registers with RPS and requests parameters from RPS.

4. *LAN Bridge Server (LBS)*: Maintains a set of statistical counters on frame traffic through the bridge, and reports to management when preset thresholds are exceeded. Counts are kept, for example, on the number of frames passed through the bridge and the number of frames discarded because of congestion.

These may be located in bridges. The first three may also be located on other systems that are active full time. The LAN Bridge Manager receives and assembles all the *soft error* frames from multiple attached rings. Algorithms within this manager analyze the soft errors to isolate the errors to a fault domain. The two adapter addresses comprising a fault domain and the soft error count for each adapter are displayed. With *hard errors*, an adapter on the ring can be counted on to "beacon" the problem, using a signaling technique described in Section 17.3.3. The date and time of the beaconing, the address of the beaconing adapter, the address of the nearest active upstream neighbor, and the type of beaconing are all displayed.

The LAN Network Manager collects such information from each bridge manager and/or from other servers which may be located on multiple rings.

Other LAN servers.   SystemView adds to the architecture *special alerts* requested by vendors.[29] An example of this is the cooperation with Novell, resulting in the definition of alerts that are valuable to *LAN servers*, such as Novell's NetWare 386. Novell defined 110 NetView alerts that can be generated by a NetWare 386 file server or other comparable servers. These can report fifteen types of conditions (e.g., limit exceeded or out of resource) from a dozen loci (such as memory, disks, or LAN boards). Being added to the architecture,

---

28.   The Bridge Manager functions do not require the LAN Network Manager or the LAN Station Manager.

29.   Reportedly [Ziegler91a], many LAN vendors—including Banyan, 3COM, Microsoft, and Novell—have stated their intent to support NetView interfaces through the NetView/PC application program interface and/or other ways.

this family of alerts also becomes available to other vendors of LAN servers. Novell's network management system, uses a gateway called the SNA Network Loadable Module, running on the NetWare 386 server to communicate with NetView. The communication uses LU 6.2 protocols, and travels over token ring or SDLC links.

NetView evolves to become the manager of multiple LAN Network Managers. Different vendor's LAN management systems are incorporated, to the extent that they meet the NetView protocols and support NetView features.

4.8.2 X.25 Interconnection (XI) Network Managers

As another example, public and private subnetworks are parts of the whole that need to be managed. The interfaces between the two are places for data collection and management action.[30,31] A further example of this subnetwork collaboration is the **Network Supervision Function (NSF)**, a NetView application to oversee the use of an SNA network as a passthrough for X.25 traffic (the XI capability). *XI is the X.25 Interconnection program* that enables an SNA network to provide a DCE interface identical to that which a public PSDN provides to its end-systems.

The nodes at the boundary of the SNA network, that participate in this passthrough, are called XI nodes. To provide a central management, LU-LU sessions are established between each XI node and its controlling NSF located in a S/390 mainframe. One type-0 LU-LU session, between NSF and XI, carries NSF operator commands and the XI reports. A second session carries XI alerts plus standard VTAM-NCP traffic. This latter session is between the PU of the communications controller and the SSCP in the host. With all this information, NetView may then display detailed diagnostic data and recommend courses of action pertaining to the X.25 connection.

NSF operates pretty much as a relay program, relaying application or operator commands, replies, and status information between NetView and the Node Management Function (NMF) in the XI nodes. The functions of NSF include:

- Fault management
- NCP, modem, and XI diagnostic aids
- Log trace
- On line reconfiguration
- Display defined system resources
  - Add new or remove old resources
  - Modify resource parameters

---

30. For example, IBM's NPSI, for interfacing X.25 subnetworks to SNA networks has a system management component.

31. AT&T and IBM will also develop software so AT&T's ACCUMASTER Integrator and IBM's NetView and Information/Management products will work together. Existing interfaces will be adapted so as to lay the foundations for using OSI network management standards (*World News Today*, March 25, 1991).

- Gathering of activity and accounting information
  - Virtual circuit characteristics
  - Traffic volumes and call durations
- Warm or cold restart
- Remote operation (from terminal on another host)

During operation, XI continually updates a number of counters. They apply to the LAP-B operation and packet level traffic of the X.25 interface, and also the entire XI node itself. The contents of these counters are sent to NSF on the request of the operator and on the occasion of a counter overflow.

Operator control of XI. The Network Supervisory Function (NSF) enables the network operator to:

- Activate and deactivate permanent virtual circuits (PVCs)
- Enable logical channels, and spare LUs
- Test the X.25 interface, and conduct end-to-end tests
- Change resource definitions concerning window sizes, packet sizes, membership in closed user groups, and XI routing tables
- Request information about the status of the X.25 interface, permanent virtual circuits (PVCs), number of logical channels in use, and parameters of logical channels, such as window sizes and packet sizes
- Request maintenance and availability statistics, and accounting information (such as called and calling addresses, and duration of calls)

4.8.3   Voice/Data System Management

The trend is to the common management of shared data and voice facilities. The telephone company can detect if a physical communication path fails, but only the data processing components can detect if the data is coming through intact or garbled. There is an obvious need to coordinate the total physical and logical (application/session) system management. The decade of experience in anticipatory, pro-active management of data networks (rather than purely reactive management) is now being applied to the combination of voice and data. The following subsection illustrates how all this is coming together.

Voice management components.   Voice system management, illustrated in Figure 4.15, includes the following:

- *CBX and PBX alert monitors*, which poll the CBXs for problems, process the alerts, and optionally forward selected alerts to a system manager.
- *CBX/PBX alarm and traffic monitors*. These use special alarm translators (like TSB's AT1[32]) to capture alarm and traffic data from a myriad of PBX and non-PBX network

---

32.   TSB International, an IBM business partner, is located in Toronto, Canada.

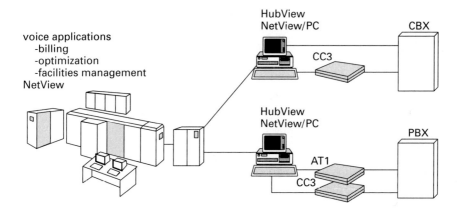

Figure 4.15 Typical components in voice system management.

equipments. Upon detecting a user-defined alarm condition, the alarm translator dials a management service point and sends the alarm data to it. The service point, in turn, may transport the alarm to a system manager.

- *PBX line fault monitors.*
- *PBX/CBX call-detail data collectors.* These use special call-detail-record (CDR) collector devices (like the TSB's CC3), to collect accounting data from PBXs and CBxs. A management service point periodically dials the CDR collector devices for its data. The accounting data, in turn, may be periodically transmitted to a system manager that supports billing, analysis, and network design.
- *Call accounting.* These applications allow the cost of the physical plant to be allocated and charged back to using individuals and/or organizations. They also provide traffic analysis, based on the call records, to give an overview of the PBX performance and the load or quality level of attached lines.
- *Bandwidth management*—e.g., more bandwidth may be allocated to voice during the day, and more allocated to data during other hours (see Section 18.5.3).
- *Facilities management*, including the management of moves, adds, and changes throughout the customer's voice system.

HubView/PC, shown in Figure 4.15, is an application for NetView/PC that centralizes voice network fault management, traffic data collection, and call detail record (CDR) collection.[33] As shown, it draws information from PBXs and CBXs[34] via special buffer devices attached to these exchanges. HubView/PC monitors alarms and filters them based

---

33. HubView/PC is licensed by TSB International Inc.

34. As of this writing, HubView/PC supports switches from AT&T, Ericsson, Fujitsu, GTE, Harris, Intecom, ITT, IWATSU, MICOM, MITEL, NEC, NT, Roadrunn Perception, ROLM, Siemens, Tadrian, TIE, and Toshiba Perception PBXs.

on customer's definition as: *critical, potential critical* (based on frequency and duration criteria), or *minor*. The first two categories are formatted as generic alerts and sent to NetView with recommended action and probable cause data. "Minor" alarms are written to a file for further processing as the customer requires.

Given the host connection, the functions of HubView can be expected to evolve. One of the valuable expected features is the ability to perform moves, adds, and changes (MACs) from a command-driven application interface. This would allow MAC transactions to be initiated from applications, such as NetView Voice Facilities Management applications.

T1 resource management.   The current IDNX[35] network (see Section 18.5.3) provides for the sharing of voice and data traffic on T1 lines. The Transmission Network Monitor (TNM) provides a single user interface from which to view and manage an entire IDNX network, using graphics and windowing software. The PS/2 workstation allows an operator to view the network topology and to zoom in on the failing card or port anywhere in the network. In addition to providing stand-alone control for IDNX networks, the TNM can forward IDNX network information to NetView applications on a host. A bidirectional command-set with NetView allows the TNM to send network alarms to the NetView host and to perform tasks based on commands sent from NetView. Access to a relational database system, using SQL, lets the Transmission Network Manager display realtime updates of network event, alarm, and configuration information.

Data from the SPE.   The service provider equipment (SPE) of the common carriers, which is dedicated to a customer, may also be of vital concern. This has been recognized by some carriers, and a suitable provision of alarm data, status indications, and call-detail records are being provided [Llana89]. An example of this is the announced *MCI Integrated Network Management Service (INMS)*, which provides a customer interface on a PS/2 or a host connection, on the customer's premises.[36] A partial list of the currently available services includes the following:

- Trouble management provides online ability to open, update, monitor, and close trouble reports.

- Configuration management allows customers to query and assess the configuration of MCI services in their network.

- Operations management provides the real-time ability to monitor the MCI portion of the customer network and view operational alarms and traffic status, perform call

---

35.   The IDNX products are made by Network Equipment Technologies, Inc.

36.   According to *Communications Week*, May 7, 1990, the first phase of INMS includes an programmable workstation at the customer premise, connected by an LU 6.2 session to MCI's VM host. The second step is a unidirectional link from the MCI host to the customer's host running NetView. The third step is a NetView (or other similar tool) application giving the ability for any workstation attached to the customer's host to communicate with MCI's host.

detail record searches, obtain call detail record statistics, and identify network problem areas.

- Performance and planning management allows customers to generate reports based on traffic and alarm data.

Carrier information from such sources significantly reinforces the capability of system management applications, particularly in voice/data communication systems.

Network operations center. The network operations staff thus acquires the information resources that are needed to effectively manage the data/voice networks. Data is drawn from a number of complementary sources. The base is the NetView facilities oriented primarily to the data network. These are augmented by the bridge to the Information Management databases concerned with trouble-ticket tracking, inventory records, and change records. These data-information sources are complemented by the NetView Voice Facilities Management for the cable system inventory and work-orders for voice related service and repair. The voice usage reports and billing are then aided by NetView Call Accounting, which draws data from the call detail records sent from NetView/PCs associated with PBXs.

4.8.4   Advanced Peer-to-Peer Networking System Management

Advanced Peer-to-Peer Networking (APPN) is an evolution of SNA wide area networking, with emphasis on minimum system definition, dynamic topology update, and nondisruptive network growth (see Chapter 14). Consistent with this evolution, the philosophy of APPN system management is the distribution of management services, so as to provide local controls where that is desirable, and to add system managers for broader management functions. Hence, there is a Control Point Management Services function (CPMS) *in each Type 2.1 node*, which collects management data regarding that node. This is true for APPN end-nodes as well as APPN network-nodes.

APPN management hierarchy. An APPN *system manager* oversees the system management for a group of network-nodes within its *sphere of control*. It receives event alerts and gathered statistics from the nodes under its control. The system manager, together with a local or remote operator, thus form a *domain system management center*. The system manager provides remote access to data and operator functions in all the APPN network-nodes that belong to that system manager. This is done via LU 6.2 sessions between the system manager and each of the network nodes within its sphere of control.

The **AS/400** provides support for system management in a stand-alone AS/400 environment for managing and controlling a network of attached workstations and printers. In addition, it provides system management capabilities to manage and control *peer-connected* systems like AS/400, S/36, S/38, PS/2, and 3174 establishment (cluster) controllers.

A set of APPN system managers, moreover, can be grouped together, to form a sphere of control. Thus, APPN system managers can also be nested to form a hierarchy of control, if that is desired. The APPN system managers can also become inputs to the higher-level SNA/OSI system managers described previously.

Integrated into an SNA subarea network, network-nodes (like the AS/400 and the PS/2) can be managed and controlled directly by NetView.[37] As an intermediary between NetView and peer-connected systems, the AS/400 can manage nodes in the APPN network independently of NetView, and it can also assist NetView to control nodes in that network. The intent is to provide (where appropriate) a seamless flow of alerts to NetView from APPN system managers.

Electronic service support connection.   The connection to the IBM electronic customer service support function can be through a single central system manager site in the APPN network.

When an `Alert` is received from a remote site, the system manager site can automatically generate a problem record or have one generated after the remote fault analysis is complete. Once this fault-record is generated, it is updated at each step through the process of managing the problem, giving a chronology of the problem. This central problem log can be searched to view problems based on the originating site, problem type, and other relevant parameters.

Requests for Program Temporary Fixes (PTFs) by the remote sites results in a search of the PTF database at the APPN central site. If there is a match found, the PTF(s) can then be automatically forwarded to the remote site for installation. If there is not a match within the central site PTF database for the service request, the request can be forwarded by the central site to the service support system.

4.8.5   DECnet Management

As discussed above, while the movement toward OSI will make multivendor management easier, accommodations for existing proprietary conventions will still be necessary. Another good illustration of single point of control, for multivendor system management, is the SNA-DECnet case described here.

Interlink Computer Sciences, Inc. provides a product[38] that allows the user to manage a DECnet Phase IV network from NetView. It allows a single network control center for both SNA and DECnet networks using NetView. In particular, it makes it possible to:

- Supply DECnet events to NetView as `Alerts`
- Allow a NetView operator to enter standard DECnet commands to display DECnet status, display usage and error counters, configure, test, and control DECnet
- Perform loop back tests to DECnet nodes

The Interlink software gateway runs on a boundary node S/390; and the physical connection to an 802.3 Ethernet is via a LAN channel station (8232) or the 3172 Interconnection Controller (see Section 17.5.2). NetView may be running on the gateway S/390 system or on another S/390 located elsewhere in the SNA network.

DECnet "events" are sent from DECnet-nodes to the boundary-node, where Interlink reformats them as SNA Network Management Vector (NMVT) RUs. These are then

---

37.   The type of session used for communication with NetView varies. The subarea network-nodes communicate via an SSCP-PU session. The direction for APPN network-nodes is to communicate with NetView via LU 6.2 sessions.

38.   The Interlink NetConnect product, and associated products, are IBM alliance offerings.

forwarded to the fault management application in NetView. On arrival, they appear as generic `Alerts`.

DECnet management commands are issued via a task running under NetView. The text of these messages is sent over an LU 6.2 session to the boundary node of the SNA network, where Interlink encodes them into DECnet's system management protocol. These are then sent to DECnet via the gateway software. Responses from the DECnet nodes are decoded and sent over a second LU 6.2 session to the NetView task for display on the operator's console.

The interoperability between SNA and DECnet nodes, for application-services, also provided by the Interlink software, is described in Section 5.9.

In addition to this Interlink facility, DEC systems and element managers within those systems, can be monitored, controlled, and automated using NetView/PC and a Cooperative Software Program called the *Network Management Access Program* from Automated Network Management, Inc.[39]

Conclusion

The architecture under discussion has the objective of incorporating, in a practical and efficient way, the coming international standards and also the diversity that is demanded by heritage systems, new technologies, and new application requirements. That scope requires a corresponding system-management capability of great breadth and depth.

The Systems Management Process is the integration of diverse system management facilities for multiple communication protocols, along with workload and economic analysis/planning functions that have characterized well-run data-processing shops. The ten years of experience with system management of complex networks based on NetView now is being reformulated to apply to the complex of LANs, MANs, and WANs, for data, image, and voice, with ever-higher performance, greater function-distribution, and more local autonomy. At the same time, there is growing cooperation among the system managers that are produced by different vendors, large and small. The base applications remain: fault, configuration, operations, performance, accounting, security, asset, and change management. Each is under pressure to expand to the broader multiprotocol, multivendor, data/image/voice areas.

The expectation is that the OSI efforts in network management will provide the common-denominator blueprint for this next stage. The movement toward that commonality is well underway.

Acknowledgments

I am particularly indebted to the following for valuable input or reviews of this chapter: R. C. Williams, M. F. Gering, W. B. Kleinoeder, P. Janson, R. M. Willett, and R. L. Sayre.

---

39. DEC systems managed from NetView via the Automated Network Management, Inc., program, include the Network Control Program, Terminal Server Manager, Remote Bridge Management System, and LAN Traffic Monitor.

TECHNICAL REFERENCE
NetView/PC Commands

- `Linkdata` requests the service point to return collected data for a link or link segment.
- `Linkpd` requests a service point to do problem determination on a link or link segment. The response includes the status of the link, a probable cause of failure, and data on the failed resource (e.g., type/name).
- `Linktest` requests service point to test a link and report results. The request can specify how many times the test is to be run.
- `Run_Command` requests that a service point run a specified command. The service point response can be used to drive an automated command list at the host.

SNA Change Management Commands

- `Accept` cancels the removability of a change installed previously at an agent, and relinquishes resources required to maintain removability.
- `Activate` causes reactivation of the agent.
- `Delete` deletes a change file at one or more agents.
- `Install` directs that a change file and its corequisites be used, by one or more agents, to alter all components necessary to effect the change.
- `Remove` returns all components previously altered to their original condition.
- `Retrieve` obtains a change file prepared at an entry point or at another system manager, for storage at a system manager.
- `Send` distributes a change file from the system manager to one or more agents or other system managers.
- `Send_And_Install` is the same as `Install` except that the system manager sends a change file in the same request.

EXERCISES

4.1   Name eight components of network management.

4.2   Name several additional functions (beyond network management) also included in system management.

4.3   What are the six basic steps commonly used in system management?

4.4   What are the three basic components of an OSI system management structure?

4.5   Name the five basic steps in fault management.

4.6   What four parameters are frequently measured in performance management?

4.7   Give four objectives of security management.

4.8   Are the following true or false?
   - Private key cryptography uses a public algorithm.
   - Secret messages can be sent under a public key and decrypted under a matching private key.

- A digital signature can be encrypted under a private key and decrypted with a matching public key.
- Once a user is certified by a Kerberos, that authentication can be sent to any application-server.
- SNA LU authentication uses passwords as keys for encrypting random data.

4.9 The integration of system management for OSI, SNA, and TCP/IP requires the convergence or accommodation in which three key areas?

4.10 How does the CAU contribute to security?

5
Distributed Resource Managers

5.1 INTRODUCTION

As speeds of LANs and WANs increase, the network offers greater opportunity for high-performance resource distribution. Conversely, the demands on communications are increasingly determined by the growing assortment of *distributed resource managers* (also called application-servers, or client–servers). These operate, for the most part, at layer 7 of the OSI structure. This chapter is devoted to giving an overview of the prime resource managers that contribute to distributed systems operation. The intent is to highlight those aspects of interest to the communications specialist, and to give further insight into the tight relationships between the distributed operating system and the communication services.

One of the most important types of servers deals with distributed data. Two distinct types of data servers are involved, for *file systems* and for *relational databases* using *Structured Query Language (SQL).*[1] Essential to both are the communication protocols for *sync points* and *back-out* capabilities, to insure data integrity in distributed operations. Hence an effort is made below to describe what the distributed data facilities are and how they cooperate in the network.

Then, we examine the operation of the general-purpose LAN server, using as examples one microprocessor system, the IBM PS/2 LAN Server and one mainframe system, the AS/400 PC Support, which provide easy-to-use application services that are important to most LAN users. This chapter also includes some discussion of the pioneering TCP/IP family of client-servers, the virtual terminal, and the way in which client–servers can function across SNA and DECnet networks.

While movements to convergence are underway, and some of these are cited, the current requirement is the support of a large diversity in function, interfaces, and protocols.

---

1. SQL is a standardized set of statements used to manage information stored in a database.

5.2 DISTRIBUTED DATA

5.2.1 Introduction

The objective of a distributed data system is to let the application programmer access I/O as if the data were local; let the system determine the actual location of the data; and let the system retrieve the data regardless of its location. The distributed data system must present the data to the application in a form that is useful for the application.

However, data systems vary greatly. File structures may be organized by bytes or records. Directories may be flat or hierarchical [Summers89],[Popek85]. Different operating environments may use different data styles, which may be foreign to the applications. For example: workstations use ASCII character coding, while some hosts use EBCDIC; different data structures are created by different programming languages; integers may have different lengths, and floating-point representations may vary.

Clearly, some consistency and interoperability is needed among the different operating environments. Within IBM products, for example, this means a need for transparent distribution at least among all SAA and AIX/OSF environments. Beyond that, it means to seek consistency with the data systems of other vendors, by agreements with members of multivendor associations, like the Open Software Foundation (OSF).

Current data classes.   In general, current data systems might be put into three classes:[2]

1. *Byte-oriented* or stream files
2. *Record-oriented* files, simple, unstructured, files, or files with relations among records in each file
3. *Databases* with relations among records in multiple files, with concurrency, integrity, and security features

Actually, the third, databases, can be built using either byte or record-oriented files. All three classes are important in their own sphere. One does not replace the other. The objective, therefore, is not only to have good data-management systems, of all three types, but also to have the architecture that permits the interchange of data in any of these categories among all workstations and mainframes that need it.

Flat (nonstructured), **byte-oriented**, ASCII files dominate the PC environment, having grown in a simple DOS world. UNIX, too, uses flat files. In stream access, the application specifies a byte location within the file and the number of bytes to access in the file. The stream (or byte) files are particularly suitable for text and for noncoded, image, and mixed-object documents. Tools are available for making the data from stream files convertible for use within record-oriented files and relational databases as well. Conversely, data from record-oriented and database files can be transformed for use in applications that only handle byte-oriented files.

In **record access**, the application reads and writes subunits of files called "records." A record-oriented file consists of a set of slots in which records can be stored. Each record consists of a set of related fields describing some real entity (or aspect of a real entity) of interest to the application.

---

2. Coming to the fore is a new development called Object-Oriented Database Management systems, which may eventually join and perhaps overshadow the rest.

The **database** is characterized by its services for integrity, concurrency, and recovery, with the ability to share at a low level (record or field) among multiple users. Database managers (DBMs) have found wide acceptance because of the efficiency of data extraction, and the ease of application programming. *Intelligent decisions can be made within the database manager, so that only the pertinent data is actually moved.* Database managers may be:

- Hierarchical databases, consisting of records that are related to each other in a tree structure, by means of pointers contained within the records

- Network databases, with pointers similar to hierarchical, but with relations other than the simple tree hierarchy

- Relational databases, with relations inferred by the values of common fields contained in the tables of the database

- Object-oriented databases, where data is stored as objects, and each object is an instance of an abstract data type defined by an application

The future DBMs are expected to be predominantly relational models, although object-oriented databases are also finding their niche. In SAA and AIX, the **SQL relational** database model is the standard.[3] One of the main reasons for this choice is that the high-level SQL is easily decomposed into relational algebraic operations *that enable parallel execution at multiple locations.* Once executed, the data can be recomposed for delivery to the user.

Distributed data system requirements.   The requirements of a distributed data system include:

- Support for *all three classes*: databases, record-oriented files, and byte stream files
- *Common programming interface* for applications access to data using higher-level language Calls
- A *naming structure* that is independent of the physical location of the data or the path to the data

Data located on workstations and mainframes must be accessible throughout the enterprise, using a common directory system to locate the files. Security and resource-recovery facilities should likewise be common, where feasible. The desired positioning of the distributed data client and the distributed data server is illustrated in the two nodes of Figure 5.1. In the ideal world, the CPI would be applicable to all of the data systems in the enterprise; and the distributed data manager would shield the user from all differences.

5.2.2   Intersystem Distribution Manager

There will always be a requirement to support multiple industry standard protocols natively. However, multiple client–server pairs that work between like data systems are not always sufficient, because of the need for transparent interoperability among different

---

3.   Some data, such as that stored in an AS/400 database, can be accessed either as record-oriented files or through SQL interfaces as a relational database.

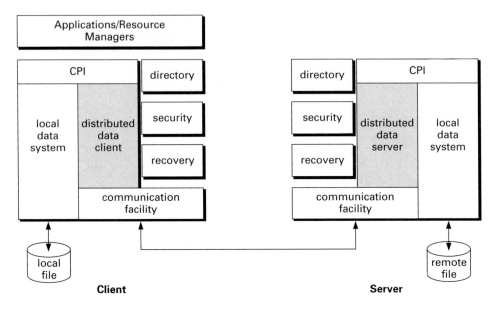

Figure 5.1 Distributed data system elementary structure.

systems. With multiple types of data systems (with database, record-oriented, and stream files), the mix and match combinations can quickly become too complex. Where feasible, there can be advantages in a common intermediate architecture. For this, another level of independence is required. *A system-independent, intermediary language, or set of data models is needed* for use by an intermediary, intersystem distribution manager. If the data systems are all identical, then the intermediary can be almost null. However, in the more general case, the intermediary must accommodate differences, and produce *standardized data system Calls*. A target data system then needs to translate only from one set of standardized calls to its own language. One example of such an intermediary distribution manager is the IBM *Distributed Data Manager (DDM)*. The relationship of that intermediary to the file systems of different operating environments is shown in Figure 5.2. The desired transparency process is basically as follows:

1. The originating system's higher-level language (HLL) file I/O Calls and/or HLL relational database Calls must be usable for remote operations, as well as local operations, in a range of higher-level languages. In SAA, the range currently includes COBOL, FORTRAN, C, and RPG. The SAA Calls have been standardized for these languages on the four sets of systems, OS/2, OS/400, VM, and MVS.

2. The Distributed Data Manager (for files and/or database), which receives these HLL Calls in an originating system, must determine whether the desired data is local or remote.

3. If the data is local, the originating DDM must translate these Calls to the access methods of the local file and database services.

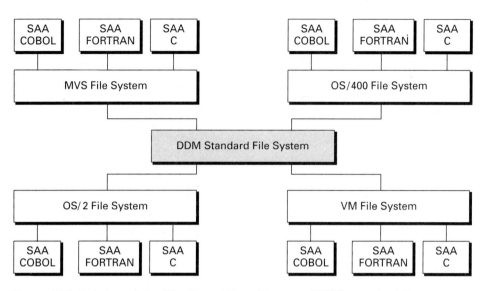

Figure 5.2 Relation of the Distributed Data Manager (DDM) standard file system to the file systems of different environments [Demers88a].

4.   If the data is remote, the originating DDM must send *corresponding but canonical DDM Calls or messages* to the DDM in the remote systems.

5.   The DDM in the remote systems must be able to translate these standardized Calls to the access methods of its local system.

SAA's DDM architecture has been evolving toward the above objectives. The distributed processing concept is illustrated in Figure 5.3. There two workstations and four mainframes are connected. The physical connections may be by LANs, WANS, or a combination of the two (the bandwidth, caching, and buffering in the design will of course affect performance). Each system, workstation, and mainframe is capable of the requester/ server function. Multiple data relationships, depending on the organization functions, can be established among all the systems.

In SAA's DDM [Demers88a], the application program uses Common Programming Interface (CPI) elements to call for distributed data. These elements are simply the existing high-level language statements for input-output or SQL statements. For example, with COBOL files, the application program begins with an `Open`, issues successive `Reads` or `Writes`, and ends with a `Close`. The DDM architecture allows for the inclusion of interfaces for database, record-oriented, and byte-oriented systems. Separate models and services are needed for each.

Both file models and relational data models are integrated into the DDM architecture. This integration is illustrated in Figure 5.4. The DDM agents are general-purpose DDM routers that allow an application to communicate with multiple servers and make sure that DDM commands get routed to the proper program in the proper server. The DDM communication manager drives the DDM protocol over a particular communication

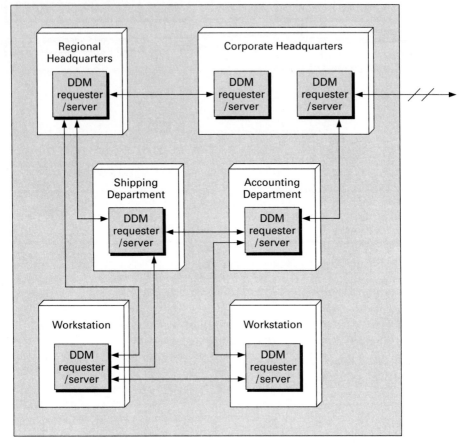

A Distributed System

Figure 5.3 DDM requester/servers in workstations and hosts [Demers88a].

facility, but is designed modularly so as to evolve to drive multiple types of communication facilities.

Each language has a runtime library that interprets the particular syntax and semantics of the CPI and converts them in a sequence of Calls to the data system. The requests to the data system are examined by the underlying data access software, which determines the location of the data from directory information. Then, if the data resides on another system, the CPI request results in the utilization of communications facilities to contact the other system. If the data is currently cached on the client system, the remote server is asked if the client cache is valid. If it is, the cached data is used. If it is not, the data is accessed on the server system using DDM protocols. In DDM, that end-to-end communication is handled by SNA LU 6.2 conversational protocols.

To illustrate further, SAA DDM systems provide file transfer as a transparent capability of the utilities for copying files within the system. For example, the AS/400

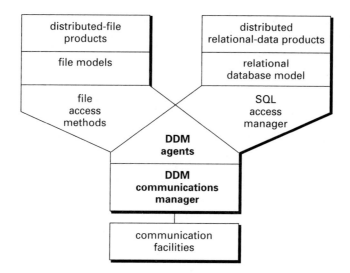

Figure 5.4 Integration of file and relational data models into DDM.

`Copy_File` command can be used to copy a file to or from a remote system with the same convenience as copying a file from one library to another library on the same system.

National language support.   A further complication is that the files and databases need to serve users in multiple national languages. Functions like `Sort` and `Select` must operate on characters in the national language, which are not the same in every language. In fact some twenty-six different languages are popular worldwide. Both the screen messages and data operations must utilize the unique characters in each language. Multinational operations are not practical without these capabilities.

5.2.3   Distributed File Systems

File transfer involves the moving or copying of the whole file from one system to another. *File access* allows one system to read or write selected, individual records of a file that is held on another system. *File serving* is another term sometimes used [Black89] to describe an extension of the former to allow one system to create, delete, and manipulate remote directory structures.

SAA Distributed File Manager.   The goal of SAA's Distributed File Manager (DFM) is transparent access to remote files through existing HLL interfaces. DFM consists of *the record-oriented file models, stream-oriented file model, and hierarchical directory model of DDM architecture.* Subdirectories can be created in or deleted from the server's hierarchical directory; files can be created, deleted, copied, renamed, locked, and unlocked in the target server. Once created, the attributes of the server's files can be retrieved and changed, and the files can be opened for data access.

OSI File Transfer (FTAM).   The OSI File Transfer, Access, and Management (FTAM) is an OSI standard, ISO 8571, that concerns three functions:

1. *File transfer function*—the movement of part of the whole of a file content between open systems

2. *File access function*—the inspection, modification, replacement, or erasure of part of a file's contents

3. *File management function*—the creation and deletion of files, and the inspection or manipulation of the files attributes

FTAM functions as an application-service–element within the OSI application layer.

A typical use would be to copy a file from one system to another. FTAM establishes an *association* to a complementary FTAM on a remote system. The association depends on the Association Control Service Element (ACSE) and the lower layers (1 through 6) of OSI. Following the successful association, the file is transferred. On completion of the transfer, the association is closed.

OSI has adopted a single intermediary data model approach. A common **virtual filestore** is defined, and each system then has the responsibility of *mapping their own real file management systems to this single conceptual model.*

The FTAM design is built around specific structures of files. The range of structures allowed includes unstructured, flat, and hierarchical structures. The FTAM files are modeled to contain zero, one, or more identifiable **Data Units** (DUs), where a DU is the smallest accessible unit of information contained in a file, and the smallest unit of transfer in FTAM. DUs are related in a tree structure; and subtrees are called **File Access Data Units (FADUs)**. The FTAM structure is the intermediary structure, into which the remote file can be transformed. In that way, the application is insensitive to the actual internal structure or access method of the remote file.

SAA FTAM functions.   *OSI/File Services*, an IBM implementation of FTAM, is one of the OSI application-services that have been included in the SAA family.[4] As in DDM, the data encoding in the two (local and remote) files may be different, the access methods may be different, and the file formats may be different in the two systems. The FTAM file is the structure understood by both systems. In the IBM OSI/File Services, the support extends to CMS files in the VM environment, and Physical Sequential files in the MVS environment. These files are mapped into the FTAM-1 (unstructured text) and FTAM-3 (unstructured binary) document types.

The "user interface" to FTAM is outside the scope of the FTAM standard. The SAA user interface for FTAM consists of an application programmer interface (API) and an interactive interface. The API complies with the SAA ground rules, providing Calls in COBOL and C. The interactive interface is a menu driven real-time interface.

---

4.   The SAA OSI/File Services are as defined by ISO 8571 (FTAM) International Standard. The first release conformed to the subset profiles of the US NBS Implementation Agreement (Phase 2 T1 and M1 profiles), and the CEN/CENELEC ENV 41-204 profile. The complexity of the issue can be grasped by the further arguments for support of the INTAP profile, the full support of the GOSIP profile, and the NBS T2/A1 and T3/A2 profiles.

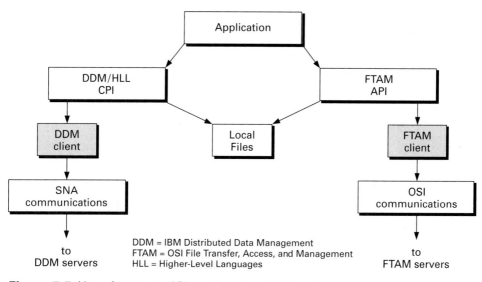

Figure 5.5 Use of separate APIs and protocol stacks.

DDM and FTAM designs.   There is a difference in the design approaches of DDM file system and FTAM. The DDM file system has been particularly designed to match the needs of major proven SAA file systems, and through them to match the high-level languages available on all SAA systems (COBOL, FORTRAN, C, RPG). *DDM accordingly has defined sets of standard file models that are each tailored to the specific requirements of these high-level languages.* The result is a high degree of local/remote file access transparency for the SAA standard languages.

FTAM, on the other hand, defines *a single hierarchical file model*, that can be constrained in various ways to meet specific access requirements.[5] FTAM's single hierarchical file model supports a rich set of attributes, ways of organizing data, and ways of accessing data. However, this model was not designed to specifically meet the file use requirements of existing programming languages and existing file system products. Applications must use special FTAM interfaces to use new file systems built to the FTAM specifications.

In general, there is little problem in creating products that support both FTAM and the DDM record file models: FTAM for new applications requiring OSI connectivity, and DDM for new and existing applications requiring transparent file access through third-generation language file interfaces.

Common file access interfaces.   There always remains the issue of coexistence or integration when still another file system arrives on the scene. Consider, as an example, the addition of the OSI FTAM to an existing DDM system. The possible integration of these two illustrates the integration of pairs of systems in general. A staged integration could take place. Initial designs necessitate *separate APIs*, for DDM-based services and FTAM, as shown in Figure 5.5. Each leads to a file client which is tailored to a separate (and probably different)

---

5.   For example, the sequential flat constraint does not allow a data unit at the root of the tree, and permits only one level below the root.

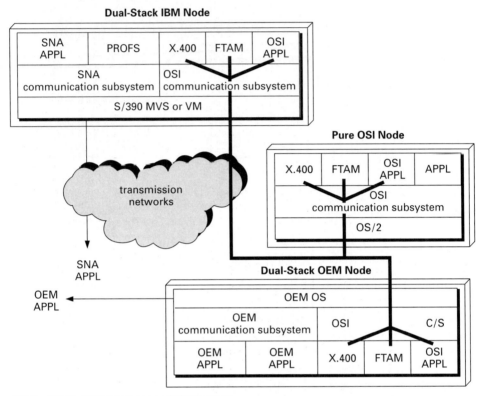

FTAM = OSI File Transfer, Access, and Management
OEM = Other Equipment Manufacturer
X400 = OSI Messaging Service

Figure 5.6 Concurrent access to proprietary and OSI application-services in a multivendor environment.

type of communications facility. This coexistence phase is further illustrated in Figure 5.6, showing exchanges among a pure OSI node and dual stack nodes of different vendors. The OSI and non-OSI services use *separate upper-layer*, end-to-end communications facilities. However, the requirement is that *common transport facilities*, at least in layers 1, 2, and 3a, can handle both the SNA and the OSI upper-layer protocols.

A longer range, technical direction needs to be a growing degree of *transparency, at the higher-level languages*, shown in Figure 5.7. It should provide transparency despite the use of different distributed-file protocols, whether they be IBM's DDM family or the OSI FTAM. This should also include transparency at the API for end-to-end data-exchange facilities, be they SNA or OSI, and any of the lower-level transport facilities like LANs, ISDN, etc. In this projection, the system determines, from the CPI Call, whether the data operation is local or remote. If remote, the interface software determines, by the destination, which communications protocols and file protocols are appropriate. The match to the different sets of higher-level languages may not be perfect, and precisely equivalent results may not always be obtained when using different models. Nevertheless,

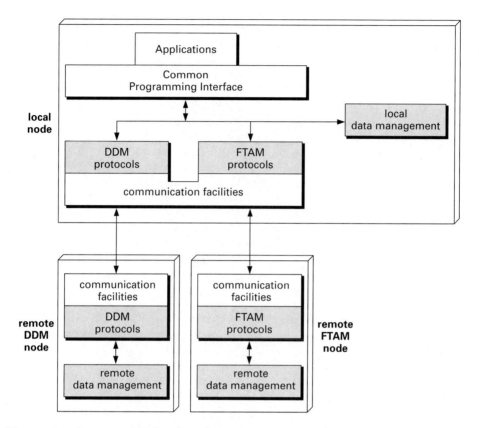

Figure 5.7 Common API for distributed data in remote DDM and FTAM nodes.

a workable common API is probably possible. There currently are no known products of this sort, but the technical feasibility appears to be there.

Finally, then, with an approach like DDM, there is the issue of *integration with commonality and interoperability* between any newcomer model and those preceding it. Recall that DDM is itself a meta-architecture, designed to incorporate multiple models. So, the judgement can be made whether such a meta-architecture is sufficiently adaptable to also incorporate each newcomer.

Andrew and multiple stream-files.   There remains, of course, the many other data systems in the marketplace. This particularly includes popular byte-oriented data systems on LANs, such as the widely used Sun Network File System (NFS), the Apple Filing Protocol (AFP), and the Andrew File system (AFS) [Satyanar90], a highly regarded relative newcomer from Carnegie Mellon University.[6] These, too, must somehow be put into the interoperability picture described above.

---

6.   The Andrew File System was originally developed at Carnegie Mellon, with funding from IBM. Andrew is now produced by Transarc, a commercial spin-off of the earlier Carnegie Mellon development.

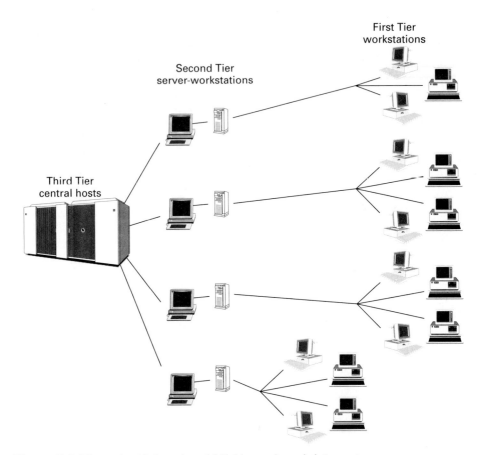

Figure 5.8 Three-tier University of Michigan shared data system.

There is the problem of multiple workgroups that have their own file systems. How far is it feasible to go in sharing data among very diverse file systems whose users are dispersed over great distances? One approach to this question can be found in the experience of the University of Michigan. In general, the university user population is often large, ranging from thousands to tens of thousands. The multicampus geography covers miles, and often an entire state. Multiple types of LANs become connected via backbone LANs and WANs. The problem is that different departments have different byte-oriented file systems, but it is desired to have general accessibility to shared files. Moreover, a requirement of the system design is often that there must be zero impact to the current end users. The current user interfaces and the current workstation communications protocols must be maintained.

While there are many network file server technologies available, few (if any) are suitable for addressing the needs of tens of thousands of client workstations, spread over large areas, while maintaining high performance. The solution chosen by the University of

Michigan is to provide a *three-tier data system*. This promising configuration is illustrated in Figure 5.8. Common, massive data storage is provided on mainframes at the third tier, using the Andrew File System.[7] The mainframes also provide centralized back-up and recovery for the second-tier servers. The second-tier servers, between the mainframes and the workstations, serve diverse other file protocols and terminal types. Terminal users at the University of Michigan can see either the Andrew File System (AFS), or Sun's Network File System (NFS)[8] or the Apple Filing Protocol (AFP). *Mapping is done only between Andrew and each of the others.* The intermediate servers provide protocol conversion for these file systems and for terminals: Apple Macintosh, Apollo, SunOS, IBM-RT, RISC System 6000, PC-DOS, DEC Ultrix, and NeXT. These intermediate servers maintain the desired transparency for the user. AFS-speaking workstations can bypass the intermediate second tier and go directly to the mainframes. Each AFS client workstation runs a high-performance disk cache that fills as files are requested from the central servers. With the client disk cache, AFS satisfies between 80 percent and 92 percent of the file requests from the local disk (once the cache is filled) [Hanss90]. The interrupt intensive work is thus done in a front-end processor instead of the mainframe. In that University of Michigan system, TCP/IP protocols are used. At the time of this writing, the mainframe is an IBM 3090 and the intermediate servers are IBM RTs. To handle the large number of queries, the 3090 has 128 I/O channels, each capable of 4.5 megabytes per second. For the storage function at the central site, the 3090 can support hundreds of gigabytes of disk storage and gigabytes of memory.

Data consistency is maintained through a callback function. *Callbacks* are promises, delivered by the central server along with a file, that the server will notify the AFS client process if another user stores a modified version of the file. The design point is to avoid validity checks, which occur too frequently with other systems. *The combination of caching and callback reduces the network load and insures high performance.*

AFS was chosen as the core technology for the Michigan project. It provides the "industrial-quality" file system on the mainframes and also can be used directly by the end users. Factors contributing to this choice were:

- AFS pushes CPU-intensive tasks to the workstations rather than the server, thus allowing more clients per server.

- AFS scales to large environments readily, without one-by-one changes as users are added. It accommodates increasing numbers of users simply by adding more file server machines and their local workstations.

- AFS is suitable for WAN use as well as LAN use, since it does not rely on timing for file integrity, and also chooses a packet size that will work well across LANs.

---

7. The University of Michigan project has ported the Unix-based Andrew to the S/370 MVS operating system.

8. The IBM statement of direction is that NFS will also be provided across all SAA and AIX systems. AIX or OS/2EE users will be able to access files that reside on remote MVS, VM, OS/400 or AIX server systems.

- AFS has a rich set of security and authentication mechanisms, essential in a common file system of large scope.
- AFS has a good set of administrative utilities that reduce the numbers of personnel needed to run the system.

OSF choice of Andrew.   The technical advantages of the Andrew File System have been recognized by the Open Software Foundation (OSF), which has specified Andrew technology for their Distributed Computing Environment (DCE). Andrew, therefore, can be expected to find wide use and be more or less integrated into each operating environment. The OSF choice of Andrew was influenced by the following [OSFDCE90]:

- AFS allows users to address files with the same pathname from anywhere in the system. It provides transparent access to local and remote files.
- Access control mechanisms (Kerberos-like, see Section 4.4.7) protect the files and directories.
- Access to files and directories inside a cell is not interrupted by single server failures. AFS makes replicated units of file systems available for read access.
- The file server is designed to serve a very large number of concurrent requests with good performance. Sections of files are transferred as needed, and can be cached on the client machine.

5.2.4   SAA Distributed Database

The Distributed Database Manager.   SAA's Distributed Relational Database Manager is defined by the IBM *Distributed Relational Database Architecture (DRDA)*. This architecture is actually a composite, consisting of the SQL language, the Relational Database, the SQL models of DDM, and the LU 6.2 support of the Logical Unit of Work and security, plus additional support for describing database data using FD:OCA (see Section 6.2.4).

The objective of DRDA is to work with different database managers on *heterogeneous systems*. These may have dissimilar catalogs, dissimilar hardware architectures, and differences in data types. Interoperability is provided initially among SAA systems, using DB2, SQL/DS, SQL/400, and OS/2 database managers. Some of the desired relationships among SAA systems are illustrated in Figure 5.9 [Reinsch88]. Interoperability is then extended to AIX/OSF systems and to systems of other vendors.

The function of the Distributed Database Manager (DDBM) is to enable a logical view of a database whose constituents are at multiple locations, and to relate that data— e.g., by multilocation joins and unions. The DDBM adds a variety of support features to the raw database. They typically provide *concurrency controls* (locking) to prevent one user from interfering with another and possibly getting inaccurate data. While update locks are held, no other program is allowed to access that data. While read locks are held, no other program is allowed to change that data. *Security controls* are imposed to insure that each user has access only to the portion of the database for which the user is authorized. *Recovery* facilities are provided on a *global transaction basis*, to permit unwinding sets of

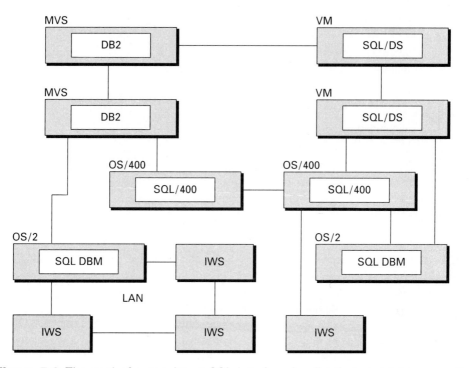

Figure 5.9 The goal of a consistent SQL interface for distributed database on all systems.

operations that encounter failures. Error reports and diagnostics are facilitated. The DDBM also schedules transactions as they are queued up and provides accounting information if required. Malfunction alerts, based on the Logical Unit of Work (LUW), using LUW_ids, are coordinated with system management.

The personal computer DDBMs often run on server workstations. They connect to each other and to requester workstations via LANs, and also may link to large-scale mainframes attached to LANs and remote WANS. In the SAA approach to heterogeneous systems, each location has its own database manager (DBM); and each DBM does data/communications management, recovery management, and logging. Each site is highly autonomous, but intimately cooperative. Thus, the DDBM is a partnership of independent, cooperating DBMs.

Performance can often be optimized for a particular operating system or particular hardware configuration. With distributed systems, however, the performance question must be addressed *across a range of operating systems* and configurations. This multienvironment performance has been a major target of SAA/AIX database managers. One of the challenging aspects of performance is the more or less dynamic moving or replication of data, to achieve locality for frequently referenced items. Another is the detection and unscrambling of deadlocks, as multiple users lock portions of the data at multiple locations.

	SQL statements per UOW	DBMs per UOW	DBMs per SQL statement
remote request	1	1	1
remote unit of work	>1	1	1
distributed unit of work	>1	>1	1
distributed request	>1	>1	>1

Figure 5.10 Distributed database definitions.

SQL API.   There must be a common, full-function interface (rather than a subset of function that constrains existing applications) in each of these distributed database systems. The **SQL interface** is the standard to which many systems are gravitating.[9] In DRDA, the elements of the SAA Common Programming Interface (CPI), for interaction with local or remote data systems [Reinsch88], are the existing statements of the IBM Structured Query Language (SQL). This is built upon the American National Standard (ANSI) database language SQL X3.135-1986. The ANSI specification includes elements like: `Select`, `Insert`, `Update`, `Delete`, `Table/View/Index`, and `Grant`. The goal is to achieve a consistent SQL interface, at least on all SAA and AIX/OSF systems, from the largest mainframes to the programmable workstation [G320-9929].[10] Globally unique object names and globally unique user-ids are involved. Full, automatic data transformation is supported in DRDA, as the data moves from one hardware platform to another. Both numeric and character data transformations are provided.

Styles of SQL database access.   Several alternative strategies and levels of access capability are possible. As charted in Figure 5.10, these styles depend on three factors: the number of statements per unit of work, the number of DBMs per unit of work, and the number of DBMs per SQL statement. The four styles of access are:

1.   **Remote requests**—(See Figure 5.11(a).) Only a single remote database manager (DBM) per SQL statement; and each SQL statement is independent. The DBM will force a commit (making a data-change a part of the database, see Section 5.3.3) after the completion of every SQL Call. The application is limited to one remote SQL Call, so there

9.   The IBM statements of direction are that SQL relational remote database capability will be provided on all SAA and AIX operating system platforms. Each will support SNA LU 6.2

10.   With that support, users will be able to access and share relational data residing in SAA or AIX databases. This will allow an AIX or SAA user to search a local database and switch to a remote database (located on either an SAA or AIX system) to accomplish a query or update (see [G320 9929]).

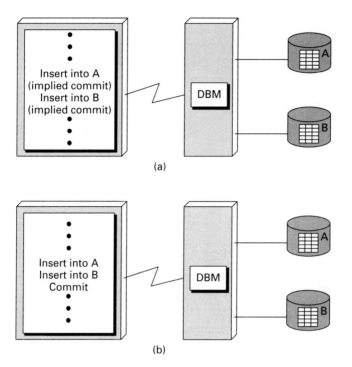

Figure 5.11 Two levels of capability with single remote DBM per SQL statement: **(a)** remote request; **(b)** remote unit of work.

cannot be related requests such as a debit/credit pair. The DBM is mostly unaware that distribution is happening.[11]

2.   **Remote unit of work**—(See Figure 5.11(b).) Provides transparent read/update at one remote location. *Multiple SQL statements* can be related in a single commit scope. The DBM commit is on a set of requests; the remote database accepts all or none. Local users and remote users share data as if they were all local.[12]

3.   **Distributed unit of work**—(See Figure 5.12(a).) As in (2), but with the ability to read/write data on *multiple remote systems*. However, each SQL statement must access only one location. The DBM knows or finds out which system manages the data to be read or changed by each request. The more mature versions of this style of distribution treat multiple updates at different systems as a single unit of work. Thus, logs and a 2-phase commit are required. The DBM must be capable of preserving integrity if failure occurs in any system or any communications. Either all of the related changes will be committed in the various databases or none of them will.[13]

---

11.   A current example of this style is the IBM Time Sharing Option (TSO)/E Server.
12.   A current example of this style is the IBM OS/2 EE remote data services.
13.   A partial example of this style is the IBM DB2 multiple read and single write.

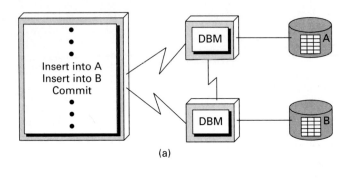

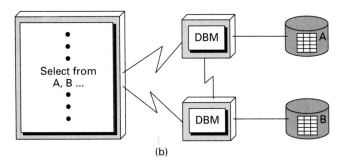

Figure 5.12 Two levels of capability with multiple DBMs per unit of work: **(a)** distributed unit of work; **(b)** distributed request.

4. **Distributed request**—(See Figure 5.12(b).) As in (3) but with the ability to use *multiple DBMs per SQL statement*. An SQL statement can `Join/Union` data across multiple DBMs. Data can be moved between systems without any effect on the user applications.[14]

Query Manager.   The SAA database managers support both interpretive and compiled SQL. The interactive environment for the database manager (DBM) is the Query Manager (QM). The Query Interface (QI) defines objects, functions, and commands that are included in the query manager. Data is retrieved by the QM from the DBM using SQL Calls.

OSI Remote Database Access (RDA).   The OSI SQL Remote Database Access (RDA), along with others, is currently under development in the standards community. The earlier IBM DRDA experience, along with others, contributes to the evolution of RDA. To the extent that they ultimately differ, it is expected that IBM will support both DRDA and RDA, will seek to make them as common as possible, and will make them largely transparent to the application development process.

Distributed CICS.   A further delineation of earlier alternatives in distributed data is in the experience of distributed CICS systems. These provide the capability for cooperative

---

14.   An example of this style is the IBM R* Prototype.

processing with access to CICS-owned data and applications on another workstation or on a mainframe. Transparent mainframe-to-PWS and PWS-to-PWS communication is provided for five variations:

1. *Transaction routing* allows a transaction to be initiated in one system and executed in another system.[15]

2. *Function shipping* allows application programs in one system to access data on another system.[16]

3. *Asynchronous processing* (another form of function-shipping) allows a program in one system to initiate a transaction which in turn initiates a subordinate transaction in another system, which functions asynchronously from the initiator.

4. *Distributed transaction processing* also allows transactions running in a workstation or mainframe to initiate transactions in another CICS system. However, in this case, the systems communicate synchronously.

5. *Distributed CICS Link* enables a CICS OS/2 transaction to *link* to programs on any connected CICS system. For example, this allows CICS in workstations (OS/2 systems) to access and use existing mainframe non-CICS database systems (e.g., DB-2).

5.2.5 Prognosis

The technology for making diverse data systems transparently available to applications has made surprising progress. The concurrent development of advanced application-development tools (e.g., the IBM AD/Cycle) makes this transparency imperative. The near-term goal, therefore, is to provide application-development tools that will transparently use data in any location, on mainframes or server workstations, whether the data be byte, record, or database oriented.

5.3 RESOURCE-RECOVERY

A distributed system contains many more components, that participate in a user's work, than in a single local system. It therefore becomes much more important to a user that all the distributed resources involved in his or her work be maintained in good working order.

A good philosophy in distributed systems is that recovery responsibility must be delegated to each distributed resource manager. This includes guarding the integrity of resources, recovering from damage, backing out incomplete changes, and retrying operations. There remains, however, the job of *synchronizing the operations of multiple resource managers who may be involved in interdependent recovery operations in multiple nodes.*

---

15.   For example, a CICS data manager on a PS/2 workstation can route transactions to other CICSs on MVS or vice versa. CICS can also send transactions to IMS.

16.   For example, CICS provides the ability to access remote services and distributed databases and files via function shipping among CICSs on MVS, VM, and OS/2 CICS systems.

The coordination of resource-recovery may be needed in many situations, involving different types of resource managers. However, maintaining the integrity of the distributed database is of special concern. Primary attention, therefore, has been given to the resource-recovery for database and file management systems, as discussed below.

5.3.1 Robustness and Data Integrity

The DBM must be able to achieve controlled updates at several different locations, all within the scope of a single transaction. For example, updates can be made on both multiple hosts and the workstation databases. Records must be moved from one to the other without loss or duplication. No updates can be lost, even when any database system or the communication system fails. Integrity must be maintained even when multiple DBMs are involved in a data request. This amounts to the coordination of changes affecting multiple resource managers within a single networkwide commit scope.

OSI and SNA have very similar facilities for resource-recovery. The SNA/SAA **Resource-Recovery (RR)** facility has its counterpart in OSI called **Commitment, Concurrency, and Recovery (CCR)**. Commitment insures that either all parts complete and all changes are made permanent, or no changes are made, and diagnostic information is passed. Concurrency insures that the desired action may proceed without interference from other external actions. Recovery insures integrity despite failure.

CCR and RR provide support for recovery. When Protected Resource Mangers (PRMs) are defined and used, the actual recovery process is specific to the PRM, not the application-process. With two-phase commit protocols, the application-process does not have to be involved in the recovery. This is particularly useful after a system crash when the application no longer exists.

Of course, one cannot guard against all occasions of data failure. Hence, it is necessary always to have *secure data* that survives any failure, and is available to the application-process after the application has been restored to normal operation. This is often equated with data written on disk, with all associated directories updated.

An obvious goal, from the user's perspective, is to have a common programming interface for resource-recovery (RR and CCR) facilities, or to have the SAA facilities as a superset of the OSI facilities. Then, a common application-service–element would suffice for the two strategic communication protocols, OSI and SNA (and perhaps for others as well).

Sync-point-manager concept.   Conceptually, the requirement is for a general-purpose sync-point-services function to insure integrity in every enterprise environment. As illustrated in Figure 5.13, each sync-point-service might involve multiple *protected-resource managers (PRMs)* using multiple communications protocols. In concept, PRMs may be needed for databases, files, messages, and conversations. PRMs contact other corresponding PRMs directly. When the Resource Manager/Database decides to distribute the work via a protected conversation, it contacts the Resource Manager/APPC.

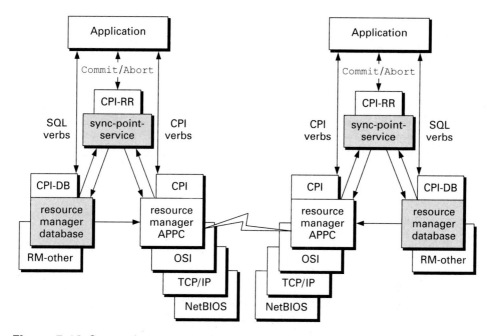

Figure 5.13 Sync-point-services applied to multiple environments.

The CPI, for resource-recovery, ideally would be defined so that the *same sync-point-service* can be in each operating environment of the enterprise. Steps towards this general concept are described below.

5.3.2 Logical Unit of Work

For both OSI and SNA, the span of a transaction between sync points is called the *Logical Unit of Work (LUW)*. Each LUW is given a unique identifier. Any failure within a LUW invalidates the entire LUW.

The communications system must support *commit* services accordingly. When access to recoverable files and databases is distributed, then the Logical Unit of Work (LUW) processing must also be distributed. All participating systems must have a say in whether the commitment of the transaction should be made, or whether the entire operation must be rolled back.

An LUW [Demers88b] begins at the beginning of a job or at the end of a previous LUW. The explicit request to commit or back-out (rollback), or the end of a job, ends the LUW. During an LUW, all requests to update are performed, but are held to be temporary and recoverable. They become permanent only at the completion of the commit request. *If there has been any failure, the commit request is not given, and the updates are backed out.* Prior to the commit request, updates can also be rolled back to the beginning of the LUW by an explicit command.

In the local system, it is usually the operating system that provides notification of the failure of an application [Reinsch88]. The local DBM then can take appropriate action to back-out any incomplete work and release the locks held by the failed application.

In the distributed case, it may be a remote operating system which discerns that an application has failed. Hence, a major requirement for the commit/back-out system to be effective is a mechanism for very timely failure notification among the nodes affected.[17] Comprehensive and timely failure notifications must be incorporated so that remote applications can be allowed to hold locks on database resources without an inordinate jeopardy to the availability of that same data for the rest of the users. When using connection-oriented protocols such as LU 6.2, the LU 6.2 PRM can also detect session failures. The PRM reports those failures to the node's synch-point-service.

SNA/APPC conversations are equipped to be part of a Logical Unit of Work. The conversation manager carries an *LUW_id* on the conversation protocols of any protected conversation.

5.3.3 Two-Phase Commit

The Logical Unit of Work may involve cascaded transactions progressing down a tree of application-processes. In such a tree, there is a master and a slave relationship for resource-recovery. One or more of the master's subordinates may need to involve other processes. In that case, the first subordinate becomes a superior to another subordinate. If the master at the top of the tree indicates that changes are to be made permanent or undone, then that request ripples down to all branches of the tree. Each node replies with its willingness to comply or otherwise. If any node receives a negative response from below, that is propagated upward till it reaches the master at the top of the tree. In this way, a request from the master is fulfilled only if all of the involved nodes agree. In summary, there are two phases:

1. The master informs all subordinates of the actions about to be requested. Each subordinate either agrees or provides a reason for not complying. Any participant in the LUW can initiate back-out up till the end of phase one.

2. The master then orders either a commitment, so all the actions are taken, or a rollback to each system's original state.

Concurrency control.   Concurrency control complements commitment. The local system that manages the database can use one of several methods. For example:

- All other users of the data can be locked out, and prevented from using the data until commitment is complete.

- All other users may continue to use the old data until commitment occurs, at which time the new data values are released.

---

17.   SNA's Advanced Program-to-Program Communication (APPC) and LU 6.2 address this need for notifications.

5.3.4   SNA/SAA Resource-Recovery

CPI-Resource-Recovery.   A significant level of transaction protection is available with very few calls through a portion of the Common Programming Interface (CPI). In an environment that has implemented **CPI Resource-Recovery (CPI-RR)**, synchronization points are established when a transaction program is started, when a program issues a CPI Resource-Recovery `Commit` call, and when a program terminates. In CPI-RR, the nature of the protection and the meaning of a sync point differ for each protected resource. In particular, we have protected databases and protected conversations as follows.

▪ *Protected database*. When a protected database is accessed, the system "remembers" what the record looks like when it is accessed. After any number of updates, any of the programs participating in a transaction may decide to make the updates permanent and advance all of the protected resources to the next sync point. If a program has made changes to the record, and then a program issues a `Commit` call to establish a new sync point, the changed records become the version of record stored in the database, and the "remembered" records are discarded.

If the program makes changes to the record and then issues a `Backout` call to return to the previous sync point, the "remembered" version of the record is retained in the database, and the changes to the record since the last sync point are discarded.

▪ *Protected conversation*. CPI-RR also "remembers" the state of a conversation, on each side, at the last sync point. Then, if a back-out occurs, each program's conversation state will be changed to the state at the time of the last sync point.[18]

In CPI-RR, a program receives a TAKE_COMMIT notification via the *status_received* parameter on a CPI-Communications (CPI-C) `Receive` call. That program eventually responds with either a `Commit` or `Backout` call. A program receives a TAKE_BACKOUT notification as a *return_code* parameter on CPI-C calls, such as `Send_Data`, `Receive`, and `Prepare_To_Receive`.

LU 6.2 cooperation.   With the cooperation of LU 6.2, SAA further makes distributed transactions feasible by facilitating distributed error recovery [SC31-6808]. Each LUW is identified by an *LUW_id*, consisting of a *network-qualified LU_Name*,[19] an *LUW instance number*, and an *LUW sequence number*. The latter is incremented by one for each successful sync point and each back-out. The critical point is that the *LUW_id is unique in the network*. The LUW_id is sent on the `Attach` header of each conversation in the distributed transaction.

Two levels of resource synchronization are provided by LU 6.2: Confirm and Syncpoint.

Confirm simply requires that the receiving program acknowledge a message. The reply takes the form of either a `Confirmed` verb or a `Send_Error` verb. The LUs serve

---

18.   The most important thing the conversation PRM remembers is the LU_name of the partner. With that, it is able to drive recovery in the event of node or link failures.

19.   The LU_name here refers to the name of the SNA Logical Unit (see Figure 3.15).

only to forward the request and the reply between the programs. No LUW_id is required; and support for system recovery provided. Recovery action, necessitated by a negative reply, is the responsibility of the partner programs.

Syncpt is the verb understood by LU 6.2 to execute the CPI-RR Commit call. The Syncpt verb can also be issued directly by some applications. The RR function, in cooperation with the LU, insures the consistency of *protected resources* across the distributed transaction. Protected resources include local databases, whose state changes are logged by the local LU, so that all changes during a transaction can be restored to a prior state in the event of a transaction failure.

The point in a transaction at which resources are synchronized is called the LU 6.2 **sync point**. When a program issues Syncpt, its LU sends a sync point request on all the protected conversations allocated to that program. Local resource managers are also asked to Prepare. Each program receiving the sync point request also issues Syncpt to its participating programs, so as to propagate the request throughout the distributed transaction.

Consistency means that if a return code of OK is received by the transaction that issued the Syncpt verb, then every other transaction program participating in the LUW, which issued a dependent Syncpt will also have received its OK.

Similarly, consistency means that if a BACKED_OUT return code is received on any protected conversation in a distributed transaction, then BACKED_OUT will be forced on every protected conversation in the distributed transaction. In addition all protected resources that participate in the LUW will be backed out to the most recent successful sync point. Occasions for instigating a Back_Out might, for example, include:

- Program checks or application Abends forced from outside the application
- Abort of the application initiated by the operator
- An operating system failure
- Back_Out requested by the application program
- Abend requested by the application program

Two-phase commit by LU 6.2.   Each *successful* sync-point request involves four commands, illustrated in Figure 5.14. Prepare and Request_Commit make up phase one. Committed and Forget make up phase two.

- **Prepare** tells the subordinate to begin to prepare the protected resources so that they may be fully committed to the changes that have been accumulated during this LUW, but also allows these changes to be reversed, or backed-out.
- **Request_Commit** informs the superior that all is ready for the command to commit.
- **Committed** informs the subordinate sync-point-services that all protected resources are to be committed.
- **Forget**. Each LU has kept a log of transactions on its protected conversations. When processing a Logical Unit of Work, whenever a transaction program issues a verb that

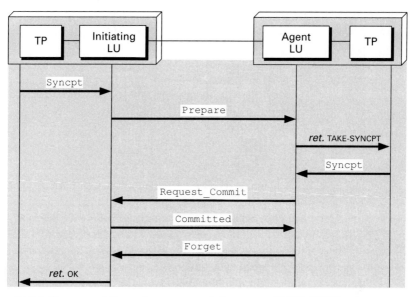

Figure 5.14 Command flows in a successful `Syncpt` [SC31-6808].

makes any changes to a protected resource, it is logged. The command `Forget` informs the initiating LU that its sync point is complete and the LU can erase its log record for this LUW.

If, on the other hand, the receiving transaction program has detected some error, the sync point will not be successful. In that case, a **Backout** verb will replace the receiver's `Syncpt` verb. The `Backout` verb causes the local LU to restore all locally protected resources to their status as of the last successful sync point, and to send a BACKED_OUT indication on all protected conversations.

RR sequences.   Illustrations of the SNA Committed and Backed-Out sequences are given in Figure 5.15. This illustration is a three-tier distribution, with node A initiating the transaction. Note that the `Prepare` command ripples down from the master (A). When (B) receives the command, (B) in turn passes it to each of its subordinates. The acceptances (`Request_Commit`) are then passed from each subordinate up to the master. Finally, the `Committed` command ripples downward to each subordinate. The first Backed-Out sequence is where a subordinate initiates the process. The second Backed-Out sequence illustrates the case where the master initiates the process.

Resynchronization.   If there is a failure of an LU, a session, or a conversation, during sync-point processing, of course, the above `Syncpt` cannot be expected to complete. In that case, a separate, architected transaction program, named `Resync`, is called upon. When a new session can be made available, the `Resync` program in one LU attaches its counterpart in the other LU, to guide recovery procedures. In the resulting conversation, the LUs are made to validate the integrity of their logs, and to determine the sync-point status at the time of failure. This information is then used to attempt to complete the interrupted sync-point

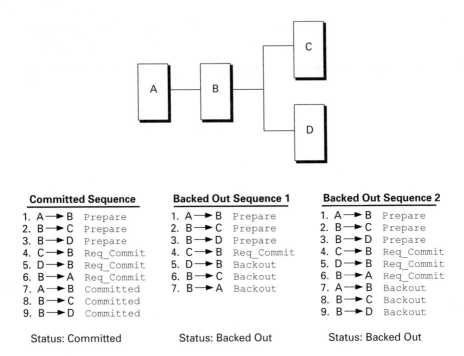

Committed Sequence	Backed Out Sequence 1	Backed Out Sequence 2
1. A → B Prepare	1. A → B Prepare	1. A → B Prepare
2. B → C Prepare	2. B → C Prepare	2. B → C Prepare
3. B → D Prepare	3. B → D Prepare	3. B → D Prepare
4. C → B Req_Commit	4. C → B Req_Commit	4. C → B Req_Commit
5. D → B Req_Commit	5. D → B Backout	5. D → B Req_Commit
6. B → A Req_Commit	6. B → C Backout	6. B → A Req_Commit
7. A → B Committed	7. B → A Backout	7. A → B Backout
8. B → C Committed		8. B → C Backout
9. B → D Committed		9. B → D Backout
Status: Committed	Status: Backed Out	Status: Backed Out

Figure 5.15 Examples of SNA Committed and Backed-Out sequences [SC31-6808].

protocol. This resynchronization procedure does not include the restarting of a failed transaction program.

Referential integrity. A related capability, included in the SAA relational-database services, is **referential integrity**. This insures integrity among multiple sets of tables, using relationships among elements in the several parts. When changes are made in one part, these relationships are used by the database manager (rather than the application) to insure consistency. For example, we do not want to delete a department while there are still employees reporting to that department. Conversely, we do not want to assign an employee to a department that does not exist.

5.3.5 OSI Commitment, Concurrency, and Recovery

CCR service primitives.   In a very analogous fashion, OSI has defined seven primitives for CCR:

1. **C-Begin**, *sent by the initiator*. It is sent to each subordinate. This primitive may use the session-layer **major-sync-point** as a starting point (see Section 9.4.3). Parameters include the **atomic action identifier**. An optional parameter indicates the time the superior will wait before issuing a `C-Rollback` to cancel the action.

2. **C-Prepare**, optional, *sent by the initiator*, to prompt a reply indicating willingness to commit.

3. **C-Ready**, *sent by the responder*, offering to commit.

4. **C-Refuse**, *sent by the responder*, along with a reason for being unwilling to commit.

5. **C-Commit**, *sent by the initiator* after receiving the necessary `C-Ready`. It must be confirmed. This primitive maps to another session level major-sync-point.

6. **C-Rollback**, *sent by the initiator*, following a `C-Refuse`. It must be confirmed.

7. **C-Restart**, *sent by both*, making each partner aware of the other's state, and identifying the point at which the action is to be restarted. It must be confirmed.

CCR sequences. Examples of the OSI CCR Committed and Rollback sequences are shown in Figure 5.16. This example concerns two processes that are subordinate to a third. The superior therefore works with each of the subordinates. In this example, the rollback is initiated by the superior; but a subordinate could initiate the rollback as well.

Comparing this with the corresponding SNA sequences in Figure 5.15 indicates the roughly corresponding commands:

SNA

- `Prepare`
- `Request_Commit`
- `Committed`
- `Backout`

OSI

- `Prepare`
- `Ready`
- `Commit`
- `Rollback`

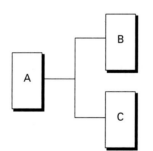

Committed Sequence		
1. A → B	`Prepare`
2. A → C	`Prepare`
3. B → A	`Ready`
4. C → A	`Ready`
5. A → B	`Commit`
6. A → C	`Commit`
7. B → A	`Commit_Confirm`
8. C → A	`Commit_Confirm`

Rollback Sequence		
1. A → B	`Begin`
2. A → C	`Begin`
3. A → B	`Prepare`
4. A → C	`Prepare`
5. C → A	`Ready`
6. B → A	`Refuse`
7. A → B	`Rollback`
8. A → C	`Rollback`
9. B → A	`Rollback_Confirm`
10. C → A	`Rollback_Confirm`

Figure 5.16 Examples of OSI Committed and Rollback sequences.

The OSI `Begin` carries the LUW_id. In SNA the LUW_id is carried in the `Attach`. OSI did not want to have implicit begins, so they invented an extra message for each LUW.

Each CCR application primitive results in one or more application-level protocol data units (APDUs), with flows in both directions. The CCR primitives at the application level then progress directly into session primitives, without any contribution from the presentation layer. The APDU exchanges produce an `S-Sync_Major`, `S-Resynchronize`, and/or an `S-Typed_Data` primitive at the session level. The consequent APDUs and session-level protocol data units (SPDUs) are carried as data or expedited data in transport-level protocol data units (TPDUs).

OSI/Transaction Processing uses CCR, and defines additional rules to support more than one protected resource.

5.3.6 Time Service

Some distributed applications need to insure the order of events, or to schedule events that are to occur in different locations. *Recovery analysis may depend on the sequence of events which is known only through time stamps.* Therefore, a time service is sometimes used to synchronize the clocks in all of the resource managers of a distributed environment, so that distributed applications can function properly.

In the OSF technology,[20] time can be obtained from primary time providers such as the Traconex/PSTI radio clock. The clocks in the network are then divided into clients and servers. Clients obtain their time from servers; and servers synchronize with each other. A client will ask time from a number of servers, and an algorithm will be used to select a correct time from among the responses.

5.4 APPLICATION MANAGERS

The availability of applications throughout the network can be baffling to the user without some comprehensive assistance. What applications are available? Where are they? What are their initiation procedures? These are some of the irritations that await a user unless assistance is provided. That assistance is the purpose of the Application Manager. The goal of the **Application Manager (AM)** is to provide a seamless facility for start-up of applications, whether they are local or on remote systems.

To do this, the AM maintains application profiles that describe the elements of each application and the users to which they are available. AM likewise handles the registration of applications, including the definition of information required to start the application. AM also retains information on how to initiate each application, when selected by a user.

The AM, as in OS/2, assists the user in selecting the application to be accessed, by presenting the user with a predefined list of application options (the OS/2 starter list group,

---

20. OFS selected the *DECdts* for its digital time service technology.

updated to include host applications). This is the user's own profile, containing applications of interest to that particular user.

The AM determines whether the selected application is local or remote, but that is transparent to the requester. If all is in order, AM establishes the necessary session and appropriate network connections for the selected application. The user is not aware of the physical location (whether in the programmable workstation or in some remote host) of the chosen application. Nor is the user aware of the steps involved in obtaining authorization and initializing the host portion of the application.

The end user should be able to access all applications in the enterprise that he or she is authorized to access. That includes OS/2 stand-alone applications and host applications accessible via terminal emulation.

This access needs to be done through a single logon and password at the workstation. Administrative functions should generate the appropriate logons to the host systems. This would go through the normal server security procedures (e.g., RACF[21] in mainframes).

SAA Delivery Manager provides the means to control and distribute software and files from hosts to workstations. It provides for preplanned download/update of applications that either operate alone in workstations or cooperatively with hosts. These can be initiated by the user or the administrator. New applications, or new versions of a current application may be installed and made ready for use during the download process.

End users can select packages to be delivered, installed, or updated on their OS/2 workstations. Or, a plan for a change can be created at the S/390 mainframe, and the changes will be distributed across the network. In addition, support has been promised for delivery to DOS workstations and from AS/400 hosts. For LAN environments, where no S/390 or AS/400 exists, the change would be delivered to the LAN server and made available to users on the LAN by code sharing [G01F-0281].

NetView Access Services.   Another beginning of a networkwide application-service can be seen in the *NetView Access Services* for mainframes.[22] Its main purpose is to provide simultaneous access to one or more applications such as a data-management system like CICS or IMS, a subsystem like the Time Sharing Option (TSO), an application like the word-processor DisplayWrite/370, or a transaction within a system. These all can be accessed on multiple MVS or VM mainframes, in multiple locations, from a single terminal, using one user-id and password, while protecting those applications from unauthorized access. Applications can be grouped, specifying which users have access to each group of applications. Customized application menus are provided for each user. After logging on the NetView access service, and selecting a number of applications, the system logs on automatically to each application on the user's behalf. A user, then, can jump between the applications, and copy, for example, data from a record in the IMS database into a DisplayWrite/370 letter. While one application is carrying out a task, another application can carry out other tasks.

---

21.   Resource Access Control Facility (RACF) is a comprehensive guardian of host resources, requiring user-id and password authorization for access to resources in a user's profile.

22.   NetView is not a prerequisite for NetView Access Services.

5.5   LAN REQUESTER/SERVER

5.5.1   Introduction

One of the fastest growing environments is that of PC or PS/2 servers on LANs, whose clients are requesters in either programmable or nonprogrammable workstations on the LAN. Such servers of multiple workstations are most feasible when the bandwidth is above a few megabits per second. Hence, the popularity of LAN servers operating on LANs in the 4–16 Mbps range.

There are many vendor offerings of LAN servers that include flat-file, printer, and messaging services. Among these are Microsoft's LAN Manager, Banyan's VINES, Novell's NetWare, and IBM's LAN Server. Currently, IBM, DEC, and others have agreed to use a common-base package provided by Microsoft, called LAN Manager. For example, a subset of the IBM LAN Server product will merge to be entirely compatible with the Microsoft product. In addition, Novell has stated its intention to implement NetWare on OS/2 and the IBM RISC S/6000 AIX platform. NetWare will be integrated with the IBM OS/2 Communications Manager and Database Manager, and will provide NetWare OS/2 customers access to SAA services. All this will considerably aid interoperability.

There are, in fact, many discreet servers for different functions, and the functions in any one server can grow. Primary functions offered by a LAN server can include shared flat files, shared SQL databases, shared printers, and messaging services. Other server functions might include FAX services and image services. The LAN server further provides facilities for defining, controlling, and managing access to the resources under its jurisdiction.

5.5.2   Requester Tasks

The client portion, residing in programmable workstations, and called the **LAN requester**, or LAN client, is allowed access to shared resources at the LAN server. The LAN requester, operating in the user's workstation, in concert with the server, can usually perform a limited number of distributed tasks, including:

- Copy and move files
- Replicate files: the user can identify files that are critical, and can periodically replicate them on any LAN server or LAN requester
- Print files on remote printers
- Send, receive, save, and forward messages
- Run a shared program
- View a list of logged-on users

File replication works by having the source of data check for changes at user-defined intervals. If there are no changes, there is no action. If there have been changes, the target is notified and the target performs the updates.

The LAN workstation user's view is object-oriented. The user sees files, databases, printers, applications, mailboxes, and individual users. Many of these objects are accessible at different servers in the network, as illustrated in Figure 5.17. The user should

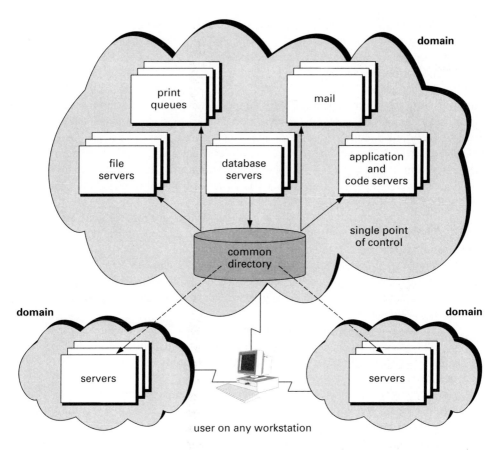

Figure 5.17 Servers in multiple domains, with a common directory, available to a workstation.

be oblivious to the location of those objects, the underlying communications protocols, and the operating systems used in different systems.

With one logon, and one user-id, the user can have access to multiple servers that handle flat files, and also to multiple database managers that handle relational (SQL) databases. These may be on multiple operating systems, in multiple domains that cut across servers. The user does not need to know where the resource is located, but asks for the resource by name. The system figures out where the resource is located.

5.5.3   The IBM LAN Server

The IBM **LAN Server** [S84-0086] is a component of the network operating system, which provides basic application-services in the LAN environment. It also provides security and administrative support.

Access control to shared resources is of growing importance. On a given LAN there may be more than one **domain**, which is a scope of administration, and a scope of authentication of shared resources. Each domain consists of a set of servers. Domains can also extend across multiple networks, and can reside in separate enterprises. The administrator can control any shared resource, such as files, disk directories, printers, print queues, and peripheral devices.

How much access is allowed to a particular user can be controlled by a **network administrator**. The network administrator defines domains, domain resources, and users. He or she defines entities with unique names within the scope of a domain. These entities include: users and groups of users, network applications, spooler queues, and serially attached devices. Administrators can define all user and user-group information at one central location. Hence, for example, there is no need to add a new user's account to each individual server. The IBM LAN Server has an access control modeled after the large system RACF security system, for SAA compatibility.

The network administrator defines which applications are to be *public*, and can be shared by whom. *Private* applications can also reside on the server. The network administrator also defines which printers are to be shared, and may establish a group of printers into a *printer pool*. Jobs that are waiting for access to a printer then are put on a *spooler queue*, which is serviced by a printer pool. Print jobs can be routed to the first available printer, or to a specifically configured printer, or can be designated for a specific time of day.

Logging on requires the use of a valid user-id and password. The requester can change the password. Logon verification of the user-id is provided with an optional encrypted password. Three levels of authority are allowed for validation: user, administrator of local files, and network administrator.

The server may be located on one of many bridged LANs, which may be token rings, Ethernets, or the PC Network. As broadband WANs become feasible, servers may also be located there. Some servers handle only ASCII byte-oriented flat files. The database component of OS/2 EE includes a relational (SQL) database server, which also may operate on OS/400, MVS, or VM operating systems, as well as non-IBM systems. The SAA LAN Requester may operate on OS/2 or DOS workstations.

Naming. A resource in the local area network is identified by a two part name: the *server name* and the *net name* which identifies a resource on a particular server. This is the Universal Naming Convention (UNC) name. The *net name* is either the directory path and filename (for a file resource) or the device name (for a printer or serial device). An alias can, however, be used, if it has been earlier defined with the server location.

For example, an administrator can assign a name to a file, and can move that file to any server in any connected domain. When a user asks for that file by its name, the user can be unconcerned with the physical location of the file. The servers will translate the filename to a pathname that permits access to the file at its current location.

5.6 MAINFRAME SERVERS

The mixture of PC, PS/2, and mainframe (e.g., As/400 and S/390) servers seeks to enable workstations to take advantage of the thousands of available applications and the distributed data in each of these operating environments. It is desirable to use all of the resources of these environments where each is best suited. The full integration of PC, PS/2 and mainframe LAN servers is still underway. The accelerating data rates of both LANs and WANs drives LANs and WANs together. However, some good illustrations of the trend are available.

AS/400 PC support.   Consider, as an example the foundation of cooperative processing found in the PC Support on the AS/400 mainframe. That support includes:

- A seamless view (using tailorable menus) of AS/400 and workstation applications.
- SQL-like commands to transfer data between AS/400 database files and programmable workstations.
- Sharing and simultaneous access of workstation files by multiple users. Data and applications can then be accessed by OS/2 and DOS users as though that data or application resided on a normal fixed disk at the programmable workstation.
- A set of APIs for application-to-application interaction.
- Use of any AS/400 or workstation printer in the network.
- A close integration of word-processing (DisplayWrite) and office systems (Office/Vision) facilities, with the ability to send messages to anyone on the WAN/LAN network.
- Communications serving, particularly including WAN access to other hosts.

LAN mainframe.   It is reasonable to expect a variety of servers to be developed for use in both LANs and mainframes. One worth mentioning as an indication of trends is the licensing of Microsoft's LAN Manager to Micro Tempus to port that product to an MVS mainframe. Running, as far as the LAN PCs are concerned, like any other LAN server, the MVS version is planned to provide virtual disks on the host storage devices. Similarly, users of Phaser System's Netware for VM or Netware for MVS can add S/390 capability to their Novell LAN Server. The Phaser System products use software in both the PC and the mainframe to provide NetWare-based file services on the S/390, and routing services to other S/390s or to other NetWare LANs. This, in combination with Novell-provided SNA interfaces,[23] allows NetWare LAN Servers or its users to share S/390 capacity and resource management. They can copy files between environments bidirectionally, submit work for batch printing on the mainframe, and use the WAN for LAN-to-LAN sharing [Ziegler91].

Direction.   The objective is to use each mainframe and workstation resource where it makes sense, and to balance the distribution of function as the particular application matches the configuration possibilities. A blend of workstation and mainframe functions can often be better than either one alone. The high performance of the LAN and the simpler structure of the LAN server may provide better response times for simple queries in many applications. The more complex applications, very high transaction rates file or serving from larger databases, archiving, backup, and administration may be more appropriate from the mainframe. The application mix will be distributed between mainframes and workstations depending on their origin, their data dependencies, and their total resource needs.

---

23.   Novell provides IBM 3270 and LU 6.2 emulators. (See also Section 19.3)

5.7   TCP/IP CLIENT–SERVERS

All TCP/IP application-services also have a **client** and **server** component. Workstations, department processors, and central hosts, of multiple vendors, having multiple operating systems, may play the roles of TCP/IP client or server, if they are given the corresponding support [Reinhold].

TELNET.[24]   The client portion of TCP/IP's *TELNET*, in the user's system, is a *terminal emulation protocol, which permits users to access applications in other systems, as if directly attached to that system.* Just as with any other logon, the user (client) must provide a user-id and password, before access to the server system is granted. After a successful logon, TELNET users can act just as if their terminals were directly connected to the remote server-host.

The target host must support the server portion of TELNET; some systems will support both client and server portions; and some systems will support only the client portion.

A system containing the client support may be locally or remotely accessed (e.g., via a VM passthrough or an SNA network). Once logged on to that system, the user issues a TELNET command, with the identity of the remote TCP/IP system to be accessed.[25]

SMTP.[26]   The **Simple Mail Transfer Protocol (SMTP)** is an electronic mail protocol, also having both client (sender) and server (receiver) portions. Several "post-office" arrangements can be made. One machine may connect to another and transfer a message to a list of mailboxes on the destination machine. The format of the messages is governed by a standard (RFC 822) that defines the headers.

The receiving post office, for example, might be a UNIX or AIX/OSF system, containing a forwarding package called *POP (Post Office Protocol).* A user then might use a SMTP client protocol at the workstation to create and send mail, and use the UNIX or AIX/OSF system as the mail recipient. The UNIX or AIX/OSF system would hold the mail until requested to download it to the user's workstation.

A frequent arrangement is to use a mainframe as the intermediary. In this case, the workstation can use a variety of terminal access methods (LAN, SNA WAN, pure BSC) to access the host. At the host, the user can create the mail using an SMTP client or a host-based office system with a gateway to SMTP.

Since electronic mail is pervasive, it is important for SMTP to have gateways to other non-TCP/IP electronic mail systems. A specific example of this is the user in a VM or MVS environment, who can send and receive mail across both TCP/IP and SNA WAN or pure BSC networks. (VM includes an interface between SMTP and RSCS, the VM messaging system; MVS uses an interface to Network Job Entry (NJE), its means of

---

24.   TELNET protocol, DARPA RFC 793, 854.

25.   TCP/IP users can use TELNET to access an IBM system and then from that system use VTAM to access applications across the SNA network. Likewise, an SNA VTAM user can access a system that has both VTAM and TCP/IP, and from that system use TELNET to access applications across the TCP/IP network.

26.   Simple Mail Transfer Protocol, DARPA RFC 821.

forwarding job entry data.) The user then may therefore send mail to destinations on either the TCP/IP or the RSCS/NJE networks.

FTP.[27]   The **File Transfer Protocol (FTP)** uses a client–server pair to transfer files to or from a remote host. It also allows users with read/write access to display, define, and delete files and directories. The file transfer protocol supports a small variety of file types: ASCII, EBCDIC, binary, and paged. (A paged file type is a special mechanism for passing structured files between systems of the same type.) FTP provides password protection of files, and offers data compression, and checkpoint/restart on blocks of transmission. It does not provide any file translations or conversions.

The procedure is for the client to first establish a control connection with the server. The server then asks the client to identify a client port for the file transfer; and the server then opens a connection to that client-designated port.

It is readily feasible to arrange for file transfers across combinations of TCP/IP and other networks. For example, through the use of VM "execs," the transfer of data across both TCP/IP and SNA WAN or pure BSC networks may be automated. After an FTP logon to one remote host, and the transfer of files to that host, the execs at that host could arrange to send the files across an SNA or BSC network to yet another host.

The Trivial File Transfer Protocol (TFTP)[28] is a simpler protocol, without password protection or directory capability. It is used for the exchange of files between PCs and PS/2s, and to enable a host to obtain files from a PC server.

AIX access for DOS.   This is an IBM means for a PC-DOS user to exchange information and access applications that reside on TCP/IP-based systems such as an AIX PS/2 or AIX RISC System/6000. Communication between the two systems can be via Ethernet, token ring, or Async. Three functions include file sharing, printer sharing, and terminal emulation. The DOS user sees the AIX files as virtual disk drives. The AIX security capabilities can be used to allow multiple users access to information while protecting from unauthorized access.

Migration to OSI.   The original purpose of TCP/IP has been absorbed by later standards efforts. The later OSI application-services generally have more functionality than the earlier TCP/IP counterparts. The prognosis is for migration of TCP/IP to OSI and those proprietary architectures that include OSI as a subset. The relationship of the TCP/IP structure to that of OSI is shown in Figure 5.18. In this migration one would expect first application-level gateways,[29] and then complete replacement as follows:

- TELNET to OSI Virtual Terminal (VT)
- FTP to OSI File Transfer (FTAM)
- SMTP to OSI Messaging (X.400)

---

27.   File Transfer Protocol, DARPA RFC 959.

28.   Trivial File Transfer Protocol, DARPA RFC 783.

29.   IBM has stated that it will provide application layer protocol translation functions between SMTP and X.400, and between FTP and FTAM. A translation between Telnet and Virtual Terminal is reportedly under investigation.

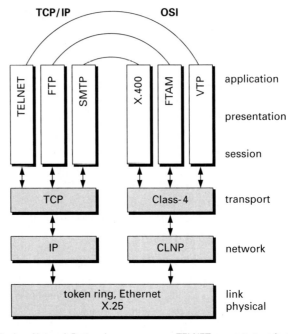

CLNP = Connectionless Network Protocol
FTAM = OSI File Transfer, Access, and Management
FTP = File Transfer Protocol
IP = Internet Protocol
TCP = Transmission Control Protocol

TELNET = remote terminal protocol
SMTP = Simple Mail Transfer Protocol
VTP = Virtual Terminal Protocol
X.400 = OSI messaging service

Figure 5.18 Relation of TCP/IP to OSI [Reinhold].

Some would argue that these transitions be accompanied by facilities that allow OSI application-services to run on top of the existing lower-level TCP/IP protocols. This approach is not favored by those who desire a rapid migration to OSI. The lifetime of TCP is obviously related to the use of mixed stacks.

The impetus for transition from TCP to OSI is strengthened by the determination of the U.S. Department of Defense (DOD) to do this quickly. The U.S. Government OSI Profile (GOSIP) V 1.0, called for OSI as a mandatory requirement beginning in August 1990. GOSIP V 2 is effective December 1991, and GOSIP V 3 is effective December 1992. For example, the DOD Computer Aided Logistics Support (CALS) Initiative requires that defense contractors use GOSIP beginning in 1992. CALS will be used to transmit documents and drawings of contracted equipment. The DOD recommended transition strategy is in five parts:

1. *Dual hosts and end-systems.* These provide both DOD and OSI protocol suites that are used in native mode without a gateway.

2. *Layer 7 gateways.* These can be provided to permit interoperation between TCP and OSI application-services. For example, gateways for mail and file transfer between the respective TCP and OSI application-services can be developed. The gateway is really a

host or end-system supporting both the DOD and OSI protocol suites, plus a protocol converter sitting on top of those stacks to map between the highest-level DOD and OSI protocols.

3. A preference for "*pure stacks.*" This means that interoperation can be achieved by application-level gateways, but newer OSI application-services, like X.400 message systems would run on pure OSI protocol stacks and not on TCP stacks.

4. An *Internet gateway*. This gateway operates at level 3c (Internet sublevel). Except for the richer addressing capabilities of the OSI CLNP, it and the IP protocol are functionally equivalent. Therefore, the gateway at this level is fairly simple. When a packet arrives at one of the gateways, the network layer protocol determines whether it is a DOD or OSI packet and passes it on to the appropriate internetwork protocol.

5. *Remote logon capability.* A user connected to a host with only DOD protocols can remotely logon to an end-system with only OSI protocols. This is done by first using TELNET on the originating DOD protocol host to logon to an intermediary dual-protocol machine. Then the OSI Virtual Terminal on the dual-protocol machine can be used to remotely logon to the destination OSI end-system. Either an application program or a gateway performing the same function, on the dual-protocol machine, would be used.

5.8   VIRTUAL TERMINAL CLIENT–SERVER

The ISO Virtual Terminal Protocol (VTP) is intended to relieve the problems of protocol conversion for the multitude of different terminal types. Because of the growing number of different terminal facilities, this has proven to be a difficult task. The VTP goals included a limited set of terminal classes:

- *Basic class*—simple character-oriented devices with scroll mode, DIS 9040 and 9041. Basic class is intended to support both IBM 3270 type synchronous terminals and ASCII terminals such as the DEC VT-100.

- *Forms class*—which added the ability to define display fields to the basic class virtual terminal.

- *Graphics class*—supporting vector graphics in devices.

- *Image class*—to accommodate bit-mapped images.

- *Text class*—capable of handling word processing and messaging displays.

- *Mixed class*—to handle combinations of the above.

The virtual terminal model is shown in Figure 5.19. The standard provides a protocol for the exchange of messages between two virtual terminal entities. Both ends of the connection must map their actual terminal operations to and from this virtual terminal. The virtual terminal model is a tool for the definition of a large variety of virtual terminal types. Defining a virtual terminal means assigning values to a set of virtual terminal parameters. However, because there are so many types of terminals and applications, many terminal profiles must be defined.

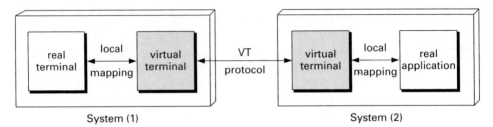

System (1)   System (2)

Figure 5.19 The virtual terminal model.

Continuing technical advances seem to outdistance many of the efforts at agreement on standards. We currently have new emphasis on windows, tailorable icons, multilevel color, highlighting, advanced graphics, moving video, programmable functions, and so forth. Nevertheless, the standards work continues, and many of the virtual terminal classes will find good value.

5.9   DECNET–SNA CLIENT–SERVERS

Another type of client–server pair exists in the exchange of services between nodes in DECnet and SNA subarea networks.[30] The possible configurations of a family of such products, made by Interlink Computer Sciences, Inc., are shown in Figure 5.20. The functions provided include:

- Shared data sets, files, and applications
- VT type terminals and 327x terminal emulation
- Interprogram communications
- Bridged electronic mail systems (IBM's PROFS[31] and VM Notes users are linked with DEC's VAX Mail or ALL-IN-1)
- Cooperative network management with NetView (see Section 4.8.5)
- DECnet to DECnet via SNA subarea network

All of the *Interlink* gateway functions run as a started task in MVS or a disconnected virtual machine in VM. In MVS systems, interfaces exist to IBM application and communications services including: JES (for remote printing or batch job submission), TSO (for user-initiated file transfer or terminal emulation), and VTAM (for routing over SNA, connection to NetView, or terminal emulation). VM systems provide comparable services.

Further, the *Interlink* support allows client and server programs (operating in layer 7) to coprocess in either direction across the gateway with complete transparency to the end

---

30.   DECnet to SNA linkages are provided by a number of companies, including: Interlink Computer Sciences Inc., Intel (FlexLINK), Joiner Associates Inc. (Jnet), Soft-Switch Inc., and Digital Equipment Corp. (Message Router/PROFS).

31.   PROFS is an IBM Office System that operates on VM, a S/390 operating system.

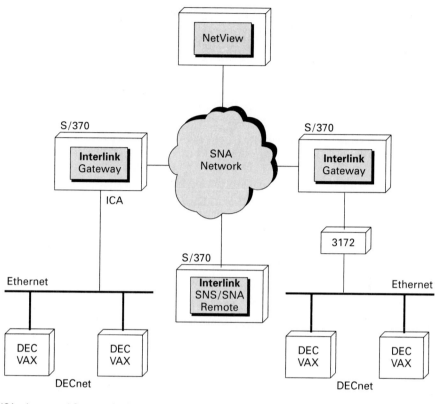

ICA = Integrated Communications Adapter
3172 = LAN Interconnect Controller

Figure 5.20 The Interlink SNS/SNA Gateway family. [Courtesy of Interlink Computer Sciences.]

user. *It implements on the IBM host the callable routines of DECnet task-to-task verbs.* Alternatively, it allows the use of IBM's *LU 6.2 for coprocessing*, via an interface between VTAM and the DECnet.

For the DEC user, all of the standard commands that he or she would expect to apply to a remote VAX node now apply to the IBM host. For example, with the `EDIT` command, the DEC user can apply his editor to a file resident on an IBM mainframe, without moving it to his local node. As far as the IBM user is concerned, his file-transfer functions are controlled by native format TSO or CMS commands. In both directions, the translation of data and file types is handled transparently.

The network interface (the physical connection) between a S/390 and an Ethernet is provided by the 3172 Interconnection Controller (see Section 17.5.2) or by the integrated adapter of a 9370. The interface from the SNA network is to an 802.3 LAN (that uses DECnet higher layer protocols). However, the LAN, in turn, may also be connected to a DECnet WAN. If the *Interlink* software is at two gateway nodes of the SNA network, as

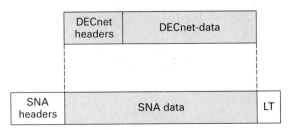

Figure 5.21 Encapsulation of DECnet message in SNA message.

shown in Figure 5.20, then users on the two separate DECnets can apply their same native command sets to address any node on the two DECnets.

Interlink has, in effect, written layers 3 through 5 of DECnet for the *IBM mainframe, which then looks just like another DECnet node*. Since the Network layer of DECnet is running in the IBM host, it can be configured as a routing node. This enables the *Interlink* software in one IBM host to route DECnet traffic over an SNA network to another IBM host (also containing *Interlink* software). Thus both IBM systems appear as DECnet nodes.

The actual handling of the DECnet traffic is *via a pair of LU 6.2 sessions* (to simulate the full duplex nature of a DECnet link). The DECnet messages (data plus DECnet headers) are simply *encapsulated (*as SNA data) into LU 6.2 messages, as shown in Figure 5.21. At the receiving end, the DECnet packets are removed from SNA and delivered to the *Interlink* software on the receiving node. If the actual destination is a node in the DECnet attached to the receiving IBM host, the packet will be forwarded on to its destination.

Conclusion

This chapter has illustrated some of the many ways in which distributed resource managers have begun to take advantage of the growing networking capabilities. These sophisticated and distributed resource managers of many kinds become the companions and replacements of the early file and print servers. Their steady conversion of the network into a distributed operating system with increasing transparency can clearly be seen.

Distributed data is becoming a practical reality, particularly with the ability to transparently use both SQL data and file data from local and remote sources, on LANs and on WANs. The sophistication of this service is illustrated by the progression of styles from one SQL statement in one unit of work on one database, to multiple SQL statements per unit of work with multiple databases per unit of work, and still later adding multiple databases per SQL statement. For both files and databases, transparency regardless of location has been approached in a systematic way using the family of models that are tailored to the higher-level language APIs. The two-phase commit procedures prove to be relatively simple ways of insuring data integrity across the network.

The LAN servers, in both powerful workstation-class (PS/2) computers and mainframes (e.g., A/400s and S/390s), are growing in capability and in the ability to jointly serve the LAN user where each is best suited.

The demonstrated ability to share data, share applications, submit jobs, and inter-change mail, across SNA and DECnet systems also attest to the progress made in upper-level client–servers for multiple-architecture interoperability.

We can expect further technical progress in these areas to lead to a broadly transparent accessability of data, regardless of location or whether it is byte, record, or database oriented, on different vendor systems.

All these pieces are fitting into a more systematic multiprotocol, multivendor communications architecture, whose mission includes the support of the types of distributed resource managers shown above. The implementations of many of these facilities are being pursued in a spirit of cooperation among many vendors acting in business partnerships.

Acknowledgments

I am particularly indebted to R. A. Demers, A. P. Citron, Stefano Zatti, M. D. Ayres, C. J. Bontempo, J. W. Gura, and K. Albert for valuable input or reviews of this chapter.

EXERCISES

5.1 What are the three classes of data systems in common use?

5.2 What is the purpose of generating standardized calls in an intermediary like DDM?

5.3 True or false: Both the IBM Distributed Data Management (DDM) and the OSI File, Transfer, and Access Management (FTAM) architectures use distinct models that are each designed to precisely match the needs of a higher-level language.

5.4 What is the meaning of "callback" in the University of Michigan three-tier data system?

5.5 Name the four styles of distributed database, and give a distinguishing characteristic of each.

5.6 Define a Logical Unit of Work.

5.7 Summarize the two phases of a two-phase commit.

5.8 Explain the difference between an LU 6.2 Confirm verb and an LU 6.2 syncpt verb.

6
Information Interchange

6.1 INTRODUCTION

The information interchange between two partners implies not just transmission but also understanding. For that, the partners must speak the same language or have facilities for interpretation. This information has a variety of forms, including text, graphics, image, voice, and sometimes video. It may arrive by phone, hard copy, electronic mail, facsimile, or other computer network services.

This diversity is driven by certain types of applications that are built into cooperating systems. These applications are distributed between *programmable workstations (PWSs) and servers (or hosts), which may be anything from a PS/2 on up to a mainframe.* A good example of this diversity is in the modern office, as illustrated in Figure 6.1. In the office environment, the correspondence and the library use a growing assortment of types of information, including letters, charts, forms, calendars, reports, spreadsheets, newsletters, and messages on paper, FAX, and electronic mail.

The integrated office is a concept whereby business communications, administrative services, and decision support systems can all have consistent user interfaces for text, graphics, and image. The applications can be supported in a PWS, and yet have various functions distributed differently between the PWS and hosts. One example of the wide range of related applications that could be distributed, and function cooperatively, is illustrated in Figure 6.2. These applications need to interact with one another, regardless of distance (recall the progression of transmission speeds illustrated by Figure 2.3). That distribution of function between cooperating systems is illustrated in Figure 6.3. Note that in this example, the business communications applications have their user interface in the PWS, but most of their function is located in a host. On the other hand, the administrative service and decision support applications have a majority of their functions in the PWS. Their common data and its processing are in the hosts.

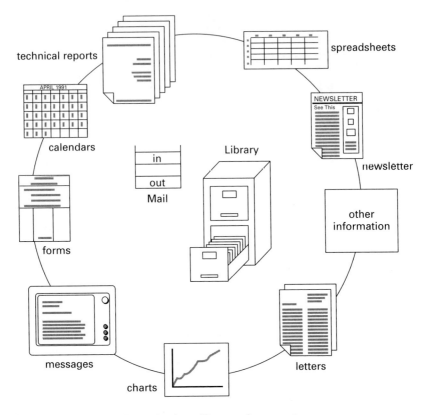

Figure 6.1 Information flows in the office environment.

An early implementation of this concept is OfficeVision. Fundamentally, a system like **OfficeVision** takes advantage of the compute-power in programmable workstations to create friendly, i.e., easy-to-learn, and easy-to-use interfaces, for a variety of types of information. That same workstation may also do most or all of the application-processing, as in spreadsheet and word-processing applications. The system furthermore uses the facilities of shared-logic hosts (small and large) to allow sharing of data and resources among the user population. Other application areas often follow the same pattern of distributed function. Multivendor systems of all sizes need to participate in many of these information exchanges. In many cases, therefore, there is a growing need for standards of information interchange for a widening spectrum of types of information.

Our objective in this chapter is to introduce the realm of Information Interchange Architectures, and to provide an understanding of their functions, and the roles they play in the Enterprise Information Network.

6.1.1 Architecture Families

Accordingly, we first provide an overview of the architectures and services that have been devised to facilitate the precise interchange of information in its various forms. Particu-

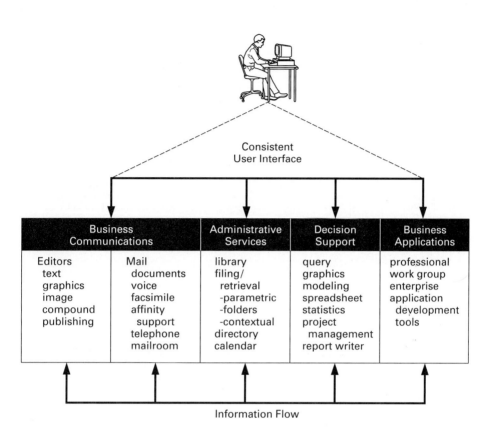

Figure 6.2 Office applications family.

larly, this includes three steps in the processing of text, graphics, and image documents:

1. *To create, edit, format, revise*, and *present* documents, using **Information Interchange Architecture (IIA)**. IIA records the structure and layout of a compound document, and makes intelligible the text, graphics, or image being transmitted. This creates the document content data stream.

2. *To distribute, file, search, browse, retrieve,* and *print* the document, using the **SNA Document Interchange Architecture (DIA)**. Alternatively, the handling and delivery of documents can be done using the **OSI X.400 Interpersonal Messaging System.** The *envelope* for the data stream tells what distributed application-services are to do with the document. That envelope in SNA is the encapsulation provided by the headers of the SNA Document Interchange Architecture (DIA) and SNA Delivery Service (DIA/ SNADS headers). The OSI envelope is the header of the OSI X.400 Interpersonal Messaging System.

3. *To transmit the envelope and its contents.* This is done by their further encapsulation in the headers of the *SNA or OSI communication protocols.*

The IBM IIA is a superset of the OSI Office Document Architecture (ODA). IIA includes both formatted (presentation) and processable (revisable) forms. The revisable

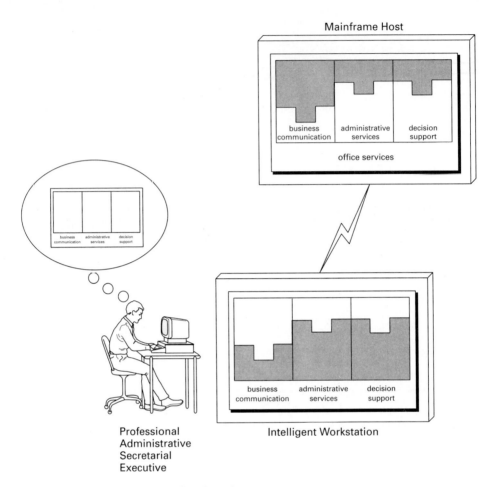

Figure 6.3 Distribution of office functions.

form of IIA is identically the ISO ODA. The SNA DIA roughly corresponds to the OSI Interpersonal Messaging System using X.400. These, in turn, are all independent of the connect, communicate, and transport functions of OSI and SNA.

There is still another dimension to information interchange. While documents are the primary means of information interchange, work is progressing on mixing *voice* (recorded and live) with information in the text, graphics, and image forms. A useful tool in this area is the architecture for *voice/data systems*, using the **CallPath Services API**, which allow application programs to interact with and control voice PBXs and CBXs, along with voice response units.

All of these facilities are described in more detail in the following sections of this chapter.

6.2 DATA STREAMS

6.2.1 Introduction

Applications increasingly use multiple types of data (e.g., text, graphics, image) in a single document. These **compound documents** are distributed across diverse systems and are passed among different applications at many locations. Also, new applications are constantly in need of joining in the sharing of data. It is necessary that data descriptions and content be precisely understood by all of these applications that receive and process the data. *A detailed set of descriptors is needed to accompany the document in storage, transmission, and processing.* The creation of commonly understood data streams that can handle compound documents is designed to further this understanding.

Current document-architecture development recognizes the diversity of using products and the rapid advances in technology. For general communicability, it is desirable that the data stream be *device independent.* This is needed if we are to service increasingly diverse types of devices (e.g., displays, printers, plotters, graphics, audio, and video devices), made by different vendors. Device controls are technology- and design-dependent and are best added separately as needed. The attempt is made, therefore, to create architectures that are as independent as possible from products and technology. These device-independent architectures within IIA can involve two layers [GG24-3503]:

- First there is the broad-scope **document content architecture (DCA)** (where the word "*document*" has to be considered in a broad sense, including text, graphics, image, video, and voice). This DCA includes the overall *structure* of the document being handled, its *layout*, and the *objects* carried in the data stream. Layout pertains to how the document content is divided into pages (or equivalent), and how portions of the content are positioned within the pages. A document content architecture allows one to *create, edit, format, and present* various kind of documents.

- Second, there is the architecture of *each type of object* carried by the document, including objects like *text*, *image*, and *graphics*. A supporting type of object deals with fonts. Each such **object content architecture (OCA)** gets down to details of data encoding and data formatting controls, for a particular type of information. An *object*, then, is a named collection of data and controls which conforms to one object content architecture. Objects can be transmitted in data streams and stored in libraries.

As in other aspects of communications architecture, the essential requirement, to accommodate diversity and change, is a *building-block structure, with independence among its parts.* For data streams, this means separating from each other: (a) the document's *logical structure* (chapters, paragraphs, etc.), (b) its data *objects* (text, image, graphics), and (c) its *physical layout* structure (placing objects on a page and layout within objects). Then, changes in any of these three components do not affect the other components.

The above focuses on the development of device-independent document data streams. On the other hand, a number of very popular data streams have earlier been devised for particular devices (or classes of devices). Examples, are the 3,270 display data streams and programmable printer data streams. *These contain device controls specific to the intended targets* (and are described further in Section 6.2.5).

Data streams can be very complex, full of detailed information that describes the objects and their relation to each other. Fortunately, the user can be largely unaware of this complexity. As documents are created, with friendly user interfaces, the underlying systems can help to provide the architected descriptors for the document being created. The following discussion of these architectures is offered, nevertheless, to provide some understanding of the underlying processes, particularly those which are used by compound-document systems.

6.2.2 Office Document Architecture (ODA)

Compound documents include things like spreadsheets, word-processing files, engineering drawings, pie charts, graphs, FAX images, and electronic mail. It is often a lot more efficient, for example, to devise a work plan, or a report, with the inclusion of such "natural" means of communication, rather than to rely only on words.

The external standards communities have made progress with the **Office Document Architecture (ODA)** [ODA88], and the **Standard General Markup Language (SGML)** [SGML86]. The Office Document Architecture (ODA) standard defines the representation of office documents; the format of the data stream for the interchange; and specific architectures for character (text) content, geometric graphics, and raster graphics (image) [Codes85], [Codes87], [Codes88], [FAX88a], [FAX88b], [Graph87].

ODA model and structures. The ODA model [Dawson89] for document processing includes three processes: *editing, layout, and imaging.* The successive stages are portrayed in Figure 6.4:

1. The *editing* process includes the creation of document logical structures (e.g., chapters, sections, paragraphs) and content. The resulting intermediate form of the document is the *processable document*. This is a revisable form. Even after being transmitted to another location, the logical structure and content can be changed.

2. The *layout* process formats the document into a page-based form. ODA layout structures include page sets, pages, and two subsets of pages called frames and blocks within frames. Illustrations, captions, running headers, footers, and body areas are examples of their use. The resulting intermediate form is either the *formatted document*, which is not revisable, or the *formatted processable document*, which is revisable.

3. The *imaging* process produces the final presentation of the document suitable for printing or transmission or storage.

Distinct from the layout view of a document (pages, frames, and blocks), is the logical view, having to do with the intellectual elements of a document. The structure of the logical view might include:

- *Front matter*: title page, table of contents, etc.
- *Main matter*: chapters, paragraphs, figures, footnotes, etc.
- *Back matter*: appendix, index, etc.

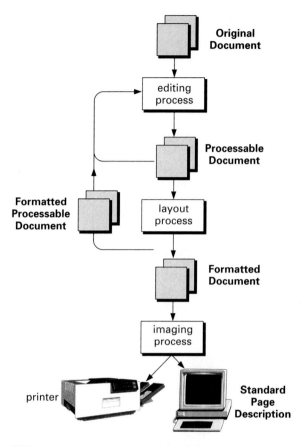

Figure 6.4 The ODA document-processing model.

The capability to define a logical view, in addition to the layout view, differentiates the ODA structure from precursor types of architecture.

Tower constructs.   Like in all architectures, some grouping of allowable functions are needed. Recognizing that, in general, different applications will support different document-content-architecture (DCA) functions, a scheme is needed to minimize the number of possible combinations. A base level has been defined in the architecture that is to be consistent for all participating applications. Then, on top of this base, there are "towers" for function classes.

Subsets of function within each tower are arranged hierarchically. For example, there is a tower for different subsets of drawing orders, and another tower for subsets of symbols. Then the ground rule is that any product which supports a tower at a given level must also support all lower levels of that same tower.

Applications that support a particular function set can interchange data with all other applications that support that same function set, or a superset of that function set.

Moreover, if a product receives constructs that it does not recognize, it must still preserve them if the data stream is to be round-tripped back to other applications. This preserves the integrity of the interchange document, and may allow some documents to be interchanged among products that support different levels of function.

The National Institute of Standards (NIST) Level 2 Document Application Profile (DAP) aids this process by defining a basic set of ODA functions.

ODA consortium.   A multivendor consortium, initially including Groupe Bull, DEC, IBM, ICL, Siemens, and UNISYS, is working cooperatively to develop a worldwide solution for the interchange of documents based on ODA revisable form. The consortium will develop an openly licensed software toolkit, with consistent interfaces, for document transmission among different types of computers.

6.2.3   Information Interchange Architecture (IIA)

As mentioned above, IBM's compound document architecture is called Information Interchange Architecture (IIA). It supports the interchange of processable (i.e., revisable) compound documents, composed of text, images and graphics, and also nonrevisable, formatted (presentation) documents. The revisable component of IIA is exactly built on the ISO Office Document Architecture (ODA).

A nonrevisable, formatted (presentation) component is also standardized as a part of ODA, but that part apparently is less well accepted in the industry. The IBM presentation option, is called **Mixed Object Document Content Architecture/Presentation (MO:DCA/P)**. It is designed to be device independent.

IIA remains compatible with the evolving standard. IIA, however, has to address a broader range of requirements than was formulated for ODA. Examples of these extensions include things like image compression, audio content, other multimedia support, and full national language support.

No transformations are needed when an ODA revisable document enters an IIA environment. ODA presentation documents, moreover, can use a subset of the features of the MO:DCA presentation capabilities.

ODA revisability.   Having a *processable document* (and revisability) means that the data you have is in a form so that you can read it into an editor and work on it. To permit revision, the intended logical structure must be explicit and modifiable. The logical structure defines and relates the parts of the document, such as chapters, paragraphs, lists, tables, figures, artwork, and footnotes, to give the document meaning. ODA *(revisable form)* contains *tags* (comparable to SGML tags) to define the logical structure.

A *live document* recognizes that there are pieces of the document (such as the data in a spreadsheet) that is going to change. It means that not only is the data revisable but there are links or pointers to the source of that data. The hooks for this in ODA are very flexible, and those pointers could actuate a variety of things. They could, for example, point to a REXX procedure, that starts a program that updates the data. They could even invoke an

Electronic Data Interchange (EDI) application that asks for updated data from some remote enterprise function.

Revisability is an expansion of the stylesheet concept, prevalent in word processors, to apply not only to text, but also to graphics, image, and other types of information. ODA has the ability to tag portions of the processable data, and to *bind particular methods (or styles) to the data*. For example, a spreadsheet could have one or more methods (styles) applied to it. One method could generate a bar chart; another method could generate a pie chart.

Styles can specify such parameters as color, highlighting, font attributes, arcs, line-type, character precision, chart-type, chart element attributes, hyphenation, tab stops, tab alignment, and justification. When applied, these are carried in a data stream as the revision descriptor function of a processable object.

Presentation architectures.   Today, users have a wide variety of presentation architectures to choose from. These include ASCII,[1] ODA, IBM's device-independent MO:DCA/P, and IBM's device-dependent Intelligent Printer Data Stream (IPDS), plus those in a range of products, including Postscript and PCL. Screen presentations are built using Windows Metafile, and the Presentation Manager Metafile (which is based on MO:DCA/P). Currently, it is often necessary for a print server to be able to handle a number (if not all) of these candidates, as their use can vary from department to department.

In addition to the ODA presentation component, the standards organizations are also working on a compound document presentation standard called **Standard Page Description Language (SPDL)**. That is not, however, expected to be fully device independent. Its development is reportedly based largely on Postscript, a product produced by Adobe Corp.

To see the nature of a *device-independent presentation architecture*, we describe the current IBM architecture for compound document presentation: MO:DCA/P.

MO:DCA presentation functions.   MO:DCA/P includes a variety of page layout features. Logical pages can be positioned anywhere on the medium. A page can consist of multiple blocks of text, image, graphics, and bar-code data. Data blocks and text can be presented at different orientations, Segments within a page may be electronically merged on logical pages. Overlays may be electronically merged on logical pages and the medium.

The basic organization of a MO:DCA/P document is shown in the sample of Figure 6.5. A specific example of MO:DCA/P data stream components is shown in Figure 6.6. Each page may contain multiple objects (of different types, such as image, text, or graphics). Each object is separately defined. A simple hierarchical nesting is employed. More complex structures are, however, also feasible. For example data objects may be nested to include other data objects. Overlays (such as an invoice form) may be combined with the data from the data stream. Resource groups can also be formed, for later reference, composed of data objects, fonts, overlays, etc. Such resource groups can appear in a document, page, overlay, or data object.

---

1.   ASCII is the American Standard Code for Information Interchange, based on ANSI X3.64.

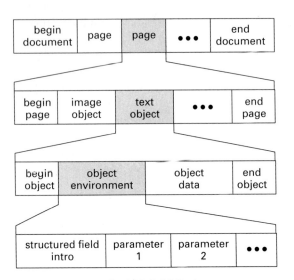

Figure 6.5 Sample organization of a MO:DCA/P data stream.

All function and data in a MO:DCA/P data stream is built up in **structured fields**. Each has the structure shown at the bottom of Figure 6.5, having an introduction or command part and zero or more parameter fields. Then, as also shown in Figure 6.5, related fields are grouped together and bounded by unique *begin* and *end* field pairs. In this manner, the hierarchy is built for the objects, pages, and document.

The interchange of MO:DCA/P documents imposes no special requirements on the underlying communication protocols. However, there may be application sensitivity to data syntax, particularly the code points (e.g., ASCII or EBCDIC) in use. Interchange among such applications requires the use of a *Coded Graphical Character Set Global Identifier (CGCSGID)*, that is to be interpreted by the interacting applications.

6.2.4   Object Content Architectures (OCA)

Both ODA and MO:DCA/P should be viewed as *carriers* of the object content architectures (OCAs). Thus, Information Interchange Architecture (IIA) contains MO:DCA/P, a *Document Content Architecture (DCA)*, which in turn carries *Object Content Architectures (OCAs)* for formatted (presentation) documents. Figure 6.7 illustrates a very simple letter using four types of objects.[2] The OCA list is extendable as new requirements emerge. To permit growth, each object type is treated equally, and document description is kept strictly separate from object data and its format controls. Functions are also kept

---

2.   As another example, the family of MO:DCA/P, Image (IOCA), Presentation Text (PTOCA), Graphics (GOCA), and FONT (FOCA) are used in the IBM IMAGEPLUS product. Using optical storage, scanners, and processors, the system captures, stores, retrieves, displays, processes, distributes, and prints visual information.

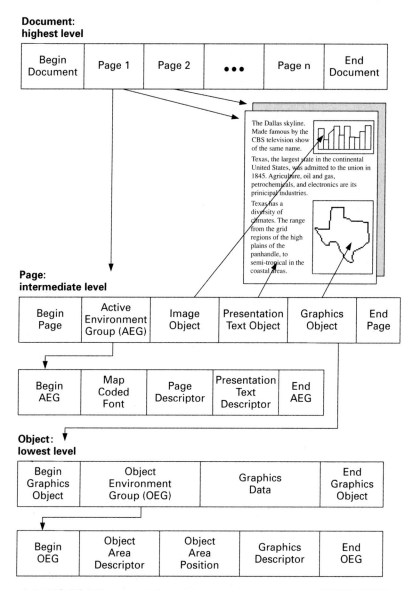

Figure 6.6 MO:DCA/P presentation data stream components [GG24-3503].

independent of device characteristics and application data formats. This single data stream architecture is thus designed to grow and to embrace all appropriate object types.

Objects contain the *x*, *y* location of the object, the data representations, and the presentation capability. The data of objects can be of different forms. It is coded characters for text, drawing orders (lines, arcs, circles) for graphics, and noncoded bits for raster

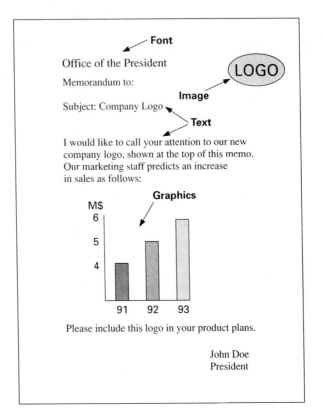

Figure 6.7 Simple letter using four content types.

graphics (image). Formatting controls of each OCA specify appropriate data characteristics and formats. This may include, for example, things like character set, compression algorithm, line type, margin settings, orientation, and line direction. Most of the OCAs have a descriptor part that addresses the space needed for the object. MO:DCA/P currently carries four types of objects: presentation text, graphics, image, and font, as follows.

Presentation Text Object Content Architecture (PTOCA).   PTOCA concerns text objects that are structured by components such as chapters, sections, paragraphs, headers, titles, footnotes, figures, and captions. The presentation text is self-describing by means of the structured fields. Contents of these fields are control sequences, parameters, and graphic character data. A descriptor subfield carries the size and shape of the object space. Graphic characters can be placed at addressable positions, and rotated relative to a baseline. These positioning specifications are given by control sequences that are carried with the data.

The Character Content Architecture (CCA) is a supporting ISO standard, ISO 8613, 1989, Part 6, that defines the syntax and semantics of text (character) objects within an ODA document. This is incorporated in the revisable component of IBM's IIA (based on ODA), but as of this writing, it is not incorporated in the PTOCA of MO:DCA/P.

Graphics Object Content Architecture (GOCA). GOCA typically involves graphical pictures that are built up from primitives, such as lines, arcs, characters, symbols, shaded areas, and point arrays. Each primitive may have attributes, such as line width, orientation, shading pattern, or resolution. Colors are another variable. GOCA is concerned with the graphics data involved in using such primitives to construct line-drawn graphics.

Segments are self-contained groups of primitive *drawing orders* and attributes. Presentation processes use drawing orders to draw graphic pictures, incorporate raster images and produce character strings. Facilities are provided for chaining segments together to describe a complete picture. One segment can also call another segment, temporarily transferring control to that called segment.

The Geometric Graphics Content Architecture (GGCA) is a complementary standard defined by ISO for a computer graphics picture in a binary encoded format, as specified by Computer Graphics Metafile (CGM). This is described in ISO 8632. It is incorporated in the revisable component of IBM's IIA (based on ODA), but as of this writing, it is not incorporated in the GOCA of MO:DCA/P.

Image Object Content Architecture (IOCA). IOCA typically involves images that are scanned, with the data sampled at regular intervals. With a value given to each sample, we obtain a digital signal representing the image. The image points are called *pels* or *pixels*. Standard image parameters include size (number of image points), resolution (pels per inch), compression algorithm, scan direction (e.g., left-to-right; top-to-bottom) and data element size (bits per pel). Color structure is given in either of two ways: the bits for each element of a color model, such as red, green, blue, or use of a look-up-table-id, whereby the pel value is the index for the table and the data at the indexed location in the table is the color value for the pel [Hakeda90].

Font Object Content Architecture (FOCA). FOCA uses font resource information to determine the shape of the character images to be generated on the media. Since formatting and presentation of documents takes place on different systems, it is important to preserve presentation consistency. FOCA provides common font and character definition models for this purpose. [3]

The Font Information Interchange Standard has been defined by ISO for specifying the architecture and interchange format of font resources and font references [ISO9541]. The semantics of ISO-9541 are incorporated in IBM's IIA (both revisable and presentation components).

Formatted Data Object Content Architecture (FD:OCA). FD:OCA *describes data* from files, databases, and applications for interchange within or across environments. Because every database or file can have its own convention about data representation and meaning, an architecture is needed to describe the syntax and semantics of any given set of data items. Such descriptive information can then accompany the data when it is communicated. The data itself can be communicated "as is"; if any transformation of the data is needed,

---

3. IBM also supports the popular ADOBE System Type 1 font technology. This provides a base for using outline technology to generate fonts at any desired resolution.

that can be done by the receiving station with the help of the descriptors that accompany the data.

A formatted data object consists of two parts:

- The *descriptor* describes the object. It expresses what format and what data type is used. It further tells how parts are grouped together into rows or arrays of data.

- The *described data*, just as it would have been read from a database, or as it would be expected by an application program.

Both the descriptor and the data part each begin with a format field called an *introducer*. The *data types*, part of the descriptor, can, for example, be bit and byte strings, character strings, or numeric data. Integers might be decimal numbers in zoned or packed format, or signed or unsigned binary numbers. Fractional numbers might be decimal or binary fixed point, hexadecimal floating point, or IEEE binary floating point.

Data arrangements might be single fields or tabular arrays, or collections of records from traditional databases. These seemingly different arrangements are treated as variations of a single general concept. All are a special case of a multidimensional, more or less regular, array of elements whose formats may not be identical.

FD:OCA is used in the Distributed Relational Database Architecture (DRDA), for data interchange, but as of this writing, it is not incorporated into MO:DCA/P.

Communication of document objects.   This is illustrated by the case of an image object, as follows. The image object is produced by scanning and compressing a document. Figure 6.8 illustrates the wrapping of the object with the necessary headers for transmittal [Morris90].

1. The compressed image of each page is first wrapped in an Image Object Content Architecture *(IOCA) envelope*, consisting of header and trailer fields around the object.

2. The collection of IOCA-wrapped page images is then put in a document-level wrapper that is the *MO:DCA/P envelope*. This adds header and trailer fields to the whole document.

3. For transmission, the *SNA headers and trailer* are then added.

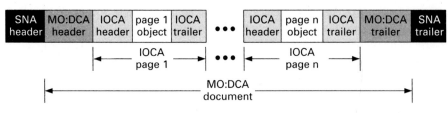

MO:DCA = Multiple Object Document Content Architecture
IOCA = Image Object Content Architecture

Figure 6.8 Packaging of page objects for communication.

6.2.5   Device-Specific Data Streams

MO:DCA/P is device independent. It does not address the controls unique to a device, such as paper load and font load. Device-specific data streams, such as the **3270 data stream** and the **Intelligent Printer Data Stream (IPDS)** therefore need device-specific inputs in addition to the input of MO:DCA/P.

IPDS is a printer data stream that contains the information necessary to identify, monitor, and control the functions of the printer. It uses a two-way dialog between the printer and its management system that provides cooperative resource management, cooperative recovery, and restart management.

For example, a product called *Print Services Facility (PSF)* takes a MO:DCA/P input in presentation form (already formatted for presentation), looks out at the printers attached to it, finds out the characteristics of those printers, and decides which attached printer is best suited to the needs of the document (e.g., color, fonts, etc.). PSF then adds device controls by building device-specific IPDS wrappers for that printer. For example, if this is a color print, it might have to order a turn-on of a color chip, or it might replace the logical indication of a page with a command to feed from a particular paper drawer. It might also retrieve appropriate fonts from its library and download them to the printer.

Figure 6.9 illustrates this process. A PSF function, separate from the printer, accepts the MO:DCA/P and produces the IPDS. PSF (operable in all four SAA environments) performs a variety of useful functions. Nevertheless, if present trends continue, one can imagine, in the future, some programmable printers that can perform the PSF function for themselves. In that case, the printers would be able to receive MO:DCA/P data streams directly.

Similarly, in the display area, a device-dependent data stream, the 3270 data stream, has been used for nonprogrammable displays. Figure 6.10 illustrates that operation. Note that the device driver has been located in the host. Now, with the advent of the programmable workstation (e.g., the PS/2), all the functions shown could be replaced by a combination of OS/2, the Presentation Manager, and the Dialog Manager, all within the PS/2. No 3270 data stream, per se, need be involved. With such intelligence, it should thus be possible for that type of unit to accept a device-independent data stream, like MO:DCA/P, and perform all the necessary interpretations and additions of device controls. For that to be achieved, however, it would be desirable for the Presentation Manager Common Programming Interface (CPI) to include the semantics of MO:DCA/P. The host would have to

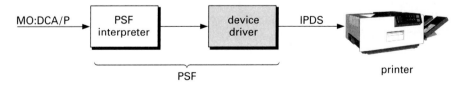

IPDS = Intelligent Printer Data Stream
MO:DCA = Multiple Object Document Content Architecture
PSF = Print Service Facility

Figure 6.9 MO:DCA/P and device-specific IPDS.

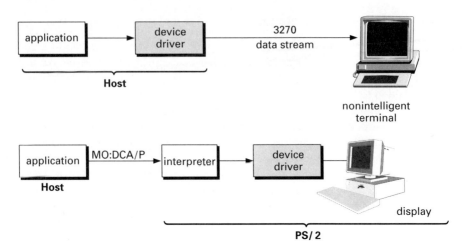

Figure 6.10 Evolution of display data streams.

generate the MO:DCA/P syntax; and the workstation Presentation Manager would have to accept as input the MO:DCA/P syntax.

Thus, MO:DCA/P has been developed in anticipation of the programmable printers and workstations of tomorrow, and the advantages accruing from the use of device-independent data streams for intersystem communication.

6.2.6 Print Management

Communication technology has made it possible to distribute electronically the printed message to any point on the globe. Low-cost computer technology and laser print technology has made it possible for the printing function to migrate out of the central data processing complex and onto the desks of the enterprise staff. The resulting requirement, in the networked enterprise, is the ability to send a print job anywhere in the organization without knowing which type of printer is at the target location or its features. This has been called *printer independence*.

A corollary requirement is *programmer independence*, the separation of the programming and the print-formatting tasks. Printer and programming independence are both essential to cooperating systems. They also ensure the ability to develop applications today for printers that will come to market in the future, with features such as on-board image decompression. We discuss two steps along this road: the current IBM Advanced Function Printing and the projected OSF print service.

Advanced Function Printing (AFP)   is a composite system of print-related components. The AFP data stream (AFPDS) uses MO:DCA/P as its device-independent format. AFP uses IPDS as its device-dependent data stream. AFP also includes facilities to handle earlier data streams, such as the 1403 printer data stream. The device-independent MO:DCA/P data stream is converted into the IPDS printer data stream by the system print management software product, Print Services Facility (PSF), as illustrated in Figure 6.9.

AFP, like other SAA architectures, is an open architecture, and both the printer (IPDS) and the application (MO:DCA/P) data streams have been published. As a result, AFP is becoming a de facto standard for electronic printing.[4] Programs that are part of the AFP solution today provide bridges between AFP and other data streams such as PostScript and ASCII.

OSF Print Management.   The preceding discussion illustrates the variety of options in presentation architecture and the difficulty of providing a universal capability for printing any document from any source. A major step towards this objective is being taken, however, in the OSF distributed management project. OSF is undertaking a multivendor cooperation to provide a set of client–server applications for managing a distributed computing environment. This includes a client–server print service that can accommodate multiple presentation architectures.

The OSF specification is based on the ISO document printing standard, ISO 10175, which concerns print job management. The objective is to provide a vehicle for print management that is independent of the actual data stream used. The standard defines an API that provides the basic requirements to request print, prioritize print, schedule print, cancel print, and distribute print. Supplementary operations would include things like collating, three-hole punching, stapling, etc.

The print manager will be an application-service, and should be independent of the communication protocols used. The client portion would be independent of the data stream being used, as would the interaction between the client and the print server (which is basically a print spooler and scheduler). A separate print supervisor performs the function of print driver for selected print architectures. Transformations of different print data streams can be added to the basic print-driver functions. This gives the ability to manage the printing of multiple printer architectures.

Several submissions to OSF (including one by DEC, MIT, and IBM) are based on earlier work on the Palladium project at the Massachusetts Institute of Technology. Candidates for the data stream architectures this OSF project might accommodate are many, but a high degree of interoperability would be obtained if it included ASCII, PostScript, SPDL, MO:DCA/P, and ODA/P. If this OSF project is successful, another bottleneck in multivendor cooperating systems will have been lessened.

6.3 MESSAGE HANDLING SYSTEMS OVERVIEW

6.3.1 MHS Purpose

The basic purpose of a **message handling system (MHS)** is to allow applications to communicate without requiring that the origin and destination applications be active simultaneously. Hence, the system must store the messages when necessary, and deliver the information when the resources become available. For example, the time for sending data may be when lower-cost transmission facilities become available (e.g., at night), or

---

4.   For example, non-IBM products, such as: printers, computer output microfiche devices, and software for word-processing, spreadsheet applications, font and image creation tools, and print distribution packages, have been announced that support AFP architectures.

after compensating for time differences, when destination nodes are activated. Various levels of priority, security, or integrity may be required for each distribution. Architecturally, an MHS is considered to lie in the application layer (layer 7), and should ultimately be accessible through the Common Programming Interface (CPI). The important elements of such systems are the standards that specify the structure of messages being sent between dissimilar systems, and the means for transferring these messages over public or private networks.

6.3.2   Common Message Handling System Structures

As shown in Figure 6.11 the heart of the message system, in both OSI and SNA, is a *store and forward*, asynchronous message transfer system, whose OSI **Message Transfer Agents (MTAs)** or SNA **Distribution Service Units (DSUs)** are distributed throughout the network. At each of these store and forward nodes, a distribution is either queued to a *local delivery queue* or to the appropriate *next-node queue*. Communication among these nodes is via either the LU 6.2 program–program protocols of SNA or the corresponding OSI layers. Routing among these nodes contrasts with routing performed by lower layers (see Section 12.4). For example, APPN routing identifies the network-nodes to be traversed *by a single session*; in the store and forward nodes, routing identifies the *multiple, independent sessions* to be traversed by a distribution. In OSI, this asynchronous transfer service is called the **Message Transfer System (MTS)**, while in SNA, a comparable service is called the **SNA Distribution Services (SNADS)**.

In both the OSI and SNA message handling systems, the message transfer system, or distribution services, are separated from the user by an intermediate set of message processing services. These are called **user agents** (UA) in OSI. In SNA, the equivalent of the user agent is split into two nodes, the *Source/Recipient Node (SRN)* and a server *Office Systems Node (OSN)* that can handle more than one Source/Recipient Node. The SNA and OSI versions are closely functionally equivalent, and the SNA version can be considered to be a distributed UA.

Communications services independence.   As noted earlier, we have three distinct sets of architecture and services:

1. *Document content architectures*, like ODA and MO:DCA/P (in IBM under an umbrella architecture called IIA)
2. *Message handling systems*, with protocols like X.400 and SNADS/DIA (SNA Distribution Services and Document Interchange Architecture, see Section 6.5.1)
3. *Communications systems*, with protocols like OSI, SNA, TCP/IP, and NetBIOS

In principle, these three types of service should be independent of each other. Either SNA, OSI, TCP/IP, or NetBIOS communications services can carry any application message such as the content of a SNADS/DIA document interchange unit or an X.400 envelope. These contents should be completely independent of the medium and protocol that transports it. Furthermore, the content architectures, MO:DCA/P and ODA could be carried by either the SNA message handling system or the X.400 message handling system.

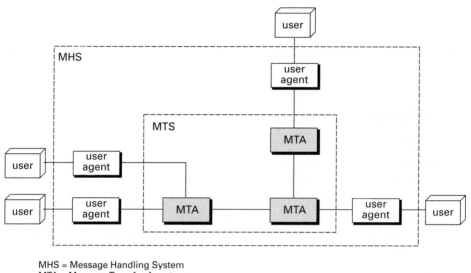

MHS = Message Handling System
MTA = Message Transfer Agent
MTS = Message Transfer System

(a)

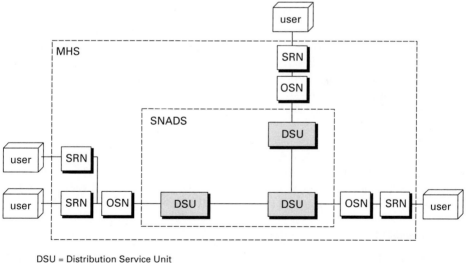

DSU = Distribution Service Unit
OSN = Office System Node
SRN = Source/Recipient Node

(b)

Figure 6.11 The structures of the message handling systems: **(a)** The structure of the X.400 message handling system, **(b)** The structure of the SNA message handling system.

6.4   OSI MHS DESIGN (X.400)

The CCITT has issued a set of MHS recommendations in the X.400 series, which are only outlined in the following. It is expected that these will be incorporated into the emerging Message Oriented Text Interchange System (MOTIS) standards, which are being developed under ISO auspices (and are essentially identical to X.400).

6.4.1   User Agents

User agents may provide a set of services to individual users, such as the ability to:

- Edit and compose messages
- Perform message filing and retrieval
- Perform message arrival notification
- Use nicknames and local distribution list expansion
- Interface to the Message Transfer System (MTS), so as to submit messages and receive and view messages from others

User agents may have specialized functions that are user-written. The structure of X.400 is such that the message sent could, with suitable facilities at both ends, be composed of binary files (including executable programs and spreadsheet data), or data that represents graphics, telematics, facsimile, or digitized speech. User agents may also be agents for connection to other message handling systems, such as the TELEX network, the Postal System, or IBM's DISOSS, PROFS, and OfficeVision systems[5] that are linked to the Message Handling System. Such interactions with the Message Transfer System (MTS) are not standardized.

The **form** of the message given to the user agent consists of data for an *envelope* (a header) and the message *contents*. The envelope contains the addresses of the originator and the recipients, plus other information like whether the originator wants confirmation of delivery. The envelope that accompanies the contents actually changes somewhat in its submission to the MTA, the inter-MTA transmissions, and the final delivery to the destination UA.

The **content** of the message has two parts, the *heading* and the *body*. As you would expect, the heading contains the names of the originator and recipient, a unique message-id, the subject of the message, and any references to other messages. The body of the contents may be coded in various ways, including the International Alphabet, IA5 Text (very similar to ASCII), Teletex, and Group 3 Facsimile.

6.4.2   Message Transfer Agents

The Message Transfer System is composed of a network of **Message Transfer Agents (MTAs)**, (see Figure 6.11(a)). Each MTA acts like a local post office to:

- Accept *responsibility for delivery* of messages given by various local UAs

---

5.   DISOSS, PROFS, and OfficeVision are IBM office systems products. DISOSS runs on MVS S/390 systems. PROFS runs on VM S/390 systems, OfficeVision is an SAA product.

- Act as a *relay station*, in a store-and-forward mode, so as to move messages toward the MTAs of the intended recipients
- *Deliver* messages to the appropriate local UAs

The MTA also must manage the associations among MTAs, maintain a directory of routing information, and provide delivery reports.

Within the MTA is a function called the **Reliable Transfer Service** (RTS) to establish associations (i.e., sessions) and coordinate the reliable transmissions between MTAs. For this, the RTS makes direct use of the lower-layer services.

The originator and recipients are each identified by an **Originator/Recipient name** (O/R name), having two possible forms. The first form consists of a subset of the following:

- Country name
- Administration domain name
- Organization name
- Organization unit name

- Private domain name
- Domain defined terms
- Personal name

The second form of the O/R name is the X.121 worldwide address (see Section 12.3.3) or a telematic terminal identifier.

6.4.3   Inter-Node Protocols

Three peer protocols have defined in X.400: P1, P2, and P3. As illustrated in Figure 6.12(a), these pertain to:

- *P1*: MTA to MTA protocol.
- *P2*: UA to UA protocol for Interpersonal Messages.
- *P3*: UA to MTA. In the 1988 model, P3 is also used between a message store and the MTA, when the message store is remote from the MTA. (This protocol is the subject of still further revisions.)

The X.400 functions reside as application-services in the application layer. MTAs communicate with each other using the X.400 P1 protocol, and UAs communicate with each other using the X.400 P2 protocol. The formats for the P1 and P2 flows are shown in Figure 6.13(a).

User agents may be of many types, and the header information will vary accordingly. The X.420 recommendation concerns the *Interpersonal Messaging (IPM)* user agent, for electronic mail. IPM user agent services are made available to users by a local editor. The *P2 protocol* concerns the header and content exchanged between peer IPM UAs.

All the services offered by the IPM UA to the user are reflected in the P2 header. These include the following:

- IPM message-id
- Authorizing user

- Obsoletes
- Subject

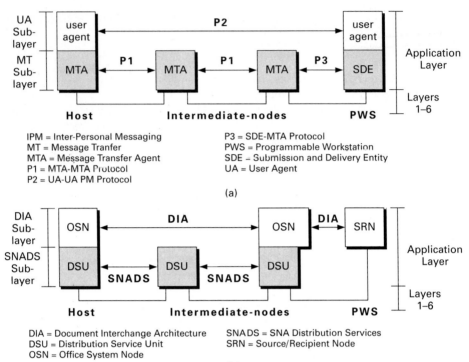

IPM = Inter-Personal Messaging
MT = Message Tranfer
MTA = Message Transfer Agent
P1 = MTA-MTA Protocol
P2 = UA-UA PM Protocol

P3 = SDE-MTA Protocol
PWS = Programmable Workstation
SDE = Submission and Delivery Entity
UA = User Agent

(a)

DIA = Document Interchange Architecture
DSU = Distribution Service Unit
OSN = Office System Node

SNADS = SNA Distribution Services
SRN = Source/Recipient Node

(b)

Figure 6.12 The three peer protocols of **(a)** X.400; **(b)** SNADS.

- Originator
- Primary recipients
- Copy recipients
- Blind copy recipients
- In reply to
- Cross reference

- Importance
- Sensitivity
- Reply by (time)
- Reply to users
- Expiration date
- Autoforwarded

The *P1 protocol* is used for communicating between Message Transfer Agents (MTAs). The P1 message content is both the header and the body of the service data unit received from the UA, as shown in Figure 6.13(a). The P1 peer *message protocol data units (MPDUs)* are of three types: for user messages, for delivery reports, and for probes. The P1 header (or relaying envelope) has three forms: the submission (or user) envelope, the relay envelope, and the delivery envelope. For example, the user envelope, or header for the user MPDU, has the following fields:

- Message PDU-id
- Originator O/R name
- Recipient O/R name

- Priority
- Deferred delivery time
- Trace information

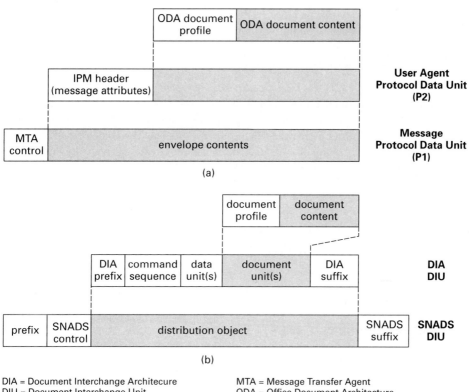

Figure 6.13 OSI X.400 and SNA document interchange formats: **(a)** protocol data units for P2 and P1 protocols; **(b)** document interchange units for DIA and SNADS protocols.

6.4.4 Programmable Workstation as User Agent

When a user agent (UA) is located in a programmable workstation, it can communicate with a remote Message Transfer Agent (MTA). This UA-MTA remote communication is handled in the workstation by a **Submission and Delivery Entity** (SDE), which submits and receives messages from an MTA. The SDE and the MTA are architectural peers, and communicate using a special interactive, transaction oriented, *P3 protocol*. All the service primitives, between a UA and its MTA, are mapped to one Operation Protocol Data Unit (OPDU).

In the 1984 version of X.400, a UA must be continuously available if it is to be assured of receiving its messages. In the 1988 version of X.400, ISO and CCITT have eliminated this constraint, by including the concept of an optional **Message Store (MS)**. *The Message Store is inserted between the MTA and the UA.* The protocol between the MS and the MTA remains the P3 protocol. However, the protocol between the MS and the UA is a new protocol called the **P7 protocol**. This protocol is never initiated by the MS; hence, the UA can be switched off when it is not in use.

The X.400-1988 recommendations also specify security services that are based on cryptographic techniques and digital signatures.

6.4.5 X.400 Management Domains

An Administrative Management Domain (ADMD) is a group of MTAs that is managed by a government telecommunications agency (e.g., a Post Telephone and Telegraph, PTT, agency) or a Recognized Private Operating Agency (RPOA), such as a local network provider or common carrier. A Private Management Domain (PRMD) is a group of MTAs maintained by an organization other than an administration (e.g., a private organization or company). The CCITT view has been that PRMDs:

- Attach peripherally (and only) to ADMDs
- Will not span country boundaries
- Will not act as relays between ADMDs
- May not be allowed to interconnect to one another, depending on country regulations

The ISO version of MHS (MOTIS), on the other hand, imposes no constraints on PRMD interworking.

6.5 SNA MHS DESIGN (SNADS)

SNA Distributed Services (SNADS) is likewise a store and forward service that delivers documents to nodes throughout the network. In addition to office systems services, SNADS serves the change-distribution application of network management, file transfers, job networking, print services, electronic data interchange, and other functions.

SNADS uses the SNA LU 6.2 protocols, but it does not require the prior establishment of all end-to-end sessions. If a given destination node does not have a session (or may not even be powered on) SNADS delivers the document to a point closest to the destination node, and stores it temporarily there. Delivery is guaranteed, with either a confirmation of delivery or a notification of failure.

SNADS allows files to be sent from any origin to many destinations on any node in the network. Locations can change without requiring a name change, rather than fixed addresses, because is uses names. It offers routing, copying, and storage efficiencies when a document is to be sent to multiple destinations. This asynchronous, delayed delivery applies to documents and messages. Referring again to Figure 6.11, the primary differences between the X.400 and SNADS designs are:

- The Office System Node (OSN) serves multiple end users (SRNs), whereas an X.400 UA serves only one end user.
- The OSN must coreside with the SNADS Distribution Service Unit (DSU). The SRN or the OSI user agent may be separate from the DSU or MTA.
- DIA/SNADS and MHS are roughly equivalent in the functions of document distribution. The DIA, however, also supports additional functions, such as library services, which are not yet included in X.400.

The SNADS functions operate in Office Systems Nodes (OSNs). SNADS uses SNA to transmit Document Interchange Units (DIUs) provided by Document Interchange Architecture (DIA). SNADS offers other services, such as the replication of copies when there are multiple recipients attached to it.

Both DIA/SNADS and X.400 MHS are modeled as sublayers of the application layer in the SNA and OSI architectures.

6.5.1   Document Interchange Architecture

Document Interchange Architecture (DIA) controls the flows of documents throughout the network. The DIA **document distribution service** enables the source node to *request distribution* of information, *request status* of information, *request delivery* of queued information, and *cancel delivery* of queued information. It enables the sender to know who has actually received sent documents.[6] The **document library service** allows documents to be *filed, searched, retrieved,* or *deleted* from the library, using arguments like name, date, author, and recipient.

DIA inter-node protocols.   For SNADS, three inter-node protocols have been defined (see Figure 6.12(b)):

- The SNADS protocol for distribution service unit DSU-DSU communication
- The DIA protocol for office system node–to–office system node (OSN-to-OSN) communication
- The DIA protocol for source/recipient node–to–office systems node (SRN-to-OSN) communication

The formats for these flows are shown in Figure 6.13(b).

6.6   MAIL SYSTEM INTEROPERABILITY

A number of approaches and products have been devised to achieve interoperability among the mail systems from different vendors. Some of these are described in the following.

6.6.1   Open Network Distribution Service

The *interoperation of the OSI X.400 and the IBM PROFS and DISOSS systems* is achieved via a gateway at the OSI application level [Capodil89]. It further involves a common user interface, so that either system or a cascade of several systems can be used transparently. The destination name then allows the system to determine whether X.400 or SNADS is the proper vehicle.

---

6.   Some implementations, particularly DISOSS, also maintain a queue of both text and image documents, keeping transmitted documents until notified that all the persons on the distribution list have in fact received the document.

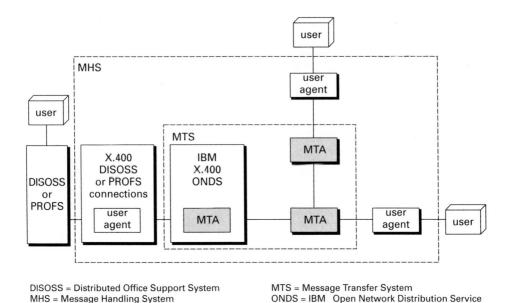

DISOSS = Distributed Office Support System
MHS = Message Handling System
MTA = Message Transfer Agent

MTS = Message Transfer System
ONDS = IBM   Open Network Distribution Service
PROFS = Professional Office System

Figure 6.14 Using a special MTA and user agent to connect DISOSS or PROFS to an X.400 MHS.

The *Open Network Distribution Services (ONDS)* product acts as a specialized MTA in an X.400 network. The role of the ONDS is illustrated in Figure 6.14 and Figure 6.15. Acting as an MTA within the X.400 Message Transfer System, the ONDS provides connection services to proprietary electronic mail systems. This can be to either user-written UAs or to vendor-provided UAs, such as the IBM OfficeVision.

ONDS uses the OSI/Communications Subsystem (see Chapter 11) for the communication via X.25 to other OSI-based nodes. On the S/390 mainframes, the X.25 interface is provided by the NPSI feature on the communication controllers (see Section 19.5). These relationships are shown in Figure 6.15. As indicated there, users attached to the X.25 network can exchange X.400 type messages, through the ONDS gateway, with:

- Users similarly attached to other X.400 ONDSs on the network

- Users attached to PROFS or DISOSS systems, via PROFS or DISOSS Connections

The *DISOSS and PROFS Connections, with ONDS*, provide an *application level gateway* to allow users of DISOSS and PROFS systems to exchange messages with users of public and private electronic mail facilities based on the CCITT X.400 recommendations. Using the ONDS and its associated Connection products, users of DISOSS and PROFS can exchange messages with each other and with X.400 users.

OfficeVision/VM and OfficeVision/MVS, the SAA Office Systems, support X.400 connectivity via the X.400 PROFS Connection Program Offering and the X.400 DISOSS

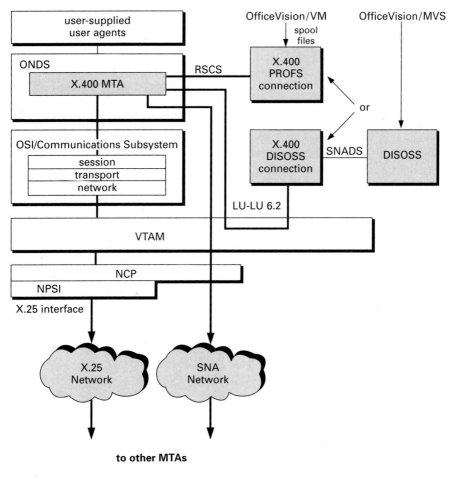

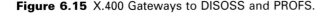

ONDS = IBM's Open Network Distribution Service   RSCS = VM message protocol
NPSI = NCP Packet Switching Interface   VTAM = Virtual Telecommunications Access Method
NCP = Network Control Program

Figure 6.15 X.400 Gateways to DISOSS and PROFS.

Connection Program Offering. ONDS also provides a VTAM/APPC interface (in the MVS environment only) that uses LU 6.2 to transfer data to other MTAs via SNA links.

ONDS uses the directory provided by OSI/Communications Subsystem, and provides extensions to that directory including ISO-defined objects for X.400 addressing. X.400 PROFS Connection accesses this directory in order to translate addresses between X.400 originator/recipient conventions and addresses in the OfficeVision/VM or PROFS network. The ONDS also maps the X/400 O/R addresses to the SNADS address used by DISOSS. If the sender of a message requests a delivery report, the MTA must report (with a message) to the sender when that message was delivered or not delivered.

6.6.2 IIN and X.400

An example of the use of X.400 and the IBM Open Network Distribution Service (ONDS) is the worldwide **IBM Mail Exchange** services of the IBM Information Network (IIN).[7]An illustration of such an interconnection with IBM office systems, via IIN and diverse value-added carriers, is shown in Figure 6.16. The common transport facility for switching purposes uses OSI X.25. IBM office system users address users via standard IBM address formats, while X.400 users use X.400 standard address formats. Mail Exchange is a composite that provides for address translation, as well as the message header and transmission envelope translation between X.400 and both IBM formats, PROFS and DISOSS. Private mail formats are converted by the user agent into the X.400 format illustrated in Figure 6.17.[8]

Mail Exchange provides a directory facility that can be used to store details of system users, and to search through directory entries for the electronic address of the parties to be communicated with. This directory will be evolved to compatibility with multivendor X.500 directories.

6.6.3 A Central Soft Switch Mail Gateway

When more than two different mail systems need to interoperate, and different vendor's office systems are involved, separate gateways for each possible pair may become difficult to manage. A common switching arrangement is helpful. An interesting approach to the marriage of different electronic mail systems is the multiprotocol, application-level mail switch made by Soft Switch. The Soft Switch approach is modular so as to accommodate the electronic mail systems of different subnetworks, such as X.400, IBM SNADS, TCP/IP SMTP,[9] and others.[10] The exchange of mail among three systems, SNA-based OfficeVision, TCP/IP-based SMTP, and OSI-based X.400, can be achieved by Soft Switch

---

7. Mail Exchange's X.400 service is available on the IIN networks in over sixteen countries, and via public packet switched networks from over seventy other countries. Mail Exchange provides the facility to connect an office system that supports X.400 to a public messaging domain (such as MCI, U.S. Sprint, GE Information Services, and AT&T) for communicating with other X.400 systems. Connections also can be made to existing IBM office systems users of Mail Exchange.

8. Proprietary mail systems thus communicate with each other. These include AT&T Mail, SprintMail, BT Tymnet's Dialcom, Netherland PTT's, Memocom GE's QUICK-COMM, Western Union's EasyLink, and MCI Mail, as well as IBM's PROFS, DISOSS, and S/36 or S/38 with Personal Services.

9. The Simple Mail Transfer Protocol (SMTP) is widely used on TCP/IP-based communications networks. The specific formats are specified in RFC821 and RFC822 SMTP. SAA, AIX, and other UNIX systems providing this level of formatting are able to exchange mail. In general, SMTP functions are a subset of both X.400 and PROFS/DISOSS.

10. Soft Switch's Central cooperates with diverse systems. It supports access to and from the backbone for systems that include: DEC ALL-IN-1, Novell MHS, Dialcom, HP DeskManager, MCI Mail, Banyan Mail, Wang MaiLWAY, Data General CEO, and 3COM 3+Mail, in addition to the IBM mail systems.

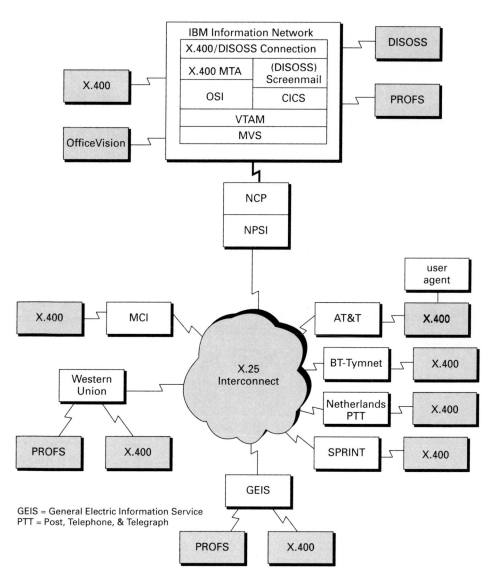

Figure 6.16 X.400 and IBM office systems interoperation via IIN and other VANs.

gateways, as shown in Figure 6.18.[11] Specific vendor protocols, such as IBM's PROFS, DEC Message Router, and various LAN-based protocols can also be handled by Soft Switch. The Soft Switch mail switch (called *Soft Switch Central*) can be used, for example,

---

11. For example, bridge functions running on MVS, VM, and OS/400 will allow users on any system having TCP/IP and SMTP (such as AIX) and SAA OfficeVision users to exchange mail and notes. Officevision users on OS/2 workstations get access to SMTP mail by connection to an OfficeVision host. OSI/X.400 users and SAA-OfficeVision users will similarly exchange mail.

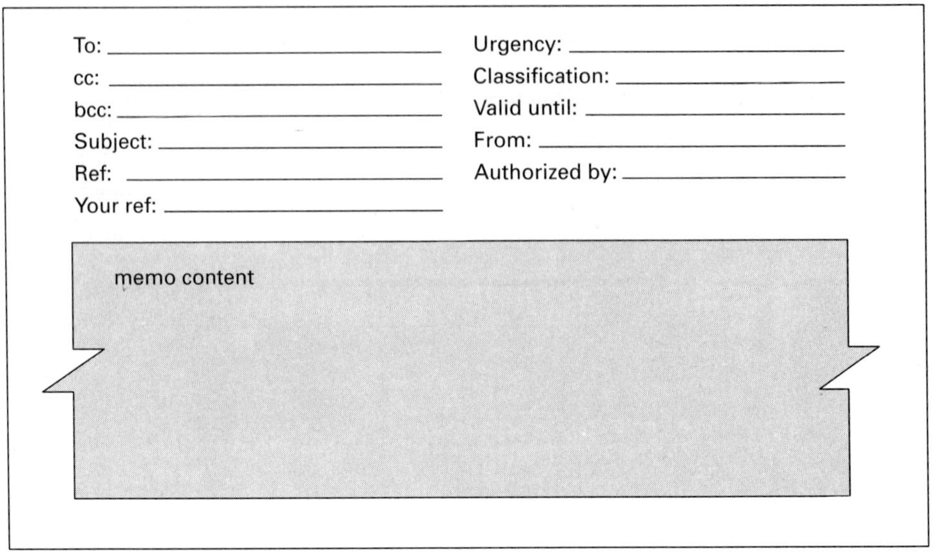

To:
cc:
bcc:
Subject:
Ref:
Your ref:
Urgency:
Classification:
Valid until:
From:
Authorized by:
memo content

Figure 6.17 X.400 message format.

SNA
OfficeVision-
SMTP
Gateway
OfficeVision-
X.400
Gateway
SMTP
mail
X.400
mail
TCP/IP
X.400
mail
OSI

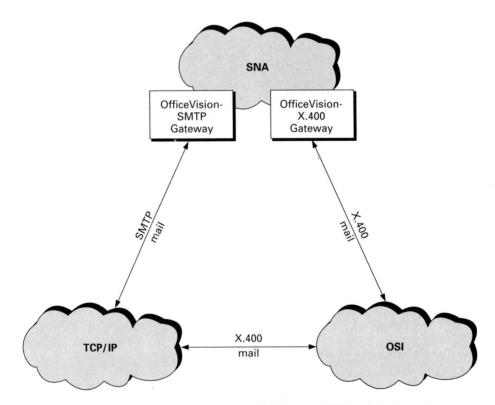

Figure 6.18 Mail exchange among SNA- TCP/IP-, and OSI-based systems.

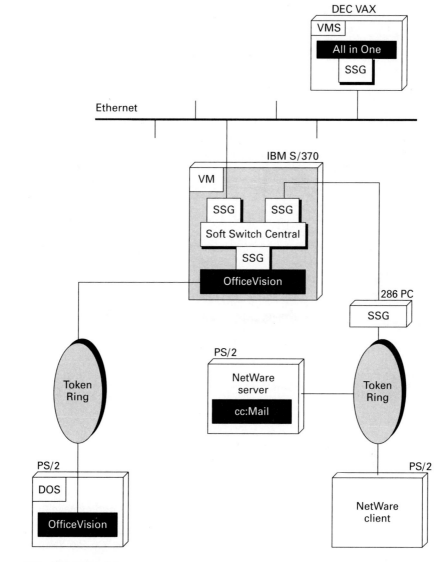

SSG = Soft Switch Gateway

Figure 6.19 Joining DEC's All in One, IBM's OfficeVision, and NETWARE's cc:Mail.

to connect an IBM PROFS system through an X.400 gateway to a public mail network. It can be used, as shown in Figure 6.19, to join different vendor's mail systems on LANs. On a larger scale, a wide area backbone can be used to integrate a worldwide network of IBM, DEC, Wang, and LAN-based mail systems, as illustrated in Figure 6.20. On the backbone, X.400 and SNADS protocols are used.

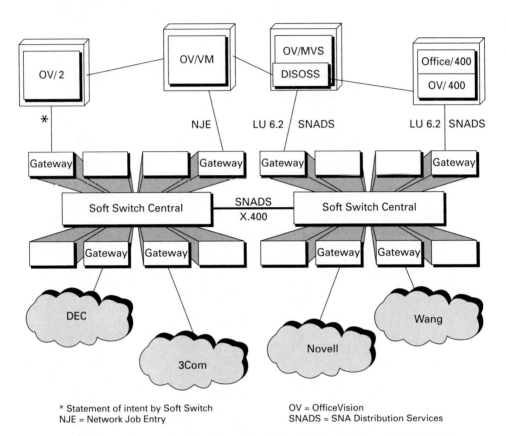

* Statement of intent by Soft Switch   OV = OfficeVision
NJE = Network Job Entry   SNADS = SNA Distribution Services

Figure 6.20 OfficeVision Connectivity: The Soft Switch Solution [SoftSwitch].

Soft Switch Central currently executes on an IBM host, under MVS or VM [SoftSwitch]. Key features of the system include:

- *Gateways* that implement standard and proprietary protocols and manage the flow of traffic into and out of Central.

  - The *X.400 Gateway* implements the X.400 P1 protocol. On the SNA side, the Gateway communicates with the Central using a standard LU 6.2 session. On the X.25 side, the Gateway connects to a public packet switch network, like Telenet, AT&T, and MCI.
  - The *SMTP Gateway*.
  - The *SNADS Gateway* uses LU 6.2 to communicate with IBM office systems such as DISOSS. Some non-IBM office systems use non-IBM implementations of SNADS.
  - *LAN connectivity* is provided for proprietary mail systems such as 3Com's *3+ Mail*, Banyan's *Banyan Mail*, Enable Software's *Higgins*, and Consumers

Software's *Network Courier*. These LAN gateways reside on a PC and interface the local mail system protocol to SNADS. These LAN gateways then connect to the Central through the above mentioned SNADS gateway.

- DEC, Wang, and Hewlett Packard systems connect to the Central through software that resides in a single node of these vendor's networks.

- *Translation Services*, in the Central, which translate word-processing documents whenever a document is sent between incompatible systems.

- *Printing Services*, in the Central, that may route documents to a printer near the destined user.

6.7   ELECTRONIC DATA INTERCHANGE (EDI)

A series of standards have emerged, both nationally and internationally, which facilitate the computer-to-computer exchange of common business transactions. That exchange is known as *Electronic Data Interchange (EDI)*. These business transactions can be as simple as purchase orders, invoices, and remittance/payment authorizations, or as complex as an advanced shipping notice or request for quote with a CAD binary drawing included.

These documents can be created by computer systems in one enterprise and exchanged, *along with the standards-defined structural syntax information*, with the computer systems of another enterprise. The structural syntax identifies the nature of the document and identifies the format of each data item within the document. The receiving computers will use the structured syntax to interpret and process the document.

The *American National Standards Institute (ANSI)* in 1979 chartered the Accredited Standards Committee (ASC) X.12, to develop uniform standards for Electronic Data Interchange. ANSI X.12, as it is generally called, is the most commonly used EDI standard in North America. ANSI X.12 is based on earlier work by the Transportation Data Coordinating Committee (TDCC). In addition, the Uniform Code Council's (UCC) Uniform Communications Standard (UCS), commonly used in the grocery and wholesale distribution industry, has been moved under the auspices of ANSI.

EDIFACT.   EDI For Administration, Commerce, and Transport (EDIFACT) is a blending of the North American ANSI X.12 standard and the United Nations for Trade Data Interchange. EDIFACT is an international set of recommendations that allows worldwide trading partners to define the format and structure of trading documents. EDIFACT and ANSI are working to make the two standards into one worldwide standard. EDIFACT syntax rules became a full international standard (ISO 9735) in 1988.

Different message types, for different types of transactions, correspond to the business forms customarily used for those transactions. A data segment is composed of a defined sequence of data elements, such as price or date of shipment. The position of an element in the segment determines its function. A comprehensive data element dictionary defines the composition of each such element. Each data segment, such as a purchase order, is encapsulated in a transaction header and trailer. Multiples of such encapsulated segments can, in turn, be enclosed in a functional groupheader and trailer. Finally, there is an interchange control header and trailer around the multiple functional groups. That composite becomes the data for the communications system.

Many companies that use EDI have found that trying to manage the electronic connections and communications to their hundreds and potentially thousands of businesses and trading partners is difficult. This has led many companies, large and small, to use the services of a *Value Added Network (VAN)* that provides EDI Services. Using an EDI Service VAN isolates the user from multiple protocol dependencies, problem determination, and security problems.[12]

All EDI Service VANs provide an electronic "mailbox" as the temporary storage point for EDI transactions as they are moving between enterprises. The EDI user submits messages to the EDI VAN and these messages are distributed by the VAN to the addressees' mailboxes. Recipients can check and retrieve the contents of their mailbox at any time.[13] Most EDI Service VANS also provide interconnection to other VANs, reducing or eliminating the need to connect to multiple VANs to reach all EDI partners.[14]

Translators are available[15] that can translate application data formats into or from national EDI standards such as ANSI X.12, and international EDI standards, such as UN/EDIFACT. They can allow one to enter transactions interactively or to write transactions in a file, and then transfer the data to other systems.

The 1984 and 1988 versions of X.400, being designed for relatively small interpersonal messages between humans, are not yet ideal for EDI. Further work on X.400 support for EDI is underway. The X.435 EDI standard will, among other things, provide true end-to-end receipt notifications between the originator and the final recipient.

6.8 VOICE/DATA COMBINATIONS

Information interchange often benefits from a combination of voice and data. Many voice/data applications make use of the combination of large database transaction processing, voice response units, voice mail, and both voice and data transfer. A typical voice/data complex is illustrated in Figure 6.21. The CBX/PBX is connected, as another "I/O controller," to an application host. Conceptually, the host can be any size, from PS/2s on up. Voice response units provide the programmed segments of voice messages that are assembled and controlled from the host.

---

12. The traffic carried by VANs is increasing, and is already awesome. For example, it is estimated that the worldwide IBM Information Network (IIN) currently transports about one thousand gigabytes of data per month.

13. IIN's *Information Exchange (IE)* is such a mailbox service. IE supports all popular EDI standards and can be accessed using one of the IBM expEDIte software products (expEDIte/CICS, expEDIte MVS, expEDIte 400, expEDIte/36, expEDIte/PC, expEDIte OS/2 or expEDIte AIX), or from a 2780/3780 Remote Job Entry station.

14. For example, IIN's *IBM expEDIte Interconnect* allows IE users to connect to EDI partners on 13 other EDI VANs.

15. EDI translators such as the IBM expEDite DataInterchange Series.

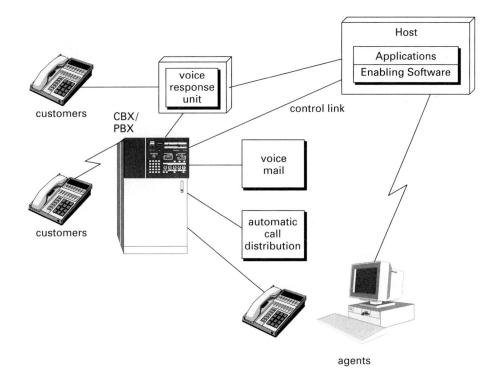

Figure 6.21 Some typical voice/data configurations.

6.8.1 Technology Trends

Computer-to-PBX links are being developed by PBX manufacturers in cooperation with computer vendors. These links enable applications to track PBX events, to instruct the PBX to make calls, transfer calls, and generally integrate the PBX into a voice/data system.

Storage of voice has been made more economical by voice compression techniques. Digital Signal Processors (DSPs) remove speech pauses and repetitive pitch patterns, and encode the result in 15 to 20 percent of the pulse code modulation (PCM) de facto standard of 64 kbps, while still maintaining voice-grade quality. DSP components the size of a PC plug-in board can handle the voice compression of thirty-two conversations, at a cost of under 5 dollars per conversation channel.

At the same time, the cost of hard disk storage continues to plummet, enabling the economical storage of many hours of speech. One 3 1/2-inch disk, for example, holding 320 megabytes of formatted storage, is adequate for about seven hours of compressed voice storage.

New services provided by some carriers include:

- *Dialed Number Identification Service (DNIS)*, which enables users with multiple telephone numbers directed to the same incoming trunks to identify the *called number*
- *Automatic Number Identification (ANI)*, which identifies the billing *number of the calling party*

6.8.2   Voice/Data Applications

The objective of many voice/data applications is, in effect, to provide the interface between many thousands of potential telephone callers and the data-processing complex. Information from the PBX or CBX is forwarded to the CPU, and processed there, resulting in (a) application processing, (b) direction given to the voice response unit, and/or (c) information provided to a human agent.

In some telephone networks, the *caller's identity* can be inferred from the CBX information on the caller. Data about an incoming call, such as the trunk it arrived on, or the dialed extension, or the dialed telephone number (Dialed Number Identification Service, DNIS), is transferred from the CBX to the host. Some carriers also can provide the calling party's telephone number (Automatic Number Identification/Calling Line Identification, ANI/CLID). Information relevant to a particular caller can then be made immediately available.

Voice-answer-back units can be programmed to respond in a manner dependent on the phone number of the caller. Once his identity is known by the computer, each caller can be given a set of subject areas to choose from, which have been tailored to that caller. The Voice Response Unit (VRU) can then respond to a range of queries, made by the customer with touch tone. Predefined decision trees can guide the inquirer to different banks of information and different voice-answer-back segments.[16]

Computer analysis of the identity of the caller and queries can either provide information from the database or direct the query to an appropriate intermediary. If a caller needs to be transferred, information entered at one stage of the call can be passed on to the next agent. Consultation features enable an agent to consult with a specialist or supervisor in a three-way call, as both the agent and the specialist view the customer's information screen at the same time. Calls can be directed to queues of the least busy agents. Call traffic can also be managed according to priority of the caller and the subject involved.

Conceptually, a series of information sources can be connected, and a composite result presented. One can foresee an iterative interaction between persons and the system, without losing track of who the caller is, why he or she called, and the state of the issue.

Call-out procedures, as in telephone marketing, can be similarly made more efficient. The number being called can be used to bring forth relevant information tailored to that destination.

---

16.   As an example, IBM voice response units, at this writing, handle four to thirteen telephone channels, store 3,000 to 16,000 words, on only 80 Megabytes of hard disk, and can be networked for up to 600 lines.

In either case, the computer can provide the record of relevant prior transactions. Since these may be on different subjects, the data can be organized and displayed as time/subject maps.

6.8.3   Telephony Application-Services

All this is facilitated by application-services that are oriented to telephony. The **CallPath Services**[17] [GC31-6824], for example provide four types of service:

- Program-initiated telephone call establishment

- Program-initiated redirection of inbound calls

- Program manipulation of existing telephone calls, such as transferring an existing call to another party

- Program monitoring of the progress of a telephone call via switch messages, such as CALL_CONNECTED, CALL_TRANSFERRED, and DISCONNECTED

The parties involved in such telephone calls may be of four types:

- An extension on a telephone

- A switched data terminal

- A recording device or record-playing device

- A pilot number for an automatic call distribution (ACD) group[18]

6.8.4   Telephony Switch Programming Interface

The **CallPath Services API,** is an interface that shields the application from both the host's communication subsystem and the format and protocols details used by the telephone switch. This API has been designed to give an application program access to telephony functions supported by a variety of telephone switches.

The telephony switch API concept is illustrated in Figure 6.22. The application may invoke a function relating to the switch by *issuing a program-call*[19] *at the CallPath Services API*. The CallPath Services subsystem, residing in the computer, checks the call for errors. If none are found, the information from the program-call is put into the format understood by the selected switch. The CallPath service then returns control to the program, returning information, such as a return code, to the program by means of the appropriate parameters on the program-call.

---

17.   The stated intent of IBM is to make these CallPath services available on S/390s and PS/2s, as well as on the AS/400.

18.   ACD is a service that allows incoming calls directed to the same dialed number, the pilot number, to be routed to one of multiple agents in the ACD group.

19.   A program-call brings a subroutine into effect, by specifying the entry conditions of the subroutine.

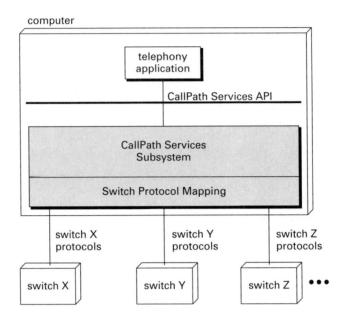

Figure 6.22 Computer-to-telephony-switch communication via the CallPath Services API.

Depending on the function requested by the program, the switch may send one or more messages, such as call progress event messages, to the program in reply. These messages are received asynchronously to the processing of the program-call.

If the application issues a call that requests a function not supported by a particular target switch, a negative response will be returned by either the subsystem or the switch. Also, the application does not need to know about the communication protocols that a given switch supports.[20] The communications transport used to transfer messages between the application-service (e.g., CallPath Services) and the switch can be, in general, any communication facility supported by both the computer and the switch.

The CallPath Services API enables applications to communicate with many different switch types, made by different vendors.[21] The stated IBM strategy is to provide worldwide multiple vendor switch support for both customer premise and central office centrex.

20.   Today, the protocols used for control of telephony switches vary with different manufacturers. Work is underway in standards bodies like the American National Standards Institute (ANSI) and the European Computer Manufacturers' Association (ECMA) towards common, standardized protocols. IBM participates in this work. The CallPath Services API has been designed such that a minimal amount of change will be required to use the standardized protocols when they are completed.

21.   Initially including Northern Telecom, Siemens, Rolm and IBM.

The mapping functions are designed to facilitate the evolution to standards on computer-switch communications that are currently under development.[22]

Call model. A call can be simple, involving only two parties, or it may involve multiple parties in a simultaneous conference call, or it may require sequential handling by multiple parties. To accommodate different situations, each unique party's participation in a given call is given a *connection_id* by CallPath Services, in one of two ways.

1. If a program-call results in one or more new connections, the CallPath subsystem returns the applicable *connection_ids* to the program in the appropriate returned parameters of the program-call. If a calling party is placed in a queue and is sequenced through various devices (such as recorded music, recorded announcements, and messaging devices) a new *connection_id* is generated for each new device.

2. If the program is monitoring call activity, rather than initiating it, the program will be informed of new *connection_ids* as part of the information contained within *switch messages*. An example is where the program is monitoring a party and an incoming call arrives for that party. The CallPath subsystem will generate, and place into the message sent from the switch, two *connection_ids*, one for the called party and one for the calling party.

If a program needs to know whether the `Make_Call` is successfully performed, it must issue a `Monitor_Program_Call`, specifying the resource whose call activity it wishes to monitor. This Monitor call requests that *call-progress-events* (one of the categories of messages that a program can receive) be sent to the program from the switch. A list of such resources may be specified by a *group definition id*.

A summary of the key calls available at this CallPath API is given in this chapter's Technical Reference section.

6.8.5   Voice/Data Illustration

An illustrative voice/data installation [G521-1210] is shown in Figure 6.23. The computerized branch exchange (CBX) there is an all-digital controller[23] that provides switching and interface functions for end-to-end digital communications of voice and data from desktop-to-desktop on a single twisted pair telephone wire. The primary purpose of the CBX usually is to provide voice connectivity for the establishment. However, for a small incremental cost, those without other connectivity can obtain data connectivity through the CBX. Terminals connected to the CBX or to one of the department LANs (token ring or Ethernet) have access to applications on a variety of hosts. For example, the CBX terminals have access to the mainframes (via the cluster controller), the ASCII hosts, the departmental LAN servers (via the Remote NetBIOS Access Facility-RNAF), the regional data network (via the terminal server and routers), and external asynchronous or X.25 networks (via the modem pool or X.25 packet assembler-disassembler-PAD).

---

22. The European Computer Manufacturer's Association (ECMA), Technical Committee 32 reportedly hopes to have an approved ECMA standard for a computer/switch interface by the end of 1991.

23. For example, the ROLM 9751 CBX.

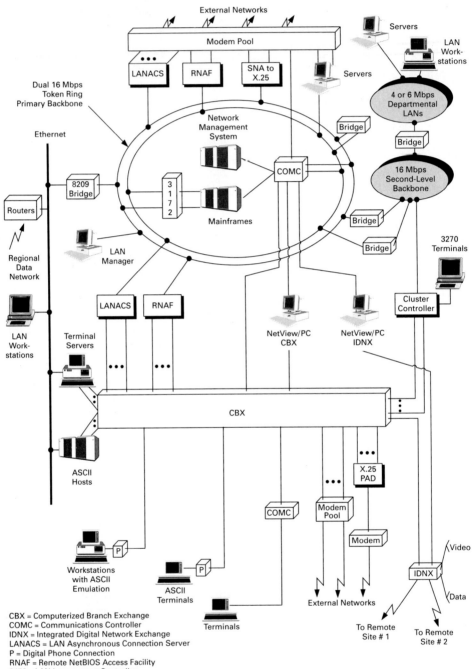

Figure 6.23 Voice/data network [G521-1210].

Conclusion

The field of multimedia information interchange is developing very rapidly, thanks to the combination of broader bandwidth from optical fiber, high-resolution displays, lower-cost storage, and PCs with ever-greater processing capability. Information now includes graphics, image, video, and voice, as well as text, and dramatic tools for their combined use are already appearing in the marketplace.

There is a current need for standard ways to express, combine, transmit, and control these various forms. The ISO *Office Document Architecture (ODA)* for revisable documents, and the IBM *Multiple Object: Document Content Architecture (MO:DCA/P)* for formatted (nonrevisable) documents, enable useful specifications of compound documents involving these diverse forms. Much will be learned in the coming decade to evolve these standards further.

To be revisable, such documents carry indicators of their structure and layout; moreover, each type of information (e.g., text, graphics, and image) uses defined encoding and formats. These compound document architectures are now ready for use. They are complex, however, and application-services must shield the typical user from this complexity by automated interpretation of the user interface.

The CCITT X.400 Message Handling System and the corresponding SNA/Distributed Service (SNADS) are almost identical in concept and structure. Application-layer gateways are therefore feasible, as is integration of the two. Cooperation with the X.500 directory system is a natural follow-on. The technical feasibility of mail system interoperability among SNA, TCP/IP and OSI systems is assured and well demonstrated. Electronic Data Interchange (EDI) services will also be able to build on the message handling systems. Compound documents and electronic messaging combine to broaden the information interchange possibilities.

The linking of the data-processing and voice systems, via the telephone switch programming interface, is a reality and will shortly be standardized. Another dimension for voice/data applications is opened.

Acknowledgments

I am particularly indebted to P. F. Heffner, J. Mosher, D. S. Camm, R. A. Bostick, M. E. Ferree, J. K. Crutcher, and Chip Lawson for valuable input or reviews of this chapter.

TECHNICAL REFERENCE

CallPath Services Program-Calls

The CallPath Services program-calls are designed to be made from higher-level languages, including C, COBOL, FORTRAN, REXX (the SAA procedures languages), CSP (the SAA application generator), and RPG. The call format varies slightly with each language, but is close to the form:

```
CALL <name of call> (parm0, parm1, ...parmN)
```

There are thirty-seven CallPath calls defined. To illustrate, some of the key calls are:

- `Add_Party`—add a new party to an existing telephone call

- `Alternate_Call`—alternate between two existing calls, an active and a held call
- `Conference_Call`—retrieve a held call and join with parties in a second active call
- `Hold_Call`—place an existing call on hold
- `Invoke_Feature`—invoke a feature for the phone associated with a specified party
- `Make_Call`—establish a telephone call
- `Monitor`—register interest in receiving specified events for specified resources
- `Redirect_Call`—change the destination of an incoming call from one party to another
- `Register_Ownership`—establish ownership of a specified resource
- `Transfer_Call`—transfer an existing call from a party that is currently taking part in the call to a new party
- `Trigger`—trigger an action in the target switch when the switch encounters a specified event

EXERCISES

6.1   Identify the IBM and ISO architectures to: create, edit, format, revise, and present a document.

6.2   What are the OSI and SNA facilities that provide for document or message delivery?

6.3   What is meant by a processable or revisable document?

6.4   What are the two basic components of the OSI X.400 message handling system?

6.5   Where are the three X.400 protocols, P1, P2, and P3 used?

6.6   What is Electronic Data Interchange (EDI)?

6.7   What is the purpose of the CallPath Services API?

Part 3
End-to-End Data-Exchange Facilities

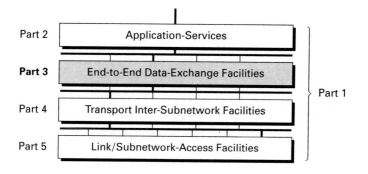

Part 2	Application-Services
Part 3	End-to-End Data-Exchange Facilities
Part 4	Transport Inter-Subnetwork Facilities
Part 5	Link/Subnetwork-Access Facilities

Part 1

Part 3 addresses the second macro-layer dealing with end-to-end data-exchange facilities. It first describes the concept of the Common Programming Interface, and end-to-end facilities that ease the work of the application programmer in conducting a dialog. Locating the named destination, using X.500, and then making the end-to-end logical connection are explained. Also described are the services, in layers 5 and 6, at the two ends of a communication which directly support application-processes and help to maintain orderly operations of a particular communication. Specific implementations, namely LU 6.2 and OSI/Communications Subsystem are examined. The emphasis in these chapters is on the functions provided and the key interfaces involved.

   Chapter 7, Communication APIs, discusses the SAA Common Programming Interface for communications (a set of APIs common across all SAA platforms), and the important concept of network independence at that level. The three major communications models, conversation, remote procedure call, and transaction messaging, are described.

   Chapter 8, Directories and Logical Connections, summarizes the use of X.500 for common directory services. The potential integration of OSI and SNA directories is examined. The evolution of control points is reviewed. The facilities for end-to-end logical-connections using OSI and SNA are described.

   Chapter 9, Presentation and Session Services, then describes the layer-6 (presentation) and the layer-5 (OSI session and SNA data-flow control) services. Synchronization, chains, and brackets in SNA, and tokens and activities in OSI are reviewed. Approximate correlations of OSI and SNA terms and functions in layers 5 through 7 are discussed.

Chapter 10, SNA Logical Units, presents an overview of the SNA LU 6.2 implementation of end-to-end functions. The SNA session and conversation are further explained. The example of the APPC/MVS implementation is outlined.

Chapter 11, OSI/Communications Subsystem, then briefly describes the function and structure of the IBM OSI/Communications Subsystem. This is an implementation of OSI layers 4 through 6 plus the ACSE of layer 7. Its design facilitates incorporation in systems with different architectures.

Both LU 6.2 and OSI/Communications Subsystems contain a layer-4 component, the discussion of which is deferred till Part 4.

7
Communication APIs

7.1 INTRODUCTION

A high percentage of the customer's investment goes into the applications that use the distributed network. Hence, the ease of programming, and the stability and portability of applications is of great economic importance. The industry accordingly seeks a consolidation of the Application Programming Interfaces (APIs) used for communications and cooperative processing. At the same time, it is necessary that the APIs that are used will facilitate the distribution of function.

This chapter first focuses on the concept of a Common Programming Interface (CPI), as a set of common APIs developed in SAA. The prospects for *network independence* at the SAA CPI for Communications (CPI-C), with a common API for both SNA and OSI communication protocols, are further explored.

The requirements for and nature of multiple communications APIs, including conversational, remote procedure calls, and messaging are discussed. The specific operation of the CPI for communications in the conversational mode are described. Discussions of lower-level APIs, such as those of NetBIOS and the X-Open Transport Interface (XTI), are discussed in Chapter 13.

7.2 SAA COMMON PROGRAMMING INTERFACE

Primary purposes of the *Common Programming Interface (CPI)* are to simplify the programming effort and to *increase the portability of both programs and trained programmers from system to system*. By offering a CPI-C across different protocol stacks that provide the same communication semantics, applications can be written without concern for syntactic differences of the underlying communication protocols. Identical APIs, matching each of the languages made a part of SAA, and usable in all SAA, AIX/OSF, *and other operating environments*, are major steps in this direction.

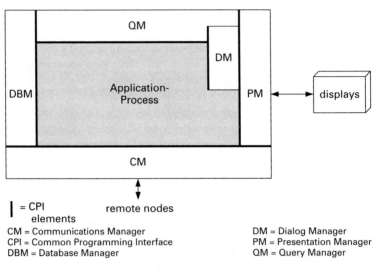

Figure 7.1 CPI element relationships.

7.2.1 Application-Services and the CPI

There are distinct *elements* in the CPI, including the elements for transaction communications, file transfer, distributed database, resource-recovery, and information presentation. Any application-service conceivably can provide a component of the CPI. Moreover, some application-services can both provide a component of the CPI and in turn use the CPI offered by some other application-service. Some of the possible relationships are illustrated in Figure 7.1. Application-services may use the communications portion of the CPI, for inter-node communications; or, they may use some other portion of the CPI, to access another application-service, which may then use the communication portion of the CPI.[1]

7.2.2 Gradual CPI Expansion

The CPI cannot be static. The C language, for example, was not widely used (outside of the UNIX community) until recently. Knowledge-based languages are evolving and growing in importance. Higher-level, easier-to-use extensions to an API are always expected. The important thing is that for a given language, there is one programming interface for the range of systems found in the enterprise.

Other elements in the CPI will be needed, as new application-services arrive. The CPI allows the development of distributed resource managers (clients and servers) that will

---

1. Note, therefore, that Figure 7.2 shows a simplification of the Common Programming Interface. In reality, some of the CPI elements appear at application-services and some appear at the end-to-end communication facilities.

take advantage of the consistency offered by SAA. The CPI should evolve to also treat newer common functions in the OSI and SNA environments in a transparent manner. The CPI thus can provide a high degree of stability to the programming community by its common use even in growing languages and systems.

7.2.3   Network Independence via the CPI

The general objective is to provide an API whose elements are insulated from the protocols and semantics of the underlying communication services being utilized, and to enable the *transparent* support of *multiple transport networks* under that interface.[2] Within that broad scope, a primary SAA objective is to allow transaction-processing (TP) applications to communicate with either a remote OSI or SNA partner, without requiring a knowledge of the underlying protocols used. Such **network independence** can be provided via the CPI and its associated mappings.

This evolution to common functions [Ahuja88], however, cannot occur overnight. Moreover, requirements and technology are varied and constantly changing, so that uncommon facilities will always be with us. An idealized picture of the objective, therefore, is that shown in Figure 7.2.

1. A *Common Programming Interface* that is independent of the underlying OSI or SNA facilities.

2. A selection of optional *application-services*, such as distributed file services and distributed database services, a growing number of which are *commonly used with both OSI and SNA* communications.

3. End-to-end *data-exchange facilities*, where selections could be made from either OSI sets or SNA sets of options.

4. *Common transport facilities*, which can service either the OSI or SNA end-to-end data-exchange facilities. All of the OSI link/subnetwork facilities will be common. Subnetworks, like X.21 circuit switched networks, X.25 PSDNs, SDLC/HDLC wide area networks, multiple LANs, and ISDN would be available to all applications, whether they used OSI or SNA option sets in the upper layers.

The movement to Open Systems Network Architecture (OSNA) thus includes movement toward increasing breadth of the CPI, common application-services, and common subnetworks for data transport. In time, this commonality will predominate. However, there also are shown the uncommon OSI, SNA, and non-SAA components, some of which may be transitional, and others of which may satisfy newer needs.

Multivendor use of CPI-C.   The communications element of the CPI-C, incorporated into higher-level languages is available to all. The implementation of the CPI in non-IBM systems is encouraged through licensing agreements on the interface copyright. X/Open Company

---

2.   A sometimes overlooked requirement of transparency is that the communications services must operate at the same priority as the user-task being served.

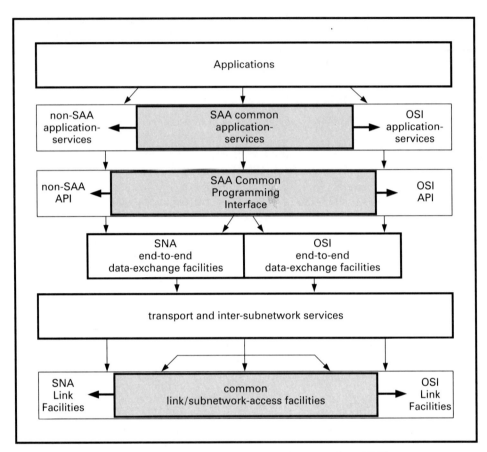

Figure 7.2 Evolution of the Common Programming Interface (CPI), common application-services, and common link/subnetwork-access facilities.

Ltd.,[3] an independent, nonprofit consortium of international computer system vendors, who are developing the *vendor-independent Common Application Environment (CAE)*, has licensed IBM's CPI-C for incorporation in the CAE. This is intended to make CPI-C available for TCP/IP-based systems.[4] Since more than one hundred software companies intend to adhere to the X/Open specification for UNIX-based Common Application Environment, which includes the IBM CPI-C, one can expect its wide use. As a participant in X/Open,

---

3. X/Open is an independent, nonprofit consortium of international computer systems vendors, including AT&T, Bull, DEC, Fujitsu, Hewlett Packard, Hitachi Ltd., IBM, ICL, NCR Corp., Nixdorf, Nokia Data, Olivetti, Open Software Foundation, Philips, Prime Computer, Siemens, Sun Microsystems, Unisys, and Unix International Inc.

4. E. Robert Roth, of IBM, stated in a presentation to SAA World, April 11, 1990, that it is not unreasonable to expect to have communications initiated through CPI-C, flow across SNA, OSI, or even TCP/IP or local protocols like NetBIOS.

IBM's AIX/OSF systems (as well as its SAA systems) will likewise use CPI-C. Finally, it is hoped by many that the CPI-C, or a very close relative, will become an international standard.

The CPI-C can, therefore:

- Be consistent across all SAA and AIX/OSF computing environments and others that will implement the CPI

- Be accessed at least via all SAA high-level languages

- Offer network independence, as seen by the applications, for both OSI and SNA communications subsystems (and any other protocols that might similarly be supported under the CPI with appropriate mappings)

- Enhance the portability of applications across all SAA and AIX/OSF operating environments, and others that support the CPI

7.3 CONVERSATION, MESSAGE, OR REMOTE PROCEDURE CALL (RPC)

A number of different API models, with corresponding API services, have been used successfully for interaction between applications (and between application-services). Prominent among these are three types of APIs: **conversation**, **remote procedure call (RPC)**, and **message queues**. All three methods can effectively hide the details of the communications process. All three methods can also hide the heterogeneity of the operating systems and the data formats used. Each of the three APIs can also be employed in client–server communications.

The state of development of these models varies greatly. The *SNA conversational model* (Advanced Program-to-Program Communication, APPC) is a very widely used de facto standard, adopted by many vendors. The corresponding *OSI conversational model* has only recently been defined as a standard, and awaits wide testing and evaluation. *RPC models* have also been widely used, particularly including the NCS model from Apollo, and the Sun RPC from Sun Microsystems. However, the industry standard proposed by OSF, built upon the NCS, was only recently implemented. As of this writing, there is not yet an industry standard for the *messaging model*. Nevertheless, all three models are promising, and so some of their features are described in the following.

In all three methods, the parameters carried or other procedures must be sufficient to activate the remote process, carry on the interaction, and terminate it. The conversation model provides a tight control for relatively detailed interactions. Both the remote procedure call and the message queue technique provide a simpler interface to the application program. However, the controls built into the conversational facilities are valuable for a wide range of applications.

Each of these APIs requires a set of presentation services and interaction controls in layers 5 through 7 of the architecture. Their position in the node structure is within the end-to-end data-exchange facilities shown in Figure 7.2. The CPI-C (for conversational communications) is shown there with both an SNA APPC stack and an OSI Transaction Processing (TP) stack. As explained below, the transparent mapping from a common API to either the OSI or the SNA stack can be achieved.

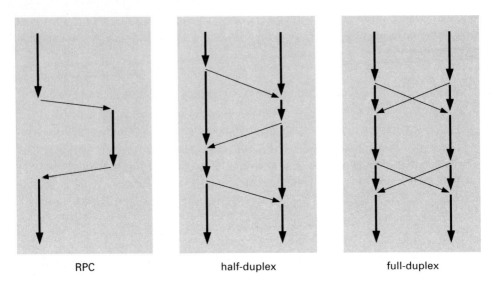

RPC   half-duplex   full-duplex

Figure 7.3 Three common data-exchange modes.

If the principles of a layered architecture are adhered to, any of these three APIs, with their associated dialog controls, should be independent of the underlying transport-service-providers shown in Figure 2.2, and so should be able to utilize any of them. So long as the two communicating ends have the *same API model*, many combinations of upper-level data-exchange facility and lower-level transport-service-provider are possible. In practice, however, each combination costs something, and so the degree of mix and match becomes an economic issue.

7.4 CONVERSATIONS

7.4.1 Introduction

The *conversational model is basically Send/Receive*, but a wide range of supplementary facilities are available. A logical connection (called a conversation or dialog) is established between the two partners, and multiple conversations between partners are possible. The conversation method is especially suitable when there are many interactions per transaction between paired end points. The conversational model implements coroutines that enable overlapped execution in the distributed transaction (unlike RPC, which usually is fully synchronous). This comparison is illustrated in Figure 7.3, which shows concurrent operations at the two communicating partners in both half-duplex and full-duplex modes.[5] The conversational model is designed for both short- and long-running message exchanges (unlike message queueing, which usually does not correlate messages). It is, accordingly,

5.   Full-duplex mode is not currently supported in SNA's LU 6.2, but full duplex is specified for OSI transaction processing and is a known requirement for LU 6.2.

meant to be the natural "interactive" model. The following addresses the conversational elements of the CPI. The underlying LU 6.2 functions in support of conversations is given in Chapter 10.

7.4.2   CPI-C for OSI and SNA Conversational Applications

Conversational communication uses the communications element of the CPI known as *CPI-C*. It is suited to all SAA languages (and usable by non-SAA languages as well), and it isolates its applications from the protocols used to implement the data-exchange facilities.

Though the formats and protocols for the end-to-end data-exchange facilities in SNA and OSI[6] are significantly different, the semantics of the service requests for the two communications architectures are so close, that the mapping of the CPI-C to both is a feasible task. Hence, it is possible to have a very high degree of transparency at the CPI for conversations using either OSI TP service or SNA APPC service. To the extent that CPI-C will be provided on other vendors' processors supporting OSI, CPI-C also provides an excellent platform for OSI program interoperability.

Research has shown that the symbolic_destination_names (sym_des_name) can be mapped, using side information, to OSI or SNA names [Janson91]. In the case of SNA, the sym_dest_name can be mapped to a Transaction-Program name and an LU_name (TP_name.LU_name). In the case of OSI, the sym_dest_name is mapped to a Transaction-Processing Service-User name and the title of an application-entity (TPSU_name.AE_title).

One would not expect a perfect match between the current SAA Common Programming Interface and the more recently defined OSI TP Services. However, the match is very good, because work was done in the standards organizations to make it so. A few less important capabilities in the CPI (like log-data under `Deallocate`) may not get a mapping. Other minor inconsistencies may later be eliminated by enhancements to either the CPI or OSI TP services. Otherwise, a fairly complete mapping is possible now, and one is given in this chapter's Technical Reference section. Because the standards work on OSI/ TP is, as yet, much less complete than the SNA work, in the following we will compare the two and then go into more detail on the existing CPI-C.

7.4.3   Conversations and Dialogs

A distributed application consists of the sum of all of its distributed application-processes, and the interactions among them. In SNA, a **conversation** is the communication that exists between peer application-processes. *The roughly comparable OSI function is called the* **dialog**. Conversations (dialogs) are never shared by more than two application-processes. However, application-processes may have multiple conversations (dialogs) with many other application-processes. A distributed transaction having multiple conversations is illustrated in Figure 7.4. These relationships among application-processes may be serial or

---

6.   APPC, using LU 6.2, and the OSI Application-Service–Element.

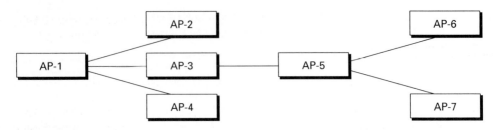

Figure 7.4 Six conversations linking application-processes in a distributed transaction.

simultaneous. They may be hierarchical or networked. Multiple parties may interact either synchronously or asynchronously.

The starting call[7] to the CPI is usually to establish a conversation with another application-process. The statements of the CPI are interpreted by service elements of the communications subsystem. Each conversation uses a set of such service elements. In SNA, the aggregate of these service elements at each end of the logical connection is called a **Logical Unit (LU)**, whose position is illustrated in Figure 7.5. Each LU communicates with its partner at the other end of the connection, in support of the application (the LU is analyzed further in Chapter 10).

---

7.   The calls associated with the CPI are local calls, not to be confused with the remote call of the remote procedure call (RPC) facility.

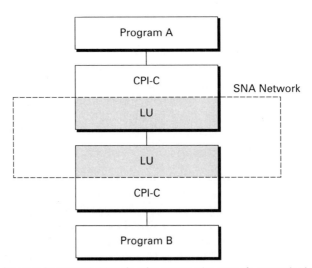

CPI-C = Common Programming Interface for conversation-type of communications
LU = Logical Unit

Figure 7.5 Programs communicating via SNA network using the services of CPI-C and LUs.

For each conversation, in SNA, the LUs at each end establish a set of end-to-end resources, in layers 4 through 7, to support that conversation. In SNA, each such resource set, including both ends, comprises a **session**. In OSI, an **association** is analogous to (but not in all respects identical to) a session. An association is defined as a relationship between entities at the application layer. However, *the association also triggers a set of relationships, and the setting up of resources, in layers 4 through 7. In this sense, the association is similar to the session.* At any given time, SNA conversations are assigned to sessions, and OSI dialogs are assigned to associations. SNA also uses the term **half-session**, meaning the resources needed at one end to maintain the session; a half-session exists at each partner (the SNA session is explained further in Section 9.3).

Though these session (and association) resources are put in place for it, the conversation (or dialog) never needs to refer to a session (or association) in particular. SNA Transaction Programs see only the conversation; OSI Transaction Processing Service Units (TPSUs) see only the dialog. Once a conversation or dialog is set up, all subsequent verbs referring to it can use a conversation (or dialog) identifier, which is by then tied to either an LU 6.2 stack or the corresponding OSI upper-layer stack. Then, during the data-transfer phase, the protocols of the underlying communication subsystems are not visible to the applications.

7.4.4   Initiating a Conversation

Program-to-program communication is initiated through the use of high-level language statements that are defined as part of the CPI-C.

At program execution time, when an SNA protocol stack is used, these CPI statements result in the utilization of SNA formats and protocols defined in LU 6.2 for communication with other applications. For example, statements in the communications portion of the CPI might be used to establish a conversation between two programs, synchronize the processing between programs, send and receive data between these two programs, determine transmission status, notify a partner of errors in the communication, and then terminate the conversation.

In SNA, the CPI-C supports two types of conversations:

- **Mapped** conversations use **data records** having formats that are agreed to by the application programmers.
- **Basic** conversations exchange **logical records** whose formats have been standardized. Each logical record consists of a 2-byte length field and a data field.

Mapped conversations are the easiest way of communicating because the data record is extracted from the data stream and given to the application. The programmers do not need to be concerned with the record size actually transmitted, or the format of the data stream. Mapped conversations are recommended for application programs. Basic conversations are more for service programs, because they make it possible to access the SNA General Data Stream (GDS); this can be useful for systems and management programs.

To identify the remote partner, the originating program submits a *symbolic_destination_name* to CPI-C. The latter, in turn, obtains further *side information* about the destination and the desired conversation. This information is obtained from either an application-level directory or local storage. The data had to be supplied earlier by a systems administrator. Side information for this conversation would include the name of the partner program *(TP_name)*, the name of the LU to be used by the partner *(partner LU_name)*, and some properties of the session that will be allocated for this conversation *(mode_name)*. The LU_name may have to be a fully qualified LU_name,—i.e., prefixed by the Net_id. These properties can determine the characteristics of the session, including the security of the session (e.g., by using encryption or not).

7.4.5 CPI-C Program Calls

Programs using CPI Communications converse with each other using program **calls**. These calls are used to establish the full characteristics of the conversation, to exchange data, and to control the information flow between the two programs.

Program calls are a preferred mechanism because they are well known and well understood. It is felt that they can perform well across a network, as well as within a single system. When a remote procedure is invoked, the calling procedure is usually suspended[8] only until the local operation is complete. A given transaction can continue to execute other procedures while the call procedure awaits a response. The two transaction programs run as coroutines with as much overlapped execution as they desire. For example, a program could issue a `Prepare_To_Receive` and continue doing a lot of processing before issuing a `Receive` verb.

Many conversations will use only the simple *starter set calls*. More specialized processing can be done using the *advanced function calls*. The advanced function calls are in three sets: for improved performance and notify of error, to set parameters, and to extract information. Both sets are briefly described below [SC26-4399].

Starter set calls.   Many applications can be written with only these few calls:

- `Initialize_Conversation`—initialize the conversation characteristics
- `Accept_Conversation`—accept an incoming conversation
- `Allocate`—establish a conversation
- `Send_Data`—send data
- `Receive`—receive data
- `Deallocate`—end a conversation

Advanced function, performance-oriented calls.

- `Confirm`—send a confirmation request to the partner program
- `Confirmed`—send a confirmation reply to the partner program
- `Flush`—send all items in the buffer immediately
- `Prepare_To_Receive`—change a conversation from the send to the receive state, in preparation to receive data

---

8.   Several products (including VTAM) have nonblocking interfaces that return to the application even before the local operation is complete.

- `Request_To_Send`—notify its partner that it would like to send data
- `Send_Error`—inform the remote program that the local program detected an error
- `Test_Request_To_Send_Received`—determine whether the remote program is requesting to send data (like a poll)

Advanced function, set-operations.   Set-operations enable the programmer to set parameters dealing with a conversation or a type of conversation that will be repeated often. They include:

- `Set_Conversation_Type`
- `Set_Deallocate_Type`
- `Set_Error_Direction`
- `Set_Fill`
- `Set_Log_Data`
- `Set_Mode_Name`
- `Set_Prepare_To_Receive_Type`

- `Set_Receive_Type`
- `Set_Return_Control`
- `Set_Send_Type`
- `Set_Sync_Level`
- `Set_TP_Name`
- `Set_Partner_LU_Name`

Advanced function, extract operations.   These calls enable a programmer to retrieve the values of parameters that the programmer may want to examine and possibly change. They include:

- `Extract_Partner_LU_Name`
- `Extract_Conversation_Type`

- `Extract_Mode_Name`
- `Extract_Sync_Level`

7.4.6   States and Transitions

To keep the two partners to a conversation in synchronism with each other, CPI Communications uses the concept of a **conversation state**. The state of each partner must have a known relation to the state of the other partner, although the two states need not always be the same. The state of each partner determines what the next sequence of actions may be. The defined states are:

- **Initialize**—the call `Initialize_Conversation` has been completed, and a *conversation_id* has been assigned
- **Send**—able to send data
- **Receive**—able to receive data
- **Send-Pending**—both data (to be processed) and send capability have been received
- **Confirm**—a confirm request has been received
- **Confirm-Send**—both a confirm request and permission-to-send have been received
- **Confirm-Deallocate**—both a deallocate call and a confirm request have been received
- **Reset**—no conversation

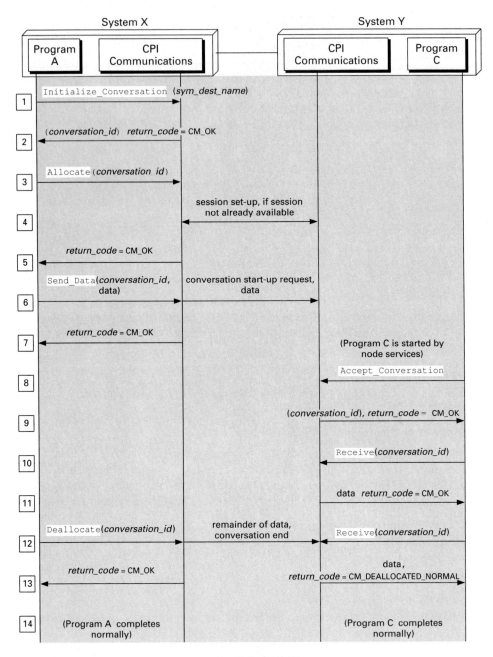

Figure 7.6 Data flow in one direction [SC26-4399].

7.4.7   CPI-C Data Flow Illustrations

Example 1: establish conversation

The sequence of steps in the data flow is shown in Figure 7.6, and described below.

1. The `Initialize_Conversation` call identifies the conversation partner (in *sym_dest_name*).

2. CPI Communications returns a *conversation_id*, and a return code indicating that no errors were found. Program A must store the *conversation_id* and use it on all subsequent calls intended for that conversation. At this point, two tasks have been accomplished:

- CPI-C has established a set of conversation characteristics for the conversation, based on the *sym_dest_name*, and uniquely associated them with the *conversation_id*.
- The default values for the remaining conversation characteristics have been assigned.

3. Allocate call asks that conversation be started, using the *conversation_id* previously assigned.

4. LU-LU session is established, if not already existing.

5. A *return_code* of CM-OK indicated that the `Allocate` call was completed and an LU-LU session is activated. Program A's end of the conversation is now in **Send** state, and Program A can begin to send data.

6., 7. The `Send_Data` call hands the data to CPI Communications, which returns a *return_code* of CM-OK. Any number of `Send_Data` calls can be issued before the buffer actually is full. When the local LU's send buffer reaches a preset level, the conversation startup request and data are sent to the remote node.[9]

8., 9. Once the conversation is established, the system services in the remote node will start Program C. Initially, Program C's end of the conversation is in the **Reset** state. Program C then delivers an `Accept_Conversation` call, and so gets its own unique *conversation_id*, with a set of conversation characteristics (some of Program C's defaults are based on information contained in the conversation startup request). Program C's end of the conversation is then in the **Receive** state.

10., 11. Once its end of the conversation is in **Receive** state, Program C begins whatever processing role it and Program A have agreed upon. In this case, Program C accepts data with a `Receive` call. Program A could continue to make `Send_Data` calls, and Program C could continue to make `Receive` calls. However, for the purpose of this example, assume that is all Program C wants to do.

12. Program A issues a `Deallocate` call, which sends any data buffered in the local LU and ends the conversation. Program C issues a final `Receive` call to insure that it has collected all the data.

---

9.   Some products may choose to transmit the conversation startup request as part of the `Allocate` processing.

13., 14. The *return_code* for the final `Receive` call is CM-DEALLOCATED_NORMAL, which simply tells Program C that the conversation is deallocated.

Example 2: data flow in both directions

Figure 7.7 illustrates the flow of data in both directions, with a transfer of control over who is allowed to send data. The conversation in this example is already established. Program A's end of the conversation is in **Send** state, and Program C's is in **Receive** state.

1.–4. Program A is sending data, and Program C is receiving data.

5. When Program A finally wishes to receive data, it issues a `Receive` call. This causes

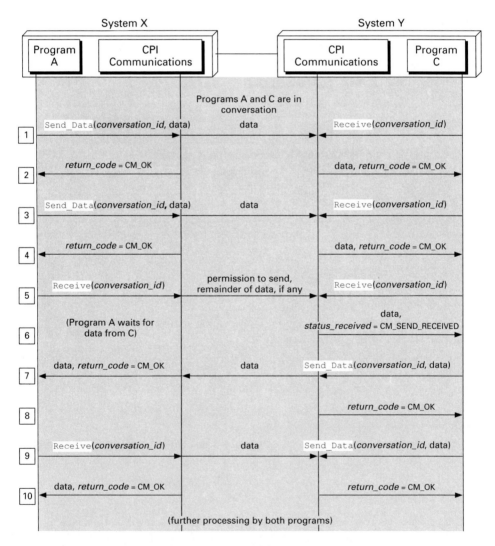

Figure 7.7 Data flow in both directions [SC26-4399].

the remaining buffered data at System X to be sent. Also, a permission to send is sent to Program C. Program A's end of the conversation is then placed in the **Receive** state, and Program A waits for a response from Program C.

6.   Program C issues `Receive` calls. Finally, a *status_received* parameter arrives set to CM-SEND_RECEIVED. This indicated that Program C's end of the conversation is now in the **Send** state.

7.   Program C therefore is free to issue a `Send_Data` call. The data from this call, on arrival at System X, is returned to Program A as a response to the `Receive` it issued in step 5.

At this point, the flow of data has been completely reversed, and the two programs can continue whatever processing their logic dictates. Program C can send data and Program A can issue its `Receive` calls.

To give control of the conversation back to Program A, Program C would simply follow the same procedure that Program A executed in step 5.

8.–10. Program A and Program C continue processing. Program C sends data and Program A receives the data.

These two examples use only the starter set of available calls. For illustrations of more advanced facilities, see the SAA CPI Communications Reference [SC26-4399].

7.5   REMOTE PROCEDURE CALL

7.5.1   Introduction

The remote procedure call (RPC), used for process-to-process communication, has been popular in the industry and a number of new designs have been proposed [Yemini89]. The RPC hides low-level details of each system's run-time environment and communications support, making it possible to use RPC over multiple transport-service-providers. It also hides the differences in the two systems data formats, hardware architecture, and operating systems.

RPC is essentially one request, followed by one response. It usually is synchronous, in that the client waits for the response, rather than going on with other work. It is a natural complement to the use of other calls in programming with higher-level languages.

The *RPC model is basically call/return,* like a familiar subroutine call. *The requester issues a call as if it were local.* The client part has a call resolution process that determines if the call is for a local or remote instance of the resource manager. The RPC facility locates the target system and communicates with the RPC counterpart in the target system. The latter passes the call to the resource-manager server-part. The RPC does all the distribution work, and the target resource manager ordinarily has no awareness of distribution (except for things like recovery and security).

7.5.2   Interface Definition Language

With RPC, it is necessary to have a compile-time definition of the interface used in particular systems. Corresponding **stubs** at both ends then bind the application-process to a run-time service.

The application programmer first uses an **Interface Definition Language (IDL)** to define the operations that a server exports to clients. An IDL is a language that describes remote interfaces that are callable by clients and provided by servers. An interface definition written in an IDL contains information about operations that can be called remotely, including the arguments that can be used. It is thus used by programmers to define the scope of the call and the syntax of parameters. The programmer then compiles this definition to produce code (stubs) for use by both the client and server of the RPC. During data transfer, the client program calls the stub, which packages the arguments of the call, and transmits the data to the server. Stubs also handle data representation issues, calling a data conversion engine if the selected transfer syntax specifies the caller stub to do conversions. The server stub unpacks the arguments, calls the application subroutine that actually does the work, packages the results of that work, and sends the reply to the client stub. The results are returned to the calling program in the same way as local results are.

7.5.3 OSF Remote Procedure Call

A good illustration of an RPC is the one selected by the Open Software Foundation. Based on the Hewlett-Packard RPC, the main components of this RPC are as follows [OSF89]:

1. The *run-time library* (sometimes simply called the *run-time*) implements the RPC protocol. These functions largely correspond to those in the end-to-end data-exchange facility in the prior structures. The RPC run-time has a set of interfaces (the run-time API) for use by stub code. It provides for looking up a callee in side information or a system directory, establishing a connection to the callee, sending call requests and responses, etc. A key responsibility of the run-time is to maintain control of state-conditions on behalf of callers and callees during an association, which is the time when a caller process is bound to a callee. Finally, run-time builds the appropriate headers for the RPC packets, as required by the transport-service-provider, and invokes the transport-service-provider on behalf of the caller or callee.

2. The *Network Interface Definition Language (NIDL)* [Dineen88], for defining the RPC interfaces and producing stubs, is strictly a declarative language. It contains only constructs for defining the constants, types, and operations of an interface; it has no executable constructs. (NIDL is considered to be an OSI layer-7 function.)

The NIDL source is composed of declarations from a higher-level language, augmented with interface definitions, and indications for the use of each parameter. There can be a NIDL for each higher-level language for which RPC support is desired. Other information in the NIDL specify where data conversion is to be done, types of parameter marshalling (i.e., copying the input arguments into a buffer) to be used, server authentication support, and if the run-time will support two-phase recovery protocols.

3. The *NIDL compiler* (sometimes known as the NIDL processor, or stub generator), checks syntax, translates NIDL definitions into declarations in languages such as C, and generates **stub code** for use in the client and the server. The compiler produces the "stubs," which are language modules.

4. The *stubs*, in concert with the RPC run-time library, connect program calls to the run-time environment (see Figure 7.8). The "caller stub" will first issue an `RpcBindToInterface` command, including a proposed transfer syntax and transport scheme, to attempt the binding. The information returned may indicate a choice of transfer syntaxes and/or transport addresses to be used. The caller stub would select one of each, and then go ahead with the actual call processing.

An `RpcSend` (by the caller stub) commands the transmission of a requester's call to the callee node. An `RpcReceive` command will obtain the results from the callee. An `RpcUnbind` command terminates the bind.

5. The *Network Data Representation (NDR)* [Dineed88] protocol defines how the structured values that are supplied in a remote procedure call are encoded for network transmission. The purpose of NDR is to enable machines with different local data representations to communicate typed values to one another. The NDR protocol specifies a set of data types that can be used to specify sets of typed values. It also defines a way to represent scalar formats. NDR represents a sequence of values as a format label plus a byte stream.

OSF specifications require that the RPC run-time libraries be supported using XTI (X/Open Transport Interface) or socket interfaces over TCP and UDP (the connection-oriented and connectionless interfaces of TCP/IP, respectively). Other standard or proprietary transport-service-providers may, of course, be added by individual vendors. The NCS/RPC connectionless protocol assumes the existence of an underlying datagram transport, such as UDP/IP. The connection-based RPC package assumes the existence of a connection-based protocol, such as TCP/IP. The connection-oriented version can take advantage of the connection-oriented natures of X.25, NetBIOS and SNA.

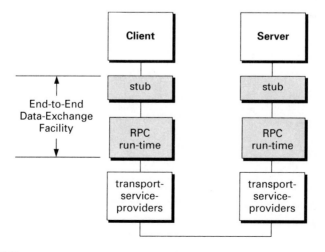

Figure 7.8 RPC structure.

7.6 TRANSACTION MESSAGE QUEUEING

The management of message queues between processes has often been used as the data-exchange facility. For example, the TeleCommunications Access Method, TCAM, (a predecessor of VTAM) is basically message-queue-oriented. The UNIX inter-process-communication is message-queue-based. Also, the current SAA Presentation Manager, uses message queues between the display user interface and the multiple window processors.

The *message model is basically enqueue/dequeue*. If the data-exchange facility is by messaging, queue managers are needed at both the client and the server ends. The requester formulates a request in the form of a message.

The message-queues concept is simple, as shown in Figure 7.9. `Getmsg` and `Putmsg` are the primary commands, issued by an application-process to a message-delivery-system. The queue managers deliver the message to the proper queue associated with the destination resource manager.

The online transaction-processing world has developed this approach fully, for high-performance applications that transmit mostly small objects. It has been found useful to

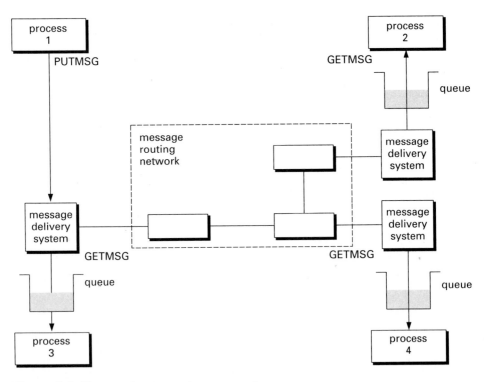

Figure 7.9 Message/queue system-concept.

regard each request as an isolated packet; to judge which packet should be worked on next, using queues to arrange the work order; to distribute packets among processors, depending on both the packet priority and the processor workload; or to split packets into multiple workscopes, so as to process them differently or simply in parallel. Such message services were built into subsystems like IMS and CICS.

Different queue management approaches have been used in clients and servers, too.

- The client process may be event-driven, as in the window-facility of presentation management. There keyboard and/or pointer events, perhaps involving icons and a mouse, are the events that are coded and placed in the input queue.

- The content of a message received by a client or server may initiate a process leading to another message being queued for transmission. Hence some form of inter-message-queue communication is fundamental to message driven processing.

In OS/2 [Duncan89], for example, queues are named-global-objects. Any process that knows a queue's name can write into it. However, only the process that created the queue can read from it or destroy it. The entries in a queue can be ordered in three ways: FIFO (first in, first out); LIFO (last in, first out); or according to the priority of the entry.

The information unit is usually made up of a header and data. Message queue approaches are usually asynchronous. They therefore can use connectionless or connection-oriented message-routing networks. However, sequential delivery is often important, and should be assured. Message-routing facilities can be built atop any network protocol.

Conclusion

The concept of the Common Programming Interface (CPI), suitable for most if not all of the major higher-level languages, promises major advantages. Different elements of this interface meet the needs of different application-services. The network *independence*, at this level, from the particulars of SNA conversational or OSI transaction-processing protocols seems assured. The licensing of this same communications element, CPI-C by X/Open raises the hope that the CPI-C will similarly become available for TCP/IP protocols.

The improvements underway in remote procedure call protocols promise that RPC will be a preferred protocol in many client–server applications, where tight or extended interaction is less important. More specialized transaction-oriented applications will find a message queue the most efficient.

In each case, the application programming interfaces are evolving to further distributed processing, with transparency to location of resources at the API. The maturing of cooperating systems depends heavily on this continuing progress.

Acknowledgments

I am indebted particularly to the following for their input and reviews of this chapter: L. M. Rafalow, M. R. Jones, Jr., O. K. Baek, Philippe Janson, and E. C. Broockman.

TECHNICAL REFERENCE

Mapping of SAA CPI to OSI TP Primitives

Without going into further details on each command, the following mapping is shown to illustrate the correspondence between calls at the CPI-C interface and verbs used within OSI.

CPI-C	OSI TP
Accept_Conversation	Mapped from TP-Begin_Dialog indication
Allocate	Maps to TP-Begin_Dialog request
Confirm	Maps to TP-Handshake request

Confirmed	Maps to one of the following:
	    to TP-Handshake response, or
	    to TP-Handshake_And_End response, or
	    to TP-Handshake_And_Grant_Control response

Deallocate	Mapping depends on Set_Deallocate_Type:
	
	CM-DEALLOCATE_FLUSH maps to TP-End_Dialog request
	CM-DEALLOCATE_CONFIRM maps to
	    TP-Handshake_And_End request
	CM-DEALLOCATE_ABEND maps to TP-U_Abort request
	CM-DEALLOCATE_SYNC_LEVEL depends on Set_Sync_Level:
	    CM-NONE maps to TP-End_Dialog request
	    CM-CONFIRM maps to TP-Handshake_And_End request
	    CM-SYNC_POINT maps to TP-Deferred_End_Dialog request

Prepare_To_Receive	Mapping depends on Set_Prepare_To_Receive_Type:
	CM-PREPARE_TO_RECEIVE_FLUSH maps to TP-Grant_Control request
	CM-PREPARE_TO_RECEIVE_CONFIRM maps to
	    TP-Handshake_And_Grant_Control request
	CM-PREPARE_TO_RECEIVE_SYNC_LEVEL also depends on
	    Set_Sync_Level:
	    CM-NONE maps to TP-Grant_Control request
	    CM-CONFIRM maps to TP-Handshake_And_Grant_Control
	        request
	    CM-SYNC_POINT maps to TP-Deferred_Grant_Control request

Receive	Will complete when a wide variety of OSI events occur such as TP-Data indication, TP-End_Dialogue indication, and TP-Commit indication
Request_To_Send	Maps to TP-Request_Control request
Send_Data	Maps to TP-Data request, possibly followed by other actions, depending on Set_Send_Type and Set_Prepare_To_Receive_Type
Send_Error	Maps to TP-U_Error request

EXERCISES

7.1 What is the SAA Common Programming Interface?

7.2 What are the three areas where commonality is sought in OSNA?

7.3   What are the characteristics of a conversation or dialog?

7.4   What is a remote procedure call?

7.5   What is the role of the remote procedure call stubs?

7.6   How does an application use a queued message API?

8

Directories and Logical Connections

8.1 INTRODUCTION

We come now to the need to establish end-to-end logical connections that will facilitate communication between two application-entities. To do that, we first need some mechanism for finding the location of the desired named entity. A universal, worldwide directory, usable by multiple communications architectures, is needed. The *CCITT X.500 directory services* provide the future direction; it is general enough to have the potential of accommodating multiple communication protocols. Specifically, the potential merger of SNA and OSI directory services at the application layer is discussed. The relationships to directory services at lower layers is noted.

Then some *agreement* must be reached on the types of facilities at the two ends which best serve the projected communication. Those facilities must be set in place. The knowledge and authority for these actions needs to reside somewhere, and so we are faced with the question of control points. Regionalized and peer-to-peer control points are examined. The establishment of OSI associations and SNA sessions are then explained.

8.2 NAMING

8.2.1 Introduction

There may be three tokens involved in the process of locating and reaching a destination: a name, an address, and a route. A name conveys a sense of "what;" an address conveys a sense of "where;" and a route has a sense of "how to get there from here." At least two of these three tokens are essential. Some networks do not use names, but do use addresses and routes.[1] Others use names and routes. Others use all three tokens. In all cases, the route

---

1. Telephone systems and packet networks function without names, but in general, users prefer to have a name space as well.

is the desired result. The route is found from the name or the address either by directories of some sort or by an algorithmic mapping.

The distinction between names and addresses has often been obscure, as both names and addresses have been used to uniquely identify an object. The term *name* may simply mean the highest level of identifier used by humans to denote something [Patel90]. More generally, the name is what is passed to identify that which is of mutual interest. When that name (like Delancey Street) refers to a location, or more typically when it consists of numeric or alphanumeric characters meant for machine use rather than human use, we call it an address. In a network, an *address* (sometimes another name) is often an intermediate form of location identifier; it is intermediate between the name of an object commonly used by humans and a route to the object [Zatti88a].

A primary purpose of names is to give independence from implementation structures. By using names, a program need not be concerned with details, such as permanent network locations or transport characteristics. A level of indirection exists, so that by simple table-look-up or directory action, a further determination of location can be made. Then, if an object's name is used, many changes can take place without disruption.

8.2.2 TCP/IP Name Service

Before looking at the OSI (X.500) directory services, it may be instructive to look briefly at the TCP/IP naming method and its associated directory service. The TCP/IP Internet naming method is called **domain naming**. The directories, where a name can be exchanged for an Internet address, are located at **domain name servers**. Only the Internet addresses are used across the network. To insure uniqueness, Internet *domain names* and standard *network addresses* may be assigned by the network coordinator, at SRI International, Menlo Park, CA. There is also a "yellow-pages" type of directory, in some installations. This is a generic look-up facility, which can be used to find resources within categories. That facility is included in some Network File System (NFS)[2] products.

The domain name is a concatenation of naming levels. The first naming category is for major-user communities, such as EDU for educational institutions, GOV for government agencies, and COM for commercial users. Successive name components further refine the name. For example, IBM would have a directory at IBM.COM that would have the Internet addresses for multiple locations within IBM. Examples would be Yorktown.IBM.COM and Raleigh.IBM.COM. Then, within IBM.COM or at the particular location, there might be separate directories for multiple systems at each location, such as VM3.Raleigh.IBM.COM. The OSI X.500 directory, described below, extends this hierarchical naming concept.

8.2.3 OSI and SNA Names

The world is already full of different naming and addressing conventions. The standards bodies have sought to incorporate the major naming and addressing schemes under universal naming and addressing conventions. This is no small task, and must result in

---

2. Network File System was originally developed by SUN Microsystems Inc.

fairly complex and lengthy conventions. The approach taken by OSI in naming is similar to that of TCP/IP in having structured names of variable length, with a hierarchy of authority levels. Each authority level is then responsible for uniqueness of the names of its immediate children—i.e., those names within its immediate area of authority. This universal naming convention is broad enough to include SNA names, as well as the OSI names. Note that these X.500 name components form a tree structure, much like that of TCP/IP names. However, the TCP/IP components are ordered "leaf-to-root," whereas the X.500 name components are ordered "root-to-leaf."

Names are often unique only in a particular environment. It is further desirable, therefore, to allow for aliases and nicknames. Then a given object may be known by different names in different environments, and the "system" can keep track of the transformations needed. Thus, local application-processes can be made insensitive to name changes elsewhere in the network.

In SAA, the **symbolic_destination_name** is such a nickname for the destination. This is the primary SAA means for identifying a destination application-process at the Common Programming Interface (CPI); and each application-process may have multiple symbolic_destination_names. Note that the symbolic_destination_name is independent of any underlying communication protocol.

In OSI, each application-entity (see Section 3.5.2) also has a name, called the **application_entity_title (AE_title)**. Aliases and group names are also permitted. An application-process (named by an application-process-title) may have multiple application-entities, each with its own application_entity_title.

What about SNA names? **LU_names** are given to **LUs** (see Section 3.5.1). *LUs are aggregates of end-to-end function located within an end-node.* Each SNA network can have a separate naming authority, and LUs need only be unique within an SNA network. When there are multiple interconnected SNA networks, therefore, the network itself needs to be identified by a **Net_id**. When prefixed with a Net_id qualifier, these Net_id.LU_names then uniquely identify the destination. In APPN, a special LU, associated with a control point in a node, has a corresponding **CP_name**. A CP_name thus refers to the node, and therefore the Net_id.CP_name uniquely identifies the node represented by that name.

8.2.4   X.500 Naming Structure

In an integrated naming scheme *(which respects existing structures)*, names are structured into components reflecting the hierarchy of administrative boundaries around objects. Then names can be assigned independently within each boundary by the relevant authority according to its own criteria [Zatti88b]. For example, if "IBM" is part of a naming structure, then IBM is responsible for the uniqueness of all names of objects within IBM. This is roughly analogous to the methods used in the existing worldwide direct-dial telephone network.

An **entry** in the directory tree is a collection of attributes related to an object (objects exist in the real world; entries describe them in the tree). In the X.500 structure, all entries are ordered in a hierarchy, illustrated by the global naming tree in Figure 8.1. OSI refers to this tree as the **Directory Information Tree (DIT)**. Such a hierarchical name structure

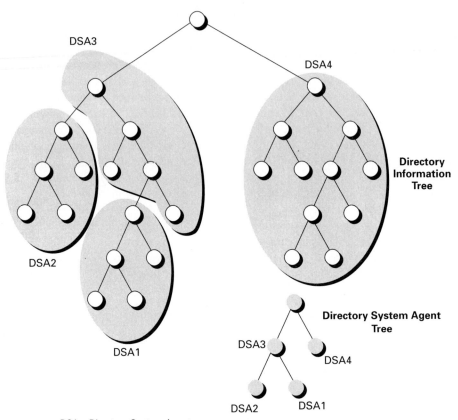

DSA = Directory System Agent

Figure 8.1 Directory Information Tree and corresponding Directory System Agent tree.

facilitates the delegation of naming authority. As new names are added, each node in the tree only needs to guarantee that the names in the next lower level (its logical children) are unique. Access to the directory information is through a **Directory System Agent (DSA)**. DSAs are interconnected, typically as shown in Figure 8.1. Note, however, that the relations among DSAs are not limited to the simple tree structure.

Each object in the directory tree belongs to an object class, such as country, organization, organizational unit, department, application-process, or application-entity. Not all entries at the same level need belong to the same class, however. The entry for each object in the directory is structured, as shown in Figure 8.2, as a set of attributes. Each attribute has an attribute-type field, followed by a set of attribute values. The attribute type indicates the class of information given by that attribute (for example, telephone number); the attribute value is a particular instance of the attribute (for example, 232-7959). One of the attributes may be the common name of the object. Thus, the directory information tree has three elements: it contains entries, which have parameters, which have parameter values.

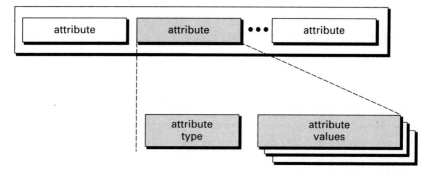

Figure 8.2 Format for X.500 directory entry.

Each object that has an entry in this directory information tree has a name, called the **Relative Distinguished Name (RDN)**, composed of one or more distinguished attributes of the object entry. The RDN, for example, may be the name, "Sweden" at the country level.[3] That RDN, however, is also allowed to have multiple attributes (e.g., location=Stockholm, common-name=Smith, representing both locality and a name). Some of the attribute types are standardized, but administrators can also create additional types for use within a domain.

The **distinguished name** of an object includes the object RDN plus the RDN of all the objects in its upper hierarchy. For example, that hierarchy can include the hierarchical classes: **country, organization, organization unit**, and so forth. To illustrate, an object's distinguished name might be country=Sweden; company=IBM; department=742; person-name=Smith.

Typically, the object that has been named is a person or a communications system component like an application-entity; however, any kind of object can be named. Directory entries for each object, consisting of a set of attributes, are open ended. However, preferred attribute types can be established by a "naming authority." The X.500 recommendation does define some **object classes**. These recommended classes, for example, include: alias, application-process, application-entity, directory system agent (DSA), and device.

Name changes are easily accommodated. At each of the levels in the object naming tree, the local naming authority has to insure the uniqueness of its "children," and has to accept as a prefix the names of the higher-level objects in the tree above. (Note that in different domains of the object naming tree, identical application-processes at different locations could have the same relative distinguished name, but different prefixes in their distinguished name.) Because these prefixes can become very long, local systems may devise nicknames for the prefix. Once the name has been selected, it must be registered in the directory.

---

3.   Countries are identified by 2-digit country IDs from ISO 3166.

8.3   NAME TO ADDRESS RESOLUTION

8.3.1   SNA_Names and OSI NSAPs

Each LU, in SNA, has an **LU_name**, which is unique only within its network. This is sometimes called the SNA_name. The SNA name space contains LU_names; and, in Advanced Peer-to-Peer Networking (APPN), there are also **CP_names**, which are the LU_names of APPN control points in nodes. To establish totally unique SNA_names (i.e., LU_names and CP_names), a network qualifier (uniquely identifying the network) is prefixed, to give: **Net_id.SNA_name**. Hence, LU_names and CP_names can become globally defined. The LU_name is a true name, often used by humans. Like "Delancey Street," it also has some properties of an address.

To clarify the significance of LU_names, we need to discuss the relation between SNA LUs and OSI service-access-points (SAPs) [Janson91]. The upper boundary of the LU provides for application access to the end-to-end data-exchange facilities. The OSI presentation service-access-point (PSAP) does the same thing. The lower boundary of the LU provides it with access to the layer-3c services of SNA path control. This is similar to the way that the OSI network service-access-point (NSAP) provides access for the OSI transport-layer entities to the OSI layer-3c network services.

Note that, in effect, in SNA a connection point analogous to *one PSAP* is tied one-for-one to a connection point analogous to *one NSAP*, whereas in OSI many PSAPs may be tied to one NSAP. In SNA (unlike OSI), therefore, the PSAP and the NSAP are tied together and given a common name, the LU_name.

To find an approximate relationship between OSI and SNA names and address conventions, one needs a starting point. *The starting point is to recognize that the unique identifier, seen by layer 3c, in OSI is the NSAP;*[4] *and the corresponding unique identifier in SNA is the network qualified LU_name.*

With the net_id qualifier, the SNA_names, as well as the OSI NSAPs, can be globally defined, as shown further in Section 12.3.4. Once the correspondence of NSAP and Net_id.LU_name is accepted, the rest is more easily understood.[5]

8.3.2   Directory Actions

Directory-type functions for name to address resolution can exist at one, two, or three levels. The possibilities are:

- The **application-layer directory (A-directory)** provides the globally unique destination address, or an equivalent globally unique identifying name that is understood by layer 3c.

- The **network-directory (N-directory)** can (in APPN and subarea networks) provide the identity of the destination's serving-network-node or subarea-node.

---

4.   The NSAP is the service-access-point of the network layer.

5.   The equivalence between NSAP and LU_name is not complete, however. For example, the LU retains some ability to physically move to another end-system, and end-systems can move to other intermediate-systems, without affecting the bulk of the routing process.

- The **link/subnetwork directory (L/S-directory)** may provide the link-station address, the subnetwork point of attachment address or the LAN address.

First, in this chapter, we examine the global application-level directory, based on X.500. The roles of the more specialized lower-layer directories are discussed in Sections 14.4 and 16.9.

A key function of the application-layer directory (A-directory) is to locate named destination application-entities. The OSI information desired from the directory is the presentation layer service-access-point (PSAP) address in the destination node. This PSAP address consists of the NSAP and all of the higher-level selectors. Thus, the A-directory provides the information needed for the routing through the OSI network (the NSAP) and also the information for routing up through the higher-layer destination layers (the selectors).

Conceptually, the A-directory could handle either the OSI AE_title or the SAA symbolic_destination_name, as inputs. It could provide the PSAP (with NSAP) for OSI destinations; and it could provide the Net_id.LU_name for SNA/Subarea or SNA/APPN destinations. That concept is illustrated in Figure 8.3. This assumes that an SNA network-layer directory function completes the action to obtain the information needed for routing (the continuation of the level-3 directory and routing process is presented in Section 12.4.2 and Figure 12.7).

A further possibility would be for an integration of these multilayer-directory functions. The A-directory in that case would, for example, provide the combination *Net_id.CP_name.LU_name* for the APPN.

For simplicity, each PSAP normally connects to one and only one application-entity. The OSI standard allows an application-entity to have more than one PSAP. However, if that were ever implemented, the directory could return the several PSAPs for a given application_entity_title. The directory user would then have to make the decision of which

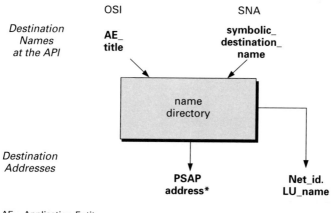

AE = Application-Entity
*PSAP = address includes the NSAP address

Figure 8.3 Inputs and outputs of name directory.

one to use. Selection could be based on different classes of service or lower-layer transmission technology. Most implementations, including the IBM OSI/Communications Subsystem, support only one PSAP per application-entity.

8.4   X.500 DIRECTORY SERVICES

The OSI application-layer-directory (A-directory) provides a structure for unambiguous identification of distributed resources on a global scale.[6] Its basic function is the resolution of "user-readable" object names to information required for effective communication. It is a reference source, used by distributed services to locate elements, along with their associated parameters, which are important for communications.

The complete hierarchical name, with all of its components from the root, can obviously become lengthy. Hence, prefixes are often omitted, as the system would add them back automatically, or nicknames for prefixes are used, where they are understood by the system.

Attributes of a name can be of different types, including such things as phone numbers, postal addresses, or presentation (PSAP) addresses. A print service, for example, would list as attributes the formats it accepts and its print speeds. Destination names might include as attributes the types of protocol stacks they can cope with. While some attribute types have been standardized by OSI, owners of application-entities can register whatever attributes they like, in accord with the directory standard.

Given a name, the attributes can be found. Given a name and particular attribute types, as parts of a query, the directory will return the values of those attributes. If a query is only a generic attribute (e.g., printer type font), the directory will return the names of objects having the specified attribute. The user can then browse the list, looking for a particular item. Thus, there could be three basic modes of interaction with the directory:

- Directory assistance—simple name resolution for a single named object (e.g., "Taxes," the name of an accounting program)
- White pages—the ability to browse the directory (at any level) as if alphabetically leafing through the white pages of a phone book (e.g., checking all entries beginning with "T")
- Yellow pages—the ability to search for objects in the directory related by a common characteristic of the objects (e.g., all accounting programs)

8.4.1   X.500 Operational Structure

As noted above, the access to the OSI **Directory Information Base (DIB)** is provided by the **Directory System Agent (DSA)**, as shown in Figure 8.4. Each DSA understands a defined protocol for directory searches. Any local or remote application-process commu-

---

6.   The initial OSI/Communications Subsystem from IBM implemented a subset of the X.500 standard at a single site, without the distributed data feature.

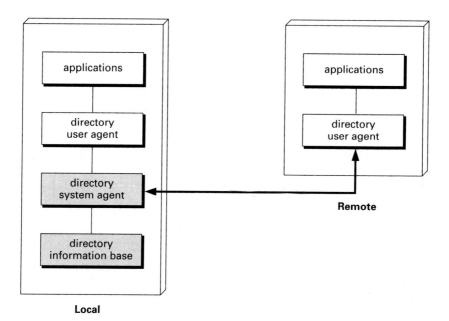

Local

Figure 8.4 Local and remote access to the OSI directory.

nicates with this directory system agent via an intermediary, the **Directory User Agent (DUA)** in that application-process's system. The DUA is a module that understands the directory protocol, and shields the application from details of the directory process. The DSAs may be distributed, forming a network of DSAs, as shown in Figure 8.5. Each DSA has an associated directory information base. A DUA interacts with one or more DSAs. Each DSA and DUA is an application-entity at the application layer.

Two directory protocols have been provided. The DSAs communicate among themselves using the **Directory System Protocol (DSP);** and the DSA's are invoked (through directory user agents) using the **Directory Access Protocol (DAP).** Using the DAP, a user agent can update the directory information base, and receive a confirmation. Using the DAP, a user agent can also request information from a DSA and receive a reply. The DAP service elements are in three groups:

- **Read category**:
  - `Read`—aimed at a particular entry, causing the values of some or all of the attributes to be returned
  - `Compare`—aimed at a particular attribute of a particular entry, to check whether a supplied value matches a value of that attribute
  - `Abandon`—meaning the originator of the request is no longer interested in the result

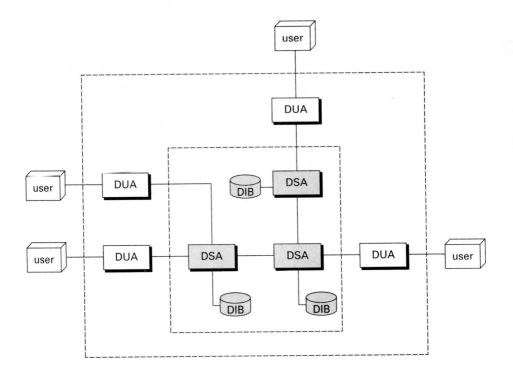

DIB = Directory Information Base
DSA = Directory System Agent
DUA = Directory User Agent

Figure 8.5 The structure of the X.500 directory system.

- **Modify category**:
  - `Add_Entry`, `Delete_Entry`, `Modify_Entry`
- **Search part**:
  - `Search`—returning information from all of the entries within a certain portion of the DIT that satisfy some filter
  - `List`—returning the list of immediate subordinates of a particular named entry in the DIT

Some implementations, like the first release of the IBM OSI/Communications Subsystem, have facilities for only a single DSA, and do not support the search commands.

Replication for availability, and caching for performance, are parts of a directory design philosophy. These both, however, complicate the data update process. To relieve this problem, updates in some implementations may be propagated only at intervals selected by the administrator.

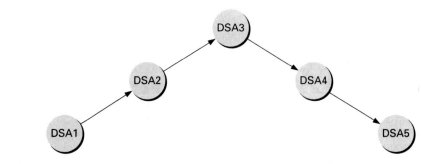

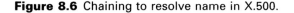

DSA = Directory System Agent

Figure 8.6 Chaining to resolve name in X.500.

8.4.2   X.500 Search Process

The directory information tree (DIT) is divided into nonoverlapping segments, called *directory domains (or subtrees)*, as shown in the DSA tree of Figure 8.1. As a general rule, the *resolver portion of the DSA*, which performs the lookup function, understands the overall namespace structure and the naming relationships of one domain to another. It maintains information about domains, such as: domain identifiers and domain parents and children (superior and subordinate references).

The mechanism of name-resolution uses the name itself in the navigation procedure. The structure of the name guides the directory search, and DSAs responsible for each of the name's components are visited successively in the search.[7] To avoid endless searches, with the possibility of loops, a search can be limited to a certain time duration, or to a certain size of result (number of entries) to be returned.

When a local DSA cannot resolve the name in the query, it may thus seek the help of other DSAs. It can do this in several ways.

- The local DSA may *refer* the calling DUA to another DSA; or, the local DSA may itself seek the help of another DSA.

- It may do this by *chaining* from one DSA to another, as shown in Figure 8.6, using the naming structure itself for navigation among the DSAs. Note, however, that since the relations among DSAs are not limited to the simple tree structure, more complicated chaining than that shown can result.

- A DSA may also use *multicasting*, as illustrated in Figure 8.7, where a DSA "fans-out" a request to multiple DSAs for parallel processing. A broadcast type of communication would be appropriate for this mode, such as is found in LANs. The DSA performing the fan-out is responsible for result consolidation.

---

7.   There is concern that this approach may sometimes prove to be quite inefficient. If so, variations can be expected.

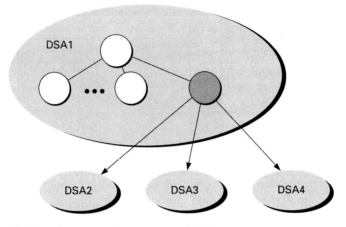

Figure 8.7 Multicasting to resolve name in X.500.

8.5   COMMON OSI/SNA DIRECTORY

While OSNA will have to handle multiple protocols, in an integrated directory besides OSI and SNA (e.g., TCP/IP and LAN-oriented protocols), the place to start is the integration of OSI and SNA directories. This is our long-range direction, and some of the problems faced there will benefit the broader integration.

Earlier implementations of the X.500 directory reserved its use for name to address transformations of OSI subsystems. One possible scheme for using the X.500 directory as a basis for common OSI/SNA services is illustrated in Figure 8.8. There, side information at the application programming interface would be used to convert the symbolic_destination_name (nickname) to either the Net_id.LU_name or the OSI application_entity_title. More precisely, the side information would yield either:

- TP-Name, Net_id.LU_name, and mode-name
- TPSU-name, AE-title, and mode-name

Then the X.500 directory could be used to find the presentation (PSAP) address, and an SNA network-layer directory (N-directory) could be used to retrieve the identity of the destination serving network-node.

Recall that the symbolic_destination_name (an 8-character nickname) usually has no global meaning. The application_entity_title will have a global meaning, including the entire prefix of the directory's distinguished name (including terms like country, organizational unit, etc.). The AE_title also includes the application-process common name, and the application-entity common name.

8.5.1   Integrated Directory Concept

There is a recognized ultimate requirement for an application-layer-directory that provides a common image and common services for OSI, SNA, TCP/IP, and NetBIOS-based systems. For SAA and AIX/OSF systems, this directory must be scalable across the

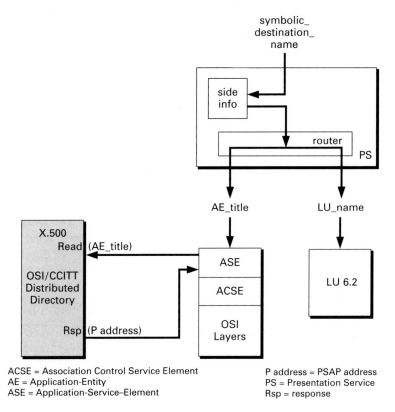

Figure 8.8 Use of X.500 to retrieve OSI presentation address.

combined SAA and AIX/OSF product set and be applicable to small networks as well as a large, multivendor, interconnected network environment. An SAA-distributed directory will thus have to evolve with X.500, and yet incorporate, advanced and high-performance functions. A theoretical model for an integration of SAA and OSI directories is illustrated in Figure 8.9. The common directory API and the resource location functions would include a correct subset of the X.500 directory standard. In effect, the combined directory service would include at least an X.500 directory-user-agent (DUA) function (as part of the node control point). Information stored in the integrated directory could be used to select the appropriate communications support, depending on the destination and the quality of service desired. Such an approach would allow for the rapid introduction of new facilities as needed. In this way, too, a distributed directory for SAA and AIX/OSF systems could be fully interoperable with other-equipment-manufacturer (OEM) systems that follow the base X.500 directory.

Common directory API.   A single API is needed for both OSI X.500 and SAA-Distributed Directory–based applications. The OSI *local-alias* corresponds to the SAA *symbolic_destination_name*. An OSI local-alias, for example, might include all or only small parts of the country code/organization/location/local-name, prescribed for the OSI AE_title.

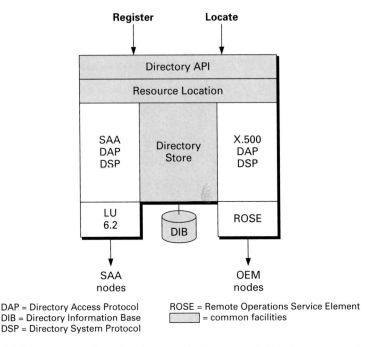

Figure 8.9 The common function in the X.500 superset directory concept.

An SAA symbolic_destination_name, similarly, might be the locally understood nickname. The SAA symbolic_destination_name could be generalized to be an alias for either a transaction program located at some LU (having an LU_name) on an SNA network or an OSI TPSU located within some application-entity (having an application_entity_title) in an OSI network [Janson91].

The namespace, however, must be expressed in multiple national languages, if the names are to be user-friendly in today's worldwide environment. The requirement is that the directory be enabled to deal with both left-to-right and right-to-left languages, and with both character and idiogram-based languages. In addition, for operations that cross national boundaries, a single directory will need to handle several of the above combinations simultaneously.

Relation to resource managers.   Ordinarily, the objects placed in the A-directory are those that would change relatively infrequently. For example, it probably would not contain the parameters of files. Rather, the resolution of a filename would be only partially completed in the A-directory, down to a level where parameters indicate a file server name, location, and protocol. That file server would then be depended on to use its own file subdirectory or catalog to locate the path to the desired file. Files could be made known to the application-layer name directory by externalizing the local directories as subdirectories of the application-layer directory.

A generalization of this type of situation is the concept of directory-active resource managers. Any resource manager that has an inherent and specialized directory can function in cooperation with the application-layer name directory. In these cases the resolution of a resource name can proceed into the sphere of control of the cooperating resource manager. Logically, this can be viewed as the application-layer directory having subordinate references to the subtrees contained in the cooperating resource manager. The end result provides visibility to all resources via a consistent set of directory mechanisms.

Network-layer directories.   In a layered-network architecture, there may actually be several directories at different layers which must cooperate with each other. The application layer is where humans interact; the A-directory is therefore well suited to name-to-address mapping. On the other hand, the name/address-to-route mapping is intimately involved in the network-layer functions. Therefore, it is in a network-layer directory (N-directory) and route-selection services where the name/address-to-route mapping can best be done.[8]

SNA control points have used an N-directory for transformation of an LU_name into an identifier for a destination serving node. In subarea networks, these N-directory services are contained in the *System Services Control Points (SSCPs)*, which are control points for a region of a network, and are located in each type-5 node (usually S/370 and S/390 hosts). The subarea directory services map the LU_name to a two-part destination address (subarea and element addresses). In APPN, the N-directory services are associated with the control points of each network-node. The APPN N-directory maps the LU_name to the identity of the destination serving network-node. In each case, protocols have been defined for the interrogation of the N-directories.

The APPN N-directory function is closely linked to the dynamic network topology-update and route-selection processes. Therefore, it must be designed for high performance. A search by the APPN N-directory services then locates the destination network-node server, which is identified by that node's CP_name.

An overall directory concept also includes the incorporation of *lower layer (1–3a) directory* searches (such as TCP/IP's Address Resolution Protocol, ARP, NetBIOS' Name-Query, and SNA's Token Ring Discovery Protocol; see Section 16.9). These take advantage of the broadcast facilities inherent in LANs to search for local facilities on the LAN that translate global identifiers (e.g., NSAPs) to LAN-specific station addresses.

Each of these lower layers in the transport-service-provider has a distinct service to perform that is characteristic of the layers it serves. The design task is to relate the upper-layer directory services with the lower-layer directory services so as to create, in effect, a distributed and partitioned directory service.

8.5.2   Alternative Design Approaches

One other possible and more integrated approach is shown in Figure 8.10. The side information only translates the symbolic_destination_name (a nickname) into a universal name which the directory can recognize. Then, depending on whether the destination uses

---

8.   It can be argued that the route-selection/mapping is not strictly a directory function, since it changes depending on where the question is being asked, that is, the mapping is not source-independent.

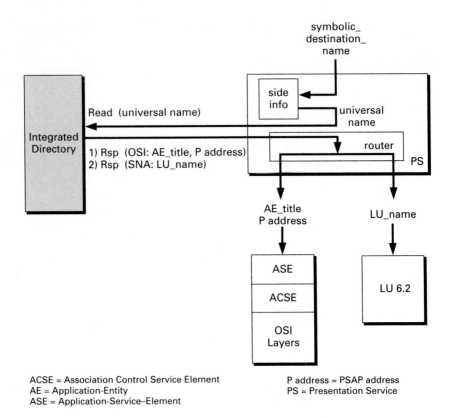

ACSE = Association Control Service Element
AE = Application-Entity
ASE = Application-Service–Element

P address = PSAP address
PS = Presentation Service

Figure 8.10 Use of directory to retrieve both OSI presentation and SNA address.

OSI or SNA end-to-end protocols,[9] the directory would respond with either:

- AE-title, P-address
- LU_name

Given that the integrated directory should provide the LU_name (as described above), two strategies for APPN are possible:

1. The integrated directory could provide:

    Net_id.LU_name

in which case, a *broadcast-search* by the APPN N-directory could find the CP-names (of the network-nodes adjacent to the destination end-node) and TVs (Tail Vectors)[10] corresponding to the LU_name. Sometimes, the destination end-node is connected to more than one network-node. In those cases, the distributed N-directory service would provide

---

9. The directory can contain almost any kind of information about the named destination. One piece of information could pertain to its preferred end-to-end communication facilities.

10. TVs are information about all the links between the subject end-node and one or more adjacent network-nodes.

the CP_names of all of the connected network-nodes, and the tail vectors leading from them to the destination end-node.

2.   Alternatively, the integrated directory could provide:

Net_id.CP-name.LU_name

in which case a *directed-search* by the APPN N-directory services, to the found CP_name, could confirm the location of the named LU, and that the named network-node is still the serving node for that LU. This strategy, using a directed-search, avoids the traffic occasioned by broadcast searches. If, moreover, the destination is not an ordinary LU, but is a control point, then another short cut is possible. Then, the directory service might avoid any further searching by looking into the topology data base to simply see if the CP is currently active.

When the destination is an LU, the found CP_name does not have to be that of the destination end-node. The size of the N-directory is substantially reduced by the ability of server network-nodes to know the way to multiple attached end-nodes. Hence, only the CP_name of the server nodes adjacent to the desired end-node needs to be kept in the N-directory. The remainder of the path, from the server node to the destination end-node, is known as the **Tail Vector**. That information can be provided by the server node as it confirms the location of the desired LU_name.

Separate from this N-directory, is the APPN topology database, which keeps track of the status of links and network-nodes in the APPN network. This information is deliberately kept invisible to the user. It is described in Section 14.6.

8.5.3   Directory Services Transport

The distributed A-directory services are layer-7 application-services. The directory user agents (DUAs) and the directory system agents (DSAs) communicate using the layer-7 OSI Directory Access Protocol (DAP) and the Directory System Protocol (DSP). As with many transaction-oriented application-services, these layer-7 protocols can be independent of the underlying layer 1 through 6 communication protocols. As discussed previously, the API can shield the application from these underlying communication protocol differences. It follows that the distributed directory services can also be designed to use diverse communication services, including, for example: (1) SNA LU 6.2 services over an SDLC WAN, an X.25 WAN, or a LAN, or (2) OSI/Communications Subsystem or TCP/IP services over an X.25 PSDN or a connectionless network.

8.6   CONTROL-POINT DISTRIBUTION

8.6.1   Introduction

We see the necessity for control points, of sorts, in all types of management, whether we are using OSI, SNA, TCP/IP, or some other set of protocols. The control point exercises control over a **control domain**, which is the administrative bounds for management of a portion of the network. The bounds of the domain correspond either to resource ownership or to special agreements among the owners. Domains may be disjoint, nested, or overlapped. Multiple domains then must be coordinated, or must cooperate with each other, to permit cross-domain communication. Theoretically, there are at least four possible control-point arrangements for the provision of directory and logical connection services:

1. A *single, centralized* set of services, provided for all nodes within a large control domain

2. Multiple instances of *regional control domains*, as in (1), operating as *peers* of one another

3. Local control points *in all nodes*, operating autonomously *as peers* of one another

4. Local control points as in (2) or (3), but also operating hierarchically under one or more *higher-level control points*

We often have had separate sets of control points for directories, security, logical connections, configuration services, and system management. Some are best separate, but all must be related to each other, to have a robust network.

Each protocol suite has had a management philosophy within these four options. The SNA management evolution is perhaps the longest and most comprehensive. Historically, the directory and connection services in SNA networks have evolved from (1) and (2) to (3) and (4) for various circumstances. The driving forces for this evolution have been the growth in the size of networks, and the absolute need for nondisruptive operations, coupled with minimum skilled resources for large network operations. At the same time, in SNA, a two-level configuration of end-systems and intermediate-systems has been maintained. The combination of these two philosophies has determined the definitions of various types of nodes in SNA Subarea and APPN configurations.

8.6.2   Subarea Control-Point Services

Basic network services require the cooperation of all the nodes in a network. Hence, the operation of these services is inherently distributed to some extent. However, in the 1970s, hardware costs were relatively high, and it was more economical to draw all the information for these services to a central or regional point. In a single host system, with distributed terminal subsystems, this concentration of services was called the **Systems Services Control Point (SSCP)**, which was located in the central processor. The function of the SSCP is the general management of a control domain,[11] such as bringing up the network, helping to establish logical connections between LUs, and helping in recovery and maintenance, when necessary. It also provides the interface to the network operator for that domain.

Each SSCP establishes a liaison with its representatives, called **Physical Units (PUs)** in each and every box within the control domain of the SSCP. The PU provides a location

---

11.   *Control domain* is a term used to indicate the scope of control of a particular resource manager across a subset of the nodes of a distributed system.

for configuration-related services which must be performed at a particular node. An SSCP and PUs together control the network configuration and the data-transportation resources provided by the nodes in the domain of the SSCP. For example, the PU understands how to activate a link, and the SSCP determines that a link should be activated.

Similarly, the SSCP is connected to all the Logical Units (LUs) within its domain. Thus, both the individual boxes and the individual ends of each logical connection (or session) are connected to and require services of the central SSCP. The operations are distributed, but the control is central.

In subarea networks, SSCP-to-LU and the SSCP-to-PU sessions both are prerequisites to an LU-LU session. An SSCP-PU session, in turn, is a prerequisite for any SSCP-LU sessions (with LUs in the node of that PU).

As multiple-host systems grew, there were multiple SSCPs, with multiple control domains. These SSCPs, therefore, became *regional service controllers*, and the SSCPs had a peer relation to each other. The SSCPs together controlled cross-domain LU-LU sessions. The assignment of resources to different SSCPs is flexible. For example, each SSCP in the network might control (activate and deactivate) about an equal number of resources; or one SSCP might control most of the network resources; or more than one SSCP might share control of some resources.

8.6.3   Peer-to-Peer

The power and sophistication of individual units continued to grow, as hardware costs fell (thanks to dramatic technological advances), to the point where a desktop PC now has the function and power of a former large-scale host. The next logical step in this evolution, therefore, is the treatment of each such processor as a suitable control point. Topology, session, directory, and routing services all have been evolving from a central or regionalized control concept to a peer-to-peer relationship. **Advanced Peer-to-Peer Networking (APPN)** provides this decentralized control. In APPN networks, there is no SSCP. Instead, similar control functions are distributed among control points (CPs) in each node. Such control points now exist, for example in PS/2's, as well as in AS/400 intermediate (departmental) processors, and 3174 cluster (establishment) controllers. No session with a remote SSCP is needed. Instead, any inter-node cooperation is coordinated via inter-node CP-CP communication.

At the same time, this further decentralization facilitates other improvements in dynamic reconfiguration, reduction of coordinated systems definitions, higher availability, and ease of use (see Chapter 14). Such peer-to-peer networking has been adopted by IBM as an across-the-board strategy.[12] Nevertheless, a two-level relationship is maintained between end-nodes and network-nodes. For economy and performance reasons (e.g., reducing broadcast traffic) end-nodes can be like "leaves" attached to network-nodes, and can economize by depending on adjacent network-nodes for services.

---

12. "We understand what peer to peer means, and we're going to get there across the board," Rick McGee, manager of IBM's communications systems architecture, quoted in *Information Week*, February 19, 1990.

8.6.4   Node Types

Nodes are, first of all, classified in OSI as *end-systems* and *intermediate-systems*, as described in Figure 3.5. To identify nodes as specifically APPN nodes, the corresponding terminology of *end-nodes* and *network-nodes* has been used. Beyond that, node types in a network are usually characterized by the nature of the transport services at layers 4 and 3c, plus the node's control-point capabilities. In OSI, for example, we have five options at the transport layer and both connectionless and connection-oriented services at the network layer. Nodes in a protocol-converged network, (as OSNA evolves) are primarily of four types:

- Pure SNA nodes, including both subarea and APPN types
- Pure OSI nodes
- Combined OSI and SNA nodes
- Other combined nodes, to include TCP/IP and NetBIOS services

Within IBM, there are two kinds of networks: the Advanced Peer-to-Peer Networking (APPN) and the subarea networks. Simple examples of these networks are shown in Figure

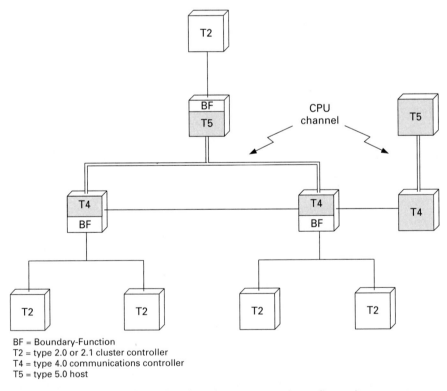

BF = Boundary-Function
T2 = type 2.0 or 2.1 cluster controller
T4 = type 4.0 communications controller
T5 = type 5.0 host

Figure 8.11 Node types in a simple subarea network configuration.

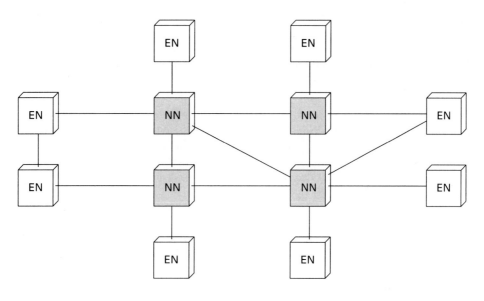

EN = End-Node
NN = Network-Node

Figure 8.12 Node types in a simple Advanced Peer-to-Peer Network (APPN).

8.11 and Figure 8.12. The corresponding types of nodes we need to introduce now are:

- *Type 2.1:* network-nodes and end-nodes in APPN (see Figure 8.12). *Both contain APPN peer control points.*[13]

- *Type 2.1 LEN:* nodes are simpler, low-entry end-nodes, which do not have CP-CP sessions with an associated network-node.

  - Type 2.1 nodes can also attach to subarea networks as peripheral nodes. In that case, they can appear to the subarea as either simpler (Low-Entry Networking, **LEN**) type 2.1 nodes or as type 2.0 nodes.

- *Type 2.0:* peripheral-nodes in subarea networks; similar in role to an end-node, but *with no control point.*

- *Type 4:* intermediate-node in subarea networks (e.g., a communications controller, see Figure 8.11); offloads the routing functions from the mainframes; similar in role to an APPN network-node, but *with no control point.*

- *Type 5:* a host-node in a subarea network; *contains an SSCP.*

---

13. Not all end-nodes contain control points which can establish sessions with other control points. In particular, the simpler, low entry networking (LEN) end-nodes do not.

8.6.5   SNA Configurations

Consider further the SNA subarea network shown in Figure 8.11. The hosts, type-5 nodes, can provide a boundary-function for a channel attached cluster (establishment) controller, a type-2.0 node. The type-5 nodes also contain a control point, called a Systems Services Control Point (SSCP) for all the nodes assigned to its domain. Three communication controllers, type 4, are also shown, two of which are channel attached to one host. Each of these, in turn, might be connected to other remote communication controllers. A local or remote communication controller might also attach additional type-5 hosts. Each communication controller, type 4, also provides boundary-functions to attached type 2.0 cluster controllers. Type-4 and type-5 nodes can also attach type-2.1 nodes that operate in a type 2.0 mode or as LEN type-2.1 nodes.

Now consider the Advanced Peer-to-Peer Network (APPN) shown in Figure 8.12. All the nodes in this configuration are type 2.1. Those whose primary function is to provide intermediate routing services are the network-nodes. Those whose primary function is to service their own end users are end-nodes.

8.7   OSI CONNECTION SERVICES

8.7.1   Introduction

A logical connection, in any architecture, involves a definition of the characteristics of the communication between two application-processes. Now, the logical-connection characteristics could be identified in the headers associated with each and every data unit to be transmitted. Some teleprocessing systems have been built largely on this principle. However, most of the communication characteristics do not change from message to message and can be recorded at the initiation of the logical connection. Certain other characteristics that do change from time to time can still be included within message-control headers. Thus, the design of the logical-connection mechanism depends on the judgment as to which communication characteristics can appropriately be established at the beginning of a logical connection, and which need a flexibility for modification during the conduct of the logical connection. The data flow for a given logical connection, then, is directed by the set of control tables that contain the agreements made at connection initiation time, augmented by a supplementary degree of control from the bits in the headers.

8.7.2   Establishing an Association

As noted in Chapter 3, two remotely located OSI application-entities can establish an *application association,* usually called simply, an *association,* with each other. For each association, each application-entity will have a set of functions, at the application layer, that pertain to that association. This is illustrated, conceptually, in Figure 8.13, where each association makes use of some set of application-service–elements.

The association operates in concert with pairs of entities at the presentation, session, and transport layers, and so (in a limited way) is comparable to the SNA session. Multiple

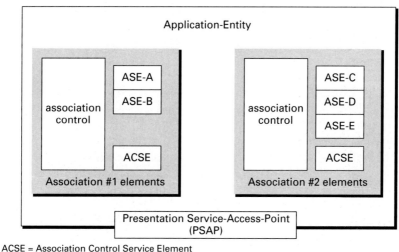

ACSE = Association Control Service Element
ASE = Application-Service–Element

Figure 8.13 Conceptual structure of application-entity.

associations among the several processes of a distributed application may be necessary. That situation is illustrated in Figure 8.14. Note that each application-process may have multiple application-entities, each of which is devoted to communications on a different association. It is also possible to have different associations between the same pair of application-entities.

The OSI Association Control function is a common service for multiple application-entities. Each OSI association makes use of an **Association Control Service Element**

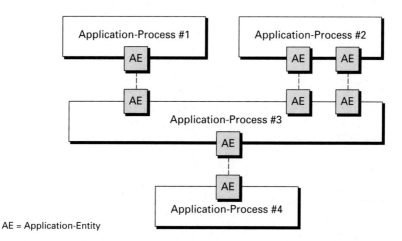

AE = Application-Entity

Figure 8.14 Associations of application-entities linking application-processes.

(**ACSE**) [IS 8649], [IS-8650] whose function is to assist in establishing and terminating a particular association.

In OSI, the connection of an application-entity to these other end-to-end services, is via a particular *presentation layer service-access-point (PSAP)*, shown in Figure 8.13. Each application-entity is unambiguously associated with a PSAP. The latter, in turn, is connected, one-to-one, to a session service-access-point (SSAP). An application-entity may have multiple associations, using multiple connection-end-points, in the same PSAP and SSAP pair.

During the establishment of an association, for a calling application-entity, the PSAP address of the *called* application-entity must be used to establish a presentation-layer connection. That destination PSAP address is obtained either from side information, or from an application-layer directory. That directory provides this PSAP address in exchange for the called application_entity_title.

The association supports the cooperation between two application-entities within a defined **application context**. This is a mutually agreed to relationship between the application-entities. In particular, it includes a specification of the *Application-Service–Elements (ASEs)* and related options that will be employed in the association. (The primary application-services are discussed in Chapters 4 through 8.) The application context also includes coordination and sequencing information on which ASE to invoke when a particular protocol data unit (PDU) arrives. Each application context has a *named application-context definition*. In general, the application contexts will be developed by the users of OSI, rather than by the standards groups.

The association also operates within a defined **presentation context**. This is a negotiated agreement on the syntax to be used by the two partners in their communication. It includes a list of sets of *data types*, along with *encoding rules* for the data (see Section 9.2).

The side-information or directory also can provide other descriptors of an application-entity, in addition to its PSAP address, such as the AE nickname and the AE_title. The descriptor of the local initiating AE may contain an **application mode** for that AE [SL23-0191]. The application mode specifies various association attributes that the local initiator desires when it establishes an association, such as:

- Session-layer functions
- Initial *permission_to_send* level
- Transport layer *quality_of_service*
- *Application_context_name*
- Default *abstract_syntax_nickname*
- List of abstract syntax names

Setting-up sequence [Davison90].   The sequence of activities involved in setting up an OSI association are summarized as follows:

1. The application-process, through its application-entity, identifies the *AE_title* of the desired destination. That title is mapped (by side information or an application-layer

directory) to a *PSAP address* of the destination. The PSAP address is used to establish the lower-layer connections.

2.   The initiating application-entity (AE) proposes an *application context*. The responding AE can accept or propose an alternative. The initiating AE then either accepts the alternative or aborts the association.

3.   The specifications for the presentation, session, and transport services are passed to the lower layers via *primitives*, and the connections at each underlying layer are established.

This sequence is started with the **A-Associate** primitive, which drives logical connections at the application, presentation, session, and transport layers. The ACSE service-primitives, the ACSE protocol data units, and the parameters associated with each, are presented in this chapter's Technical Reference section. The interplay among the primitives and PDUs is fairly complex. An overview follows.

Multilayer connects.   The application, presentation, and session connections are tied together and are negotiated and established simultaneously. There is a one-to-one correspondence between an application association, a presentation connection, and a session connection.

To explore this further, we need to recall the flows between layers. Figure 8.15 illustrates how an A-Associate request results in the flow of parameters and data through the application and presentation layers to the session layer. The flow between layers is in the form of **service-primitives**, such as an A-Associate request at the application layer, and P-Connect or S-Connect at the presentation or session layers. Certain parameters contained in application primitives are also contained in presentation primitives and are mapped directly to presentation services. Certain other parameters contained in application primitives are passed first into presentation primitives and then into session primitives. *The Connect SPDU thus incorporates the information contained in the Associate APDU and the Connect PPDU.* What gets instantiated dynamically at the time of setting up a connection are the connection-end-points within the SAPS of each layer.

8.7.3   Transaction-Processing Application-Service–Element

The OSI **Transaction-Processing Application-Service–Element (TP-ASE)** provides the management of the dialog between two transaction programs. The *Association Control Service Element (ACSE)* is responsible for establishing and terminating the association, which is serially used by a dialog (see Section 9.4). That pair TP-ASE and ACSE is therefore responsible for establishing, maintaining, and terminating *dialogs and associations* (roughly analogous to SNA conversations and sessions) for transaction programs. The structure is illustrated in Figure 8.16. Once the association is established, the data has a direct path around the ACSE to presentation services (PS). Other (nontransaction) OSI applications, on the other hand, can function without a dialog, and can have a direct path to the ACSE for association establishment, and thereafter directly to presentation services. For those applications, the application-entity needs only the ACSE and any involved application-service–elements (like FTAM or Virtual Terminal).

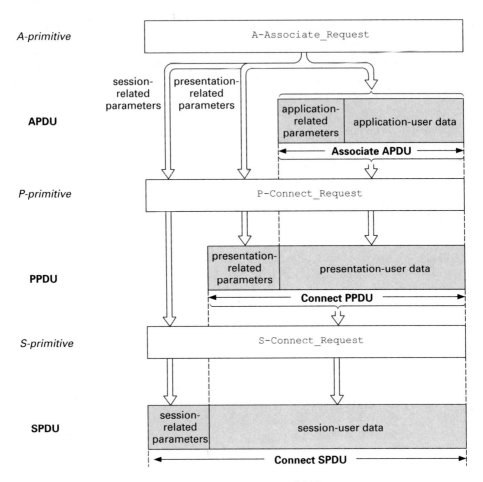

Figure 8.15 Embedding of three connects in one PDU.

8.7.4 Remote Operations Service Element

One of the commonly used OSI application-service–elements is the **Remote Operations Service Element (ROSE)**, used to invoke an operation in a distant node.[14] ROSE invokes a remote operation, and receives replies or errors related to the invoked operation. The invocations are correlated with the replies using an invoke id. ROSE is used only after an application association has been set up between two application-entity invocations. A remote operation is defined by an action-name, arguments, a success result, and a failure

---

14.   ROSE was originally designed as a basic request/reply protocol, for use between a user agent and a message transfer agent in the X.400 Message Handling System. It bears a distant relationship to remote procedure calls.

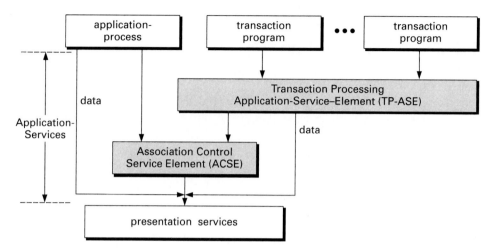

Figure 8.16 Application-services for OSI applications and transaction programs.

result. The three parts of the **ROSE Invoke PDU** are:

- Invoke *id*
- The *action* to be performed
- The *arguments* required for the specified operation

ROSE classifies the operations according to how the performer is expected to report its outcome: operations involving a systematic reply, or a reply indicating failure, or a reply indicating success, or no reply at all. ROSE PDUs for this result and abnormal conditions are:

- `RO-Result` informs the invoking application-entity of the successful completion of an invoked operation.
- `RO-Error` informs the invoking application-entity of an error.
- `RO-Reject_U` lets the ROSE user reject a request (or a reply) from its peer.
- `RO-Reject_P` lets the ROSE service provider inform the ROSE user of a provider-detected problem.

The presentation service primitive, related to the ROSE commands, is the *P-Data*.

8.7.5   End-System-to-Intermediate-System Protocols

We need to note at this point the **end-system-to-intermediate-system (ES-IS)** protocols that are used at lower layers in a complementary fashion. OSI ES-IS protocols are intended to aid connection-establishment and routing by providing network-layer directory services at a special serving node within the originating subnetwork. The OSI ES-IS standards are specified in two documents. ISO 9542, for connectionless-mode service, and ISO 10030, for connection-oriented service (see Section 16.9).

8.8   SNA CONNECTION SERVICES

8.8.1   Establishing an LU-LU Session

Session services (a component in the control point) establish the logical connection between the two end partners of a communication. This logical connection is based on an agreement between the two partners as to the end-to-end facilities they are prepared to share. Included are such things as send/receive controls, end-to-end flow controls, and error-recovery procedures.

The Bind command.   In subarea networks, either of two LUs first contacts a third party, an SSCP, which then assists in the logical connection (or Bind) between the two LUs. In APPNs, on the other hand, the connection between any two LUs is done by the dialog between the services in the nodes of the two LUs, with the help of the control point in the immediately adjacent server network-node. *The Bind command is largely common to both APPN and subarea networks.* The Bind is fully interoperable with APPN and subarea networks. However, in APPN, the Bind also carries the route set-up information.

Let us assume that two LUs exist and that one wants to initiate a session with the other. A single command, called Bind in SNA, must be sent by one LU to the other, proposing the session and requesting agreement on a set of ground rules for the session. The Bind command contains multiple fields that specify the selection of options at SNA layers 4, 5, 6, and parts of 7. It also carries class of service and priority information used at layer 3.

There could be more than one type of Bind contract, so the initiator of the Bind must advise what type of Bind contract it has in mind. The format (FMT) field specifies the format of the Bind RU, and so tells the other LU what meaning to give to the various fields in the RU. A type field further specifies whether the Bind is negotiable or nonnegotiable.

The receiving LU does not necessarily reject a Bind because of any incompatibility with the Bind parameters. Some parameters are negotiable. The protocol anticipates that a "down-level" end-system may not understand the meaning of some fields in the proposed Bind, and enables the up-level box to negotiate down to the level of service provided by its back-level partner. To negotiate, the receiving LU returns a positive response that carries a complete set of session parameters that can differ from those suggested in the Bind. The sender of the Bind checks the parameters in this response. If acceptable, they are used for the activated session. If not, an UnBind is sent. A successful Bind causes the knowledge of a session and a group of session resources to be created in both partners.

8.8.2   APPN Approach

Design features [GG24-3287]. Advanced Peer-to-Peer Networking (APPN) is a network design in which ease of use and simplicity were sought by (1) decentralizing control so that each node maintains its own responsibility for entering or leaving the network, (2) further automating the processes of directory lookup, route finding, session bind, and congestion control in such a way as to make them as invisible as possible to users of the network, and (3) using network control and data transport algorithms that minimize control message overhead and maximize the robustness of the connection between end users [Green87]. *The control point (CP) design of APPN provides some of the basis for a new generation of networks.* There is also an expectation that some of these approaches can be extended to apply to multiple transport protocols in an integrated network. The primary APPN design features associated with the control points are:

- Dynamic resource registration and directories
- Dynamic topology changes
- Local, rather than networkwide coordinated system definition
- Automated route selection (by class of service and current network status)
- Adaptive pacing
- End-node access to multiple network-nodes

The APPN session services, network-layer directory services, topology database, configuration services, and route selection are all functions of the control points located in each APPN network-node and end-node. For example, the local system definitions are spread, as necessary, to other nodes by control-point mechanisms.

APPN peer control points. In APPN, each node of the network retains a high degree of autonomy, even though part of a coordinated network. Aside from the need to keep LU_names unique, no central authority, with responsibility for coordinating network definitions, needs to be consulted prior to network participation. Rather, each node owner retains control over that node's membership in the network, and network operations are conducted by peer-to-peer interactions.

CP-CP sessions are those sessions that are established between control points in adjacent network-nodes, and between control points in APPN end-nodes and network-node servers. These sessions are used for N-directory, topology-update, and routing services. These sessions use LU 6.2 protocols, which has the advantage of a robust, general-purpose service.[15]

End-Node-to-Network-Node (EN-NN) protocols, using CP-CP sessions, include the ability to *register* LUs and a *locate* function that calls for network-layer directory and route services. These provide a complementary function to the application-layer directory discused above. Lesser types of end-nodes are accommodated without the benefit of CP-CP sessions between them and network-nodes. A Low Entry Networking (LEN) end-node has a minimum control-point function, and does not have a CP-CP session with a network-node. CP-CP sessions never exist between end-nodes, or between a network-node and a subarea node.

---

15. LU 6.2 may, however, be more than necessary for this specialized service. More limited, and higher-performance control sessions are probably feasible.

Conclusion

Directory services, control points, and logical-connection establishment are thus inter-twined. The X.500 *universal naming structure* can incorporate SNA, OSI, and other protocol naming methods. The X.500 application-layer directory provides the way for integration of SNA, OSI, and probably other protocol's upper-layer directory services. A worldwide, multiprotocol naming and directory service is promised.

The X.500 directory services, in combination with APPN-type of dynamic network-layer directory services and LAN discovery protocols have a clear potential to provide the future mechanisms for multisubnetwork *destination-location and route-determination*. End-to-end logical connections then can be established for SNA, OSI, or other upper-layer end-to-end protocol systems.

The *peer-to-peer* control-point philosophy of APPN sets the direction for future evolution of the OSNA topology update facilities. New high-speed technologies for routing at layer 2 (see Section 18.5) will complement the current layer-3 routing facilities.

Acknowledgments

I am particularly indebted to the following for input and reviews of this chapter: Philippe Janson, K. Britton, Y. M. Cheung, Mark Pozefsky, Stefano Zatti, E. C. Broockman, Tony Rego, and Jerry Mouton.

TECHNICAL REFERENCE

The following summaries are presented to aid understanding. Because standards change, however, the reader is cautioned to consult up-to-date standards for all implementation work.

ACSE Primitives

Only three types of service-primitives are needed for association control: associate, release, and abort. In the lists below, each primitive is followed by its parameters. Those ACSE primitive parameters that are marked (Pres) map directly to *presentation service*. Those that are marked (Sess) map to session service. Those that are marked (Cont) pertain to the ACSE's negotiation of the application and presentation contexts. The columns on the right indicate whether a parameter is carried in the request (Req), indication (Ind), response (Rsp), or confirm (Conf) flows at the service interfaces.

	Req	Ind	Rsp	Conf	
A-Associate					
• *calling_AE_title*	x	x			
• *called_AE_title*	x	x			
• *responding_AE_title*	-	-	x	x	
• user information	x	x	x	x	
• *application_context_name*	x	x	x	x	(Cont)
• *single_presentation_context*	x	x	-	-	(Cont)
• *presentation_context_definition_list*	x	x			(Cont)
• *presentation_context_definition_result*		x	x	x	(Cont)
• *calling_PSAP*	x	x	-	-	(Pres)

	Req	Ind	Rsp	Conf	
▪ *called_PSAP*	x	x	-	-	(Pres)
▪ *responding_PSAP*	-	-	x	x	(Pres)
▪ *default_presentation_context_name*	x	x	-	-	(Pres)
▪ *default_presentation_context_result*	-	x	x	x	(Pres)
▪ *presentation_requirements*	x	x	x	x	(Pres)
▪ *quality_of_service*	x	x	x	x	(Sess)
▪ *session_requirements*	x	x	x	x	(Sess)
▪ *initial_serial_number*	x	x	x	x	(Sess)
▪ *initial_tokens*	x	x	x	x	(Sess)
▪ *session_connect_id*	x	x	x	x	(Sess)
▪ *result*	-	-	x	x	
A-Release					
▪ *reason*	x	x	x	x	
▪ user information	x	x	x	x	
▪ *result*	-	-	x	x	
A-Abort					
▪ user information	x	x			
▪ *abort_source*	-	x			
A-P-Abort					
▪ *reason*	-	x	-	-	(Pres)
▪ *data*	-	x	-	-	(Pres)

The *result* parameter, in the response and confirm of A-Associate, is provided by the responding user of the association, or by the application control service element, or by the presentation service provider. It may be used to convey one of the following:

▪ ACCEPTED

▪ REJECTED_BY_RESPONDER (reason unspecified, transient, permanent, or unrecognized AE_title)

▪ REJECTED_BY_ACSE

▪ REJECTED_BY_PS (transient or permanent)

ACSE Protocol Data Units (PDUs)

Corresponding to the three types of ACSE primitives, there are three types of association control PDUs. These, with their parameters, are:

A-Associate_Request
- ▪ *protocol_version*
- ▪ *called_AE_title*
- ▪ *calling_AE_title*
- ▪ *application_context_name*
- ▪ user information

A-Associate_Response
- ▪ *protocol_version*
- ▪ *result*
- ▪ *responding_AE_title*
- ▪ *application_context_name*
- ▪ user information

A-Release_Request
- ▪ *reason*
- ▪ user information

A-Release_Response
- ▪ *reason*
- ▪ user information

A-Abort
- ▪ *abort_source*
- ▪ user information

EXERCISES

8.1   Give a simple definition of a name, an address, and a route.

8.2   Construct a TCP/IP domain name for a host that is owned by the Digital Equipment Corporation (DEC), is located in Boston, and has the designation of Boston host number 5.

8.3   In SNA and OSI, what uniquely identifies the location of the destination?

8.4   What is a relative distinguished name?

8.5   True or False: (a) In SNA the connection point analogous to a PSAP and the connection point analogous to an NSAP are tied together and have a common name, the LU_name. (b) In OSI, there is a one-to-one correspondence between an NSAP and a PSAP.

8.6   Give some examples of the roles of the application-layer directory, the network-layer directory, and the link/subnetwork-directory.

8.7   What is the purpose of the directory user agent?

8.8   True or False: (a) In a multimainframe SNA subarea network, the SSCPs cooperate as peers. (b) In an SNA APPN network the peer-peer control points coordinate topology updates, session establishment, N-directory services, and route selection. (c) Peer-Peer control points are not practical for PWS-to-PWS communication on a LAN.

8.9   What layers are involved in an OSI association?

8.10   What are the main functions of the two contexts for an association?

8.11   How does the A-Associate primitive affect the setup of the upper layers?

8.12   What does the SNA `Bind` command do?

8.13   What are CP-CP sessions, and what are they used for?

9
Presentation and Session Services

9.1 Introduction

The similarity of data-exchange facilities in OSI and SNA layers 5 and 6 gives encouragement to the plans for a Common Programming Interface. This chapter provides a tutorial on the SNA and OSI end-to-end data-exchange facilities in those layers.

To recapitulate, a view of the major components in the evolving Open Systems Network Architecture (OSNA) was summarized in Figure 3.14. Earlier chapters covered the overall architecture (Chapter 3), application-services for system management (Chapter 4), distributed data (Chapter 5), and information interchange (Chapter 6). The Common Programming Interface (CPI), which serves both application-processes and application-services, was covered in Chapter 7. Directories and logical connection services were explained in Chapter 8.

As a subset of the broader Figure 3.14 concept, a focus on the integration of SAA, SNA, and OSI facilities was shown in Figure 7.2. This is the long-range, core-integration direction, around which other integrations revolve. In the midlayers of Figure 7.2 we see a pair of SNA and OSI facilities for end-to-end data-exchange. These reside in the presentation and session layers 5 and 6. OSI and SNA functions in these two layers are different and yet very similar. This chapter focuses on these two layers:

- *Layer-6 (presentation) services*, which help to make the presentation of information match the facilities of the end-system, and, in OSI, also arrange agreement on the syntax to be used.

- *Layer-5 services*, which govern the conduct of a conversation or dialog in an orderly way. The functions of the SNA data flow controls (synchronization, chains, and brackets) and the function of the OSI session layer (synchronization, tokens, and Activities) are reviewed.

Discussion of two specific implementations of these layers (5 and 6) is provided in the next two chapters.

Then, having gone through the architectures of layers 5 through 7 in the chapters thus far, a reflection is given at the end of this chapter on the comparable SNA and OSI terms and functions. The rough analogs between the basic LU functions and corresponding functions in OSI are identified and qualified. By these analogs, it is hoped that the reader can see the approximate equivalence, despite differences, in the two higher-layer architectures.

9.2 PRESENTATION SERVICES

9.2.1 Introduction

The presentation layer is concerned with the way in which information must be presented, in order to be understandable to the application and to application-services. The two partners may live in different syntax worlds. It is often impossible for the programs of one operating system, one hardware system, or one programming language to use the information produced by the programs of another. This may simply be caused by different coding schemes (e.g., ASCII, IA5, or EBCDIC). There may be different ways of representing types of information (e.g., floating point, integers, text, image, or sequences of text or image). It may be necessary for each to use certain presentation formats on display screens or printings. To overcome these problems, it often is necessary to resort to a uniform and precise way of describing information and providing means for data conversion. There are different approaches to doing this.

The **transfer syntax** is a set of rules for the representation of user information while it is in transit between two presentation entities. Defining a transfer syntax has not been a major issue in SNA networks, because only a small number of different syntaxes are usually employed and mapping among them is well defined. Data conversion is almost always performed at the sending end, so that the transfer syntax is the syntax of the receiver. In contrast, OSI allows a negotiation of the transfer syntax to be either that of receiver or the sender, or something else that is agreed upon.

One approach, of course, is to require that all applications use common representations for all data that might be exchanged, by any pair of application-processes. This is, then, a **common data syntax**, and no syntax conversion is needed anywhere. Presentation services then could be virtually a null service. SAA, for example, provides a number of data streams that can be used by both parties in different circumstances. This common user language, unfortunately, is not always possible.

The second approach is to plan the data conversions between commonly used pairs of environments, a C language and a COBOL language pair, for example. Precise descriptors and conversion plans can be made in advance for each such combination.

Still another approach is to use a **standard transfer syntax** as the *intermediary* for the physical data transfer between partners, and to *convert any local representation to and from the standard form*. OSI supports any of the above approaches, but the last, standard transfer syntax, is commonly used in current implementations.

The transfer syntax to be used in a particular conversation could be anything, but it must be agreed to by both partners. If that common syntax is to change during the life of a connection, the two partners again have to agree. The presentation services have a role to play in the negotiation of these agreements. Otherwise, a default transfer syntax may be assumed. If necessary, then, the presentation services at each end must also provide the transformation between the common transfer syntax, and the local syntax.

9.2.2 Abstract Syntax

An abstract syntax is a means for assigning meaning to a collection of data values. *It does this by providing a description of the types of data to be transmitted*, without specifying any particular representation for the data being described. It does not specify any coding of those values. For example, two applications may simply decide to use integers and character strings. The abstract syntax would consist of only those two types. As another example, consider that we have a data type called "Name," containing two data values: Bob and Smith. An abstract syntax in this case would be:

"The Name data type consists of a first name followed by a second name."

Often the meanings of data are specified in such text descriptions and are easily reflected in the application. Of course, such text statements could be expressed by some more compact convention, and this is sometimes advantageous when the expression must be interpreted by a program. For such purposes, OSI offers the Abstract Syntax Notation (ASN.1).

Abstract Syntax Notation (ASN.1) is a language for describing data types and values [Chappell]. As defined in ISO 8824 [ISO-8824], it is used in many of the OSI application-layer standards that have been issued by CCITT SG VII and ISO SC 21, to define the data structures they use.

As an example, the above illustration of the "Name" data structure, in ASN.1 would be:

Name ::= SEQUENCE {First_Name, Second_Name}

The symbol ::= is interpreted: "is defined as." ASN.1 includes the concept of **tags**— identifiers that indicate the type of each data element. These tags are used in the standard encoding of data described by **ASN.1 Basic Encoding Rules (BER)**.

ASN.1 tagging.   Each data element in a data stream is identified with a **data element tag**. This tag has only two parts: *class* and *number*. There are four defined classes:

- *Universal* tags, defined in ASN.1 standards, ISO 8824. Common types such as boolean, integer, sequence, and character string are included.

- *Application* tags, reserved for other ISO application-layer standards, such as FTAM or JTM.

- *Private-use* tags, for nonstandard use.

- *Context-specific* tags, that are unique only within an immediate context.

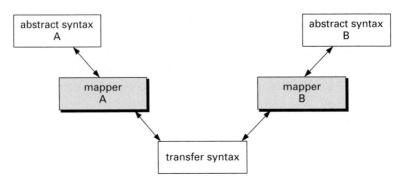

Figure 9.1 Mapping between user's abstract syntax and common transfer syntax.

   These four classes are identified in the first half of the tag. The second half of the tag, its number, then specifies a specific type within one of these four classes. The currently assigned ASN.1 Universal tags are listed in this chapter's Technical Reference section. For example, the tag whose class is Universal and whose number is 3 denotes the type BITSTRING. Note that ASN.1 is case sensitive. The basic types are all uppercase; and all types begin with an uppercase. An ASN.1 illustration is given in this chapter's Technical Reference section.

9.2.3 OSI Presentation Services

Transfer syntax.   The representation of the *value* of a date type follows a set of encoding rules. The Basic Encoding Rules (BER), which are recommended by OSI for the transfer syntax, apply the ASN.1 tag, consisting of class and number, to each data element. The BER formats are further described in this chapter's Technical Reference section. The standards say little about the techniques for converting to and from the transfer syntax. This is a local issue for each implementation.

   OSI thus offers a way to both *describe data independent of how it is represented* in any particular product, and a *standardized transfer syntax* for the transmission of data between systems. The approach chosen is to negotiate a transfer syntax for each abstract syntax, either the standard transfer syntax (BER) or a private one. The syntax used by the originating and receiving application-entities may be the same as or different from the transfer syntax. For example, one partner might use 1's complement notation; and the other might use 2's complement notation. The agreed-upon transfer syntax might be absolute values with sign. If either end uses some syntax, other than the transfer syntax, then a mapping function must be provided to map the user syntax into and/or out of the intervening transfer syntax (see Figure 9.1).

Negotiating the transfer syntax.   The presentation entity at each end is responsible for negotiating an *agreement on the transfer syntax*. During the connection phase, a proposed *context_list* and a counter-proposed *context_result_list* (accepting or rejecting each item in the proposed list) are used for this negotiation. There are two key parts to this negotiation: selection of *abstract syntaxes* to be used, from those proposed in the context list; then for each selected abstract syntax, selection of a *transfer syntax* to be used, from the list proposed for that abstract syntax. Those syntaxes proposed by the initiator of the connection, and also accepted by the responder, will be the basis of the *defined_context_list*. The combination of the two user's abstract syntax and a transfer syntax is called the **presentation context**. The contexts are identified by integers (presentation context identifiers) that are used with each transferred data value. User-defined names are one possible user interface, but are not part of the standard.

A **default_context** is one that is always known, and is resorted to when the *defined_context_list* is empty. During the data transfer phase, the data is passed between application-entities using the *defined_context* set. This becomes the *default_context* set if the defined set is empty. In the case of expedited data, however, the data always is passed using the *default_context*.

OSI presentation functions.   Only three functional units are unique to the OSI presentation services:

1. *Presentation Kernel*—Kernel is most of the presentation layer. It makes it possible to negotiate a set of presentation contexts at association set-up time, and to perform syntax conversion on user data of all session primitives. *Each context specifies the abstract syntax of the user's data and the transfer syntax to be used in transmitting that user data.*

2. *Context management*—This makes it possible to change the context set during the course of a connection.

3. *Context restoration*—This arranges the restoration of the appropriate context after resynchronization. Allowance is made for the changes in context during the life of the connection, so the correct context is applied to the restored dialog.

Presentation primitives and Protocol Data Units (PDUs).   The OSI presentation primitives, with their parameters, and the presentation PDUs are listed in this chapter's Technical Reference section. Note that the presentation-context parameters are carried in the P-Connect primitives and the connection PPDUs. Most of the other presentation primitives are session related and are passed through the presentation layer to the session layer. The related primitives of the Association Control Service Element (ACSE) are given in the Technical Reference section of Chapter 8.

9.2.4   SNA Presentation Services

In the following, we discuss those parts of the SNA presentation services that deal with information interchange.

Data mapping.   The SNA approach is simply to allow users to transmit data in the network data format that is most suitable to them. If the receiver needs a different data format, only then is a data mapping made. Typically, no mapping at all is required; often mapping occurs at only one end, and rarely is mapping needed at both ends. However, SNA also allows a standard transfer syntax, such as ASN.1 BER.

User-supplied maps to transform the data as the application needs it, can be simple (like converting ASCII to EBCDIC) or highly complex. Only the access to the mapping function is architected, not the maps themselves. The mapping function is carried out by a presentation services component, appropriately called the *mapper*.

To identify the map to be used at the sending end (prior to transmission), a **map_name** is supplied by the sending transaction program. The sending-end mapper performs the corresponding data transformations. The further mapping at the receiving end also needs an identification of which map to use there. That might, in simpler cases, be the same name used at the sending end, which can be transferred on the conversation. The GDS representation of the map name is called a *map_name_GDS-Variable* (with the corresponding *GDS_id* field).

Mapping continues until the map_names are changed. The mapper at each LU retains and uses the most recent map_names, which remain valid until changed by another *map_name_GDS-variable*.

General Data Stream (GDS)   [SC31-6808]. In SNA, the application program typically uses whatever record size makes sense for the application and the buffers available to the application. Moreover, application records may be of diverse formats, from noncontiguous data to noncoded data to digitized voice. To facilitate full connectivity among programs written for different applications in different processors, *the inter-node data transfers are made independent of the application record size and format variations* (as is done in OSI also).

GDS-Variables enable all kinds of transaction programs to interpret the records they transfer in the same way. When user data cannot fit in the biggest buffer that the mapper can send, the mapper splits the one record into many logical records. The logical records with a GDS type-id is called a *GDS-variable*.

The *GDS-Variable* is formed as in Figure 9.2. The **General Data Stream** format is primarily a length indicator, a type-id field, and a data field. The 2-byte type-id field tags the data and specifies whether the record contains user data or a *map_name*. The record is subdivided into smaller segments, called logical records. As shown in Figure 9.2, each logical record is then given its own 2-byte *Logical-record Length-indicator* (LL field).

The first record contains the LL field with the continuation bit set on, the user-data type-id, and the first part of the user data. After that, the mapper sends the rest of the data as LL and data. If there is more data, the LL has the continuation bit set on.

The transformation from application data records to GDS-Variables is performed by the mapped-conversation component of the LU. That is done after first performing any program-specified mapping of the data record. All this transformation, from application records to GDS-variables, is, however, mercifully hidden from the application programmer.

The SNA GDS-variables and OSI ASN.1 BER encodings are very similar. Both are tagged, length-specified representations, and they differ mainly in the details of representation. ASN.1 does define universal types, but that could also be done for GDS.

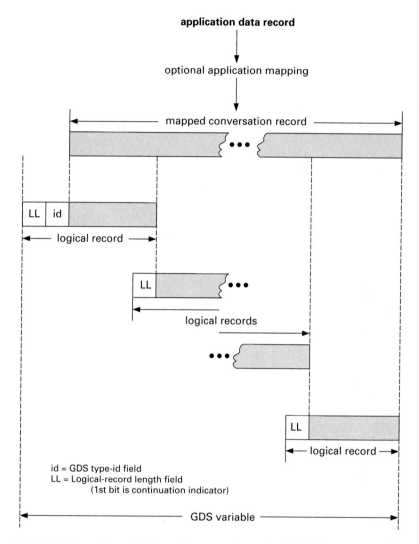

Figure 9.2 Relation of application data records to the GDS data stream [SC31-6808].

PS headers.   When the LL field of a logical record contains a unique value, it can signal that the contents of the following logical record contain control information. One of the uses made of this so-called *PS header* is to indicate that the following record contains sync point related commands,[1] used in resource-recovery (see Section 5.3.).

---

1.   Examples of sync-point-related headers are: `Committed`, `Prepare`, `Request_Commit`, and `Forget`.

9.3   SNA SESSIONS

9.3.1   Session Overview

Purpose.   The execution of a session is analogous to a communication between two or more people *who are equipped to understand each other*. Multiple serial conversations may be carried out in this communication. Eventually, one of the two groups decides to terminate the connection, and perhaps start a communication with some other group of persons.

An example of this is the case of a bank official at a branch location, who initiates a session with an application program for new accounts at a central location. The official processes a whole series of different new account transactions (each one involving a short conversation) over an extended period of time. The official might then terminate that session and initiate a different one, to a different application, dealing with a loan or investment. Another series of different loan transactions may proceed within the second session. It should be emphasized that a new session is not always required for a new transaction program. In many cases, an application subsystem (such as IMS or CICS) provides access to multiple transaction programs without requiring the establishment of a new session. Multiple conversations can then be held, serially, with multiple transaction programs, on the same session.

Session content.   The SNA session is characterized by the sets of functions chosen to provide end-to-end services. A user of LU 6.2, for example, chooses options at session establishment time and by using certain verbs or parameters on verbs at the LU API.

The session protocols.   Because each session may serve very different users, the functions that help effective data exchange often need to be unique for each session. A partial list of such options (for which protocols are needed) includes the following.

1.   Presentation services
     - Data conversion (data syntax translation)
     - Mapping
2.   Data flow control
     - Sequence number assignment
     - Brackets around a work scope (e.g., a transaction)
     - Chaining of requests, after which an acknowledgment is required
     - Request/response correlation
     - "My turn, then your turn" send/receive controls
3.   Transmission control
     - Maintenance of proper sequence (via numbering of messages)
     - Encryption and decryption
     - Control of expedited and normal flows
     - Pacing (that is, message flow-rate control)

Transmission control, a layer-4 function within the SNA session, is discussed in Chapter 14 when we discuss the SNA transport-service-provider.

9.3.2   Synchronization

Every message entering or exiting the layer-3 network is referred to in SNA as a *request (RQ)* or a *response (RSP)*. For each request there *may* be a *response*. The response message may only acknowledge receipt of a request; however, the semantics is entirely up to the application. The response can mean much more if the application wants it to. The response does not reply to a request. The reply to the request (if there is one) will take the form of a new request, sent back to the originating LU.

The acknowledgment (positive or negative) is not limited to an acknowledgment of mere reception by the **half-session** (a term meaning the combination of the data-flow-control and transmission-control layers at one end of a session). Further checking may be involved at higher layers prior to sending a response. Some responses must await authorization from application-services or the application-process. The checks made at these levels are open-ended. In some cases, for example, validity checks on the format might be made; in other cases, the response may be negative because of an inability to accept a command. The response, therefore, is used as a general-purpose acknowledgment from the receiver that the sender of the request may (or may not) proceed. A negative response returns sense data.[2]

Each request or response contains a **Request/Response Header (RH)** and the unit of information that is intended to flow between the two LUs. In SNA this latter unit of information is called the **Request/Response Unit (RU)**. Thus, the request or response generally consists of an RH and an RU.

All the protocols that accompany each request and each response are governed by the contents of the RH. The RH contains the protocol indicators for both data flow control and transmission control. By careful bit encoding, these controls are packed into only three bytes. (The format of the RH is given in Figure 9.7 in this chapter's Technical Reference section.)

Definite response.   Recall from Section 5.3.4 that the Common Programming Interface CPI-C includes a `Confirm`, which requires an acknowledgment. The execution of this call, within the LU, causes the sending of a *definite response indicator (DRI)* in the request header (RH). The request receiver must return either (1) a positive response to accept the request or (2) a negative response to reject the request.

Exception response.   If a request specifies an exception response, the request receiver returns a negative response for any unacceptable requests, and does not return any positive responses. The exception response protocol is identified by an *exception response indicator (ERI)* in the RH.

---

2.   The sense data may identify the reason for a negative response. However, with LU 6.2, if the negative response was sent because of a `Send_Error` verb (issued by the application), the application should issue `Send_Data` to indicate the real reason for the negative response.

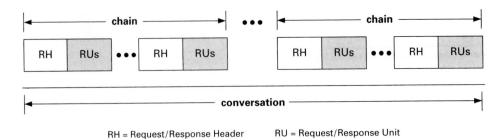

RH = Request/Response Header   RU = Request/Response Unit

Figure 9.3 A series of chains within a conversation, as seen by a Logical Unit.

9.3.3 Chains

Chains are a series of requests that are treated as a unit of recovery. An LU sets indicators in the RH to identify the beginning and end of a chain. The *begin chain indicator (BCI)* is set in the RH of the first request; and the *end chain indicator (ECI)* is set in the RH of the last request of a chain. Both the *BCI* and *ECI* are set in the RH of a single-element chain. Figure 9.3 illustrates a series of chains in a conversation, as seen by an LU.

In a **definite response chain**, the sending LU sets the *ERI* in the RH of all but the last request of a chain; it sets the *DRI* in the RH of the last request in a chain. After receiving the last request in a chain, the receiving LU returns there a positive response to acknowledge that the entire chain is acceptable, if the receiving application issued the verb `Confirmed`. If any one of the chain elements is unacceptable, a negative response is returned.

In an **exception response chain**, the *ERI* is set in the RH of every request in a chain. No positive responses are sent; but a negative response is sent if any of the requests in a chain are unacceptable.

9.3.4 Brackets

Brackets identify a sequence of request chains and responses exchanged in either direction. Brackets are used to mark the beginning and end of conversations, discussed in Section 7.4. Following the `Initialize_Conversation` and `Allocate` calls at the Common Programming Interface, CPI-C, an LU sets a *begin bracket indictor (BBI)* in the RH of the first request of the first chain of a bracket. This identifies the beginning of a conversation. Following the `Deallocate` call at the CPI-C, an LU 6.2 sets the *conditional end bracket indicator (CEBI)* in the RH of the last request in the last chain of the bracket.[3] This identifies the end of the conversation.

---

3.   LUs other than type 6.2 use end bracket indicators (*EBIs*), not conditional end bracket indictors (*CEBIs*) to identify the end of a bracket.

9.3.5   Function Management Headers

A Function Management (FM) header is an optional field at the beginning of a request unit (RU) that carries control information from logical units. LU 6.2 uses three types of FM headers:

- An *Attach FM header* to specify the name and required characteristics of a target transaction program

- A *security FM header* to carry LU-LU session password verification data

- An *error-description FM header* to describe a transaction program error or an attach failure

- A *Backout FM header*, used with resource-recovery (see Section 5.3) is one of the error-description FM headers

A *format indicator (FI)* in the request header (RH) identifies whether the request unit contains any FM headers. (The format of the FM header itself is given in Figure 9.8 in this chapter's Technical Reference section.)

Presentation headers.   In the case of sync point, the FM header format is not used. Instead, the format of the GDS variable is used with the LL field set to a value of 1. All LLs that indicate a length less than 2 are reserved for use by the LU. (The format of the PS header is shown in Figure 9.9 in the Technical Reference section for this chapter.)

9.4   OSI SESSION LAYER

9.4.1   Primary Session Functions

The OSI session layer contains functions that are partially comparable to those in the SNA Data Flow Control layer. The primary OSI session-layer functions (which OSI only helps the user to perform) are:

- Managing the *direction of data flow*, using half-duplex (two-way alternate), or full-duplex (two-way simultaneous) interaction

- Helping the user to set *message synchronization-points in a data stream*, and to resynchronize to those points when necessary

- Managing the interruption of a dialog, and the later *resumption of a dialog* at a pre-arranged point

The message flows are controlled by session services in a conservative manner. For example, though the release of a connection may be abrupt at the lower layers, the session-layer release is meant to be more orderly. When a release of a connection is requested, it is delayed until all outstanding Session Service Data Units (the flows across the PS-Session boundary) have been delivered, in both directions, if possible.

The session connection establishes the session-layer services to be employed in an association. At any instant, each session connection has one and only one transport connection. However, different session connections can sequentially use the same transport connection, and each session connection could sequentially make use of different transport connections.

9.4.2   Tokens

There are situations where it is best if only one of the two partners in an interchange has the right to take certain actions, at a given time. For example, half-duplex flows is a mechanism to enforce the behavior where only one partner may send at one time. In OSI, these situations are managed by the use of **tokens**. Only one of the two partners in a conversation can have a particular token at one time. Possession of a token by an entity means that it is permitted to do the associated action. The token may be passed, however, from one partner to the other. The four types of tokens are:

- *Data token*: used to manage one-at-a-time transmissions, in half-duplex connections
- *Minor-synchronization token*: giving one partner the ability to set minor message-synchronization-points for the conversation
- *Major-sync/Activity token*: giving one partner the ability to set major message-sync points, and to manage the grouping of messages, called an **Activity**
- *Release token*: used to govern the release of a connection

Three Session Protocol Data Units (SPDUs) provide flexibility in the use of tokens:

- Give_Token—allows a user who is a holder of a token to pass it to the other user
- Please_Token—allows a user who does not have a token to request it
- Give_Tokens_Confirm—allows the transfer of all tokens to the other partner

Any token can be present or absent from an association, depending on the functions of the session layer that have been selected for use on the association. Tokens are possessed at four levels: (1) data, (2) sync-minor, (3) sync-major/Activity, and (4) release. Control is conveyed by this hierarchy. That is, to use the function permitted by a given token, the local application-process must own it and all tokens that are present below it.

9.4.3   Synchronization

OSI sync points are mechanisms for the synchronization of data flows between two communicating partners. Acknowledgments at sync points, using sequence numbers of messages, are involved. (Note that this corresponds to *definite response* in SNA, see Section 9.3.2.)

Minor synchronization point.   This facility supports the end user in establishing synchronization points within the sequence of message flows. The decision as to where a sync point should be established is a user decision. If the user desires, *an acknowledgment from the receiver may be required at a minor synchronization point*.

Major synchronization point.   With this facility, the user can completely separate the flow into a series of units, each of which is ended with a major sync point. An example of such a unit would be a transaction, a file being transmitted, or a chapter of text. *Each such unit must be explicitly acknowledged* after a major sync point. Further data flows cease until this is accomplished. Both major and minor sync points have an associated serial number, to maintain sequence synchronization.

Resynchronization. Upon the request of either user of session services, the session flows can be re-established starting at some prior message-sync point. This may be at the last major sync point or one of the later minor sync points. The session resynchronization service is only an aid to the user. It does not save transmitted messages; and it does not manage recovery. It primarily provides a marking facility for the user, as an aid for recovery procedures in the application or the application-services. Session services marks the data stream, as directed by the user, and applies a serial number. When resynchronization occurs, the serial number is reset back to the resynchronization point. The session layer service primitives for resynchronization are derived from the corresponding presentation-layer service primitives, whose parameters are listed in the Technical Reference section.

9.4.4 Activities

A series of message units, separated by major sync points, can be grouped into an **Activity**, as illustrated in Figure 9.4. *The significant characteristic of an Activity is that it may be interrupted and continued at a later time.* The sync point sequence numbers will be remembered, so that data flows will remain synchronized. The Activity can be resumed at the last sync point. For example, if a large file is being sent, and one end of the Activity needs to interrupt the process, then the Activity can be resumed later at the last major synchronization point. However, it is still the responsibility of the session-user to save data or context needed for the resumption. Multiple sequential Activities can be held within a single session connection. The standard also allows an Activity to span multiple sessions. The session-layer service primitives for Activity control (`Activity_Start`, `Interrupt`, `Resume`, `End`, and `Discard`) are derived directly from the corresponding presentation-layer service primitives, whose parameters are listed in this chapter's Technical Reference section.

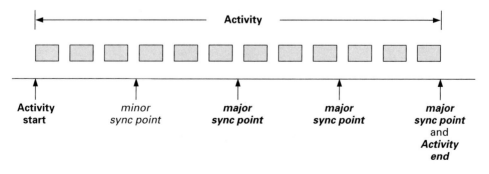

Figure 9.4 Major sync points within an Activity.

9.4.5 Data

Four data variations have been defined. In addition to the commonly understood **normal data** and **expedited data**,[4] there are **typed data** and **capability data**. Typed data is used for control messages that will be sent even when the data token (giving permission to send) is with the other end. Typed data may be required, for example, on the occurrence of an event that needs immediate attention, such as system management alerts. Capability data applies when partners are using the *Activity* facility. Capability data enables users to avoid the overhead of always setting up an Activity, and instead, allows users to send small amounts of data when no Activity has been arranged.

9.5 OSI PRIMITIVES AND PDUS

Flows of primitives.   Primitives are the semantically defined flows of information across layer boundaries—for example, between the presentation and session layers. Presentation service must offer the application all features needed by the application, regardless of which lower layer actually implements these features. Presentation-layer primitives therefore must contain information that is needed for operations in lower layers. These primitives include session-control actions, such as tokens, synchronization, Activities, and exception reports. Starting as presentation primitives, information progresses to and through the presentation and session layers all the way to the transport layer. While the presentation layer transforms data on every primitive, only a minority of its primitives involve presentation protocols and thus deserve PPDUs. For most primitives, the presentation layer transforms the user data, if any, and passes the request through to the session layer. There, the Session Protocol Data Units (SPDUs) reflect the control functions done in the session layer.

The `S-Connect` primitive contains parameters for synchronization and token management initialization. The `S-Connect` also inherits as parameters all the information that must be passed down to make a Transport Connection. This includes parameters for a *quality_of_service*. They are defined almost identical to the parameters in the `T-Connect` primitive for the connection-oriented transport services. For the most part, these parameters are simply passed down to the transport service.

Session PDUs.   The session PDUs come in six categories: a kernel set concerned primarily with session connections, a token set, a set of special data PDUs, synchronize PDUs, those for control of Activities, and exception-reporting PDUs. A complete list of SPDUs, with the parameters in each, is given in this chapter's Technical Reference section.

9.6 OSI/SNA COMPARABLE FUNCTIONS

It is not possible to make very precise correlations between OSI and SNA end-to-end functions. For every similarity, one can find some exceptions or other differences. The following analogs, therefore, are not the only possible ones; and the corre-

---

4. Expedited data carries an implied request that it be placed ahead in intervening transmission queues when possible.

sponding functions are not always identical to each other. Nevertheless, the functions are very similar in some very important ways. Consider the following approximate analogs:

- *A name that identifies an application-process*:
    - *SAA*: **symbolic_destination_name** (a local alias)
    - *SNA*: **Network-qualified LU_name** (global Net_id.LU_name)
    - *OSI*: **application_entity_title**
    - These names can be used by applications to refer to a partner. However, the SAA sym_dest_name is only a local alias, whereas the application_entity_title and the Net_id.LU_name are globally unique. The sym_dest_name could be used as an alias for either an SNA LU_name or an OSI application_entity_title.

- *An interactive communication between two transaction programs*:
    - *SNA*: **conversation**
    - *OSI*: **TP dialog**
    - From the viewpoint of transaction processing, the SNA *conversation* is analogous to the OSI *dialog*. A conversation couples two transaction programs, which then have a peer relationship for a synchronous exchange of data. A dialog similarly connects TP-Service-Users. The IBM OSI/Communications Subsystem assigns dialogs to associations (and so stimulates P-Connects, S-Connects, and T-Connects, at the corresponding three layers). This is similar to the way in which SNA assigns conversations to sessions dynamically. There is a one-to-one correspondence between dialog and association, just as between conversation and session, *at any given time*. The dialog or conversation may end, and the association or session lives on, to support another dialog or conversation at a later time.

- *An end-to-end logical connection, whose use requires the establishment of two sets of end-to-end data-exchange facilities* (which are then available for sequential use by conversations or dialogs):
    - *SNA*: **session**
    - *OSI*: **association**
    - From the viewpoint of the service each provides, the analog of the SNA *session* is the OSI *association*. The user achieves an end-to-end logical connection by requesting this service. This appears to be an intuitive and very useful analogy. However, from a total protocol point of view, the SNA session is more analogous to a combination of the OSI A-association, P-connection, S-connection, and the T-connection. One can argue that the association needs all these end-to-end connections in order to function, just as the session needs corresponding relationships in each of its layers 4 through 7.

    There are other differences. Strictly speaking, the association can exist without a transport connection; and the transport connection can live on beyond the end of an OSI session-layer connection and be reused by a different session-layer connection later on. There is no corresponding characteristic in SNA.

- *Commands that trigger the set-up of the end-to-end services for a session or association*:

  - *SNA*: **Bind** request
  - *OSI*: **A-Associate** plus P-Connect, S-Connect, and T-Connect request
  - The SNA Bind asks for the establishment of an SNA session, which is analogous to the transport-connection-request asking for a transport connection. The transport connection, moreover, is followed by upper-layer connections as well. Therefore, the completion of the Bind is analogous to completion of the T-Connect, *plus the following* S-Connect, P-Connect, *and* A-Associate.

- *A command that identifies and may load a remote transaction program as target for a conversation or dialog:*

  - *SNA*: **Attach**[5]
  - *OSI*: **TP-Begin_Dialog**
  - The resources allocated in SNA at Attach are roughly comparable to the resources assigned in OSI at TP-Begin_Dialog.

- *A mechanism for requiring a response from the partner, at the end of a series of messages, before proceeding further*:

  - *SNA*: **end-of-chain**
  - *OSI*: **sync point**
  - SNA *end-of-chain* and OSI *sync point* are comparable in that they both can require a response before continuing further.[6] Note that the term *sync point* is used differently in the two architectures. Both SNA and OSI synchronize the flow of *messages*. OSI uses the term sync point on this occasion, but SNA does not use the term sync point in that context. Both SNA and OSI synchronize the flows to *resources* such as databases. Both use sync points for this occasion.

- *A mechanism for requesting a turn to speak, in half-duplex operation:*

  - *SNA*: **Signal**
  - *OSI*: **Please_Data_Token**

- *A mechanism for giving the other partner a turn to speak, in half-duplex operation*:

  - *SNA*: **Change_Direction_Indicator**
  - *OSI*: **Give_Data_Token**

- *A set of commands for synchronizing, insuring integrity, and facilitating recovery, in distributed operations*:

  - *SNA*: **Resource-Recovery and sync point**
  - *OSI*: **Commitment, Concurrency, and Recovery**
  - See Section 5.3

---

5. The Attach command has an implied "load and execute" semantic to it, but some products implement the capability to have the program instance predetermined and preloaded.

6. The term *dialog-unit* is used for a number of Session PDUs that is terminated by a major sync point (or Activity-end), and always requires a definite response at its completion.

Conclusion

End-to-end communication is only possible if both ends partake of like functions and architecture at layers 5 and 6. The SNA and OSI *end-to-end data-exchange architectures* are both comprehensive and strong. Each has a multitude of options. Although concentration on fewer options occurs, and increased commonality can be foreseen, there will have to be multiple options and multiple optimizations for specific circumstances. Parts of the architectures, for example, become incorporated into the four approaches of Figure 3.14: APPC (conversational), OS/TP (dialogs), Remote Procedure Call (RPC), and Messaging.

The upper boundary of these layer 5 and 6 facilities is the Application Programming Interface (API) at the presentation service interface. The development of the *Common Programming Interface* (see Section 7.4.2) for multiple-communication stacks is accordingly key to reducing the burdens on application programmers. In general, there is a set of very similar capabilities in the data-exchange facilities of SNA and OSI facilities. These similarities support the feasibility of network independence at the Common Programming Interface for Communications (CPI-C).

Some of the key features of these two data-exchange layers (5 and 6) are:

- The OSI *presentation context* helps to insure understanding between dissimilar end users. Each context, agreed upon at the time an association is established, specifies the abstract syntax of the user's data and the transfer syntax used in the transmission of that data.

- The SNA functions (synchronization, chains, brackets, PS headers, and FM headers) support the CPI-C and CPI-RR calls for robust conversations of distributed application-processes.

- The OSI session-layer functions (tokens and sync points,) manage the flows and synchronization in a manner very similar to that in SNA. The Activity function is more distinct.

Acknowledgments

I am particularly indebted to Jerry Mouton and A. P. Citron for valuable input or reviews of portions of this chapter.

TECHNICAL REFERENCES

The following summaries are presented to aid understanding. Because standards change, however, the reader is cautioned to consult up-to-date standards for all implementation work.

Abstract Syntax Notation 1 (ASN.1) Tags

- Universal 1 *BOOLEAN*
- Universal 2 *INTEGER*
- Universal 3 *BITSTRING*
- Universal 4 *OCTETSTRING*
- Universal 5 *NULL*

- Universal 6 *OBJECT IDENTIFIER* (associated with an information object)
- Universal 7 *OBJECT DESCRIPTOR*
- Universal 8 *EXTERNAL* (externally defined)
- Universal 9 *REAL*
- Universal 10 *ENUMERATED*
- Universal 11–15 *Reserved for future use*
- Universal 16 *SEQUENCE* and *SEQUENCE OF* (a structured type, referencing an ordered list of types)
- Universal 17 *SET* and *SET OF* (a structured type, referencing an unordered list of types)
- Universal 18–27 Character string types:

18 - *NumericString*;	19 - *PrintableString*;
20 - *TeletexString*;	21 - *VideotexString*
22 - *IA5String*;	25 - *GraphicString*;
26 - *VisibleString*;	27 - *GeneralString*

- Universal 23 *UTCTime* (Greenwich mean time)
- Universal 24 *GeneralizedTime* (date, time of day, local time differential)
- Universal 28 *Reserved for future use*

ASN.1 Definitions

ASN.1 definitions have the general form:

```
<module name>DEFINITIONS::=BEGIN<module body>END
```

where module name and module body are place keepers to be filled with the actual name and the actual text definition. For example, part of a module body might be:

```
ConfirmPDU ::= SEQUENCE {SessionID INTEGER,
Result INTEGER {completion(0), error(1) }}
```

There, the type name is ConfirmPDU, and the definition is SEQUENCE, with a list of two types. Not only is the "result" defined as an integer, but meaning is given to two values of that type. The "named number list" in the inner brackets provides mnemonic identifiers for particular values (0 and 1) of the result.

Basic Encoding Rules (BER)

In this encoding scheme [ISO-8825], each data element has three components, shown in Figure 9.5: the identifier, length, and contents.

The *identifier* octets are used to encode the ASN.1 tag assigned to the type of data value being encoded. The first two bits of the octet (bits 8 and 7) are used to denote the *class* of the tag. Bit 6, a form field, tells whether the element being encoded is primitive or constructed. A primitive element has no further nested elements. A constructed element contains a series of subelements. The *number* of the tag is encoded in bits 5 through 1. That subdivision of the BER identifier is also shown in Figure 9.5. If the tag number is less than or equal to 30, only one identifier byte is needed.

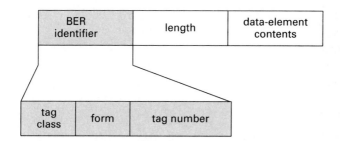

Figure 9.5 Structure of BER encoding.

However, if the tag number is more than 30, then multiple bytes are used. The first bit of each successive id byte indicates whether it is the last id byte, and 7 bits of each byte are used for the tag number.

The *length indicator* is one byte, unless bit 8 is 1, indicating a string of bytes for the length indicator. In that case, the 7 bits of the first byte tells the number of bytes in the length indicator.

The *contents field* of the BER encodes the value of the data element. The data value may be an arbitrary complex, with nested structure, as shown in Figure 9.6. Note that an id field and a length field precedes each encoding of a data-element segment.

OSI Presentation Service-Primitives

All the presentation service-primitives, except `P-Connect`, `P-Release`, `P-Abort`, and `P-Alter_Context`, correspond to session-layer primitives of the same name. These session-layer primitives concern data, tokens, synchronization, resynchronization, exception reports, and activities. In the following, each presentation service-primitive is listed along with its parameters. The columns on the right indicate whether a parameter is carried in the request (Req), indication (Ind), response (Rsp), or confirm (Conf) flows at the service interfaces of the presentation layer.

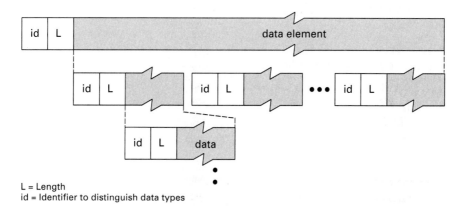

L = Length
id = Identifier to distinguish data types

Figure 9.6 ASN.1/BER encoding of the data element.

	Req	Ind	Rsp	Conf
CONNECTION PRIMITIVES				
P-Connect	X	X	X	X
▪ *calling_PSAP*	X	X		
▪ *called_PSAP*	X	X		
▪ *responding_PSAP*			X	X
▪ *mode*	X	X		
▪ *context_definition_list*	X	X		
▪ *default_context_name*	X	X		
▪ *context_definition_result_list*		X	X	X
▪ *default_context_result*			X	X
▪ *presentation_requirements*	X	X	X	X
▪ *result*			X	X
▪ *session_id*	X	X	X	X
▪ *serial_number*	X	X	X	X
▪ *token_assignment*	X	X	X	X
▪ *session_requirements*	X	X	X	X
▪ *quality_of_service*	X	X	X	X
▪ data	X	X	X	X
P-Release	X	X	X	X
▪ *result*			X	X
▪ data	X	X	X	X
P-U_Abort	X	X		
▪ data	X	X		
P-P_Abort		X		
▪ *reason*		X		
CONTEXT PRIMITIVE				
P-Alter_Context	X	X	X	X
▪ *context_addition_list*	X	X		
▪ *context_deletion_list*	X	X		
▪ *context_addition_result_list*		X	X	X
▪ *context_deletion_result_list*			X	X
▪ data	X	X	X	X
DATA PRIMITIVES (session related)				
P-Typed_Data	X	X		
▪ data	X	X		
P-Data	X	X		
▪ data	X	X		
P-Expedited_Data	X	X		
▪ data	X	X		
P-Capability_Data	X	X	X	X
▪ data	X	X	X	X
TOKEN PRIMITIVES (session related)				
P-Token_Give	X	X		
▪ *tokens*	X	X		

	Req	Ind	Rsp	Conf
P-Token_Please	x	x		
▪ *tokens*	x	x		
▪ data	x	x		
P-Control_Give	x	x		

SYNCHRONIZE PRIMITIVES (session related)

	Req	Ind	Rsp	Conf
P-Sync_Minor	x	x	x	x
▪ *type*	x	x		
▪ *serial_number*	x	x	x	x
▪ data	x	x	x	x
P-Sync_Major	x	x	x	x
▪ *serial_number*	x	x		
▪ data	x	x	x	x
P-Resynchronize	x	x	x	x
▪ *type*	x	x		
▪ *serial_number*	x	x	x	x
▪ *tokens*	x	x	x	x
▪ *context_id_list*		x		x
▪ data	x	x	x	x
P-U_Exception_Report	x	x		
▪ *reason*	x	x		
▪ data	x	x		
P-P_Exception_Report		x		
▪ *reason*		x		

ACTIVITY PRIMITIVES (session related)

	Req	Ind	Rsp	Conf
P-Activity_Start	x	x		
▪ *activity_id*	x	x		
▪ data	x	x		
P-Activity_Resume	x	x		
▪ *activity_id*	x	x		
▪ *old_activity_id*	x	x		
▪ *serial_number*	x	x		
▪ *old_session_id*	x	x		
▪ data	x	x		
P-Activity_End	x	x	x	x
▪ *serial_number*	x	x		
▪ data	x	x	x	x
P-Activity_Interrupt	x	x	x	x
▪ *reason*	x	x		
P-Activity_Discard	x	x	x	x
▪ *reason*	x	x		

Most parameters of the presentation-service primitives are passed to the session layer. The quality of service parameter is passed first to the session layer and then to the transport layer. The parameters used by the presentation layer, and not passed to the session layer, are:

- *context_definition_list*: lists the identifier and name of each context to be used
- *context_definition_result_list*: indicates acceptance or rejection of each item in the context_definition_list
- *multiple_defined_contexts*: notes that the defined context set may contain more than one context at one time
- *default_context_name*: identifies the context to be used in the absence of a selection, and for expedited data
- *default_context_result*: identifies the context that was agreed to or rejected by the other partner
- *presentation_requirements*: selects the context management and context restoration functional units

OSI Presentation PDUs and Parameters

Following the practice in the standards, we list below the PPDUs, their parameters, and also the related parameters, marked with an asterisk, that are passed directly to the session layer.

CONNECTION PDUs
Connect

- *calling_PSAP*
- *called_PSAP*
- *multiple_defined_contexts*
- *context_definition_list*
- *default_context*
- *protocol_version*
- *presentation_requirements*
- *user_session_requirements*
- user data

- *calling_SSAP**
- *called_SSAP**
- *session_connection_id**
- *serial_number**
- *token_assignment**
- *revised_session_requirements**
- *quality_of_service**
- *mode*

Connect_Accept

- *responding_PSAP*
- *multiple_defined_contexts*
- *context_result_list*
- *default_context_result*
- *protocol_version*
- *presentation_requirements*
- *user_session_requirement*
- user data

- *session_connection_id**
- *responding_SSAP**
- *serial_number**
- *token_assignment**
- *revised_session_requirements**
- *quality_of_service**
- *mode*

Connect_Reject

- *responding_PSAP*
- *context_result_list*
- *default_context_result*
- user data

- *responding_SSAP**
- *quality_of_service**
- *session_requirements**
- *protocol_version*

Abnormal_Release_User

- *context_identifier_list*
- user data

Abnormal_Release_Provider

- *provider_reason*
- *abort_data*

CONTEXT PDUs

Alter_Context

- *context_addition_list*
- *context_identifier_deletion_list*
- user data

Alter_Context_Ack

- *context_addition_result_list*
- *context_deletion_result_list*
- user data

DATA PDUs

Typed_Data

- user data

Data

- user data

Expedited_Data

- user data

Capability_Data

- user data

Capability_Data_Ack

- user data

SYNCHRONIZE PDUs

Resynchronize

- *context_identifier_list*
- *type**
- *serial_number**
- *tokens**
- user data

Resynchronize_Ack

- *context_identifier_list*
- *serial_number*
- *tokens**
- user data

SNA Request/Response Header (RH)

The format of the Request/Response Header (RH) [LY43-0081] is given in Figure 9.7. To distinguish between a request and a response, examine bit 0 of byte 0 of the RH.

Request

| RR1 = 0 | RU category | r | FI | SDI | BCI | ECI | DR1I | r | DR2I | ERI | r | RLWI | QRI | PI | BBI | EBI | CDI | r | CSI | EDI | PDI | CEBI |

Response byte 0 · · · · · · · · · · · · byte 1 · · · · · · · · · · · · byte 2

| RR1 = 1 | RU category | r | FI | SDI | 1 | 1 | DR1I | r | DR2I | RTI | r | r | QRI | PI | r | r | r | r | r | r | r | r |

r = reserved

Field   Description

BBI = Begin Bracket Indicator
BCI = Begin Chain Indicator
DR1I = Definite Response 1 Indicator
DR2I = Definite Response 2 Indicator
CDI = Change Direction Indicator
CEBI = Conditional End Bracket Indicator
CSI = Code Selection Indicator
EBI = End Bracket Indicator
ECI = End Chain Indicator
EDI = Enciphered Data Indicator
ERI = Exception Response Indicator

Field   Description

FI = Format Indicator (FM header or NS header)
PDI = Padded Data Indicator
PI = Pacing Indicator
QRI = Queued Response Indicator
RLWI = Request Larger Window Indicator
RRI = Request/Response Indicator
RTI = Response Type Indicator
RU category = Request/Response Unit category (FM, network control, data flow control, session control)
SDI = Sense Data Included Indicator

Figure 9.7 RH formats [LY43-0081].

FM and PS Header Formats

The formats for the function management headers and the related presentation services headers are shown in Figures 9.8 and 9.9.

Session PDUs

KERNEL PDUs

Connect (Initiate session connection)

- *calling_SSAP*
- *called_SSAP*
- *connection_id*

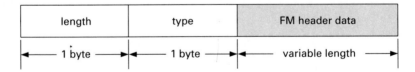

| length | type | FM header data |

|←—— 1 byte ——→|←—— 1 byte ——→|←—— variable length ——→|

Figure 9.8 Function Management (FM) header format.

Figure 9.9 Presentation services (PS) header format.

- *serial_number*
- *token_setting*
- *user_requirements*
- *protocol_options*
- *version_number*
- *maximum_TSDU_size*
- user data

Accept (Accept session connection)

- same as Connect

Refuse (Refuse to accept connection)

- *version_number*
- *transport_disconnect*
- *connection_id*
- *reason*
- *user_requirements*

Finish (Request orderly termination)

- *transport_disconnect*
- user data

Disconnect (Agree to orderly termination)

- user data

Not_Finished (Reject orderly termination)

- user data

Abort (Unplanned connection release)

- *transport_disconnect*
- *protocol_error_code*
- user data

Abort_Accept (Accept the Abort initiative)

Data_Transfer (Normal data transfer)

- *enclosure_item*
- user data

TOKEN PASSING PDUs

Give_Tokens (Pass token to partner)

- *tokens*

`Please_Tokens` (Request passing of token)

- *tokens*
- user data

`Give_Tokens_Confirm` (Transfer all tokens)

`Give_Tokens_Ack` (Acknowledge all tokens)

SPECIAL DATA PDUs

`Expedited_Data` (Expedited data transfer)

- user data

`Typed_Data` (Typed data transfer)

- *enclosure_item*
- user data

`Capability_Data` (Capability data transfer)

- user data

`Cap_Data_Ack` (Capability data acknowledge)

- user data

SYNCHRONIZE PDUs

`Minor_Sync_point` (Set minor sync point)

- *confirm_flag*
- *serial_number*
- user data

`Minor_Sync_Ack` (Acknowledge minor sync point)

- *serial_number*
- user data

`Major_Sync_point` (Set major sync point)

- *end_Activity_flag*
- *serial_number*
- user data

`Major_Sync_Ack` (Acknowledge major sync point)

- *serial_number*
- user data

`Resynchronize` (Serial numbers)

- *token_settings*
- *resync_type*
- *serial_number*
- user data

`Resync_Ack` (Acknowledge resynchronize)

- *token_settings*
- *serial_number*
- user data

`Prepare` (Notifies of immanent arrival of SPDUs)

- *type*

ACTIVITY MANAGEMENT PDUs

`Activity_Start` (Start of Activity)

- *Activity_id*
- user data

`Activity_Resume` (Resumption of Activity)

- *connection_id*
- *new_Activity_id*
- *old_Activity_id*
- *serial_number*
- user data

`Activity_Interrupt` (Interrupt Activity)

- *reason*

`Activity_Interrupt_Ack` (Acknowledge interrupt)

`Activity-Discard` (Terminate Activity)

- *reason*

`Activ_Disc_Ack` (Acknowledge termination)

`Activity_End` (Signal Activity end)

- *serial_number*
- user data

`Activity_End_Ack` (Acknowledge Activity end)

- *serial_number*
- user data

EXCEPTION PDUs

`Exception_Report`

- reflect parameter values

`Exception_Data`

- *reason*
- user data

EXERCISES

9.1 Define a transfer syntax.

9.2 What is an abstract syntax?

9.3 What is the purpose of the ASN.1 tags?

9.4 Of what is the presentation context composed?

9.5 In SNA, what Call at the CPI triggers the sending of a definite response indicator to get an acknowledgment?

9.6 Give a primary use of the SNA bracket.

9.7 What are the four OSI tokens, and what does possession of a token mean?

9.8 Analogs can be made between which items in the left column and which items in the right column?

Net_id.LU_name	association
A-Associate	*Bind request*
dialog	sync point
Attach	*change_direction_indicator*
session	application_entity_title
Give_Data_Token	*TP-Begin_Dialog*
end-of-chain	conversation

9.9 How are the SNA GDS-variable and the OSI BER encodings similar?

10
SNA Logical Units

10.1 INTRODUCTION

Referring back to the components of an Open Systems Network Architecture (OSNA), in Figure 2.2, we now consider a concrete design of the conversational support shown there as APPC. The architectures of the preceding chapter find practical realization there.

The term *Advanced Program-to-Program Communications (APPC)* refers to the verbs and services embodied in the SNA Logical Unit, *LU 6.2.* That LU supports program-to-program communication in a conversation mode and is a fully developed industry standard. It is the SNA workhorse for synchronous communication. Its verbs are the SNA implementation of the SAA Common Programming Interface CPI-C, plus some other more specialized verbs.

The viewpoint of the LU taken in this chapter is primarily that of the user or the CPI, and other externals, particularly the inter-node protocol data units. While the total LU encompasses a set of end-to-end functions in layers 4, 5, 6, and parts of 7, this chapter primarily focuses on the *end-to-end data-exchange facilities*, which are architected in layers 5 and 6 (see the preceding chapter and Figures 2.2 and 7.2).

An illustration using one particular implementation of LU 6.2, namely APPC/MVS, showing how LU 6.2 is used, is included.

10.2 SNA LOGICAL UNITS

Function of the LU [SC30-3084]. The LU may be thought of as a *location in the SNA network that supports one or more ports for communication via the network.* The LU is relatively fixed, although new ones may be dynamically added. An application-process may always interface to the network through the same LU, or the application-process may move from one LU to another. In more sophisticated situations, an application-process might interface to several LUs concurrently. The position of an LU in the SNA node structure is

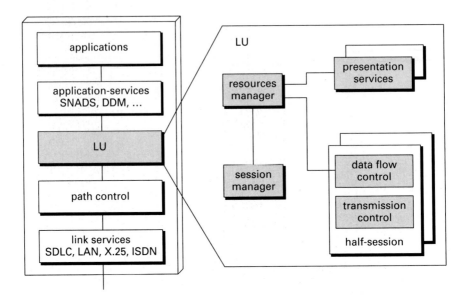

Figure 10.1 Position of an LU in the SNA node structure.

shown in Figure 10.1 [SC30-3269]. The LU content includes:

- *Presentation services*, which are intimately tied to the application-process
- *End-to-end controls*, which are the data flow and transmission controls
- *Session manager*, which is coordinated by a resources manager

Types of LUs.   Early SNA products produced a variety of LU types, each tailored to a particular set of user requirements. These included:

- LU 1—host program to keyboard, printer, card unit, or disk drive
- LU 2—host program to 3270 display
- LU 3—host program to 3270 printer
- LU 4—host program to text processor
- LU 6—general purpose program-to-program

The growth of distributed processing has brought a spectrum of new requirements, such as remote program activation, file transfer, distributed databases, data-update synchronization, document distribution, system management, security, and peer connection among diverse processors. These requirements have been converged, and a new LU 6.2 was created to meet these program-to-program needs [Cypser78].

LU_names.   Each LU has an LU_name. The LU user requesting establishment of a network connection may know the LU_name or a recorded symbolic name of the destination LU (the **symbolic_destination_name**). In the latter case, side information or application-layer directories will provide the LU_name. Since LUs may be in different networks, the network can be identified by a Net_id prefix, giving Net_id.LU_name as the complete identifier.

LU's operating-system support.   Logical Units (LUs), in SNA, are addressable ports in the network. More than that, however, they provide communications-oriented services, much like an operating system, to one or more local application programs. Like other operating system facilities, the LU must perform or arrange for resource allocation. A primary concern is the resources necessary for a session to be established and conducted between two or more partners. The LU may schedule allocation to its own (wholly owned) resources, or coordinate the allocation of shared resources, or arrange for the creation of new copies of resources. The LU may help to control the commitment of the partners to resource changes, such as updates to distributed databases. The LU may, moreover, help to exercise security controls and perform formatting services for its program clients.

10.3   SNA/LU 6.2

While many of the earlier LUs used subsets of SNA functions that were needed for a particular product type, such as printers or displays, LU 6.2 is designed to be generic and independent of product types [SC30-6808]. For the first time, the boundary between the LU and the application is formally defined, using an architected set of **verbs**. Mandatory base functions guarantee connectivity. All optional functions are grouped into a limited number of option sets; and a product implementing any member of an option set must implement all functions in that option set. Providing a single, standard LU, that can be used on all products, thus eliminates many incompatibilities that inhibit intercommunication [GC30-3084]. Designed specifically for program-to-program communication, LU 6.2 contains additional features to make that practical. For example, since in the case of a program, there is no human to perform error recovery (as in the case of a terminal), LU 6.2 provides more dynamic, program-controlled error recovery [GG24-1584].

10.3.1   LU 6.2 Services

An LU is defined by the services it provides to a user. The primary services of an LU 6.2 are:

- Program initiation and termination—remote programs are selected, started up, and deactivated. As an option, programs can exchange arbitrary, program-defined data (Program Initialization Parameters) when a conversation is established.
- Resource allocation and deallocation.
- Commitment control (sync point).
- Synchronization control.
- Outage and error notification.
- Mapped conversation support.
- Security—access controls involving remote LU authentication, verification of user-ids, and cryptographic services.

LU 6.2 supports a peer-to-peer relationship between partner **transaction programs**.[1] Either partner can initiate a session. LU 6.2, moreover, can support multiple parallel sessions between any two partners, or with multiple different partners.[2]

A transaction program can be invoked by another transaction program using an LU-controlled mechanism called **Attach**. The invoking transaction program calls for the establishment of a conversation with another named transaction program. An instance of a transaction program is created for each conversation. Then, each transaction program communicates with the other by issuing Calls, which are interpreted as verbs understood by the supporting LU.

Conversations use an LU-LU session in a serial fashion, effectively time slicing the session. By this means, logical connections for a conversation can be established quickly, without the overhead of always creating a new session for each conversation. Conversations are frequently of short duration, while sessions are typically of longer duration. A conversation is deallocated by either partner, which then frees the session for use by some other conversation.

SNA refers to two types of transaction programs, the **application-transaction program**, of end users, and **service-transaction programs**, which are architecturally defined for network services. OSI uses the term **transaction-program service-users** (**TPSUs**) for both types. Each of these is a particular case of the more generic OSI *application-process*.

10.3.2   Sender/Receiver Concurrency

Three degrees of concurrency are used by different applications:

1. *Synchronous transfer*—involving real-time interaction between two transaction programs.[3] That conversation is active for the duration of the transaction. This has been the dominant mode for interactive conversations. LU 6.2 was designed for synchronous, half-duplex (one way at a time) operation. However, there is no fundamental reason why a conversation could not be full-duplex.

2. *Datagram-type*—involving immediate transmission but no response. This requires a special one-way conversation.

3. *Asynchronous transfer*—where the sending and receiving transaction programs generally are not active at the same time.

Datagrams.   LU 6.2, strictly speaking, does not support datagrams as they are commonly understood. LU 6.2 does, however, include a **one-way conversation**, which is suitable for

---

1.   LU 6.2 architecture refers to the target program of an `Allocate_Conversation` request as a *transaction program*. This does not imply that all applications using APPC are transactions, as defined by the metrics associated with database systems like CICS and IMS.

2.   Parallel sessions have required that multiple network addresses be allocated for the same LU.

3.   There is a difference between "synchronous transfer" and "synchronized transfer." The LU 6.2 conversation model has the primitives to synchronize the distributed transaction program using the `Confirm` verb, but the programs do not have to operate in a synchronous fashion in real-time lock-step.

datagram types of communication. The sending application-entity issues a single verb, a `Send_Conversation` verb (or `MC-Send_Conversation`), which is a composite of other verbs. This single verb allocates a conversation (issues the verb `Allocate`) and names the target LU and partner program. It sends the data, and follows immediately with a deallocation of the conversation and flush option. The flush option forces an immediate ending without waiting for any response from the partner LU or partner program. The result is a one-way flow of packets. If the amount of data is small enough, there is only one packet sent, as in a datagram.

Asynchronous transfer. For this case, the LU uses SNA Distributed Services (SNADS), which is explained in Section 6.5. Since the destination transaction program is typically not active at the time the data is sent, the data is stored at one or more service transaction programs (TPs) at locations en route. Then, at an appropriate later time (e.g., when low-cost transmission is available) the data is sent to a service TP at the destination. Finally, an application TP at the destination retrieves the stored information.

10.3.3   LU 6.2 Verbs

The LU protocol boundary is the service interface that isolates the application program from the network. This LU interface uses a set of **verbs** to represent the LU 6.2 functions available to the applications. These verbs, and the associated handling of the verbs for LU 6.2, have been referred to as *Advanced Program-to-Program Communication (APPC).* LU 6.2 verbs have more options and features than CPI-C. These may be useful to systems programmers, while application developers in general would rely on CPI-C. The LU 6.2 verbs include functions for opening and closing the communications, sending and receiving data, and support for security, synchronizing programs, synchronizing data-bases, and error handling. The semantics of the verbs define the functions. The syntax can vary with the particular programming interface. *The semantics of the conversation Calls, of the SAA Common Programming Interface (CPI-C), for example, are exactly the same as a subset of the LU 6.2 verbs, even though they are packaged somewhat differently.*[4]

    The APPC architecture does not limit a data record either in format or content. With the well-defined LU 6.2 verbs, the program-to-program communication also becomes independent of the operating systems, hardware types, and languages used. For example, a COBOL program on an IBM PS/2 can communicate with a C language program running on a non-IBM UNIX machine,[5] if both use the LU 6.2 verbs (or CPI-C).

Basic conversation verbs. Most of the LU 6.2 verbs correspond to the CPI-C calls described in Chapter 7. More specific definitions of the LU 6.2 **basic conversation verbs** are provided in this chapter's Technical Reference section. As noted in the discussion of the CPI-C, the states of the lower-level communication subsystem determine conditions at the protocol boundary, and so determine the verbs which may then be issued.

---

4.   IBM's statement of future direction is for still more complete support of the LU 6.2 verbs at the SAA CPI-C interface.

5.   LU 6.2, for example, will be available on the AIX PS/2 and the AIX/6000, as well as on all SAA systems.

In basic conversations, there is a standard format for all of the data transmitted by the application-process. The data transmitted with these basic conversation verbs must be by records with a header, called the *GDS-variable header*. This header specifies the total length of the logical record, and also includes an optional identification *(GDS id)* that specifies the type of data being sent.[6]

Mapped conversation verbs.   Applications written in higher-level languages, however, can benefit from a modified set of verbs that give greater flexibility in application-record format and hide certain options and details of the basic conversation verbs. This modified set is called the *Mapped Conversation Verbs*. The name derives from the fact that these verbs provide optional data-mapping support, which helps to make programs independent of the data structures on which they operate. User-defined mapping can be done by LU 6.2 on the sending side, on both the sending and receiving sides, on only the receiving side, or on neither side. **Mapped conversations** allow the transaction programs to exchange arbitrary data records *in any format set by the programmers.* With a mapped conversation, the transaction program sends just data. *There is no header.* APPC adds the header automatically. Thus, use of mapped verbs hides from the programmer the details of the underlying data stream used by LU 6.2.

The set of mapped conversation verbs corresponds to the basic conversation verb set, and includes the following:

- `MC-Send_Data`
- `MC-Prepare_to_Receive`
- `MC-Send_Error`
- `MC-Confirmed`
- `MC-Allocate`

- `MC-Receive_and_Wait`
- `MC-Flush`
- `MC-Confirm`
- `MC-Request_to_Send`
- `MC-Deallocate`

These are essentially the same as the basic verbs. There are some minor differences in return-codes. Two significant differences are:

- `MC-Receive_And_Wait` functions like its basic counterpart, but receives application-specific data records rather than logical records having the GDS-variable header.

- `MC-Send_Data` sends one application-specific data record. The length and GDS id fields are inserted by presentation services. An optional parameter of this Call is *map_name*, which specifies the name of a user-defined map that identifies the format of the record being sent, and how that record is to be transformed (mapped) before it is sent.

Control verbs.   While a few of the functions within the LU can be considered to be application-services, there are many other application-services that reside outside the LU and use the LU. These create a conversation with a partner service program at the partner LU. They cooperate to perform the desired service.

---

6.   An exception to this is if the data is long enough to be split up into multiple records; then only the first record has a GDS id, and the high-order bit of the LL field indicates that more data follows (see Figure 9.2).

An example of such an application-service is SNADS, the asynchronous distribution service. Service transactions, distributed between the partner LUs are also needed to exchange resynchronization data after failures of conversations that were protected by a resource sync point.

For such privileged services, and for network operators, LU 6.2 includes control verbs that provide LU-LU control and coordination. Chief among these control verbs are **session-control verbs** for activation and deactivation of sessions:

- `Activate_Session` and `Deactivate_Session`.

- `Initialize_Session_Limit` verb determines the number of parallel sessions to be permitted, per mode name, between two LUs.

- `Change_Session_Limit` alters the maximum allowable number of sessions.

- `Reset_Session_Limit` returns the session limit to zero. It also deactivates the sessions, under a given mode name, to a partner LU. Options allow queued requests for conversations to be satisfied before the reset is completed.

Another set of control verbs is the **LU definition verbs**, to define, modify, examine, or delete local LUs:

- `Define_Local_LU` enters the network-qualified LU_name (Net_id.LU_name), the total LU-LU session limit for this LU, security information to check incoming allocation requests, and names of maps to be used for local data transformations.

- `Define_Remote_LU` enters the local name of remote LUs, along with that LU's network-qualified name. It also includes the LU-LU password to be used during session activation, and whether parallel sessions are supported.

- `Define_Mode` concerns the local LU support for the partner LU. It includes the mode names, which are tied to class-of-service, and optional session parameters such as maximum RU size, pacing counts, and cryptography.

- `Define_TP` enters parameters of a transaction program (TP) at a local LU. This includes the transaction program name, optional functions it supports, such as resource sync point and map_names, conversation-level security information, and whether any `Attach` parameter information is required. This verb also defines which control-operator verb privileges may be used (such as session control), and whether the TP may allocate conversations with certain service programs.

Four **display verbs**, to view the parameters of these and other control verbs, are also provided.

10.3.4   LU 6.2 Operations

Assigning conversations to sessions.   When an application-entity asks that a conversation be provided for its use, the resource manager in the local LU first tries to use an existing active session. If no sessions are available, then a new session will be bound. If no session is available and none can be added because the session limit has been reached, the

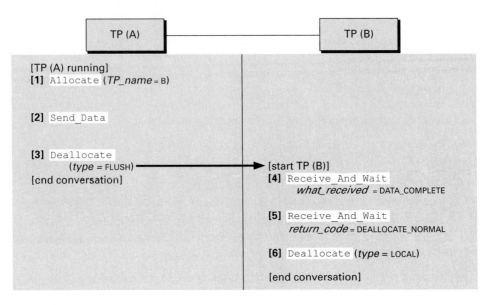

Figure 10.2 A one-way conversation [Gray83].

session request will be denied if immediate allocation is requested. If `Allocate` *(when_session_allocated)* is used, the request can be queued if there are no sessions available and no sessions can then be bound.[7]

Buffering.   The LU does not necessarily send one message for each verb. A more efficient mapping of verbs to messages can save considerable communication expense. Programs that issue LU 6.2 verbs assume the existence of a **send-buffer** and a **receive-buffer** in the LU. Data sent by the program is first accumulated in the send-buffer. The LU will transmit the data on the session when the accumulation reaches the amount of the *maximum_RU_size* for the session, or when the program issues a verb that explicitly tells the LU to flush its send-buffer. Similarly, incoming data is accumulated in the receive-buffer until the program issues a verb that receives data.

Illustrative sequences.   The simplest way to get an understanding of the details in LU 6.2 operation is to follow the sequence of commands in typical exchanges. Following Gray et al., one-way and two-way conversations, with an accumulation of messages, are illustrated in the two examples, shown in Figure 10.2 and Figure 10.3 [Gray83]. These show the details of what is happening in the LU, whether or not CPI-C is used.[8]

---

7.   The queuing of requests using the *when_session_allocated* parameter must be done with care to avoid deadlock.

8.   In Figure 10.3, the transaction program split a logical record over two `Send_Data` commands, and set the high order bit of the first LL field to indicate a continuation.

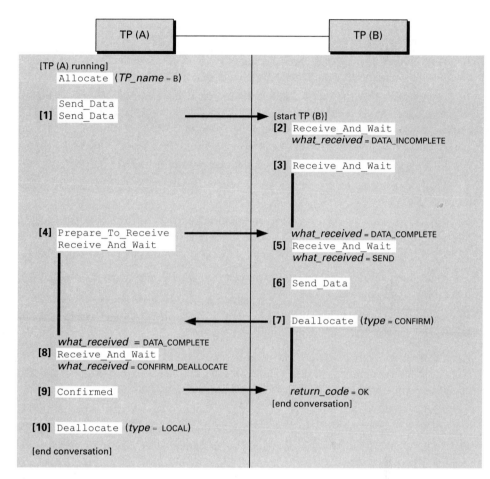

Figure 10.3 A two-way conversation with confirmation [Gray83].

Illustrative one-way conversation.   In this first example, transaction program (A) initiates a conversation, sends a message to transaction program (B), and terminates the connection. The verbs in Figure 10.2 have the following effects:

1.   TP(A) issues the LU 6.2 `Allocate` verb (or achieves this via the CPI-C), that names the remote transaction program, to request a conversation with partner program (B). The LU creates an allocation request, using the information provided in the `Allocate` verb.

To initiate the conversation, the LU sends the remote LU an `Attach` request, using an Attach FM header. (An FM header is a coded field placed at the beginning of an RU.) When the target LU receives the FM header, that LU sends it to its LU resources manager (RM). This RM checks parameters, including the security parameters in the `Attach`. If no problem is found, the LU selects and loads the specified transaction-program code, and calls it, placing it initially in **receive** state for the conversation.

The LU for TP(A) places the allocation request in the send buffer and returns control to TP(A), with the conversation in the **send** state. No data is sent.

2. TP(A) issues `Send_Data`, which causes the LU to place the data in its buffer behind the allocation request. The data are short enough that nothing is sent.

3. TP(A) issues `Deallocate` with *type*=FLUSH, which means that the deallocation is to be immediate. The LU sends the contents of its buffer with a Deallocate indication. The conversation is now completed at TP(A). The session flow, consisting of one message, starts TP(B), with the conversation in **receive** state.

4. TP(B) issues `Receive_And_Wait` and receives all the data.

5. TP(B) issues another `Receive_And_Wait` and receives the DEALLOCATE_NORMAL return code.

6. TP(B) issues `Deallocate` with *type*=LOCAL, causing the LU to discard its control information for the conversation. This ends the conversation for TP(B). Both TP(A) and TP(B) continue in execution until they end themselves, or are otherwise terminated.

Thus, three verbs were compressed into one message. If the message is short enough, it can flow as one packet.

Illustrative two-way conversation.   Next, both TP(A) and TP(B) send data to each other. Figure 10.3 shows additional features of the APPC verbs:

1. The first two verbs are the same as in the previous example, except that this TP(A) must send a larger amount of data. These data are long enough that the LU has to send some data while retaining a portion of the data in its local send buffer.

2. TP(B) issues `Receive_And_Wait`, thereby obtaining the first portion of the data.

3. TP(B) issues `Receive_And_Wait` again, thereby causing the LU to suspend the execution of TP(B) until the remaining portion of the data has been received by the LU.

4. TP(A) issues `Prepare_To_Receive`, later followed by `Receive_And_Wait`, which causes the LU to send the contents of its buffer, together with the SEND indication, to TP(B).[9] The execution of TP(A) may have been delayed because of the execution of other programs at its LU, or because the LU may have been doing other processing that did not result in activity on this conversation. The LU suspends execution of TP(A) until it receives data to satisfy the `Receive_And_Wait`.

Control is returned to TP(B) as soon as the remaining portion of data is received by its LU. Note the opportunity for execution overlap. The `Prepare_To_Receive` turns the session around and, until TP(A) issues the `Receive_and_Wait`, TP(A) is free to continue processing in parallel with TP(B).

5. TP(B) issues another `Receive_And_Wait` and receives the SEND indication.

6. TP(B) issues `Send_Data`, causing the LU to place the data in its buffer. Nothing is sent.

7. TP(B) issues `Deallocate` with *type*=CONFIRM, which implies confirmation processing and causes the LU to send the contents of its buffer together with a

---

9.   The `Prepare_To_Receive` is optional. It may be used because it does not block and allows the issuing transaction program to do other work.

`Confirm_Deallocate` request. The CONFIRM causes the LU to suspend execution of TP(B) processing until it receives an affirmative or negative response.

The LU returns control to TP(A), indicating that the program has received all the data.

8. TP(A) issues another `Receive_And_Wait` and in return receives the CONFIRM_DEALLOCATE request.

9. TP(A) responds affirmatively by issuing `Confirmed`, thus causing its LU to send an affirmative response. A `Send_Error` can be issued instead of `Confirmed`, in which case the conversation remains allocated at both programs.

The LU returns control to TP(B) to indicate successful completion of the `Deallocate`. The conversation is complete for TP(B).

10. TP(A) issues `Deallocate` with *type*=LOCAL, which causes the LU to discard its control information for the conversation. The conversation ends for TP(A).

Performance.   The performance of LU 6.2, like any software, is dependent on the implementation as well as the architecture. It is fair to say that initial implementations did not optimize LU 6.2 performance. Subsequent implementations have improved performance almost 100 percent.

On local area networks, the chief competitor to LU 6.2 are simple LAN protocols like NetBIOS. For LAN attached PS/2s, doing small transactions, later LU 6.2s seem to perform comparably to NetBIOS. For large transactions, that is, transfers of 100Kbyte files, the LU 6.2 performance is often superior while providing more function.

10.3.5   LU Sending Sequence

A fuller understanding of the data flows, at a still further level of detail, can be obtained by considering the header indicators and flow sequences in the following tracing of a message through one LU and into another.

The sending half-session (HS) sends each message, complete with its request header (RH), plus corresponding parameter values for use in building the transmission header (TH), to path control. Path control is then responsible for delivering the complete message to the receiving half-session in the remote LU. Messages are sent by path control in the same order as they are received. Each half-session can assume that the messages arrive in the same order as the partner half-session sent them.

Mapping.   Each `MC-Send_Data` verb sent to the LU includes a data record. If mapping is being performed, presentation services (PS) maps the data record into a mapped-conversation-record. The LU segments this record into a sequence of logical records, according to the rules of the General-Data-Stream architecture. These logical records, plus FM headers, become a complete *conversation-message*.

Chaining.   That conversation-message, then, is converted into a chain of smaller messages which the other partner can handle (depending on buffer sizes). To build these chains, the presentation service assembles the FM headers and logical records into RU-sized units (the maximum RU size for a session is determined by `Bind` negotiations). When the RU-size buffer is full, PS transfers the data to the half-session, with an indication of whether it is the last of the data in the chain for a conversation-message. The sending PS detects the end of a conversation-message by verbs like `Prepare_To_Receive, Receive_and_Wait,`

`Confirm`, `Syncpt`, or `Deallocate`. Upon receiving any of these, it then sends its remaining accumulated data.

RH header.   When PS sends the data, the HS adds the RH (request/response header), adds a sequence number, and enciphers the data if cryptography is used. The RH indicators are determined by the LU actions or by parameters in the verbs that have been received from the application interface. For example, HS sets the chaining indicators *(BCI, ECI)* to indicate the first and last elements of each chain. It sets the bracket indicators *(BB, CEB)* to indicate the first and last messages in a conversation. It sets the *change-direction (CD)* indicator when the `Prepare_To Receive` verb was issued, *RQD 2 or 3* when `Confirm` was issued, and *conditional_end_bracket* *(CEB)* when the `Deallocate` verb was issued. The *change_direction(CD)* bit is set when `Receive_And_Wait` is issued. Also, when needed, the LU generates FM headers, such as an Attach or Error-Description FM header *(FMH-5 or FMH-7)*.

To path control.   The combination of the max_RU and the RH is called the **basic-information-unit (BIU)**. The chain of BIUs is the conversation message. The half-session (HS) passes each completed BIU (including the RH) to path control. For all but the last BIU of a conversation message, the encoding in the RH is *RQE1* (respond only in case of detected error). For the last BIU in a chain, at the end of a conversation message, HS encodes the RH with *EC (end_of_chain)*.[10] The last element of the chain may be set to either *definite response (RQD)* or *exception response (RQE)*, depending on the verbs the transaction program issued. After receiving the entire chain, the receiver will send a negative response if any element of the chain is unacceptable. The receiver of an *RQD* will send a positive response to acknowledge that the entire chain is acceptable.

The corresponding address information for the TH is sent as control data across the PC interface. Path control then has the assignment to carry each BIU to the receiving half-session, in the destination LU. The rate at which HS sends BIUs is determined by end-to-end pacing. HS may enforce either fixed pacing or adaptive pacing (see Sections 14.2.2 and 14.7), depending on which was determined at session initiation.

10.3.6   LU Receiving Sequence

From path control.   At the receiving end, the HS receives BIUs and TH information from path control. The receiving half-session deciphers the data, if session cryptography is specified. It checks the sequence numbers to detect lost or duplicate messages. If no errors have been detected, the half-session sends any messages containing the `Attach` or security FM headers to a resource manager. All others are routed to presentation services.

RH indicators.   Presentation services also is sent significant RH indicators such as: end-of-a-message *(end_of_chain)*, enter-**send**-state *(change_direction)*, confirmation-request *(definite_response 2/3)*, and end-of-conversation *(conditional_end_of_bracket)*.

To the TP.   When the transaction program (TP) issues a `Receive_And_Wait` verb, presentation services (PS) passes the data and protocol information back to the TP. For

---

10.   After the last BIU of a conversation message, the sender will go into **receive**, **confirm**, or **deallocate** state.

mapped conversations, PS strips the LL and ID fields of the General Data Stream (GDS header), reblocks the data into a data record for the TP, and passes the data record to the TP in receive-buffer-size segments.

When PS receives an end-of-conversation message, it forwards this only after all incoming messages have been successfully received by the TP. It then provides the end of conversation indicator as a return for the next `Receive_And_Wait` verb.

10.3.7 Local/Remote Transparency

Distributed processing among cooperating systems makes local/remote transparency highly desirable. The direction is to achieve that at the Common Programming Interface CPI-C. Side information, associated with the CPI-C can determine if the call is local or remote, and direct it accordingly. The additional requirement, however, is that the performance be optimized for the local case. Memory-to-memory transfer, for example, avoiding much of the communication protocols, is the fast route. This is the approach, for example, in the MVS implementation of CPI-C.

10.4 APPC/MVS—AN ILLUSTRATION

A good illustration of an LU 6.2 implementation is the APPC/MVS available on S/390s.[11] In concert with the SAA Common Programming Interface CPI-C, the application developer uses program-name references for transparent application-to-application connectivity. A client–server relation can be established between application-processes on an MVS system and application-processes on any system that supports the industry standard LU 6.2 formats and protocols. The client application as well as the server may reside on either the MVS system or its partner. Usually, however, because of its compute and data facilities, MVS lends itself as an environment for application-servers.

APPC/MVS is an application-service that uses VTAM. APPC/MVS schedules a suite of application-processes or servers in response to connection requests. Each such application-process is scheduled by a conversation that was requested (a) by another application-process located in any other system in the APPC network, or (b) by an application-process running on the same MVS system. This allows multiple-application-process relationships both across systems and within MVS systems.

Server styles. Consider that a client–server relationship is to be set up between two application-processes. Two basic server styles are supported. In the simplest case, each client's request results in a unique copy of the server application. This results in *multiple instances* of the server. For example, if five different users concurrently requested the same application, there would be five pairs of processes in execution. Also, the same or different users can use *multiple copies* of the same application-process.

On the other hand, it is also possible to have multiple requests scheduled to a *single server instance*. The single server is started by an operator or automated command, and

---

11. Recall that *APPC* is the term referring to the LU 6.2 verb set and associated functions.

remains active to receive concurrent requests from many different users.[12] Of course, that more sophisticated server must be capable of handling multiple conversations concurrently. This approach is used by the IMS database subsystem to handle APPC requests for database transactions in the MVS environment.

Connectivity.   At a single workstation, therefore, a user can simultaneously work with application-processes in different locations *throughout the enterprise*. Transparency of server location is managed by the operating systems supporting APPC. Windowing can aid the coordination of operations in the multiple conversations. Other SAA systems participating in this APPC network include OS/2EE, OS/400, and VM. Via APPC/MVS application-processes, connectivity is provided directly to DB2 and IMS databases, and by internal conversation to CICS-managed data also. In the CICS case, a CICS transaction would be needed to either extract or update CICS-managed data records. APPC/MVS connectivity also includes services like TSO-interactive[13] and batch environments. A large and growing number of software vendors also now support APPC, further broadening the APPC network.

Conclusion

APPC and the underlying LU 6.2 are seen as a practical implementation of CPI-C, and a supporter of CPI-RR. They have become an industry workhorse for conversational, interactive communications.[14] LU 6.2's stable, well-defined verbs permit effective and robust interactions among cooperating application-processes. These can be distributed throughout the enterprise on a broad variety of different systems, from different vendors, from workstations to mainframes.

Acknowledgments

I am particularly indebted to L. R. Parker, A. P. Citron, L. M. Rafalow, Philippe Janson, and F. Voss for valuable inputs or reviews of this chapter.

TECHNICAL REFERENCES

LU 6.2 Conversation Verbs

A brief description of the LU 6.2 verbs follows [Gray83],[GG24-1584]:

- `Send_Data` moves data into a buffer, and returns control to the transaction program. Arbitrary amounts of data can be sent, structured as a series of variable length records, delimited by 2-byte length-fields. The data is actually sent on the occasion of a subsequent verb (e.g., `Confirm`) or when the buffer is filled.

---

12.   Since non-CPI-C verbs are used, this approach does not lend itself to the complete portability objectives of SAA.

13.   Once logged onto TSO/E via LU 2 protocols, the user can invoke applications that then utilize APPC/MVS communication services. Hence, TSO/E applications can access IMS and CICS managed data via internal conversations to transactions which can extract data and send the data to the TSO address space for processing.

14.   Reportedly, more than seventy vendors use LU 6.2, facilitating communications between IBM and OEM facilities.

- `Receive_And_Wait` delivers data and/or control information to the issuing transaction program. Once issued, the transaction program is in a wait state until some message arrives.

- `Receive_Immediate` receives any information that is then available, but does not wait for information to arrive.

- `Post_On_Receipt` requests posting of that conversation when information is available to receive.

- `Prepare_To_Receive` is issued at the end of a message, and indicates that no further messages will be sent. It further causes control information to be sent to the other partner, indicating that the other partner now has send control.

- `Flush` directs that all buffered data and control information be sent.

- `Request_To_Send` asks the partner program for the right to send. That information is passed to the opposite partner as a returned value on a subsequent verb which that partner issues.

- `Send_Error` reports to the sending partner that an error occurred in the data being received. The receiving partner purges the pieces that are buffered. The flow is also reversed, so that the partner issuing the `Send_Error` obtains **send** control. Having thus gotten **send** control, that partner can optionally use a data transfer to convey further information about the error, and to trigger recovery programs. In a similar manner, if the sending partner discovers an error which should interrupt a message, the sending program can issue a `Send_Error`. In that case, the sending partner retains **send** control.

- `Confirm` is sent at the end of a message, and asks the receiving partner to confirm that no errors have been detected in it. The receiving partner can reply with either a `Send_Error` if errors were found, or with a `Confirmed` if no errors were detected. `Deallocate` *type*=ABEND* is also permitted as a reply.

- `Allocate` requests that the remote partner LU build a new conversation with a named program. The `Allocate` also has an implicit request for a new session if needed. The response of the remote LU is to arrange for the named program to be placed in execution and associated with the new conversation. To accomplish this, the `Allocate` verb carries the following parameters:

  - *LU_name* is the name of the LU at which the desired new partner program is located.
  - *TPN* is the Transaction Program Name of the new partner program with which the conversation is desired.
  - *mode_name* specifies the class of service (quality of transportation service) that is to be provided for the new conversation. The *mode_name* might, for example, call for a SECURE, BULK, or LOW DELAY conversation.[15]
  - *sync_level* specifies the highest sync level applicable to the conversation (NONE, CONFIRM, or SYNCPT).
  - *type* specifies whether the conversation is basic or mapped.
  - *security* provides a user-id, password, and a profile that the remote LU uses, to verify the identity of the user, and to validate authority to access desired resources.
  - *PIP* provides program-initialization-parameters to be passed to the target program.
  - *return_control* relates to waiting for an available session. The program can (a) relinquish control until a session is established, or (b) regain control before a session is established.

---

15.   The three parameters, LU_name, TP_name, and mode_name may use locally defined names. For LU 6.2 alone, only the LU_name will be translated from a local value to a network value. When using CPI-C, the LU_name, TP_name, and mode_name are encoded locally with the symbolic_destination_name.

- *resource* is a return parameter in which the LU provides the conversation identifier. That *resource_id* is supplied with all future verbs in that conversation.

- `Deallocate` terminates the conversation that resulted from an `Allocate`. To reduce the volume of exchanges, the FLUSH, CONFIRM, and SYNCPT functions may be combined with the `Deallocate`. The transaction program that was activated by an `Allocate` is not ended immediately by the `Deallocate`. It continues until it terminates its own execution or it is terminated by operator action.

- `Test` lets the program find out whether a `Request_To_Send` notification has been received or if it has been posted as a result of a preceding `Post_On_Receipt`.

Type-Independent LU 6.2 Verbs

- `Backout` rolls back all changes to a protected resource since the last sync point. This is done for all protected resources throughout distributed transactions, in multiple remote nodes. (Resources used in a conversation are protected when the conversation is allocated with a synchronization level of SYNCPT.) When multiple programs in multiple nodes are involved in a distributed transaction, they, too, must be advised of the backout. That is done with a BACKOUT return code, which requires each recipient, in turn, to also issue a `Backout`.

- `Syncpt` (sync point) makes the accumulated changes to multiple resources permanent. Remote programs receive the sync point request through TAKE_SYNCPT indications returned in the *what_received* parameters. Each program's LU cooperates in propagating the sync point request throughout the transaction. Alternatively, the application can choose to not make the changes permanent, and, instead, to roll back to the state of the resources at the time of the previous sync point. Thus, the return code will be either OK, or BACKED OUT.

- `Wait` is used to allow programs to receive information from more than one conversation. It indicates that the program waits for posting to occur on any of a list of conversations, for which a `Post_On_Receipt` has previously been issued. The return code tells whether posting has occurred, and why.

EXERCISES

10.1 In what layers are the functions of the LU?

10.2 Name six primary services provided by LU 6.2.

10.3 What is the primary advantage of the mapped conversation verbs?

10.4 What is the relation between the LU 6.2 verbs and the CPI-C calls?

10.5 What are the LU verb and LU request that establish a conversation with a partner program?

10.6 In LU 6.2 client–server operations, what are the two styles of server instantiation?

11
OSI/Communications Subsystem

11.1 INTRODUCTION

We now look at a concrete implementation of the OSI protocols, the IBM OSI/ Communications Subsystem. It is an implementation of OSI layers 3, 4, 5, and 6, plus the Association Control Service Element (ACSE) of layer 7. Referring again to Figure 7.2, the OSI/Communications Subsystem includes the OSI end-to-end data-exchange facilities and the transport and intersubnetwork services.

This OSI design is modular so as to facilitate porting the subsystem to the SAA and AIX/OSF families of systems. This promises to insure the consistency and interoperability among all these systems, and to reduce the learning time for installations having multiple types of systems within the SAA and AIX/OSF families. A description of this design is presented as both a summary of the OSI facilities and a practical illustration of their implementation.

11.2 FUNCTIONAL OVERVIEW

The OSI/Communications Subsystem supports the following OSI profiles:[1]

- National Institute of Science and Technology (formerly NBS) Stable Implementation Agreements

- US GOSIP (U.S. Government OSI Profiles) version 1

- UK GOSIP (United Kingdom Government OSI Profiles) version 3.0

- European Norms: ENV 41-104 part 2, 41-204, and 41-205

- Interoperability Technology Association for Information Processing (INTAP) profile definitions

---

1. The stated IBM intent is that the same OSI/Communications Subsystem functions will be provided on all SAA and AIX/OSF systems.

OSI/Communications Subsystem is a package embracing the following OSI functions:

- ACSE
- Presentation layer
- Session layer
- Transport layer

- Internet Protocol
- X.25 Packet Level Protocol
- 802.3/4/5

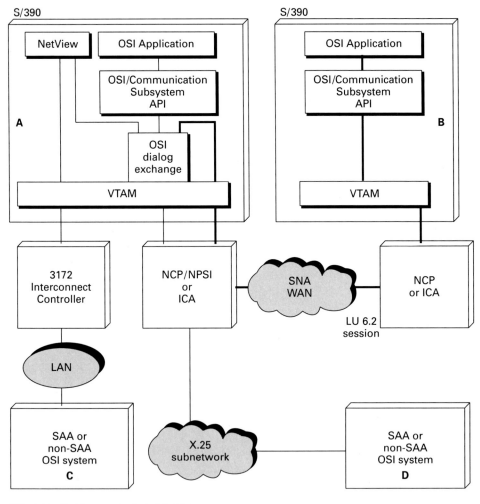

ICA = Integrated Communications Adapter
NCP = Network Control Program
NPSI = Network Packet Switch Interface

Figure 11.1 Local and remote OSI applications using the OSI end-to-end Communication Subsystem.

As illustrated in Figure 11.1, OSI/Communications Subsystem currently links applications in SAA systems to applications in SAA or non-SAA systems via X.25 public packet switching data networks or LANs.

Not every node needs to have an OSI subsystem for communicating with other OSI systems. An arrangement is provided whereby, through the services of an intervening SNA network, *using LU 6.2 sessions*, an OSI application in one location (A) can use the OSI/Communication Subsystem at a different location (B) to talk to locations C and D. This is illustrated in Figure 11.1, showing the remote OSI/Communications Subsystem API connected to the OSI communication facilities in another node, via an LU 6.2 session.

The two applications using the OSI/CS API, in Figure 11.1, can also communicate using the intervening SNA WAN (or LAN).

As shown in Figure 11.2, the OSI/Communications Subsystem protocols of layers 4 through 7 extend end-to-end, while the X.25 packet-layer protocols are used between the X.25 network and each end-system. The lower-layer transmission could, in fact, be via an X.25 network, as illustrated, or via a LAN, or, conceivably, via an SNA network (as described in Section 19.6).

The OSI protocols that are implemented in each layer of the OSI/Communications Subsystem are cited in this chapter's Technical Reference section.

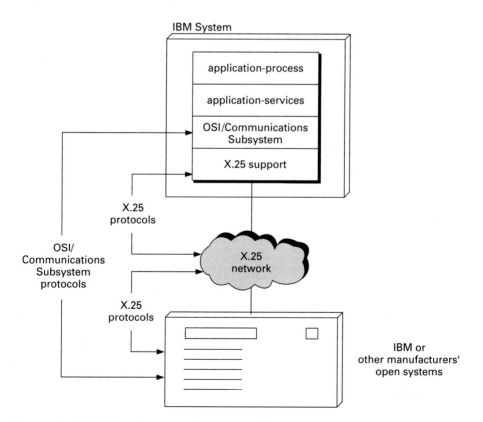

Figure 11.2 Multivendor connection using OSI/Communication Subsystem.

11.3   SUBSYSTEM STRUCTURE

The OSI/Communications Subsystem architecture has some interesting aspects [Mouton89], [Goldberg91]. A view of its structure is shown in Figure 11.3. The design attempts to make the **base** shown there independent of the host or workstation in which it is placed. The base interfaces to different system environments through Boundary Units. The boundaries connect to applications, access methods, and local management functions, in different workstations and mainframes.

The categories of service provided by the base are:

- *Control block management*—manages control blocks representing the OSI concepts of *n*-entity, service-access-point, and connection-end-point
- *Finite state machine services*
- *Work management*
- *Buffer management*, across layers
- *Resource management*—provides early warning of low storage conditions
- *Message logging and tracing*

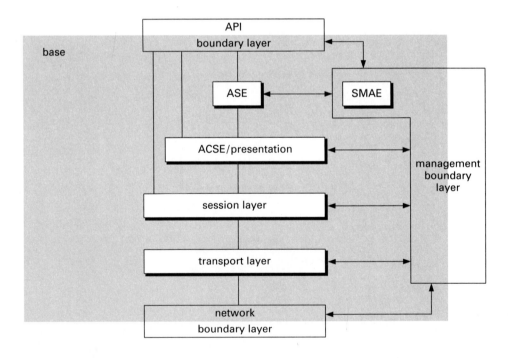

ACSE = Association Control Service Element
API = Application Program Interface
ASE = Application-Service–Element
SMAE = System Management Application-Entity

Figure 11.3 An overview of the IBM OSI/Communications Subsystem.

Each OSI layer is supported as called subroutines, which are coded in Pascal. All interface operations are handled as work requests which contain the OSI primitives. A layer-oriented work-manager controls the assignment of tasks to each layer. This isolates the layers from the operating system tasking structure, and so minimizes queuing and task switching. Nevertheless, multiple invocations are allowed per layer. The work-request design makes the operation relatively independent of the physical location of an adjacent layer. Hence, it could allow layers that currently run together on the same base to be later distributed over a system with multiple bases connected by high-speed media. Subsystem *Boundary Units* are of three types:

- The *management boundary* is a Boundary Unit that integrates this portable subsystem into the local management services. This unit provides for management of the subsystem, access to configuration and directory information, and reporting of events and statistics. Whenever a new layer is activated, an interface with this manager is automatically activated also.

- The *network boundary* is designed to facilitate routing between the subsystem and a variety of subnetworks. Currently, support is provided for both connection-oriented services, using the X.25 interface, and connectionless service using the ISO CLNP protocol over 802.2 LANs.

- The *API boundary* interfaces to the Common Programming Interface of SAA and other APIs. The Common Programming Interface provides a set of library routines usable by COBOL and C applications. These routines convert the services provided by the OSI layers into an interface that is easily usable by application programmers. Since these routines are consistent across all the SAA environments, application portability is enhanced.

The portable base, plus the Boundary Units of a particular system constitute an OSI/ Communications Subsystem for that system. Thus, for example, the architecture can facilitate an OSI/Communications Subsystem for MVS, VM, OS/400, and OS/2.

11.4   SUBSYSTEM PROGRAMMING INTERFACE

11.4.1   Language Needs

OSI/Communications Subsystem needs three distinct application program interfaces:

1. A *high-level language API*, for portable applications of a general character. Generally, when using this API, ease of use is more important than performance.

2. A *high-performance API* for complex applications, and commonly used application-services. This is needed for systems programmers, to minimize path length and data movement. Asynchronous operation and full negotiation capability are required. The applications using this API are usually written in assembler or in C language.

3. A *transaction-processing API* with full service and performance for transaction type of applications. Facilities here are comparable to those provided by the SNA LU 6.2, designed for application-to-application communications.

The first is for general use. The second is mostly for privileged system-type of processes. The third is still, at this writing, in the final stages of the ISO standards development process. Nevertheless, the direction is clear, and the definition of this API can be anticipated (see the Technical Reference section in Chapter 7 for the possible mappings between the SAA CPI-C and OSI-TP services).

11.4.2 Subsystem High-Level Language API

The OSI/Communications Subsystem high-level API, like the SAA Common Programming Interface (CPI), is based on a call interface. The "look and feel" is the same as that of the SAA CPI. The general form of the call is:

```
CALL function-name (association_id, parameter_1,
...parameter_n, return_code)
```

The last parameter is a return-code, to indicate the success or failure of the call processing. 0 indicates success; 1–9 is a success with qualifications; 10–N is failure. Called routines have 6 character names beginning with "OS." The Calls are kept simple, with few parameters. *Set* (to pass parameters) and *Extract* (to read parameters) routines are used for optional parameters. These are used only as needed. These calls are supported in compilers and libraries of both COBOL and C languages. This API can access either the ASCE/ presentation layer or the session layer. (The ASCE is used to establish and terminate connections.)

For portability, this Call interface is identical across SAA systems (MVS, VM, OS/ 400 and OS/2), including identical subroutines and identical names for options. The Calls, further, have been made as alike as possible across the supported languages.

Some special features can be added to facilitate program development, without affecting interoperability. Examples of this, in OSI/Communications Subsystem are:

1. **Process suspension**—the programmer can operate in either of two modes:
    - *Call complete*—control is not returned to the program that issued the call until the call completes. This completion depends on the type of call, and may occur when:
        - The request or response initiated by the call has been sent
        - An indication or confirmation has been received from the partner
        - A time-out has been reached
    - *Call validated*—the application may continue during request processing. The application regains control as soon as the call has been received and validated by the subsystem, and before the call is complete.

2. **Receive-Any**—the application receives an indication or confirmation from any association in progress. This reduces the complexity of program design when the program is handling many connections.

Presentation layer encoding/decoding.   The OSI/Communications Subsystem programming interface supports the encoding and decoding functions of the presentation layer as defined by ISO 8825. An **Abstract Syntax Checker (ASC)** utility is used to compile the abstract syntax definitions to produce *C or COBOL data structures* that are placed in the application-entity (AE) source code. The data structures enable data in the local representation to be exchanged between the AE and the presentation layer. The presentation layer converts fields of the data structure to and from the prescribed transfer syntax (see Section 9.2).

11.4.3   Starter Call Set

Many programs will need only the OSI/Communications Subsystem starter set, consisting of 15 Calls at the higher-level language API. All told, the subsystem supports 128 Calls, for those that need detailed control and higher performance. A partial description of the starter set, in five categories, follows:

1. **Enrollment**

   - `Build_Application_Entity_Environment`: builds control blocks and data areas for application-entity within the application-process; returns *application-entity-id*.
   - `Register_Application_Title`: contains *application-entity-id* and external nickname of application-entity; registers application-entity and its OSI address; builds OSI/Communications Subsystem control blocks for the application-entity. The SAP string, from the NSAP to the PSAP is assigned at this time.

2. **Association Establishment**

   - `Build_Association_Environment`: contains *application-entity-id*; builds control blocks and data areas for an association; returns *association-id*.
   - `Associate`: contains *association-id* and symbolic_destination_name, the nickname of the remote application-entity; sends associate request to target partner program.
   - `Receive_Associate_Confirm_Specific`: contains *association-id*; waits for and receives specific *association-result* (ACCEPT or REJECT); receives user data, if any.
   - `Invite_Association`: contains *association-id*; waits for incoming associate indication; receives user data, if any.
   - `Respond_to_Association`: contains *association-id*; sends *association-result* (ACCEPT or REJECT).

3. **Data Transfer**

   - `Receive`: contains *association-id*; receives user data, if any; also indicates any tokens received.
   - `Get_Data_Structure`: contains *association-id*; gets one data structure from a received buffer at offset; identifies abstract-syntax-name used (from header); identifies structure received (from header).
   - `Put_Data_Structure`: contains *association-id*; puts one data structure into a buffer at offset; specifies abstract-syntax-name used (for header); specifies structure to be moved (for header).
   - `Send_Data`: contains *association-id*; sends a normal data request.

4. **Association Release**

   - `Release`: contains *association-id*; sends a release request to partner.
   - `Respond_To_Release`: contains *association-id*; sends a release response to partner.
   - `Free_Association_Environment`: contains *association-id*; frees control blocks and data areas of an association.

5. **Deregister**

   - `Deregister_Application_Entity`: contains *application-entity-id*; deregisters application-entity and its OSI address from OSI subsystem; frees control blocks and data areas of the application-entity.

11.5   DEFINING THE SUBSYSTEM RESOURCES

Another good overview of the OSI stack can be obtained by considering how the OSI/Communications Subsystem must be provided with information about the resources in the network. The subsystem information base must contain data on:

- Network topology
- Transport options
- Application-entities
- Directory service
- System management

In addition, at subsystem startup, an initialization file must contain information about:

- Lines to activate
- Thresholds

Further discussion of these subsystem definitions can be found in this chapter's Technical Reference section.

11.6   OSI-SNA SHARED RESOURCES

The number of possible OSI/SNA configurations is large. The objectives of a distribution of OSI standards throughout a mixed SNA/OSI configuration is partially conveyed in Figure 11.4. This figure includes:

- Common System management: NetView can be used to manage the common OSI and SNA network resources.
- OSI and SNA communications take place over the three types of LANs (802.3/4/5), plus the FDDI.
- Using the remote API, OSI applications can transmit over an SNA WAN to a boundary-node having the OSI/Communications Subsystem.

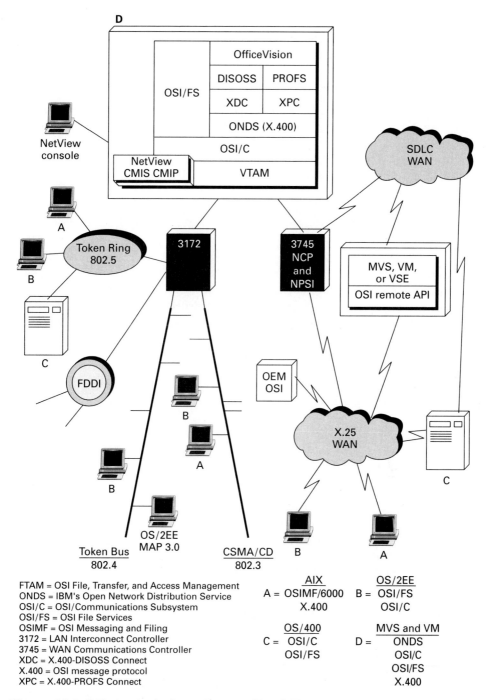

Figure 11.4 OSI standards throughout an SNA/OSI configuration.

- SNA WANs can be shared as an SNA and X.25 backbones; and X.25 WANs can carry SNA traffic (see Chapter 19).

- OSI file services and message handling services interact among SAA and AIX/OSF systems. The OSI Message Handling Service interoperates with OfficeVision, PROFS and DISOSS (see Section 6.6).

In general, transport facilities (layers 1 through 3) can be shared flexibly. The possible structures of an integrated SNA(APPN)-OSI node, with common functions is discussed in Section 14.8.

In addition, as noted in Section 7.2.3, it is expected that a common API will be forthcoming, to provide *network independence* at this CPI for SNA conversational and OSI TP applications.

Conclusion

The OSI/Communications Subsystem provides the OSI communications for OSI-based applications in many sizes of SAA and AIX/OSF systems. It also provides the basic component for the further integration of OSI and SNA, involving the use of many links and subnetworks in common. A common network-independence at the CPI-C is also expected. The evolving architecture thus places this subsystem as a key module in a flexible structure that facilitates growth in multiprotocol, multivendor facilities.

Acknowledgments

I am particularly indebted to Liba Svobodova, Jerry Mouton, L. L. Hale, and Philippe Janson for valuable input and reviews of this chapter.

TECHNICAL REFERENCES

OSI/Communications Subsystem Standards

- Layer 7, **Application**
    - Common Management Information Protocol (ISO 9596)
    - Association Control Service Element (ASCE) Protocol (ISO 8650)
    - Directory Access Protocol (DIS 9594)
- Layer 6, **Presentation**
    - KERNEL (ISO 8823), ASN.1 (ISO 8825)
- Layer 5, **Session**
    - Versions 1 AND 2, All Functional Units, (ISO 8327)
- Layer 4, **Transport**
    - Class 0, 2, 4 (ISO 8073)
- Layer 3, **Network**
    - Connectionless Network Protocols using X.25, (ISO 8473)
    - Connection-Oriented Network Protocols using X.25, (ISO 8878)

Defining OSI resources

Network topology. The subsystem definitions pertaining to network topology, in the case of attachment to an X.25 network, include the following:

The *local network address* for a subsystem is the Network Service-Access-Point (NSAP) address. This NSAP forms the bottom part of the unique presentation address for each local application-entity. Each PSAP address is then the concatenation of the NSAP address and the selectors of the upper layers in the subsystem.

The subsystem must be advised of the *standards level* of the attaching X.25 subnetwork. It may correspond to the 1980 or the 1984 standard, which would affect the protocols that can be used.

The *lines* between the subsystem node and the X.25 network must be defined. Depending on the implementation, this definition may include the DTE address, packet size, and window size to be used.

Transport modes. The subsystem must be advised which of the five transport classes to use (which are described in Chapter 13). Classes 0, 2, and 4 are supported in the OSI/Communications Subsystem. For each class, one or more outbound transport modes must be selected. An application-entity uses the mode when initiating a connection. Multiple application-entities can share a single outbound transport mode. In OSI/Communications Subsystem a single inbound mode supports classes 0, 2, and 4. The mode parameters include the following:

- *Class 0*—size of TPDU, which determines the amount of data that an application-entity can transmit at one time; connection-oriented or connectionless network service; and the duration of the timer that waits for confirmation of a successful connection.

- *Class 2*—in addition to the above: whether to negotiate down to class 0, whether to use explicit flow control, and values for multiplexing.

- *Class 4*—in addition to the above: whether to negotiate down to class 0 and/or 2, flow control values, additional timers like retransmit time, inactivity time and give-up time; and whether to use a checksum.

The definition of application-entities includes means to locate them and their lower-layer services. AEs to be defined include customer written AEs as well as those for directory services, system management, and other system provided application-services.

For locating application-entities, the customer usually employs a 1- to 8-character application-entity *nickname*. The API can handle this, and must convert it to the formal OSI *distinguished name*. The latter is then used by the directory services to find the destination presentation address. The application_entity_title is a part of the distinguished name.

Local application-entities that initiate associations need an application mode to specify the lower layer services. These can include:

- *Presentation layer*—application context, including the named local syntax used by the application and named mapping functions used to convert data into a common transfer syntax.

- *Session layer*—initial token assignments for sending data, synchronizing data sent thus far, and initiating a release of a connection. These tokens specify which partner can perform the indicated service. Selection of version 1 (512 bytes) or version 2 (10K bytes) regulates the amount of data sent at one time.

Directory services.   The preferred mode is to use a central or distributed directory service. Without such a service, all such information must be maintained in the local node.

- *Local directory*—including local application-entities and remote application-entities with which the local AEs wish to communicate. In this case, the local node must maintain this information as it changes.

- *Central/distributed directory services*—requires the definition of application-entities for the Directory User Agent (DUA) and the Directory System Agent (DSA). (The first release of IBM OSI/ Communications Subsystem supports that subset of the Directory Access Protocol specified by MAP 3.0.) With this service, the DSA acquires the responsibility to update the OSI-wide information as it changes, so the local DUA can always get current information.

System management domains.   As an OSI application, the system management function relies on the use of System Management Application-Entities (SMAEs) for communication between management processes and agent processes. A given node may contain both managing and agent functions. All communication is between a manager and an agent. A subsystem node must use an administrative facility to define the SMAEs that support local and remote managing and agent processes which need to communicate in this manner.

EXERCISES

11.1   The OSI/Communications Subsystem interfaces to which environment boundaries?

11.2   The OSI transaction-processing API is comparable to what set of verbs in SNA?

11.3   Give six examples of shared resources or interoperation between OSI and SNA systems.

Part 4
Transport-Service-Providers: Transport/Inter-Subnetwork Facilities

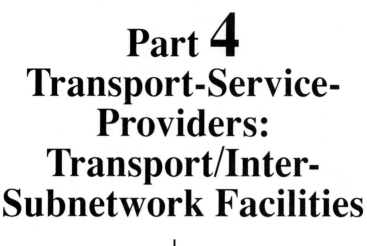

Part 2	Application-Services	
Part 3	End-to-End Data-Exchange Facilities	Part 1
Part 4	Transport Inter-Subnetwork Facilities	
Part 5	Link/Subnetwork-Access Facilities	

Part 4 addresses the mid portions of the overall structure in Figure 3.14. It introduces the concept of the *multiprotocol transport-service-provider*, at layers 1 through 4, capable of carrying traffic from different end-systems and over multiple subnetworks. It then focuses on the layers 3c and 4 macro layer concerned with end-to-end transport control and *inter-subnetworking*. After a general discussion of inter-subnetworking, attention is given to OSI, TCP/IP, NetBIOS, SNA/APPN, and SNA/subarea-network, in layers 3c and 4.

 Chapter 12, Transport-Service-Provider (TSP) Structures, first examines the *addressing*, at layers 1 through 3, the place of SNA addressing in the OSI scheme, and the routing that takes place at multiple layers. The roles of *bridges and routers* are discussed, with emphasis on routing among multiple subnetworks. The concept of *internetworking* is broadly generalized. The concepts and options for multiple-protocol backbone-subnetworks are examined.

 Chapter 13, TSPs: OSI, TCP/IP, NetBIOS, provides a tutorial on the protocols used in OSI and TCP/IP at layers 3c and 4. The OSI transport layer classes, the connectionless network service, and the X.25 connection-oriented service are explained. The basic TCP/IP services, and the X/Open Transport Interface (XTI) for OSI and TCP/IP are reviewed. NetBIOS is briefly explained.

 Chapter 14, TSP: APPN, looks in some depth at the objectives and approaches of *Advanced Peer-to-Peer Networking*. Ease of installation and ease of use are the key attributes. The reduction of system definition, automatic topology updating, nondisruptive reconfiguration, and dynamic route selection are detailed.

Chapter 15, TSP: Subarea-Networks, reviews the SNA Subarea network briefly, including cross-domain and cross-network operations. It then focuses on the manner in which the APPN and subarea networks can coexist and cooperate dynamically.

Chapters 16–18 in Part 5 then discuss the sharing, by each of the above layer-3c and -4 facilities, of lower-layer services of the transport-service-provider. These are the link/subnetwork-access facilities in layers 1 through 3a.

12
Transport-Service-Providers

12.1 INTRODUCTION

At this point, we begin looking more deeply at the lower four layers that comprise the **transport-service-providers**. What should these four layers do for us, and what structures are needed? As noted in Chapter 1, market requirements call for a transport-service-provider offering easy-to-use, multiprotocol, scalable, wide-area-network and local-area-network services. Referring to Figure 3.14, these transport-service-providers must (a) interconnect the various links and subnetworks in layers 1 through 3a, and (b) accept and transmit the multiple upper-layer protocols in layers 5 through 7. These transport-service-providers must, moreover, offer the cost and performance advantages that newer, high-speed technologies make possible. The requirements appear to be in roughly the following priority:

1. Reduction of operational complexity and cost in large networks. This involves reduced system definition, dynamic topology updates, and nondisruptive changes in the network.[1]

2. The ability for major end-systems to optionally connect to multiple types of transport-service-providers.

3. The ability of a transport-service-provider to connect to end-systems that were designed for different transport facilities, so as to provide a *multiprotocol transport service* (e.g., a backbone that can carry X.25, SNA, TCP/IP, and NetBIOS traffic).

---

1. For example, when network communication controllers must be added or removed from the network, operations outside those units should not be disrupted. There should be no need to shut the system down for redefinitions concerning the changed controllers.

4. High-performance, high-speed data routing. In the early time period, data rates of T1 (1.5 Mbps), and T3 (45 Mbps) will be common, with subsequent data rates going well beyond.

5. Voice/data/video integration.

These five topics are discussed in this and later chapters.

Chapter 12 is a network structure chapter with emphasis on the interconnection of subnetworks. In this chapter, we begin the examination of transport-service-providers by discussing the fundamentals of addressing and the use of global OSI-based addressing. SNA addressing is made an integral part of that. Routing techniques, at all layers, are key, and get special attention. The interconnection of subnetworks in many combinations, using bridges, routers, and gateways, is described. The generality of the concept of inter-subnetwork routing, at layer 3c is explained. Backbones that encapsulate "foreign" protocols and end-systems that can use different subnetworks are examined. Finally, we discuss the structures needed for the evolution of protocol-independent transport-service-providers, using combinations of bridges and routers and taking advantage of protocol-independent routing below layer 3.

In later chapters, we take up the use of these techniques in specific implementations.

12.2   THE TRANSPORT-SERVICE-PROVIDER LAYERS

What is the overall architecture of the transport-service-provider, in a multiprotocol, multivendor environment? The transport-service-provider, as seen by the upper layers in an end-system, involves data routing and transmission in layers 1 through 3, plus a supervision of these transmission services residing in layer 4. The primary transport-service-providers are in five protocol "islands," with OSI, TCP/IP, APPN and/or subarea-network, or NetBIOS, protocols as shown in Figure 12.1. Many other proprietary protocols, such as DECnet, Novell's IPX, and Apple's Appletalk may also need to be integrated in an enterprise information system, but our discussion can start with the five cited. Each of the five transport-service-providers may involve subnetworks within them, such as LANs, ISDN, or MANs, operating at layers 1 and 2. While emphasis is placed on the transition to OSI, the persistent challenge is to connect pairs of like end-systems which may be located on subnetworks that carry any of these five protocols.

Figure 12.2 shows a generalized structure of a multistack end-system. Communication is between an upper end-to-end data-exchange facility in one node and a corresponding end-to-end facility in another node. That communication is via the transport-service-provider, composed of the transport entities in the transport layer, the network entities in the network layer 3c, and the links or subnetworks in layers 1 through 3a.[2] We refer to the aggregate of facilities in layers 1 through 3a as the **link/subnetwork-access facilities**. Each link or subnetwork-access provides a *logical-link* (see Section 3.6.3) that serves a

---

2. The sublayers 3a, 3b, and 3c are explained in Section 3.2.7.

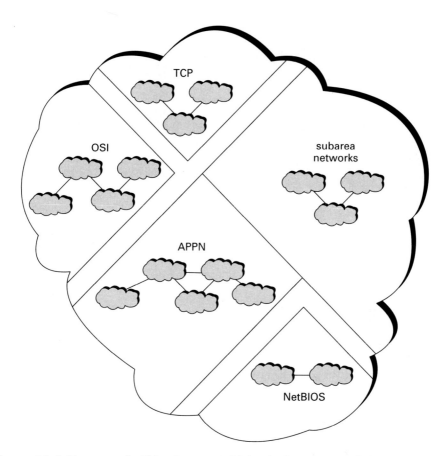

Figure 12.1 Transport facilities in protocol islands that must be linked.

network-entity at layer 3c. More completely, each logical-link serves a *protocol stack* that is tied to a network-entity.[3] Logical-links connect to network-entities in other end-systems or in intermediate-systems. The physical connection from an end-system (whether to another end-system, a subnetwork like X.25, or other subnetwork) is an **access-link**.

Typical link/subnetwork-access services with a LAN, or a point-to-point link, for example, result in traffic flowing from a network-entity in an end-system, over a logical-link to a network-entity in another end-system. However, when the end-to-end logical connection is between two end-systems, via intermediate-systems, the connection is usually accomplished by concatenating two or more logical-links via intermediary layer-3c entities.

---

3.   There are cases (as with some LANs) where the network layer is null. In those cases, the logical-link is with the next higher layer that is present.

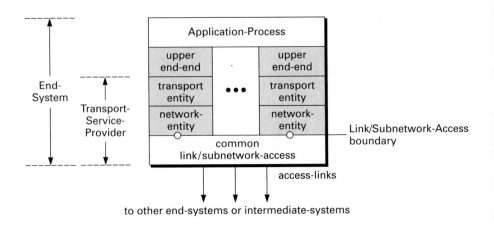

to other end-systems or intermediate-systems

Figure 12.2 Generalized structure of a multipack end-system.

12.3   ADDRESS SPACES

To achieve an integrated network, the disparate addressing schemes have to be reconciled. The following therefore examines important address components and the participation of the SNA addressing in the worldwide OSI addressing conventions.

12.3.1   Subnetwork Points of Attachment

Within specific transport facility protocols, such as the protocols in LANs, ISDN, and the X.25 packet-level protocol, the addressing mechanisms are specific to a particular link or subnetwork. Consider, as a prime example of a subnetwork, an X.25 PSDN. Subnetwork addresses in a PSDN identify only a point of attachment to the subnetwork. These **Subnetwork Points of Attachment (SNPA)** addresses have no significance beyond a particular subnetwork, unless groups of subnetworks have agreed among themselves to use a common subnetwork addressing scheme. For example, public networks may agree to use the X.121 [X.121] addressing convention for data networks, and E.164 [E.164] for ISDNs, both of which are hierarchical numerical addressing schemes (like telephone numbers). In general, however, the addressing associated with protocols below the network-3c sublayer are interpreted only within the scope of those single subnetworks. They need not be, and often are not, globally applicable.

The SNPA address is only sufficient to find the correct point of attachment of a node. Even when the destination is located in a node on that subnetwork, some further addressing is usually needed to find the destination application-process within that node. When there are multiple concatenated subnetworks, then the SNPA must be augmented to identify the correct subnetwork as well.

12.3.2   Interdomain Addressing

OSI anticipates the day when all administrative domains for subnetworks will use a common global addressing system. Either all subnetwork addresses must be modified to accommodate that global system (which is unrealistic), or the end-nodes must have some multidomain awareness, and some conversion must take place at interworking units. This brings us to two main options [Svobodova90]:

1.   *Extended address structure*: adding a Net_id (or domain_id) to existing addresses. This Net_id is then used for interdomain routing. It determines the route within each intervening subnetwork to the gateway of the next domain.

2.   *Address encapsulation*: encapsulating the remote destination address, of a node within a foreign subnetwork, in a field of a local subnetwork address. The local address directs the message to the nearest gateway. With multiple intermediate addressing domains, the process is repeated in each domain, so that the address of the gateway to the next domain is always provided. The destination address is unused until the final gateway is reached. Some X.25 networks employ this scheme.

   As described below (Section 12.3.4), the preferred SNA approach is the same as that of OSI, to provide a Net-id for each subnetwork, as in (1) above.

12.3.3   Network Addresses

A **network address**, according to ISO 7498-3 is "a name, unambiguous within the OSI environment, which is used to identify a *set* of Network Service-Access-Points (NSAPs)." Usually, however, the network address refers to only one NSAP. An **NSAP address** is a networkwide unique address used to identify a single NSAP.

   Figure 12.3 shows the points where the OSI network address and the subnetwork point of attachment addresses apply. The SNPA addresses (at the 3a–3b boundary) identify the points at which end-systems interface to the particular subnetworks. These

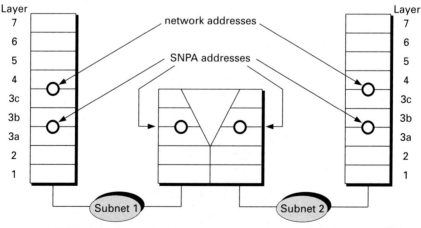

SNPA = Subnetwork Point of Attachment

Figure 12.3 Points where the OSI network address (NSAP address) and the subnetwork point of attachment address (SNPA address) apply.

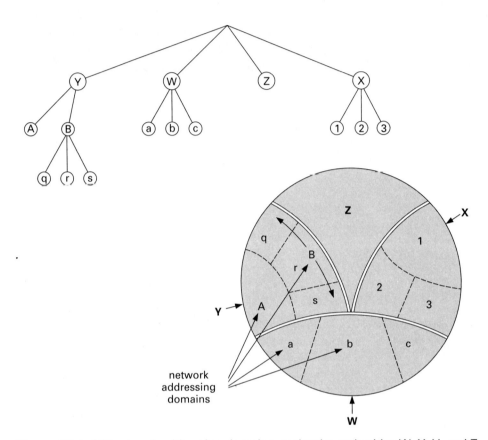

Figure 12.4 OSI network addressing domains, under the authorities W, X, Y, and Z.

SNPA addresses are often used within the subnetwork.[4] The OSI network addresses, on the other hand (at the 3c–4 boundary), identify the transport-layer entities residing inside the end-systems.

The approach taken by ISO and the CCITT for network addresses adds an extra level of hierarchy, so as to encompass the existing numbering, organizational, and geographically-based plans under a single umbrella. This amounts to new format identifiers in NSAP addresses, the **Authority and Format Identifier (AFI)**. Each format belongs to some authority. The format applies to the addresses in domains that are controlled by that authority.

Each **network addressing domain** is administered by one and only one addressing authority. That domain is a subset of the global network addressing domain, which includes all of the NSAP addresses by all addressing authorities (see Figure 12.4). The

---

4. Note that a physical box may have multiple SNPAs on the same subnetwork. For example, an X.25 end-system can have several DTE addresses, but a single physical connection to the X.25 PSDN.

addressing authorities may be hierarchical, forming an inverted tree structure, wherein each lower authority assigns addresses only within its own immediate domain.

The network address structure, as defined in ISO 8348/Add.2 is:

$$NSAP = AFI.IDI.DSP$$

where:

- AFI, the *Authority and Format Identifier*, is the code that specifies the format of the IDI, the authority responsible for allocating values of the IDI, and the abstract syntax of the DSP.

- IDI, the *Initial Domain Identifier*, either contains the actual addresses used in a subnetwork (such as a telephone number), or identifies the authority (e.g., a country or a corporation) responsible for allocating values of the DSP (see the CCITT and ISO formats below).

- DSP, the *Domain Specific Part*, has semantics that are determined by the authority defined in the IDI. In some cases, however, the DSP is null, and the IDI number is a public number (as in telephone numbers). The authority in this case is that in the AFI.

NSAP address formats.   Because NSAP addresses are used to route traffic through an OSI network, they are defined in syntax and semantics. However, variations with existing subnetworks must be accommodated. There are, therefore, three types of network-address formats:

- CCITT formats
- ISO formats
- Local formats

The *CCITT formats* use a *Public Data Number* in the IDI. The DSP may or may not be present. The following CCITT formats are specified for **subnetwork-dependent addressing**, where the IDI contains the *subnetwork address* (i.e., the subnetwork point of attachment address) for X.25, telex, telephone, or ISDN subnetworks:

- *CCITT X.121*, used in X.25 networks, has an IDI with a maximum of 14 decimal digits. It can accommodate up to 4 digits of **Data-Network Identification Code (DNIC)** and up to 10 digits of **Network Terminal Number**. The first three digits of the DNIC are a country code, and the following digit is a network number within the country (assigned by CCITT for countries with multiple public networks).

- *CCITT F.69*, used in the telex network numbering, has an IDI of 8 decimal digits.

- *CCITT E.163* format [E.163] is the numbering plan for the international telephone service. Its IDI of 12 decimal (dial) digits include 1 to 3 digits for **country code** and up to 11 digits for a **National Specific Number** (i.e., subscriber number within the same country or geographic area).

- *CCITT I.331* format (also known as E.164) is the numbering plan for the ISDN era. It has a maximum IDI of 15 decimal digits for an International Data Number. This includes a 3-digit **country code**, a **National Destination Code**, and a **Subscriber Number**. Twelve digits may be used prior to December 31, 1996. The 15-digit IDI is larger than the current 14-digit maximum of X.121. To better harmonize the ISDN and X.121 codes, there are proposals to extend the X.121 definition from 14 to 15 digits [Matsubara89].

Two ISO **subnetwork-independent addressing** formats are:

- *ISO 6523 ICD* (International Code Designator) format, which allows 4 digits for the IDI. The DSP is always present.
- *ISO 3166 DCC* (Data Country Code) format, which allows only 3 digits for the IDI country code.

The ICD is used for nongeographic address assignment authorities. It may be used where the authority is international, rather than being associated with a single country.

The *subnetwork-independent formats* are preferable when multiple subnetworks of various kinds may be encountered. In this mode, at each subnetwork to be traversed, the NSAP is used as the index to a routing table to determine the subnetwork address (SNPA address) of the gateway to the next subnetwork. Once at the final subnetwork, the mapping is from the NSAP to the SNPA address of the destination node—e.g., on a LAN, the MAC (Media Access Control) address and a link SAP address. The price to be paid for this generality, however, is the need for directory look-ups to map NSAPs to SNPA addresses.

The maximum allowable length of an NSAP is 40 decimal digits. This translates to 20 bytes of binary-coded decimal digits [X.213]. Both X.25 call-set-up packets and the ISDN Q.931 SETUP are capable of conveying a full length NSAP (up to 40 digits). The Technical Reference section gives the NSAP formats and dimensions for some of the acceptable NSAP addresses [Patel90], [EWOS89b].

Alternative DSP formats.   In general, the DSP may be subdivided into any number of components; and each component may be a different size, as long as the total allowable size of the DSP is not exceeded, as specified in ISO 8348/Addendum.2. Some of the allowable DSP formats are shown in Figure 12.5. Format (a) follows an *organizational hierarchy*; format

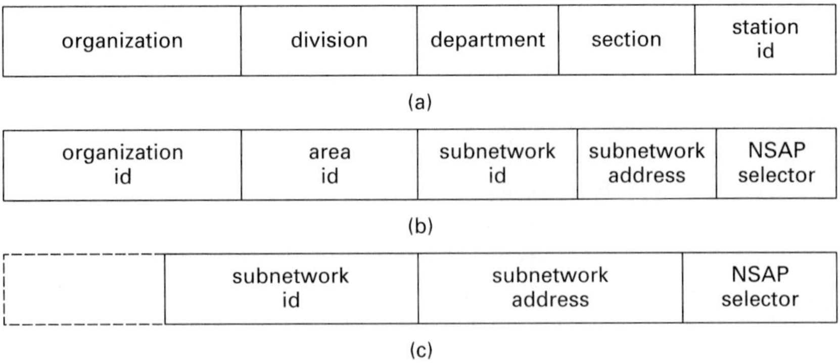

organization	division	department	section	station id

(a)

organization id	area id	subnetwork id	subnetwork address	NSAP selector

(b)

	subnetwork id	subnetwork address	NSAP selector

(c)

Figure 12.5 Examples of allowable DSP formats.

(b) follows a combination of an organizational hierarchy and a *subnetwork hierarchy*; format (c) is based only on subnetworks. Note that subnetwork format (c) has three components: a subnetwork identifier, which must be worldwide unique within the address space of the authority defined by the IDI, a subnetwork address like an address in an X.25 subnetwork),[5] and the NSAP selector which need be unique only in the end-system.

The *subnetwork-address* in the above formats may, moreover, have a variety of meanings; it may be:

- A *real address of a node with a single real point of attachment* to a subnetwork
- A *virtual address, of a node with a single point of attachment*, to ensure that any future changes in the attachment of end-systems do not mean that the network address must change.
- A *virtual address, representing an end-system with multiple attachments to the same subnetwork*. In this case, a mapping must be done, by the end-system and/or intermediate-systems to map the virtual address to one of the real subnetwork addresses.
- A *virtual address, representing an end-system with attachments to multiple subnetworks*. In this case, the "subnetwork-id" must represent all the subnetworks to which the end-system belongs; and the "subnetwork-address" represents all the end-system's attachments. A mapping is then required to map both the subnetwork-id and the subnetwork-address into suitable information for further routing.

12.3.4   IBM-Specified NSAPs

Resource_names.   LU_names serve a dual purpose. They are a convenient unique name for a port into the path control layer. Therefore, like the name Delancey Street, they also have the properties of an address.

In SNA, a network resource is given a **network-qualified SNA_name**. The SNA resource can be a logical unit (LU), a control point (a CP in APPNs), or physical unit (a PU, in subarea networks). For example, an LU is given a *network-qualified LU_name*, Net_id.LU_name. This consists of a network identifier (Net_id) followed by an LU_name. The LU_name is unique within a particular SNA network. If the Net_id is registered in the **SNA Registry**,[6] then it will be made unique worldwide. The preferred structure for the eight character Net_id is: Net_id = CC EEEE NN.

- CC = country code (as per ISO 3166)
- EEEE = owning enterprise code
- NN = network suffix, for the specific network of the enterprise

In making a comparison with OSI, LU_names serve as both PSAP addresses and NSAP addresses. Recall that multiplexing and splitting occurs in OSI layers 4–7, but not in the corresponding SNA layers. Different applications never share the same LU_name,

---

5.   An end-system attached to an X.25 subnetwork is called a *Data Terminal Equipment* (DTE). The end-system address is accordingly called the DTE address.

6.   The SNA Registry is arranged through IBM branch offices.

and different applications never share the same PSAP address. However, different applications may share the same OSI NSAP address because of the multiplexing and splitting in OSI.

Transport-provider addressing.   The IBM-specified NSAP takes its place as a layer 3c address in a multi-subnetwork addressing structure. To get an overall view of this addressing, we now need to recall the headers for each layer, shown in Figure 3.23. Going a step beyond that, we allow the existence of layers 3c and 3a, each with its own headers. A resulting picture is shown in Figure 12.6, where the headers are grouped to emphasize the layer 3c inter-subnetwork header and the layer 1–3a link/subnetwork headers. In the layer 3c header there is the layer 3c NSAP address, which we now focus on.

   SNA registered resources are included in the OSI address space as a part of an NSAP address, in the ICD (International Code Designator) format. The Net_id.SNA_name is in the DSP (Domain Specific Part) of the ICD address. To be a fully legitimate OSI NSAP address, a registered AFI code (47) is used, signifying that the next field, the IDI (Initial Domain Identifier), uses an ICD format that indicates how the remainder of the NSAP is formatted. The ICD designator for IBM is 0018.

   Now, let us look at the possible make up of the IBM-specified DSP, illustrated in Figure 12.6. 9 bytes of the DSP are for the subnetwork _id, consisting of 8 bytes for the Net_id defined above and one additional byte for further network subdivision. That additional byte (called network suffix extension) can identify a subnetwork like, for example, a LAN within an SNA network. Since multiple protocols need to be handled in an enterprise network, one other byte of the DSP may be a protocol type field designator. The last (low-order) byte of the NSAP is not used in routing, but is left for local significance in the end-system (see Figure 12.5(c)). That leaves 6 bytes for the resource_name. This is adequate for SNA resource_names since they are encodings only of characters A–Z, and 0–9, and can readily be compressed to 6 bytes.

   In the layer 1–3a headers there are one or more subnetwork point of attachment (SNPA) addresses, such as the LAN, X.25 DTE, and link addresses. These SNPA addresses are discussed further in Chapters 16 through 18.

12.3.5 TCP/IP Addresses

The addresses of the service-access-points (SAPs), of the layers 3 and 4 in TCP/IP, provide components of the TCP/IP address. The SAPs of the TCP layer are called **ports**. The TCP layer SAP address, or **port_id**, is a 16-bit binary number that identifies to which higher-level process it must deliver incoming messages. Some port_ids, for common application-services, have been standardized among locations. These include, for example, common port_ids for file transfer data (20), file transfer control (21), TELNET (23), simple mail transfer (25), X.400 (103), and remote procedure call (111).

   The SAP addresses of the IP layer are called **Internet addresses** (or IP_addresses), which are 32 bits. The IP layer is equivalent to a layer 3c in OSI. The Internet address is, accordingly, analogous to the OSI NSAP.

   The combination of the port_id and the Internet address is called a **socket**: socket = IP_address.port_id.

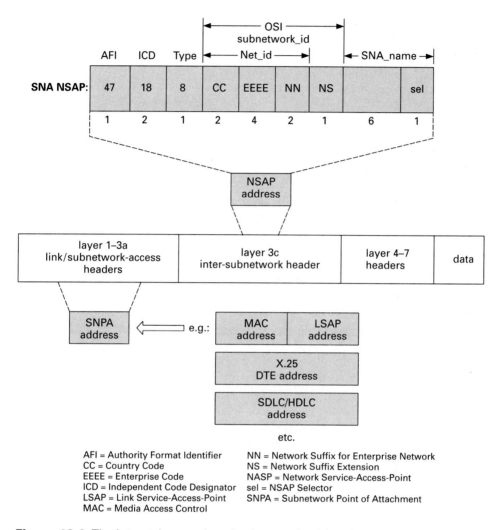

AFI = Authority Format Identifier   NN = Network Suffix for Enterprise Network
CC = Country Code   NS = Network Suffix Extension
EEEE = Enterprise Code   NASP = Network Service-Access-Point
ICD = Independent Code Designator   sel = NSAP Selector
LSAP = Link Service-Access-Point   SNPA = Subnetwork Point of Attachment
MAC = Media Access Control

Figure 12.6 The inter-subnetwork and subnetwork addressing and headers.

The IP_addresses are usually specified as four numbers separated by periods (W.X.Y.Z), where each number is the decimal value of 8 bits in the 32-bit IP_address. This IP_address has two parts, the Net_id and the **host_id**: IP_address = Net_id.host_id. The number of bytes assigned to each part (Net_id and host_id) varies, depending on the class of network.

- *Class A*: a few very large networks; leading edge bit =0; 7 other bits in Net_id; 24 bits host_id.

- *Class B*: moderately large networks; leading edge bits are 10; 14 other bits in Net_id; 16 bits host_id.

- *Class C*: many small networks; leading edge bits are 110; 21 other bits in Net_id; 8 bits host_id.

- *Class D*: reserved for multicasting, a form of broadcasting in a limited area; leading edge bits are 1110; remainder is a multicast address.

As an example, a Class C Internet address, with 24 bits for Net_id, would be built up as follows:

company: 194.032

local-network: .016

Net_id = company.local-network: 194.032.016

host_id: .100

IP_address = Net_id.host_id: 194.032.016.100

A node has a unique Internet address for each network that it is attached to. Hence, an IP router node has multiple addresses—one for each attaching subnetwork. The Net_ids for TCP/IP networks are assigned by the Network Information Center (at SRI). The host_id is always assigned by local authority.

12.4   ROUTING FUNCTION

The concepts of routing are extremely important in the three lower layers. Therefore, at this point, we examine the basics of routing approaches, the separation of routing into domains, and the practices of routing in different layers. Routing, as defined by the OSI reference model, is:

A function within a layer which translates the address of a service-access-point to which an entity is attached into a path (route) by which the entity can be reached. A route consists of a chain of entities that enables data to be relayed from one correspondent entity to another correspondent entity.

12.4.1   Routing Approaches

A primary function in the transport-services-provider is routing of packets from source to destination, both within subnetworks and among subnetworks. One finds at least three distinct design approaches (each of which has been given multiple names) for routing from source to destination. These approaches vary in where the route-selection decisions are made and how the route information is carried.

- *Source routing* (or contents-guided routing) requires that the source provide each packet with all the information needed to define the route, such as a list of the successive links to be traversed. Although every packet must carry considerable route information, a claimed advantage is that reconfiguration after a fault can be faster with source routing.

- *Label-based routing* (or address-swapping routing) is a variation of source routing. It first involves the sending of a single source-routing packet from source to destination, so that switching tables can be set up at each intermediate-node. Thereafter, each data packet sent to a node contains only a label to serve as an index into that node's table. That table determines the next link and supplies a new label for the next node.

▪ *Destination routing* requires that each intermediate-node make a decision *based on examination of the layer-3 packet header* containing the address of the desired destination. The intermediate-node may base its decision purely on its current assessment of the topology and congestion conditions, or it may use a prior set of decisions for each destination which has been stored at that node.

Source routing and label-based routing may each be done *at layer 3 or at layer 2*. When implemented at layer 2, the hop-by-hop error-recovery and flow-control facilities are usually eliminated. Error recovery and flow control are then relegated to end-to-end functions operating at higher layers. The switching at layer 2 is usually implemented in hardware for high performance (the protocol and formats have to be shaped so that it is easy to implement them in hardware). Because the upper part of DLC, involving link controls, is thus not used in the hop-by-hop process, this routing is sometimes named after the lower part of DLC, and referred to as source routing or label-based routing at the media access control (MAC) layer. It may simply be called MAC layer switching or *frame relaying* (see Chapter 18).

If, however, the recovery and/or flow control functions of the upper part of the DLC layer (called the Logical-Link Control, or LLC) are used on each physical link, and if the switching is not complete until after those functions are done, then one is inclined to associate the routing with that upper part of DLC. Then the source routing or the label routing is said to be at the LLC layer. This is called *frame switching.*

Similarly, if the DLC functions are fully used and, in addition, layer-3 flow controls are essential to the switching process, then one is inclined to refer to source routing or label routing at layer 3.

The SNA subarea networks have used connection-oriented destination routing, where explicit routes have been predefined for each destination. APPN currently uses connection-oriented label-based routing at layer 3, for each session. However, the routing discipline is independent of the network-directory and topology services, so that a combination of routing disciplines is conceivable with common directory and topology services. In the world of interconnected subnetworks, in fact, it is quite ordinary for nested subnetworks to have different and independent routing disciplines, as well as separate directory and topology services.

There are many *algorithms for finding the optimum route,* with given topology and congestion information. Note that the algorithm for route selection is separate from the issues of where the selection is made and how the route information is carried. It is interesting that the same route-selection algorithm can be used with different routing methods. For example, the same (or a very similar) routing algorithm could be used for connection-oriented label-based routing at both layer 3 and layer 2. These routes might, for example, be calculated at the beginning of every session. Moreover, *that same algorithm could be used for either connection-oriented or connectionless destination routing.* In the connectionless case, the algorithm would be used repeatedly, as the message arrives at each intermediate-node, always projecting the route from there to the destination. In the *connection-oriented case*, the same algorithm is used once, and the entire route is usually selected at the beginning of a session.[7] Nearly the same routing algorithm, based on a modified Dijkstra "shortest-path-first" algorithm, is used in both the SNA APPN networks and the OSI intermediate-system routing.[8] A long-term objective would clearly seem to be an integrated routing implementation.

Topology updates.   When topology tables in intermediate-systems (used for route determination) are dynamically updated, two basic updating methods are used.

- *Distance vector protocols* involve frequent recalculation of routing tables, and the *passage of the entire routing table* among neighboring layer-3 routers. The adjacent routers update their tables and pass the results on to other neighbors. In time, the network arrives at "convergence" when all routers agree on a network configuration. As network size increases, the convergence time also increases.

- *Link-state protocols* require the distribution of information on *changes* to the network, rather than complete routing tables. Topology information is distributed when a change occurs, rather than at preset time intervals.

There is still much debate on topology update protocols, but the newer proposals favor the link-state approach. The APPN topology updates as well as the current OSI IS-IS proposals and the newly proposed TCP/IP OSPF (Open Shortest Path First) protocol all use the link-state approach.

12.4.2   Routing Levels

As the number of end-systems in a network increase, the work involved in topology updates and route determination increases. In order to reduce the overhead associated with these functions, it is often useful to divide the network into a hierarchy of routing levels [ISO9575]. This is particularly useful when intermediate-systems at the boundary of the network must accommodate multiple end-systems. Each routing subdomain, associated with a boundary-node, maintains routing information about its own internal composition. The benefit of this technique is that the number of entries in the routing information base may be reduced. This also results in a proportionate reduction in the exchange of topology update information.

SNA routing levels.   In order to reduce the size of the topology directory (which must contain information on all the nodes in the network that are concerned with routing) and to make the topology update and routing processes more efficient, SNA divides its address space into two levels. This division is done differently in the APPN and subarea networks.

---

7.   In connection-oriented routing, it is possible to compute the route either once by the first node or piecemeal by every successive node.

8.   However, APPN adds features to the Dijkstra "shortest-path-first" algorithm, to allow weightings for class-of-service parameters.

In APPN, for example, a distinction is made between *network-nodes*, which primarily have intermediate routing capability, and *end-nodes,* which primarily house the destination LUs and provide end-user interfaces. Multiple end-systems may attach to network-nodes. Hence, there can be many more end-systems than there are network-nodes. An end-node (and its LUs) can move from one network-node to another. That is, an LU can initially get services from one network-node, and then change so as to get its services from a different network-node. It is up to the network-nodes to keep track of their attached end-nodes.

The two route components in APPN are determined by the address of the last network-node along the route to the destination, and the "*tail vectors*" which identify the links between that destination network-node and the attached destination end-node. *SNA therefore needs to perform network topology updates only for these intermediate network-nodes.* This greatly reduces the effort needed for dynamic topology update and the size of the topology database. The determination of the best route for session traffic, however, does take into account the characteristics of the entire end-node to end-node route, including the characteristics of the tail vectors.

The identity of that destination network-node is similar in form to the Net_id.LU_name discussed above. Each APPN network-node contains a control point, which has a *control point_name (CP_name).* The corresponding unique network-node name is:

$$NN\_name = Net\_id.CP\_name$$

That would result, for example, in the composite identifier:

$$NN\_name/TV/LU\_address = Net\_id.CP\_name.TV.LU\_name$$

where the Net_id and control point name identify the network-node capable of serving the end-node, and the TV refers to the tail vector, which is the link or other address information for attachments of the end-node to the serving network-node.[9]

A similar breakdown of the route into two components occurs in subarea networks, with a similar simplification for topology updates and routing. There, the serving intermediate-nodes are called *subarea-nodes,* and the attaching nodes are called *peripheral-nodes.* The two corresponding route components are determined by the *subarea address* of the last subarea-node along the route, and the *element address* which determines the link from that subarea-node to the destination peripheral-node.

Three-stage route determination.　　SNA routing, accordingly, is first to the destination network-node (or subarea-node), and then to the attached destination end-node (or peripheral-node). To preserve this independent movability of end-nodes and LUs, a network layer directory service is needed to map LU_names into the address of the destination network-node (or subarea-node). APPN, however, has a capability not possessed by subarea networks—namely, an end-node can be serviced by any one of a number of network-nodes. Hence the APPN route-selection process must know all the possible serving network-nodes, to select the best end-node to end-node route. As illustrated in Figure 12.7, SNA route

---

9.　End-nodes can attach to multiple network-nodes, therefore the best route selection has to also be aware of the characteristics of alternate tail vectors.

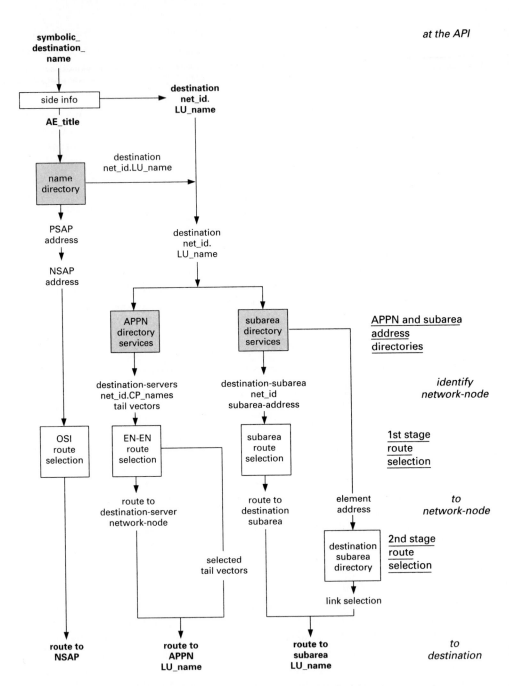

Figure 12.7 The OSI, APPN, and subarea route determination processes.

determination therefore occurs in stages:

1. The *identity of the destination-serving network-node* (or subarea-node) is obtained from an SNA layer-3 directory service. The input to the directory is the LU_name; and the output is either the subarea address or the Net_id.CP_name for the destination-serving network-node. In the case of APPN, the selection of the destination-serving network-node takes into account the multiple connections that may exist between the destination end-node and more than one network-node.

2. A first stage of route selection determines the route to the destination-serving network-node (or subarea-node).

3. A second stage of route selection identifies the "last mile" path from the destination-serving network-node (or subarea-node) to the destination end-node. This is referred to as the *tail vector* for network-nodes or the *link address* from subarea-nodes.

This "tail vector" can pertain to a variety of physical connections for the "last mile" to the destination end-node. It might be a point-to-point link, or a LAN, a dial up of a switched telephone connection, or a set up of a switched virtual circuit on an X.25 subnetwork. In APPN, that tail-vector information is not kept in the topology database, but it is known to the serving network-nodes. That information is made known to the directory services as part of the directory search process.

The **OSI route selection** is not usually thought to have a two-stage process. However, current OSI IS-IS proposals do include routing at two levels, for comparable reasons. Otherwise, the consequence would be that all OSI end-systems (and their movements) would have to be included in the network topology database. This would considerably increase the size of that database and reduce the performance of the route-selection process.

12.4.3   Roles of Layer 3

The role of layer 3 of the architecture is varied, depending on the nature of the transmission facilities being served in layers below. First, refer back to the subdivision of layer 3 into three sublayers, as described in Section 3.2.7. The upper layer, 3c, called the independent convergence sublayer, has a dominant role. One view is to consider that everything connected at the upper sublayer, layer 3c, is (to it) a subnetwork (as OSI defines it), whether that subnetwork be a LAN, an X.25 subnetwork, a voice/data broadband subnetwork, an ISDN subnetwork, or just a point-to-point connection between layer-3 intermediate-nodes. The primary layer-3c function thus becomes a multipurpose inter-subnetwork protocol which may:

1. Provide the *intermediate function* among point-to-point-links (and parallel-links)[10] of a WAN

2. Perform the *inter-subnetwork function*
   a)   Connecting *its own* network's X.25, LAN, and ISDN subnetworks
   b)   In participation with a *worldwide* private and public inter-subnetwork system

---

10.   A transmission group is a number of subnetworks or point-to-point links between the same pair of nodes, and the capability to balance the load among them.

12.4.4 Routing in Layers 1 through 3

The advent of very high speed and very high reliability optical fiber links is changing the judgments on how routing functions are best distributed. On lower speed links—say, up to 50 kbps, there is general agreement that software-governed switching at layer 3, with error detection and retransmission on each link at layer 2, is a good design. With highly reliable links, at speeds of T1 (1.544 Mbps) and above, the judgments tend to favor hardware-governed switching at the DLC or physical layer, based on self-routing headers, sometimes with error detection, but with no error correction on individual links. The infrequent retransmission is then left in the hands of end-to-end software. If resources at the intermediate-nodes are to be further conserved, the intermediate-nodes would do no layer-3 flow control and would even discard packets when the node becomes congested. With such layer-1 or layer-2 routing in intermediate-nodes, the layer-3 examination of the destination address is confined to the nodes at the boundary of the subnetwork.

Layer-3 routers.   Inter-subnetwork routing at layer 3c is based on establishing a logical-link between layer-3c entities in adjacent routing nodes. The intervening subnetworks may be connection-oriented or connectionless. At the layer-3 inter-subnetwork router, packets are routed from one incoming logical-link (terminating at an LSAP or SNPA in one subnetwork) to the second outgoing logical-link (beginning at an LSAP or SNPA in the second subnetwork). This inter-subnetwork routing can be determined by one of several schemes, usually by source routing, label-based routing, or destination routing. When we have connectionless internet-routing, the routing is usually determined by an internet destination address (involving a Net_id) that is carried in each packet. CLNP does, however, also allow for a source route to be carried in the network protocol data unit (NPDU).

Nodes containing inter-subnetwork routers are, at the same time, participants in (1) the subnetworks to which they are attached and (2) the network composed of inter-subnetwork routers. These router-nodes, therefore have both Subnetwork Point of Attachment (SNPA) addresses for each attaching subnetwork, and also inter-subnetwork addresses.

Lower-layer routing.   As link and subnetwork services become more and more reliable and of high speed, the functions at layer 3 and layer 2 can and should become simpler. Less attention can then be paid to error handling, and (for performance reasons) less processing per message should be the rule.

A sending layer 4 communicates with a receiving layer 4, using the services of layers 1 through 3. The intervening layers 3, 2, and 1 are the transportation mechanism that must be transparent to the information being communicated between the two layer 4s. In some implementations, the layer-3 controls have the sole responsibility of routing the packet, perhaps along multiple data links and through multiple nodes, from the originating layer 4 to the destination layer 4. Layer 3 adds the packet header to the message unit it receives from layer 4, to achieve this routing. In other implementations, layer 3 depends on lower layers for routing among certain nodes, as in local area subnetworks and broadband subnetworks using DLC layer or physical layer switching. In these latter implementations, the layer-3 header is examined only at the edge of the subnetwork. In these cases, the routing function in the intermediate-nodes of the subnetwork is done at layer 2 or layer 1, without examining a layer-3 header in each such node.

Routing at five sublayers.   In summary, the literature has explored routing (sometimes called switching) at five sublayers, as follows [Deaton90]:

- *Physical layer switching*—traditionally used by modems and digital network adapters for circuit-switched connections.

- *Fast packet switching, Frame Relay*, or *MAC-layer switching*. Switching at the medium access control sublayer (2a) of DLC exists in WANs (see Section 18.5), and in bridged LANs (see Chapter 17). MAC-layer switching may use source routing (contents-guided routing) [Dixon88] or label-based routing (address-swapping) [Cherukuri89]. There is no recovery or flow control at the switch points. If frames are discarded because of congestion or link errors, the protocols at the end-devices must detect the lost frames and perform retransmission. The frame-relay is limited to environments in which frame loss due to transmission errors and congestion is "acceptable."

- *Frame switching* or *LLC switching* occurs at the DLC logical-link control (or Recovery Protocol) sublayer. Recovery is performed on a hop-by-hop basis; and switching can occur between heterogeneous links and protocols.

- *Packet switching* occurs at layer 3, within a subnetwork, as in the OSI X.25 [Ahuja79] packet switched data networks, and also SNA path control.

- *Internet switching*, at layer 3c, between subnetworks, as in the IP layer of TCP/IP and the IP layer of OSI. OSI X.25, SNA/APPN, and SNA subarea path control likewise can operate at layer 3c and perform switching across subnetworks. Current APPN uses a combination of switching (via address-swapping) at layer 3 and adaptive pacing at layer 4.

The consequence of the movement to switching at lower layers, for performance at high speeds, may be the *nesting of two levels of wide area networks*. The inner (sub)network, for T1 and higher speeds, is today within the generally lower-speed wide area network. The corresponding possibility is for the existing WANs to adopt lower-layer routing. APPN, for example, conceivably could adopt lower-layer routing without fundamental changes to its directory, topology-update, and route-selection capabilities.

12.4.5   Routing in Layers 5 through 7

In every architecture, we need addresses or other identifiers to find our way, not merely to the destination LU, but all the way to the proper application-entity. This involves routing to the correct end-system, and then routing through the upper-layer stack (layers 5 through 7) to the connected application-entity. In OSI, a given application-entity can have multiple associations. In SNA, a given application-entity can have multiple sessions. Therefore, the route through the upper layers must correspond to a particular association or session. To differentiate among multiple associations or multiple sessions, some form of addressing or identifiers, beyond that provided by NSAPs, is needed.

Thus, in moving data from one application-process to another in a distant node, two levels of address are needed.

- First the address of the end-system itself, or a processing system within the end-system, is required. That, for example, is the job of the NSAP, or its SNA equivalent, the Net_id.LU_name.[11] These must be worldwide unique.
- Second, each application-entity within that end-system must have addresses or connection_ids, that are unique within that end-node, to identify each path from the NSAP to the AE.

The latter intra-node path identifiers are quite different in SNA, OSI, and TCP/IP; but similarities exist. We next consider each one, in turn. First, however, its necessary to detour a bit to review the use of service-access-point (SAP) selectors at each OSI layer.

1.   In the case of **OSI**, the service-access-point (SAP) of the network layer (the NSAP) can be made unique and provides the address of the destination node. Hence, the NSAP can determine the routing to carry a message to the destination node. The SAPs of the transport, session, and presentation layers, then, serve to identify a path to a particular application-entity (AE) of a particular application-process.

The PSAP has multiple components, including the NSAP, at the network layer, and the selectors which identify the SAPs in each of the upper layers. At each higher layer, a selector_id is added to the NSAP address:

TSAP address = NSAP address + transport selector
SSAP address = TSAP address + session selector
    = NSAP address + transport selector
    + session selector
PSAP address = SSAP address + presentation selector
    = NSAP address + transport selector
    + session selector
    + presentation selector

The SAP at each layer connects to one entity in the above layer; it identifies the layer entity used in that connection. The PSAP thus identifies both the end-system and the particular upper-layer stack (layers 5 through 7) used by its application-entity. Only one part of the PSAP, namely the NSAP, is used for routing to the proper end-system. The remainder, the upper-layer selectors, are used for routing within the end-system. Each application-entity usually has one PSAP, although the standards allow multiple PSAPs per application-entity. *The AE address is the same as the PSAP address.*

So, having reviewed the SAPs and their selectors, how do they relate to a route through the upper layers (5 through 7)? Multiple associations (roughly analogous to SNA sessions) that a given application-entity may have, are assigned to different connection-end-points (CEPs) within the SAPS on the path to that AE. That chain of CEPS, then, is the path through layers 5 through 7.

2.   In the case of *SNA/APPN* or *SNA/Subarea*, as discussed above, the LU_name gets us only to the LU within the destination node. Beyond that, one needs to identify the path for

11.   The equivalence really comes with the addition of an IDI and AFI to the Net_id.LU_name.

specific sessions of that LU and the corresponding AE. In some older LUs, only one session per LU is allowed. In LU 6.2, a *session_id* is provided at the initiation of each session (in the `Bind` command). That session_id identifies the entities involved for that session. Each conversation that uses that session gets a *conversation_id*. Certain verbs at the Application Programming Interface (API) then carry that unique conversation_id back and forth across the API. The combination of conversation_id and session_id are used to identify the path through the SNA layers 5 through 7.

3.   In the case of *TCP/IP*, as discussed above, the **Internet address** corresponds to the OSI NSAP address. The second level of the TCP/IP address is the SAP of the TC layer, called the **port_id** within a host. Port_ids may be local to a machine and unique within that machine. The combination of the Internet address and the port_id is called a socket. Applications generally employ sockets. No further addressing or session identification is specified in TCP/IP. Any further differentiation among data streams is the responsibility of the application.

12.5 BRIDGES, LAYER-3 ROUTERS, GATEWAYS

The industry and the standards bodies have chosen to give distinct names: *bridges, routers,* and *gateways*, to subnetwork connectors, depending on the layers at which they are used. In this section, we consider the differences among these connectors, and we begin to examine the fundamentals of their use (this analysis is carried further in the LAN Chapter 17). We find seven classes of linkages for similar or dissimilar subnetworks:

1.   A **repeater** operates at the physical layer, simply extending the physical character of the subnetwork. Repeaters can sometimes also provide media conversion between optical fiber and copper, with associated distance extensions. However, a repeater normally does not change any of the really fundamental distance limitations inherent in a subnetwork with a given media.

2.   A **bridge** operates at the second, data link control (DLC), layer. Bridges usually operate at the media access control (MAC), the lower sublayer of DLC. The consequence is that the link-layer elements-of-procedure (at the logical-link control, LLC, the upper sublayer of DLC) are performed end-to-end, rather than at each physical link. In the case of bridged, 802-type LANs, for example, these error-control and flow-control protocols of LLC operate across the multiple, bridged LANs. All the addresses in the bridged network must be unique. Bridges operate independent of the layer-3 and higher protocols (i.e., SNA/APPN, SNA/Subarea, OSI/X.25, OSI/CLNP, TCP/IP, NetBIOS).

3.   An **LLC switch** is a bridge that operates at the LLC sublayer of DLC. These are sometimes called link relays. An LLC switch involves the termination of the full DLC function at the bridge. A separate 802.2 protocol is active within each LAN that is bridged.

4.   A **router** works up through layer 3, using the network layer addresses of different subnetworks as well.[12] Layer-3 routers can interconnect and route across many physical subnetworks, including LANs and WANs. The layer-3 router often uses a protocol in

---

12.   The term *router* is often reserved for routing at layer 3 even though a routing function of some kind may be done at many different layers. The term *layer-3 router* is more definitive.

common with other layer-3 routers, forming a network of layer-3 routers. The use of layer-3 routers thus often results in various kinds of internetworking. Routers used to interconnect multiple subnetworks (e.g., LANs and backbone subnetworks) are also called *inter-subnetwork routers*. Layer-3 routers are sensitive to the layer-3 protocols. Hence, multiple modules of layer-3 router function (e.g., one each for SNA, TCP/IP, OSI) are sometimes used, either separately or in a combined package.

5.   A **brouter** (a nonstandard term) is a bridge plus some functions of the network layer at layer 3. It may, for example, provide routing for the set of layer-3 protocols it understands, and provide bridging for all others.

6.   A **gateway** operates above layer 3, and may convert all layers. Examples of this are often found in protocol conversions at the transport and application-services layers.

7.   A **grouter** (a nonstandard term) is a layer-3 router plus some functions of a gateway. For example, the grouter term would apply to a layer-3 router which uses a layer-4 gateway.

Another term, used in some OSI documents is the **InterWorking Unit (IWU)**. This applies to any real piece of equipment that is used to interconnect multiple subnetworks. It may operate at various levels, and may function as a bridge, router, or gateway. However, it is usually shown as a layer-3 inter-subnetwork router. An IWU may be a multiprotocol unit, containing multiple layer-3 inter-subnetwork routers and layer-2 bridges.

Bridges have found extensive use in connecting LANs, and this topic is therefore covered further in Chapter 17, along with LAN descriptions.

In an LLC switch, *two* logical-links are bound together for an extended period of time. In the layer-3 router, on the other hand, the mechanism inherently depends on the examination of a routing (layer-3) header in each packet. The layer-3 router not only terminates the logical-links, but also performs a routing of packets from one logical-link to *one of many* other logical-links, based on information in the layer-3 header.

The gateway, by definition, performs some relay functions above layer 3. Often, this is at the application layer. Some examples of this are given in the X.400 to PROFS (an IBM office system) gateways described in Chapter 6. Gateways also could be used to match different transport-layer facilities, if one were going, for example, from NetBIOS transports to SNA/APPN, OSI, or TCP/IP transports. Another example is the PS/2 SNA LAN Gateway between LANs and S/390 and AS/400 hosts. This unit performs emulation of the 3270 data stream (as a gateway) and passage (as a layer-3 router) of multiple LU-LU sessions. That unit is discussed further in Chapter 17.

These various relays are illustrated in Figure 12.8. As one proceeds from repeaters at layer 1 to gateways involving all seven layers, the intermediate relay requires packets to traverse more and more layers. Latency, the delay in transaction responses, can become a problem as one goes higher in the stack. Hence, the lower the relay function, the higher the performance, and the more independent the relay can be of the higher-layer protocols. However, the lower the relay function, the more similar the two subnetworks have to be.

To illustrate, two LANs might be connected in a number of ways:

1.   They may be connected by a layer-2 MAC bridge.

2.   If the two LANs are connected by a dedicated line, then split bridges can be used.

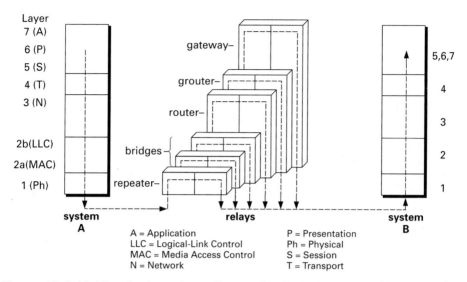

Figure 12.8 legend:

A = Application	P = Presentation
LLC = Logical-Link Control	Ph = Physical
MAC = Media Access Control	S = Session
N = Network	T = Transport

Figure 12.8 Multilevel relays, depending on the dissimilarities of two systems.

3.   If end-systems on the LAN have layer-3 routing capability, then traffic between LANs can be layer-3 routed between LANs.

   ▪   A layer-3 router can be used, with both LANs connected to that one router, or
   ▪   Traffic can be routed first to a boundary layer-3 routing node on each LAN (designed to control inter-subnetwork flows) and then through a connecting bridge (or a split bridge) to a similar boundary layer-3 routing node on the other LAN.

Other configurations would replace the dedicated line in the split bridge with high speed IDNX-type voice/data networks or with high speed links in an all-data WAN.

12.6   PROTOCOL ENCAPSULATION VERSUS PROTOCOL CONVERSION

There often are two basic choices in the design of layer-3 routers and gateways, when faced with multiple protocols. We next examine these two approaches and give some significant examples.

Protocol *conversion* has the task of relating two architectures that have been designed separately with different objectives. The problems in doing this (cited below) may be formidable. Nevertheless, protocol conversion, sometimes with compromises, often leads to a lower-cost and more efficient solution. An alternative approach is *encapsulation*. In this approach, one network protocol (e.g., at layer 3c) is enclosed by another network protocol (say, at layer 3a). This means that the data and headers from the upper layers are all simply treated as data by the lower layer. All upper-layer data and controls are encapsulated by the headers of the lower layer. (In general, encapsulation has been the approach blessed by internetworking standards, and is widely used in OSI, TCP, and SNA.)

12.6.1   Types of Protocol Conversion

Protocol conversion between two architectures can be done in two ways [Svobodova90]:

1. *Service-interface-mapping*: The conversion takes place between functionally compatible service-primitives of a corresponding layer in each architecture.

2. *Protocol-flow-mapping*: The conversion takes place at the level of the individual protocol data units (PDUs) used by the two architectures.

Service-interface-mapping may be much simpler, particularly when the service interfaces in the different architectures are similar. The corresponding primitives may be simply swapped. This can be the case, even though the lower intralayer protocols (PDUs) of the two architectures may be very different.

On the other hand, when the protocols of the connecting subnetworks are sufficiently close, a translation of addresses and conversion of protocols is feasible within the relay. This approach is more feasible, for example, in cases of similar architectures, like the interconnection of SNA APPNs with SNA subarea networks.

Conversion limitations.   Protocol conversions are obviously more feasible when one of the two architectures involved has been drawn from the other, so that the semantics and syntax are compatible. A completely compatible mapping is only possible when the semantics in the two protocols are truly equivalent. Otherwise, approximations are needed. A number of difficulties can be encountered, like the following.

-   One architecture may have no counterpart at all for some feature in the other.
-   A feature may be mandatory in one architecture and optional in the other.
-   Differences in syntax may include things like different field sizes, and allowable character sets.
-   Error recovery features in one may not be provided in the other, or may not be as effective.

In the design of the relay, therefore, some subjective judgments may have to be applied in arriving at reasonable equivalents or tolerable compromises.

Beyond these protocol conversions, linking separate subnetworks also raises important issues relating to overall addressing, system management, and security. In these areas, too, common facilities and format conversions need to be sought for practical and effective operations.

12.6.2   An Example for Comparison

Consider, for example, the problem of communicating APPC end-to-end, across two dissimilar networks: between an end-node using NetBIOS on a LAN and an SNA node using APPN on a WAN.[13] A gateway is proposed between the two networks. A straightforward approach, using *encapsulation*, is shown in Figure 12.9(a). The features of this

---

13.   A related problem was addressed by Johannsen, Lamersdorf, and Reinhardt who reported on a layer-3 gateway connecting NetBIOS with X.25, assuming a common transport class 0 at both ends [Johannsen88].

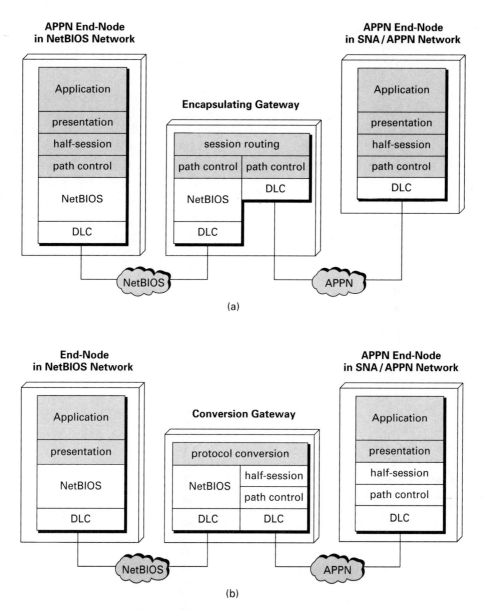

Figure 12.9 NetBIOS/APPN gateways using encapsulation and conversion: **(a)** LU 6.2 and APPN network protocols encapsulated by NetBIOS; **(b)** gateway with protocol conversion.

solution are:

- The upper-layer protocols are LU 6.2, at both ends.
- The APPN path control exists in both the end-nodes and the gateway. The APPN protocol is thus the common *inter-subnetwork* or *encapsulated* protocol.

- Traversing the NetBIOS network is accomplished by placing the NetBIOS layer "under" the APPN layer. This results in the NetBIOS protocols encapsulating all of the layers above it, including the APPN protocols.

Thus, NetBIOS is used in a connecting subnetwork within the larger network that uses the APPN inter-subnetwork protocol. This approach would not work for the inverse, NetBIOS over SNA, because NetBIOS does not possess an intermediate routing capability. The primary disadvantage of this encapsulation approach is that the two protocol systems (APPN path control and NetBIOS) consume larger amounts of memory in the end-node, where cost is usually a prime consideration. The *protocol conversion* approach is shown in Figure 12.9(b). The features of this approach are:

- There is no common layer 3 or layer 4 in both end-nodes and the gateway.
- In the gateway, protocol conversion is needed between the NetBIOS protocols on the one hand, and part of the SNA half-session and the path control protocols on the other.
- There remains the problem of having either an LU 6.2 application programming interface (API) at both ends, or having an NetBIOS API at both ends, so they will understand each other. In either case, a mapping is necessary from that API to a "foreign" underlying transport at one end.[14]

Both conversion and encapsulation are often feasible. Conversion (by either *service-interface-mapping* or *protocol-flow-mapping*) is necessary if the transport protocol is different in the two end-systems. Conversion by service-interface-mapping can be very effective in those cases where a high degree of commonalty in service-interfaces can be found.

Encapsulation of one network-layer protocol by the other is feasible if the transport-layer protocols in the two end-systems are the same. Because of the lack of comparable features in different protocols, and the changes that take place in protocols, the encapsulation strategy is often more practical than conversion. With the greater availability of bandwidth, the extra transmission burden is not high. In the case of a common backbone network, for example, all the protocols of the end-system and attached subnetwork, at layer 3c and above, are then simply carried as data in the backbone. There remains, then, the accommodation of the connect and termination phases, which can be done by protocol mapping.

Both approaches (conversion and encapsulation) have their price. Depending on available technology and design ingenuity, both have their place [Caldwell88].

12.6.3 Transport-Service-Gateways

A significant illustration of protocol conversion by service-interface-mapping, occurs at the transport-service boundary. It may be surprising to realize that two pure OSI hosts cannot interoperate if one host uses class 0 transport protocol (TP-0), which is common in countries having X.25, and the other uses class 4 (TP-4), which is common for users of

14. This *mapping* is an accommodation by the API of a transport protocol that it ordinarily does not work with.

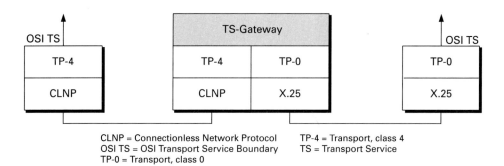

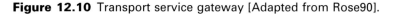

CLNP = Connectionless Network Protocol   TP-4 = Transport, class 4
OSI TS = OSI Transport Service Boundary   TS = Transport Service
TP-0 = Transport, class 0

Figure 12.10 Transport service gateway [Adapted from Rose90].

connectionless network protocol (CLNP). The *Transport Layer Gateway*, discussed by Johannsen et al. addresses this problem [Johannsen88]. The *transport service bridge* (more properly called a gateway), described by M. T. Rose, also addresses this type of problem [Rose90]. As shown in Figure 12.10, a relay is introduced above the OSI transport service.[15]

The transport-service-gateway (TS-gateway) uses service-interface-mapping. It basically copies service-primitives from one transport-services (TS) stack to another. For example, upon receiving a connection indication from one TS stack, the TS-gateway will issue a connection request to the other TS stack. This works except for slight differences in the two transport services that cannot be correlated with functions in the other service. One such issue is the carrying of user-data on connection establishment. TP-0 does not support this; and TP-4 does. So, connections with such data may have to be refused or handled with special procedures. A similar problem pertains to expedited-data. TP-0 does not support it; TP-4 does. That facility must be down-negotiated. Fortunately, neither facility is essential.

Another example of a transport gateway is obtained if X.25 is replaced by TCP/IP, as shown in Figure 12.10 [Rose90]. The result is a proposal for split stacks, involving OSI-based applications at both ends, with one end using its TCP/IP subnetwork, and the other end using its OSI CLNP subnetwork. To accommodate this mismatch, RFC1006[16] defines the way to produce OSI transport services on top of TCP [Simpson90]. There is also a clear similarity between these two examples of transport gateways and the example given in Figure 12.9(b), where the concatenation was between NetBIOS and SNA transport systems.

---

15.   Rose calls this a transport-service-bridge. Since it is above layer 3, it also qualifies for the gateway terminology; and since it must also pass layer-3 address information, this type of function has also been referred to as a *grouter*.

16.   RFC1006 is part of the International Standards Organization Development Environment (ISODE), which is a publicly available collection of library routines and programs that implement OSI upper-layer services. ISODE provided an early example of TCP/IP to OSI coexistence based on transport-service-bridges.

Thus, the TS-gateway (or a close relative) has applicability to OSI/OSI, OSI/TCP, and NetBIOS/APPN. Similar options can be considered for other pairs of transport systems, such as SNA/OSI and SNA/TCP. The use of service-interface-mapping opens the possibilities that the upper portion of one protocol stack might use the lower portion of another one, effectively enabling the lower-layer networking mechanisms of the latter to transport the higher-layer end-to-end protocols of the former (see also the XTI in Section 13.7). As Rose notes, moreover, a single TS-gateway can contain more than two stacks, although only two stacks are in use for any given connection. *The logical extension of this concept leads to the possibilities that an end-system may be given access to multiple types of subnetworks; and a given subnetwork may attach multiple types of end-nodes.*

12.7 SUBNETWORK COMBINATIONS

There are many possibilities of interconnecting subnetworks of the same or different types. But first, recall what is meant by the term subnetwork. The ISO 8648 definition of a **subnetwork** is "a collection of equipment and physical media which forms an autonomous whole, and which can be used to interconnect other real systems for purposes of communication" [ISO-8648]. Thus, a subnetwork can be anything from a point-to-point line to a LAN or an X.25 PSDN, so long as it is part of some larger network concept. Many such autonomous subnetworks exist; and some of the prominent candidates are sketched in Figure 12.11. Some larger enterprises will probably employ all of these types. They will, moreover, be interconnected in more ways than shown there.

In the following, we examine a general concept of subnetwork interconnection. Subnetworks can be used in many parallel, nested, and cascaded combinations, as illustrated in Figure 12.12. In each case, messages flow between applications A1 and A2.

(a) *Single subnetwork*—Figure 12.12(a). This could be any of the "networks" identified in the preceding chapters. The subnetwork includes layers 1 through 3, particularly the path control or OSI network layer and the underlying link layer. At the end-systems, a pair of layer-4 entities oversees the operations.

(b) *Parallel subnetworks*—Figure 12.12(b). This is an example of an OSI X.25 subnetwork in parallel with a proprietary network like APPN. In general, this is the case of an end-system having capability to communicate via multiple transport systems.

(c) *Two-level nested*—Figure 12.12(c). The outer subnetwork here might be APPN, X.25, or one using the OSI connectionless protocol. The nested subnetwork might, for example, be an X.25, ISDN, metropolitan area network (MAN), local area network (LAN), or analog dial network. Higher speed subnetworks, operating at layer 2, will also be prevalent as broadband facilities become more widespread. In the case shown, the inner subnetwork acts, in effect, as a link-layer support of the path control layer in the APPN subnetwork. In any case, the upper end-to-end layers see only the outer network (APPN in the case shown).

(d) *Parallel nests*—Figure 12.12(d). There are three parallel subnetworks, each of which can act, in effect, as a link-layer support of the APPN network.

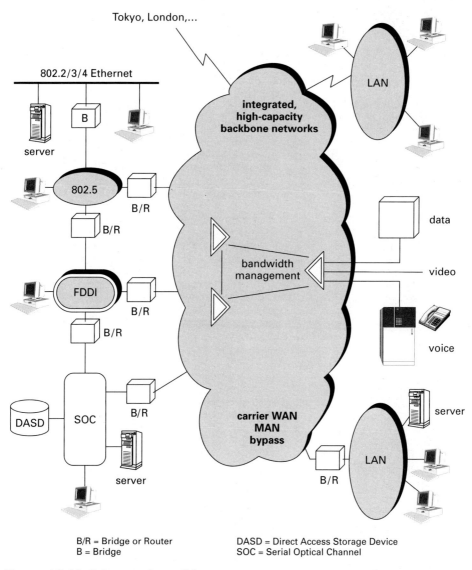

Figure 12.11 Subnetwork candidates.

(e) *Cascaded nests*—Figure 12.12(e). Multiple LANs and a backbone fast packet switch (FPS) are connected together in cascade. That combination subnetwork (LAN/FPS/LAN), then, acts at a link layer for the APPN network.

It is important to recognize that system management and control should extend across the combinations of subnetworks. This includes cooperation among functions like:

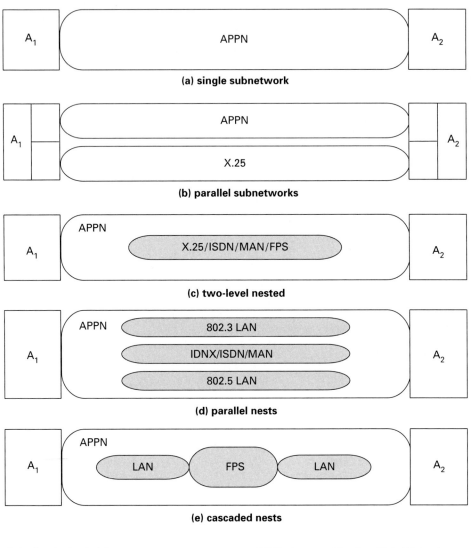

(a) single subnetwork

(b) parallel subnetworks

(c) two-level nested

(d) parallel nests

(e) cascaded nests

FPS = Fast Packet Switch   ISDN = Integrated Services Digital Network
IDNX = Integrated Digital Network Exchange MAN = Metropolitan Area Network

12.12 Parallel, nested, and cascaded subnetworks.

directory, topology, and routing services, fault-determination, and change management. With this cooperation, effective communications can be achieved across these combinations, even though the individual subnetworks may:

- Use different protocols
- Use distinct addressing
- Be managed with a high degree of autonomy

The generalized concept of subnetworks is rather fundamental and helps one to think in terms of a modular construction of networks. Considering the examples in this section and the preceding section (on transport-service-gateways), the necessity of an architecture for heterogeneous subsystems becomes apparent. Some end-nodes may have multiple interfaces to different subnetworks, as in Figure 12.12(b); some subnetworks may have multiple interfaces for different types of end-nodes; and in addition subnetworks may be nested in various ways. An overall architecture, then, is needed to provide the efficient integration of these many types of subsystems, both within and without the standards. The right blend of semi-autonomy and overall coordination and control must be sought in each case. System management, directory services, dynamic topology update, and route-selection services are needed throughout. The result must be a transparent network from the user's perspective, which also can meet the user's changing needs for distributed applications and application-services.

12.8   INTER-SUBNETWORKING

Because of its wide use, we now look more deeply at encapsulation to achieve inter-subnetwork operations. In particular, we look at the generality of inter-subnetworking, subnetwork passthrus, and interoperability of like nodes attached to dissimilar subnetworks. Then we examine in more detail the operations of inter-subnetwork layer-3 routers.

12.8.1   Inter-Subnetworking—A Definition

Inter-subnetworking is a particular use of layer-3 routers to connect multiple subnetworks. It usually involves at least four things:

1.   A consistent inter-subnetwork address-space among the layer-3 routers that interconnect the involved subnetworks.

2.   Means for correlating subnetwork-addresses (SNPA addresses) with inter-subnetwork addresses.

3.   A *routing mechanism* among the multiple inter-subnetwork routers, each of which connects a pair of subnetworks.

4.   An interface or boundary to a higher layer in the end-systems.

One example of many types of inter-subnetworking is the familiar internet protocol of TCP/IP.

12.8.2   Generality of Inter-Subnetworking

The concept of inter-subnetworking, described above, applies to many pairs of subnetworks. OSI, to date, has blessed both the connectionless network protocol (CLNP) and the X.25 packet-layer protocol as legitimate OSI Internet Protocols.[17] The U.S. De-

---

17.   The term *Internet* has been reserved for the special cases of inter-subnetwork protocols that are recognized by TCP/IP or ISO standards organizations. Otherwise, we use the lowercase internet or the more general term *inter-subnetwork* protocol.

partment of Defense (along with many others) has, of course, long used its own Internet protocol, as part of TCP/IP for this purpose. IBM, also, has long used SNA as an inter-subnetwork protocol for transmissions across LANs and X.25 networks (via its NPSI product). In a comparable way, IBM has used its *X.25 Interconnect (XI)* facility to treat the X.25 protocol as an inter-subnetwork protocol, to achieve a passage through an SNA-subnetwork for X.25 data.

Even as the industry moves toward the OSI Internets in the coming decade, a still more general approach to internetworking is needed. That approach must be able to harmonize the multiplicity of standards and maintain continuity with the diverse subnetworks in our heritage and with new technologies.

LAN-to-LAN routers.   Figure 12.13 illustrates the common use of layer-3 routers, with one of several protocols (CLNP, IP, or SNA-PC) used as the common layer-3c protocol across LANs and an intervening backbone. For generality, we call this protocol the **Inter-Subnetwork Protocol (ISP)**.

The case where the intervening backbone is an X.25 PSDN is shown in Figure 12.13(b).[18] As shown, we can consider the layer-3 routers X and Y to be parts of the overall Inter-Subnetwork Protocol (ISP) network, within which the X.25 PSDN and the two LANs are subnetworks. Two levels of addressing are involved. Consider, for example, that a Call_Request is made from an end-system on the X.25 subnetwork. If that request is for a logical-link to an end-system on that same X.25 subnetwork, then only the X.25 address (called a Data Terminal Equipment, DTE, address or Subnetwork Point of Attachment, SNPA, address) is needed to get the message to that end-system. If, on the other hand, the request is for a logical-link to an end-system attached to a different subnetwork, like one of the LANs in Figure 12.13, then the X.25 DTE address is insufficient. The Call_Request must contain two addresses. One is the X.25 subnetwork address of a node on that subnetwork, like Router X or Router Y, which understands the ISP (layer-3) addressing. The second address is the layer-3 (ISP) address of the desired end-system. The final layer-3 router node may then use LAN-broadcast address-resolution facilities to find the corresponding LAN station and link-layer SAP addresses of the destination end-system.)

On the other hand, if the backbone is a high-speed LAN or a fast packet switch whose routing is also at layer 2, then the encapsulation is simplified to that shown in Figure 12.13(a).[19]

In configurations like Figure 12.13, the intermediate (ISP) routers (e.g., routers X and Y in Figure 12.13), may be any one of several protocols, such as CLNP, TCP/IP, SNA-subarea, or SNA-APPN. In any case, there would have to be consistency between the layer-3 capabilities of the end-systems and the intermediate routers. Several different sets of such ISP protocols can coexist, each having its own intermediate routers.

---

18.   The DLC in the LAN is the LAN logical-link control (LLC) and the media access control (MAC) sublayers.

19.   As explained in Chapter 18, however, the DLC headers in the fast packet switch must now carry additional information.

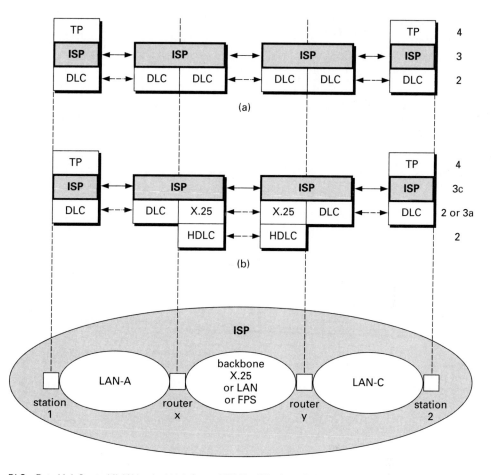

DLC = Data Link Control [LAN Logical-Link Control (LLC)   ISP = Inter-Subnetwork Protocol (e.g., CLNP, IP,
      and Media Access Control (MAC)]   SNA-PC)
FPS = Fast Packet Switch   TP = Transport Protocol (layer 4)
HDLC = High-Level Data Link Control   X.25 = X.25 Packet Level Protocol (PLP)

Figure 12.13 Routers based on an inter-subnetwork protocol as the encapsulated layer-3c protocol; **(a)** backbone is layer-2 LAN or FPS; **(b)** backbone is X.25.

The ISP routers of a given protocol, together with the origin and destination nodes that have that same layer-3 protocol, comprise a *network* in themselves. As in any network, one wants to avoid the necessity of coordinated systems definition in the nodes of that network. Dynamic, automatic definition, with nondisruptive growth, are needed, as other inter-subnetwork nodes are added, are removed, or fail. Other network facilities, such as directory services and system management that include the inter-subnetwork nodes, are also needed. In short, the kind of dynamic directory, topology, and routing facilities that WANs like APPN were designed to provide are also needed for any inter-subnetwork capability. (Some of these facilities are discussed in Chapter 14.)

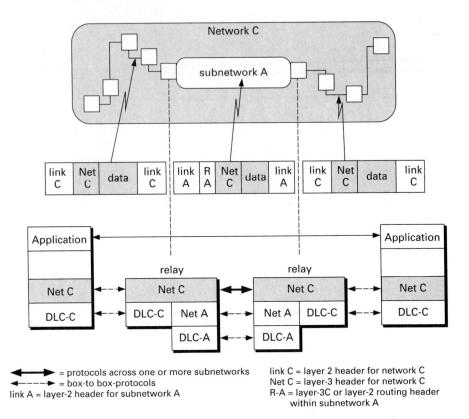

Figure 12.14 Encapsulating subnetwork headers when internetworking.

Subnetwork passthru. We next examine in more detail the encapsulation of protocols involved in some subnetwork combinations. The basic case of inter-subnetworking is illustrated in Figure 12.14. Network C and subnetwork A have different network-layer protocols. Network C includes subnetwork A, and has subnetwork A within it. In one sense, subnetwork A acts as a link within network C. This is the case whether subnetwork A uses layer-3 routing (as in an X.25 PSDN) or uses layer-2 routing (as in a fast packet switch subnetwork).

Imagine a message going from the leftmost node to the rightmost node. The headers in the three sections of the path are shown in Figure 12.14. In the central subnetwork, the network-layer header and the data of network C have been encapsulated within two headers of subnetwork A. The nodes at the boundaries between network C and subnetwork A must contain the relays that perform the encapsulation and decapsulation. In this example, we could also say that subnetwork A is used as a subnetwork passthru for network C.

Let us next relate this subnetwork passthru to the sublayers in layer 3. As discussed earlier, the OSI network layer is divided into three sublayers, shown in Figure 3.8.

Conceptually, these three sublayers apply to many combinations beyond the specific protocols that have been standardized. In the terms of these sublayers, the network-layer protocols of network C can be referred to as the independent-convergence protocol, operating in the *independent-convergence sublayer, layer 3c*. The terminology is appropriate because we are maintaining end-to-end consistency, independent of the intermediary subnetworks. Further, the access protocol to subnetwork A, in Figure 12.14, is appropriately called the subnetwork-access protocol, operating in the *subnetwork-access sublayer, layer 3a*. If there is some inadequacy in the functions of subnetwork A, then some "glue" must be provided between them; this intermediary sublayer can be called the *dependent-convergence sublayer, or 3b*.

How does this relate to the familiar "Internet"? Referring to Figure 12.14, the data and the network-C layer-3 header are encapsulated within the subnetwork-A headers. With multiple, cascaded subnetworks (like subnetwork A), with one or more inter-subnetwork routers between each pair of subnetworks, that encapsulation process is repeated at each subnetwork. In such cases, the strings of nodes within network C, in Figure 12.14, may collapse to only one node between each pair of subnetworks. This is then the more familiar Internet configuration.

Examples of subnetwork passthru. With subnetwork passthru, both end-systems are connected to one network, which in turn contains a subnetwork. Two such passthru subnetworks are discussed below.

1. *Passing through an SNA WAN*: Here, the boundary nodes of an SNA subarea subnetwork can envelope messages with SNA protocols, for passage through the SNA subnetwork. This is a degenerate version of Figure 12.14, where, for example, two end-systems are pure OSI nodes (using the X.25 protocol), and both are directly connected to an SNA subnetwork (see Figure 12.15). The "foreign" end-systems use a different layer-3 protocol than the subnetwork to which they are attached. In this case, the job of enveloping and de-enveloping is done in the boundary SNA nodes. The latter must provide the X.25 DCE interface, (that is, the data-circuit-terminating-equipment interface, which is that shown by an X.25 packet network). The enveloped protocol in this case is a reformatted X.25.[20] The DCE interface, provided for the attaching X.25 nodes, is found in the IBM XI product. The SNA-provided DCE is discussed further in Chapter 18. Figure 12.15 can be further generalized if the SNA subnetwork shown there is replaced by a high-speed subnetwork, such as one using fast packet routing. In that case, the two layers PC/DLC become compressed, and the routing is done in the DLC layer.

2. *Passing through an X.25 WAN:* In this case, the boundary-nodes of an SNA Subarea WAN can envelope messages (which use SNA protocols) with X.25 protocols, for passage through the X.25 subnetwork. This capability (called Network Control Program, Packet Switching Interface, NPSI) is described in Chapter 19.

---

20. The encapsulated protocol is that of a reformatted X.25 protocol. The reformatting is needed because the X.25 interface is not symmetrical. The reformatting may, for example be to an intermediate format of the X.75 protocol, which was designed to couple separate X.25 networks.

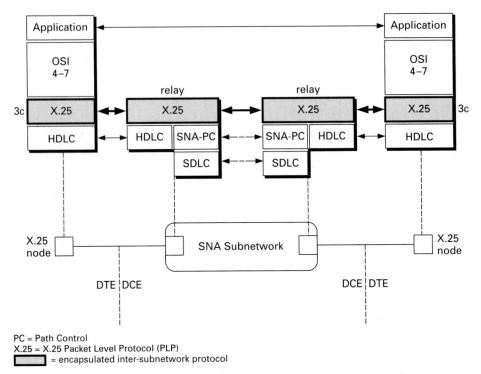

PC = Path Control
X.25 = X.25 Packet Level Protocol (PLP)
■ = encapsulated inter-subnetwork protocol

Figure 12.15 SNA subnetwork passthru by stand-alone X.25 end-nodes.

A generalization of this same passthru concept would be to provide a multiprotocol backbone WAN network, having conversion or encapsulation facilities for different types of subnetworks and programmable end-systems. Such a backbone, for example, might carry traffic for multiple end-systems whose layer-3c and higher protocols are SNA, OSI, TCP/IP, or NetBIOS. The subnetworks connecting to the backbone might be X.25 wide area networks. Or, that attaching subnetwork could be one of the 802.2 family of LANs or the wideband FDDI LAN. This generalized backbone WAN possibility is discussed further in Section 12.9.

Subnetwork interoperability. With interoperation, one end-system is attached to one subnetwork and the other end-system is attached to another subnetwork with a different architecture. Such interoperation is a degenerate case of the example in Figure 12.14, when only one of the end-systems is directly connected to subnetwork A, and the other end-system is connected to network C, and the higher-layer protocols of both end-systems are designed to work with network C. Examples would be an OSI-based application, attached to an X.25, LAN, or TCP/IP subnetwork, communicating with another OSI-based application that is attached to an SNA/SDLC wide area subnetwork (both applications employ OSI end-to-end controls). These are common examples of subnetwork interoperability.

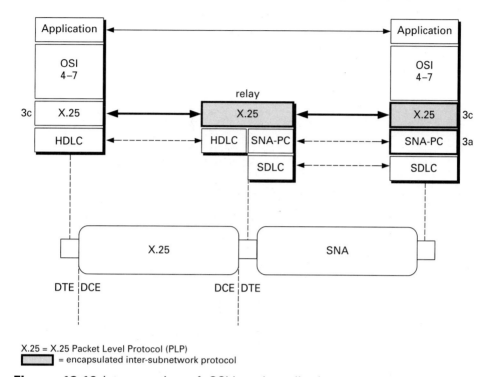

X.25 = X.25 Packet Level Protocol (PLP)
▨▨▨▨ = encapsulated inter-subnetwork protocol

Figure 12.16 Interoperation of OSI-based applications across X.25 and SNA subnetworks using X.25 as the encapsulated protocol.

Figure 12.16 illustrates the interoperation of OSI-based applications across X.25 and SNA/SDLC subnetworks.[21] Note that here the X.25 is the inter-subnetwork protocol that is encapsulated, and the SNA subnetwork is the subordinate, acting as a sort of link-layer connection. The SNA path control function is also, in effect, a sublayer 3a. The OSI message is carried within SNA path control protocol headers as it traverses the SNA subnetwork. At the boundaries of the SNA subnetwork, these SNA headers are added or removed. Of course, the SNA subnetwork shown could be replaced by other types of subnetworks, such as one using fast packet routing at layer 2. The OSI message (including its OSI layer-3 controls) would then be encapsulated as data in layer-2 headers.

In Figure 12.17, on the other hand, we illustrate *SNA-based applications* operating across these same networks. Here, the SNA-PC is the inter-subnetwork protocol. Then, the X.25 subnetwork plays the role of a subordinate subnetwork. Now, at the boundaries of the

---

21. Note that we loosely refer to a network as an X.25 network. In reality, the X.25 interface applies only to the DTE/DCE interface of that network. The protocols used within the network are proprietary to the network vendor.

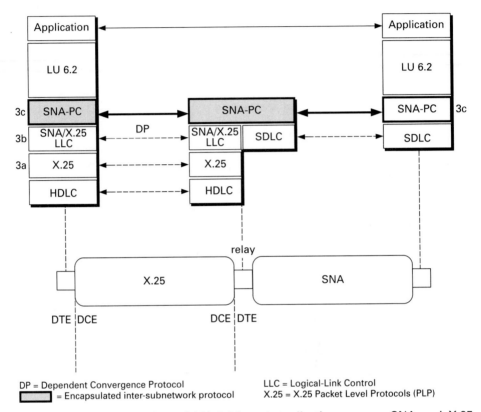

Figure 12.17 Interoperation of LU 6.2-based applications across SNA and X.25 subnetworks, using SNA path control as the encapsulated protocol.

X.25 subnetwork, we add and subtract enveloping X.25 headers as the message enters and leaves the X.25 subnetwork.

In order to provide full SNA service across the two subnetworks, however, an augmented X.25 protocol, transparent to the X.25 PSDN, must be used, to enhance the X.25 subnetwork capability. Called the SNA/X.25 Logical-Link Control (LLC), this is (in OSI terminology) a nonstandard function in the middle sublayer, the dependent convergence *sublayer 3b*. The X.25/LLC is the "glue" that makes the two subnetworks more functionally compatible.

If the relay of Figure 12.17 is packaged within a node of the SNA subnetwork, we have the IBM NPSI product. This product provides a DTE (terminal) interface to the X.25 network. The SNA/X.25 LLC and NPSI are described further in Chapter 19.

Note that in the figures involving X.25 subnetworks, the CCITT X.25 (DTE-DCE) interface appears only at the subnetwork boundary, between end-systems and intermediate-systems. That protocol does not necessarily appear between intermediate-systems within the X.25 subnetwork.

12.8.3   Inter-Subnetwork Layer-3 Routers

The routers in between subnetworks are the keys to multi-subnetwork interconnections.[22] The operation of these routers is examined here in more detail.

Inter-subnetwork router functions.   Routers between subnetworks have many of the functions of bridges, but, in addition, must cope with a variety of subnetwork differences. Some of these are [Stallings89]:

- *Addressing*: The subnetworks being connected may use very different addressing schemes for their attached end-systems. For example, a type 802.2 LAN may use a 48-bit binary station address. The subnetwork it connects to might be an X.25 PSDN, which also may use a 48-bit address, but that may be 12 decimal digits coded 4 bits per digit. There probably is no coordination in the assignment of these addresses. Some higher-level address convention, common to both subnets, and an associated directory service is therefore needed to tie these together.

- *Packet sizes*: The maximum allowable packet sizes vary with different subnetworks. Therefore, another service, to segment packets, may be needed.

- *Variable quality*: The networks being interconnected may have different levels of reliability, assured sequence, and recovery capabilities. End-to-end transport control (at layer 4) is usually relied on, instead. The requirement on the router is to accommodate reliability problems and changeability in independent subnetworks. This may be aided by participating in dynamic topology updates (on the occasion of inter-subnetwork-node failures, additions, or removals), associated directory updates, and network-management's problem-determination.

Routing decisions.   Consider the case where the inter-subnetwork routing uses the globally unique OSI network address (described in Section 12.3). Using this address, and stored topology data, inter-subnetwork procedures must be able to derive the subnetwork point of attachment (SNPA) address of the next "hop" enroute to the final destination. That next hop may be to the final destination or only to the next inter-subnetwork node. Once the address in the next hop is known, the routing within the subnetwork takes over, to traverse the subnetwork.

    The inter-subnetwork routing-node process can be seen clearly in the example in Figure 12.18. Two LANs are connected, via routers X and Y and an intervening subnetwork B. A host (or workstation) on LAN A talks to a host (or workstation) on LAN C. The nodes host 1, host 2, router X, and router Y all understand the inter-subnetwork addressing. They thus are participating in internet D. As far as they are concerned, the three subnetworks provide logical-links between adjacent nodes in internet D. Each of the three subnetworks (A, B, and C) receives, as input information, the data originating from a host, plus the internet-header. Within each of the subnetworks A, B, and C, this entering

---

22.   As an example, a PS/2 or PC workstation can function as a TCP/IP router interconnecting Ethernet, token ring, and PC Network LANs. Depending on the model of the workstation, up to five LANs can be so connected.

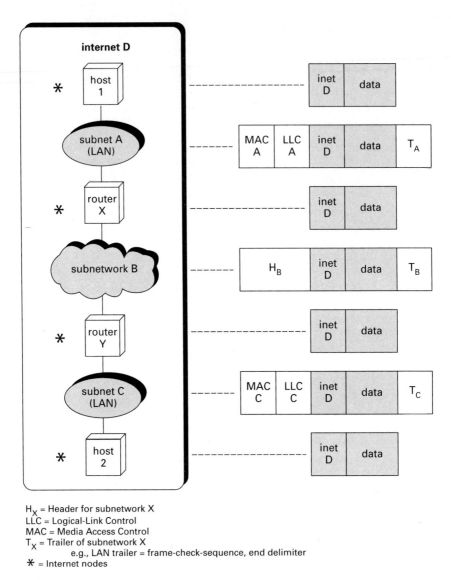

H$_X$ = Header for subnetwork X
LLC = Logical-Link Control
MAC = Media Access Control
T$_X$ = Trailer of subnetwork X
        e.g., LAN trailer = frame-check-sequence, end delimiter
✻ = Internet nodes

Figure 12.18 Routers for three subnetworks in an internet.

information is encapsulated within the headers of that subnetwork. The two hosts must speak the same language at the upper layers 4 through 7. However, the routers X and Y do not have any functions above layer 3.

The addressing within each subnetwork is at a lower layer than the addressing in the internet. The subnetwork internal addressing, such as within a LAN or an X.25 PSDN, may be unique to that subnetwork and may not be globally meaningful. The passage of a message from host 1 to host 2, therefore, *proceeds in two stages.*

- First the message must get to the correct router (internet-node) at the destination subnetwork. To do this, the message must cross intermediate subnetworks, going from router to router.

- Then, in a second stage, the message is directed from the final router across that destination subnetwork to the destination host.

As discussed in Section 12.3, many network addresses are made hierarchical. In this example, the first stage of routing uses a prefix that gets the message to the destination subnetwork. The second stage is the subnetwork addressing within, for example, a LAN or an X.25 subnetwork.

The way in which the internet-nodes determine the routes among the routers, and across the subnetworks, can be varied. One route selection procedure may be best for determining the path among internet-nodes. A different procedure may be best for the leg within each subnetwork.

Hence, at each router (which is an internet-node) a different procedure may be used, depending on whether (a) the next hop is to another router (internet-node) that is adjacent to a different subnetwork, or (b) the next hop is to the destination-node on the current subnetwork. Only when the message has arrived at the destination subnetwork need that final router concern itself with the subnetwork addresses of nodes other than routers. In fact, that last router may have to perform some special search procedures (such as the address resolution procedures discussed in Chapter 16) to find the subnetwork address of the destination-node.

Subnetwork header encapsulations.   This same encapsulation process can be used by many types of subnetworks. Subnetwork B, in Figure 12.18 can, accordingly, be a variety of things, involving different encapsulations. Some illustrative cases, and the corresponding contents of H_B and T_B of Figure 12.18, are presented in Figure 12.19:

(a) When subnetwork B is another *LAN*, the router on subnetwork B encapsulates the **input** (data plus internet header) with the LLC header and trailer, and then the MAC header (as in Figure 12.19(a); see Figure 17.25 for further detail).

(b) If subnetwork B is a *WAN* (different from the internet), then the layer-3 header for that WAN, and a DLC header and link-trailer, are wrapped around that same input (as in Figure 12.19(b)). The internet, for example could be the TCP Internet or the OSI (layer-3c) Internet. The WAN layer-3 header could, for example, be an SNA path-control header; and the DLC could be SDLC.

(c) If subnetwork B is an *X.25 PSDN*, then the router would provide the packet level protocols, for *access* to the PSDN. The router may establish and release virtual circuits through the WAN, segment and reassemble packets, and provide congestion control when the throughput of the two subnetworks is significantly different. For passage across the X.25 interface, the router encapsulates the internet protocol and the data in the X.25 packet-layer protocols (as in Figure 12.19(c)). These, however, would be replaced within the PSDN by whatever headers the internal transmission of the PSDN happened to use.

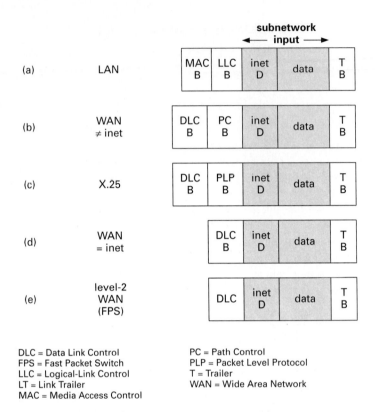

DLC = Data Link Control
FPS = Fast Packet Switch
LLC = Logical-Link Control
LT = Link Trailer
MAC = Media Access Control

PC = Path Control
PLP = Packet Level Protocol
T = Trailer
WAN = Wide Area Network

Figure 12.19 Alternative formats **(a)** through **(e)**, in subnetwork B of Figure 12.18.

(d) If the internet D protocol is, instead, a full-function inter-subnetwork protocol, with system management, directories, dynamic-reconfiguration, etc., then subnetwork B might use the same layer-3 protocols as the internet D. Subnetwork B, even as a large mesh of interconnected nodes, would, in that case, be a part of the internet D. No further encapsulation is then needed, except for the link-layer protocols between adjacent nodes of that subnetwork (as in Figure 12.19(d)). That inter-subnetwork protocol for example, could be from an architecture like SNA/APPN.

(e) If subnetwork B is a WAN that uses layer-2 routing, as described in Chapter 18, then the packets would be segmented at the edge of the WAN into mini-packets, and given a mini-packet DLC header containing the layer-2 routing information (as in Figure 12.19(e)).

End-system servers.   In the above, we assumed that the end-systems, host 1 and host 2, understood the inter-subnetwork routing protocols, and were therefore participants in internet D. On the other hand, the origin and destination end-systems may be outside the internet D, and depend on an intermediate internet-nodes X and Y to service them as attachments.

Routers may, for example, be capable of activating and using switched circuits. For this, the router must know which network layer addresses are accessible via the circuit switched service. It must then be able to determine corresponding dialing codes and to perform appropriate dialing

The origin and destination hosts, on LANs in Figure 12.18, may use no layer-3 header at all. In these cases, the adjacent intermediate-system routers, X and Y, have more work to do. Then these adjacent routers must be able to in effect, create the internet header.

In still other cases, multiple layer-3 protocols, such as TCP/IP, ISO/CLNP, and SNA/ APPN might be used on a LAN (provided that the two end-systems use the same layer-3 headers). These LAN protocols might be different from the inter-subnetwork protocols used in X and Y. The adjacent routers X and Y then would be called upon to encapsulate those LAN layer-3 headers.

12.8.4   Specific Router Architectures

We have today a wide variety of routing architectures. A very brief overview follows.

TCP/IP routers

Within a TCP/IP network, there are autonomous networks that are independently managed and need to be interconnected. An autonomous network may contain multiple subnetworks (e.g., LANs). Each autonomous network has a unique system number assigned to it by SRI. Routers interior to these autonomous networks and exterior routers between networks are needed.

TCP/IP Interior Gateway Protocols (IGP).   Within an autonomous network, there are layer-3 routers, which generally use one of a family of routing protocols. These include:

- RIP (Routing Information Protocol) [RFC1058], based on a protocol originally used for XNS (Xerox Networking)
- GGP (Gateway-to-Gateway Protocol), which was designed for use within the ARPANET
- OSPF (Open Shortest Path First), a proposed new routing protocol

Still another under development is the IS-IS (Intermediate-System-to-Intermediate-System) routing protocol to be used in OSI. All of these IGP routing protocols use different sets of messages for exchanging topology information between routers.

TCP/IP Exterior Gateway Protocols (EGP).   These are the routing protocols that interconnect the autonomous networks [RFC901]. These routers exchange and maintain information on their own autonomous network and on how the various other autonomous networks can be reached. EGP protocols only exchange information about the subnetworks (e.g., LANs) within their respective autonomous networks. They do not exchange specific system topology information. This isolates detailed changes within the autonomous networks.

TCP/IP Core Networks.   TCP/IP wide area networks, sometimes called *core networks*, attach autonomous TCP/IP networks using Exterior Gateway Protocols discussed above. The National Science Foundation NSFNet is one such example. Connectivity to the core network can be by direct point-to-point link connection or by an X.25 connection (effectively used as a link connection). The U.S. Department of Defense Network (DDN), the Computer Science Network (CSNet), and the European networks generally use X.25.

SNA routing

There are two distinct connection-oriented approaches taken by SNA, to date, in the path control layer. These are label-based routing in the Advanced Peer-to-Peer Networks (APPN), and destination routing in the SNA subarea networks (see Sections 14.6 and 15.7, respectively).

OSI routing

The inter-subnetwork routing protocol specified by OSI is the Connectionless Network Protocol (CLNP). It is patterned largely after TCP/IP (see Section 13.4).

Other proprietary routers

Four other routers are in common use, as follows:

- *DECnet router*. The Digital Equipment Corporation (DEC) Digital Network Architecture includes routing based on administrative *Areas* [Malamud89]. An Area can contain up to 1024 nodes, and up to 63 Areas can be connected together to form a DECnet. Within an area, the routers are called layer-1 routers. Routing between Areas is performed by layer-2 routers. When a layer-1 router receives a packet headed for another Area, the layer-1 router sends that packet to the nearest layer-2 router.

- *XNS router*. This is also a hierarchical routing scheme, originally developed by Xerox Network Systems. It includes an XNS level-1 Internet Datagram Protocol (IDP) and an XNS level-2 Routing Information Protocol (RIP). The corresponding XNS layer-4 protocols are the Sequenced Packet Protocol (SPP) and the Packet Exchange Protocol (PEP).

- *IPX router*. The Novell-defined Internet Packet Exchange Protocol (IPX) supports dynamic routing through the Routing Information Protocol (RIP), and also can use static routing tables that are under operator control. The corresponding Novell layer-4 protocol is the Sequenced Packet Exchange (SPX).

- *AppleTalk Router*. The AppleTalk Phase 2 Protocol was introduced by Apple Computers, Inc., in 1989. It includes a set of routing-related protocols: Datagram Delivery Protocol (DDP), Routing Table Maintenance Protocol (RTMP), Name Binding Protocol (NBP), AppleTalk Echo Protocol (AEP), Zone Information Protocol (ZIP) and the AppleTalk Address Resolution Protocol (AARP).[23]

---

23. Interoperation of AppleTalk LANs with other LANs is also feasible so long as the upper-layer protocols are consistent. For example, a Macintosh on a Localtalk network using TCP/IP can be connected to an Ethernet LAN via an IP router such as FASTPATH by Kinetics, Inc.

12.8.5   Public/Private Internetworking

The ground rules for the interoperation of public and private subnetworks continue to evolve. As the OSI addressing becomes more universally accepted, the opportunities for efficient interworking increase. A somewhat idealized objective is portrayed in the following.

A relatively simple case of global multidomain internetworking is the proposed two-level scheme illustrated in Figure 12.20. At the center is a public or private high-speed backbone. This might be a wide area fast packet switched network, a high-speed LAN, a metropolitan area network, or an X.25 PSDN. Connecting to it, and to each other, are various private domain networks (A, B, C, and D). These might each, in turn, be composed of multiple subnetworks, using combinations of X.25, SNA/WAN, LAN, or other technologies. Each pair of adjacent networks (e.g., A and D) are connected by internetwork layer-3 routers. ISO documentation sometimes refers to these as *Interworking Units (IWUs)*. Each network is also connected by a layer-3 router to the high-speed backbone (e.g., D-BB).

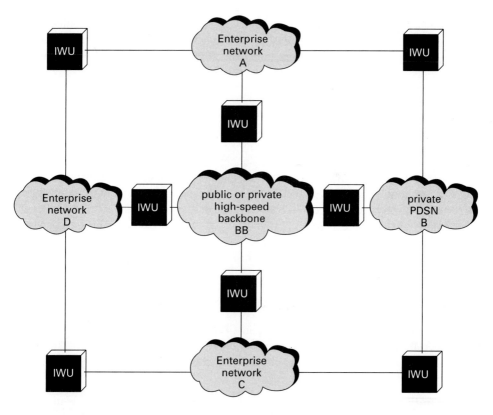

IWU = Inter Working Units (level-3 routers)

Figure 12.20 Two-level hierarchical internet topology.

First, we need to have a consistent OSI-type of addressing, as described in Section 12.3, for the aggregate. This means unique IDIs for different authority domains, and unique Net_ids (one or more) for each network in the same authority domain.

So long as any two adjacent networks are within a common authority, they have the same IDI in their NSAP addresses. The Net_id part of the DSP, however, would be different for the two networks. That, then denotes the access port on the IWU leading to the next network.

On the other hand, if an IWU connects two different authorities, then the IDI in the connecting networks would be different. In that case, the IDI part of the NSAP address denotes the access port on an IWU leading to the next network.

In the destination network, the complete DSP of the address then identifies the destination address within the destination network.

Unfortunately, this world of universal NSAP addressing is only part of the picture. The reality, for the foreseeable future, is the presence of multiple network architectures, particularly including OSI, TCP/IP, NetBIOS, and SNA layer-3c functions, as well as the multitude of lower layers such as ISDN, X.25, and LANs. Hence, a still broader concept is needed. The evolving OSNA must accommodate this diversity even as it optimizes for the strategic OSI direction. Designing with a flexible base and tower architecture to accommodate diversity where needed is the challenge. An OSNA WAN then must provide the backbone for transporting data for both "foreign" end-systems and "foreign" subnetworks. This is further analyzed in the following section.

12.9   THE MULTIPROTOCOL BACKBONE

12.9.1   Objectives

This chapter has examined a variety of subnetworks and the use of bridges, routers, conversion, and encapsulation to achieve interoperation of different subnetwork combinations. We can now bring it all together to get an overview of the functions involved, and to review the many factors that are involved in the design of a multiprotocol, multivendor enterprise communication system [Deaton90]. To do this, we first examine the concept of a *multiprotocol backbone operating at layers 1 and 2*, which could be implemented in a structure as simple as a LAN. Then we address a hypothetical universal WAN that is also protocol independent.

12.9.2   Multiprotocol Layer-2 Backbone

A frequently encountered need is in two parts: (1) use a high-speed LAN (or other layer-2 transport facility) as a protocol-independent backbone for some number of subnetworks, and (2) limit and control the inter-subnetwork traffic. To achieve the two, we need a combination of bridges and routers.

Configuration.   Figure 12.21 shows one basic approach to this problem. The configuration is fairly general. All the subnetworks (A thru N) and the backbone could be bridged LANs in themselves. Moreover, each subnetwork shown there could also be a similar hierarchy of LANs. The backbone could also be made of T1 or T3 lines. We assume that multiple

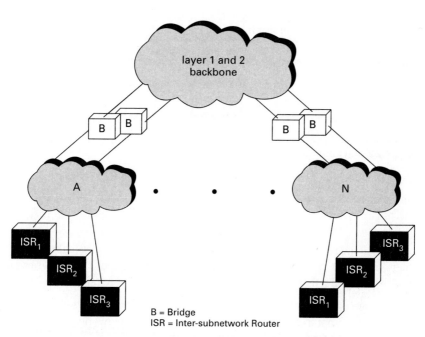

Figure 12.21 Bridge/router network.

protocols, such as OSI, SNA, and TCP/IP are used in each of the subnetworks (A through N). End-systems (or end-system controllers), accordingly, have a layer-3 capability. An end-system, for example, might be structured as a *subset* of Figure 3.14.

A layer-3c network may exist, therefore, for one or more of the eight forementioned protocols,[24] across the entire multi-subnetwork configuration. In Figure 12.21, we assume there are three such layer-3c protocols. The inter-subnetwork traffic is routed via bridges and the backbone, and the backbone is protocol-independent. The backbone (in effect) appears in each such layer-3 network as a point-to-point link-layer connection.

Control.   It is generally held that congestion control, traffic filtering, and security management can best be done when *intermediate layer-3 routers* are used for the inter-subnetwork traffic control. Without routers, and only 802.X bridges, there is no way for the bridge to negotiate to reduce congestion. The alternative then is to discard packets that exceed the acceptable bandwidth, and require retransmissions. Layer-3 routers also can better cope with topology changes and take advantage of switched services than bridges can. At times, the router may also have to adjust packet sizes to conform to the abilities of each subnetwork. Accordingly, two steps can be taken:

1.   In each subnetwork, one node having intermediate-node layer-3 routing capability, is designated as an **Inter-Subnetwork Router** (ISRs in Figure 12.21) for each of the three

---

24.   TCP/IP, CLNP, SNA subarea, SNA APPN, DECnet, XNS, IPX, and AppleTalk.

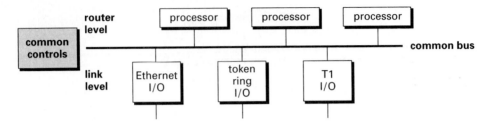

Figure 12.22 Packaging of multiple routers.

protocols. For APPN, for example, this ISR would be a node having APPN network-node capability. Each ISR can be connected anywhere on a subnetwork LAN (A…N), and the ISR need not be connected to the backbone. For availability, a second set of ISRs could be similarly designated.

2.   Any special inter-subnetwork filtering or security controls are placed there in the ISRs. To further limit and control the inter-subnetwork traffic, the bridges may be defined to pass only ISR-to-ISR traffic, that is, between routers designated as inter-subnetwork routers.

Thus, the network is managed as a layer-3 router network, even though the routers are used only for routing and not as the connecting links between subnetworks.

The management functions of the layer-3 network (such as an APPN which spans the multiple subnetworks shown), also apply well to the entire configuration. If an ISR in any subnetwork should fail, the topology update process is immediately aware of that, and a route to an alternate ISR will be selected. The bridges would, of course, have to be defined to also include the alternate ISRs as allowable destinations. Similarly, directory functions, such as the APPN `Locate` functions, can be used to find a named destination, across the entire network (see Chapter 14).

Alternate router packaging.   A further step is to consider packaging the multiple layer-3 routers in one node. For example, layer-3c functions for OSI, APPN, and TCP/IP might be present in one workstation. That multiprotocol node, first of all, could be attached at any point on each LAN subnetwork. The next alternative is to replace the bridges with this multiprotocol router. Either of these combinations (multiple routers in one package located either on the LAN or between the LAN and the backbone) can be cost effective, so long as they do not create too vulnerable a single point of failure for the system.

A rough idea of a multiprotocol multiprocessor router is sketched in Figure 12.22. A common bus can join the layer-1 through -3a input/output elements (for various types of LANs and high-speed lines) and the processors that are capable of doing the layer-3c routing function. A bridging function for some protocols might also be included in the software of the processors.

12.9.3   Multiprotocol WAN

We now explore a broader problem of a **Multiprotocol-Wide Area Network (MP-WAN)**. This is defined to both serve *a wide variety of types of end-systems*, and be able to interoperate with *a variety of subnetworks*.

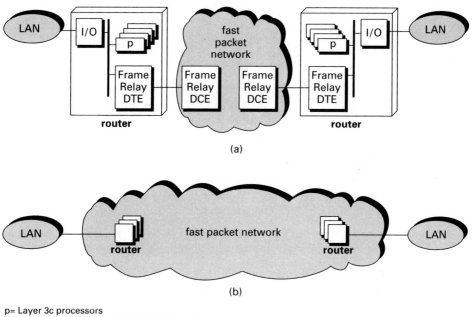

p= Layer 3c processors
I/O = Input/Output (layer 1 and 2 LAN access)

Figure 12.23 Providing LAN access to a fast packet network: **(a)** interfacing to a fast packet network via external routers and an I.122 interface; **(b)** connecting directly to a fast packet network with internal routers.

First of all, Figure 12.23 illustrates two approaches to packaging a multiprotocol capability for LAN-LAN communication via a fast packet[25] backbone. The illustration assumes a frame-relay interface, but others (e.g., a MAN interface or a broadband ISDN interface) could have been assumed. In Figure 12.23(a) a stand-alone router (i.e., a network-access facility containing both layer-1 and -2 input/output units and layer-3c inter-subnetwork routers) is used at each end. In Figure 12.23(b) the same router functions are incorporated into the interface of the fast packet network.

The requirement, however, is broader than just LAN-LAN communication. In particular, the goal of the illustrative MP-WAN is to:

1. Accommodate different types of *end-systems*, which

    a) have different layer 1 through 3a interfaces, such as Frame Relay, ISDN, X.25, SDLC/HDLC/PPP,[26] and S/390 channel)

---

25.   Fast packet here refers to any layer 1 to 2 packet switching system, as described in Chapter 18.

26.   SDLC, HDLC, and PPP are layer-2 protocols. SDLC and HDLC are well-established standards (see Figure 19.31). PPP, the Point-to-Point Protocol, is an emerging HDLC-like protocol for point-to-point communication between routers [RFC1171], [RFC1172]. It includes a 16-bit field that identifies which higher-level protocol is encapsulated in the information field of the frame.

b) had been designed to work with different layers 3–4 of transport-service-providers, such as those of OSI, SNA, TCP/IP, and possibly others

2. Interoperate with *subnetworks*, including the LAN family (Ethernet v 2, 802.X and FDDI), X.25, SNA Subarea, SNA APPN, MAN, and ISDN subnetworks

In the following, we will discuss a hypothetical MP-WAN meeting these requirements. By examining this hypothetical MP-WAN, we can review the various layer-2 and layer-3 interfaces, the possible conversions or encapsulations, and the alternative packagings of these functions. That synthesis will serve to review some of the prior discussion and to introduce topics that will be discussed in more detail in subsequent chapters.

Network-access facilities.   To accommodate this diversity, the Multiprotocol-Wide Area Network (MP-WAN) must provide **network-access facilities** that are tailored to the attaching units. From the preceding discussion, those network-access facilities would include:

1. The appropriate link and subnetwork access-interfaces at layers 2 and 3a, to accept, for example, X.25, HDLC, SDLC, PPP, ISDN, and frame-relay inputs

2. The appropriate bridges for layer-2 protocols

3. The appropriate inter-subnetwork router functions for protocols of layer 3c

To illustrate a generalization of Figure 12.23, units of these network-access facilities are variously positioned in Figure 12.24. As shown there, the network-access units involve input/output (I/O) facilities that are essentially layer 1 through 3a link/subnetwork-access facilities. The network access units also involve processors that provide layer-3c router services[27] and/or layer-2 bridge services. End-devices[28] might connect to a network-access unit by various means:

- Directly
- Through a LAN
- Through a cluster (establishment) controller
  - through a cluster controller on a LAN
  - through LAN and then a cluster controller
- Through an SNA/SDLC (subarea or APPN) subnetwork
- Through an X.25, TCP/IP, or OSI/IP subnetwork

Network-access layer-2 and layer-3a interfaces.   There are many optional types of network-access units that the MP-WAN might provide. To look more closely at these possibilities, a hypothetical and somewhat idealized MP-WAN network node, is shown in Figure 12.25. It offers a variety of optional layer-2 and layer-3a interfaces, as part of the network-access facilities. These include interfaces to end-systems that use ISDN, Frame Relay, X.25 packet level protocols, S/390 channels, or one of the standard link-access-

---

27. The aggregate of network-access units has also been called an Interworking Unit (IWU).

28. An end-device is all or part of an end-system. A good example of the latter is the nonprogrammable workstation attached to a cluster (establishment) controller. The former is an end device, and the combination is the end-system.

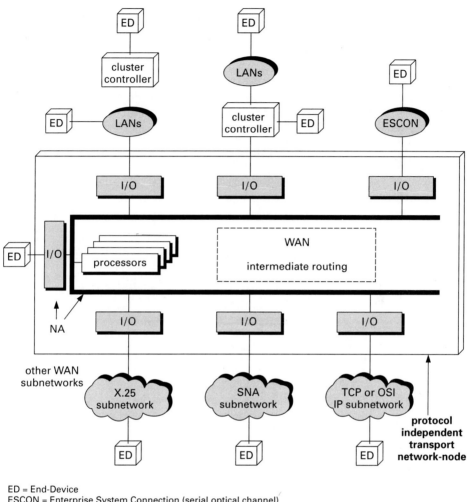

ED = End-Device
ESCON = Enterprise System Connection (serial optical channel)
I/O = Input/Output (layer 1–3a Link/Subnetwork-Access)
NA = Network Access facility
processors = layer-3c router and/or layer-2 bridge services

Figure 12.24 Matching diversity to a particular transport service using boundary network access units.

procedures (e.g., LAP-B of HDLC). When providing an interface to an end-system that performs as an X.25 DTE, the network-node must provide the complementary appearance of an X.25 DCE (see Chapter 19).

Also illustrated in Figure 12.25 is the use, in effect, of either LANs or X.25 packet switching data networks or SNA networks as pseudo access-links to the WAN. For this purpose, the MP-WAN network-node would need the 802.X interface to the LAN and an Ethernet v2 interface as well. The network-node would also need to provide the appearance of an X.25 DTE for connection to the X.25 PSDN.

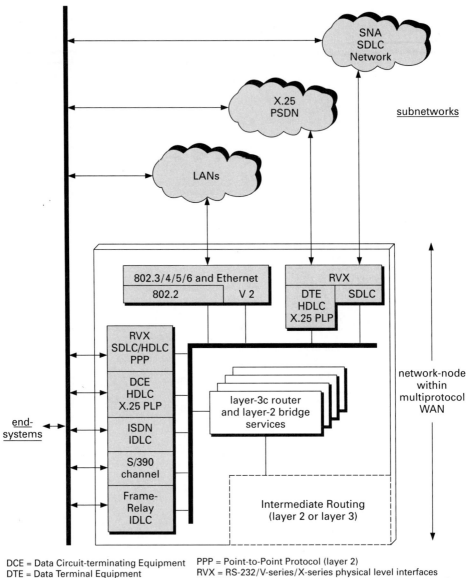

DCE = Data Circuit-terminating Equipment   PPP = Point-to-Point Protocol (layer 2)
DTE = Data Terminal Equipment   RVX = RS-232/V-series/X-series physical level interfaces
PLP = Packet Level Protocol (layer 3)   ▭ = Input/output (layer 1–3a link/subnetwork-access)
IDLC = ISDN Data Link Control

Figure 12.25 Optional end-system and subnetwork connections to idealized, multiprotocol, network-node.

Network-access inter-subnetwork services.   Besides the link/subnetwork-access interfaces, the network-access facility may offer address resolution, inter-subnetwork routing, protocol conversion and/or protocol encapsulation, filtering, and security services in appropriate bridges and routers, at layers 2 and 3.

If, as shown in Figure 12.25, there is a LAN *bridge* located in the network-node, it would enable devices attached to one LAN to establish 802.2 logical-links with devices attached to a second LAN. If the network-node is attached to both LANs, the network-node serves as a simple bridge. If the two LANs are connected to different network-nodes of the WAN, the two network-nodes provide the function of a split bridge (see Chapter 17).

In addition, there can be many sets of layer-3c services. Two different approaches are viable, depending on whether the internal protocols of the MP-WAN provide routing at layer 3 or at layer 2. To illustrate, assume first that the MP-WAN uses an SNA layer-3 protocol for Intermediate-System-to-Intermediate-System (IS-IS) within the MP-WAN. Then, the following protocol conversions or encapsulations may be used:

▪   If the MP-WAN is to connect an APPC-based application on a *NetBIOS-based LAN* with an SNA/APPC-based application on an *APPN WAN*, then the MP-WAN needs to offer a suitable NetBIOS/APPN gateway function. Then a gateway protocol conversion, similar to that in Figure 12.9(b) might be offered by the MP-WAN.

▪   If, moreover, OSI-based end-systems attached to the MP-WAN are to interoperate with *OSI-based end-systems on X.25 PSDNs*, then the X.25 protocol is the inter-subnetwork protocol. Hence, protocol encapsulations similar to those in Figure 12.16 might be offered by the MP-WAN.

▪   If, in addition, the MP-WAN is to be a passthru for the *direct attachment of X.25 based end-systems*, the X.25 protocol is still the inter-subnetwork protocol. Then, encapsulations similar to those in Figure 12.15 are options.

The handling of TCP/IP based end-systems can be handled similarly. Each of these conversions or encapsulations can (in principle) be a module of the network-access facility of the MP-WAN.

If, on the other hand, the MP-WAN uses a fast packet switching technique internally, then there is no layer-3 operating IS-IS within the MP-WAN. Instead, the layer-3 addressing or circuit identifier is put into layer 2 (see Section 18.5). That mapping of information from layer-3 headers to layer-2 headers is likewise a job for the network-access facility. The inter-subnetwork protocol (ISP) is encapsulated within the DLC protocol, as shown in Figure 12.13(a).

Signaling.   Before data transmission can start in our hypothetical MP-WAN, however, the destination in the MP-WAN has to be established. For connection-oriented WANs, the network-access facility will need to understand connection-establishment (signaling) procedures of the attaching end-systems and subnetworks.

Separate modules are needed for each signaling system. For example, in the ISDN case, this signaling is at layer 3, while the subsequent data transmission is at lower layers. High-level signaling and low-level routing also may occur in the case of LAN-to-LAN transmission via the WAN. The subsequent LAN transmission is at layer 2, and the WAN routing (switching) may be either at layer 3 or layer 2 (see Chapter 18).

Also, the MP-WAN has to understand the *addressing* information provided by the attachments. This might, for example be that of TCP/IP, X.25, an SNA network, or NetBIOS. Each is different. This address interpretation and the location of the destination-

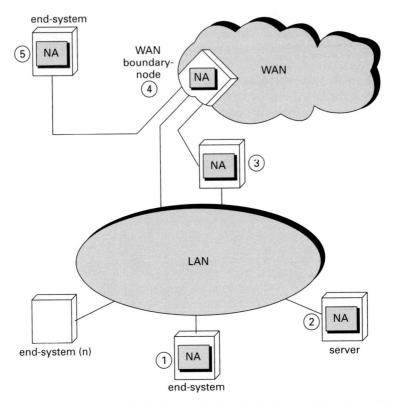

NA = Network-Access facility (layer 1–3a link/subnetwork-access plus router and/or bridge services)

Figure 12.26 Alternative locations for network-access facilities in a multiprotocol world.

node within the WAN involve the WAN *directory services*. Beyond that, the connection also involves the *WAN topology services*, and the *WAN route selection services* (see Chapter 14).

12.9.4   Network-Access Packaging

In these illustrations of the MP-WAN, we have assumed that the network-access facilities would all be packaged either in stand-alone routers (Figure 12.23(a)) or within the nodes at the boundary of the MP-WAN (Figure 12.23(b) and Figures 12.24 and 12.25). Putting them all within the boundary-node of the WAN might be desirable, if only to insure that the total design effort sought efficiency in the use of network-access facilities. However, there are other options available to the system designer for the location of some network-access facilities.

The intended result in any case is the appearance, to the user, of a multiprotocol transport service. Figure 12.26 illustrates possible configurations for achieving this, with different locations of portions of the network-access facilities. Thus, some network-access facilities might be executed:

- In *end-systems (1) attached to LANs*. Each end-system then carries any conversion or encapsulation burden.

- In a *LAN Server (2)*. This NA facility is connected *only* to the LAN. A WAN boundary-node must also connect to that LAN. This NA facility thus also serves many end-systems on the LAN (see also Figure 12.21).

- In a *subnetwork connector (3)*. This NA facility is connected to *both* the LAN *and* the boundary-node of the WAN. Each NA facility therefore also serves many end-systems on the LAN (see also Figure 12.23(a)).

- In *boundary network-nodes* (4) *of the MP-WAN*. This makes sense particularly for the frequent types of attachments (see also Figures 12.24 and 12.25).

- In the *end-systems (5) directly attached to the MP-WAN*.

The important goal of the architecture is that, regardless of the diverse packaging, all the network-access facilities complement each other in a way that minimizes cost and maximizes performance.

Conclusion

Structure of transport-service-providers. Looking back at previous chapters, we saw, in Figure 2.9, how end-systems might use multiple types of transport-service-providers: interconnected LANs and FDDI, Metropolitan Area Networks (MANs), SDLC WAN, X.25 PSDN, ISDN, and Frame Relay, or the private broadband subnetwork for voice and data, with bandwidth management. As in Figure 2.9, different end-systems might have link/subnetwork-access facilities for any one, or for more than one, of these subnetworks.

The groupings of sublayers of the transport-service-provider, and the use of the transport-services (TS) and link/subnetwork-access (LSA) boundaries, as shown in Figure 2.2 and Figure 3.14, are keys to future interoperability possibilities.

TS boundary. In Section 12.6.3, proposals were discussed for split-stack interoperability between some of the transport-service-providers below the transport service boundary (layer 4 and below) and some of the end-to-end data-exchange facilities (layers 5 and 6) above the transport services boundary. One example given was OSI applications, based on OSI layers 5 and 6, running on TCP/IP layer-4 transport. In Section 12.6, the possibilities of conversion and encapsulation of transport layer protocols were discussed, with a NetBIOS to APPN gateway at the transport layer as another example. These indicate the potential feasibility of other split stacks near the transport services boundary.

LSA boundary. The inter-operability direction is for all the link/subnetwork-access facilities (of layers 3b, 3a, 2, and 1) to be commonly available to the OSI, SNA, and TCP/IP protocols (in layers 4 and 3c). Moreover, though NetBIOS is used primarily on LANs, NetBIOS may also cross other subnetworks like X.25 and SDLC WANs, with the help of appropriate network-access facilities (see Section 19.2.3).

Inter-subnetworking.   We saw, too, in Figure 12.12, how subnetworks might be used in parallel, nested, and cascaded combinations. Link and subnetwork facilities may be interconnected by *inter-subnetwork protocols*, such as the Internet protocols of TCP, (e.g. recall Figure 12.18). Other layer-3c protocols (like OSI/CLNP, X.25, and SNA Path Control) also have this capability. They may also link subnetworks and/or provide a WAN capability of their own.

- Addressing in the multi-subnetwork world is a fundamental problem. Addressing will evolve to the OSI globally unique NSAP structure. This has been designed to incorporate existing addressing schemes, including that of SNA.

- Routing has been essential at layer 3, but higher performance at higher speeds often benefits when routing *within subnetworks* gravitate to lower layers, with minimum processing at intermediate nodes.

- Bridges, Routers, and Gateways all are important in fully connected, multiprotocol networks. Encapsulation and conversion, including service-primitive switching, are key techniques being used.

Multiprotocol transport.   This is made possible by the use of the TS and LSA boundaries, combinations of bridges and routers, and by taking advantage of layer-2 routing, which is protocol transparent. Backbone subnetworks are advantageously made using high-speed LANs and/or fast packet switching at layer 2.

Acknowledgments

I am particularly indebted to Philippe Janson, J. P. Gray, G. A. Deaton, Mark Pozefsky, V. Hoberecht, and Refik Molva for valuable input or reviews of this chapter.

TECHNICAL REFERENCE

NSAP Sizes

AFI values and corresponding IDI formats and DSP lengths (IDP = AFI + IDI) are as follows:

AFI (dec)	IDI format	IDP length (decimal)	DSP length
36	CCITT X.121	up to 16 digits	24 decimal digits
37	CCITT X.121	up to 16 digits	9 binary octets
38	ISO 3166-DCC	5 digits	35 decimal digits
39	ISO 3166-DCC	5 digits	14 binary octets
40	CCITT F.69	up to 10 digits	30 decimal digits
41	CCITT F.69	up to 10 digits	12 binary octets
42	CCITT E.163	up to 14 digits	26 decimal digits
43	CCITT E.163	up to 14 digits	10 binary octets
44	CCITT I.331	up to 17 digits	23 decimal digits
45	CCITT I.331	up to 17 digits	9 binary octets
46	ISO 6523-ICD	6 digits	34 decimal digits
47	ISO 6523-ICD	6 digits	13 binary octets

AFI	IDI format	IDP length	DSP length
48	Local	2 digits	38 decimal digits
49	Local	2 digits	15 binary octets
50	Local	2 digits	19 ISO646 characters
51	Local	2 digits	7 national characters

A further recommendation on field sizes comes from ECMA. ECMA 117 DSP format is shown in Figure 12.5(c), with the following sizes:

- binary abstract syntax
  - subnetwork identifier—2 octets
  - subnetwork address—0–6 octets
  - NSAP selector—1 octet
- decimal abstract syntax
  - subnetwork identifier—5 digits
  - subnetwork address—0–15 digits
  - NSAP selector—3 digits

EXERCISES

12.1 What are the two boundaries of the transport-service-provider at which split stacks can be facilitated?

12.2 What is the difference between the subnetwork point of attachment (SNPA) address and the NSAP address?

12.3 Name the three parts of the OSI NSAP address.

12.4 What are the format and components of the IBM-specified NSAP in OSI?

12.5 What are the formats and components of the TCP/IP Internet address and socket?

12.6 Name three types of routing disciplines.

12.7 Name the types of routing or switching that can occur at layers 2a, 2b, 3a, and 3c.

12.8 What names are appropriate for relays at layers 2, 3, and 7?

12.9 What is primitive swapping or service-interface mapping?

12.10 What might be the inter-subnetwork protocol, operating at layer 3c, when the subnetworks are LANs, X.25 PSDN, or ISDNs?

12.11 What are some of the services that can be provided by an inter-subnetwork router?

12.12 What are three different types of functional components in network access facilities for a multiprotocol WAN?

13

Transport-Service-Providers: OSI, TCP, NetBIOS

13.1 INTRODUCTION

Transport-Service-Providers (TSPs) offer the combined services of layers 1 to 4. Figure 3.14 shows two groupings of sublayers below the transport-services boundary:

- The transport services of layer 4 and the inter-subnetwork services of layer-3c

- Link/subnetwork-access services of layers 3b, 3a, 2, and 1

This chapter begins the deeper examination of the functional content and key protocols of layers 4 and 3c in the transport-service-provider. These layer descriptions show important distinctions between OSI, SNA, TCP/IP, and NetBIOS. Essentially all of the functions below these layers are already common to OSI, SNA, and TCP/IP. A major part of the functions above these layers can also become common. The nature of these layers 4 and 3c, and the potential for their interoperation, are therefore very important parts of the multiprotocol approach to networking.

- First, we examine the OSI components, including the five classes of OSI transport services, the Connectionless Network Protocol (CLNP), and the Connection-Oriented Network Protocol (X.25). These are the evolutionary targets for many networks, so a tutorial with considerable detail and explanations are presented. The prospects for higher-performance OSI-like protocols are also noted by using the Express Transport Protocol (XTP) as an illustration.

- The issue of a programming interface at the transport-services boundary is noted with a review of the X/Open transport interface (XTI), which has been designed for use with both OSI and TCP systems.

- The important coexistence of OSI and TCP/IP systems, and the transition to OSI has been discussed earlier. In this chapter, the TCP/IP protocols, and their close relationship to the OSI class-4 transport and the CLNP protocols are reviewed in more detail.

- The NetBIOS protocols, as an example of LAN-oriented protocols, are reviewed.

- Finally, the means for protocol stack selection, in a multiprotocol transport-service-provider, are examined.

The layer 3c and 4 functions in SNA will be covered in Chapters 14 and 15.

13.2   OSI TRANSPORT LAYER

The transport layer can be viewed as an agent of the upper layers (5 through 7) to direct the work of the transport-service-provider in layers 1 through 4. It can play a key role in making it possible for diverse upper and lower protocols to interoperate with each other. Hence, an understanding of its functions and its service-boundaries is very important. Both connection-oriented and connectionless transport services are defined in standards. We will cover only the connection-oriented transport layer standard, since that is by far the most commonly used. When using a connection-oriented transport layer, the lower layers (2 and 3) may provide connectionless or connection-oriented services.

13.2.1   Transport Requirements

The transport layer's primary responsibility is the control of the lower-layer transportation functions, so as to match the **Quality of Service (QOS)** that is offered by the layer-3 network service provider, to the quality of service required by the user. The objective is to provide a sufficiently reliable end-to-end data transfer, taking into account the possible shortcomings of the intermediate subnetworks. By using supplementary end-to-end controls, the transport layer may shield the upper layers from deficiencies in the lower data-delivery layers.

The various classes of transport-layer services may perform the following functions:

1. Receive *quality of service* requirements from the user (via the session layer), and negotiate these with the network layer

2. Where possible, *augment the network layer* abilities to provide the desired quality of service

3. Receive from above, and provide the network layer with necessary *destination address* information

4. Provide *connection-identification*, when different connections use the same network service-access-points. A system of *addressing* must allow transport service users to refer unambiguously to one another

5. Decide whether to *multiplex* multiple transport connections onto a single network connection

6. Provide *end-to-end flow control*, so as to meet the needs of the distant transport entity

7. Respond to requests from above, and arrange for the use of *expedited data* units

8. Establish the optimum *data-unit size*

9. *Segment* single data units into multiple data units, so as to meet the buffer needs of the network layer

10. Optionally, provide *concatenation* (several data units into a single data unit), or *splitting* (multiple network connections for a single transport connection), as appropriate

11. Provide *end-to-end sequencing*, *error detection*, and *recovery* facilities, where appropriate

Not all of these capabilities are necessarily used.

Two basic types of transport service are possible: connection-oriented and connectionless.

▪ In connection-oriented mode, the transport service (provided by the four lower layers) is a reliable and sequenced message flow between a pair of end-to-end data-exchange facilities in the upper three layers. Before data flows, however, a connection is established between peer entities in the transport layer. During the connection-establishment phase, negotiations determine parameters and functions that will govern subsequent data transfers. That connection then receives an id, which facilitates subsequent data transfers within that connection.

▪ In connectionless mode, individual data transfers, called *datagrams*, are sent with no relationship among them. There is no guarantee of reliable delivery. There is no negotiation of options that govern the transport.

13.2.2 Transport Protocol Classes

Different types of service (e.g., teletex and data processing) require different degrees of reliability, which are available from different transport providers. No one end-to-end transport-layer service can therefore be best for all situations. There has resulted, therefore, a set of five classes of OSI transport-layer facilities. The selection of functions, from the above list (in Section 13.2.1) depends on the class of service chosen in the initial connection-establishment phase. Three levels of reliability of subnetworks are handled:

▪ **Type A**—*Good reliability*: acceptable residual error rate,[1] and acceptable rate of signaled errors[2]

▪ **Type B**—*Not so good reliability*: acceptable residual error rate, but high signaled error rate

▪ **Type C**—*Poor reliability*: high residual error rate

For the networks with poorer reliability, a transport class with greater recovery capability is needed. Since types A and B may be either multiplexed or nonmultiplexed, we get the

---

1. *Residual errors* are undetected by the network and if detected must be detected by the user, such as by checksum on end-to-end data.

2. *Signaled errors* are those detected by the network and signaled to the affected users.

five classes of transport layer protocol:

	Nonmultiplex	Multiplex
▪ Network **type A**:	Class 0	Class 2
▪ Network **type B**:	Class 1	Class 3
▪ Network **type C**:		Class 4

These five classes are defined as follows:

▪   **Class 0**, *for type A* networks, is oriented to CCITT recommendation S.70 for teletex, which is a text transmission upgrade of telex. It is the simplest class, and provides no significant enhancement of quality of service (QOS). Functions for connection-establishment, data transfer with segmenting, and error reporting are available.

▪   **Class 1**, *for type B* networks, was designed to provide minimal error recovery for an X.25 network. It has capability to recover from some errors that are signaled by the layer-3 network service. *The TPDUs are numbered*, so that one can resynchronize after an X.25 reset and better cope with a disconnect. Expedited data is provided; and data may be exchanged during connection-establishment.

▪   **Class 2**, also *for type A* networks, is an enhancement of class 0, to allow multiplexing, but still no QOS enhancement. Multiplexing may be useful when public network duration charges apply to each network connection, even when no data is flowing. By-products are an optional flow control capability, and expedited data transfer.

▪   **Class 3**, also *for type B* networks, provides the recovery capabilities of class 1 plus the multiplexing and flow control capabilities of class 2.

▪   **Class 4** is designed *for type C* networks. It can detect errors that are not signaled by the network service. The objective is to detect lost, mis-sequenced, or duplicated TPDUs. It contains class 3 functions plus additional recovery capabilities, a checksum and time-out procedures. The resequencing capability enables the support of connectionless (datagram) networks.

The TPDUs employed by each class are listed in the Technical Reference section.

13.2.3   Transport-Service Primitives

The transport-service primitives are the data units at the transport-service (TS) boundary. There are only four types of OSI transport primitives:

▪   T-Connect is used to make the connection to the peer transport entity.

▪   T-Data is used by both entities to send data.

▪   T-Disconnect (with its confirmation) clears the connection.

▪   T-Expedited_Data is used to send limited amounts of data without being restricted by flow control (whenever this is possible).

The OSI TS boundary is thus relatively simple. The parameters sent with each of these primitives are listed in this chapter's Technical Reference section.

13.2.4   Transport-Service Addressing

The calling network address and the called network address, in OSI, are the Network Service-Access-Point (NSAP) addresses of the network layer. These are globally unique addresses that identify a transport entity in an end-system. It is possible, moreover, that the transport layer will multiplex more than one session on a connection to a network address. To identify individual sessions (of layer 5), therefore, the transport layer uses another level of addressing called Transport Service-Access-Points (TSAPs). Each user of the transport layer accesses the transport services via a unique TSAP. *The user is thus identified by the TSAP.* To establish the right connections, the calling TSAP and the called TSAP are included in the connection-request that initially establishes the transport-layer connection.

The transport layer then maps TSAPs to NSAPs, the network addresses. This NSAP address is not used in any TPDUs, but it must be passed on to the next lower layer, the network layer, for its use.

The TSAPs, however, are not carried in all TPDUs. Rather, a simple connection-identifier is assigned by each transport entity. One or both of these identifiers (called Source Reference and Destination Reference) are carried by most TPDUs *after* the connection-request is sent.[3] The exception is the simple Data TPDU for class 0 and 1 (see the Technical Reference section). Thus, a transport connection involves three identification or addressing components:

- Transport connection-identifiers, which identify the unique connection
- NSAPs, which identify the source and destination systems
- TSAPs, which identify the transport users

13.2.5   Transport-Layer Functions

Segmenting.   If the message received by the transport layer exceeds the maximum allowable TPDU size, the transport entity must segment the message before transmission. These segments must be reassembled, in the correct order, at the receiver. The *transport layer sequence-number*, applied to each segment, facilitates this process. Also needed is the end-of-transmission (EOT) flag, which marks the beginning and end of a set of segmented TPDUs.

Quality of Service (QOS).   The quality of service desired by the user can be requested of the transport layer. It is usually pre-arranged or, if negotiated, it can be agreed to by the transport-service provider. ISO 8072 calls for the following *QOS parameters*:

1. Speed:
    - *Throughput*—the smaller of octets sent per second or octets received per second, during a measured transmission sequence
    - *Transit delay*—the elapsed time between a `T-Data` request and the corresponding `T-Data` indication

---

3.   The reference number really identifies the connection-end-point (CEP) in the transport-service-access point (TSAP).

- *T-Connect-release delay*—the delay between a transport-service-user-initiated T-Disconnect request and the successful release of the T-Connect at the peer transport-service-user

2. Reliability:
   - T-Connect *establishment failure probability*
   - *Residual error rate*—the ratio of totally incorrect, lost, and duplicate Transport Service Data Units (TSDUs)[4] to total TSDUs transferred across the TS boundary during a measurement period
   - *Transfer failure probability*—the ratio of total failures (failure to deliver the octets in a transmitted TSDU), to the total attempts to deliver, during a measurement period
   - T-Connect *release failure probability*
   - T-Connect *protection*—to prevent unauthorized monitoring or manipulation of TS user information
   - T-Connect *priority*—on having a T-Connect QOS degraded, if necessary
   - *Resilience*—the probability of having the transport-service-provider initiate a T-Connect release in a specified time interval

The quality of service requested by the calling TS user may be lowered either by the TS provider or by the called TS user.

End-to-end flow control.   OSI uses a *flow control credit* protocol, that is built upon the use of sequence numbers for error control.

Initially, at connection-establishment time, the sender is given a credit equal to the sequence number modulo count. The window, indicating the number of allowable transmissions is thus initially equal to that count. No messages may be sent beyond the leading edge of the window. The trailing edge of the window is advanced each time another message is sent. This progressively narrows the window. Then, *means must be provided for the receiver to grant new flow control credits*, or permission to advance the leading edge of the window. The amount of the credit tells the sender how far the leading edge of the window may be advanced. The receiver, on the other hand, can withhold sending additional credits (along with its acknowledgments) when its buffers are filling; and in this way, the sender is prohibited from advancing the leading edge of the window and sending more.

Acknowledgments and credits are independent of each other. A credit may be given without any new acknowledgments, and acknowledgments may be given without any new credits.

End-to-end recovery.   The sequence numbering mechanism provides for detection of lost messages and their recovery. Cumulative acknowledgments are periodically required. A timer, associated with each TPDU sent, provides an upper limit to the waiting time for an acknowledgment. Beyond that, the sender must retransmit. Because acknowledgments may also get lost, duplicates are possible. These will be recognized by their identical sequence

---

4.   A Transport Service Data Unit (TSDU) is simply a data unit that passes across the transport-service boundary, which is the boundary between the transport layer and the session layer.

numbers, so long as the sequence numbers do not repeat in less than the maximum possible TPDU lifetime. Also, the sender must not be confused by multiple acknowledgments of the same TPDU.

13.3   OSI INTER-SUBNETWORKING

In the previous chapter, considerable emphasis was put on the concept of inter-subnetworking, including the flow of information across a wide variety of subnetworks that use different protocols. As application requirements multiply and technologies expand our options, this inter-subnetwork capability becomes increasingly vital. Both connection-oriented and connectionless protocols can be used to accomplish this. It is the common, worldwide NSAP addressing, discussed in the previous chapter, which now becomes common to the connection-oriented and connectionless inter-subnetwork capability. Under OSI, both the connectionless network protocol (CLNP) and the connection-oriented X.25 protocol are offered as standards. Both are examined in the following sections.

The key to *internetworking* is the role of a layer-3c protocol, which, in effect, handles the lower subnetwork as it would a link (see Figure 3.8). The lower layer-3a protocol headers envelope the user-data and also layer-3c and higher layer headers. As shown in Figure 12.14, the end points must share a common layer 3c. The intervening subnetworks can be of different kinds, such as an X.25 PSDN or one of several types of LANs (see also Figure 12.13).

13.4   OSI CONNECTIONLESS (INTERNET) LAYER

The standard connectionless protocol, under OSI, is the **Connectionless Network Service (CLNS) protocol, CLNP**, which is a direct descendent of the TCP/IP protocol.[5] Semantically, the CLNP is very similar to the IP protocol of TCP/IP. The major difference between the two protocols is in the extensive addressing capability of CLNP.

The term *connectionless* primarily connotes an absence of error recovery and flow-control facilities within the protocol, and the presence of some form of destination address or route information in each PDU. A connectionless protocol depends on higher-layer protocols to maintain message sequence and to recover from any lost or damaged packets. In the case of CLNP, this dependence is usually placed on the end-to-end transport-layer functions.

13.4.1   CLNP Functions

The standard divides CLNP functions into three types:

1. Mandatory
2. Optional and essential if requested
3. Optional but can be ignored if requested

---

5. The CLNP was originally called the "Connectionless Internetwork Protocol." Because it is not the only approach to interworking, and because the protocol can also be used with a single subnetwork, the name was changed to "Connectionless Network Protocol."

Type 1 functions are mandatory. They include:

- *Header format analysis.* If the protocol-identifier field indicates that this is the standard version of the protocol, then header analysis determines whether or not the protocol data unit (PDU) has reached its destination subnetwork. That is, if the destination address field provides an NSAP that is served by this network-entity (perhaps in an attached subnetwork), then the PDU has reached its internet destination. If not, it shall be forwarded to another Internet-node.

- *Route PDU.* Based on the destination address, the route is determined, and the underlying service is selected, to forward a PDU to the next network-entity. The appropriate primitive (SN-UnitData request) is issued by the network-entity.

- *Segmentation.* The maximum packet size may be different in different subnetworks. The Internet relay therefore may have to segment packets before passing them on. Four parameters are involved in the segmentation:

  - *Data_Unit_id*—to uniquely identify the initial PDU.
  - *Data Length*—the length of the data in bytes.
  - *Offset*—the position of the segment, as it was in the original data, expressed in multiples of 64 bits.
  - *More Flag*—to indicate whether or not all segments have been sent.

The header of the datagram (shown in Figure 13.12 in the Technical Reference section) is applied to each segment. The header contains a 6-byte segmentation part, for the data-unit-identifier, the segment offset, and the total length of the original PDU, including header and data. Segments are first made, with the *More flag* set to 1. The last segment has its *More flag* set to 0. If all segments do not arrive at the destination, the entire data unit is discarded after a waiting time period.

- *PDU lifetime.* Due to malfunctions, it can happen that packets wander in the connectionless network indefinitely. To prevent this, datagrams must be discarded after having been in the network for a predetermined lifetime. One approximate way of doing this is to count the number of times a datagram passes through a gateway (i.e., an inter-subnetwork router), and to make some upper-bound estimate (usually 500 ms) of the probable time between such encounters. Each time a datagram passes an inter-subnetwork router, the original lifetime figure is decremented. When the accumulated transit times exceed the predetermined lifetime, the packet is discarded.

- *Discard PDU.* A PDU is discarded, and associated resources are freed, when, for example:

  - A violation of protocol has occurred
  - A checksum fails
  - Local congestion prevents processing
  - A PDU's destination address is unknown or unreachable
  - A source route is incorrect or invalid
  - A PDU lifetime has expired

Two other functions are mandatory in implementations, but are used only at the discretion of the sending network service user. These are error reporting when a PDU is discarded, and the use of a checksum on the entire PDU header. That checksum would be verified every time the PDU header is processed, and updated every time the header is modified.

Type 2 functions are those optional functions that, *if requested*, are considered essential to the successful delivery of the PDU. If such a function is requested, the PDU is discarded by any receiving system that does not support the needed functions. Each option is described by a *parameter code*, a *parameter length*, and a *parameter value*. These type 2 functions are:

- *Security.* The standard does not specify the way in which protection services are to be provided. The protocol provides only for the encoding of security information in the PDU header. Security services may include, for example, data origin authentication, data confidentiality, and data integrity of a single data unit (see Section 4.4.7).

- *Source routing.* The originator may specify the complete path a PDU shall take. Source routing uses a list of network-entity–titles of the intermediate systems along the route. This list is held in a parameter within the options part of the PDU header. *Complete source routing* does not allow other, nonlisted, entities to be traversed.

- *Route recording.* A record is made of the complete path taken by a PDU as it traverses a series of intermediate-systems. A recorded route consists of a list of network-entity–titles held in a parameter list within the options part of the PDU header. Each intermediate-system adds its own network-entity–title at the end of the list. *Complete route recording* requires that all segmented PDUs take the same path.

Type 3 functions are those that are desirable but not essential. An intermediate-system may process a PDU even if the system does not possess the optional functions requested. Type 3 functions include:

- *Partial source routing.* As in complete source routing, above, a list of intermediate network-entities is provided by the source. A PDU may, however, take any path to visit the next entity on the list, including a path that contains other, nonlisted entities.

- *Partial route recording.* A list of the network-entities traversed along the route is accumulated. However, segments may each take different paths. When reassembly of segments occurs, the route recorded in any of the segments may be placed in the reassembled PDU.

- *Priority.* The resources of end-system and intermediate-system network-entities (such as outgoing transmission queues and buffers) can be used preferentially to process higher-priority PDUs ahead of lower-priority PDUs.

- *Quality of service.* QOS information is provided to network-entities along the route, in the options part of the PDU header. This information may be used to help make routing decisions. It may also be used to request a quality of service from a subnetwork.

- *Congestion notification.* Intermediate-systems may inform the destination network-entity of congestion. This is done through the use of a flag in the quality-of-service parameter in the options part of the PDU. That information may be provided to the network service user.

- *Padding.* Space can be reserved in the PDU header to align the data field to a convenient boundary (e.g., a computer word boundary).

13.4.2   OSI CLNP (Internet) Addressing

At layer 3 and above, there are three levels of addressing to consider:

- The id of the *subnetwork*
- The address of a destination-node in that subnetwork
- The address of an *application-process* within the destination node or station

In the earlier TCP Internet protocol, this was expressed in the form *Net_id.host_id.port_id.* In OSI, the NSAP address is universally defined (see Section 12.3.3), and includes the equivalent of Net_id and host_id. In OSI, the port_id corresponds to the TSAP address. The OSI PSAP address, in turn, includes both the TSAP address, the SSAP address, and the NSAP address. Therefore, in OSI, the PSAP address is sufficient and encompasses the three levels of addressing that were separately identified in TCP/IP. For routing among the various subnetworks, the components of the NSAP must be accessible to the routing function.

In some very simple nodes, the SSAP and TSAP addresses will not be needed; and in a single network, the Net_id is not needed. Since the destination is frequently known only by name, and since named destinations may move from location to location, a directory service (see Chapter 8) is needed to translate from names to location addresses.

CLNP PDU formats.   The formats and contents of the CLNP Protocol Data Units (PDUs) are given in this chapter's Technical Reference section.

13.4.3   Provision of the Underlying Service

The *subnetwork points of attachment* addresses are defined by each individual subnetwork authority (public or private). Hence, the source and destination addresses sent by the inter-subnetwork router to the subnetwork (in the *SN-UnitData* primitive), specify the subnetwork point of attachment addresses, which are unique to that subnetwork.

In the *SN-UnitData* primitive are *quality_of_service* parameters, whose content is based on prior knowledge of the service available from the subnetwork. These parameters may include:

- *Transit_delay:* the elapsed time between an *SN-UnitData* request and the corresponding indication.
- *Residual_error_probability:* the ratio of lost, duplicated, or incorrectly delivered data units to total data units transmitted to the subsystem during a measurement period.
- *Cost determinants:* constraints imposed by the user. These are satisfied by the Route PDU function, in accord with tariff information. The mechanism by which this is accomplished is a local matter.

If the attaching subnetwork is an 802.2 LAN, the SNPA addresses used in the *SN-UnitData* request and indication primitives are the seven-octet station addresses—that is, the 6-octet *MAC address* plus the 1-octet *LLC SAP address*.

If the attaching subnetwork is an X.25 PSDN, then a virtual circuit must be made available following the generation of an *SN-UnitData* request by the connectionless layer. The mechanisms for the call setup are a local matter. The *SN-destination_address* and the *SN-source_address* parameters in the *SN-UnitData* request and indication are often the X.121 DTE addresses used by the X.25 subnetwork. Other subnetwork addressing schemes (e.g., CCITT E.163 and E.164) may also be used.

13.5 OSI X.25 PACKET-LEVEL INTERFACE

13.5.1 Introduction

In this section, we will again adopt the terminology of the communications carriers shown in Figure 13.1. The *Data Terminal Equipment (DTE)* can be any type of user facility, from a large computer system to a very simple terminal. The *Data Circuit-terminating Equipment (DCE)* terminates the access line from the carrier's Data Switching Exchange (DSE) and performs any signal conversions necessary to the operation of the carrier.

The connection-oriented X.25 packet level protocol has been designed to operate as: (a) a self-sufficient network, (b) an internet capable of connecting multiple subnetworks, and (c) as a subnetwork operating under some other layer-3c inter-subnetwork protocol. In each case, a packet switching network provides a connection-oriented network service. We first examine the meaning of these terms.

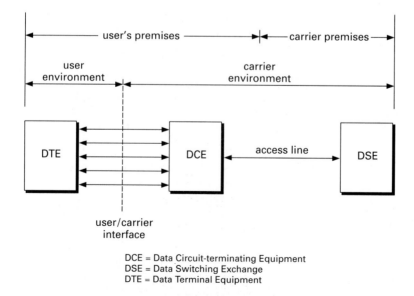

Figure 13.1 Interfacing to a communications carrier.

Packet switching networks.   In packet switching, all messages (both user information and network call-control information) are formed into discrete units called *packets*, which contain a header to specify packet control functions and packet network destination. *The packet network provides a* **virtual circuit**, *that is, one that appears to be a point-to-point connection for a pair of DTEs.*[6] *Actually, the physical lines are shared by many DTEs through multiplexing (asynchronous time-division multiplexing) provided by the packet carrier.* These virtual circuits may be switched (in which case, a virtual-call set-up and clearing procedure is required of the DTE) or permanent (in which case a permanent association is maintained between the DTEs and no calling procedure is needed).

The simple purpose of the X.25 packet switching network is to provide one or more *logical-links* between two X.25 end-systems (DTEs). This provision of a logical-link, you will recall, is the common purpose of all the services within the link/subnetwork-access facility, whether we are talking about LANs, WANs, or channels. The X.25 PSDN, however, can serve in two ways. It can be a layer 1 through 3a logical-link for layer-3c CLNP entities, or it can itself be the only layer-3 entity, fulfilling the roles of both layer 3c and 3a. Here, again, however, the terminology changes. The X.25 standards use a special term, *virtual circuit*, for the X.25 logical-link. The **logical channel id** is the identifier of the virtual circuit at each DTE/DCE interface, and is locally assigned at each interface.

X.25 does not define the packet network, only the DTE-DCE interface. It does not provide end-to-end communication for data-format compatibility, the logical grouping of data, end-to-end data flow control, end-to-end recovery, or system management.[7] Higher-layer protocols (in layers 4 through 7), such as are found in SNA or OSI, must be added to the lower-layer X.25 functions to achieve communicability.

Connection-oriented network service.   The connection-oriented services provided by the X.25 network layer (3c or 3a), to the controlling transport (or other 3c) layer, are as follows:

1.   *Address control.* The network layer, distributed throughout the transport provider, can uniquely identify each destination transport-entity in the network.

2.   *Route execution.* The network layer, active in every network-node in the transport provider, can establish an appropriate route so that messages are directed to their proper destination address.

3.   *Flow control.* The controlling transport-entity, at the receiving end, will avoid having its buffers over-run. This will be accomplished by requiring the network-layer functions to throttle input to the layer-3 network, as necessary. The network layer also will maintain adequate flow controls within its network to avoid congestion.

4.   *Sequence maintenance.* The network layer will maintain the correct sequence of messages delivered within a given connection to the destination.

5.   *Delivery options.* The network layer may provide expedited delivery and confirmation of delivery of selected messages.

---

6.   The virtual circuit extends end-to-end, including the layer-3a services at both ends.

7.   Some limited end-to-end communication is provided in X.25 via the Q-bit, as noted in Section 13.5.3.

6. *Error detection and recovery.* The network layer will acknowledge receipt of sequenced messages as appropriate and require retransmissions as needed.

7. *Quality of Service.* The network services (as observed by a network services user) are provided in accord with an agreed-to level of quality, including parameters such as:

- *connection_time*
- *residual_error_rate*
- *transit_delay*
- *signaled_error_rate*
- *throughput*
- *cost*

These definitions of QOS parameters are almost identical to those for the ISO connection-oriented transport service (layer 4), with the substitution of network for transport. The definitions do vary, however, in the case of throughput, protection, and resilience. Throughput of the network services is specified as desired and minimum values. For the transport services, it is specified as average and maximum values. Of all these network QOS parameters, *only throughput and flow control (packet size and window size) are negotiated during connection-establishment time.* The remainder are chosen or agreed upon by other means not specified in the standard.

13.5.2   X.25 Layers and Time Phases

The CCITT view is of protocols that span the DTE/DCE interface. However, the carriers are free to, and usually do, locate their protocol functions in the DSE rather than in the DCE. The figures of this chapter illustrate that fact. These protocols operate at several layers and in several time phases.

Layers.   The interface between the DTE and the DCE is served by protocols at three layers, as follows:

- *Layer 1.* The physical connections and the establishment of real circuits. For analog and for some early digital networks, this is the EIA RS 232-C or the equivalent CCITT V.24 electrical interface. For digital synchronous networks this is the CCITT X.21 interface (although many packet switching networks use X.21 BIS, which is basically the same as V.24). X.21 includes protocols for call establishment and clearing, which are DTE/DSE protocols (see Figure 13.2).[8]

- *Layer 2.* The HDLC data-link control provides a protocol for the simultaneous bidirectional flow of data blocks called "frames" (including an address field, a control field and a frame check sequence, as well as an information field). Note that in the case of digital synchronous networks (Figure 13.2(a)), a flow using HDLC (or some other data-link control) is between two or more DTEs. This DLC protocol is a DTE/DTE protocol and is *not* part of the X.21 DTE/DCE interface. However, in the case of packet switching networks (Figure 13.2(b)), this HDLC flow is between a station in a DTE and a station in a DSE. This *is* part of the X.25 DTE/DCE interface.

---

8.   1988 CCITT X.25 defines only nonswitched attachment at the physical layer. X.25 relies on X.32 and X.31 for switched call establishment at the physical layer.

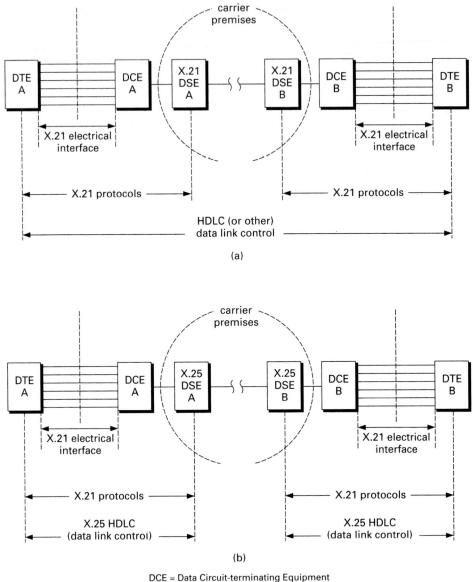

DCE = Data Circuit-terminating Equipment
DSE = Data Switching Exchange
DTE = Data Terminal Equipment

Figure 13.2 (a) X.21 and DTE/DTE data-link control in a synchronous digital network; **(b)** X.21 and the X.25 DTE/DSE data-link control in a packet-switching network.

- *Layer 3*. A third set of DTE/DSE protocols, at a third level, is needed in X.25 to support the DTE/DCE interface for packet switching networks in order to subdivide or form messages into packets with the appropriate packet headers and to provide DTE/DSE packet flow rate control.

Time phases.   Now let us look at how X.25 communication facilities perform in four time phases of a virtual call:

1. The *call-establishment phase* concerns the "setup" of the communications carrier facilities so as to provide communication between a calling DTE and a called station.
2. The *data transfer phase* is when the connection is established and data may be transferred.
3. The *call-clearing phase* concerns the release of the communications carrier facilities.
4. The *idle phase* equates to the *on-hook* condition in telephone network, but may further indicate that the DTE is not ready to accept a call.

Figure 13.2 illustrates the differences between an X.21 synchronous digital network and an X.25 packet switched network. In the former, a DLC connection exists DTE-to-DTE. In the latter, this is not true. How then do these time phases (cited above) relate to the X.21 and X.25 interfaces? We find three different situations regarding the call establishment and clearing phase:

1.   These establishment and clearing phases *do not exist at layer 1* if the DTE uses a nonswitched (leased) circuit of an X.21 digital network. They also do not exist at layer 1 if the DTE uses a nonswitched (leased) access line and a **Permanent Virtual Circuit (PVC)** of an X.25 packet switched network. A PVC becomes active when the link layer at both DTE/DCE interfaces becomes operational.

2.   These phases *do* provide a direct DTE-to-DTE connection and disconnection when the DTE use an X.21 switched, digital network.

3.   When using an X.25 interface and switched virtual circuits, one can think of a combination of two networks, each of which has distinct time phases. In *packet switched networks,* call establishment and clearing phases for virtual circuits are evidenced by special packets formed *at layer 3*. In addition in packet switched networks, there may be other completely separate call establishment/clearing phases *at (the X.21) layer 1* if the access to the packet switched network is via a real switched circuit.

Protocols.   Note that in case of *circuit switching* (of real circuits) between DTEs, there is no protocol involving interaction between the DTE and the carrier network during the data transfer phase. The only protocol during the data transfer phase is a DTE-DTE protocol spanning the entire real circuit. *Virtual circuits*, on the other hand, do require a protocol between the DTE and the packet-carrier network during the data transfer phase.

13.5.3   X.25 Interface Operations

Given the preceding structures, we now review the use of logical channels and control packets in the call-establishment and the normal data flows at the X.25 interface.

Logical channels.   One of the things desired in some data-processing systems is to be able to multiplex many different (layer-5) sessions on a given virtual circuit, across a single interface. The designers of the X.25 interface chose to aid this multiplexing by creating a **logical channel id** *to locally designate each virtual circuit*. For this, each virtual call or permanent virtual circuit is *locally assigned a* **logical channel group number** (less than or equal to 15) and a **logical channel number** (less than or equal to 225). The combination of group and channel number, called the *logical channel id*, constitutes a virtual circuit number. Since the logical channel id is assigned locally, it usually is different at the two DTE/DCE interfaces of a virtual circuit.

For virtual calls, these channel ids are assigned during the call set-up phases. For permanent virtual circuits, these are assigned at the time of subscription to the service. The logical channel id then must be carried in every packet header (except those for restart packets where these id fields are zero). Note that a virtual circuit may carry many different OSI associations concerning different application-entities. Similarly, a virtual circuit may carry different SNA sessions.

X.25 protocols enable X.25 DTEs to establish multiple concurrent logical channels on the access link to an X.25 network. According to the standard, a DTE is allowed to establish 4095 simultaneous virtual circuits (to other DTEs), over a single physical DTE-DCE link.[9] The DTE-DCE interface is defined to provide full-duplex statistical multiplexing, so at any one time, packets on many of the 4095 circuits may be flowing in either direction.

Packet headers.   The Data Switching Exchanges (DSEs) of packet switching networks are built to recognize packets. *Every data packet sent between DTEs includes packet headers. In addition, all of the network control messages are also contained in packet headers.* Each packet is then enclosed in the data-link control header and trailer.

Packet types are indicated by the low order bits of byte 3 in the header. In the 4 high-order bits of the first byte of each header for the data packet, the **Q or data qualifier bit** indicates that some special processing of that packet is needed by the DTE (for example, for device control messages). The Q-bit is transparent to the DSE network. Other than the Q-bit, these 4 bits are usually fixed. However, other identifier codes are used when the sequence numbering of data packets is performed modulo 128. Still other codes can be assigned.

Each packet header also includes the local *logical channel id* for that virtual circuit and also a packet type indicator. The *packet type indicator* for the data packets is only a 0 in the low-order bit of the third byte, but is a full byte in the other packet types. (In the latter cases, there is a 1 in the low-order bit.)

The `Call_Request` packet includes space for the destination address (SNPA address) plus an indication of its length. The `Incoming_Call` packet may contain the address of the calling DTE. The facility field in the `Call_Request` packet may optionally be used for facilities like reverse charging.

The third byte of the data packet header is similar to the control byte of HDLC (data link control) information frames except that the polling (P/F) bit is replaced by

---

9.   Logical channel 0 is reserved for control packets such as `Restart` and `Diagnostic`.

the **Mor more data bit**. The M-bit is used to indicate, in a full data packet, whether there is a logical continuation of data in the next data packet on a particular virtual circuit.

The send P(S) and receive P(R) sequence-numbers are defined to create *a "sliding window" that only allows a predetermined number of frames to be outstanding on a given logical channel at a given time*. Acknowledging each packet individually, would require excessive traffic and lost channel capacity during waits for each acknowledgment. Rather than doing that, the sliding window allows the sending of multiple packets before waiting for an acknowledgment. For example, if the window size is 7, the sender may send 7 packets before waiting for an acknowledgment. The lowest-numbered packet in the window is the first packet in the transmitted sequence that has not been acknowledged. Once an acknowledgment is received for the first packet sent within the window, the window slides forward, allowing another packet to be sent.

The maximum allowable number of outstanding frames, called window size, W, is set for each virtual circuit either at subscription time or at call-establishment time, but it can never exceed a system parameter modulus of 7 or 127.[10,11] *The P(S) and P(R) sending and receiving sequence numbers, sent with most packets, are used primarily for controlling the data flow on each logical channel* to or from the packet switching network, rather than for providing acknowledgements between stations for error control. The objective is to have an ability to throttle the flow on each logical channel (to prevent overdriving the packet network).

Some packets are not sequenced. One of these is the `Interrupt` packet, which will be transmitted by the network without waiting for all other previously sent packets to be delivered. Moreover, it will be delivered to a DTE even when it is not accepting data packets. The `Interrupt` packet can carry user data. An example of its use is to transmit a terminal break character.

Also there are `Receive_Ready` (RR) packets and `Receive_Not_Ready` (RNR) packets for flow-control, which contain a receive-count, P(R), but not a send-count. When there is no data packet to carry the receive sequence-number P(R), the RR packet is used by the DTE or the DSE to indicate that it is now ready to receive data packets on a given logical channel with the indicated P(R). (The number of packets to be sent without a response will be less than 8 or less than 128 depending on the modulus used for sequence numbering.) An RNR packet, on the other hand, tells a DTE or a DSE of an inability to accept additional data packets on a given logical channel. The RNR can be cleared by an RR packet sent in the same direction. A DTE or a DCE can also simply withhold acknowledgments in order to shut off flow beyond the current window.

Access links to a packet network.   The access line between the DCE on customer premises and the data switching exchange (DSE) of the carrier network is always a real (rather than

---

10.   The P(S) and P(R) numbers in the X.25 header roughly correspond to the Ns and Nr sending and receiving sequence numbers of HDLC.

11.   The window W is always equal to or less than the modulus minus 1.

virtual) circuit. The following four cases have to be architected:

Access link	Virtual circuit
1. Nonswitched	Permanent
2. Nonswitched	Switched
3. Switched	Permanent
4. Switched	Switched

A switched, real access circuit might be either an analog circuit or a digital circuit. Switched access is defined by Recommendation X.32.

Call establishment and clearing. The sequences in X.25 for virtual circuit call-establishment phase, data-transfer phase, and clearing phase use packets for information exchange. A simplified illustration of this is given in Figure 13.3. The packets for virtual circuit establishment and clearing are formed at layer 3 and flow at layer 2. The characters of the virtual circuit call-progress signals are placed in the cause fields of the `Clear_Request` or `Reset` packets.

The sequence shown in Figure 13.3 is as follows:

1. The calling DTE indicates virtual call request by transferring a `Call_Request` packet across the DTE/DCE interface. This packet includes the called DTE address and a logical channel number selected by the calling DTE.

2. The destination DSE indicates that there is an incoming call by sending to its DTE an `Incoming_Call` packet, using the logical channel there that is in the ready state and has the lowest available logical channel number.

3. The called DTE enters the virtual call data transfer state after it indicates its acceptance of the call by sending a `Call_Accepted` packet. The latter specifies the same logical channel as that of the `Incoming_Call` packet.

4. The calling DTE enters the data transfer state after it receives (from its DSE) a `Call_Connected` packet that specifies the same logical channel as in the `Call_Request` packet. (Note that the logical channel numbers at the two ends are usually different.)

5. In the data phase, traffic can flow in either direction at any time. `Data`, `Interrupt`, `Flow_Control`, and `Reset` packets may be exchanged in the data transfer state.

6. A DTE may request that the virtual call be cleared by sending a `Clear_Request` packet. However, the logical channel will not be returned to the ready state until the local DSE returns a DCE `Clear_Confirmation` packet.

7. The remote DSE in turn can advise the other DTE by sending a `Clear_Indication` packet. That DTE responds by sending a DTE `Clear_Confirmation` packet and the DTE then returns to the ready state. The *cause-code* field of the `Clear_Indication` packet may, for example, be coded to indicate one of the following:

- number busy
- access barred

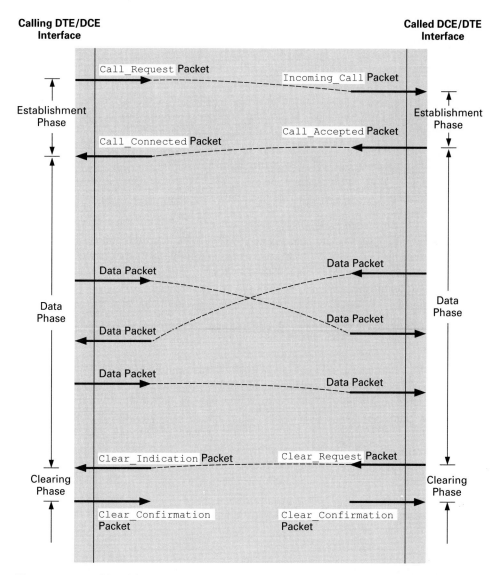

Figure 13.3 Simplified illustration of call establishment, data transfer, and call clearing [Cypser78].

- network congestion
- out of order
- invalid call
- not obtainable
- number refuses reverse charging

- local procedure error
- remote procedure error

End-to-end recovery.   When the network determines that it has possibly lost some packets, it will send a `Reset` or `Clear` to the attached DTEs. That `Reset` is handled by the transport entity. At that time, the two partner transport entities must acknowledge to each other that a `Reset` exists, and inform each other of the last TPDU received. Resumption of transmission begins from that synchronization point.[12]

When all connections are lost, the network sends a `Restart`. The `Restart` applies to all virtual circuits on the DTE/DCE interface. Virtual calls disappear, and sequence numbers for permanent virtual circuits are reset. It is then necessary for a partner to ask for a new connection. Control packets then must be used to identify the new connection and resynchronize as described above.

X.25 addressing.   The *calling_address* and the *called_address* (sometimes called DTE-addresses) are what OSI also calls the **Subnetwork Point of Attachment** (SNPA) addresses. This address may or may not be the same as an NSAP. The *called_address* is necessarily unique at least to that one network. It primarily provides the address of a station in a PSDN destination-node. An NSAP, on the other hand, refers to points where the service of the network layer is made available to its users. The NSAP, moreover, is universally unique. An end-node may have more than one NSAP address and may be attached to more than one subnetwork.

Thus, the X.25 *called_address* is *not* necessarily the same as the destination NSAP. With cascaded subnetworks (see Figure 12.13, for instance), the NSAP is in the final destination-node on a remote subnetwork. The way in which the cascaded networks arrange the hand-over of the destination address is up to the administrators of the two networks. The *called_address*, in the intermediate X.25 subnetwork, may be only the station address of an intermediate router, between subnetworks. (In the example of Figure 12.13, the inter-subnetwork routing depends on the information contained in the layer-3c IP header, not the LAN or X.25 headers.) In general, therefore, the X.25 *called_address* can be considered to be the station address of a destination node on a particular subnetwork; and only sometimes does that equate to an NSAP address (or part of an NSAP) in that same node.

13.5.4   Fast-Select Facility

As X.25 evolves, new facilities are needed and added. The standard includes a large number of facilities dealing with call-restrictions (e.g., closed-user-groups), charging (e.g., reverse charging), quality of service, reliability (e.g., DTE-DTE acknowledgement), call-destination management (e.g., call-redirection), and fast-select. The latter is worthy of special attention.

---

12.   In SNA use of X.25, the ELLC (layer-3b) function allows "riding over" certain resets and clears, because of the recovery capabilities provided.

There are transaction-type applications in which only one message (and perhaps a reply) constitutes the whole transaction. A very fast set-up and destruction of a virtual circuit is needed. The **fast-select facility** does this.

To use fast-select, the DTE requests it in the facilities field of the `Call_Request` packet. The allowable user data field is accordingly increased from 16 to 128 bytes. This larger data field is delivered to the destination DTE in the `Call_Indication` packet.

If the virtual circuit is not to be established after the response, the restricted mode is chosen. Then the destination DTE immediately responds with a `Clear_Indication` packet, also containing up to 128 bytes of user data. Thus, with one exchange, up to 2 x 128 bytes of user data was exchanged.

If, on the other hand, a normal virtual circuit is to be continued after the fast select, then the unrestricted mode is selected. The destination DTE then has the option of replying as above, or replying with a normal `Call_Accepted` packet (augmented by up to 128 bytes of user data). The virtual circuit then remains in normal operation.

13.6 EXPRESS TRANSFER PROTOCOL (XTP)

As available bandwidth increases and the volume of data increases, nodes are hard pressed to keep up with message processing. More efficient protocols become necessary [Hiles89]. XTP is a good example of *techniques that go beyond the OSI standards for special situations that require very high performance* [Cohn88],[Chesson]. XTP obtains higher performance by simplifying the OSI protocols, using simple PDU formats, and reducing the number of messages exchanged to set up a connection and deliver short messages at high speed. It is not a standard, but draws key parts from standards. We summarize it here as an indication of *the type of evolution OSI may need for high-performance systems.*

XTP transfer layer.   XTP defines a new transfer layer, which is a unification of the network and transport layers of OSI. A comparison of the OSI and XTP packet exchanges is given in Figure 13.4. To initiate a connection, transfer a single packet message, and terminate the connection requires only three packets in XTP but requires six packets in OSI TP-4. This type of optimization is achievable when one knows and limits both the application and the configuration. The approach is tailored to one type of subnetwork, a high-speed LAN. It depends on high reliability in that subnetwork, and a high probability of successful connection. These are characteristic of optical fiber in general.

Contexts.   The OSI transport protocol connections require an explicit request/response exchange in order to initiate and terminate connections. The XTP, on the other hand, uses an implicit connection set-up mechanism to minimize the overhead.

Separate **Context Records** are maintained by the originator and destination XTP entities. Context Records contain sequence number information, XTP PDU fields, error control data, and those parameters necessary to manage XTP operations. The Context mechanism allows a connection to be established with a single PDU. Unlike OSI TP-4, no negotiation takes place between originator and destination when establishing a Context. If a single message transfer is required, the Context is automatically terminated upon completion of the transfer.

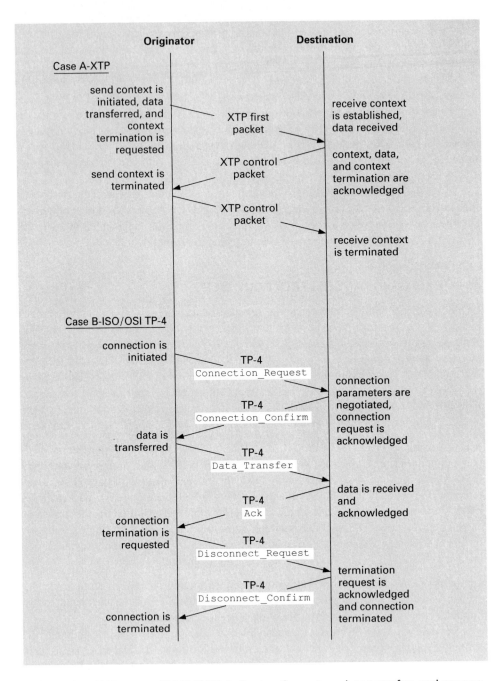

Figure 13.4 XTP versus ISO/OSI TP-4: Connection setup, data transfer, and connection termination [Cohn88].

End-to-end control.　Sequence numbers are used in XTP to keep the correct order of the packets. Sequence numbers refer to the number of the data bytes in the data stream. Hence, the end-to-end protocol works even in the presence of segmenting or blocking of packets. A rate-based flow control, using the sequence-numbers, regulates the sender, and allows a receiver to dynamically throttle senders when necessary. The rate control can specify an interpacket spacing as well as the aggregate rate.

Selective retransmission.　XTP uses a selective retransmission scheme that will retransmit only those packets that were not received. In contrast, OSI TP-4 uses a roll-back retransmission scheme, that retransmits all packets after the lost one. Selective retransmission requires that the receiver track gaps in the sequence numbers. Up to 16 gaps can be reported to a sender for retransmission.

Datagram versus connection.　The same real-time packet processing mechanism is used for datagrams and connections. In fact, there is not the usual distinction between these two. *A datagram can be seen as a short-lived connection*. A connection can be seen as a long-lived datagram. Hence, datagrams are reliable, and benefit from the same rate, flow, and error control mechanisms as do connections.

13.7　X/OPEN TRANSPORT INTERFACE (XTI)

ISO does not specify the syntax of a *programming interface at the transport-services boundary*. However, many manufacturers are cooperating to establish such a common API under the umbrella of the X/Open Company Limited. The interface known as the **X/Open Transport Interface (XTI)** [Richter89] was first published in the X/Open Portability Guide Issue 3.[13] *It is concerned primarily with the services of CLNP, specified in ISO 8072, but it supports TCP/IP as well*, and, in principle is adaptable to services provided by other transport systems. X/Open reportedly is also about to publish a document called *The Use of XTI to Access NetBIOS*.[14] XTI, therefore, is another good candidate for future accommodation in a multiprotocol architecture.

The XTI is expressed in function Calls of the C programming language. Those XTI Calls defined to be mandatory are sufficient to utilize the service primitives of either the OSI or the TCP transport service.

XTI operations.　At the XTI interface, a *transport-end-point* of a transport-service-provider must be **opened** by a transport-service-user, before any service request. The transport-end-point is also closed explicitly by the transport-service-user (or by the transport-service-provider if the connection is abnormally terminated). Multiple transport-service-users can share a transport-end-point, but each transport-end-point can support only one established transport connection at a time. To the transport-service-provider,

---

13. *X/Open Portability Guide*, issue 3, volume 7, Transport Interface.
14. Reported in *Data Communications*, March 1991.

all users of the same transport-end-point appear to be a single transport-service-user. The primary XTI functions can be seen in a typical six-step procedure of the connection-oriented mode:

1. *Open a transport-end-point* (T-Open)

2. *Associate an address* with the transport-end-point (T-Bind)

3. *Establish a transport connection* (T-Accept, T-Connect, T-Listen, and T-RcvConnect)

4. *Exchange data* (T-Send and T-Rcv)

5. *Release transport connection* (normal: T-SndRel and T-RcvRel) and (abnormal: T-SndDis and T-RcvDis)

6. *Close transport-end-point* (T-Close)

-   T-Open creates a transport-end-point, and returns a file descriptor that serves as the local identifier of the end-point.

-   T-Bind associates a protocol address with a given transport-end-point, thereby activating the end point.

-   T-Connect requests a connection to the transport user at a specified destination and waits for the remote user's response.

-   T-RcvConnect is used with T-Connect to establish a connection in an asynchronous manner. It allows an active transport user to determine the status of a previously sent connect request. If the request is accepted, the connection phase will be complete on return from this function.

-   T-Listen enables the passive transport user to receive connect indications from other transport users.

-   T-Accept is issued by the passive user to accept a particular connect.

-   T-SndDis can be issued by either transport user to initiate an abortive release of a transport connection.

-   T-RcvDis identifies the reason for an abortive release, when the connection is released by the transport provider or another transport user.

In contrast, the XTI connectionless mode has no step 3 (above) for connection-establishment or step 5 for connection release. In step 4, data transfer is done with other Calls (T-SndUData, T-RcvUData, and T-RcvUDerr).

The X/Open Portability Guide lists fourteen such Calls as mandatory for connection-oriented transport service, and nine Calls as mandatory for connectionless transport service, of which six Calls are common to both.

XTI synchronous calls poll for completion rather than using a posted event-handle or invocation of an asynchronous post routine. XTI does not support either a broadcast or a multicast function.

13.8 TCP/IP

The desire for an inter-subnetworking capability, with an addressing structure that enables one to traverse different subnetworks having different architectures, led at an early date to the development of the TCP/IP protocols. These are now in wide use. The OSI CLNP described above is a direct outgrowth of the pioneering TCP/IP, sponsored originally by the U.S. Department of Defense. Although, in general, there will be a movement from the TCP/IP protocols to OSI, we can expect the TCP/IP protocols to remain in wide use for years to come. We now look more closely at the protocols of the TCP and IP components [Comer88].

13.8.1 TCP/IP API

Three application program interfaces are in common use for TCP/IP applications:

1.   The *User Datagram Protocol (UDP)* provides a layer-4 access to the connectionless service of IP. There is no connection establishment between the two applications that use UDP. Accordingly, there is no acknowledgment of receipt of a packet, and no indication from the receiver if errors occurred during transmission. There is no assurance that packets will be received in the order that they were sent.

2.   The *Transmission Control (TCP) API* establishes a layer-4 logical circuit connection between two application programs. A full-duplex byte stream of data is transferred between the applications. Error checking and retransmission of data are provided, without involvement of the application program.

3.   The *Sockets API* is a higher-layer interface. It was originally used on UNIX systems for interprocess communication within the system. TCP/IP applies it to communication between systems. Application programs create a socket, specifying which low-level transport protocol to use, and connect the socket to the partner application. The application program then can read and write, in a duplex byte stream, without having to handle the overhead of processing a specific protocol.

13.8.2 Transmission Control Protocol (TCP)

The basic purpose of TCP, like that of OSI transport class 4, is to provide an end-system-to-end-system reliable stream delivery. A connection is therefore made, at the transport layer, between the two end-systems. That connection enables error control and flow control, which are briefly described below.

Prior to any information flow, the two applications need to take some action to establish a transport-layer connection. Each application works with its own operating system to this end. One application indicates that it desires a *passive open*, which means that it is ready to accept an incoming connection. The other partner requests its operating system to perform an *active open*, which requests the connection. A three-way handshake between the two TCPs is then sufficient to establish the connection. That sequence (A to B), (B to A), and (A to B), confirms that both sides are ready and both sides agree to an initial pair of sequence numbers, to be used in acknowledgments and flow control.

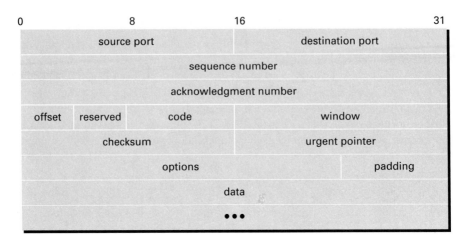

Figure 13.5 Format of the TCP packet with the TCP header.

TCP headers.   TCP receives a stream of bytes, which it divides into packets for transmission. Each packet consists of data plus a TCP header. The format of that TCP header is shown in Figure 13.5. That same format is used for both data packets and connection-establishment packets. Each packet travels through the Internet in connectionless mode, as a datagram. The end-to-end TCP layer is then responsible for the end-to-end ordering and safe delivery of these datagrams.

Note that the TCP header does not contain the address of the source or destination end-systems. That is the job of the Internet Protocol. The TCP header only contains the TCP port numbers that identify the application programs within the end-systems.

Error control.   The sequence number, acknowledgment number, and window fields in the packet header are used for error control and flow control, all based on a simple sliding-window technique.

Whereas X.25 uses the simple sliding-window technique for flow control, the acknowledgments in that same technique are used by TCP for error control. In effect, the sender also keeps a timer for each packet sent. If the acknowledgment for that packet is too long delayed, the packet is assumed lost, and the packet is retransmitted.

Sequence numbers are used to maintain order and to insure that every packet is acknowledged. However, the sequence numbers actually apply to bytes in the data stream rather than the packets they form. The sequence number in the TCP header identifies the position in the sender's byte stream of the data in the packet. The acknowledgment number in the packet header identifies the highest byte that the source of that packet has received. Thus, the sequence number refers to the data stream flowing in the same direction as the packet carrying the sequence number. The acknowledgement number, on the other hand, refers to the data stream in the direction opposite to that of the packet carrying it.

The *options* field varies in length, so the *offset* field is used to specify the offset of the data portion of the packet. The *code* field is a format indicator for the packet, identifying the type of packet it is. The *res* (reserved) field is reserved for future use.

Flow control.   *TCP allows the window size to vary* at the discretion of the receiver. Each acknowledgment, which specifies the number of bytes received, is accompanied by a window-size-indicator (in the *window* field of the TCP header) that specifies how many additional bytes of data the receiver is prepared to accept. As buffers fill up, for example, the receiver can reduce the window-size-indicator. The sender should reduce the window size accordingly.

TCP can also collect data on round-trip delays, by timing the wait for acknowledgments. The calculation of an average round-trip delay can be another factor in estimating congestion and hence in determining window size.

13.8.3   Internet Protocol

The layer-3c Internet Protocol (IP) is connectionless, meaning that it does not establish a layer-3c connection for error recovery or flow control. The IP header is shown in Figure 13.6. (Note that its contents are very close to those of the OSI CLNP header in Figure 13.12.) The IP has the important job of analyzing the address of the destination end-system and routing accordingly, across intermediate subnetworks. The IP also controls fragmentation, and can use a number of options that help to monitor and control the network. These and other functions described in the following bear a close resemblance to those of CLNP.

Format controls.   The *version* field specifies the IP protocol version, which must be common to the sender, receiver, and inter-subnetwork routers. Mismatches will result in rejected datagrams. The *length* field tells how long the IP header is, in multiples of 32 bits.

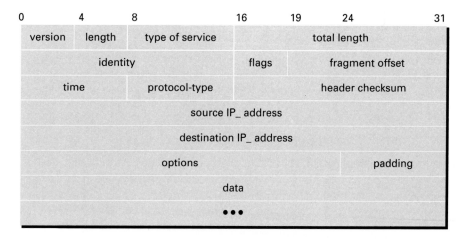

Figure 13.6 Format of the Internet Protocol (IP) datagram with the IP header.

The *total length* field then gives the total length of the IP datagram, in bytes, including both the header and the data.

Fragmentation.   Because different LANs, X.25 subnetworks, and others have different limitations on the size of message they can handle, the layer-3c interworking units located between subnetworks often have to divide the messages into fragments, to meet the requirements of a subnetwork. Once so divided, the fragments are carried through the network to the destination end-system.

Three fields in the IP header, *identity, flags,* and *fragment-offset,* manage the fragmentation process. The *identity* field uniquely identifies the datagram. Every fragment of a packet receives the *ident* field of the parent packet. The *flags* field tells whether the datagram may be fragmented, and whether this is the last fragment of a packet. The *fragment-offset* field specifies the offset of this fragment in the original datagram, measured in units of 8 bytes.

Lifetime.   Because a datagram sometimes can be the victim of loops in the network and other malfunctions, a time limit is placed on the life of each packet. The *time* field specifies how long, in seconds, the datagram should be allowed to exist in the network. The source of the datagram sets this timer. Whenever a datagram passes through an inter-subnetwork router, the timer is decremented.[15] When the timer has been decremented to zero, the packet is discarded.

Monitoring options.   As in OSI, the TCP/IP *option* field has three interesting possibilities (which can be specified by the setting in the *code* field at the beginning of the *option* field).

▪   The *Record Route Option* allows the source to create an empty list of IP addresses, so that each inter-subnetwork router can insert its address as the datagram passes through.

▪   The *Source Route Option* allows the sender to dictate a path through the network. The source provides the sequence of Internet addresses along the route. In *single source-routing,* only one subnetwork is allowed between successive Internet addresses. In *loose source-routing,* multiple subnetwork hops are allowed between a pair of specified Internet addresses.

▪   The *Timestamp Option* (like the Record Route Option) allows the source to create an empty list of IP addresses. In the timestamp option, however, each successive inter-subnetwork router puts an entry in the list containing the time and date at which the router handled the datagram.

13.8.4   Internet (IP) Routing

The all-important routing addresses are the source IP_address and the destination IP_address. These internet addresses correspond to the OSI NSAPs, and they, too, must be globally defined. The routing from inter-subnetwork router to inter-subnetwork router, across diverse subnetworks, is discussed in Section 12.8.3).

---

15.   For example, the unit of decrement might be the average length of time, in seconds, for a packet to traverse a subnetwork, between inter-subnetwork routers.

Internet routing is primarily concerned with routing through gateway (inter-subnetwork router) nodes to a destination network. The routing mechanism accordingly uses the Net_id portion of the internet address, rather than the host_id, until the destination network is reached. The routing in each gateway is based on tables which provide the address of the next inter-subnetwork router (gateway), depending on the Net_id of the destination network.

The *type of service* field is broken down into subfields. These provide hints to the Internet routing algorithm that help it choose one path over another. A precedence subfield, with values 0 through 7, indicates the relative importance of the datagram. Three bits can then be set to request particular characteristics in a route: a D-bit requests low delay; a T-bit requests high throughput;. an R-bit requests high reliability.

An inter-subnetwork router (gateway) is basically a normal host running TCP/IP, as the gateway function is included in the base IP protocol. Incoming datagrams to any host will be checked to see if that host is the IP destination host [GG24-3376]:

- If yes, the datagram is passed to the higher-layer protocols.
- If no, the datagram is treated as an outgoing datagram, and the IP routing service will determine where to send it for the next hop.

When a small host has more than one gateway to choose from, a common practice is to always send to a default gateway. That gateway, in turn, is expected to reroute the message in a correct direction.

Subnetworks, such as LANs and X.25 networks may be crossed as intermediate subnetworks in a route. In those cases, the internet gateways (inter-subnetwork routers) turn over to the subnetworks the job of routing through the subnetwork. If, for example, the route includes a series of bridge-connected LANs, the entire set of bridged LANs (a LAN region) is treated as one subnetwork. As shown in Figure 13.7, the inter-subnetwork router ISR(B), where a message first enters the LAN, determines that the inter-subnetwork router ISR(C) is the proper exit from an interconnected LANs. After ISR(B) specifies the station address of ISR(C), it is up to the LAN subnetwork to route the message through the LAN bridges to ISR(C). As far as the Internet layer is concerned, the entire set of bridged LANs is only an effective link connection. Inter-subnetwork router ISR(C) finally uses Net-4 to route to the destination host. A similar procedure applies to any other self-contained subnetwork, such as an X.25 PSDN or an SNA/APPN subnetwork.

13.8.5   X Window System

The X Windows System allows a user to view several programs simultaneously on a bit-mapped high-resolution display. These programs may be operating on the workstation or on a remote host connected to the TCP/IP network.[16] The part that manages the user's display is called the X Window Server. The application program is called the X Window Client.

---

16.   The IBM X Window System for TCP/IP on MVS and VM, and the AIXwindows for RISC System/6000 and AIX PS/2, include an API based on the OSF/Motif User Interface Toolkit. The Toolkit function enables the application programmer to invoke high-quality graphic designs that have a bevelled appearance [Reinhold91].

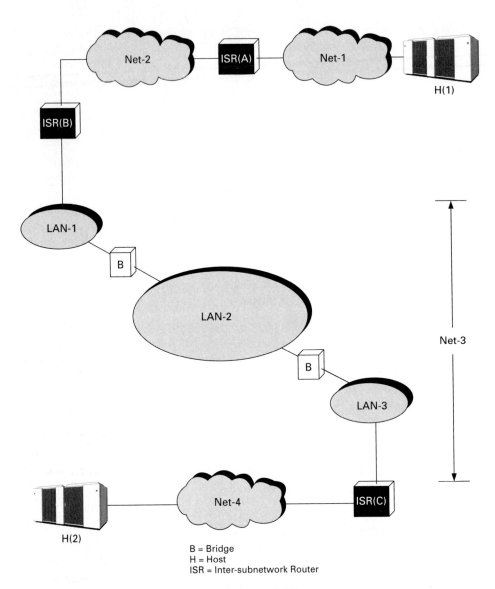

Figure 13.7 Internet routing across bridged LANs.

13.9 NETBIOS

The LAN protocols have developed almost independently of the wide area network protocols. The result is a present-day proliferation of de facto standards and proprietary protocols. Among these, for example, are the NetBIOS protocols developed by IBM, the IPX/NetBIOS protocols developed by Novell, and the TCP/NetBIOS and OSI/NetBIOS protocols developed by 3Com. Beyond these are the broader XNS protocols of Xerox, the

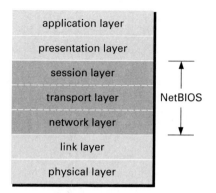

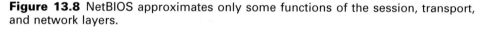

Figure 13.8 NetBIOS approximates only some functions of the session, transport, and network layers.

AppleTalk protocols of Apple Computer Co., and the NetWare (SPX/IPX) protocols of Novell. These, too, can be expected to remain for the foreseeable future. The longer-term goal, however, must be to integrate the LAN, WAN, and MAN areas into a multiprotocol network with full interoperability. To understand this problem we examine, in the following, the IBM NetBIOS, one of the LAN-oriented protocols.

The **Network Basic Input/Output System (NetBIOS)** is only one of the commonly used application programming interfaces for the LAN environment today. It is supported in the Ethernet, token ring, and IBM PC Network environments. IBM introduced NetBIOS originally for use on the PC Network, an early LAN. Actually, it was defined as only an interface between the application programs and the network adapter to local area networks (LANs). However, some LU-like and transport-like functions have been added. Current applications and services, using LANs via PC-DOS, MS-DOS, and OS/2 operating systems, frequently use some form of NetBIOS. It is one of the de facto standards in the LAN environment, although several variations of NetBIOS are used.

NetBIOS layers.   NetBIOS provides a name-oriented connection between LAN adapters. Multiple applications can use the NetBIOS interface concurrently. Connection is on a peer-to-peer basis. As Figure 13.8 indicates, NetBIOS provides functions that logically fall within the realm of three OSI layers: the session, transport, and network layers. The NetBIOS interface, in effect, is at the top of a very slim session layer. That places it just above the transport layer. In the pure LAN world, there need be minimal network-layer function, and the transport layer may be simple. Though it is hard to correlate with the other transport-service-providers, we consider NetBIOS here because it, too, needs to be one of the protocols participating in split-stack combinations near the transport-services boundary (see also Section 13.7).

Frequently, NetBIOS support uses the 802.2 interface to provide datagram or session-layer communications between applications executing from different machines in the network. It is also possible for NetBIOS to access the network without going through the 802.2 interface.

Network control blocks.   Calls to NetBIOS involve the use of a *Network Control Block (NCB)* within an application. The NCB is simply the format in which instructions are given to NetBIOS. It contains, for example, fields for the command, local session number, number of the application, pointer to a message buffer address, a name on the local NetBIOS interface, and another name on a local or remote NetBIOS interface. The command field tells NetBIOS what the application wants to do. When the application then issues a command, control is transferred from the application to the software associated with the LAN adapter. The subsequent communication between the application and the adapter software is via the network control block for that interrupt.

NetBIOS sessions.   NetBIOS session establishment requires a preordained cooperation between the two stations [Thomas89]. One application must have issued a `Listen` command when another application issues a `Call` command. The `Listen` command references a name in its NetBIOS name table, and also the remote name an application must use to qualify as a session partner. If the receiver (listener) is not already listening, the Call will be unsuccessful. If the Call is successful, each application receives notification of session establishment with a 1-byte *session-id*. `Send` and `Receive` commands then transfer data. At the end of a session, either application can issue a `Hang_Up` command.

Datagrams require no preliminary commands to set up a session. It is necessary, however that the receiving node have issued a `Receive_Datagram` command. Otherwise the data is simply lost. In general, there is no assurance of delivery of datagrams. Also, the size of a datagram is limited to 512 bytes. This is in contrast to the 131,072 bytes that could be transferred with a single `Chain_Send` command.

A summary listing of the NetBIOS commands and illustrative NetBIOS command flows are given in this chapter's Technical Reference section. Further illustration of NetBIOS setup is given in Section 19.2.2, with the LAN-LAN via WAN Program.

WAN environment.   NetBIOS alone is insufficient for general communication across a WAN. Its name space is limited. It lacks support for subnetworks (e.g., X.25 and ISDN) other than LANs. It does not have the same recovery capabilities that an APPC has. Moreover, in the absence of architected protocols below the NetBIOS interface, different manufacturers have implemented it in different ways. Hence, for communication from LAN workstations to remote hosts via WANs, APPC (or equivalent) is often preferred. The use of LU 6.2 as an intermediary between two NetBIOS-based LANs is given in Section 19.2.2.

13.10   PROTOCOL STACK SELECTION

A growing requirement arises in this multiprotocol world, when a message needs to be routed to one of several *protocol stacks* in a destination-node. For example, an incoming frame coming off a LAN might be routed, within a destination-node, to either an SNA, OSI, TCP/IP, or NetBIOS protocol stack.

If that frame contained an X.25 packet or an OSI datagram, *it would have to be routed to the appropriate network-entity*. Supposing it were an X.25 packet, there is the question of routing it to a pure OSI path or to an SNA destination which uses X.25 as a pseudo-link. Or, the desired path might be to an ASCII-based application that uses an ASCII/X.25

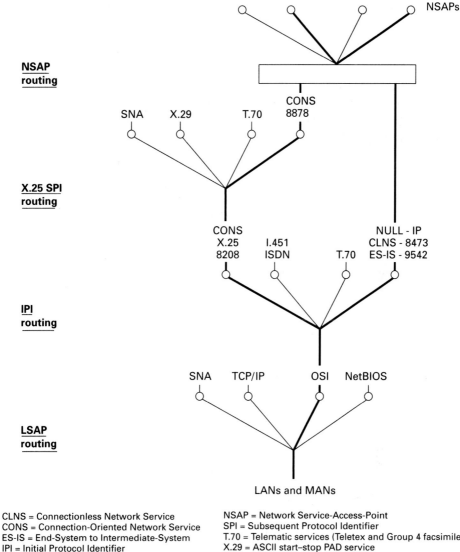

CLNS = Connectionless Network Service
CONS = Connection-Oriented Network Service
ES-IS = End-System to Intermediate-System
IPI = Initial Protocol Identifier
LSAP = Link Service-Access-Point

NSAP = Network Service-Access-Point
SPI = Subsequent Protocol Identifier
T.70 = Telematic services (Teletex and Group 4 facsimile)
X.29 = ASCII start–stop PAD service

Figure 13.9 Routing within an end-system.

converter. Some early possibilities are illustrated in Figure 13.9.

■   For LANs (and MANs), the link layer SAPs provide the first level of selection, as shown in Figure 13.9.

■   If OSI is selected by the LSAP routing, then further levels of protocol selection may be made by *two kinds of Protocol Identifiers (PIDs)*, the Initial Protocol Identifier and the Subsequent Protocol Identifier.

- The protocol operating directly over the data link layer is termed the initial protocol, and is identified by the **Initial Protocol Identifier (IPI)**. For X.25, the IPI is in the GFI (General Format Id) field of each packet.[17] The IPI is used to select a specific network layer protocol machine, as shown in Figure 13.9. That IPI selection might be to a network-entity for connection-oriented or connectionless service, or one of the others shown.
- The protocol that is carried by the initial protocol is termed the subsequent protocol, and is identified by a **Subsequent Protocol Identifier (SPI)**. Connection-oriented data packets have an SPI (established in Draft Technical Report DTR 9577) in the *first octet of layer-4 data*. If the input message is an X.25 *Call-Establishment* request, then the SPI (which is then the *first octet* of the *Call_User_Data field*), is used, along with the NSAP, to select an X.25 user. This SPI selection could be to the ISO 8878 (X.25 connection-oriented service) or to one of the other protocols that used X.25 as a carrier, such as SNA or X.29 (ASCII).

Following call-establishment, the virtual circuit's **logical channel number** is used to find the pre-established path. The SPI does not apply to connectionless, where there is no call-establishment. The NSAP is used for still further user selection. Each NSAP may support both connection-oriented and connectionless service.

Conclusion

Referring back to Figure 3.14, we see the four sets of protocols at layers 4 and 3c: SNA, OSI, TCP/IP and NetBIOS. All are important. Particularly OSI, SNA, and TCP/IP increasingly share the other facilities of an integrated architecture illustrated by Figure 3.14. The OSI protocols described in this chapter promise to become the common denominator in many multivendor networks of the future. Key aspects of these OSI protocols are:

- OSI offers five classes of end-to-end transport protocols, for three different reliabilities of the supported networks, with and without multiplexing capability.
- Both connection-oriented and connectionless OSI network services can be provided at layer 3c. Both can provide inter-subnetwork services. The X.25 PSDN can operate at layer 3c, or at layer 3a under some other layer-3c protocol.

TCP/IP is a close relative of OSI layer 3c and part of OSI layer 4. Coexistence and close interoperation of TCP/IP with OSI and SNA will be with us for years to come.

LAN-oriented protocols, like NetBIOS, are of many breeds. They are widespread, and key ones must be integrated into the broad LAN/MAN/WAN enterprise network.

Acknowledgments

I am particularly indebted to G. R. Shelton, G. A. Deaton, and E. B. Taylor for valuable input or reviews of this chapter.

---

17. ISO DTR 9577, section 5, explains the relationship between the GFI and the IPI. Bits 2 and 3 of the first byte of the X.25 packet select ISO 8208 and either modulo 8, modulo 128, or GFI extension.

TECHNICAL REFERENCES

Transport-Service Primitives

There are only four types of transport-service primitives: `T-Connect`, `T-Disconnect`, `T-Data`, and `T-Expedited_Data`. The parameters for each are given below. The columns on the right indicate whether a parameter is carried in the request (Req), indication (Ind), response (Rsp), or confirm (Conf).

	Req	Ind	Rsp	Conf
`T-Connect`	x	x	x	x
• *called_address (TSAP)*	x	x		
• *calling_address (TSAP)*	x	x		
• *expedited_data_option*	x	x	x	x
• *quality_of_service*	x	x	x	x
• *responding_address (TSAP)*	x	x		
• user data	x	x	x	x
`T-Data`	x	x		
• user data	x	x		
`T-Expedited_Data`	x	x		
• user data	x	x		
`T-Disconnect`	x	x		
• *reason*		x		
• user data	x	x		

Transport PDU Types

Ten PDU types are needed to handle the connection-establishment, data, and termination phases at the transport layer. As shown below, these are fairly uniformly used in all five transport protocol classes, except for class 0, which uses a minimum number of TPDUs.

	Class				
	0	**1**	**2**	**3**	**4**
CR: `Connection_Request`	x	x	x	x	x
CC: `Connection_Confirm`	x	x	x	x	x
DR: `Disconnect_Request`	x	x	x	x	x
DC: `Disconnect_Confirm`		x	x	x	x
DT: `Data`	x	x	x	x	x
ED: `Expedited_Data`		x	f	x	x
AK: `Data_Acknowledgment`		r	f	x	x
EA: `Expedited_Data_Ack`		x	f	x	x
RJ: `Reject`		x		x	
ER: `TPDU_Error`	x	x	x	x	x

f not available when *not_explicit_flow_control* is selected.
r not available when *receipt_confirmation* is selected.

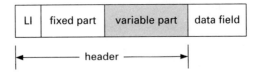

Figure 13.10 Transport PDU format.

TPDU Formats

The structure and content of the TPDUs is summarized below. As shown there, each TPDU contains a length indicator, a fixed part, a variable part (when present), and a data field (when present). The first octet of the fixed part contains the TPDU *type_code*. This *type_code* determines the structure of the fixed part and the allowable parameters of the variable part.

All TPDUs will contain an integral number of octets. TPDUs shall contain the header and the data field, if present. The header shall comprise (1) the length indicator (LI) field, (2) the fixed part, and (3) the variable part, if present, as shown in Figure 13.10.

The length indicator (LI), in the first octet of the TPDU, contains the length of the header, in octets, excluding the LI field itself. Header length may be 0-254. The value 255 (11111111) is reserved for possible extensions.

TPDU fixed part. The fixed part includes the TPDU *type_code* (4bits), and frequently used parameters. The length and structure of the fixed part are determined by the TPDU *type_code*. Other contents of the fixed part may include the following parameters, distributed as shown in Figure 13.11:

- *credit* (CDT); in CR, CC, AK and RJ, flow control credit allocation
- *source_ref/dest_ref*; two unique numbers, selected at each end, which associates the TPDU with a specific transport connection
- *class*; preferred transport class, 0–4
- *option*; in CR and CC, selects normal flow control fields (7 bit sequence number and 4 bit credit) or, in classes 2, 3, and 4, extended flow control fields (31 bit sequence number and 16 bit credit); also selects explicit flow control in class 2
- *reason*; in DR, the reason for disconnecting a transport connection or rejecting a connection request
- *EOT*; one bit in DT and ED, set in the last TPDU when a TSDU has been segmented into multiple TPDUs
- *TPDU_NR*; in DT, the send sequence number
- *EDTPDU_NR*, in ED, the send sequence number of a EDTPDU
- *TR_TU_NR*; in AK, and RJ, the next expected sequence number
- *YR_EDTU_NR*; in EA, the next expected ED sequence number
- *cause*; in ER, the reason for rejecting a TPDU

TPDU variable part. The variable part is used to define less frequently used parameters. It need not be present. When it is, it has the format of parameter-code, parameter-length-indicator, and parameter-values, for each parameter.

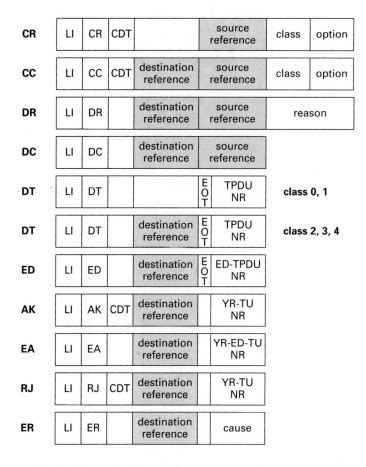

CDT = Flow Control Credit
ED-TPDU-NR = Send sequence number of
    an Expedited Data (ED) TPDU
EOT = Segmenting bit set to 1 on the last TPDU
TPDU-NR = Send sequence number of a data
    (DT) Transport Protocol Data Unit

YR-ED-TU-NR = The next expected Expedited
    Data (ED) sequence number
YR-TU-NR = The next expected DT sequence
    number

Figure 13.11 Parameters in the fixed part of the TPDU headers.

Transport Connection Request

As an illustration, the variable part of the `Connection_Request` TPDU is the most complex, and may contain the following parameters:

- *calling_TSAP_id;* Transport Service-Access-Point that identifies the calling transport user
- *called_TSAP_id;* Transport Service-Access-Point that identifies the called transport user
- *maximum_TPDU_size*
- *version_number* (not class 0)

- *security parameters* (not class 0)
- *checksum* (class 4 only)
- *option selections* (e.g., *expedited_data*, *receipt_confirmation*, and *checksum* in class 4) (not class 0)
- *alternative protocol classes* (not class 0)
- *maximum_acknowledge_time* (only class 4)
- *maximum_* and *average throughput* (not class 0)
- *target_* and *minimum_acceptable_residual_error_rate* (not class 0)
- *priority* (not class 0)
- *target_* and *maximum_acceptable_transit_delay* (not class 0)
- *reassignment_time* (not class 0, 2, or 4)

Negotiable during connect.   Of the above TPDU components, the following options and parameters are negotiable downwards only:

- *extended_formats* and *normal_formats*
- *TPDU_size*
- *alternate acceptable protocol class(es)*
- *option selections* (*expedited_data*, *receipt_confirmation*, and *checksum*)
- *throughput*
- *residual_error_rate*
- *transit_delay*
- *priority*

CR data part.   The `Connection_Request` may also contain up to 32 octets of user data (except in class 0, where no user data is permitted).

OSI CLNP PDU Formats

There are, in CLNP, only two PDU types, the `Data` PDU and the `Error_Report` PDU. These two PDU formats are shown in Figure 13.12 and Figure 13.13. Both headers are followed by a data field. The data PDU header is truncated to only the first byte when the source and destination are both in the same subnetwork. Otherwise, the **Data PDU header** includes:

- *protocol_identifier*—identifies the CLNP protocol
- *length_indicator*—for only the header, in bytes
- *version*—to indicate successive versions of a given CLNP protocol
- *PDU_lifetime*, given in multiples of 500 ms., and decremented once each time the packet passes through an inter-subnetwork-router (gateway)
- *flags*
  - SP tells whether or not segmenting is permitted
  - MS is the More flag
  - ER tells whether or not the source desires an error report when a packet is discarded
- *type*—tells whether this is a `Data` packet or an `Error_Report` packet

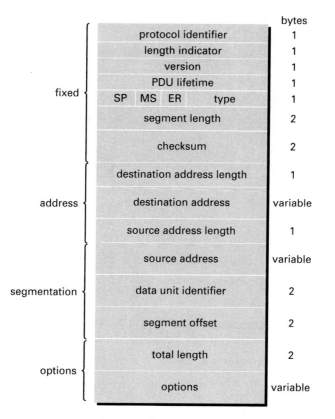

Figure 13.12 ISO Connectionless network protocol header format.

- *segment_length*—gives the total length of the segment, including header length, in bytes
- *PDU_checksum*—the result of a checksum calculation, computed on the header
- *destination_* and *source_addresses* are of variable length, so each is provided with an address length field
- *segmentation*—used if the SP flag is set to 1. This then includes: *data_unit_identifier*, *segment_offset*, and *total_length* parameters
- *options*—the last part of the header describes the options supported. Each option is described by a parameter code, a parameter length, and a parameter value. Parameters may include:
  - *quality_of_service*—concerning allowable delays and reliability
  - *source_routing*—with a list of the subnetworks to be traversed from source to destination
  - *recording_of_route*—actually traces the route taken thus far, so that the route taken can be learned during problem determination
  - *priority*—in the range of 0–14
  - *security*—as defined by the users
  - *padding*—to lengthen the PDU header to a standard size

The **Error_Report PDU header** is the same as that for the data PDU except that (a) there is no segment part, and (b) the three flags in the fixed part, SP, MS, and ER are set to 0, and a

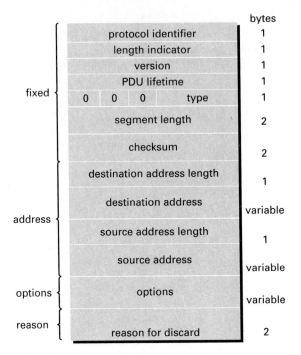

	bytes
protocol identifier	1
length indicator	1
version	1
PDU lifetime	1
0 0 0 type	1
segment length	2
checksum	2
destination address length	1
destination address	variable
source address length	1
source address	variable
options	variable
reason for discard	2

fixed, address, options, reason

Figure 13.13 ISO CLNP error-report header.

reason_for_discard is added. The *source_address* tells who generated the error report, and the packet is sent to the originator of the discarded PDU. The error report is placed in a data part following the header. This data part contains the entire header of the discarded Data PDU, and may also contain some or all of the data field of that discarded PDU. The path taken is a retrace of the path taken by the discarded PDU, using source routing.

OSI Network Service Underlying Primitives

	Req	Ind	Rsp	Conf
SN-UnitData	x	x		
• *SN-source_address*	x	x		
• *SN-destination_address*	x	x		
• *SN-quality_of_service*	x	x		
• SN-user data	x	x		

NetBIOS Commands

The four categories of NetBIOS commands are:

Datagram Support
- Receive_Datagram
- Receive_Broadcast_Datagram
- Send_Datagram
- Send_Broadcast_Datagram

General Commands
- Reset
- Cancel
- Adapter_Status
- Unlink

Session Support
- Call
- Listen
- Send
- Chain_Send
- Receive
- Receive_Any

Name Support
- Add_Name
- Add_Group_Name
- Delete_Name

NetBIOS Flows

In this example, shown in Figure 13.14, a PC logs on to the network, sends a message to another station on the network, and then logs off the network [GG24-3360]. The following commands are used:

- Reset—to initialize the environment (adapter) for an application
- Add_Name—to add its unique network-name to the network
- Listen—to allow other network stations to establish a session with this name/station
- Call—to open a session with another network station
- Send—to send data to the partner that the Call command established a session with. An acknowledgement of data received will be returned since Send_No_Ack was not specified
- Receive—receives the data from a session partner (not from just any opened sessions, as in Receive_Any)
- Hang_Up—to close the session with this partner
- Delete_Name—to delete this user's unique network name from the network

EXERCISES

13.1 List seven services provided by the transport layer.

13.2 (a) Which transport class provides the least recovery facilities and can be used with X.25 networks, and (b) which class is suitable for low reliability networks and connectionless (datagram) networks?

13.3 What uniquely identifies a transport entity?

13.4 What uniquely identifies a user of the transport layer and a session at layer 5?

13.5 What is the *credit* as used in the transport layer flow control?

13.6 What is meant by a connectionless protocol?

13.7 What is PDU lifetime?

13.8 What are the addresses in OSI and TCP/IP that encompass the id of the subnetwork, the address of the node in that subnetwork, and the address of the application-process?

13.9 Describe a virtual circuit of a packet switching network.

13.10 What are some of the services of an X.25 connection-oriented network?

13.11 When is the X.25 packet-level window size established?

13.12 Is the X.25 DTE address always the same as the OSI NSAP address?

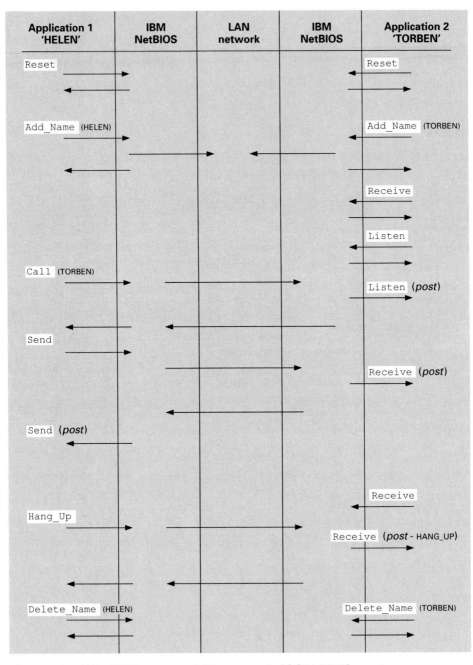

Figure 13.14 NetBIOS command flow example [GG24-3360].

13.13 How can the overhead of X.25 connection set-up be reduced when one wants to send only one packet?

13.14 What is the X/Open Transport Interface (XTI)?

13.15 How does TCP/IP enable the window size to be adjusted by the receiver?

13.16 How is source-routing facilitated in TCP/IP ?

13.17 What does NetBIOS provide, and where does it sit in the architecture?

14

Transport-Service-Provider: SNA/APPN

14.1   INTRODUCTION

In the past fifteen years, SNA has gone through several major growth stages, evolving from a single-host environment to multiple-host mesh networking and then Advanced Peer-to-Peer Networking (APPN). This chapter focuses on that latter stage, after first introducing the transmission control layer, which is the upper layer of the SNA transport-service-provider.

What is APPN, and how does it fit into OSNA? APPN is IBM's extension to SNA that provides self-defining networks for *ease of use in network operations*. Dynamic definition of new (or deleted) resources, dynamic topology updates, dynamic reconfiguration in the event of failures, and dynamic route selection based on class of service are the primary features. To keep pace, some dynamic definition features have been added to the SNA subarea-network architecture as well, as discussed in the following chapter. However, the APPN clearly sets a new standard for SNA.

In the broad picture of OSNA, illustrated by Figure 3.14, APPN is intended to be the *ease-of-use* pacesetter. This is one of five discernible threads in the ongoing OSNA evolution. The other four are the expansion of common application-services, end-to-end system management, integration of multiple communication protocols, and the incorporation of higher-speed facilities.

APPN's place in Figure 3.14 is at layer 3c, as an inter-subnetwork protocol, joining together point-to-point links, and diverse subnetworks such as LANs, MANs, X.25, ISDN, and frame-relay. The OSNA goal is to obtain full interoperability in an easy-to-use information utility, and APPN is an important part of that movement. *Facilities both above and below layer 3c are common to APPN and subarea networks.* Moreover, the potential integration of APPN and OSI is clear,[1] aided by the common addressing, under the OSI NSAP umbrella, discussed in Section 12.3.3.

---

1.   The potential integration of APPN and OSI is based on IBM research projects described in Section 14.8.1.

14.2   SNA TRANSMISSION CONTROL

14.2.1   Introduction

In SNA, the end-to-end controls for the transport-service-provider are called *transmission control*. SNA's transmission control function is located between data flow control and path control (see Figure 3.2). The instance of transmission control for one session is sometimes called a Transmission Control Element (TCE). One transmission control element is assigned to each half-session. The TCE is the "front office" for the half-session, providing a session-oriented entry to the path control layer.

Whenever two LUs wish to establish a session with each other, they must each use a transmission control element for that session. It then becomes a connection point for that session to the common path control layer, which is shared by all sessions. Thus, each TCE is a "user" of the path control layer.

14.2.2   Congestion Control

Pacing of the end-to-end data flows is a primary responsibility of transmission control.[2] Congestion in the network must be prevented if data loss and/or inefficient retransmissions are to be avoided. To prevent congestion SNA uses pacing at both the transmission control layer and, in some cases, in the lower layers. In all SNA pacing, a window is agreed upon between sender and receiver. The window specifies the number of messages (of some maximum size) that may be sent before another window is agreed to. A request is sent for permission to send the next pacing window, and a response gives the permission. The general sequence is:

1.   Sender sends first data of window 1, and requests pacing window 2.
2.   Receiver grants pacing window 2.
3.   Sender sends rest of window 1's data.
4.   Sender sends first data of window 2, and requests pacing window 3.
5.   Receiver grants pacing window 3.
6.   Sender sends the rest of window 2's data.

Thus, the next pacing window is requested when the current window is started. This reduces the waiting periods for permission to send. A sender may, in fact, be in possession of almost two windows at one time. In both APPN and subarea networks, however, the pacing window size need not be fixed but can be altered as congestion requires it. The APPN pacing is described in Section 14.7.

14.2.3   Bind Options

The initiation of a session is ordered by the `Bind` command. It must contain all the information needed by the two ends for effective data exchange. Because it also serves to pull together an overview of the end-to-end data-exchange facilities, a summary of the

---

2.   No pacing at this level is also an option.

principal options that might be selected for a session, and proposed in a `Bind` command, is given in this chapter's Technical Reference section.

New requirements can be expected continuously. As new facilities are provided, new `Bind` formats can be defined accordingly. On the other hand, some implementations have no need of all the options available. Moreover, the number of possible combinations of these many options is very large. Hence, a relatively small number of *Presentation Service (PS) profiles, Function Management (FM) profiles,* and *Transmission Service (TS) profiles* have evolved that are commonly used subsets of the available `Bind` options. Each profile identifies a prescribed subset of the architecture. In the `Bind` command, the session is defined by three profile fields and three usage fields (that provide information on the profiles).

TS profile and TS usage fields specify facilities that are primarily in the transmission control layer. These include pacing counts, maximum RU sizes, and information as to whether sequence numbers (or ids) and certain TC commands will be used. (LU 6.2 uses TS profile 7.)

FM profile and FM usage fields specify facilities that are primarily in the data-flow control layer. These include the request/response mode (e.g., definite or exception responses), the send/receive mode (e.g., half-duplex or duplex), chaining, brackets, and the allowable data-flow-control commands. (LU 6.2 uses FM profile 19.)

PS profile and PS usage fields specify the characteristics of the presentation services in each half-session.

Extended bind.   For system management purposes (particularly problem determination), it is helpful to know all the resources associated with a particular session; so some permanent end-to-end session-id is desired. That session-identifier is called the **Fully Qualified Procedure Correlation Identifier (FQPCID)**. It is carried on `Locate`, `Bind`, and `UnBind`, so all control-flows associated with a session establishment are permanently identified. So that it will be unique for correlations in problem determination, that number should not be duplicated. `Binds` carrying the FQPCID are called **extended `Binds`**, which also include the *class of service/transmission priority* field. Newer APPN and subarea network products all use the extended `Bind`. All independent LUs, defined as those which do not have SSCP-LU sessions (e.g., those having sessions within APPN networks) establish LU-LU sessions using extended `Binds`. The extended `Bind` is now also used for all sessions between up-level type-5 and type-4 nodes. The extended `Bind` is used whenever the destination-node is capable of handling the extensions.

14.3 APPN OVERVIEW

The evolution of Advanced Peer-to-Peer Networking (APPN) began with its introduction on midsized processors like the system 36 and the AS/400. The primary objectives were operational-ease and high availability, particularly including the reduction of system-definition workloads, dynamic reconfigurability, and nondisruption during network changes. *With APPN, no definition of partner resources is required, and no definition of network routes is required.* With the addition of APPN in the PS/2, the 3174 cluster (establishment) controller, and DPPX/370, plus improvements in linkages between APPN and subarea networks, APPN has become a full participant in SNA LANs and WANs.[3] For example, an OS/2 LAN workstation can act as an intermediate-node to route traffic between OS/2 and/or DOS workstations and one or more remote AS/400s.

APPN architecture extends SNA in two dimensions. First, it completes the ability of two end-systems to establish peer-to-peer logical connections with each other independently, without recourse to a centralized System Service Control Point (SSCP).[4] Second, it provides a distributed control-point structure with comprehensive functions. Key attributes of APPN networks thus include:

▪ *Dynamically-updated network topology database services*, for automatically recording network topology changes, and making these changes immediately known throughout the network.

▪ *Distributed, network-layer directory services* for automatically registering and locating both end-system and intermediate-system resources. For example, the current node location can be determined for any remote LU which is identified only by name.

▪ *Route selection services*, to select the best available route to the remote LU. This selection is based on the continuously up-to-date topology database and a *class of service* specified by the LU initiating the session.

▪ *Adaptive pacing and transmission priority*, to control the flow of traffic for each session, and to jump ahead of lower priority traffic at queuing points in the network.

These distributed services are used for two related purposes:

1. To reduce the need for coordinated network definitions, thereby simplifying network installation, additions or deletions of nodes, and reconfiguration

2. So that end-systems can enter a network, become dynamically registered, and communicate across the network without the aid of any remote SSCP

The nodes in an APPN network use a distinct architecture, and are called type 2.1 nodes. Three sets of protocols differentiate three types of 2.1 nodes. These are called **network-nodes, APPN end-nodes** and **Low Entry Networking (LEN) end-nodes**. Figure 14.1 illustrates a simple APPN, involving network-nodes and end-nodes. Also shown there are the various LU-LU sessions possible. Other configurations might use a local area network (LAN) to interconnect all the nodes. Also, SNA subarea networks can connect to APPN networks and can be intermediary between two APPN networks.

APPN networks have given particular attention to full function LU 6.2 operations within T 2.1 nodes. This means that an LU 6.2 within a T 2.1 node may have multiple and

---

3. E. Robert Roth, of IBM, in a presentation to SAA World, April 11, 1990, further stated, regarding APPN, that "We expect to provide similar, consistent support on all SAA platforms and the network components like communication controllers that connect the environments."

4. Such "independent LUs" do not need to receive session set-up commands from a remote SSCP. On the other hand, such LUs currently cannot receive some of the SSCP services, such as having a session cryptography key generated by the SSCP.

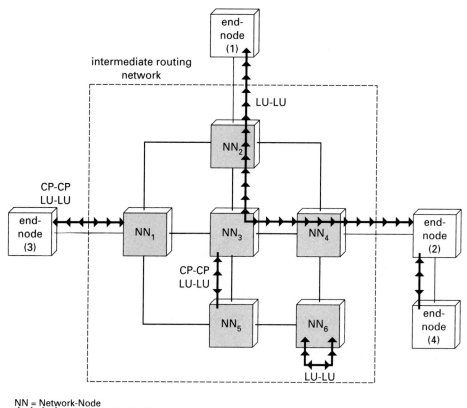

Figure 14.1 Sessions among APPN end-nodes and network-nodes.

parallel sessions with mainframe applications across a subarea network, as well as the same functions when communicating with other T 2.1 nodes across the APPN network.

14.3.1　Control-Point Functions

Every APPN node (end-nodes and network-nodes) contains a control point (CP) that manages and coordinates certain services with other nodes in the network. This is done through CP-CP sessions that use LU 6.2 protocols. Adjacent APPN nodes use a pair of parallel CP-CP sessions to exchange network information. The services thus coordinated include:

- *Connection*—connecting a new node or link into an existing network
- *Directory*—building and maintaining a network-layer directory of local and remote logical units (LUs), and participating in the distributed APPN directory services to locate session partners

- *Route selection*—primarily a network-node service for maintaining the network topology database and determining the preferred route through the network to a remote resource, based on the desired class of service
- *Sessions*—initiating, negotiating, and activating sessions between two LUs
- *System management*—performing fault-determination and sending alerts to a system manager when the node detects programing or machine problems

14.3.2   Type 2.1 Nodes

Type 2.1 nodes differ from the earlier nodes in that T 2.1 nodes support peer-to-peer communications (even though they may also perform as peripheral nodes in an SNA subarea network). Having control points in each T 2.1 node, they do not need the services of a central (SSCP) control point to coordinate basic network services, such as establishing LU-LU sessions between T 2.1 nodes. When T 2.1 nodes are connected to a subarea network, they can nevertheless elect to have SSCP-PU sessions in order that system management alerts may be forwarded to an SSCP and hence to a NetView manager.[5]

T 2.1 nodes can have multiple links attached, including SDLC, X.25, and LANs. In keeping with the peer philosophy, link stations decide the role (primary or secondary) that they will assume. This is negotiated by the exchange of link-level commands called Exchange id (XID).

Similarly, a T 2.1 node can have LUs which have either primary or secondary roles. An LU 6.2 in a T 2.1 node may have sessions with more than one partner LU, and also may have multiple sessions with one partner LU. These T 2.1 LUs can act as either primary or secondary LUs, or both at the same time.

Figure 14.2 illustrates that a type 2.1 node can be either an end-node or a network-node. End-nodes, in turn, can be of two types, an APPN end-node or a Low Entry Network (LEN) end-node. These are explained in the following.

APPN network-nodes provide route selection services, directory services, intermediate routing, and management services to end-nodes. They participate in distributed searches to locate destination LUs. They assist in passing a given message from node to node, along a chosen route, to the destination. In addition, they provide distributed flow controls for session traffic.

End-nodes, on the other hand, are simpler nodes, which primarily serve end users (i.e., application-processes). All sessions that enter an end-node terminate in that node.[6] An end-node does not provide any network-services to other nodes. End-nodes can, however, have varying capabilities for cooperating with network-nodes, and a limited capability of communicating with other end-nodes. In the case of end-node-to-end-node communication, there is no CP-CP session between the end-nodes.

---

5.   A preferred technical direction is to communicate with NetView via LU 6.2 sessions. However, this transition is not yet complete, and SSCP-PU sessions still predominate.

6.   Locally attached terminals and LUs are considered part of the end-node, as far as the network structure is concerned.

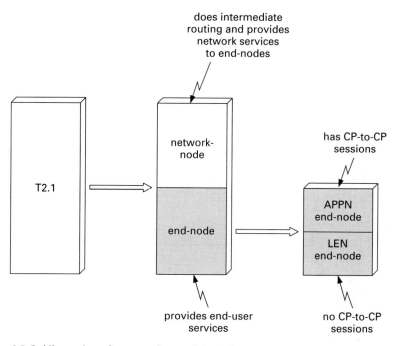

Figure 14.2 Hierarchy of types of type 2.1 nodes.

Two types of end-nodes can connect to an APPN network. An **APPN end-node** has full end-node functions, and may have multiple connections into the APPN network to multiple network-nodes. It uses the services of one adjacent **Network-Node-Server (NNS)** via CP-CP sessions. For example, an APPN end-node can *register* its local LUs with its serving network-node, without operator action. It can ask its serving network-node to *locate* a remote LU.

A simpler end-node type, called **Low Entry Networking (LEN) end-node** has also been defined.[7] This node also supports Advanced Program-to-Program Communications (APPC), and SNA type 2.1 transport services, like the APPN end-node. However, the LEN end-node does not have CP-CP sessions to other nodes, and therefore cannot directly request services such as `Register` and `Locate`. It can, however, achieve a modified `Locate` function indirectly, with the help of a serving network-node.

Common functions.   Figure 14.3 indicates the control-point services that are common to the type 2.1 nodes. The network-nodes are distinguished from the end-nodes by having

---

7.   Examples of LEN end-nodes include printers (like the 3820 page printer), workstations (such as those supported by Displaywriter, OS2/EE, and APPC/PC) and input devices (like the Scanmaster). The Network Control Program in communications controllers, and VTAM in mainframes also have the LEN functions.

CP services	T2.1 base	LEN EN	APPN EN	APPN NN
configuration services	X	X	X	X
session services	X	X	X	X
address space manager	X	X	X	X
directory services		X	X	X
management services		X	X	X
CP-CP sessions			X	X
topology and route selection				X
intermediate routing				X

Figure 14.3 Common control-point services.

topology, route selection, and routing services. To fully provide these services, CP-CP sessions exist among APPN end-nodes and APPN network-nodes. LEN end-nodes do have control points, but they do not participate in CP-CP sessions.

Both APPN end-nodes and network-nodes can contain LUs (LU 6.2 or older types). A network-node may perform all the functions of an end-node; both node types perform the same services to local LUs, and establish connections to other nodes.

Each T 2.1 node is identified by a unique name consisting of two parts: a network identifier (Net_id) and a control-point name (CP_name). This network-qualified name, Net_id.CP_name, is defined in the T 2.1 node at system definition time. It is provided by an administrator to make sure it is unique. Within an APPN network, all network-nodes share a common Net_id. End-nodes, however, can dial into separate APPN networks, and therefore may not always share a common Net_id with the network to which it is attached.

Different products will have different link-level features. Hence, T 2.1 nodes will sometimes have internode links using a channel (e.g., connecting a mainframe to an establishment-controller), an X.25 packet switching network, a token ring, an Ethernet, or an SDLC switched or leased connection.

The formats of the transmission headers for the T 2.1 and other types of SNA nodes are discussed in this chapter's Technical Reference section.

14.3.3 APPN End-Node Functions

The APPN end-node protocols provide the following functions:[8]

- *Selecting* an attached APPN network-node as a network services provider (a serving network-node), and activating CP-CP sessions between the APPN end-node and the serving network-node.

- *Registering*, dynamically, local logical units (LUs) with the serving network-node. A network-node becomes aware of the resources in its client end-nodes either by sending search requests to them or by receiving registration requests from them.

- *Requesting* the serving network-node *to locate* a desired communications partner LU.

- *Responding to network searches* for local logical units (LUs).

- *Activating LU-LU sessions* via a `Bind` on routes provided by the serving network-node.

- *Supporting parallel connections* to multiple APPN nodes in an APPN network.

Thus, when attaching to an APPN network, the end-node automatically registers its location and resources with the serving network-node. Resource locations are discovered dynamically in the network, so there is no requirement for definition of partner resource location.

The APPN end-node-to-network-node (EN-NN) protocols are an open and published architecture.

14.3.4 Low Entry Networking (LEN) End-Nodes

A LEN end-node does not support control-point-to-control-point (CP-CP) sessions. Hence, the `Locate` function is not available to the LEN end-node, and all potential connections with remote destination LUs are predefined via system definition. The LEN system definition specifies the destination LU_name, the CP_name of the LEN's adjacent network-node through which the LU can be accessed, and the identification of the link directly attaching the LEN end-node to that adjacent network-node. This is just as if the remote LUs all existed at the LEN's adjacent network-node. A serving network-node then can determine the actual location of the destination LU and select the best route to it.

Since LEN end-nodes are not equipped to have CP-CP sessions with a network-node (NN) server, a modified procedure is used in which the NN server takes on some additional responsibilities for these simpler nodes, as follows.

1. Since the NN server cannot automatically pick up the LU_names in the attaching LEN end-nodes (without a CP-CP session), the NN must have these LEN LU_names *registered by its local administrator*.

---

8. In addition, IBM has stated its intention to facilitate the interconnection of two adjacent AS/400 APPN networks that have different administrations, and to allow dynamic switching to another APPN network-node server when a link failure occurs between an APPN end-node and its existing network-node server.

2.   The LEN end-nodes (being without a CP-CP session) also need the help of the NN server to search for the location of a desired LU, and to send the *extended* `Bind` through the network. These LEN nodes need only send a `Bind` command to the NN server. That `Bind` contains the desired class of service (COS) and priority, or simply a mode name from which the network-node can deduce the COS and priority. The `Bind` does not yet contain route information.

3.   Once the origin's NN server receives the `Bind`, identifying the desired LU and the desired mode, that NN server will proceed to locate the NN server for the destination LU. The origin NN server then calculates the preferred route, from itself to the target end-node, and *attaches to the original* `Bind` *a list of nodes and links to be traversed in the route.*[9] The origin NN server then forwards that expanded `Bind` through the network, along the selected route, to the desired LU.

14.3.5   Cluster Controller Type 2.1

One of the currently available T 2.1 nodes that is *capable of being a network-node* is the **3174 cluster controller** (often called *establishment controller* or *display controller*). The 3174 provides high-performance channel connectivity and APPN network-node services for LAN attached APPN workstations. (The workstations use the **Networking Services/2 (NS/2)** software to provide the APPN support.)

In addition, a separate 3174 Peer Communications feature enables communication between DOS workstations that are coax attached (with 3270 wiring) to the 3174.[10] These workstations can further communicate with workstations that are attached to the same 3174 via a token ring LAN, and with workstations connected by coax to another 3174 on that same LAN (see Section 17.5.3).

The cluster controller also provides a variety of terminal support functions, including:

- Concurrent multiple-host connections
- Concentration and routing of traffic from lower speed links to higher speed links, and vice versa
- Support for a variety of terminal types, including ASCII and 3270 data streams
- Shared terminal control electronics for economy
- Both local (coax) attachments and LAN attachments
- System-management support

NetView operators have remote console services available for NS/2 nodes and 3174 nodes. For example, the NetView operator can query the network-node for APPN topology information, start traces, and view logs.

Display terminals attached to T 2.1 cluster controllers may be of several types. The type where keystroke interpretation is provided by the cluster controller have been called **Control Unit Terminals (CUTs)**. Or, terminals may be **Distributed Function Terminals**

---

9.   This list is called a *route-selection-control-vector (RSCV)*.

10.   As a statement of direction, IBM has indicated its intent to also provide the Peer Communications support for OS/2 EE workstations that are coax attached to a 3174.

(DFTs), which provide their own keystroke interpretation. DFTs also provide functions such as windowing, graphics, and imaging capability, and a more functional user interface. The PCs and the PS/2s, attached to a controller, of course, have still greater versatility. The PS/2 workstation can be attached as either 3270 or ASCII terminals, or as APPN end-nodes or network-nodes, and can therefore participate fully in cooperative processing. The 3174 with APPN therefore provides the base for *very general workstation-to-workstation communication along with workstation-to-mainframe communication.*

Comparison with type 2.0.   The cluster controller is defined architecturally as a type 2.0 node or a type 2.1 node. Currently, only the type 2.1 cluster controller can participate in an APPN network. A type 2.1 node is very similar to a type 2.0 node except that there is a control point (CP) in the type 2.1 node. As described above, this CP provides a subset of the SSCP functions, and allows type 2.1 nodes to communicate with each other on a peer-to-peer basis. On the other hand, type 2.0 nodes can only communicate with subarea nodes. Type 2.0 nodes depend on a boundary-function in a serving node for certain control-point functions. In subarea networks, that serving node would be a type 4 (communications controller) node, providing address translation and routing functions, or a type 5 (mainframe host) node, which also provides control-point functions.

14.3.6 Configurations

A LEN or APPN end-node can fit into a larger network context in three ways:

1.   Attached to another LEN or APPN end-node as a peer

2.   Attached to an APPN via a serving network-node, which is part of a larger complex of network-nodes

3.   Attached to a subarea network via a boundary-function in the subarea network

The end-node could, moreover, attach to multiple networks—for example, to all three of these cases over different links. The end-node sees cases 1 and 3 as being very similar, since the subarea-node containing the boundary-function appears to the network-node like another end-node. The difference is that case 3 also permits SSCP-dependent protocols to be used. Case 3 is discussed further in Section 15.5.

Figure 14.4 illustrates LAN-oriented APPN networks. The emphasis there is on PS/2 interoperation, with inter-LAN connections via some high-speed link. That might be a leased line, an SNA WAN, or an X.25 WAN. However, interactions with the mainframes (on a WAN or LAN) are also increasingly important. Figure 14.5 illustrates these and other types of APPN transport connections that are feasible.

The *network-node (NN)* capability, which includes the intermediate routing function, now exists in the DPPX/370, important midrange processors (like the S/36 and AS/400), down to the PS/2, and the 3174 establishment (cluster) controller. The PS/2, AS/400 and DPPX/370 can also function as an *APPN end-node (EN)*. S/390s with MVS, VM, or VSE operating systems, and communication controllers (like the 3745) can appear (to an attaching network-node) to be an end-node.[11]

---

11.   However, the communication controllers and mainframes (T4 and T5 nodes) do also provide the intermediate function.

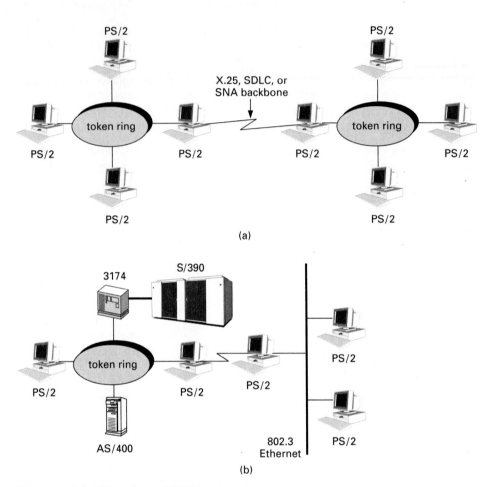

Figure 14.4 LAN-oriented APPN networks.

Multiple type 2.1 end-nodes (and network-nodes) can communicate with each other when attached to the same LAN, to interconnected LANs, or to SNA WANs. As Figure 14.5 shows, any network-node, such as the PS/2, the AS/400, or the 3174 Establishment Controller can connect to the APPN and subarea networks. Then:

- Programmable workstations and mainframes, attached to either a subarea network or an APPN WAN or an APPN LAN can establish sessions with other PS/2s and mainframes on these interconnected WANs and LANs.

- LAN/WAN/LAN passthru is also feasible. Programmable workstations and AS/400s can establish sessions with each other when they are located in separate APPN networks

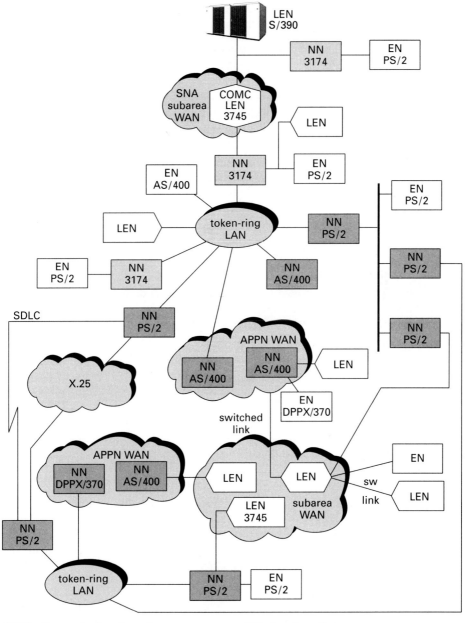

COMC = Communications Controller   LEN = Low-Entry Node
EN = APPN End-Node   NN = APPN Network-Node

Figure 14.5 Subarea host, LAN, and WAN connections using APPN.

on either side of the subarea network. The intermediate subarea network, moreover, could be a set of independent, interconnected subarea networks.[12]

Thus a wide range of possibilities already exists for common transport services across LANs and WANs, with combinations of APPN networks and subarea networks, involving terminals, workstations, and mainframes. Applications using either product-specific APPC interfaces or the SAA Common Programming Interface, in mainframes, in APPN nodes, and in LEN nodes can communicate with each other via LU 6.2 sessions across all these configurations.

LUs in the APPN nodes can be dynamically registered with SSCPs in the subarea network; and LUs in separate APPN networks can dynamically communicate across subarea networks, with little systems definition in the subarea network (see Section 15.5).

14.4   APPN NETWORK-DIRECTORY SERVICES

14.4.1   Functions

As the name suggests, directory services help to locate a named resource. The system needs to know where the destination LU is located now. That destination may have moved recently, perhaps as part of a departmental relocation or company reorganization. Directory services then has the job of determining where the named destination LUs are now located, and what their serving network-nodes are.

The application-layer directory was discussed in Chapter 8. When a conversation is requested, it is often done using the symbolic_destination_name of the desired resource. The application-layer directory or side information then provides the LU_name (alternatively, the application-process might itself know the destination LU_name). The network-layer directory picks up the task from there, to relate the LU_name to a destination-serving network-node. In APPN, the primary purpose of the network-layer directory services is to identify the name of the control point in the network-node that currently provides service to the requested LU.

Each network-node is responsible for maintaining a directory of its local resources, including those of all its attached end-nodes. These entries can indicate either that they are stable and need not be verified, or they need to be verified before each reference. There is an entry somewhere in the distributed directories for every resource (e.g., LU) in the network which end-nodes wish to have registered.[13] The source of that entry is the network-node where that resource is *registered and served.*[14]

---

12.   The interconnection of multiple subarea networks is with the SNA Network Interconnect (SNI) feature discussed in Chapter 15.

13.   End-nodes have the option to register or not to register each LU in the end-node.

14.   For example, on a LAN, there may be multiple network-nodes, but only one network-node is designated (at any one time) to be the registrar and server for a particular end-node on that LAN, even though that end-node may use all the network-nodes for communication purposes.

Thus, the directory services are distributed throughout the network. They are distributed in all the network-nodes and (to a lesser extent) in end-nodes. A LEN or APPN end-node maintains a local directory containing entries for locally resident LUs, and for those residing in an adjacent node connected as a peer—such as another end-node.

In a LEN end-node the names of all possible destination LUs (those LUs that the LEN probably will want to communicate with) are entered in the LEN directory. Those not in an adjacent peer end-node, but out in a connected APPN or subarea network, are nevertheless assumed to be adjacent. Upon receiving the `Bind` from the LEN end-node, a serving network-node will determine the actual location of the destination LU and will forward the `Bind` appropriately.

An APPN end-node, on the other hand, does not need to maintain a complete directory of all LUs with which it initiates sessions. It can initiate a search into the APPN network to find a desired LU by invoking the services of its serving network-node.

Each such directory in a network-node is built and maintained by: (a) automatic resource registration from the APPN end-nodes to their serving network-nodes, (b) dynamic caching within the network-nodes as the results of directory searches, and (c) system definition via local operator input.

14.4.2 Searching

Since the directory information is distributed, as described above, an efficient means is needed for searching the distributed databases. Searches are local or remote. In Figure 14.1, for example, if end-node (1) initiates a session, the LU-LU session between end-node (1) and end-node (2) will use network-node (NN_2) as an origin-serving network-node, and network-node (NN_4) as a destination-serving network-node. NN_2 would first perform a *local search* for the destination LU and, if necessary, would also coordinate a *remote search* for that LU.

Local search. To locate a destination LU, directory services in the origin-serving network-node first checks its local directory, to see if the LU is in the originating node or in one of the locally attached end-nodes. If that fails, the next place to look is the **local cache**. If the desired LU is found there, the originating directory may nevertheless send a probe or directed search to the expected destination-node, to confirm that the desired LU is still there. The directory cache thus provides an educated guess of where the LU is located.

The customer is given the ability to predefine the locations of commonly used resources, so they never have to be discovered. Directory entries can only be removed by an explicit delete command. However, when the cache is full, an aging algorithm is used to free up more space. Those LUs not used in a long time will tend to disappear from the cache.

The directory cache is an essential element of network performance, even though it can be rebuilt in normal operations. For this reason, safe-store of the directory cache, saving of the cache information across system outages, is desirable.

Remote search.   If the desired LU is not found in either the local cache or the local directory,[15] then a **broadcast search request** is sent. Different algorithms may be used for this search, so long as it is consistent across all nodes. The simplest (adequate for all but the largest size networks) is to send the broadcast to all adjacent network-nodes to which a CP-CP session is active. These search messages are then propagated outward further from the adjacent nodes. The search for a resource cascades through the network, creating a spanning-tree search. Each node retains information about the search until all of its children reply. This continues until a network-node is found which has the desired LU within itself or within one of its end-nodes. Even then, the search is propagated further to check that no other node has the same LU-name defined as being local. The overhead for this search has been limited to no more than two messages per CP-CP session pair [Jaffe86]. A limited search, limited to a specific group of nodes, or a certain number of hops in the search, is optionally available also.

Another future possibility, in network-layer directory services, is to have one or more **central (or regional) directories** for the network. If that existed, then a network-node could first send a directed search to that central directory. If the search in the central directory reveals the location of the desired LU, then the central directory, in turn, could send a directed search to the control point of the resource, to confirm the location. The use of a central directory (or multiple regional directories), in addition to the broadcast search technique, may be preferable for very large networks, because of the volume of search traffic as the network size increases.

General LU_naming.   While APPN end-nodes can define their LUs dynamically to their serving network-nodes, the LEN end-nodes cannot. Their LUs must all be given to their serving network-node by explicit operator action. To reduce this burden of generating LU definitions in the serving network-node, *general names* can be used for the LEN LUs. General names can all have a common stem with an asterisk (*). Then, any LU_name being searched for, starting with that stem, will match this general name. The serving network-node would, in that case, provide a positive response to the search.

Moreover, an entry in the directory can be an asterisk alone. This is called a **wild-card** entry. A wild card is useful for a node attached to a subarea boundary-node. Then, when a node sends a `Locate` for an LU that is physically in the subarea network, no node in the APPN network will find it, except that the node attached to the subarea can send a special indication of a wild card in its positive response.[16] Subsequent `Binds` can be sent into the subarea by that node attached to the boundary-node (see also Section 15.5).

14.5   APPN EN-NN PROTOCOLS

The *APPN end-node to network-node* (EN-NN) protocols (a) advise the server network-node of the LUs that are in the end-node, and (b) request the assistance of the network-node in locating, and establishing a route to, a named destination. For the APPN end-node,

---

15.   If the end-system chooses not to register some of its LUs, a query by the serving network-node to the end-node sometimes may be appropriate.

16.   If multiple network-nodes reply with a wild card, the originating network-node uses the first one received.

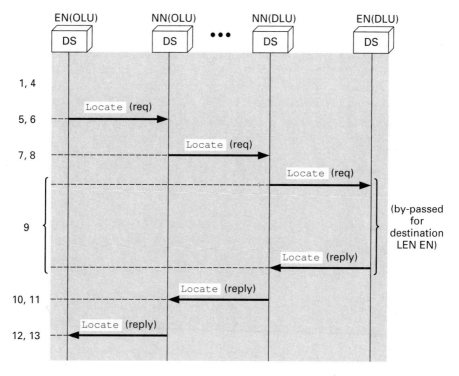

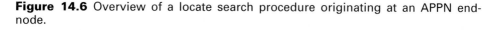

DLU = Destination LU
NN(DLU) = Network-Node serving the destination LU

NN(OLU) = Network-Node serving the origin LU
OLU = Originating LU

Figure 14.6 Overview of a locate search procedure originating at an APPN end-node.

the principal CP-CP commands are `Register`, `Delete`, and `Locate`. The EN-NN protocols are an open, published architecture. The end-node uses the *extended* `Bind` command to establish the LU-LU session. Using the EN-NN protocols and `Bind`, the APPN end-node can initiate a session, by itself and its serving network-node, to any other LU in the network (APPN and/or subarea). In these EN-NN protocols, there is no dependence on the availability of a remote control point (SSCP) or on the links to it.

An illustration of the APPN `Locate` function at the time of session initiation follows. Figure 14.6 shows a typical message flow [SC30-3422]. Recall that both the origin and destination end-nodes use adjacent network-nodes as servers.

1. The origin end-node may have a choice of network-nodes to use as a server. After making a selection of a *network-node server*, the end-node control point establishes a session with the control point of that server node (for full duplex operation, the network-node also establishes a session with the end-node).

2. Each time that the end-node establishes a CP-CP session with a network-node server, the end-node sends and **registers** the names of the end-node LUs that the end-node wants

to make known to the serving network-node. Registration can also occur each time that an LU is activated.

3.   Directory actions proceed in two stages. First, side information in the end-node or an *application-layer directory (A-directory)* translates the symbolic_destination_name of the destination application into the corresponding LU_name of the destination (if the LU_name is not already specified).

4.   The second stage involves the distributed network-layer directory (N-directory), which operates in several steps as follows. Directory Services (DS) in the origin end-node searches its local directory for the destination LU. If it is found, DS returns the CP_name of the destination-serving network-node.

5.   If the LU_name is not found, directory services in the origin end-node sends a `Locate` request to the adjacent NN server. This includes a unique session_identifier, a `Cross_Domain_Initiate` command, the origin end-node tail vectors,[17] the local CP_name, and the names of the origin and destination LUs. This request may optionally also include the *class of service* (obtained from the mode_name) that is desired for the connection. The origin and destination LU_names are included in the `Locate` request.

6.   The *network-layer directory (N-directory) service* then finds the *CP_name* for the network-node that is a server for the destination end-node. This is done by a local or remote search.

7.   Network-layer directory services in the origin NN server first searches its local directory (which includes the registered LUs of all its attached end-nodes) and its local cache. *The serving network-node seeks the name (i.e., the CP_name) of the network-node that is server for the destination LU*. If that LU_name and CP_name are found in the local directory or cache, then a directed search is sent to the destination network-node, to confirm that the desired LU is still served by that control point. If the desired LU_name is not found, in the local directory or cache, the origin NN server proceeds with a remote (broadcast) search, starting with its adjacent neighbors.

8.   As part of the remote search, a Directory Services (DS) in a distant network-node finds the desired LU_name in its directory. That network-node would be the serving network-node for the destination end-node.

9.   Directory services in that serving network-node forwards the `Locate` request to directory services in the destination APPN end-node. A `Locate` reply is then returned by the end-node DS to the destination-serving network-node. This contains the identity of all the final links (tail vectors) from multiple network-nodes to the destination end-node.[18,19]

---

17.   The origin APPN end-node generates as many tail vectors (i.e., link descriptors) as it has links leading to adjacent network-nodes or to LANs that can be used for sessions.

18.   A destination end-node generates the same types of tail vectors as the origin end-node, but also includes any links that lead directly to the origin APPN node.

19.   The destination network-node may itself contain the destination LU, in which case no tail vectors are returned.

10. The destination-serving network-node sends the `Locate` reply to the origin NN server with a positive response. The `Locate` reply indicates whether the found entry was a *wild-card* entry or an explicit entry.

11. The NN server of the origin node then calculates the *best route*, all the way from the origin end-node to the destination end-node. The calculation takes into account the class-of-service information provided earlier by the origin end-node.

12. The NN server then returns the search request to the origin end-node, adding a specification of the selected route in the form of the *Route Selection Control Vector (RSCV).*[20]

13. The origin end-node is then in a position to send an *extended* `Bind` request, including the RSCV (also the class of service and priority), via the selected route, all the way to the destination end-node, and the session proceeds to be established.[21]

Of course, the remote (broadcast) search is not always necessary. For destinations already in the local directory or cache of the origin's NN server, session set-up can be very rapid—with half the control-flows required in subarea networks.

   If the origin end-node had been a LEN end-node, it would have simply sent the `Bind` without the RSCV. The origin-serving network-node would have originated the search upon seeing a `Bind` without an RSCV. After finishing the search, computing the RSCV, and adding it to the `Bind`, the origin-serving network-node would then have forwarded the completed `Bind` to the destination.

   If the destination end-node had been a LEN end-node, step 9 would have been by-passed, assuming that the LUs in the LEN node had been defined to the destination-serving network-node.

14.6 APPN TOPOLOGY AND ROUTE SERVICES

14.6.1 Dynamic Topology Update

As intelligence moves into workstations, and more and more employees have workstations and participate in networking, peer-to-peer networks with *dynamic reconfiguration* become more desirable. As the network grows, moreover, the number of experienced, well-trained operators and system programmers cannot grow proportionately. Rather, the customer must be able to install or change a network with minimal or no involvement of network personnel in the definition process. The objective is to connect a wide variety of terminals without requiring a central point to contain up-to-date definitions of their functions or addresses.

   A prime requirement of the network is *nondisruption of service* at the time of network configuration changes. Additions or deletions of network-nodes, in particular, must not affect the operation of the remainder of the network. The addition or removal of end-nodes

---

20. The session route need not share any of the path that had been used by the prior `Locate` message.

21. Note that the originating LU always becomes the primary LU in the LU-LU session.

or network-nodes must therefore be dynamic, without any shutdown of any other network-nodes.[22]

Under APPN, each node is manually defined only to itself [SC30-3422]. It enters the network by activating its communication adapter(s). If it is an end-node, it automatically registers its resources (e.g., LUs) with its serving network-node.[23] Network topology is automatically discovered as network-nodes enter and leave the network. Resources (e.g., end-nodes) can move from network-node to network-node in the network. The resources defined in each network-node can be found automatically without any operator action in other nodes.

We now consider how APPN has addressed this challenge. In particular, let us first consider the case where the network-node to which the requesting end-node is attached, is not yet connected to the APPN network. An illustration of this would be if NN_1, in Figure 14.1, were not yet functioning as part of the APPN.

Link activations.   A network-node (such as NN_1 in Figure 14.1) may be entered into the network by an operator action or simply on the occasion of a user seeking to communicate from an end-node. In either case, the *entering network-node* will initiate the necessary configuration services by activating its links to some number of its immediately adjacent network-node neighbors. This might be a dial connection, if leased lines are not in place.[24]

As part of the link activation process, the two stations (on a link) exchange identification information, using the XID3 link-level commands (see Figure 14.7). These exchanges include the following indicators:

1.   Whether the sender supports CP-CP sessions

2.   Whether the sender wants to receive a `Bind` for a CP-CP session, in order to get access to network-node services

3.   Whether the sender can provide network-node services (via a CP-CP session)

4.   Whether the sending node needs support for a dependent LU[25]

By thus identifying capabilities, or lack of same, back-level boxes that do not support APPN architecture extensions can be protected, a suitable `Bind` structure (extended or not) can be selected, and fuller services can be provided when appropriate.

After exchanging identification information, the data-link control becomes active. Once the links to adjacent network-nodes are activated, the *control point* in the *entering end-node* will establish LU 6.2 sessions (by the exchange of `Bind` and its response) with the control points in the adjacent network-nodes. At the start of the CP-CP session, the two

---

22.   For example, with Networking Service/2, the operating system that provides APPN functions on the PS/2, the user can dynamically add, change, and delete local LUs, modes, and other system definitions while the system is running. There is no need to take down the OS/2 Communications Manager while performing these tasks. Of course, sessions may still be interrupted by an unplanned failure of a node.

23.   If an end-node chooses not to register its resources, it is not required to do so. The end-node can indicate to its serving network-node that it prefers to be searched for its resources.

24.   It is also possible to have dial lines and leased lines in parallel.

25.   A dependent LU needs an activation command (`ACTLU`) from a remote control point (SSCP).

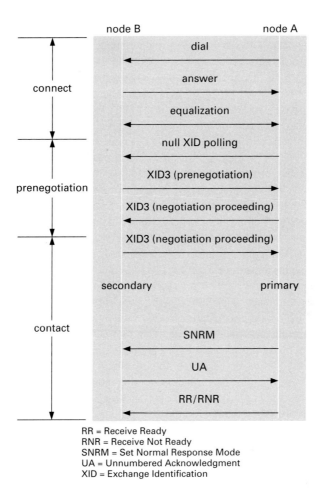

RR = Receive Ready
RNR = Receive Not Ready
SNRM = Set Normal Response Mode
UA = Unnumbered Acknowledgment
XID = Exchange Identification

Figure 14.7 Activation of a switched link between two type 2.1 nodes.

CPs inform each other of their capabilities for network services. The *entering network-node* then will proceed to propagate enough information to control points in all the other nodes in the network, so that all network-nodes then have an up-to-date picture of the network topology, including the newly entered network-node. This topology update process is described in the following.

Topology database.   The network topology database contains information on all network-nodes, and the transmission groups[26] interconnecting them. This database does not include information on end-nodes or the transmission groups attached to them. Unlike the directory database, which is distributed among network-nodes, the topology database is fully replicated at each network-node.

---

26. Transmission groups may consist of point-to-point links, LANs, X.25 subnetworks, etc.

`Topology_Database_Update` messages (TDUs) flow on all the CP-CP sessions between network-nodes. This occurs at the time of a node entry into the network, as noted above, and also when any other change to the network occurs. A link or node failure, for example, can cause that element to be removed from the network, with a consequent topology update. In this case, the topology update TDUs fan out from the adjacent nodes that detect the failure.[27]

APPN end-nodes contain only a small topology database, containing information about itself and its adjacent links. LEN end-nodes contain no topology database at all.

Part of each node's topology database is the local resources, particularly: (a) the node and all of its properties, and (b) the locally attached links, and all of their properties. Whenever a network-node has a change in its local network configuration, the control point is required to store the updated information in its local database, and to propagate the change via an update message to all adjacent network-nodes. This update information, called a **Resource Control Vector (RCV)**, is created by the network-node that owns the resource. Generally, a TDU will contain multiple RCVs, each of which must be processed separately.

The RCV contains a resource identifier, and a set of resource characteristics. Also, an updated sequence number is applied for each new RCV update message that a topology database manager originates. This indicates the "age" of the resource information, as it is propagated to all the neighbors. When receiving such a numbered RCV, the control point compares the arriving sequence number with that already stored for the particular resource. That way, only more recent information is accepted and propagated further.

Each network-node preserves its topology database on nonvolatile storage, so as to save it across system outages. Nevertheless, after a failure, and a disconnect of a node, there is the problem of bringing its topology database up to date. Rather than have all network-nodes involved in this, the immediate neighbors help out. Upon establishment of CP-CP sessions, each adjacent node sends the returning node all of the TDUs it received from its other neighbors while the connection was down. This is done by sequence number exchanges. If necessary, the entire topology database of a returning node can be regenerated.

Note that the APPN topology and routing databases need to describe only network-nodes and transmission groups (i.e., links and subnetworks) between network-nodes. The computation of a route between end-nodes then involves getting tail vectors from these end-nodes, and concatenating them with possible routes across the network. If the entire end-to-end route, including all end-node connections, had to be included in the databases, the database would have to be dramatically larger.

APPN thus minimizes the need for coordinated system definition. Network resources (e.g., logical units, links, etc.) are defined only at the node where they are located. APPN distributes information about these resources through the network dynamically, as needed. Logical units, in a network-node or in APPN end-nodes attached to a network-node, need be defined in only a single network-node. (That definition of resources at one node is not

---

27. The using application program is alerted to a session failure by a suitable return code. The application can then issue an appropriate call to establish a new session on an alternate path, if one exists.

eliminated by the dynamic network topology updates.) If a resource moves to another network-node, taking its name with it, APPN will find that resource by performing a network search transparent to the requesting application. With dynamic reconfiguration and the topology database functions, system definition is dynamic, resulting in a much easier to use system, with real-cost savings in both systems definition and system management.

14.6.2   Class of Service

The `Bind` sender requests a type of service by specifying a **mode name**. This mode name is associated with a class of service (COS) definition that is used to determine the most desirable route for the session. The COS definitions identify the characteristics that nodes and links must possess to be included in the route selected for the session. These characteristics might include response time, bandwidth, or security, for example. Cost and congestion of nodes along some routes are other important considerations. *Source-routing can take all such requirements into consideration in selecting and then maintaining the optimum route.*

The user can choose to rely on a default class of service chosen by the system, or the user can indicate the application preference via a "mode" selection. Usually, five classes of service suffice:

1. Batch oriented
2. Batch oriented with high security
3. Interactive oriented
4. Interactive oriented with high security
5. Network service messages on CP-CP sessions

Also associated with the class of service is a **transmission priority**. APPN networks (like subarea networks) allow the user to define a network priority and (via the class of service description) three session-level priorities: *high, medium*, and *low*. Control flows, for network services, have the highest priority. Highly interactive, short transmissions, for example, could be given a higher transmission priority than batch or messages from less important applications. Priority is the same for the entire route, in a given session. The transmission priority is carried in the `Bind` request at session establishment, allowing the two halves of the session and the intermediate-nodes along the path to store the priority for the session.

Path control maintains priority queues for each link. It places data for each session in the appropriate priority queue. To insure that lower-priority messages are not preempted indefinitely by higher-priority messages, an aging mechanism is also used.

14.6.3   APPN Route Selection

There is no need to precompute routes through an APPN network. Instead, routes are dynamically generated as required, using information about the network's topology and the desired class of service. APPN determines a best route from end-to-end. This may be directly from end-node to end-node, across a single shared facility (e.g., a link or a LAN), or it may be via intermediate network-nodes.

Remember that end-nodes and network-nodes connect to each other across "subnetworks" in the OSI sense, whether they be LANs, X.25 subnetworks, or point-to-point links. Any of these subnetworks can also be referred to, in SNA, as a *transmission group*. In this sense, the APPN network-nodes function as inter-subnetwork routers, which is analogous to the TCP/IP router-to-router function.[28]

In APPN a "least-weight" path is dynamically calculated for the Bind and subsequent session traffic. This depends on the characteristics of all candidate transmission groups and nodes. Those node and link characteristics had been previously exchanged among all APPN nodes. Route selection capabilities are resident in every network-node. Once the topology of the network has been updated, during the connectivity phase, the originating network-node can calculate an optimum route for the session from the origin end-node to the destination end-node. It does this using the updated topology database, the specified class of service, information on tail vectors gathered during the Locate process, and an optimum-route-finding algorithm. If multiple routes are of equal weight, a random distribution is used. Taking advantage of the fact that end-systems can connect to multiple network-nodes, the optimum route may not pass through the destination-serving network-node.

Using class of service coefficients.   The route selection process is based on an algorithm that considers the qualities of all the nodes and transmission groups along alternate routes. The nodes and transmission groups in the network have a small number of properties that are considered to be relevant to route selection. Node properties to be considered might include its operational-status, congestion, and capacity. Transmission group properties might include operational-status, congestion, security, propagation-delay, cost/packet, cost/connect time, utilization, and queueing-delay. Each class of service then involves the definition of a relative-importance-coefficient, or property-weight, for each selected property of the nodes and transmission groups.

For each class of service, the *property-weights* for each node and transmission group are combined to a corresponding *node weight* and *transmission group weight*. Lower weights indicate better conditions. These node and transmission-group weights, then, give a relative measure of the "goodness" of that node or transmission-group for that specific class of service.

Given the current network topology information, and the "goodness-weights" (for each node and transmission group) for each class of service, each network-node can calculate an optimum (least weight) route to each other network-node, for each class of service. This calculation is done each time there is a change in topology and there is a request for a session. The calculation results in a "tree" of paths, rooted at the origin of the session, to destination network-nodes. The calculation uses "shortest-path" algorithms, where "shortness" is defined as the lowest composite weighted sum, for the class of service desired [Baratz85]. For response time, for example, the path length calculation

---

28.   The same analogy applies to the intermediate function in the path control layer of subarea networks.

might include the sum of the delays in the connected links and nodes. In the algorithms, different weights can be given to different factors. Once constructed, the entire "tree" is stored. It is then available for future route requests from that node for that class of service.

Finally, a measure of node congestion is needed. One indication is the closeness to the maximum number of intermediate sessions that are allowed in a given node. This limit may depend on the capacity of the node, and on the noncommunication processing-load that may be reserved for the node. As an example, the node might be considered "congested" when the number of intermediate sessions reaches 90 percent of the maximum, and "uncongested" when the number again falls below 80 percent. This, too, can be taken into account in selecting the preferred route.

For route calculation, the topology database provides the current status of the nodes and transmission groups in the network. *Subnetworks*, such as public switched dial networks, X.25 and X.21 networks, and local area networks (LANs), act as transmission groups within an APPN network. When such a route is calculated, the topology database must know the dial digits, or equivalent Subnetwork Point of Attachment (SNPA) addresses to connect across the intervening link or subnetwork to other APPN nodes. The SNPA address (e.g., MAC address on a LAN) for the "last mile" across a subnetwork, to a destination end-node on that subnetwork, is obtained as the tail vector during the Locate phase.

Source and destination routing. There has been much debate about source routing versus dynamic destination routing, which is calculated dynamically by every intermediate-node along the way. Connectionless networks usually use dynamic destination routing; they may also have source routing, but this is currently uncommon. Some (of many) considerations follow.

Connectionless, dynamic destination routing is best where messages are short and usually to a different destination each time. This saves the expense of setting up a session for one or only a few packets.[29] Expendable messages, such as stock market quotes, because they are constantly replaced, is another case where dynamic destination routing is very acceptable. However, connectionless, dynamic destination routing systems have a variety of uncertainties, besides the well-known temporary loops, which may form until a route finalizes. These loops occur when some intermediate-node erroneously claims a link to some part of the network, but in reality only has a bit bucket there. Connectionless, destination routing makes it very hard to localize such problems, because there may be no feedback as to where the message has actually been sent. With source routing, fortunately, the sender has full knowledge of the route followed by his data. And if, for reasons of error or congestion, a message cannot be forwarded by some network-node, a notification can be returned to the sender along the reverse route.

With connectionless, destination routing, moreover, the intermediate-nodes have a considerable additional storage requirement. They must maintain, at all times, even in the absence of any traffic, the routes to other nodes.

---

29. Note, however, that if a session exists between two locations, the Send_Conversation verb of LU 6.2 allows a one-verb transmission of a datagram.

Source routing and a virtual-circuit philosophy were selected in APPN, rather than connectionless, constantly varying, destination routing, to avoid the problems of message throw-aways, and reduce the difficulties of problem determination, the workload on the intermediate-nodes, and the inefficiency of regular resequencing. The design rather seeks to be able to operate efficiently at high-usage levels and speeds.

In the APPN designs, one can set up routes selectively, at the time sessions are set up. In the APPN design, too, the burden of calculating routes is not carried by all network-nodes, but only by those network-nodes that are the servers of session originators. Time is not spent doing route calculations for each and every packet.

What is the relation between the APPN source-routing algorithm and the OSI IS-IS connectionless algorithm? The path-determining algorithm used in APPN source routing is the well-known Dijkstra SPF algorithm. That same algorithm can be used to either:

(a) Specify the entire route (as in source routing)

(b) Estimate the entire route but specify only the path to the next node (as in destination routing)

While the final outcome cannot be predicted, this same algorithm is currently favored in the discussions of a new standard for the proposed IS-IS (intermediate-system-to-intermediate-system) OSI protocol. If that algorithm were adopted, then *with both using essentially the same routing algorithm*, interoperation would be facilitated between a connection-oriented subnetwork (like APPN) having source routing, and a connectionless OSI subnetwork having dynamic destination routing.

Route selection control vectors.   The APPN source-routing calculation concerns two kinds of routes. One is for a route of the `Locate_Search` request that is directed to the network-node of the destination LU. The other is for a route of the `Bind` request. In both cases, the topology database is used to construct a *Route Selection Control Vector (RSCV)*, which is appended to the `Locate_Search` or `Bind` request. The RSCV in a `Locate_Search` request is a list of contiguous network-nodes along the route from the origin-serving network-node to the destination-serving network-node. This represents the minimum spanning tree (most direct route) using adjacent CP-CP sessions. The RSCV in the `Bind` request is a list of contiguous transmission groups along the route from the node containing the origin LU to the node containing the destination LU (a transmission group may actually be fairly complex, such as a group of parallel lines, a local area network, or a public PSDN). This RSCV represents the optimal route based on the requested class of service.

The route for the `Bind` is calculated in the CP of the network-node that serves the originating end-node. Once that is done, session services provide the LU in the origin APPN end-node with the information to create the `Bind` command, including the destination and mode information in the original conversation request, plus the RSCV. An option in APPN is *RSCV caching*. This eliminates the need for the control point to recalculate a route every time one is needed. By saving a previously calculated route, and reusing it for some amount of time, session set-up time can be improved.

The RSCV is attached to the `Bind` and sent along the selected route, to the destination LU (attached to the destination-serving network-node). If the parameters in the proposed

`Bind` are acceptable to the destination LU, a positive response is sent, and the session is established. Otherwise, some negotiation on the `Bind` parameters, via the `Bind` response, can take place.

14.6.4 APPN Routing

Introduction. IS-IS routing is another area where rapid evolution is taking place, encouraged by the advances in fiber technology. As discussed in Section 12.4.4, the movement of routing to lower layers and the simplification of IS-IS protocols is a clear trend. The high-speed technologies discussed in Chapter 18 illustrate this. However, we still will need a mixture of layer-3 and layer-2 routing, with the high-speed subnetworks within or interoperating with the current speed networks. The current APPN internode routing and pacing techniques, described below, are a step forward in layer-3 routing at moderate speeds. The approach *eliminates the need for coordinated system definition in the intermediate-nodes*. The key is that the topology updates and route calculations, or variations thereof, can be applied at layer 2 or layer 3 and over a wide speed range. The particular source routing with label swapping technique used in APPN and described below, is therefore only one part of this larger picture.

NN session connectors. As the *extended* `Bind` command flows from the source to the target end-node, each intervening network-node makes note of the session being established, and sets up appropriate **line-connection tables** for it. At a given network-node, these tables determine the outgoing line for each session. Therefore, all subsequent messages in that session can flow along that same optimum path. Thus, a single command flow activates both the route and the session.

The **session-connectors** in each network-node swap a 17-bit **Local_Form-Session_Identifier (LFSID)** in the Transmission Header (TH) of the incoming message for a different LFSID in the TH of the outgoing message. Each intermediate-node picks its next available 17-bit number for its outgoing LFSID on that link, at the time the `Bind` passes through. Although the LFSID changes value in each node, as a message passes through, the session-connector tables relate the incoming identifier on one link to the outgoing identifier on another link. This technique gives us 17 bits of addressability *per link*, rather than per network. Later, when an `UnBind` passes through, all the LFSIDs along the route are freed.

One bit of this *LFSID* field is used to indicate which of the two communicating nodes is the originator of the `Bind`. The other 16 bits are broken up into two 8 bit fields.[30] Each node along the path creates its own *LFSID*. The contents always determine, for each node, the next link and next destination along the route for that particular session.

---

30. These two fields are called *Session id High (SIDH)* and *Session id Low (SIDL)*. In the `Bind` request, and in all subsequent messages for the associated session that flow in that same direction, the destination address field (DAF) of the FID 2 TH contains the *SIDL*, and the origin address field (OAF) of the TH contains the *SIDH*. For the `Bind` response, and for all subsequent messages associated with that session, in that same direction (opposite to the `Bind`), the fields are reversed. That is, the OAF contains the *SIDL*, and the DAF contains the *SIDH*.

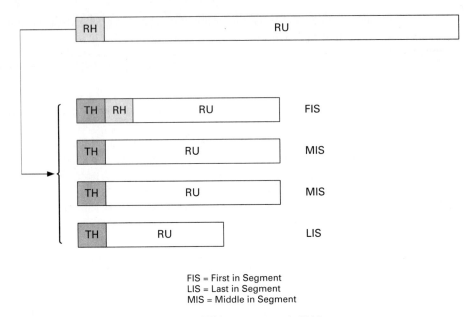

FIS = First in Segment
LIS = Last in Segment
MIS = Middle in Segment

Figure 14.8 Segmentation of an SNA request unit (RU).

Segmentation. Segmenting, to control usage of buffer space at each node, is done as shown in Figure 14.8. The segments are each identified, in the TH header, as First in Segment (FIS), Middle in Segment (MIS), or Last in Segment (LIS).

Segmenting may occur between an end-node and a network-node, and between two end-nodes, as well as between network-nodes. The maximum LU size is specified LU-to-LU, and the segment size is specified node-to-node. The maximum request unit (RU) size is negotiated between LUs at Bind time, and any RU that exceeds this maximum length will be immediately segmented.

14.6.5 APPN Connection Network

We now consider the routing between two APPN nodes when both are attached to a common subnetwork, such as a LAN. The APPN architecture refers to this capability as a **connection network** for a **Shared Access Facility (SAF)**. This general terminology was chosen because the concept is potentially applicable to several types of subnetworks, such as LANs and switched (dial) networks, which have the ability to directly access multiple destinations from one output port.

The LAN is an example where subnetwork point of attachment (SNPA) addresses must be found, if we are to communicate with nodes attached to the subnetwork. In the LAN case, these SNPA addresses consist of two parts: the LAN station address and the link service access point (LSAP) address. Chapter 16 discusses facilities for finding these addresses, by using a variety of special LAN-oriented discovery protocols, when LANs operate independent of WANs. When a LAN is a subnetwork within an APPN network, however, these special protocols have a more limited utility. When APPN exists in the origin and destination nodes, the determination of the origin and destination SNPA addresses is done by the serving network-nodes as a normal part of the APPN `Locate` function.

Recall from the session establishment example of Section 14.5 that both the origin and the destination APPN end-nodes provide their serving network-nodes with their tail vectors as part of the `Locate` process. These tail vectors include descriptions and SNPA addresses of all the links between the end-node and adjacent network-nodes, plus any connections to a shared access facility like LANs. Without the connection-network feature, the subsequent data path between end-nodes could be via its serving network-node. This trip via the serving network-node is unnecessary in a LAN. Another unsavory alternative would be to have every LAN-attached node define every other LAN-attached node in its directory (since they are, in effect, adjacent). That is obviously unsatisfactory, too.

The solution is for the network-node doing route calculation to know that two end-nodes are attached to the same LAN (or other SAF), and to specify the RSCV (route selection control vector) accordingly. So, a special naming scheme is needed so that all end-nodes on a given LAN can be so identified. All connections to a given LAN are therefore indicated as a connection to a named Connection Network (CN).[31]

During LU-LU session activation, the CN_name is used. When an LU in an APPN end-node attached to a CN initiates an LU-LU session, it reports the CN_name, and its own MAC address to its network-node server, in the session-initiation request. If the serving network-node then determines that the destination end-node can be reached through the same CN, the serving network-node calculates a route for the session that traverses the CN. The serving network-node returns the appropriate routing information (including the destination SNPA address) in the RSCV to the origin node.

14.7 ADAPTIVE PACING

In APPN, during the data-transfer phase, special congestion controls using adaptive pacing are applied to each session individually. Such individual session control is deemed to be fairer than allowing one session to impact other sessions. Adaptive session-level pacing provides a node (that supports many sessions) a dynamic means to allocate resources to a session that has a burst of activity, and to reclaim unused resources from sessions that have no activity. The controls are designed (a) to avoid congestion at intermediary and end buffers, (b) to eliminate any need for throwing away messages, and (c) to eliminate

---

31.   One can also think of the Connection Network as all the nodes on the shared access facility defined as having a connection to a common **virtual routing node**. Similarly, ISO/IEC DIS 10589 defines a **pseudo-node** where a broadcast subnetwork has *n* connected intermediate-systems, and the broadcast subnetwork itself is considered to be a pseudo-node. Each of the ISs has a single link to the pseudo-node (rather than *n*-1 links to each of the other intermediate-systems).

possibilities of deadlock. (The last occurs when node A holds packet x until node B sends packet y; but conversely, node B holds packet y until node A sends packet x.) As the name implies, deadlocks are particularly deadly, as manual intervention by a skilled person is usually necessary.

APPN pacing is applied independently, for each direction of data flow, in each hop in the session route. The sender requests the right to send messages; the receiver sets up buffers, and responds to the sender. Thus, each receiving node along the session path tells each sending node that a specific number of messages (RUs) may be sent. To insure that there will be sufficient buffer space available upon arrival, the receiver allocates enough space to handle the maximum allowable size of RUs.

To economize on buffer space, adaptive window sizes, rather than fixed windows, are used in APPN. That window size is calculated by the receiver depending on the sender's utilization of previous windows, remaining availability of buffers, and congestion in the receiving node.[32] The sender, too, provides an input to this calculation. If the sending queue grows beyond a certain point, the sender can ask for a larger window. By all these means, the distribution of buffers among sessions is dynamic. Resources are allocated to sessions that have a high amount of activity, and buffers are reclaimed from sessions with low activity. High buffer utilization can thus be achieved.

Also, the APPN adaptive pacing (unlike virtual-route pacing in subarea networks) allows arbitrary changes in the size of the pacing window—to any value. The receiver returns (in the pace response) the window size for the next window. To speed the reaction, in case of congestion, a node can even request its partner to not send the unused portion of the current window, and to change the size of the next window.

Global flow control, along the entire route is effected by the phenomena of *back-pressure*. If a receiving end-node reduces the window it will accept, buffers in an intermediate-node will begin to fill up. That sign of impending congestion will motivate the intermediate-nodes to likewise reduce their window sizes. This backward pressure will fairly quickly reach the source of the data.

Real buffer storage is, of course, more efficient than virtual storage, on disks. Hence, as a threshold of real-storage use is reached, some further throttling is appropriate. Rather than penalize the innocent new sessions, a search is made to find the session holding the largest window. The next time that session requests a window, it will be reduced by one. In this way the successive window sizes are gradually reduced until the operation is below the real-storage threshold.

To get the adaptive pacing started, both sides say whether they support adaptive pacing and what the initial window size should be. For this, the *extended* Bind command includes: (a) an adaptive pacing indicator, to confirm that adaptive pacing is supported, (b) a primary receive-window, and (c) a secondary receive-window. Fixed window pacing will be used if either end does not support adaptive pacing. Values in the Bind change at each hop, to reflect needed sizes at each hop, rather than only end-to-end.

---

32. One measure of congestion, for example, is the number of received messages that have not yet been processed.

14.8   APPN-OSI INTEGRATED NODES

With the burgeoning importance of communications in multivendor environments, an increasing number of OSNA nodes will need to have capability for communicating to both SNA and OSI nodes. *IBM's integration strategy is to implement native, fully compliant OSI products while maximizing interoperability, resource sharing, and the value added functions of SNA.* Making use of the Common Programming Interface described in Section 7.2, there can be a high degree of flexibility and programmer productivity. Customers will be able to transparently use whichever protocol stack satisfies the business requirement for application integration, interoperability, performance, and/or system management.

A simple three-way conversation among an integrated node, a pure OSI node, and a pure SNA node is illustrated in Figure 14.9. Dual control stacks are in the integrated node. The application in the integrated node has access to both protocol stacks. Communication takes place via both the APPN path control and the X.25 subnetwork. An application pair communicates using corresponding end-to-end controls.

Sharing of the layer 1 through 3a facilities is also of great economic importance, as illustrated in Figure 14.10. Where both OSI and SNA protocols are desired, two parallel networks (OSI/SNA) at the layers 1 through 3a should not be required.

14.8.1   Commonality of Node Functions

Still further integration, in the coming years, can take a variety of forms. Which will best succeed is a matter of conjecture. However, the technical feasibility of two very attractive directions has become clear, and are discussed in the following.

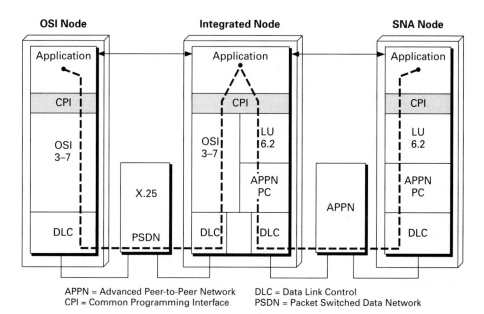

Figure 14.9 OSNA transparent application example, with three applications conversing via APPN and X.25 PSDN and dual-stack node.

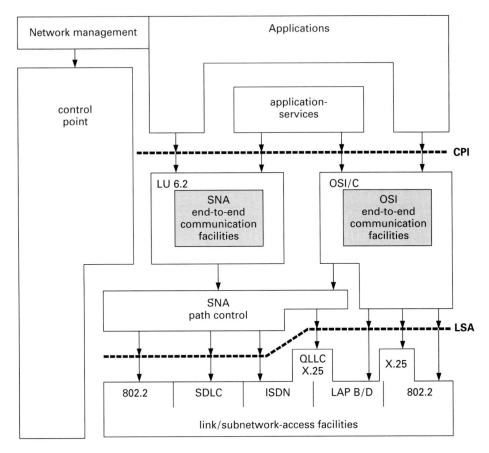

LAP B/D = Link-level procedures, types B and D   QLLC/X.25 = SNA Qualified Logical-Link Control for X.25
OSI/C = OSI Communications Subsystem

Figure 14.10 Potential OSNA integrated-node structure.

The first set of concepts for the integration of OSI functions and SNA functions can be illustrated by Figure 14.10 [Janson91]. Separate end-to-end data-exchange facilities, in the upper layers, are provided for SNA and OSI. Three important areas, nevertheless, can be common, regardless of whether the applications involved are OSI-based or SNA-based:

1.   The *link/subnetwork-access facilities*, including the LANs, X.25, ISDN, SDLC, and voice/data subsystems with bandwidth management, can be commonly available to all applications.[33]

---

33.   All the Link/Subnetwork-Access facilities shown in Figure 14.10 should be shareable by both OSI and SNA protocol stacks, layers 3c through 7. (The two instances of 802.2 shown in the diagram is only because the sharing of all facilities is difficult to draw.)

2. The *Common Programming Interface* (CPI) should be common and transparent to the underlying communication protocols, where feasible. A common programming interface should apply to key application-services (such as asynchronous-messaging and distributed data services) as well as transaction applications.

3. Economy, as well as ease of use, requires *shared services* among different architectures wherever appropriate. Candidates for such sharing include:

- *System management services*, both within the combined node and at higher-level focal points
- *Control point functions* of network-layer directory services, topology database, configuration services, and route selection

Boundary mapping. Stack-switching may require mapping, at the boundary, from one stack to another. In Figure 14.10, for example, a current APPN path-control layer expects to handle SNA sessions. However, each session has to be anchored in the lower part of an LU. A non-SNA protocol from another protocol stack, such as that of OSI layer 3c, cannot just drop packets into the SNA path control. It must first pass the packet through an LU session anchor. Since that anchor is only a small part of the LU, a mapping function is needed that will allow the OSI component to access only the session anchor part of the LU. Research projects [Janson91] have shown that the LU 6.2 can be divided into upper (LU 6.2A) and lower (LU 6.2B) parts in a way that:

- The upper and lower combination performs fully as the LU 6.2 architecture
- The lower part only provides the full-duplex logical-connection support that is needed by non-SNA protocols to cross APPN path control networks

According to this research, when the OSI upper stack is attached to APPN path control, via an LU 6.2B, path control accepts the OSI stack as a legitimate LU. The LU 6.2B, therefore has been referred to as an **OSI-LU**. The OSI stack, on the other hand, sees below it a legitimate subnetwork access protocol, acting in its sublayer 3a. Two such OSI-LUs in different integrated nodes, could thus communicate with each other, exchanging OSI layer-3c (X.25 or CLNP) PDUs across the SNA network.

OSI-SNA addressing. The incorporation of SNA addresses into the OSI structure was described in Section 12.3.4. This facilitates the mapping of SNA addresses into ones that an OSI network will understand. It does not do the job for the reverse, that is: converting an OSI address into one an SNA network will understand.

This is a requirement, for example, in the situation shown in Figure 14.11, where two end-systems (NSAPs 37'1'M and 37'41'N) on two different OSI networks (1' and 41') want to communicate using an SNA network as an intermediary or backbone. The networks are joined by OSI/SNA integrated nodes called Interworking Units (IWUs). This is a simple directory problem at the IWUs analogous to finding the subnetwork point of attachment (SNPA) address for a destination on a subnetwork. In this case, however, we need to find, for each destination NSAP, the two-level APPN address of the OSI/SNA interworking units. That IWU address is the combination of the IWU CP_name and the name for the OSI-LU in that node. Figure 14.11 gives the example of the contents of the directory

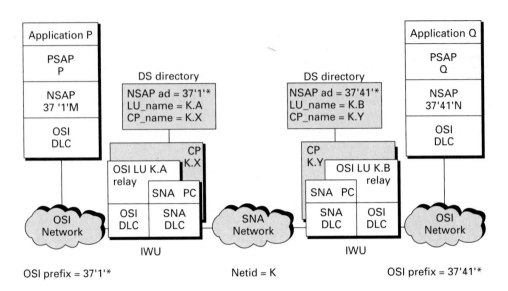

Figure 14.11 OSI internetworking over SNA subnetwork [Janson91].

service at the two IWUs, for the two NSAPs, 37'1'M and 37'41'N. These IWU directory entries might be manually entered. However, when the OSI Inter-Domain Routing Protocol (IDRP) is finally in place, it is expected that IWUs will be able to dynamically learn the address through which each distant domain or subnetwork can be reached.

TS boundary usage.   A second, companion approach to integration adds to the first by using all three boundaries in Figure 3.14 (CPI, TS, and LSA). The addition of split stacks at the TS boundary (see Section 12.6.3) places a burden of TS mappings on the transport-service-provider, but it offers additional generality, and can sometimes eliminate the need to have layers 3 and 4 in the end-system.

14.9   APPN INTEROPERATION EXAMPLES

The integration of APPN and OSI was discussed in the previous section. The integration of APPN and SNA subarea is treated in Chapter 15. In addition, there is the question of APPN interoperation with other leading protocols, particularly IPX, AppleTalk, DECnet, and the TCP/IP of UNIX systems. Perhaps a hopeful trend can be seen in the early statements of intent (in March 1991) for the following:

- *Apple and APPN*. APPN support on the Macintosh will enable AppleTalk, Apple's networking protocol, to be integrated into wide-area SNA networks. Any Macintosh on an AppleTalk network will have full access to any resource in the SNA network. It also will allow the SNA network to be used as a backbone, transparently, connecting remote AppleTalk networks into a single network.

- *Novell and APPN.* With APPN support in Novell products, Novell systems will be able to interconnect two or more workgroup local area networks (LANs) across an SNA network without requiring mainframes to set up the connections.

- *Siemens/Nixdorf and APPN.* Siemens Nixdorf is the largest computer company in Western Europe. APPN end-node support of Siemen's SINEX/UNIX products will enhance the already wide connectivity of Siemens Nixdorf and IBM systems. Already over 2000 of these systems are connected to SNA networks.

- *System Strategies and APPN.* This company (a subsidiary of NYNEX Corp.) offers EXPRESS and ezBRIDGE product lines that will support the APPN end-node architecture. These products thereby will provide communications capabilities between IBM APPN networks and DEC VAX/VMS and UNIX systems.

Conclusion

The projected role of the APPN in the OSNA can be seen by referring back to Figure 3.14. The APPN service at layer 3c, along with OSI layer-3c services, can utilize all of the lower transport facilities at layers 1 through 3a. Moreover, all of the applications and application-services that use the Common Programming Interface (CPI-C) can use either the APPN or OSI transport services.

APPN has taken major strides toward ease of use by dynamic topology update, distributed directory services, dynamic route selection by class of service, and the overall reduction of coordinated system definition. All this, however, is still only part of a broader evolutionary process that has been gathering steam for several years. The ease of use thread is joined by several others.

Research on the integration of OSI and APPN has also shown how the OSI upper stack and the SNA upper stack can both share the common layer 1 through 3a transport facilities. With the advent of the SNA addressing incorporated in the OSI NSAP formats, the layer-3 addressing is compatible between APPN and OSI. One can therefore foresee the possibility of a high degree of integration and interoperation between these two.

Another thread is also clear. As higher-speed links (above T3) become more prevalent, one expects further evolution in that direction, too. The diverse approaches to the accommodation of broadband facilities, including high-performance routing at layers 1 and 2, are treated in Chapter 18.

Another evolutionary thread involves the accommodation of multiple protocols. There is a well-known requirement for any transport-service-provider, like APPN, to be able to attach a variety of types of end-systems and subnetworks. Different end-systems may expect to see transport services based on TCP, OSI, SNA, or NetBIOS. The design approaches in such an evolution toward protocol independence were discussed in Chapter 12.

One has to conclude, therefore, that the technologies for ease of use in APPN are important planks in a larger OSNA edifice that is now taking shape.

Acknowledgments

I am particularly indebted to E. C. Broockman, M. Pozefsky, J. E. Drake, G. R. Shelton, O. Choi, and P. Immanuel for valuable input and reviews of this chapter.

TECHNICAL REFERENCES

SNA Transmission Headers

The types of formats for the SNA transmission headers (THs) are:

- FID-1 TH is used in subarea networks, between subareas that do not use virtual routes.

- FID-4 TH is used in subarea networks, between subareas that do use virtual routes.

- FID-2 TH is used without the Origin/Destination Assignor indicator (ODAI) between a T4 or T5 node and an adjacent T-2.0 or T-2.1 node, in subarea networks.

- FID-2 TH, with an Origin/Destination Assignor Indicator bit, is used between APPN network-nodes, between network-nodes and end-nodes, and also between APPN nodes and LEN nodes in subarea networks.

The format for the type FID-2 TH is given in Figure 14.12. The ODAI indicates which node (at session-activation time) assigned the OAF'-DAF' values that are carried in the TH. Together with the OAF' and DAF' values, the ODAI value forms a 17-bit Local-Form Session_Identifier (LFSID). The OAF' and DAF' values used in the TH in one direction are reversed in the other direction.

Bind Options

When options are limited in LU 6.2, the selected options are noted by an asterisk (*).

1. Transmission Control Facilities:
   - *Pacing* on normal flow will be one of the following:
     - no pacing,
     - primary to secondary only,
     - secondary to primary only, or
     - both directions.*

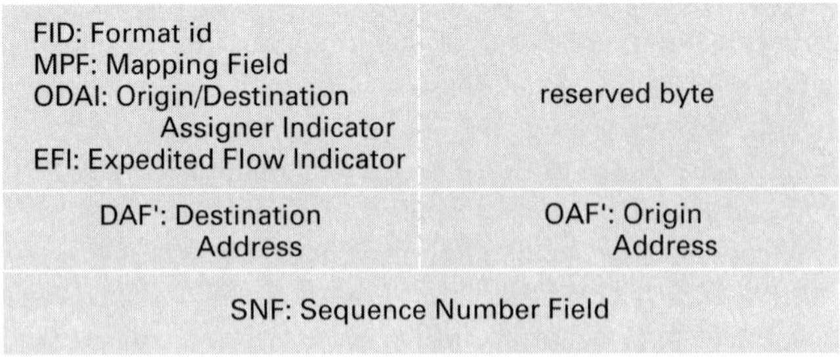

FID: Format id MPF: Mapping Field ODAI: Origin/Destination Assigner Indicator EFI: Expedited Flow Indicator	reserved byte
DAF': Destination Address	OAF': Origin Address
SNF: Sequence Number Field	

Figure 14.12 SNA type FID-2 TH format [LY43-0081].

- *Pacing* parameters will be:
  - primary send window size = $n1$,
  - primary receive window size = $n2$;
  - secondary send window size = $n3$,
  - secondary receive window size = $n4$;
  - adaptive pacing will* (will not) be used.
- A *maximum RU* that will be sent this session (and policed by TC) is
  - K bytes from the primary half-session,
  - L bytes from the secondary half-session.
- *Sequence numbers* (or ids) are used on the normal flow.
2. Data Flow Control Facilities pertaining to both half-sessions:
   - Normal-flow *send/receive mode* will be:
     - duplex (FDX),
     - half-duplex (HDX) contention, or
     - half-duplex flip-flop (HDX-FF).*
   - *Contention resolution*: One half-session speaks first in HDX-FF mode and wins contention in the HDX contention mode. This will occur when either:
     - the secondary speaks first and wins, or
     - the primary speaks first and wins.
   - *Recovery responsibility* will be in either:
     - the primary half-session, or
     - the sender of the negative response.*
   - *Brackets* will be used* (or not).
   - *First speaker* (one having the freedom to begin bracket without first asking permission of other half-sessions) will be either:
     - the secondary half-session, or
     - the primary half-session.
   - *Bracket termination* will be either by
     - rule number 2 (terminated on last request of last chain), or
     - rule number 1 (termination depends on response to end-bracket indicator).*
   - Only certain *data flow control RUs* will be allowed in this session. Examples might be one of the following:
     - none,
     - `Signal, Logical_Unit_Status, Shutdown, Shutdown_Complete,` and `Request_Shutdown,`
     - the above plus `Quiesce_At_End_Of_Chain, Quiesce_Complete,` and `Release_Quiesce,` or
     - the above plus `Ready_To_Receive.`
3. Data Flow Control Facilities for each of the two half-sessions (each half-session may be different):
   - *Chaining* use either:
     - multiple RU chains are allowed,* or
     - only single RU chains are allowed.
   - *Waiting rules*, either:
     - only one definite response can be outstanding,* or
     - multiple definite responses can be outstanding.

- *Chain response* protocol will be one of the following:
  - no response,
  - exception-response,
  - definite-response, or
  - definite-response or exception-response.*
- *Responses* will be in the same order as requests received (or not).
- *End-bracket indicator* may (or may not*) be sent by the primary LU.

4. Presentation Service Facilities:

- *FM headers* may be used* (or not).
- *Security manager* can receive:
  - a user-id,
  - password,
  - already verified indication,
  - profile id on FMH-5 `Attach` commands.
- *Alternative codes* will be used (or not) (for example, ASCII and EBCDIC).
- *Data compression* will be used (or not) when sending (may be different for each half-session).
- *Synchronization level*:
  - none,
  - `Confirm`,
  - `Confirm`, `Sync_Point`, and `Backout`.
- *Parallel sessions* between the two LUs will (will not) be supported.
- *Change Number of Sessions* is (is not) supported.
- *Cryptography* option is:
  - none,*
  - mandatory,*
  - selective.
- *User data*:
  - unformatted data,
  - mode-name,
  - session instance id,
  - network-qualified PU name,
  - random data.

5. Extended `Bind` also includes:

- *Control vectors*:
  - Fully Qualified PCID, to uniquely identify the session,
  - class of service/transmission priority.

EXERCISES

14.1   Name four key attributes of APPN networking.

14.2   What are the two basic types of nodes in an APPN network? What are the two types of end-nodes?

14.3   How are destination locations defined in an APPN network?

14.4   What technique is used to reduce the frequency of dynamic network search for destinations?

14.5   How can one reduce the burden of defining LUs in a LEN end-node?

14.6   What are the three primary commands used in the published EN-NN interface?

14.7   How is the size of the APPN topology database kept smaller?

14.8   When is it necessary for APPN topology database update messages to flow?

14.9   Name some of the properties of nodes and transmission groups that might be used in route selection.

14.10   How does route selection take into account both the class of service needed and the node and TG properties?

14.11   How is the most direct route through a shared access facility (like a LAN or a switched network) selected?

14.12   OSI/APPN integration first of all involves commonality in what two areas?

15

Transport-Service-Provider: SNA/Subarea and APPN

15.1 INTRODUCTION

The SNA subarea networks are also participating on the previously mentioned five evolutionary tracks.[1] Some current examples are:

1. Ease of use:
    - Independent LUs in connected APPN networks or attached LEN end-nodes, *having dynamic LU definition in the subarea network*
    - Dynamic attachment of channel-connected control units
2. Multiple subnetwork capabilities within subarea networks:
    - X.25 PSDN
    - LANs 802.3/4/5
    - FDDI
    - Serial Optical Channel (ESCON)
3. Use of the subarea network as a backbone with multiple-protocol passthrus for:
    - X.25 end-systems and PSDNs
    - TCP/IP
    - APPN networks
    - NetBIOS on LANs

If past history is any indication, we can expect a continuing transformation of subarea networks, as well as APPN networks, following these trends. The APPN extensions to SNA are important components of this movement. The corollary is to inject some of the

---

1. Five evolutionary tracks of OSNA: expanded application-services, end-to-end system management, ease of use—including programming independence at the API, incorporation of multiple communication protocols, and use of high-speed facilities.

APPN dynamics into subarea networks themselves. Then, the combination of APPN and subarea networks stays on these tracks. The APPN/subarea evolution proceeds, even as APPN grows in significance, and the integration with OSI also proceeds.

Most of the seven-layer architectural structure is *common to APPN and subarea networks*. This commonality includes:

- All the upper layers, 5 through 7

- All of the links and subnetworks (in layers 1, 2, and 3a, including X.25, LANs, MAN, FDDI, ISDN, Frame Relay, SDLC, and channels), described in Chapters 16 through 19

The key differences between APPN and subarea networks are in the distributed directory, dynamic definition, dynamic topology update, and dynamic routing capabilities. Of less significance are other differences in the transmission control and path-control layers.

In this chapter we discuss the addition of some dynamic configurability to subarea networks, and the interoperation of APPN and subarea networks. The unique subarea-node-types are first examined. Then we examine *the capability for having sessions established across combinations of APPN and subarea networks, without prior system definition*. The few other unique parts of the subarea network, primarily in the path-control layer, are also summarized in this chapter.

15.2   SUBAREA-NODES, TYPES 5 AND 4

The bulk of the present-day SNA networks use a set of layer-3c inter-subnetwork protocols with a numerical, hierarchical addressing scheme. The addressing has a *subarea* part (corresponding to the telephone company's area code) and an *element* part (corresponding to the user's local number). These SNA networks have, accordingly, been called subarea networks.

In a subarea network, the *subarea-nodes* are those that use these numeric addresses as the primary means for route expression. Subarea-nodes provide intermediate routing services, and also provide mapping between local addresses and network-wide addresses. Communication-controllers having these capabilities are called *type 4 nodes*. Mainframe hosts having these same capabilities plus a central (or regional) Systems Service Control Point (SSCP) are designated *type 5 nodes*.

Communication controllers can be interconnected by many types of subnetworks—e.g., point-to-point links, LANs, and X.25. They also attach a wide variety of terminals and programmable end-systems.[2]

An illustrative subarea network is shown in Figure 15.1. The two hosts are type 5 nodes. The three communications controllers are type 4 nodes. These five nodes are all subarea-nodes to which peripheral-nodes (e.g., cluster controllers) can be attached.[3]

---

2.   A typical 3745 mod 170, for example, can handle 2 token rings, 2 T1 lines, and 112 medium speed lines.

3.   These peripheral-nodes, in turn, can attach a wide variety of terminals, workstations, printers, and other devices.

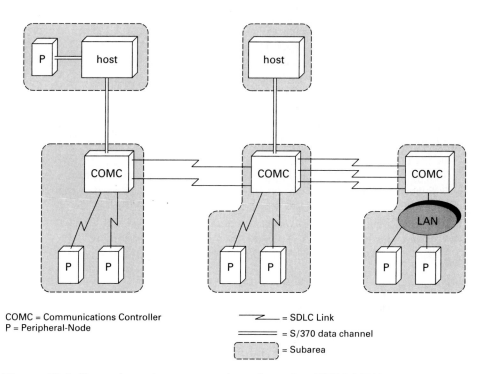

COMC = Communications Controller
P = Peripheral-Node

⎯⎯⎯⎯⎯ = SDLC Link
⎯⎯⎯⎯⎯ = S/370 data channel
⌐ ⌐ ⌐ ⌐ = Subarea

Figure 15.1 Illustrative subarea network configuration [GC30-3073].

15.2.1   Boundary-Functions

The boundary-function exists in type 4 and type 5 nodes to serve peripheral-nodes attached to these subarea-nodes. These *peripheral-nodes are type 2 nodes*. They are "owned" by an SSCP, on whom it depends for directory and session set-up services. A key point is that the type 2 peripheral-nodes do not, in themselves, have peer-to-peer capability. (This lack has been overcome with the advent of the type 2.1 node described in the preceding chapter.) Since the SSCP is not located within the type 2 node, communication to the SSCP is via a session with the SSCP. At the transmission-control layer, the two boundary-functions, are:

1.   Providing pacing of the data flows for half-sessions in connected peripheral units
2.   Performing some session control functions in cooperation with the half-sessions that are in the connected peripheral units

Other boundary-functions, concerned with address translation, are performed at the path-control layer. The boundary-function also serves to assist the connection between subarea networks and APPN networks.

Not all sessions employ pacing, but if they do, a pacing queue for that session will exist in the sending Connection-Point-Manager (CPMGR). An RU on the expedited flow, on the other hand, need not wait for pacing; it can be advanced (in the CPMGR) ahead of normal flow requests that are waiting (in the queue) for a pacing indicator in a response.

The job of the boundary-function at the path-control layer is the transformation of network addresses to local addresses, and vice versa, for type 2 nodes such as a cluster (establishment) controller. The local addresses are shorter addresses, which are adequate for the smaller domain of a subarea.

Finally, the boundary-function must support interactions between subarea networks and peripheral APPN networks. The boundary-function acts as a surrogate for an LU in the APPN network, and communicates with its SSCP to obtain the assistance of the SSCP. This is needed when an APPN LU wants to establish a session with an LU in the subarea network, or wants to establish a session that crosses the subarea network. These roles of the boundary-function are discussed in Section 15.5.

15.3   CROSS-DOMAIN LU-LU SESSIONS

One of the major steps, to make the network easier to use, is to reduce the amount of coordinated system definition for LUs. We first examine the cross-domain LU-LU session creation in subarea networks, as the forerunner of the method for dynamically creating APPN to subarea LU-LU sessions.

Of course, with APPN, two control points are always involved in every LU-LU session between two nodes. Similarly, in the subarea network cross-domain case, the destination LU is not under the control of the same SSCP that controls the originating LU. We therefore see a peer relationship between SSCPs, with SSCP-SSCP sessions, which are a forerunner of the Control-Point-to-Control-Point sessions in APPN.[4] The exchange of SSCP-SSCP cross-domain commands gathers from the two SSCPs the information that is needed by the LUs for session initiation. This is illustrated in Figure 15.2:

1.   SSCP-A receives a `Session_Initiation` (INIT_SELF) request from LU-X.[5] SSCP-A checks its directory and may determine that LU-Y resides in another domain, under the control of SSCP-B. If SSCP-A does *not* find LU-Y in its local directory, SSCP-A will sequentially search the directories of other SSCPs (i.e., in the distributed multidomain directory) until LU-Y is found.

2.   SSCP-A sends a `Cross_Domain-Initiate` (CD-INIT) request to SSCP-B. The CD-INIT request identifies both the requesting LU-X and the destination LU-Y. The

---

4.   Functionally, therefore, subarea SSCPs and APPN control points are peers of each other, although they do not now communicate directly.

5.   The INIT_SELF may result from a logon. The INIT_SELF includes the name of the destination LU, and may also include a mode-name identifying the preferred session characteristics, an indication of how the session request might be queued, and user data such as a user-id and password.

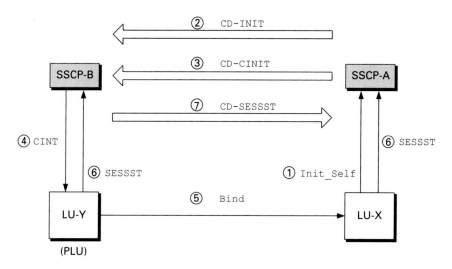

Figure 15.2 Cross-domain session initiation.

CD-INIT is roughly similar to the APPN Locate, in that it seeks confirmation from a distant control point concerning the ownership of a destination LU.

3. Next, SSCP-A sends a Cross_Domain-Control_Initiate (CD-CINIT) request to SSCP-B. The CD-CINIT request passes further information about LU-X (including the Bind image) to SSCP-B.

4. SSCP-B then is able to send a Control_Initiate (CINIT) to LU-Y. The CINIT includes the network addresses of the two LUs, a proposed Bind image, and the name of LU-X. LU-Y then has all the information needed to activate the session.

5. LU-Y sends a Session_Activation (Bind) command to LU-X.

6. To confirm to its SSCP that the session has been started, LU-Y sends a Session_Started (SESSST) command to its SSCP-B. After a Bind response is received, LU-X also sends a SESSST to SSCP-A.

7. SSCP-B, in turn, advises SSCP-A of the same thing by a CD-SESSST command.

In all of this, the two LUs have had dialogs with their respective SSCPs, unaware that any cross-domain signaling between SSCPs was involved.

Once the session is established, the peer-to-peer protocols, at layers 5 through 7, only affect the end-nodes in the end SNA domains, as shown in Figure 15.3, even though they may cross multiple intervening domains. The intermediate-nodes are not involved with these upper-layer protocols. An exception to this is the end-to-end flow control provided by virtual-route control. That end-to-end congestion control is affected by the discernment of congestion at intermediate-nodes (see Section 15.7.2). The protocols at layers 1 through 3 basically interact with multiple intervening nodes in the intervening SNA domains, as illustrated in Figure 15.3.

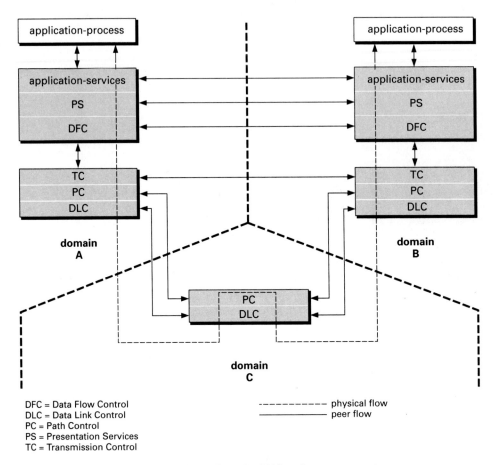

DFC = Data Flow Control
DLC = Data Link Control
PC = Path Control
PS = Presentation Services
TC = Transmission Control

– – – – – – – – – – physical flow
———————— peer flow

Figure 15.3 Peer flows in a three-domain SNA subarea network.

15.4 CROSS-NETWORK LU-LU SESSIONS

Different SNA networks have different sets of LU-names and network addresses. Still, they can be joined with cross-network sessions. To initiate a session between LUs in different networks, an exchange again takes place between control points, but this time through a gateway. Multiple gateways can also connect two networks. Because LU_names need not be unique across the two networks, aliases are used to avoid duplicates in any one network. Therefore some name-to-alias conversions are needed as cross-network sessions are set up.

Gateway-nodes contain one subarea path control instance for every interconnected network. The gateway function acts as an intermediary between the two network path control elements, similar to the way the boundary-function acts as intermediary between subarea and peripheral path-control elements. The boundary-function translates a network

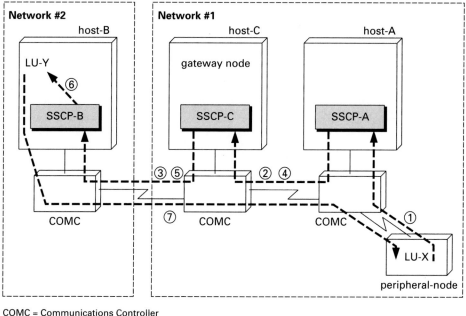

COMC = Communications Controller
LU = Logical Unit
SSCP = Systems Service Control Point

Figure 15.4 Initiating a cross-network LU-LU session.

address that subarea path control uses into a local address that peripheral path control uses. Similarly, the gateway function translates a name that one network uses into an alias name that an interconnected network uses.

Consider the situation in Figure 15.4, where there are two separate networks, network # 1 and network # 2. Each is a network of mainframe hosts; each mainframe contains an SSCP; and each mainframe uses an attached communications controller. An LU-X, under the control of SSCP-A wishes to initiate a session with LU-Y, under the control of SSCP-B. Each LU has a real name in its own network. If the two networks use the same name (for different LUs), then an alias name will be assigned in the other network. The mainframe containing SSCP-C, at the boundary of network #1, and its connected communications controller, contain the gateway function. The directories of each network give the appearance of a single network, of which the gateway is a part. From an addressing standpoint, LU-Y appears to SSCP-A, to be in the domain of the gateway SSCP-C. To SSCP-B, LU-X also appears to be in the domain of the gateway SSCP-C.[6] The two LUs are unaware of the separation of the LUs in different networks. Again, the SSCPs communicate among themselves (via the intermediary gateway) as necessary. The

---

6. However, each SSCP has other information that may tell the true domain of partner LUs.

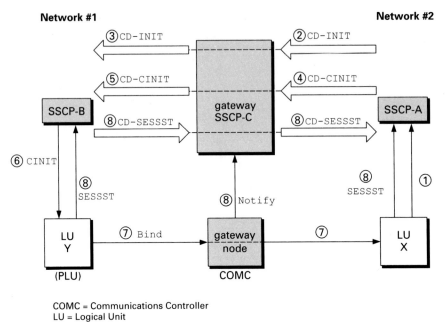

COMC = Communications Controller
LU = Logical Unit
SSCP = Systems Service Control Point

Figure 15.5 Initiating a session across a network gateway.

cross-network sequence is shown in Figure 15.5, which should be compared with the cross-domain sequence in Figure 15.2. The cross-network sequence is as follows:

1.   The initiating LU-X sends its SSCP-A a `Session_Initiation` requesting that a session be established to LU-Y. SSCP-A uses its local directory services to locate LU-Y. If necessary, SSCP-A also uses a sequential search of other SSCPs to find LU-Y, as described below.

2.   SSCP-A accordingly sends a `Cross_Domain-Initiate` (CD-INIT) request to gateway SSCP-C, identifying LU-X and LU-Y as prospective partners.

3.   The gateway SSCP-C knows that LU-Y is really in the domain of SSCP-B. The gateway SSCP-C may translate the alias name of LU-Y to its real name in network #2; and it may translate the real name of LU-X to its alias name in network #2. Then SSCP-C sends a `CD-INIT` on to SSCP-B.

4.   SSCP-A follows this by sending a `Cross_Domain-Control_Initiate` (CD-CINIT) to SSCP-C.

5.   Accordingly, SSCP-C forwards the CD-CINIT to SSCP-B.

6.   SSCP-B now is able to send the `Control_Initiate` (CINIT) request to LU-Y.

7.   LU-Y then has all the information it needs to send the `Session_Activation` (Bind) request to LU-X.

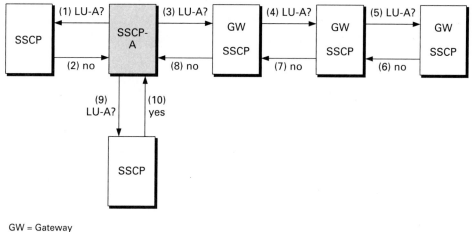

GW = Gateway
SSCP = Systems Service Control Point

Figure 15.6 Directory search in interconnected subarea networks.

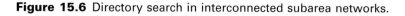

8.   The establishment of the session is confirmed to all involved SSCPs (A, B, and C) via `SESSST` and `CD-SESSST` commands. After it has seen the `Bind` and `Bind` response, the gateway-node notifies the gateway SSCP that the session has started and identifies the virtual route used for the session in both networks.

Directory searches.   There are some underlying directory searches involved in the above. There may, in fact, be multiple gateways, connecting multiple subarea networks. Gateways need not have defined all the LUs in cascaded remote networks. A *dynamic search capability* is provided instead, and directory searches may be needed in all of the connected networks. The process is illustrated in Figure 15.6. There, SSCP-A wants to find LU-A. SSCP-A may find LU-A in its directory as a result of a prior system definition. Or it may be found in the cache of SSCP-A as a result of a prior directory search. If LU-A is not thus found, SSCP-A sequentially interrogates the other SSCPs with which it has established control sessions, including one (or more) gateway SSCPs. Each gateway passes the query on to the next gateway. As shown, this search could cascade through any number of gateway SSCPs, in the search for LU-A. As that search cascades across a gateway, name translation may be performed.

Note that this, too, is a distributed directory. However, the SSCP search process is different from the control-point searches in APPN. In subarea networks, the initiating SSCP must communicate directly with all SSCPs in its multidomain network, so these SSCPs must all be in session with one another.[7] In the subarea network (see Figure 15.6), cascading of the search does occur, but only among linearly connected network *gateways*. In APPN, on the other hand, there is no requirement that all the control points in an APPN network be in session with each other. Instead, the search cascades in a spanning tree

---

7.   The SSCPs are not, however, in session with SSCPs in the connected networks.

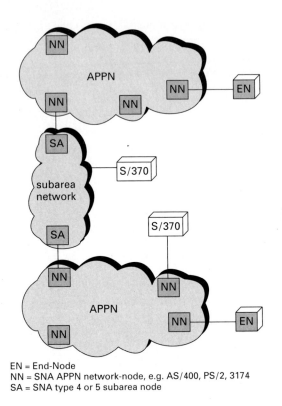

EN = End-Node
NN = SNA APPN network-node, e.g. AS/400, PS/2, 3174
SA = SNA type 4 or 5 subarea node

Figure 15.7 Joining of APPN and subarea networks.

throughout the APPN network. Each network-node retains information about the search until all of its children in that tree reply.

15.5   DYNAMIC APPN-SUBAREA LU-LU SESSIONS

15.5.1   Introduction

Ease of use for combinations of APPN and subarea networks continues to receive much attention. Simple ways are now available for using independent LUs.[8] *Sessions can now be dynamically established*, with little or no systems definition, between independent LUs in APPN nodes and either (a) mainframe LUs in subarea networks or (b) other independent LUs in other APPN networks that are also attached to subarea networks.

APPN network-nodes can effectively tie together subarea networks and APPN networks through their intermediate-routing services. To the subarea network, the APPN network appears simply as a single, composite LEN peripheral-node. To the APPN network, the entire subarea network appears simply as a single, composite LEN end-node.

8.   An independent LU does not require SSCP-LU sessions and an activation command (ACTLU) from a remote control point. Independent LUs can be either primary or secondary LUs.

The objective is to make the combination of subarea and APPN networks, joined at one or more subarea boundary-functions, to appear to be seamless, as illustrated in Figure 15.7. Moreover, a subarea network can act as an intermediate stage between two APPN networks. These operations are explained in the following.

15.5.2 Boundary-Node Surrogate

Transmission through a subarea network always requires the assistance of one or more SSCPs. One major reason for this is that the SSCP translates LU_names to network addresses, and provides the network addresses for inclusion in the transmission headers (THs). Nevertheless, this does not mean that the independent LUs had to be defined in the SSCP beforehand. The SSCP is able to dynamically support a `Bind` request from an independent LU in an APPN network, and to facilitate operation of the `Bind` in the subarea network.

How is this possible, if the independent LU does not have a session with an SSCP? The answer is that it can borrow one from a boundary-function when it wants to use the subarea network. Just as there were cross-domain SSCP-to-SSCP sessions to facilitate cross-domain LU-LU sessions, so also there can be BF-to-SSCP sessions to facilitate independent LU use of subarea networks. The borrowed session used for this communication is the SSCP-PU session for the node in which the boundary-function is located.

For this purpose, three new SNA commands were added to the SNA request repertoire so that the boundary-function could communicate with its SSCP while helping to establish an LU-LU session. These all correspond to requests in a single network [SNAPersp90] :

- `BF-INIT` corresponds to `Initiate`
- `BF-CINIT` corresponds to `Control_Initiate`
- `BF-SESSST` corresponds to `Session_Started`

Four other commands were also added to assist in termination of a session or takeover of an SSCP: `BF-TERM`, `BF-SESSEND`, `BF-CLEANUP`, and `BF-SESSINFO`.

Recall that within an APPN network, sessions may connect independent LUs (which use their local control points, and do not require any assistance from any SSCP). Now, using the boundary-function, sessions may connect mixed pairs of LUs (one independent of an SSCP and one dependent on an SSCP). The independent LU initiates the session. Three cases of boundary-function assistance are shown in Figure 15.8. These are:

- An APPN end-node attached to a boundary-function in a subarea network, as in Figure 15.8(a). For example, a T 2.1 PS/2 attached to a BF in one subarea can communicate with a host in another subarea. An independent LU in the PS/2 is thus in session with a mainframe's LU.

- A similar case, in Figure 15.8(b), but with the APPN end-node attached to an APPN network, and still communicating with a subarea network LU. Again, the internetwork connection is by an APPN network-node connected to a subarea boundary-function.

- As shown in Figure 15.8(c), two T 2.1 nodes, each attached (via different APPN networks) to different boundary-nodes in the subarea network. Independent LUs in these two end-nodes may have sessions using the subarea network as an intermediary backbone. To the T 2.1 nodes that are attached to boundary-functions, these sessions appear as if the

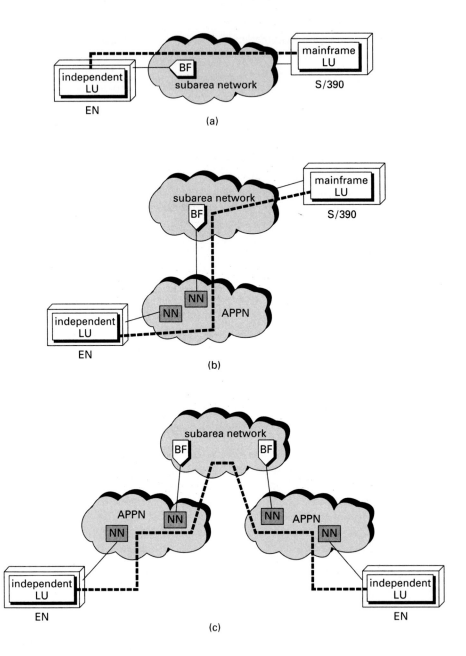

BF = Boundary-Function
NN = Network-Node

Figure 15.8 Independent LUs and subarea networks; **(a)** independent LU-to-mainframe LU with APPN end-node attached to subarea network; **(b)** independent LU-to-mainframe LU via APPN and subarea network; **(c)** independent LU-to-independent LU via two APPNs and subarea network.

T 2.1 nodes were adjacent to each other. The backbone, in fact, can be a single-domain or multiple-domain network, or it can be multiple subarea networks.

15.5.3 Dynamic Subarea-Network Access

Sessions in the three cases of Figure 15.8, described above, can be established dynamically, without any prior systems definition of the independent LUs that are attached to subarea networks. The way this spontaneous session establishment works is shown in Figure 15.9.

Binding an independent LU and a mainframe LU.   The sequence for the two cases of Figure 15.8(a) and Figure 15.8(b) is given in Figure 15.9(a) as follows:

1.   The boundary-function (BF) in a subarea-node, with a link to an adjacent APPN node, receives an unsolicited `Bind`. It comes from an independent LU in the type 2.1 end-node that wants to establish a session with a mainframe LU located in the subarea network. As far as the attached T 2.1 node is concerned, the entire subarea network appears to be just another T 2.1 node.

2.   The boundary-function recognizes this `Bind` as an extended `Bind` from an independent LU. It therefore seeks help from its SSCP because it lacks a network address for the destination LU, and it also needs some routing information. The BF sends a `BF-INIT`, containing a copy of the `Bind`, to its SSCP.

3.   The originating LU is not included in the SSCP directory. The SSCP will therefore get a network address for a surrogate LU that appears to be located with the BF. The SSCP accordingly issues a `Request-Network_Address-Assignment` (RNAA) request to the PU in the BF's node. The response to the `RNAA` contains an address relative to the BF subarea (i.e., including the subarea address for that subarea-node). The SSCP then proceeds to use its normal techniques for checking the destination LU location and availability. If the destination LU is located in another domain or in another SNA network, cross-domain SSCP-SSCP interactions are executed as discussed previously.

4.   The SSCP is then able to send a `BF-CINIT` to the BF. This contains the network addresses and virtual-route information. This, in effect, tells the BF to forward the `Bind` on toward the destination mainframe LU. If a virtual route is not available, the PU of the subarea-node containing the BF is asked to activate one.

5.   The BF then has all the information it needs to send a `Bind` to the mainframe LU, using the subarea type of transmission header (FID-4), including the appropriate network addresses.

6.   After a positive response to the `Bind`, BF advises its SSCP of the activation of the session by sending a `BF-SESSST`.

Binding two independent LUs.   The sequence for the case of Figure 15.8(c), two APPN nodes with independent LUs, *connected through a subarea network*, requires a few additional steps. These are shown in Figure 15.9(b). This sequence is the same as in Figure 15.9(a), except that the `Bind` (step 5.1) is forwarded from BF #1 to BF #2, instead of directly

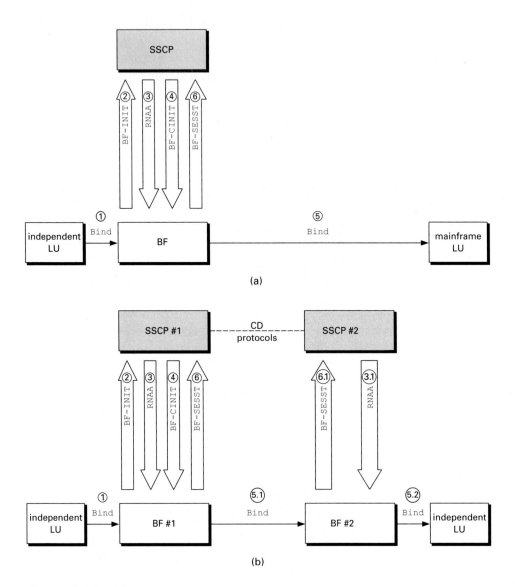

BF = Boundary Function
CD = Cross Domain

Figure 15.9 Session initiation between independent LU and subarea mainframe LU and another independent LU: **(a)** Independent LU to subarea dependent LU; **(b)** independent LU to independent LU via subarea network.

to the destination LU. Also, steps 3.1, 5.2, and 6.1 are added as follows:

- 3.1   The BF #1 needs a subarea-network address for the destination LU, which in this case is also an independent LU. That must be obtained by the SSCP that controls BF #2 (to which the destination LU is connected). BF #2's SSCP sends an `RNAA` request to the BF # 2, via its PU, to have an address assigned. That address is returned in the response to the `RNAA`.[9]

- 5.1   The `Bind` is sent from BF #1 to BF #2, which converts the subarea type FID-4 transmission header of the subarea network to a type FID-2, which the attached APPN node can accept.

- 5.2   The BF #2 forwards the `Bind` to the destination LU in the attached APPN node.

- 6.1   BF #2 also advises its SSCP of the session activation by sending a `BF'-SESSST`.

Session termination uses an `UnBind` on the LU-LU session. The intervening boundary-functions note such `UnBinds`, and notify their controlling SSCPs by sending a `BF-SESSEND`. The SSCPs then can send `Free_Network_Address` (FNA) requests to the relevant subarea PUs.

Remembering an LU.   We have seen the situation where an originating independent LU makes itself known to an SSCP by submitting a `Bind` via a boundary-function. However, in the above we did not ask how the SSCP knew where the destination independent LU was. What is the ability of an SSCP to know about an independent LU in a connected APPN network? Of course, those LUs could be system-defined, with the apparent location in the APPN node attached to the boundary-function. That often is the desirable approach. In general, however, one wants to reduce the system definition burden. Moreover, one needs to be able to accommodate changing conditions dynamically. The SSCP accordingly is able to *remember an independent LU for a specified time period*, once it has requested a session in or through the subarea network, as described above. *Thus, the independent LU is dynamically defined when it first uses the subarea network, and that definition remains for some specified time thereafter.* During that time period, mainframe LUs within the subarea network and independent LUs looking for a session across the subarea network, will be able to find the dynamically defined destination LUs in the SSCP directories.

While these approaches to APPN-subarea cooperation are very helpful, there is a known requirement for still further improvements. There are ample opportunities for further control-point cooperation to facilitate still easier LU-LU session establishment across combinations of subarea and APPN networks. When VTAM/NCP is enhanced with APPN function, allowing APPN control points to operate within the subarea nodes, then the APPN and subarea directory functions will cooperate fully.[10]

---

9.   The `RNAA` would not be needed if the address of BF # 2 had already been established as a result of an earlier LU-LU session through that same BF.

10.   IBM also intends to put APPN on its mainframes (e.g., S/390s), according to Ellen Hancock, vice president and general manager, IBM Communication Systems, as reported in *Communications Week*, March 11, 1991.

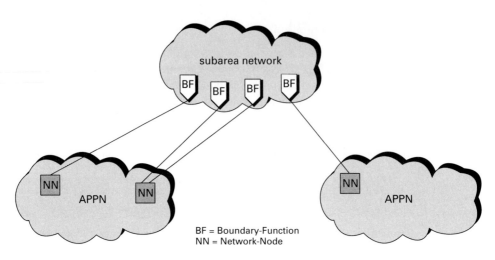

Figure 15.10 Multiple APPN–subarea connections.

15.5.4 Multiple APPN-Subarea Connections

Availability, throughput, and congestion-reduction require multiple connections between networks. Then, if one of the link connections that an independent LU may use is down, or if the connecting communications controller is down, the LU may choose another link for a session restart or for subsequent sessions. Accordingly, an APPN network can have multiple tails connecting it to the same or multiple communication-control-units of the subarea network, as shown in Figure 15.10. A given network-node can also have tails to multiple disconnected subarea networks. Given the dynamic definition of independent LUs described above, users in an APPN network can dynamically access applications in the subarea network across different connections. These APPN-to-subarea network connections may be to different subareas in different domains, in the same or different subarea networks. This provides flexibility while still providing greatly reduced system definition.

VTAM achieves both the dynamic definition of independent LUs and the multiple-tails ability by capitalizing on the fact that the cross-domain protocols had earlier been built to dynamically define cross-domain LUs. The simple expedient was to have all APPN independent LUs defined as cross-domain resources. This is also consistent, considering that the APPN independent resource is controlled by the remote control point in the node of the independent LU.

Inter-network logon filters. Not all distant LUs may be welcome in a given subarea network, however. For security reasons, a systems programmer can limit the acceptance of `Binds` from connected APPN networks. The acceptable `Binds`, for example, may be only those (a) from APPN LUs that are previously defined in the subarea network, or (b) from LUs that are dynamically defined in the subarea network and send a `Bind` over a predetermined connection between the APPN and the subarea network, or (c) a combination of these two limits. By the use of session-management exits in VTAM, the acceptance of incoming

`Binds` can be further screened by various criteria. For example, `Binds` might be accepted only from 9 A.M. to 3 P.M. Similarly, outgoing `Binds` can be restricted to certain links on one or more connected subarea networks. Of course, the other security provisions, discussed in Section 4.4.7, also apply.

15.5.5   Finding the Inter-Subnetwork-Node

There is one other piece to the multi-subnetwork picture. How does an APPN end-node find the network-node that can forward its `Bind` to a subarea network? The destination LU might be in the subarea network or in some other APPN network. To find the LU, a `Bind` has to find its way *via an inter-subnetwork node into the connected subarea network*.

   We will see in Chapter 16 that several *ES-IS protocols* are being defined in OSI for finding serving nodes. We will also see there that various *LAN discovery protocols* are similarly in use. However, in the specific case of connecting APPN and subarea networks, some simple solutions are currently available, as follows. There are three ways to do this:

1.   In each APPN network, one or more network-nodes that is connected to the subarea network can use the *wild card* (see Section 14.4.2). The wild card LU-Name is just an asterisk (*). Then, when an APPN directory search is being made, and no other node has found the desired LU, the wild card will indicate that the destination might be obtained via that network-node with the wild card. That network-node then forwards the `Bind` to the subarea network.

2.   Other *general names*, system-defined in the connecting network-nodes, can be similarly used (see Section 14.4.2) to indicate that LUs with a particular name-stem can be obtained via a network-node connected to the subarea network.

3.   Certain destination LUs can be system-defined in the network-nodes connected to the subarea.

In each of these cases, the `Bind` is sent via a network-node to a boundary-function in the subarea network. Then the procedures described earlier are followed, to get the `Bind` to the destination LU in the subarea network or to the next boundary-function. In the latter case, when the `Bind` is passed by the next boundary-function to a network-node in the destination APPN network, normal APPN directory procedures are followed. These are roughly the same procedures as when a serving network-node receives a `Bind` without an RSCV (i.e., a directory search and route calculation, as in Sections 14.4 and 14.6).

15.6   OTHER DYNAMIC SUBAREA DEFINITION

Full APPN capabilities are not yet available in the interaction between APPN and subarea networks. This would involve full dynamic topology exchange, dynamic directory flows, and dynamic route setup. A significant step has been the dynamic definition of independent LUs in subarea networks, described above in Section 15.5.3 In addition, several other small steps have been taken recently to develop dynamic systems definition in subarea networks, as follows.

Dynamic configuration of channel-attached devices.   VTAM, under MVS, supports the dynamic, less disruptive addition of communication controllers (e.g., 3745) and cluster (establishment) controllers (e.g., 3174, 3274) to existing networks. With this capability, the user can define and activate such units attached to the channel interface. This becomes even more significant with the Establishment System Connection (ESCON), an optical fiber channel connection (see Section 18.10). ESCON, in effect, converts the channel connection into a local area network spanning distances of up to nine kilometers. Control units on ESCON can be attached with no disruption to mainframe services.

The definition and activation of the control units are accomplished by cooperation between the MVS operating system and VTAM, the telecommunications access method. When the control unit is physically attached, the operating system sends a `Read_Configuration_Data` channel-command to the control unit to gather vital product data (see Section 4.4.6). MVS creates an advisory message on the acquisition, which is picked up by VTAM. The information so provided is sufficient for the definition of the PU and the LUs in the control unit. Names for these are generated by VTAM, and default options are used where necessary. Control-unit definition is provided by easy-to-use panel driven functions, which removes the requirement to IML/IPL MVS in order to modify units or to add them to an existing system.

Line changes.   In subarea networks, using type 4 nodes with the Network Control Program (NCP), more planning is needed for line changes than in APPN networks. Nevertheless, considerable flexibility is obtainable. For example, one suggested line change sequence is, roughly:

1. The Network Control Programs (NCPs) of the communication controllers (like the 3745) are defined (in a process called *system-generation*) with spare line definitions.
2. Spare line-cards are included in the communication controllers, and these match the spare line-definitions.
3. When lines are to be added, the spare line-card is added to the configuration by operator console action.

Dynamic switched definition.   Adding switched devices to the network can also be nearly automatic. Dynamic definitions can be obtained for dial-in devices not previously defined to VTAM. During the system connection, the `XID` command at the link level obtains the identification of the dial-in device. This product information is in two fields of the XID: the product type is identified by the *id_Block* and the particular device is identified by the *id_NUM*, which is unique within a product type. Given this identification, the mainframe host can dynamically assign a PU_name and LU_names to complete the definition.

This dynamic assignment is done with reusable model definitions that have been built for the Physical Units (PUs) and Logical Units (LUs) of common devices. The installation can predefine a block of PU_names and LU_names for each anticipated model. These models are then used in installation exit routines for configuration services. When a given device dials in, it is recognized via the XID, and the appropriate model is used to generate the necessary PU_name and LU_names and to complete the definition.

15.7   SUBAREA PATH CONTROL

As noted earlier, of the seven layers in communications architectures, it is primarily the layer 3c that is unique in SNA subarea networks. Currently, the largest number of private subnetworks in the world are of this architecture, which was designed for customer control and high throughput. These subarea networks will continue to be the mainstay for many enterprises, fitting into and internetworking with the newer peer-oriented configurations. Some of the important layer-3 characteristics of these subarea networks are discussed below.

15.7.1   Subarea Addressing

The set of addresses within one SNA network is called an *addressing area*. In subarea networks, this addressing area is divided into a number of *subareas*. Each addressing subarea is then further divided into *elements*. A particular network address is then the combination of a subarea address and an element address.

The two parts of the address are shown in Figure 15.11. With this arrangement, *much of the routing can be handled by examining only the subarea address*. When the message finally arrives at the correct subarea, the element address is examined.

SNA subarea networks assign such numerical addresses to each SSCP, PU, and LU. The customer defines only the LU_names. The system-definition process adds the network address to each LU_name. Or, the specific address is assigned dynamically as part of a dial connection using the switched network. Independent LUs are defined dynamically in the subarea network as described in Section 15.5.3.

Older SNA networks use a 16-bit address with a variable length 1- to 8-bit subarea address and the remainder as element address. Newer subarea networks use an 8-bit

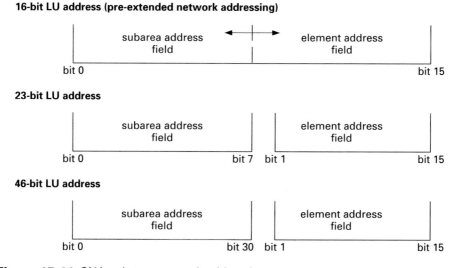

Figure 15.11 SNA subarea network addressing.

subarea address and a 15-bit element address. This allows up to 32,767 element addresses within each of the subareas. The current architecture allows up to 31 bits for subarea address, and 15 bits for element address. However, not all 31 bits are currently used in products.

The PUs in hosts and communications controllers have one (or possibly more) subarea address(es) assigned to them. Five such subareas are shown in Figure 15.1. *All LUs in peripheral-nodes (e.g., type 2 cluster controllers) adopt the subarea address of the host or communications controller to which they are attached.* However, type 2 peripheral-nodes do not understand the subarea network addresses, and depend on the boundary-function for address interpretation.

Shortened addresses.   Any node that deals with a shortened address requires that some adjacent node provide address transformation services for it. In the case of cluster controllers, for example, it seems reasonable that fewer than 256 LUs need ever be addressed within that one node. Therefore, 8 bits of address seem more than adequate; so only 8 bits need be transmitted to that node, which is designated as a type 2 node. The TH used with a type 2 node requires 8 bits for an origin address and another 8 bits for a destination address. The shortening of the address to 8 bits can and does take place in the communications controller or host that is adjacent to the cluster controller. The adjacent type 4 or type 5 node **boundary-function** performs this address translation, as noted in Section 15.2.1, so as to reduce the burden on the cluster controller.

Link addresses.   To simplify configuration system management, the current SNA network services also utilize network addresses to identify links between nodes. A link is activated via the PU services of the node that contains the primary station for that link.

When using the switched network, the physical link is provided via the dial procedure. The dial address is used to establish the physical connection. Once the dial connection is established, the same layer 3 addressing discussed above is used for communication among LUs.

Transmission groups.   This term is used in subarea networks to connote any physical connection between type 4 or type 5 nodes. It may include, for example, LANs, X.25 subnetworks, or multiple point-to-point links. The latter deserves further attention. It is very advantageous to have a number of parallel physical links act as one logical link. Multilink *transmission groups* are used to bundle links together into a single-link appearance. Messages from one or more *sessions* are distributed across the parallel links according to *priority*. This first of all provides additional bandwidth. In addition, it offers increased availability. If one of the links in a transmission group fails, the traffic simply continues to use the remaining links, without disrupting sessions. Because messages traveling on different links can arrive out of order, a sequence number on each message enables the receiver to re-sequence them and avoid duplicates.

15.7.2   Route Control

Explicit and Virtual Routes.   We found earlier that each hop between adjacent nodes can have two levels of protocols: data-link control and transmission groups. The latter applies an oversight link service, particularly including the management of priority in link services. In a similar fashion, the path between two subareas, in a subarea network, has two levels of protocol at layer 3 for route control:

1.   *Explicit route control* creates a sequence of physical links (or transmission groups). An explicit route is composed of the series of physical link connections between an origin subarea-node and a destination subarea-node.

2.   *Virtual route control* manages the flows on a route between subarea-nodes. Sessions are assigned to a virtual route. Each session is given a priority by the user at session initiation. *That priority determines the queue that is used at each transmission group.* In addition, congestion on that route is monitored and controlled by virtual-route pacing.

A virtual route is defined by the combination of a virtual route number, its priority, and the origin/destination pair. A virtual route takes on the physical characteristics of its underlying explicit route. The combination of the explicit route and virtual route characteristics constitutes a *class of service*.

Virtual route pacing.   The virtual route employs dynamic pacing, in which the window size is influenced by the nodes along the route as they detect congestion. The FID-4 Transmission Header (TH) includes a set of indicators for window control (see Figure 15.12). When the virtual route is first activated, minimum and maximum window sizes are defined, depending on the characteristics of the links in the underlying explicit route. Initially, the window size is set to its minimum value. Then, as permission is granted for each additional window, the size of the window is increased by one, up to the maximum value. At any time, however, if a node along the route detects congestion, it can reduce the window size. Depending on the node's level of congestion, it can either decrement the window size by one (using the virtual-route change-window indicator) or immediately slam it down to the minimum (using the virtual-route reset-window indicator).

   The maximum and minimum window sizes can be specified at system generation time or by an access-method exit-routine. For paths composed of TP links, the default minimum size is equal to the number of transmission groups in the explicit route. The default for the maximum window size is three times the minimum window size. The window sizes for channel connections are different.

Route selection.   The class of service specified by the user determines the routes that can be used for a given session. The class of service, for example, may pertain to a required response time, availability, or security. In the subarea network, the selection of which routes meet a particular class of service is done by the system designer. This information is defined to the system. In defining the network, the customer's system designer defines the available classes of service, the virtual routes that they map to, and the transmission groups that the underlying explicit routes traverse. An SSCP then uses this information in a class-of-service table, which lists the available virtual-route/transmission priority pairs.

   The information about allowable routes is distributed among the subarea-nodes. Each node contains only the information needed to route data to the next subarea along the path.

bytes

0	FID4—format identification (0100) TG sweep indicator (0 or 1) ER and VR support indicator (0 or 1) VR pacing count indicator network priority (0 or 1)	TG segmenting field reserved bits
2	initial explicit route number (4 bits) explicit route number (4 bits)	virtual route number (4 bits) reserved bits transmission priority field (2 bits)
4	virtual-route change window indicator (0 or 1) TG non-FIFO indicator (0 or 1) virtual-route sequencing and type indicator (2 bits) transmission-group sequence number field (bits 4–15)	
6	virtual-route pacing request (0 or 1) virtual-route pacing response (0 or 1) virtual-route change window reply indicator (0 or 1) virtual-route reset-window indicator (0 or 1) virtual-route send sequence number field (bits 4–15)	
8	DSAF—destination subarea address field (4 bytes)	
12	OSAF—origin subarea address field (4 bytes)	
16	reserved (3 bits) SNA indicator (0 or 1) mapping field (2 bits) reserved expedited flow indicator (0 or 1)	reserved byte
18	DEF—destination element field (2 bytes)	
20	OEF—origin element field (2 bytes)	
22	SNF—sequence number field (2 bytes)	
24	DCF—data count field	

Figure 15.12 Transmission header for FID type 4 [LY43-0081].

Conclusion

The more than 30,000 SNA subarea networks around the world are a highly evolved, dependable set of networks that carry a tremendous workload. They can be expected to continue to provide dependable service for the foreseeable future. The communications technology has, however, advanced rapidly. Local area networks, peer-to-peer dynamic definition technologies, international standards, the need to transport multiple protocols, and the advent of high-performance subnetworks based on optical fibers all are developing simultaneously. All need to find their place in an overall continuously evolving architecture.

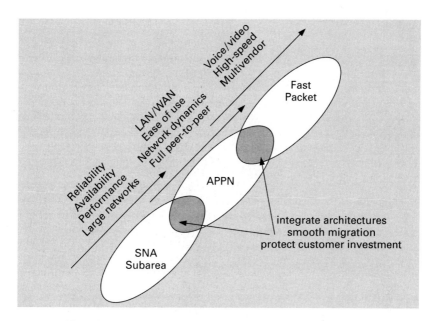

Figure 15.13 Overlapping SNA technical directions.

This chapter has shown the start of that central piece of this picture concerning the integration of APPN and subarea networks. Emphasis was placed on the approaching seamless combination as far as session initiation is concerned. Any to any LU-LU sessions, on LANs, WANs, or any combination, using higher-performance LU 6.2s are the result.

The preceding chapter described the newer APPN capabilities in dynamic network definition and reconfiguration, and projected the integration of APPN with OSI. The following chapters will show the integration of these multiple layer-3c protocols with LANs, and the projected integration of high-speed facilities now in the making. All of these movements are interrelated and fit into an overall architecture such as that depicted in Figure 3.14.

Prognosis. Under the architectural umbrella of end-to-end systems management, broader application-services, and multiple protocols, the SNA technical direction can be discerned to include three overlapping movements, shown in Figure 15.13:

1. The SNA subarea architecture has been developed for large wide area networks, with emphasis on performance, reliability, and availability, with less attention to ease of use.

2. APPN brings a practical LU-LU capability across LANs and WANs, using LU 6.2, and emphasizing ease of use, network dynamics, and full peer-to-peer operations.

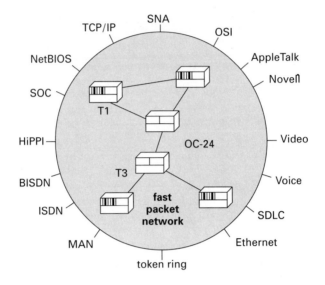

Figure 15.14 Fast packet network and its projected users.

3. Fast packet routing at the lower layers, with high-speed links, will provide efficient carriage of voice, video, and data, and multiprotocol transport. The goal is illustrated in Figure 15.14.

Each new stage overlaps with the former, requiring an integration of architectures, and a smooth migration to protect the investment in prior technologies. At the same time, this evolving SNA technology becomes more common with and integrated with OSI. Most of the diverse facilities in layers 1, 2, and 3a (LANs, FDDI, X.25, ISDN) are already common. The Common Programming Interface will in effect make upper data-exchange layers appear to be more common. The incorporation of SNA addresses within OSI NSAP structure will facilitate interoperation. Finally many application-services at layer 7 (e.g., X.400, X.500, system management) become either common or linked by application-layer gateways. Thus, we see SNA both extending and converging simultaneously.

Acknowledgments

I am particularly indebted to M. Pozefsky, O. H. Choi, J. C. Fletcher, and J. T. Carroll for valuable input or reviews of this chapter.

EXERCISES

15.1 Name three purposes of boundary-functions in subarea networks.

15.2 How does a session get established when the communicating LUs are controlled by different SSCPs?

15.3 With multiple interconnected subarea networks, how is the destination LU found?

15.4 How does an independent LU in an APPN network get assistance from an SSCP to set up a session with a mainframe LU?

15.5 Is there any way that an SSCP can know the BF location of an APPN LU, besides system definition?

15.6 How does a parallel link transmission group make use of the total bandwidth of the links?

Part 5
Link and Subnetwork
Access

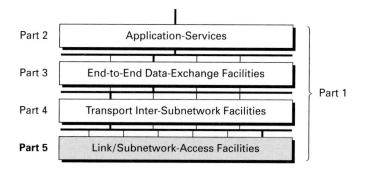

Part 5 provides an introduction to the multitude of lower-layer offerings (in layers 1 through 3a). It shows how these *Link/Subnetwork-Access* facilities can be common parts of the multiprotocol structure of Figure 3.14. It describes the important LAN facilities and the rapid movement to higher-speed, fiber-optic facilities.

Chapter 16, Link/Subnetwork-Access presents the architecture for treating the expanding universe of links and subnetworks (e.g., LANs, MANs, X.25, ISDN, and fast-packet networks) as lower-layer services that can be commonly available to multiple upper-layer protocol stacks. The various link-level directory functions for locating inter-subnetwork nodes and address resolution are reviewed.

Chapter 17, Local Area Networks, describes three members of the important local area network (LAN) family: CSMA/CD, token ring, and token bus. Bridge, router, and gateway interconections of LANs, WANs, and mainframes are described and analyzed.

Chapter 18, High-Speed Services, describes the remarkable growth of high-speed technologies. High-performance fast-packet switching in WANs, FDDI, MANs, SMDS, ISDN, Serial Optical Channels, and gigabit facilities crowd the scene.

16
Link/Subnetwork
Structures and Address
Resolution

16.1 INTRODUCTION

An important requirement of enterprise networks is that end-systems (like mainframes and establishment controllers) and intermediate-systems have transparent and extensible access to *multiple* types of transmission links and subnetworks. These lower layers should be *commonly accessible by multiple types of layer (3 through 7) protocols.* That lower-layer variety, including LANs, X.25, ISDN, frame relay, MANs, and point-to-point links, thus becomes common to OSI, TCP/IP, and SNA upper-level protocols. NetBIOS, too, gets access to a variety of LANs. The concerted management of the access to such a broad family of common links and subnetworks is here called **Link/Subnetwork-Access** (LSA).[1] This concept was introduced in Section 3.4.2, using Figure 3.14. It concerns the facilities below the LSA boundary in that figure. The *formalization of an open interface at this level* is another major step in the evolving OSNA.[2] The fundamental design approach of this concept, and its rationale, are discussed further in this chapter.

Given this flexibility in the use of multiple types of link/subnetwork facilities, a corollary requirement is the dynamic binding of these lower facilities to the inter-subnetwork facilities of layer 3c. The ease of addition and change of elements in these lower-layer facilities is aided by dynamic address resolution protocols, also discussed below.

16.2 TRANSMISSION OPTIONS

The available options in the lower layers are many, and their number is growing. Some of the transmission services that could coexist in an end-system are shown in Figure 16.1, and are reiterated below.

- X.25 packet switched virtual circuits, ISO 8208/7776

---

1. IBM documents also refer to this as "*Lower-Layer Services Architecture.*"
2. Some elements of this architecture have been published as of this writing [HLMa, HLMb].

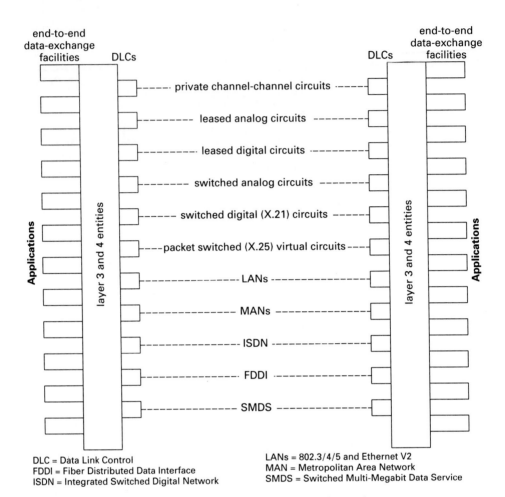

Figure 16.1 The wide range of link and subnetwork alternatives.

- Local Area Networks IEEE 802.2
  - CSMA/CD 802.3, Token-Bus 802.4, Token-Ring 802.5
- Metropolitan Area Networks IEEE 802.2, 802.6
- Fiber Distributed Data Interface (FDDI) LANs IEEE 802.2 and ANSI X3T9.5
- ISDN (Basic, Primary, and Broadband)
- Frame relay I.122
- SMDS (Switched Multi-Megabit Data Service)
- High-speed digital data circuits (T1, T2, T3, SONET)
- Enterprise System Connection (a serial optical channel)

- Link Access Procedures
  - SDLC
  - HDLC
  - IDLC (ISDN DLC, a multiplexing link standard under development in standards bodies)

Multiple protocol stacks in the higher layers of the communications systems (layers 3c through 7) must accommodate this variety of lower-layer services. Therefore each of these lower-layer services are best managed as one of a number of options, appearing to upper layers as alternative logical-links (see Figure 12.2).

16.3   LOGICAL-LINKS AND ACCESS-LINKS

There is a common way of looking at all of these options. Referring again to Figures 12.2 and 3.14, a network entity at layer 3c uses lower-layer facilities in layers 1 through 3a to communicate with a similar network-entity in another node. (A match-maker layer 3b is sometimes also needed to "glue" 3c to 3a.) This logical circuit between a pair of 3c network-entities has been called a **logical-link**. One end of the logical-link is provided by entities of a link/subnetwork-access facility. This end might, for example, be for an 802.2 logical-link in LAN attached devices, an SDLC logical-link in cluster (establishment) controllers, or an X.25 logical channel in X.25 end-systems.

Another way of stating this is that logical-links are the service provided by *any type of subnetwork*, if we define the term *subnetwork* very broadly, as in ISO 8648-3. There the term *subnetwork* can be applied to point-to-point connections, LANs, and X.25 PSDNs.[3] Any of these can participate in an "internet" that connects subnetworks in layers 1 through 3a.

The services provided by link/subnetwork-access (LSA) may be connection-oriented or connectionless. Separate logical-links are used by each type. Both connection-oriented and connectionless traffic may share the same access-link.

The protocols of links (like SDLC) and subnetworks (like X.25) encapsulate all higher-layer protocols. One can also think of this process as an internet-like process, where a higher layer-3c protocol is the *encapsulated protocol*.

16.4   SUBNETWORK TRENDS

The link/subnetwork-access facilities also are changing rapidly. Three factors will probably affect the future character of these services:

- The technologies in these transmission services will be increasingly dominated by fiber and digital technologies, offering economical high bandwidth and low error rates.

---

3.   With this broad definition of "subnetwork," the link/subnetwork-access could properly be called simply "subnetwork-access." However, for clarity, we shall stick to the more cumbersome but more explicit link/subnetwork-access terminology.

- The traffic will include expansions of current interactive traffic with a newer growth of large data transfers for image, high-resolution graphics, and data retrieval.
- The available bandwidth will increase the use of teleprocessing facilities as an extension of the local system channel or bus for cooperative processing.

There are many possible combinations of wide area networks (WANs), metropolitan area networks (MANs), local area networks (LANs), and serial optical channels. All of these can be considered to be subnetworks. An internet (at layer 3c) may be used to interconnect them. OSNA thus considers them to be available options for SNA and non-SNA upper-layer architectures like OSI, TCP/IP, and NetBIOS.

16.5   LINK/SUBNETWORK TERMINOLOGY

In following chapters, a further set of link and subnetwork terms needs to be clarified. Figure 16.2 shows the relation among lower-layer communication resources. Key terminology definitions are as follows:

- *Logical-Link:* This is a general term for the link/subnetwork-access facilities that enable an interaction between two specific network-entities. The network-entities in question can usually be considered to be at layer 3c (though if layer 3c is null, the interaction is between entities in the layer directly connected to the link/subnetwork-access facility). Logical-links use all the facilities below the link/subnetwork-access boundary. In general, the logical-link is *a set of protocol machines* that manage the end-to-end exchange of traffic over a real or virtual circuit.

- *X.25 Logical Channel:* The functions in the X.25 packet layer 3a that manages the exchange of data traffic over an X.25 virtual circuit. Essentially, it is a particular example of a logical-link that connects a pair of layer-3c network-entities.

- *SNA/X.25 Logical-Link:* This is the X.25 Logical Channel plus the special SNA end-to-end protocols (called SNA, Qualified or Extended, X.25 Logical-Link Control) that are added to the X.25 protocols when SNA data is carried. (The SNA/X.25 LLC is not to be confused with the DLC LLC.) In the SNA world, this SNA/X.25 LLC amounts to a layer 3b, and lies above the X.25 packet layer 3a. It supports the end-to-end exchange of SNA-based data traffic over an X.25 virtual circuit (see also Section 19.5.2).

- *Link:* A link represents a complete connection to an adjacent node, and includes both the link stations *and the physical media* over which data is transmitted. The link, for example, may be a LAN, an ISDN connection, a S/390 channel, or an SDLC point-to-point line. The link provides a communication between network-entities. It is, therefore, often used interchangeably with the most general definition of subnetwork.

- *Link Station:* Usually refers to a DLC function. It includes protocol machines to manage the elements of procedure at layer 2b required for the exchange of data with another link station in an adjacent node. This, for example, includes the management of instances of the LLC and MAC sublayers and the physical layer.

A link station is associated with one or more connection end-points (CEPs) within LLC-layer service-access-points (SAPs). Thus, for an SDLC primary link-station commu-

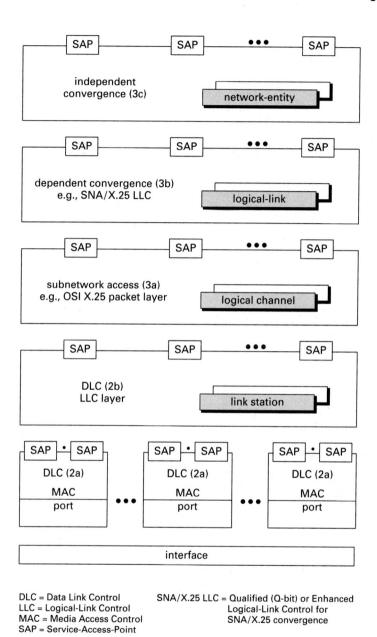

DLC = Data Link Control   SNA/X.25 LLC = Qualified (Q-bit) or Enhanced
LLC = Logical-Link Control   Logical-Link Control for
MAC = Media Access Control   SNA/X.25 convergence
SAP = Service-Access-Point

Figure 16.2 Communication resources in layers 2 and 3.

nicating with *n* secondary link-stations, the primary has *n* CEPs. Each secondary has one CEP.

- *Port:* A hardware-addressable component of an interface at layer 2a by which a node has access to a transmission medium, and through which data passes into and out of a node. There is a one-to-one correlation between DLC Media Access Control (MAC) interface and port. In most cases, the MAC interface and port are synonymous.

■ *Transmission Group (TG):* A transmission group represents a group of parallel links (or subnetworks) connecting adjacent nodes, *that is viewed as a composite unit.* A TG number is associated with each group. When more than one TG connects two adjacent nodes, they are known as parallel TGs. When a node has TGs connecting to more than one adjacent node, it has multiple TGs. A TG may, for example, consist of LANs, point-to-point SDLC lines, or a S/390 channel.

Another term that is sometimes useful is **access-link**. The information flow from an end-system, that is using one or more logical-links, flows over *physical media* sometimes called access-links. *Access-links connect one end-system to another end-system or to an intermediate-system.* Common access-links are point-to-point lines and CPU channels.

Different logical-links may need to share the full bandwidth of an access-link. For example, the X.25 protocols allow multiple logical-links to share a single access-link. Usually, this is done by a serial access to the total bandwidth of the access line.

16.6   ARCHITECTURAL RELATIONSHIPS

The link/subnetwork-access of Figure 3.14 includes and manages the services of four or possibly five layers:

■   **Physical layer**.

■   **Media access control (MAC)**: the lower sublayer of DLC that supports the media-dependent functions, and uses the services of the physical layer to provide services to logical-link control. Different MAC functions are involved for HDLC and LANs 802.3, 4, 5, and 6, but in general, MAC may perform:

  ■   frame reception/generation
  ■   data integrity/error detection
  ■   address recognition/generation

■   **Logical-link control (LLC)**: the upper sublayer of DLC, controlling the flows of frames on the links. Different frame controls are used for HDLC (SDLC, LAPB and LAPD) and the LANs (IEEE 802.2).

■   **X.25 packet layer**: (a sublayer 3a), providing the X.25 interface to a PSDN, for setting up, taking down, and communicating over X.25 virtual circuits.

■   **Convergence layer:** E.g., the *SNA/X.25 Convergence* (an optional layer 3b, also called the SNA/X.25 Logical-Link Control), to augment the X.25 protocols so as to make them compatible with SNA features.

A typical layering structure for *separate* OSI and SNA models is shown in Figure 16.3. Note that on both the OSI and SNA sides, the X.25 packet-level protocol is operating as a subnetwork access protocol (layer 3a). On the SNA side, it operates beneath the SNA path control, which operates as an internet-like layer-3c protocol for X.25.

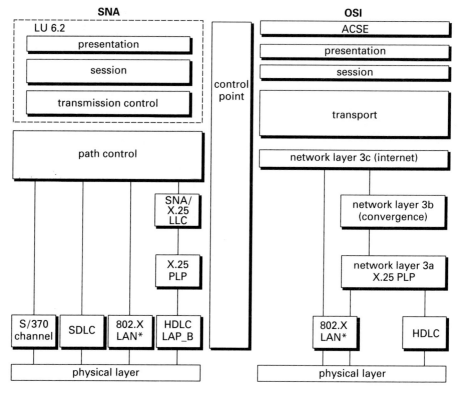

Figure 16.3 Typical layer structure for coresident SNA and OSI.

16.7   LOWER-LAYER SHARED FACILITIES

Since all link/subnetwork-access facilities are (or can be) identical in the OSI and SNA models, it is natural to expect that they could be shared by the OSI, SNA, and other stacks. The architecture for this sharing has also been called **Lower-Layer-Services Architecture (LSA)** [HLMa], [HLMb].

One possibility for such sharing is shown in Figure 16.4. In the OSI case, the path would be through the X.25 PLP, and then either to HDLC data-link control or to one of the 802.2 LANs. (The Internet and convergence sublayers may or may not be null.) Alternatively, the CLNP (Internet) layer could connect directly to one of the 802.2 LANs. Still another alternative is for the entire layer 3 to be null, in which case the 802.2 LANs are accessed by the OSI transport layer. In the LU 6.2 case, the path would be via path control and the convergence sublayer called the SNA/X.25 Logical-Link Control (LLC), to the X.25 PLP. Alternatively, in Figure 16.4, the LU 6.2 and path-control connection

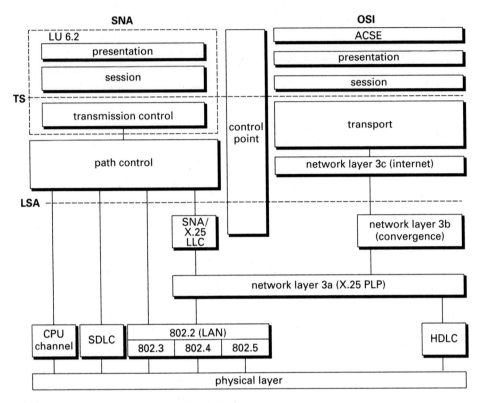

* 802.X is a common 802.2 Logical-Link Control Layer
  supporting MAC layers for 802.3/4/5/6 LANs and MANs.

Figure 16.4 Sharing multiple link services between dual stacks.

could be directly to either the CPU local channel, an SDLC subnetwork, or one of the 802.2 LANs.

The extension of this sharing concept would be for more link/subnetwork-access facilities to be shared by multiple stacks. It would provide a generalized framework for whatever lower-layer services are required by a particular node, including such optional items as: X.25, ISDN, frame relay, HDLC (SDLC, LAPB, LAPD), LAN (802.2, 802.3/4/ 5/6), FDDI, S/390 channel, and the serial optical channel. In general, the upper portion of one protocol stack (down to and including the equivalent of the OSI layer 3c) could use the lower portion of another one (up to and including the equivalent of the OSI layer 3a). This effectively would enable the lower-layer mechanisms of the latter to transport the higher-layer end-to-end protocols of the former.

The control point has the function of instructing the link/subnetwork-access to make a connection to a remote node, using a selected LSA protocol service. Once the connection was made, the control point proceeds with the link station activation (exchanging identifications, etc.).

16.8   THE LSA SWITCHING BOUNDARY

There is a recognized need for an efficient connection across the link/subnetwork-access (LSA) boundary of Figure 3.14. We thus see the opportunity for the *third fundamental switching point in the OSNA structure*. The purpose of that boundary is to readily connect a particular layer 3c–4 combination (e.g., an SNA path control and transmission control layer, or an OSI network and transport layer) to its counterpart layers 3c–4 in a destination-node, via a particular link or subnetwork. Following OSI structures, this ability to share physical links and subnetworks among colocated upper-protocol stacks is achieved by assigning different service-access-point (SAP) addresses for each upper-protocol stack.

The image then, is like another cross-bar switch, which enables two application-processes in two end-systems, to send traffic on one of several links or subnetworks by switching at this link/subnetwork-access boundary in each node so as to connect the appropriate upper-protocol stack and logical-link.

LSA routing.   Routing services below that link/subnetwork-access boundary routes the incoming and outgoing messages to and from the proper layer-3c network-entity. In OSI terms, different SAPs are assigned to different protocol stacks. A given layer-2 or layer-3a facility can thus be shared among multiple upper-layer stacks, each of which has a distinct SAP.

16.9   LINK/SUBNETWORK DIRECTORY PROTOCOLS

16.9.1   Introduction

The subject of directories was introduced in Chapter 8, and the concept of an integrated directory, with components in different layers, was discussed in Section 8.5.1. We now consider the contribution of directory services at the link/subnetwork layers (1 through 3a), in a multiprotocol environment. These are usually called **Address Resolution Protocols (ARPs)**, or **ES-IS protocols**, and they can be considered to operate at layer 3b. The primary purpose of ARPs is to find the subnetwork point of attachment (SNPA) address for an entity whose name or higher-level address is known. These address resolution protocols include:

- TCP/IP Address Resolution Protocol
- NetBIOS name resolution scheme
- ES-IS protocols developed for the OSI connection-oriented X.25 PSDNs
- ES-IS protocols for OSI connectionless network service (CLNS)
- A known requirement for comparable protocols for all 802 LANs

This important area is still in a state of flux. Further developments and consolidations are probable, so the following is only a current snapshot of the problems and possible approaches.

LAN directory services may be used solely for LAN operations or to operate in conjunction with WANs in a multi-subnetwork environment. LAN directory services have grown in these different environments, and they are still evolving [Dixon87]. In general,

ES = End-System

Figure 16.5 Typical configuration requiring dynamic definition.

they work by taking advantage of the LAN broadcasting capabilities. A query is broadcast
to all stations on a subnetwork; the station that can satisfy the query returns a response. A
discussion of the use of ARPs in LAN/WAN/LAN configurations, using Figure 16.5,
follows.

The backbone of Figure 16.5 could use one of a growing variety of link/subnetwork
technologies. It could, for example, be:

- A high-speed (16 Mbps) LAN or a (100 Mbps) FDDI
- A T1 or T3 mesh using data-only or voice-data bandwidth managers
- A Metropolitan Area Network (MAN)
- A fast-packet subnetwork using frame relay, ISDN narrow band, or ISDN broadband
  (ATM) interfaces
- A mesh of intermediate-systems, using layer-3 protocols such as TCP/IP, APPN, or
  X.25

Each of these except the last can operate below layer 3 in the data-transfer phase.
Considering Figure 16.5, and recalling the inter-subnetwork units defined in Section 12.5,
the inter-subnetwork units "C" can be one of three types:

1. *Bridges*, which connect at the MAC sublayer of layer 2, and allow a single logical-link
   from end-system to end-system.
2. *LLC switches*, which connect at the LLC sublayer of layer 2, terminate the logical-
   links at each switch, and require a concatenation of logical-links across the three
   subnetworks, without recourse to layer 3 services.
3. *Routers*, which terminate the logical-link at each inter-subnetwork router (ISR),
   employ layer-3 services at each ISR, and use three logical-links: ES-ISR, ISR-ISR,
   and ISR-ES.

Another configuration is where the inter-subnetwork units "C" are bridges, but the inter-
subnetwork traffic is controlled by inter-subnetwork routers located on each LAN at "D"
in Figure 16.5.

For all of these configurations, the purposes of the address resolution protocols are of two classes:

1.   In any case, the address resolution protocols are desirable so that end-systems can find servers (such as print servers), or any other end-system, or an intermediate-system that leads to a destination end-system. This is needed to eliminate the administrative burden of system definition in an end-system that is newly attached to the LAN. Without an address-resolution process, the attaching node must be told by an administrator the MAC/LSAP addresses of destination-nodes (such as serving-nodes). In addition, it is desirable to allow logical entities to move from one physical MAC/LSAP address to another, without requiring a change to the system definition.

2.   If the inter-subnetwork units (C) are routers, the ARP is, in addition, desirable so that end-systems can find an inter-subnetwork router that can forward data to a destination on another subnetwork.

16.9.2   TCP/IP Address-Resolution Protocol

The broadcast abilities of LANs have been used in many protocols to resolve a name (usually a network layer title or address) into an appropriate subnetwork point of attachment (SNPA) address. The TCP/IP protocol, for example, uses its *Address Resolution Protocol (ARP)* to enable a node to dynamically map between an Internet Protocol (IP) address to the appropriate MAC address [RFC829]. When node X wants to resolve Internet address *IA1*, it broadcasts a special packet, an address-resolution packet, that asks the node whose Internet address is *IA1* to respond with its *SNPA address*. A response packet is returned by the station that recognizes as its own the specific Internet address that was sent. Each node (such as node X) gradually builds a table, adding items gathered through the use of address-resolution packets, containing the target Internet address.

If the sought Internet address is on a distant subnetwork (rather than the current one receiving the ARP broadcast) then some IP router (IP gateway) on the current subnetwork may recognize the prefix of the destination Internet address. That IP router would then respond, identifying its MAC address, LSAP, and a Route Information Field (RIF). When TCP/IP protocols are supported on a multisegment, bridged Token-Ring Network, the *bridge routing information* for each Internet address is simultaneously collected and saved, along with the MAC address. The ARP sender's SNPA address is included in every ARP that is broadcast. Therefore receivers of the ARP can also update the binding of the sender's Internet address-to-SNPA address in their cache.

A related situation is when a workstation (or host), at start-up, needs to determine its own Internet address. In that case, the workstation in question sends a broadcast for help, containing its SNPA (MAC) address. That protocol is called the *Reverse Address Resolution Protocol (RARP)*. Some **RARP server** connected to the LAN will translate the station address to an Internet address, and send back the reply.

16.9.3   NetBIOS Directory

NetBIOS also has an interesting *name-discovery* feature. It is strictly LAN-oriented. There are multiple versions of NetBIOS by different vendors. In the IBM version, NetBIOS LAN adapters are given 16-bit network names to identify each other (1 bit is reserved). An application tells the adapter to register a network name by one of two commands: `Add_Name` (a request for a unique name) or `Add_Group_Name`. The adapter broadcasts a network petition (a name-claim packet) to use a selected name. If a requested unique name is already in use, the affected adapter issues a complaint, and the pending name registration command is refused. In the absence of network complaints, the selected name is placed in the NetBIOS name table. NetBIOS then reports the success to the application, along with a 1-byte name-number. That number is subsequently used in various NetBIOS commands.

The NetBIOS protocol then can use a `Name_Query` packet to resolve a NetBIOS name to the appropriate MAC address. That packet is sent, by a group address, to all active NetBIOS stations on the network. The station that currently supports the named entity will respond by sending a `Name_Recognized` packet. This packet contains the desired addressing information. As it returns, it also discovers the possible bridge routes between the two stations. For session traffic (not datagram traffic) appropriate session identifiers are also exchanged within these two types of packets.

Assuming a network name is deleted and re-registered with each physical move, the associated application-process can move from one LAN node to another, and the network will find it.

16.9.4   Connectionless ES-IS

In a similar manner, the OSI protocols for connectionless network service (CLNS) provide for a dialog between an end-system and an intermediate-system (an *Inter-Subnetwork Router, ISR*) that is already participating in an Internet. The protocols provided for this dialog are the end-system to intermediate-system (ES-IS) protocols, ISO 9542, which address the following problems:

- How do *end-systems* discover the existence and reachability of *intermediate-systems* (ISRs) that can route messages to destinations on *other subnetworks*, other than the one(s) to which the end-system is directly connected?
- How do *end-systems* discover the existence and reachability of *other end-systems* on the same subnetwork (when the known destination NSAP does not contain the subnetwork point of attachment address)?
- How do *intermediate-systems* (ISRs) discover the existence and reachability of *end-systems* on the subnetworks to which they are directly connected?
- How do end-systems decide *which* intermediate-system (ISRs) to use to forward a message (when more than one intermediate-system is available)?

Configuration and routing information.   The solutions to these problems involve the transmission of configuration and routing information between network-entities residing in end-systems and intermediate-systems.

- Configuration information permits end-systems and intermediate-systems to discover each other.
    1. End-systems are informed of two things:
        a) The name of a network-entity (called the *network-entity–title*)[4] for each intermediate-system (inter-subnetwork router) on the subnetwork.
        b) The *subnetwork-point-of-attachment address* of each ISR.
    2. Intermediate-systems are informed of the *NSAP addresses* supported by each end-system, and the subnetwork-point-of-attachment address(es) of the end-system.
    3. End-systems can obtain information about each other in the absence of an intermediate-system. End-systems may query, over a broadcast subnetwork, to discover whether a particular *NSAP* is reachable on the subnetwork, and, if so, what *subnetwork-point-of-attachment address* to use.
- Route redirection information allows intermediate-systems to inform end-systems of better paths to use, when alternate paths are better known to the intermediate-system.

Protocol functions.   A brief summary of the key connectionless ES-IS protocol functions is given in the following:

- **Timers** determine the frequency of execution of some functions. The *Configuration Timer (CT)* determines how often a system reports its availability to other systems on the same subnetwork. The *Holding Timer (HT)* determines how long received information is held before discarding it.
- **Report-configuration** is used by ESs and ISs to inform each other of their reachability and current subnetwork addresses.
    - *End-systems broadcast* `ES-Hello` *PDUs* to all ISs, to inform other systems about the NSAPs it serves. On receipt of an `ES-Hello`, an IS stores the NSAP, subnetwork-point-of-attachment pairs.
    - *Intermediate-systems broadcast* `IS-Hello` *PDUs* to all ESs. The `IS-Hello` contains the IS's network-entity–title. On receipt of an `IS-Hello`, an ES stores the network-entity–title, subnetwork-point-of-attachment pairs.

The report-configuration function is invoked each time the local CT expires. An IS may optionally suggest a value for end-systems on the local subnetwork to use, as the setting of the configuration-timer, by including the ES-CT option in the transmitted `IS-Hello` PDU.

- **Query-configuration** is used when there is no IS currently reachable on the subnetwork, and a subnetwork-point-of-attachment address is needed, to which to forward a PDU destined for a certain NSAP. This occurs when the local cache (or other table-look-up) does not contain the desired address. *The query is sent to all ESs on the subnetwork.* Subsequently, an `ES-Hello` may be received, from a responding ES, containing the NSAP address along with the corresponding subnetwork-point-of-attachment address.

---

4.   Network-entity–titles are like NSAPs with a zero selector byte.

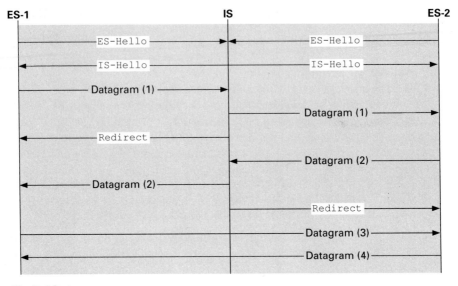

Figure 16.6 Connectionless ES-IS protocols [ISO 9542].

- **Configuration-notification** may be used by an ES or IS to quickly send configuration information to *a system that has newly become available*. Upon detecting the new arrival, an ES or IS can send its own `Hello` message to the new arrival. That permits the new arrival to quickly build up its routing information base.

- **Request-redirect (RD)**, from an IS to an ES, tells if the source ES could have sent the message more directly to the network-entity the IS is about to send it to.[5] Providing that the quality-of-service constraints permit the message to by-pass this IS, the IS informs the source ES of the "better" path. The source ES receiving such a redirect will record the suggestion in its routing database. In practice, an end-system may transmit a datagram to any active intermediate-system. That intermediate-system forwards the data and may issue a redirect packet (see Figure 16.6).

- **PDU header error detection** performs a checksum on the entire PDU header, at each point where the header is processed. If the checksum calculation fails, the PDU is discarded.

The formats of the connectionless `IS-Hello`, `ES-Hello`, and `Redirect` PDUs are given in this chapter's Technical Reference section.

---

5.   This is done only if (a) the next hop is to the destination system, and the destination is on the source ES subnetwork, or (b) the next hop is to an IS that is connected to the same subnetwork as the ES.

16.9.5   Connection-Oriented ES-IS

The connection-oriented ES-IS protocol, given in ISO IS 10030, addresses how connection-oriented end-systems on X.25 subnetworks discover the existence and reachability of intermediate-systems (inter-subnetwork routers) that can route to destinations on subnetworks other than the one to which the end-system is directly connected. IS 10030 performs logically the same functions specified above, in ISO 9542. However, the lack of a broadcast environment in X.25 prompted the following modifications. The specification has two subsets:

- The *Configuration Information* enables an ES to discover the subnetwork point of attachment (SNPA) addresses of systems on the local subnetwork through which packets may be routed to a destination on a remote subnetwork.

- The *Redirection Information* enables an ES *that is already attempting to establish a connection* to be redirected to a specific appropriate SNPA address, via which the connection preferably should be routed.

The **Subnetwork Address Resolution Entity (SNARE)** is a supplier of information concerning routing within a single subnetwork. It may be in one or more Data Terminal Equipment (DTEs), which are end-systems attached to an X.25 network. In order to use the ES-IS protocol, each end-system must have knowledge of at least one SNPA address that can be used to access a SNARE.

For *Configuration Information*, the ES establishes an X.25 connection to a SNARE by issuing an X.25 `Call_Request`. For each requested network address, the SNARE supplies details of the SNPAs on the subnetwork via which the network address can be reached, and the associated quality of service.

The Redirection phase is used when an ES does not know the subnetwork address of the inter-subnetwork router by which its `Call_Request` should be transmitted, and instead simply uses the address of a SNARE. A `Clear` indication in response to such a `Call_Request` can contain user-data with an appropriate subnetwork address via which a connection could be established. The ES then can retry the connection-establishment.

The expanded set of PDUs in ISO IS 10030 is illustrated in Figure 16.7. The PDUs are as follows:

- SNARE
    - `SHL—SNARE-Hello` PDU
    - `SRH—SNARE-Request_Hello` PDU
- Configuration Notification
    - `ESC—End-System-Connect` PDU
    - `SNC—SNARE-Notification_Complete` PDU
    - `ESH—End-System-Hello` PDU
    - `ENC—End-System-Notification_Complete` PDU
    - `SRN—SNARE-Received_Notification` PDU
- Configuration Collection
    - `ESC—End-System-Connect` PDU

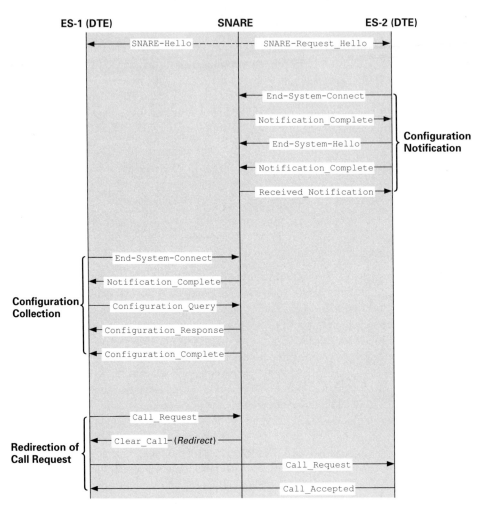

DTE = Data Terminal Equipment
SNARE = Subnetwork Address Resolution Entity

Figure 16.7 X.25 connection-oriented ES-IS protocols.

- SNC—SNARE-Notification_Complete PDU
- ESQ—End-System-Configuration_Query PDU
- SCR—SNARE-Configuration_Response PDU
- SCC—SNARE-Configuration_Complete PDU
- Redirection of Call Request
  - RD—Redirect PDU

The formats for these PDUs are given in this chapter's Technical Reference section.

16.9.6   802.2 LAN Discovery

There is also a known requirement for a common process that provides name to address resolution specifically for IEEE 802.2 LANs. A common process is needed to eliminate the administrative burden of system definition for an end-system when it is newly attaching to the LAN. Without such a "discovery" process, the attaching node must be told by an administrator the MAC/LSAP addresses of serving-nodes and/or inter-subnetwork-nodes. In addition, it is desirable to allow logical entities to move from one MAC/LSAP address to another, without requiring a change to the system definition. Fulfilling this requirement, moreover, would permit dynamic cooperation between LAN (layer-2) directory services for 802.2 LANs and directory services for inter-subnetwork (layer-3c) operations. The end-to-end directory and route-selection processes in LAN/WAN/LAN configurations can then be integrated effectively and dynamically.

The IBM discovery function provides LAN stations with such a directory service by providing a name (network-entity–identifier) to address resolution. There are two types of network-entity–identifiers: single and group.

- A *single identifier* refers to an individual network-entity. In APPN, for example, this identifier would be a unique identifier of an APPN network-node, while in the OSI world, this may be a network-entity–title or an NSAP address.

- A *group name* refers to one or more single entities that are associated to one another. A group might, for example, include all APPN network-nodes on a LAN. Enabling an end-system to find a member of a group, using the group identifier, allows further choices of connection, which may be important for availability or throughput improvements.

In the discovery process, the requesting LAN station sends out a frame containing the desired single or group identifier. A response is then received indicating the MAC and LSAP addresses of the desired entity. If a group identifier is used, then multiple responses will be received with the required information.

To illustrate further, when APPN nodes are located on a LAN, end-nodes will use the discovery function to dynamically find a network-node server. APPN network-nodes will respond to the discovery requests from APPN end-nodes with their MAC and LSAP addresses. The end-nodes will then use this information to contact the network-node. In a similar way, the APPN network-nodes can dynamically locate other network-nodes to establish APPN network-node-to-network-node connectivity.

Conclusion

The lower-layer services architecture, providing link/subnetwork-access to a broad range of common facilities, adds to the foundation for multiprotocol networks. The structure lends itself to a wide variety of options at layers 1 through 3a, and facilitates the incorporation of new facilities as they are developed. The discussion of this common link/subnetwork-access concept, with its LSA boundary, completes the picture of the three switching boundaries (CPI, TS, and LSA) introduced in Chapter 3 (see Figure 3.14). Particular features of many of the link/subnetwork-access facilities, including LANs and high-speed services, are discussed in the following chapters.

Address-resolution protocols make possible the dynamic addition of diverse types of link/subnetwork facilities to work with inter-subnetwork (layer-3c) protocols. They provide the binding between layer-3c inter-subnetwork addressing and subnetwork addressing. These lower-layer directory functions can be made to work cooperatively with the dynamic directory and topology services provided by control points in layer-3 networking (discussed in Chapter 14). In multiprotocol environments, multiple sets of ARP-type protocols can function side-by-side for their respective protocol suites.

Acknowledgments

I am particularly indebted to G. A. Deaton, J. J. Lynch, R. C. Dixon, and J. H. Ragsdale for valuable input or reviews of this chapter.

TECHNICAL REFERENCES

Connectionless ES-IS PDU Formats

The formats for the two `Hello` Protocol Data Units (PDUs) are given in Figure 16.8 and Figure 16.9. The type field identifies the type of PDU, whether an `ES-Hello`, an `IS-Hello`, or a `Request_Redirect` PDU. The `ES-Hello` carries one or more source-NSAP addresses. The `IS-Hello` carries an IS network-entity–title (NET).

The `Redirect` (RD) PDU carries a destination *NSAP address (DA)*, a *better subnetwork address (BSNPA)*, and possibly a *network-entity–title (NET)*. The destination address is the NSAP address of a destination associated with some message being forwarded by the IS sending the RD.

The format of the RD PDU is shown in Figure 16.10, for the case when the redirection is toward an IS. When the redirection is directly to a destination ES, the format is the same except that the *NETL* field is zero, and there is no *network-entity–title* field.

	octet
network-layer protocol identifier	1
length indicator	2
version/protocol id extension	3
reserved (must be zero)	4
0 0 0 type	5
holding time	6, 7
checksum	8, 9
number of source addresses	10
source address length (SAL) indicator	11
source address (SA)	12
SAL	
SA	m – 1
	m
options	p – 1

Figure 16.8 End-System–Hello (ESH) PDU format in connectionless ES-IS [ISO 9542].

octet

network-layer protocol identifier	1
length indicator	2
version/protocol id extension	3
reserved (must be zero)	4
0 0 0 type	5
holding time	6, 7
checksum	8, 9
network-entity–title length (NETL) indicator	10
. network-entity–title (NET) .	11 m – 1
. options .	m p – 1

Figure 16.9 Intermediate-System–Hello (ISH) PDU format in connectionless ES-IS [ISO 9542].

octet

network-layer protocol identifier	1
length indicator	2
version/protocol id extension	3
reserved (must be zero)	4
0 0 0 type	5
holding time	6, 7
checksum	8, 9
destination address length (DAL) indicator	10
. destination address (DA) .	11 m – 1
subnetwork address length indicator (BSNPAL)	m
. subnetwork address (BSNPA) .	m + 1 n – 1
network-entity–title length (NETL) indicator	n
. network-entity–title (NET) .	n + 1 p – 1
. options .	p q – 1

Figure 16.10 Redirect (RD) PDU format when it is sent to an IS in connectionless ES-IS protocol [ISO 9542].

octet

	octet
network-layer protocol identifier	1
version number	2
PDU type	3

ENC = End-System Notification_Complete
ESC = End-System Connect
PDU = Protocol Data Unit
SNARE = Subnetwork Address Resolution Entity
SRH = SNARE Request Hello

Figure 16.11 ENC, ESC, and SRH PDU-structure in connection-oriented X.25 ES-IS [ISO 10030].

Connection-Oriented ES–IS PDUs

The format for three Protocol Data Units (PDUs), the ENC, ESC, and SRH PDUs, is given in Figure 16.11. Building on that base:

- The SNC PDU format is that of the ENC plus a 1-byte *request_time* field.

- The SRN PDU format is also that of the ENC, only adding a 2-byte *notification_required* field.

- The ECQ PDU format is also that of the ENC, plus a 1-byte *network_address_length* indicator, and a variable length *network_address* field.

- The ESH PDU format is that of ECQ plus a variable *quality_of_service* field.

- The SCC PDU is also built on the ECQ format, only adding a 1-byte *query_limit* field.

The RD format is shown in Figure 16.12; and the SCR format is shown in Figure 16.13.

	octet
network-layer protocol identifier	1
version number	2
PDU type	3
holding time	4 5
address mask length indicator	6
address mask parameter value	7 k – 1
SNPA mask length indicator	k
SNPA mask parameter value	k + 1 m – 1
SNPA address length indicator	m
SNPA address parameter value	m + 1 n – 1

Figure 16.12 Redirect (RD) PDU-structure in connection-oriented X.25 ES-IS [ISO 10030].

octet

	octet
network-layer protocol identifier	1
version number	2
PDU type	3
holding time	4
	5
address mask length indicator	6
	7
address mask parameter value	
	k – 1
SNPA mask length indicator	k
SNPA mask parameter value	k + 1
	m – 1
network address length indicator	m
network address	m + 1
	n – 1
SNPA address length indicator	n
SNPA address parameter value	n + 1
	p – 1
QOS	p
	p + q

PDU = Protocol Data Unit
QOS = Quality of Service
SCR = SNARE Configuration Response
SNARE = Subnetwork Address Resolution Entity
SNPA = Subnetwork Point of Attachment

Figure 16.13 SCR PDU-structure in connection-oriented X.25 ES-IS [ISO 10030].

EXERCISES

16.1 Complete the following: (a) A logical-link is the service provided by a _____. (b) The logical-link provides communication between _____.

16.2 What is a transmission group (TG)?

16.3 Give an example of five layers (or sublayers) that may be included in the link/subnetwork-access facility.

16.4 What is the mechanism for connecting a link/subnetwork-access facility to an upper-layer (3c–7) protocol stack?

16.5 A CLNS ES-Hello informs the other systems about _____.

16.6 On receipt of a CLNS IS-Hello, an ES stores _____.

16.7 In connection-oriented service, what configuration information does the SNARE provide?

16.8 What happens when an end-system sends a NetBIOS Name_Query packet on the LAN?

17

Local Area Networks

17.1 INTRODUCTION

This chapter provides an overview of the primary LAN subnetworks. It highlights the common boundary, provided by five types of LANs, for use by upper-layer stacks of different protocols. It then goes into further depth to show the network designs that incorporate LANs. The practical use of bridges and routers, and the integration of LANs with WANs and mainframes, are analyzed and illustrated.

Why do we have LANs? As the trends continue, for almost every worker to have access to computing facilities, and also to be able to communicate electronically with each other, the cabling problem grows in importance. The concept of a "wall outlet" that provides high-performance access to diverse computing facilities is therefore very attractive. Wiring the building once with high-capacity cable, and then permitting all kinds of physical and logical reconfigurations, without affecting cabling, becomes a great cost saver and lost-time saver. Hence, we are seeing a rapid growth in the local area network (LAN).

The geographic coverage of many LANs initially was relatively small, confined to a building or a campus-like complex of buildings. Relatively high bandwidth, over these relatively short distances, can be obtained. Usually, the media can be selected to provide more bandwidth than the foreseeable requirements. Low error rates, (typically 10^{-9} to 10^{-10}) can be obtained in these controlled environments.

Newer optical fiber and broadband technologies, on the other hand, are greatly expanding the range of LANs. The orientation for LAN use has been shifting from the department to the establishment, and then to the entire widespread enterprise. (FDDI and metropolitan area networks, MANs, are covered in Chapter 18.)

A LAN has three primary components. First, there is a wiring system to facilitate comprehensive, one-installation service to all parts of a building, campus, or area. Second, there is an access protocol to manage the communication among units on the LAN. And third, there is the set of practical communication adapters to make the physical connections feasible. The combination becomes an effective subnetwork, and is so called in some ISO documents.

Architecturally, LAN convergence is a reality, thanks largely to the adoption of a common sublayer (IEEE 802.2) for a broad variety of types of LANs. The integration of LANs and WANs likewise progresses steadily, with the development of multiprotocol routers, discussed in previous chapters, and the wide use of bridges, routers, and gateways, discussed in this chapter. The management of LANs, from a system management perspective, is covered in Section 4.8.1.

17.2   LAN STANDARDS

17.2.1   The Five LAN Sisters

The standards organizations have focused on a common service boundary at the logical-link control (LLC) sublayer of layer 2, defined by IEEE 802.2. This common boundary applies to five LAN MAC-layer protocol standards. These are:

- CSMA/CD (collision detection) 802.3
- Token-Bus 802.4
- Token-Ring 802.5
- Fiber Distributed Data Interface (FDDI) X3T9.5
- Metropolitan Area Network 802.6

The relationship among the IEEE standards is shown in Figure 17.1. FDDI is handled by the ANSI standards group, rather than the IEEE group, and so FDDI has a different number series. Nevertheless, 802.2, logical-link control, is intended to be the common

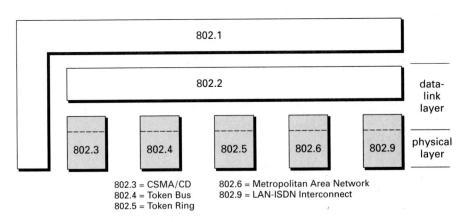

Figure 17.1 Family of IEEE LAN standards.

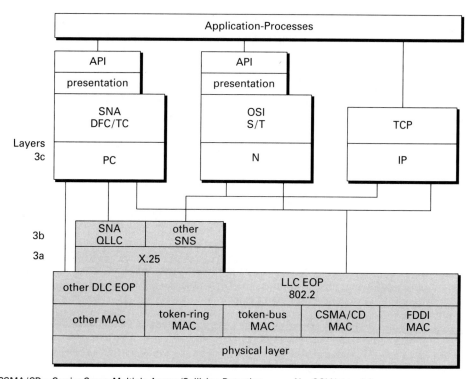

CSMA/CD = Carrier Sense Multiple Access/Collision Detection   N = OSI Network Layer
DFC/TC = SNA Data Flow Control/Transmission Control Layers   PC = SNA Path Control
EOP = Elements of Procedure   QLLC = Qualified Logical-Link Control
FDDI = Fiber Distributed Data Interface   SNS = Subnetwork Services
MAC = Media Access Control   S/T = OSI Session/Transport Layers

Figure 17.2 Multiple links serving multiple stacks.

interface to all five of these standard LANs (802.3/4/5/6 and FDDI). 802.1 describes the
relationship among the IEEE standards, and their relationship to the ISO reference model.

IEEE 802.3, the collision detection technology, was derived from Ethernet version 2,
which was used extensively in the earlier LANs. A high percentage of existing LANs stem
from this technology. The latter three LANs, however (802.4/5 and FDDI), all use the later
token technology.

A major benefit from these standards activities is that multiple upper-layer protocols
can now coexist on the same physical LAN. Furthermore, the common upper layer of
802.2 in many cases facilitates the interoperation of the different types of LANs.

17.2.2   The Common 802.2

The general applicability of the 802.2 elements of procedure is illustrated in Figure 17.2.
Each LAN has a separate lower sublayer, for the media access control. The common 802.2
sublayer can be employed directly by any of the three upper stacks, OSI, TCP/IP, or SNA.

Logical-link control.   Recall that the data link control (DLC) in layer 2 has two sublayers: the media access control (MAC) and the DLC logical-link control (LLC). The media access control (MAC) sublayer handles the tasks of frame delimiting and error checking. The LLC, then, controls the sending and receiving of the frames on the LAN, in accord with the IEEE 802.2 standard. The services provided by the 802.2 can be seen in its service-primitives. The OSI LLC primitives (at the LLC service-interface) are given in this chapter's Technical Reference section, for unacknowledged connectionless and connection modes. There also is an acknowledged connectionless mode.

A station may have multiple LLC sublayer instances that all interface to the same MAC sublayer. LLC protocols thus allow any two workstations or hosts attached to a LAN to operate with multiple concurrent logical-links. Since the LAN can also be used as access-links to intermediate-nodes of a WAN, 802.2 protocols similarly allow attachments on the LAN to have multiple concurrent logical-links to any host or workstation that is on a local or remote LAN. 802.2 supports three types of LLC service:

- **Type 1** provides HDLC-like *connectionless* service (i.e., unnumbered information link frames). No flow control or error recovery is supported. This type may be appropriate when higher layers provide any essential sequencing and recovery services.

- **Type 2** provides full HDLC-like *connection-oriented* services, such as data sequencing, flow control, and error recovery [Gerla 88].

- **Type 3** provides *acknowledged connectionless* service.

The LLC protocol procedures use the concepts and commands of the earlier balanced DLC known as *Asynchronous Balanced Mode (ABM)*, defined in ISO 7809. This same procedure was also the basis for the X.25 LAP-B. These LLC protocols include, for example, commands for station activation, the exchange of sent and received sequence numbers, frame rejection, and disconnect.

The LLC examines the address information of incoming messages, and (if a link station has been opened) routes the data to the upper layers via the LLC connection-end-points (CEPs) and service-access-points (SAPs). If no link-station has been opened, the message is passed to a manager that matches the Destination SAP (DSAP) in the incoming message with an LLC SAP (LSAP).

The LLC also provides configuration and network management services. Connection services establish and terminate CEPs at LLC-layer SAPs for network users. XID (Exchange id) is an unnumbered command used by LLC to convey the types of LLC services supported and the receive-window size. Network management services provided by the LLC include:

- Acquisition, accumulation, and reporting of status and/or statistics
- Routing of statistics logs, threshold logs, and error logs or reports to the node communications system manager
- Execution of LLC peer-to-peer tests
- Tracing of the protocol-data-unit data

LAN frame formats.   The frame formats of the 802.3, 4, and 5 LANs are all very similar (see Figure 17.25). Each has a MAC header and trailer, surrounding the LLC fields. The 802.3 and 802.4 MAC headers have a preamble needed to insure synchronization. The 802.3 format also includes a PAD (insertion of extra bits) that enlarges the message when necessary to insure that its transmission is greater than the time to travel to the furthest node. Within the MAC header is the destination and source MAC address. In the token-ring (802.5) format, routing information (up to 18 bytes in the IBM implementation) can be inserted between the source address and the DSAP of the LLC.

Universal address.   The 802.1 standard, that is common to all the above LANs, allows a 48-bit LAN station address. This allows registration of a unique adapter card address for every LAN station anywhere. The first 3 bytes are assigned by IEEE to manufacturers of adapter cards. The possibility exists, therefore, for a universal addressing structure among interconnected LANs of the different types (802.3, 4, 5, FDDI). Unfortunately, the standard also allows for locally administered addresses. Therefore this commonality is not assured—only allowed.

Address fields.   Addressing for the LAN is actually in two parts. The MAC sublayer uses two *MAC address fields* (2 or 6 bytes) for destination and source MAC address. The LLC, in addition, uses two 1-byte address fields for the *LLC-layer SAPs* of the destination and source. These LLC-SAPs are also called *LSAPs*. The destination LSAP is also called a DSAP; and the source LSAP is called an SSAP. 802.2 link activation protocols establish the LSAPs for a logical-link between network-entities in two nodes. That two-level address allows multiple simultaneous logical-links to be maintained through one physical port. (The format of the control field of the LLC sublayer is given in Figure 17.26 in this chapter's Technical Reference section.)

The first bit of the DSAP indicates whether the address is an individual or a group address. The first bit of the SSAP indicates whether the frame is a command or a response. The *remainder of the LSAP identifies the appropriate network-entity within the end-system*. The LSAP selector is used, for example, to select among OSI, TCP/IP, SNA, and NetBIOS. (A given network-entity type, however, may use more than one LSAP.) Some codes for use in LSAPs are given in the Technical Reference section.

The earlier Ethernets (version 2) used a format different from that of 802.3, involving a Type field that differentiated one higher-layer Ethernet protocol from another (e.g., an IP packet, X.75 packet,[1] or an address-resolution packet). (That de facto Ethernet standard is shown in Figure 17.27, in the Technical Reference section, along with the hybrid of the old Ethernet and 802.3 standard that IBM uses on the older Ethernets for SNA traffic.)

802 APIs.   As shown in Figure 17.3, two 802 application programming interfaces (APIs) can be used [GG24-3360]. Most programs use the **802.2 LLC API**. In the OS/2 imple-mentation, for example, the APPC, NetBIOS, and terminal emulation programs all use the LLC API. Other applications, or system services, may use the MAC layer interface, known as the **direct API**.

---

1.   X.75 is a protocol used for interconnecting two public X.25 subnetworks.

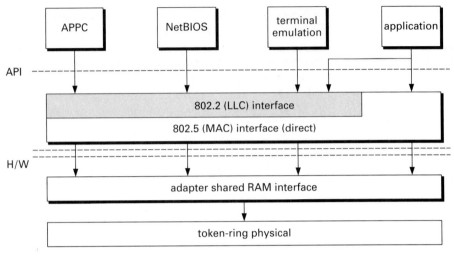

H/W = Hardware Implementation

Figure 17.3 802 token-ring adapter structure [GG24-3360].

Interoperability.   SNA nodes on the ring, using node type 2.1 and *connection-oriented* LLC support, can initiate sessions with a peer type 2.1 node on the same or a different LAN. Using node type 2.0 or type 2.1, they can also establish sessions with any SNA mainframe node attached to an SNA wide-area backbone. The upper-layer (layer 4 through 7) protocols, of course, have to be compatible. OSNA nodes, which may also include OSI, TCP/IP, or NetBIOS protocols, may use *connection-oriented* or *connectionless* protocols on the LAN— provided, again that the two ends are compatible.[2]

17.3   LAN FEATURE OVERVIEW

The following sections (17.3.1 through 17.3.5) are introductory overviews of the currently popular 802.3, 802.4, and 802.5 LANs.

17.3.1   LAN Characteristics

The differences in the five LAN subsystems, 802.3/4/5/6, and FDDI, and hence the selection of a particular LAN, have to do with:

- Transmission media, and hence bandwidth and performance
- Topology, and adaptability to change
- Reliability and recovery from malfunction
- Predictability of performance under heavy load conditions

---

2.   TCP/IP does not normally use connection-oriented LLC protocols.

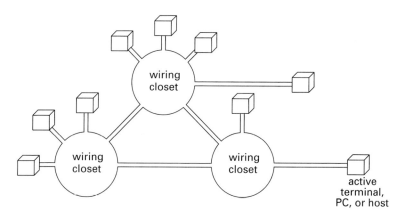

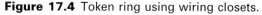

Figure 17.4 Token ring using wiring closets.

- Installation costs

Topologies.   The two primary topologies used in the standards are ring topology and bus topology. The ring topology is essentially a series of individual point-to-point links, between successive stations on the ring, without taps on the line. This, therefore, lends itself to optical fiber transmission, where taps are somewhat difficult. For the ring to operate, all intermediate stations must be functioning, or must have a reliable facility for being by-passed. For ease of installation, maintenance, and change, the most popular configuration is a set of wiring closets, with radial loops emanating from each closet.[3] This is shown, for a token-ring configuration, in Figure 17.4.

Media.   Transmission media in wide use now include shielded twisted pair, unshielded twisted pair, coaxial cable, and optical fiber. Twisted pair has the economic advantage that much of it has been previously installed for telephone and other services. Type and quality of the twisted-pair wire determines the allowable operating speeds. Generally, these are limited to the 1 to 16 megabits per second, although for short distances, higher speeds are feasible.

Coaxial cable has greater bandwidth (in the 300-500 Megahertz realm) and can have lower radiation and noise susceptibility. Coax is, of course, more expensive than twisted pair, and installation costs are usually a major consideration.

Optical fiber has the advantage of still higher bandwidth (hundreds to thousands of Mbps) to meet evolving requirements. It has lower attenuation per mile, and also lower radiation and noise susceptibility. Optical fiber, moreover, is smaller and lighter than comparable copper. With its tremendous bandwidth, existing conduits (often underground or in walls) can be used to obtain much higher capacity. Because of its low radiation properties, security is enhanced. Connector losses can be a problem. While the material costs are not high, installation costs are relatively high, because considerable skill is required.

---

3.   It has also been observed that as intelligent access units proliferate, with multiple attachments to each, all LANs acquire more of a tree topology.

Modulation. LAN systems are either *baseband*, using single-channel digital transmission, or *broadband*, using frequency division multiplexing to obtain multiple channels. In baseband, signals are repeated (and hence reconstructed), while in broadband, the signals at different frequencies must be amplified.

With broadband, modems are used for transmission and reception. Two-way connectivity involves retransmission by some "head-end" that operates on a different channel. Each two-way communication thus involves a "forward-channel" and a "reverse-channel." Many separate channels can be allocated to different purposes, such as data and video. The price for this flexibility is a somewhat more complex system with associated maintenance burdens.

Performance predictability. Analysis and modeling are usually used to predict the performance of the subsystem under peak load conditions. With token-passing systems, a specific response time and throughput can be predicted for a specific load situation. With collision detection systems, probabilities estimates can be made, based on probable distributions of loads. Of course, in any case, unpredictable transmission errors always introduce an element of uncertainty, particularly with low-quality media.

17.3.2   Token Passing

The *token* in a ring LAN is a particular bit pattern that is never allowed in the data being transmitted. The token, then, is the permission to send, when a particular station receives that token. In earlier designs, only one token is circulating at any one time.

A station that receives a message may:

- Copy the message if the address in the message is that of the receiving station
- Retransmit the received message

17.3.3   Token Rings (802.5)

In rings, the access protocol controls transmission through the use of the token that is passed from station to station. Multiple rings can be interconnected via architected bridges or routers, to provide very extensive complexes of logically connected LANs, as shown in Figure 17.5. Bridges can provide, for example, connections among 16 Mbps and 4 Mbps token rings, as well as to token-bus and Ethernet LANs. Connections can further be to directly attached hosts, and through routers to more remote hosts and other LANs.

The technical reasons for a choice of a ring design was summarized by the vice chairman of the X3T9.5 standards committee on FDDI, as follows [Ross 89]:

- A ring can be shown to offer superior reliability, availability, and serviceability, even in the face of physical damage to the network.

- The point-to-point connections around the ring not only provide an easy focus of standardization, but also allow different ring links to have different characteristics and optimization points. Optical fiber, which does not adapt well to bus configurations, can be easily accommodated.

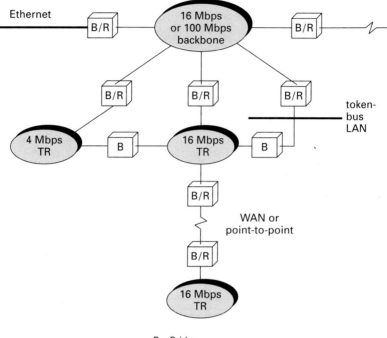

B = Bridge
B/R = Bridge or Router
TR = Token Ring

Figure 17.5 Multiple LAN interconnections via a high-speed backbone.

- Ring topologies offer advantages in the ease of initial configuration and reconfiguration as the network requirements change. Failing stations on fiber links can be isolated through the use of appropriate protocols. These protocols also provide for the logical addition and deletion of stations without detrimental effects on existing ring traffic.

- Ring topologies, and the protocols supported by them, offer significant performance advantages. These include insensitivity to load distribution, the ease of fairly allocating the available bandwidth, low arbitration times, bounded access delay, and no requirement for long preambles.

As noted above, since a ring is not "tuned," different media can be incorporated as physical segments of the ring. Optical fiber, for example, can be used for the intercloset wiring, while a different media is used for the loops to terminals.

The number of stations that can be tolerated on a ring depends on the speed of the ring and the wire used. The 16/4 token-ring adapter supports 260 stations at 4 Mbps on shielded, twisted-pair, but only 72 stations at 4 Mbps on unshielded twisted-pair. Up to 260 stations can be supported on a 16-Mbps ring using shielded, twisted-pair wire. Unshielded twisted-pair wire is generally not recommended at 16 Mbps.

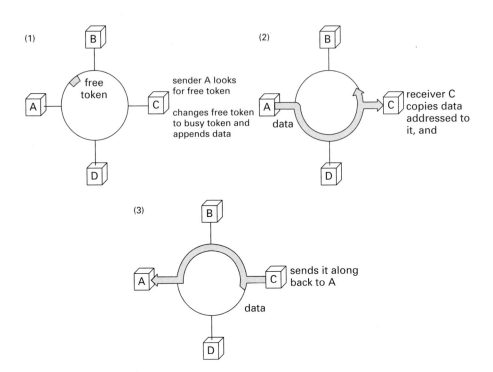

Figure 17.6 Token circulation on the ring.

Ring Media Access Control.   Tokens on a ring can be handled in several ways. Consider, for example, in Figure 17.6, that station A sends a message to station C. The address of C is in the message. Two courses of action may be taken, depending on the ring design.

- In some rings, C will copy the message for its own use, and then put the same message back on the ring. Only when the originator, station A receives the leader of the same message, will the data be removed and the token freed.
- In higher-speed rings, (e.g., the IBM 16 Mbps ring), station A will release the token as soon as it has finished its transmission (early token release).

Addressing.   In the token ring, addressing is independent of physical location, and may contain three classes of address. A *specific address* identifies the station, regardless of its location. A *group address* identifies the station as a member of a group, such as a member of a department. A *functional address* allows frames to be sent to a particular service, regardless of where that service is located on the ring. A functional address is really only a special case of a group address.

Priority with fairness.   To obtain quicker access to the ring, at times, eight priority levels are available. If a station has a priority message, and no token is available, it can make its need known to the transmitting station. The waiting station does this by putting a reservation for a priority in any passing frame. When the transmitting station for that frame receives a higher priority reservation, it must retain information on the current priority; and a new token is issued at the requested priority.

Availability. High availability is achieved in the token ring by a combination of:

- Error detection on both the ring path and within the adapter
- A ring diagnostic program to provide intermittent error analysis and probable cause information
- A manual reconfiguration procedure, supported by bypass capability in the lobe cable,[4] ring cable, and multistation access units
- A ring recovery protocol to provide recovery from solid failures

Active monitor. One station on the ring is automatically selected to act as the "active monitor." Its jobs include: clocking the ring's signal, compensating for phase jitter, providing buffer space for tokens, and generating the first token on the ring. All other stations check that the active monitor is operating, and that the clock is operating at the specified frequency. If these checks fail, another station is automatically selected to be the active monitor.

Ring poll and beacons. Each station monitors the activity of its nearest upstream neighbor. Periodically, the active monitor initiates the *ring poll*, which serves to obtain the address of each **Nearest Active Upstream Neighbor (NAUN)**. Hence, the upstream address is regularly refreshed, as stations insert and remove themselves, without interfering with normal ring operation.

If a station detects a failure (e.g., loss of signal), it begins transmitting a special *beaconing frame*. This frame contains the address of the transmitting station and its NAUN. As the beacon frame is repeated by each successive station, it soon reaches the NAUN. Recognizing its own address as the NAUN, it proceeds to take recovery actions. The NAUN removes itself from the ring and conducts diagnostics. If the NAUN finds no fault within itself, it reinserts itself into the ring, and the beacon-transmitting station takes recovery action. That station similarly removes itself from the ring and takes diagnostics. If either station finds a fault within itself, it remains off the ring. Meanwhile the domain of the fault is known to all other stations, and manual or other remedies can be provided.

Soft errors, such as a nonverified frame-check-sequence, are recorded in the frame-status field of the concerned frame. Periodically, a station that has detected soft errors will issue a soft error report to LAN Network Management. The use of such reports, and LAN Management in general, is discussed in Section 4.8.1.

Transmission frames. Higher transmission efficiencies are obtainable with larger frame sizes. Applications such as graphics, imaging, and high-speed bulk data transfer require both higher-speed LANs and larger-frame sizes. Newer adapters follow this trend, but not all adapters are yet consistent. For example, at the time of this writing:

- PC 16/4 Adapters attach PCs and PS/2s to token rings operating at either 16 or 4 Mbps. At 4 Mbps, the maximum frame size is 4501 bytes, and at 16 Mbps, the maximum frame size is 17,997 bytes.

4.　The lobe cable is the loop between the wiring closet and the attaching system.

- Establishment (cluster) controllers (e.g., IBM 3174) can handle 4 Kbyte frames through its 16 Mbps adapter.
- Communication controllers (e.g., IBM 3745) can handle frame sizes up to 8 Kbytes at 16 Mbps, and 2 Kbytes at 4 Mbps.

Early token release.   Without early token release, the token is not freed for another's use until the transmitted message completes an entire circuit of the ring. Only then does the sending station recognize its own address in the header of the returning frame, and free the token. The propagation delay through a ring takes a finite amount of time. As the bit rate of a ring increases, such idle time on the ring means a significant loss of ring capability.

This loss is reduced by the early token release feature. Here, the transmitting station releases the token as soon as it completes the data frame transmission. Hence, multiple frames (i.e., units of data) can be on the ring at the same time.

Illustration.   The design for the local area network at the IBM Research Triangle Park (RTP) facility at Raleigh is shown in Figure 17.7 [Campbell]. It illustrates the design practices that make very large, high performance, bridged, token-ring networks feasible. A single-level backbone structure is often used for a small campus (a mini-campus) consisting of less than six buildings. Each floor of each building may be a distinct LAN segment. Dual mini-campus backbone segments (for high availability) then are bridged to each LAN segment. A two-level backbone structure has been used for a large campus with six or more buildings. Each cluster of one to four buildings has its local LAN segments (e.g., one per floor) bridged to dual mini-campus backbones. The multiple mini-campus backbones, in turn, are bridged to dual higher backbones. The main reason for the two levels of backbones is for problem isolation and backbone-traffic reduction.

The IBM Research Triangle Park (RTP) campus had grown to use a token-ring network consisting of 57 interconnected rings, supporting 11,000 terminals and 48 host computers. Fifty-five percent of the terminals are 3270 displays and 45 percent are programmable workstations. The network appears as a single logical LAN with host access provided by the communication controller gateway feature. By using token-ring–attached control-units and communication controllers, users get essentially local response times and access to any host.

Token-ring–attached control-units are used to connect the 3270 family workstations to the network. The programmable workstations are directly connected to the LAN via token-ring adapter cards, to allow peer communications. Each building typically has a ring per floor. The local rings on each floor are connected to parallel mini-campus rings via two bridges (PS/2 model 50s installed in racks). Many of the mini-campus rings have fiber-optic repeaters. The mini-campus rings are connected via bridges to parallel 16-Mbps backbone rings. The backbone rings are extended via fiber-optic repeaters over the entire site. With the intermediate mini-campus rings, the backbone ring only terminates in four buildings.

The parallel mini-campus and backbone rings serve two purposes. First, if there is a single failure of a bridge or a mini-campus or a backbone ring, there will be an alternate

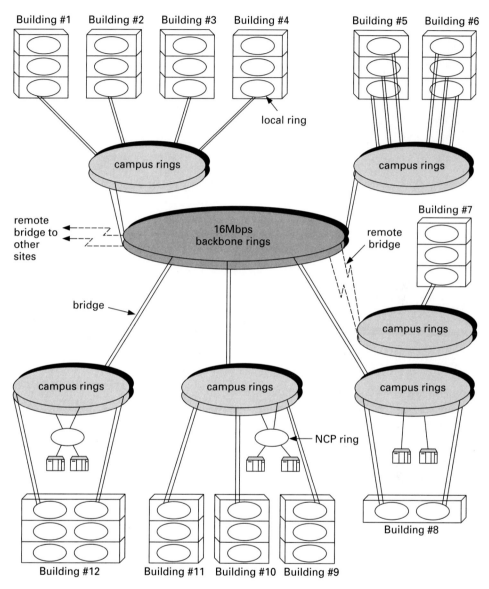

Figure 17.7 Local area network design [Campbell].

path through the network. Since the token-ring architecture uses a source-routing mechanism, the parallel rings also provide load distribution. As network usage increases further, both the backbone and the mini-campus rings can be operated at 16 Mbps, with minimum change (altering existing cards to run at 16 Mbps) for the users.

17.3.4   Token Bus (802.4)

The broadband cable has the unique advantage of allocating different frequency channels to different types of services, such as data, voice, and video. The IEEE 802.7 Broadband Recommendation provides a method of sharing a broadband cable system among such services. Split bandwidth allocation allows, for example, a combination of:

- Three 10 Mbps MAP 3.0 channels, using 802.4
- Three 2 Mbps IBM PC Networks
- Five 10 Mbps IEEE 802.3 LANs
- Many other services to share the same cable, such as:
  - Alarm circuits
  - 6 MHz videos
  - Voice circuits
  - Asynchronous, bisynch, or SDLC links

The token-bus architecture is designed to use some of these cable channels. In the 802.4 Token Bus, there is a fixed transmission order that is pre-established, independent of the physical positioning on the bus. After each node hears its predecessor node, it must transmit to the next node in the logical sequence. The function is thus as if there were a physical ring.

17.3.5   CSMA/CD LANs (802.3)

Carrier-Sense, Multiple-Access, with Collision-Detection (CSMA/CD) is a bus-oriented LAN technology. 802.3 is the IEEE standard version for that approach. An illustration of a large 802.3 multiple-bus network is shown in Figure 17.8. The facilities provided vary with each vendor, but a representative description follows. The *transceiver interface* provides recognition of the destination address and performs error detection by a cyclic redundancy check. Each station, in addition, contains a *network processor* board that establishes and terminates circuit connections, and builds the packets for transmission.

The original physical layer specification for Ethernet is 10Base5, which stands for 10 Mbps baseband with a maximum segment distance of 500 meters. 10Base2 uses a thinner, less expensive coaxial cable and provides for a maximum segment distance of 200m. The 1Base5 (StarLAN) option was created to allow Ethernet systems to use existing phone lines. The IEEE 802.3 10baseT standard allows Ethernet LANs to transmit data at 10 Mbps over most of the installed telephone lines. The maximum length of twisted pair cable that 10baseT standard allows is 100 meters. The 10BaseT standard uses a star topology suitable for the use of wiring closets. The standard requires transceiver interface and control electronics at both ends of the twisted pair cable emanating from such a closet.

Collision avoidance.   In a bus using collision detection, there is no pre-established sequence, and any station may transmit at any time. Obviously, then, collisions may occur; and there will be more collisions at higher loads. Since collisions require retransmissions, when a collision is detected, then each collision further increases the system load, and the effects

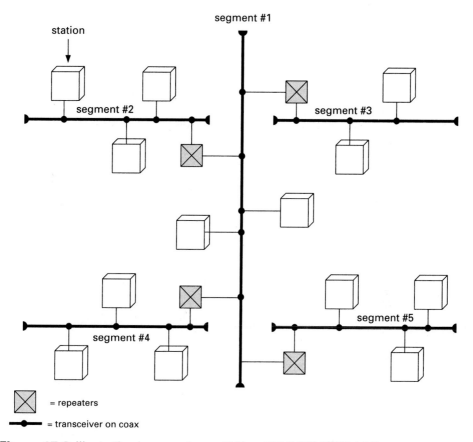

Figure 17.8 Illustrative large-scale, multi-bus, 802.3 CSMA/CD LAN.

can be cumulative. The success of collision detection systems, therefore, depends on the systems being relatively lightly loaded, and/or on using further algorithms to minimize the probability of collisions.

The probability of collision is reduced if a station "listens before talking." The *Carrier Sense/Multiple Access* systems require that a station talk only when it discerns that the medium is quiet. There still will be collisions, because messages can be traveling on the bus, but not yet arrived at the receiving station. Nevertheless, the probability of collision is greatly reduced by the listening requirement.

Collision detection systems (CSMA/CD) further can "listen while talking." If the sender detects a collision during her transmission, the damage is reduced by immediately stopping that transmission.

The probability of collision and the variations in arrival rates depend on the number of devices, the physical length of the network, the activity of each device, and the nature of the traffic. Because of the above uncertainties in the collision process, the delay in transmission can only be statistically predicted. Nevertheless, with good design, relatively high utilization can be achieved, and the probabilities of delays can be satisfactory.

Frame format.   (The frame format for 802.3 is shown in Figure 17.25, in this chapter's Technical Reference section.) The 64-bit Preamble is used to establish synchronism between the sender and the receiver. The 48-bit destination address field and the 48-bit origin address field allow for a very large address space. The data-type field is application dependent. The cyclic-redundancy-check (CRC), of 32 bits, applies to the entire frame except the preamble and the CRC field.

17.4   LAN BRIDGES AND ROUTERS

The enterprise network is increasingly dependent on multiple LANs and the interconnection of LANs to WANs. Bridges, and routers therefore play key roles in network integration. The broad use of bridges, routers, and gateways was discussed in Chapter 12. In Section 12.5, their definitions, limitations, and design advantages were presented. Routers (at layer 3) were discussed in connection with inter-subnetwork connections, in Sections 12.8 and 12.9. Some of the common objectives in using bridges and routers in LANs pertain to the following:

- *Physical LAN size:* effectively increasing the allowable physical length of the LAN.
- *Performance*: address-filtering, so that local traffic is confined to the local network, rather than flooding all connected LANs.
- *Reliability*: creation of self-contained units, so that a fault may not disable communication for all devices.
- *Security:* keeping different types of traffic (e.g., product development, planning, personnel, and accounting) confined to certain media.
- *Management:* cooperation with a LAN network-management function.

17.4.1   Designing with Bridges and Routers

Though it might be euphoric to think of the whole world as one big LAN, or sets of transparent bridged LANs, reality drives us to a combination of bridges and routers. A common conclusion is that bridges are suitable for connecting a considerable number of LANs, particularly those that are relatively homogeneous; and routers play an important role in connecting such clusters of LANs to each other and to WANs. We next examine why this is so.

Protocol sensitivity.   More and more, there is the necessity for living in a multivendor world, with ever-evolving communications facilities. Hence, multiple layer-3 protocols appear to be a long-term necessity. Different protocol stacks will often be built into different workstations. For example, a relay between LANs may have to accommodate NetBIOS, TCP/IP, and SNA traffic. Routers must cope with multiple layer-3 protocols, while bridges are in general insensitive to them. This makes the bridge considerably simpler and less costly.

Where the bridge is not adequate, the modular design of the router, to handle multiple protocols efficiently, then becomes economically important.

Traffic isolation.   One of unique characteristics of LANs is their ability to *broadcast* to all stations. One of the uses of this ability is to find the location of a destination, when only its name is known. That is a form of distributed directory service (see Section 16.9). Individual users, too, can send messages to small or large groups of users. With bridging, the range of such broadcasts gets multiplied. That is satisfactory until we discover that the broadcast traffic load can become oppressive very quickly. With larger networks, bridges tend to suffer from *broadcast storms*. Broadcasts might also be occasioned by the frequent transmission of information on the status of some networks, or by some malfunction on a workstation. Machines tend to synchronize on broadcasts, so you can get a spike of traffic. On bridged Ethernets, spiking can lead to increased collisions, which cause packets to be dropped, necessitating retransmissions. Spikes thus could widen up and tend to clog the network [Hunter 89].

Further intelligence is therefore needed to control the possibility of a growing problem. It turns out that the examination of the layer-3 address, as in routers, can help greatly. Routers can provide a higher degree of traffic isolation, and create *"firewalls"* between LAN segments, so the broadcast traffic is stopped at the router. Wasteful traffic is thus reduced, and processing resources are conserved.

Congestion.   Another problem is that of *traffic congestion* caused by the volume of traffic and speed mismatches or bottlenecks in the network. When the rate of flow through a MAC-layer bridge exceeds its capacity or that of the receiving subnetworks, the bridge has no alternative but to discard the messages. A stormy buildup of retransmissions can result. MAC bridges have no flow control capabilities. Again, more intelligence is needed. Logical-link control and layer-3 routers can have *flow control abilities*. Congestion feedback messages of different types can be used (e.g., the ICMP Source Quench messages in TCP/IP).

Depending on the options selected in communicating LAN stations, the congestion control is performed at different sublayers [EWOS89]. In Figure 17.9, for example, MAC relay congestion can be controlled from two layers. If the communicating LAN stations implement the 802.2 logical-link control (LLC) Type 2, which does include flow control, the congestion control may be operated at the LLC sublayer, as shown in Figure 17.9(a). If only LLC type 1, having no congestion control, is implemented in the concerned LAN station, and if the communicating end-systems support the connection-oriented transport service (e.g., OSI transport protocol type 4), then this control is performed in an end-to-end way at the transport layer, as shown in Figure 17.9(b).

Throughput.   At times there is a great surplus of bandwidth, and we do not mind spending it lavishly. At other times, particularly with expensive wide area links, *bandwidth conservation* and *link utilization* are very important. With some bridges, particularly with some using the transparent bridge spanning tree algorithm, one must deactivate all but one link between subnetworks, keeping others in idle standby, ready when the first fails. Other bridges (like source routing bridges) and routers in general do not have this limitation, can use parallel bridges, and hence can use bandwidth more efficiently. All links in the network are used for

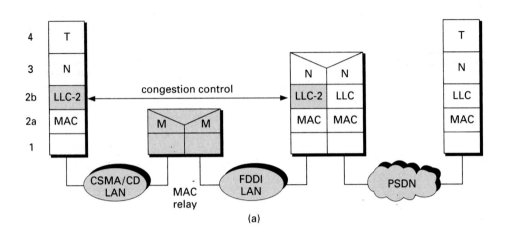

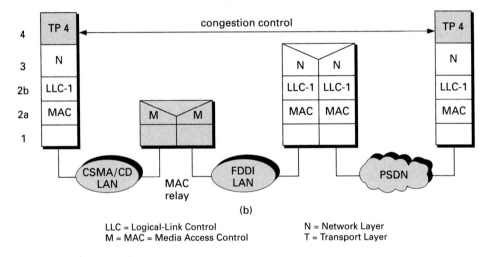

Figure 17.9 MAC relay congestion control from **(a)** the DLC/LLC layer and from **(b)** the transport layer.

traffic; and traffic can be more balanced with a fuller topology. A router, in addition, can select an optimum path based on parameters like transit delay, congestion, the hop-count, or security of the path. *Priority* facilities can insure higher performance for higher-priority traffic. On the other hand, a router will tend to introduce transit delay due to network layer processing. Implementations must keep this to a minimum.

Reliability/availability.   Intelligence can, in principle, be built into both bridges and routers to reduce frame loss, misordering, duplication, and undetected errors. In addition, routers that are part of a layer-3 network also are tolerant of failures in links or other routers. Alternate paths, dynamic topology updates, and intelligent path selection can be part of the router design.

Management.   System management is often a neglected but vital consideration. Multiple organizational entities need to communicate. However, the *administration* of the joined networks may need to be partitioned among these organizational entities. A degree of intelligence and control can be built into both bridges and routers; however, the more sophisticated routers often have a superior set of facilities. *System management* can then be partitioned in flexible ways, with responsibilities for problem determination, access control, and configuration updates properly governed.

Price.   There is, of course, a price for everything [McQuillan89]. Routers were, in general, considerably more expensive than bridges. This difference in price is, however, narrowing. The value of the router functions increase as the size of the network increases, as the diversity of subnetworks increases, and as the diversity of connected organizational entities increases. The network designer therefore needs to consider the optimum combination of bridges for some clusters of LANs and routers for the interconnection of these LAN clusters and other types of subnetworks.

17.4.2   LAN Bridge Functions

The bridge function enables a workstation or host attached to one LAN to establish logical-links with workstations or hosts attached to another LAN. Multiple LANs, with multiple bridges can be cascaded, providing logical-links across multiple LANs. The remote (or split) bridge provides logical-links between workstations or hosts on two LANs that are connected by a long distance leased or switched link.

The transformation functions that a bridge must perform obviously depends on the differences in the architectures of the two LANs being connected. A checklist of the possible functional differences that might need to be considered follows:

- MAC layer:
    - Group address map
    - Address bit swap
    - Source routing emulation (when converting from a source-routing to a transparent bridging LAN)
    - Priority
    - Frame size
    - Frame format conversion
- LLC layer:
    - LLC emulation for XID or TEST commands
- Network layer (at route set-up time):
    - MAC address (in data field) bit swap for noncompliant implementations
    - Address resolution (NSAP to MAC address)
    - Route discovery

When a LAN is divided by the insertion of a bridge, the filtering process of the bridge can improve the throughput by reducing congestion. It effectively divides a LAN into two pieces, and isolates the traffic of each LAN from the other. The bridge must examine all frames arriving from both LANs, and, through reference to internal routing tables, forward to the adjacent LAN only those frames that are destined for the adjacent LAN.

17.4.3   Source Routing and Transparent Bridges

There has been some controversy about how bridges should operate. Two approaches, the *transparent bridge* [Perlman84] and the *source-routing bridge* [Saltzer81] have vied for favor. The former was first designed for Ethernets; the latter for token rings. The designs, however, apply to either type of LAN. The standards organization has provided a combination of these two approaches, called the SRT (Source-Routing/Transparent) solution.

The **simple bridge** listens "promiscuously" to all packets, on each connected LAN [Seifert88]. Static tables in the bridge determine which frames are to be passed through the bridge to other LANs. Configuration changes therefore requires system-definition changes to all the simple bridges. **Learning bridges**, on the other hand, learn which addresses are on which side of the bridge. They modify their address tables automatically, as each packet is received. Whenever a packet arrives that is not already in the bridge tables, the bridge "floods" all LANs other than the one from which the packet arrived, to discover the appropriate route.

Learning bridges, with their broadcasts, rely on a loop-free topology. Hence, no active alternate paths can be allowed. Stand-by paths are permitted, but these can carry traffic only after the failure and elimination of the priority path. The protocol used to compute the single-path topology is known as the *spanning tree protocol* [Perlman84], [Bridge87]. Learning bridges are also called **transparent bridges** because no change is required of old end-stations when the bridge is installed. An illustration of the use of transparent bridges is given in Figure 17.10(a), where several bridges are blocked to prevent looping, and each active bridge has recorded the stations on each side of the bridge.

For the **transparent bridges**, each bridge initially enters the network and periodically transmits a `Hello` message carrying an id, timer values, path cost parameters and flags associated with the spanning tree algorithm. The `Hello` message is received by other bridges attached to that segment, and a *root* bridge on the originating LAN is selected for a *least-cost* path. A `Hello` message is then transmitted on the adjoining LAN segments, with the id of the root, and the process is repeated. In this way, the identity of the root bridge is propagated across the network, along least-cost paths. The "loser" bridges enter the blocking-state, and the "winners" enter the learning-state.

In **source-routing**, a Routing Information Field (RIF) within each frame contains a sequence of bridge_numbers and LAN_ids.[5] Each frame, accordingly, will be passed from

---

5. The IEEE 802.1 international standard specifies that a *routing field* may be inserted (only in routed frames) following the MAC header. The *routing field* consists of a control-field and the sequence of bridge-segment numbers specifying the route. The existence of the *routing field* in the frame is indicated by setting the first bit of the source-address to 1.

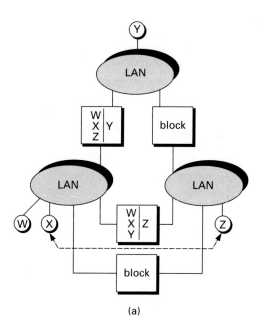

(a)

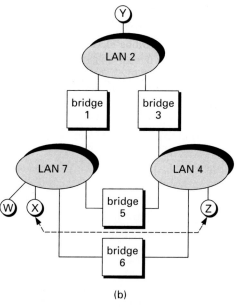

(b)

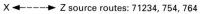
X ◀----▶ Z source routes: 71234, 754, 764

Figure 17.10 (a) Transparent and **(b)** source-routing bridge operation.

LAN to LAN, through the chain of bridges and LANs specified by the transmitting station in the RIF. Figure 17.10(b) illustrates the use of bridge_numbers and LAN_ids (assigned by a LAN Network Manager) and the source routes using them.

This scheme requires a prior path-search, by the end-stations, to determine the desired route. Several search approaches can be used. In an earlier approach, an originating station sends an *all-routes explorer frame* to find the destination.[6] Bridges receive the search frame, and update it with the bridge_number and LAN_id that it is forwarded on. Multiple copies, coming via parallel paths may exist. As each copy is received by the destination station, a response is sent back the way it came. The source station thus obtains information about multiple routes, and a preferred route is selected by the source station. In an alternative and *preferred* approach, the multiple copies of the all-routes explorer frame arriving at the destination can be avoided by designating a subset of the bridges as "**spanning tree explorer bridges**," so that only one route exists between any two LANs, as far as the explorer frame is concerned. This configuration can be automatically accomplished by using the *spanning tree algorithm* where bridges communicate with each other to establish and maintain a single-route explorer path through the network. This prevents a target ring from receiving duplicate frames. Then, the target station will return the discovery frame to the originating station by an *all-routes explorer*, so as to traverse all routes back to the originating station. Bridges can be defined to limit the forwarding of explorer traffic through a maximum number of bridges (**max-hop count**). Before forwarding an all-routes explorer frame, each bridge can check the routing information field to see if the max-hop count has been exceeded. If "yes," the frame will not be forwarded. This helps to limit the proliferation of messages in multi-hop configurations.

The source-routing protocols thus allow for active alternate paths through the network, as well as parallel paths between any two rings of the network. This alternate and parallel path approach increases throughput, improves traffic distribution to reduce congestion, and improves availability in case of failures. For instance, the network backbone can be duplexed to ensure that service is never disrupted. These same considerations apply when multiple LAN clusters are connected via WANs, where alternate/parallel paths in the WANs are likewise relevant.

Two arguments are often cited. Transparent bridges have the advantage that the end-stations do not have to add the routing field to the frame format. This makes it easier to incorporate transparent bridges in existing LANs. Cascading many LANs also could result in a build-up of search messages multiplied by active parallel paths. Advocates of source-routing claim that it will be applicable to much higher speed LANs of the future. These arguments oversimplify the situation, however. Some of the more interesting facets are summarized below.

Simplicity.   Tables in the source routing bridge (SRB) are limited to knowledge of the *LAN-ids* for adjacent LAN segments. Current designs of the transparent bridge, on the other hand, require it to maintain table entries of all active *stations* in the network. Source routing bridges are therefore designed to copy and process only frames that need routing to another segment, as opposed to transparent bridges (TB) that currently need to copy and process *all* frames on

---

6.   The explorer frames are not *broadcasts* because they are not sent to multiple destinations.

each segment. Unless this TB design is improved, the processing in the SRB will be considerably less than in the TB. This is always a performance issue, but it becomes crucial as the speed of LANs increases, and the processing power of bridges becomes the limitation. Delays are introduced by the processing time required to make forwarding and filtering decisions. The arrival of frames into a bridge at a rate exceeding the processing rate will cause additional congestion of links and bridges [Seifert88].

Active alternate paths.   A strong requirement exists for active parallel bridge paths. With source routing, this capability can be achieved with less complex bridges. Parallel paths also provide high throughput, since the relay decision is based on known routing information. This performance of parallel paths, of course, becomes more important with higher-speed LANs, since then the processing at either bridges or intermediate nodes in a WAN can rapidly become the bottleneck.

Route discovery.   The discovery process enables the station to learn about the character- istics of the path, such as maximum frame size. Source routing thus enables the end-station to determine the best possible bridge route meeting a minimum class of service, such as a specific frame size. This is possible even when workstations are moved, which can be done without hardware or software changes.

Flooding the network with discovery messages has been said to be a problem with source routing. Unrealistic and poorly designed configurations, with large numbers of cascaded LANs, can be imagined to create such possibilities. With practical hierarchical configurations, often using backbone LANs, and routers between very large LAN clusters (for other good reasons, see Section 17.4.1), the possibility of discovery flooding is made sufficiently small. With a network designed to be robust (rather than collapse) in periods of very high usage, an improbable momentary peak load results in a momentary delay and does not significantly affect the network capacity.

To support multicast (i.e., frames with group destination addresses), with minimum flooding of the destination-node, source routing has introduced the concept of **single- route broadcast**. This is a configuration parameter associated with each bridge. It can be managed through different mechanisms, ranging from manual configuration to automatic configuration by bridges, with or without direct communication between the bridges.

Path recovery.   Since each station using source routing is aware of its frame's path through the bridged local network, that path can be reported to system management on the occasion of a path failure.

The SRT solution.   The problem has been that LAN networks are partitioned into transpar- ent and source-routing parts, as depicted in Figure 17.11. The source-routing bridges forward source-routing frames only, and form a network with source-routing bridges only. Similarly, transparent bridges forward transparent bridge frames only, and form a spanning tree with transparent bridges only.

A simple solution to this undesirable partitioning between transparent and source- routing elements was approved by the IEEE 802.2 standards committee.[7] A bridge was

---

7.   IEEE P802.5M/P802.1X/D2 is the draft amendment to ISO 10038 due to become an ISO standard in 1992.

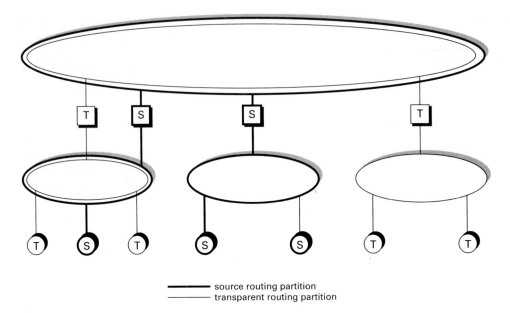

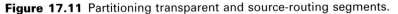

──────── source routing partition
──────── transparent routing partition

Figure 17.11 Partitioning transparent and source-routing segments.

defined that can accept either approach, *allowing interoperability between SR and TB end-stations*. The logic for this **SRT bridge** is shown in Figure 17.12. The SRT bridge simply asks if there is a routing information field present or not, in each received frame, and acts accordingly. It acts as a transparent bridge if no routing information is present, and acts as a source-routing bridge if routing information is present. *With this approach, a heterogeneous mix of systems requiring source routing or transparent bridges can be supported.* This is another breakthrough. It facilitates interoperation among diverse workstations and

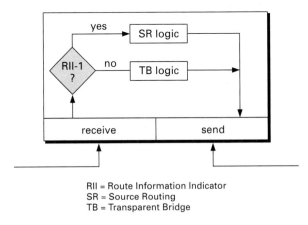

RII = Route Information Indicator
SR = Source Routing
TB = Transparent Bridge

Figure 17.12 Bridge logic.

servers on different LANs such as Ethernet, token ring, and FDDI. Existing systems can interoperate without change, although software upgrades may further improve performance.

17.5 LAN SYSTEMS

17.5.1 The IBM Bridge Family

The IBM family of bridges is illustrated in Figure 17.5 [Beumeler89]. It currently has four primary components:

- Bridges among local 16 Mbps and 4 Mbps token-ring LANs
- Bridges between local 4 Mbps token-ring LANs and PC Network LANs
- Bridges between *remote* 16 Mbps or 4 Mbps token-ring LANs
- Bridges between token-ring and Ethernet (v2 or 802.3) LANs

For the remote token-ring network bridge, adapter cards are needed in PCs attached to each of the remote rings. Frames are then sent over a telecommunications link without the intervention of higher-layer protocols. For the local bridge, both LAN adapters are in one PC, which is directly connected to both local rings.

The remote token-ring bridge.   Two remotely located token rings can be connected through leased or switched long-distance lines, using the remote bridge facility in two PS/2s. Smaller PCs and PS/2s can support line speeds ranging from 9.6 to 64 kbps, depending on the physical interface. The larger PS/2s can support line speeds ranging from 9.6 to 1.544 Mbps, depending on the physical interface. The communications adapters can attach to either a synchronous modem, a multiplexer such as the Integrated Digital Network Exchange (IDNX), or a ROLM PBX.

Except for the delay of the phone line itself, the remote bridge is essentially invisible to the LANs. However, for consistent response times, and throughput, the remote bridge is best with a T1 line. Software that operates across a local bridge can, with no change, operate across a remote bridge. Also, the LAN Network Manager can communicate with the remote bridge and stations on its rings as it would with a local bridge. This aids network management of the multiring environment, including error and failure detection and problem isolation.

A terrestrial link between LANs can be of any distance—e.g., as much as 3,000 miles. Parallel bridge links can be active simultaneously, either for additional bandwidth or for backup. However, delays in satellite service or in some store-and-forward packet services could introduce delays that exceed protocol tolerances. In such cases, protocol timers would have to be matched to the communication circuit delays.

Token-ring bridge software.   As shown in Figure 17.13, the software in the (PC or PS/2-based) remote network bridge has three components:

1. The *communications adapter* software, executed on the communications adapter card, handles the transmitting and receiving of synchronous data across the telecommunications link.

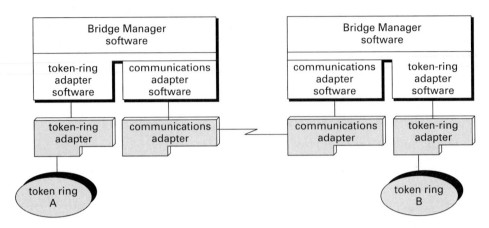

Figure 17.13 The token-ring remote bridge components [Beumeler89].

2. The *bridge-manager*, executed on the PS/2 processor, provides network management services for the interconnected LANs. These include problem determination, aiding inserting stations, and communicating with the parent LAN Network Manager.

3. The *token-ring network adapter* software, executed on the PS/2 processor, provides the interfaces among the bridge-manager, token-ring adapter, and communication adapter.

Token-ring to Ethernet bridge.   The 8209 bridge connects the 4 and 16 Mbps 802.5 token-ring LANs to the 802.3 CSMA/CD LANs and many of the earlier Ethernet (version 2) LANs as well.[8] Routing is done at the MAC layer. Supporting functions, however, require a layer-3 awareness. In particular, many LAN protocols send MAC addresses as part of the information field (e.g., ARP). Different vendors have encoded these addresses differently. Hence, at least in the short term, the 8209 will perform bit swapping of addresses in certain selected frames, like ARP.

The transparency is extensive, even though it is limited by nonstandard formats of the older implementations, as shown in Figure 17.14.

- In connecting *token rings* to the *802.3* LANs, the 8209 can accommodate a wide variety of upper layer protocols, including, SNA, OSI, TCP/IP, and NetBIOS. IBM and Novell have also announced their cooperation to implement Novell IPX protocols on the 8209.

- That generality also applies to like-like passthru situations (*Ethernet to token ring to Ethernet*), where communicating devices on Ethernets use the same LAN MAC protocol (e.g., Ethernet v2, or 802.3).

---

8. A statement of direction has also been issued by IBM for an interconnection product for the 802.5 token-ring and the 802.4 token-bus LAN.

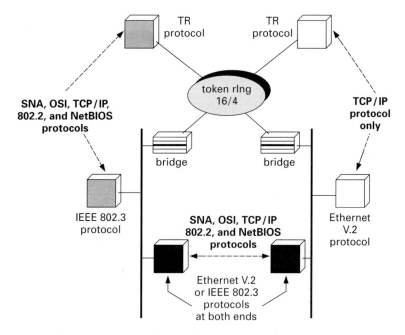

Figure 17.14 Protocol independence of the 8209 LAN bridge.

- However, when one device is on a *token ring*, and the other device is on the older *Ethernet v2*, the LAN bridge is sensitive to the upper-layer protocols. Then only the TCP/IP protocol has thus far been supported.

The token-ring and Ethernet LANs use different routing algorithms. The 8209 therefore supports both the source routing protocol of the token ring and the transparent bridge protocol of Ethernet, and converts from one to the other when crossing the bridge. Because of the Ethernet and 802.3 bridging methodology, only one 8209 bridge (between an Ethernet and a token ring) can forward data at a time. The transparent protocol automatically selects which bridges are blocked and automatically reactivates them when the primary bridge fails.

With the upgraded 8209, to also handle IPX, one can have a mixture of Novell and IBM servers, on 802.3 Ethernets and 802.5 token rings, which are connected by 8209s, as shown in Figure 17.15. An interoperating, dual-client requester workstation then has access to servers from both vendors on token-ring networks and Ethernets (see also Section 19.3). Note, however, that the Novell as well as IBM machines on the token ring all must have source routing drivers in order to pass through the current 8209 bridge, which converts source routing to transparent routing.

17.5.2   LAN to Host Connections

In this section we look at a variety of types of products for LAN to host connections, and then consider some theoretical alternatives for LANs with NetBIOS and APPC.

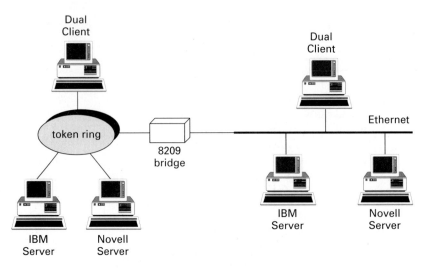

Figure 17.15 Coexistence with dual clients to Novell and IBM servers, via 8209.

Some hosts are directly connected to LANs. Other hosts can only be reached via the wide area network (WAN). In the latter cases, a special router or relay function is needed to provide entry into the WAN. Such relay functions can be performed by other hosts directly attached to the LAN, by communications controllers, by cluster (establishment) controllers, and by PCs and PS/2s.

In today's multivendor, multiprotocol environment, both the direct connections and the routers between LANs and hosts must also face the need to accommodate multiple sets of network-layer and higher-layer protocols.

LAN attachment possibilities. Nearly universal LAN attachment facilities are available, to connect LANs to hosts and SNA WANs. For example, these include the following product capabilities:

- *Outboard DLC units* on S/390s, like the 3172 Interconnect Controllers.
- *Cluster (establishment) controllers* can attach 4 or 16 Mbps LANs, and can also be used as a LAN relay to a System 390, via either SDLC or X.25 and a local, channel-attached communication controller.
- *Communication controllers*, channel-attached to hosts, also can support multiple LANs (e.g., up to eight 16-Mbps LANs with up to 9,999 physical units, on a 3745). LANs on remote communication controllers can also connect via SDLC and a local, channel-attached communication controller to hosts.
- *Intermediate-size systems* (like the IBM 9370 and AS/400) are attached to LANs via an integrated communications adapter (ICA).
- The PC can be used as a LAN gateway. The PS/2 EE *SNA Gateway*, for example:
  - Connects Ethernet (v2.0 or 802.3), token rings, or PC Networks, via either SDLC,

X.25, or an intermediary token-ring LAN, to a channel-attached communication controller and hosts

- Carries multiple concurrent SNA sessions, via up to 254 LUs (LU 0, 1, 2, 3, and 6.2)
- Acts as a single PU 2.0 to one host, and as spokesperson for multiple LAN attachments
- Coresides with other servers (file, printer, database, and/or network manager)
- Supports programmable workstations using DOS or OS/2 EE each having APPC and/or 3270 emulation
- Supports OS/2 EE having 802.2 and/or NetBIOS API

The use of the SNA gateway in a multivendor (NetWare/IBM) configuration is illustrated in Section 19.3.

Multi-LANs to S/390-Channel. The *S/390 outboard DLC units* have acquired broad capabilities. The S/390 I/O channel is not usually thought of as a subnetwork, because its distance capabilities have been relatively small. It is, however, a well documented "open architecture" at the link layer, whose capabilities have been greatly increased with the advent of optical fiber (see Chapter 18). The **3172 Interconnect Controller** is, in effect, an LLC switch between channels and many different LAN protocols, with S/390 hosts as destinations. It operates at layers 1 and 2, with no processing at layer 3. It is, however, limited to LAN-mainframe connections; it is not, in itself, a LAN-LAN or LAN-to-WAN or host-host bridge.

Figure 17.16 illustrates a multiprotocol, multioperating system, multivendor configuration, with four types of LANs feeding multiple hosts via the 3172. The three-tiered 3172 illustrated there could handle up to 6 channel attachments and 12 LAN attachments. Alternatively, the channel connections for twelve LANs could be daisy-chained so as to all use only two channels. In still another case, the twelve LANs could be distributed among a cluster of three different hosts.

These LANs may be 4 and 16 Mbps token-ring, Ethernet,[9] PCNet, FDDI, or MAP 3.0 Token-Bus LANs. These LANs can all be channel-attached to hosts (e.g., AIX/370, MVS, VM) using a single, shared, interconnect controller. The design of this 3172 bridge is such that multiple higher-layer protocols, including TCP/IP, SNA, and OSI can be passed through from LANs to hosts. As of this writing, for example, the 3172 supports OSI and SNA flows over 802.3/4/5 and FDDI. It also supports TCP/IP flows over Ethernet version 2.0, 802.3, 802.5, and FDDI. For example, a variety of PCs (AIX/RT, AIX/PS-2, OS/2), connected to these LANs, and supporting TCP/IP protocols, thus can communicate with host applications also using TCP/IP. Workstation-to-host as well as workstation-to-workstation communication is thus obtainable using the TCP protocol. With the addition of a DOS server program, any of these same host applications can be accessed by PC-DOS workstations on the LAN, too.[10]

---

9. Ethernets connected to a 3172 may be version 2 standard and thin wire, 802.3 10base5 wire and 802.3 10base2 wire.

10. Newer versions of cluster controllers (Establishment Controllers like the 3174) also connect to the ESCON. The intent was also announced by IBM to provide attachment of the 3745 family of communication controllers to the ESCON channel.

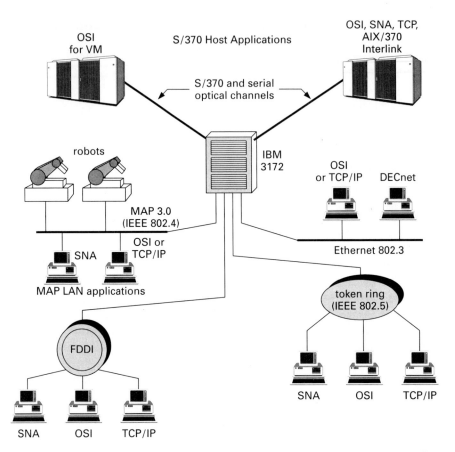

Figure 17.16 Multiprotocol, multioperating system, multivendor 3172 configuration.

The control program in the 3172 does not look inside the received frame to perform any protocol operations. It does allow the host program to set filters so that a frame containing specified patterns will be sent across the channel to the host. All other received frames are discarded.

PS/2 SNA Gateway.   The PS/2-based *SNA Gateway* [GG24-3552] provides SNA session connectivity between S/390 or AS/400 hosts and units on LANs, X.25 PSDNs, and SDLC lines. Figure 17.17 illustrates that connectivity. 3270 emulation services are provided in the gateway. Both DOS- and OS/2-based workstations are accommodated. These attachments to token-ring, Ethernet (version 2.0 and 802.3), and PC Network (baseband and broadband) LANs are all given SNA LU-LU facilities via the gateway. The connection between the gateway and the hosts can also have variations. That connection may be via token-ring LAN, X.25 PSDN, or an SDLC line.[11]

---

11.   Currently, some restrictions apply; see [GG24-3552].

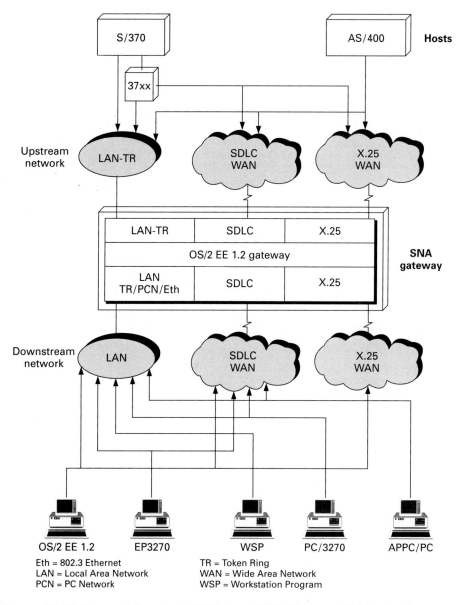

Figure 17.17 Connectivity via the PS/2-based SNA Gateway [GG24-3552].

To the host, the LAN Gateway appears as an SNA type 2.0 control-unit. To the stations on the LAN, the gateway looks like an SNA type 4 communications controller, providing 802.2 connectivity. The gateway operates in two modes. It implements the LU functions (LU 0, 1, 2, 3, and 6.2) as dependent LUs in the gateway as long as the corresponding workstation is offline. However, as soon as a workstation is online, the

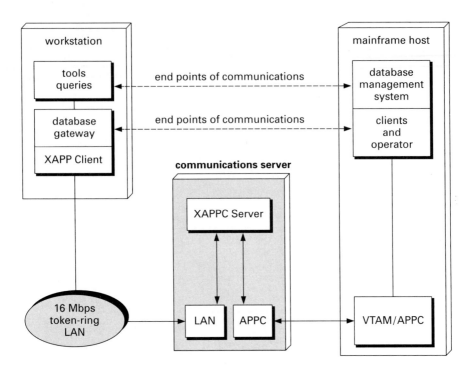

Figure 17.18 Data flow, LAN to host, using APPC carriage [SH21-0438].

gateway steps aside and lets the workstation assume the responsibility of supporting the LU functions. All subsequent LU-LU and LU-SSCP traffic exchanged with the host is simply passed through the gateway transparently.

By pooling LUs, the gateway can require the definition of fewer LUs at the host than are actually defined at the LAN. At logon, the gateway can choose an LU from the pool. Dedicated LUs (outside the pool) are also available. The end-user can use any PC software that offers SNA downstream support. For example, LAN-attached PCs running OS/2 EE, DOS APPC/PC, and DOS 3270 software products can simultaneously use the same gateway. The multitasking facilities of OS/2 provide the capability to run these gateway facilities and other tasks of the LAN Network Manager at the same time.

APPC Host Gateway.   A special case, but also an interesting illustration, is the gateways used in the IBM Data Interpretation System [SH21-0438]. Advanced Program-to-Program Communications (APPC), using LU 6.2, is the carrier for LAN to host communications, *even when the LAN workstation upper-layer protocols (layers 4 through 7) are different from those on the host.* Figure 17.18 shows a two-step client–server process to connect a query application to a host Database Management System (DBMS), such as SQL/DS. This particular offering (the Data Interpretation System) uses *XNS protocols*[12] on the LAN. An

---

12.   XNS is based on the Xerox Corporation LAN protocols.

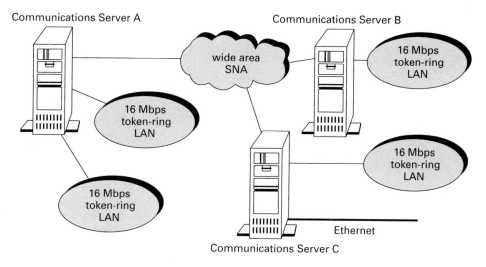

Figure 17.19 LAN-to-LAN via APPC on a wide area SNA network [SH21-0438].

application-layer gateway then places the message from the workstation into an APPC (LU6.2) packet, for transmission to the host. That host client program then makes the query to the DBMS. The effect is as shown, with the workstation client communicating with the host client to achieve communications between the queries application and the DBMS.

That same communications server can also provide *APPC carriage for the XNS-based data between LANs*, and across an SNA WAN, as in Figure 17.19. Similarly, APPC carriage can be used to connect adjacent LANs (up to thirteen intervening LANs can separate two communicating LANs). The communications servers establish APPC conversations with each other over the SNA network (using leased or switched lines) and any intervening LANs. The XNS-based data is thus routed among the token-ring and Ethernet LANs over the APPC conversations.

LANs with NetBIOS and APPC.   We frequently encounter multiple protocols, such as NetBIOS and APPC/APPN or OSI on LANs. In the following we discuss some design alternatives for handling these protocol combinations.

For example, NetBIOS may be used for LAN client to PS/2 LAN server, and APPC may be used for LAN client to S/390 server communications. Workstations come in various sizes, however, and the luxury of both NetBIOS and APPC/APPN protocol sets is sometimes something that the limited memory of a workstation can ill afford. We next consider various options.

The simplest approach (though somewhat more expensive in memory) is that shown in Figure 17.20. The LAN server and the workstation can both handle two protocol sets, NetBIOS and APPC/APPN. The SNA unit on the LAN is only an intermediate-node for the host APPC session. No protocol conversion is needed anywhere.

In the next possibility, shown in Figure 17.21, the LAN units are trimmed down to one transport-provider. This is the currently common use of NetBIOS on the LAN. The server

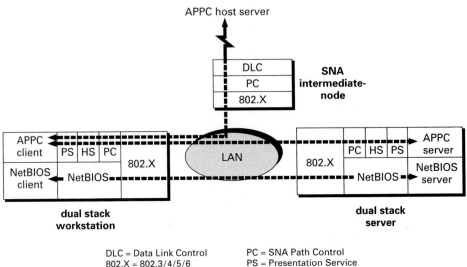

DLC = Data Link Control   PC = SNA Path Control
802.X = 802.3/4/5/6   PS = Presentation Service
HS = SNA Half-Session

Figure 17.20 Dual protocol stacks in both workstation and server.

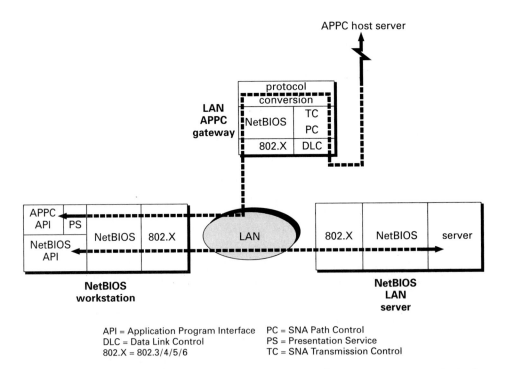

API = Application Program Interface   PC = SNA Path Control
DLC = Data Link Control   PS = Presentation Service
802.X = 802.3/4/5/6   TC = SNA Transmission Control

Figure 17.21 Dual API but single-transport protocol in workstation; and single-protocol stack in LAN server.

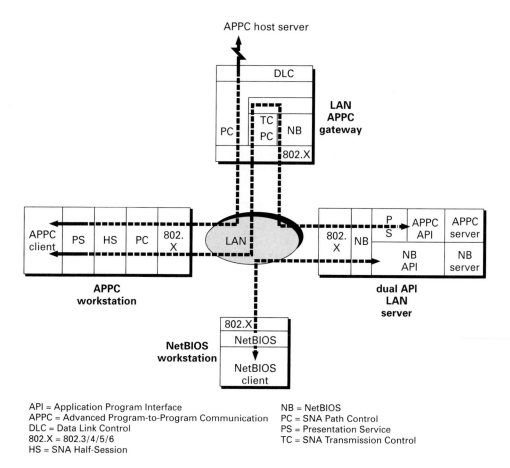

Figure 17.22 Single-protocol stacks in workstations; and dual API but single-transport in LAN server.

is reduced to only NetBIOS and its API. Also, the workstation is relieved of the two transports, allowing only NetBIOS as the transport while still allowing the two APIs in the workstation. Using only NetBIOS on the LAN then requires a mapping of the APPC API to NetBIOS in the workstation, and the conversion of NetBIOS to SNA/APPN in the gateway, for interaction with the host.

In the next scenario, in Figure 17.22, we economize in two types of workstations, and put some burden on the LAN server. The LAN server has only a single (NetBIOS) transport-provider, but has dual API. This server can have both NetBIOS-based and APPC-based application-services. Two types of workstations, either APPC or NetBIOS-based, have only one transport-provider each. The APPC-based workstation connects through an intermediate function unit on the LAN to remote APPC-based application-services. There remains the problem of granting the APPC-based workstation access to the LAN server, which only understands NetBIOS and not APPN. The burden of converting the SNA/APPN to NetBIOS is placed in the gateway; and the mapping of the APPC API to NetBIOS is done in the server.

A final scenario could combine the single transport, dual API workstation of Figure 17.21 with the single transport, dual API of the server in Figure 17.22.

DECnet connections.   A situation comparable to that of Figure 17.21 occurs when the LAN is Ethernet, rather than token ring, and the protocol stack is that of DECnet rather than NetBIOS. Again, a protocol conversion (DECnet to SNA) external to the LAN, and (logically) between the LAN and the host is needed. The 3172 provides the link-layer connection between the Ethernet and the S/390, as discussed above. The DECnet/SNA gateway is provided by host software from *Interlink Computer Sciences* (SNS/SNA GATEWAY) (see Section 5.9). The 3172/Interlink combination thus supports the interconnection of Ethernet devices running DEC communications software with host applications running SNA software. When an Ethernet supports both TCP/IP and DECnet protocols, a separate Ethernet adapter (on the 3172) is used for each type of flow. Both protocols, however, flow over the same channel adapter.

17.5.3   Coax Wiring to Token Ring

There are large investments in coaxial wiring from cluster controllers to workstations. Pending a rewiring for direct LAN attachment, an interim peer-to-peer communications among these programmable workstations is possible. The **Peer Communications** feature on the 3174, with **Peer-Station (PS)** services enable coax-attached PCs with coax-type 3270 emulator cards to run LAN software and interact with like PCs on connected token rings. Interactions may be between workstations on the same cluster controller or between workstations whose cluster controllers are connected by token-ring LANs. This PS mode is limited to applications that use either the 802.2 interface or the NetBIOS interface. It is done at some sacrifice in data-transfer performance, below that of the 4 Mbps token ring.

In effect, *the cluster controller provides the equivalent of an internal token-ring LAN*, complete with LAN adapters for the attached PCs. That internal LAN, in turn, can be bridged to other external token-ring LANs.

The 3174 cluster (establishment) controller supports a source-routing bridge function for communicating between the pseudo-LAN in the cluster controller and other 802.5 LANs. It provides basic frame-routing services, queues up and transmits frames outbound from peer stations, and monitors the token ring for MAC frames addressed to its peer stations. As with actual LAN segments, each peer station has its own MAC address.

Higher-layer protocols, such as LU-6.2, LU-2, and NetBIOS, are supported, as long as they meet the 802.2 or NetBIOS interface specifications. Peer stations (DOS or OS/2), for example, can communicate with host APPC applications or with LAN servers [Tolly90].

17.5.4   Token Ring Connection Overview

It is difficult to get a complete overview of all the current connectivity possibilities that exist today. Figure 17.23 attempts to summarize only some of the available connections to a token-ring LAN. They range from simple terminals, like the 3270, and programmable

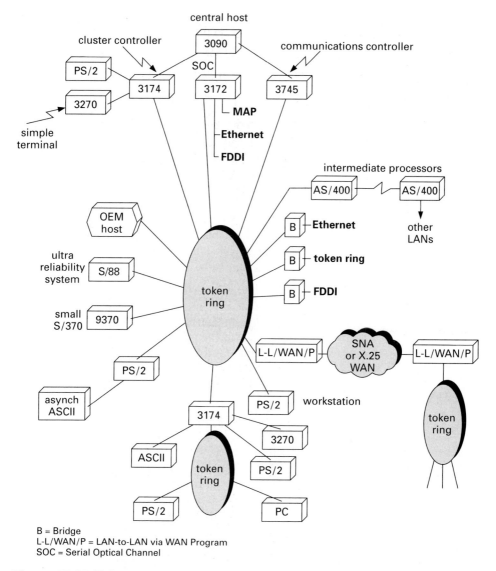

Figure 17.23 Token ring attachments of IBM and non-IBM components [G521-1210].

workstations, like the PS/2, through intermediate processors, like the AS/400 and 9370, to large central hosts like those in ES/9000. The latter connect to subnetworks via communications controllers, like the 3725, and 3745, or the direct attachment of the 3172. Cluster controllers (also called *establishment controllers*), like the 3174, gather clusters of "dumb" terminals, as well as programmable workstations. Ethernet, token bus (using MAP protocols), and fiber FDDI are joined via bridges to the token ring. They are also joined via the 3172 to the mainframe. So, too, are the wide area networks connected to mainframes via the communications controllers such as the 3745 or the integrated communications adapters of the AS/400 or 9370.

Software support. Beyond connectivity, of course, is the question of communicability. For that, the higher layers of protocols (layers 3 through 7) are provided in OSI, SNA, TCP/IP, or NetBIOS, as described in earlier chapters.

APIs appropriate to LAN operations are readily available in software-support packages. For DOS-based workstations, for example, the IBM LAN Support Program provides the 802.2 interface as well as a NetBIOS interface. The API for use of LU 6.2 is provided in the APPC/PC software, which in turn uses the 802.2 interface of the LAN Support Program. The LAN Support Program is not needed for workstations using OS/2 EE, as equivalent functions are incorporated in the OS/2 communications subsystem.

Systems like PS/2, with multitasking OS/2, then enable a user to (a) communicate with servers on the LAN, (b) execute local applications, (c) execute applications split among multiple (PS/2 or mainframe) processors, and (d) execute a local application while other software monitors or intercepts incoming messages. Other PS/2s and mainframes may act as servers. As an example, a PS/2 on a LAN, with type 2.1 node capability, can use LU 6.2 program-to-program capability to communicate with host or other PS/2 applications. Concurrently, in another task, it may emulate a 3278 "dumb" terminal for interaction with other host programs. Concurrently, it may use NetBIOS to communicate with other PCs on the LAN. One of those might be a PS/2 server on the LAN, which might also be able to fetch relevant data from a mainframe host.

17.5.5   A Campus Illustration

As a further example, LANs are widely used in university campuses to interconnect independent department subnetworks [G521-1210]. Initial growth is often in isolated department LANs, using different network software (such as Novell's Netware, 3Com's 3+ Open, IBM's LAN Server, and so forth). The department LANs may be of different types, such as token ring, Ethernet, or the Apple LocalTalk. When the need for a campus-wide communications leads to the installation of a backbone network, those department LANs are connected to the backbone.

Figure 17.24 illustrates different kinds of interconnections to the backbone: Ethernet, token ring, a second-level Ethernet, and connections to a host and a WAN gateway. By these connections, both primary and satellite buildings are connected to a dual backbone ring. A fiber-optic ring will support either a 16 Mbps token ring network or a 100 Mbps FDDI network. Relative to FDDI, the 16 Mbps token ring network is a low-cost, mature technology. Later, when the need for a higher bandwidth backbone develops, it would be a natural migration to an FDDI backbone.

Recalling the discussion of Section 12.9, regarding multiprotocol backbones, bridges and routers can be used variously to make these connections and to control the flows among the subnetworks. Bridges provide a low cost, simple solution. Routers are used (either as shown in Figure 17.24 or as inter-subnetwork-routers attached to each subnetwork as in Figure 12.21) when the broadcast and other traffic between subnetworks need to be further controlled.

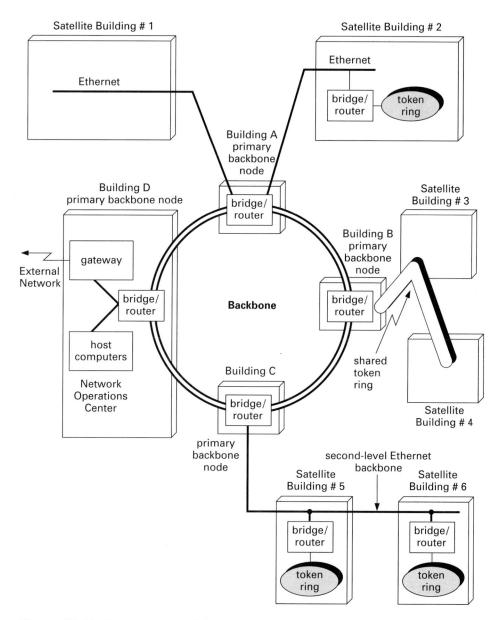

Figure 17.24 Campus connectivity.

Prompted by such environments, there is a trend in the computer industry to provide for the attachment of workstations to any of several types of LANs. For example, Apple and other vendors have announced Ethernet and token ring adapters for the Macintosh. IBM, Sun, and Apollo workstations support token ring and Ethernet connections. Also, IBM PCs can attach to LocalTalk via an adapter made by TOPS.

Conclusion

LANs have become an integral part and often the key part of many enterprise networks. They interconnect terminals, workstations, establishment (display) controllers, communications controllers, and mainframes. LANs and WANs (particularly higher-speed ones) are rapidly becoming integrated, providing ready access to all applications and application-services. The empowerment provided by the PC is augmented by the ability to *share the services of diverse servers on LANs and WANs that have very good response times.*

The integration of the LAN and WAN facilities, creates a broad spectrum of hosts and servers that includes mainframes as well as PC, PS/2 and RISC S/6000 class machines. The any-to-any capability, across LANs and WANs is also brought closer by the extension of Advanced Peer-to-Peer Networking to the LAN, as discussed in Chapter 14. The upper layers see a common LAN service, through the common 802.2 interface, whether the lower layer be for Ethernet 802.3, token ring, token bus, or FDDI.

The LANs that are interconnected by layer-2 bridges are protocol-independent, easily extending communicability across departments and work groups. The interoperation of systems on Ethernets, token rings, and FDDI is now becoming a practical reality. Protocol converting bridges like the 8209 are accompanied by the SRT bridge technique that easily handles both transparent and source routing. The need for a degree of isolation and control among very large LAN clusters then leads to the growing roles of layer-3 routers, which must likewise become multiprotocol capable, as discussed in Chapter 12.

The use of high-speed WANs for LAN-to-LAN connection is addressed in Chapter 18. LAN-to-LAN connections for NetBIOS and the LAN/WAN interactions with NetWare are discussed in Chapter 19.

Acknowledgments

I am particularly indebted to R. C. Dixon, J. J. Lynch, K. A. Preiss, and J. L. Smith, for valuable input or reviews of this chapter.

TECHNICAL REFERENCES

LAN PDU (Frame) Formats

In Figure 17.25, the first bit of the DSAP, within the 802.3/4/5 LLC header, indicates whether the destination is an individual or a group. The DSAP for the global destination (all active stations) is all one's.

In Figure 17.26, the control field, within the 802.3/4/5 LLC header, has one of three formats. When the first bit is 0, the format is that for information transfer. When the first two bits are 10, the format is for supervisory commands. When the first two bits are 11, the format is for unnumbered commands. The 7-bit sequence numbers N(S) and N(R) come from modulo 128 counters.

LSAPs

Figure 17.27 shows the older de facto Ethernet v2 format and a hybrid that IBM uses on the older Ethernets for SNA traffic. Half of the LSAP address space is reserved (by the IEEE standard) to identify which higher-layer protocol stack is to be used (e.g., SNA or OSI or TCP/IP). IBM has

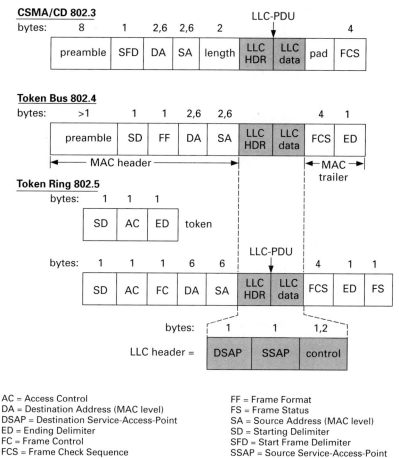

Figure 17.25 802.3/4/5 LAN frame formats.

defined some SAP uses, also. For example, some of the SAP addresses in use are [GG24-3376]:

LSAP Addresses	Name	Defined by
X03	Network Management	IEEE
X06	DOD INTERNET	IEEE
XFE	ISO Network Layer	IEEE
XAA	SNAP	IEEE
X04	SNA Path Control	IBM
XF0	NetBIOS	IBM

For historical reasons, two LSAPs can be used for OSI services: *7E* for 8208 CONS and *7F* for either CONS or CLNS.

The SNAP (Subnetwork Access Protocol) code point AA is used in both the DSAP and SSAP fields when TCP/IP uses either an 802.3 or 802.5 LAN, to indicate that additional fields (the SNAP header) have been added to the standard formats. Those extended formats are shown in Figure 17.28.

Destination Service-Access-Point

bit 0 = individual or group address
bits 1 through 7 = 7-bit address

Source Service-Access-Point

bit 0 = command or response indicator
bits 1 through 7 = 7-bit address

Logical-Link Control

The control field follows the CCITT LAP-B definition

byte 0								byte 1	
0	1	2	3	4	5	6	7	0	1–7

0				$N_{(S)}$				P/F	$N_{(R)}$	information transfer
1	0	S	S	X	X	X	X	P/F	$N_{(R)}$	supervisory commands
1	1	M	M	P/F	M	M	M			unnumbered commands

information and supervisory		unnumbered	
commands	responses	commands	responses
I	I	UI	UA
RR	RR	SABME	DM
RNR	RNR	DISC	FRMR
REJ	REJ	XID	XID
		TEST	TEST

DISC = Disconnect
DM = Disconnected Mode
FRMR = Frame Reject
I = Information
M = Modifier function bits
N(R) = Receive Sequence Number
N(S) = Send Sequence Number
P/F = Poll/Final Bit
REJ = Reject

RNR = Receive Not Ready
RR = Receive Ready
S = Supervisory Function Bits
SABME = Set Asynchronous Balanced Mode Extended
UA = Unnumbered Acknowledgment
UI = Unnumbered Information
X = Reserved
XID = Exchange Station Identification

Figure 17.26 Service-access-point (SAP) and logical-link control (LLC) header fields.

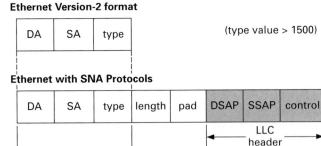

Ethernet Version-2 format

DA	SA	type

(type value > 1500)

Ethernet with SNA Protocols

DA	SA	type	length	pad	DSAP	SSAP	control

LLC header

DA = Destination Address (MAC level)
DSAP = Destination Service-Access-Point
LLC = Logical-Link Control
SA = Source Address (MAC level)
SSAP = Source Service-Access-Point

Figure 17.27 Ethernet addressing formats.

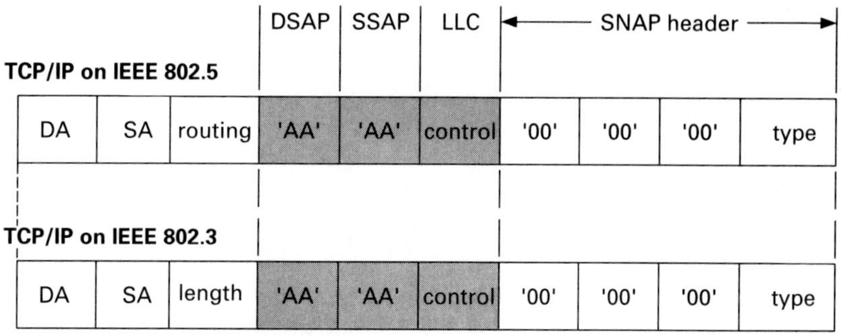

DA = Destination Address (MAC level)
DSAP = Destination Service-Access-Point
LLC = Logical-Link Control
SA = Source Address (MAC level)
SSAP = Source Service-Access-Point

Figure 17.28 TCP/IP addressing on IEEE 802.3/5 (RFC-1042 recommend use of SNAP headers).

(TCP/IP uses only connectionless (type 1) LLC. The LLC control byte therefore usually indicates only Unnumbered Information (UI) (set to 03), although the standard allows TEST and XID commands as well.)

OSI LLC Primitives

Listed are the OSI LLC primitives and their parameters for two modes: unacknowledged connectionless and connect. The columns on the right indicate whether a parameter is carried in the request (Req), indication (Ind), response (Res), or confirm (Conf).

	Req	Ind	Rsp	Conf
UNACKNOWLEDGED CONNECTIONLESS MODE				
DL-UnitData	X	X		
source_address	X	X		
destination_address	X	X		
data	X	X		
priority	X	X		
CONNECTION MODE				
DL-Connect	X	X	X	X
source_address	X	X	X	X
destination-address	X	X	X	X
priority	X	X	X	X
DL-Data	X	X		
source_address	X	X		
destination_address	X	X		
data	X	X		

	Req	Ind	Rsp	Conf
DL-Disconnect	X	X		
source_address	X	X		
destination_address	X	X		
reason		X		
DL-Reset	X	X	X	X
source_address	X	X	X	X
destination_address	X	X	X	X
reason		X		
DL-Connection_FlowControl	X	X		
source_address	X	X		
destination_address	X	X		
amount	X	X		

EXERCISES

17.1   What are the five limited area networks that use the common 802.2 interface?

17.2   What are the three primary components of every LAN?

17.3   What are some of the functions of the DLC logical-link control?

17.4   What does the token-ring *active monitor* and its *ring poll* do?

17.5   What happens after a token-ring station detects a loss of signal and begins transmitting a beacon frame with the address of the NAUN?

17.6   What is meant by *early token release*?

17.7   How is the probability of collision reduced in CSMA/CD LANs?

17.8   What is the spanning tree used by transparent bridges?

17.9   In source routing, how does the originating station get information on possible routes without sending multiple route messages to the destination?

17.10   How does the SRT bridge work?

18
High-Speed Services

18.1 INTRODUCTION

A large new set of high-speed transmission facilities, at layers 1 and 2, are becoming available. These include FDDI—a high-performance LAN, Metropolitan Area Networks—for public, citywide communication, ISDN WANs, frame-relay interfaces with fast packet switching networks, and Serial Optical Channels for the extended data center. Referring back to our basic Figure 3.14, *these all fit below the link/subnetwork-access boundary*. The trend of architectures in this area was discussed in Chapter 16, where common use of components at this level, and *common access by upper protocol stacks* (OSI, TCP/IP, SNA, NetBIOS) was emphasized. The link/subnetwork-access boundary, and the growing number of high-speed options, enlarges the opportunities for sharing lower-layer facilities among multiple-protocol stacks, which has been a basic theme in this view of Open-Systems Network-Architecture (OSNA).

This chapter provides a highly compressed overview of this rapidly growing area. Key characteristics, basic operations, and architectural structures are briefly described.

18.2 THE BANDWIDTH EXPLOSION

The economics of transmission is now dramatically affected by the prevalence of optical fiber. T1 links at 1.54 Mbps are followed by T3 links at 44.73 Mbps. Each of these offer major reductions in price per unit of bandwidth.[1] That pattern is followed as the **SONET (Synchronous Optical NETwork)** unfolds. SONET specifies the transmission encoding and multiplexing scheme for the fiber optic backbone network. The operation is defined in the United States, for speeds from 51.84 Mbps to 2.4 Gbps (with extensions possible to

---

1. The breakeven points for converting to T1 and T3 have been estimated to be: the cost of 5 to 6 56 kbps lines equals the cost of one T1 (@ 1.544 Mbps), and the cost of 4 to 5 T1 lines equals the cost one T3 (@ 44.736 Mbps).

13.2 Gbps), using byte interleaved multiplexing. The unit of bandwidth, 51.84 Mbps, is planned in multiples of 1 to 48 units. Bit rate families are simply multiples; that is, OC-n has a bit rate of n times 51.84 Mbps. The earlier offerings, first up to OC-3 at 155 Mbps and then up to OC-12 at 622 Mbps are major milestones to enable data/voice/image communications.

The advent of optical pipes across the country will thus open up new options for broadband transport. The anticipated bit rates in the public network digital hierarchy for the U.S., Canada, and Japan, include:

DS0	64 kbps	1 DS0
T1= DS1	1.544 Mbps	24xDS0
DS1C	3.152 Mbps	48xDS0
T2= DS2	6.312 Mbps	96xDS0
T3= DS3	44.736 Mbps	672xDS0
DS4	274.176 Mbps	4032xDS0[2]
STS-1 and OC-1	51.840 Mbps	
STS-3 and OC-3	155.52 Mbps	
STS-12 and OC-12	622.08 Mbps	
STS-24 and OC-24	1244.16 Mbps	
STS-48 and OC-48	2488.32 Mbps	

The STS/OC family is the SONET physical layer ANSI standard. STS refers to the interface for electrical signals; and OC (which stands for Optical Carrier) is the light or photonic equivalent.

The hierarchy used in Europe and elsewhere includes:

E0	64 kbps
E1	2.048 Mbps
E2	8.448 Mbps
E3	34.368 Mbps
E4	139.264 Mbps

At OC-3 (155.52) and above we get worldwide commonality under CCITT standards for the Synchronous Digital Hierarchy (SDH):

SDH-1	155.52 Mbps (same as OC-3)
SDH-4	622.08 Mbps (same as OC-12)
SDH-16	2488.32 Mbps (same as OC-48)

In addition to all these plans, much of the literature suggests that 10 gigabits per second per fiber is a reasonable goal by the year 2000 (see Section 18.12). Beyond that, research on wave-length division multiplexing in fiber promises many times that speed.

---

2. Note that framing bits overhead account for the fact that the bit rates are not exact multiples of DS0=64 kbps.

18.3 HIGH-SPEED OPTIONS

Introduction.   LAN speeds (in FDDI) have already increased to 100 Mbps. With the above prospects, WAN speeds will dramatically increase also. These developments can dramatically change the communications scene. New applications are prompted by the available bandwidth. Taking advantage of the improving economics, message lengths for images, animation, and compound documents will probably increase greatly. More workstations will appear per establishment; and shorter response times will be routine. Wider use of image storage, FAX, electronic mail, and new forms of interaction, such as video telephonics and workgroup video, are probable.

An early and major thrust in the use of high-speed, wide-area facilities is the interconnection of LANs and widely separated data centers. The enterprise network takes on the appearance of Figure 18.1. Local communications, using sets of LANs and subnetworks with traditional multidrop concentration, are linked by high-speed WANs. Local interactive traffic, especially that on LANs, comes in bursts—it can consume the full network capacity for brief moments and then be minimum for long periods. Hence meeting the needs of 100 Mbps LANs requires WANs with at least T3 (i.e., 45 Mbps) capability. As bandwidth becomes more available, performance comparable to that in the LAN will be obtainable across interconnected, widely separated regions. Full connectivity will need the OC-3 at 155 Mbps. The new fiber optic transmission facilities have also given carriers and companies the opportunity to save expenses by sharing these WAN facilities among voice, data, facsimile, image, and video.

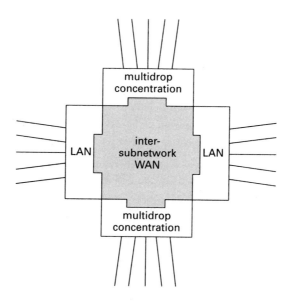

Figure 18.1 Multidrop and LAN concentration feeding the intersubnetwork WAN.

Seven options emerge.   Amid the very intense research and development in the high-speed arena, the following major thrusts are evident:

- *ISDN*: Public and/or private ISDN, using basic and primary interfaces, for voice and data, at 64 kbps and 1.544 Mbps in the U.S., and 2.048 Mbps in Europe
- *Frame-relay* data interface and associated fast packet networks at 1.544 Mbps and higher
- *FDDI*: High-speed (100 Mbps) LANs
- *Private bandwidth management* of the new facilities for voice/data/image, at T3 (45 Mbps) and higher
- *MANs*: Public and/or private Metropolitan Area Networks at 45 Mbps and higher
- *SMDS*: Switched Multimegabit Data Service (SMDS), providing a backbone service for MANs
- *Broadband ISDN*: Public and/or private ISDN using Asynchronous Transfer Mode (ATM) at 150 Mbps and higher

In a different category is an eighth option, the Serial Optical Channel (SOC), at 200 Mbps, and the High-Performance Parallel Interface (HiPPI), at 800 Mbps, which greatly extend the range of channel-connected computers, devices and workstations.

Fast-packet switching.   In the metropolitan and wide area networks, techniques called *fast-packet switching* are in rapid evolution. This term is generally applied to two different approaches:

1.   **Frame relay** operates with a *variable length frame* (which could, for example, be compatible with those used in LANs or current WANs). Frames are relayed at layer 2 or layer 1, rather than at layer 3. The CCITT I.122 recommendation, for a frame-relay interface, uses a Link-Access-Procedure based on LAP-D, as in the ISDN recommendation I.441, Q.921/Q.922.

2.   **Cell relay** works with *small, fixed-length packets* that contain a 48-byte payload and a 5-byte header. These cells are relayed at layer 1, the physical layer, in a manner similar to a multiplexor. Two standards based on cell-relay have been defined: IEEE 802.6 for MANs and Asynchronous Transfer Mode (ATM) for WANs.

Both types of relay derive from the fact that networks using fiber are highly reliable and run at very high speeds. Both take advantage of the fact that the end-systems using the WAN are usually programmable and powerful enough to perform any necessary error correction and end-to-end flow control. Both, accordingly, perform routing below layer 3, and minimize error control and flow control within the subnetwork switch-nodes.[3]

---

3.   Routing in variable-length fast-packet and cell-relay networks is clearly below layer 3 (many people prefer to call this *switching*). Whether we consider the routing to be in an upper sublayer of layer 1 or a lower sublayer of layer-2 hinges on new definitions of these layers, which are still being debated.

Note that both frame-relay and cell-relay techniques can be used in interfaces for access to networks which may or may not use the same architecture within the network.[4]

Switched facilities.   Switched, rather than, or in addition to, leased high-speed facilities are increasingly attractive. Switched back-up to a private leased network is often essential. Switched T1 and T3 services are available. Bandwidth on demand, in increments of 56 kbps, up to 448 kbps, has also been offered.[5] This trend can be expected to continue, as more carriers complete their high-speed switching systems.

Structure.   All of these new directions fit within the link/subnetwork-access macro-layer of Open-Systems Network-Architecture (OSNA) described previously. The universal addressing structures of OSI, incorporating subnetwork addresses within a general NSAP structure, as described in Section 12.3.3, apply to each. Some, for example, like MANs and ISDN, which are carrier-oriented, will use the E.164 (CCITT I.331) numbering scheme, which in turn fits within the OSI NSAP structure. Each can make use of an internetworking layer 3c where address resolution may be needed between subnetworks. Some, like FDDI and MAN fit easily under the same 802.2 interface that the LANs (802.3/4/5) fit into. Some, like X.25 may need a convergence sublayer 3b to fit more perfectly under a particular layer 3c.

Moreover, these layer-1 and -2 services are, in principle, usable by each of the upper-layer protocol stacks shown in Figure 3.14: including the inter-subnetwork facilities at layer 3c and the end-to-end data-exchange facilities like APPC, OSI transaction-processing, and remote-procedure-call, at layers 5 through 7. Each can carry the application-services like file transfer, distributed database, and asynchronous messaging. In each case, therefore, these new directions provide cost and performance opportunities, as options to be used by multiple upper-layer protocols within the OSNA structure.

18.4   FDDI

18.4.1   Introduction

FDDI is a major step upward in LAN performance, using fiber. It has been developed in the Accredited Standards Committee (ASC) X3T9 (the relevant ISO standards are IS 9314/1 2 and DIS 9314/3). Following the architectural concepts of IEEE 802, the committee chose the token ring protocol of IEEE 802.5 as the starting point for the FDDI MAC protocol [Ross89]. Since *FDDI is also compatible with the common 802.2 interface*, upgrades to FDDI should be relatively easy.

---

4.   IBM plans to start using fast-packet technology in 1993, adding features to APPN that take advantage of high-speed transmission links by eliminating hop-by-hop flow control, according to Rick McGee, IBM's manager of communications systems architecture, reported in *Data Communications*, March 1991.

5.   Switched T1 and switched T3 offerings were announced by the Williams Telecommunications Group, and Bandwidth on Demand was announced by U.S. Sprint, at the Telecommunications Association Annual Conference, Sept. 23–28, 1990, in San Diego, CA.

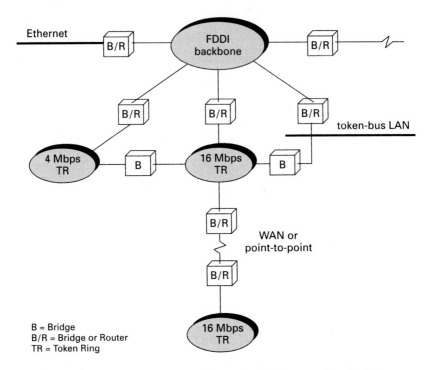

Figure 18.2 Multiple LAN interconnections via a high-speed backbone.

The FDDI network is a 100 Mbps token ring[6] using optical fiber, with dual counter-rotating rings. One ring is used for data transmission, and the other remains as backup in case of link or station failure. The FDDI can be used as a high-speed backbone for lower speed 4, 10, and 16 Mbps LANs, as shown in Figure 18.2. Its high speed will also be valued in file and bit-mapped graphics transfers, as interconnects among mainframes, and as an access point for overall system management. An enhancement to FDDI, called FDDI-II, adds a time-division-multiplexing capability, to accommodate mixtures of voice, video, and sensor data.

A functioning FDDI network will, however, require a family of high-speed components. Recalling the discussion in Section 12.9, concerning the use of bridges and/or routers for a multiprotocol backbone, a variety of components is needed. A possible combination of elements is shown in Figure 18.3. It includes, for example: single-unit stations, concentrators, mainframe host gateways, bridges/routers to LANs (4/16 Mbps token rings, Ethernet and FDDI), remote FDDI-to-FDDI bridges/routers, and routers between FDDI and WANs.

---

6. The FDDI link rate is 125 Mbps, but due to the 5/4 coding scheme, the effective bit rate is 100 Mbps.

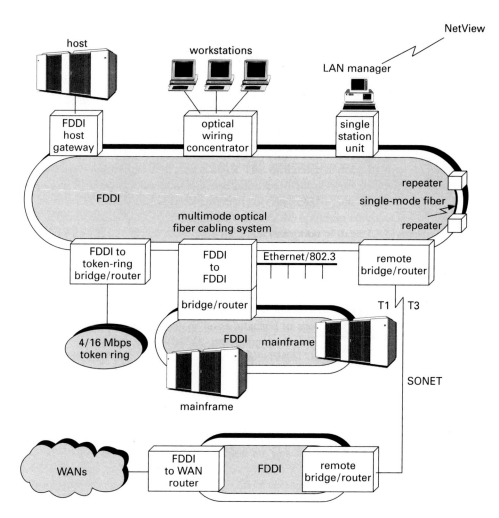

Figure 18.3 Elements of a high-performance LAN/WAN configuration.

Key FDDI features.   In summary, key characteristics of FDDI include:

- Fiber optic medium[7]
    - LED-based technology
    - Duplex cable and connectors

---

7.   The FDDI standard specifies 62.5/125 micron multimode optical fiber media as the reference media. The standard also provides information for attaching FDDI cable plants using 50/125, 100/ 140, and 85/125 micron multimode optical fibers as alternatives. The FDDI standard will also specify a single-mode optical fiber for extending the transmission distances from 2 km to up to 20 km. IBM recommends 9/125 or 10/125 micron single-mode fibers for this application.

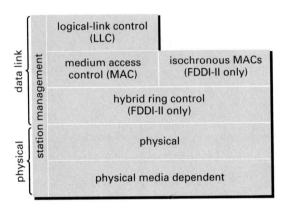

Figure 18.4 FDDI architecture sublayers.

- Token-passing architecture
- High speed (100 Mbps)
- Dual ring connection for redundancy and dual access
- Networks of up to 500 stations on a 100 km duplex cable
- Up to 2 km between stations

Sublayers.   The sublayers of the FDDI architecture are shown in Figure 18.4.

- The *Physical-Media-Dependent (PMD)* sublayer concerns the electrical and optical link connections. It characterizes the fiber-optic drivers and receivers, the cables, and the connectors. The physical media is two strands of optical fiber, driven by light emitting diodes, which operate at a wavelength of 1,300 nanometers.

- The *physical sublayer (Phy)* handles the clocking, encoding, and decoding functions. It serves to synchronize the data and its clocks.

- *Medium Access Control (MAC)* handles packet framing, token control, and address recognition/generation. It also verifies frame check sequences.

- *Logical-Link Control (LLC)*, which provides data assurance services, is outside the FDDI standard. The FDDI MAC, however, is specified to be compatible with a superset of the logical-link control (LLC) protocol developed by IEEE 802.2.

  FDDI-II adds two other distinct sublayers to handle the special clocking and access controls for isochronous data (see Section 18.4.3). The station-management standards provide for station participation in station-initialization, error-recovery, and configuration-management.

18.4.2 Operations

The FDDI LAN uses two counter-rotating 100 Mbps token rings [Thurber89]. Each station on the loop regenerates and repeats each symbol it receives. The nature of the clocking system limits the *variable length* frame sizes to a maximum of 4500 bytes.

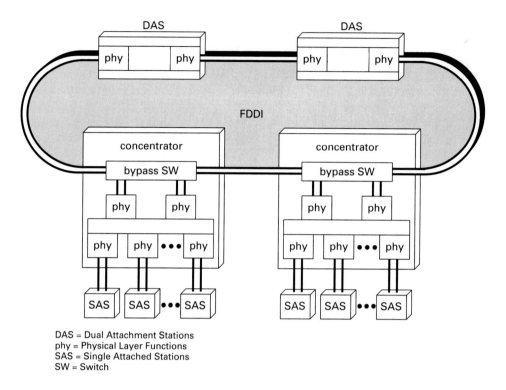

DAS = Dual Attachment Stations
phy = Physical Layer Functions
SAS = Single Attached Stations
SW = Switch

Figure 18.5 FDDI using concentrators.

Wrapping. In normal operation, data is transmitted on the primary ring. The secondary ring is provided for fault tolerance and reconfiguration. If there is a break in a cable, or if one station on the ring fails or is powered off, the station adjacent to the interruption "*wraps*" the secondary and primary rings together, to form a new continuous ring. In case of multiple failures, the wrap process continues, forming multiple disjoint rings.

Stations may also offer *by-pass capability*, whereby an optical switch by-passes a station's receiver and transmitter connections. The signal from an upstream station is passed directly to the next station downstream from the one by-passed. By-passing may be initiated by the station itself, by a neighboring station, automatically at the removal of power, by a human operator, or by some network configuration function.

Concentrators. Individual (dual-attachment) stations on the ring must have two physical-layer entities to accommodate the two counter-rotating rings. However, a more economic approach than direct station attachment is to use concentrators, as shown in Figure 18.5, to which multiple devices can be attached [Juenzel89]. A concentrator can monitor all of its attached stations. If a single attached station, or its cable, fails, the by-passing of the failure can occur electronically within the concentrator. Single station adds and deletes need not affect the backbone loop. The optical spurs from the concentrators also increases the distances that can be handled. Still more complex configurations are allowed in the standard.

A dual attachment concentrator can attach *a tree of single attachment concentrators*, with single attachment stations as the lowest leafs of the tree.

Token operations.   A unit on the FDDI LAN can release a free token immediately after transmitting a message on the ring. Therefore, one or more frames and a free token can exist at the same time on the ring.

A given MAC will transmit a frame only after it has captured a token. After capturing a token, a station may continue to transmit until its token-hold timer expires, or it has no more information to transmit. After transmitting its frames, the station issues a new token. A frame travels around the ring, back to the station that placed it on the ring. Recognizing its own source address, the MAC of the origination station strips its frame from the ring. The contents of the frame-status (FS) field indicate the success (or failure) of the transmission.

Synchronous service, in FDDI, is an optional service, not required for interoperability. It is defined as a level of service that is needed, regardless of the load on the ring, by applications with predictable bandwidth and response-time limits. This service would be used, for example, for voice, real-time data, and video. Those *stations allocated synchronous service may use an available token whenever the station has messages queued for transmission. It may transmit, however, only for an agreed upon length of time.* The allocation of synchronous bandwidth to each station is managed by station management, in response to requests from stations. *Those stations can then transmit a prenegotiated amount of data with each captured token.*

Maintaining fairness.   FDDI uses a unique measure of LAN utilization to enforce fairness of access for all stations. As more and more frames are added to the ring, by successive stations, the token, as seen by the down-stream node, in effect continues to be bumped to the rear, and it takes increasingly longer for the token to get around. Hence that time (the **token-rotation-time**) is directly related to the load on the ring. Note that token-rotation-time is the time between the appearance of successive tokens at a particular station. It is not the time for one physical token to travel unimpeded around the ring, because each token is removed and replaced with another when data is inserted.

Accordingly, each station measures the time between appearances of a token. As this time (and the load on the ring) increase, only higher-priority traffic may be placed on the ring (as described further in the following sections).

Asynchronous service is when the level of *service for a given priority will be deferred until the load drops below a prescribed level.* Asynchronous transmissions can be grouped into eight priority levels.

To establish asynchronous access control, each station bids a needed maximum token-rotation-time, depending on the dominant application at that station. The initialization procedure then sets a *Target Token Rotation Time (T-TRT)* for all stations, equal to the lowest value that is bid by any of the stations. (The station bid may be half the "worst case" time, since the FDDI design guarantees no more than twice the T-TRT.)

Asynchronous service may use a token only to the degree that total load permits. A Token-Rotation-Timer (TRT) is set to the T-TRT when a token is captured. TRT then begins to count down. The TRT is reset to T-TRT when a token returns or when the TRT counts all the way down. Whenever a token is captured, the value of the TRT is saved. *Asynchronous traffic may be sent only if the TRT did not expire and there is time left in the TRT. That will be the case so long as the actual token-rotation-time is less than the target token-rotation-time that was set in the timer.* Then, the remaining time in the TRT is the amount of time still allowed for the station to transmit asynchronous data on the captured token [Mazzafero90]. Each station sends its highest-priority data first, and continues until the rotation timer expires or all queued data is sent.

Restricted asynchronous service also guarantees a certain bandwidth and response time, but only after their restricted service begins. There is no guarantee on how long it will take for their restricted service to begin. (FDDI token and frame formats are given in Figure 18.32 in this chapter's Technical Reference section.)

18.4.3 FDDI-II

FDDI-II, a future development, uses a *time-division-multiplexing approach* to *divide the bandwidth between voice and data* [Ross87], [Hehmann90]. FDDI-II can create up to sixteen separate and equal isochronous, duplex channels which operate in increments of 6.144 Mbps, up to a maximum of 99.072 Mbps. To satisfy both European and North American phone systems, each of these channels can be reallocated into subchannels in increments of 8 kbps. Several isochronous channels may be combined to form a larger channel for video and other applications.

The circuit-switched service provides a continuous connection between two stations. Instead of using addresses, the connection is established by knowing the location of time slots that occur regularly, relative to some timing marker.

Frame structure.   A fixed FDDI II frame structure is used. Every 125 usec a new frame is inserted by a station called *cycle master*. Each 125 usec cycle contains a chain of 97 fixed size *cyclic-groups* or slots. One of these is always reserved for token data, providing a minimum bandwidth for data. Each of the 96 other cyclic-groups (slots) in a cycle is available for either isochronous data or token data, with the former taking priority.

Each of the 96 cyclic-groups contains 16 bytes, each of which is available for assignment to one of the 16 isochronous channels. One byte per cycle-group and 96 cycle-groups per 125 usec yields 6.144 Mbps per channel. If an isochronous channel is not assigned, the corresponding data byte in each cyclic-group is integrated as part of the packet (token) data channel [Ross87], [Ross89].

Priority.   Priority in an FDDI II channel is given in four levels:

1.   Circuit-switched data in an isochronous channel
2.   Synchronous traffic, where fixed units of data are to be delivered at regular intervals, with a delay not exceeding twice the T-TRT
3.   Asynchronous traffic that may use either a restricted or nonrestricted token
4.   Asynchronous traffic that may only use a nonrestricted token

All stations on the ring must have FDDI-II capability, for the assignment of isochronous channels.

18.5   HIGH-PERFORMANCE ROUTING (SWITCHING)

18.5.1   Introduction

We next examine techniques for high-performance routing (often called switching) at layers 1 and 2 in WANs. This can be particularly important for LAN-to-LAN via WAN operations. In earlier times, the bandwidths of the communicating media were the limiting factor in throughput. With the fire-hose of data now becoming available over optical fibers, the limiting factor becomes, instead, the processing cycles that are needed in the intermediary-systems and end-systems to simply process each packet going through. As data rates rise above the T1 or T3 level, the processing involved in routing must be reduced, in order to efficiently handle the high volumes of data flowing.

As discussed in Section 12.4.4, this is facilitated if the routing is pushed down from layer 3 to layer 2 or layer 1. A corollary advantage of lower-layer routing (switching) is that such routing can be made essentially transparent to all protocols above the MAC layer. Thus, the multiprotocol transport is facilitated for flows such as OSI, TCP/IP, SNA, NetBIOS, and other protocols. To achieve the performance needed, *routing protocols and formats must also be tailored to hardware, rather than software implementations*. The hardware designs must have structural regularity so as to exploit VLSI wherever possible.

At the same time, the reliability of the media is improving greatly. This can be taken advantage of to reduce the processing load on intermediate-nodes. Most of the transport-layer functions like flow control and error recovery for data, packetization and reassembly, can be performed on an end-to-end basis, or at least at the edges of a subnetwork. This reduction of recovery facilities should not be taken too far, however; error recovery is still needed. Bit Error Rates (BER) of 10^{-12} to 10^{-14} for short haul and 10^{-9} for long haul (50+ km between repeaters) can be reasonably expected. Then, when one has 10^{14} pixels per picture to transmit, we may still have too many errors per picture. At one gigabit per second and 10^{-9} BER, we still have one error per second.

One approach to this reliability issue is to have only end-to-end (or subnetwork edge-to-edge) error recovery during normal operations but to revert to a hop-by-hop error recovery when an error threshold on a particular hop is exceeded. When the error rate again falls below a threshold, then unrecovered flows are used on that hop again. This is the adaptive approach used with *Checkpoint Mode* data link control [Deaton90], [Brodd84], [Bux89].

With the lower-layer routing, multiple media can also be more readily handled. In the past, the voice and video transports have favored circuit switching while the data transports have favored packet switching. The widespread use of digitized voice and video, coupled with large-scale chip integration, offers opportunities for very fast switching fabrics which can accommodate both circuit-switched and packet-switched traffic in a unified manner.

In the following, we illustrate all these possibilities by referring to several experimental examples of fast packet switching. These use VLSI components for very fast *automatic network routing* at lower layers, and offer the options of fixed or variable length packets.

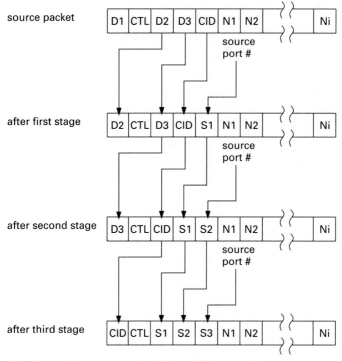

CID = Channel id used by the destined switch fabric adapter
Di = Destination address used by the *i*th stage
Ni = Information field
Si = Source addresses identifying path through the network

Figure 18.6 Example of header modification in three-stage switch configuration [Ahmadi88].

18.5.2   Automatic Network Routing

Automatic network routing (ANR), at layers 1 and 2, is designed to use VLSI fully and to minimize processing in intermediate-nodes. Very high performance results. An example of automatic network routing is shown in Figure 18.6 [Ahmadi88]. This illustrates the way in which the headers are modified, as a packet traverses the switch fabric. The length of the routing address, shown as *D1, D2, D3*, actually would depend on the size of each stage and the number of stages in the switch system. *The Di is the routing address used by the ith stage to route the packet*. The *CID* is a Channel Identification Address that is used by the destined **Switch Fabric Adapter (SFA)** to finally connect to an interface such as ISDN or LAN. A control field, shown as *CTL*, identifies the length of the address, and the priority of the packet.

Assuming a routing address of 1 byte per stage, for example, would allow 256 output lines per stage. In order that each stage can interpret the header identically, the *first* byte of the header always will be the routing address of the destined output link of that stage. The second byte will always be the control field.

At each stage, a shifting of the address is therefore needed. After the first byte, *D1*, has been used by the first stage, to route the packet to its output link, *the whole address field is shifted to the left*, as shown in Figure 18.6. The *D1* is discarded, but the control field retains its position behind the first byte (now *D2*). This process is repeated at each stage. The leading edge byte is always what is needed at each stage. After the last stage, the first byte will be the *CID*, for use by the destination Switch-Fabric-Adapter (SFA).

In order to construct a history of the path taken, the vacant positions (resulting from discarding a byte at each stage) will be filled by the source address at each stage. This is also illustrated in Figure 18.6. Knowledge of such a path has a number of uses. It may, for example, be used by fault management to isolate intermittent failures. It may also be used as the reverse path for fast set-up operations.

In a bandwidth-managing subnetwork where all the nodes had a uniform switch fabric (all of this type), the user packets could be segmented once upon entry into the subnetwork of such nodes. They would not need to be recombined until they reached the other "edge" of the subnetwork. Designs of this nature allow the building of VLSI based switches having large numbers of ports and high total capacity.

The automatic network routing scheme, at layers 1 and 2, requires no software table look-up or storage. Hence, *no routing tables need be updated or used at intermediate-nodes*. Calls can therefore be set up and taken down much faster than in conventional switched systems. Changing routes (e.g., because of malfunctions) during an ongoing call, without disruption to the end user, becomes more feasible. The practical elimination of a set-up phase also facilitates the handling of single datagram packets. In the following, two experimental switches using automatic network routing will be briefly described.

The Zurich switch.   The Zurich switch configuration [Ahmadi88], for integrated circuit and packet switching, is a good illustration of the concepts of switch fabrics with automatic routing at layers 1 and 2. It is shown in Figure 18.7. The *Switch Fabric (SF)* of the switch system contains *Switch Fabric Elements (SFEs)* that can be grouped together to form one or more stages of a multistage fabric. The aggregate of the distributed switch fabric elements, in multiple interconnected nodes, constitutes the subnetwork routing capability. Nodes at the periphery of the switch system may also contain SFAs. At these peripheral SFAs, user information from both circuit switched and packet switched interfaces are converted into *uniform length packets*, with a header containing routing information. The SFA interfaces might, for example, be to ISDNs and LANs. The switch fabric elements route the packets, using a source-routing mechanism, from any input to any output switch fabric adapter. Multiple switch systems (of the type shown in Figure 18.7) can be connected via their SFAs and intervening ISDN or LAN facilities. ANR then operates at successive intermediate nodes, as shown in Figure 18.6, each node picking up a subsequent part of the address field.

PARIS.   The PARIS project, an acronym for *Packetized Automatic Routing Integrated System*, for integrated voice, video, and data, achieved comparable fast routing, but with variable length packets [Cidon88]. In many ways, PARIS is like the Zurich switch.

Integrated Switch System

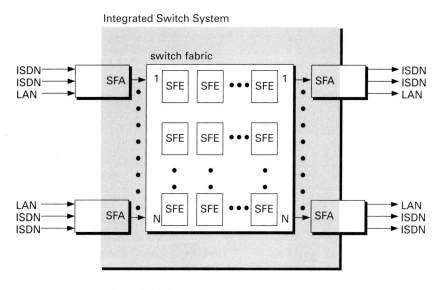

Figure 18.7 Basic switch configuration [Ahmadi88].

Most of the transport-layer functions such as flow control and error recovery for data, and packetization and reassembly for voice and video, are performed on an end-to-end basis.

At call set-up time, a network control function selects the optimum path using an updated topology database. From this it determines the ANR field from source to destination and back. In addition, an alternate route may also be selected in advance. Then, if failure is detected, the call can be rapidly switched to the alternate with minimum disruption.

As in the Zurich switch, the ANR field is composed of a number of small words. In PARIS, this is equal to the number of hops that the packet has to travel. Each word, then, represents an outgoing link on the packet's path. The ANR packet header routes the packet across an entire general topology network rather than within a single node. Thus, each packet header contains enough information to control all of the routing within intermediate nodes along the path.

The major difference, then, is in *the ability of PARIS to handle variable length packets.* Transmission efficiency can thereby be increased (and transmission costs can be accordingly lowered) substantially. It does this at a cost of more queueing. In PARIS, each adapter has a set of high-speed FIFO queues, which interface to the PARIS bus. There are both "to the bus" and "from the bus" FIFOs. With these queues, the variable length packets can be accommodated, and the automatic network routing is done much like that described above for the Zurich switch.

In PARIS, the intermediate-node functions include packet buffering, determination of the outgoing link, the actual switching function of transferring the packet from the incoming to the outgoing link, congestion control to prevent excessive packet queueing, and priority functions.

We note that a disadvantage of the pure ANR approach is the size of the address that must be carried with each packet. A compromise that can be considered is the ANR analogy of APPN routing, namely, a combination of ANR within each node, as described above, and some form of label swapping (see Sections 12.4.1 and 14.6.4). In effect, the label swapping must retrieve the ANR set needed at the following node. The tradeoff is the call set-up process required to establish the label swapping information at each node.

18.5.3   Bandwidth Managers for Voice/Data/Image

Let us now take a closer look at some of the current voice/data/image networks. Multimedia transport, including voice, image, video, and data, as illustrated in Figure 18.8, is becoming increasingly advantageous as broadband facilities become more available. In many corporations, the mergers of data-processing and voice communications departments has made evident the savings that are possible by the use of common transmission facilities for these different media. Subnetworks, with fast packet switching of broadband links, carrying multiple media, can become subnetworks within layer-3 types of WANs

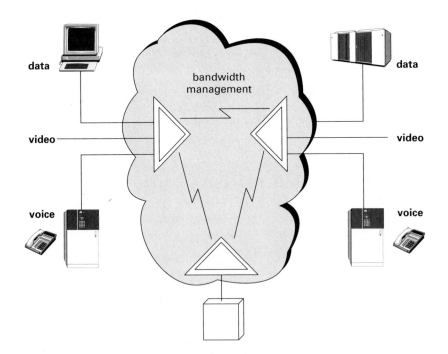

Figure 18.8 Bandwidth management of multimedia carriage.

described earlier. These subnetworks may be private or public, and may follow the pattern of private subnetworks with bandwidth management, or use the ISDN or MAN facilities, or (more likely) a combination of these.

A basic difference with voice/data networks is that it usually is not possible to slow down the voice input through input-throttling mechanisms. Therefore, some guarantee of available bandwidth must be given before the call is accepted.

Private bandwidth managers.   The management of bandwidth can be a cooperation among the end users and the system manager. If an end user (e.g., an application-process) anticipates a need for more bandwidth, the end user should be able to request it. If, on the other hand, the network manager discerns that congestion is building up, the manager should be able to suggest a change in bandwidth allocation. Products like the IDNX[8] *dynamically* allocate appropriate amounts of bandwidth, on high-speed lines, among the voice, data, and image streams. Such managers can be access-protocol-independent.[9]

Private bandwidth managers have proven to offer substantial efficiencies and line cost savings. As volumes grow, we can expect the bandwidth managers to apply their management to the higher bandwidths of T3 and SONET links. The amount of economic advantage, however, depends heavily on tariffs. The trend is to make these private, broadband, bandwidth-managed subnetworks an integral part of the larger network by their close cooperation with the larger directory, routing, and system management functions.

IDNX.   The **Integrated Digital Network Exchange (IDNX)** is a good example of a *resource manager* for networks of leased T1 lines carrying both voice and data. A typical configuration is shown in Figure 18.9, which, by fully using T1 lines, might replace hundreds of voice and data circuits. Use of T3 lines is similarly advantageous. Bandwidth can be allocated to voice or data on demand, by time of day, or by permanent allocation.

As the IDNX subnetwork grows or has malfunctions, the topology is automatically updated. Topology update packets are broadcast on the signaling channel to neighboring nodes, which update their topology maps, and in turn broadcast this information to the rest of the network.

When the IDNX determines that a trunk has reached a threshold level of errors, the IDNX takes that trunk out of service, and reroutes the traffic on alternate paths through the network—with little or no disruption to the calls (voice or data) on that trunk. Data is not disrupted because retransmission can bridge the short interruption. Voice may be disrupted for some seconds. An alert monitor, running on a NetView/PC, collects events and alarms from the IDNX network, and can transmit them up to NetView at a mainframe host (see T1 Resource Managers in Section 4.8.3).

---

8.   The Integrated Digital Network Exchange (IDNX) is a bandwidth manager product of Network Equipment Technologies, Inc.

9.   Though able to carry multiple-access protocols, each bandwidth manager mesh uses some (often proprietary) protocol for the internode operation and management.

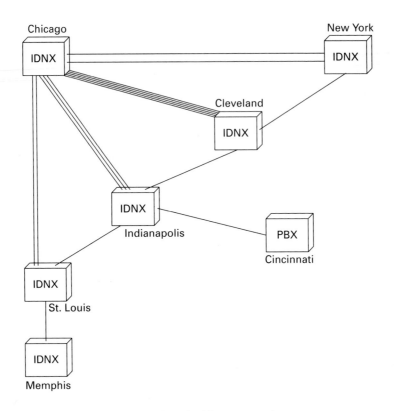

Figure 18.9 Using IDNX in a mesh voice/data network.

18.5.4   Fast Packet Network Access Units

In Section 12.9 we discussed having a subnetwork perform as a backbone for other subnetworks. The fast packet subnetwork is a natural for that backbone role. Operating at layers 1 and 2, it has excellent properties for a multi-protocol backbone. Then, there is a need for *Network-Access (NA) units* (see Figure 12.24) that can accommodate diverse "foreign" architectures by performing any necessary protocol conversions or encapsulations. These network-access units may accommodate multiple types of LANs, other WANs, or end-systems.

One prime NA candidate would adapt LANs to WANs for *LAN/WAN/LAN* interoperation. For example, with suitable network-access units, the 100 Mbps FDDI LANs and the WAN using SONET 155 Mbps and 622 Mbps facilities should provide a compatible, high-performance combination. At the same time, there can be a mixture of voice and data on the SONET lines.

There is a potential for bridging, at layer 2, between LANs and a fast packet subnetwork that operates at layer 2 or layer 1. On the other hand, *LAN/WAN/LAN connectivity is usually via layer-3 routers*, for reasons cited in Section 17.4.1. To illustrate, consider that the subnetwork B in Figure 12.18 is now a fast packet subnetwork. LAN/

WAN/LAN operations then require cooperation among the LAN routing (in subnetworks A and C), the inter-subnetwork (layer 3c) routing in X and Y, and the routing over a fast packet mesh of SONET lines, in subnetwork B. The IP routers of TCP/IP (or comparable layer-3c inter-subnetwork routers for SNA and OSI WANs) need to handle the *address resolutions from subnetwork addressing to inter-subnetwork addressing*. From the viewpoint of the fast packet subnetwork these layer-3c routers, including address-resolution capabilities, provide a *network-access* function for the fast packet subnetwork.

To make such a fast packet subnetwork a general purpose backbone, capable of handling diverse architectures as illustrated in Figure 12.24 and 12.25, still other network-access units for other WANs and end-systems may need consideration. Network-access units for X.25, SNA/APPN, SNA/Subarea, TCP/IP, and NetBIOS are early candidates. The MAN interface, the ISDN interface, and the I.122 frame-relay user-network interface, described in Sections 18.6.2, 18.7.2, and 18.8, respectively, are other candidates for network-access units to a fast packet backbone network.

Because the fast packet subnetwork routes at layer 2 or layer 1, it acts very much like a link connection between the layer 3 routers in its access units. Multiple data streams can be multiplexed on the access lines to the fast packet subnetwork. The layer-3 routers can have multiple logical-links (one to each destination layer-3 router) on a single physical access link.

18.6   METROPOLITAN AREA NETWORK (802.6)

18.6.1   Introduction

The basic purpose of the Metropolitan Area Network (MAN), is to provide high-speed, public, integrated transmission services, such as voice, data, and video *over a large (but limited) geographic area, of at least 50 kilometers* in diameter [Pr802,89]. Using IEEE 802.6, MAN is another MAC-layer architecture that is *designed to be largely consistent with the IEEE 802.2 standard* at the DLC logical-link control layer. Some carriers also see this as a technology stepping stone to full Broadband ISDN, using Asynchronous Transfer Mode cells.

Increasing speed causes difficulties with earlier technologies. The token rotation time in token rings became a limiting factor in token rings, as the clock rate increased. The solution was the *early token release*, which permitted multiple tokens on the ring at one time. This technique was successfully used on 16 Mbps rings, and was also adopted in the FDDI. As speeds increase beyond 100 Mbps, the time for the token to travel between stations amounts to dead time and this also becomes a significant performance problem. Therefore, to allow nodes to access the network simultaneously, in a nonsequenced manner, the time-slotted ring or bus is used. There, fixed size slots parade along the ring or bus and stations can simultaneously access whatever slot is near them. To ensure fair access for all stations, some form of slot reservation is also needed.

The slotted bus with reservation technology that is being pursued for the MAN is known as **Distributed Queue Dual Bus (DQDB)**. Typically, a MAN could consist of interconnected DQDB subnetworks, within a metropolitan area, as illustrated in Figure 18.10. Both public and private DQDB subnetworks are envisioned. Each of these DQDB

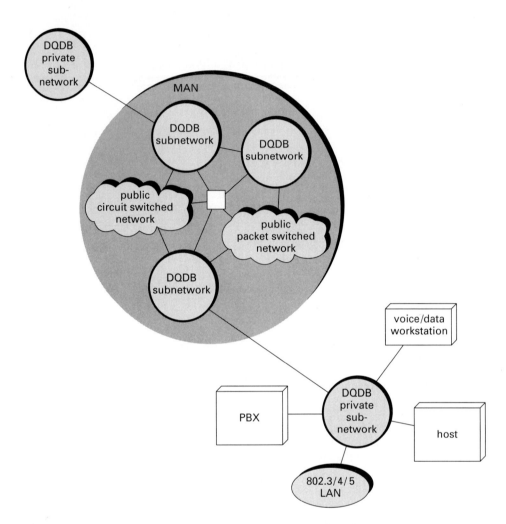

Figure 18.10 DQDB as both public and private subnetworks.

subnetworks could serve a variety of PBXs, voice/data workstations, mainframe hosts, and LANs. Various high-speed subnetworks could use the MAN as the metropolitan distribution backbone. As illustrated in Figure 18.11, this could include FDDI LANs, broadband segments of the voice/data WAN, Serial Optical Channels of host complexes, private DQDB subnetworks, and other higher-speed LANs.

Key MAN features.   Key characteristics of the Metropolitan Area Network (MAN), using DQDB, include:

- Packet- and circuit-switched (voice) capability
- Sharing between packet and isochronous capacity

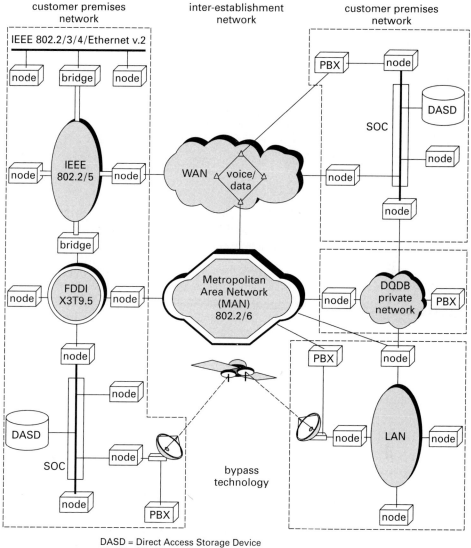

Figure 18.11 Metropolitan area network (MAN) in voice/data system.

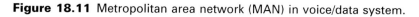

- Two active unidirectional busses
  - Opposite directions of transmission
  - Protocol-based on cooperation of both buses
  - Slots originate at head end of bus, and may be used only once
  - Transmit-node determines which bus direction to use

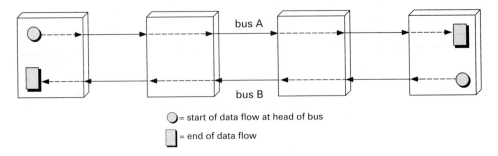

= start of data flow at head of bus

= end of data flow

Figure 18.12 Dual bus flows [Pr802,89].

- Auto-reconfiguration in presence of faults
- A distributed queueing packet access protocol
- Ultimately, an integrated voice/data network

Compatibility between MAN and B-ISDN is being sought. The concept involves the use of MANs as access-links to B-ISDN. A station on the MAN would be located at a local exchange serving the ATM-based B-ISDN. Consistent with this, addressing based on CCITT Recommendation E.164,[10] the ISDN numbering scheme, is used in MANs to identify customer interfaces, with an additional provision for group-addressing.

Three MAN services.   The standard specifies three services:

1. *Connectionless* MAC sublayer service. (This transports frames up to 9188 bytes, thus accommodating all 802 LAN frames except the 18K byte frame allowed in 802.5.)

2. *Connection-oriented* data service.

3. *Isochronous* service.

18.6.2 DQDB Dual Bus Architecture

The dual bus architecture of a DQDB subnetwork [Pr802,89b] consists of two unidirectional buses and a multiplicity of nodes along the buses as shown in Figure 18.12. A given node may want to send data in one direction on one bus and in the other direction on the other bus. The structure of each DQDB node is shown in Figure 18.13. The writing to the bus is the logical OR of the data from upstream and the data from the access station. An access station can fail, or be removed, with no consequence to the operation of the subnetwork.

All data is carried in *fixed size data units called* **slots**. The fixed length (52 byte) *slot payload on the bus is called a* **segment**. Two types of slots are queued arbitrated and pre-arbitrated.

---

10.   E.164 uses addresses of 15 decimal digits, which include country code, area (city) code, and local number.

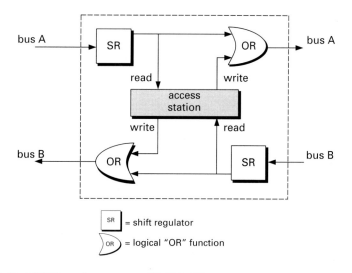

Figure 18.13 DQDB node structure [Pr802,89].

Queued arbitrated.   This access-method has three data priority queues for medium-access arbitration, and fixed-length slots for data transfer. Slots have 53 bytes, including a 52 byte slot payload (segment) and a one byte access control field. This slot is the same length as the B-ISDN ATM cell. Each priority level provides distributed queue access for the support of connectionless and connection-oriented data service.

Separate distributed queues are made for each level of priority. Segments with a higher priority will always gain access ahead of segments at all lower levels. The queues of a given data priority at all the nodes are treated like *one* distributed queue. Segments of a given priority entering any part of this distributed queue, for access to a bus, are processed first-in, first-out (FIFO). For this to work, each node must know where each segment sits in the one distributed queue for its data priority.

Each node tells its upstream nodes of its intent to send data at a specified priority; it does this by setting the request bit of a slot on the bus opposite from the one on which it wants to send data. Each node keeps a count of the downstream requests for each bus; it does this by monitoring the request field of slots that pass by on the other bus.

For access to the queued-arbitrated slots, each node then keeps an up-down counter for each direction of travel. Each counter counts the number of requests for access that it receives on one fiber and the number of unused slots that pass on the other. This difference count is the number of unfilled requests for slots on that bus. With these counters, the node can thus determine the number of segments that are queued ahead of it (awaiting access to the bus) in each direction. Each node thus is able to determine the position in the distributed queue of a given priority for each of its segments awaiting transmission.

The distributed queue protocol operates at the media access control (MAC) layer in the architecture. The current standard supports an LLC sublayer in a manner consistent with the other IEEE 802.2 standards. Each 125 usec frame consists of a frame header,

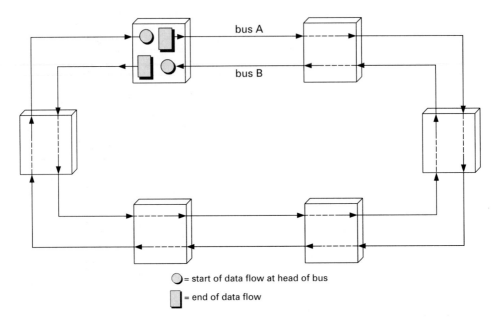

= start of data flow at head of bus

= end of data flow

Figure 18.14 DQDB looped bus topology.

followed by fixed length cells (one cell per slot, the number of cells depending on the bit rate of the link used), and then an end of frame field. Each cell is 48 bytes plus a 5-byte header. The cell formats for carrying the segmented LLC-PDU of the MAN are given in this chapter's Technical Reference section.

Pre-Arbitrated (PA).   This access method uses assigned octet positions in particular slots for the transfer of individual octets of data. It supports isochronous connection-oriented services.

   The pre-arbitrated slots are designated by the node at the head of the bus; only nodes that were previously assigned these slots can use them. An access station may only write into designated positions of a PA segment payload. The access station is notified of the offsets for its data (relative to the start of the PA segment payload).

Looped bus topology.   In the looped bus topology, the end points of the two busses are colocated, as shown in Figure 18.14. Note, however, that, as before, data does not flow from the end of a bus through to the head of a bus. There is a natural break between the head and the end, and the topology is not that of a ring. In case of a bus fault, the network can be reconfigured by re-establishing the natural break adjacent to the fault, as shown in Figure 18.15. If the node adjacent to the fault does not support the Head of Bus capability, then reconfiguration would be completed by the node closest to the fault with that capability. Multiple bus failures will result in a subnetwork being split into isolated islands.

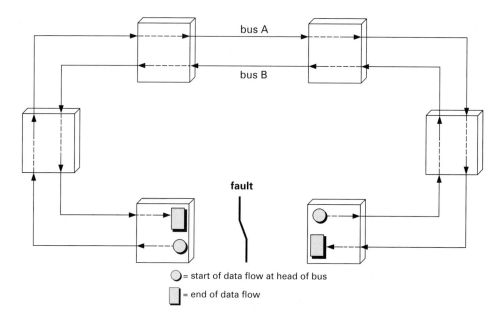

Figure 18.15 Reconfigured DQDB loop.

Some users will be directly connected to the MAN bus. Others will be connected to other subnetworks, such as LANs, which in turn are connected to a MAN bus. The total configuration therefore can resemble Figure 12.21, with multiple subnetworks connected to the backbone MAN by bridges or routers.

Security. With the DQDB MAN, every user's data might pass through every other subscriber's node. This would pose security issues. For security reasons, the MAN might be separated into a public transport portion and a private access subnetwork. A bridge between the two would filter out only traffic destined to other access subnetworks. Data destined for users within the access subnetwork would be ignored.

Fairness. At the time of this writing, the proposed 802.6 standard appears to be still somewhat flawed. Under heavy loading, in larger networks, the attachments closest to the head-end get a higher portion of the available bandwidth. Several proposals to correct this shortcoming are now under consideration.

One other promising reservation scheme, that addresses the fairness issue, is worth a brief mention. In the *Cyclic-Reservation Multiple-Access (CRMA)* scheme, a slotted bus periodically collects reservations. Numbered reservation commands periodically issued by the head-end collect requests for slots as they pass nodes wanting to transmit. The collected requests are entered in a head-end FIFO queue. Entries percolate through the FIFO, to generate as many slots as are needed for that cycle. On matching a passing cycle number with one associated with a previous reservation, a node begins transmitting in the first free slot it finds in that cycle. Fairness can be achieved by imposing a bound or window on the number of slots reservable in one reservation command [Mueller87], [Zafiropulo90].[11]

18.6.3   SMDS

Introduction.   The *Switched Multi-Megabit Data Service (SMDS)* is yet another near-term offering, defined in the *Bellcore Digest of Technical Information* [Bellcore-a]. As its name states, it is a high-speed digital data service. It is also *a partial introduction to MANs.* The following provides only the briefest description, to position SMDS relative to other services.

A packet-switched, SMDS access-means, called the **Subscriber Network Interface (SNI)**, provides single-customer access. Subscriber access to the network supporting SMDS is by means of a dedicated line from the subscriber system to a **MAN Switching System (MSS)**. This line initially will be T1 at 1.5 Mbps or T3 at 45 Mbps, and eventually will be 155 Mbps. An optical SONET (Synchronous Optical Network) interface is also planned, as equipment conforming to the SONET standard is available [Hemrick88]. SMDS will appear as a subnetwork in each customer's overall networking scheme, much as a LAN does today.

One initial set of relationships among the DQDB/802.6 access protocols, the public network supporting SMDS, and the metropolitan area network is sketched in Figure 18.16. *The DQDB/802.6 protocol operates in subnetworks that provide the access from the customer premises equipment,* through the Subscriber Network Interface, to the public network supporting SMDS. The composite of these functions is the MAN. Unlike the MAN, however, SMDS ultimately has no distance.

If a customer has access to an 802.6 MAN, then his attachment to SMDS could be just another peer node within an 802.6 access-subnetwork. In the simplest case, the customer could have a two-node SMDS access-subnetwork. One node would be at the service provider's point of presence; the other node would be at the customer's premises. There, for example, the customer could connect a local area network to the 802.6 access-subnetwork through a bridge or a router.

SMDS protocols.   The SMDS protocol stack, and its relationship to an OSI stack such as 802.5, is shown in Figure 18.17. In this example, with two subnetworks (a LAN and an SMDS) the upper-layer protocols go from end-system to end-system; and both subnetworks are oblivious to the upper-layer protocols. The layer-3 Internet Protocols (IPs) cross each subnetwork: from one end-system to a midway router, and from there to the other end-system. The subnetworks themselves are oblivious to the Internet Protocols. The router must translate

---

11.   The Distributed-Queue Multiple-Access (DQMA) and Cyclic-Reservation Multiple-Access (CRMA) proposals are also based on slotted unidirectional bus structures. They have two significant advantages over DQDB. First they provide throughput fairness, even at high speeds and large distances. Secondly, by allowing reservation of multiple consecutive slots, they make segment labeling unnecessary and facilitate segment reassembly.

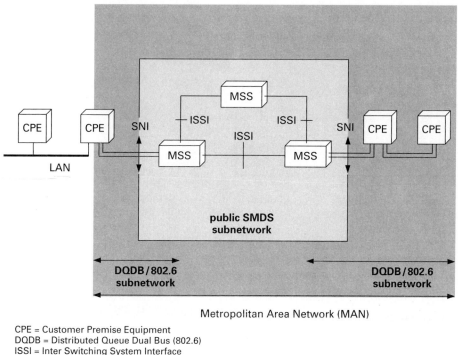

Metropolitan Area Network (MAN)

CPE = Customer Premise Equipment
DQDB = Distributed Queue Dual Bus (802.6)
ISSI = Inter Switching System Interface
MSS = MAN Switching System
SNI = Subscriber Network Interface
SMDS = Switched Multi-Megabit Data Service

Figure 18.16 Relationships among 802.6, SMDS, and MAN.

IP addresses into subnetwork addresses, which are the only addresses a subnetwork understands. *The IP router thus appears to the SMDS subnetwork as a network-access unit that provides protocol transformation.* The SMDS Interface Protocol (SIP) exists between the router and the Switching-System (SS) of the SMDS subnetwork, and similarly between the end-system and a switching-system. (This is roughly analogous to the X.25 interface between end-systems and a Data-Switching-Exchange (DSE). The interface to the SMDS has three layers:

- *SIP level 3*: SMDS address association; and error detection

- *SIP level 2*: Segmentation/reassembly; distributed queue protocol (a subset of the 802.6 protocol); framing; and error detection at the segment level

- *SIP level 1*: Physical layer; bit-level transmission

(Preliminary versions of the formats for the protocol data units at SIP-2 and SIP-3 are given in Figure 18.34 in this chapter's Technical Reference section.) Before being given to the physical layer, the variable-length MAC data units are segmented into fixed-length slots of 53 bytes as in 802.6 [Cox 91].

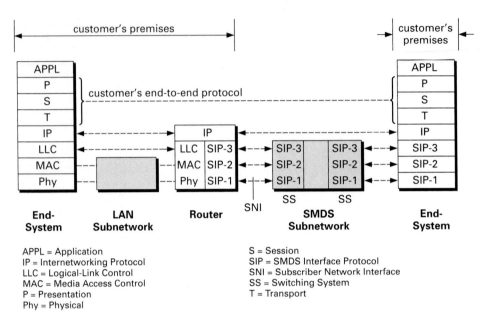

Figure 18.17 Example of use of SMDS with LAN.

Services. The focus of the associated SMDS MAN switching system is solely on providing "data-only" service, and thus any capability of the MAN technology for supporting voice traffic is not exploited in providing SMDS [Hemrick88]. SIP is connectionless in nature; no explicit flow control, sequencing, or retransmission procedures for errored data units are defined in the protocol. No guarantee exists for delivery of packets in order.

18.7   ISDN

18.7.1   Introduction

Technological advances now make it possible to have 64 kbps and higher-speed links from the customer premises to the local exchange. That bandwidth can be used in a variety of ways, and in particular, to multiplex digitized voice, data, high resolution images, group-4 facsimiles, high-fidelity sound, videotex, teletex, or telex on the same line. This *single-access-interface* and *a single-access-line*, coupled with a digital network capable of integrating voice and data, is known as an **Integrated Services Digital Network** (ISDN). The initial ISDN, known as Narrowband ISDN, offers digitized service to customer premises at 144 kbps and 1.54 Mbps in the U.S., and 2.048 Mbps in Europe and elsewhere, with multiple subchannels in each.

ISDNs support both switched and nonswitched connections. The switched connection may be either circuit-switched (the common telephone connection) or packet-switched.

ISDN services.   A number of ISDN services are being defined [Bellcore]. Not all services will be provided by all carriers. Several of the more interesting services are summarized in the following.

- *Calling line identification* provides the calling party's ISDN number to the called party. A calling party can restrict this feature.[12]

- *Connected line identification* provides the connected party's ISDN number to the calling party. (The called party can restrict this feature.)

- *Multiple subscriber number* allows the assignment of multiple ISDN numbers to a single interface. The digits significant for terminal differentiation are an integral part of the ISDN numbering scheme.

When the calling party number identification is generally available, it can become a part of diverse applications, such as: automatic call-back when busy, selective call-forwarding and distribution, call-trace, and electronic-data-interchange.

ISDN standards.   The CCITT has been developing an extensive set of standards for ISDN as follows:

- I.100—ISDN concepts and structure
- I.200—Services supported by ISDN
- I.300—Overall network aspects
- I.400—ISDN user-network interfaces
- OSI Physical layer
  - I.430—Basic user-network interface specifications
  - I.431—Primary rate user-network interface specifications
- OSI DLC layer
  - I.440, Q.920—User-network interface; general aspects
  - I.441, Q.921, Q.922—User-network interface specifications
- OSI Network layer
  - I.450, Q.930—User-network interface; general aspects
  - I.451, Q.931—User-network interface; specifications for basic call control
  - I.462, X.31/X.32—Packet mode (X.25)
- I.500—ISDN internetwork interfaces
- I.600—ISDN maintenance

Thus, the standardization efforts apply to

- *Services* offered to subscribers, so the services will be internationally consistent

---

12. Calling line identification has been challenged in the U.S. courts as a possible violation of privacy.

- The *user-interface*, so terminal equipment can be portable and compatible with each other
- *Network capabilities*, so that networks can talk to each other

18.7.2   ISDN Interfaces

Basic and primary rate interfaces.   The basic rate interface provides *two "B" channels, each at 64 kbps and one "D" channel at 16 kbps*. The data rate before overhead is therefore 144 kbps.

The **B (Bearer) channel** is intended for user information streams, and does not usually carry signaling information.[13] Each B channel may be used in a circuit-switching mode or in a packet-switching mode. Multiple information streams may be multiplexed together in the same B channel. However, for circuit-switching, an entire B channel will be switched to a single-destination user-network interface. Each B channel can carry point-to-point 64 kbps full-duplex data. Both B channels can be combined to carry 128 kbps full-duplex in a switched circuit. Each B channel can carry one PCM 64 kbps voice or two adaptive differential PCM (ADPCM) 32 kbps voice channels.

The **D channel** is, first of all, intended to carry signaling information for circuit-switching by the ISDN. However, in addition to signaling information, a D channel may also carry packet-switched data.

The **primary rate interface** comes in two sizes: 1.544 Mbps in North America and Japan (based on the existing T1 transmission standards), and 2.048 in most other countries. In North America and Japan, the primary rate supports *23 B channels, each at 64 kbps, and 1 D channel at 64 kbps*. The European primary rate supports 30 B channels and 1 D channel.

Currently agreed to in standards bodies is the ability to have multiple point-to-point primary rate interfaces to the network, and to have a D channel in only one of them for signaling for all of them. This, in effect, considers all of the channels from all of the interfaces as one logical port group.

H (high-speed bearer) channels.   A primary rate **H0 channel**, of 384 kbps, likewise is intended for user-information streams, and does not carry signaling information. At the U.S. 1544 kbps primary rate interface, one can have 4 H0 channels, if a D channel can be provided from another interface. Alternatively, a single primary interface can yield 3 H0 plus 1 D channels. At the European 2048 kbps primary rate interface, one can have 5 H0 plus 1 D channels. A primary rate interface may have a single 64 kbps D channel and any mixture of B and H0 channels.

The U.S. 1536 kbps **H11 channel** consumes a primary interface. Signaling for the H11 channel, if required, is carried in a D channel on another interface. The European 1920 kbps **H12 channel** structure is composed of one 1920 kbps H12 channel and one 64 kbps D channel.

---

13.   The B channel may carry signaling information for certain modes of X.25 packet services.

Thus, the bandwidth of a U.S. primary rate interface can be arranged[14] in many ways, such as:

- 23 B + D   (24 x 64 kbps)
- 24 B   (24 x 64 kbps)
- 4 H0   (4 x 384 kbps)
- 3 H0 + 1 D   (3 x 384 kbps + 1 x 64 kbps)
- 1 H0 + 17B + 1D   (1 x 384 kbps + 18 x 64 kbps)
- 1 H11   (1 x 1536 kbps)

Similarly, in Europe, the primary rate payload could be allocated as:

- 30 B + D   (31 x 64 kbps)
- 5 H0 + D   (5 x 384 kbps + 1 x 64 kbps)
- 1 H0 + 24 B + 1 D   (1 x 384 kbps + 25 x 64 kbps)
- 1 H12 + 1 D   (1 x 1920 kbps + 1 x 64 kbps)
- 1 H11 + 6 B + 1 D   (1 x 1536 kbps + 7 x 64 kbps)

ISDNBIOS. This is an application programming interface (API) that is provided with the PS/2 ISDN support.[15] It is consistent with the existing NetBIOS API. Existing NetBIOS applications can be run in ISDNBIOS compatibility mode. Commands not supported in ISDNBIOS include `Send/Receive_Datagram`, `Send/Receive_Broadcast_Datagram`, `Add_Group_Name`, and `Unlink`.

18.7.3 ISDN Components

Physical configurations. Some of the possible configurations are shown in Figure 18.18. The computer systems shown there might be individual computers (e.g., a mainframe), or they might be the gateway to a network of computer systems. The trend will be to simplify the current disorder in local exchanges, combining the voice switches, data circuit switches, and packet switches. Gradually, then, the ISDN switch would be able to feed a variety of digital subnetworks, which might be circuit-switched or packet-switched, public or private.

At the customer's premises, the ISDN access-interface may be provided by a *controller*, to which terminals are attached, or by a *PBX*, to which terminals and/or phones are attached. In either of these cases, the terminals or phones need have no awareness of the ISDN connection. They could simply rely on the controller or PABX to function as an adapter, and provide the proper multiplexing and ISDN access-interface. On the other hand, terminal equipments that meet the ISDN interface might also attach to such a PABX. If there is no PABX on the customer's premises, the equivalent function can be provided by a *Centrex* in the local exchange.

---

14. For example, in SNA, by a parameter in the `Setup` message, the Connection Manager is able to identify the type of channel that is desired, for the call that is being established.

15. ISDNBIOS is provided with the ISDN Co-Processor Support Program, which supports the IBM ISDN Interface Co-Processor/2 and runs on PC/DOS and OS/2 SE.

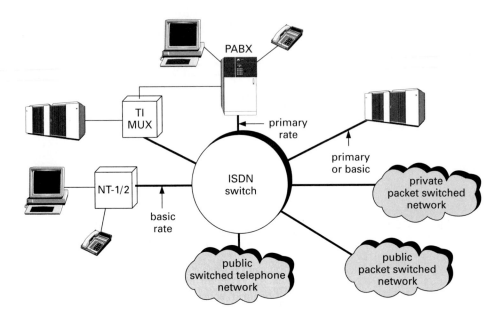

Figure 18.18 Multiple subnetworks fed by an ISDN switch.

CCS-7. Most of world's carriers are undergoing a technology upgrade in their signaling systems. The signaling within the toll network is migrating to a common system known in the U.S. and Canada as **Common Channel Signaling #7 (CCS-7)**. Sometimes also called SS 7, this system *takes the initial dial or pulse information, routes the call, connects to the called party, and rings the destination terminal.* CCS-7 is designed for digital transmission on 56 kbps or 64 kbps. It can support variable message lengths to 272 octets.

CCS-7 signaling is not unique to ISDN, but it is essential to ISDN operations. In an ISDN, for example, the signaling path might extend from a class 5 switch at the originating local exchange to a similar switch at the destination local exchange. In between, the signaling path would include a series of *signal-transfer-points*, illustrated in Figure 18.19, whose function is to control an associated *toll switch* along the route of the call. Figure 18.19 shows how the operation appears from the perspective of the CCS-7 signal transfer point. Actually, the user data and the CCS-7 signaling would, in most cases, share a single line from the customer's premises.

ISDN user premises reference points. The possible interfaces within the user premises have been identified as in Figure 18.20. These interfaces are called, in the standard, *user premises reference points*. They may or may not exist in a given configuration.

- *Network Termination Type-2 (NT2)* corresponds to equipment such as a PBX or a terminal cluster (establishment) controller. It might also represent a local area network.

- *Terminal Equipment Type-1 (TE1)* provides an interface (S) that complies with the ISDN user-network interface definition. The "S" reference point, for basic

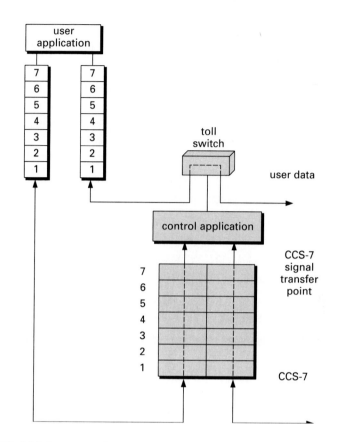

Figure 18.19 CCS-7 perspective.

rate, is 2B + D (two 64 kbps channels plus one 16 kbps channel) clocked at a rate of 192 kbps.

- *Terminal Equipment Type-2 (TE2)* has some other interface (e.g., V or X series), and needs an adapter to interface to ISDN.

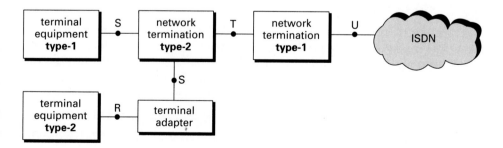

Figure 18.20 User premises reference points.

- *Terminal Adapter (TA)* allows equipment with a non-ISDN interface to become compatible.[16] The adapter may be packaged within the NT2 (PABX or terminal controller).

- *Network Termination Type-1 (NT1)* provides functions that map to the physical-layer characteristics of a particular ISDN.

Different PTTs and telephone companies may make different reference points available to customers. In some networks, the "T" interface, rather than the "U" interface could be supplied by the network. In different implementations, we may also have some of the components in Figure 18.20 packaged together, such as:

- (NT2 + NT1) packaged: physical interface occurs at "S" but not "T"

- (NT2 + TA) packaged: physical interface occurs at "T" but not "S" to adapter

- No NT2 or TA: physical interface occurs where "S" and "T" coincide

Terminal Equipment type 1 uses the D channel for signaling. When using multibutton terminals, two forms of signaling are possible:

- Stimulus signaling—as in the past, where the PABX has to interpret what a particular button (or key) on a particular set means.

- Functional signaling—where the terminal and switch dialog as partners to convey the message.

Rate adaption.   A further *multiplexing function* must be inserted when the bit rate of the terminal equipment is less than that of the B channel. For binary rates of 8, 16, and 32 kbps, a straightforward multiplexing scheme is specified.

For other rates, detailed procedures are given in the standards for handling X-series circuit-mode DTEs (I.461-X.30), X-series packet-mode DTEs (I.462-X.31), and V-series DTEs (I.463-V.110 and I.465-V.120).

Rate adaption functions may be packaged within the terminal adapter (which, in turn, might be packaged in the PABX or terminal controller). A peer entity at the other end must understand the adaption process.

ISDN interface data rates and ISDN wiring are summarized in this chapter's Technical Reference section.

18.7.4   ISDN Layers

It may be helpful, next, to relate the ISDN to the WAN and the LAN in terms of the OSI layers. The end-to-end flow via an ISDN is shown in Figure 18.21, involving at each end a terminating equipment (TE), an NT1 (which accepts the terminal's ISDN S/T interface), and an Exchange Termination (ET) that accepts the ISDN line at the local exchange. (It is assumed that any NT2 functions are incorporated in the terminal equipment.)

---

16. A Terminal Adapter (TA) (like the IBM 7820) can replace a modem or a Data Circuit terminating Equipment (DCE), making the installation to the ISDN transparent and without other system modifications.

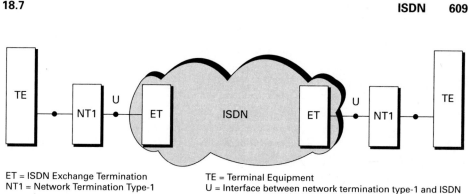

ET = ISDN Exchange Termination   TE = Terminal Equipment
NT1 = Network Termination Type-1   U = Interface between network termination type-1 and ISDN

Figure 18.21 Major components in an end-to-end ISDN flow.

Recall the DTE/DCE interface of X.25 shown in Figures 13.1 and 13.2. Although the defined X.25 interface is between the DTE and the DCE, the layer-2 HDLC protocols (as well as the layer-3 packet protocols) are between the DTE and the DSE. The DSE is within the network and on the carrier premises. In a similar fashion, the ISDN interface is defined between the terminal equipment (TE) and the NT1 of Figure 18.21. The ISDN protocols similarly extend beyond the NT1 as follows:

- *D channel*—Layer-2 LAP-D protocols and the layer-3 signaling (e.g., call establishment) protocols are between the terminal equipment (TE) and the exchange termination (ET).

- *D or B/H channel, packet mode*—Layer-2 LAP-B and layer-3 packet protocols are between the TE and the ET.

- *B/H channels, circuit mode*—Layer-2 IDLC (or other DLC) protocols are between the two communicating TEs.

In all cases, the layer 3c and higher protocols are between the two communicating TEs.

SNA-APPN/ISDN connections.   If we first consider the B channel operating in the circuit-switch mode (rather than the packet-switch mode), and zoom into one end of Figure 18.21, we find the layers shown in Figure 18.22. The NT1 operates at layer 1, for both the D and the B channels. On the D channel, the ISDN protocols operate at layers 1 through 3, between the terminal equipment (TE) and the exchange termination (ET). The B channel can use a variety of protocols at layers 2 and above. Shown is IDLC at layer 2 and APPN at layer 3. In the circuit mode, the ISDN ETs (and all the intermediate toll switches) operate only at layer 1.

If the B channel operates in the packet-switch mode, then we have the familiar DTE-DCE interface of X.25, and the ISDN ET interoperates with the terminal equipment using the X.25 protocols at layers 1 through 3.

LAP-D.   A part of the ISDN standard is the link-access procedure (at the DLC layer) to be used on the D channels. It provides control for a time multiplexed link between a network subscriber and an ISDN central office. *It provides for multiple logical-links in the D channel,* detection and recovery of transmission errors, flow control, sequence numbering, and sequence control.

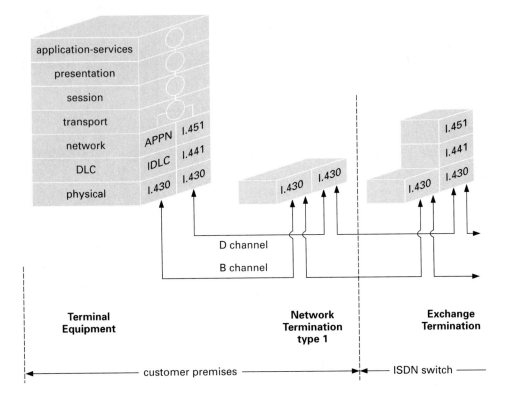

Figure 18.22 One end of an ISDN connection, using SNA on the B channel, in circuit mode.

LAP-D is based on the ISO LAP-B (balanced mode) link standard, which, in turn, is a variation of HDLC. The format is the familiar: flag, address, control, information, frame-check-sequence, flag. (This is illustrated in Figure 18.35 in this chapter's Technical Reference section and in Figure 19.31.) LAP-D employs a two-part address: a Terminal Endpoint Identifier (TEI), and a Service-Access-Point Identifier (SAPI). The TEI identifies a specific connection-end-point (CEP) within a service-access-point, and typically identifies a particular user device that shares the interface. However, a single device can be assigned more than one TEI. The TEI (and each CEP in a SAP) thus distinguishes among multiple logical-links to a particular network-entity. The SAPI identifies the protocol operating over the data link service, as provided by the LAP-D protocol (e.g., SAPI=16 for X.25, SAPI=0 for signaling). It thus also effectively identifies the source within the device, particularly the type of traffic, such as packet-switched data or control signaling. The C/R bit indicates whether the frame is a command or a response. The control field, for the logical-link control (LLC) sublayer, is either 1 byte (for modulo 8 sequence numbers) or two bytes (for modulo 128 sequence numbers).

IDLC.   ISDN Data Link Control (IDLC) is IBM's interpretation of the Q.921/Q.922 data link controls, at layer 2, designed and optimized for ISDN applications. IDLC is consistent with the emerging CCITT recommendation Q.922, which is only a small delta on the ISDN I.441/Q.921. (The protocols in Q.922 have also been referred to as LAP-F.) Used on the ISDN channel B, IDLC (Q.922) is a superset of Link Access Procedure-D (LAP-D), while maintaining the basic functions that are provided in IEEE 802.2 for LANs and LAP-B for X.25. In IDLC, the 13-bit SAPI and TEI fields of LAP-D (see Figure 18.35) are replaced by a 10-bit **Data Link Connection Identifier (DLCI)** and 3 reserved bits. The other minor differences pertain to the use of the command/response (C/R) bit, allowing responses to information frames, and providing for frame reject in the control field.

IDLC is also, in many respects similar to SDLC. However, IDLC is a peer-to-peer full-duplex protocol, whereas SDLC is a primary to multiple secondary stations polling protocol. A key difference is in the address field. SDLC uses an 8 bit address field while IDLC (Q.922) uses a 10 bit address field with the ability to expand it still further when required. It is important to note that this address field is consistent with the newly emerging frame relay standards (CCITT Recommendation I.122) that rely on Q.922 as well.

The ISDN B channel can use a variety of link access procedures (so long as the two ends agree). Thus, SDLC, LAP-B, and IDLC all have been used there. However, the strategic direction would seem to be to a common IDLC (based on Q.922).

LAN/ISDN connections.   Consider, first, Figure 12.13. It shows that *the inter-subnetwork protocol is encapsulated by the protocols of the subnetworks being traversed*—that is, by protocol headers of the LANs and the X.25 subnetworks. Figure 12.18 better shows how this encapsulation occurs. Our question now is, what happens when the center subnetwork in Figure 12.18 is an ISDN, and the internet protocol is either OSI CLNS or TCP/IP?

Let us look more closely at the TCP/IP layers in Figure 3.26. The Internet Protocol (IP) functions as a layer 3c, X.25 then is at layer 3a, and the LAN 802.2 is at layer 2. If the X.25 is absent (on the LAN side), then the layer 3a is null, and IP communicates directly with the LAN 802.2. If, now, we assume that the ISDN is to operate in packet mode, then the routers X and Y, in Figure 12.18 would look like Figure 18.23. Both B channels and

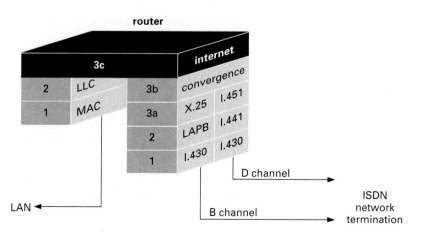

Figure 18.23 Router facing a LAN on one side and an ISDN on the other.

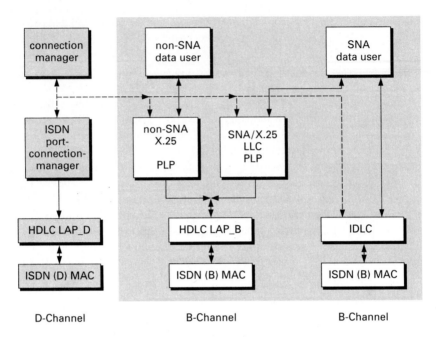

Figure 18.24 Key elements of the basic rate (2B+D) ISDN process.

a D channel are involved on the ISDN side. The B channel uses the X.25 and LAP-B protocols. The D channel uses the I.441 (LAP-D) and I.451 protocols. If, on the other hand, the X.25 is absent on the ISDN side, then the B channel in the router has no layer 3a, and layer 2 can be SDLC or IDLC or LAP-B. The Internet protocol (whether CLNP or IP) is connectionless. Before any ISDN data transmission can occur, one must open a B channel, as in a connection-oriented service. Therefore, a layer 3b signaling layer is needed to manage the opening of a B-channel when it is needed and to close it after an idle-period time [Brusseau89].

18.7.5 Signaling by I.451/Q.931

For the user, the protocols standardized in ISDN for making calls are some of its most important features. The D channel functions described in Q.931 (I.451) pertain to the establishment and termination of circuit-switched and packet-switched connections across an ISDN. In the standard, these are considered to be layer-3 functions (just as the X.25 call set-up is considered to be layer 3 in the standards). The messages defined in Q.931 occupy the *information field* of the D channel LAP-D protocol [Q.931,88].

SNA/ISDN signaling. In SNA, the functions of Q.931 are performed by the ISDN port-connection-manager. The position of this function is shown in Figure 18.24. At the lowest layer (not shown) is the physical interface. Above that are the three MAC layer services. Above that is the DLC/LLC function, including HDLC/LAP-D for the D channel and either

HDLC/LAP-B or SDLC or IDLC for the two B channels. Providing information fields for the D channel, is the ISDN port-connection-manager. Note that there are also connection-manager functions to coordinate the establishment of data paths in the B channels as well.

The B channel information is provided by either an SNA data user or a non-SNA data user. Each of these would use a different upper-layer protocol stack. Either could employ the X.25 packet-layer protocols on a B channel. However, the SNA user would interpose the SNA X.25/LLC (as a layer-3b convergence) discussed in Section 19.5.2.

The ISDN port-connection-manager performs the signaling protocols required to create the switched end-to-end physical connectivity through an ISDN network to a remote peer node. Basic port connection management uses the D channel for sending or receiving circuit-switched signaling-messages to establish a B channel.

Permanent (leased-like) connections do not use ISDN signaling messages to establish calls on B channels. Instead, these calls are arranged at subscription time. Semipermanent (leased-like) connections may or may not use signaling protocols, depending on how the provider sets up the service at subscription time.

18.8   FRAME RELAY (I.122)

Frame relay is the interface for *high-performance routing of variable length frames* over WANs at layer 2. **CCITT I.122** is *an adaptation of the ISDN interface* for this purpose [I.122,88] [ANSI,88]. It (like X.25) is first of all a *standard user-network interface to a WAN*. It does not necessarily determine the protocols used within the WAN. The I.122 Recommendation states that it is aimed at data services up to 2 Mbps.[17]

Frame relay can be considered to be a streamlined version of the X.25 packet switching data network. The goal of I.122 frame relay is, in effect, to move the virtual circuit identifier, implemented in an X.25 layer 3, down to layer 2. Processing-intensive functions such as level-3 addressing, packet sequencing, and error correction, are moved to the end-systems connected to the network. Errors detected by the network are simply dropped. Frame relay is attractive in its simplicity. Its implementations can use much the same switching hardware as today's packet switching equipment, providing through software upgrades a convenient increase in network speeds. However, the frame-relay interface also has potential for use as the interface to fast packet networks such as those described in Section 18.5.

The term *relay* connotes that the layer-2 frame is not terminated by the logical-link control (LLC) at each switching node, but is relayed to its destination. While different LLC protocols (SDLC, HDLC, etc.) can be used at the two ends, the preferred direction is for common use of the evolving Q.922 standard, which is a superset of I.441/Q.921.

The key aspects of a frame relay service are:

- Data transfers at least up to 2 Mbps (frequently at T1, 1.544 Mbps, and possibly much higher)

---

17. The upper limit of 2 Mbps is not a technical limit, as frame-relay technology is applicable to higher speeds. It is, however a policy limit relative to ATM technology that is designed for the higher speeds.

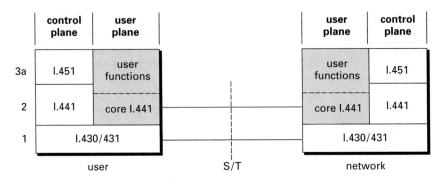

Figure 18.25 User/network interface with I.122 [I.122].

- Protocol transparency regarding upper layers
- Multiplexing of channels on a given access-link
- Reliance on higher-layer protocols for error recovery and flow control

User-network interface. The I.122 user/network interface is sketched in Figure 18.25. The I.122 frame formats are shown in this chapter's Technical Reference section. A frame (shown in Figure 18.37) consists of an opening flag followed by a 2-byte address field, a user data field, a frame check sequence, and a closing flag. This is as seen at the MAC layer. At this level, any end-to-end controls, such as logical-link control (LLC), are included within the user data field.

Except for the 2-byte address field, these frame-relay formats are those defined in Link Access Procedure-D (LAP-D) as per I.441, Q.921 (see also Figures 18.35 and 19.31). The frame-relay format and protocol are a superset of LAP-D, built upon Q.921, and are specified in Q.922. (A proposed 2-byte address field for frame relay is illustrated in Figure 18.38 [FRSpec90].) *It is made up of a 10-bit Data-Link-Connection-Identifier, called DLCI, a 1-bit command/response indicator, and bits that indicate congestion and echo the indication.* The 2-byte address field is the same as that in the IDLC previously discussed except that in the latter the three congestion-oriented bits are instead reserved.

In frame relay, each DLCI value defines a logical channel within the underlying physical channel. Each logical channel has its own DLC elements of procedure at the LLC layer, and its own set of protocols at layer 3 and above. Special values of DLCI (such as all zeros) are used to indicate that the information field contains control information. In frame relay, the DLCI value has only local significance. The network associates the two DLCIs (at the two communicating end-systems) with a virtual circuit. Frame relay can be considered to be a MAC level connection-oriented service for which the virtual circuit and DLCI values are established.

The core I.441, Q 921, and also Q.922, employed by the user at the MAC layer of DLC, includes things like:

- Frame delimiting and frame alignment

- Frame transparency

- Frame multiplexing and demultiplexing using the DLCI address field

- Insuring the frame has an integer number of octets and is not too long or too short

- Detection of transmission errors (but no correction by retransmission)

Frame-relay signaling.   Initially, many frame-relay installations will use the simpler permanent virtual circuit (PVC) without signaling for a switched virtual circuit (SVC). However, the infrequent user needs SVCs. The frame relay signaling is based on the ISDN Q.931 signaling. Some additional information elements are being added for frame relay, however. These include parameters for frame size, transit delay, bandwidth, and the data link connection identifier (DLCI).

Applications.   Planners see many roles for frame relay, including LAN/WAN/LAN communication and end-system/WAN connection, as shown in Figures 12.23 and 12.25. As noted earlier, the I.122 frame-relay interface can be used for WANs whose internal protocols. As described by Lippis, that WAN might for example be broadband (T1 on up) nodal processors in which virtual channels can be routed across the wide area network [Lippis90]. The nodal processors deliver dynamic routing at layer 2 or layer 1, with bandwidth on demand, between network-access units, thus creating a logical mesh topology. Every network-access unit is then logically adjacent to every other network-access unit.[18]

18.9   BROADBAND ISDN

The term *Broadband ISDN (B-ISDN)* is used to indicate the use of bandwidths above those in the Narrowband ISDN offerings. The initial B-ISDN offerings are expected, in the second half of the 1990s, to be in the range 150 to 600 Mbps. While the Narrowband ISDN is almost exclusively provided over copper wiring, the Broadband ISDN uses optical media in at least one part of the network. The B-ISDN services are expected to include: high-speed data transfer, video teleconferencing, video telephony, high-quality audio, and video distribution. Thus, Broadband ISDN is one hope for full utilization of the capabilities of the SONET family. The B-ISDN standards, however, in CCITT Study Group XVIII, are still in the early stages of formation. Two user interfaces are being standardized: one at 155.52 Mbps, and one at 622 Mbps.

18.9.1   Asynchronous Transfer Mode (ATM)

B-ISDN will use a specific packet-oriented mode, based on asynchronous time division multiplexing. This has been called **Asynchronous Transfer Mode (ATM)**. ATM is meant to provide unified switching for voice, data, and image in public networks. ATM multiplexing does not dedicate time slots to individual services, as in time division

---

18.   As another example, *Data Communications*, of October 1990 reports Rick McGee, manager of communications system architecture at IBM, saying that IBM researchers are working on ways to enable customers to build frame-relay networks that provide equal performance for TCP/IP, OSI, and NetBIOS protocol stacks.

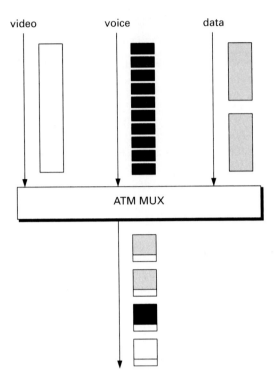

Figure 18.26 Multiplexing voice, video, and data in asynchronous transfer mode.

multiplexing. Instead, the information in each data stream is packetized and placed in small, fixed-length cells. Figure 18.26 illustrates the principle. ATM fills each cell with traffic from only one circuit, be it video, voice, or data. Each cell (or packet) contains the address and control information needed to route through the network according to packet priority. The cell or packet nature of ATM promises customizing of function, performance, and quality to individual needs.

Principle ATM characteristics. The principle characteristics of ATM include the following:

- All types of information are acceptable, narrowband and broadband, information coming in bursts or in more continuous flows.
- The user can interface the network at the highest possible bit-rate.
- All of the bandwidth is used by all of the services for part of the time.
- The information is transferred via virtual channels set up on labeled cells, which are directly multiplexed into the output stream.
- Framing is not required.

ATM cells.   In ATM, the transport carries fixed size (53 byte) blocks, called cells. Each cell consists only of a 48-byte user information field and a 5-byte header. Like X.25, ATM is

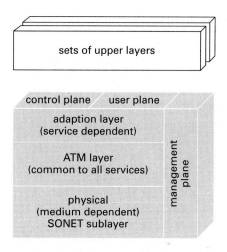

Figure 18.27 The layers of asynchronous transfer mode.

connection-oriented. *Each cell contains a header that identifies the virtual connection to which the cell belongs.* The ATM header (illustrated in Figure 18.39 in this chapter's Technical Reference section) contains identifiers for both the virtual channel and the virtual path.[19] These headers control the asynchronous switching. The signaling, however, is carried in a separate virtual circuit. ATM also supports real-time isochronous services, in circuit-mode emulation.

Cells belonging to different communications can be multiplexed on the same link. Cell sequence integrity on a virtual circuit is guaranteed. However, when the network becomes congested, it discards the ATM cells of lower priority.

B-ISDN layers. The ATM functions are layered as shown in Figure 18.27. The control-plane, the elements and protocols responsible for transferring control information, is identical, at layers 2 and 3, to those elements in Narrowband ISDN. An extension of Q.931 sits atop LAP-D. The M-plane, including the elements and protocols responsible for system management, is based on the current OSI management standards for layers 2 through 7.

In the user plane, ATM is the highest sublayer of the physical layer (although some argue that it is also a lowest sublayer of layer 2) [Vorster88]. Thus (assuming we include ATM in the physical layer), intermediate-nodes would not need to implement a protocol stack above the physical layer.

The **adaption layer**, above the ATM at the end-systems, maps the outgoing information into ATM cells, and collects ATM cells as they arrive.

---

19.   Both MAN and ATM have a 5-byte header, but the headers are not exactly the same. The MAN header differs from the ATM header in that (a) only 20 bits of VCI address field are used by MAN, and (b) the ATM generic flow control (4 bits) and the 4 bits of ATM VPI are replaced by a byte of MAN access control field.

18.10   ENTERPRISE SYSTEM CONNECTION (ESCON)

Optical fiber is also extending the broadband capability of mainframe channels. Fiber is, in effect, creating a local area network extending for kilometers the connections among mainframes and communications or device controllers. The architecture of this channel subnetwork is tailored to the serial optical channel, using fiber.

The many broadband channels of a mainframe or intermediate-size processor are the funnels through which a wide variety of network-based end-stations find access to the databases and processing power of these hosts. A multiplicity of logical-links, for 802.2 LANs, FDDI, and SDLC protocols, can be constructed. These logical-links can thus extend via copper and fiber from widely scattered end-systems to network entities in the host.

ESCON features.   A current example of this trend is the *Enterprise System Connection (ESCON)*, an optical channel connection for mainframes that extends the dimensions of the channel-connected environment to a radius of 9 kilometers [GA23-0383]. With ESCON:

- Multiple mainframe systems can communicate (channel-to-channel) with each other
- Many device or communication control units can share a single optical link to a mainframe channel
- Multiple mainframe systems can gain access to multiple device or communication control units

Up to 60 channels and control units can thus be interconnected, of which any 30 can be connected concurrently. ESCON's key features are:

- Fiber optic distribution system
- 200 Mbps link rate
- Star and switched star topologies
- Up to 3 kilometers without repeaters; and cable distances up to 9 kilometers
- Channel-to-channel and channel-to-control-unit connections (e.g., mainframes, LANs, terminal-controllers, DASD, tape, printers)
- Nondisruptive installation and removal

By attaching a 3172 Interconnect Controller (see Section 17.5.2) to a parallel-to-serial protocol converter, the 802.2/3/4/5, and FDDI LANs can be connected via an optical channel to mainframes within the 9 km range of the ESCON system (see Figure 18.28).

Two functional entities at layer 2 are defined by the architecture. The device layer provides functions and protocols equivalent to the earlier S/390 channel-to-control-unit operation. The link layer essentially defines a packet-switching operation, whose function is to transport information between units in a point-to-point star or switched star network. The link layer is symmetrical. That is, operations viewed from either end of a link appear identical.

The physical link consists of two fibers, one for sending and one for receiving. Information on the link is transmitted in a special 10-bit code (8 of 10 code), giving an

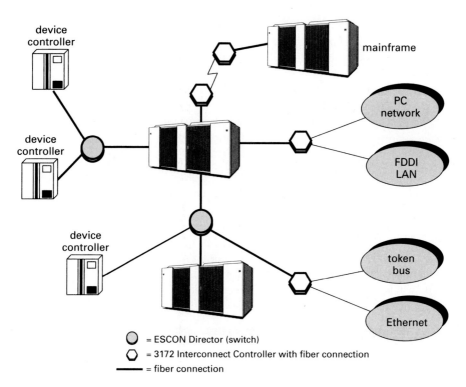

Figure 18.28 LANs, mainframes, and devices in the Enterprise System Connection (ESCON).

instantaneous link rate of 20 megabytes per second. After deducting for control (e.g., pacing bytes) and data encoding overhead, a channel data rate, for real application data, of 10 megabytes per second is achieved. Power in attached units is remotely controlled using the same fiber link that is used for the transmission of data.

Dynamic switch characteristics. ESCON connections can be established or removed dynamically, with no effect on other connections. A short-duration connection, for example, involves:

1. A channel or control unit sends a connection frame to the switch (called the Enterprise System Connection Director, ESCD).
2. The switch interprets the request and activates the connection if the desired port is available. Communication then proceeds between the identified ports.
3. One of the two units sends a frame containing a request to remove the connection.

The switch does not recognize differences between channels and control-units. Among these it supports multiple concurrent connections.

Frames can vary in size from 7 bytes to 1035 bytes. Each frame includes both the frame source address and its destination address. These addresses are used to route frames through the network. The switch examines the destination address and dynamically connects the port receiving the frame to the destination port (if not busy). In addition, the device-level portion of the frame carries a device address which is equivalent to the address used on the earlier S/390 I/O interface.

The source and destination addresses are broken up into an 8-bit link address and a 4-bit logical address. The link address is used for routing through the dynamic switch. The logical address is used to select "logical-systems." For example, the logical addresses might be used to select one of sixteen possible guest machines in a VM environment.

Reliability/availability.   Cyclic redundancy checking, the redundant 8/10 code, and disparity checking, in combination, assure the detection of (almost) all errors. Because of the extremely low error rates, frame retry procedures are not justified, and the rare recovery procedures are allocated to the receiving control units.

For availability, control-units can provide at least two fiber optic channel adapters, providing dual links to the ESCON switch. Likewise, a system can configure at least two dynamic switches, with control-units and hosts attached to more than one switch. This guarantees that single failures cannot cause system failure.

CPU-CPU coupling.   The ESCON Serial Optical Channel (SOC), at 200 Mbps, is used for channel-to-channel connections. Multiples of these channels can be multiplexed to yield higher data rates. The distances for ESCON links are currently limited; however, with the advent of SONET capacity lines there will be new possibilities for linking multiple channels between ESCON switches on very remote CPUs via the SONET lines. Remote memory-to-memory and channel-to-channel connections will make good use of the new bandwidths.

18.11   NSFNET

The technology trends in high-speed networks can also be seen in the current efforts to develop nationwide broadband networks for science and education. The National Science Foundation Network (NSFnet) was originally funded to establish a 56-kbps and then a T1 (1.544-Mbps) backbone linking research and education centers across the nation.[20] The next, current step is a T3 (44.736-Mbps) upgrade. Further upgrades are planned. Toward the end of 1989, the traffic approximated two billion packets per month. The number of active users is expected to grow from the one million in 1989 to four to six million within ten years. The number of computer connections will increase from over 100,000 in 1989 to 500,000, according to EDUCOM predictions [GK21-0104].

NSFnet is a packet-switching network based on TCP/IP. It is expected that OSI protocols will be used in tandem with and ultimately replace TCP/IP. The *Nodal Switching Subsystem (NSS)* routes packets between a midlevel network and other nodes in the

---

20.   MCI, the University of Michigan, and IBM have been key contractors in the development of NSFNet.

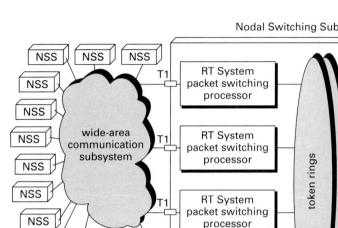

Figure 18.29 NFSnet's nodal switching subsystem [GK21-0104].

NSFnet backbone. One NSS is located at each of the backbone node sites. Each NSS currently includes multiple IBM RTs,[21] loosely coupled with token-ring networks into a multiprocessing system, as shown in Figure 18.29. Each NSS consists of three major elements:

1. Packet Switching Processors (PSPs), that switch packets to or from the wide area communications subsystem or a colocated LAN.

2. Routing Control Processor (RCP), that determines the routing information that is loaded into the PSPs. There is one RCP per node, and all RCPs communicate with each other to determine the best routing.

3. Statistics gathering: One IBM RT system is dedicated to gathering network traffic statistics.

For availability reasons, processors and LAN elements can be replicated. These components can be serviced or replaced without taking the entire switch down.

---

21.   The IBM RT is an IBM microprocessor using TCP communications.

MCI operates the lines connecting the NSFnet nodes. MCI interfaces with NetView, using a system management application called MCI View (see Section 4.8.3). Data is also sent to NetView by NetView/PCs, which poll each nodal switching system. Another tool, called Internet Rover, developed by Merit, continually queries nodes in the network. Data gathered from each NSS are reported to a workstation, which displays information about abnormalities in the Network Operations Center.

18.12 GIGABIT NETWORKS

Bandwidths of a gigabit per second, and more, are not now needed in most networks. They are essential, however, for a growing number of applications. These include scientific applications, archival systems, and some distributed processing applications. In the scientific arena, visualization of huge amounts of data, in animated fashion, requires very large bandwidths. This need is acute, for example, in large projects like those of the mapping of the human gene structures, the Hubble space telescope, and the superconductor supercollider (SSC) for nuclear research. The gigabit links are therefore sometimes very important elements of future planning, but only a brief mention of them is possible here.

Gigabit/sec NREN.   The program plan submitted to Congress, on September 8, 1989, by the Office of Science and Technology Policy called for the *National Research and Education Network (NREN)* to grow NSFnet in a third stage. This would upgrade NSFnet to 1 to 3 gigabits per second, to selected research facilities, and 45 megabits per second to approximately 1000 sites nationwide. The proposed deployment of stage 3 includes a specific, structured process resulting in transition of the network from a government operation to a commercial service.

High-Performance Parallel Interface (HiPPI).   The 800 Mbps HiPPI was an early advance toward meeting the need for gigabit interprocessor links. It provides 25 Mbps per line on a 32-bit parallel bus, for a total of 800 Mbps. A 64-bit parallel bus has also been defined, which could double the data rate. Its distance, by itself, is limited to 25 meters, in a point-to-point connection. In connection with optical fiber extenders, however, the distances are expanded up to 2 kilometers. HiPPI has been proposed as an ANSI standard, X3T9 [HiPPI90]. In relation to the OSI model, HiPPI covers the physical layer and a small portion of the data link control layer.

   Each packet consists of one or more bursts. A *burst* is a fixed length sequence of 256 4-byte words. Bursts, then are grouped in multiples of four to make up a 4096-byte *page*. This is the granularity of the IBM implementation of HiPPI. With very high speed transmission, buffering is even more key than usual. For example, incoming HiPPI data fills the inbound HiPPI buffer one burst at a time, until a 4-kilobyte page is waiting. Then, HiPPI issues a page-waiting software signal. Any additional bursts continue to queue up in the 32-kilobyte inbound buffer until the buffer is full. When the application issues a read request, the HiPPI Program Base is given control and loads the first page from the HiPPI inbound buffer into main storage. HiPPI continues to place pages into main storage until the hardware buffer is empty or the read request is satisfied. With still higher speeds, then, much larger buffers are needed. Fortunately, as the cost of memory continues to decline, very large fast buffers become practical.

Ultranet Network Technologies, Inc., provides a related connectivity hub that supports multiple HiPPI interfaces (each at 100 Mbps) plus a number of others, including the Cray HSX interface (100 Mbps), the IBM channel interface (4.5 Mbps), and the VME (IEEE 1014) interface (20 Mbps). The Ultranet hub can be used to interconnect mass storage, special purpose processors, and general purpose processors, and to provide HiPPI ports to high-speed communications servers.

Fiber Channel Standard.   A subsequent effort of the ANSI X3T9.3 standards group concerns the *Fiber Channel Standard*, which is being optimized for serial transfers of large blocks of data such as used for file transfers and output to printers and graphics terminals [Tolmie89]. The Fiber Channel Standard is being specified in three speed and distance ranges:

Low end	50 Mbps	0.1 km
Mid range	250 Mbps	2–10 km
High end	1000 Mbps	2–10 km

The Fiber Channel has been defined in four layers:

1. FC-3 consists of a set of "bridge" facilities that define how existing protocols (e.g., HiPPI and block multiplexing) are to be carried on the fiber channel.

2. FC-2 defines the framing protocol and the control of the interconnection fabric. The proposed frame structure resembles that of SDLC/HDLC, with start-of-frame and end-of-frame delimiters surrounding a frame header, data field, and cyclic redundancy check field.

3. FC-1 defines the encoding and decoding scheme (8B/10B), and the special characters used to form frame delimiters.

4. FC-0 defines the physical interface, including fibers, connectors, and transceivers.

General.   Other specialized optical links have proven feasibility [Eng88]. From 1 Gbps traveling over 1 kilometer a decade ago [Bergman85], [Baack83], [Baack86] to 16 Gbps traveling over 60 kilometers [Tucker88], [Cochrane88]. In addition, coherent transmission schemes have demonstrated 2 Gbps over 200 kilometers [Kwashita86]. Eng and Bergman [Eng88b] conclude that the evolutionary improvements in present (incoherent) LAN technology will permit speeds of tens of Gbps to be achieved in this decade.

Beyond that is the future challenge to use the full bandwidth of optical fiber amounting to thousands of gigabits per second (terabits per second). Optical amplifiers and filters are already feasible. Since electronics, rather than optics, will be the limiting factor, the use of slices of the available bandwidth by frequency division multiplexing is attractive. One can foresee up to gigahertz electronics accessing terahertz optical bandwidths, with aggregation of lower-speed inputs.[22]

---

22.   Drawn from presentation by Robert S. Kennedy, "Symposium: From Servo Loops to Fiber Nets," MIT, October 25, 1990.

Conclusion

FDDI at 125 Mbps link rate, ESCON (serial optical channel) at 200 Mbps, and HiPPI at 800 Mbps, are today's high-speed capabilities. Frame-relay techniques are also on the fast track. Fast packet switching systems using layer-2 routing are also becoming operational. Much will be built on these and their extensions in the next few years. Narrowband ISDN, SMDS, MAN, and Broadband ISDN also will be contending for overlapping markets. All will offer improved transmission services with reduced processing at higher speeds.

All of these link/subnetwork-access facilities in Chapters 17 and 18 operate at layers 1 through 3a. All are commonly available to any of the layer 3c and higher protocol stacks, as illustrated in Figures 2.2 and 3.14. FDDI and MAN join the LANs of Chapter 17 in providing the common 802.2 interface. MAN, SMDS, and Broadband ISDN (ATM) improve interoperability by using a common 53 byte cell.

Figure 18.30 provides a comparison of the lower layers needed for ATM, frame-relay, frame-switching, and X.25 PSDNs. ATM itself uses only the physical layer. I.122 frame relay, in addition, needs segmentation and error detection. Frame-switching needs all of that and, in addition, needs flow control, windowing, and retransmission at the LLC sublayer of layer 2. X.25 needs all of that and, in addition, needs the packet-layer functions of layer 3.

A multiprotocol *Transport-Service-Provider (TSP)* must consider the customer needs for many of these options. Many of them, (ISDN, frame-relay, frame-switching, and X.25) first of all affect the user-network interface. That user-interface can determine the nature of the network-access units in order to gain access to the transport-service-provider. Within that TSP, the architecture may be very different from that of the user-interface. A frame-relay interface, for example may connect to a network of node-processors with bandwidth management, which uses automatic network routing and/or address swapping entirely at layer 1. Hence, we can expect steady evolution of high-performance subnetworks, while offering a variety of network-access interfaces.

Many evolutionary scenarios are possible. One probable scenario for broadband network evolution calls for three phases as follows [Materna89]:

1.   A growth in private broadband subnetworks (T3 and above), complements the advent

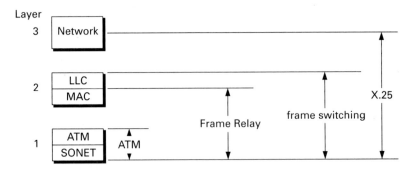

Figure 18.30 Protocol span using four techniques.

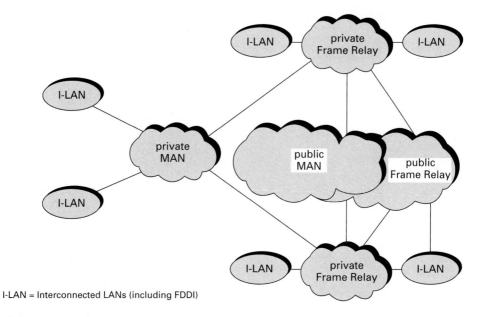

I-LAN = Interconnected LANs (including FDDI)

Figure 18.31 Possible scenarios.

of public broadband facilities. This has three components: *FDDIs, fast-packet WANs,* and *MANs,* as shown in Figure 18.31.

2. As in (1) above, and with public MANs connected *by ATM switches* to other (distant) public MANs. An interworking unit (IWU) provides the interface between the DQDB medium and the ATM medium.

3. As in (1) above, and with both public and private subnetworks (MANs and fast-packet WANs) *connected to Broadband ISDN networks.*

Acknowledgments

I am particularly indebted to E. C. Broockman, C. A. Murphy, J. J. Lynch, N. L. Golding, J. L. Frantz, M. Demange, P. Chimento, V. J. Buberniak, E. Loizides, E. Sussenguth, and F. Corr for valuable input or reviews of this chapter.

TECHNICAL REFERENCES

FDDI Frame Formats

Figure 18.32 shows the FDDI token and frame formats. A comparison of these with the LAN formats in Figure 17.24 reveals a great similarity except for the absence of LLC in the FDDI frames. Any LLC headers would be part of the LLC-PDU.

Another difference is the coding using symbols in FDDI rather than bytes in the other LANs. Data transmitted on the fibre is encoded in a scheme where every 4 bits from MAC is transmitted as

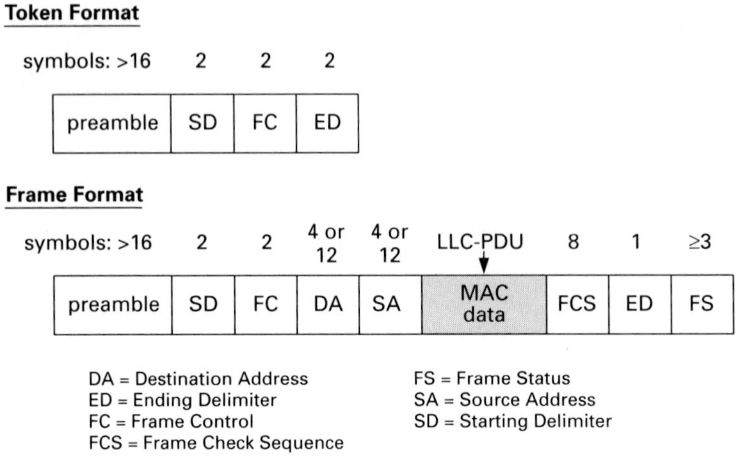

Token Format

symbols: >16   2   2   2

preamble	SD	FC	ED

Frame Format

symbols: >16   2   2   4 or 12   4 or 12   LLC-PDU   8   1   ≥3

preamble	SD	FC	DA	SA	MAC data	FCS	ED	FS

DA = Destination Address   FS = Frame Status
ED = Ending Delimiter   SA = Source Address
FC = Frame Control   SD = Starting Delimiter
FCS = Frame Check Sequence

Figure 18.32 FDDI token and frame formats.

a 5-bit symbol. The 4 bits from MAC have 16 possible data values. Since there are 32 5-bit symbols, some of these are theoretically available for control symbols.

The synchronization preamble contains 16 or more idle symbols (each idle=11111). The pattern of the starting delimiter starts with the symbols JK (J=11000; K=10001). The ending delimiter of the token is two T symbols (T=01101).

Frame control (FC) distinguishes synchronous and asynchronous frames, restricted and nonrestricted tokens, the length of the address field (16 or 48 bits), the type of frame, and the control functions for that type. The types of frames are:

- *MAC beacon frame*: an alert for a ring failure, and an aid to its location.
- *MAC claim frame*: used during start-up and recovery to select one station to start issuing a token.
- *LLC frame*: used to assure frame delivery and correct sequence.
- *Station management frame*: used for various station management functions, such as reconfiguration, error control, and bandwidth allocation.

Three indicators in the frame-status field indicate (a) whether an error has been detected (b) whether a station has recognized its own address in that frame, and (c) whether a station also makes a copy of that frame. When the originating station recognizes its own address as the source address, it checks to verify that no errors were detected, and that the frame was copied by a receiving station.

MAN Cell Format

The logical-link control PDU becomes the data for the MAC layer. The successive encapsulation of this data [Le], [Littlewood89] in three sets of headers/trailers is shown in Figure 18.33.

- First the *LLC PDU* is encapsulated in a header and trailer to form a datagram at the MAC layer. This header includes a 64-bit destination address, a 64-bit source address, a beginning-end tag, and a quality of service class. Routing is based on this destination address, which is formed according to the E.164 standard. A 1 octet *protocol identifier* indicates the higher-layer protocol being used.

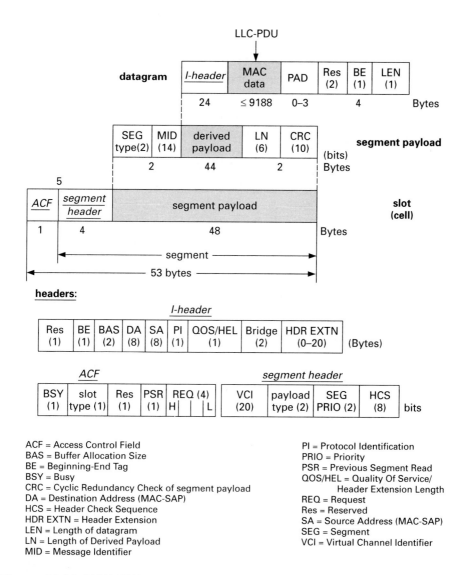

Figure 18.33 MAN PDU structures [Le].

- That *datagram*, then, must be *sliced into segments* that later fit into the 52-byte slot-payloads. Each slice of the IM-PDU is 44 bytes, which are surrounded by a 2-byte header and a 2-byte trailer, producing a 48-byte segment-payload. A *segment-type* indicates whether the segment is the first, last, sole or middle segment of a datagram. A *message-identifier* accompanies each segment-payload, to permit reassembly of the datagram from the incoming segments.

- That *segment-payload*, in turn, is given a 4-byte segment header, to form a **segment**. The segment header contains a *virtual channel identifier*.

• That *segment* is a fixed size (52-byte) slot-payload that is given a 1-byte slot header (ACF, the access control field) and transmitted on the bus as the cell in the MAN slot. The segment header and the slot header add up to a 5-byte header for the 48-byte segment-payload. The 53-byte MAN cell is consistent with the 53-byte cell of Broadband ISDN ATM.

When segmenting, the MAC source and destination addresses appear only in the first segment of the message. The destination address is checked by all nodes on the network. When a match is found, the message is read; subsequent segments are then accepted based on the message identifier label.

The *Previous Slot Received (PSR)* bit makes it possible to re-use slots immediately. The receiver of a slot sets the PSR bit. There is not time to set the bit while the header is available; therefore, the policy is to set the bit in the next slot instead.

A slot may also be reserved repetitively, in each 125 usec frame, for synchronous information. Each 48 byte segment payload is then devoted to 64 kbps channels. The 4 bytes of the segment header are not used.

SMDS Frame Formats

The SMDS SIP-3 format is shown in Figure 18.34(a). The *Control Indicator* field is used to indicate whether the destination-address pertains to a single user or a group of users. The *Carrier Indicator* and *Carrier Select* fields are used to select various service providers or carrier networks. Up to eight Carrier Select fields may be included. The large allowable size of the *Information* field was chosen to accommodate the largest information fields in standard LANs. Hence, no segmentation of LAN information usually will be needed when interconnecting LANs to SMDS.

The format of the SIP-2 protocol data unit is shown in Figure 18.34(b). The SIP-3 PDU becomes the information field of this frame. The frame-check-sequence field is used for a 32-bit CRC on the information field only. The length check field then facilitates a 16-bit check on the information length field. While this protocol level thus checks for error, it does no error correction, or frame retransmission.

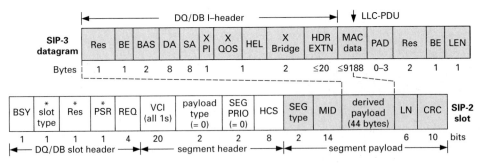

Figure 18.34 SMDS data formats: **(a)** SIP-3 Protocol Data Unit format; **(b)** SIP-2 format [Dix 88].

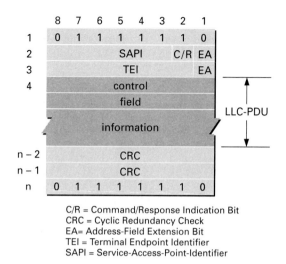

C/R = Command/Response Indication Bit
CRC = Cyclic Redundancy Check
EA= Address-Field Extension Bit
TEI = Terminal Endpoint Identifier
SAPI = Service-Access-Point-Identifier

Figure 18.35 Frame format for ISDN LAP-D.

HDLC Frame Formats

The HDLC format is: flag, address, control, information, frame check sequence, and flag. The HDLC/LAP-D format, used in the signaling on the ISDN D channel, is shown in Figure 18.35. The LAP-D address field is extendable. The cyclic redundency check (CRC) may be 16 or 32 bits. (See also Figure 19.31.)

The 2-byte control field format (for the extended, modulo 128 operation) is the same as in the LAN 802.2 logical-link control, shown in Figure 17.26. For the modulo 8 operation, the sequence numbers N(S) and N(R) are only 3 bits each, so the control field can be compressed into 1 byte.

The HDLC classes of procedure are shown in Figure 18.36. There are basic and optional commands. Three classes are:

1. *UNC*—Unbalanced operation Normal response mode Class, involving the polling of the secondary by the primary station (used, for example, in SDLC).

2. *UAC*—Unbalanced operation Asynchronous response mode Class, where one secondary station can speak without being polled (this class is rarely used).

3. *BAC*—Balanced operation Asynchronous balanced mode Class, which avoids the primary–secondary asymmetry, and two stations have equal abilities (used, for example, in X.25).

The HDLC commands are:

- RR—Ready to receive; acknowledges received I frames.
- RNR—Not ready to receive; acknowledges received I frames.
- DISC—Terminates the link connection.
- FRMR—Reports receipt of a frame that was not acceptable.
- UA—Acknowledges acceptance of a set-mode command.

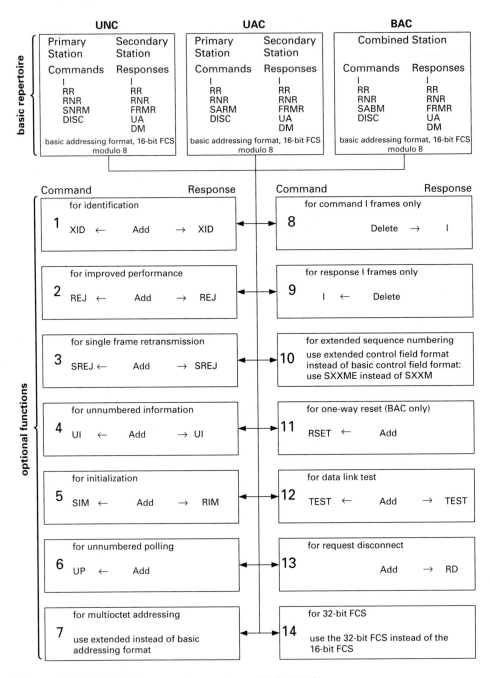

Figure 18.36 HDLC classes of procedures [ISO 7809].

- DM—Reports that a station is in a disconnected mode.
- XID—Exchanges identification and operational parameters.
- UI—Sends information without regard to sequencing.
- SIM—Sets initialization mode (e.g., program load).
- RIM—Station requests to be sent a SIM.
- UP—Polls station without regard to sequencing.
- SNRM, SARM, SABM—Sets the operational mode.
- SNRME, SARME, SABME—Sets mode with the extended (2-byte) control field.
- REJ—Requests retransmission of all I frames that had an N(S) value equal to or higher than the N(R) in the REJ frame.
- SREJ—Requests retransmission of a single frame with an N(S) equal to the N(R) contained in the SREJ.
- TEST—Exchanges information fields for test purposes.
- RSET—Permits reset of link sequence numbers for one direction of interchange. Receiving station resets its N(R), and sending station resets its N(S).

SDLC is a conforming subset of HDLC, providing the basic repertoire of commands for normal response mode (UNC) and a selection of the allowable options.

ISDN Interface Data Rates

The basic data rate, without overhead (2B+1D) is 144 kbps. The overhead, on the customer side of NT1, at the "S" or "T" interface, is 48 kbps. When added to the 144 kbps, the total "S/T" basic bit rate is 192 kbps.

With a different format, the overhead at the network side of the NT1, at the "U" interface, is only 16 kbps. Adding this to the 144 kbps gives a total basic bit rate, at the "U" interface, of 160 kbps. (If line coding is used, with two bits per baud, then the total baud rate at the "U" interface would be only 80,000 baud.)

The bits of *the D and the B channels are multiplexed on the line*. In the basic rate, for example, the 16 kbps D and two 64 kbps B channels are multiplexed, repetitively, on the NT to TE line in the following sequence: 8xB1, 1xD, 8xB2, 1xD, 8xB1, 1xD, 8xB2, 1xD, with frame and balancing bits in between.

In the primary rate interface, all B and D channels are 64 kbps, so they can be uniformly time-division multiplexed. In the U.S. primary rate, for example, the twenty-three 64-kbps B channels and one 64 kbps D channel are time-division-multiplexed, with each channel sending 8 bits in its time slot. The frame is 193 bits (24 eight-bit time slots and one framing bit).

ISDN Terminal Bus and Wiring

The interface at the S/T reference point has also been specified as a bus to which a number of terminal equipments can be attached. The *short-passive-bus* allows an NT1 or NT2 to support up to eight terminal equipments. ISDN uses CSMA/CR (carrier sense multiple access with collision resolution) to control access to the bus. (With both voice and data applications on each terminal, the busy times with eight terminals could be appreciable.) The maximum length of the bus should not exceed 100 to 250 meters, depending on the impedance of the cable. The *extended-passive-bus*

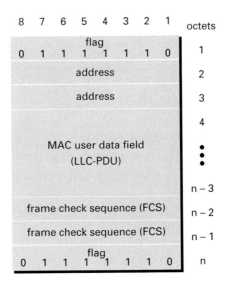

Figure 18.37 Frame-relay frame format.

allows a bus length of up to 500 meters, assuming all terminal equipments are within the last 25 to 50 meters.

The *ISDN physical connector*, specified for the "S" or "T" interface is an 8-wire interface. This I.430 interface uses the ISO DIS 8877 plug (which differs slightly between Europe and North America). Two pins are the Receive pair; two pins are the Transmit pair; and the other four pins are for power (in some applications, no power feeding across the interface may apply). Only the four wires needed for reception (pins 3, 4, 5, and 6) are mandatory. It is recommended, however, that any premise wiring should include all 8 wires.[23]

Frame-Relay Frame Format

The format for the I.122 frame-relay user-network interface is shown in Figure 18.37. A proposed 2-byte address field is shown in Figure 18.38. Key items include:

▪   The *Data Link Connection Identifier (DLCI)*, of 10-bits, identifies the bidirectional frame relay connection at the interface between the user-device and the network. The DLCI has only local significance, and may be reused on nonoverlapping virtual circuits (those not sharing end-points).

▪   The *Discard Eligibility (DE)* bit, if set to "1" indicates a request that a frame should be discarded in preference to other frames in a congestion situation, when frames must be discarded to ensure safe network operation.

▪   The *Backward Explicit Congestion Notification (BECN)* bit may be set by a congested network to notify the user that congestion avoidance procedures should be initiated where applicable for traffic in the opposite direction of the transmitted frame.

---

23.   The inner four prongs of the eight-prong ISDN connector exactly match the four prongs of the standard telephone connector. Hence a four-prong plug can be inserted in an eight-prong jack.

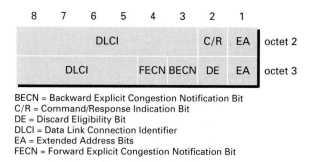

8	7	6	5	4	3	2	1	
DLCI						C/R	EA	octet 2
DLCI			FECN	BECN		DE	EA	octet 3

BECN = Backward Explicit Congestion Notification Bit
C/R = Command/Response Indication Bit
DE = Discard Eligibility Bit
DLCI = Data Link Connection Identifier
EA = Extended Address Bits
FECN = Forward Explicit Congestion Notification Bit

Figure 18.38 Frame-relay link-layer address field format.

- The *Forward Explicit Congestion Notification (FECN)* may be set by a congested network to notify the user that congestion avoidance procedures should be initiated where applicable for traffic in the direction of the transmitted frame.

ATM Header Format

The ATM cell format, with its 5-byte header, is illustrated in Figure 18.39. Note that the cell size (53 bytes) and information field (48 bytes) correspond to the slot size and segment-payload of the MAN format shown in Figure 18.33.

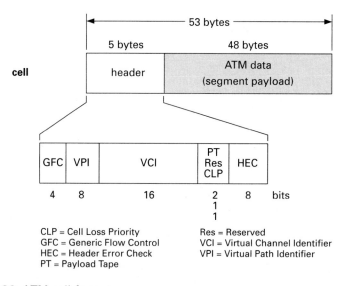

CLP = Cell Loss Priority
GFC = Generic Flow Control
HEC = Header Error Check
PT = Payload Tape

Res = Reserved
VCI = Virtual Channel Identifier
VPI = Virtual Path Identifier

Figure 18.39 ATM cell format.

EXERCISES

18.1 SONET uses data rates in multiples of what base data rate?

18.2 Worldwide commonality between SONET and the CCITT Synchronous Digital Hierarchy (SDH) begins at what data rate?

18.3 Identify seven major options for high-speed local area, metropolitan area, and wide area networks.

18.4 Name two types of fast packet switching and a characteristic that distinguishes them from each other.

18.5 Define the parameter used to measure the load on the FDDI ring.

18.6 How does checkpoint mode adjust to changing link error conditions?

18.7 How does automatic network addressing provide the addresses for successive stages?

18.8 What technique is used in high-speed MANs to allow multiple nodes to have simultaneous, nonsequenced access?

18.9 How does a MAN station know how many messages are queued ahead of it in downstream stations?

18.10 What channels are supported in the ISDN basic rate?

18.11 What channels are supported in the ISDN primary rate in the U.S. and in Europe?

18.12 Where does the frame relay PDU carry the virtual circuit identifier?

18.13 What indicators do frame relay use to help control network congestion?

18.14 What is an ATM cell like, and what can it be used for?

18.15 What makes ATM connection-oriented?

18.16 What does optical fiber and ESCON do for channel connections?

Part 6
Working Together

The preceding 18 chapters have taken us from the top down through each of the layers of the communications architecture. We close this book with one final chapter that first reflects on the directions being pursued towards an open systems network architecture for cooperating systems, and then adds a wide variety of concrete examples of systems and subsystems working together.

19
Multiprotocol
Interconnections

19.1 INTRODUCTION

To recap, as stated in Chapter 1, the foundation for OSNA involves communication via OSI, SNA, TCP/IP, and NetBIOS:

1. Among applications in both SAA and AIX/OSF systems

2. Between applications in these systems and applications in other systems, such as those of DEC, NetWare, SUN, Apple, and Hewlett Packard

Key to this is transparent access to common data, including access to distributed files and SQL databases *with full preservation of data integrity.*

The underlying infrastructure for such cooperation has been outlined in the preceding chapters. A top down summary of all chapters indicates that the infrastructure is being built in the following directions:

▪ *Enterprise system management*: SystemView strategy; OSI management framework; problem management for OSI, TCP/IP, and SNA; security facilities; heterogeneous LAN management; data/voice management; OSF/Distributed Management Environment.

▪ *Multiprotocol and multivendor networking*: Transparency at the Common Application Programming Interface (CPI-C); OSI, TCP/IP, and SNA-LU 6.2 across all platforms; dynamic location and topology updates, with minimum system definition; common link/ subnetwork facilities; use of high speed services; continued standards emphasis; multivendor LAN and WAN transport facilities; NetWare, Apple, DECnet, and other vendor connectivity.

▪ *Transparent database access*: Standard SQL programming interface; Distributed Relational Database Access (DRDA) across SAA and AIX platforms; support of ISO/ RDA standard.

- *Transparent file access:* Andrew File System in OFS; OSF/Distributed Computing Environment (OSF/DCE) for SAA and AIX; multiple remote file access via NFS, FTAM, and DDM.

- *Transparent remote application access*: X.500 directory support; SAA CPI-C; conversation, remote procedure call, and messaging paradigms; X Windows, TELNET, and terminal emulators.

- *View and print anywhere*: Multimedia information interchange; ODA, MO:DCA/P, and SGML; heterogeneous printer support over the network; ADOBE fonts on SAA and AIX.

- *Multivendor office support*: X.400 support; OfficeVision for SAA, AIX, DOS, and non-IBM platforms; TCP/IP mail bridges; Soft Switch Central.

- *Value-added networking*: IIN applications and interenterprise connectivity.

Much of this book has been about multiprotocol network interoperation. This actually has been evolving for years, and the current facilities are part of the evolving structure. The challenge of an architecture like OSNA is to integrate these early and future developments into an efficient system rather than a mere collection.

In this final chapter, we look at many current and concrete examples of multiprotocol communication facilities and interoperation. Some of these possibilities are illustrated in

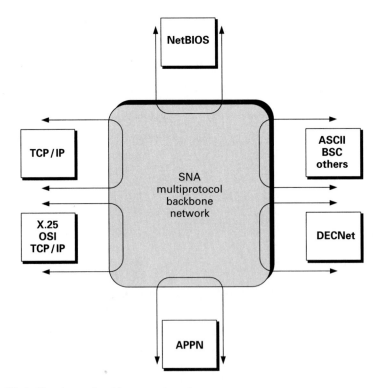

Figure 19.1 Sharing a backbone network.

Figure 19.1, showing a backbone carrying NetBIOS, ASCII, BiSynch, DECnet, APPN, X.25, and TCP/IP. Interoperation with DECnet was discussed in Chapters 4 and 5. We will look here at interoperation of SNA with other protocols.

These examples include the transport of NetBIOS traffic across SNA WANs. We then note the interoperation of SNA-based servers with NetWare servers (using IPX), and the connection of LANs using Apple Company's AppleTalk protocols. The interoperation of X.25 networks and TCP/IP networks with SNA networks are further described. Finally, we review the attachment of diverse terminals and multiprotocol end-systems.

19.2 LAN/WAN/LAN CONNECTIVITY

19.2.1 Introduction

LAN-to-LAN connectivity via a wide area backbone network offers a number of choices. One could connect at the link level via *leased lines*, as in the remote bridge described in Section 17.5.1. One could use, instead, a *switched network*, such as an ISDN, which would also appear simply as a link-level connection. Finally, one could use a *packet-switched WAN*, such as an X.25 or an *SNA subnetwork*. A private subnetwork like SNA could have within it several components, such as the SNA subarea network, the APPN subnetworks, and/or fast packet switching subnetworks.

Issues.   The choice of LAN-LAN connection depends on the performance of the intervening subnetwork and the functions desired in the end-systems. Subjects that need to be addressed include:

- Handling multiple upper-layer protocols
- Handling multiple connection (signaling) protocols
- Locating destinations in different address spaces
- Handling different subnetwork routing techniques
- Security
- Flow control
- System management participation

While lesser solutions are certainly possible, handling all of the above requirements tends to favor the layer-3 router, with full intermediate-node support at the edge of the backbone subnetwork.

Layer-3 protocol compatibilities.   The simplest *"one-protocol" layer-3 connection* of LAN-to-LAN via a WAN requires that the LAN and WAN layer-3 protocols be compatible. In one approach, it requires that:

a) The LAN is connected to the WAN by a node having layer-3 intermediate routing capability for that WAN

b) The sending and receiving end-systems on the LAN have compatible layer-3 through -7 protocol stacks (though their layer 3 may be null)

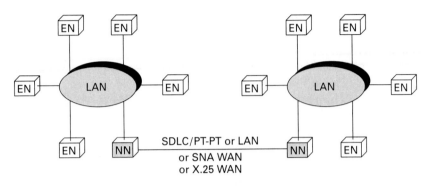

Figure 19.2 APPN network-nodes connecting two LANs.

c)   If the sending and receiving end-systems on the LAN do have a layer 3 then their layer 3 is compatible with that of the WAN

An illustration of such a LAN-to-LAN connection, in the case of APPN end-nodes and network-nodes, is shown in Figure 19.2. Separate, parallel connections of this nature can be made for multiple protocols. A variation of this approach is that shown in Figure 12.21, and discussed in Section 12.9. The requirements of this common-layer-3 protocol connection, however, are not always met. Particularly with NetBIOS, which does not have the usual layer-3 capability, an approach is needed, which provides WAN encapsulation of LAN-unique protocols.

19.2.2   LAN to WAN Routers

The principles of LAN-to-WAN routers were addressed in Chapter 12. Most current WANs use layer-3 routing, so this will be a common mode for some time. For example, the IBM 3745 provides connection between remote token-ring LANs via high-speed links that operate at up to 2 Mbps. APPN network nodes also can be the intermediate WAN link. An example of the use of APPN network-nodes as routers between two LANS is illustrated in Figure 19.2. The logical-links between the pair of network-nodes could use, for example, a dedicated SDLC line, a high-speed LAN, or a mesh network of an SNA or X.25 WAN.

Using source routing throughout each subnetwork, the entire route through the WAN, and the LANs at both ends, could be made into one integrated route. The total route information would have to include the addresses of any bridges in the origin and destination LANs, layer-3 address information for switching at the intermediate WAN nodes, and the final station address on the destination LAN. LAN-to-LAN routing via the WAN could then be very efficient.

19.2.3   NetBIOS LAN-to-LAN via WAN

One of the pressing requirements in the area of multiprotocol transport has been the carrying of NetBIOS sessions across a wide area network. SNA subarea networks, APPNs, and X.25 PSDNs currently offer this capability, as described in the following.

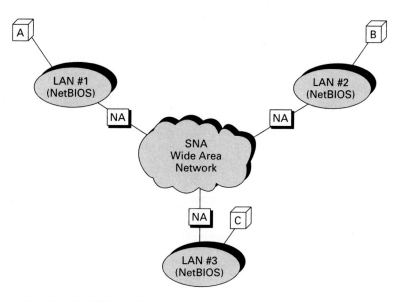

A, B, and C are NetBIOS-based workstations
NA = Network Access Unit

Figure 19.3 NetBIOS LAN-to-LAN via WAN.

LANs are frequently interconnected by MAC-layer bridges forming a larger network with a single address space. This connected set is sometimes called a **region**. MAC addresses, ring numbers, and bridge numbers must be unique within a region. The 802.2 LLC protocols are (by definition) used within a region, but not across regions. This is because regions may be interconnected by mechanisms of various speeds—some of which are not capable of upholding the LLC timers. The LAN-to-LAN connection issue, therefore, is really the region-to-region connection issue.

The "one layer-3 protocol" requirement (discussed above) is not met when the protocols used on the LAN are NetBIOS, and the WAN is SNA/SDLC (subarea or APPN) or OSI/X.25. Then, some special mechanism, for handling dissimilar protocols is needed. That situation is shown in Figure 19.3, where A, B, and C are workstations, on different LANs, which need to communicate with each other using NetBIOS. One or two of these might also be a server. The LANs are interconnected by an SDLC or X.25 WAN.

As one example, an IBM implementation of a WAN network-access unit for LAN NetBIOS data is called the **LAN-to LAN via WAN program (L-L/WAN/P)**. As previously noted (see Figure 12.26), network-access units may be packaged in a variety of ways, including packaging in a server on the LAN. That is the case for the L-L/WAN/P, in the configuration shown in Figure 19.4. The network-access functions of the L-L/WAN/P, particularly the interpretation of names/addresses and the encapsulation of the LAN protocols, are done in a LAN-attached PS/2. That PS/2 acts as a communications server for the NetBIOS-oriented LAN end-systems. All inter-subnetwork traffic is routed through these L-L/WAN/P units. At each L-L/WAN/P, the layer-2 protocols of the LAN are

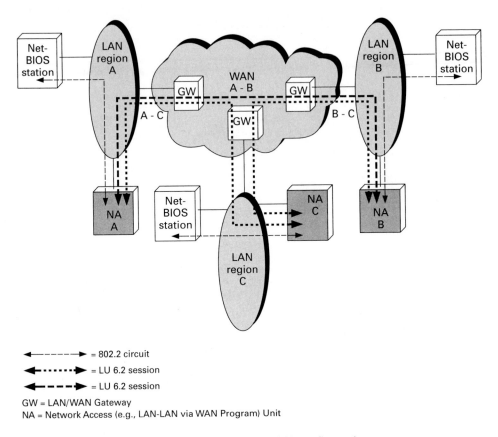

= 802.2 circuit
= LU 6.2 session
= LU 6.2 session

GW = LAN/WAN Gateway
NA = Network Access (e.g., LAN-LAN via WAN Program) Unit

Figure 19.4 One-to-many LAN-to-LAN via WAN configuration.

terminated, and the LAN information and upper layer headers are *encapsulated and transported across the backbone within LU 6.2* and WAN packet headers.

That backbone may be an X.25 WAN, an SNA WAN, or a point-to-point SDLC line. The gateway provides the entry to the particular type of WAN. For example, the gateway to an SNA WAN could be a 3745 communications controller or a channel-attached 3174. In the SNA WAN case, the PS/2 containing the L-L/WAN/P appears as a type 2.1 end-node to the WAN gateways (see Section 15.5). The NetBIOS session runs from the originating end-system to the target end-system, and not from end-system to the L-L/WAN/P. It may, however, be necessary to increase any application or NetBIOS timers to accommodate the WAN delays. Multiple regions can be interconnected, with one L-L/WAN/P per region.

The key to such an arrangement, is an *address-resolution function* at the L-L/WAN/P. They interpret NetBIOS session activation and datagram frames, and act on the names in these frames to determine the target LAN.

Filtering.   The WAN is typically unable to support the same amount of traffic that circulates in a LAN. Hence, another key feature of the L-L/WAN/P is the filtering of broadcast traffic to keep from overloading the limited bandwidth of the intervening WAN. In the L-L/WAN/P, all general broadcast traffic is terminated, but broadcast traffic to a group entity will be forwarded to a single remote LAN.

Further control can be obtained by keeping a list, in the L-L/WAN/P, of servers or requesters in a given region that should be accessible to other regions through the router. In doing this, the L-L/WAN/P allows wild-card strings, so that exact matches are not needed, and a class of destinations can be allowed. For example, if the name "BILL" were configured, the destination names of "BILLY" and "DomainxxBILL" would find a match. To avoid the requirement that all allowable names be configured, another capability is used in which a region-qualifier is permanently imbedded in the name of a station being accessed through the router. A region qualifier can then also be used to create a match.

NetBIOS circuit establishment.   Refer again Figure 19.4, recalling that the network-access (NA) units contain the LAN-to-LAN via WAN Program (L-L/WAN/P). LU 6.2 sessions are set up between the various L-L/WAN/Ps. The desired circuit involves the concatenation of an LU 6.2 session in the WAN with NetBIOS connections in the two LANs. The general sequence for bringing up such a circuit, for a NetBIOS region-region session, is as follows.

1. The source station application issues a `Call` request to NetBIOS.

2. The NetBIOS code in the source station sends a `Name_Query` on the LAN looking for the name.

3. L-L/WAN/P receives the `Name_Query` frame.

4. L-L/WAN/P searches the caches for a match on the name. If the name is in the positive (previously found) cache, it will be forwarded to the target region found in the cache. If the name is in the negative cache (previously not found) it will be discarded. If not in either cache, all names in all target regions' names lists will be searched for a match. Again, if found, it will be forwarded; otherwise, discarded.

5. If the frame is to be forwarded, L-L/WAN/P passes the `Name_Query` to the filter routine to determine whether it should be filtered.

6. If the request is not filtered, it is forwarded directly to the target L-L/WAN/P that supports the target region, with a special header indicating that it is a `Name_Query` verses a normal forwarded frame.

7. The target L-L/WAN/P, upon receipt of the request, sends the `Name_Query` out on the target LAN.

8. The target station, upon receipt of the `Name_Query`, recognizes its name and sends a `Name_Response` back to the target L-L/WAN/P.

9. The target L-L/WAN/P, upon receipt of the `Name_Response`, forwards it directly to the source L-L/WAN/P, with a special header indicating that it was a response.

10. The target L-L/WAN/P will also, if necessary, *initiate a connect to establish a type 2 link* between the target L-L/WAN/P and the target station. It will use the destination MAC SAP address, and bridge-route contained in the response frame.

11. The source L-L/WAN/P, upon receipt of the response, sends the `Name_Response` back to the source station.

12. The source station, upon receipt of the first response, now knows that the target station exists and has a route to the L-L/WAN/P that supports the region it is in.

13. The source station will then, if necessary, *establish a type 2 link* using the destination SAP address, and the route to the source L-L/WAN/P received on the response frame.

14. Upon receipt of the successful connect complete, the source station will then send a `Session_Initialize` frame on the established circuit and the target station will respond with a `Session_Confirm` on the established circuit.

15. The `Call` request is now complete.

19.3   MULTIVENDOR CONNECTIVITY

The use of SNA/APPN by Apple, Novell, Siemens/Nixdorf, and System Strategies (NYNEX) was noted in Section 14.9. The stated intentions, to include CPI-C and APPC as well as APPN, by Novell and Apple further enlarges the sphere of common advanced application development. Other proprietary protocols, however, must also be accommodated. There are numerous arrangements for connecting LANs using non-IBM proprietary protocols to IBM networks. A few current examples of such interoperation are given below, to indicate the range of approaches and functions achieved, and the directions for future multivendor cooperation.

Multivendor LAN Servers.   A client workstation needs to be able to access multiple servers from different vendors transparently. A major step in that direction has been taken with the interoperability of Novell NetWare servers and IBM OS/2 LAN Servers [Starkovich91]. IBM and Novell local area networks can coexist on the same token ring. From a single DOS requester, a user can log on to both servers and access all resources available on both servers. At the same time, Novell users gain functions such as IBM emulators to access IBM mainframes. Figure 19.5 illustrates the common use of the 802.2 service by the NetBIOS, IPX, and PC/3270 data streams. Similarly, gaining access through an OS/2 requester to both IBM Servers and Novell Servers can be achieved with a small amount of definition work, without any special software. A second phase of development will enable a DOS or OS/2 client to access both LAN Server and NetWare servers concurrently without the need for the user to log in to both servers [Novell91].

Multivendor LAN and mainframe servers.   The mainframe can provide an extension of the LAN server services. The IBM *LANRES/VM* product, for example, allows a S/390 VM system to be coupled with a NetWare server to provide disk, print, administrative, and software distribution services to a NetWare environment. Communication between the two is via a S/390 channel attachment.

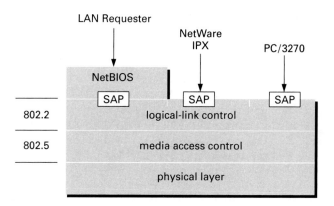

Figure 19.5 Shared 802.2 interface for IBM and NetWare protocols.

LANRES/VM extends NetWare disk volumes to include disks on the mainframe, which can be accessed using standard NetWare client software. NetWare workstations can also send print jobs to IBM host-attached printers. VM administrators can perform NetWare administrative functions such as adding and deleting users on the multiple NetWare servers, setting passwords, limiting disk space utilization, and controlling file and directory access.

Technology demonstrations have also been made for the simultaneous access of the midrange AS/400 PC Support (see Section 5.6) and NetWare servers [Starkovich91].

Novell also has indicated it will implement NetWare on the OS/2 platform, and integrate it with the IBM OS/2 Communications Manager and the IBM Database Manager. This will provide NetWare OS/2 customers with access to SAA services.

Multivendor LAN Servers and mainframe applications. An illustration of the use of the *SNA gateway* in a multivendor configuration is shown in Figure 19.6. The IBM LAN Server contains both the LAN Server code and the Communications Manager configured for an SNA gateway. The 3174 and the SNA gateway are recognized by the mainframe as PU type 2 devices with multiple LUs defined to the PS/2 SNA gateway. The Requester function in the DOS or OS/2 workstation uses protocol stacks for both Novell's IPX and IBM's NetBIOS [Starkovich91]. The Requester, therefore, can be logged on to the NetWare server, the IBM LAN server, and the S/390 mainframe concurrently.

For connections to multiple SAA mainframes, via token-ring LANs or SDLC, there also is the *NetWare for SAA* communications facility in the NetWare product. It can distribute as many as 1000 simultaneous host display, printer, and LU 6.2 sessions to LAN users. LAN users can also access host applications such as OfficeVision and DB2 from their workstations.

Novell servers on mainframes. Still another example, shown in Figure 19.7, illustrates the ability of workstations using NetWare SPX/IPX protocols to obtain access to *NetWare*

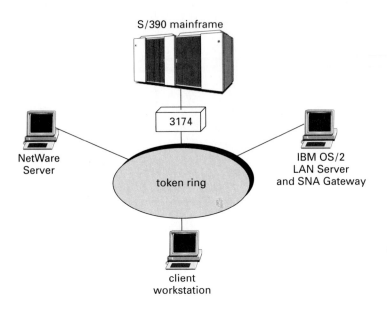

S/390 mainframe

3174

NetWare
Server

IBM OS/2
LAN Server
and SNA Gateway

token ring

client
workstation

3174 = Cluster (establishment) controller

Figure 19.6 Three-way service for client workstation [G325-5010].

server functions located in IBM S/390 mainframes. The software located in the VM mainframes is Phaser System's *NetWare for VM.* Through the use of this product, a Novell NetWare LAN user can connect to a local or remote S/390, as well as to remote NetWare LANs, via SNA networking [Zeigler91]. Through NetWare, DOS, and NetWare-for-VM

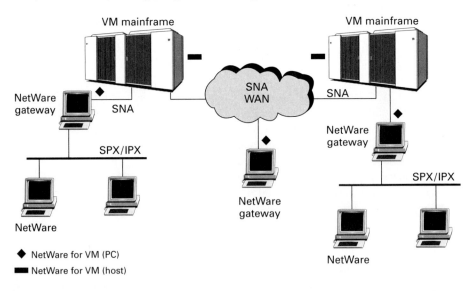

VM mainframe   VM mainframe

NetWare
gateway   SNA

SNA
WAN   SNA

NetWare
gateway

SPX/IPX

SPX/IPX

NetWare

NetWare
gateway

NetWare

◆ NetWare for VM (PC)
▬ NetWare for VM (host)

NetWare

Figure 19.7 VM mainframe services for NetWare users.

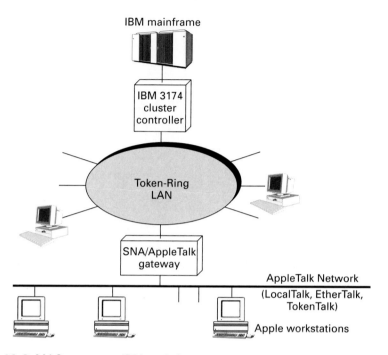

Figure 19.8 MAC access to IBM mainframes.

commands, the user can attach to the remote file server and process requests as if the remote LAN server were local. NetWare requests are transparently routed by VTAM through multiple mainframes to the designated remote NetWare file server. As shown in Figure 19.7, *NetWare for VM* software is also located in gateways between the LANs and the SNA network.

Both *NetWare for VM* and its MVS counterpart product, *NetWare for MVS*, provide NetWare based file services on the S/390, batch services, and routing services to other S/390s or other NetWare LANs [Phaser90].

AppleTalk to mainframe applications. Figure 19.8 illustrates the connection of workstations using Appletalk (LocalTalk, EtherTalk, or TokenTalk) protocols to access applications in an IBM mainframe. A *gateway* provides the communication protocol conversion to that of SNA.[1,2] Most of these gateways support token ring, as shown. Some also support SDLC and coax connections to the IBM 3174 cluster (establishment) controller.

---

1. AppleTalk to SNA gateways are produced by a number of vendors, including Tri-Data Systems Inc. (makers of Netway 2000), Avatar (makers of MacMainFrame Gateway), and DCA (makers of MacIRMALAN gateway) [Kosiur90].

2. Another approach to such gateway services is through a NetWare/386 server. Since Macintoshes have access to the NetWare/386, they also can take advantage of the IBM mainframe services through Netware's SAA Services feature. The latter enables a Macintosh user to access IBM mainframes via a token-ring connection [Kosiur90].

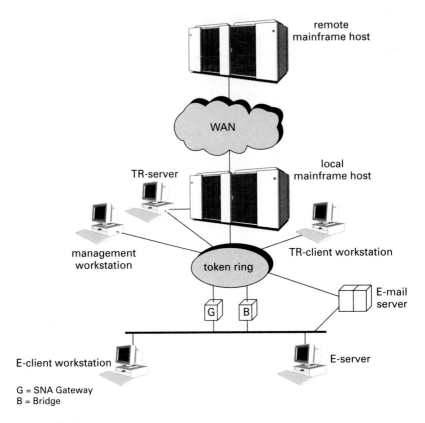

remote mainframe host

WAN

TR-server

local mainframe host

management workstation

token ring

TR-client workstation

E-mail server

E-client workstation

E-server

G = SNA Gateway
B = Bridge

Figure 19.9 Multivendor client–server configuration.

In addition to terminal emulation, Apple's support of SNA includes APPC and LU 6.2. MacAPPC consists of a communications coprocessor card and a communications card for the SNA network, housed in a Macintosh II. Linking the Macintosh II running MacAPPC to an AppleTalk network delivers APPC support to the rest of the Macintoshes on the network [Kosiur90].

In addition, The Apple Database Access Language (DAL) client–server software provides access to the SQL Data System (SQL/DS) on an IBM VM mainframe. The DAL server in the mainframe receives requests from the application in the workstation, carries out the requests against SQL/DS, and sends the desired data back to the application for workstation processing.

Multivendor configuration potentials. Considering some of the above possibilities, one finds a broad range of configuration potentials, sketched in Figure 19.9. Referring to that figure, multiple communications protocols can coexist, so that, with appropriate bridges, routers and gateways, some of the present-day concurrent possibilities include:

- Token-ring client workstations:
  - NetWare 386 client

- IBM OS/2 LAN client
- Dual client; DOS or OS/2, client for NetWare and IBM LAN Server
- AS/400 client
- AIX client

- Ethernet client workstations:
  - Macintosh client
  - SUN client
  - DEC Microvax client

- Servers:
  - NetWare 386 Server
  - IBM OS/2 LAN Server
  - Microchannel 370 E-mail server
  - AS/400 PC Support
  - LANRES/VM NetWare extensions
  - Phaser NetWare for VM and MVS
  - NetView

- Management workstations:
  - LAN Network Manager
  - NetView/PC
  - NetView Graphic Monitor Facility
  - Distributed Console Access Facility
  - NETremote and NetWare 386 Help Desk

In such configurations, there are increasing opportunities of cooperation. Common E-mail, using Soft Switch Central can tie together multiple mail systems. LAN and mainframe data sharing can become commonplace. Apple, NetWare, IBM, and other vendors will interact in advanced program-to-program communications (APPC), with APPN and the Common Programming Interface (CPI-C). Distributed Remote Database Access (DRDA) using SQL will also increase in capability and usage.

19.4   SNA/X.25 CONNECTIVITY OVERVIEW

The OSI X.25 packet level interface was described in Section 13.5. SNA end-systems provide the X.25 DTE interface using either the Network Control Program Packet Switching Interface (NPSI) feature on communications controllers or an integrated Network Interface Adapter (NIA) on other units. We now will examine some of the many ways in which SNA and OSI X.25 networks can interoperate.

An overview of some of the desired X.25 connectability is shown in Figure 19.10. The X.25 *interface* provides a standard way of connecting to packet-switching networks, whether, internally, they be SNA networks or non-SNA public PSDNs. An SNA network can provide the X.25 DCE interface (called the XI feature), making it appear like an X.25 PSDN. Moreover, an end-system having an X.25 DTE can have upper-layer protocols of OSI, TCP/IP or SNA, as in nodes A, B, and C of Figure 19.10. Therefore, referring to Figure 19.10, it is entirely feasible, today, to provide *layer 3c through 7 like-to-like (SNA-*

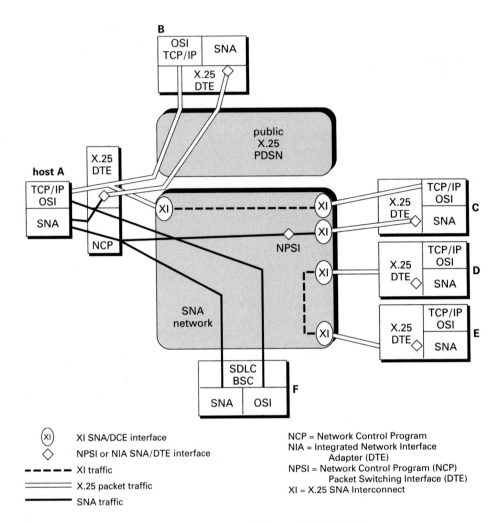

Figure 19.10 General connectivity with SNA and X.25 PSDNs.

to-SNA, OSI-to-OSI, TCP/IP-to-TCP/IP) connectibility between:

1. Applications in an integrated *host A*; and
2. Either (a) *X.25 DTEs (B)* attached to the public PSDN, or (b) *X.25 DTEs (C)* attached to the SNA network

Moreover, that same triple like-to-like capability exists for two communicating X.25 DTEs, (D) and (E), both attached to the SNA network via XIs.

Also, hosts A and F of course have SNA-to-SNA communicability via the SNA network, without using any X.25 facilities.[3]

---

3. They could also have the OSI-to-OSI connection via the SNA network if the split-stack results of the research project discussed in Section 14.8 were applied.

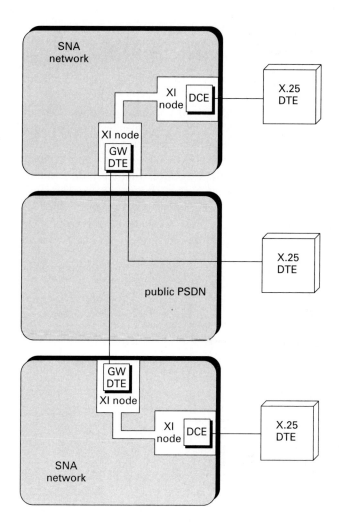

Figure 19.11 SVCs spanning SNA and public PSDNs.

Also, the X.25 DTE to X.25 DTE connection can be obtained via either an SNA network or a non-SNA public PSDN, or a cascaded combination of both, as shown in Figure 19.11. Each of these possibilities are described in the following sections.

The connection facilities described above, plus the improving economy of conversion facilities, makes general connectivity possible. This total connectability, for OSI, SNA, and TCP/IP services, can thus be obtained via either an SNA network or a non-SNA PSDN, or a combination of both. Moreover, these same concepts can apply as new and higher performance technologies are applied to the layer 1 through 4 transport-service-providers.

19.5   THE SNA-X.25 DTE INTERFACE

19.5.1   SNA-to-SNA via a Public PSDN

There is the need for SNA-based units to attach to a non-SNA Public Packet Switched Data Network (P/PSDN) *as an X.25 DTE*. SNA S/390 hosts can use the **NCP Packet Switching Interface (NPSI)** feature on the communications controller for this purpose. The NPSI encapsulates and decapsulates SNA message units with packet headers, so the message conforms to the X.25 interface. The message then can be transported through the P/PSDN. Figure 19.12 shows the NPSI feature located in a communications controller acting in concert with a **Network Interface Adapter (NIA)** within a cluster controller (also known as an establishment controller), to add and subtract these headers. The consequent enveloping of SNA headers with X.25 headers is shown in Figure 19.13.

In order to avoid sending a large number of costly nondata packets through the network, no polling messages are passed through the PSDN. Instead, the remote NIA internally polls the peripheral node.

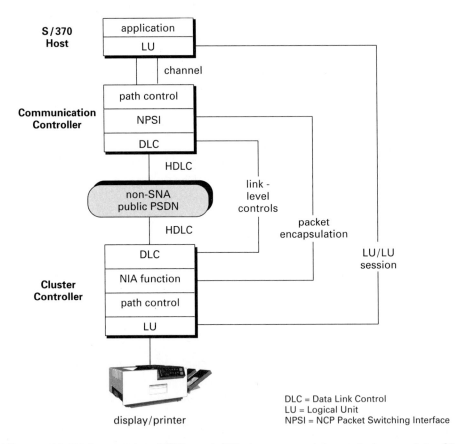

Figure 19.12 Interposing NPSI and NIA to encapsulate and decapsulate SNA message units with X.25 packet headers.

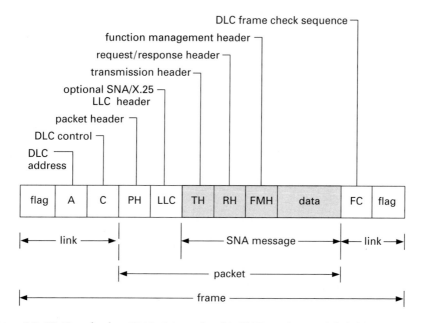

Figure 19.13 Enveloping SNA data unit with X.25 packet and link headers.

Also included in the communications controller features is the use of *switched virtual circuits* across a public PSDN. Thus, public PSDNs can effectively provide additional switched links within an SNA network.

The AS/400 (with APPN) similarly incorporates the equivalent of the NPSI to allow the transport of APPN traffic through X.25 networks. A NPSI-like interface for the APPN is illustrated in Figure 19.14. This is a simplification of the case illustrated in Figure 12.17. For an LU-LU flow across the X.25 subnetwork, the APPN path-control protocol would be the encapsulated (layer-3c) protocol. The X.25 packet-layer protocol would be the layer-

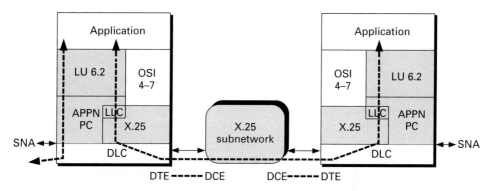

Figure 19.14 Carrying an SNA data unit and APPN transport protocol through an X.25 transport subsystem.

3a subnetwork-access protocol, and the SNA/X.25 LLC function would be the layer 3b (the glue) that makes the set work well together.

19.5.2   SNA X.25 Uniqueness

SNA-to-SNA connections across a P/PSDN use SNA upper-layer (3c through 7) protocols at both ends. We refer to these end-systems as **SNA X.25 DTEs**. In these cases, the SNA X.25 interface uses a CCITT approved set of packet types. However, when connecting to SNA X.25 DTEs, certain other unique facilities are employed, as a convergence layer 3b, as follows.

SNA/X.25 Logical-Link Control (LLC).   In permitting concurrent use of SDLC data-link control and X.25 virtual-circuit protocol services, it is desirable to add certain useful properties of the former to the latter. These include SDLC data-link control functions such as exchange identification (XID), operational mode selection, link testing, and link disconnect, none of which are provided by X.25. SNA DTEs employ several kinds of SNA/X.25 LLC protocols to do this. Each is distinguished by a unique value in the first byte of the X.25 `Call` user data field.

Types of SNA/X.25 LLC.   Virtual circuits entering an SNA network are classified (in the `Call` user-data field) into different types, depending on the type of logical-link control (LLC) required:

- LLC *type 0,* for connections between NPSI and native X.25 equipment.
- LLC *type 2,* for connections to SNA PU type 2 terminals. This older feature uses a Physical Services Header instead of qualified data packets for LLC.
- LLC *type 3*, or Qualified Logical-Link Control (QLLC) is the common implementation.
- LLC *type 4*, for NPSI/GATE support (see Section 19.8.2).
- LLC *type 5*, for NPSI PAD support of ASCII terminals.
- LLC *type 6,* for Enhanced LLC (ELLC), to compensate for poor network reliability.

Further definition of the unique SNA X.25 facilities are given in this chapter's Technical Reference section.

19.6   SNA-WAN AS PASSTHRU FOR X.25

19.6.1   Introduction

Major advantages accrue if most of the enterprise communications can be operated and managed as a single network. Links and nodes can be shared between different functions, and system management can be done by one well-trained staff, instead of by several groups. Figure 19.15 illustrates the desire to have "a network" that can service end-systems with different sets of higher-layer protocols, particularly including the SNA, OSI,

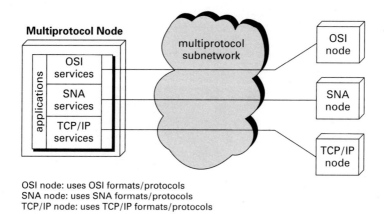

OSI node: uses OSI formats/protocols
SNA node: uses SNA formats/protocols
TCP/IP node: uses TCP/IP formats/protocols

Figure 19.15 Desired multiprotocol connection through a single backbone subnetwork.

and TCP/IP sets. In Section 19.5, the X.25 network carried SNA. Now we look at the SNA network carrying X.25 and other protocols.

Toward this end, the **XI function** is an early illustration of methods that provide the effect of operating an SNA network and an X.25 network as essentially one network. TCP/IP over X.25 also can be carried. XI is an interesting illustration of feasibility, despite the fact that the particular technique of using an LU-LU session for the transport, and layer-3 routing throughout, would probably be replaced as higher-speed lines and fast packet networks become prevalent. In the following, therefore, the reader can understand the use of network-access functions that provide DCE interfaces, and consider the alternative transport-service-providers that may use similar interfaces.

19.6.2 The SNA Subarea XI Function

The XI function, in an SNA communications controller (e.g., 3745) provides the appearance of an X.25 DCE—that is, the appearance presented by an X.25 packet-switching network. Any X.25 terminal equipment (an X.25 DTE) can receive full X.25 network service when attached to this SNA/XI interface. Since most end-system vendors now provide an optional X.25 interface, the X.25 interface can be installed on the DTE and connected to the SNA communications controller.

This use of an SNA network as an X.25 backbone may sound surprising, but in fact, the protocols used within an X.25 PSDN are not standardized and are not specified by the X.25 interface. In general, moreover, the layered architectures of SNA, OSI, and TCP/IP deliberately keep the upper layers relatively independent of the lower subnetwork layers.

The fundamental idea of encapsulating one set of protocols within those of an intervening subnetwork was shown in Figure 12.14, as part of the general discussion of internetworking. The particular case of X.25 protocols within SNA protocols was illustrated in Figure 12.15. A particular implementation of this concept, the IBM XI, is

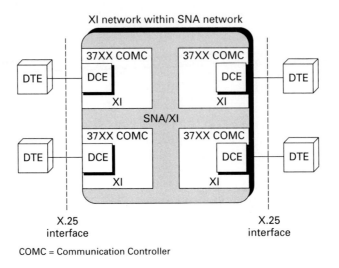

COMC = Communication Controller

Figure 19.16 XI subnetwork within an SNA network [GH19-6575-1].

sketched in Figure 19.16, where the XI allows an SNA network to be the transport for X.25 data. Thus, through XI interfaces in the peripheral SNA communications controllers (e.g., 3745s), one X.25 DTE can communicate with another X.25 DTE. If those DTEs follow the OSI (or TCP/IP) protocols in their higher layers (above layer 3a), the XI thus provides an OSI to OSI (or TCP/IP to TCP/IP) transport through the SNA network. An illustration of using the SNA backbone between two TCP/IP systems on Ethernet LANs [GG22-9125], is shown in Figure19.17. The XI feature is needed only in those communications controllers

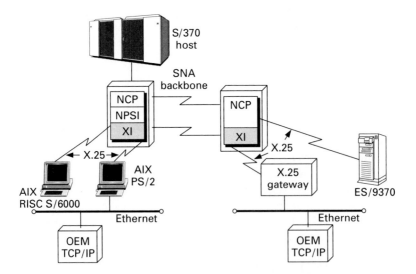

Figure 19.17 SNA/X.25 backbone between two TCP/IP subnetworks [GG22-9125].

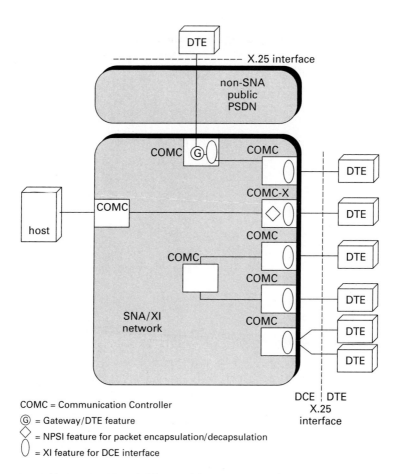

Figure 19.18 Using the X.25 DCE interface of SNA networks.

to which the X.25 DTEs are attached. Intermediate routing nodes may be pure SNA nodes or XI nodes.

The XI nodes and the NPSI nodes are particular examples of interworking units (IWUs) that facilitate the traversal of a subnetwork. It is worth noting that in general IWUs establish IWU-to-IWU connections on which they multiplex multiple end-to-end connections. This multiplexing can be particularly important if there is a charge per connection.

Connectivity.   Thus, as shown in Figure 19.18, the SNA/XI type of network adopts X.25 DTEs as users of the SNA network, allowing data exchange between:

1. Two X.25 DTEs connected to the same XI node.
2. Two X.25 DTEs connected to two different XI nodes in the same XI network.

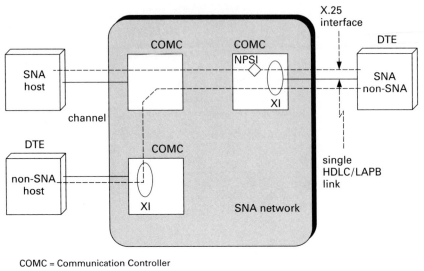

COMC = Communication Controller
◇ = NPSI DTE interface
() = XI DCE interface

Figure 19.19 Simultaneous connection of DTE to SNA and non-SNA (e.g., OSI) hosts.

3. One X.25 DTE connected to an XI node of an SNA network and another X.25 DTE connected to a public packet switching X.25 data network (P/PSDN). An XI node having the Gateway DTE function serves as the intermediary point between the two networks.

4. An X.25 DTE connected to an XI node, and thence to an SNA host, using the NPSI feature.

All of these connections of X.25 DTEs say nothing about the higher-layer protocols. *They can, in fact, be either pure SNA, OSI, or TCP/IP upper-layer protocols*, so long as both ends understand the same protocols.

19.6.3   X.25 End-System to S/390 Application

With both NPSI and XI features, as in one communications controller (COMC-X) in Figure 19.18, we have the further capability for an X.25 DTE to attach to the SNA/XI network and communicate with an SNA applications in SNA hosts. The higher-layer protocols can be SNA protocols at both ends. NPSI can be placed in any communications controller. A calling DTE selects the XI-NPSI bridge by specifying its address within the X.25 `Call` packet.

The DTE-DCE link at the X.25 interface multiplexes Logical Channels (LCs), and hence virtual circuits on that single line. Each of these LCs is able to be connected anywhere in the XI network. In Figure 19.19, one LC is able to communicate with a NPSI

DTE, and hence the data traverses the SNA network and ultimately is sent to or from the SNA host. A different LC from that same X.25 access line traverses the XI network (also via non-XI SNA intermediate-nodes) to communicate with a DTE on a non-SNA host.

19.6.4 X.25 Connectivity via PNA

Using software in a PS/2 provides a still more flexible approach to multiple-protocol accommodation and diverse device attachments. In this next example, the attachments are first made to the PS/2, which provides all the interfaces to the SNA network. The potential of this approach can be seen from the Programmable Network Access (PNA) product, which provides:

- X.25 *connectivity*, including:
  - *X.25 DTE* connected to PNA via a line or an X.25 PSDN
  - Data transfers between locally attached *X.25 terminals* through PNA
  - Concentration of *ASCII terminal* data streams through a CCITT X.3 PAD
  - *SNA host* connectivity for X.25 terminals through XI and NPSI
  - *Concentration of all X.25 downstream traffic* onto a single upstream line
- *Concentration of traffic of multiple SNA terminals* onto a single SDLC or X.25 link to the backbone network
- Terminal identification and a user authorization procedure for *dial-in* connections
- *System management* facilities, in collaboration with NetView, including diagnostics for downstream modems, and file transfer and retrieval for program, configuration, and maintenance data

Thus, the PNA approach is still another example of a multiprotocol network-access unit. It similarly enables network consolidation through the use of a common backbone as a transport for multiple data streams and multiple protocols. It also provides concentration of data traffic from multiple types of devices (e.g., ASCII and X.25) for transmission over the backbone.

19.7 SNA/TCP/IP CONNECTIVITY

For many enterprises, sharing resources with TCP/IP is of the utmost importance. In fact, much can be done along this line in networks with mixed SNA and TCP/IP protocols. We now look at some further examples of such TCP/IP connectivity.

19.7.1 TCP/IP and SNA Connection Mechanisms

Some of the existing TCP/IP and SNA connectivity options are shown in Figure 19.20. These include direct attachment of TCP/IP nodes to:

- Token Ring (802.5), Ethernet (802.3), PC Network, and FDDI
- X.25 and SNA/XI WANs
- Hyperchannel

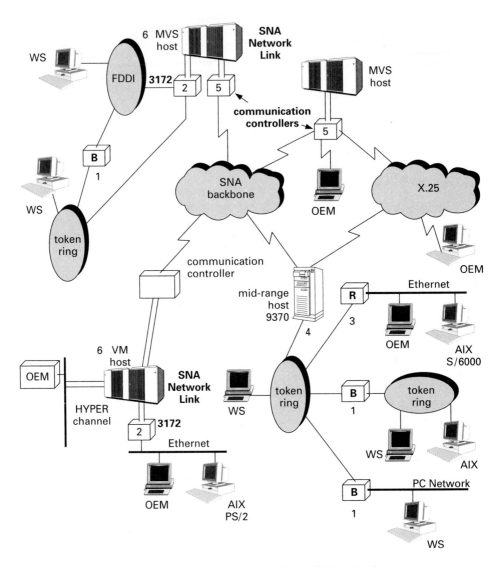

Figure 19.20 Enterprise connectivity using TCP/IP [GG22-9125].

19.7.2   SNA Network Link for TCP/IP

One of the early approaches to using the SNA backbone is illustrated in Figure 19.21, showing the **SNA Network Link**, which is part of MVS and VM TCP/IP software. This approach is attractive when one also has TCP/IP messages that pass between MVS and VM hosts, which support TCP/IP and are connected to the SNA backbone. In this design, TCP/IP is declared as an application to VTAM (a TP access method). Each TCP/IP host

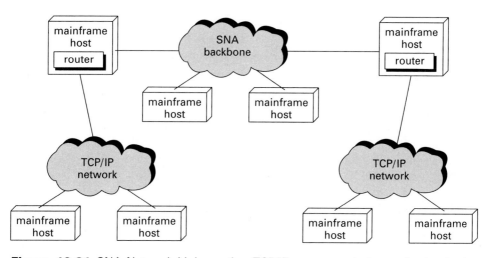

Figure 19.21 SNA Network Link, routing TCP/IP messages between hosts via the SNA backbone [GG22-9125].

sets up an SNA session (type LU-0) with other TCP/IP hosts that are connected to the SNA backbone. These paired systems establish an SNA communications path that the TCP/IP support in each host can use. As an example, if there were four hosts on the SNA backbone, each could have three SNA sessions, one to each of the other hosts.

The TCP/IP network shown in Figure 19.21 could be a token-ring network with AIX/ TCP/IP workstations. Alternatively, that could be a cluster of Ethernets, token rings, and FDDIs, with a 3172 Interconnect Controller that connects them all to a S/390 host. They have complete interoperability; that is, any TCP/IP users on any LAN or the host may access any other so connected.

As still another variation, the XI facility, described earlier, could be used with the SNA link of Figure 19.21. In that case, TCP/IP messages would be routed from a TCP/IP workstation via an X.25 PSDN, and an SNA communications controller containing the XI facility, to a host containing the SNA Network Link facility. That host could then route the TCP/IP messages to other hosts, on the SNA backbone, that also support TCP/IP.

Each of these Network-Link for TCP/IP approaches has overhead and performance limits as traffic increases, but they are very adequate in many circumstances.

19.7.3   TCP/IP Scenarios

To illustrate further, consider an IBM S/390 host that supports TCP/IP, connected to another TCP/IP host or workstation (e.g., AIX/TCP/IP system or a non-IBM TCP/IP system). The connected user can [GG24-3376]:

- Use TELNET to *simulate a 3270 terminal* attached to the IBM system, and thus access applications on the IBM system.

- Use TELNET similarly to *access IBM databases*, via a subsystem like CICS.

- Use the File Transfer Protocol (FTP) (or TFTP) to access flat files on the IBM system and *transfer files* to the AIX/OSF or non-IBM system (and vice versa).

- *Access files* on S/390s that support TCP/IP and NFS/RPC. When connected to a host supporting SNA Link (described above), the AIX/OSF or OEM unit can access the files of all the S/390 hosts using SNA Link.

- Use the TCP/IP simple mail service, SMTP, and an interface to the corresponding IBM PROFS messaging system, to *exchange messages* with the IBM system. Electronic mail can be exchanged between any user of the IBM (RSCS/NJE) mail services, on an SNA network, and TCP/IP users on, say, an Ethernet. The gateway in this case can be a VM/390 supporting TCP/IP and SMTP.

Thus, a high degree of TCP/IP interoperability is available, by a variety of means.

19.8   ATTACHMENT OF DIVERSE DEVICES

Devices using diverse protocols (such as asynchronous binary communication) abound. We will be faced with conversion problems, for a variety of device types, for the foreseeable future. *An SNA application, for example, needs to see SNA logical-links to the five types of simple devices* shown in Figure 19.22. Enveloping, conversion, and padding, (plus NPSI), of the non-SNA devices makes them all manageable. In the following we review some of the primary facilities in common use.

19.8.1   Non-SNA Nodes to X.25 PSDN to SNA Network

Non-SNA nodes.   The terminal may have no upper-layer protocols (like a start-stop terminal) or may have non-SNA and non-OSI proprietary protocols. Our particular example

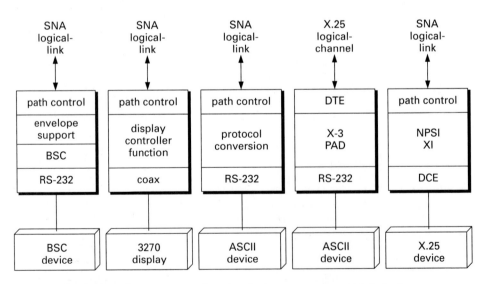

Figure 19.22 Transform support for simple (nonprogrammable) devices.

of a non-SNA node is now a simple terminal whose layers 1 through 3 obey the X.25 protocol. The question is, how do they communicate with an SNA-oriented application?

Using the LU-LU pipe.　Within the SNA nodes (with which non-SNA nodes are to communicate), the means of communication is via LU-LU sessions. At some point, there must then be a conversion between the SNA protocols and what is required for interfacing to the X.25 PSDN. To perform the conversion of protocols, a software companion to NPSI is provided in the communications controller, called **Protocol Converter for Non SNA Equipment (PCNE)**. As shown in Figure 19.23(a), a non-SNA X.25 device, using a virtual circuit across a public PSDN, connects through the NPSI and the protocol converter, to an LU. That LU then is the representative of the non-SNA node, and might be called a *Virtual-Circuit's Surrogate LU*.

The PCNE maps SNA session flow control protocols and X.25 flow control protocols. However, still higher layer protocols remain the joint responsibility of the two end users [Deaton81]. The PCNE in the communications controller acts as a simple LU type 1 (corresponding to a 3767 printer terminal) for the non-SNA terminal it is representing. The host LU therefore believes it is communicating with that type of SNA device.

Then, in order for the message to traverse the P/PSDN, the headers have to be changed. Instead of encapsulating SNA headers with packet headers, the PCNE/NPSI strips off the SNA headers, and *converts the SNA headers into packet headers*. That is what happens when data is sent from the host through the P/PSDN to the remote non-SNA X.25 DTE. In the reverse direction, packet headers are *converted* into SNA headers. It can be specified that NPSI use the delivery confirmation bit (D bit) to map the definite response mode of SNA.

Asynch and other devices on X.25 PADs.　The asynchronous/ASCII devices use a link-layer protocol that is not compatible with the X.25 packet-level protocols. As shown in Figure 19.23(b), the X.25 PAD service is provided to give these terminals access to packet-switching data networks. An X.25 virtual circuit then carries the ASCII data. NPSI then interfaces to this X.25 network at the host end. It provides a protocol conversion function that allows communication between an SNA host and these start stop terminals (connected to an X.25 PSDN), using an X.28/X.29/X.3 PAD device (see Figure 19.24). X.29 defines how the DTE uses X.25 qualified data packets to control the PAD and hence control the start–stop terminal. X.28 defines how the start–stop terminal communicates with the PAD to establish an information path, initiate the service, and exchange control information or user data. X.3 defines the operation of the PAD. The NPSI PAD support includes two subfunctions (XPAD) that are extensions to the PCNE: Integrated Pad (*IPAD*), and Transparent or nonstandard PAD (*TPAD*).

IPAD supports a subset of CCITT Recommendation X.29 for communication with TTY 33/35 and similar start–stop DTEs. This means that an ASCII terminal that conforms with Recommendation X.28 can access an SNA host via an X.3 PAD and NPSI. As shown in Figure 19.23(b), the data again passes between the communications controller (COMC) and the host application via an LU-LU connection, as in the basic PCNE case. (The figure uses XPAD to represent either IPAD or TPAD.) With IPAD, the application is oblivious of the PAD.

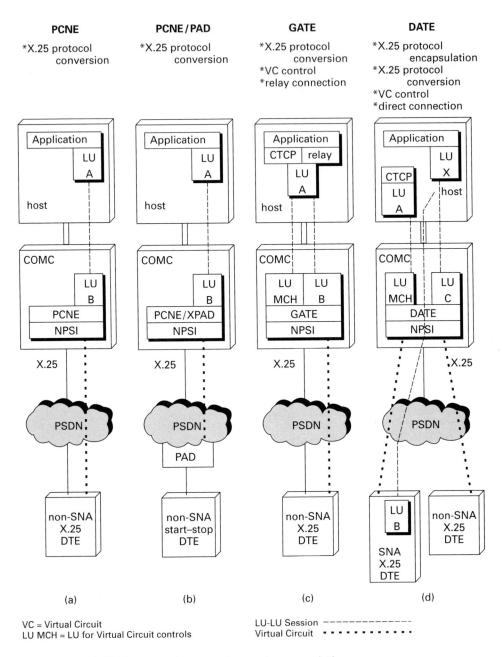

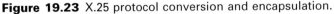

Figure 19.23 X.25 protocol conversion and encapsulation.

TPAD, on the other hand, is provided to facilitate support for PADs that are inconsistent with Recommendations X.3/X.28/X.29. In this case, the host application-program may communicate with, and control the remote PAD by sending four types of packets from TPAD to the remote PAD. Qualified data packets, interrupt packets, and

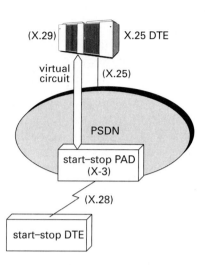

Figure 19.24 Start–stop DTE attached to X.25 PDSN.

reset packets can be sent, as well as data packets. An example of a non X.3 PAD is a bisynchronous PAD.

Again, as shown in Figure 19.23(b), a proxy LU in the communications controller has a session with the application in the host. TPAD support determines which type of packet is to be sent from the host by examining the first byte of the SNA message, which must contain a packet identifier. PCNE accordingly replaces the SNA header with the appropriate packet header. For traffic in the opposite direction, PCNE replaces the packet header with an SNA header and identifies the packet type received by inserting the packet identifier in the first byte of the SNA request unit.

Code translation. Whether or not code translation occurs between EBCDIC and the International Alphabet No. 5 depends on prior system-definition.[4] When translation is requested, data is translated for unqualified packets and for RUs beyond the first byte.

In all of these cases, Figures 19.23 (a–d), the user is responsible for insuring that the application and the X.25 terminal employ compatible data streams (see Chapter 6).

19.8.2   Switched Virtual Circuit Control

It is further desirable, in some cases, that the application program have control over switched virtual circuits. `Call`, `Clear`, `Interrupt`, and `Reset` packets, as well as *qualified* `Data` and `Data` packets, are involved. A host program called the **Communication and Transmission Control Program (CTCP)** establishes sessions with and works with either a *GATE* or a *DATE* program associated with NPSI in the communications controller [Deaton83].

The function associated with NPSI, called **GATE**, allows the host-resident CTCP application program to monitor PSDN virtual circuits. *GATE* responds to host commands

---

4.   This is determined by the value of the PAD keyword in the X.25 MCH statement.

to activate and deactivate virtual circuits, by transmitting certain types of control packets. It enables the host to send and receive the contents of *qualified* `Data`, `Interrupt`, `Call` set-up, call `Clear`, and `Reset` packets.

As shown in Figure 19.23(c), the *GATE* virtual-circuit controls are handled by an LU-LU session between the *CTCP* and the LU for virtual circuit controls, called MCH LU. Data packets are sent to LU-B which is the surrogate of the non-SNA X.25 DTEs. Both user data and control data pass through the host-control program *CTCP*.

Another NPSI associate, called **DATE**, allows the *CTCP* to monitor and control virtual circuits to both non-SNA X.25 DTEs and SNA DTEs. As shown in Figure 19.23(d), with *DATE*, the control packets are handled by a separate LU-LU session between the MCH LU and the LU for the *CTCP*, which does the virtual-circuit management. Unlike *GATE* (but like PCNE), *DATE* maps packets to SNA session data without having to include virtual-circuit control parameters in the application data stream. The contents of the data packets are transferred directly on sessions between the application and the terminal's LU. This is either a surrogate LU for the remote non-SNA X.25 DTE, or an LU in an SNA peripheral-node. In the latter case, this session extends from the host through the public-packet network to the SNA peripheral-node.

Thus, with NPSI/*DATE*, SNA headers are *encapsulated* and decapsulated for SNA peripheral-nodes attached to public PSDNs; and SNA headers and packet headers are *converted* for non-SNA X.25 DTEs attached to public PSDNs.

19.8.3   Terminal Emulation

The world remains heavily populated with nonprogrammable (and low-cost) devices, which must be kept as active participants in the network. These particularly include synchronous terminals (like the IBM 3270), ASCII terminals (like the IBM 3101 and the DEC VT100), and ASCII printers (like the IBM Proprinter and the Okidata printers).

Establishment (cluster) controllers, like the IBM 3174, and communication controllers like the IBM 37xx, provide for direct attachment of such devices, and connection to either 3270 or ASCII oriented host programs. Four types of protocol accommodation have been used:

1. *Protocol conversion*: This allows ASCII devices to *emulate 3270 devices attached to 3270-oriented programs* in hosts. The ASCII start–stop data format is changed into a 3270 data stream, and vice versa. Similarly, 3270 data stream devices emulate ASCII data stream terminals that are to be connected to ASCII-oriented programs in hosts.

2. *Protocol enveloping*: This transmits the ASCII device data stream unchanged, while adding the host protocols (e.g., SNA LU type 1 headers, in an SNA environment). This mode is used to provide communication between an ASCII device and *an SNA oriented host that is running an ASCII oriented application*.

3. *Transparency mode* is very similar to protocol-enveloping, but the data contains control information that identifies which data is not to be converted.

4. *ASCII passthru* transmits unmodified data between an ASCII device and an *ASCII-oriented program* in a remote ASCII-oriented computer.

Of these types, the protocol conversion and the ASCII passthru are used in the 3174 establishment (cluster) controller, to connect a wide variety of ASCII and 3270 devices to either ASCII hosts or 3270 hosts.

ASCII conversions.   ASCII is defined in an ANSI document known as ANSI X3.4-1977. There ASCII is defined as a 7-bit coded character set, including 33 control characters and 95 graphic characters. A set of extended controls is included in ANSI X3.64. The list of functions is large, and vendors can choose among many options. Seven- and 8-bit codes, with and without parity are in common use. Many products now emulate other products, without a single rigorous standard.

Nevertheless, a reasonable degree of compatibility has been achieved. Conversions to a non-ASCII protocol are therefore feasible. Diverse configurations, using protocol converters, are available to provide full-screen SNA benefits to users of ASCII devices. These include:

- Stand-alone converters, such as the IBM 3708, which converts the ASCII data stream to a 3270 data stream

- Cluster controllers, such as the IBM 3174, which provide:
  a) ASCII to 3270 data stream conversion
  b) ASCII passthru to ASCII hosts
  c) Reverse conversion from 3270 to ASCII
  d) Attachment of ASCII devices directly or via leased or switched lines

- Host (S/390) protocol converters, in relay programs, such as are possible in IBM's GTMOSI software

- Communications controller converters, such as IBM's NTO option in 37xx controllers

- Programmable Network Access via software in a PS/2

3270 emulation connectivity.   Programmable workstations, like the PC or PS/2 can also function as simple displays, in emulation mode, when that is what the application-process expects. Figure 19.25 shows the multiple ways in which the emulating workstation could be connected to a S/390 host. Two basic environments can be used.

1. The workstation is directly connected to a cluster controller, such as the 3174.
   - The cluster controller, in turn, may be directly channel attached to the S/390 host.
   - The cluster controller may be remotely connected via a communications controller to the channel.

2. An SNA LU type 2 and a PU type 2.0 or 2.1 are created in the workstation.
   - The workstation may then be remotely connected via an SDLC line and a communications controller to the channel.
   - The workstation may be connected to a token-ring LAN, which, in turn, is connected via either a communications controller or a cluster controller to the channel.

A brief summary of the 3270 data stream facilities is given in Section 6.2.5.

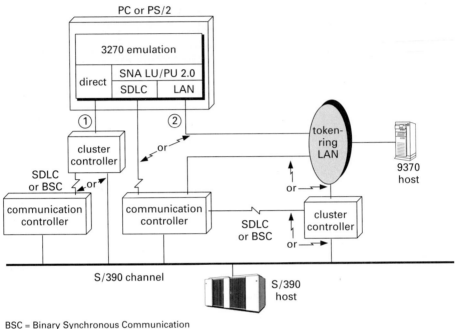

BSC = Binary Synchronous Communication
SDLC = Synchronous Data Link Control

Figure 19.25 Alternative connections of 3270 emulator (in workstation) to hosts [GG24-3359].

LAN asynchronous connection.   Another illustration of data stream conversion, and broad connectability, is shown in Figure 19.26. Three types of terminals are shown: 3270, asynch/ASCII, and PS/2 (PC). Three types of data streams are accommodated: 3270, ASCII, and 5250. These different data streams may be expected by applications in IBM S/390, OEM, or IBM AS/400 types of hosts. ASCII and 3270 terminals may need access to any of these hosts. Thus, the possible combinations include:

1. *3270 terminal access* to:
    - 3270 data stream application
    - ASCII data stream application
    - AS/400 5250 data stream application
2. *ASCII terminal access* to:
    - 3270 data stream application
    - ASCII data stream application
    - AS/400 5250 data stream application

LANACS.   Also noted in Figure 19.26 are *LAN Asynchronous Connection Servers (LANACS)*. These units manage multiple (up to 32) asynchronous communication lines and modems, for use by other LAN stations and for connection to multivendor hosts. Three

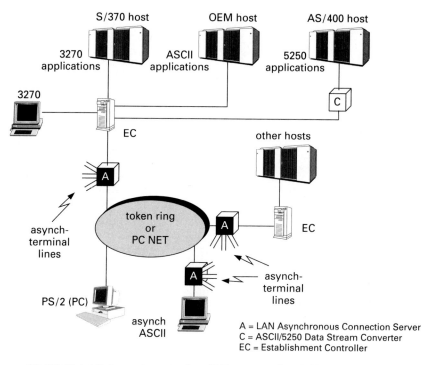

Figure 19.26 Establishment controller (EC) connecting LANs to hosts that expect three types of terminal data streams: 3270, ASCII, and 5250.

functions are needed:

1.   *Dial out.* The user LAN workstations can connect to the server first, acquire a modem, and then dial out to a remote service. Acting like a client–server for communications, the workstation and LANACS exchange ASCII data by NetBIOS protocols.

2.   *Dial in.* A remote user can dial into the LANACS, respond to a menu prompt, and get connected to a LAN-attached PC providing some service. The LANACS also provides connection between a remote host and any ASCII terminal on the LAN or a line. A version of the LANACS contains a protocol-converter so that the ASCII terminal can appear like a 3270 to the remote host.

3.   *TCP/IP encapsulation.* The ASCII or 3270 data stream is encapsulated in a TCP/IP protocol, if the host application uses TCP/IP. The LANACS supports the TCP/IP TELNET protocol as client or server. Thus, any of the LANACS clients on the LAN or asynch lines or incoming TELNET sessions can get 3270 emulation and connect to a mainframe.

As shown in Figure 19.27, ASCII data comes to LANACS in three ways:

1.   From Async terminals that dial into LANACS.

2.   From LAN terminals, via NetBIOS, into LANACS.

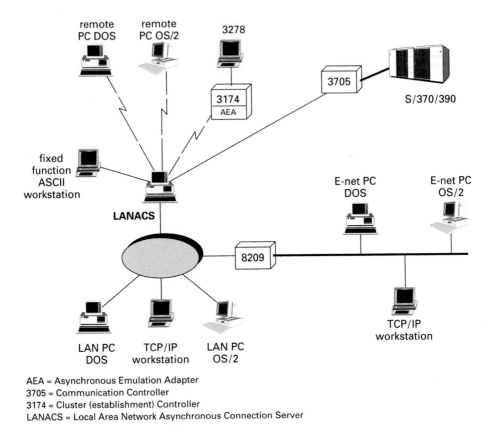

AEA = Asynchronous Emulation Adapter
3705 = Communication Controller
3174 = Cluster (establishment) Controller
LANACS = Local Area Network Asynchronous Connection Server

Figure 19.27 Connections through LANACS to an IBM S/390 host [GG22-9489].

3.   From 3278 terminals that are coax attached to a 3174 cluster controller, and appear to LANACS as a DEC VT100. Protocol conversion from 3270 data stream to ASCII is done in the Asynchronous Emulation Adapter (AEA) of the 3174.

LANACS encapsulates ASCII data in TCP/IP protocols, and it also does NetBIOS to TCP/IP protocol conversion. It then forwards that data to any type of TCP/IP host.

LANACS then supports the connection of ASCII, 3270, and TCP/IP terminals to the following seven types of hosts [GG22-9489]:

1.   *IBM S/370/390 SNA hosts* (see Figure 19.27). LANACS does no protocol conversion in this configuration. For LAN workstations running TCP/IP, LANACS will strip off the TCP/IP encapsulation and present ASCII data to the IBM host's ASCII protocol converter.

2.   *TCP/IP hosts* (see Figure 19.28). The target TCP/IP hosts can connect to either the token-ring network or the Ethernet. If the workstation also runs TCP/IP, and if a TCP/IP host supports 3270 protocol, then the LANACS is used for 3270 protocol conversion.

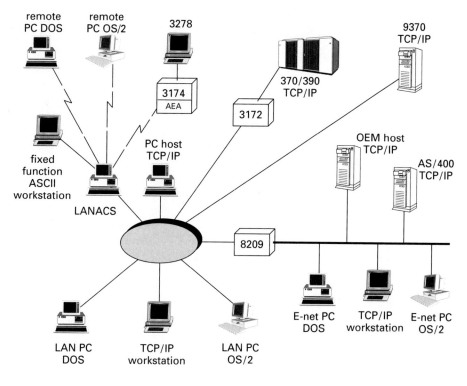

3172 = LAN Interconnect Controller

Figure 19.28 Connections through LANACS to a TCP/IP host [GG22-9489].

3. *Asynchronous ASCII hosts* (same as Figure 19.27, but with ASCII host as the target, instead of S/370/390 and 3705). These ASCII hosts may, for example, be IBM Series/1, DEC, Hewlett Packard, or Prime computers that are attached through ASCII ports to the LANACS.

4. *AS/400 through a 5208 Protocol Converter* (same as Figure 19.27, but with 5208 and AS/400 as the target, instead of the S/390 and 3705). The AS/400 applications expect the 5250 data stream, so a front-end 5208 converter is provided to convert from ASCII to the 5250 data stream.

5. *ASCII host on Ethernet* (same as Figure 19.27, but with the terminal server on Ethernet, which serves as a front-end for an ASCII host on Ethernet. A switched link is between the LANACS and the terminal server.) LANACS strips off the TCP/IP encapsulation coming from a TCP/IP workstation and presents only ASCII data to the terminal server.

6. *PC hosts on the LAN* (token ring, Ethernet, or PC Network). LANACS sends data within NetBIOS or TCP/IP as needed by the PC host.

7. *Remote PC running DOS or OS/2* (same as Figure 19.27, but with a switched line between the LANACS and the remote PC target). The connection is through a LANACS Async port that can be dialed to the remote PC. If the same terminal emulators are being used at both ends, file transfer is possible. If different emulators are being used, file transfer is still possible if the same file transfer protocols are supported. Otherwise, only typing messages back and forth is possible. Some emulators support remote printing (file to print). The remote PC is in answer mode.

19.9 MULTIPROTOCOL END-SYSTEMS

19.9.1 Multiprotocol Workstations

With the continuing diversity of device types and communication protocols, the communication manager in a workstation needs to have considerable adaptability. The communications manager also becomes the middle function for a variety of workstation facilities. Figure 19.29 illustrates the workstation communications manager tying together the key aspects of an SAA workstation:

- Common User Access (Presentation Manager)
- Common Programming Interfaces (CPI)

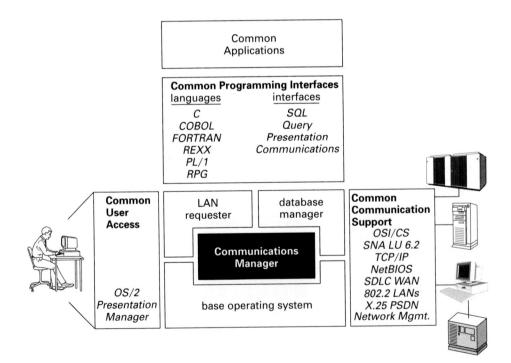

Figure 19.29 Central role of a PS/2 communications manager.

- ▪ Communications, Presentation, SQL, and Query
- ▪ Distributed Application-Services
  - ▪ LAN Requester (file/print/message services)
  - ▪ Database Manager (SQL service)
- ▪ Common Communications Support
  - ▪ OSI SNA, TCP/IP, and NetBIOS services
  - ▪ WAN, X.25, and LAN (802.3/4/5,FDDI)
- ▪ Integration in overall network management

The growing power of programmable workstations makes it feasible to accommodate multiple sets of communication protocols with improving transparency for the user. This capability can be put into three shells:

1. SAA systems, including SNA and OSI
2. TCP/IP systems
3. NetBIOS systems

The **first shell**, the *SNA/OSI* combination, with a gradual merging of the two, will often be considered the long-range strategic shell for applications distributed across LANs and WANs. Network independence for these two, at the Application Programming Interface (API), is the immediate goal. In addition, the workstation can utilize a variety of link/subnetwork-access facilities. Provided the same protocols exist at both ends, either SNA LU 6.2 or OSI protocols can be used over SNA WANs, X.25 PSDNs, or any of the LANs.

The **second shell** adds *TCP/IP*, and often the AIX/OSF (or UNIX) operating system. This shell seeks commonality with the OSI function, and a gradual transformation into OSI function.

The **third shell**, using *NetBIOS*, is primarily used for communication within the LAN, by application-services (like the LAN server) as well as LAN-based application-processes. For those workstations that do not support SNA or OSI protocols, NetBIOS/APPC gateways are needed to enable their communication with hosts that expect upper-layer protocols like LU 6.2.

PS/2 Communications Manager. An illustration of the structure of the Communications Manager in a PS/2 is shown in Figure 19.30. For the programmer, the Communications Manager has multiple Application Programming Interfaces (APIs), including SAA/CPI-C, APPC, NetBIOS, 802.2 LLC, and others (Asynch and Server/Requester) designed for ease of use. LU types 2 and 6.2 are supported. Emulators for Asynch, 3270, and 5250 devices are also provided.

This node can function as both a type 2.1 and a type 2.0 node [GG24-3359]. A wide variety of optional device drivers include drivers for Asynch terminals, 3270 terminals, SDLC lines, token-ring LANs, Ethernet 802.3, X.25, and PC Networks. Each X.25 link may be configured as DTE (an end-system attaching to a PSDN) or as a DCE (receiving the attachment of a DTE). In the latter case, two end-systems can become connected back to back, without any intervening X.25 network.

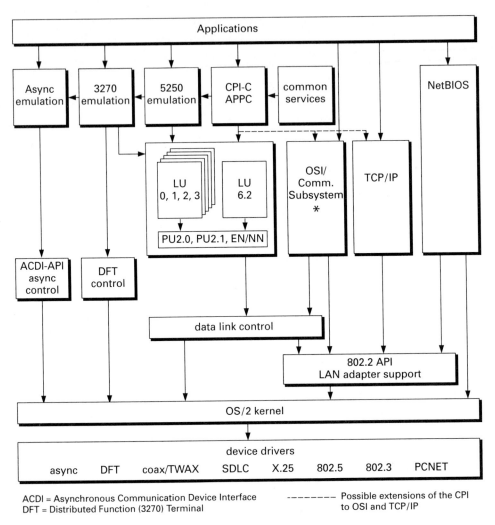

Figure 19.30 Communications manager structure in PS/2 type 2.1/2.0 node.

19.10   VALUE-ADDED NETWORKS

X.25 networks, SNA/SDLC, Async (asynchronous line protocol), LANs, high-speed lines, 3270 terminals, start–stop terminals, and different hosts whose applications may expect OSI, SNA, TCP/IP, NetBIOS, or other protocols, all can add up to considerable complexity. Once operational, the system management, involving all the factors cited in Chapter 4, can be another challenge. With limited staffs and lengthening development backlogs, outsourcing a portion of the enterprise network to a *value-added network (VAN)* is therefore often becoming part of the overall network design process.

The use of a VAN for electronic mail and Electronic Data Exchange (EDI) was discussed in Sections 6.6 and 6.7. Another aspect of the VAN is the ability to provide the protocol conversions needed to interoperate with a multitude of different systems. Some VANs do this, moreover, with fully redundant, disaster backed-up, secure, high-performance networks.

As an example, the IBM Information Network (IIN) already provides, or is in a good position to provide, many of the multiprotocol facilities described in this chapter. Aided by the economy of scale, the VAN can effectively move toward any-to-any capability. Currently, IIN offers X.25, asynchronous, bisynchronous, and SDLC connections. Dial, as well as leased line options, are facilitated by over 400 dial-in nodes around the world.

IIN has long interconnected SNA subarea networks. When the end-systems on LANs[5] use APPN, a LAN-to-LAN connection via the IBM Information Network is another option. IIN provides a leased line connection to the nearest APPN network-node, point-to-point, or multipoint. Different APPN networks, with distinctly identified Net_ids, can be thus interconnected using the APPN network-node products for the router and IIN as the intermediary transport. Connection is thereby also provided to other enterprise locations and business partners that are attached to IIN.

IIN's NetView-based system management centers are located in seventeen countries. These sites are connected by a combination of satellite, microwave, fiber, and digital terrestrial links at speeds up to T3. Small aperture (1.2 or 1.8 meter) customer premises terminals for satellite reception can be implemented. Each IIN boundary node has a minimum of two alternate paths throughout the network. Usually at least one alternate path uses an alternate common carrier, and in many cases uses a different transmission media. Automatic backup and recovery is facilitated by sharing the ownership of network resources among multiple communications management sites. Thus, dependable transport, with alternate routing, through a fully meshed T1-T3 backbone, with optional connections to multiple data centers, is already available in many parts of the world.[6]

Conclusion

The preceding 19 chapters have described the multiprotocol and multivendor networking of OSNA. This network architecture provides support for:

- Enterprise system management
- Common application-services

---

5. To date, APPN network-nodes include the AS/400, PS/2, and the 3174 establishment controller. A variety of APPN end-nodes and Low Entry Networking (LEN) nodes attach to the AS/400 and 3174.

6. The data flows are awesome. IIN is connected to over 2000 enterprise networks, many of which are themselves multiple interconnected networks. Over 5000 large hosts, each capable of serving tens to thousands of terminals, are connected. Besides the many users of IIN electronic mail and EDI, over 600,000 groups of users (each with a group id) have access to the IIN data centers.

- Transparent file and database access
- Transparent remote application access
- View and print anywhere
- Multivendor office support
- Value-added networking

This chapter has provided an overview of a large collection of facilities for interoperation among subnetworks using different communication protocols. Much has already been accomplished along these lines. Concurrent access to multiple-vendor LAN servers, both LAN and mainframe servers, and mainframe applications are readily feasible. TCP/IP and SNA use of X.25 transport facilities; NetBIOS, X.25 and TCP/IP use of SNA transport facilities; and the accommodation of diverse devices, like ASCII/async devices, on SNA and other systems, all are commonplace.

In retrospect, the wide variety of facilities in this and preceding chapters evidences a wealth of technical experience and know-how. This leads to the orderly integration of subnetworks into a cooperating whole (see Figure 3.14). The evolution of a multiprotocol macroarchitecture, called in this text OSNA, stems from these experiences.

This *evolutionary process* involves the acceptance of heterogeneity as a normal occurrence. It promotes commonality of language and function as seen by the user. It fosters common application-services and cooperation among remote systems of different sizes and architectures. It shields the user from much of the underlying complexity, and yet provides a consistent, easy to use, and extensive set of user operations. The process seeks and finds commonality of boundaries and interfaces at multiple levels. These interfaces use international standards or are otherwise made publicly available to all vendors; they are used as means for the sharing of common facilities among heterogeneous elements. The process also makes accommodations for differences through intermediary convergence functions. All this has rapidly progressed as art and discipline, so that one can appropriately refer to the process as the development of an Open Systems Network Architecture that has been the subject of this book.

Acknowledgments

I am particularly indebted to T. B. McNeill, G. Deaton, R. Kersey, and C. Lawson for valuable input or reviews of this chapter.

TECHNICAL REFERENCES

Link-Layer Formats

Formats for Lap-B with X.25 ELLC, IDLC, HDLC, and SDLC are given in Figure 19.31.

XI Optional Facilities

Optional facilities of CCITT X.25 included in SNA X.25 XI DCE interface:

- *Extended Packet Sequence Numbering:* Sequence numbering of packets modulo 128.

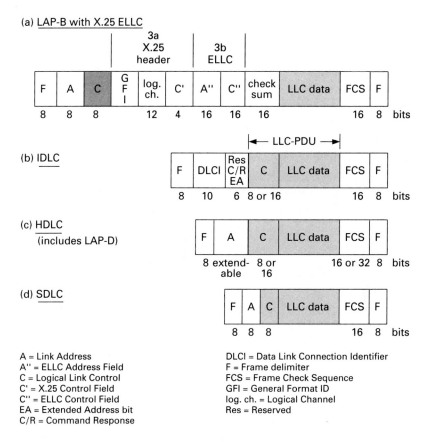

Figure 19.31 Link-level frame formats.

- *Incoming Calls Barred*: Prevents incoming virtual calls from being presented to the DTE.
- *Outgoing Calls Barred:* DCE rejects outgoing virtual calls from the DTE.
- *One Way Logical Channel Outgoing:* Logical channel used only for outgoing virtual calls.
- *One Way Logical Channel Incoming:* Logical channel used only for incoming virtual calls.
- *Nonstandard Default Packet Sizes:* Packet size optimized for the application. If the default packet sizes are different at the two ends of a virtual circuit, the XI node at the receiving end must block or segment the packets.
- *Nonstandard Default Window Size:* Window size optimized for the application.
- *Flow Control Negotiation:* Negotiation, on a per call basis, of packet and window size, for each direction of transmission.
- *Closed User Groups:* Restricts communication to authorized members of a group.
- *Reverse Charging:* Assigns accounting information to the called DTE.
- *Reverse Charge:* Authorizes the DCE to accept reverse charge Acceptance calls for this DTE.

- *Call Redirection:* Redirects incoming calls when DTE is unable to receive them.

Two other useful XI optional user facilities, not included in the 1984 version of X.25 are:

- *Direct Call:* Automatic connection of a DTE to a predefined DTE, as soon as the former is switched on.
- *Call Transfer:* Either one of the DTEs using a switched virtual circuit can clear the call and redirect the call to a third DTE.

SNA-Unique X.25 Facilities

SNA/X.25 logical-link controls. *LLC-3 (QLLC)* uses Qualified `Data` packets (`Data` packets with 'Q=1') to transfer data-link control information between adjacent SNA nodes. These commands are passed through the PSDN using qualified `Data` packets. Data are sent as normal, unqualified `Data` packets.

   LLC-6 (ELLC) employs LLC headers carried in the User Data field of DATA packets. The purpose of ELLC is to provide additional circuit assurance and data integrity. The ELLC protocol can detect lost SNA messages (or segments of messages) and recover them when signaled failures occur in the PSDN, without interrupting the SNA session user. Residual (undetected) errors in the PSDN are detected by the ELLC checksum, allowing retransmission of the erroneous message (or message segment). It allows recoverable call clearing, virtual circuit restarting, and interface restarting. The special user data fields that each packet carries for ELLC purposes are:

- A 2-byte address field
- An extended (2-byte) control field
- A 2-byte frame-check-sequence field

The resulting LAP-B link-layer format is included in Figure 19.31.

The Call user data field.   As discussed in Section 13.10, the first part of the *Call User Data (CUD) field* of `Call_Request` packets is used as a protocol control. A Subsequent Protocol Identifier (SPI), is carried in the first octet of this User Data field to:

- Distinguish between SNA-to-SNA connections and SNA-to-non-SNA connections
- Select the particular SNA/X.25 LLC protocol to be used in SNA-to-SNA connections

SNA's unique use of packet types.

1.   Packet segmentation and concatenation are sometimes needed to avoid exceeding the maximum user data. These functions use the X.25 defined *"More Data Mark" (M-bit)* to signal concatenations.

2.   The *"D" bit* in the packet header indicates that a confirmation of delivery is needed. When D=0, acknowledgment (of sequence-numbered packets) is between the sending DTE and the network. When D=1, acknowledgments come from the remote DTE. The former is useful and therefore is supported in SNA only in the case of non-SNA connections. For SNA-to-SNA communications, D=1, since the end-to-end delivery confirmation is already built into SNA, with its `Definite_Response` and `Exception_Response` facilities.

3.   In `Call_Request` and `Incoming_Call` packets, the undefined bits 1 through 6 of the first octet of the user data field are used to distinguish between SNA-to-SNA and SNA-to-non-SNA connections.

4. All DTEs on SNA-to-SNA connections use a consistent set of diagnostic codes as a result of clearing, resetting, or restarting. Higher SNA layers are notified of each error condition, so that recovery procedures can be undertaken.

EXERCISES

19.1 In the LAN-LAN via WAN program, how is the NetBIOS PDU transported across an SNA network?

19.2 How does LAN-LAN/WAN/P keep the WAN from being flooded by LAN traffic?

19.3 How does NPSI allow SNA traffic on the X.25 PSDN?

19.4 What does the SNA/X.25 LLC do?

19.5 How is X.25 data carried through an SNA WAN?

19.6 What does the X.25 ASCII PAD do?

19.7 Identify four important application programming interfaces that are found in programmable workstations.

Answers to Exercises

CHAPTER 1

1.1 Broad application-services, end-to-end system management, common APIs, multiple protocol stacks, common addressing structure, and common transport facilities.

1.2 Application, application-services, data-exchange facility, and transport-service-provider.

1.3 Network independence is the independence, at the application programming interface, of the nature of the underlying communications protocols.

1.4 Common application-services, common programming interfaces, and common transport-service-providers.

1.5 (a) End-systems capable of using multiple types of transport-service-providers; (b) transport-service-providers capable of handling multiple types of end-systems; and (c) application-services that can function with multiple operating systems.

1.6 OSI networking, TCP/IP networking, APPN networking, SNA subarea networking, Local Area Networks, X.25 Packet Switched Data Networks, ISDN, Frame Relay, Fast Packet Networks, and SDLC links.

CHAPTER 2

2.1 Cooperating systems refers to applications running on two or more computer systems working together to accomplish a single work scope.

2.2 Program instantiation, security, resource-recovery, directory, data conversion, system management, file transfer, SQL database, application manager, multimedia information interchange, print services, store and forward messaging, telephony services, and application development.

2.3 Conversation, message, and remote procedure call interfaces.

2.4 The multi-gigabit plane, the multi-megabit plane, and the multi-kilobit plane.

2.5   A cooperative processing domain is a collection of networked computers that provide a common directory and permit transparent access to secure data and to other services.

2.6   Loose workgroups, front-end processing, distributed processing, interactive processing, and transaction processing.

2.7   A client is a local function that facilitates the use of a remote server, often by means of an easy-to-use interface.

2.8   Common system management, directory services, security services, recovery facilities, application programming interfaces, and lower-layer transport facilities.

CHAPTER 3

3.1   The lower macro layer: transport-service-providers in layers 1–4, and the upper macro: end-to-end dialog-exchange facilities and application-services in layers 5–7.

3.2   A subnetwork is a collection of equipment and physical media that form an autonomous whole, and which can be used to interconnect other real systems for purposes of communication. Examples are LANs, X.25 packet switching networks, and point-to-point links.

3.3   (a) Ethernet, token ring, token bus, FDDI, and MAN; and (b) X.25 PSDN, SDLC WANs, ISDN, Frame Relay, and bandwidth managed voice/data subnetworks.

3.4   Conversational, remote procedure call, and message queues.

3.5   Subnetwork independent convergence, subnetwork dependent convergence, and subnetwork access.

3.6   The Common Programming Interface, the transport services boundary, and the link/subnetwork-access boundary.

3.7   An *entity* is any collection of services, in a particular layer, that is capable of sending or receiving information. It is composed of *service elements.*

3.8   A *service-access-point* is the means by which a user entity in layer $n+1$ accesses a service of a provider entity in layer n.

3.9   Transmission control, data flow control, presentation services, and part of the application layer.

3.10 They both lead to the establishment of a set of peer entities in the end-system's layers 4–7.

3.11 A *peer protocol* is a language used by peer entities, which may be in different nodes, to exchange instructions and data.

3.12 In connectionless operation, there is no explicit activation process to establish the logical-link between peer entities. Each data unit contains all the information needed for delivery. Ordered delivery, flow control, and error control are not provided.

CHAPTER 4

4.1   Fault, configuration, operations, security, performance, accounting, asset, and change management.

4.2   Coordination of installation, data resources, usage of all resources, planning, inventory control, and financial management.

4.3   Collecting, transforming, transporting, storing, analyzing, and acting.

4.4   Managed objects, agents, and system managers.

4.5   Fault detection; problem diagnosis; bypass and recovery; problem resolution; and tracking and control.

4.6   Response time, availability, utilization, and component delays.

4.7   User authentication, resource access control, confidentiality, and data integrity.

4.8   All are true.

4.9   Event data formats, formats and protocols for management functions, and APIs for management applications.

4.10   The *CAU* reports the identity of station insertions on the token ring, and can remove a station when so directed by the LAN Network Manager.

CHAPTER 5

5.1   Byte oriented or stream files, record oriented files, and databases.

5.2   So that the target data system needs to translate from only one set of standardized calls to its own language.

5.3   False. Only DDM is so designed.

5.4   With callback, the AFS server will notify the AFS client if any other user stores a modified version of the file being used by the client.

5.5   *Remote Requests*: one SQL statement per UOW; one DBM per UOW; one DBM per SQL statement. *Remote Unit of Work*: more than one SQL statement per UOW. *Distributed Unit of Work*: more than one DBM per UOW. *Distributed Request*: more than one DBM per SQL statement.

5.6   A *LUW* is the span of a transaction between sync points.

5.7   In the first phase, the master informs all subordinates of the actions about to be requested. Each subordinate either agrees or provides a reason for not complying. In the second phase, the master orders either a commitment, so all the actions are taken, or a rollback to each system's original state.

5.8   The `Confirm` verb simply requires that the receiving program acknowledge a message. The `Syncpt` verb directs the execution of the function of a CPI-RR `Commit` call.

CHAPTER 6

6.1   The IBM Information Interchange Architecture (IIA), which includes the revisable portion of the ISO Office Document Architecture (ODA) and the IBM MO:DCA/P architecture for formatted (presentation) documents.

6.2   OSI X.400 Interpersonal Messaging system and the SNA Document Interchange Architecture.

6.3   A processable (revisable) document has an explicit and modifiable logical structure that can be readily worked on by an editor.

6.4   User agents and message-transfer agents.

6.5 P1: MTA to MTA; P2: UA to UA; and P3: UA to MTA.

6.6 EDI enables standard formatted documents to be created by one computer system in one enterprise and exchanged, along with the standards-defined structural syntax information, with the computer system of another enterprise.

6.7 The CallPath Services API enables a computer program to invoke a function relating to a PBX/CBX by issuing a program-call at the CallPath Services API.

CHAPTER 7

7.1 The SAA CPI provides identical APIs, matching each of the higher level languages of SAA, for all SAA and other operating system environments. The objective is productivity and portability relative to both application programs and programmers.

7.2 Movement towards a Common Programming Interface, common application-services, and common subnetworks for data transport.

7.3 In a conversation or dialog, a logical connection is established between two partners, supporting multiple interactions between them, with overlapped executions in the distributed transactions, which use Send/Receive program calls.

7.4 Remote procedure call is essentially one request, followed by one response, like the calls in a higher-level language, with the client usually waiting synchronously for the response.

7.5 RPC stubs stand in, at the client's end, for the procedure being called; they stand in, at the server's end, for the client making the call. They, in effect, make the remote calls look like local calls.

7.6 The application program uses `GetMessage` and `PutMessage` commands to queues associated with a destination resource manager. Each message is usually a self-contained packet, logically independent of other packets in the data stream.

CHAPTER 8

8.1 A name connotes "what"; an address connotes "where"; and a route connotes "how to get there from here."

8.2 Host5.Boston.DEC.COM.

8.3 Net_id.LU_name in SNA and the PSAP address in OSI, which contains the NSAP address.

8.4 A *relative distinguished name* is a single token from a distinguished name, and it contains a set of attribute values concerning a particular entry in an X.500 directory.

8.5 (a) True; (b) False.

8.6 The A-directory provides a globally unique destination address or destination name that is understood by layer 3c. The N-directory (in SNA) provides the identity of the destination's serving network-node or subarea node. The L/S-directory may provide the SNPA address (e.g., the link station address, the DTE address, or the LAN address).

8.7 The directory user agent interfaces to the user, understands the directory protocol, and shields the user from the details of the directory process.

8.8 (a) True; (b) True; (c) False.

8.9 An *association* is a connection at the application layer which then acts in concert with pairs of entities at the presentation, session, and transport layers.

8.10 The *application context* specifies the application-service–elements to be employed, and the *presentation context* determines the data types and the coding to be used in the association.

8.11 The `A-Associate` request results in the flow of parameters and data through the application layer to lower layers. At the time of setting up an association, connection-end-points are set up within the SAPS of each upper layer.

8.12 The `Bind` command contains multiple fields that specify the selection of options at SNA layers 4 through 6 and parts of 7, and triggers the activation of a session using these options.

8.13 CP-CP sessions are established between control points in adjacent APPN network-nodes, and between control points in APPN end-nodes and network-node servers. They are used for N-directory, topology-update, and routing services.

CHAPTER 9

9.1 The *transfer syntax* is a set of rules for the representation of user information while it is in transit between two application-entities.

9.2 An *abstract syntax* is a means for assigning meaning to a collection of data values without specifying any particular representation for the data.

9.3 ASN.1 tags identify the type of each data element, such as boolean, integer, and character, and variations of the same.

9.4 The *presentation context* is the combination of the two users' abstract syntax and a transfer syntax.

9.5 The `Confirm` call at the CPI causes the sending of a *definite response indicator* in the Request Header (RH).

9.6 *Brackets* mark the beginning and end of a sequence of chains called a conversation.

9.7 Tokens for data, minor synchronization, major synchronization, and token release. Possession of a token by an entity means that it is permitted to do the associated action.

9.8 Analogs can be made for the following OSI and SNA terms:
- application_entity_title and network-qualified LU_name
- dialog and conversation
- association and session
- `A-Associate` and `Bind` Request
- `TP-Begin_Dialog` and `Attach`
- sync point and end-of-chain
- `Give_Data_Token` and `Change_Direction_Indicator`

9.9 Both are tagged, length-specified representations, and they differ mainly in the details of representation. ASN.1 does define universal types, but that could also be done for GDS.

CHAPTER 10

10.1 The LU includes functions in layers 4 through 6 and parts of 7.

10.2 Program initiation and termination, commitment control, message synchronization control, outage and error notification, mapped conversation support, and security.

10.3 Mapped conversation verbs give greater flexibility in application record format.

10.4 Sematically, the LU 6.2 verbs are a superset of the CPI-C calls.

10.5 The `Allocate` verb causes the LU to send an `Attach` request.

10.6 One can have multiple instances of the server or have multiple client requests scheduled to a single server instance.

CHAPTER 11

11.1 The *base* interfaces through boundary units to the management boundary, the network boundary, and the API boundary.

11.2 The OSI transaction processing API is comparable to the verbs of LU 6.2.

11.3 Common system management, common LANs and FDDI, remote OSI API via SNA WAN, SNA WANs carrying X.25 traffic, X.25 PSDNs carrying SNA traffic, interoperation of file handlers and message handlers.

CHAPTER 12

12.1 The transport service boundary and the link/subnetwork-access boundary.

12.2 The *SNPA address* pertains to a subnetwork at the service-access-point (SAP) of layer 2 or 3a; and the NSAP address is worldwide unique at the SAP of layer 3c.

12.3 NSAP = AFI.IDI.DSP, including the Authority and Format Identifier, the Initial Domain Identifier, and the Domain Specific Part.

12.4 AFI of 1 byte=47, IDI of 2 bytes (ICD)=18, type of 1 byte=8, Net_id of 8 bytes network suffix of 1 byte and SNA_name of bytes, and end-system selector of 1 byte.

12.5 IP_address = Net_id.host_id; socket = IP_address.port_id.

12.6 Source routing, label-based routing, and destination routing.

12.7 Fast packet switching or frame relay at layer 2a, frame switching or LLC switching at layer 2b, packet switching at layer 3a, and internet switching at layer 3c.

12.8 Bridges at layer 2, routers at layer 3, and gateways at layer 7.

12.9 With service-interface-mapping, protocol conversion takes place between service primitives of a corresponding layer in two different architectures.

12.10 The inter-subnetwork protocol might be CLNP, TCP/IP, SNA-PC or other proprietary routing protocols.

12.11 Inter-subnetwork data filtering, congestion control, security, address resolution, topology changes, switched services, and participation in problem determination.

12.12 Link and subnetwork I/O interfaces, layer-2 bridge functions, and layer-3c inter-subnetwork router functions.

CHAPTER 13

13.1 Negotiate quality of service with the network layer, provide connection identification, provide end-to-end flow control, segment data units, and provide end-to-end sequencing, error detection, and recovery facilities.

13.2 (a) Transport class 0; (b) Transport class 4.

13.3 The NSAP address.

13.4 The TSAP address

13.5 The *credits* are sent by the receiver to give the sender permission to advance the edge of the flow control window.

13.6 Connectionless connotes an absence of error recovery and flow control facilities within the protocol, and the presence of some form of destination address or route information in each PDU.

13.7 *PDU lifetime* is the amount of time a PDU can travel in a connectionless network before being discarded.

13.8 The OSI PSAP address, which includes the universally defined NSAP address, the TSAP address, and the SSAP address; and the three addressing levels of Net_id, host_id, and port_id, in TCP/IP.

13.9 A *virtual circuit* appears to be a point-to-point connection for a pair of DTEs, but actually shares lines with many DTEs through asynchronous time-division multiplexing.

13.10 Network layer flow control throttles input to the layer-3 network; message sequence is maintained; errors are detected and recovery is executed; and an agreed to quality of service is provided.

13.11 The X.25 fixed window size is set at subscription time or at call-establishment time.

13.12 No. The DTE address is the SNPA address of the X.25 subnetwork. In a multi-subnetwork environment, the NSAP is at a higher level.

13.13 With the X.25 fast-select facility, data is carried by the `Call_Request` command. A connection between two DTEs is made and immediately broken. 128 bytes of data can be sent in each direction, with the transmission of only two packets at the network layer.

13.14 The XTI is an Application Programming Interface at the transport service boundary, expressed in function Calls of the C programming language. It is designed to use both OSI and TCP/IP transport services.

13.15 Each acknowledgment is accompanied by a window-size-indicator that specifies how many additional bytes of data the receiver is prepared to accept.

13.16 The source-route option in the Internet Protocol allows the source to provide, in each datagram, the sequence of Internet addresses along the route.

13.17 NetBIOS provides a name-oriented connection between LAN adapters. Its API can be considered to be near to (and not fundamentally different from) the transport services boundary, at the top of a very slim session layer.

CHAPTER 14

14.1 Dynamically updated topology database, distributed directory, route selection by class of service, and adaptive pacing.

14.2 Network-nodes and end-nodes. APPN end-nodes and Low-Entry Networking (LEN) end-nodes.

14.3 When attaching to an APPN network, the APPN end-node automatically registers its location and resources with the serving network-node. There is no requirement for definition of partner locations.

14.4 Dynamic caching of search results.

14.5   Use a common stem with an asterisk or simply an asterisk for all LUs in the LEN end-node.

14.6   `Register`, `Delete`, and `Locate`.

14.7   The topology database need not contain information on the end-nodes and their transmission groups. That information is only gathered during a `Locate` process.

14.8   Topology update messages flow only when a node enters the network or any other change to the network occurs.

14.9   Node operational status, congestion, and capacity. TG operational status, congestion, security, propagation delay, cost, utilization, and queueing delay.

14.10 Each class of service involves a relative-importance coefficient, or weight, for each property. The property weights for each node and TG are then combined to give a relative measure of "goodness" for that class of service.

14.11 A *Connection Network* name (e.g., a name for bridged-LANs) is provided with the end-node's tail vectors during the `Locate` process, so the selected route can simply use the shared access facility.

14.12 A Common Programming Interface and shared layer 1 through 3a facilities.

CHAPTER 15

15.1   Pacing of flows to peripheral-nodes, address translation for peripheral-nodes, and assisting in the logical connection of APPN and subarea networks.

15.2   The SSCPs in the two domains communicate with each other to gather all the information needed for the `Bind` command.

15.3   The search for a destination LU cascades from gateway to gateway, in a distributed directory search.

15.4   Following reception of the `Bind` from the independent LU, the boundary-function gets its SSCP to aid in the session establishment.

15.5   An SSCP can remember (for a specified period) the BF location of any APPN LU that previously had a session with a mainframe LU.

15.6   Messages from one or more sessions are distributed across the parallel links according to priority, and are re-ordered as necessary at the receiving end.

CHAPTER 16

16.1   (a) Subnetwork; (b) network-entities.

16.2   A *TG* represents a group of parallel links (or subnetworks) connecting adjacent nodes, that is viewed as a composite unit.

16.3   Physical layer (1), media access control (2a), DLC logical-link control (2b), X.25 packet layer (3a), and SNA/X.25 convergence (3b).

16.4   Each upper-layer (3c through 7) protocol stack can have a separate service-access-point (SAP) at the LSA boundary.

16.5   The NSAPs that the ES serves.

16.6   The network_entity_title and SNPA of the IS.

16.7   For each requested network address, the SNARE supplies the SNPA addresses on the subnetwork via which the network address can be reached, and the associated quality of service.

16.8 The station that currently supports the named entity will respond with the desired MAC addressing information and the routes between the two stations.

CHAPTER 17

17.1 Ethernet 802.3, token bus 802.4, token ring 802.5, FDDI, and metropolitan area network 802.6.

17.2 A wiring system, an access protocol, and a set of communication adapters.

17.3 Station activation, exchange of sequence numbers, flow control, error recovery, and network management.

17.4 The active monitor clocks the ring's signal, and periodically initiates a ring poll that serves to obtain the address of each node's nearest active upstream neighbor.

17.5 The nearest active upstream neighbor (NAUN) receives the beacon frame, removes itself from the ring, and conducts diagnostic tests. If these are successful, it reenters the ring and the station that issued the beacon does likewise.

17.6 The transmitting station releases the token as soon as it completes the data frame transmission. Hence multiple frames can be on the ring at the same time.

17.7 By listening before talking and talking only when the medium is quiet; and by listening during talking, and stopping if a collision is detected.

17.8 A single path topology among the bridged LANs, where only one bridge between two LANs is used to carry traffic, and other bridges between those LANs are blocked to prevent looping.

17.9 An explorer frame travels to the destination by the single route spanning tree bridges, and an all routes explorer frame is returned to the originating station.

17.10 The SRT bridge acts as a source routing bridge if a routing information field is present, and it acts as a transparent bridge if no routing information is present.

CHAPTER 18

18.1 51.840 Mbps.

18.2 155.52 Mbps.

18.3 FDDI, MANs, ISDN, Frame Relay, SMDS, Broadband ISDN, and Private bandwidth management.

18.4 Frame Relay has variable-length packets, and cell relay has fixed-length packets.

18.5 *Token rotation time (TRT)* is the time between the appearance of successive tokens at a particular station. TRT increases as the ring load increases.

18.6 By normally using end-to-end error recovery, but reverting to hop-by-hop error recovery when an error threshold on a particular hop is exceeded.

18.7 The addresses for each stage are concatenated. After the address for the current stage has been used, the address field is shifted, discarding the current address, so that the address for the next stage is then at the leading edge of the concatenated addresses.

18.8   The slotted bus with reservation procedures.

18.9   Each station tells its upstream nodes of its intent to send data of a given priority. It does this by setting a request bit in a slot on the bus with traffic going in a direction opposite to the direction that the station wants to send data.

18.10 The *basic rate* has two B channels each at 64 kbps for data, and one D channel at 16 kbps for signalling and perhaps some packet traffic.

18.11 The *primary rate* in the U.S. supports 23 B channels and 1 D channel. The primary rate in Europe supports 30 B channels and 1 D channel. All channels are 64 kbps.

18.12 Frame Relay moves the virtual circuit identifier down to layer 2, and places it in the data link connection identifier (DLCI) within the two byte address of the MAC protocol.

18.13 The backward and forward explicit congestion notification bits and the discard eligibility bit, all in the address fields of the MAC header.

18.14 Each ATM cell has a 48-byte user data field and a 5-byte header. A cell can be used by any kind of information, up to the maximum data rate, bursty or continuous.

18.15 ATM is connection oriented since each cell contains a header that identifies the virtual channel and the virtual path, which are pre-established.

18.16 LANs, communication controllers, and device controllers can be connected at data rates of 80 Mbps to hosts within 9 kilometers.

CHAPTER 19

19.1   The NetBIOS PDU is encapsulated within an LU 6.2 header.

19.2   By filtering all general broadcast traffic but forwarding broadcast traffic to a group entity on a single LAN.

19.3   NPSI encapsulates the SNA protocols within the X.25 headers, so the SNA data can be carried on an X.25 PSDN.

19.4   SNA/X.25 LLC adds some SLDC functions such as exchange identification (XID).

19.5   The XI feature provides an X.25 DCE interface and encapsulates the X.25 PDU within SNA headers for transmission through the SNA WAN.

19.6   The X.25 PAD for Async devices established a virtual circuit to carry the ASCII data through the X.25 PSDN.

19.7   CPI-C, APPC, NetBIOS, and 802.2.

Glossary

abstract syntax.   A means of expressing the semantics of data, without describing the representation of that data.

access-link.   The physical link used to connect or attach end-systems to wide area networks.

ACF/NCP.   Advanced Communication Function/Network Control Program. A program product that provides communication controller support in an SNA network.

ACF/VTAM.   Advanced Communication Function/Virtual Telecommunications Access Method. A program product that provides host processor support in an SNA network.

ACK.   Acknowledgement.

ACSE.   Association Control Service Element. A set of facilities for controlling an application association between two applications that communicate using a presentation connection. It provides means to establish and release an association between the applications (OSI).

Activity.   A logical unit of work into which peer applications can separate the data that they exchange (OSI).

ACTLU.   Activate Logical Unit (SNA).

ACTPU.   Activate Physical Unit (SNA).

adaptive pacing.   See *adaptive session-level pacing*.

adaptive session-level pacing.   A form of SNA session-level pacing in which session components exchange pacing windows that may vary in size during the course of a session. Session-level pacing occurs within independent stages along the session path according to local congestion at the intermediate-nodes.

adjacent link station.   A link station that is directly connected to a given node by a link connection, over which network traffic can be carried.

adjacent node.   Two nodes that are connected by one or more links with no intervening nodes.

Advanced Peer-to-Peer Networking (APPN).   Data communications support that routes data in a network between two or more peer systems that are not directly attached.

Advanced Program-to-Program Communications (APPC).   Data communications support that allows programs on one system to communicate with programs on other systems having compatible communications support. For example, APPC is the method of using LU 6.2 session protocols.

AE.   See *Application-entity*.

AE_Title.   See *Application_entity_title*.

AFI.   Address Format Indicator. A 1-byte prefix in every OSI NSAP address, specifying the internal structure of the subsequent IDI and DSP fields.

AIX.   Advanced Interactive Executive (IBM UNIX offering).

alert.   A record sent to a manager to identify a problem or an impending problem.

alias.   An alternative name that is not known outside of the local systems on which it is used.

ANSI.   American National Standards Institute.

ANR.   Automatic Network Routing.

API.   Application Program Interface. A formally defined programing language interface.

APPC.   See *Advanced Program-to-Program Communication*.

application context.   An explicitly identified set of application-service–elements, related options, and any other necessary information for the interworking of application-entities on an association (OSI).

application-entity.   An individually identifiable OSI application component referred to by its own name(s)—(title(s))—and PSAP address(es).

application_entity_title.   The name of an application-entity. It can be used to locate a particular application.

application layer.   OSI's layer 7, supporting standardized communication applications such as electronic mail, file transfer, etc.

application-layer directory.   A directory implemented at the application layer and mapping objects names, such as application_entity_titles, to object attributes such as addresses, etc.

application-process.   An element that performs information processing for a particular application.

application program.   A program written for or by a user to perform the user's work; an end user.

application-service–element.   That part of an application-entity which provides an OSI environment capability, using underlying services when appropriate.

application transaction program.   A program written for or by a user to process the user's application; an end user of a type 6.2 logical unit. Contrast with *service transaction programs*.

APPN.   See *Advanced Peer-to-Peer Networking*.

APPN end-node.   A type 2.1 end-node that provides full SNA end-user services and supports sessions between its local control point (CP) and the CP in an adjacent network-node, to dynamically register its resources with the adjacent CP (its network-node server), to send and receive directory search requests, and to obtain management services; it can also attach to a subarea network as a peripheral-node.

APPN network-node.   A type 2.1 (T2.1) node that, besides offering full SNA end-user services, provides intermediate routing services within a T2.1 network, and provides network services to its local LUs and attached T2.1 end-nodes in its domain; it can also attach to a subarea network as a peripheral-node.

APPN node.   An APPN network-node or an APPN end-node.

ARP.   Address Resolution Protocol (TCP/IP).

ASCII.   American Standard Code for Information Interchange. A set of 7-bit coded characters (8 bits including parity). The set includes control characters and graphic characters.

ASM.   Address Space Manager.

ASN1.   Abstract Syntax Notation One.

association.   A relationship between two or more application-entities. Each association has an application context associated with it, which defines the rules within which each application must act.

ATM.   Asynchronous Transfer Mode.

authorized APPN end-node.   In APPN, an end-node that is "trusted" by its network-node server to supply information about its resources that will affect the network directory database. If a node is authorized, all information it sends about itself is accepted. The authorization status of an end-node is system-defined in its network-node server.

basic conversation.   A temporary connection between an application program and an APPC session in which the user must provide all the information on how the data is formatted. Contrast with *mapped conversation*.

begin bracket.   The value (binary 1) of the begin bracket indicator in the RH of the first request in the first chain of a bracket; the value denotes the start of a bracket (SNA).

BER.   Basic Encoding Rules. The particular transfer syntax defined in ISO 8825. These rules provide a representation of the abstract syntax ASN.1.

BF.   See *Boundary-Function* (SNA).

bidder.   The LU-LU half-session defined at SNA session activation as having to request and receive permission from the other LU-LU half-session in order to begin a bracket. Contrast with *first speaker*.

bind session (Bind).   A request to activate a session between two logical units (SNA). See also *session initiation request*.

Boundary-Function (BF).   A capability of a subarea-node to provide protocol support for attached peripheral-nodes, such as: (a) interconnecting subarea path control and peripheral path control element, (b) performing session sequence numbering for low-function peripheral nodes, and (c) providing session-level pacing support.

boundary-node.   A subarea node with boundary-function.

bracket.   One or more chains of RUs and their responses that are exchanged between two LU-LU half-sessions and that represent a transaction between them. One bracket must be completed before another one can be started. Examples of brackets are database inquiries/replies, update transactions, and remote job entry output sequences to workstations (SNA).

bracket protocol.   A data flow control protocol in which exchanges between the two LU-LU half-sessions are controlled through the use of brackets; one LU is designated at session activation as the first speaker and the other LU as the bidder. The bracket protocol involves bracket initiation and termination rules (SNA).

bridge.   A unit that connects two subnetworks, usually at the MAC (Media Access Control) layer. For example a bridge connects LANs that use the same Logical-Link Control (LLC) procedure but may use different MAC procedures. See also *LLC switch*.

broadcast. The transmission of data packets to all nodes on a network or subnetwork simultaneously.

BSC. Binary Synchronous Communications. A line control using a standard set of transmission control characters and control character sequences, for binary synchronous transmission of binary coded data.

cache. A fixed area of main storage that is continually updated with the most recent information.

Call. The action of bringing a computer program, routine, or subroutine into effect, usually by specifying the entry conditions and entry point.

CCITT. Comité Consultatif International Télégraphique et Téléphonique. Sets international standards for data communication.

CEN/CENELEC. European Committee on Norms/European Committee on Electrotechnical Norms.

CEPT. Conference of European Postal and Telecommunications Administrations.

change direction protocol. A data flow control function in which the sending logical unit stops sending requests, signals the receiving logical unit using the change direction indicator in the RH, and prepares to receive.

checksum. The sum of a group of data, used for error-checking purposes.

CICS. Customer Information Control System. A program that enables transactions entered at remote terminals to be processed concurrently by user-written application programs. It includes facilities for building, using, and maintaining databases.

Class of Service (COS). The priority level (high, medium, or low) assigned to the transmission groups and intermediate routing nodes included in a session after the session is established. A COS may also be distinguished by the security and the bandwidth that it offers.

client. A function that requests services from a server and makes them available to a user.

CLNP. Connectionless Network Protocol. OSI's connectionless protocol for use at the internetwork layer (SNICP).

CMAE. Common Management Application-Entity. An application-entity implementing OSI system management.

CMIP. Common Management Information Protocol. OSI's application protocol for transporting network management information such as performance measurement, problem determination, configuration, accounting, or security data.

CMOT. CMIP over TCP/IP.

CMS. Conversational Monitor System (VM).

CNM. Communication Network Management.

CNOS. Change Number of Sessions (SNA).

commit. A process that causes data changed by an application or user to become part of a database.

communication controller. An IBM term designating products that implement the switching or network function in SNA subarea networks.

communications adapter. A part that electrically or physically connects a computer or device to a data communications network.

communications line. The physical media (such as a wire or a telephone circuit) that connects one node (or system) to another node (or system).

configuration services.   One of the types of network services in the System Services Control Point (SSCP) and in the PU; configuration services activate, deactivate, and maintain the status of PUs, links, and link stations. Configuration services also shut down and restart network elements and modify path control routing tables and address transformation tables (SNA).

Connection-End-Point (CEP).   The representation of one end of a connection between two peer service-user *n*-entities within the OSI environment.

connection network.   A representation within an APPN network of a shared access transport facility, such as a LAN.

connection-oriented service/protocol.   A service/protocol including the notions that a set-up and a take-down phase delimit an operational phase during which data are transferred in a more or less controlled and orderly fashion (sequenced, paced, error-free). OSI recognizes the concept of a connection-oriented service/protocol at any of layers 2 through 7. SNA provides connections at the link and transport (SNA session) levels.

connectionless service/protocol.   A service/protocol including the notions that individual data units, messages, or packets are transferred one after the other without any relation to one another, without any prior connection set-up or subsequent take-down, and typically, with a high probability but no guarantee of delivery, no sequencing, flow or error control (e.g., like unregistered letters in a postal system). OSI recognizes the concept of a connectionless service/protocol at any of layers 2 through 7 in principle, though it is not actually defined at each layer.

control point (CP).   A collection of tasks, which provide directory and route selection functions for APPN. An end-node control point provides its own configuration, session, and management services with assistance from the control point of its serving network-node. A network-node control point provides session and routing services (SNA).

conversation.   The logical connection between a pair of transaction programs for serially sharing a session between type 6.2 logical units from transaction to transaction. While a conversation is active, it has exclusive use of an LU-LU session as delimited by a distinct bracket; successive conversations may use the same session.

COS.   (1) Class of Service. (2) Corporation for Open Systems. A corporation focusing on the promotion of selected subsets of OSI standards.

CP.   See *Control Point*.

CPI.   Common Programming Interface. An SAA term designating programming interfaces that have been standardized across systems for accessing specific subsystems from applications.

CPI-C.   Common Programming Interface for Communications. The SAA CPI specifically defined for accessing the communication subsystem implementing network protocols.

CPI-RR.   Common Programming Interface for Resource-Recovery. The SAA CPI specifically designed for accessing the resource-recovery subsystem fundamental for transaction processing.

CPMS.   Control Point Management Services.

CRC.   See *Cyclic Redundancy Check*.

CRV.   Cryptography Verification.

cryptography.   The transformation of data to conceal its meaning.

cryptography key.   A binary value that is used as a data encrypting key to encipher and decipher end-user data that is transmitted over a session or association that uses cryptography.

CSMA/CD.   Carrier Sense Multiple Access/Collision Detect (e.g., Ethernet).

CUA.   Common User Access (SAA).

CUT.   Control Unit Terminal. An SNA terminal that can run only one session at a time.

CV.   Control Vector (SNA).

cyclic redundancy check (CRC).   A block-checking procedure for error detection.

DAP.   Directory Access Protocol. One of OSI's application-layer standards, specifying a protocol for access to the application-layer directory update and query functions by a DUA.

Data Circuit-Terminating Equipment (DCE).   The network equipment installed at the user's premises that provides all the functions required to establish, maintain, and end a connection, and the signal conversion and coding between the DTE and the network. See also *Data Terminal Equipment (DTE)*.

Data Flow Control (DFC) layer.   The SNA layer within a half-session that (1) controls whether the half-session can send, receive, or concurrently send and receive RUs; (2) groups related RUs in RU chains; (3) delimits transactions via the bracket protocol; (4) controls the interlocking of requests and responses in accordance with control modes specified at session activation; (5) generates sequence numbers; and (6) correlates requests and responses.

datagram.   A completely self-contained unit of data. A datagram is routed as an independent unit.

data link.   Synonym for link.

Data Link Control (DLC) layer.   The layer that consists of the link stations that schedule data transfer over a link between two nodes and perform error control for the link. Examples of data link control are SDLC for serial-by-bit link connection and data link control for the System/370 channel.

data stream.   A continuous stream of data elements being transmitted, or intended for transmission, in character or binary-digit form, using a defined format.

Data Terminal Equipment (DTE).   That part of an end-sytem's data link that sends data, receives data, and provides the data communications control functions according to a prescribed set of protocols. It also interfaces to the user application.

DCA.   Document Content Architecture.

DCE.   See *Data Circuit-Terminating Equipment*.

DCF.   Data Count Field.

DDM.   See *Distributed Data Management*.

decipher.   To return enciphered data to its original form.

definite response.   A protocol requested in the form-of-response-requested field of the RH that directs the receiver of the request to return a response unconditionally, whether positive or negative, to that request chain. Contrast with *exception response*; *no response*.

delayed request mode.   An operational mode in which the sender may continue sending request units after sending a definite response request chain on that flow. The sender does not have to wait for a response to that chain. Contrast with *immediate request mode*.

delayed response mode.   An operational mode in which the receiver of request units can return responses to the sender in a sequence different from that in which the corresponding request units were sent. Contrast with *immediate response mode*.

DES. Data Encryption Standard.

DFC. See *Data Flow Control layer* (SNA).

DFT. Distributed Function Terminal. A terminal that can run multiple sessions concurrently (SNA).

DIA. Document Interchange Architecture.

dialog. An OSI term denoting a connection between two communicating Transaction-Processing-Service-Users (TPSU's) at the application layer.

DIB. Directory Information Base. An OSI/CCITT term denoting a database storing X.500 directory information.

Directory Services (DS). Services for resolving user identifications of network components to network routing information.

DIS. Draft International Standard.

DISOSS. Distributed Office Support System (SNA).

distinguished name. A sequence of relative distinguished names that uniquely identifies an object instance (X.500).

Distributed Data Management (DDM). A function of the operating system that allows an application program or user on one system to use data stored on remote systems. The systems must be connected by a communications network, and the remote systems must also be using DDM (SAA).

DIT. Directory Information Tree. An OSI/CCITT term denoting the tree of information about objects registered in an X.500 directory.

DIU. Document Interchange Unit (X.500).

DLC. Data Link Control.

Document Interchange Architecture (DIA). The rules and structure for the exchange of information between office applications. Document Interchange Architecture includes document library services and document distribution services.

DOS. A PC operating system.

DQDB. Distibuted Queue Dual Bus.

DRDA. Distributed Relational Database Architecture (SAA).

DS. See *Directory Services*.

DSA. Directory Service Agent. An application-entity supporting the OSI directory service (X.500).

DSP. Directory Service Protocol. One of OSI's application-layer standards, specifying a protocol for directory update and query functions between DSAs (X.500).

DSP. (NSAP). Domain Specific Part. The least significant part of an NSAP address, whose content is determined and used by the authority administering the local domain within which the addressed NSAP resides. The DSP may itself be structured into further subfields administered by lower-level authorities. See *AFI* and *IDI*.

DTE. See *Data Terminal Equipment*.

DUA. Directory User Agent. An application-entity's interface to the OSI directory service.

duplex. Pertains to communications in which data can be sent and received at the same time. Contrast with *half-duplex*.

EBCDIC.   Extended Binary-Coded Decimal Interchange Code. A coded character set consisting of 8-bit coded characters.

EDI.   Electronic Data Interchange.

EGP.   Exterior Gateway Protocol (TCP/IP).

Electronic Mail.   Documents sent through the system from one user to another.

element address.   A value in the SNA network address that identifies a particular resource within a subarea. See also *subarea address*.

ELLC.   Enhanced Logical-Link Control (SNA).

EN.   See *End-Node*.

encipher.   To scramble data or convert it, prior to transmission, in order to mask the meaning of the data to any unauthorized recipient. Contrast with *decipher*.

End-Node (EN).   A particular end-system, and a node in an APPN network that can be a source or target node, but does not provide any routing or session services to any other node.

End-System (ES).   A system at the periphery of a network, which is a communication end point and source and/or sink of data flow (OSI).

entity.   An OSI term referring to a component implementing some protocol at some level. Entities are defined at all seven layers. They are reachable through the SAPs of the immediately inferior layer, and offer SAPs to entities of the immediately superior layer.

ERP.   Error Recovery Procedure.

ES.   See *End-System*.

ESCON.   Enterprise System Connection.

ES-IS Routing Protocol.   A standard OSI protocol for exchanging routing information between adjacent ES's and IS's.

EWOS.   European Workshop for Open Systems.

exception request.   A request that replaces another request in which an error was detected (SNA).

exception response.   A protocol requested in the RH that directs the receiver to return a response only if the request is unacceptable as received or cannot be processed; that is, a negative response, but not a positive response, may be returned (SNA). Contrast with *definite response, no response*.

exchange identification (XID).   A data link control command and response passed between adjacent link stations that allow the two link stations to exchange identification and other information that is necessary for further operation over the data link (SNA).

explicit route.   The end-to-end physical connections in SNA into which the virtual route is mapped.

F.   See *flag*.

FCS.   See *Frame Check Sequence*.

FDDI.   Fiber Distributed Data Interface.

FDX.   Full-Duplex.

FF.   Flip-Flop.

FID.   Format Identifier.

first speaker. The LU-LU half-session defined at session activation as able to begin a bracket without requesting permission from the other LU-LU half-session to do so. Contrast with *bidder*.

flag. A bit field to delimit the data that precedes or follows it (SDLC).

flow control. The process of managing the rate at which data traffic passes between components of the network. Flow control optimizes the rate of flow of message units with minimum congestion in the network. Flow control allows the receiver to receive message units at the rate at which it can process them without overflowing its buffers or the buffers at intermediate routing nodes. See also *pacing, session-level pacing, virtual-route (VR) pacing*.

FMH. See *Function Management (FM) Header*.

FQN. Fully Qualified Name (SNA).

FQPCID. Fully Qualified Procedure Correlation Identifier. A network unique identifier that is used for (a) correlating messages sent, such as a `Locate` search request and its replies, and (b) identifying a session for problem determination, accounting, and performance monitoring purposes (SNA).

frame check sequence. A field that contains error checking (e.g., cyclic redundency check) information, and is appended at the end of a frame.

FTAM. File Transfer, Access, and Management. One of OSI's application-layer standards, specifying a service and protocol for file transfer and management.

FTP. File Transfer Protocol. (TCP/IP).

Function Management (FM) Header. Optional control information, present in the leading RUs of a chain (SNA).

gateway. A unit that operates above layer 3 to facilitate interoperation between different protocols.

GDS. General Data Stream (SNA).

GDS Variable. A type of RU substructure that is preceded by an identifier and a length field (SNA).

GGP. Gateway-to-Gateway Protocol. (TCP/IP).

GOSIP. Government OSI Profile.

half-duplex (HDX). Pertaining to data communications that can be sent in only one direction at a time. Contrast with *duplex*.

half-session. A component that provides data flow control and transmission control at one end of a session (SNA).

HDLC. High-level Data Link Control.

HDLC LAP B. High-level Data Link Control, Link Access Procedure B. The link-layer protocol used in X.25 networks.

HDX. See *Half-Duplex*.

HDX-C. Half-Duplex Contention.

HDX-FF. Half-Duplex Flip-Flop.

hop count. The number of networks or subnetworks through which a packet passes on the way to its destination node.

host.   A computer connected to a network that provides services to users in other nodes. A host may be of any size, from a PC to a mainframe, but the term is usually applied to larger computers.

HS.   See *Half-Session*.

HSID.   Half-Session Identification.

ICD.   International Code Designator. A code point in the ICD space administered by ISO to identify NSAP registration authorities under NSAP format 47.

ICMP.   Internet Control Message Protocol (TCP/IP).

id.   Identifier.

IDI.   Initial Domain Identifier. The more significant part of an NSAP address, whose content defines the authority administering the DSP portion of the NSAP address. See *AFI* and *DSP*.

IDLC.   ISDN Data Link Control. Extended version of LAP-D for data uses on a B or H channel.

IDNX.   Integrated Digital Network Exchange (Network Equipment Technologies, Inc.).

IDRP.   Inter-Domain Routing Protocol. An OSI protocol still under development, designed to allow gateways between heterogeneous routing domains to exchange routing information in a meaningful way.

IGP.   Interior Gateway Protocol (TCP/IP).

IIN.   IBM Information Network.

immediate request mode.   An SNA operational mode in which the sender stops sending RUs after sending a definite response request chain until that chain has been responded to. Contrast with *delayed request mode*. See also *immediate response mode*.

INN.   Intermediate Network-Node.

intermediate routing function.   A routing function that allows a network location to receive session data from an adjacent location and route it to the next location on the session path.

internetwork.   A network built from subnetworks attached to one another through interworking units (inter-subnetwork routers) performing an internet relay function in the upper part of the network layer (SNICP). See also *inter-subnetwork router*.

inter-subnetwork router.   A router designed for routing at level 3c between subnetworks such as LANs and backbone subnetworks.

inter-working unit (IWU).   A layer 1 through 3c unit that interconnects multiple subnetworks. An IWU includes at least one inter-subnetwork router. It may service multiple protocols.

IP.   (1) DARPA Internet Protocol. The internetwork layer (SNICP) connectionless protocol used in the DARPA internet. (2) Internet Protocol (TCP/IP).

IPDS.   Intelligent Printer Data Stream.

IPL.   Initial Program Load.

IPR.   Isolated Pacing Response.

IPX.   Internetwork Protocol Exchange. Novell's implementation of XNS protocols in Netware.

IS.   Intermediate-System. A term denoting a switching node inside a network, used to route and relay communication between end points (OSI).

ISDN.   Integrated Services Digital Network.

isochronous.   (1) Transmissions in equal time increments. (2) A timing scheme in which the modem clock depends on the terminal clock.

IWU. See *Inter-Working Unit*. A layer 1 through 3c connection unit (which includes an inter-subnetwork router).

JTM. Job Transfer and Management. One of OSI's application-layer standards, specifying a service and protocol for job transfer and management.

Kerberos. An authentication system.

LAN. Local Area Network.

LAP-B. Link Access Procedure-Balanced.

LEN. Low-Entry Networking (APPN).

LFSID. Local-Form Session Identifier. A dynamically assigned value used at a type 2.1 node to identify traffic for a particular session using a given transmission group (APPN).

link. An assembly of two or more layer-2 termination installations and the interconnecting communications channel operating according to a particular method that permits information to be exchanged. A link may represent a complete connection to an adjacent node, and include both the link station and the physical media over which it is transmitted. The link may, for example, be a LAN, an ISDN connection, a S/390 channel, or an SDLC point-to-point line.

link station. The combination of hardware and software that allows a node to attach to, and provide control for, a link.

Link/Subnetwork-Access. The aggregate of protocols, at layers 1, 2, and 3a, such as X.25, ISDN, LANs, channels, and HDLC/SDLC, in an end-system or an intermediate-system, which control access to the corresponding links and/or subnetworks.

LLC. Logical-Link Control. The upper part of the data link control (DLC) layer, dealing with the procedural (as opposed to format and coding) aspects of the link protocol.

LLC switch. A bridge that operates at the logical-link control sublayer of DLC. An LLC switch involves the termination of the full DLC function at the bridge.

local address. An address used in a peripheral-node in place of a network address and paired with a network address by the boundary-function in a subarea-node (SNA).

logical channel number. Virtual circuit identified at the packet level of X.25.

logical-link. The set of protocol machines used to connect network-entities in two systems, and to manage the exchange of traffic over a real or virtual circuit.

logical unit (LU). A port through which an end user accesses the SNA network in order to communicate with another end-system.

LSAP. Link SAP. An addressable service-access-point at which network entities can access link services.

LSID. Local Session Identifier (APPN).

LU. Logical Unit. An SNA term designating a network addressable entity equivalent to a multilayer entity in the OSI sense.

LU_name. A name and an address designating an LU in an SNA or APPN network.

LU 6.2. An SNA term designating LUs of type 6.2, designed for program-to-program communication in a transaction processing environment.

MAC. Media Access Control. A sublayer of the data link control layer.

mainframe. A multiuser, multipurpose computer system, such as the IBM S/390 and AS/400 systems.

MAN. Metropolitan Area Network.

managed object. An abstracted view of a resource that represents its properties as seen by (and for the purpose of) system management.

management services. One of the types of SNA network services. Management services provide functions for problem management, performance and accounting management, configuration management, and change management.

MAP. Manufacturing Automation Protocol. An enhanced subset of OSI standards defined for the purpose of manufacturing automation by a group of industries following an initiative of General Motors Corp.

mapped conversation. A mode of operation, with SNA LU 6.2, which hides from the programmer the details of the underlying data stream.

message unit. A generic term for the unit of data processed by any layer.

MIB. Management Information Base. All of the informational aspects of a system. The MIB is composed of all object instances that exist on that system (OSI and TCP/IP).

mode name. The name used by the initiator of a session to designate the characteristics desired for the session, such as traffic pacing values, message length limits, sync point and cryptography options, and the Class of Service within the transport network (SNA).

modem. A device (*modulator-dem*odulator) that converts data from the computer to a signal that can be sent over a communications line, and converts the communications signal to data for the computer.

MOTIF. A graphic user interface developed by OSF.

multipoint. In data communications, pertains to a network that allows two or more stations to communicate with a single system on one line.

MVS. Multiple Virtual Storage, an S/370 or S/390 operating system.

NCP. Network Control Program. A program that provides communications-controller support (SNA).

NCS. Network Computing System (Hewlett Packard).

negative response. A response indicating that a request did not arrive successfully or was not processed successfully by the receiver. Contrast with *positive response*. See also *exception response*.

negotiable Bind. A capability that allows two LU-LU half-sessions to negotiate the parameters of a session when the session is being activated (SNA).

network. A collection of data-processing products connected by communications lines for exchanging information between stations.

network-access facility. An aggregate of network-access units that provide entry to a transport provider. When packaged separately, the network-access facility is also sometimes called an interworking unit.

network-access unit. A unit that provides an entry to a transport provider. It is a connection between a subnetwork and either another subnetwork or attaching end-systems. A network-access unit may contain both layer 1 through 3a (input/output) services and layer-3c inter-subnetwork routing services.

network directory. A network-layer directory function for deriving routing information from layer-3 addresses.

Network-Entity–Title (NET). Used when there are no upper (4–7) layers, instead of the NSAP. The network-entity–title has the same format and comes from the same namespace as the NSAP. The NET uses a selector byte with value 0.

Network Management Vector Transport (NMVT). The request unit format used in management services data flow (SNA).

network-node. A node that can define the paths or routes, control route selection, and handle directory services for APPN.

network-node server. A network-node that is directly connected to an end-node or a low-entry networking end-node and has been assigned to service the end-node session request.

network-qualified name. A SNA resource_name composed of a Net_id and an unqualified resource_name. The resource_name may, for example, be a logical unit name or a control point name.

NFS. Network File System (TCP/IP).

NN. See *Network-Node*.

no response. A protocol requested in the RH that directs the receiver of the request not to return any response, regardless of whether or not the request is received and processed successfully. Contrast with *definite response, exception response* (SNA).

node type. A designation of a node according to the protocols it supports and the network addressable units that it can contain. Four types are defined: 2.0, 2.1, 4, and 5. (SNA).

nonswitched link. A connection between two nodes that does not have to be established by dialing. Contrast with *switched link*.

NPD. Network Problem Determination.

NPSI. An IBM software product allowing communication controllers to attach to X.25 networks (SNA).

NREN. National Research and Education Network.

NSAP. Network SAP. An addressable service-access-point at which transport entities can access network services.

ODA. Office Document Architecture.

ODA/ODIF. ODA/Open Document Interchange Format.

OEM. Other Equipment Manufacturer.

OSF. Open Software Foundation.

OSI/Communications Subsystem. The generic name for IBM's implementation of OSI, which is the basis for its OSI product family, across all system platforms.

OSI LU. A term used to refer to OSI/Communications Subsystem instance appearing as a SNA LU within a system implementing both OSI and SNA.

OSNA. Open Systems Network Architecture. A term coined for this book to describe the evolving multiprotocol architecture that incorporates SNA, OSI, TCP/IP and NetBIOS facilities.

OSPF. Open Shortest Path First (TCP/IP). A routing algorithm.

P-selector. The selector field specific to the presentation layer, which is appended to a SSAP address to constitute a PSAP address.

pacing. A technique by which a receiving component controls the rate of transmission by sending a component to prevent overrun or congestion.

pacing group. The requests that can be transmitted in one direction over a session before a session-level pacing response is received, indicating that the receiver is ready to accept the next group of requests. Synonymous with *window*.

pacing group size. The number of requests in a session-level pacing group. The pacing group size is set at session activation. Synonymous with *window size*.

pacing response. An indicator that signifies a receiving component's readiness to accept another pacing group; the indicator is carried in a RH for session-level pacing, and in a TH for virtual route pacing (SNA).

packet. A sequence of binary digits, including data and control signals, that is transmitted and switched as a composite whole.

parallel links. Two or more links between adjacent nodes.

parallel sessions. Two or more concurrently active sessions between the same two logical units using different pairs of network addresses. Each session can have independent session parameters (SNA).

Path Control (PC) layer. The layer that manages the sharing of link resources of the SNA network and routes message units through it. Path control routes message units between LUs in the network and provides the paths between them.

path control network. The part of the SNA network that includes the physical control, data link control, and path control layers.

PBX. Private Branch Exchange. A switching system located on a customer's premises that consolidates the number of inside (extension) lines into a smaller number of outside lines (trunks).

PC. Path Control. The name of the network layer in SNA.

PCID. Procedure Correlation Identifier (SNA).

PDN. Public Data Network.

PDU. Protocol Data Unit. A unit of data or packet at some (context dependent) layer of protocol.

peer-to-peer. A relationship in which all parties are equal in stature (none control the others or are more capable than the others).

peripheral-node. A node that uses local addresses for routing and therefore is not affected by changes in network addresses. A peripheral-node requires boundary-function assistance from an adjacent subarea-node (SNA).

physical layer. OSI and SNA layer 1, defining the mechanical format of cables and connectors used in a network, and the electrical format of the coded signals exchanged through them.

physical unit (PU). The component that manages and monitors the resources (such as attached links and adjacent link stations) of a node, as requested by an SSCP via an SSCP-PU session. Each node of an SNA subarea network contains a physical unit.

PING. The process of sending an ICMP Echo Request packet to a host or gateway, with the expectation of receiving a reply (TCP/IP).

PLU. See *Primary Logical Unit.*

PM. Presentation Manager. The program that presents, in windows, a graphics-based interface to applications and files.

PNA. Programmable Network Access.

POP. Post Office Protocol. Allows an AIX-based system to act as the receiver for mail destined for a user of TCP in another computer (TCP/IP).

positive response. A response indicating that a request was successfully received and processed. Contrast with *negative response.*

POSIX. Portable Operating System Interface for Computer Environments (an IEEE project).

presentation address. An address that uniquely identifies an application. It consists of an NSAP address, a TSAP address, an SSAP selector, and a PSAP selector.

presentation context. The combination of a transfer syntax and the transformation necessary for mapping from abstract syntax to transfer syntax.

Presentation Services (PS) layer. The layer that provides services for transaction programs, such as controlling conversation-level communication between them.

primary logical unit. The LU that sends the `Bind` request for a particular LU-LU session. Contrast with *Secondary Logical Unit.*

PROFS. Professional Office System (VM).

protocol. The meanings of, and the sequencing rules for, request and responses used for managing the network, transferring data, and synchronizing the states of network components.

PS. See *Presentation Services layer.*

PSAP. Presentation SAP. An addressable service-access-point at which application-entities can access presentation-layer services.

PSH. Presentation Services Header (SNA).

PTF. Program Temporary Fix.

PU. See *Physical Unit.*

QLLC. Qualified Logical-Link Control. A special-purpose SNDCP function inserted between the X.25 and path control layer of SNA internets to raise the functionality of X.25 connections to that expected by SNA path control.

RACF. Resource Access Control Facility. Allows access to data and system components based on authorization levels (VM and MVS).

RDA. Remote Database Access. One of OSI's application-layer standards, specifying a service and protocol for remote database access.

Recommendation X.25. A CCITT recommendation for the interface between a DTE and a DCE.

relative distinguished name. A single token from a distinguished name. A set of attribute values concerning a particular entry in an X.500 directory.

relay function. The function performed by intermediate-systems within a subnetwork, and by IWUs within an internetwork, to pass information coming in on one link or subnetwork out to another link or subnetwork.

reply. A request unit sent only in reaction to a received request unit.

Request (RQ). A message unit that signals initiation of a particular action or protocol.

Request/Response Header (RH). Control information preceding an RU that specifies the type of RU and contains control information associated with that RU (SNA).

Request/Response Unit (RU). A generic term for a request unit or a response unit (SNA).

Response (RSP). (1) A message unit that acknowledges receipt of a request; a response consists of a response header, a response unit, or both; (2) in SDLC, the control information (in the C-field of the link header) sent from the secondary station to the primary station.

RFC. Request for Comments. A series of documents that address a broad range of topics affecting internetwork communications (TCP/IP).

RH. See *Request/Response Header* (SNA).

RIP. Router Internet Protocol (TCP/IP).

RJE. Remote Job Entry.

ROS. Remote Operation Service. One of OSI's application-layer standards, specifying a service and protocol for remote procedure calling.

router. A device that connects networks or subnetworks at the network layer. It is protocol-dependent and connects only networks operating with the same level-3 protocol. Routers also select the best transmission paths and the optimum sizes for packets. See also *inter-subnetwork router*.

routing. The forwarding of a message unit along a particular path through a network as determined by parameters carried in the message unit, such as the destination network address in a TH.

RPC. Remote Procedure Call.

RQ. See *Request*.

RQD. Request for Definite response (SNA).

RQE. Request for Exception response only (SNA).

RQN. Request No response (SNA).

RSCS. Remote Spooling Communications Subsystem. The program that transfers spool files, commands, and messages between VM user-ids (VM).

RSCV. Routing Selection Control Vector. A source routing vector included in APPN Bind PDUs to describe the route to be taken by the Bind and the subsequent LU 6.2 session.

RSP. See *Response*.

RU. See *Request/Response Unit*.

RU chain. A set of related RUs that are consecutively transmitted in one direction over a session. Each RU belongs to only one chain, which has a beginning and an end indicated by control bits in RHs within the RU chain (SNA).

SAA. System Application Architecture. An IBM architecture for allowing the design of applications for distributed systems.

SAP. See *Service-Access-Point*.

SAPI. Service-Access-Point Identifier.

SDH. Synchronous Digital Hierarchy.

SDLC. See *Synchronous Data Link Control*.

Secondary Logical Unit. The LU that receives the Bind request for a particular LU-LU session. Contrast with *Primary Logical Unit* (SNA).

segmentation.   The process of dividing a unit of data into smaller units in order to send it across a network.

server.   A function that provides services for users in another node. There may be multiple servers in a host machine.

Service-Access-Point (SAP).   The point at which services are provided by an *n*-entity to an *n+1* entity, in a layered communication system.

service-primitive.   A particular invocation of a service element across its service interface.

service transaction programs.   IBM–supplied programs that are defined by SNA for providing transaction services. See also *transaction program*. Contrast with *application transaction program*.

session.   A connection between communicating session-layer entities in an OSI context; a connection between communicating LU's in a SNA or APPN context. A logical connection between two LUs that can be activated, tailored to provide various protocols, and deactivated, as requested. The SNA session activation request and response can determine options relating to such things as the rate and concurrency of data exchange, the control of contention and error recovery, and the characteristics of the data stream.

session cryptography.   The process of providing security for end-user data by enciphering and deciphering the data.

session initiation request.   An INIT or logon request from a LU to a control point that asks for the LU-LU session to be activated. See also `Bind`, a consequent activation command.

session layer.   OSI's layer 5, defining the structure of the dialog between two applications.

session-level pacing.   A flow control technique that permits a receiving half-session to control the data transfer rate (the rate at which it receives request units). It is used to prevent overloading a receiver with unprocessed requests when the sender can generate requests faster than the receiver can process them (SNA). See also *pacing*.

session limit.   The maximum number of concurrently active LU-LU sessions a particular LU can support (SNA).

session services.   One of the types of network services in the SSCP and in a LU. These services provide facilities for a LU or a network operator to request that the SSCP initiate or terminate sessions between LUs (SNA).

SGML.   Standard Generalized Markup Language.

SID.   Session Identifier.

SIP.   SMDS Interface Protocol.

SMTP.   Simple Mail Transfer Protocol. A TCP/IP application protocol used for transferring mail between users on different systems.

SNA Character String (SCS).   A data stream composed of EBCDIC controls, optionally inter-mixed with end-user data, which is carried with a RU.

SNA Distribution Services (SNADS).   An IBM architecture that defines a set of rules to receive, route, and send electronic mail in a network of systems.

SNA/FS.   SNA/File Services. File transfer services in a SNA network.

SNAcP.   The subnetwork access protocol implemented by the lower sublayer (3a) of OSI's network layer.

SNADS.   See *SNA Distribution Services*.

SNDCP. The subnetwork-dependent convergence protocol or function implemented by the middle sublayer (3b) of OSI's network layer to match the service offered by the lower SNAcP sublayer to that expected by the higher SNICP sublayer.

SNI. SNA Network Interconnect. An architecture for interconnecting individually administered SNA networks.

SNICP. The subnetwork-independent convergence protocol implemented by the higher sublayer (3c) of OSI's network layer.

SNMP. Simple Network Management Protocol. A management process for TCP/IP networks.

socket. An end point for communicating between processes; a pair consisting of TCP port and IP address, or UDP port and IP address (TCP/IP).

SONET. Synchronous Optical NETwork.

span of control. A collection of network-node control points for which another system is acting as a system manager.

SQL. Structured Query Language.

SSAP. (1) Session SAP. An addressable service-access-point at which presentation entities can access session-layer service primitives. (2) Link SAP. The source service-access-point.

SSCP. See *System Services Control Point.*

start–stop. Asynchronous transmission such that a group of signals representing a character is preceded by a start element and followed by a stop element.

subarea. A portion of the SNA network consisting of a subarea-node, any attached peripheral-nodes, and their associated resources. Within a subarea-node, all LUs, links, and adjacent link stations that are addressable with the subarea share a common subarea address and have distinct element addresses.

subarea address. A value in the network address that identifies a particular subarea. See also *element address* (SNA).

subarea network. A connected collection of PU type 4 and type 5 nodes, their peripheral PUs (excluding PU type 2.1 nodes) and the communications facilities interconnecting them (SNA).

subarea-node. A node that uses network addresses for routing and whose routing tables are therefore affected by changes in the configuration of the network. Subarea-nodes can provide boundary-function, gateway-function, and intermediate routing function (SNA).

subnetwork. Any collection of equipment and physical media that form an autonomous whole, and can be used to interconnect other real systems for purposes of communication. LANs and X.25 packet switched data networks are examples of subnetworks.

switched link. A link between two nodes that is established by dialing.

synchronization point (sync point). (1) An intermediate or end point during processing of a transaction at which an update or modification to one or more of the transaction's protected resources is logically complete and error free; (2) a point at which the processing of end-user data is checkpointed.

Synchronous Data Link Control (SDLC). A discipline for managing synchronous, code transparent, serial-by-bit, information transfer over a link connection. Transmission exchanges may be duplex or half-duplex over switched or nonswitched links. The configuration of the link connection may be point-to-point, multipoint, or loop. SDLC conforms to subsets of the Advanced Data Communication Control Procedures (ADCCP) of the American National

Standards Institute and High-level Data Link Control (HDLC) of the International Standards Organization (SNA).

system definition.   The process of coding and loading resource definition statements and macro instructions that describe the network's configuration and operation to the network's software. The system definition process includes system generations.

system generation.   The process of selecting optional parameters for software and tailoring the software to the requirements of the network. See also *system definition*.

System Services Control Point (SSCP).   A control point within an SNA subarea network for managing the configuration, coordinating network operator and problem determination requests, and providing directory services and other session services for end users of a network. Multiple SSCPs, cooperating as peers with one another, can divide the network into domains of control, with each SSCP having a hierarchical control relationship to the PUs and LUs within its own domain.

tail vector.   A representation of a transmission group available at an end-node for use by sessions that terminate in that node. Such a TG is not in the network topology database, and one of the purposes of the Locate/CD_Initiate search is to obtain the tail vectors of the nodes containing the origin and destination LUs. These tail vectors are sent to the origin LU's network-node server, which combines these with the node and TG data in the topology database to compute a preferred session route (APPN).

TC.   Transmission Control (SNA).

TCE.   Transmission Control Element.

TCP.   Transmission Control Protocol (TCP/IP).

TDB.   See *Topology Database*.

TDU.   See *Topology Database Update*.

TEI.   Terminal End point Identifier.

TELNET.   Remote terminal access for TCP/IP.

TG.   See *Transmission Group*.

TH.   See *Transmission Header*.

Topology Database (TDB).   A fully replicated distributed database maintained by APPN network-nodes. It contains a listing of the nodes, interconnecting links, and their various characteristics within an APPN topology subnet. It is used to describe the topology of an APPN network and to perform class-of-service-based route calculations.

Topology Database Update (TDU).   A unit of information containing topology database information that flows between APPN nodes. TDU's are used to synchronize the topology database among a number of nodes within an APPN Topology Subnetwork.

TP.   Transaction program in an SNA context. The entity using the LU 6.2 services in a SNA network, akin to a TPSU in an OSI network.

TP or TPC.   Transaction processing in an OSI context. One of OSI's application-layer standards, specifying a service and protocol for distributed transaction processing. The TP service is similar to the service provided by LU 6.2 instances to SNA transaction programs across the CPI-C interface.

TPF.   Transmission Priority Field.

TPN.   Transaction Program Name (SNA).

TPSU.   Transaction Processing Service User. An OSI term akin to a TP in SNA, denoting the process or procedure that uses the OSI TP service.

transaction.   An exchange between (1) a workstation and a program, (2) two workstations, or (3) two programs that accomplishes a particular action or result; for example, the entry of a customer's deposit and the updating of the customer's balance.

transaction program.   A program that processes transactions. There are two kinds of transaction programs: application transaction programs and service transaction programs.

transfer syntax.   The syntactic structure and ordering of data units as they are transferred between systems.

transmission control layer.   The SNA layer within a half-session that synchronizes and controls the speed of session-level data traffic, checks sequence numbers of requests, and enciphers and deciphers end-user data.

Transmission Group (TG).   A group of links between adjacent nodes, appearing as a single logical link for routing of messages. A transmission group may consist, for example, of one or more SDLC links (parallel links), a LAN, or a single System/370 channel (SNA).

Transmission Header (TH).   Control information that is created and used by path control to route message units and to control their flow within the network (SNA).

transport layer.   OSI's layer 4 offering a full-duplex transport service between logical transport entities located in physical stations attached to the same network or internetwork.

TRS.   Topology and Routing Services. The topology tracking and route computation services of APPN, collectively implemented by the TRS components in every APPN network-node.

TSAP.   Transport SAP. An addressable OSI service-access-point at which session entities can access transport services.

TSO.   Time Sharing Option (MVS).

UDP.   User Datagram Protocol. A connectionless datagram protocol that requires minimal overhead, but does not guarantee delivery (TCP/IP).

UNIX.   An operating system originally developed by AT&T.

VAN.   Value Added Network.

Virtual Machine (VM).   A functional simulation of a computer and its associated devices. Each virtual machine is controlled by a suitable operating system.

virtual route.   A logical connection between two subarea-nodes that is physically resulted as a particular explicit route (SNA).

VM.   See *Virtual Machine*.

VPD. Vital Product Data.

VRU.   Voice Response Unit. A product that fields incoming calls by playing one or more prerecorded messages. The messages may require the caller to input additional information on the telephone keypad. The sequence of messages may be determined dynamically by this additional input.

VT.   Virtual Terminal. One of OSI's application-layer standards, specifying a service and protocol for terminal access.

VTAM.   Virtual Telecommunications Access Method.

WAN.   Wide Area Network. A network or subnetwork that provides communication services to a geographic area larger than that served by a local area network or a metro area network.

window.   (1) Synonym for pacing group; the number of data packets that can be sent before waiting for an authorization to send another packet. (2) An area of the screen through which a panel or portion of a panel is displayed.

window size.   Synonym for *pacing group size*.

X/Open.   Consortium promoting the practical implementation of standards in support of open systems.

X-Windows API.   An application program interface designed as a distributed, network-transparent, device independent, multitasking windowing and graphics system.

X.25 PLP.   Packet-Level Protocol. OSI's connection-oriented protocol for use at the internetwork level (SNICP). It may also be used at the Subnetwork Access level (SNAcP).

X.25.   CCITT Recommendation X.25.

X.400 MHS.   Message Handling System. One of OSI's application-layer standards, specifying a service and protocol for electronic mail.

X.500 Directory.   The joint CCITT-ISO standard fro the OSI application-layer directory, allowing users to register, store, search, and retrieve information about any objects or resource in a network or distributed system.

XI.   An IBM software product allowing communication controllers to offer an X.25 interface on a SNA network.

XID.   Exchange Identification command (SNA).

XID3.   XID format 3 (SNA).

XNS.   Xerox Network Services. A distributed file system that lets workstations use remote resources as if they were local.

Cited References

[Ahmadi88] H. Ahmadi, W. E. Denzel, C. A. Murphy, and E. Port, "A High-Performance Switch Fabric for Integrated Circuit and Packet Switching," *IEEE Communications Society INFOCOM '88*, March 27–31, 1988. (Figures 1 and 6, © 1988 IEEE, reprinted by permission of IEEE.)

[Ahuja79] V. Ahuja, "Routing and Flow Control in Systems Network Architecture," *IBM Systems Journal*, vol. 18, no. 2, 1979, pp. 298–314.

[Ahuja88] V. Ahuja, "Common Communications Support in Systems Application Architecture," *IBM Systems Journal*, vol. 27, no. 3, 1988, pp. 264–280.

[ANSI,88a] *Frame Relay Bearer Service: Architectural Framework and Service Description*, ANSI document T1S1/88–185, December 1988.

[ANSI,88b] *Signalling Specifications for Frame Relay (rev. 6)*, ANSI document T1S1. 2/88–440, December 1988.

[Autru89] Pasquale Autru and Christopher Ballard, "NetView Distribution Manager: An Update," GG23-0002, *Interface*, April 1989; available through IBM branch offices.

[Baack83] C. Baack, G. Elze, G. Grosskopf, and G. Walf, "Digital and Analog Optical Broad-Band Transmission," *Proceedings on the IEEE*, vol. 71, no. 2, February 1983, pp. 198–208.

[Baack86] C. Baack, *Optical Wideband Transmission Systems*. Boca Raton, Fla.: CRC Press, 1986.

[Ballard89] C. P. Ballard, L. Fartara, and B. J. Heldke, "Managing Changes in SNA Networks," *IBM Systems Journal*, vol. 28, no 2, 1989, pp. 260–273.

[Baratz85] A. E. Baratz, , J. P. Gray, P. E. Green, J. M. Jaffe, and D. P. Pozefsky, "SNA Networks of Small Systems," *IEEE Journal on Selected Areas in Communications,* May 1985, pp. 416–426.

[Bellcore] *ISDN Basic Access Call Control Switching And Signaling Requirements*, Bellcore Technical Report TR-TSY-000268, Bellcore Communications Research, Inc., Morristown, N.J.

[Bellcore-a] *Metropolitan Area Network Generic Framework System Requirements in Support of Switched Multi-Megabit Data Service*, Bellcore Technical Advisory, TA-TSY-000772, issue 1, Bellcore Communications Research, Inc., Morristown, N.J., February 1988.

[Bellcore-b] *Generic System Requirement in Support of Switched Multi-Megabit Data Service*, TA-TSY-000772, issue 3, Bellcore Communications Research, Inc., Morristown, N.J., October, 1989.

[Bergman85] L. A. Bergman and S. T. Eng, "A Synchronous Fiber Optic Ring Local Area Network for Multi-Gigabit Mixed Traffic Communications," *IEEE Journal on Selected Areas in Communications*, vol. SAC-3, no. 6, November 1985, pp. 842–848.

[Beumeler89] Mark Beumeler, "Token Network Bridges," *Interface,* March 1989, GG23-0001; available from IBM branch offices. (Figure 4, IBM © 1989, reprinted by permission of IBM).

[Black89] William Black, "File Access and Serving in an OSI Environment," *Computer Networks and ISDN Systems*, vol. 17, 1989, pp. 294–299.

[Bridge87] Draft IEEE Standard 802.1: Part D, "MAC Bridges," *IEEE Computer Society*, May 1987.

[Brodd84] W. D. Brodd and R. A. Donnan, "Data Link Control Requirements for Satellite Transmission," *Proceedings of the Ninth International Conference on Computer Communications*, North Holland, Publ. Co., New York, pp. 251–258.

[Brusseau89] Philippe Brusseau, "Interconnection of LANs, using ISDN, in TCP/IP Architecture," *Proceedings of the Autumn 1989 European UNIX System User Group Conference*, 1989, pp. 189–196.

[Burg89] Fred M. Burg and Nicola Di Iorio, "Networking of Networks: Interworking According to OSI," *IEEE Journal on Selected Topics in Communications*, vol. 7, no. 7, September 1989. (Figures 4, 5, 6, © 1989 IEEE, reprinted by permission of IEEE.)

[Bux89] W. Bux, P. Kermani, and W. Kleinoeder, "Performance of an Improved Data Link Control Protocol," *Proceedings of the Ninth International Conference on Computer Communication*, October 1988, North Holland Publ. Co., New York, pp. 251–258.

[Caldwell88] Caldwell, L. G. "Untangling the Network Jungle," *CIPS Edmonton '88 Proceedings*, 1988, pp. 294–300.

[Campbell] Randall G. Campbell, "A Communications Strategy for Growth," *Personal System Technical Solutions Journal*, G325-5005; available through IBM branch offices. (Figure 6, IBM © 1990, reprinted by permission of IBM.)

[Capodil89] Giorgio Emo Capodilista and Ron Bostick, "IBM X. 400 Programs," *Interface,* January 1989, IBM Corp., Raleigh, N.C.

[Case90] J. Case, J. Davin, M. Fedor, and M. Schoffstall, "Keeping It Simple," *Unix Review*, vol. 8, no. 3, March 1990, pp. 60–66.

[Chappell] David Chappell, "Abstract Syntax Notation One (ASN. 1)," *Communications Standards Management*, New York: Auerbach Publishers, 1989.

[Cherukuri89] R. J. Cherukuri and J. H. Derby, "Frame Relay: Protocols and Private Network Applications," *Proceedings IEEE INFOCOM '89*, vol II, April 1989, Ottawa, Canada, pp. 676–685.

[Chesson] Greg Chesson, "XTP/PE Overview," *IEEE CH2613*, August 1988, pp. 292–296.

[Cidon88] Israel Cidon and Inder S. Gopal, "PARIS: An Approach to Integrated High-Speed Private Networks," *International Journal of Digital and Analog Cabled Systems*, vol. 1, no. 2, April/June 1988, pp. 77–85.

[Cochrane88] P. Cochrane and M. Brain, "Future Optical Fiber Transmission Technology and Networks," *IEEE Communications Magazine*, vol. 26, no. 11, November 1988.

[Codes85] *Information Processing: Coded Character Sets for Text Communication*, ISO 6937 Parts 1–3, International Standards Organization, 1985.

[Codes87] *Information Processing—8 Bit Single Byte Coded Graphic Character Sets*, ISO 8859 Parts 1–3, International Standards Organization, 1987.

[Codes88] *Character Repertoire and Coded Character Sets for the International Teletex Service*, CCITT Recommendation T. 61, 1988.

[Cohn88] Marc Cohn, "A High-Performance Transfer Protocol for Real Time Local Area Networks," *1988 IEEE Military Communications Conference*, Conference Record, vol. 3, pp. 1041–1047. (Figure 2, © 1988 IEEE, reprinted by permission of IEEE.)

[Comer88] Douglas Comer, *"Internetworking with TCP/IP."* Englewood Cliffs, N.J.: Prentice Hall, 1988.

[Cox9] Tracy Cox, Frances Dix, Christine Henrick, and Josephine McRoberts, "SMDS: The Beginning of WAN Superhighways," *Data Communications*, April 1991, pp. 105–110.

[Cypser78] R. J. Cypser, *Communications Architecture for Distributed Systems.* (Figure 17.13, copyright © 1978, Addison-Wesley Publ. Co., Reading, Mass., reprinted with permission.)

[Davison90] Wayne Davison, "Application Associations: The Key to Establishing OSI Conversations," *Communications Standards Management.* New York: Auerbach Publishers, 1990.

[Dawson89] Frank Dawson, "Opening Your Office with ODA," *UNIX Review*, March–April 1989.

[Deaton81] G. A. Deaton, Jr., and A. S. Barclay, "IBM Gives U. S. Users Ticket to X.25 Networks," *Data Communications*, September 1981.

[Deaton83] G. A. Deaton, Jr. and R. O. Hippert, Jr. "X. 25 and Related Recommendations in IBM Products," *IBM Systems Journal,* vol. 22, nos. 1, 2, 1983, pp. 11–29.

[Deaton90] G. Deaton. "Considerations for Advanced Networking in the 1990's," *Tenth International Conference on Computer Communications, ICCC '90*, New Delhi, India, November 1990.

[Demers88a] R. A. Demers, "Distributed Files for SAA," *IBM Systems Journal*, vol. 27, no. 3, 1988, pp. 348–361. (Figures 3 and 10, IBM © 1988, reprinted by permission of IBM.)

[Demers88b] *Loc. cit.*, p. 359.

[Dineen88] T. H. Dineen, P. J. Leach, N. W. Mishkin, J. N. Pato, and G. L. Wyant, *The Network Computing Architecture and System: An Environment for Developing Distributed Applications*, 33rd IEEE Computer Society Conference, San Franciso, February 1988.

[Dix88] Frances R. Dix and Edward J. Isganitis, "Access and Internal Network Protocols for Providing Switched Multi-Megabit Data Service," IEEE CH2535 3/88/0000-1235, Globecom 88 IEEE Global Telecom. Conference. (Figures 5 and 6 © IEEE, reprinted with permission of IEEE.)

[Dixon87] Roy C. Dixon and Michael Willett, "Enhancing Connectivity for Token-Ring Networks," presented at *Localnet East*, June 1987, and *FOC/LAN 87*, October, 1987.

[Dixon88] R. C. Dixon and D. A. Pitt, "Addressing, Bridging, and Source Routing," *IEEE Network Magazine*, vol. 2, January 1988, pp. 25–32.

[Duncan89] Ray Duncan, "Interprocess Communications in OS/2," *Dr. Dobb's Journal*, June 1989, pp. 15–25.

[E. 163] *Numbering Plan for the International Telephone Service*, CCITT Recommendation E. 163, *Red Book*, 1984; Proposed Revision to E. 163, International Telephone and Telegraph Consultants Committee, 1988.

[E. 164] The Numbering Plan for the ISDN Era; CCITT Recommendation E. 164; Revised Recommendation E. 164, International Telephone and Telegraph Consultative Committee, 1988.

[Eng88] S. T. Eng and L. A. Bergman, "Gigabit Fiber Optic Computer Networks: Technology and System Considerations," *EFOC/LAN 88, Sixth European Fibre Optic Communications and Local Area Networks Exposition*, Amsterdam, the Netherlands, June 29, July 1, 1988.

[Eng 88b] *Loc. cit.*

[EWOS89] *EWOS Technical Guide on Relays, Draft 2* ECMA/TC32 - TG6/89/342, European Computer Manufacturer's Association, Geneva, Switzerland, October 16, 1989.

[EWOS89b] *EWOS Technical Guide, OSI Layers 1 to 4 Addressing, Draft 6:* ECMA/TC32, European Computer Manufacturer's Association, Geneva, Switzerland, October 4, 1989.

[Farber73] D. J. Farber and J. J. Vittal, "Extendibility Considerations in the Design of the Distributed Computer System (DCS)," *Proceedings of the National Telecommunications Conference*, Atlanta, Georgia, November 1973, pp. 15E–1 to 15E–6.

[FAX88a] *Standardization of Group 3 Facsimile Apparatus for Document Transmission*, CCITT Recommendation T. 4, International Telephone and Telegraph Consultative Committee, 1988.

[FAX88b] *Facsimile Coding Schemes and Coding Control Functions for Group 4 Facsimile Apparatus*, CCITT Recommendations T. 6, International Telephone and Telegraph Consultative Committee, 1988.

[Font] *Information Processing—Font and Character Information Interchange*, ISO 9541, International Standards Organization.

[FRSpec90] *Frame Relay Specification with Extensions Based on Proposed T1S1 Standards,* Cisco Systems, StrataCom, DEC and Northern Telecom, September 18, 1990.

[G01F-0281] *SystemView and the OS/2 Environment*, IBM Corp.; available through IBM branch offices.

[G320-9929] *IBM Enterprise Solutions for the 1990s*, IBM Corp., available through IBM branch offices.

[G325-5010] *IBM PS/2 Technical Solutions*, January 1991. (Figure on p. 18, IBM © 1991, reprinted with permission of IBM), available from IBM branch offices.

[G521-1210] *IBM Solutions for Campus Communications Systems*, IBM Corp.; available from IBM branch offices. (Figures 11 and 15, IBM © 1990, reprinted with permission of IBM.)

[GA23-0383] *Introducing Enterprise System Connection*, IBM Corp.; available through IBM branch offices.

[GA27-3136] *SNA Formats*, IBM Corp.; available through IBM branch offices.

[GC23-2002] *AIX Family Definition Overview*, IBM Corp.; available through IBM branch offices.

[GC26-4341] *Systems Application Architecture—An Overview*, IBM Corp., May 1987; available through IBM branch offices.

[GC30-3073] *SNA Technical Overview*, IBM Corp.; available through IBM branch offices. (Figures 1–5, IBM © 1991, reproduced with permission of IBM.)

[GC30-3084] *Systems Network Architecture: Transaction Programmer's Reference Manual for LU Type 6. 2,* IBM Corp.; available through IBM branch offices.

[GC31-6824] *CallPath Services Programmer's Reference*, IBM Corp.; available through IBM branch offices.

[Gerla88] Mario Gerla and Leonard Kleinrock, "Congestion Control in Interconnected LANs," *IEEE Network*, vol. 2, no. 1, January 1988, pp. 72–76.

[GG22-9125] Alan Reinhold, *Communications Systems Bulletin, TCP/IP,* IBM Corp.; available from IBM branch offices. (Figures from pp. 21, 63, 65, 73, and 89, IBM © 1988, are reprinted by permission of IBM.)

[GG22-9489] *Local Area Network Asynchronous Connection Server (LANACS) Version 2 Connectivity,* IBM Corp.; Telecommunications Systems Center, Dallas, available through IBM branch offices. (Figures 3 and 4, IBM © 1991, reprinted with permission of IBM.)

[GG24-1584] *An Introduction to Advanced Program to Program Communication,* IBM Corp.; available through IBM branch offices.

[GG24-3052] *Integrating X. 25 Function into SNA Networks,* IBM Corp.; available through IBM branch offices.

[GG24-3503] *Information Interchange Architecture,* IBM Corp., available through IBM branch offices. (Figure 16, IBM © 1990, reprinted with permission of IBM.)

[GG24-3287] *Advanced Peer to Peer Networking,* International Technical Support Centers, IBM Corp.; 1988; available through IBM branch offices.

[GG24-3359] *IBM OS/2 Extended Edition Communications Manager, Version 1.1 Cookbook,* vol. 1, IBM Corp.; available from IBM branch offices. (Figure 5, IBM © 1989, reproduced with permission of IBM.)

[GG24-3360] *IBM OS/2 EE Communications Manager, Version 1.1 Cookbook,* vol. 2, IBM Corp.; available through IBM branch offices. (Figure 519 and 536, IBM © 1989, reprinted by permission of IBM.)

[GG24-3376] *TCP/IP Tutorial and Technical Overview,* IBM Corp.; available from IBM branch offices.

[GG24-3503] *Information Interchange Architecture,* IBM Corp.; available through IBM branch offices. (Figure 16, IBM © 1990, reprinted by permission of IBM.)

[GG24-3552] *IBM OS/2 Extended Edition, Version 1.2 Cookbook: Communications Manager Design and Implementation,* IBM Corp.; available from IBM branch offices. (Figures 19 and 21, IBM © 1990, reprinted with permission of IBM.)

[GH19-6575-1] *X.25 SNA Interconnection, General Information Manual,* IBM Corp.; available through IBM branch offices. (Figure 1.1, IBM © 1988, reprinted with permission of IBM.)

[GK21-0104] *NSFnet—The National Science Foundation Computer Network for Research and Education,* IBM Corp.; available from IBM branch offices. (Figure "Nodal Switching System," IBM © 1990, reprinted with permission of IBM.)

[Goldberg91] S. H. Goldberg and J. A. Mouton, "A Base for Portable Communications Software," to be published in *IBM Systems Journal.*

[Graph87] *Information Processing Systems—Computer Graphics—Metafile for the Storage and Transfer of Picture Description Information,* ISO 8632 Parts 1–4, International Standards Organization, 1987.

[Gray83] J. P. Gray, P. J. Hansen, P. Homan, M. A. Lerner, and M. Pozefsky, "Advanced Program-to-Program Communication in SNA," *IBM Systems Journal,* vol. 22, no. 4, 1983. (Figures 9 and 10, IBM © 1983, reprinted with permission of IBM.)

[Green87] P. E. Green, R. J. Chappuis, J. D. Fisher, P. S. Frosch, and C. E. Wood, "A Perspective on Advanced Peer-to-Peer Networking," *IBM Systems Journal,* vol. 26, no. 4, 1987, pp. 414–427.

[Hakeda90] Y. Hakeda, "The Image Object Content Architecture," *IBM Systems Journal*, vol. 29, no. 3, 1990, pp. 333–342.

[Hanss90] Ted Hanss, "Institutional File System Overview," draft copy of paper dated July 11, 1990.

[Hehmann90] Dietmar B. Hehmann, Michael G. Salmony, and Heinrich J. Stuttgen, "Transport Services for Multimedia Applications on Broadband Networks," *Computer Communications*, vol. 13, no. 4, May 1990.

[Hemrick88] C. F. Hemrick, R. W. Klessig, and J. M. McRoberts, "Switched Multi-Megabit Data Service and Early Availability Via MAN Technology," *IEEE Communications Magazine*, vol. 26, no. 4, April 1988, pp. 9–14.

[Hemrick88b] *Loc. cit.*

[Hiles89] W. Hiles, D. Marlow, and J. McDearman, "A Systematic Method for the Selection of a Transport Level Protocol," *Proceedings of the 1989 IEEE Southeastcon*, pp. 709–712.

[HiPPI90] *High-Performance Parallel Interface Framing Protocol*, working draft, American National Standard for Information Systems, *X3T9/89-146, X3T9. 3/89-013*, February 15, 1990.

[HLMa] *IBM/3Com Heterogeneous LAN Mangement Architecture Reference*, IBM Corp.; December 3, 1990; available from IBM, Dept. C13/B002, P. O. Box 12195, Research Triangle Park, N.C.

[HLMb] *IBM/3Com Heterogeneous LAN Management Application Program Interface Technical Reference*, IBM Corp.; December 3, 1990; available from IBM, Dept. C13/B002, P. O. Box 12195, Research Triangle Park, N.C.

[Hunter89] P. Hunter, "Bridging the LAN Gap," *Communications Management*, July 1989, pp. 42–44.

[I. 122,88] "Framework for Providing Additional Packet Mode Bearer Services," ISDN General Structure and Service Capabilities, CCITT Recommendation I. 122, vol. III, fascicle III. 7, International Telephone and Telegraph Consultative Committee, 1988.

[IS 8649] *Association Control Service Element*, IS 8649, International Standards Organization.

[ISO 8650] *Protocol Specification for Association Control*, IS 8650, International Standards Organization.

[ISO 7809] *Information Processing Systems—Data Communication—High-level Data Link Control Procedures—Consolidation of Classes of Procedures*, ISO 7809, International Standards Organization.

[ISO 8648] *Information Processing Systems—Open Systems Interconnection—Internal Organization of the Network Layer*, ISO 8648, International Standards Organization.

[ISO 8824] *Information Processing Systems—Open Systems Interconnection—Specification of Abstract Syntax Notation One (ASN. 1)*, ISO 8824, International Standards Organization, 1987.

[ISO 8825] *Information Processing Systems—Basic Encoding Rules for Abstract Syntax Notation One (ASN. 1)*, ISO 8825, International Standards Organization, 1987.

[ISO 9541-1] *1991 Information Technology—Font Information Interchange: Architecture*, ISO/IEC 9541-1, International Standards Organization.

[ISO 9541-2] *1991 Information Technology—Font Information Interchange: Interchange Formats*, ISO/IEC 9541-2, International Standards Organization.

[ISO 9542] *Information Processing Systems—Telecommunications and Information Exchange Between Systems—End System to Intermediate System Routing Exchange Protocol for Use in*

Conjunction with the Protocol for Providing the Connectionless-Mode Network Service (ISO 8473) ISO 9542, International Standards Organization.

[ISO 9575] *OSI Routing Framework—Type 3*, ISO/IEC DTR 9575, International Standards Organization, April 18, 1988.

[ISO 10589] ISO/IEC DIS 10589, International Standards Organization, October 24, 1990, p. 5.

[ISO 10030] *Information Processing Systems—Data Communications—End System Routing Information Exchange Protocol for Use in Conjunction with ISO 8878*, ISO DIS 10030, International Standards Organization, July 1989.

[Jaffe86] J. M. Jaffe, A. E. Baratz, and A. Segall, "Design Issues in the Implementation of Distributed Dynamic Routing Algorithms," *Computer Networks and ISDN Systems,* vol. 12, no. 3, 1986, pp. 147–158.

[Janson90] P. Janson, R. Molva and S. Zatti, "Security in Open Networks and Distributed Systems," IBM Internal Report.

[Janson91] P. Janson, R. Molva, and S. Zatti, "Architectural Directions for Opening IBM Networks: The Case of OSI," IBM research report RZ2131; available from IBM branch offices. (Figure 12, IBM © 1991, reprinted with permission.)

[Jerves89] Wayne Jerves, "Network Management," *Interface,* IBM Raleigh, January 1989.

[Johannsen88] W. Johannsen, W. Lamersdorf, and K. Reinhardt, "Architecture and Design of an Open Systems LAN/WAN Gateway," *IEEE Computing Society, Proceedings of the Computer Network Symposium,* 1988, pp. 112–119.

[Juenzel89] James Juenzel, Anand Parikh, and James Marsh, "FDDI Dual Ring of Trees Topology," *Telecommunications,* October 1989, pp. 75–78.

[Kosiur90] Dave Kosiur, "Corporate Connectivity Gets Macs off SNA Sideline," *Data Communications,* August 1990, pp. 101–106.

[Kwashita86] K. Kwashita et al., *Electronics Letters,* vol. 22, 1986, p. 79.

[LANTech89] "Standard Lets NetBIOS Applications Run Over OSI Protocols," *LAN Technology,* December 1989, p. 10.

[Le] My T. Le and Russ Pretty, "The IEEE P802. 6 Metropolitan Area Network Distributed-Queue, Dual-Bus Protocol," *Communications Standards Management,* New York: Auerbach Publishers. 1990. (Adaptation of Exhibit 17, © 1990 Warren, Gorham, & Lamont, Inc., used with permission.)

[Leet89] Jim Leet and Mike Errico, "Network Asset Management," *Interface,* April 1989, GG23-0002, IBM Corp.; available through IBM branch offices.

[Lippis90] Nick Lippis, "Frame Relay Redraws the Map for Wide-area Networks," *Data Communications,* July 1990, pp. 80–94.

[Littlewood89] M. Littlewood, "Metropolitan Area Networks and Broadband ISDN: A Perspective," *Telecommunication Journal of Australia,* vol. 39, no. 2, 1989.

[LLana89] Andres Llana Jr., "Inside MCI's Network Management Offering," *Communications in Banking,* vol. 6, no. 9, September, 1989, pp. 16–18.

[LY43-0081] *SNA Network Protocols and Formats* LY43-0081-0, IBM Corp.; available through IBM branch offices. (Figures 3-2, 3-4, and 4.1, IBM © 1988, reproduced by permission of IBM.)

[Malamud89] Carl Malamud, *DEC Networks and Architectures.* New York: Intertext Publications/ Multiscience Press, Inc., 1989.

[Materna89] Bogdan Materna, Brian J. N. Vaughan, and Charles W. Britney, "Evolution from LAN and MAN Access Networks Towards the Integrated ATM Network," *Conference Record, IEEE Global Telecommunications Conference and Exhibition*, vol. 3, pp. 1455–1461, Dallas, Texas, November 27–30, 1989.

[Matsubara89] M. Matsubara, "Evolution of CCITT Numbering Plans and Network Interworking," *Computer Networks and ISDN Systems*, vol. 17, 1989, pp 47–57.

[Mazzafero90] John F. Mazzafero, "An Overview of FDDI," *Communications Standards Management*, New York: Auerbach Publishers, 1990.

[McGurrin88] Michael F. McGurrin, "Religious Wars: A Defense of the Connection-Oriented Network Service Heresy," *Proceedings Interface '88*, Chicago, March 1988, pp. 306–313.

[McQuillan89] John M. McQuillan, "Routers as Building Blocks for Robust Internetworks," *Data Communications*, September 21, 1989, pp 28–33.

[Moore88] R. E. Moore, "Utilizing the SNA Alert in the Management of Multivendor Networks," *IBM Systems Journal*, vol. 27, no. 1, 1988.

[Morris90] H. M. Morris and R. H. Orth,"Image System Communications," *IBM Systems Journal*, vol. 29, no 3, 1990, pp. 371–383.

[Mouton89] J. Mouton, "Open Systems Interconnection Communications Subsystem" *Interface*, January 1989.

[Mueller87] Hans R. Mueller, M. Mehdi Nassehi, Johnny W. Wong, Erwin Zurfluh, Werner Bux, and Pitro Zafiropulo, "DQMA and CRMA: New Access Schemes for Gpbs LANs and MANs," *IBM Research Report RZ 1987*, September 6, 1989.

[Needham78] R. M. Needham and M. D. Schroeder, "Using Encryption for Authentication in Large Networks of Computers," *Communications of the ACM*, vol. 21, no. 12, December 1978, pp. 993–999.

[NMF90] OSI/Network Mangement Forum: Forum Architecture, issue 1, January 1990.

[Novell91] *Guide to IBM Interoperability*, Novell, Inc., Provo, Utah, 1991.

[ODA88] *Information Processing—Text and Office Systems—Office Document Architecture (ODA) and Interchange Format*, ISO 8613, International Standards Organization, 1988.

[OSF89] "Distributed Computing Environment," a proposal presented by Hewlett-Packard Co., IBM Corp., Locus Computing Corp., and Transarc Corp., jointly with DEC and Microsoft Corp. to the Open Software Foundation (OSF), October 6, 1989.

[OSFDCE90] "Distributed Computing Environment Rationale," *Open Software Foundation*, Cambridge, Mass., May 14, 1990.

[OSINMF] *OSI/Network Management Forum: Forum Architecture*, issue 1, January 1990, Bernardsville, N.J.

[Patel90] Ahmed Patel and Vincent Ryan, "Introduction to Names, Addresses, and Routes in an OSI Environment," *Computer Communications*, vol. 13, no. 1, January/February 1990, pp. 27–36.

[Perlman84] R. Perlman, "An Algorithm for Distributed Computation of a Spanning Tree in an Extended LAN," Digital Equipment Corp., 1984.

[Phase90] *Netware for VM v2.15, and NetWare for MVS v2.15*, Phaser Systems, Inc., San Francisco.

[Popek85] G. J. Popek, "Heterogeneity," *The LOCUS Distributed System Architecture*, pp. 98–105. The MIT Press, Cambridge, Mass.: MIT Press, 1985.

[Pr802,89] *Project 802—Local and Metropolitan Area Networks, Proposed Standard: Distributed Queue Dual Bus (DQDB) Metropolitan Area Network (MAN)*, unapproved draft, June 23, 1989, *IEEE*. (Figures 2.1 and 2.2, © 1989 IEEE, reprinted with permission of IEEE.)

[Q. 931,88] *ISDN User-Network Interface Layer 3 Specifications for Basic Call Control*, CCITT Recommendation Q.931 (I.451), *CCITT Blue Book*, International Telephone and Telegraph Consultative Committee, 1988.

[Reinhold] Alan Reinhold, *Communications Systems Bulletin, TCP/IP*, GG22 9125, IBM Corp.; available from IBM branch offices. (Figures on pp. 21, 63, 65, 73, and 89, IBM © 1988, reprinted by permission of IBM.)

[Reinhold91] Alan Reinhold and Erik Burgdorf, Charlie Cobleigh, and Raymond Kressmann, *TCP/IP*, GG22-9125-02, IBM Corp.; available through IBM branch offices.

[Reinsch88] R. Reinsch, "Distributed Database for SAA," *IBM Systems Journal*, vol. 27, no. 3, 1988, pp. 362–369.

[RFC768] *User Datagram Protocol*, DARPA RFC 768, Defense Advanced Research Projects Agency, Arlington, Va.

[RFC791] *Internet Protocol*, DARPA RFC 791, Defense Advanced Research Projects Agency, Arlington, Va.

[RFC792] *Internet Control Message Protocol*, DARPA RFC 792, Defense Advanced Research Projects Agency, Arlington, Va.

[RFC793] *Transmission Control Protocol*, DARPA RFC 793, Defense Advanced Research Projects Agency, Arlington, Va.

[RFC829] *Address Resolution Protocol (ARP)*, DARPA RFC 829, Defense Advanced Research Projects Agency, Arlington, Va.

[RFC901] *Exterior Gateway Protocol (EGP)*, with precedence rules defined in RFC 911, DARPA RFC 901, Defense Advanced Research Projects Agency, Arlington, Va.

[RFC1058] *Routing Information Protocol (RIP) with RIP Extensions*, DARPA RFC 1058, Defense Advanced Research Projects Agency, Arlington, Va.

[RFC1171] *The Point-to-Point Protocol for the Transmission of Multi-protocol Datagrams over Point-to-Point Links*, DARPA RFC 1171, Defense Advanced Research Program Agency, Arlington, Va.

[RFC1172] *The Point-to-Point Protocol (PPP) Initial Configuration Options*, DARPA RFC 1172, Defense Advanced Research Program Agency, Arlington, Va.

[Richter89] N. Richter, "Transport Interfaces in SINIX Systems," *Proceedings of the Spring European UNIX Systems User Group (EUUG) Conference*, 1989, pp. 95–102.

[Rose90] Marshall T. Rose, "Transition and Coexistence Strategies for TCP/IP to OSI," *IEEE Journal on Selected Areas in Communications*, vol. 8, no. 1, January 1990. (Figure 8, © 1990 IEEE, reprinted by permission of IEEE.)

[Ross87] Floyd E. Ross, "FDDI—An Overview," *IEEE CH2409*, January 1987.

[Ross89] Floyd E. Ross, "An Overview of FDDI: The Fiber Distributed Data Interface," *IEEE Journal on Selected Areas in Communications*, vol. 7, no. 7, September 1989.

[S84-0086] *IBM Operating System/2 Local Area Network Server, User's Reference*; IBM Corp.; available from IBM branch offices.

[Saltzer81] J. H. Saltzer, D. P. Reed, and D. D. Clark, "Source Routing for Campus-Wide Internet Transport," *Local Networks for Computer Communications*, New York: North Holland Publishing Company, 1981, pp. 1–23.

[Satyanar90] Mahadev Satyanarayanan, "Scalable, Secure, and Highly Available Distributed File Access," *IEEE Computer*, May 1990, pp. 9–21.

[Savage91] Patric Savage, "Impact of HPPI and Fibre Channel Standard on Data Delivery," *Digest of Papers—Tenth IEEE Symposium on Mass Storage Systems*, IEEE Service Center, Piscataway, N.J., pp. 186–187.

[SC26-4399] *Common Programming Interface Communications Reference*, IBM Corp.; available through IBM branch offices. (Table 2, Figure 3, and Figure 4, IBM © 1988, reprinted by permission of IBM.)

[SC30-3084] *SNA Transaction Programmer's Reference Manual for LU type 6. 2*, GC30-3084, IBM Corp.; available through IBM branch offices.

[SC30-3269] *SNA Format and Protocol Reference Manual: Architecture Logic for LU Type 6. 2*, SC30-3269, IBM Corp.; available through IBM branch offices.

[SC30-3346] *SNA Format and Protocol Reference Manual: Management Services*, IBM Corp., available through IBM branch offices.

[SC30-3422] *Systems Network Architecture Format and Protocol Reference Manual Architecture Logic for Type 2. 1 Nodes,* IBM Corp., December 1986; available through IBM branch offices.

[SC31-6808] *SNA LU 6. 2 Reference: Peer Protocols*, available from IBM branch offices. (Figures 2-5, 5.3-3, and 5.3-12, IBM © 1988 and 1990, reprinted with permission of IBM.)

[Seifert88]. William M. Seifert, "Bridges and Routers," *IEEE Network*, vol. 2, no. 1, January 1988, pp. 57–64.

[SGML86] *Information Processing—Text and Office Systems—Standard Generalized Markup Language (SGML)*, ISO 8879, International Standards Organization, 1986.

[SH21-0438]. *Data Interpretation System Communications Services*, SH21-0438, IBM Corp.; available from IBM branch offices. (Figures 1–2 and 1–10, IBM © 1989, reprinted with permission of IBM.)

[Simpson90] David Simpson, "TCP/IP-OSI 5 Routes to Coexistence," *Systems Integration*, April 1990.

[SL23-0191] *MVS and VM OSI/Communiations Subsystem Programming Concepts and Guide*, IBM Corp.; available through IBM branch offices.

[SNAPersp90] *SNA Perspectives*, vol. 11, no. 1, January 1990, pp. 11–15.

[SoftSwitch] "Soft.Switch Product Overview," *Soft. Switch*, Wayne, Pa. (Figure in centerfold reproduced with permission of Soft.Switch.)

[Stallings89] William Stallings, "Internetworking: A Guide for the Perplexed," *Telecommunications*, September, 1989, pp. 25–30.

[Starkovich91] *IBM/Novell Local Area Networking Interoperability*, IBM National Distribution Division, Boca Raton, Fla., March 1991.

[Steiner88] Jennifer G. Steiner and Daniel E. Geer, Jr., "Network Services in the Athena Environment," *Proceedings of the August 1988 EUUG Conference*, 1988, pp. 63–72.

[Summers89] R. C. Summers, "Local-Area Distributed Systems," *IBM Systems Journal,* vol. 28, no. 2, 1989.

[Svobodova90] L. Svobodova, P. Janson, and E. Mumprecht, "Heterogeneity and OSI," *IEEE Journal on Selected Areas in Communications*, vol. 8, no. 1, January 1990, pp. 67–79. (Figures 2, 3, 4, © 1990 IEEE, reprinted by permission of IEEE.)

[Taber89] Dave Taber, "Alert Focal-Point," *Interface,* April 1989, GG23-0002; available through IBM branch offices.

[Thomas89] Stephen A. Thomas, "The NetBIOS Interface," *Communications Standards Management*, section 63-20-30, New York: Auerbach Publishers, 1989.

[Thurber89] Kenneth J. Thurber, "Getting a Handle on FDDI," *Data Communications*, June 21, 1989, pp. 28, 30, 32.

[Tolly90] Kevin Tolly, "IBM Liberates Coax-Attached PCs," *Data Communications*, July 1990, pp. 115–122.

[Tolmie89] Don Tolmie, "The High-Speed Channel (HSC) and Ultra-High-Speed Networks," *Proceedings, Broadband FOC/LAN '89*, the First Broadband Networks Exposition, and the Thirteenth Fiber Communications and Local Area Networks Exposition, 1989, pp. 421–426.

[Tucker88] R. S. Tucker et al., "16 Gbit/s Optical Time-Division Multiplexed Transmission System Experiments," *Optical Fiber Conference '88 (OFC)*, New Orleans, La, January 25–28, 1988.

[Vig89] Deepak Vig, "Local Area Network (LAN) Management," *Interface*, March 1989, GG23-0001, available through IBM branch offices.

[Vorster88] J. Vorstermans and A. Vieeschouwer, "Layered ATM Systems and Architectural Concepts for Subscribers' Premises Networks," *IEEE Journal on Selected Areas in Communications*, vol. SAC-6, no. 9, December 1988, pp. 1545–1555.8

[Willett88] Michael Willett and Ronald Martin, "LAN Management in an IBM Framework," *IEEE Network*, vol. 2, no. 2, March 1988.

[X.121] "International Numbering Plan for Public Data Networks," CCITT Revised Recommendation X. 121, International Telephone and Telegraph Consultative Committee, 1988.

[X.213] Section A.8.4. *Maximum Network Address Length*, CCITT AP IX 52-E Annex A to Recommendation X. 213, International Telephone and Telegraph Consultative Committee.

[X/Open] *X/Open Portability Guide*, issue 3, volume 7, Transport Interface.

[Yemini89] Yemini et al., "Concert: A High-Level Approach to Heterogeneous Distributed Systems," *Proceedings of the 9th International Conference on Distributed Computer Systems*, Newport Beach, Calif., June 1989.

[Zafiropulo90] Pitro Zafiropulo, "On LANs and MANs: An Evolution from Mbit/s to Gbit/s," EFOC/LAN 90, *Proceedings, Eighth European Fibre Optic Communication and Local Area Networks Exposition*, Munich, June 27–29 1990, pp. 15–22.

[Zatti88a] Stefano Zatti and Philippe Janson, "Interconnecting OSI and Non-OSI Networks Using an Integrated Directory Service," *North Holland Computer Networks and ISDN Systems*, vol. 15, North Holland Publ. Co., New York, pp. 269–283, 1988.

[Zatti88b] *Loc. cit.*

[Ziegler91] Kurt Ziegler, Jr., *Distributed Computing and the Mainframe*. New York: John Wiley, 1991.

[Ziegler91a] *Loc. cit.*, p. 246.

General References

Advanced Function Printing Software Data Stream Reference, SH35-0073, IBM Corp., 1988; available through IBM branch offices.

Ahuja, V., "Common Communications Support in Systems Application Architecture," *IBM Systems Journal*, vol. 27, no. 3, 1988, pp. 264-280.

Backes, Floyd, "Transparent Bridges for Interconnection of IEEE 802 LANs," *IEEE Network*, vol. 2, no. 1, January, 1988.

Baratz, A. E., J. P. Gray, P. E. Green, J. M. Jaffe, and D. P. Pozefsky, "SNA Networks of Small Systems," *IEEE Journal of Selected Areas in Communications,* vol. SAC-3, no. 3, May 1985, pp. 416–426.

Bellcore Technical Advisory, TA-TSY-000772 and TA-TSY-000773, Bellcore Communications Research, Inc., Morristown, N.J.

Benjamin, J. H., M. L. Hess, R. A.Weingarten, and W. R.Wheeler, "Interconnecting SNA Networks," *IBM Systems Journal,* vol. 22, no. 4, 1983, pp. 344–366.

Bernsten, J. A., J. R. Davin, D. A. Pitt, and N. G. Sullivan, "MAC Layer Interconnection of IEEE 802 Local Area Networks," *Computer Networks ISDN Systems*, vol. 10, no. 5, December 1985, pp. 259–273.

Bux, W., and D. Grillo, "Flow Control in Local Area Networks of Interconnected Token Rings," *IEEE Transactions in Communications,* vol. COM-33, no. 10, October 1985, pp. 1058–1066.

Cherukuri, Rao J., and Jeffrey Derby, "Frame Relay: Protocols and Private Network Applications," *IEEE Infocom '89, Proceedings of 8th Annual IEEE Computer and Communications Societies*, vol. 2, April 1989, pp. 676–675.

Codes for the Representation of Names of Countries, ISO IS 3166, International Standards Organization, 1981.

Comer, Douglas, *Internetworking with TCP/IP*. Englewood Cliffs, N.J.: Prentice Hall, 1988.

Communications Standards Management. New York, Auerbach Publishers, 1990.

Cypser, R. J. *Communications Architecture for Distributed Systems.* Reading, Mass.: Addison-Wesley Publ. Co., 1978.

Deaton, G. A., "Flow Control in Packet-Switched Networks with Explicit Path Routing," *Proceedings of the Flow Control in Computer Networks Conference*, Paris, France, February 1979.

Deaton, G. A. Jr., and R. O. Hippert, Jr., "X.25 and Related Recommendations in IBM Products," *IBM Systems Journal*, vol. 22, nos. 1, 2, 1983, pp. 11–29.

Document Composition Facility, Introduction to the Generalized Markup Language: Using the Starter Set, SH20-9186, IBM Corp., 1980; available through IBM branch offices.

Document Content Architecture: Revisable-Form-Text Reference, SC23-0758, IBM Corp.; available through IBM branch offices.

Document Interchange Architecture: Concepts and Structures, SC23-0759, IBM Corp.; available through IBM branch offices.

Domain Specific Part of Network Layer Addresses, ECMA 117, European Manufacturers Association (ECMA), Geneva, Switzerland, 1986.

DTE/DCE Interface Description, GH19-6576, IBM Corp.; available through IBM branch offices.

Encoding of NSAP Addresses in Network Layer Protocols, ISO/TC97/SC6/WG2 N10, International Standards Organization, June 1985.

End-System to Intermediate-System Routing Exchange Protocol for Use in Conjunction with ISO 8473, ISO 9542, International Standards Organization, 1987.

Format and Protocol Reference Manual: Architecture Logic for Type 2.1 Nodes, SC30-3422, IBM Corp.; available through IBM branch offices.

Franccois, P., and A. Potocki, "Some Methods for Providing OSI Transport in SNA," *Journal of Research and Development*, vol. 27, no. 5, September 1983, pp. 452–463.

Franklin, S., and T. Peters, "Graphical Interface Services for Application Integration," *Graphics Interface '89 Proceedings*, Canadian Information Processing Society and Canadian Man-Computer Communications Society, June 1989, pp. 105–112.

Gerla, M., and L. Kleinrock, "Congestion Control in Interconnected LANs," *IEEE Network*, vol. COM-2, no. 1, January 1988, pp. 72–78.

Gerla, M., and L. Kleinrock, "Flow Control: A Comparative Survey," *IEEE Transactions on Communications*, vol. COM-28, April 1980, pp. 553–574.

Gray, J. P., and T. B. McNeill, "SNA Multiple System Networking," *IBM Systems Journal*, vol. 18, no. 2, 1979, pp. 263–297.

Gray, J. P., P. J. Hansen, P. Homan, M. A. Lerner, and M. Pozefsky, "Advanced Program-to-Program Communication in SNA," *IBM Systems Journal*, vol. 22, no. 4, 1983, pp. 298–318.

Green, P. E., and R. J. Chappuis, J. D. Fisher, P. S. Frosch, and C. E. Wood, "A Perspective on Advanced Peer-to-Peer Networking," *IBM Systems Journal*, vol. 26, no. 4, 1987, pp. 414–428.

IBM 3270 Information Display System Data Stream, GA23-0059, IBM Corp., 1986; available through IBM branch offices.

IBM Implementation of X.21 Interface—General Information Manual, GA27-3287-2; IBM Corp., February 1986; available through IBM branch offices.

IBM Systems Journal, vol. 27, no. 1, 1988. Special issue on Network Management.

IBM Systems Journal, vol. 27, no. 3, 1988. Special issue on SAA.

Information Processing Systems—Open Systems Interconnection—Distributed Transaction Processing, Parts 1, 2, 3, ISO TC97/SC21 N2272, International Standards Organization, September 1988.

Integrating X.25 Function into SNA Networks, GG24-3052; IBM Corporation, March 1988; available through IBM branch offices.

Intelligent Printer Data Stream, S544-3714, IBM Corp., August 1987; available through IBM branch offices.

IPDS Architecture Reference Manual, S544-3417, IBM Corp.; available through IBM branch offices.

Kanyuh, D., "An Integrated Network Management Product," *IBM Systems Journal*, vol. 27, no. 1, 1988, pp. 45–59.

Maxemchuk, Nicholas F., and Magda El Zarki, "Routing and Flow Control in High-Speed Wide Area Networks," *Proceedings of the IEEE*, vol. 78, no. 1, January 1990.

"Metropolitan Area Network Generic Framework Systems Requirements in Support of Switched Multi-Megabit Data Service," *Technical Advisory TA-TSY-000772*, Bell Communications Research, Inc., Morristown, N.J, issue 1, February 1988.

Moore, R. E., "Problem Detection, Isolation, and Notification in Systems Network Architecture," *Proceedings of IEEE Infocom '86*. Miami, Fla., April 1986, pp. 377–381.

NETBIOS Application Development Guide, SG8X-2270-00, IBM Corp., July 1987; available through IBM branch offices.

NPSI (X.25 NCP Packet Switching Interface) General Information, version 3, GC30-3469-02, IBM Corp., December 1989; available through IBM branch offices.

Overview of Advanced Peer-to-Peer Networking, GC38-7026, IBM Corp.; available through IBM branch offices.

Pitt, D. A., and F. Farzaneh, "Topologies and Routing for Bridged Local Area Networks," *Proceedings of IEEE Infocom '86*, Miami, Florida, April 1986.

Pitt, D. A., and J. L. Winkler, "Table-Free Bridging," *IEEE Journal on Selected Areas of Communications*, vol. SAC-5, no. 9, December 1987, pp. 1454–1462.

Pozefsky, Diane, and Daniel A. Pitt, and James P. Gray, "IBM's Systems Network Architecture," *Computer Network Architectures and Protocols*, 2 ed., edited by Carl A. Sunshine, New York: Plenum Publishing Corp., 1989.

Rudin, H., and H. Muller, "On Routing and Flow Control," *Proceedings of the Flow Control in Computer Networks Conference*, Paris, France, February 1979.

Rutledge, J. H. "OSI and SNA: A Perspective," *Journal of Telecommunication Networks,* 1982, pp. 13–27.

Schick, T., and R. F. Brockish, "The Document Interchange Architecture: A Member of a Family of Architectures in the SNA Environment," *IBM Systems Journal*, vol. 21, no. 2, 1982, pp. 220–244.

SNA Format and Protocol Reference Manual: Architecture Logic for Type 2.1 Nodes, SC30-3422, IBM Corp.; 1988, available through IBM branch offices.

SNA Technical Overview, GC30-3073, IBM Corp., 1991, available from IBM branch offices.

SNA Transaction Programmer's Reference Manual for LU type 6.2, GC30-3084-03, IBM Corp.; September 1990; available from IBM branch offices.

Soha, Michael, and Radia Perlman, "Comparison of Two LAN Bridge Approaches," *IEEE Network*, January 1988.

Stallings, W., *Handbook of Computer Communications Standards,* vol 1. New York: Macmillan, 1987.

Sullivan, T. P., "Communications Network Management Enhancements for SNA Networks; An Overview," *IBM Systems Journal*, vol. 22, nos. 1, 2, 1983, pp.129–142.

Sultan, R. A. and P. Kermani, G. A. Grover, T. P. Barzilai, and A. E. Baratz, "Implementing System/36 Advanced Peer-to-Peer Networking," *IBM Systems Journal,* vol. 26, no. 4, 1987, pp. 429–452.

Sundstrom, R. J., and J. B. Staton, G. D. Schultz, M. L. Hess, G. A. Deaton, L. J. Cole, R. M. Amy, "SNA: Current Requirements and Direction," *IBM Systems Journal,* vol. 26, no. 1, 1987, pp. 13–36.

Svobodova, Liba, "Implementing OSI Systems," *IEEE Journal on Selected Areas in Communications,* vol. 7, no. 7, September 1989.

Sy, K. K., et al., "SNA-OSI Interconnections," *IBM Systems Journal,* vol. 26, no. 2, 1987, pp. 157–173.

System Application Architecture, Common Programming Interface, Communications Reference, SC26-4399-02, IBM Corp., August 1990; available through IBM branch offices.

Systems Application Architecture Common Programming Interface Dialog Reference, SC26-4356, IBM Corp.; available through IBM branch offices.

Systems Application Architecture Common Programming Interface Presentation Reference, SC26-4359, IBM Corp., October 1987; available through IBM branch offices.

Systems Network Architecture—Format and Protocol Reference Manual: Architectural Logic, SC30-3112, IBM Corp.; available through IBM branch offices.

Systems Network Architecture Format and Protocol Reference Manual: Management Services, SC23-0757, IBM Corp., March 1986; available through IBM branch offices.

Systems Network Architecture Formats, GA27-3136, IBM Corp.; available through IBM branch offices.

Systems Network Architecture, Technical Overview, GC30-3073, IBM Corp., 1991; available through IBM branch offices.

TCP/IP Domain Names—Concepts and Facilities, RFC 1034, November 1987.

TCP/IP Tutorial and Technical Overview, GG24-3376-01, IBM Corp., July 1990; available through IBM branch offices.

Token-Ring Access Method and Physical Layer Specifications, ANSI/IEEE Standard 802.5, 1985.

Token-Ring Network Architecture Reference, SC30-3374, IBM Corp.; available through IBM branch offices.

Wakahama H., et al., "Application of OSI Protocols as Intermediary for DCNA-SNA Network Interconnection," *Proceedings of the Third International Conference on Introduction of OSI Standards,* Cambridge, England, September1985, pp. 312–344.

The X.25 1984 Interface for Attaching SNA Nodes to Packet Switched Data Networks - General Information Manual, GA27-3761-0; IBM Corporation; Nov., 1986; available through IBM branch offices.

X.25 1984/1988 DTE/DCE and DTE/DTE—General Information Manual, GA27-3761, IBM Corp.; available through IBM branch offices.

X.25 1984/1988 DTE/DCE and DTE/DTE Interfaces—Architecture Reference, SC30-3409, IBM Corp.; available through IBM branch offices.

X.25 1984/1988 DTE/DCE and DTE/DTE Interfaces—General Information Manual, GA27-3761, IBM Corp.; available through IBM branch offices.

X.25 SNA Guide, GG24-1568; IBM Corp., July 1987; available through IBM branch offices.

X.25 SNA Interconnection—General Information Manual, GH19-6575-1; IBM Corp.; available through IBM branch offices.

X.25 SNA Network Supervisory Function, GH11-3033, IBM Corp.; available through IBM branch offices.

X.25-SNA Interconnection (XI), G511-1087-00, IBM Corp.; January 1988; available through IBM branch offices.

Zafiropulo, Pitro, "On LANs and MANs: An Evolution from Mbit/s to Gbit/s," *Proceedings of the Eighth European Fibre Optic Communication and Local Area Networks Exposition,* 1990, pp. 15–22.

Zatti, S., and Janson, P., "Interconnecting Heterogeneous Networks to OSI with a Global Naming Scheme and Gateway Address Mapping," *Proceedings of the International Zurich Seminar*, March 1988; also IBM Research Report RZ-1651, August 1987.

Zatti, S., and P. Janson, "Internetwork Naming, Addressing, and Directory Systems: Towards a Global OSI Context," *Computer Networks and ISDN Systems,* vol. 15, 1988, pp. 269–283.

Communications Standards

OSI REFERENCE MODEL

ISO 6523	Data Interchange—Structure for the Identification of Organizations
ISO 7498	Open Systems Interconnections (OSI) Basic Reference Model
ISO 7498-1	Connectionless Model
ISO 7498-2	Security Architecture
ISO 7498-3	Naming and Addressing
ISO 7498-4	Management Framework

APPLICATION LAYER

ISO 8571	File Transfer and Management
ISO 8649	Service Definition for the Association Control Service Element (ACSE)
ISO 8649-1	Peer Entity Authentication during Association Establishment
ISO 8649-2	Connectionless Mode ACSE Service
ISO 8650	Protocol specification for the ACSE
ISO 8832	Job Transfer and Manipulation
ISO 9040, 9041	Virtual Terminal Protocol
ISO 9072	Remote Operations Service Element
ISO 9595	Common Management Information Service Element
ISO 9596	Common Management Information Protocol Specification
ISO 10040	System Management Overview

ISO 10164-1	Systems Management, Part 1, Object Management Function
ISO 10165-2	Structure of Management Information, Part 2, Definitions of Support Objects
X.400–X.430	Data Communication Networks, Message Handling Systems, *CCITT Red Book vol. VIII–fascicle VIII.7*, 1984
X.400–X.420	Data Communication Networks, Message Handling Systems, *CCITT Blue Book vol. VIII–fascicle VIII.7*, 1988
X.500–X.521	Data Communication Networks—Directory, *CCITT Blue Book vol. VIII–fascicle VIII.8*, 1989

PRESENTATION LAYER

ISO 8822	Connection-Oriented Presentation Service Definition
ISO 8823	Connection-Oriented Presentation Protocol Specification
ISO 8824	Specification of Abstract Syntax Notation One (ASN.1)
ISO 8825	Specification of Basic Encoding Rules for ASN.1

SESSION LAYER

ISO 8326	Basic Connection-Oriented Session Service Definition
ISO 8327	Basic Connection-Oriented Session Protocol Specification

TRANSPORT LAYER

ISO 8072	Transport Service Definition
ISO 8072/Add 1	Connectionless Mode Transmission
ISO 8073	Connection-Oriented Transport Protocol Specification
ISO 8073/Add 2	Operation of Class 4 over Connectionless Network Service
ISO 8602	Protocol for Providing the Connectionless Mode Transport Service

NETWORK LAYER

ISO 8208	X.25 Packet Level Protocol for Data Terminal Equipment
ISO 8348	Network Service Definitions
ISO 8348-1	Connectionless Mode Transmission

ISO 8348-2	Network Layer Addressing
ISO 8473	Protocol for Providing Connectionless Mode Network Service
ISO 8648	Internal Organization of the Network Layer
ISO 8878	Use of X.25 to Provide Connection Oriented Services
ISO 8881	Use of X.25 Packet Level Protocol in Local Area Networks

DATA LINK CONTROL LAYER

IEEE 802.2	Local Area Network (LAN) Logical-Link Control
IEEE 802.3	CSMA/CD LAN Protocol
IEEE 802.4	Token-Bus LAN Protocol
IEEE 802.5	Token-Ring LAN Protocol
IEEE 802.6	Metropolitan Area Network Protocol
ISO 3309	High-level Data Link Control Procedures Frame Structure
ISO 4335	High-level Data Link Control Procedures Consolidation of Elements of Procedures
ISO 7776	CCITT X.25 LAP-B Procedures
ISO 7809	High-level Data Link Control Procedures Consolidation of Classes of Procedures
ISO 8802	LANs, Part 2, Logical-Link Control
ISO 9542	Connectionless End-System–Intermediate-System (ES-IS) Routing Exchange Protocol
ISO 10030	Connection-Oriented ES-IS
ISO 9314-1	FDDI Token Ring Physical Layer Protocol
ISO 9314-2	FDDI Token Ring Media Access Control
ISO 9314-3	Physical Layer Medium Dependent
DP ANS ASC X3T9.5–6.2	FDDI Token Ring Station Management

ADDRESSES OF STANDARDS ORGANIZATIONS

American National Standards Institute (ANSI)
1430 Broadway
New York, NY 10018

Institute of Electrical and Electronic Engineers (IEEE)
IEEE Service Center
445 Hoes Ln
P.O. Box 1331
Piscataway, NJ 08855

International Standards Organization (ISO)
1 Rue de Varembe
Case Postale 56
CH-1211 Geneva 20
Switzerland

International Telephone and Telegraph Consultative Committee (CCITT)
2 Rue Varembe
CH 1211 Geneva 20
Switzerland

Open Software Foundation (OSF)
11 Cambridge Center
Cambridge, MA 02142

U. S. Government OSI Profile (US GOSIP)
The U. S. Government's OSI Advanced Requirements Group
National Institute of Standards and Technology
Gaithersburg, MD 20899

Index

Abstract syntax   283
Access authorization   110
Access-link   341, 413, 514
Accounting   108
ACSE   74, 271
Active monitor   541
Activity   293
Adaptive pacing   469
Address   250, 342
  format indicator   344
  resolution protocols   517
Advanced Interactive Executive; *see* AIX
Advanced Peer-to-Peer Networking; *see* APPN
AE-address   358
AFI   344
Agent   97
AIX   12
Andrew   151
APPC   309
APPC Host Gateway   562
APPC/MVS   321
AppleTalk   647
Application association   270
Application context   272
Application_entity_title   251, 295
Application-layer directory   458
Application Managers   168
Application-services   8, 25, 34
APPN   267, 276

connection network   468
end-node   447
routing   467
OSI integrated nodes   471
subarea connections   490, 496
ASCII conversions   667
ASN.1   283
Association   73, 270, 295
Association Control Service Element; *see* ACSE
Asynch   663
Asynchronous processing   159
Asynchronous Transfer Mode; *see* ATM
ATM   615
Attach   296
Authentication   109
Authority and Format Identifier; *see* AFI
Automated Network Management Inc.   137
Automated recovery   103
Automatic Network Routing (ANR)   587

Bandwidth managers   591
Base   328
Basic conversations   235
Basic Encoding Rules; *see* BER
Basic-information-unit; *see* BIU
Basic rate   604
Beacon   541
BER   283

Bind   276, 442, 476
BIU   320
Boundary-functions   483
Brackets   290
Bridge   359, 546
    parallel paths   553
Bridge Manager   130
Broadband ISDN   615
Broadcast search   456
Broadcast storms   547
Brouter   360
Byte-oriented, ASCII files   142

Cache   455
CallPath Services   219
Capability data   294
CCITT
    E.163   345
    F.69   345
    I.331   345
    X.121   345
CCR   160, 166
CCS-7   606
Cells   29, 578, 616
CEP   69
Certificates   112
Chains   290, 319
Change management   106
Checkpoint mode   586
CICS   158
Class of network   349
Class of service; see COS
Clients   35
CLNP   403
    (Internet) Addressing   406
    PDU formats   434
Cluster controller   450
Clusters   29
CMIP   100
Coax wiring   566
Collection point   98
Collision detection   544
Command lists   115
Commit   161
Commitment, concurrency, and recovery; see
CCR
Common Communications Support   85

Common Management Information Protocols;
see CMIP
Common Programming Interface; see CPI
Communication architecture independence   17
Communications Manager   673
Compound documents   187
Concurrency   162, 312
Configuration control   104
Confirm   76, 163
Congestion   442, 547
Connection-end-point; see CEP
Connection-oriented   79
Connection-oriented network service   408
Connectionless   79
    network protocol   403
    network service   403
Context management   285
Context restoration   285
Control domain   265
Control point   265, 445
Control point_name   353
Control unit terminal; see CUT
Controlled Access Unit   129
Conversation   231, 295, 315
Conversation_id   359
Conversational communication   233
COS   463
Country code   345
CP-CP sessions   277
CP_name   251, 353
CPI   227
    Resource-Recovery   163
CPI-C program calls   236
Cross-domain   484
Cross-network   486
CSMA/CD   544
CUT   450
Cyclic-groups   585

Data Country Code; see DCC
Data circuit terminating equipment   39
Data exchange   49, 55
Data exchange facilities   27
Data integrity   160
Data-Network Identification Code; see DNIC
Database   143
Datagrams   312

DATE   666
DCC   346
DCE   39
DDM   144
DECnet
    connections   566
    management   136
DECnet-SNA   178
Defining   332
Definite response   289
Definite response chain   290
Dependent-convergence sublayer   373
Destination routing   351
DFT   451
Dialog   233, 295
Digital signature   111
Directory
    Access Protocol   257
    Information Tree   251
    searches   489
    services   454
    System Agent   252
    System Protocol   257
DISOSS   208
Distance vector protocols   352
Distinguished name   253
Distributed Computing Environment; *see* DCE
Distributed Console Access Facility   104
Distributed data   142
Distributed Data Manager; *see* DDM
Distributed File Manager   147
Distributed function terminal; *see* DFT
Distributed processing   31
Distributed Queue Dual Bus; *see* DQDB
Distributed relational database architecture; *see* DRDA
Distributed request   158
Distributed resource managers   141
Distributed transaction processing   159
Distributed Unit of Work   157
Distributed function terminals   450
DNIC   345
Document Content Architecture   187
Document Interchange Architecture   185, 207
Domain naming   250
Domain Specific Part   345
Domain system manager   96
Domains   29

DQDB   593
DRDA   154
DSP formats   346
Dynamic subarea definition   497
Dynamic switched definition   498
Dynamic topology update   459

E.163   345
E.164   345
Early token release   542
EDI   215
EDIFACT   215
Electronic Data Interchange; *see* EDI
Electronic Service Support   136
Emulation   666, 667
EN-NN Protocols   456
Encapsulations   379
Encryption   110
End-of-chain   296
End-nodes   446
Enterprise system connection; *see* ESCON
Enterprise-system-manager   96
Entity   68
Environments   10
ES-IS   520, 523
ESCON   618
Ethernet   544
Exception response   289
    chain   290
Exchange identification; *see* XID
Explicit route   501
Explorer frame   552
Express Transfer Protocol; *see* XTP
Extended Recovery Facility   106
Exterior gateway protocols   381

Fast packet switching   357, 578
Fast select   416
Fault management   101
FDDI   579
FDDI-II   585
Fiber Channel Standard   623
Fiber distributed data interface; *see* FDDI
File Transfer Protocol; *see* FTP
Filestore   148
Financial services   108
Flow control   402

FM headers   291
Font   195
Formatted data   195
FQPCID   443
Fragmentation   424
Frame Relay   357, 578, 613
Frame switching   351, 357
FTAM   148
FTP   175
Fully Qualified Procedure Correlation
Identifier; *see* FQPCID
Function distribution   24
Function management (FM) header   291
Function shipping   159

GATE   665
Gateway   359, 360
GDS-Variables   286
General Data Stream   286
General LU_naming   456, 497
Generic alerts   115
GOSIP   61
Graphics   195

Heterogeneous networks   5
Heterogeneous systems   13
Hierarchical databases   143
HiPPI   622
HubView/PC   133

IBM Information Network; *see* IIN
ICD   346
IDLC   610
IDNX   591
IIA   190
IIN   210, 675
Image   195
Independent-convergence sublayer   373
Independent LU   493
Indication   76
Information Interchange Architecture; *see* IIA
Initial Domain Identifier   345
Initial Protocol Identifier; *see* IPI
Integrated Services Digital Network; *see* ISDN
Intelligent Printer Data Stream; *see* IPDS
Inter-subnetwork
    protocol   369, 370, 403

node   497
router   360, 385
Interactive   31
Interconnect Controller   559
Interface Definition Language   241
Interior gateway protocols   381
Interlink Computer Sciences   136
International Code Designator; *see* ICD
Internet-address   348, 359
Internet (IP) Routing   424
Internet Protocol   84, 423
Interoperability   16
Interpersonal Messaging   203
Interpersonal Messaging System   185
InterWorking unit; *see* IWU
Inventory   108
IP-address   349
IPDS   197
IPI   430
IPX router   382
ISDN   602
ISDNBIOS   605
IWU   360

Label-based routing   350
LAN
    asynchronous connection   668
    data link control   610
    discovery   525
    frame formats   535
    Network Manager   127
    Requester/Server   170, 171
LAN to host connection   557
LAN-to-LAN routers   370
LANACS   668
LAP-D   609
Layer Management Entity; *see* LME
Layers   49
Learning bridges   550
LEN   447
LFSID   467
Lifetime   424
Line changes   498
Link   512
    activations   460
    state protocols   352
    station   512

link/subnetwork-access   340, 509
LLC switch   359
LME   99
Local-Form Session_Identifier; *see* LFSID
Local search   455
Locate   447
Logical channel   412
    group number   412
    number   412
Logical-channel-id   408
Logical connection   49
Logical-link   74, 511
Logical-link control   534
Logical problems   103
Logical records   286
Logical unit of work   161
Logical units   267, 309
Logon filters   496
Looped bus topology   598
Low Entry Networking; *see* LEN
Lower layer routing   356
Lower-layer-services architecture (LSA)   515
    switching boundary   517
LSAPs   535
LU authentication   114
LU_names   251
LU 6.2   311
    verbs   313

MAC address   535
Macro layers   47
Mainframe servers   172
Major synchronization point   292
Major vector   115
MAN   593
Managed objects   117
Management databases   126
Management Information Base; *see* MIB
MAP   61
Map_name   286
Mapped conversations   235
    verbs   314
Mapping   285
Message handling system   199
Message queues   231, 244
Message Transfer Agents   202
Metropolitan Area Network; *see* MAN

MIB   99
Microsoft's LAN Manager   173
Migration to OSI   175
Minor synchronization point   292
Mixed Object Document Content Architecture
Presentation; *see* MODCA/P
MODCA/P   190
Mode name   463
More data bit   413
Multiprotocol backbone   384
Multiprotocol WAN   386
Multivendor systems   5

Name-discovery   520
Naming   172, 249, 250
National Destination Code   346
National language support   147
National Research and Education Network; *see*
NREN
National Science Foundation; *see* NSF
National Specific Number   345
NDR   243
Nearest active upstream neighbor   541
Net_id   251
NetBIOS   426
    and APPC   563
    circuit establishment   643
    commands   436
    flows   437
    LAN-to-LAN   641
    sessions   428
NetView
    Access Services   169
    Distribution Manager   107
    OSI Role   121
    TCP/IP Role   124
NetWare for VM   646
Network
    access units   388, 592
    addresses   343
    administrator   172
    control blocks   428
    data representation; *see* NDR
    databases   143
    independence   229
    interface definition language; *see* NIDL
    layer directory   458

management   89
operations center   135
service underlying primitives   436
supervision function   131
terminal number   345
Network-node   446
Network-node-server   447
Network-qualified LU_name   295
Network-qualified SNA_name   347
NIDL   242
Node types   268
Novell   130
Novell NetWare servers   644
NREN   622
NSAP-address   343
NSAP sizes   394
NSF   131
NSFnet   620

Object classes   253
Object content architecture   187
Object-oriented databases   143
ODA   186, 188
Office Document Architecture; see ODA
OfficeVision   184
ONDS   208
One-way-conversation   312
Open Network Distribution Services; see
ONDS
Open Software Foundation; see OSF
Open Systems Interconnection; see OSI
Open System-Management Architecture   95
Open System Network Architecture; see
OSNA
Operating systems   10
Originator/recipient name   203
OSF   9, 39
OSF remote procedure call   242
OSI   11
    session layer   291
    TP Primitives   246
OSI-SNA addressing   473
OSI-SNA shared resources   332
OSI/Communications Subsystem   325
    Manager   119
OSI/File Services   148
OSI/SNA directory   260
OSNA   10, 13

Packet headers   412
Packet level interface   407
Packet switching networks   408
PARIS   588
Path control   499
PC Support   173
PDU lifetime   404
Peer entities   77
Performance management   107
Peripheral-nodes   353, 483
Permanent virtual circuit; see PVC
Persistent sessions   105
Physical units   266
PNA   659
Port_id   348, 359
Ports   348, 513
Pre-arbitrated   598
Presentation architectures   191
Presentation context   272, 285
Primary rate interface   604
Private-key cryptography   110
Profiles   59, 443
PROFS   208
Programmable Network Access; see PNA
Protected conversation   163
Protected-resource managers   160
Protocol
    boundaries   64
    conversion   361
    converter   663
    data unit   77
    encapsulation   361
    stack selection   428
PS header   287
PSAP   358
    address   358
Public Data Number   345
Public-key cryptography   110
Public/Private internetworking   383
PVC   411

QOS   398, 401
qualifier bit   412
Quality of service; see QOS
Query Manager   158
Queued arbitrated   597

Rate adaption   608

RDA   158
Record access   142
Recovery   402, 416
Reference points   606
Referential integrity   166
Register   447
Relational databases   143
Relative distinguished name   253
Reliability   399
Remote Data Access; *see* RDA
Remote operations   103
Remote Operations Service Element; *see* ROSE
Remote procedure call; *see* RPC
Remote requests   156
Remote search   456
Remote unit of work   157
Repeater   359
Request   76
Request/response unit   78
Requirements   4, 339
    operations   6
Resource control vector   462
Resource managers   36
Resource recovery   159
Response   76
Response time measurements   107
Restricted asynchronous service   585
Resynchronization   165, 293
Revisability   190
REXX   115
RH header   320
Ring poll   541
ROSE   274
Route
    determination   353
    discovery   553
    recording   405
    selection   463, 501
        control vectors   466
Routing   350, 356, 359
    decisions   377
    levels   352
RPC   231, 241

SAA   12
    Delivery Manager   169
SAP   69

Searching   455
Security   109
Segmentation   401, 404, 468
Selectors   69
Servers   35
    styles   321
Service-Access-Point; *see* SAP
Service-interface-mapping   362
Service point   98
Service primitive   75
Session   73, 288, 295
    connectors   467
    cryptography   114
    protocols   288
    services   276
Session_id   359
Shared access facility   468
Signalling   391, 612
Simple Mail Transfer Protocol; *see* SMTP
Simple Network Management Protocols; *see* SNMP
SIP   601
Slots   596
SMAE   100
SMAP   100
SMDS   600
    interface protocol; *see* SIP
SMTP   174
SNA
    gateway   560, 645
    names   254
    Network Link   660
    NSAPs   347
    registry   347
    routing   382
    sessions   288
    transmission headers   476
SNA-X.25 DTE   652
SNA/OSI convergence   19
SNA/OSI integration   40
SNA/X.25 connectivity   649
SNA/X.25 Logical-Link Control   654
SNADS   206
SNARE   523
SNMP   98, 123
SNPA   342
Socket   348, 359
Soft-Switch   210

Software serviceability   104
SONET   575
Source and destination routing   465
Source routing   350, 405
Source-routing bridge   550
Spanning tree protocol   550
Speed planes   28
SPI   430
SQL API   156
SQL relational database   143
SRT bridge   554
SSCP   266
Standards   9
Station manager   128
Stubs   241
Styles of SQL database access   156
Subarea
    addressing   499
    networks   481
    nodes   353, 482
Subnetwork   52
    access protocol   56
    address resolution entity; *see* SNARE
    dependent convergence protocol   56
    independent convergence protocol   56
    interoperability   374
    passthru   372
    points of attachment; *see* SNPA
Subnetwork-access sublayer   373
Subnetwork-address   347
Subsequent Protocol Identifier; *see* SPI
Switched Multi-Megabit Data Service   600
Symbolic_destination_name   251, 295
Sync point   296
Sync-point-manager   160
Synchronization   289, 292
Synchronous Digital Hierarchy   576
Synchronous Optical Network; *see* SONET
Syncpt   164
System Management   89
    APPN SM   135
System management application-process; *see*
SMAP
System Management Application-Service–
Element   100
System manager   96
System structures   25

Systems Management Application–Entity; *see*
SMAE
Systems Services Control Point; *see* SSCP
SystemView   91

T1 resource management   134
Tail vectors   353
Target token-rotation-time (T-TRT)   584
TCP/IP   421
    Address-Resolution Protocol   519
    Addresses   348
    API   421
    client–servers   174
    connectivity   659
    name service   250
Technical and office protocol; *see* TOP
Telephony application-services   219
TELNET   174
Text   194
Tiered systems   37
Time phases   409
Time service   168
Token   292, 538
Token bus   544
Token ring   538
Token ring to ethernet bridge   556
Token-rotation-time   584
TOP   61
Topologies   537
Topology database   461
Topology and route services   459
TP-ASE   273
TPDU Formats   432
Transaction
    processing   32
    programs   312
    routing   159
Transaction-Processing Application-Service–
Element   273
Transfer syntax   282, 284
Transmission control   442
    protocol   421
Transmission group   464, 500, 514
Transmission headers   476
Transmission network monitor   134
Transmission priority   463
Transparency   34

Transparent bridge   550
Transport
    boundary 63
    layer   398
    PDU Types   431
    protocol classes   399
    service addressing   401
    service bridge   365
    service gateways   364
    service primitives   400, 431
Transport-service-providers   18, 47, 339
Two-phase commit   162
Type-4 nodes   482
Type-2 nodes   451, 483
Type-2.1 nodes 446
Typed data   294

Universal address   535
UNIX 12
User Agents   202
User authentication   113

Value added network; *see* VAN
VAN   216, 675
Verbs   311, 313
Virtual circuit   408

Virtual route   501
    pacing   501
Virtual terminal   177
Vital-product-data   108
Voice/data   216
    SM   132

Wild card   456, 497
Workgroups   31
Workstations   672

X Window   425
X.25   407
    Addressing   416
    DCE   655
    Logical Channel   512
    PAD   663
X.400   185, 202
X/Open   419
    Transport Interface; *see* XTI
XI   131, 655
XI function   655
XID   105
XTI   419
XTP   417

Zurich switch   588

A HISTORY OF
RHODESIA

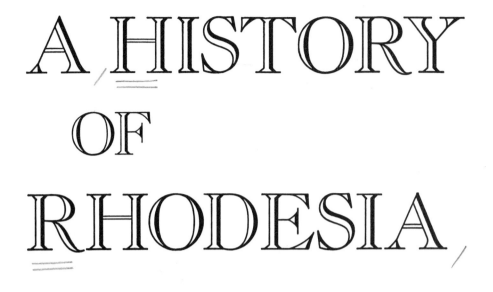

A HISTORY OF RHODESIA

Robert Blake

 Alfred A. Knopf, New York, 1978

THIS IS A BORZOI BOOK
PUBLISHED BY ALFRED A. KNOPF, INC.

Copyright © 1977 by Robert Blake
All rights reserved under International and Pan-American Copyright Conventions.
Published in the United States by Alfred A. Knopf, Inc., New York.
Distributed by Random House, Inc., New York.
Originally published in slightly different form in Great Britain by Eyre Methuen Ltd, London.

Library of Congress Cataloging in Publication Data
Blake, Robert, Baron of Braydeston, [date]
A history of Rhodesia.
Bibliography: p.   Includes index.
1. Rhodesia, Southern—History.   2. Africa, Southern—History.   I. Title.
DT962.5.B55   1978   968.9'1   77—20363
ISBN 0—394—48068—6

Manufactured in the United States of America
First American Edition

To Letitia

Contents

ACKNOWLEDGEMENTS   xv

INTRODUCTION   xvii

CHRONOLOGY   xxi

MAPS   xxiii

Part 1: The Chartered Company

1   THE LAND AND THE EARLY CONQUERORS
5000 BC—AD 1700

    3

The British occupation in perspective – The land and climate – Victoria Falls – Bushmen's paintings – The Great Zimbabwe – Rhodes's grave – The Bantu – The Monomatapa and the Changamire – Arrival and expulsion of the Portuguese.

2   THE NDEBELE KINGDOM 1700–1886   14

Rozwi rule – The Zulu explosion – The Ndebele move north – Clash with Boers – Their origin and character – British policy in Cape Colony – Mzilikazi in Bulawayo – The Moffat Mission – White hunters – Lobengula, a Dark Age monarch – Gold in 'Zambesia' – Diamonds in Kimberley – The Patterson affair – The 'Voortrekker'.

3   CECIL RHODES 1853–89   29

Confederation in South Africa – 'Colonialism' v. the 'imperial factor' – Foreign rivalries – Gold on the Rand – Rhodes – His early life – His health – Kimberley – Oxford – His friendship with Alfred Beit – His character and mode of life – His ideals – The struggle for South Africa – Significance of southern Zambesia – The Moffat Treaty – The dilemma of Lord Salisbury.

4   THE CONCESSION AND THE CHARTER 1888–89   42

Rhodes's problem – The Rudd Mission – Lobengula's difficulties – The discomforts of his court – A frock-coated envoy – The Rudd Concession – Its dubious morality – Maund and other rivals – Visit of indunas *to England – Rhodes 'squares' his rivals – Selous – The charter sealed – Trouble in Bulawayo – Character of Dr Jameson – His friendship with Lobengula – Execution of Lotje, 'Strafford of the Ndebele dynasty' – Jameson's second visit – Lobengula fails to ratify Rudd Concession.*

5 THE PIONEER COLUMN 1889–90   62

*Frank Johnson – His proposed coup against Lobengula – Selous' alternative –
Johnson's contract and misleading account of it – The Pioneers – The military
escort – Jameson threatens Lobengula – Departure of the Column –
Pennefather, Jameson and Colquhoun – Column reaches Salisbury.*

6 THE MAP IS DRAWN 1890–91   76

*'Effective occupation' – Nyasaland and Harry Johnson – Lord Salisbury's
ultimatum to Portugal – Nyasaland secured – Barotseland, the Ware Concession – Failure to gain Katanga – Need of an eastern port – Colquhoun's secret
instructions – Coup in Manicaland against 'Gouveia' – Forbes abandons bid for
Beira – Colquhoun unfairly blamed – Failure to acquire Gazaland – Sir John
Willoughby – Skirmish at Choua Hill – Settlement with Portugal – the
Adendorff trek rebuffed – Portuguese and Boer ambitions frustrated – Rhodes
and Harry Johnston part company.*

7 SETTLEMENT AND WAR 1890–93   93

*The Pioneers discharged – Legality of their rewards – A torrential rainy season –
Hardships of settlers – Malaria, beetles, bullfrogs, rats and snakes – Visit of
Lord Randolph Churchill – Arrival of Rhodes – Jameson, Chief Magistrate –
Colquhoun sacked – Economic depression – Black-White relations – The
juridical situation – Irreconcilable claims – Origins of Matabele War – The
Victoria Incident – War propaganda – Defeat of Lobengula – The Shangani
Patrol, a Rhodesian symbol.*

8 CONQUEST 1893–95   111

*Lobengula's fate assessed – Force the basis of company rule – Contrast with other
colonies – Rhodes at his apogee – Powerlessness of Whitehall – Land and cattle
– Indefensible policy of Jameson – Brutality and sexual exploitation by police
– Boom in Bulawayo.*

9 REBELLION 1896–97   123

*Rinderpest – The Jameson Raid – 'Rebellion' in Matabeleland – Atrocities on
both sides – Divergent Ndebele aims – Millenarian fanaticism – Burnham
shoots the 'Mlimo' – Course of campaign – Rhodes arrives – Plumer's Column –
Lord Grey succeeds Jameson – Relief of Bulawayo – Shona revolt – The
Mazoe Patrol – Defeat of Ndebele – Rhodes's indabas in the Matopos –
Chamberlain and the Charter – The Shona rebellion crushed – A vignette by
Lady Grey.*

10   THE AFTERMATH 1897–1902   144

*White conquest reaffirmed – The railroad revolution – Grey's view of the
Shona – His mode of life – Rhodes seeks to allay settler discontent – Sir
William Milton succeeds Grey – The new Constitution – Imperial control – A
Legislative Council – Powers of the Administrator – The Rhodesian Civil
Service – The South African War – Death and funeral of Rhodes – Question
mark over Rhodesia.*

11   THE RULE OF THE COMPANY 1902–18   155

*Drastic impact of white rule on black life – Black passivity – Assimilation v.
segregation – Observations of Henri Rolin – Sexual relations – Missionaries'
limited success – Compromises in Native Policy – Ndebele grievances over land
– Urban problems – Passes and registration – The Native Department – The
debate on Rhodesia's future – Changes in the Legislative Council – The impact
of the 1914–18 war.*

Part 2: A Self-Governing Colony

12   RESPONSIBLE GOVERNMENT 1914–23   173

*Sir Drummond Chaplin succeeds Milton – Amalgamation with north, or union
with south – The Privy Council's decision on land – Cave Commission's award
– Sir Charles Coghlan – Responsible Government v. union – Legco elections –
Funeral of Jameson – Churchill at the Colonial Office – The Buxton Committee
– A new Constitution – Smuts's rival offer – The referendum decides for
Responsible Government – Analysis of voting – Analogies with UDI.*

13   THE NEW ORDER 1923–31   189

*The end of 'greater South Africa' – Smuts fails to turn the tide – Expro-
priation of BSA Company – Analysis of new Constitution – Coghlan as
'Premier' – 1924 elections – The political pattern – A one-party system –
Coghlan's outlook – Shirley Cripps and the evils of the settlers – African voices
– Native reserves and native purchase areas – The Coryndon Commission – Its
dubious predictions – The Carter Commission – African reactions – The Land
Apportionment Act of 1931.*

14   THE DECLINE OF THE RHODESIAN PARTY 1927–33   205

Relations with South Africa – Settler grievances against Whitehall – Economic

*problems – Death of Coghlan – Moffat's premiership – The Meikle affair –
The Hilton Young Commission – Amalgamation recedes – The Copper Belt –
Paramountcy – The slump – Huggins crosses the floor – The Reform Party –
Huggins and racialism – Mineral rights – Moffat buys out the company – The
1933 election – Huggins in office.*

15   THE HUGGINS ERA 1933–39   217

*Character and attitude of Huggins – The Industrial Conciliation Act – A
political convulsion – Huggins easily wins 1934 election – The economic
problems; minerals, tobacco, agriculture – Amalgamationists press their case –
African opposition – The Bledisloe Commission – The native problem –
African attitudes – The fight against African urbanization – Huggins compromises – The native problem unsolved.*

16   WAR AND AFTERMATH 1939–48   231

*Election of 1939 – Outbreak of war – Huggins creates Defence Committee with
Guest and Tredgold – The colony's war effort – RAF training ground –
Domestic politics – 'Socialistic' measures – Labour divisions healed – Party
genealogies – The Central African Council – Huggins becomes more 'liberal' to
anger of Liberal Party – The 1946 election – A minority government – Huggins
buys out the railways – An African strike – Huggins wins election of 1948.*

17   THE ORIGINS OF FEDERATION 1945–51   243

*Diverse characteristics of the Rhodesias and Nyasaland – Constitutional
developments – Roy Welensky – 1948, a turning point – Effect of the
Northern Rhodesian and South African elections – Amalgamation vetoed – The
move towards Federation – The Conference of Officials 1951 – The Role of Sir
Andrew Cohen – Details of the proposals.*

18   FEDERATION ACHIEVED 1951–53   255

*Reactions to the Officials Conference – The Africans – The Liberal Party – Sir
E. Guest – Sir R. Tredgold – Self-government or 'civilized standards' – Visit
to Central Africa by Griffiths and Gordon Walker – Conference at Victoria
Falls – Defeat of Labour Government – Oliver Lyttleton finally vetoes
amalgamation – Mounting Labour and African opposition to Federation –
Banda's tour of Scotland – The Capricorn Africa Society – The Lancaster
House Conference – Constitutional disputes and agreements – The debate in
Southern Rhodesia – Reports of the specialist commission – Huggins wins his
referendum – The Federation inaugurated.*

Part 3: Federation and the White Backlash

19 SOUTHERN RHODESIAN SOCIETY 1946–53   273

Quality of the immigrants – Umtali described as 'Poonafontein' – Myth that most Rhodesians 'have no other home' – An urban society, but rural social ascendancy – 'The planter interest' – 'Surbiton in the Bush' – High standard of living – African servants and bad race relations – A cultural desert – Sense of insecurity – Relations with South Africa – Sexual taboos – Problems of prostitution – White social distinctions – Ignorance about Africans – Rigid separatism – Illiberalism of immigrants.

20 THE HEYDAY OF FEDERATION 1953–57   284

Complexities of the Constitution – Rivalry of Dominion and Colonial Offices – Huggins as Federal Prime Minister – Wins 1954 election – Southern Rhodesia now a 'territory' – Rise of Garfield Todd – His antecedents and character – Wins territorial election – Federal prosperity – Roads and planes – 'Partnership' and its problems – Africans called 'Mr' and 'Native' abolished – Liberal measures – Todd's efforts to break down barriers – Kariba – Dominion status for the Federation refused – Sir Roy Welensky succeeds Huggins.

21 A TURNING POINT 1957   296

The franchise – The Tredgold Report on Southern Rhodesia – A parallel with the past – Welensky and the Federal Constitution – African disapproval – Ascendancy of Todd – White misgivings about his 'style' – The Immorality Act – Modifications to Tredgold Report – Todd's threat to resign – The Party Congress – A Cabinet revolt quelled.

22 THE FALL OF TODD 1957–58   307

A second Cabinet rebellion – Todd forms a new Government – Repudiated by caucus and Congress – Whitehead becomes Prime Minister – Wins election of 1958 by narrow margin – Todd's new party loses every seat – Reasons for Todd's fall – Welensky not involved – Nature of 'liberalism' – Difference between that of Todd and Whitehead – A personal recollection.

23 THE DECLINE OF THE FEDERATION 1956–60   319

Character of Whitehead – Alienation of Africans – Repercussions of Suez – Change of course in UK – Extension of African self-government – Implications

*for Federation – African unrest – Emergence of Nkomo and the Congress Party –
Bad relations between Welensky and Whitehall – Macmillan takes an interest –
State of emergency in Central Africa – The Devlin Report – The Monckton
Commission set up – 'The wind of change' – Ian Macleod becomes Colonial
Secretary – Macmillan's defence of British colonial policy – De Gaulle and the
French Empire – The Congo crisis – The Monckton Report.*

24 THE ECLIPSE OF WHITEHEAD 1960–62   333

*A new Constitution for Southern Rhodesia – Volte-face by Nkomo – White-
head wins referendum for 1961 Constitution – Central African politics in
London – Macleod 'too clever by half' – Dissension between Colonial and
Commonwealth Relations Offices – Macmillan becomes bored – Welensky con-
templates UDI – The Plewman and Quinton Reports on land – Whitehead
forces the pace – African Nationalist misjudgements – ANC banned –
Foundation of ZAPU – Violence – ZAPU banned – The Rhodesian Front –
Winston Field – Defeat of Whitehead – Responsibility of Nkomo and Sithole.*

25 THE RHODESIAN FRONT 1962–63   345

*R. A. Butler takes charge of Central Africa – Dissolution of Federation
inevitable – Rage of Welensky – Northern Rhodesia granted right to secede –
Field's Cabinet – He aims for independence on 1961 Constitution – British
refusal – Victoria Falls Conference – Ought Field to have gone? – Myth of
promise of independence – Federation dissolved – Divisions in African
Nationalism – Sithole founds ZANU – Rhodesian Front gains ground – Ian
Smith returns from London empty-handed.*

26 THE FALL OF FIELD 1964   356

*Field visits London – No change from Sir Alec Douglas-Home – An interview
with Wilson – Contingency plans for UDI – RF caucus ousts Field – He
declines to fight back – Ian Smith becomes Prime Minister – His deviousness –
His identification with white ascendancy – His Rhodesian 'patriotism' –
Advantages and drawbacks.*

27 SMITH 1964–65   363

*Clamp-down on African agitation – Renewed negotiations with Whitehall –
Welensky tries to return to politics – Smith goes to London and withdraws
threat of UDI – Welensky heavily defeated at by-election – Smith argues for
an indaba of chiefs as test of African opinion – Preparations for UDI – Van
der Byl deals with the media – Armed forces and civil service under control –*

The indaba *held – Sir Alec refuses to accept its verdict – Labour wins the election – Wilson's strong warning – European referendum on independence on 1961 Constitution – Smith goes to London for Sir Winston's funeral – His strange conduct – Rhodesian general election May 1965 – Ought the dissolution to have been granted? – Overwhelming victory for RF – Final defeat of the 'old establishment'.*

28 UDI 1965   374

Ideology of the RF – Smith committed to UDI – Dismissal of Evan Campbell – An envoy to Portugal – Further negotiations with Britain – The Five Principles – Smith's last visit to London – Deadlock over franchise, African opinion, and retrogressive amendments – Wilson flies to Salisbury – His fury at treatment of Nkomo and Sithole – His chilly reception of Lord Graham's post-prandial humour – Renewed deadlock – Archbishop of Canterbury hints at force – Rhodesians burn Bibles – Wilson back in London – Final effort to dissuade Smith – UDI declared on November 11 – The reasons behind it – A rush of blood to the head? – Or a calculated move towards segregation and white consolidation?

EPILOGUE 1965–77   385

Constitutional questions – 'OAG' – Dupont – Effort to involve the Queen – 'Smith's Crispins' – Treatment of the Governor – The opposition in Rhodesia – Life after UDI – African docility – Question of 'force' – Wilson's rejection of it – Oil sanctions – Conservative attitude – Ill-founded optimism of Wilson – Financial skill of Wrathall and Bruce – Portugal and South Africa – Beira Patrol – Byrd Amendment – State of the economy – The Tiger talks 1966 – Beadle's backbone – Smith pulls out – 'NIBMAR'– Judicial battles – Execution of three Africans – Beadle ejected from Government House – The Fearless talks 1968 – New constitution – Smith declares a republic 1969 – Conservatives back in office 1970 – Smith accepts Home/Goodman proposals – Pearce Commission finds them unacceptable to Africans – Portuguese revolution 1974 – Independence for Angola and Mozambique – Kissinger's intervention – Smith agrees to 'majority rule' on conditions – Geneva Conference – Smith's attitude – Bishop Muzorewa – The Patriotic Front – Power bases of Nkomo, Sithole and Mugabe – Chances of a peaceful settlement – A tribute to the Europeans who tried to make multi-racialism work.

APPENDIX: THE BEIT TRUST   415
SELECT BIBLIOGRAPHY   417
INDEX   422

Acknowledgements

The idea of writing this book was suggested to me by Mr Harry St J. Grenfell who till his retirement held a prominent position first in the British South Africa Company and then in Charter Consolidated, the London end of the Anglo-American Corporation of South Africa which absorbed the old BSA Company. The original plan was to write a history simply of the Company, but this was changed to a history of Southern Rhodesia and the history of the Company appears in these pages only insofar as it overlaps with that of the Colony. I planned to finish it at the Declaration of Independence in 1965, but I later decided to include an Epilogue to bring the story to the present day. It is only an outline and I must emphasize that many years will elapse before a proper history of that period can be written.

I am most grateful to the Anglo-American Corporation and to Charter Consolidated for their help which has been indispensable in producing this book, and I would in particular like to thank Mr Harry Oppenheimer and Mr Grenfell for their advice and support. I would also like to thank Sir Keith Acutt, Mr Tim Birley, Sir Frederick Crawford, Mr Adam Payne, Mr John Richardson, Sir Albert Robinson and Mr Robin Rudd.

I have had many conversations with people who have participated in recent Rhodesian affairs. The list is too long to give in full and some of them, both African and European, prefer to remain anonymous; in particular I have not thought it right to mention by name any of the members of the present government since several of them gave me interviews on that assumption. I would particularly like to mention the help I have had from the late Lord Malvern, the late Mr Winston Field, Mr Garfield Todd and Sir Roy Welensky. Others who have been most helpful were the late Sir Ernest Guest, the late Sir Robert Tredgold, Sir Hugh Beadle, Sir Humphrey Gibbs, Mr Julian Greenfield, Sir Cornelius Greenfield, Sir Andrew Strachan, Mr Jack Quinton, Mr Evan Campbell, Mr Hardwicke Holderness, Mr Ellman-Brown, Senator Sam Whaley, Mr Stan Morris, Mr Abrahamson, Sir Ray Stockil, Mr George Rudland, Sir Patrick Fletcher, Mr and Mrs Richard Acton (Judy Todd), Sir Henry McDowell, Mr Donald Low, Dr Craig and Sir Robert Birley. One cannot write about Rhodesia without entering into the area of modern political controversy. I do not expect those whom I have consulted to agree with my judgement of events, and I must take full responsibility for it.

One of my most useful sources has been the transcripts taken by Mr Rex Reynolds of his conversations with Lord Malvern who was in the unusual position of being able to comment on his own biography by Professor Gann and Dr Gelfand – itself, of course, a valuable work. I am very grateful for his help.

No one can write about Rhodesia without acknowledging his debt to Professor Gann whose histories of Southern Rhodesia to 1933 and Northern Rhodesia to 1953 are books of major importance. The same can be said of Dr Gelfand whose many books on the medical history of the country and the religious beliefs of the Shona are indispensable. I also owe a heavy debt to Professor Ranger's *Revolt in Southern Rhodesia* – a remarkable study of the rebellions of 1896.

I have found the unpublished thesis by Mr Malcolm Rifkind, MP, *The Politics of Land*, very helpful in understanding one of the most puzzling aspects of Rhodesian history and I have also had the advantage of reading some of the draft chapters of Mr Richard Wood's forthcoming history of the Federation.

I would like to thank Miss Doreen Mackay, Mrs M. A. Read and Miss Sarah King-Turner for typing and retyping my chapters with such exemplary skill and patience. Finally, I would like to thank Miss King-Turner and my daughter, Deborah, for correcting the proofs, Mr F. T. Dunn for compiling the index and Miss Elsbeth Lindner for copy-editing my typescript and seeing it through the press.

Introduction

This is a history of the origins and course of the modern European occupation of 'Southern Rhodesia' – 'Rhodesia' as it has been termed since the old 'Northern Rhodesia' became independent under the name of Zambia in 1963. Rhodesian history is a strange and intriguing compound of romance, idealism, courage, arrogance, avarice and accident. Moreover it involves, even if on a miniature scale, some of the most intractable problems of the twentieth century: the relations between the races, the nature of political power, the limits of constitutional loyalty, the conflict between ideology and economics, the future of 'White Africa'.

The country's history has, however, aroused only limited international interest. The drama of its beginning is, of course, famous – Cecil Rhodes, the Pioneer Column, the settlement of Salisbury, the war with Lobengula, the Shangani Patrol, the 'rebellions' in Matabeleland and Mashonaland. But, for many years after that, the history of the country is almost unknown except to specialists. A few people are aware that Rhodesia, like India, was governed by a chartered company – the last example in British history of this kind of regime. Fewer still have studied the hybrid constitution which followed the end of the British South Africa Company's rule in 1923, though it is the key to the understanding of much that has happened recently. Some echoes of the Rhodesian contribution in two world wars may linger in some ears. A fair number of people know that Sir Godfrey Huggins (Lord Malvern) held the premiership of his country for longer than anyone in the history of the British Empire since Sir Robert Walpole.

But in general it would be true to say that until the 1950s very little interest has been taken in the contemporary politics or past history of Southern Rhodesia. Then the colony became quite suddenly a subject of major attention. The creation of the Federation of the two Rhodesias and Nyasaland was a matter of burning political controversy in Britain. There were those who saw it as the foundation of a great multi-racial Dominion which would be a counterpoise to a South Africa increasingly dominated by the principles of apartheid and only too likely to draw Southern Rhodesia into the same orbit. Others saw in it a bold but impracticable attempt by the white settlers to extend their power at precisely the moment when African nationalism was challenging white rule all over the continent. Whether the Central African Federation was regarded as a manifestation of idealistic multi-racialism or of Southern Rhodesian imperialism, it was a subject of much publicity and fierce debate. Its origins, its heyday, its dissolution with consequences, not least of which has been Southern Rhodesia's unilateral declaration of independence, are matters of high controversy still.

To some extent this book reflects these contrasts in the interest taken from outside in the various periods of Rhodesian history. In the story of a nation, as in the lives of most individuals, there are long passages when nothing very much happens. These cannot be ignored, for they may contain the causes of later events which have a much greater significance, but there is no need to devote to them the same space which one gives to those events themselves. If the outside world has taken little interest in the history of Southern Rhodesia from the end of the rebellions to the beginning of federation this is largely because much of it is not very interesting.

What matter in the history of a country are the turning points – the moments of decision when a different line of action might have changed the course of events. There are at least five in the modern history of Southern Rhodesia. The first is of course the European occupation itself. The second is the ending of Company rule in 1922 and the choice of 'Responsible Government' rather than adherence to the Union of South Africa. The third is the decision to opt for federation. The fourth is the dissolution of the Federation. The fifth is UDI. In between these there are less decisive episodes which none the less involved some change of course if not a sharp turn: the settlement after the rebellions; the Land Apportionment Act; the political crisis of 1933; the ousting of Garfield Todd in 1958; the general election of 1962; the fall of Winston Field in 1964. It is these major and minor turning points, their nature, causes and effects, which this book endeavours to discuss and analyse.

The story of a country is not only the story of the economic, political, ideological and external forces which have shaped it, but also that of the individuals who made – or failed to make – decisions. An attempt has been made to portray such figures as Rhodes, Lobengula, Jameson, Coghlan, Lord Malvern, Roy Welensky, Garfield Todd, Edgar Whitehead, Winston Field, Ian Smith and others who played a crucial part in events. Many of them are still alive or were when I began this book. I am very grateful to them for allowing me to talk to them, but they should not be regarded as in any way endorsing what I have said. Indeed some of them will certainly disagree with some of my conclusions.

Chronologically the story of Southern Rhodesia divides into three parts: Company rule from 1890 to 1923; 'Responsible Government' 1923 to 1953; federation, its dissolution and consequences 1953 to 1965. The book was intended to end with UDI. What has happened since is too recent to have become 'history'. Nevertheless, an attempt has been made in a brief epilogue to survey the principal events, in full consciousness that the future historian will have a great deal more to say about them.

I have had the advantage of access to many collections of papers not normally available to historians. I have spent considerable periods of time in Rhodesia and have got to know most of the leading figures in the country's recent history, also to understand something of the outlook of the white settlers which has a remarkable resemblance to that of the southern secessionists before the American Civil War (cf. R. Hofstadter, *The Paranoid Style in American Politics* and David Davis, *The Slave Power Conspiracy and the Paranoid Style*). I have also tried, though this is less easy, to get some insight into the mentality of the Rhodesian Africans, which is not quite the same as that of the Africans in neighbouring countries, for a host of historical reasons.

The Queen's College, Oxford
June 1977

Robert Blake

Chronology

1509	Portuguese discover 'Rhodesia'.
1652	Dutch land at the Cape.
1693	Portuguese expelled from Rhodesia.
1815	Cape becomes a British colony.
1822	Mzilikazi flees from Shaka.
1822–36	*Mfecane.*
1836	Great Trek begins.
1840	Mzilikazi reaches Bulawayo.
1853	Rhodes, Beit and Jameson born.
1854	Moffat Mission.
1868	Lobengula succeeds Mzilikazi.
1870	Rhodes arrives in Natal.
1881	Majuba.
1886	Gold discovered on Rand.
1888	Rudd Concession.
1889	British South Africa Company incorporated under Royal Charter.
1890	Pioneer Column reaches Salisbury.
1893	Defeat of Lobengula. Shangani Patrol.
1895	Jameson Raid.
1896	Grey succeeds Jameson as Administrator. Rebellions in Matabeleland and Mashonaland.
1898	Milton becomes Administrator. Southern Rhodesia Order-in-Council passed.
1900	Boer War begins.
1902	Death of Rhodes. Peace of Veereniging.
1906	Death of Alfred Beit.
1907	Settler majority in Legislative Council.
1914	Drummond succeeds Milton.
1917	Death of Jameson.
1918	Privy Council decides ownership of 'unalienated land'.
1919	Cave Commission reports.
1922	Referendum favours Responsible Government.
1923	Chartered Company accepts Colonial Office terms. Constitution of Southern Rhodesia promulgated General election. Coghlan Premier.
1925	Morris Carter Report published.

1927	Death of Coghlan. Moffat Premier.
1928	Moffat wins general election.
1931	Land Apportionment Act passed.
1933	Chartered Company sells its mineral rights to Southern Rhodesian Government. Moffat replaced by Mitchell. Huggins narrowly wins general election.
1934	Second general election. Landslide for Huggins.
1939	Bledisloe Commission reports. Huggins wins general election. War-time government formed.
1940	Air Training Scheme begins in Rhodesia.
1946	General election. Huggins forms minority government.
1948	Huggins dissolves and wins general election easily.
1951	Conference of Officials on Federation. Conservatives win British general election.
1953	Federation of Rhodesia and Nyasaland inaugurated. Huggins becomes its first Prime Minister.
1954	Garfield Todd wins Southern Rhodesia general election.
1956	Welensky succeeds Lord Malvern (Huggins).
1957	New franchise in Southern Rhodesia. Nkomo founds new ANC.
1958	Fall of Todd. Whitehead wins general election.
1960	Macmillan makes 'wind of change' speech.
1961	Referendum confirms new Southern Rhodesian constitution. Monckton Report. ZAPU founded.
1962	Rhodesian Front wins general election. Field Prime Minister.
1963	Split between Nkomo and Sithole/Mugabe. ZANU founded.
1964	Federation dissolved. Field ousted. Smith Prime Minister.
1965	Smith wins every 'A' Roll seat at general election. Independence declared on November 11.
1966	Talks on HMS *Tiger* breakdown.
1968	'The Constitutional Case'. Abortive talks on HMS *Fearless*.
1969	New constitution. Rhodesia declared a republic.
1970	Conservatives win British general election.
1971	Home/Goodman proposals accepted by Smith.
1972	Pearce Commission finds terms unacceptable to Africans.
1974	Revolution in Lisbon leads to independence for Angola and Mozambique.
1976	Kissinger and Vorster persuade Smith to agree to 'majority rule'. Geneva Conference. Carter wins US Presidential election.
1977	Geneva Conference breaks down. Dr Owen proposes a fresh Anglo-American initiative.

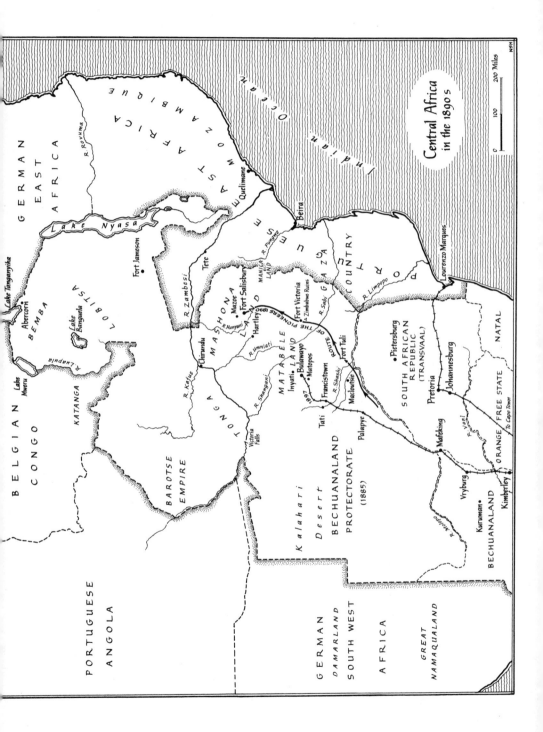

Central Africa
in the 1890s

0   100   200 Miles

BELGIAN CONGO

PORTUGUESE ANGOLA

GERMAN EAST AFRICA

R. Rovuma

Lake Tanganyika

Abercorn

BEMBA

Lake Mweru

R. Luapula

KATANGA

Lake Banguela

LOBITSA

LOZI

BAROTSE EMPIRE

R. Kafue

TONGA

Victoria Falls

R. Shangani

Chirundu

MASHONALAND

R. Zambesi

Tete

Fort Jameson

Lake Nyasa

PORTUGUESE EAST AFRICA

MOZAMBIQUE

R. Hunyani

Mazoe

Fort Salisbury

Hartley

R. Umniati

MANICA LAND

R. Punwe

Quelimane

Indian Ocean

Beira

GAZA

R. Sabi

Zimbabwe Ruins

Fort Victoria

MATABELELAND

ROUTE OF THE PIONEERS 1890

Inyati

Bulawayo

Matopos

1897

Francistown

R. Shashi

Fort Tuli

Macloutsie

Tati

R. Limpopo

GAZA COUNTRY

Lourenzo Marques

PORTUGUESE

Pietersburg

SOUTH AFRICAN REPUBLIC (TRANSVAAL)

Johannesburg

Pretoria

Palapye

Kalahari Desert

BECHUANALAND PROTECTORATE (1885)

R. Molopo

Vryburg

Mafeking

R. Vaal

ORANGE FREE STATE

NATAL

Kimberley

Kuruman

BECHUANALAND

To Cape Town

GERMAN DAMARLAND SOUTH WEST AFRICA

GREAT NAMAQUALAND

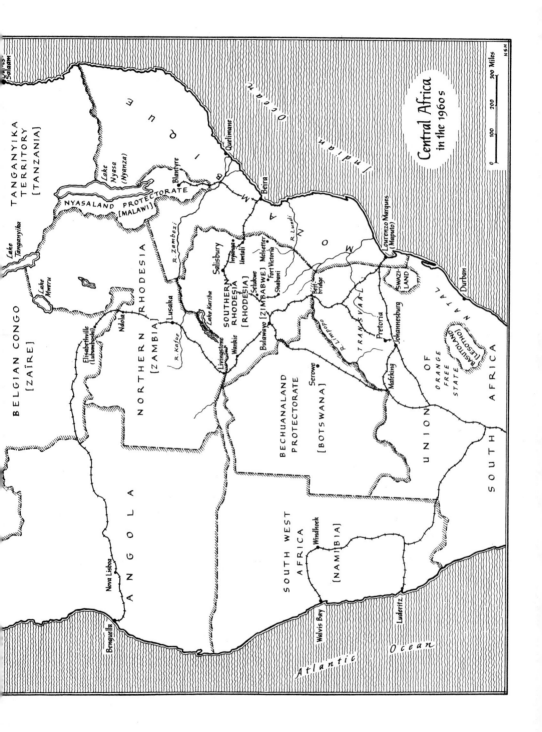

Central Africa
in the 1960s

0   100   200   300 Miles

TANGANYIKA TERRITORY
[TANZANIA]

BELGIAN CONGO
[ZAÏRE]

Lake Tanganyika

Lake Mweru

Elisabethville
(Lubumbashi)

Ndola

NORTHERN RHODESIA
[ZAMBIA]

Lusaka

R. Kafue

Livingstone

Wankie

R. Zambezi

Lake Kariba

Lake Nyasa
(Nyanza)

NYASALAND PROTECTORATE
[MALAWI]

Blantyre

Quelimane

Beira

SOUTHERN RHODESIA
[RHODESIA]

Salisbury

Inyanga
Umtali

Melsetter

Selukwe
Fort Victoria

Bulawayo [ZIMBABWE]

Shabani

R. Lundi

Birchenough bridge

Lourenço Marques
(Maputo)

SWAZI-LAND

Durban

R. Limpopo

TRANSVAAL

Pretoria

Johannesburg

Mafeking

BECHUANALAND PROTECTORATE
[BOTSWANA]

Serowe

ORANGE FREE STATE

BASUTOLAND
[LESOTHO]

NATAL

UNION OF SOUTH AFRICA

ANGOLA

Nova Lisboa

Benguela

SOUTH WEST AFRICA

Windhoek

[NAMIBIA]

Walvis Bay

Lüderitz

Atlantic Ocean

Indian Ocean

Mozambique

Part 1

THE
CHARTERED
COMPANY

1

The Land and the Early Conquerors 5000 BC – AD 1700

In the perspective of history the British occupation of 'Zambesia', as the area north of the Limpopo River was vaguely described, can be regarded as one of the last scenes in the European partition of Africa, and that partition itself as the final act in the astonishing drama of European expansion all over the world from the days of Vasco da Gama onwards. Like waves produced in ever widening circles by some vast sub-oceanic convulsion, the Portuguese, Spanish, Dutch, French and English spread first to America and Asia, then to the Antipodes, finally to Africa. And in 1890 the last ripple of all, even as the effects of that convulsion were dying away, carried the Pioneer Column into Mashonaland and three years later into Bulawayo. For over half a century the waters remained calm, almost stagnant. Then they began to ebb with ever increasing speed.

This double transformation has been amazingly rapid. In 1870 less than one-tenth of Africa was occupied by Europeans. By 1914 less than a tenth remained independent. Yet by the middle of the 1960s the only area governed from a European capital was the anachronistic Portuguese empire. British, French, German and Belgian colonial rule had vanished. With the Lisbon revolution of April 1974 the Portuguese empire vanished too. Today the only countries to be ruled by Europeans are those where the Whites have established themselves as autonomous indigenous élites – the Republic of South Africa and the self-styled Republic of Rhodesia. This is the framework within which Southern Rhodesia's eighty-seven years of existence has to be set.

It was not for lack of interest that Africa was the last of the great continents to be explored by the Europeans. Its fascination has been perpetual. From classical antiquity people dreamed of its strange marvels, mysterious wealth and magical possibilities. But the peculiar geographical configuration of the continent made penetration from outside a formidable task. Most of Africa consists of a high plateau of ancient rock (immensely rich in minerals) stretching from the

Cape to the Atlas Mountains, surrounded by a narrow low-lying coastal belt. The rivers which would be the normal approach to the interior are nearly everywhere broken not far from the sea by unnavigable cataracts as they flow down from the plateau. The coast is inhospitably devoid not only of natural harbours, but of bays, inlets and channels. The coast line is no longer than that of Europe, but it encompasses a continent three times the size. The coastal belt, hot and steamy, has been from time immemorial until very recently the haunt of malaria and other lethal fevers. Tsetse fly, the killer of transport animals, was, and in great tracts still is, a deadly obstacle to movement both on the coast and further inland.

Although the approach to the interior was so formidable, the climate and vegetation are by no means unpleasant for those already there. The latest theories suggest that mankind may originally have evolved on the plateaux of eastern and southern Africa. Whatever the truth of this, the great area of bush and grassland which runs up from South Africa, encircling the Congo basin and ending in Tanzania and Kenya, has been for thousands of years a corridor for the movement of men. Countless generations of nomadic peoples have moved along it from north to south, though sometimes there have been back eddies; indeed one of these accounts for the Ndebele who live in the western part of Southern Rhodesia today, another for the Whites who have ruled the land since 1893.

Very little is known about the past history of southern and central Africa. The indigenous peoples never discovered the wheel nor did they evolve a written language. They experienced neither of the two great revolutions which have transformed the Euro-Asiatic world: the urban revolution of Mesopotamia; the industrial revolution of England. This does not mean that the social order which prevailed among the African tribes when the European impact first occurred was at all simple. On the contrary, it was subtle and highly complicated – an elaborate web of hierarchical, spiritual and diplomatic relations. But it is true that the system had emerged largely in isolation. Even the Ndebele state, the most highly developed in Southern Africa, was no more than an Iron Age monarchy when it was finally destroyed by Cecil Rhodes in 1893.

Southern Rhodesia constitutes a small section of this vast plateau of Southern Africa. Its area is three times that of England, i.e. about 150,000 square miles (the whole area of Africa is 11,000,000 square miles). The maximum distances from east to west and north to south are rather less than 600 miles, and the country lies almost wholly within the southern tropics. The cliché, 'a land-locked island', is no less true for being a cliché. Unlike so many of the states created by the European partition of Africa, it is not an artificial entity owing its shape merely to the political bargains of the chancelleries of Europe. On the contrary, it has had for centuries a geographical unity of its own and it possesses natural frontiers; on the north the formidable barrier of the Zambesi; on the south what Kipling erroneously called 'the great grey-green greasy Limpopo River, all set about with fever trees'; on the west the dry sands of the Kalahari desert; on the east the mountains which divide Rhodesia from Mozambique and provide the pleasantest scenery and climate in the country.

Most of Southern Rhodesia lies within the Tropic of Capricorn, but the climate is far from 'tropical' in the ordinary sense of the term. This is because of its altitude. A quarter of its surface lies between four and five thousand feet above sea level; by far the greater part is over two thousand feet and scarcely any of it is below one thousand. Yet, although so much of Southern Rhodesia is above the top of Ben Nevis, one has no sense of height. The impression is one of a rolling plain with long vistas and endless blue horizons. On the high veld Europeans can live without discomfort. The best time of year is the early winter'– late April to the end of June. The rainy season is over, and the dusty aridity of the year's third quarter is yet to come. By day the temperature, even in April, is not very much hotter than in a hot English summer. The sky is a deep blue and the fleecy clouds never bring rain. One can fix a date for a picnic years in advance. By night it is cool and in June and July there can be frosts, sometimes severe. The champagne quality of the air, the brilliant glitter of the stars in the vapourless night sky, the sense of illimitable space all combine to produce a feeling of euphoria and boundless possibilities.

Yet it is well to take with a grain of salt the modern Rhodesian's praise of what he calls his 'wonderful climate'. The rainfall, averaging twenty-five to thirty inches a year, is confined to the summer (late November to early March). It is thundery and torrential, but there seldom seems to be enough of it, and complaints of droughts are endemic. Even on the high veld the temperature in October and November can be 100°F or more in the shade; the visitor is ill-advised to forget that he is in the tropics and that the almost vertical noonday sun really can burn. At the end of the long rainless winter the savannah vegetation is parched, brown and lifeless under the flaring October sun and under a sky cloudless but white and hazy, not from moisture, as at the corresponding time of year in England, but from the dust and fine ash produced by innumerable bush fires. A similar 'double-take' is the flaming red and gold of the Msasa and other indigenous trees at this time – the Rhodesian spring – their colours resembling in sharpened degree those of the autumnal beech woods of England in the same month. The arid atmosphere dries up the European skin and the dust produces symptoms rather like hay fever. Conditions away from the high plateau, whether one descends north into the Zambesi valley or south towards the low veld and the Limpopo, are much hotter and anything but agreeable.

There are four notable sights for which Rhodesia is rightly famous, one of them natural, three of them man-made. The Victoria Falls in the extreme north west corner of the country, discovered by David Livingstone in 1855, are one of the wonders of the world. The Zambesi, after flowing in a leisurely way through some 800 miles of bush from its source in the north of Zambia, suddenly plunges over a huge basalt rock cliff into a series of narrow zigzag gorges. The falls are one and a quarter miles wide and their greatest height is 355 feet. An average over the year of 47 million gallons of water flows down every minute. At the flood season the figure rises to 120 million. The spray can be seen like a great plume of steam as far as twenty miles away on land – much further from the

5

air – and the roar is tremendous. Hence the Makololo name which is translated as 'the smoke that thunders'. The scene has a magnetism that draws even the most blasé of visitors to return to it, and more than compensates for the damp enervating heat of the Zambesi valley. The exotic rain forest, the lunar rainbow, the grandeur of the gorge and the hypnotic noise of falling water are experiences which no one who has been there can ever forget. Oddly enough, Cecil Rhodes never saw it.

The three man-made spectacles for which Southern Rhodesia is celebrated symbolize three eras in the history of the country. The Bushmen's rock paintings are the earliest. No one has ever seen them all. Over two thousand have been discovered. Some of the finest are in the caves of the Matopos near Bulawayo. They are the work of a primitive tiny yellow-skinned hunting people. The Bushmen supplanted whoever were the previous inhabitants of the plateau at a time probably between 6000 and 5000 BC. The pictures are works of art and amazingly vivid. From them one can reconstruct, if only in shadowy outline, the way of life – its heyday, decline and twilight – of a race now vanished except for a few pathetic survivors who still eke out a precarious existence in the desiccated wastes of the Kalahari desert. At a date not known with any precision they were driven out by the Bantu, a race unmistakably negroid, more advanced, formidable and aggressive – the forebears of the Shona-speaking peoples who constitute three-quarters of the African population today.

Mention of the Bantu leads naturally to the second of the great man-made monuments for which Southern Rhodesia is famous – the celebrated dry stone ruins of Zimbabwe a few miles south of what is now Fort Victoria. The Great Zimbabwe (the word simply means 'burial ground of the chiefs') is spread over some sixty acres. It probably originated as a shrine of 'Mwari' and later became a political capital.[1] The main features which still stand above ground are the 'Acropolis', a series of immensely thick walls built on a giant granite hill or 'kopje'; and, below it in the valley, the 'Great Enclosure' or 'Temple' with free-standing, elegantly patterned walls thirty-five feet high and a curious conical tower believed by some experts to be a fertility symbol. The Great Enclosure may have been a royal residence. The purpose of the Acropolis, which commands extensive views in every direction, is uncertain – perhaps a fortress which would have been almost impregnable in the hands of determined defenders against the weapons of its day. These remarkable buildings are constructed from granite slabs laid upon each other without mortar or cement – resembling, though on a far grander scale, the stone walls which still divide fields in the Cotswolds. The Great Zimbabwe was built and rebuilt over many hundreds of years. The latest part was probably constructed in the early fifteenth century, after which the archaeological evidence suggests an abrupt social and economic decline.

Zimbabwe was first 'described' in the archaeological sense by one Karl Mauch,

[1] P. S. Garslake, 'Zimbabwe Ruins re-examined', *Rhodesian History*, Vol. I, 1970, 17–29, gives the latest archaeological opinion.

6

a German schoolmaster and geologist with a taste for adventure. He was guided
to it in 1871 by an American hunter–prospector by the name of Adam Renders
(or Render) who believed, as many did, that there had once been some long-
vanished 'white' – or at any rate non-negroid – civilization in central Africa. Could
this strange ruin be one of King Solomon's fortresses? Renders thought that it
was. Mauch concluded, less improbably though not less erroneously, that it was
built by Phoenician artisans under Hebrew influences, that 'the Temple' was a
copy of the palace where the Queen of Sheba stayed when she visited King
Solomon and that Zimbabwe was the capital of Ophir from which Hiram, the
Phoenician ally of the Jewish monarchs, sent 420 talents of gold.

This theory is now totally exploded. No serious modern student of the subject
doubts that Zimbabwe was the work of the ancestors of the Shona-speaking
peoples now inhabiting the eastern half of Southern Rhodesia. European travellers
and explorers of the 1870s, confronted with the primitive condition of the Shona
tribes whom they met, were understandably reluctant to believe that this could
be so. Today, thanks to archaeological and other forms of research, we are more
aware that civilizations can decline as well as rise and there seems nothing odd
in the notion, supported by all the available evidence, that Zimbabwe was built
by black men and was for a time the political and religious capital of a highly-
developed Bantu monarchy.

The third symbolic man-made monument is the tomb of Cecil Rhodes who
founded and gave his name to the modern colony. It is a plain slab on a kopje
in the Matopos a few miles south of Bulawayo. Rhodes called the place 'World's
View' and he loved to sit there brooding about his plans and hopes, surveying the
strange panorama – a seemingly endless prospect of grotesquely shaped granite
hills with huge rocks perching on their tops at improbable angles that appear to
defy the ordinary rules of balance and gravity. When there is rain in the air and
clouds are building up and thunder reverberates far off, one need not be over-
imaginative to catch something of the sense of fear and magic which this queer
region has inspired in generations of Africans. Similar slabs commemorate Dr
Jameson – forgivably perhaps as he was Rhodes's closest friend – and Sir
Charles Coghlan, the not very memorable first Prime Minister of Rhodesia. But
the least happy feature of this otherwise impressive setting was the direct result
of Rhodes's own instructions. He wished that the bodies of the Shangani Patrol –
heroes of the Rhodesian Valhalla, courageous victims of military ineptitude –
should be re-interred near his grave. Their collective tomb is not worthy of their
courage. It is perhaps as well that no more man-made monuments are to be
imposed on this naturally impressive scene.

The Bushmen, the early Bantu, the British … two significant sets of invaders
are omitted. Neither the Portuguese nor the Ndebele left any monuments worthy
of note, but they are important nevertheless, especially the latter. To survey in
detail the history of Rhodesia from the arrival of the Bantu to the arrival of
Cecil Rhodes does not come within the scope of this book. But some account,
however brief, is essential, if the story of subsequent events is to make sense.

A great deal of our knowledge of early Rhodesian history must be based on conjecture. There is a world of difference between the reliability of history founded on written documents and history dependent upon oral tradition or archaeological evidence, however good. The first written documents on Rhodesia date from the Portuguese landings in the early sixteenth century. It is, however, generally agreed that several centuries before that an Iron Age negroid civilization was to be found over most of Central Africa; the peoples concerned not only knew how to smelt iron, but also to mine gold, though their techniques seldom allowed them to dig deeper than 100 feet. By this time there had been some contacts, however tenuous, with the outside world. Indonesian sailors had colonized Madagascar and reached the East African coast. From a very early stage Arab navigators and traders sailed to the same shores. The idea, current in late Victorian times, that the country was the Ophir of Biblical fame and contained fabulous quantities of gold, probably stems from travellers' stories going back to remote antiquity when Muslim voyagers traded their goods for gold objects. It was a delusion. Although Rhodesia does have deposits of auriferous ore, no great lode has ever been discovered. Yet delusions can shape history as potently as reality. The lure of Ophir drew adventurers, explorers, invaders to Rhodesia over many centuries, and indeed led directly to the creation of the modern state.

At a time which is uncertain, the Iron Age peoples inhabiting the Rhodesian plateau developed into primitive monarchies. We know nothing directly of the cause, but we can guess that the necessities of war, conquest and trade operated in much the same way as they did upon the Teutonic tribes of northern Europe and the Hebrew tribes of Biblical Palestine. There were evidently several of these monarchies, but the one about which we know most – or are least ignorant – is the kingdom of the Monomatapa which first impinged on European consciousness at the time of the Portuguese invasion. The tribe that formed the basis of this monarchy was known as the Karanga, who are believed to have come from somewhere in the vicinity of Lake Tanganyika. Exactly when their monarchy became established it is impossible to say. It was apparently centred originally on the Great Zimbabwe, although by the time of the Portuguese the capital had been moved to Chitako, over 200 miles north at the foot of the escarpment which leads down to the Zambesi valley. This move occurred in the fifteenth century and various explanations for it have been given: new discoveries of gold; exhaustion of the land near Zimbabwe; the search for salt, which is a rare and precious commodity for an inland people subsisting largely on cereals and vegetables.

The original title of the paramount chief or King of the Karanga was the Mambo. It was their northern conquest which gave him his new name. Mutota, the King, who led his armies to Chitako and destroyed the rule of the indigenous tribes, was called by them 'Mwene Mutapa', which means 'master of the ravaged land'. The title may well have been conferred in a spirit of irony; but it became adopted first as the 'praise name' of Mutota himself and later, in the corrupted form of Monomatapa, as the hereditary title of the dynasty, like Tsar or Kaiser. According to oral tradition, the rule of the Monomatapa reached its zenith under

Mutota's son, Matope, who reigned over what was probably a loose tribal confederacy said to extend to the shores of the Indian Ocean. His death at some date in the late fifteenth century began a series of dynastic feuds and wars of succession. The only one of his many sons who had inherited his ability was called Changa. According to one tradition his mother was a slave. Another says that he was not a son of Matope at all, but a grandson in the female line and that his father was a chief of the Rozwi, an important Karanga clan. In either case he was not in the line of succession, but at the time of his father's death he was acting as a sort of viceroy at Zimbabwe. He soon proclaimed his own independence and symbolized his alliance or connection with the Rozwi by calling his kingdom Urozwi. He personally assumed the Arab title of Amir – Arab influences were strong both at Zimbabwe and Chitako – and before long his own name and that of his title were amalgamated into 'Changamire'. This in its turn became a title, like Monomatapa. Changa did not last long himself, but the struggle he started developed into deadlock. The Monomatapa could not dislodge the rebel dynasty from Zimbabwe. Equally the successors of Changa failed in their efforts to subdue the Monomatapa.

The kingdom of the Monomatapa at the beginning of the sixteenth century was a well-organized hierarchical society. The monarch was supported by a military aristocracy, a priesthood and a large number of high-sounding office bearers. The system as described by the Portuguese chroniclers bears some faint similarity to European feudalism, though technologically far inferior. The Karanga, like all the Bantu people of south central Africa, knew the use neither of the cart, the plough, nor the draught animal. Human labour was their sole source of power. They had a certain skill in the useful arts – weaving, pottery, carving in wood or stone, welding, and building. They had a primitive calendar which divided the month into three ten day weeks, but they had no accurate system of dating the years. All their knowledge was based on oral tradition which, handed down by the old, tends to create a highly conservative social order. No people in this part of Africa discovered the secret of transferring spoken words into visible symbols. The art of writing remained unknown until it was taught by the Europeans at the end of the nineteenth century. The primitive nature of Bantu husbandry meant that only the barest reserve of food could be produced. There was no possibility of stock-piling grain as the Pharaohs of Egypt had done. Survival depended upon strict adherence to a traditional village system of agricultural co-operation. Although the upper classes of the Monomatapa kingdom seem to have been able to accumulate a certain amount of individual property, the general emphasis was on communal ownership.

This rigidly traditional society, however resistant to innovation, was not necessarily an unhappy one. The Karanga were, after all, ignorant of the vast new horizons which were opening up in contemporary Europe of the Renaissance; they knew nothing of the rediscovered glory that was Greece and the grandeur that was Rome. Their religious beliefs, if one can judge from the extreme difficulty encountered by Christians of every denomination down the centuries in converting them, must have been spiritually satisfying. They believed in an all embracing deity, a Creator whom they called Mwari. But he was too remote to deal with individuals; their fortunes were guided by an elaborate hierarchy of tribal and ancestral spirits to be wooed and propitiated through spirit mediums or divines. The monarch himself possessed spiritual powers and he was aided in his authority by the advice of a priestly caste who proclaimed the judgement of ancestral rules and were repositories of the ancient traditions of the tribe. The witchcraft, human sacrifice and superstitious fraud which characterized this barbarous religion may not have irked unduly a society which had never known anything else.

This then was the nature of the Bantu kingdoms encountered by the first Portuguese visitors at the beginning of the sixteenth century. We can be sceptical of the grandiose descriptions of the state kept up by Monomatapa and the eloquent accounts of his wealth, which some of these travellers sent to Lisbon; they had their own motives for exaggeration. Nonetheless with every allowance made, it is clear that the Shona-speaking tribes of eastern Rhodesia were organized on a far higher level than their demoralized descendants whom the British hunters, missionaries and traders discovered some three hundred and fifty years later.

The Portuguese colonization of Rhodesia has never been adequately dealt with by historians. This may be because there is little satisfaction in tracing the story of an enterprise which failed so completely and left so little behind it. The Portuguese endeavoured for nearly two centuries to establish their dominion in what is now Mashonaland, and to gain the heathen Bantu for Christianity. They had some notable successes; one Monomatapa professed to be converted, and a son of his actually became a Dominican monk, ending up as vicar of the Convent of Santa Barbara in Goa. At the height of their power the Portuguese effectively controlled the eastern part of Mashonaland, but by the end of the seventeenth century there was not one Portuguese outpost on the plateau, and when the first missionaries came up from the south 150 years later, they did not find a single indigenous Christian. Like the Latin kingdom of the Crusaders, the Portuguese rule in Rhodesia bequeathed nothing to posterity save the ruins of its fortresses and churches.

The motives behind the Portuguese bid for Central Africa in the sixteenth century were similar to those of the British bid in the nineteenth century – religion, adventure, trade, above all gold. At one stage they even contemplated a colony of settlement and assembled a suitable collection of colonists, but in the end diverted them to Goa, thus narrowly failing to create a precedent for Rhodes's Pioneer Column. It is unlikely that such a project would have succeeded. The gap between Portuguese military technology and that of the Karanga Chiefdoms was large, but not as large as the gulf between nineteenth-century Britain and the kingdom of Lobengula. The Portuguese could win battles – though not always. It was another thing to establish their rule. Communications with the metropolitan power were infinitely slower and more precarious. Portugal was herself a declining power for much of the period of her African venture, and in 1580 fell under the rule of Spain for the next sixty years. Above all there was the problem of disease – especially malaria. Even in Rhodes's day its cause was still unknown, but its cure, quinine, had been discovered. The Portuguese had no such remedy nor any knowledge of the sanitary precautions which were taken for granted three centuries later.

Like the British, the Portuguese occupation was a by-product of a wider imperial policy; in the case of Britain the struggle with the Afrikaners for the domination of Southern Africa; in the case of Portugal the struggle to share in and ultimately control the trade of the Indian Ocean and to oust the Muslims who had held a monopoly since the triumph of the Ottoman Empire in the Middle East. In 1488 Bartolomeu Dias rounded the Cape and sailed as far as the Fish River, proving that Africa did not, as some feared, extend indefinitely southward. In 1497 Vasco da Gama set out on one of the most famous expeditions in the history of oceanic exploration. He sailed round Africa putting in at places which are now called Natal (so named because he landed on Christmas Day), Lourenzo Marques, Quelimane, and the island of Mozambique. Thence he went to Mombasa, one of the most flourishing Muslim ports, and eventually across the Indian Ocean to Calicut. He returned in triumph to Lisbon in September 1499, having been away for twenty-six months. The wider implications of this extraordinary feat do not concern us. It is sufficient to say that the Portuguese interest in the east coast of Southern Africa began then.

In 1505 the Portuguese sent out a much larger fleet under Francisco d'Almeida with the object of establishing themselves beyond dispute in the Indian Ocean. Rumours of the Monomatapa's gold were already rife, and d'Almeida was instructed to set up *en route* a station on the African coast. This he did at Sofala, a few miles south of the modern Beira. The object was to intercept, or participate in, the trade in gold carried on between the Monomatapa and the Arabs of the coast. But the Muslims were powerful at court and they had little difficulty in diverting their commerce to ports further north.

Lisbon therefore decided to send an emissary to the Monomatapa in person, and this dangerous office fell to a 'degregado' or condemned criminal called Antonio Fernandes, who was thus given an opportunity of redeeming himself. Fernandes accomplished his mission some time between 1509 and 1512. The dates are obscure and it is not easy to deduce from the terse notes of his report exactly what route he took. But he evidently met the Monomatapa and at least set foot in the kingdom of the Changamire. He can certainly claim the distinction of being the first white man to penetrate into what is now Southern Rhodesia.

Viewed in one aspect, the history of the Portuguese venture is a tale of brutality, bigotry and rapacity, viewed in another, one of heroism, faith and devotion. At first they were content with a few posts on or near the coast, while their traders endeavoured to establish themselves at the Karanga court. Goncala da Silveira, a Portuguese Jesuit of aristocratic descent, in 1560 actually converted

Nogomo, the young Monomatapa, to the Christian faith. Muslim influences, however, soon induced him to revert to paganism and cause da Silveira to be strangled. A series of natural disasters – locusts, floods, disease, famine – ensued, and convinced him he had made an unfortunate mistake. His Muslim counsellors were in their turn put to death, and he sent a message of contrition to the Portuguese. The new King of Portugal, Sebastian, who was half-mad, would not accept this olive branch and insisted on sending in 1569 an expedition to avenge the martyr's death.

It was led by Francisco Barreto, an experienced general. His sensible plan was to go overland from Sofala to the Mashonaland plateau. This was a reasonably healthy route, but he was persuaded by the expedition's spiritual adviser, Father Monclaro, who had the ear of King Sebastian, to travel up the malarial Zambesi. Disease resulted in a heavy toll of deaths including in the end that of Barreto himself, though by then he had sufficiently alarmed the Monomatapa to extract a treaty ceding the Zambesi valley from Tete to the sea – a concession which was all the easier for the Bantu monarch to make since the area was not actually his to concede.

The Portuguese authorities evidently believed that the Monomatapa was more like an Aztec Emperor than a Bantu Paramount Chief. His wealth was greatly exaggerated. Fernandes Homer, who succeeded Barreto and marched from Sofala to Manica by the healthier upland route in a second bid for gold, soon discovered that Ophir was a fable. He established posts in Manicaland, and a certain amount of gold began to trickle through, but never in large quantities.

The rest of the story of the Portuguese in Zambesia need not detain us. Nogomo died in 1596. His successor but one, Kaparavidze, in 1629 tried to eject the European colonists, but was defeated temporarily, and a puppet Monomatapa was installed in his place. Two years later, however, he led an uprising which wiped out the entire Portuguese garrison and all the settlers in Mashonaland and Manicaland. But the Portuguese, displaying that extraordinary tenacity which right up to the revolution of 1974 characterized their attitude to their colonial possessions, refused to give in. They sent a punitive expedition which on July 24, 1632 annihilated Kaparavidze's forces and installed the previous puppet for another twenty years.

After the middle of the century Portuguese power began to wane. For a time they sought to preserve it by a policy of divide and rule, supporting the Monomatapa against the Changamire. Portuguese troops may even have reached the Great Zimbabwe and temporarily ejected the monarch from his capital. But in 1693 Dombo, the reigning Changamire, joined the Monomatapa, wiped out the Portuguese forces, massacred the settlers at the station of Dambarare, and flayed alive two friars in order to discourage missionary zeal. This was the end of the Portuguese presence in what is now Rhodesia. Their stations, with the exception of one or two in Manicaland, were abandoned. A series of defeats by the Arabs, culminating in the fall of Mombasa in 1698, had by the end of the century greatly weakened their position in the Indian Ocean.

At home the exhausting effects of the war with Spain continued for many years. Lisbon decided to throw such resources as it still possessed into opening up Brazil, which was less inaccessible and had a healthier climate than south east Africa. The Portuguese still clung to their coastal settlements and a few fever-ridden outposts on the Zambesi, such as Quelimane, Sena and Tete, which is one of the hottest and most disagreeable places in Africa. But by 1700 no white man was living on the Rhodesian plateau.

2

The Ndebele Kingdom 1700–1886

The Monomatapa did not gain from his temporary alliance with his hereditary foe. The Rozwi state was an expanding power, and the Changamire's troops soon over-ran the older kingdom. By 1720 the Monomatapa had moved his capital to the Tete district to be under Portuguese protection. There the dynasty lingered on as shadowy Portuguese puppets until 1917 when their last monarch, Chocko, revolted against the Mozambique government and was deposed. They had long ceased to have any relevance to Rhodesian history.

We know very little about events during the hundred and forty years which followed the defeat of the Portuguese. Most of what is now Rhodesia together with parts of what is now Mozambique came under the sway of the Rozwi Mambo (the title of Changamire seems to have fallen into disuse). The Rozwi clan was supposed to have magical powers and the Mambo himself, ruling from the Great Zimbabwe, the place where the voice of Mwari was believed to be heard, was a cross between King and High Priest.

There was a certain amount of barter trade with Arab merchants, but in general this Bantu monarchy was as much cut off from the rest of the world as the kingdom of the Monomatapa had been before the coming of the Portuguese. All recollection of the techniques brought by the white man appears to have faded. The wheel, the draught animal, written language were none of them to be found by the next wave of European conquerors.

Before their arrival, however, the Rozwi regime had been completely destroyed. At the beginning of the nineteenth century an extraordinary convulsion occurred among the Nguni people in what is now the northern part of Natal. It was initiated by Dingiswayo, Chief of a Nguni tribe called the Mthethwa, who was evidently a great organizer and built up a formidable army; with this base he set out on a course of territorial expansion. No one knows quite what the forces were behind this movement; whether it was a combination of population growth and soil exhaustion, or desire to control the trade in gold and ivory with the Portuguese at Delagoa Bay or an indirect consequence of the arrival of white settlers in the south and west. Whatever the cause, the results were cataclysmic.

The key figure was not Dingiswayo but Shaka, the illegitimate son of Senzanogakona, the chief of the Zulus who were then a relatively unimportant appanage of Dingiswayo's confederacy. Aided by Dingiswayo, Shaka after his father's death arranged the murder of his brother and succeeded to the chieftainship in 1818. He was a military genius and created what has often been described as a 'Black Sparta'. He formed a standing army quartered in barracks and forbidden marriage till forty. He invented the technique of the short stabbing assegai used at close quarters with the protection of a huge shield, and he gave his troops mobility by insisting on bare feet instead of sandals. After the death of Dingiswayo, Shaka became ruler of the Mthethwa as well and embarked on a series of conquests which made him master of most of northern Natal. He was a bloodthirsty tyrant whose reign was one of terror and he took a sadistic pleasure in slaughter for its own sake. Eventually in 1828 he came to a well-deserved end, being murdered by another of his brothers, Dingane, himself destined to give his name to 'Dingaan's Day' – the annual celebration by the Afrikaners of his crushing defeat at Blood River on June 16, 1837 in revenge for the murder of Piet Retief and his followers.

Long before Shaka's death his course of massacre and pillage had set the whole of the Bantu peoples of the area on the move. This process known as the *mfecane* (the crushing) or *difaqane* (forced migration) caused untold deaths and reshaped in the course of a few years the whole tribal pattern of Southern Africa. By the end of it the high veld from the Orange River to the Limpopo was a devastated and depopulated area, and when the Great Trek began in 1835 the Boers found only whitening bones and burned-out kraals. The movements of tribes which resulted from the *mfecane* and the Great Trek are immensely complicated to follow – rather like movements of fleets and squadrons in a huge naval battle.

Of the many currents set in motion by the turbulent whirlpool of the *difaqane*, two directly affected Southern Rhodesia. In each case, as with many other such movements, a relatively small force of Zulu 'Kumalo' or kindred warriors set out for the north or west to escape from Shaka's vengeance. Like black snowballs, as they moved down they grew in size, encountering less martial tribes, massacring their men, forcibly enlisting their boys, carrying away their women and cattle. The first of these ferocious hordes was led by a sub-chief of the Ndandwe, a tribe which Shaka had defeated. About 1821 – no dates in this story are certain – Zwangendaba, as he was called, fled northwards. His followers confusingly called themselves Ngoni although the name is normally used as a generic term for the tribes living in the east of South Africa. Some ten years later he crossed the Limpopo and descended upon the unfortunate Rozwi. Zimbabwe was sacked. The last Rozwi Mambo according to one tradition was flayed alive, according to another threw himself to his death from the belea-guered citadel. Zwangendaba did not stay, but continued northwards across the Zambesi in 1835, eventually establishing the Ngoni kingdom on the west of Lake Malawi.

In 1822 one of Shaka's ablest generals, Mzilikazi, was rash enough to hold on to some captured cattle. This was regarded as a heinous crime since Shaka's power and wealth depended largely on his successful claim to be sole owner of the enormous herds acquired in his wars of conquest. When he heard that Shaka was accusing him, Mzilikazi fled west and then north with two or three hundred men into the high veld across the Vaal River. The familiar process soon began. Before long he had an army of 5,000 whose tactics he modelled on those of Shaka, and his kingdom with a capital near modern Pretoria had become by 1825 the dominant power in what is now the eastern Transvaal. His people were called the Ndebele (or Matabele), meaning 'people of long shields'. Seven years later he moved further west to the Marico valley in order to be out of range of continued Zulu reprisals. He was soon to meet a far more for-midable foe.

The Dutch had been established at the Cape ever since the arrival of Van Riebeeck at Table Bay in 1652. He was a ship's surgeon, the first of many medical men to play a role in southern Africa – Livingstone, Jameson, Rutherfoord Harris, Godfrey Huggins, Hastings Banda. The original settlement was intended to provide fresh vegetables and water for ships on the way to and from the East Indies. From a very early stage it was considered necessary for this purpose to have a permanent farming community there. The word Boer strictly means farmer, though it came to be applied after the Great Trek to all Republican Afrikaners. The frontier of this colony of settlement gradually advanced, despite the intention and wishes of the Dutch East India Company. By the end of the eighteenth century the eastern frontier had reached the Great Fish River and the colonists had penetrated 300 miles north. The white population was 22,000. Non-Whites, mainly Hottentots – or Khoikhoi, as they should strictly be called – outnumbered Whites by 2 to 1, some 25,000 being slaves. In 1795, as a move in the Napoleonic wars, Britain seized the Cape, fearing that the pro-French 'Batavian Republic', as Holland had now become, would hand it over to their enemy. By the Treaty of Amiens it was restored to the Dutch in 1803. The resumption of war resulted in a renewed British occupation three years later, and this was confirmed at the Congress of Vienna. The Cape was to be a part of the British Empire for the next century and a half, and there began a conflict between Briton and Afrikaner which only ended in 1961 with the final departure of the Union from the Commonwealth.

Rhodesia was in one sense destined to originate as a sub-colony of Cape Colony. Why were the British in the Cape at all? What made successive govern-ments of different political complexion not only hang on to but expand this most refractory, most difficult, least predictable and least rewarding of all their overseas possessions? No doubt there were many reasons for individual Britons to go out there – religion, adventure, gain, escapism and others. No doubt ministers and the officials who advised them were conscious of these motives. But the decisions of the government were not primarily affected by such considerations. The Cape was important to Whitehall because of the route to India. That was why it was acquired in the first place. That was why official opinion for over a century regarded it as one of the keys to British imperial supremacy. To quote one of the best recent books on imperial history, 'To all Victorian statesmen India and the British Isles were the twin centres of their wealth and strength in the world as a whole'.[1] In 1881 the Carnarvon Commission declared that the Cape was 'indispensable to your Majesty's Navy' and 'the integrity of this route must be maintained at all hazards and irrespective of cost'. The opening of the Suez Canal a dozen years earlier had made no difference at all to this assessment. It was taken for granted that in the event of war our most likely enemy, France, would be able to use her fleet to make the Canal useless.

If Cape Town could have been treated as a sort of Gibraltar the situation would have been different, but it could not. Official opinion accepted as axiomatic the proposition that paramountcy throughout Southern Africa was an indispensable corollary of paramountcy at the Cape. 'It is an entire delusion', wrote Lord Kimberley, 'to imagine that we could hold Cape Town abandoning the rest. If we allow our supremacy in South Africa to be taken from us, we shall be ousted before long from that country altogether.' The problem, therefore, became the problem of an ever receding frontier. 'South Africa', as Sir Charles Dilke wrote, 'is a Dutch colony which we have conquered in the Stadholder's name from his soldiers, then conquered a second time, and lastly bought; all three against the will of the Dutch population.' The Dutch pastoralists on the frontier never accepted this situation. They detested imperial rule. It provided a further reason for their longing for *lebensraum*. The Boer republics, created as a result of the Great Trek to the north of the Orange River, could neither be curbed nor assimilated. Yet their existence seemed a perpetual menace to British paramountcy. Where would it all end? There was force in the argument of the London *Times* in February 1853 (quoted by Derek Schreuder in his able study, *Gladstone and Kruger*):

Once embarked on the fatal policy of establishing a frontier in South Africa and defending the frontier by force there seems to be neither rest nor peace for us till we follow our flying enemies and plant the British standard on the walls of Timbucktoo.

The Afrikaners by the end of the eighteenth century constituted a nation

---

[1] Ronald Robinson and John Gallagher, *Africa and the Victorians*, 1961.

of their own and were ceasing to have links of any real significance with Holland whence they had originally stemmed, but whither they had long ceased to wish to return. One author has seen in them the last and most formidable of the nomadic tribes which swept across the southern veld in those endless migrations which constitute so much of African history; a white tribe possessing the weapons of another technological world and endowed with a faith in their own mission and purpose equal to those of any rival. Whatever the virtues of this comparison may be, it at least emphasizes a point: the Afrikaners are a unique phenomenon, and there is nothing quite parallel to them in modern history.

Conquering races have in the past usually become assimilated in the course of time – though in varying degrees – with the conquered. Thus the Normans in England, the Spaniards and Portuguese in South America, the succession of northern invaders in India. The Afrikaners have by contrast placed a rigid barrier against what is sometimes termed 'miscegenation'. Reinforced by their interpretation of the Old Testament, this 'people of the book' treated the Africans from the start as hewers of wood and drawers of water. They were not necessarily cruel. In a curious way there was a sort of love/hate relationship between the races. In certain respects the Afrikaner understood better than other Europeans what made up the African mentality. He was, after all, in one sense an African. But he was at best paternalist; there could never be any question of equality or of political rights.

British governments, in contrast, though far from liberal by modern standards, were at least influenced by some ideas which post-dated seventeenth-century Dutch Calvinism. Likewise the first wave of English settlers who arrived in 1820. Moreover, from the beginning the latter tended to be artisans and traders, to be urban rather than rural – and town dwellers are seldom as rigid in their views as those brought up on the land. Their attitude towards non-Whites was never as repressive as that of the Dutch, and they brought some of the notions of the Enlightenment with them. The arrival of British missionaries was another element in the new situation.

But the main effective pressure for reform stemmed from the British Government which in 1825 imposed an advisory council and in 1832 executive and legislative councils on the hitherto autocratic governor. In 1828 the pass laws and other restrictions on the Khoikhoi were removed. In 1834 slavery was abolished throughout the British dominions. This came as the last straw for many Afrikaner farmers, especially as the compensation turned out to be considerably less than they had been led to expect. In 1835 the Great Trek began and during the ten years course of this remarkable exodus 14,000 or something like one-sixth of the white population of Cape Colony left for the interior. The women and children travelled in those ships of the veld, slow-moving wagons drawn by oxen. The men rode on horseback. They were crack shots. Provided that they were not taken by surprise they had a fire power and mobility which made them certain victors against apparently overwhelming numbers of Africans, even when these employed the hitherto invincible tactics invented by Shaka. For defensive purposes the Boer wagons drawn up in a circle or *laager* protecting families and stores were an impregnable bulwark from which to shoot down the charging black warriors.

Mzilikazi clashed with the Voortrekkers in 1836. It soon became clear that he had met his match. Early in 1837, after a number of skirmishes, his main force was attacked and heavily defeated by Hendrick Potgieter, one of the ablest Voortrekker commandants. The Ndebele monarch himself survived along with some ten thousand followers, but he knew that this could not last, and he decided to set out on yet another stage in his amazing *Anabasis*. He crossed the Limpopo and, after various vicissitudes which included an abortive attempt to settle north of the Zambesi and the reduction of the last strongholds of the Rozwi in what is now Wankie, he established in about 1840 a mobile capital which he called Matlokotloke in the Bulawayo–Inyati area. His kingdom and dynasty were to be safe for the next half century.

The district within a radius of about fifty miles of modern Bulawayo was fully settled by the Ndebele, but their raiding parties dominated a far larger territory than that. The tribes known as the Makalanga in the south and west of Rhodesia came largely under their control, though oddly enough the conquerors seem to have been influenced in no small degree by the religious beliefs of the conquered. These were similar to those of the Rozwi, and the priests of Mwari were allowed to continue their ministrations. The tribes inhabiting the nearer parts of the east and north east plateau, collectively called the Mashona, were likewise subject to continuous raids. But it is important not to exaggerate the extent of these depredations. White settlers in the early 1890s had a double reason for pitching it high. The Chartered Company's claims in Mashonaland were believed to depend on concessions from Lobengula, Mzilikazi's successor. It was to the Company's interest to accept Lobengula's own version of his sovereignty, which according to him extended at least as far as the Sabi and Hunyani rivers, if not beyond. In the second place a part of the moral *ex post facto* justification of the destruction of the Ndebele kingdom in 1893 came to be the argument that it saved the Mashona and Makalanga from impending extermination by the assegais of Lobengula's *impis*. This made the 'ingratitude' of the Shona rising three years later all the more outrageous, and seemed to excuse the severity of its repression.

There can be no question that the life of the Shona-speaking tribes after the *mfecane* was in every way worse than it had been under the relatively placid and prosperous rule of the Rozwi Mambos. But this was not solely due to the raids of the Ndebele, which never reached beyond the Sabi–Hunyani line and seldom as far. In the area between these rivers and the modern frontier with Mozambique there dwelt Shona chiefs who had scarcely heard of the Ndebele and recognized no suzerain whatever. They had their own troubles as the century wore on with the Portuguese and other enemies, but they were not affected at all by Mzilikazi or Lobengula. Nor is it right to believe that even those within the Ndebele raiding area were the victims of totally arbitrary slaughter for the sake of slaughter. What prevailed was a tributary system, harsh, cruel and no doubt bitterly resented, not unlike an American mafia 'protection' racket. If tribute in terms of cattle, etc. was not paid, punitive action of a ruthless nature ensued. But this is not quite the same thing as the lurid picture of perpetual massacre drawn by the early European historians.

After the rule of the Monomatapa and the Changamire, the Ndebele monarchy can be regarded as the third attempt to bring modern Rhodesia under a unified authority. It covered a much smaller area than its predecessor. Yet its very compactness made it a more formidable power. Unlike its predecessors it was a rigidly centralized military monarchy, not a loose confederation ruled by a priestly king with limited powers. Nor was it much concerned with trade. It was designed for war and the herding of cattle. At the top of the social and military hierarchy was the King, whose authority was absolute. He owned all the people, the land, the cattle and the ivory. There were only two Ndebele rulers in the history of the kingdom, both of them highly capable administrators, men of formidable ability by any standards.

Beneath the King were the original Zulus or the descendants of Zulus, who had set out in 1822 to escape from Shaka. They were known as the *Abezansi*. Next came the *Abenhla*, those conscripted from the Swazi and Sotho peoples in the course of the long journey. Finally, there were the *Amaholi*, Shona-speaking peoples willingly recruited into the system after Mzilikazi's arrival in Rhodesia. These castes were not completely rigid and, after the settlement in Matabeleland, the *Abenhla* rose in status and were on occasion given quite responsible posts. Both castes regarded the *Amaholi* as far inferior. The key commanders, the *indunas*, were almost always *Abezansi*. What is more, they were royal appointees who owed nothing to any hereditary right. The Ndebele territory was divided into four provinces, each under a senior *induna*. These in turn were subdivided into regimental areas, some forty altogether. There was rigorous military training, and the army totalled 15,000 to 20,000 men. Marriage was not permitted to members of a regiment until it had proved its valour in battle. Such a system presupposed continuous warfare and it was this need which the regular raids on the neighbouring tribes supplied.

We have no reliable descriptions of Mzilikazi's rule in Matabeleland before 1854. In that year the celebrated Methodist missionary Robert Moffat, Livingstone's father-in-law, paid a lengthy visit to the capital. It was not their first meeting. In 1829 the curiosity of Mzilikazi, still in the Transvaal, had been aroused by reports of Moffat's charismatic activities at Kuruman, his famous mission station on the Bechuanaland frontier of Cape Colony. He sent emissaries. They were treated with hospitable courtesy. Moffat personally escorted them back. Mzilikazi was immensely impressed by the personality of this striking figure whose friendship seems to have filled some curious psychological need. They met again in 1835. Soon afterwards the Ndebele were driven across the Limpopo by Potgieter. Nearly twenty years passed before the incongruous couple saw each other again.

In 1852, by the Sand River Convention, Britain reluctantly recognized the independence of the South African Republic, as the Voortrekkers of the Transvaal called themselves – a fateful decision in the light of hindsight. Two years later the Orange River Sovereignty was accorded the same status. The history of South Africa thus moved on a course which, though not indeflectible, became far more difficult to change, and in the end, despite many a twist and turn, never was changed. The effects on Zambesia were to be long delayed, but profound.

The first result of Transvaal independence was a *détente* with the Ndebele kingdom. Mzilikazi signed a treaty in 1853 with the Boers; he agreed to stop traffic in arms and to give protection to travellers, foreign traders, and hunters from the Transvaal so long as they adhered to the recognized and well-guarded route via the Mangwe Pass. It was a turning point in Ndebele history. From 1840 to 1853 the King had pursued a policy of diplomatic isolation. This now ended, less by consent than from prudent recognition of an ultimately irresistible military threat. The white man with gun and Bible had arrived. Nevertheless, for various reasons in which, as with all treaties, expediency played a larger part than morality, the Transvaalers stuck to their bargain. It was not they who were to destroy the Ndebele – which is not to say that they would have hesitated to do so if the political situation had turned out differently.

In 1854 Robert Moffat, who was an explorer as well as a missionary, made a remarkable journey by compass across the uninhabited country between Shoshong, in what is now Botswana, and Mzilikazi's capital. The King was delighted to see him, but he made it clear that there would be no encouragement for him to convert the Ndebele. From his own view Mzilikazi was quite right. He must have seen that the whole social and political order on which his own power depended would be destroyed by the Christian faith. The religion of the Prince of Peace ill-accorded with a system based on perpetual war; the Ndebele way of life involved the consistent breach of most of the ten commandments, not merely as a matter of backsliding but of principle. Moffat had to content himself with dispatching supplies to Livingstone, then engaged in one of the greatest of all his expeditions, which resulted in his becoming the first Briton to see the Victoria Falls and to cross Africa from coast to coast.

Three years later Moffat returned to Matabeleland and persuaded Mzilikazi to allow him to set up a mission station at Inyati. There was strong opposition from some of the King's advisers, who saw the missionaries not only as a threat to their social order, but as the advance fifth column of an occupying power. But the King recognized the advantages of the presence of white men. They could act as interpreters, they knew how to mend wagons and weapons and they could perform other technical skills, for a missionary had to be a handyman in those days if he was to manage at all. Most important asset of all – they had medical knowledge, even if they were not all qualified doctors.

Mzilikazi had personal reasons to value this. 'He is much more aged than I expected to find him,' wrote Moffat in 1854, 'and on examination I found his disease to be the dropsy.' A diet of huge quantities of beef washed down by pot after pot of 'Kaffir beer' had damaged the King's health. Not only did he display many of the symptoms of the chronic alcoholic, but he suffered acutely, as his son Lobengula was to suffer too, from 'the statesman's malady' – the gout. He and Lobengula were thus interestingly paired with their respective contemporaries in England, the 14th Earl of Derby and Joseph Chamberlain, who, though from different causes, were martyrs to the same complaint. Moffat could ease Mzilikazi's pain even as Dr Jameson was to alleviate the distress of Lobengula. Medicine, politics and religion are closely entwined in the history of Southern Africa.

The mission at Inyati was an almost unredeemed failure. It has been so deeply revered in Rhodesian mythology as the first white Christian settlement in the country that its lack of success tends to be forgotten. Both Mzilikazi and Lobengula may have been moderate by the standards of Zulu Kings – though it is well to remember what those standards were – but they were autocrats whose single word could be death. None of their subjects who valued his life was likely to go over to Christianity in the knowledge of royal dis-approval. For a whole generation hardly a single convert was made. Nor did the missionaries have the consolation of moral solidarity and personal friendship. Robert Moffat departed in 1860. He left a party consisting of his son John, a tough extrovert Welshman called Morgan Thomas and the Rev. William Sykes, a pessimistic figure who suffered from indifferent health and the early loss of his wife.

Life at Inyati was harsh, the climate exhausting. The supplies upon which even the most frugal white man depended were scarce and very expensive. The mere process of keeping alive left little time to sow the seeds of the gospel. In any case the soil on which it had to be scattered was even more barren than the dry veld where the missionaries tried to grow their crops. The missionaries were appalled at the *mores* of the Ndebele. Robert Moffat described them on one occasion as 'an army of whoremongers ... a nation of murderers whose hand. is against every man'.[2] On another he wrote that they worshipped 'the god of war, rapine, beef-eating, beer-drinking and wickedness'. The Mashona, he continued in the same letter 'are a more civilised and industrious tribe than these leonine mortals among whom I sojourn and are a very superior race'.[3] This latter opinion would have been shared by few other white men.

It is not surprising that life on the isolated mission station was marked by explosive quarrels and bitter resentments, often about matters of the utmost triviality. The tragi-comical story is far too long to recount here. By July 1865 the missionaries living in adjacent huts were communicating with each other

[2] Quoted in Oliver Ransford, *The Rulers of Rhodesia*, 1968, 102.
[3] Rhodesian National Archives MO5/1/1, to Mary Moffat, August 1854.

by letter only, copies being duly sent on a journey of many months and several thousands of miles to the metropolitan headquarters of the London Missionary Society. 'The Directors must have sometimes wondered', Dr Ransford writes, 'whether their brethren at Inyati were living in reality or in a confused dream world brought on by the African climate.'[4]

John Moffat decided that he could stand it no longer. In 1865 he left for the station at Kuruman. Fourteen years later he resigned from the LMS to carve out a new career for himself as a native commissioner in the Transvaal and Bechuanaland. But he was destined to see Matabeleland again. In the late eighties his role in negotiations with Lobengula was to be crucial. Meanwhile Sykes and Thomas were left to fight it out at Inyati. At first the battle went in favour of Thomas, partly because his letters to the LMS were at least legible. But he fatally blotted his copy book during the interregnum after Mzilikazi died. Not only did he establish himself as a sort of prime minister to the regent, who was in temporary charge till a successor could be found[5] – an action which contravened all the Society's rules against interference in politics, though Thomas justified it on the ground of preventing a bloodthirsty war of succession. He also took some part in the highly unchristian rites with which Lobengula was installed as the new Chief. In July 1870 he was dismissed by the Directors. A welter of recriminatory letters and appeals for justice followed. Thomas wrote a best-seller called *Eleven Years in Central South Africa*. He set up a station of his own at Shiloh twenty miles from Inyati. Sykes, victorious but as gloomy as ever, remained at Inyati. When he died there in 1887 there was not a single Christian convert in Matabeleland.

Missionary activity was not the only manifestation of white interest. The quarter of a century after the Transvaalers' treaty with Mzilikazi saw the heyday of the mounted white hunter. There was a large though fluctuating demand for ivory in Britain and Europe. It was the raw material for many a hideous piece of ornamental Victoriana, and for piano keys, billiard balls (until composition substitutes became more popular) and cutlery handles. The huge herds of elephants which from time immemorial had roamed the central plateau were almost exterminated. Black hunters, with guns obtained by barter despite the treaty, played their part in this disastrous slaughter. By the late seventies the surviving herds had made their way to remote tsetse fly areas where men on horseback could not pursue them. Although elephant shooting as a carefully controlled 'sport' continues to this day, the great period of the ivory trade was over.

Frederick Selous, said to be the original of Rider Haggard's Allen Quartermaine in *King Solomon's Mines* and destined later to guide the Pioneer Column to Salisbury, saw the end of it. He arrived at Tati in August 1877 to seek his fortune, but in October we find him writing to his father from Daka, south

[4] Op. cit., 158.
[5] See below p. 25.

of the Zambesi, 'on this side of the river elephant hunting is virtually at an end, all the elephants being either killed or driven away'. Selous did indeed manage to make a living, though not·a fortune, but as a guide to prospectors and sportsmen and a collector of specimens, not as a commercial hunter.

In 1868 Mzilikazi died. He was eighty, and given his mode of life it was remarkable that he survived as long as he did. One cannot withhold admiration for the military and political skill which had enabled a man who in European eyes was a mere savage to bring his people safely to their destination after such extraordinary vicissitudes and so long a journey.

His death created a complicated problem of succession. Under Ndebele law the heir was the son of the 'senior' queen, i.e. the queen whose father was a higher ranking chief than any of the others whose daughters Mzilikazi had married. The late King was a great believer in dynastic alliances and had a large number of wives. The 'senior', however, was the daughter of a chief, Uxwiti, who back in the days when they were still in Natal had murdered Mzilikazi's father. This gave the King an irrational dislike of her son, Kulumana; the story is that he had him secretly put to death. After a prolonged interregnum under an elderly regent by the name of Nombate, Lobengula, a son by a lesser queen, was persuaded to accept the Chieftainship. He was installed in March 1870. Lobengula had himself, according to tradition, been at one time the object of his father's wrath, but had been smuggled away and brought up by priests in the Matopos. He was an intelligent man with an acute political sense. His career in many ways resembles that of certain Dark Age European monarchs educated under the auspices of the Church, and ruling a turbulent, ferocious, military aristocracy. His position was at first far from secure, for the Uxwiti family were not reconciled to the succession and it had been by no means established that Kulumana really was dead. In June one of the best fighting regiments rebelled in favour of a Ndebele Perkin Warbeck claiming to be Kulumana. Lobengula crushed them with the utmost ruthlessness, slaughtering every man. His claim to the Chieftainship was never seriously threatened again.

Nevertheless Mzilikazi's death marked another turning point in the fortunes of the Ndebele state and the role of the King. Not only did it coincide with the first European discoveries of gold in Southern Rhodesia and hence with the arrival of increasing numbers of white prospectors, traders and adventurers, but the interregnum caused a permanent shift in the balance of power within the monarchy. Lobengula does not seem to have succeeded to the same absolute authority that Mzilikazi possessed. He could not disregard – at least to begin with – the advice of the councillors who had conferred the Chieftainship upon him. Nor did he inherit one of his father's vital assets, the great wealth derived from possession of all the cattle in the realm. By some process not wholly clear, the leading *indunas* acquired a share of the royal herds and the King was relatively hard up in the early years of his reign. Moreover, the iron military discipline which had, during their wanderings, been essential to the very survival of the Ndebele began to slacken in a period of relative security. The destruction of one of the most formidable fighting regiments in the army was another source of weakness. Personally Lobengula, a man of immense size and imposing demeanour, seemed a much more formidable figure than his father, who was not only small, but soft-voiced almost to the point of effeminacy. In reality he never had quite the same degree of power.

The first discovery of gold in Southern Rhodesia since the days of the Portuguese occurred in 1867. There is a dispute as to whether Karl Mauch was the actual discoverer, or Henry Hartley, a celebrated hunter who was with him. The place was near the Umfuli River, seventy miles south west of modern Salisbury. Mauch gave the discovery some picturesque publicity in the *Transvaal Argus* and also referred to another gold-bearing area found by Hartley at Tati which lies in what is now Botswana. Lobengula laid claim to the area but his claim was disputed by the Bamangwato, an important Bechuana tribe. There was a minor gold rush to this region, and in 1870 Lobengula granted what came to be known as the Tati concession to a body called the London and Limpopo Mining Company, represented on the spot by Sir John Swinburne, a relation of the poet. The Concession, like all such documents, gave away no land. It simply conferred the right to mine precious metal. In 1871 Lobengula granted a similar concession in the north to the South African Goldfields Exploration Company which employed Thomas Baines, the painter and explorer, as its agent. In the event little came of either of these ventures. Money was hard to raise. There was far less gold than expected.

Baines, who had hoped to make his fortune, died in 1875 leaving something more valuable to posterity than wealth – the most famous paintings ever made of the contemporary Southern African scene. Mauch's high-flown nonsense about the land of Ophir did indeed implant in romantic minds an image which was to have a cogent effect two decades later, but for the moment the eyes of every prospector and speculator turned to the new diamond fields of Griqualand West where in 1869 the celebrated stone, the 'Star of Africa' had been found.

The discovery of diamonds at what became Kimberley had important political implications for the whole future of Southern Africa. The ownership of Griqualand West was disputable, though not disputed as long as it was empty veld. The bankrupt Transvaal Republic laid claim to one part of it, the Orange Free State to another. The British government had long regarded a confederation of the Boer republics with Cape Province and Natal, on the Canadian model, as the only satisfactory means of achieving a strong self-governing South African dominion under the Crown capable of dealing with the African Chiefs on its own, of coping with the endless problems of the moving frontier and above all ensuring the security of Cape Town and Simonstown. The snag was money, but if the Cape acquired the wealth of the diamond fields, confederation became a fiscal possibility. If on the other hand the Boers, with their latent hostility to England, succeeded in their claim, confederation would never come off. There had, furthermore, always been shadowy plans in the Cape to open a northern route into the 'far interior' at some future date. Griqualand West lay across that route. In October 1871, having obtained a favourable arbitration award, Sir Henry Barkly, Governor of the Cape, annexed the territory, but the price was further consolidation of Boer hostility.

Britain now seemed embarked on a 'forward' policy, and Lobengula began to feel the effects. In 1876 a mission under Alexander Bailie, a surveyor by profession, reached his court with the object of securing labour for the diamond diggings 600 miles south. The King agreed to this, but he was probably less happy when the thirty or so white traders at Bulawayo petitioned for a permanent British representative to be stationed there. Sir Bartle Frere, the new Governor of the Cape, sympathized with this request: he was a firm believer in 'forward' and he was strongly backed by Disraeli's Colonial Secretary, Lord Carnarvon, a keen imperialist and believer in confederation, who had been Colonial Secretary in 1867 when Canada had been united. In 1877 Carnarvon authorized the annexation of the Transvaal and in 1878 a British force entered Bechuanaland. The English were now on the southern frontiers of Lobengula's realm. The same year, with Frere's approval, an embassy under a Captain R. R. Patterson was sent to Bulawayo by Sir Theophilus Shepstone, the Administrator of the Transvaal. The Captain, alas, lacked tact. So did Shepstone. Seven years earlier the latter in a message to Lobengula had imprudently referred to Kulumana as the rightful heir to the Chieftainship. He could have touched on no more sensitive spot. Apparently Patterson followed suit, only in more threatening terms. He then insisted, against Lobengula's will, on making a trip to the Victoria Falls. He and his companions, who included a son of Morgan Thomas, the missionary, never returned. They were almost certainly murdered on the King's orders.

This was the classical recipe for expansion; murder of an emissary or resident followed by a punitive expedition and advance of the frontier. In 1879 war broke out between the English and the Zulus under Cetewayo, who had been given a deliberately unacceptable ultimatum to dismantle the whole military system upon which his regime depended. In the ensuing campaign, after a fearful set-back at Isandhlwana, Lord Chelmsford, the British Commander, extinguished Zulu power for ever at the battle of Ulundi. These events on the face of things boded ill for Lobengula. He was saved by two episodes which lay quite outside his knowledge, comprehension or control.

In 1880 Disraeli dissolved Parliament. The election was mainly fought on the Government's policy in India and Africa. The Liberals were victorious and Gladstone took office with a strong commitment to Treasury economy and to the reversal of an imperial policy alleged to be alike extravagant and immoral.

He had been in office less than a year when South African affairs blew up into a crisis yet again. The Transvaal Boers had bitterly resented annexation. The defeat of Cetewayo removed the only consideration which made it tolerable, the need for the help of British arms against the Zulus. Early in 1881 the Boers rose in rebellion and inflicted a humiliating defeat on the British at Majuba, the precursor of their successes two decades later at the beginning of the second

South African War. The Liberals, who had never approved of the original annexation, were disinclined to persist; they restored independence to the Transvaal Republic subject to a rather shadowy British claim of 'suzerainty'. The decision was probably inevitable in the political circumstances, but it looked too much like conceding to force what would not be conceded to justice, for anyone to feel comfortable about it, and the consequences of the first Boer War for future relations between English and Afrikaner were to be baleful.

As far as Matabeleland was concerned, the effect of British military ineptitude and Gladstonian fervour was to discredit the 'forward' policy and to leave the Ndebele state undisturbed for the time being. No more was heard of the Patterson affair. White traders, concession hunters and missionaries displaying considerable nerve continued to cluster around Lobengula's kraal. The King, with subtle diplomacy, continued to play off one white interest against another, and to govern his country by a skilful blend of conciliation and ferocity. The scenes of slaughter and superstition regularly enacted at the Ndebele court continued to horrify white observers. Whereas most Europeans looked on the Mashona and Makalanga with mere contempt, they regarded the Ndebele with fear of their cruelty and hatred of their arrogance. 'Never till I saw these wretches', wrote Sir Sidney Shippard, Administrator of Bechuanaland, in October 1888, 'did I understand the true mercy and love of humanity contained in the injunction given to the Israelites to destroy the Canaanites.'[6] The sentiment was worthy of the Voortrekkers. It made certain that when the final crunch came, the Ndebele kingdom would be crushed without misgiving or remorse.

Meanwhile, the Boers, who ruled the two ramshackle republics constantly teetering on the verge of bankruptcy, jogged along much as they had ever since the Great Trek; they led the same rough, independent, pastoral, semi-nomadic lives; they had the same rigid caste attitude; their politics were no less parochial, their administration no less deplorable; and their outlook – that of fundamentalists and flat-earthers – was almost as remote from the currents of the modern world as the minds of the Blacks and Coloureds who worked for them. But they hated England, they were deadly marksmen, they knew the veld like the backs of their hands and so they had for the moment put themselves beyond the long arm of London. But ... could it last? As Kipling wrote in *The Voortrekker*, one of his best poems:

> His neighbour's smoke shall vex his eyes, their voices break his rest.
> He shall go forth till south is north, sullen and dispossessed.
> He shall desire loneliness and his desire shall bring,
> Hard on his heels, a thousand wheels, a People and a King.
> He shall come back on his own track, and by his scarce cooled camp
> There shall he meet the roaring street, the derrick and the stamp:

[6] Rhodesia National Archives NE1/1/9, Shippard to Sir Francis Newton, October 29, 1888.

There he shall blaze a nation's ways with hatchet and with brand,
Till on his last-won wilderness an Empire's outposts stand.

In 1886 gold was discovered on the Witwatersrand in the Transvaal. The
world of Southern Africa could never be the same again.

3

Cecil Rhodes 1853–89

The effect of the discovery of gold on the Rand has to be seen in the context of British objectives in the 1880s. These had not basically changed for twenty years. Gladstone's decision to cede the Transvaal made no difference in that respect. The aim was still confederation on the Canadian model, the problem of the Boers being regarded as similar to that of the French Canadians and amenable to a similar solution. The differences among various Colonial Secretaries were of method not purpose. That continued to be the creation of a loyal self-governing union which could keep the Bantu chiefs in order, reconcile British and Afrikaners, and hence provide, without too much expense, a stable hinterland for the naval bases on the southern coast upon which Britain's imperial security was believed to depend.

There were two possible ways of achieving the needed union of South Africa. One was peaceful persuasion based on the economic and cultural drawing-power of the Cape, by far the largest and most populous of the potential components of such a federation. This in the language of the day was 'colonialism' or 'the colonial factor' – the words had a meaning different from their modern usage. The idea was that a self-governing Cape Colony under the British flag would by its own volition and momentum pull the Boer republics peacefully into a union based on mutual consent. In pursuance of this purpose the Cape, after receiving 'representative government' in 1853, was granted 'responsible government' nineteen years later. The Colonial Office hoped that it would now take the initiative.

Unfortunately 'colonialism', whatever its success had been in Canada and would be in Australia, came up against two great snags in South Africa; first, the Boers of the republics had no intention of giving up their autonomy; and secondly the Cape Afrikaners had a great deal of sympathy with them. As Leonard Thompson puts it, 'The Cape Colony was not fitted to play the crucial role in which it was cast by Britain'.[1] Not only was the white population very thinly spread over a vast area, but it was uneasily divided. The Afrikaners may have regarded the Boers of the Transvaal with a certain sophisticated contempt as parochial, narrow-minded country cousins, but they also felt a sense of kith-and-kin. Carnarvon's annexation brought out these feelings to a high degree. The *Afrikaner Bond*, their political organization founded in 1879, though never a majority, controlled a large block of seats in the Cape parliament. No government could afford to ignore their sentiments. Cape 'colonialism' backed by Rhodes was in the end to colonize Rhodesia; it never managed to absorb the Boer republics.

The alternative way of achieving South African union was direct intervention from London – 'the imperial factor', to use the language of the day. Eventually this was what succeeded, but there were only two Colonial Secretaries who can be regarded as 'activists' in the sense that they took positive steps to determine events. One was Lord Carnarvon whose coup of 1877 was reversed at Majuba four years later. The other was Joseph Chamberlain who first tried 'colonialism' through Cecil Rhodes and then, thwarted by the fiasco of the Jameson Raid, asserted the 'imperial factor' through Lord Milner in no uncertain way. Eighteen years after Majuba a second Boer War revenged the first – a pyrrhic revenge perhaps in the longer perspective of history, but one that served its purpose for half a century. And as Lord Salisbury in a different context had observed, 'fifty years ... that period is something in the lifetime of a nation'.

From the British point of view 'activism' and the 'imperial factor' may have proved in the end to be the right answer. The Colonial Office could hardly have accepted them in the aftermath of Majuba. The fourteen years from then till Chamberlain became Colonial Secretary in 1895 saw the eclipse of 'activism', and the creation of Rhodesia owed nothing to it. This was in part because British governments were worried by more serious matters than South Africa. The 'eighties' were a critical decade in British history. Ireland, the rise of radical democracy, the Egyptian imbroglio, the Penjdeh Incident – these were the issues that perturbed English statesmen. As for South Africa, they were content to hope against all probability that union would somehow happen and that the Boer republics would accept the reality as well as the outward form of British suzerainty.

The hope, such as it was, depended on two assumptions: that Britain remained the only European power of the first magnitude in the area; and that the Cape retained its economic supremacy and political drawing-power *vis-à-vis* the two republics. At the beginning of the decade both these assumptions were correct. Well before the end they had ceased to prevail.

Until 1880 the only other European country with an interest anywhere near was Portugal, which possessed the coast line of Mozambique and Angola and

[1] Monica Wilson and Leonard Thompson (eds), *The Oxford History of South Africa*, Vol. II, 1870–1966, 1971, 249.

laid shadowy historical claims to the whole hinterland. The next to enter the scene was Belgium, or rather its King Leopold, who proceeded to carve out a huge personal empire in the Congo. Neither of these for the moment mattered greatly as far as Britain was concerned. But it was a different matter when in May 1883 Germany hoisted her flag at the port of Angra Pequena in South West Africa and a year later proclaimed a protectorate over the whole of that vast but mainly arid area.

The complex reasons for Bismarck's initiative have been brilliantly analysed by A. J. P. Taylor.[2] They related to the European balance of power and stemmed from the breakdown of Anglo–French relations after the British occupation of Egypt in 1882 rather than any real desire to build up a colonial empire; Germany had neither the inclination nor the naval resources to make herself into a serious rival to Britain as the paramount power in South Africa. No one, however, could be sure of this at the time and the government of the Transvaal under Paul Kruger, its tough and determined President elected in 1883, was quick to play off Germany against Britain in order to strengthen the republic's position.

The immediate threat to Cape 'colonialism' was the extension of the Transvaal westwards across the 'missionary road' to the north until the Boer frontier became contiguous with German South West Africa. The 'missionary road' running through the eastern edge of Bechuanaland was the traditional route to the 'far interior' which, with varying degrees of enthusiasm, had been long regarded as the natural hinterland for the Colony's eventual expansion. Not surprisingly the Transvaalers regarded it as their hinterland too. British governments, ready to bend over backwards since Majuba in order to placate Cape 'colonialism', could not afford to let the missionary road go to a hostile power. But the attitude of the *Bond* was uncertain. Its leader, Hofmeyr, was inclined to allow the Transvaal to absorb the two miniature Boer republics of Stellaland and Goshen, which had half-established themselves in Bechuanaland. Faced with this hesitancy, London acted.

In January 1884 the Colonial Secretary, Lord Derby, arrived at an agreement with Kruger under what came to be known as the London Convention. This superseded the Pretoria Convention of 1881. Britain abandoned her right to have a say in the Transvaal's native policy, and there was no mention of suzerainty, but the western frontier of the Transvaal was defined, and its line was drawn well short of the missionary road. When a few months later Kruger seemed to be breaking the Convention by declaring a protectorate over part of the forbidden territory, the 'imperial factor' at once came into play. Sir Charles Warren with 4,000 men went out as a Special Commissioner in January 1885. He annexed the southern part of Bechuanaland, which became a crown colony. Ten years later it was incorporated into the Cape. Over the northern part, the modern Botswana, he declared a British protectorate. 'The Suez Canal to the interior', as Cecil Rhodes called the missionary route, was secure for the moment.

[2] *Germany's First Bid for Colonies*, 1938.

In fact the German initiative did not amount to much. Born of diplomatic considerations relevant to the balance of power in Europe, it faded away when those considerations changed. But any feeling on the part of the Cape Government or the Colonial Office that they might have over-reacted was speedily dissipated by an occurrence of which the consequences were more far-reaching than any other single event in the history of Southern Africa. In 1886 vast gold-bearing deposits were discovered on the Witwatersrand south of Pretoria and deep into the Transvaal – an area of 100 miles by 170, which seemed to possess almost inexhaustible supplies of ore. Nothing like them had ever been known before. Within fifteen years 'the Rand' was to be producing one quarter of the world's entire output of gold. It is true that the auriferous content of the ore was lower than anywhere else and the reefs were deeper, but the necessary engineering techniques, chemical knowledge and foreign capital were available on a scale which could not have been obtained a generation earlier.

The Transvaal was thus transformed almost over-night into a country of great wealth. Moreover, the site of the gold fields, unlike the diamond mines of West Griqualand, was one to which no other nation could make even a faintly plausible claim. The economic ascendancy which diamonds had given to Cape Colony was at once challenged. The prospect of South African federation under the British flag abruptly receded. The Transvaal was now a magnet rivalling the Cape. It was by no means certain which would prevail.

It is in the context of the portentous changes produced first by diamonds then gold that the founder of modern Rhodesia appears on the stage of history. Cecil John Rhodes, whom a few of the older white Rhodesians still quaintly call 'Mr Rhodes' (even as he was called half in hest, when scarcely out of his teens, by his rough companions at Kimberley), was born on July 5, 1853 in the vicarage of Bishop's Stortford in Hertfordshire. His father, the Rev. Francis William Rhodes, who was the incumbent, had been educated at Harrow and Trinity College, Cambridge. He was a man of comfortable private means. By his first wife, who died in childbirth, he had one daughter. By his second, Louisa Peacock, he had nine sons, two of whom died in infancy, and two daughters. Cecil was the third surviving son. His two elder brothers, Herbert and Frank, went respectively to Winchester and Eton after early education at a small grammar school at Bishop's Stortford, now extinct; the present school has no connexion with it. Cecil, possibly because of poor health, stayed on at the grammar school. He was a delicate looking, fair-haired boy, rather frail and gangling in appearance, at times thoughtful and slightly dreamy, at others full of fun and gaiety. His father hoped he would go into the Church. Indeed he rather surprisingly destined all his sons for this career, but in the end none of them took Orders. Cecil hankered after the Bar, but both sides were agreed on Oxford first. At sixteen he left school to be coached by his father. At this juncture he was taken seriously ill. All his plans were changed for the time being and he was sent out to South Africa in the (English) summer of 1870.

Seldom has a personal malady had more drastic effects on the affairs of a nation – or rather of the three nations which uneasily co-existed in Southern Africa. What exactly was it? Rhodes's biographers have always assumed 'T.B.' or 'consumption', the popular name in those days for pulmonary tuberculosis. It seemed natural that he should be ordered out to the dry sunny uplands of the veld in order to avoid the English winter. His death thirty-three years later is usually attributed to an aortic aneurysm developed in later life.

Certain papers discovered a few years ago at the Rhodes-Livingstone Museum at Livingstone in Zambia suggest a different explanation. Dr Charles Shee of Bulawayo, in a fascinating piece of medical detective work,[3] concludes that the illness had nothing to do with the lungs, but was the first sign of a congenital deformity known to doctors as 'atrial septal defect' and to laymen as 'a hole in the heart'. What Rhodes's doctor advised was rest, a change of air, and a sea voyage, adding that 'the lungs were sound, but the heart though not diseased was seriously over-taxed'.[4] The choice of South Africa can be explained by the fact that a fairly long sea voyage was needed and that Cecil's brother was already out there; he would thus have someone to look after him and not be cast among strangers.

At that time atrial septal defect was extremely difficult to diagnose, but the explanation certainly fits in retrospect with Rhodes's symptoms – recurrent heart attacks, becoming more frequent as he grew older; alternate phases of extreme pallor and cyanosis (the blue appearance caused by unoxygenated blood) which eventually became permanent; falls from his horse probably caused by syncope; and his terrible end as he slowly suffocated through lack of oxygen. 'Death from the heart ... there is nothing repulsive or lingering about it; it is a clean death, isn't it?' Rhodes asked Dr Jameson a few months before his final illness. The doctor, no sentimentalist, could not meet his eye as he returned an evasive answer, and Rhodes knew what lay ahead. Before modern surgical techniques were developed, sufferers from this deformity were reckoned to have a maximum life expectation of forty-nine. Rhodes was some three months short of that when he died on March 26, 1902.

This posthumous diagnosis may well account for another odd feature of Rhodes's health, his ability in spite of heart attacks to engage in strenuous activity and to perform remarkable feats of physical endurance. It is a characteristic of the malady that for long periods the unoxygenated blood is pumped into the lungs in the ordinary way. The sufferer can conduct his life normally and if he happens to be a person of great drive and energy there is nothing to stop him displaying these qualities until his disability takes over, when he falls into a phase of exhaustion and inertia.

[3] J. Charles Shee, 'The Ill-Health and Mortal Sickness of Cecil John Rhodes', *Central African Journal of Medicine*, Vol. 11, No. 4, April 1965, 88–93.

[4] Ibid. 91, quoting an anonymous fragment of biography in the Rhodes-Livingstone Museum.

It was agreed that the young Cecil Rhodes should make his sea voyage to Durban and join his elder brother, Herbert, who was growing cotton in Natal. What he did thereafter would depend on chance and health. He arrived just when the discoveries at Kimberley had excited the whole of South Africa and drawn adventurers, sometimes of highly dubious character, from all over the world. In March 1871 Herbert made his way to the diggings. At the end of the year Cecil followed him. He must have seemed an incongruous figure, a slim, blue-eyed boy in white flannel trousers sitting pensively on an upturned bucket, sometimes sorting diamonds, sometimes deep in Gibbon's *Decline and Fall* or the *Meditations* of Marcus Aurelius, sometimes just dreaming – and all the while seemingly oblivious of the cosmopolitan collection of prospectors, miners, thieves, crooks, swindlers and confidence men who surrounded him. Kimberley was a shanty town, one of the rowdiest places in the world. Drink and prostitutes abounded, gambling was on an heroic scale, shootings were frequent, and the general atmosphere, though not quite so lawless, was reminiscent of the Wild West of America. Cecil Rhodes was unperturbed by all this; he made money steadily, though at first not on a scale that could be called startling, and he remained determined to go to Oxford.

Herbert Rhodes, perpetually restless, soon returned to Natal, leaving his claims to be looked after by his brother. Cecil went into partnership with an older man, Charles Rudd, who was born in 1844 and had been educated like Rhodes's father at Harrow and Cambridge where he distinguished himself in athletics. He had come out to South Africa in 1865, also for reasons of health. The partnership proved satisfactory. In 1873 Cecil felt safe enough to leave Rudd in charge and departed to England to read for a pass degree at Oriel College, Oxford.

He must have been among the oddest undergraduates that the ancient University of Oxford has ever known. Instead of paying or drawing money by cheque, he obtained cash by selling uncut diamonds, of which he kept a supply in a small box in his waistcoat pocket. On one occasion, when bored at a college lecture, he caused an accidental diversion by dropping them on the floor after surreptitiously showing them to his neighbours. His academic career was much interrupted. The authorities were more tolerant than now of such interludes – or more lax. After keeping Michaelmas Term of 1873 he went back to Africa for over two years. The reason was a recurrence of heart trouble. The doctor he consulted thought he had only six months to live.

He returned in 1876 and kept seven consecutive terms till June 1878, devoting the summer vacations to his interests in South Africa. He was a member of Vincent's, and of the Bullingdon Club. He was Master of the Oxford Draghounds and he played polo. He joined the Freemasons as a member of the University's Apollo Lodge. In May 1876 he entered as a student of the Inner Temple, but he was never called to the Bar. He kept his final Oxford term, the last needed to qualify for a degree, in the autumn of 1881. By then he was twenty-eight, a millionaire and a member of the Cape Parliament.

Oxford's influence on him was lasting and profound. He was greatly impressed by Ruskin's famous inaugural lecture delivered two years before he went up. It is quoted often in books on Rhodes, but it deserves to be quoted again, for it so vividly illustrates the way in which attitudes have changed in the last hundred years.

> We are still undegenerate in race; a race mingled with the best northern blood . . .
> Will you youths of England make your country again a royal throne of Kings, a
> sceptred isle . . . ? This is what England must either do or perish; she must
> found colonies as fast and as far as she is able, formed of her most energetic
> and worthiest men; seizing every piece of fruitful waste ground she can set her
> foot on, and there teaching these her colonists that their chief virtue is to
> bear fidelity to their country, and that their first aim is to be to advance the
> power of England by land and sea: and that, though they live on a distant plot
> of land, they are no more to consider themselves therefore disfranchised from
> their native land than the sailors of her fleets do because they float on distant
> seas.[5]

This belief in a racial hierarchy with the 'Anglo-Saxons' at the top, in an imperial mission to colonize 'fruitful waste ground' and in the creation of a politically unified empire was a common feature of the younger generation of the 1870s. Ruskin was preaching to a receptive audience. Rhodes was by no means unusual in absorbing the sermon with enthusiasm. Where he was unusual was in his ability to translate these visions into a measure of reality. This was partly because of his wealth, for by the end of the eighties his fortune was vast. He had, with the help of Alfred Beit, a German Jewish financier of genius, obtained a near monopoly in the diamond industry at Kimberley. He was also one of the greatest 'magnates' of the Rand, though Diamonds (which he always spelt with a capital D) were his real expertise and he claimed that he never understood gold. His biographers reckon that in 1887, when he was only thirty-four, he had an income of £200,000 a year from diamonds and something between £300,000 and £400,000 from gold.[6]

Money did not matter to him for its own sake. He lived simply, and had no expensive tastes. Anyone who interprets his political aims in terms of his economic interests put the cart before the horse. His wealth was useful to him as a means of power and he employed it as ruthlessly as he had gained it. Power to him was primarily the means to a political end, though no doubt like all who are lucky enough to possess great power he came to enjoy it for itself. Yet his huge fortune was not enough to give him his extraordinary position. He might half in jest talk about 'squaring' the Mahdi, the Pope, the Kaiser. But he possessed another gift no less valuable than gold and diamonds. He could, as was said of Lloyd George, 'charm a bird out of a bush'.

This talent of Rhodes is hard to recapture today. His speeches as printed are

---

[5] Quoted in J. G. Lockhart and C. M. Woodhouse, *Rhodes*, 1893, 62, 63.
[6] Op. cit., 128.

dull and verbose, his letters slangy, unpunctuated, repetitive and at times barely comprehensible. Yet he had the personality, the magnetism, the conviction and the plausibility which can in some strange way persuade the most unlikely people and recruit the most improbable allies. Some people, it is true, refused to be convinced. One would expect the little-Englanders and the opponents of Empire to be hostile, but Lugard and Harry Johnston were two great imperialists who came to distrust him deeply; Joseph Chamberlain was only half-persuaded; Milner admired him in the end, but for long was sceptical; Lord Salisbury was highly resistant. It is probably right to say that most of the English establishment felt misgivings about him even when they admired him. They sensed that he was not one of them – and they were right. Socially, however, he could hold his own. He was not a parvenu. He spoke in the accents of an upper-class Englishman. He recruited noblemen, from dukes downward, to his company boards. The doors of the Kimberley Club opened at once for him, and he did not hesitate to use this bait when trying to 'square' a flamboyant bounder like Barney Barnato, his great rival in the diamond industry.

Rhodes was much loved by a few. He was also greatly hated by many, most of whom had never met him. The business methods of the 'great amalgamator' were very rough. 'So many done, so few to do' was the malicious parody of his famous last words. There would have been no lessons for him to learn from the tycoons in the modern jungle of take-over bids. Naturally he had a host of enemies. His style of life made him the target of malignant rumours. He never married. He was surrounded by an entourage of young bachelors. When excited he would laugh or shout in a high falsetto. 'Who do you think you are talking to, squealing at me like a damned rabbit,' Arthur Lawley once cried when repelling what he thought to be unjust abuse from Rhodes.[7] Was he a homosexual? Was he impotent? Or did he perhaps suffer from a then unmentionable disease which rendered marriage out of the question? The last of these allegations gained a certain plausibility when Sir Edmund Stevenson, one of the doctors present at his death, stated nearly a quarter of a century later in a book of memoirs that an aortic aneurysm was found at Rhodes's autopsy. There is a well known connexion between this and syphilis. Dr Shee, however, points out that the contemporary post-mortem notes do not refer to any such defect.[8] It is hard to believe that it would not have been mentioned had it existed.

As for the other rumours, plenty of people have squeaky voices without being impotent or homosexual – Bismarck, for example. Rhodes was certainly not an Oscar Wilde. His rather emotional friendship with younger men, especially with his secretary, Pickering – to whom he had left all his fortune and whose death was a great blow to him – might perhaps suggest some sort of repressed inclination in that direction, but nothing more. The matter is of no importance. Some people – perhaps more then than now – do not marry for the simple reason that they do

[7] See below p. 92.
[8] Shee, op. cit., 92.

not want the bother. Rhodes himself said that when he was young he was too busy to look for a wife, and when he was older marriage would have been a distraction from his great objective. Why not leave it at that?

His adversaries had a stronger case when they alleged that he drank too much. There is a conflict of evidence, but it does seem true that he imbibed freely – at least towards the end of his life; the reason may well have been the worry caused by his ailing heart. His favourite refreshment, like Bismarck's, was champagne mixed with stout – a combination which to the taste of some drink-lovers, including the great Saintsbury, spoils both beverages.

Whatever the reason, he aged prematurely. Lean and spare as a young man, he became thick and paunchy by forty. In his last years he looked at least a decade older than he really was. It is impossible to say with certainty whether this was caused by self-indulgence – he was also a heavy eater – or by his innate cardiac deformity, but the latter explanation seems more probable.

Rhodes could be arrogant, autocratic and rude when he saw no reason to be charming. He talked endlessly himself and disliked listening to others. He could fly into a temper and use brutally scathing language. He could also be generous, kind and considerate – especially to young men of no importance, whose support did not matter to him in the least. He was intensely loyal to his friends, some of whom scarcely deserved his trust, but he never forgave an enemy nor forgot an injury. He could be very vindictive. If on the debit side he was unscrupulous in his dealings, harsh to his opponents, reckless in taking the short cut to his objective, much can be forgiven to a man conscious that his time was running out and obsessed by the goal he had set himself.

Rhodes's ideas were a strange hotchpotch of adolescent fantasy and grandiose realism. The provisions of his successive wills attest to the former, the story of what he achieved to the latter. The obvious nickname which was given to him corresponds to the truth. He always thought and acted on a colossal scale. Southern Africa in the 1880s and 1890s was perhaps the latest place in the history of the world where a single individual could operate in this way. Rhodes believed that 'the Anglo-Saxon race' and the British Empire were the heirs to the future. The heady atmosphere, the vast empty spaces, the unknown mysteries of the north, the reality of one new El Dorado, the prospect of another – all contributed to an almost unlimited optimism and self-confidence.

If only the opportunities were seized, might there not be a British dominated belt running from the Cape to the Nile valley? This was Rhodes's obsession, his dream, his success and his failure. In the splendid phrase of Mr Frank Clements, 'Cecil John Rhodes was an Elizabethan – the endless rolling plains of Africa his sea'.[9]

Ironically in one sense, the man who has come to be regarded as the arch-imperialist was a strong opponent of the 'imperial factor'. Rhodes was a 'colonialist'. This did not mean that he was anti-British, though for a time he had this

[9] *Rhodesia, Course to Collision*, 1969, 14.

reputation. 'Who is Mr Rhodes?' Salisbury asked once of Harry Johnston, and answering himself went on, 'Rather a pro-Boer MP in South Africa, I fancy'.[10]

Rhodes certainly believed in co-operation between Afrikaners and British, but he never deviated from the object of a Southern Africa united under the British flag. This was quite compatible with acute dislike for what he regarded as the ham-handed, fussy, ignorant attitude of Whitehall. He believed in the wisdom of the man-on-the-spot, which he contrasted with the allegedly doctrinaire attitude of the Colonial Office under the pressure of a host of 'do-gooding' influences, missionaries, humanitarians, economizers, little-Englanders. He correctly saw that the cautious mandarins who advised ministers in London would never, if they could help it, take the risks involved in realizing his Cape-to-Cairo dream. The initiative would have to come from the Cape itself.

From 1886 onwards the struggle for the supremacy in South Africa intensified. The Cape and Natal on the one side, the South African Republic (the Transvaal) and the Orange Free State on the other, waged a war of tariffs, railway concessions and claims to their respective hinterlands. The conflict was personified in the rivalry of Rhodes and Kruger. In this struggle Zambesia was a vital factor for two reasons: its alleged wealth in gold, and its geographical significance – gold or no gold – in the future pattern of Africa. Clearly there would be no Cape to Cairo railway, no broad red band traversing the continent from one end to the other, if the Boers moved into southern Zambesia and cut the access to the north. More significantly as far as London was concerned, the triumph of Kruger would be a fatal blow to British supremacy at the Cape and would bring the hesitant *Bond* down on the wrong side.

In 1887 this possibility seemed all too likely to be realized. Lobengula was persuaded in July by an emissary of Kruger, one Piet Grobler, to sign a treaty of friendship with the Transvaal and to allow Grobler himself to take up residence as the South African Republic's Consul at Bulawayo. The treaty was later denounced by Marshall Hole, the first official historian of Southern Rhodesia, as an imposture.[11] There is no real reason to believe this,[12] even though Grobler was a shady character. Clearly, however, Lobengula soon regretted signing it. Kruger's power to make such a treaty was very doubtful under the terms of the Pretoria and London Conventions. Lobengula would not have known this, but he may well have become uneasy about Boer ambitions, and he could not have forgotten that they were the people who had driven his father out of the Transvaal into Zambesia fifty years earlier.

The Grobler treaty was not at first made public, but rumours of its existence soon reached Rhodes and he was disturbed at its implications. He promptly saw

[10] Quoted Woodhouse and Lockhart, op. cit., 164.

[11] *The Making of Rhodesia*, 1926, 61–2.

[12] See L. H. Gann, *A History of Southern Rhodesia, Early Days to 1934*, 1965, 72–3 for a discussion of the question.

Sir Hercules Robinson and urged him to declare a protectorate on the Bechuana-land model over southern Zambesia. Robinson knew that the Colonial Office would never swallow this, but he was prepared to accept Rhodes's alternative proposal and send someone to negotiate with Lobengula. The man chosen for this task was John Moffat, now Assistant Commissioner to Sir Sidney Shippard in Bechuana-land. Moffat of course knew Matabeleland well from his missionary days and was liked, trusted and respected by Lobengula who called him 'Joni'. The King would not have been so friendly if he had known that Moffat regarded the destruction of Ndebele power as the prerequisite for any improvement in 'this gloomy land of sin and violence'.[13]

He arrived in Bulawayo in December and on February 11, 1888 obtained the King's signature to what has come to be known as 'the Moffat Treaty'. The text is set out in numerous books.[14] The gist of it was that Lobengula, 'ruler of the tribe known as the Amandebele, together with the Mashona and Makalaka tributaries of the same', promised to give no part of his territories to anyone 'without the previous knowledge and sanction of Her Majesty's High Commissioner in South Africa'. If taken seriously this meant the abandonment of the right to conduct an independent foreign policy; and there was no quid pro quo in the form of British protection.

But what did Lobengula and his *indunas* really understand by it? The question must often recur to any historian of this strange impact between two alien worlds. It comes up again with the even more controversial matter of the Rudd Concession a few months later. How far could a Matabele Chief and his advisers appreciate what was implied in the documents to which they put their marks – implied, that is to say, in the minds of the sophisticated Europeans with whom they were dealing? Lobengula must have believed that he was getting something in return when he undertook not to alienate his lands without the British Government's consent. Why was this not in the treaty? It is clear that Moffat and the Rev. C. D. Helm, a missionary to whom Lobengula also listened, encouraged the belief that British protection was being granted. It is also clear that no such undertaking was ever made. Lobengula's later appeals to London or the Cape fell on deaf ears.

In April the treaty was ratified by Lord Knutsford, the Colonial Secretary, and the fact duly appeared in the *London Gazette*. It created a sensation. Kruger promptly published the Grobler treaty and the Portuguese Consul in Cape Town protested with some justice at the inclusion of the Shona tribes as vassals of Lobengula. When Lord Salisbury declared the whole of southern Zambesia to be 'exclusively within the British sphere of influence', both Portugal and the Transvaal refused to accept the claim. Relations with the latter were made no better by the murder in slightly obscure circumstances of Grobler himself early

[13] Quoted in Ransford, *Rulers of Rhodesia*, 156.
[14] See Sir Lewis Michell, *The Life of the Rt. Hon. Cecil Rhodes*, 1910, Vol. 1, 240-1; Marshall Hole, op. cit., 54 and Lockhart and Woodhouse, op. cit., 139.

in July, while returning from Bulawayo to the Transvaal via Bechuanaland. Kruger believed that Rhodes was responsible, but there is not a scrap of evidence to support the charge.

The British Government was in something of a dilemma as regards colonial policy. Salisbury could not afford to let southern Zambesia go by default to the Portuguese or to Kruger – especially the latter. It would ruin the British aim of paramountcy in southern Africa if the Cape Colonials were to be baulked of their northern ambition. On the other hand, it was clear enough that occupation of the territory was the only successful way of asserting that ambition, and it was no less clear that the 'colonial factor', if left solely to the Cape Parliament, would achieve nothing of the sort. Even the prolongation of the Cape/Kimberley railway – the 'Bechuanaland extension' designed to run west of the Transvaal frontier – was the subject of endless dispute, for there was a party which preferred to build the shortest line to the Rand. If that came off, the chances of Zambesia falling to the Transvaal would be greatly increased.

The alternative course of bringing in the imperial factor and declaring a protectorate was equally unsatisfactory. The British tax-payer, at least as interpreted by the Treasury, had a great aversion to paying for such seemingly barren additions to British rule. Lord Salisbury's peculiar political position must not, in this context, be forgotten. His first Chancellor of the Exchequer, Lord Randolph Churchill, resigned on a point of Treasury economy at the end of 1886. He was replaced by Goschen, a Liberal Unionist, and it was on the votes of the Liberal Unionists that Salisbury depended. The new Chancellor was a particularly strict exponent of Treasury dogma. Whether or not there is any truth in the famous story about Lord Randolph, it is quite certain that Salisbury could not afford to 'forget' Goschen. A protectorate, therefore, was to be avoided as long as possible.

A further difficulty was the position of Portugal – an element in the situation too often omitted in the treatment of this complicated story. The Portuguese, however dubious their claim to a broad band of Africa running from coast to coast, had managed to get it accepted by France and Germany in 1887. They too could only make it good by occupation, and the British counterclaim seemed suddenly to have awakened them from an age-long torpor. They became unexpectedly active, especially in relation to the area that was later to become Nyasaland and is now Malawi.

This was embarrassing because of the position of the Scottish missionaries there. It was a legacy of Livingstone and much religious zeal had been invested in it and in its subsidiary, the Lake Company (though not enough cash for the latter was nearly bankrupt). Salisbury did not wish to alienate the Scottish voters, who would be deeply incensed if their missionaries became subjected to Portuguese Papist bigotry. He therefore tried to fob off England's oldest ally in October 1888 by offering, subject to the acquiescence of the Cape, a free hand in northern Zambesia in return for agreement to leave Nyasaland and southern Zambesia alone. Lisbon, perhaps unwisely in view of later developments, refused. Negotiations continued for the rest of the year and on into 1889, but no agreement could be reached.

Salisbury is sometimes depicted as a lethargic figure who needed to be prodded into activity by the energetic and dynamic 'Colossus'. This is unfair. He was well aware of what was at stake. Unlike his predecessors at Ten Downing Street, he had actually seen the Cape. Indeed, he spent three months there in 1853 on his way to Australia and he knew personally something of the Colony's problems, opinions and aspirations. But there were many constrictions on his freedom of action and there were other places besides southern Africa to draw his attention: Egypt, Russia, France, India, Ireland. Let us leave him for the moment in his Jacobean palace at Hatfield, heavy-bearded, silent, enigmatic, tireless, working through his red boxes, weighing this course against that, always aware of the limitations imposed by Cabinet colleagues, Parliament and public opinion upon the choices open to a statesman – even to one who combined, as he did, the Foreign Office with the Premiership.

He is waiting upon events, looking for an opening. He could not take the initiative, but he would seize the opportunity when it came his way. And at the end of April 1889 it came. As a result of a complicated series of transactions which will be described in the next chapter, Cecil Rhodes was in a position to take the first step in his campaign for the 'far interior'. He arrived in London and applied to the Colonial Office for a royal charter for a company which he proposed to form with no less an object than the development and colonization of north and south Zambesia, together with the extension of the Bechuanaland railway.

British policy in Southern Africa had reached an impasse. Now there was a chance to get out of it.

4

The Concession and the Charter 1888–89

The Moffat Treaty had given the British government a negative hold over Lobengula; it excluded the political intervention of other powers. But the situation from Rhodes's standpoint remained precarious. It was clear that neither Whitehall nor the Cape would act on their own to secure effective occupation of the vast area north of Bechuanaland and the Transvaal. They would not indeed stop Rhodes from doing so, but he had somehow to raise the money either to add further funds to an established company or, as in fact he chose, to float a new venture. For this purpose a mineral concession from Lobengula – 'the gold of Ophir' – was essential.

At this juncture, early in 1888, Rhodes paid a fleeting visit to London. He was disturbed to find that two other companies, the Exploring Company and the Bechuanaland Exploration Company, were in the field lobbying the Colonial Office. They were closely connected and had interlocking directorships. The key figures were George Cawston, a financier, and Lord Gifford who was just under forty, had won the VC in the Ashanti War of 1873–74 and had been Colonial Secretary first for Western Australia, then for Gibraltar. He was clearly *someone*, and his influence would not be negligible. Their 'managing director' was a young adventurer, Frank Johnson, who in a different capacity was to be deeply involved in the creation of Rhodesia. The Colonial Secretary, Lord Knutsford, received their overtures with non-committal courtesy; he rightly doubted their ability to raise the money. The Exploring Company's ambassador in Bulawayo was Lieutenant E. A. Maund, a man of self-confidence, good appearance, much charm and some deviousness. He established a close *rapport* with Lobengula.

Clearly Rhodes needed to act quickly on his return to South Africa, but he sent an odd triumvirate to Bulawayo. His partner of early days, Charles Rudd, was the leader – a tall, bearded, rather melancholy-looking person. He was reliable, efficient, loyal, businesslike and very discreet. Years after Rhodes's death he threw a chest containing all his papers into the sea from his yacht off the Hebrides, declaring, 'There go the secrets of the Jameson Raid'.[1] He died in 1916 and something of South African history died with him. The next man in the party was J. Rochfort Maguire, an Irishman who had obtained three firsts at Merton College and had struck up a warm friendship with Rhodes when the latter was an undergraduate at Oriel. Maguire was a barrister and a Fellow of All Souls. Lastly there was F. R. ('Matabele') Thompson, a South African who had reorganized the compounds at De Beers. He was supposed to understand the African mind and some African languages. But he had as a boy seen his father murdered in an African revolt by having a ramrod hammered into his throat till it came out through his back; he was not the ideal choice for a role which required an iron nerve in dealing with Africans.

They were an ill-assorted trio. Rudd was a man of experience in Africa and well qualified to deal with the business side of the affair, but he lacked imagination. Maguire was a neat, slightly donnish little man who prided himself upon cleanliness and correctitude; he treated everything with a dead-pan 'Oxford manner' which at least gave nothing away. His job was to see to the legal drafting of the concession. He was, however, hopeless in the practical problems of life in Zambesia and, according to Thompson, could not even use a tin opener. Rhodes, however, thought that he had one important asset beside his legal expertise; he could teach the classics to Thompson on the long journey and sojourn in Bulawayo. Thompson had missed a university education (later, like Rhodes, he became an elderly Oxford undergraduate), and Rhodes was a passionate believer in the importance of the Greek and Roman authors. Maguire's success or otherwise is not recorded, but we do know that the trio passed the weary days waiting upon Lobengula's pleasure in backgammon and whist rather then Aeschylus and Livy.

They set out from Kimberley on August 15, ostensibly as a big-game hunting expedition. Their baggage included an introductory but uninformative letter from Sir Hercules Robinson, £10,000 in gold sovereigns, together with appropriate quantities of brandy, champagne and stout to assuage their own thirst and that of Lobengula who had become highly partial to these non-African beverages. Other white men in the party were Rudd's son, Frank, a friend by the name of Denny and a Dutch transport rider called Dreyer. The journey took ten weeks. Lobengula tried to stop them on his frontier, but they persisted and he received them civilly when they arrived on September 20. As Rhodes had expected, the situation was anything but clear. A host of speculators and concession-seekers already hung around the Chief's kraal, and others were hot on their heels.

The doyen of the trading corps was S. M. (Sam) Edwards, born in 1827 who lived to the age of ninety-five. He was the principal inheritor of what was known as the Tati Concession acquired from Lobengula by Sir John Swinburne in 1869.

---

[1] Private information. It is odd that someone whose name will always figure in the history books is recorded neither in the *Dictionary of National Biography* nor in *Who was Who*.

Even better established were James Fairbairn, the custodian of Lobengula's great elephant seal which alone validated treaties, contracts and concessions, and William Usher, another confidant of the Chief. They were regarded as members of the tribe and were the two Europeans to remain in Bulawayo during the Matabele War of 1893. They did not welcome the arrival of Rudd. There was also present Thomas Leask who, along with Fairbairn, L. C. Phillips and W. S. Tainton, had obtained in July exactly the concession from Lobengula sought by Rudd and his companions, but they lacked money, and in the end were easily bought out by Rhodes. Messrs Alexander Boggie, Cooper-Chadwick and Benjamin ('Matabele') Wilson, who defeated even Sam Edwards in longevity and died in 1960 at the age of ninety-nine, constituted another group. They too found it prudent to come in on the side of Rhodes at an early stage.

Finally – and more formidable – were Messrs E. R. Renny-Tailyour, Frank Boyle and Riley. This trio, perhaps luckily for Rhodes, arrived after Rudd and his party. Renny-Tailyour was acting on behalf of E. A. Lippert, a German banker recently established in the Transvaal. He was a cousin of Rhodes's business friend and partner, Alfred Beit, but he had quarrelled with Beit and was very willing to put a spoke in the wheel of the partnership. For the time being Renny-Tailyour was frustrated. Three years later, again on behalf of Lippert he was able to cause Rhodes much trouble.

The power of Mammon was thus well represented at Lobengula's court – only Maund being absent – but that of God should not be forgotten. There was Dr Knight Bruce, Bishop of Blomfontein who, with a German count, was engaged on an inspection of the mission stations in Zambesia. There was the Rev. C. D. Helm of the London Missionary Society, presumably one of those being inspected. He was much trusted by Lobengula and was a witness of the signature of the Moffat Treaty. Finally there was Moffat himself, who could be said to represent church and state, a former missionary and now Assistant Native Commissioner for Bechuanaland – officially accredited as British representative at Bulawayo. With both Helm and Moffat on his side Rudd had important advantages over his rivals when dealing with the Ndebele King.

As for their rivals, Rudd, or rather Rhodes had one supreme asset – gigantic wealth. The articles of association of De Beers, thanks to remorseless pressure by Rhodes on Barnato, Joel and their associates, had been drawn up in the widest possible terms. The company was legally entitled to do almost anything. Rhodes had taken the same precaution with his second great financial empire, Consolidated Goldfields of South Africa. The combined capital at this time of the two enterprises is estimated by his official biographer as thirteen million pounds.[2] None of the other concessionaires, actual or potential, could lay their hands on resources remotely approaching such a figure. Rhodes was in a position to buy them out with ease and he did so, often spending extravagant sums on claims of a dubious nature.

[2] Lockhart and Woodhouse, op. cit., 158.

Money, however, was not in itself particularly relevant to the problem of Lobengula. The Chief lived in a style and on a level where gradations of wealth which meant a great deal in European terms meant nothing at all to him. Even if every rival concession-seeker vanished, it did not follow that Rudd would be successful. Lobengula, whom all accounts agree to have been a shrewd and perceptive ruler, was well aware of the constraints upon his action, and was in a dilemma. He knew that in a battle with European forces he was bound to lose. He could see everywhere the threat of European advance, apparently in peaceful form, but ultimately backed by armed strength – the Portuguese from the east, the British and the Boers from the south.

He was faced with another problem. The Ndebele were no longer the all-conquering soldiers that they once had been, even in combat with other tribes. Only three years earlier in 1885 one of his *impis* received a crushing defeat from the forces of Khama, the Chief of the Bamangwato. Armed with modern rifles, they destroyed the Ndebele army near the Okovango River. The Ndebele had failed to secure adequate firearms, nor did they possess any cavalry – again unlike Khama who had some 300 horsemen in his numerically inferior but technically superior army. Khama's ascendancy was due to his prudent espousal of British protection, and to long-established trade relations which supplied him with the weapons he needed. His dynasty still survives. Why could Lobengula not achieve a similar relationship with the British? In fact he would probably have preferred it, but he was not an absolute monarch. He might move preceded by a grovelling claque proclaiming his praise in stylized but fulsome language; he might mete out arbitrary and unchallenged justice under the immense tree which still stands in the grounds of Government House outside modern Bulawayo; he might throw his assegai to indicate the direction of the next season's raids and be obeyed to the letter. But he depended, as perhaps all apparent tyrants do, on a certain degree of consent. Lobengula always consulted his principal *indunas* on matters of importance and often accepted their advice. The social structure of the Ndebele state militated against just those changes which were needed for political and military survival. Its economic bargaining power was on the decline with the exhaustion of its ivory. It could not easily obtain the modern rifles needed to replace the elephant guns and blunderbusses which constituted the army's only alternative weapons to the assegai. Worse still, the whole mentality of the Ndebele military leaders was resistant to reform. Like the Prussians before Jena or the French before Sedan, they were rigid conservatives who thought in terms of the tactics of a vanishing world.

There were clashes of interest within the state. The army was bitterly opposed to European penetration. Its hot-heads clamoured for the slaughter of every white man in the country – a demand which Lobengula knew would be fatal if conceded and which he continued to repulse with ironical contempt. On the other hand there existed among the *indunas* a group which profited from dealings with prospectors and traders, as indeed Lobengula did himself. They saw at least some hope for the future in a deal with the British whose attitude was to their minds,

45

even at worst, preferable to that of the Boers. Their leader was a rich and elderly *induna* by the name of Lotje who had much influence on the King and was a quasi-prime minister. Yet this party was not strong enough nor was Lobengula to take the path of Khama and put the country under British protection. It was hardly surprising that the King hesitated and vacillated, made promises first to one then to another European supplicant, granted concessions which contradicted previous concessions, and generally behaved erratically and incalculably. Nor was his judgement improved by liberal potations from the numerous cases of champagne and brandy presented to him by aspiring concessionaires.

Most contemporary accounts agree that the Ndebele Chief was intelligent, subtle, dignified and every inch a monarch (and there were a great many inches, for he was very tall, very stout and weighed twenty stone). But they agree too that negotiation with him was a trying experience. September and October are months of rapidly rising temperature, preceding the rainy season which usually begins some time in November. Ndebele court etiquette required the King's visitors to squat (no chairs were provided) on their haunches before him in the royal goat kraal and eat large quantities of half cooked meat usually covered with fat flies, the unsavoury repast being washed down with pot after pot of luke-warm 'Kaffir' beer. Maguire must often have sighed for the delicate viands and well-stocked cellar of All Souls College. The heat was intense, the smell overpowering, and the discussions or *indabas* – conducted for hours on end under the almost vertical sun – seemed interminable and often incomprehensible. Matters were made more difficult to bring to a head on account of Lobengula's preoccupation with various magical activities in connexion with rain-making, which required lengthy and unpredictable periods of solitude.

About the middle of October Maund arrived, bent on the purpose of securing a rival concession for Lord Gifford's companies, but his nose was put out of joint two days later by the appearance of Sir Sidney Shippard, Deputy Commissioner of the Bechuanaland Protectorate, with an escort of sixteen troopers from the British Bechuanaland Police. His ostensible object was to enquire further into the circumstances of Grobler's death, but he was also an ally of Rhodes. Having arranged for chairs, to avoid the humiliating posture normally required of the King's visitors, he appeared before Lobengula in a tightly buttoned frock coat with the Star of the Order of St Michael and St George, grey kid gloves and patent leather boots. He carried a silver-headed malacca cane and wore a white solar topee. Since it was by now almost the hottest season of the year – well over 100° in the shade – such garb required no small devotion to duty, but it was rewarded. Lobengula was much impressed and listened carefully. Sir Sidney then departed. At the end of the month, after two days of prolonged discussions with his *indunas* at which Rudd and party were present, Lobengula at last took a decision and on October 30 set his seal to a document drawn up in legal language by Maguire. It is in Rudd's handwriting, signed by Rudd, Maguire and Thompson, and witnessed by the missionary Helm and by C. D. Dreyer, a Dutch transport rider in Rudd's party. Helm, moreover, certified that he had explained the document to Lobengula and his council of *indunas* and that it had been executed in accordance with 'all the constitutional usages of the Matabele nation'.

The Rudd Concession[3] gave the grantees 'complete and exclusive charge over all metals and minerals situated and contained in my Kingdom, principalities and dominions together with full power to do all things that they may deem necessary to win and procure the same'. There was also authorization from the King to exclude, with his assistance if necessary, 'all persons seeking land, metals, minerals or mining rights', and an undertaking 'to grant no concessions of land or mining rights ... without [the grantees'] consent and concurrence'. The rights under the Tati Concession were expressly reserved. The Rudd Concession made no positive grant of land, though negatively it precluded other people from securing such grants. In return for these rights the grantees undertook to supply the King with £100 a month, 1,000 Martini-Henry breech-loading rifles, 100,000 rounds of ammunition and a steam boat on the Zambesi armed with 'guns suitable for defensive purposes', or, if the King should prefer, £500 in lieu.

It is doubtful whether Lobengula would have agreed at all but for certain oral promises made by the trio. The most important of these is mentioned by Helm who was only prepared to lend himself to the transaction on that basis. He wrote to the London Missionary Society on March 29, 1889:

> They [Rudd and party] promised that they would not bring more than ten white men to work in his country, that they would not dig anywhere near towns, etc. and that they and their people would abide by the laws of his country and in fact be as his people.[4]

If this undertaking really was given as an inducement – and there is no need to doubt Helm's word – then Rhodes's representatives were being disingenuous, to put it no more strongly. They were well aware that he planned a settlement in Mashonaland. Occupation of land was as much the object of the enterprise as extraction of minerals. Even if mining had been the sole purpose, there could never have been the slightest possibility of thus limiting the number of men. However that may be, the fact remains that this and other oral promises were not written into the concession. It is unlikely that the omission was accidental.

The urgency which Rhodes impressed on his emissaries is shown by Rudd's immediate action. The King's seal was set on the document at noon on October 30, and Lobengula 'gave Rudd the road', as the expression was. Four hours later he departed post haste for Kimberley with the concession and £2,500 in gold, partly to bring the document to Rhodes as soon as possible and partly to get it away from Bulawayo before his numerous rivals could discover what had happened and

---

[3] The full text is in Sir Lewis Michell, *The Life of the Rt. Hon. John Cecil Rhodes,* Vol. I, 1910, 244–5.

[4] Printed in V. W. Hillier (ed.), *Gold and Gospel in Mashonaland 1888,* 1949, Oppenheimer Series 4, 227–8.

persuade the King to change his mind. Except for agreement that he nearly lost the concession, the gold and his life, accounts differ about what followed.[5] He set out either on his own with a Kaffir driver, or with Dreyer, or with his son and Denny, from whom he became separated. Lost in the waterless, burning wastes of Bechuanaland he collapsed either under a tree, in a fork of which he placed the concession, or near an ant-bear hole where he buried the concession and/or the gold. He either remained there till he was rescued by some Bechuanas or he wandered onwards on horseback or on foot having left a letter fastened to a tree indicating the whereabouts of the gold and the concession,[6] collapsing in a delirium later and being rescued by Bushmen or stumbling into a Bushmen camp. In one or other of these situations he was revived and recovered his precious possessions.

He reached Kimberley without further mishap. Rhodes was cock-a-hoop when he saw the document. 'With this signature and the certificate of the missionary', he cried, using the jargon of a now obsolete card game, 'I'm ready to go nap, double-nap, Blucher, or anything.'[7] Early in December Rudd arrived in Cape Town with a copy for Sir Hercules Robinson. The High Commissioner, like most of the Crown officials in the Colony, was a Rhodes man. On December 15 he wrote to Lord Knutsford at the Colonial Office, forwarding the copy and adding his hope that 'the effect of the concession to a gentleman of character and financial standing will be to check the inroad of adventurers as well as to secure the cautious development of the country with a proper consideration for the feelings and prejudices of the natives'.[8]

Rhodes was well aware that securing the concession was only the first stage in his campaign. Apart from other problems, there was the danger that Lobengula might repudiate it at any time before the rifles arrived – which could not be soon. True to his favourite shibboleth – 'Nature abhors a vacuum' – he had insisted on keeping some representatives at the royal kraal until the deal could be finally ratified. Marshall Hole, author of the best account of these events, rightly considers, however, that Rudd had made a tactical blunder in leaving with the concession and not remaining in Bulawayo himself.[9] Rudd was an old South Africa hand with long experience. Maguire and Thompson, who were left behind, lacked the knowledge, authority, hardiness and nerve needed to cope with the Ndebele monarch and the importunate crowd of rival suitors endeavouring to upset the concession.

---

[5] Compare the differing versions to be found in Basil Williams, *Cecil Rhodes*, 1921, 127; Marshall Hole, *The Making of Rhodesia*, 1926; J. G. Lockhart and C. M. Woodhouse, *Rhodes*, 1963, 147; Colonel Ferris, *Draft History of the British South Africa Company* (unpublished), 31–2.

[6] This at least appears to be correct for the paper has survived and is in the Salisbury Archives, RU2/1/2.

[7] Ferris, op. cit., 32.

[8] Quoted Lewis Michell, *Cecil J. Rhodes*, I, 247.

[9] Op. cit., 76.

The two most formidable opponents of Rhodes, representing different interests it is true, but ready to enter into a temporary alliance, were Maund on behalf of the Gifford group and Renny-Tailyour on behalf of Lippert. Rumours spread by various interested parties had questioned the very existence of the 'Great White Queen'. Renny-Tailyour put the idea in Maund's head of persuading Lobengula to send personal emissaries accompanied by Maund to London to clear up this question. His motive was in part to remove Maund from the scene. Both of them were seeking personal mineral concessions, and it is possible, but non-proven, that Maund obtained one, although any such document must have been invalid if the Rudd Concession stood. Late in November Maund departed from Bulawayo with two elderly *indunas* and two letters alleged to be from Lobengula to Queen Victoria. One, authenticated by Helm, was a declaration dated November 24, 1888 of Lobengula's territorial claims *vis-à-vis* the Portuguese in Mashonaland and in effect an appeal to the Queen under the Moffat Treaty for protection.[10] It was if anything helpful to Rhodes, for it reaffirmed Lobengula's dubious claim to rule over those areas. This was a vital point in the effectiveness of the Rudd Concession as far as London was concerned. It was of course also equally vital for anyone who wished to substitute another concession from Lobengula for Rudd's.

The second letter was more questionable. It merely had the King's elephant seal for authenticity and since the trader, Fairbairn, to whom this object was entrusted was by now in the pocket of the anti-Rhodes faction, one cannot be sure that it really represented Lobengula's mind. The gist of it[11] was that the King was sending his *indunas* as 'his eyes to see whether there is a Queen', that he was 'much troubled by white men who come into his country and ask to dig gold', that 'there is no one with him he can trust, and he asks that the Queen will send someone from herself'. There is no mention of the Rudd Concession. On the way south at Kimberley Maund was to meet Rhodes who strongly pressed him to show the letter, but Maund refused. Later, in Cape Town, according to one account, Maund having heard of the possibility of a merger between Rhodes and the Gifford companies did agree to show the better authenticated of the two letters.[12] Early in February he sailed for London with the two *indunas* and John Colenbrander, an expert interpreter.

Rhodes was by now aware that Lord Gifford and Cawston had early in January put in an application on behalf of the Exploring Company for a charter to settle and trade in Bechuanaland, together with a strong suggestion that they had acquired concessions in Matabeleland which might shortly justify a similar application.[13] What with this development and Maund's mission, Rhodes saw that it was time to weigh in heavily. The visit of the *indunas* held out boundless possibilities of sentimental agitation by British 'do-gooders'. He had better be on

---

[10] For text see J. G. Macdonald, *Rhodes, a Life*, 1927, 104–5.
[11] For text see Hole, op. cit., 79.
[12] Lockhart, op. cit., 150.
[13] Hole, op. cit., 85–6. Knutsford replied in non-committal terms.

the spot as soon as possible. He sailed shortly after Maund and in May he was followed by the High Commissioner, Sir Hercules Robinson, who had a considerable pull with Lord Knutsford at the Colonial Office, and was able to be of much assistance in the matter of the charter. Unfortunately just before leaving Cape Town Sir Hercules made a speech in which he referred to 'the amateur meddling of irresponsible and ill-advised persons in England which makes every resident in the Republics, English as well as Dutch, rejoice in their independence, and converts many a Colonist from an Imperialist into a Republican'.[14] There was a storm in Parliament. Sir Hercules felt obliged to resign, and on August 20 was replaced by Sir Henry Loch, a believer in the 'imperial factor' and far less favourable than Robinson to the policy of Rhodes.

Maund and the *indunas* were suitably fêted. The two elderly chiefs (the oldest, Babyan, was seventy-five, his colleague, Mshete, ten years younger) were vouchsafed an audience with Queen Victoria to assure them of her existence. They were also treated to a military display at Aldershot where the Gatlings jammed with deplorable frequency, and to a grand breakfast with the Aborigines Protection Society whose chairman, Sir Fowell Buxton, hoped that before long 'Englishmen and Matabeles would meet in the valleys of the Limpopo as happily as they did that day in Westminster'.

On March 26 Lord Knutsford wrote a reply on behalf of the Queen to the letters delivered by Maund and the *indunas*. He dealt primarily with the less authentic of the two, not even mentioning the Portuguese claims to Mashonaland. The operative words were that Englishmen who asked leave to dig in Matabeleland had no authority from the Queen, and that she advised Lobengula 'not to grant hastily concessions of land or leave to dig'. Then came the key paragraph:

It is not wise to put too much power into the hands of the men who come first, and to exclude other deserving men. A King gives a stranger an ox, not his whole herd of cattle, otherwise what would other strangers have to eat?[15]

This was bound to be read as a clear warning against the Rudd Concession, and it is hard to believe that it was not inspired by Maund.

However, on the surface Maund and Rhodes, who saw much of each other, were friendly enough, and indeed the whole situation as between the rival interests was changing. Rhodes soon 'squared' Lord Gifford and Cawston who probably never had any serious expectation that their resources – a mere £50,000 – could compete with the millions at Rhodes's command, and were chiefly engaged in raising the price at which they could be bought out. A suitable amalgamation having been arranged, Lord Gifford as Chairman of the Exploring Company made formal application to the Colonial Secretary on April 30 for a charter to develop Bechuanaland 'and the countries lying to the north'. His letter was accompanied by one

[14] Quoted Basil Williams, op. cit., 81.
[15] Hole, 82.

signed by Rhodes and Beit on behalf of Gold Fields of South Africa pledging their co-operation.

Maund who ought, as far as his employers were concerned, to have moved over to the side of Rhodes, had departed early in April with the *indunas*, carrying the letter from Lord Knutsford and another from the Aborigines Protection Society equally inimical to the Rudd Concession, though obviously less authoritative. Maund later maintained that he had shown Lord Knutsford's letter at once to Rhodes, who sent him back to persuade the Colonial Secretary to alter it, but Knutsford refused because the Queen was abroad and he would not do so on his own responsibility. According to Maund, Rhodes then suggested that he should drop it overboard 'by accident' on the return voyage, but Maund refused.[16] Rhodes's account is quite different. He maintained that Maund never told him of the vital passage in the letter. 'You remember how he hid in that room of mine and said that there was no such message in the Queen's letter,' he indignantly wrote to Cawston six months later.[17] He described Maund as a liar[18] and some of his coadjutors used even stronger language. It is hard to believe that Maund was not playing some crooked game of his own. If so, he did himself and his employers nothing but harm. The letters did not reach Lobengula until August and their effect was nearly fatal to the whole enterprise.

Meanwhile Rhodes was busy in London on many other 'squaring' operations. There were a host of dubious claims and alleged concessions to be bought out. This was not too difficult, for he was prepared to pay lavishly in order to purchase peace. More serious were the forces that opposed the grant of a charter on grounds of principle. The London Chamber of Commerce saw it as a monopoly deal in favour of a rich Cape mining group and in contravention of the doctrine of free trade. The South Africa Committee, composed of such reputable parliamentary figures as Albert Grey, who succeeded as 4th Earl Grey in 1894, the Duke of Fife who was a son-in-law of the Prince of Wales, J. Arnold Foster, who was a future Conservative War Minister, and the formidable Joseph Chamberlain, feared that the Company would seize the land of the natives. They were backed by the Aborigines Protection Society, and their fears were fully justified by the event. Colonial Office officials anticipated a Matabele war, and they too were to be proved right. Disagreeable questions were asked in the House by Labouchère and others who deeply distrusted Rhodes. Underlying all these objections was the profound apprehension felt by missionaries, philanthropists and imperial paternalists that 'the natives' would get short shrift from the 'colonists' and needed to be protected.

At this juncture in his fortunes Rhodes displayed to the full his magical power of persuasion, that mysterious charm with which he was able to convert the seemingly inconvertible. It has to be remembered that he was not yet quite the

---

[16] Lockhart, op. cit., 111.
[17] Quoted Robert Cary, *Charter Royal*, 1970, 65. Lockhart, ibid.
[18] Lockhart, ibid.

celebrity that he soon became. Lord Knutsford appears to have been under the impression that he was Sir Hercules Robinson's secretary. Salisbury, as we saw earlier, thought of him as 'rather a pro-Boer MP in South Africa'. His achievement is therefore the more remarkable. He had been given a strong hint from Salisbury that a charter would not be granted unless some reputable non-South African names were on the Board. Believing in carrying the war into the enemy's camp he approached Albert Grey, his opponent on the South Africa Committee. Grey, a man of the utmost probity, consulted Joseph Chamberlain who said, 'I only know three things about Rhodes and they all put me against him: (1) he has made an enormous fortune very rapidly, (2) he is an Afrikander,[19] (3) he gave £10,000 to Parnell'. Grey joined nevertheless, and so did the Duke of Fife, another member of the Committee, while Rhodes put the seal of respectability on his venture by recruiting the Duke of Abercorn as chairman. He could not have achieved what he did without some strong cards in his hand, the two strongest being his vast wealth and his knowledge that the occupation of Zambesia was, though for different reasons, as necessary to the Government as to him, and that Whitehall could not or would not pay the cost from its own resources. But it was a remarkable performance all the same.

In the realm of what would now be called the 'media' he was equally successful. W. T. Stead, the colourful and celebrated editor of the *Pall Mall Gazette*, was an 'imperialist' who took an unfavourable view of the Rudd Concession, but after a luncheon followed by three hours talk he was won over, and eventually became a trustee of Rhodes's will. He was, however, not a total convert; he later spoke his mind in no uncertain way on the Jameson Raid and eventually Rhodes put him out of the trusteeship in a codicil 'on account of the extraordinary eccentricity of Mr Stead'. Another of his converts was *The Times* colonial correspondent, Flora Shaw. She later married Frederick Lugard, but Lugard, who had cause to feel badly let down by Rhodes, was never converted and always deeply distrusted his wife's hero.

In the journalistic world Rhodes received one slight set-back. Among the many people whom he saw in London was F. C. Selous, whom he had never met before. They got on well enough but Selous had been in Mashonaland four years earlier and was contemplating another visit in June to secure concessions for his newly formed Selous Exploration Company in which Frank Johnson was closely involved. Selous was not only highly sceptical of Rhodes's plan, vaguely outlined at that time, to occupy Mashonaland via Bulawayo, he was also convinced that Mashonaland was not in Lobengula's gift at all – or at least that a large part of it was not; and in May he wrote an article to that effect for the *Fortnightly Review*.[20] Most modern historians would agree with Selous[21] but it was an essential point in the case for the charter that the Rudd Concession covered all the lands claimed by

[19] Chamberlain meant by this a 'colonialist' as opposed to an 'imperialist'.
[20] *Charter Royal*, 49.
[21] See above, Ch. 2, pp. 19–20.

Lobengula and so included the whole of Mashonaland. Rhodes was to have some difficulty over this with Selous later, but for the moment he let it pass.

Despite the arrival in London on June 18 of a fraudulent letter allegedly emanating from Lobengula and denouncing the concession, but in fact concocted by Fairbairn in the anti-Rhodes interest, progress continued smoothly towards the grant of the charter. It was a slow business. The petition was formally submitted on July 13. The approval of the Colonial Office was needed, then that of the Foreign Office and also of the Prime Minister – a process not necessarily expedited by the fact that he was Foreign Secretary as well. The charter had to go to a committee of the Privy Council which heard objections – and there were quite a number. Then it went to the whole Council. In the end the petitioners were able to show an unencumbered title to the satisfaction of the lawyers. On October 29, 1889, three hundred and sixty-four days after the signing of the Rudd Concession, the charter was duly sealed under Letters Patent signed by the Queen.[22]

Its scope was immense, though not quite all that Rhodes and his friends asked for. The Bechuanaland Protectorate, perhaps as a sop to the humanitarians, was not at once put into the Company's hands, though there was a virtual promise that it soon would be. On the other hand, no northern frontier was placed on the Company's operations, despite strong objections in the Colonial Office which favoured the Zambesi. Salisbury evidently felt no need now to placate the Portuguese. Acquiescence in this demand of Rhodes is surprising. Hitherto Salisbury's policy had been to buy off Portugal with northern Zambesia. Now by agreeing to the revised territorial provisions of the charter he was in effect staking a British claim (which might or might not be enforceable) over a vast new area of which very little was known. His decision has never been adequately explained, nor is it known just how Rhodes managed to persuade him. The upshot was that the Company could operate anywhere in 'the region of South Africa lying immediately to the north of British Bechuanaland [the colony, not the protectorate], and to the north and west of the South African Republic [the Transvaal], and to the west of the Portuguese dominions'.

Yet one should not overstate the power thus granted. The preamble states:

the Petitioners desire to carry into effect divers concessions and agreements which have been made by certain of the chiefs and tribes inhabiting the said region and such other concessions, grants and treaties as the Petitioners may hereafter obtain ... with a view of promoting trade, commerce, civilisation and good government.

Whatever the Company did depended, legally at least, on agreements with local

[22] The original directors were the Duke of Abercorn (chairman), the Duke of Fife (deputy chairman), Albert Grey, Cecil Rhodes, Alfred Beit, Lord Gifford, George Cawston. The full text of the charter is in Michell, op. cit., 331–42.

chiefs or rulers. The Crown could not and did not purport to confer more than this. The most important clause was number 3, which authorized the Company, subject to the approval of the Colonial Secretary,

> to acquire by any concession agreement grant or treaty, all or any rights interests authorities jurisdictions and powers of any kind or nature whatever, including powers necessary for the purposes of government, and the preservation of public order in or for the protection of territories, lands, or property, comprised or referred to in the concessions and agreements made as aforesaid or affecting other territories, lands, or property in Africa, or the inhabitants thereof, and to hold, use and exercise such territories, lands, property, rights, interests, authorities, jurisdictions and powers respectively for the purposes of the Company and on the terms of this Our Charter.

This was certainly a very wide authority, but it could not be exercised except on the basis of concessions present or future, and the only existing one was Rudd's. On this narrow and insecure basis there balanced a vast inverted pyramid of potential future power.

The charter contained many other points of substance, some permissive, some restrictive. The Company could raise its own police force and fly its own flag. It could make roads, railways, telegraphs and harbours. It could establish banks and conduct mining operations. It could settle territories that it acquired and it could irrigate and clear land. It could make loans for any of its purposes.

The Colonial Secretary, however, had a veto on most of its actions, and, in the event of disputes between chiefs, dealings with foreign powers or adverse claims, the Company had to accept his ruling. It was obliged, 'so far as may be practical' – a proviso which enraged the humanitarians – to abolish the slave trade and the sale of liquor to natives. It had to respect the customs, laws and religion of the peoples who might come under its jurisdiction, and if the Colonial Secretary dissented from its policy in this respect, his word prevailed. The Company had to furnish him with accounts and an annual report of its administrative, though not its commercial, activities. After twenty-five years the charter could be replaced or amended by the Colonial Secretary, and would be subject to similar review at ten year intervals thereafter.

One important point not mentioned in the charter itself was an undertaking by the Company to push ahead with the railway from Kimberley first to Vryburg then to Mafeking, and to extend the telegraph from Mafeking to Shoshong.

Salisbury seems to have regarded the new company with some misgivings. He considered that its functions would be more appropriately performed by the Government. It was true that in theory the Government could control most of the Company's actions, but there was a gulf between theory and practice, and the fact that Rhodes was picking so many of Whitehall's chestnuts out of the fire gave him a hold which no amount of legal provisos would in practice easily slacken. For there was no other way out of Salisbury's dilemma. He had to keep the Cape Colonists on his side by preventing the Transvaalers from seizing the 'far interior', but both he and the Cape lacked the means. Treasury economy and the exigencies of colonial policy were alike satisfied by Rhodes's offer. There was no obvious alternative, and any doubts about the grant of a charter were removed by Lord Knutsford's argument that the position would be even worse

> if it were left to these gentlemen to incorporate themselves under the Joint Stock Companies Act as they are entitled to do. In the latter case Her Majesty's Government would not be able effectually to prevent the Company from taking its own line of policy which might possibly result in complications with native chiefs and others, necessitating military expenditure and perhaps even military operation.[23]

The original share capital of the Company consisted of one million £1 shares. De Beers subscribed for 200,000, the promoters reserved 90,000 for themselves, and the public rushed eagerly for the rest. There was, however, a certain *suppressio veri* involved, which must be regarded as one of Rhodes's least creditable actions. The public and indeed the Government assumed that the Rudd Concession belonged to the Chartered Company. This was not so. It was owned by an ephemeral body called the Central Search Association formed in April 1889. The directors were Rhodes, Beit, Gifford, Cawston, one A. O. Maund and Charles and Thomas Rudd. They agreed at the end of 1889 to let the Chartered Company have the use of the Rudd Concession in return for half the profits. In July 1890 the Central Search Association turned itself into the United Concessions Company with a capital of four million £1 shares based on its claim on the Chartered Company's profits. The United Concessions was happy to be bought out for one million specially created shares in the Chartered Company. Since these stood at £3 to £4 each and were to go higher, the potential windfall for the principal holders was enormous. When the facts emerged in 1891 there was something of an uproar, and in 1892 Lord Ripon, Colonial Secretary in the new Liberal Cabinet, receiving the Company's report about the concession, formally put on record that 'it is clear that Her Majesty's late Government was unaware of it when they advised the grant of the Charter. Whether knowledge of the arrangement would have influenced their action is a question which they alone could answer ...'

Since the departure of Rudd on October 30, 1888 much had happened in Bulawayo. The Maund mission has already been described. In itself it was a sign of increasing doubt on the part of Lobengula. Maguire was still in sufficiently good odour to accompany an *impi* sent early in the New Year in order to turn back a party heading for Tati and led on behalf of the Austral Company by

[23] Hole, op. cit., 100.

Alfred Haggard, the brother of the famous novelist.[24] Thereafter, however, things went badly. Maguire, after cleaning his teeth with scarlet toothpaste in what he took to be quiet, secluded waters some miles from the King's kraal, stripped and was about to take a bath when he was apprehended by a group of furious Ndebele and hauled naked before Lobengula. It was a sacred pool of vital importance in Ndebele religious and medical practices. The sinister colour of the toothpaste told its own tale. Poisoning and witchcraft could alone explain his conduct. He was let off with a warning and a heavy fine in cloth which he happened and was known to possess, and his toilet accessories including a much prized bottle of Eau-de-Cologne were confiscated.[25] Understandably, Maguire became impatient to get out, while Thompson grew ever more jittery.

Rhodes was worried about his representation in Bulawayo even before he sailed to England in February (1889). A notice had appeared in *The Bechuanaland News and Malmani Chronicle* on January 18 purporting, under Lobengula's signature, to suspend the concession. Its authenticity was dubious, but clearly all was not well. Early in February Rhodes persuaded two Kimberley doctors to visit Lobengula on his behalf. One, Dr Jameson, was to play a major role, partly good and partly evil, in Rhodes's career and in the affairs of Rhodesia. The influence of the other, Dr Rutherfoord Harris, was to be wholly baleful.

Leander Starr Jameson had become Rhodes's closest confidant after the death of his secretary, Neville Pickering, in 1886. He was an exact contemporary and, after a brilliant start to his medical career in England, he left for South Africa in 1878 because of the strain of overwork when he was only twenty-five. He set up his plate in Kimberley and in that cosmopolitan, easy-going ambience his charm, *bonhomie* and genuine medical ability soon gave him a large practice and great popularity. 'The Doctor', as he was called ('Dr Jim' is a subsequent invention of the English press), became one of the 'characters' of Kimberley. He was a notable gambler, particularly at whist which he played for large stakes badly. He never married but, unlike Rhodes, he had the reputation of being, in the phrase of the day, 'a lady's man'. In some ways he was a cynic. He would listen to Rhodes's endless monologues in silence broken only by an occasional deflatory interpolation. Yet at heart he was a romantic adventurer, and he fell totally under the magician's wand.

In spite of all that has been written about him, this mercurial, unscrupulous, intrepid, reckless, restless, tireless medical man is one of the great enigmas of his time. His career was extraordinary on any view. The man who won over Lobengula, made possible the success of the Pioneer Column, shattered Ndebele power (and was rewarded with a CB), was a hopeless administrator, provoked a rebellion, committed the crowning folly of the raid (and was rewarded with a prison sentence). Yet he recovered, became Prime Minister of Cape Colony,

[24] Williams, op. cit., 127; Hole, op. cit., 75 n. 1; Lockhart, op. cit., 148. It is amusing to note the different versions.

[25] Lockhart, op. cit., 148–9; Ferris, op. cit., 32.

a Privy Councillor and a Baronet, and is buried on World's View near Rhodes as one of Rhodesia's heroes. All this is on the record, but what were his 'springs of action'? Most of his papers have disappeared, as seems so often to be the case with Rhodes's closer colleagues (e.g. Rudd and Frank Johnson). His official biography is adulatory and unrevealing. No one has adequately analysed his personality. Perhaps the materials do not exist. Rhodes depended greatly on him and up to a point his flair was an invaluable aid. In the end he let his master down disastrously, not only over the raid, but in his deplorable administration of Rhodesia which led directly to the 'rebellion' of 1896. To him Gladstone's phrase applied to Disraeli's relationship with his leader, Lord Derby, might be justly adapted – 'Dr Jameson, at once Mr Rhodes's necessity and his curse'.

Rutherfoord Harris was a less important character. A born gas-bag, he talked incessantly and too much. He was unstable, impetuous, and anything but straightforward. His part in the Jameson Raid was very shady. Jameson himself in retrospect had little use for him: 'a muddling ass – on the surface a genius but under the crust as thick as they are made'.[26] Flora Shaw described him as a born intriguer and a mischief maker. One can only marvel at the lack of judgement which Rhodes could sometimes display when he made him some months later the Chartered Company's Secretary at Kimberley.

The two doctors arrived in Bulawayo on April 2, accompanied by a contractor bringing goods of the utmost importance, the first half of the consignment of arms and ammunition promised under the concession. If Lobengula accepted this – he was already taking the £100 per month – it would be a clear sign that the concession was ratified. The King, however, was still torn by doubts. He placed the weapons in charge of a guard of his soldiers under J. C. Chadwick, one of the traders who had plumped for Rhodes, but he did not formally take possession and, though Maguire and Thompson claimed that he had thus ratified the concession,[27] this was clearly not correct.

Jameson stayed for only ten days, but he at once established a close *rapport* with Lobengula, whose gouty pains he was able to alleviate and whom he delighted by his breezy charm and genial bedside manner. However, he had his practice to look after in Kimberley, and he left on April 12. He was accompanied by Maguire who understandably felt he had had enough of Bulawayo. The only survivor of Rudd's party was now Thompson, whose nerves cannot have been strengthened by the nightly adjuration in a low whisper from his trusted servant, 'Ou Master we never come out of this country alive'.[28] By now there was a horde of white concession hunters and the anti-Rhodes party was soon in the ascendancy again. They hinted that the King had been tricked into giving away the whole country. It was at this stage that the bogus letter which reached London

---

[26] Ian Colvin, *Life of Jameson*, Vol. I, 1922, 239.
[27] J. G. McDonald, *Rhodes, a Life*, 1927, 108.
[28] Lockhart, op. cit., 148.

on June 18 denouncing the concession was concocted and dispatched.[29] Yet, though a fraud, the letter did express something of Lobengula's uneasiness. The younger and more militant of his *indunas* had always detested the concession. Their fears were exacerbated by Renny-Tailyour and his minions, and the King found himself on the defensive against a powerful element of his own people.

Lobengula consulted the local missionaries, in whom he had much faith. Had he really given away his land under the concession (the original document was not available)? Could the white men dig anywhere in search of gold? Were there any limits? Their replies did not reassure him. The months of the South African winter passed uneasily. Then in August Maund arrived with two *indunas*, carrying the letters from Lord Knutsford and the Aborigines Protection Society. Just before setting off from Cape Town at the end of April he had been informed by telegraph of the amalgamation of the Gifford/Cawston interests with those of Rhodes and Beit. He was instructed henceforth to use all his efforts in favour of the Rudd Concession.[30] But he did not feel able to suppress a letter written in the name of the Queen. As for the Aborigines Protection Society, it took no risks and had already had its missive published in a Mafeking newspaper.[31]

The immense delay between the sending and receipt of letters from London or even Cape Town to Bulawayo is one of the most confusing features of this narrative. The railway had not gone beyond Kimberley. A thousand miles of parched semi-desert lay ahead. It could take as long as three months to cross by slow bullock-wagon. Knutsford had written on March 26 under the influence of an anti-Rhodes group before its subsequent amalgamation with Rhodes and their joint request for a charter. The letter was – if one can imagine such a thing – like an accidentally constructed and long delayed time bomb, and it was to kill a good many people.

It was read out at an audience with the King attended by Maund, Moffat and all white men in Bulawayo, together with the two *indunas*, one of whom was drunk and alleged that he had been advised in London to tell the Chief to allow no white men to dig for gold except as his servants. On August 10 Lobengula dictated a letter to Moffat who used an empty champagne case for a table. He took up the point about 'servants', which was indeed one of the oral provisos confirmed by Helm as an inducement to sign the Rudd Concession. But the letter did not reach London till November 18 and much had happened by then.

The prospect for the pro-Rhodes party now darkened. Knutsford's letter could be readily interpreted as a warning from Queen Victoria against the Rudd

---

[29] See p. 53. The letter was dated April 23, 1889 and was not witnessed by Helm or anyone of repute. Nor was it sent, as would have been normal, via Moffat. See Hole, op. cit., 107–9.

[30] Hole, op. cit., 110.

[31] Lockhart, op. cit., 151.

Concession. Early in September Lobengula summoned a council of *indunas* at which he denounced Helm for deceiving him. Then he rounded on the unfortunate Lotje, leader of the pro-concession party among the Ndebele, whom he accused of 'blinding his eyes'. Accounts of what followed differ in detail, but not in substance. Lotje was either strangled or had his skull beaten in by a knobkerry that night or a few days later. His wives, descendants and dependants – sixty according to one version, three hundred according to another – were slaughtered. Even his animals were exterminated and all that remained of his kraal was a heap of smouldering ash. Thus perished the Stratford of the Ndebele dynasty – victim partly of the caprice of a tyrant, partly of a letter written by a well-meaning English peer thousands of miles away and many months earlier in obsolete circumstances.

These events finally broke the nerve of 'Matabele' Thompson. Returning from a visit to Helm's mission station the day after the slaughter, he was given an ominous message – 'Tomoson, the King says the killing of yesterday is not over'. Simultaneously he observed a crowd of Ndebele warriors whose attitude seemed threatening. He unharnessed and jumped on to the nearest of his horses, borrowed a saddle[32] from Fairbairn's store and rode hell for leather south. The horse, 'Bulawayo', was a notorious bolter. Four years later in the first Matabele war it ended its own and its rider's life by heading straight into the middle of an *impi*.[33] But on this occasion its vice was a virtue. Thompson rode for two days till 'Bulawayo' foundered, and then continued on foot till, exhausted and thirsty, he reached Shoshong, proceeding thence at a more leisurely pace to Mafeking.

The vacuum, abhorred by Rhodes if not by nature, had now been created. Apart from Maund who, having been hitherto on the other side, carried little weight with Lobengula, and Moffat who was tied by his semi-official position, the pro-Rhodes faction had wholly vanished. Nor can there be any serious doubt that Lobengula and his councillors regarded themselves as rid of the concession. True, the King, with his remarkable capacity for procrastination and his extraordinary dislike of ever actually saying no to anything, never formally repudiated it, but he did not need to. He had never accepted the rifles. Until he did so the concession had no validity.

At this juncture Rhodes intervened. He had left England in August, leaving negotiations for the charter in the hands of his agents. He was weary of being fêted. Feeling rather like those American senators who in recent years have complained of being 'steaked to death' by Washington hostesses, he declared that he 'saw no reason to make my interior a dustbin for anyone'. On receiving the news at Kimberley of Thompson's flight, he realized that urgent action was needed. Once again he switched on all his charm. Once again Jameson responded. Along with Denis Doyle, an interpreter – and picking up a very reluctant Thompson at Mafeking *en route* – 'the Doctor' arrived in Bulawayo on October 17.

[32] Hole's version, op. cit., 114. Other accounts say that he rode bare-back.
[33] Ibid., n. 1.

He was to stay in those insalubrious surroundings for the next four months.

The saga of Jameson's sojourn has often been told. Hastiness and impatience were to be the defects with which later he ruined both himself and Rhodes. On this occasion his conduct was precisely the opposite. Thompson had wanted Rhodes to come in person, and Lobengula seems to have expected his arrival, for which there was on the face of things much to be said. In fact Rhodes would never have put up with the seemingly interminable *indabas* in the goat kraal. Nor of course did he possess the medical knowledge of Jameson who with his syringe and his morphia could relieve the King's gout and with various ointments alleviate his sore eyes – and could do so moreover with inexhaustible good humour, great charm and infinite patience.

One of Lobengula's demands was to see the original concession. Jameson had brought it with him and he handed it to the Chief, taking the risk that it would be at once torn up. Lobengula, however, scarcely glanced at it, and handed the paper to Moffat for safe-keeping.[34] A dangerous fence had been jumped. Jameson's purpose now was to have the concession ratified – or at least stop positive repudiation – and to 'get the road' for the expedition planned by Rhodes for the occupation of Mashonaland. It was not a simple operation and it was made no easier by the numerous white rivals whom he had to buy off or otherwise placate. Early in December he managed a preliminary break-through. Lobengula gave permission to mine for gold north of Tati. He still thought in terms of a few white men 'digging a hole'. Happy to go along with this idea, Jameson at once dispatched a small party of prospectors. It was the first mining operation of the Chartered Company and as such one of the least successful, but it served a purpose.

The warm, wet, weary weeks of the Rhodesian summer passed slowly, but although Lobengula continued to treat Thompson with sarcastic contempt, he became more and more cordial to Jameson. He even made him an honorary *induna*, which necessitated dressing up in a cloak of ostrich feathers and other paraphernalia for a grand army review. On January 27, 1890 a party as incongruous as could well be conceived turned up at Bulawayo. On November 15, 1889, only three days before the receipt of Lobengula's reply to his letter of March 26, Lord Knutsford had dispatched a lengthy missive to the Chief intended to undo the effects of that earlier letter. At Rhodes's instigation and as a riposte to Maund and his two *indunas*, the letter was entrusted to a party consisting of two officers, a corporal-major and a trooper of the Royal Horse Guards in full uniform. The physical discomfort of the four military men in the heat of Bulawayo must have equalled if not surpassed that of Sir Sidney Shippard in his frock coat, and their appearance had a similar effect. Lobengula was much impressed by the scarlet coats, the glittering brass, the polished leather. The dispatch itself was worded in the worst Whitehall jargon and made no mention

[34] According to Hole, op. cit., 116, this episode occurred on Jameson's arrival. J. G. McDonald, *Rhodes, a Life*, 117, dates it on November 28.

at all of Rhodes, referring only to the now almost forgotten names of Rudd's mission. But any doubts that Lobengula might have had about its meaning were forestalled by Jameson, who substituted a version of his own. In this the unqualified support of the Queen for Rhodes and the charter was strongly emphasized. Moreover, rumours of a Portuguese incursion from the east and a Boer *trek* from the south were made the most of by Jameson to influence the King's mind.

A day or so later 'the Doctor' informed the Chief that the operations north of Tati had yielded no result. Lobengula replied that he had better look somewhere else. Might he go east, asked Jameson, since any move further north would inconvenience the Ndebele kraals? Aware by now of Selous' plan for the Pioneer Column[35] he showed on a map the proposed north east route to Mashonaland. The King, unpredictable as ever, agreed. Would he supply some of his own men to help to cut the road for the wagons? Again the surprising answer was yes.[36] The only condition was that Jameson should himself accompany the party. After four exhausting months Jameson had now got as much as he could expect. 'Given the road' on February 13, he departed next day with Thompson for the south.

Within twenty-four hours the King appeared to vacillate once more. He summoned his *indunas*, the military envoys, Moffat, Colenbrander and Doyle. How, he grumbled, was he to answer the contradictory letters of March 26 and November 15 from the Great White Queen? In the end he sent a temporizing reply which neither confirmed nor denied the Rudd Concession, but he still declined to take over the arms and ammunition.

[35] See Chapter 5.
[36] Hope, op. cit., 125.

5

The Pioneer Column 1889–90

When Rhodes returned to South Africa in September 1889 it was clear that he had to act as quickly as possible to occupy Mashonaland. His vast plans for Barotseland, Katanga, Nyasaland, Manicaland and a sea port in Mozambique depended on this break-through. But he could not move in before the dry season of the following year. At first, doubtless for financial reasons, he envisaged a comparatively modest expedition. He recruited an élite group of twelve men of character and ability as the nucleus; they were known as Rhodes's 'apostles'. Obviously they could not go alone without an armed escort. Temporarily enrolled in the British Bechuanaland Police, they were to be protected, so Rhodes planned, by a specially raised troop of one hundred of that corps financed by the Chartered Company. The 'apostles' arrived at the police training centre at Elebe in Bechuanaland on November 9.

Other counsels soon prevailed. A new character at this juncture appears on the scene. Frank Johnson, son of a Norfolk country doctor, was only twenty-three, but he had already had an adventurous career. He had served on the Warren Expedition at the age of eighteen. Along with three friends, Henry Borrow, Maurice Heany who was American, and Ted Burnett, he had formed in 1887 a syndicate called 'the Great Northern Trade and Gold Exploration Company', with the object of obtaining concessions from Khama and Lobengula. He succeeded with Khama, but six months of weary waiting at Bulawayo produced nothing except a fine of £100 for witchcraft. From that moment onwards Johnson had it in for Lobengula, whom he regarded as treacherous, murderous, unreliable – and formidable. Subsequently he and his friends were involved in various complicated company transactions and he became Managing Director of the Bechuanaland Exploration Company, one of the two commercial concerns through which Cawston and Lord Gifford operated. In the course of their sell-out to Rhodes, Johnson found himself jettisoned without compensation for his own claims.

He was furious, but meanwhile early in 1889 he had joined up with Selous in the Selous Exploration Syndicate, the object of which was to secure concessions in Mashonaland direct from the chiefs concerned. Selous set out by boat from Cape Town to Quelimane in July 1889, and thence to Tete, Zumbo and the mountain which he named Mount Darwin. He obtained mineral concessions in the Mazoe valley area from two leading headmen of the Makorikori tribe. Part of his purpose was to discover whether Mashonaland could be occupied from the east via the Zambesi. We have seen how, earlier in the year, while in London, he had poured cold water on Rhodes's admittedly very vague plan of entering via Bulawayo. Selous was still sure that this would be disastrous, but he now realized that the Zambesi was not a possible alternative. He returned to Cape Town at the beginning of December convinced of three things: first, that the alternative route must be found from the south; secondly, that the Portuguese had penetrated much further west than had hitherto been appreciated; thirdly, that the area of Mashonaland which he had visited recognized no allegiance whatever to Lobengula.

During Selous' absence Johnson, Heany and Borrow from mid-November onwards were in close touch with Rhodes, who saw that they could be useful to him. He offered to reserve 3,000 shares for them in the Chartered Company and to buy them plus Selous out of the Selous Exploration Syndicate. The great man was in a state of anxiety. Jameson had been at Lobengula's kraal since late October, but no clear news had arrived. Rhodes was unsure how to proceed. Johnson convinced him that Lobengula's military power was too strong to risk a peaceful expedition to Mashonaland via Bulawayo. Instead Johnson proposed a military coup – 500 trained ex-members of the South African police and other forces to be raised at Rhodes's expense in order to make a dash for Bulawayo and either kill the King or hold him as a hostage; the joint reward of success for Johnson and Heany was to be £150,000 and 50,000 morgen of land together with all captured horses and cattle. The 500 were also to receive various land and prospecting rights.

This crazy scheme was taken sufficiently seriously by its two promoters to have it all set out in a rather loosely worded contract, a copy of which survives in the National Archives at Salisbury.[1] In the same place can be found Johnson's own account of the episode[2] intended as a part of his autobiography, *Great Days*, which came out in 1940. The passage was suppressed at the request of Sir Godfrey Huggins, the Prime Minister of Southern Rhodesia, on the ground that it would do harm at a moment when Germany was trying to stir up African opinion against the British.[3] According to Johnson the contract, which is dated December 7, was actually signed by Rhodes and witnessed by Rutherfoord

[1] NAR JO3/2. The document and the names of the witnesses and signatories are typed.
[2] Ibid., JO3/6.
[3] Johnson had in fact published this story in the *Cape Times* of September 12, 1930, but it attracted no particular attention.

Harris. He claims that the scheme was only frustrated by Heany, who talked too loudly in his cups in the presence of the Rev. E. D. Hepburn, Khama's missionary at Shoshong. Hepburn passed it on to Sir Sidney Shippard, who rushed to Cape Town to inform Sir Henry Loch, who summoned Rhodes, who denied all knowledge in public but privately told Johnson that the deal was off.

This story has been closely analysed by Robert Cary in *Charter Royal*, pages 54–8. It is clearly a fabrication. The dates do not fit and journeys of impossible celerity have to be presupposed. Moreover, the original contract has never been recovered from its burial place along with Johnson's other papers in the garden of his house in Jersey, whence he fled to escape the Germans in 1940. So there is no evidence beyond Johnson's word that it was ever witnessed and signed. Mr Cary considers that it almost certainly was not. The contract purports to be with Rhodes as representing the Chartered Company. Rhodes could be very reckless, but it is scarcely credible that even he would have committed without consultation such pillars of respectability as Grey and the two ducal directors to an illegal foray involving the likelihood of a major political scandal and the certainty of spending more than a seventh of the whole capital of the Company.

As Mr Cary suggests, it is much more likely that the contract was a very rough draft, formulated by two over-enthusiastic young men as a result of frequent talks with Rhodes in which many hypothetical plans were tossed into the arena. There is no need to doubt that a filibustering expedition was one of these. Six years later the Jameson Raid showed that such an idea was by no means alien to Rhodes's moral outlook, but it also showed the limits to his imprudence. There were no contracts signed, sealed and delivered; and, far from having committed the Chartered Company, Rhodes had to resign his post as Managing Director and his place on the Board when the raid failed. There is other evidence that a military solution was being talked about at the end of 1889. J. G. M. Millais in his *Life of F. C. Selous* (1918), which is based on personal knowledge as well as Selous' papers, states 'Rhodes' original plan was to attack Lobengula with a small force. This, Selous pointed out to him, would be certain to lead to disaster since Rhodes' information as to the strength of the Matabele was obviously incorrect.'[4]

Whether Rhodes, if left to himself, would ever have taken the risk of a military coup is doubtful. The chances are that he would not, but it was Selous' advice, not alcoholic boasting by Heany, which finally put a stopper on Johnson's plan; and Mr Cary may well be right in surmising that Johnson's dislike of Selous and his subsequent efforts to diminish the part played by Selous in the story of the Pioneer Column were caused by being thus overruled. For Selous, who arrived in Kimberley on December 6 or 7, came up with a solution of his own – a peaceful expedition with a military escort following a route which would give the widest possible berth to Bulawayo and the Ndebele villages. His plan

[4] 174, n. 1.

was to cut a road eastwards from the Macloutsie river to Tuli. From there the party would bear north east through the high plateau. Once on the plateau it would head north for Mount Hampden – an eminence already familiar to Selous from a previous expedition. As far as possible, hostilities with Lobengula were to be avoided, but for the sake of security a military escort considerably larger than the hundred men envisaged earlier would be needed – not less than two hundred and fifty.[5] Selous offered to lead the expedition himself, and by December 9 the broad outline had been agreed between Selous, Johnson, Heany and Borrow on the one side and Rhodes on the other.

The plan had obvious advantages over anything else hitherto proposed. Selous was a semi-legendary figure, well known and much admired both in South Africa and Britain. His book, *A Hunter's Wanderings in Africa* published in 1881, had been a best-seller. He seemed the personal embodiment of the contemporary romantic attitude towards the far flung bounds of empire; the crack shot, the big game hunter, the self-sufficient hero who could spend months on his own in the bush, courageous, chivalrous, imperturbable – in fact just the man whom Englishmen liked to regard as typical of their nation, though in reality nothing of the sort. If the names of Grey and the two dukes added respectability to the Chartered Company, that of Selous gave glamour and éclat to the Pioneer Column. Rhodes could not have been unaware of this aspect when he made his choice, but there was of course an even more important point. No other man possessed the prestige, confidence or expertise to lead an expedition through country which had been so little explored and was so little known.

There was one minor difficulty. Selous, whether from conviction of the truth or from a desire to enhance the value of the concessions which he had obtained, persisted in arguing that Lobengula had no suzerainty over the eastern part of Mashonaland and even proposed to write a series of newspaper articles to that effect. Rhodes had to do much work 'on the personal', as his phrase was, to persuade Selous to the contrary. But he succeeded at the modest cost of £2,000 from his private funds. Johnson, Heany and Borrow also agreed to abandon their rights in the Selous Exploration Syndicate in return for suitable compensation.

It was at this stage that Johnson entered into his celebrated contract with the Chartered Company. His published version of this affair is no less dubious than his unpublished story of the military coup, although it has been repeated in book after book about Rhodes and Rhodesia. According to *Great Days*[6] Johnson was breakfasting in the Kimberley Club on December 22 when Cecil Rhodes, arriving a few minutes later, 'looked vaguely at me and then suddenly recollecting me, silently sat down at my table'. They discussed, so Johnson says, the problem of occupying Mashonaland. Sir Frederick Carrington had told Rhodes that 2,500 men was the minimum military force needed. This

---

[5] This was at any rate better than the figure advised by Sir F. Carrington – 2,500 – which Rhodes rejected as financially ruinous.

[6] 94, *et sq.*

could not cost less than £1,000,000. Rhodes was in no position to raise more than £250,000. Then, Johnson says, 'purely from a desire to cheer up Rhodes I suddenly broke in ... "Why, with 250 men I could walk through the country"'. Rhodes asked him whether he meant it. 'My one idea', Johnson claims, 'had been to cheer up a worried man and I might just as well have said twenty-five men as 250.' But he replied that he did mean it. 'How much will it cost?' asked Rhodes and Johnson answered that, if Rhodes would give him a room and plenty of foolscap, he would have the figure by lunch time. Johnson continues that 'a very brief "appreciation of the situation"' convinced him that the route must avoid 'the existing trade route through the heart of the Matabele country'. It must instead go 'well to the eastward of the occupied part of Matabeleland'. After four hours of arithmetical calculation he came back with a figure of £94,000.

His story goes on that Rhodes at once agreed; but that Johnson, detesting the names of Gifford and Cawston on the Board, refused to act as a servant of the Company; that Rhodes having departed to Cape Town, summoned Johnson to see him there on December 28, and, after a long haggle, agreed to the deal on the basis of Johnson being an independent contractor rather than an employee.

It is a pity to tarnish what Sir Winston Churchill calls 'these gleaming toys of history', and no doubt there is a substratum of veracity buried somewhere in Johnson's story. He certainly did operate as an independent contractor and the sum of £94,000 was not far off the mark. But the whole impression is wrong. He had been engaged for many weeks before December 22 in negotiations with Rhodes who, far from recollecting him suddenly, must have known him very well indeed by then. The suppressed account in Johnson's own book of the proposed military coup would in itself have contradicted this part of his story. As for the idea that Johnson conceived the eastern route into Mashonaland, this was clearly an attempt to steal the credit from Selous who had successfully persuaded Rhodes to adopt that particular plan on December 9 at the latest. Indeed by that date the scheme for the occupation of Mashonaland had been largely worked out. Johnson may have done some final financial calculations after breakfast with Rhodes at Kimberley on December 22, and he may have had a row with Rhodes about Gifford and Cawston six days later in Cape Town, but this hardly justifies the romantic and egotistical version given in his autobiography.[7]

[7] That version is effectively destroyed by Robert Cary, *Charter Royal*, Chapter II. It first appeared in 1918 when Johnson wrote some reminiscences in Vol. III of the *Royal Sussex Herald* (Lahore 1918), the journal of the regiment in which he served during the First World War. It finds no place in any of the numerous books on Rhodes and Rhodesia published before that date, but it is reproduced in most subsequent books and seemed to have gained renewed authority from being repeated in Johnson's article in the *Rhodesia Herald* on September 12, 1930, and in *Great Days*, 1940. It is perhaps significant that Marshall Hole, whose *Making of Rhodesia*, 1926, is much the most reliable account of these events, makes no mention at all of the story.

However, a contract dated January 1, 1890 was undoubtedly made by Johnson with the Chartered Company. He undertook, in return for £87,500, together with 80,000 acres of land and 20 gold claims for each of 12 friends to be nominated by him, to construct a good wagon road from Palapye to Mount Hampden on or before July 15, 1890, and to occupy 'a certain portion of the territory which is included in the Company's sphere of operations until the 30th day of September 1890 at which date the said Company shall be bound to relieve the said Contractor of all further responsibilities'. The contractor's 'staff' – the technical name of the Pioneer Corps – were to receive 15 gold claims each together with the right to occupy 3,000 acres of land. Nobody seems to have bothered about the not unimportant point that the Rudd Concession, the sole authority for the whole enterprise, made no grants of land to the Chartered Company. Although the contract was in Johnson's name alone, there was an agreement to share the profits with Heany and Borrow, though not with Selous. Johnson later claimed to have made £20,000 on the deal, but whether this represented his share or had to be divided with his partners is not clear.

Whatever his defects as a chronicler, Johnson had plenty of assets as an organizer. He was a pusher and a hustler. Rhodes did not always rightly judge his man, but on this occasion he picked a winner. Dark, squat, broad shouldered, with a voice like a foghorn, Johnson set about his task of supplying men, food and transport with immense energy. He intended to keep to his contract and he succeeded. The first problem was to recruit the Pioneers themselves. This was one of Johnson's responsibilities, but Rhodes took the keenest interest in the personnel. He wanted the Corps to be a cross section of Cape Colony Society from every walk of life, with a strong emphasis on the British side, but with some Afrikaners as well. Nor was it to be confined to Cape Colony. The Boer republics and Natal were also represented. In the words of Lockhart[8] 'they included farmers, artisans, miners, doctors, lawyers, engineers, builders, bakers, soldiers, sailors, cadets of good family and no special occupation, cricketers, three parsons and a Jesuit'. There were some two thousand applicants, and less than a tenth were chosen.

Opinions about their quality differed. Marshall Hole, a sound historian but conditioned by all his past to take a benevolent view, said that 'no finer *corps d'élite* than the British South Africa Company's Police and the Mashonaland Pioneers has ever been raised'. At the opposite end of the spectrum, Labouchère, who hated Rhodes, described them as 'border ruffians of Hebraic extraction'. In between, Victor Morier, son of the British Ambassador in St Petersburg and himself a trooper, thought that they were 'on the whole an excellent body, but neither the police nor the pioneers are quite all we heard from the enthusiasts in London ... chiefly miners, etc. thrown out of employment by the smash of the Johannesburg goldfields, a sprinkling of army and navy deserters, clerks, etc.' There had indeed been a disastrous slump on the Rand,

[8] *Rhodes*, 180.

which may have explained in part the rush of candidates. Major Leonard, another participant, observed: 'Such a mixed lot I never saw in my life, all sorts and conditions from the aristocratic down to the street arab, peers and waifs of humanity mingling together like the ingredients of a hotch-potch.'[9]

Perhaps 'a mixed lot' is the best description. This was in one sense Rhodes's intention; he wished to create a colony of settlement which from artisans upwards would be self-sufficient – a microcosm of white society. Later vast areas of the African map north of the Limpopo were to be coloured red, but none of the British possessions thus transiently acquired would have quite this character; the white men who were to govern in most of the territories till the early 1960s were less differentiated socially and less dug in. Of course there were exceptions – landowners in Kenya for example – but in general it was a world of missionaries, civil servants, merchants and business executives without real roots in their temporarily adopted countries – more like the British Raj in India after the Mutiny than the American colonies or the Dominions in the Antipodes. As in those latter countries the Whites of southern Zambesia had come there to stay, but the indigenous population was there to stay too, and it was both more numerous and less vulnerable than the Red Indians or the Aborigines.

Perhaps the nearest parallel to the situation was the arrival of the 1820 settlers in the western part of Cape Colony. This too had been a planned settlement made with the authority of the British Government. This too had a basically similar purpose – to preserve a vital strategic interest on the cheap; and it was to be that very same interest, the route to India which seventy years later, indirectly and at many removes, conditioned Lord Salisbury's reaction to Rhodes's plan for the Pioneers. Finally, to make the parallel even closer, the Pioneers of 1890 did not think of themselves as agents of British global policy any more than the settlers of 1820 did. Each body of men had its own mixed and divergent motives for joining in these strange adventures.

There has been in Rhodesia and elsewhere a certain amount of hagiography about the Pioneers. This has provoked the inevitable denigratory riposte. In fact the men who marched in the column were for the most part neither heroes nor villains. A few were idealists who believed that they were bringing progress and protection to the timid Mashona, victims of Matabele ferocity – 'romantics with the strenuous Puritan romanticism of the Victorians, of Charles Kingsley and Arnold of Rugby', in the words of Philip Mason. At the other end, a very few may have been reckless adventurers of the sort immortalized by Kipling in *The Lost Legion* (1895).

[9] Arthur Leonard, *How we made Rhodesia*, 1896, 26. He is referring specifically to the British Bechuanaland and British South Africa Company Police, not the Pioneers, but all three bodies were much the same.

> We've laughed at the world as we found it –
> Its women and cities and men –
> From Sayyid Burgash in a tantrum
> To the smoke-reddened eyes of Loben,
>   (Dear boys!)
> We've a little account with Loben.

The great majority were drawn above all else by the lure of the gold of Ophir and the chance of making a fortune. No doubt the charisma of Rhodes, the sheer excitement of entering these unknown lands, the feeling that they were promoting the destiny of Britain, that they were part of a great surging movement of progress, that the future belonged to them, all played a part too.

At an early stage the question of the military escort had to be reviewed. The authorities at Cape Town were convinced that 250 was not enough. Rhodes, though acutely conscious of the cost, felt obliged early in March 1890 to double the number and also to accept Sir Henry Loch's nominee as Commander, Lieutenant Colonel E. G. Pennefather of the 6th (Inniskilling) Dragoon Guards, with Captain Sir John Willoughby, Bt., of the Royal Horse Guards as second-in-command. The detachment of 500 which guarded the Pioneer Column became the nucleus of the British South Africa Company's Police. Both corps were to be under military discipline, and Johnson, who became a Major, insisted that the Pioneer commissions should be signed by the High Commissioner representing the Queen, as well as by Rhodes on behalf of the Company.[10] The collecting of stores and transport, the recruiting of the Pioneers, the doubling of the armed escort inevitably took time, and time was precious. The dry season in Rhodesia normally lasts from late April to late November. No one could be sure how long the journey would take.

Added impetus for haste was given by rumours of a Boer *trek* from the Transvaal organized by one Louis Adendorff. This threat was to vex the Chartered Company off and on for over a year, and it was not finally scotched until June 1891 when Jameson had a confrontation with its new leader, Colonel Ferriera.[11] For the moment, however, it diminished. Loch and Rhodes met Kruger and Steyn (President of the Orange Free State) on March 12, 1890 at Blignaut's Pont on the Vaal River, and Kruger, aware that he had not got a legal leg to stand on, agreed to discourage the movement.

While the expedition was being organized, a further difficulty emerged. No one can know for certain quite what Lobengula thought was the quid pro quo for his rifles, ammunition and armed steamer on the Zambesi, none of which he had yet accepted. Probably he envisaged a relatively small number of white men digging 'a hole' in the ground rather like the miners on the Tati who had given him no particular trouble. His intelligence service – Ndebeles working

---

[10] Ferris, op. cit., 47.
[11] See Chapter 6.

for white employers on the Macloutsie – now revealed a far bigger enterprise, a white *impi* of formidable strength. He began once again to have misgivings, and his position was made no easier by the 'hawks' who had been in the ascendancy among his councillors since the liquidation of Lotje. He rounded on Doyle and Maxwell, the only remaining representatives of Rhodes and the Company after Jameson's departure in mid-February, and told them that he had been deceived. When Selous came up in March to Palapye he found no sign of the hundred Ndebele promised orally by Lobengula to Jameson. Selous promptly rode to Bulawayo, arriving on March 17 to remonstrate with the King, who denied the promise and raised numerous objections to the proposed route of the Pioneers in spite of his earlier concordat with Jameson. Selous had once shot a hippopotamus without Lobengula's consent and was therefore *persona non grata* in Bulawayo. He returned empty handed.

Clearly the answer was to send Jameson once again to Bulawayo. Not surprisingly he needed much persuasion, but Rhodes brought it off. Jameson agreed to go 'as a favour'[12] and left Kimberley on April 11. Selous accompanied him at Rhodes's behest, but Jameson who knew the form with Lobengula managed to shake him off at Tati and rode on to Bulawayo alone, arriving on April 27.[13] Two picturesque accounts, both of them from Jameson himself, describe his last interview.[14] Lobengula declared that the only route to the interior which he would allow was via Bulawayo. Jameson reminded him of his promise. Lobengula demanded a visit from Rhodes. Jameson did not commit himself on this but said that the white *impi* would fight if it was not granted the road agreed by Lobengula. 'The King told me *I* might make the road. Did the King lie?' There was a long silence. Lobengula at last replied – 'The King never lies'. Jameson answered 'I thank the King', and he departed at once for the south on May 2. He never saw Lobengula again.

By now everything was in train for the great adventure. On May 6[15] at dawn the Pioneer Corps set out from Kimberley for their long journey, the first stage being the Macloutsie River. They arrived on June 14 and camped at Grobler's Drift (so named as the site of the death of Kruger's unlucky emissary), some twenty-five miles east of the area where the five troops of the BSACP were concentrated under Colonel Pennefather.[16] At this late moment a telegram arrived for Rhodes at Kimberley from the High Commissioner giving the final go-ahead to the expedition. He insisted, however, that both corps should be inspected and certified as militarily efficient by Major General (afterwards Lord) Methuen, Deputy Adjutant-General in South Africa.

[12] Colvin, *Jameson*, I, 129.

[13] Ibid., 130.

[14] Seymour Fort, *Dr. Jameson*, 94–5; and Lockhart, op. cit., 182–3, quoting a memorandum in the papers at Rhodes House by Howard Pim, a friend of Jameson. See also Marshall Hole, op. cit., 135–7.

[15] Colvin, I, 139.

[16] Leonard, op. cit., 34.

The General had already inspected the BSACP. He now inspected the Pioneers. After putting them through various exercises he had them on parade on June 24 and addressed the officers thus.[17]

LORD METHUEN: Gentlemen, have you got maps?
THE OFFICERS: Yes, sir.
LORD METHUEN: And pencils?
THE OFFICERS: Yes, sir.
LORD METHUEN: Well, gentlemen your destiny is Mount Hampden. You go to a place called Siboutsi. I do not know whether Siboutsi is a man or a mountain. Mr Selous, I understand, is of the opinion that it is a man; but we will pass that by. Then you get to Mount Hampden. Mr Selous is of opinion that Mount Hampden is placed ten miles too far to the west. You had better correct that: but perhaps on second thoughts, better not. Because you might be placing it ten miles too far to the east. Now good-morning, gentlemen.

Encouraged no doubt by this interesting disquisition, the Pioneer Column next day ponderously lumbered forward with its hundred wagons, oxen enough to furnish two spans for each, and 'a respectable mob of slaughter cattle'.[18] Three days later it joined up with a Troop of the BSACP, a hundred strong commanded by Captain Heyman.[19] The plan was for three Troops (A, B and C) of the mounted police to accompany the expedition. The other two (D and E) remained on the Macloutsie as a reinforcement and a rearguard. The story is not made any easier to follow by the fact that the Pioneers too were divided into Troops – in this case three, also called A, B and C; and to complicate matters even further the leading Pioneer Troop for a large part of the journey was B (under 'Skipper' Hoste).

An even more difficult matter to disentangle is the precise chain of command. There were five key figures. Johnson, who had hoped to command the expedition, found himself – much to his annoyance – demoted by the 'Imperial Factor'. Loch's insistence on a large military escort meant that its commanding officer was in charge of the whole column, and Johnson merely commanded the Pioneers. He was, of course, also contractor to the expedition and there was a possibility that his own financial interests which required speed would conflict with the dictates of military prudence. The situation cannot have been made any easier if Major Leonard was correct in attributing to Pennefather 'an entire absence of tact and a furious temper'.[20] There was also Selous who was, strictly speaking, merely Intelligence Officer but whose authority as a guide

[17] Colvin, ibid., 140.
[18] 'Skipper' Hoste's Diary, Typescript NAR HO14/1/1, 32.
[19] Ibid., 46.
[20] Leonard, op. cit., 162.

was absolute. Nor was the situation made clearer by Jameson's presence. In theory he had no official position at all, but Rhodes in his capacity as Managing Director had conferred a power of attorney on the Doctor. This rather surprisingly seems to have made him a sort of arbitrator between Penne-father and Johnson. If they disagreed he would have the final say.[21]

The fifth figure of importance was Archibald Colquhoun, former explorer, colonial servant and journalist. He was to be the Administrator of the new colony. In the end he fell foul of both Jameson and Rhodes, and he tends to be de-picted as a stiff conventional bureaucrat tied up with red tape and precedents. Clearly he was nothing of the sort. What typical bureaucrat would take sixty cases of whisky and thirty of champagne with quantities of pâté de foie gras and caviare as part of his baggage on a journey like this, and demand (though it is not clear that they arrived in time) '1,000 best Havana cigars and 1,000 good Havanna cigars for entertainment'? Indeed Colquhoun's very presence on the expedition was due to an action which was not at all typical of a civil servant. In his Burma days he had accidentally put two letters in the same envelope to his official superior; one, correctly addressed, was a reply to certain criticisms; the second, intended for *The Times* correspondent, was a well in-formed attack on governmental policy concluding with an addendum: 'when reference is made to this by you ... see that the information cannot be traced to me'. Colquhoun was shunted at once into a humbler post. He was glad to take service under the Company. But he was restless and bored by having nothing to do as Administrator until there was something to administer. He was given the job of checking Johnson's 'schedules', and early on became a source of discord.

Despite the polite retrospective public observations of the members of this odd quintet, their relations were anything but harmonious at the time. If a real crisis had arisen, the obscurity of the constitutional arrangements might have been disastrous. Rhodes, the one person who in such circumstances could have given decisive orders, was, late in the day, prevented from coming. A political crisis in Cape Town had been brewing for several weeks. It resulted in an offer of the premiership. Rhodes wondered whether the post was compatible with his vast business interests, but he naturally decided that it was. The conven-tions of the time did not require the resignation of directorships. On July 17 he accepted, but there was no chance of him accompanying the Column.

Luckily, in the event all went well. On July 5 B Troop of the Pioneers under Hoste accompanied by Jameson and Selous crossed the Shashi River at Tuli. Six days later the main column followed along the road cut by the advance guard. The number of those involved varies from one account to another.[22] Something under 200 Pioneers (196 is the conventional figure), including the 'apostles' who now amounted to thirteen, escorted by 350 mounted police and

[21] Ferris, op. cit., 47.
[22] In general I have followed 'Skipper' Hoste.

followed by 400 or more Cape 'boys' and other ancilliaries, moved north – perhaps a thousand men. The residue of the BSACP, about 150, remained as a rear-guard and reinforcement at Tuli. The dangerous period was the long haul through the hot steamy low veld to the southern escarpment of the plateau. Here the thick *mopane* bush limited visibility to a couple of hundred yards. A Ndebele *impi* could have seriously damaged, if it did not destroy, the four mile train of men, oxen, horses and wagons crawling slowly through unknown country which even Selous had never traversed before. The four Maxims, the two seven pounders, the Gardner gun and the two rocket tubes which, along with Henry-Martini rifles, composed the armament of the column would have been nothing like as effective in the low veld as on the open grassland of the high plateau, and there can be no doubt that a big risk was involved.

The organizers of the expedition did, however, take some precautions. The drill for the nightly *laager* was very strict. An ingenious psychological weapon was carried by the Column as a means of striking fear into their superstitious foes. This took the form of a 10,000 candle power naval searchlight charged by a steam engine. (The earlier notion of an immense balloon had been abandoned for practical reasons.) The effect at night of these strange beams accompanied by the thud of the engine and periodic explosions of electrically fired dynamite cartridges may well have caused the Ndebele scouts, who were never far away, to pass on alarming stories of white men's magic to Lobengula.

Whatever the reason the King, though under severe pressure to go to war, never gave the order to attack. Possibly he was placated to some extent by the arrival on June 14 of two snow white pedigree bulls as a present from the Duke of Abercorn. It was a very belated present. The Duke, to the horror of 'Matabele' Thompson at Cape Town, had in the first instance sent two black bulls. These were promptly returned; black to the Ndebeles meant war, white meant peace, and Albert Grey was given the task of selecting substitutes. True, the bulls, unaccustomed to the coarse and scanty pasture of Matabeleland, expired after three months, but by then the Column had reached its objective. However, it is more likely that Lobengula was actuated above all else by the knowledge that even a victory over the Pioneers would in the end be fatal.

On June 30, while the Column was between the Macloutsie and Shashi Rivers, Jameson received a sarcastic but ambiguous letter from Lobengula, to which he returned a diplomatic answer. On August 6, however, just as the Column was nearing the end of the dangerous first phase of its journey and was near the escarpment, Colenbrander rode up from Bulawayo with a much sharper letter. Lobengula protested that he had never given permission to dig in Mashonaland. There is some evidence that the King was making a gesture of appeasement to the war party and that he knew the message would arrive too late to affect events. Pennefather replied that he had the Queen's orders to proceed and that he could not withdraw unless they were countermanded. Meanwhile, only four days earlier, Selous had solved the problem which had been worrying him all along – how to climb the seemingly impenetrable hills leading to the plateau. He discovered a narrow winding pass along which the column could safely make the thousand foot ascent. This was a great relief and he named it 'Providential Pass'. On August 14, after four days of laborious progress, B Troop of the Pioneers arrived on the high veld. Hoste writes:

> Our relief on leaving the hot steamy low veld, where for months we had seldom been able to see more than two hundred yards round us and arriving on the open veld with a cool invigorating breeze blowing may be imagined.

A place was selected to build a fort to guard the pass. It was named Fort Victoria. Next day Hoste and a party set forth to visit and photograph the fabulous ruins of Zimbabwe which so many people had heard of, so few had seen.

Compared with the first five weeks of the *trek*, all was now plain sailing. There was no longer any serious military threat. The going was much easier, and the climate must have been an agreeable contrast. It is hot, but not excessively so by day, and the heat is tempered by cool breezes; it is quite cold, with even an occasional frost, by night. A shower or two of rain might fall, but in general the weather is dry; the haze in the sky, then as now, was the result of ash dust from bush fires. The scene was one of rolling open plains covered by a golden brown savannah, far blue horizons, herds of antelope and other game. It was a fresh, entrancing, almost magical world. The morale of the Column shot up.

The rest of the journey was uneventful. Early in the morning of September 11, while the Column was crossing the Hunyani River, Pennefather, Willoughby and Captain Burnett of the Pioneers went ahead to choose a site for fortification and settlement. The story that they mistook the kopje in the middle of what is now Salisbury for Mount Hampden is a myth; there had never been any special reason for settling at Mount Hampden, which was only chosen as a general objective because it was a landmark known to Selous and identifiable on the map. Having selected what they considered a suitable site near the Makabusi River, Pennefather and his companions camped for the night. At dawn next day the Pioneers set off again. They were met by Burnett who directed them to the place of their final *laager*.[23] They arrived at 10 a.m. on September 12. The Orders of the Day announced that the name would be Fort Salisbury. Evening Orders declared that at 10 a.m. next day there would be a parade 'to celebrate the hoisting of the British Flag'. The same Orders congratulated the Column on successful attainment of its objective and expressed special appreciation for the work among others of Selous as guide and of Heany and Hoste as commanders of A and B Troops.

[23] Probably in the area where today First Street meets Manica Road. See E. E. Burke, 'Fort Victoria to Fort Salisbury ...' *Rhodesiana*, No. 28, July 1973, 12. This is the best modern account of the episode.

At 10 a.m. on September 13, the Column paraded dismounted in full dress on what is now Cecil Square. A rough flag staff had been cut by Hoste and his men. Pennefather, his ADC, Captain Shepstone, and his second-in-command, Sir John Willoughby, stood by it along with Lieutenant Tyndal Biscoe, RN, who had been in charge of the searchlight, and Canon Balfour, one of the clergy accompanying the expedition. The Canon gave a short address and an extempore prayer. The bugles sounded the Royal Salute. The Column presented arms while Tyndal Biscoe slowly ran up the Union Jack. When it reached the top the seven pounders fired a twenty-one gun salute. The bugles sounded again, and once again the Column presented arms. Pennefather called for 'Three Cheers for Her Most Gracious Majesty Queen Victoria'. The parade was dismissed, and in the words of Hoste, on whose account this description is
was now a part of the British Empire, another jewel in the British Crown'.[24]

'Pioneer Day' as it is now called has been celebrated on September 13 from that day to this amongst the budding jacarandas on Cecil Square. It is now the only place and occasion where the Union Jack flies regularly in Rhodesia – or anywhere else in Africa.

[24] Hoste's Diary, NAR HO14/1/1, 91.

6

The Map Is Drawn 1890–91

Three notables of the Pioneer Column were absent when the flag was hoisted at Fort Salisbury. Jameson, Selous and Colquhoun had left the line of route on September 3, heading east as fast as they could for Manicaland. Their foray was one part of Rhodes's grand design for Central Africa. It must be considered in relation to similar exploits destined to shape the frontiers and future of Southern Rhodesia.

Rhodes regarded the Pioneer Column in one aspect as a knife to cut through the Ndebele crust and obtain a number of juicy plums. If the Company could establish 'effective occupation', a vast area was available limited to the north only by the ill-defined borders of the Congo Free State and German East Africa, and to the east and west by the no less uncertain frontiers of Mozambique and Angola. 'Effective occupation', however, did not always mean what the words might be expected to mean. Physical occupation was not in the first instance necessary. The Pioneer Column was an exception to the general rule. What was needed were concessions and treaties with local chiefs, usually taking the form of grants of trading and mineral rights in return for cash, rifles, cartridges and a vague promise of protection against other, usually more aggressive tribes, like the Bemba or the Ngoni, whose leaders had not signed.

In the chancelleries of Europe these scraps of paper, sometimes obtained in dubious circumstances from dubious chiefs, were regarded as if they were binding agreements with monarchs whose territories, like the Balkan kingdoms, formed a static multi-coloured pattern on the map. The reality on the ground was different. The African signatories were for the most part transient if not embarrassed phantoms, tipsy unstable rulers of shifting tribes with no fixed abode, incapable of binding their unpredictable successors. The concessionaires had no delusions on that score, but they also had no delusions about the utility of the documents in the world of political and commercial diplomacy. If enough of them could be secured in a particular region, a claim would be staked, which, though not in itself conclusive, for the map in the end had to be drawn by high-level government bargaining, at least pre-empted those of other powers or commercial companies. The hands of a foreign minister would be strengthened – if he wanted them to be strengthened – by concessions in the ownership of his co-nationals. The documents were a useful form of currency when eventually a diplomatic settlement was made and spheres of influence or protectorates were established.

The map of south central Africa was drawn for the most part during the twenty-six months between October 29, 1889, when the charter was granted, and December 20, 1891, when, to Rhodes's great annoyance, the Congo Free State flag was hoisted in Katanga and that rich province finally eluded his reach. During this confused period he spread his tentacles far and wide to the north, north-east and east. By the end he had got most of what he wanted, though not all. Katanga was one of his failures, and he was unable to drive the Portuguese from the east coast and obtain either Beira or some other outlet to the Indian Ocean. Nyasaland too, though apparently secured by the end of 1891, was, by a strange chapter of accidents and conflict of personalities, destined soon to slip from the grasp of the Chartered Company, though not from British rule.

In order of time Nyasaland comes first. There had been Scottish missionary settlements inspired by the example of Livingstone in the area of Blantyre since 1875. British interest was recognized by the appointment of a consul there in 1883, but the Colonial Office, for financial reasons, had no intention of establishing a protectorate. The settlements were miserably poor. In 1878 the African Lakes Company was founded, with mixed motives of philanthropy and profit; its dividend was limited and any surplus went to the missions. In 1887 war broke out between the Company and the Arab slave traders at the northern end of the lake. The cost soon exhausted the Company's funds. By 1889 it was on the verge of bankruptcy.

The situation was made more difficult by the attitude of Portugal. Lisbon was alarmed at the rising British challenge to its own cherished dream, the claim, stigmatized by Lord Salisbury as 'archaeological', to sovereignty over the interior north of the Zambesi. It had been vividly depicted in the famous 'rose-coloured map' published by the Foreign Minister, Bocage, in 1887 showing a broad band of Portuguese territory stretching from the northern half of Mozambique to the southern half of Angola. The officials in Mozambique decided to be as obstructive as possible, and, since the only known route to the missions involved porterage across Portuguese territory, they were well placed to make trouble. True, the Zambesi could be argued to be an international waterway, but at this time its large delta was believed to be unnavigable. For a whole year arms for the Lake Company were held up and other supplies only let through after the payment of extortionate dues. Nor was this all. Early in 1889 news reached England that the celebrated Portuguese explorer Serpa Pinto was setting off in the direction of the Shiré River with a force of seven hundred armed men, which seemed somewhat excessive if, as he alleged, he was merely going on a scientific expedition.

At this juncture a new and important figure appears on the scene. H. M.

(later Sir Harry) Johnston, artist, explorer, botanist, zoologist, journalist, novelist, adventurer and empire-builder was a visionary almost as exuberant and eccentric as Cecil Rhodes.[1] His parents were typical of the prosperous middle class in most respects, apart from being adherents of the Irvingite or Apostolic Catholic Church. At the age of nineteen Johnston lost his faith – which was hardly surprising since it entailed believing that the Tsar was Anti-Christ, the second coming was imminent and that when it arrived the Irvingites, having been swept up to Heaven, would become immortal and govern the world, along with the Son of Man, for the next thousand years.[2] Johnston substituted evolution (to which he was ready to give a helping hand) for God, but he never lost the sense of being one of the elect.

His interest in Africa was stimulated by a painting holiday of seven months in Tunis. There at the age of twenty-one he heard the news of Disraeli's defeat at the general election of 1880, and he resolved to do all he could to promote the imperial cause in the face of Gladstone's policy of contraction and retrenchment. He went on a series of botanical, zoological and artistic expeditions in Angola, the Congo, Uganda and Kenya. Anyone less like an explorer it would be hard to imagine. He was five foot three inches in height, looked almost childish and spoke in a high-pitched squeaky voice. When he gave a lecture to the Royal Geographical Society Ferdinand de Lesseps, who was on the same platform, observed '*Quel pays où même les petits enfants sont des explorateurs*'.[3] Johnston compensated for these defects by talking incessantly, wittily, scandalously and outrageously. His dispatches were equally lively and unorthodox.

In 1885 he entered the Consular Service and played a much publicized and controversial role in the affairs of Nigeria. When he returned to Britain in 1888 he was a celebrity. The rumour, wholly false but denied by him with tantalizing hesitation, that he had eaten human flesh in the course of duty made him a popular guest at fashionable dinner parties. He met Lord Salisbury who was a connoisseur of eccentrics. An invitation to Hatfield followed and he regaled the little Cecils in the billiard room with stories about cannibalism. The *rapport* that he established with the Prime Minister who was also Foreign Secretary gave a decisive impetus to his career. On August 22 *The Times* published a pseudonymous article by him in which he adumbrated the idea of a continuous band of British territory from the Cape to Cairo. When Rhodes later claimed it as his, Johnston insisted that he himself was the orginator.[4]

Early in 1889 Johnston was appointed Consul in Mozambique. It did not sound much of a post, but Salisbury knew what he was doing when he offered it. At some moment during the past year he had made up his mind about Africa. He did not care a fig for Cape to Cairo but he had decided that the

[1] See Roland Oliver, *Sir Harry Johnston and the Scramble for Africa*, 1957, for a vivid portrait.

[2] Ibid., 2.

[3] Alex Johnston, *The Life and Letters of Sir Harry Johnston*, 1929, 23.

[4] Johnston to Rhodes, October 8, 1893, quoted in Oliver, op. cit., 153.

south and east were what mattered to Britain and that, if the French had a free hand in the west, they might be distracted from Egypt. The decision to concentrate on the south east meant that Portuguese pretensions must be checked. No doubt compromises and adjustments might be made to save face and keep the House of Braganza on the throne, but there must be an end for ever to the rose-coloured map. The aspirations of Cape Colony and the susceptibilities of the Scottish voter brooding about Livingstone were more important than the goodwill of 'our oldest ally'. Johnston was a tough operator, and a man of initiative was needed if the Nyasa missions were to be saved. He also had the asset of speaking fluent Portuguese.

In May, just as he was on the verge of leaving London, he met Rhodes for the first time, at a dinner party given by a clergyman who was assistant editor of the *Fortnightly*.[5] Among the other guests were Walter Pater and Frank Harris. Johnston at once fell under Rhodes's spell. They talked till midnight, when their host more or less turned them out. They continued the conversation at Rhodes's hotel till breakfast. Johnston was fascinated with the vast prospects unfolded by his companion. He learned for the first time about the proposed charter. He learned that Nyasaland, if Rhodes got his way, was to be a part of the chartered territory through the absorption of the Lakes Company. Rhodes made out a cheque for £2,000 to Johnston for expenses in securing treaties in and west of Nyasaland. A day or so later the Consul saw Salisbury and imparted some of Rhodes's plans to him. That was the occasion when, if Johnston's memory is correct, the Prime Minister asked 'Who is Mr Rhodes?'.[6] Salisbury vetoed the idea that Rhodes's money could be used for treaty-making within Nyasaland. West of it there was no objection, but he would not commit himself to handing over Nyasaland to a chartered company.

Johnston arrived in Mozambique on July 9. A navigable channel into the Zambesi had now been discovered. He went up it in a gunboat on July 28 and was soon in the lower Shiré. Serpa Pinto's forces were close to the junction of the Ruo and Shiré Rivers, the boundary as far as Whitehall was concerned between the British and Portuguese spheres of influence. Johnston warned Pinto of the danger of war and – with no authority whatever – told the Acting-Consul, John Buchanan, to declare a British Protectorate if the Portuguese crossed the Ruo. Pinto made it clear that he meant to spread Portuguese influence to Lake Bangweolo and thence westwards to Angola. But the threat caused him to pause and return for orders from higher authority. Johnston then disappeared northwards to conclude as many treaties as he could in the general direction of Lake Tanganyika, simultaneously dispatching a London solicitor turned big game hunter, Alfred Sharpe, to do the same thing westwards from the Shiré Highlands to the Loangwa River.

While he was away events moved rapidly. A skirmish between the Portuguese

---

[5] H. M. Johnston, *The Story of My Life*, 1923, 230.
[6] Ibid., 238.

and the Makololo tribe on the Ruo frontier prompted Buchanan to declare a Protectorate on September 25. On November 8, in pursuance of the same campaign, the Portuguese under Serpa Pinto's second-in-command crossed the Ruo. When the news reached Britain in mid-December there was a Protestant and patriotic outcry. Salisbury welcomed the opportunity and acted with Palmerstonian vigour. After the usual diplomatic moves he issued an ultimatum on January 11, 1890, backed by sending the Channel Fleet to the Tagus with sealed orders and a squadron from Zanzibar to Mozambique.[7] The Portuguese backed down. It was an unconditional surrender.

In Britain the ultimatum of January 1890 was soon forgotten. In Portugal it was traumatic and its shadow lies long over the years that followed. The 'insult' was remembered till very recently, and to this day the relevant papers in the Lisbon archives remain incommunicado. The government fell, the windows of the British consulate were stoned and members of the English colony in Oporto could scarcely walk abroad without insult. Mourners put black crape over the statue in Lisbon of Camões whose epic poem, the *Lusiads*, celebrated the voyage of Vasco da Gama, and who had himself sojourned in Mozambique from 1567 to 1569. It was the end of an old song. One of the few English historians who has shown some sympathy for Portugal writes:

> Essentially the conflict was between two dreams, nourished on the modern equivalent of Don Quixote's chivalric romances: small scale maps of Africa coloured in rival shades of red. Of the two, that of Rhodes and Johnston had less to commend it from an economic point of view . . . . The south to north drive of the British prevailed not because of its superior rationality but because they carried bigger guns and because an eccentric and idealist multi-millionaire was at hand to give it a forward push at critical time – a time when common sense personified by Goschen, Salisbury's Chancellor of the Exchequer, was unwilling to find a mere two thousand pounds for its incidental expenses.[8]

Many months were to elapse before a final settlement of the Anglo-Portuguese dispute, but Nyasaland was now clearly within the British sphere. It remained to be seen whether Johnston, who was back in Mozambique soon after the ultimatum, or Rhodes, who was busy weaving his plans in Kimberley, would be the dominant force. At the moment they saw eye to eye, but this harmony was not destined to last long.

Although no northern limit, apart from the frontiers of the Congo Free State and German East Africa, had been assigned to the Chartered Company, this did not mean that it could actually take possession without specific authority from the British Government. That authority would not be forthcoming unless some

[7] R. I. Lovell, *The Struggle for South Africa*, New York, 1934, 217.

[8] R. J. Hammond, *Portugal and Africa 1815–1910*, Stanford University Press, 1966, 131–2.

evidence of effective occupation could be shown. Rhodes therefore dispatched a number of emissaries to fill in the blank spaces on the map. Several foregathered at the Kimberley Club in May 1890, and a formal photograph has survived which includes some of them, along with other agents of Rhodes.[9] There we can see Colquhoun, soon to leave with the Pioneers; Joseph Thompson and J. A. Grant (son of the Grant who accompanied Speke in search of the sources of the Nile) about to depart at Rhodes's behest to Lake Nyasa and make a foray westwards to Katanga; J. W. Moir, a key figure in the Lakes Company; Harry Johnston, in a sort of smoking cap, *en route* to negotiate with the Foreign Office, having left behind him Alfred Sharpe also charged with the task of visiting Katanga; and finally, to complete the moustached, stiff-collared, heavily waistcoated octet, Rochfort Maguire (who may well have felt that his exploring days were over) and the Colossus himself.

Apart from Jameson, Frank Johnson and Selous, there were two notable absentees. One who might have been there was Aurel Schulz, a colonial doctor of giant physique who was in Kimberley making preparations for an expedition to obtain concessions from Gungunhana, Chief of Gazaland in southern Mozambique. The fact that Gazaland was regarded – and not just by Lisbon – as being well into the Portuguese sphere of influence did not of course worry Rhodes at all. The other was F. E. Lochner who had been sent months earlier in October 1889 on the thousand mile road west of Lobengula'a domains to Barotseland. In September that year Rhodes for £9,000 and 10,000[10] chartered shares had purchased a concession, rather like the Rudd Concession, secured by a Kimberley trader-cum-hunter called Harry Ware in June from Lewanika, the Barotse Chief. Lochner's task, similar to Jameson's *vis-à-vis* Lobengula, was to get it confirmed. He was also instructed if time and logistics permitted to continue northwards to Katanga.

Lochner obtained confirmation of the Ware Concession from Lewanika on June 27, 1890, aided by the famous missionary Francis Coillard. Lewanika's friendship with Khama and hostility to Lobengula contributed to the result. Lochner was too exhausted and too ill to go any further north and returned to Cape Colony. One of the terms of the treaty was that a resident should be left in Barotseland to reassure Lewanika and incidentally guard the company's interests. For various reasons this was not done, and only in 1897 did Robert Coryndon, one of Rhodes's original apostles, take up the post of resident in Barotseland. The company was lucky not to have lost it in the interval.

The three-pronged attempt to obtain Katanga ended in failure. The area was ruled by an able and ferocious tyrant called Msiri who by a combination of terrorism and military skill had built up a kingdom stretching from the Luapula River and Lake Mweru on the east to the Lualaba River on the west. Thompson never even reached Msiri's sinister kraal 'decorated with the rotting heads of decapitated

[9] Hole, op. cit., facing 131.
[10] Hole, op. cit., 214. Not 100,000 as stated in Lockhart, op. cit., 239.

victims', as Hole puts it.[11] He had to return to Nyasa, though by no means empty-handed as regards treaties with other chiefs.

Sharpe who proceeded from Karonga at the northern end of Lake Nyasa managed, after many vicissitudes, to arrive in November at Msiri's capital. He was badly received and his efforts to secure concessions and treaties were furiously rebuffed. He retired despondent to his base but he too secured many concessions from the chiefs, and the treaties obtained by Thompson, Grant and Sharpe were to be the principal basis of the Company's claim to the whole area between Nyasaland and Barotseland. The story goes that Msiri subsequently had doubts about rejecting Sharpe's offer and sent a message asking him to come back, but his letter was intercepted by a British Army officer, Captain Stairs of Nova Scotian origin, who was leading a mission on behalf of the Katanga Company, an international syndicate with a charter from the Congo Free State. Stairs destroyed the letter, and proceeded to Msiri's kraal, arriving in December. In the course of a skirmish the old Chief whose subjects were now in open rebellion was shot dead, and the whole of his domain was successfully claimed by the Congo Free State. Stairs died soon afterwards. Rhodes never forgave either him or his memory.

In fact it is doubtful whether Rhodes would have been able to hold on to Katanga even if one of his men had managed to extract a concession from Msiri. The area was almost certainly within the sphere of the Congo Free State as defined in the Berlin Treaty of 1884, and it is unlikely that Salisbury would have backed a palpable breach of that agreement. The same applies to Rhodes's other failure – the bid for a port on the east coast but the belief that a golden chance was missed is so deeply embedded in Rhodesian legend that the story needs to be told in some detail.

Even before the final confirmation of the charter Rhodes had been most anxious to ensure that the Foreign Office did not come to an agreement with Portugal. It was, from his point of view, all to the good that Lisbon had refused Salisbury's offer in 1888, and that negotiations were still in a state of suspense. On September 16, 1889 Rutherfoord Harris wrote from Kimberley a letter typical of many to the Company's Secretary in London:

> Mr Rhodes is of the opinion that *no* settlement of boundaries should be made between England and Portugal, as they (the Portuguese) are attempting to get the richest field by some artificial line. All should be left to the natural civilised development of the country when 'beati possidentes' will be the settlement.[12]

This theme is repeated in several letters and no doubt the crisis of January 1890 was highly welcome as far as Rhodes was concerned. But on August 20, just as the Column was reaching the last leg of its journey, a development took place which greatly annoyed him. An Anglo-Portuguese convention was signed, which though

[11] Op. cit., 245.
[12] NAR LO5/2/0, Harris to C. H. Weatherley.

it recognized Matabeleland, Mashonaland, the Shiré Highlands and a large slice of northern Zambesia stretching from Lake Nyasa to the borders of the Congo Free State and Angola as being in the British sphere of influence, excluded not only Barotseland west of the Zambesi but most of Manicaland. Rhodes threatened to resign his position as Prime Minister and he sent an angry letter to Harry Johnston whom he blamed most unfairly for the agreement. 'I trace your hand all through the Portuguese treaty. It is a disgraceful treaty and I will have nothing to do with it. You have given away the whole of the west, including ½ the Barotse, just ceded to me and the whole of Manika.'[13] Their relations were never the same thereafter. In fact Johnston, though not quite as extreme as Rhodes, was regarded as too anti-Portuguese to be allowed any say at all in the negotiations. Salisbury changed the subject in a marked manner when Johnston alluded to it, and the terms of the treaty were as much a surprise to him as they were to Rhodes.

We must now revert to Colquhoun. His written instructions from Rhodes contained orders to visit 'the chief of the Manica Country and obtain . . . a treaty and concessions for mineral rights in his territory'. The letter went on – 'You will endeavour to secure the right of communication with the seaboard, reporting on the best line of railway connexion with the littoral from Mashonaland'.[14] According to his widow, who subsequently remarried as Mrs Jollie, he had secret orders to seize Beira, if the opportunity arose.

> As an interesting sidelight on history it may be mentioned here that the first Administrator went up to Mashonaland with the understanding (verbal and never committed to writing) that in the not unlikely event of a conflict with the Portuguese he should make a raid on Beira, in the hope that, with a *fait accompli* staring them in the face, the Imperial Government would not interfere.[15]

Mrs Jollie goes on to say that he was reluctant to do this, and that his reluctance was the reason for his being superseded later by Jameson. Colquhoun in his own memoirs does not refer to any specific secret instructions, but he was writing in 1908 and may have felt that it would be indiscreet to spell the matter out. (Mrs Jollie wrote fifteen years later and her book is in part a polemic against the Company.) Colquhoun does, however, refer to Beira.

> It was expected by the Company that the British Government would support us in any concession we might have obtained 'even down to the sea coast', but unfortunately the position in Beira was too well defined, or at all events

[13] NAR JO1/1/1, ff. 130–3, September 22, 1890.
[14] NAR CT1/1/1, Rhodes to Colquhoun, May 13, 1890.
[15] E. M. Tawse-Jollie, *The Real Rhodesia*, 1923, Rhodesian Reprint 1971, 286.

I thought so. Had I cared to despatch a filibustering expedition to seize Beira I might have done so, but, as I was now fully aware, with the certainty that in case of accident I should be disavowed.[16]

The Administrator was being somewhat disingenuous and the story of events is more complicated than he suggests. After leaving the Column on September 3, probably unaware of the Anglo-Portuguese Convention of August 20, Colquhoun's party on September 13 reached the kraal of Umtasa, Chief of Manicaland – a mountain fastness some twenty miles north of modern Umtali. Under the convention it was well within the Portuguese sphere of influence. The Chief was a slippery trimmer who survived by playing off one powerful neighbour against another. Of these, two were particularly formidable. The first was Manuel Antonio de Sousa, ruler of the province of Gorongoza, a half caste Goanese *prazo*-holder and adventurer who had carved out a fief for himself with the assent of the Portuguese government in the northern hinterland of Beira. He was also known as 'Gouveia' which was the name of his capital. He was ferocious to a degree, had a large harem and generally behaved in the style of the freebooting Arab slave traders who had for generations past been the curse of east central Africa. In spite of these characteristics he possessed a commission from the Portuguese government. He had been rewarded personally for his services by the King in Lisbon, and his children were brought up in Portugal.

The second neighbour (of whom Umtasa was no less terrified) was Gungunhana, Chief of Gazaland, whose kraal (where he had recently moved) was some forty miles north of the upper Limpopo. He was the eastern analogue of Lobengula to whom he was related by marriage. His tribe, the Shangaans, were, like the Ndebele, an off-shoot of the Zulus and had moved north for the same reason. From the very start Rhodes had regarded Gazaland as a second possibility for his route to the sea and, as we saw earlier, one of the many emissaries that he sent all over Africa in the course of 1890 was Dr Aurel Schulz, whose object was to secure a concession from Gungunhana. Schulz arrived in June 1890, but he found negotiation difficult. The Chief lived largely on over-proof rum which had an even worse effect on him than brandy and champagne on Lobengula. He was scarcely ever sober. However, on October 4 after much effort and many a drunken *indaba* Schulz secured a concession on terms very similar to Rudd's.

As far as Manicaland was concerned, on September 4 Colquhoun obtained the usual concession from Umtasa and then returned to Salisbury. The Portuguese authorities protested on the ground that Umtasa's kraal was on their side of the frontier, but, although this was true under the Treaty of August 20, it now looked as if the Cortes would repudiate it and all would again be fluid. Rhodes authorized Frank Johnson and Jameson to reconnoitre a route from Manicaland to the sea. They set out from Salisbury on October 4. Colquhoun was furious and wrote angry letters to Rutherfoord Harris at Kimberley, thus sealing his fate as

[16] A. R. Colquhoun, *Dan to Beersheba*, 1908, 287.

Administrator. Jameson was Rhodes's *alter ego* and Rhodes expected his subordinates to know this without being told. On one of the letters Marshall Hole scribbled a marginal note: 'By this letter Colquhoun signed his death warrant.'[17] The two men reached Pungwe Bay after numerous adventures, returning by sea to Cape Town. Johnson's assessment of the economic assets of the route was ridiculously optimistic – £10 per ton from Cape Town to Salisbury; and, since the overland journey via the Missionary Road cost £70 a ton, the need for an eastern port seemed greater than ever.

On October 15 the Cortes dissolved without having ratified the Anglo-Portuguese Treaty. Colquhoun did not need Rhodes's prompting to go ahead in the process of securing treaties from the various chiefs down the Busi River to the sea. He sent a small detachment, subsequently reinforced, to Umtasa's kraal under the command of Major Forbes, Pennefather's second-in-command. Forbes, on November 15, aware that Gouveia along with the two Portuguese officials was planning to reassert Portuguese authority over Umtasa, boldly entered the latter's kraal just as that double-faced potentate was parleying the Portuguese trio. He scattered Gouveia's forces and arrested him and his colleagues. Precisely the situation envisaged in Colquhoun's unwritten instructions (which must have been passed on to Forbes) had now arisen. A conflict – probably engineered for the very purpose – had occurred with the Portuguese. The way to Beira was open. Two days before the arrival of reinforcements and the making of the arrests Forbes had written a letter to Colquhoun which plainly shows what he planned.

> Ever since Sunday [November 9] we have been so situated that within ½ hour of the arrival of a reinforcement we could by a sudden coup have decided the whole question of the E. Coast route ... I shall arrest Gouveia ... and with as little delay as possible start for Pungwe Bay via Sarmento ... I am quite confident that in arresting Gouveia we are breaking completely the Portuguese power in E. Africa ... From what I hear the Gorongoza province extends right down to the sea and as Gouveia has chosen to carry arms into our territory I think we ought to retaliate if we get him by going into his.[18]

Two days later he wrote, 'I hope to leave by the 20th at latest and should be at Beira by the 30th'. He set out with only ten men, but the demoralized condition of the Portuguese colonists was such that even a tiny force of determined troopers seemed capable of success.

Meanwhile on November 23 Colquhoun at Salisbury received from Kimberley the news that the British Government had signed an agreement with Portugal known as the 'Modus Vivendi' under which frontiers were frozen as from November 14, the day before Forbes's *coup*, pending the ratification of a permanent treaty. Colquhoun may well have already been uneasy about his unwritten orders

[17] NAR CT1/1/3, October 4, 1890.
[18] NAR A1/6/1, Forbes to Colquhoun, November 13, 1890.

to seize Beira. The latest news made the action even less defensible juridically than it had been before. He at once sent an urgent message to recall Forbes. In Rhodesian mythology his action has been condemned as the bureaucratic loss of a golden chance to secure access to the sea and a port on the Indian Ocean.

In reality it made no difference at all. Forbes had already decided, the day before Colquhoun's message had even been sent, that the risk of a filibustering seizure of Beira was too great. The euphoria which he displayed after the coup at Umtasa's kraal rapidly evaporated as he and his companions rode eastwards through the burning heat of Mozambique. On November 22 he sent a message to Colquhoun that he proposed merely to secure treaties from Chiefs. 'If I get a treaty with Sencombe on whose land Beira is ... Shall write to the Governor of Beira leaving the forcible ejection, if carried out at all, to be done later.'[19]

Forbes did not receive Colquhoun's orders till November 29. These not only called off the attack on Beira (which had been cancelled anyway), but also the plan to secure a treaty from Chief Sencombe. Forbes wrote:

> Your despatch caught me up here and only just in time to stop me going down the Pungwe. I hope to have got boats this afternoon and should have got to Sencombe's tomorrow. As you heard from my pencilled note ... we had decided not to interfere with Beira itself, but to secure a treaty with Sencombe ... Under these latest instructions I shall not go to him at all ... it is a great disappointment to the men being stopped just at the last moment.[20]

At this juncture a comedy of errors occurred. On December 3 Rhodes and Jameson at Kimberley learned for the first time, from a telegram of Colquhoun's sent on November 23, about the arrest of Gouveia, and Forbes's intention to occupy strategic points in Gorongoza (Gouveia's province), 'Note that Gorongoza reaches to sea-board including, I am informed, Beira'. There was no mention of seizing the port. Rhodes, however, was not the man to worry about the 'Modus Vivendi'. His orders can be deduced from Colquhoun's reply on December 4. 'Your wire ... instructing occupation Beira etc. arrived ... I immediately sent instructions accordingly.'

It was too late. Forbes was on his way back to Fort Salisbury when he received these new orders, only a day before his return. He told Colquhoun that they could not be carried out. The rains had set in, the swampy fever-stricken area near the port would be fatal, his troopers had no boots, and Beira was heavily reinforced. On December 17 Colquhoun wired to Rhodes for permission to abandon the attempt. The Colossus had no option but to accept.

Forbes wrote a long report for Colquhoun. One passage is slightly disingenuous and probably did much to perpetuate the myth that Colquhoun lost Beira.

[19] NAR A1/6/1, Forbes to Colquhoun, November 22, 1890.
[20] Ibid., November 29, 1890.

Although I do not think that there would have been any great difficulty in taking Beira during the dry season (and in fact I think that owing to the general panic caused by our action in Manica I could have done so, had I wished and had I not received your order of 23 November not to;) I do not think it would be practicable when once the rains have set in as they have now.

This slightly glosses over the point, one of the few on which the documents are quite clear, that Forbes had decided on November 22 not to capture Beira, although Colquhoun's order did not arrive till November 29. If anyone is to be 'blamed' for failure to occupy Beira, Forbes is the man, not Colquhoun. In fact no one should be blamed. It is in the highest degree unlikely that Salisbury, even before the 'Modus Vivendi', let alone afterwards, would have consented to such a palpable breach of international law.

The rest of the story of the attempt to secure an eastern port can be told more briefly. Rhodes was not the man to give up till events forced him. There was still the Schulz Concession from the alcoholic Gungunhana in Gazaland. Two emissaries from Schulz reached Kimberley with the news on December 3. Rhodes promptly sent one of them back with the money, while he made plans to send as soon as possible what really mattered – the arms and ammunition. Meanwhile Jameson in Manicaland decided on his own initiative (not orders from Rhodes, who had more sense) to trek with two companions, Denis Doyle and Dunbar Moodie, the whole way to Gungunhana's kraal. It was a vast journey of some seven or eight hundred miles, bold, hazardous, full of hardship – and quite unnecessary. Rutherfoord Harris had already sent the arms by sea up the Limpopo, and Gungunhana was prepared to ratify the concession on February 28, two days before the Doctor and his exhausted party arrived. The fact that Jameson personally received the concession, was arrested by the Portuguese, managed to smuggle it out through Moodie and an African courier to Lourenzo Marques and picked it up again later has masked the irrelevance of his expedition. Indeed the whole operation including the Schulz Concession was irrelevant, for there was never any chance of Salisbury claiming Gazaland as part of the British sphere, despite Gungunhana's urgent pleas, and the final treaty with Portugal in June excluded it. Four years later in 1895 the Chief was to succumb to Portuguese arms even as Lobengula had to British arms in 1893. He was imprisoned in a fortress in the Azores, was baptized in the Cathedral as Reinaldo Frederico Gungunhana in 1899 and lived till 1906.

Even before securing the Gazaland Concession Rhodes had decided on yet another attempt to obtain a route to the Indian Ocean. One of the provisos in the Anglo-Portuguese Convention of August 1890 had been the building of a railway by the Portuguese from the coast to the British sphere of influence. The general principle of freedom of transit had been confirmed in the 'Modus Vivendi'. Although the articulate element of Portugal had been in an uproar ever since the news of the arrests at Umtasa's kraal and although a battalion of 'patriotic students' (the words were not in those days self-contradictory) had sailed for Beira at the end of 1890, Rhodes decided while in London in February 1891 to offer even further provocation. Interpreting freedom of transit as the right to build irrespective of Portuguese consent a road from the head of the navigable Pungwe River to Manicaland, he sent to Beira early in April a ship, the *Norseman*, with a party of a hundred African road builders. It also contained 230 tons of food and equipment including an American stage coach.

The commander of this foray was Captain Sir John Willoughby, 5th (and last) baronet, an officer in the Blues and owner of an estate in Oxfordshire. Known for his arrogant demeanour, he was well qualified to cause the sort of 'incident' which would by the prevailing rules of the diplomatic game oblige the British Government to intervene in support of the Company. It was recognized that Willoughby might have to risk being fired upon. He might even be killed. 'Not a bit, not a bit,' Rhodes squeaked in his excited falsetto, 'they'll only hit him in the leg, only hit him in the leg.' In the event the baronet survived unscathed. The Governor of Mozambique forbade entry unless Willoughby promised not to incite the Africans of the interior against the Portuguese. This not unreasonable condition he refused to accept and on April 15 he ordered the *Norseman* with its accompanying tugs to raise steam and proceed up the river. A Portuguese gunboat thereupon fired a blank shot as a warning. The *Norseman* promptly hove to and Willoughby amidst catcalls and hoots from the Portuguese soldiery was taken to see the Governor. Meanwhile the tugs were impounded and the flags hauled down. Willoughby was at once released and allowed to return in the *Norseman* to Cape Town, having thus obtained the necessary insult to the Union Jack.

Privately Salisbury considered him entirely in the wrong and said so, giving short shrift to a protest made on his behalf by a friend (Lord Granby).[21] But the Governor's action could be regarded as a breach of the 'Modus Vivendi'. Negotiations with Portugal had reached a point where a little pressure might bring the seemingly interminable proceedings to a head. It therefore suited Salisbury to protest to Lisbon. He was reinforced by an outbreak of indignation in Cape Town. At this juncture the Portuguese really did put themselves in the wrong. Late in April 1891 the Chartered Company, after repeated adjurations beginning as early as December 18, had at last withdrawn from Massi Kessi. Their presence had all along been a palpable breach of the 'Modus Vivendi'. On May 4 a Portuguese detachment of two hundred white and three hundred black soldiers under command of Colonel Ferriera took possession of the fort. They were a detachment from a larger force which had been marching from the coast since February but had halted on the Pungwe riddled with malaria; the unfortunate students, who were unaccustomed to the deadly climate, had died like flies, and it was only a hardened body of regulars that reached Massi Kessi.

Captain Heyman with a small force was not far away protecting Umtasa's

---

[21] Lady Gwendolen Cecil, *Life of Robert Marquis of Salisbury*, Vol. IV, 1932, 74.

kraal. Colonel Ferriera had orders to expel the British from Manicaland. He presented an ultimatum, but Heyman stood his ground, and, in the ensuing skirmish on May 11 at Choua Hill some five miles from the kraal, inflicted a humiliating defeat on Ferriera, although the Company's forces consisted of only fifty men and one obsolete seven pounder gun. There is little doubt that at this juncture Heyman's troops could have reached Beira unhindered, such was the general collapse of Portuguese morale; and, having first blown up the fort at Massi Kessi, he sent a patrol under Lieutenant Fiennes for just this purpose. Fiennes, however, after only two days encountered Bishop Knight-Bruce, the Bishop of Mashonaland, who informed him that the Military Secretary to the High Commissioner and Governor of the Cape, one Major Sapte, was close behind with orders (admittedly many weeks old) to retreat at once. Fiennes felt obliged to turn back and report to Heyman. Rhodes was indignant. It is alleged that he said either to Fiennes or Heyman later – 'But why didn't you put Sapte in irons and say he was drunk?'[22] Their reply is not recorded, but they could perhaps fairly have asked whether in that case the same treatment would not have been necessary for the Bishop too.

In reality there was no opportunity missed. Rhodes could not have got away with this last effort to seize a port on the Indian Ocean any more successfully than he had with his previous efforts through Forbes, Jameson and Willoughby. Salisbury had already initialled a new convention with the Portuguese Foreign Minister who, after the disasters of the past year, was only too anxious to come to an agreement. It was ratified by the Cortes a month later, on June 11, 1891, and Rhodes's ambitions for an eastern outlet under his own control were finally extinguished. As Salisbury acidly pointed out, article I of the charter defined the Company's sphere as west of the Portuguese dominions. 'By the acceptance of that definition the company admitted the existence of Portuguese dominions between Matabeland and the sea ... If they should now attempt to deny the existence of such dominions ... they would thereby nullify their own claims to territory described as bounded by them.'[23]

The Anglo-Portuguese Convention which was formally ratified by both powers on July 3 finally settled the eastern and north-eastern boundaries of the British sphere of interest. The Portuguese gave up the corridor to Angola, which had been conceded to them in 1890, also the Manicaland plateau, though they retained Macequece. Southern Rhodesia thus acquired what has come to be one of its main holiday areas, including Umtali, the Vumba mountains and Melsetter, all of which would have gone to Portugal under the 1890 Treaty. In return, the Portuguese obtained a then useless area which, however, included the site where the Caborabassa dam was to be built over seventy years later and Britain renounced any claim to Gazaland. The Portuguese agreed to freedom of transit

[22] Colvin, *Jameson*, I, 205, n. 1.

[23] R. I. Lovell, *The Struggle for South Africa*, New York, 1934, 242 quoting *C6495*, No. 199 (Encl.).

from the coast to the interior and to the construction of a railway, but Britain dropped the humiliating clause of the earlier Treaty which gave her the right to appoint the consultant engineer. This may have been an error. It was not till 1898 that the railway – and a very unsatisfactory one – reached Umtali. Also dropped was a clause which had caused much of the trouble in Lisbon the previous year, forbidding the Portuguese to alienate any of its African territory without British consent. Instead Britain simply had the first refusal. The only frontier which remained still uncertain was the western boundary of Barotseland with Angola. Provision was made for arbitration and eventually in 1903 the King of Italy agreed to act. His decision created the line drawn on the map today, and since it gave equal dissatisfaction to both parties, it was probably not unjust.

The only remaining external threat to the company's territory south of the Zambesi was the Transvaal. The so-called Adendorff *trek* has been mentioned in an earlier chapter.[24] Kruger's official discouragement did not end the matter, although no move was made during 1890. There was much unrest in the Republic at the time. Foreigners, or *uitlanders*, to use the Afrikaans term, were buying up land on a vast scale. The Boer farmers, as so often in the past, were once again looking northwards to escape from the alien modern world and to preserve their own archaic pastoral way of life. Indeed, it is surprising that an expedition to occupy Mashonaland, or at least a part of it, had not been mounted earlier.

The area on which the *trekkers* fixed their eyes was known as Banyailand. 'Banai' is a corruption of the word *vanyai*, the name given to the people living on the northern edge of the low veld. They were in fact a branch of the Shona. It was, however, believed at this time that they were in some way separate or distinct. Adendorff and a coadjutor, one J. du Preez, on the strength of some highly doubtful concessions, tried to raise recruits in the Transvaal for a revived *trek* and the creation of an independent 'Banyailand Republic'. Their activities caused much alarm to the Chartered Company in the early months of 1891. But the danger that Hofmeyr might pledge the *Bond* in Cape Colony to support the *trek* disappeared. He was soon satisfied that legally the Transvaal Government had a duty to prevent it, and, if they did not, the British Government was entitled to repel the invaders by force. The High Commissioner at Cape Town issued a strong warning. So did Kruger, although there was a good deal of sympathy for the *trekkers* in Pretoria, and at one time it looked as if something like a thousand men with four hundred wagons were gathering for the journey.

This figure fell, however, to a hard core of a hundred with thirty or forty wagons. An attempt was made by their commander, Commandant Ignatius Ferriera, to cross the Limpopo at Main Drift on June 24, 1891. He forded the river with five companions. Inevitably the ubiquitous Dr Jameson was there to meet him. Ferriera was arrested. Jameson, releasing him on parole, crossed the

[24] Ch. 5, p. 69.

river with him and addressed the *trekkers* on the south bank of the river. They were, he said, welcome on the Company's terms, but if they tried to set up an independent republic the result would be war. A few came over on these terms. The rest melted away to the south. Their bluff had been called.

Over the years a sizeable number of Afrikaners have emigrated to Rhodesia and their descendants are still there, but no further effort was made to found a new Boer republic. The frontier was closed. Jameson had brought the end to another old dream. In the same month that the Portuguese vision of a broad trans-African band from Mozambique to Angola had vanished for good and all, the no less potent Afrikaner aspiration of an endless *trek* to the north was finally frustrated.

The British sphere of influence in Central Africa as far as foreign states were concerned had been effectively delimited by the middle of 1891, apart from the Barotseland frontier with Angola. What had not yet been settled was the allocation of authority within that sphere. Rhodes, of course, hoped to acquire the whole of it for the Chartered Company. The difficulty was the position of the Lakes Company in Nyasaland. Efforts to absorb it or take it over had made little progress during 1889 and 1890. The directors of the Lakes Company were determined to keep control in their own hands. Harry Johnston, who described them as a 'miserly, fanatical, uncultured set of Glasgow merchants', was no less determined to secure it for himself. In April 1890, however, the Chartered Company agreed to allow the Lakes Company £9,000 p.a. to administer Nyasaland, pending an ultimate amalgamation under which Nyasaland would be controlled by the Glasgow Board of the Lakes Company.

When Rhodes's solicitor, Hawksley, informed the Foreign Office in November of this arrangement, Sir Percy Anderson, head of the Africa Department, pointed out that it was illegal, for the Lakes Company as yet had no charter and therefore no administrative powers. He suggested that the Chartered Company, instead of subsidizing a body which had no power to use the money, should subsidize the British Government which had the power, but might well be unable to extract a grant from Parliament. There was to be an important *quid pro quo.* Although there was a general promise to extend in the course of time the sphere of the charter to the area north of the Zambesi, Salisbury had not yet actually authorized this step and he could have delayed it as long as he pleased. He now agreed to an immediate extension. Rhodes hastened to London early in February 1891 and after much hard bargaining he and Johnston secured an agreement with the Foreign Office on February 8 or 9 under which Nyasaland, with frontiers defined much as they are today, became a Protectorate administered by the Foreign Office, while all the British territory to the west came under the Company's charter. Johnston was not only to be Commissioner for the new Protectorate, he was also to be Administrator of the whole of the Company's territory north of the Zambesi, a position, as Professor Oliver describes it, 'both of extraordinary responsibility and extraordinary licence'.

It was perhaps inevitable that Rhodes and Johnston would quarrel sooner or later. The money for the administration of Nyasaland was never enough, even though in practice a substantial amount was added by the Treasury to the Company's subsidy. In March 1893 Johnston had to go to Cape Town and ask Rhodes for more. Rhodes agreed to raise the subsidy to £17,500 for five years and provide £4,500 towards the cost of steamers on Lakes Nyasa and Tanganyika, in return for which all Crown land and all unalienated mineral rights were to go to the Company. This agreement was sent to the Foreign Office for ratification. On August 24 the Foreign Office presented it to the London Office of the company with two important amendments, first that the subsidy should continue for ten years not five, secondly that the whole of it ahould be spent in Nyasaland. Rhodes, apparently at the suggestion of Rutherfoord Harris, that singularly ill-chosen counsellor, jumped to the conclusion that Johnston had been in secret communication with the Foreign Office behind his back. He sent an insulting message early in October to the unfortunate Commissioner, accusing him of dishonesty and disloyalty, and at once cancelled the extra subsidy. 'I am not going to create with my funds an independent King Johnston over the Zambesi,' he told Harris.

Johnston had in fact been wholly guiltless. Rhodes was in the habit of hurling wild accusations at his subordinates. The vast majority of his friends, satellites and toadies were used to this sort of treatment. Whether or not they forgave it, they were ready to forget, or to pretend to forget. Johnston neither forgot nor forgave. For him it was the end of the road. He dispatched a withering letter of 4,000 words to Rhodes with copies to Lord Rosebery, who was now Foreign Secretary, and the London Office of the company, demanding investigation, retraction and apology. He never got it, but Rhodes evidently came to the conclusion that he had been misinformed, if we can judge from a relatively polite, but brief note in February 1894, suggesting a meeting. Johnston neither answered nor met him. And at that moment, just when his seemingly hopeless deficits appeared to have put him at Rhodes's mercy, the Foreign Office, after years of ignoring every plea for funds, suddenly gave way and agreed to finance the impoverished Protectorate. Rhodes had not reckoned on this. He meant to wait till the financial position was desperate and then offer to take over the government – rather like foreclosing on a mortgage. The official volte-face, whatever its causes – which are far from clear – wrecked this plan. Rhodes no longer paid his subsidy. 'King' Johnston ceased to have any say in the vast area which constitutes modern Zambia. But Nyasaland had slipped for ever out of the Company's domain.

7

Settlement and War 1890–93

The ceremonial hoisting of the flag in Salisbury on September 13, 1890 was followed by champagne for the officers and chaplains. The preliminary stages of building the fort began that afternoon. Sunday was a day of rest. On Monday the work was continued in earnest. It was completed by the end of the month, and with the construction of Fort Salisbury Johnson had fulfilled the contract into which he had entered some nine months earlier. On September 30 the Pioneers, having been duly paid, paraded for the last time. In his Regimental Orders Johnson praised them for their loyalty and discipline, wished them success and trusted that none of them would ever regret his enlistment. On the morning of the parade he stood on a wagon and addressed them:

Officers, non-commissioned officers and men of the Pioneer Corps, with my next order you will be converted from a military force into a civilian population free from military discipline.
Parade! Right turn! Dismiss!

The Pioneers, each with three months rations, a rifle and a hundred rounds of ammunition, were now free to peg their promised fifteen gold claims and to 'ride off' their 3,000 acre farms. That evening, the sky around Salisbury was thick with the dust of the moving wagons of those who had decided to start at once on their *trek*. Few of them paused to reflect on the legal aspect of these exciting promises. The status of the farms was particularly questionable, for the Company was not in a position to give any valid title at all to land. But since farming was by far the less glamorous of the two forms of reward, and indeed was not to play any significant part in the settler economy until 1896 at the earliest, this perhaps did not matter. The gold claims were legally valid, but there were serious snags here too which might have made a prudent man pause. The Company had insisted on retaining a fifty per cent interest in all claims pegged, alternatively half the vendor's scrip in any company formed, and it reserved to itself the first right of flotation. These conditions did not appear too onerous as long as everyone believed that a vast fortune was just round the corner. Later they became very unpopular. Fifty per cent was reduced to thirty and in the end replaced by a system of royalties on a sliding scale.

The Company's title to allocate land appeared to be soon validated by the purchase in 1891 of the Lippert Concession. Renny-Tailyour had procured on behalf of Lippert a grant from Lobengula of the right to dispose of land in the latter's dominions for the next hundred years. Since Lobengula had promised under the Rudd Concession not to grant land without the consent of the Chartered Company, the grant to Lippert had a very dubious legal basis. Lobengula, convinced that Lippert was a deadly enemy of Rhodes, made it as a counter-move against the Company. There he understandably miscalculated. Rather than have an interminable and complicated juridical dispute, Rhodes bought the Lippert Concession for £30,000, although he could have argued that it was valueless anyway – which indeed was to be the decision of the Judicial Committee of the Privy Council in 1918. But in the meantime for nearly three decades the purchase was regarded as bridging an important gap between the *de facto* and *de jure* powers of the Chartered Company. It was formally approved by Lord Knutsford, and Lobengula, even if he had understood this strange legal transaction, could do nothing about it.

The Europeans during the first months of the occupation were very thin on the ground. Marshall Hole reckons that there were at most a thousand in all Mashonaland – some 190 Pioneers, 650 police (the number was reinforced to that figure in 1891 because of the Adendorff *trek*) and not more than 150 who got through from the south or east before the rainy season set in. Those who had must have regretted it. The Rhodesian summer of 1890–91 was notable for one of the heaviest rainfalls ever to be recorded (fifty-four inches at Salisbury).[1] Conditions were highly uncomfortable. Boots rotted away and clothes fell apart. The additional supplies needed to give the men a change had been left behind at Tuli – through a muddle by the contractors. The grass-roofed huts of pole and dagga (puddled mud), which seemed an adequate shelter in the dry heat of September, leaked like sieves in the first storms of October. There was a chronic shortage of supplies of every sort including axes, spades and almost all the tools needed for building. The rains reduced the road cut by the pioneers under Selous to a river of mud. Dried-up water courses with scarcely a trickle in them when the expedition had passed across on its way to the north became raging torrents four months later.

From mid-December supplies ceased entirely. The route was impassable for wagons. Before the end of January it had become impassable even for the police post-riders. The settlers were deprived of mail and newspapers as well as more

---

[1] According to 'Skipper' Hoste's diary. The average rainfall is thirty-five to forty inches and it can often be much less than that.

bulky articles. Communication with the outside world was virtually cut off until the beginning of April, when Colonel Pennefather who had been on leave in the south and had been delayed at Tuli by the floods on the Lundi became the first man since January to ride through. Unfortunately the news that he was 'delayed' at Fort Tuli, shouted across the roaring water in a colonial accent, was mis-heard as 'died'. In due course, his effects in Salisbury were sold. The Colonel was smitten with apoplectic symptoms when he observed that the astonished officer whom he first met on his return was wearing his field boots.[2]

The men who experienced the first rainy season of the occupation had to undergo much hardship. The insects were particularly odious. Termites devoured almost everything they encountered, including the poles supporting the huts. No one could move without a cloud of midges round his head. Mosquitoes multiplied in the pools of water and maddened men with their bite and their whining hum. It was not, however, realized yet that they carried a greater threat than irritation. The connexion between the *anopheles* mosquito and malaria was not established until 1898, although it had long been known that there was a relationship between the disease and marshy areas, particularly in a hot climate. The settlers had no idea of the danger of leaving the countless holes and pits, which they had dug for building purposes in the dry weather, full of stagnant water. During the wet months of 1890–91 malaria was rampant. There were not many fatalities except among those who had contracted the lethal complication which can result from frequent attacks – blackwater fever. Although the cause of malaria was not known its cure was, and thanks to the enterprise of a Doctor Rand who had procured some quinine from Macequece, official supplies being as usual inadequate, the situation was not too disastrous.

But the disease was debilitating, depressing and bad for morale, which was low enough already. The prospectors who hoped for gold soon discovered that, if obtainable at all, it could only be mined by expensive machinery non-existent in Mashonaland. The rains made further investigation impossible and they returned to Fort Salisbury for food, shelter, clothes and medicine. They found very little of any. By the end of November flour, sugar and salt had almost vanished. Not only was life very uncomfortable, it was also very boring. There were scarcely any candles or matches. It is true that a lighted candle had the disadvantage of at once attracting myriads of flying beetles, but even that was better than sitting or lying in the dark for ten or twelve hours. Rhodesia, being in the tropics, is almost equinoctial the whole year round, and there is a limit to the amount of time that can be spent in sleep, especially when the night is made hideous by the croaking of innumerable bull-frogs. Of the proverbial nocturnal pleasures of man only song was available. Colquhoun had, rather surprisingly in view of the contents of his own luggage, decreed that Mashonaland should be 'dry', and the Company had forbidden the entry of women.

One notable attempt was made to break both rules. A mysterious character

[2] G. H. Tanser, *A Scantling of Time*, Salisbury, 1965, 47.

who called himself the Vicomte de la Panouse brought out his eighteen year old mistress (a cockney maidservant whom he subsequently married in Salisbury), disguised as a boy. He arrived on Christmas Day 1890 – the last traveller to get through – with two wagons, one of which was packed with wines and spirits. But Colquhoun at once vetoed his attempts to sell whisky at £5 a bottle, and Fort Salisbury remained teetotal until St Patrick's Day (March 17) 1891 when the Administrator was persuaded to relent. The 'Count', as he was known, lowered his price and let the organizers of the party have four cases for £85. A notable beano followed, at which Forbes and Colquhoun himself were the guests of honour. The Count, who claimed to have been on Marshal MacMahon's staff in the Franco-Prussian War, also to have been a Captain in the French Navy and to have shot a hundred and three elephants in one season, became a popular figure. His name is recorded as one of founding fathers of the Salisbury Club two years later.

St Patrick's Day 1891 was an isolated celebration in a dismal period during which insects were not the only menace. Rats infested the primitive buildings. Their presence encouraged snakes which, though somewhat reducing the rat population, added a further threat to the unhappy settlers. The rats were such a pest that in the early years of Salisbury a kitten was regarded as one of the best wedding presents for the bride. Medical comforts were grossly inadequate until the arrival at the end of July 1891 of five Dominican Sisters who had volunteered to nurse the sick. This was followed by the construction of a primitive hospital with an operating theatre in which Dr Jameson himself would from time to time perform. The nursing sisters, though often ill themselves, worked indefatigably, and the fever-stricken patients of the 1891–92 season at least fared better than those of the previous year.

With the arrival of the dry weather from April onwards visitors began to appear. Four are worthy of special note. The first was Theodore Bent who was financed by the BSA Company and the Royal Geographical Society in order to investigate the ruins at Zimbabwe. In the book which resulted from his expedition – *The Ruined Cities of Mashonaland* (1892) – he argued that Zimbabwe was built by Phoenicians from Arabia. It was not till 1906 that Randall McIver put forward the now accepted view that the onus of proof lay on those who postulated an outside origin, and that in fact there was no hard evidence at all of the existence of any non-Bantu (other than Bushmen) in the area until the coming of the Arabs, which occurred after Zimbabwe had already been established.

The next visitor of note was Lord Randolph Churchill who made a tour of Southern Africa with a view to repairing his ill-health and shattered fortunes. Of the many 'candid friends' from England who have given Rhodesians the benefit of their unsolicited advice, Lord Randolph was not only the earliest but also one of the most unpopular – and that is saying something. Not that Rhodesia was the only object of his censure, for he was burned in effigy in Pretoria as a result of his remarks about the Boers. His comments appeared in a series of letters in the *Daily Graphic*, for which he was paid two thousand guineas. They were published as a book a year later under the title of *Men, Mines and Animals in South Africa*. He was in an irritable state of mind, suffering as we now know from the early symptoms of the disease which was to kill him. A diet of coarse and ill-cooked beef washed down by tepid whisky and water did not improve his temper.

Lord Randolph's observations were given wide publicity in England and carried the authority of an ex-Cabinet minister who had at one time seemed destined for the premiership. Coming just when investors were beginning to have doubts about the whole future of Mashonaland, his remarks damaged the Chartered Company and enraged the South African 'interest' in London. He was particularly scathing about the Company's police. He was also uncomplimentary about the manners and behaviour of his hosts. He regarded the prospects of gold mining and European immigration with scepticism. None of this stopped him accepting Rhodes's hospitality at Groote Schuur. When reproached by a friend, he replied, 'My dear fellow it's the only place in this God-forsaken country where I can get Perrier Jouet '74'. Percy Fitzpatrick, later author of one of the most celebrated best-sellers about South Africa, *Jock of the Bushvelt* (1907), had arranged Lord Randolph's visit, but felt obliged to repudiate some of his criticisms in a now rare book, *Through Mashonaland with Pick and Pen* (1892). One can perhaps guess that Lord Randolph was not in the frame of mind to do justice, even if some of his criticisms happened to be well-founded.

In August occurred the first visit from a director of the company. This was not Rhodes. He had travelled to Fort Tuli in November 1890 for that purpose, but had been dissuaded from going on because of the risk of being marooned during the rainy season. The first director to make his way into Mashonaland was his partner, Alfred Beit.[3] Rather oddly in view of his great posthumous generosity[4] to the country, he was destined to visit it only once again before his death. He was alarmed by the chaos, inefficiency and downright fraud which prevailed at Tuli, and as a mining expert was far from confident after his arrival in Mashonaland that the prospects for gold were as good as they were believed to be. A great deal of his time there was spent in listening to the grievances of the settlers.

There was not much that he could do. Rhodes was the key figure, and in October the Colossus arrived after a most trying journey from Beira during which he discovered for himself Frank Johnson's over-optimism about the eastern route. In view of the Portuguese hatred of him – '*homen horrivel*' was his soubriquet – Rhodes showed a certain courage, some might say insensitivity, in going that way at all. He was met at Umtali by Jameson, spent a week at Salisbury, and then travelled the country for another week, covering over 600 miles.

By the time Rhodes arrived Colquhoun had departed, ostensibly on grounds of health. In reality his position had become more and more uneasy since December 1890 when Rhodes made his personal lack of confidence obvious by appointing Jameson as Managing Director in Mashonaland with full control over policy.

[3] Among many other inaccuracies J. G. Lockhart (op. cit., 246) says that both Beit and Churchill arrived in the rainy season.

[4] See Appendix, p. 412.

The situation was not too bad for the next six months, since Jameson was hardly ever in the country, travelling as he did feverishly to Gungunhana's kraal and back – 'a seven hundred mile walking tour', as Rhodes called this superfluous expedition. Jameson hated administration and the Adendorff *trek* gave him a further opportunity to put off the evil hour, but, having settled that with characteristic aplomb, he had no option save to take up his duties as Chief Magistrate, the new title given to the ruler of Mashonaland.

Colquhoun now fades out of Rhodesian history. He has had a bad press from historians. It is true that he lacked the charm and blarney of Jameson or the thrust and energy of Johnson. It is also true that, unlike the more successful members of Rhodes's court, he had not the 'antennae' to interpret his master's wishes as it were by instinct, nor had he the sense to see how disastrous it was to pour out his woes to Rutherfoord Harris of all people. Nevertheless he had done much to lay the rough foundations of law, order and administration in the new colony, and he displayed a scrupulosity about such matters as titles and allocation of land which Jameson was far from sharing – to the lasting detriment of African interests. Indeed it was this scrupulosity which enraged Johnson and his co-adventurers who had the ear of Rhodes. Hence the latter's decision to push Colquhoun out. As for the charge of failing to secure Beira, we have seen that it is wholly baseless. Pompous, prickly and slightly obtuse though he may have been, Colquhoun for all his faults was an able man and deserves more credit than he has received.

In Salisbury and on his travels Rhodes was bombarded with complaints which he did his best to meet, and he was generous with his purse. At times however he fell back on the argument that these hardships were the price of creating a new extension to the empire, which would be a great thing for future generations. On one of these occasions he elicited a celebrated reply from a Scottish store-keeper. 'I would have ye know, Mr Rhodes, that we didna come here for posterity.'

There were bigger problems than settler discontent. Of the one million pounds capital raised to form the Company, only about half was left. £70,000 had gone on concessions, £90,000 to Johnson and his syndicate for the pioneer road. Another £50,000 had been spent on the telegraph line, now approaching Fort Victoria, and £200,000 on the police. There were many miscellaneous expenses too, and so far there had been virtually no profits. Rhodes and Jameson decided that the obvious economy was the police, which if continuing at the strength of 650 would cost at least £150,000 a year (Rhodes at a shareholders' meeting in 1892 put it at £250,000). The number was accordingly to be reduced to 150 by Christmas. To meet potential emergencies a volunteer force known as the Mashonaland Horse was recruited from the settlers. The cost of the police was thus reduced to about £50,000 a year. There was no lack of criticism at what seemed to some a reckless decision, but the Ndebele were assumed to be quiescent, the Shona tribes to be useless as fighters and in any case well disposed because of the protection afforded by the white man against Ndebele raids – assumptions which were to prove ill-founded within a very short time.

Rhodes and Jameson were both of them gamblers, and the Company's tottering fortunes seemed to necessitate a gamble. Its shares had slumped as a result of stories about the hardships during the first wet season. Matters were made even worse by the revelation in December that the Chartered Company had never owned the Rudd Concession and had had to buy out the United Concessions Company which it did with a special issue of a million chartered shares.[5] In March 1892 the Chartered Company's bankers refused to honour its cheques without a guarantee. This was duly given by De Beers, in effect Rhodes acting under another hat, but the situation was clearly one that could not continue.

Although Marshall Hole says that, apart from a few cases of violence, 'progress was unchecked and rapid' during 1891–92, his optimism seems hardly warranted by the facts. It is true that substantial buildings were erected in Salisbury, that the Standard Bank began to operate, that a printed newspaper replaced the cyclo-styled sheets of the *Rhodesia Herald*, that cricket matches were played ('extras' being often the highest score owing to the state of the wicket), that a billiard saloon was erected (in which there not only featured Gilbert and Sullivan's 'twisted cue and elliptical billiard balls', but a slanting table as well), that the first Mashonaland race meeting was held on Boxing Day 1891, that in February 1892 the telegraph line from Mafeking reached Salisbury, that in the same year the first rugby match was played and the first red light district (somewhat thinly populated) came into being on the Kopje. These signs of civilization could not mask the existence of a general economic depression throughout the two years.

Gold-mining produced negligible returns and farming none. The nearest railheads were still many hundreds of miles away and, although the distances were gradually diminishing, this was no consolation for men with very little capital which they saw dwindling rapidly with the enormous cost of bringing by primitive bullock cart most of the necessities of life. People were continually coming into the country buoyed up by stories of quick wealth to be gained. Others were continually leaving bored and disillusioned with a life of primitive hardship to which they saw no end. The shifting population was virtually static in numbers. Not even Jameson's hail-fellow-well-met manner, friendly banter and genial hospitality could allay the dissatisfaction. However, by the new year of 1893 there were signs of improvement. 'I have still to keep a fair sized pauper community', he wrote in a letter to his brother, but he thought that 'the end of the year ought to see us in a fairly good position – bar further accidents'. It was perhaps a sign of increasing confidence that on May 20 the Salisbury Club, with Rhodes as President and Jameson as Vice-President opened its premises.

In fact 1893 was to see a complete transformation in the situation. To understand what happened it is necessary to examine the problem which in one form or another has dominated Rhodesian history ever since – the relationship between the Whites and the Blacks. From 1890 till the Matabele war settled the matter

---

[5] Robert Cary, *Charter Royal*, 168; and see above, Chapter 5.

for the time being in 1893 that relationship was fundamentally ambiguous. To the Shona Paramount Chiefs, Jameson was simply another chief, head of a white tribe which did indeed possess formidable power but which would probably move on in due course and to which they owed no particular allegiance or obedience. They were glad to be relieved of the menace of Ndebele raids, or rather, to be strictly correct, those who had suffered were glad; Lobengula's forays had never penetrated to eastern Mashonaland. But this relief did not make them especially grateful to the white man. They were not so naïve as to believe that his appearance on the scene had anything to do with benevolence towards themselves. At first they were merely curious about the new arrivals and did a certain amount of friendly trade with them. Later they resented the press-gang methods of the settlers to whom cheap labour soon became essential.

The juridical position was far from clear. Until May 1891 the British Government, while conceding the Company's right to send men into Mashonaland, would not agree that the Company possessed any judicial or administrative powers over anyone, white or black, until a further concession supplementing that gained by Rudd could be secured from Lobengula. Since the Ndebele King now bitterly regretted – indeed considered that he had repudiated – the Rudd Concession, the chances of any further grant from him were nil. Inevitably in the constantly critical circumstances of the occupation the settlers tended to take the law into their own hands *vis-à-vis* the Shona. Colquhoun and Pennefather suggested as an alternative a policy of treaties with those Shona Chiefs who had been clearly outside Lobengula's sphere. There was much to be said for this, but Rhodes vetoed it on the old ground that the Company's position depended on the Rudd Concession which in its turn depended upon acceptance of Lobengula's sovereignty over the whole of Mashonaland.[6]

In May 1891 the situation was partly remedied. On April 13 the High Commissioner at Cape Town had proclaimed that the whole of the Company's area of operation was a British sphere of interest where the Crown could legislate under the Foreign Jurisdiction Acts. On May 9 an Order in Council made southern Zambesia a British Protectorate in which the High Commission could exercise 'all powers which Her Majesty had or may have ... for the peace, order and good government of all persons within the limits of this Order', subject to the rights of native rulers and their civil law as far as these were compatible with the Crown's jurisdiction. An accompanying letter made it clear that there was no intention to abridge the powers conferred on the Company by the charter. 'All persons' obviously included the Shona tribes, but they themselves recognized no such jurisdiction. Nor did Lobengula, who still claimed suzerainty over the whole of Mashonaland. In 1891 he showed the reality of the claim by sending a small *impi* to punish Chief Lomagundi who dwelt a hundred miles west of Salisbury for failing to pay tribute. The Chief was killed, his kraal left in ashes, his women and children swept off into slavery.

[6] T. O. Ranger, *Revolt in Southern Rhodesia*, London, 1967, 55–6.

The situation was therefore anything but clear and it was particularly disagreeable for the Shona who were looked on as subjects both by Lobengula and the Company. To quote Mr Philip Mason, 'to one they were a source of cattle and women, to the other a source of labour; the Mashona, reluctant to fill either role, could hardly fill both.'[7] Jameson was prudent and forebearing in his relations with the Ndebele, less so with the Shona. An episode which provoked much criticism was the action of a Captain Lendy whom he dispatched in March 1892 on an expedition to bring to trial in Salisbury Chief Ngomo, who had robbed and subsequently insulted a white trader called Bennett. Ngomo refused to move and Lendy returned to Salisbury for further orders. Jameson sent him back with reinforcements, a seven pounder, a Maxim gun, and instruction 'to take summary measures'. Lendy obeyed to the letter, bombarded Ngomo's kraal at dawn on March 17, killing the Chief, his son and twenty-one others. Rhodes strongly approved and settler opinion was delighted.

The Colonial Office took a different view. Under the legal fiction still in operation it was arguable that the Company had no right to punish Ngomo at all. Was he not theoretically under the jurisdiction of Lobengula? However, it was generally agreed that, whatever the theory, occupation by the Company gave *de facto* sovereignty in the sense that the Protectorate could not survive if it was unable to keep the peace between contending tribes or preserve the rights of property; and the only people who could do this were the Company's officers. What stuck in the throats of the High Commissioner and Lord Knutsford, the Colonial Secretary, was the severity of the action; 'utterly disproportionate to the original offence', declared Loch; and Knutsford in a dispatch considered that 'Lendy acted in this matter with recklessness and undue harshness'.

Philip Mason in a perceptive analysis of this episode suggests that it contains in embryo much of subsequent Rhodesian history – the enforcement of 'the white man's law'; the assumption (on which Lendy justified his action) that it is right to kill a large number of Blacks rather than lose a single white life; the firmness of 'the man on the spot' who has to consider that the very survival of a white island in a black sea may depend on resolute action now, contrasted with the doubts of the man in Whitehall 'who has scruples ... about common humanity and liberty and forced labour, a man who "does not know the country" and has no idea how different things are in Rhodesia'.[8]

But as the author wisely observes, it is not a simple matter of right and wrong. All depends on the standard by which one judges. Loch and Knutsford thought in terms of the military coming to the aid of the civil power at the request of a magistrate. By that standard Lendy did indeed behave with unnecessary ruthlessness. But if we look at his action as the assertion of British sovereignty over and conquest of Mashonaland – and this is undoubtedly how Jameson and the settlers did look at it – then it has to be measured by a different rule; that of the Con-

[7] Philip Mason, *Birth of a Dilemma*, Oxford, 1958, reprinted 1968, 163.
[8] Op. cit., 159.

quistadores, of Clive in India, of Napoleon, of the American frontiersmen. By that standard it seems less harsh. Moreover the censure of Whitehall and the row created by Labouchère and others in the House of Commons had an effect. Jameson stoutly defended Lendy but he was careful to avoid a repetition.

The rival claims of Lobengula and the Company upon Mashonaland were irreconcilable. Lobengula could not give up raiding. The whole economy and social structure of the Ndebele state depended upon it. But its continuance made the white development of Mashonaland impossible. Shona labour was vital, and naturally enough at the slightest rumour of the approach of an *impi* – and of course there were far more rumours than approaches – the Shona fled to their hilly fastnesses and disappeared for weeks on end. It can be fairly assumed that Rhodes and Jameson expected the matter to be settled sooner or later by war, unless Lobengula abandoned the raids. But the theory that, because of the parlous state of the Company's finances, the depression in the country, and the lure of Ndebele gold and cattle, they were deliberately planning a war for the dry season of 1893 and provoked an 'incident' will not stand up. The disbanding of the police is proof enough. Professor Ranger makes the point that a campaign of this sort would not have been a police operation,[9] but it defies belief that someone who was preparing for hostilities would have pared the only military force in the country to the bone or would have reduced the number of horses (deemed essential in a battle with the Ndebele) to less than a hundred.

The truth would seem, rather, to be that Rhodes and Jameson were waiting upon events. They were not going to start a war. Indeed Jameson's relations with Lobengula throughout 1891 and 1892 were marked by caution and restraint, and no desire at all to make a *casus belli* out of the relatively few Ndebele raids which did occur. On the other hand if something were to happen of a nature which would justify 'defensive' action in the eyes of the High Commissioner, above all if it could be conducted without bringing in the imperial factor, then they would not be backward in seizing the opportunity; and the decision, which would be Jameson's, might well be sudden and unpremeditated, given that streak of impetuosity which was to be exemplified in the raid, two and a half years later.

Lobengula for his part was no less cautious during the first three years of the Company's occupation of Mashonaland. His prudence is shown by his attitude towards the 'border' between the two countries. This was regarded by Jameson as roughly the line of the Umniati and Shashi Rivers, and he told Lobengula that only Ndebele coming to work, or sent by the King as peaceful emissaries would be allowed across. By the same token he forbade Pioneers to cross the other way and accepted Lobengula's complaint on the rare occasions when the rule was broken. It suited Lobengula to have a *de facto* border. There had always been such a line between the Ndebele state itself and its raiding areas, and he certainly did not want white men wandering across it without his knowledge and permission. But he could not acknowledge it openly without giving up his sovereignty over

[9] Ranger, op. cit., 91.

the Shona east of the Shashi river. It is probable that he did not tell his *indunas* about the 'border' at all. In correspondence with Jameson, though he never denied, he also never admitted its existence, and the Doctor probably – and not unreasonably – took silence as consent.

Because of the charges levelled at the time by Labouchère and by other enemies of the Company from that day to this, there has been an immense amount written about the origins of the Matabele war. Yet, although there are some obscurities which will never be cleared up, the essential nature of what happened is relatively simple. In May 1893 five hundred yards of copper telegraph wire between Tuli and Fort Victoria were removed – for its value, not for sabotage – by a headman called Gomalla who owed allegiance to a petty Maholi Chief named Setoutsie living on the Company's side of the border. Jameson exacted a fine of cattle which was paid by Gomalla with what Marshall Hole describes as 'an alacrity which should have aroused suspicion'. In fact the cattle belonged to Lobengula and were merely on loan to Setoutsie for milking purposes. On hearing the news from Setoutsie, who gave the impression that Jameson was aware of the true ownership, Lobengula protested strongly both to Jameson and to the High Commissioner. Jameson promptly had the cattle returned – an action which in itself suggests a pacific attitude; if he had wanted to provoke an incident over the affair it would have been easy enough to do so.

Meanwhile, a quite independent episode occurred. A Shona Chief called Bere also living near Fort Victoria stole some of Lobengula's cattle in June. Lobengula despatched a small *impi* to deal with him, but the party was met by Captain Lendy, now Magistrate, after it had crossed the border and was persuaded to return. Here again there could have been a *casus belli* if Jameson had instructed Lendy to treat it as such.

Early in July Lobengula sent a much larger *impi* across the border. Whether he meant simply to recover the cattle stolen by Bere, or to take vengeance on Gomalla and Setoutsie for double-crossing him, or to make a general example of Shona petty Chiefs who were getting above themselves, is not entirely clear. He did not intend war with the Whites or he would not have sent another *impi* simultaneously towards the Zambesi, and he made a particular point of informing Lendy that his men had strict orders not to molest the settlers or their property. It was unlucky but not his fault that the message only got through some days after July 9 when the Ndebele first began raiding the Victoria area. The spectacle of a Ndebele *impi* in full action on a primitive expedition was not a savoury one. Kraals were reduced to ashes, men assegaied and 'mutilated' (i.e. their genitals cut off), women disembowelled, children roasted alive. Whether all these things happened on this occasion is uncertain. There is no doubt that they all did at other times and places. What the settlers saw must have been nasty enough, with every allowance made for exaggeration. This was the first of Lobengula's *impis* to raid a white-occupied area. Not surprisingly it was also to be the last.

Although white lives were safe, white property, whatever Lobengula's assurances, was not. Furniture was broken, cattle were carried away irrespective of ownership, and the Shona labourers, a form of 'property' especially valuable to the settlers, indiscriminately slaughtered, save for those who fled or put themselves under protection in the fort. To the demand that the latter should be surrendered under the promise that their bodies would be left in the bush and away from the river to avoid pollution Lendy gave an uncompromising refusal, dictated alike by humanity and prestige. Moreover, as Professor Gann drily points out, if he had given them up, the wrath of the anti-Company party in London would have been even greater than it was over what actually happened. 'They would have condemned Rhodes, Beit and their friends for upholding an unholy alliance between a blood-stained feudalism and the forces of finance capitalism – a charge that would have been hard to refute.'[10] The clash symbolized the whole dispute about jurisdiction over the Shona. Lobengula and the senior *induna* Manyau, who represented him, were acting legitimately by their own lights. The Shona were their 'dogs'. What business had the white men to interfere? Equally, the representatives of the company could not tolerate an incursion which made a mockery of British rule and the *Pax Britannica*.

Nonetheless Jameson did not at first consider the matter a cause for war. He thought that the Victoria settlers had 'got the jumps', and he expected the Ndebele to disappear at once.[11] He took a more serious view when he arrived at Fort Victoria on July 17 and saw for himself what had happened. He sent for Manyau who denied all knowledge of the 'border' and for his second-in-command, Umgandan – an aggressive and 'insolent' young *induna*, described by an observer as 'the handsomest African native I have ever seen'.[12] There is no authoritative account of what was said at the meeting on July 18 but Jameson, the night before, sent a telegram to Harris: 'I intend to treat them like dogs and order the whole *impi* out of the country. Then if they do not go send Lendy out with fifty mounted men to fire into them.'[13] There is no need to doubt that he conveyed such an ultimatum, for events followed exactly that course. What is disputed is whether he gave them an hour to get moving or an hour to be across the border – which would have been quite impossible as the distance was some thirty miles.

Jameson was acquitted by F. J. (later Sir Francis) Newton in his later enquiry about the origins of the war. Though the report may be somewhat suspect, since Newton was strongly pro-Rhodes and an adverse report in the aftermath of the war and the tragedy of the Shangani Patrol would have been ill-received, there seems no reason to believe that Jameson was seeking an excuse to fire at the Ndebele. He had ample excuse to do so without holding an *indaba* at all. He undoubtedly meant simply to give the Ndebele an hour to show that they were really on the move. He gave them nearly two, and then sent Lendy with orders

[10] L. M. Gann, *A History of Southern Rhodesia to 1933*, London, 1965, 112.

[11] C7171 No. 54. Enclosure. Jameson to Harris July 10, 1973 cited by A. Dorey, 'Victoria Incident and Matabele War', *Central Africa Historical Association*, Local Series Number 16, 1966.

[12] Lockhart and Rhodes, op. cit., 255.

[13] Rhodes House Papers Mss. Afr. s228, C.3B. July 17, quoted Ranger; op. cit., 93.

that, if they were not moving off he should 'drive them as you heard me tell Manyau I would, and, if they resist and attack you, shoot them'. Lendy set off and found that they had only gone three miles in three hours and had pillaged and burned two kraals *en route*. He did not bother to 'drive' them but opened fire, killing Umgandan and some nine others. The rest fled across the border.

There can be no doubt, despite some denials, that, as Newton found, Lendy's patrol fired first. Whether he was disobeying Jameson's orders in not attempting previously to 'drive' the Ndebele it is impossible to say. Lendy died before the enquiry. Jameson's orders were oral, not written, and we only have his word for them. But the point is not relevant to the cause of war. Even at this stage war was not inevitable. Lobengula certainly did not intend to make the episode a *casus belli*. Most of the evidence suggests that his subsequent troop movements were defensive not aggressive. He was not, indeed, prepared to give up his claims on the Shona, and he now repudiated all knowledge of a 'border'. From his point of view any other action amounted to abandoning half his kingdom. He did not, however, seek a war which he knew, as he had known ever since the fate of Cetewayo fourteen years earlier, must be fatal.

What the Victoria incident did was to change Jameson's mind. He now decided that war was the best course and that this was the best moment. Whether he was swayed by the strongly pro-war sentiments of the settlers and their threats to get out unless affairs were settled with 'Loben', or whether he exploited those sentiments for other reasons is not clear. He seems to have been genuinely disturbed at Manyau's ignorance of the 'border' and at the apparent lack of control by Lobengula over his own *impi*, as evinced by the conduct of Umgandan. He also believed Lendy who falsely told him that the Ndebele had fired first. What is clear is that he now abruptly reversed his previous policy. The day after the incident he telegraphed to Rutherfoord Harris:

Rhodes might consider the advisability of completing the thing. The cash could be found and it could be done pretty cheaply if the Macloutsie Police and the High Commissioner keep out of it. I know Ferriera's terms are for 500 mounted Boers to hand over the show, a moderate sum in cash and ammunition supplied, each man to receive a farm and his loot ... I suggest the Ferriera trick, as we have an excuse for the row over murdered women and children now and the getting Matabeleland open would give us a tremendous lift in shares and everything else. The fact of its being shut up gives it an immense value both here and outside.

Ferriera had commanded the hard core of the Adendorff *trek*. After arresting him Jameson had – perhaps not very seriously – discussed with him the terms and feasibility of a *coup* against Bulawayo. The telegram quoted above, which has been ignored by all Rhodes's biographers, though available in the papers at Rhodes House, was first published by Professor Ranger in 1967.[14] It leaves

[14] Op. cit., 94.

no doubt about Jameson's deliberate decision to start a war after the Victoria incident. Rhodes was hesitant at first. Later he said that he would have preferred to postpone the matter till 1894. But as usual he backed Jameson in the end.

Rutherfoord Harris in Kimberley now proceeded to pour out pro-war propaganda. The misery of the Shona, played down in previous years, was played up with the maximum of publicity. When Moffat denounced the Company's bellicose intentions Harris privately circulated the leading British editors with copies of letters written during 1890 in which Moffat had declared that war was the only solution to the Ndebele problem.[14] The London Board of the Company was in favour – the more so when Rhodes promised to save them expense by providing £50,000 from his private fortune. On August 14 the Victoria Agreement was promulgated offering volunteers for the campaign twenty gold claims, a 3,000 morgen (6,350 acre) farm and a share of the 'loot' – an expression which received adverse comment but merely meant cattle. There was much criticism of the arrangement but these were not abnormal terms for volunteers in contemporary Southern African wars. No one expected them to fight for nothing, and the Company lacked the means to provide ordinary army pay and allowances. The military experts believed that a force of 7,000 men would be needed. Jameson, a gambler as ever and once again a winner, reckoned that the job could be done with a thousand.

Something further was needed to provide an excuse for war, which had to be authorized by the British Government. Lobengula played into Jameson's hands by denying the border, asserting his sovereignty over the Shona, refusing to accept payment under the Rudd Concession and declaring that if he had known when he sent in his *impi* what he now knew, he would have seized as much of the white people's property as he could. His troop movements too, though in the light of later evidence clearly defensive, were susceptible, like all troop movements, of different interpretations. Dawson, the trader, Helm, the missionary and Moffat, the ex-missionary, all of whom had long experience of affairs at Bulawayo, were convinced that the King did not mean war. But Colenbrander, the Company's emissary at Lobengula's court, believed that he did – and it was Colenbrander's dispatches which went to the High Commissioner and the Colonial Office.

Sir Henry Loch was in an uneasy position. Seldom had the double-hatted posture of the High Commissioner been more awkward. In theory he possessed wide powers over Mashonaland. Unlike Robinson he was very far from being a creature of Rhodes, but he had been warned by Lord Knutsford not to interfere with the administrative and fiscal arrangements of the Company – part of the tacit bargain by which Rhodes agreed to pick the imperial chestnuts from the fire. Moreover under his other hat Loch was Governor of Cape Colony which had had Responsible Government since 1872. Here his position was more analogous to that of a constitutional monarch, and he was obliged to get on as well as he could with his Prime Minister – Cecil Rhodes. Loch did his best to avoid war,

[15] Ibid., 95.

but when Lobengula sent the *induna* Umshete on a peace mission and yet still asserted his ownership of the Shona, he gave up. Meanwhile Jameson had massed, ostensibly for defensive purposes, two columns based on Salisbury and Fort Victoria, and a third at Tuli in the south.

On October 5 Ndebele troops were reported as having fired on a patrol of the Bechuanaland Border Police. Loch authorized their commander, Colonel Goold-Adams, to anticipate a possible attack on Khama's country by pushing forward onto the high veld. He was told to take command of Jameson's 200 volunteers as well as his own force of 220 police. At about the same time a similar clash was reported near the Shashi River with the Company's police. Loch was now convinced that an attack, whether or not at Lobengula's instigation, was imminent, and he authorized Jameson to push forward too. The war had begun.

Little needs to be said about it. Ndebele generalship was incompetent and resistance collapsed rapidly. It is true that with the machine gun the white volunteers and regulars possessed a new weapon of formidable power. The campaign in terms of the history of military technology deserves to be remembered as one of the first occasions for its extensive and effective use, and may well have inspired Belloc's famous couplet:

> Whatever happens we have got
> The Maxim Gun, and they have not.

Nevertheless different tactics in the form of a protracted defensive campaign, exploitation of the terrain and of their own immensely superior numbers – some 18,000 against 1,100 – might have prolonged the campaign into the rainy season with very serious consequences for the Company's finances and at least the possibility of a negotiated peace. Instead the Ndebele *impis* did the one thing that was sure to be fatal – engage in offensive set-piece battles over open ground. Their courage was immense but so were their losses. Although as a result of the Rudd Concession they had excellent rifles, their shooting was wildly erratic, and they never came close enough to use their assegais. The Victoria and Salisbury columns, soon united under the command of Major Forbes, marched steadily towards Bulawayo destroying the Ndebele *impis* in two major battles.

At an early stage Lobengula seems to have regarded the struggle as hopeless and to have decided to move the whole tribe north – a step he had contemplated more than once in the past. He was true to his word in protecting the few white men in his capital, and their lives were spared. He burned his kraal, blew up the ammunition which his troops could not carry, and left for the north a day or so before the advance guard of Jameson's columns arrived. On November 4 Forbes and the main body entered the smoking ruins of old Bulawayo to the skirl of the bagpipe. Goold-Adams followed a few days later.

Three episodes which, though they did not affect the war, had lasting consequences on Rhodesian history must be briefly mentioned. In the middle of October Lobengula had sent an embassy to interview Loch. It was escorted by

Dawson and consisted of two high *indunas* and the King's half-brother. When they reached Tati, Goold-Adams's HQ, Dawson went off for a drink leaving the trio to be looked after by a mine foreman, merely saying that they were 'three natives'. He then went on to eat his dinner. Meanwhile Goold-Adams hearing that Dawson had brought three Matabele, assumed that he had escaped from Bulawayo and that they were his guides. He did not want them to return with information and ordered them to be arrested. The bewildered *indunas* understandably panicked. One of them stabbed a guard and in the ensuing scuffle both were killed; only the King's half-brother who did not move survived. Their mission could have made no difference. The war had already begun. Yet inevitably the deaths seemed another item in the long and bitter saga, as the Ndebele saw it, of white duplicity and betrayal.

The tragedy, however lamentable an example of insensitivity and bad manners – the *indunas* after all were not just 'natives' like the rest but, in their own world, grandees – was at least the result of accident, not crime. The second episode was much worse. Lobengula fleeing north entrusted on December 3 an *induna* with a bag of a thousand gold sovereigns and a message to his pursuers: 'White men, I am conquered. Take this and go back.' The *induna* gave it to two of his men who, frightened and confused, went round to the rear of the pursuing column and after handing it to two batmen of the Bechuanaland Police, Troopers Wilson and David, who were straggling behind, disappeared into the bush. There were no witnesses. The troopers divided the cash and said nothing. A year later the story leaked out. The two were brought to trial, and sentenced to fourteen years imprisonment, though their sentences were later quashed on technicalities. History is not, however, a court of law, and there is little doubt of their guilt. It was widely believed that their conduct bore some responsibility for the third and greatest tragedy of all, the fate of the Shangani Patrol on December 4.

With the conquest of Bulawayo Jameson faced a major problem. The rainy malarial season was imminent. The torrential storms which afflict Rhodesia at that time of year have to be seen to be believed. As long as Lobengula was at large the war could not be concluded, but the Company's finances made it vital to end hostilities as soon as possible. There was a further complication. The Imperial Secretary, Graham Bower, had declared on October 23 that negotiations for a settlement with the King were to be conducted by the High Commissioner. Rhodes, now in Salisbury, received this news with great indignation, and the Company's propaganda machine was put into operation at full blast. In fact on November 4, after the occupation of Bulawayo, the Colonial Office in a letter to the London Board partly withdrew, but Jameson, out of reach until November 18 owing to a breakdown in the telegraph line to Palapye, regarded possession of the King's person not only as a means of ending resistance but as a vital bargaining counter in the battle with Whitehall and the imperial factor. He sent a message on November 7 calling on the King to surrender and received four days later an evasive reply. On November 14 he dispatched a mounted force under Major Forbes to capture the King.

By December 3 Forbes with 160 men was on the bank of the Shangani River within a day's march of Lobengula. The weather was very wet, his men were exhausted, his horses very tired. Had the message in the bag of gold been delivered as it should have been that day, he would probably have treated with the King, and the subsequent disaster might have been averted. In the event he sent a mounted patrol of fifteen men under Major Allan Wilson to reconnoitre and bring back news of Lobengula's location before dusk. Wilson duly crossed the river, but, thinking that he might by a sudden *coup* seize the King, disobeyed orders and, dark having already fallen, asked for reinforcements. Forbes, who had information which was incorrect but could not be discounted that the main *impi* had circled back to attack him, decided rightly that he could not break camp at night, but wrongly that instead of recalling Wilson he would send a second detachment of twenty-one men under Captain Borrow to reinforce the patrol. This decision made the worst of both worlds. The reinforcements were enough to encourage Wilson in his reckless course but not enough to be of any help in a crisis. The river rose during the night. At dawn and onwards on December 4 heavy firing was heard, but it was impossible to cross the Shangani. Forbes, short of food and supplies, and harassed by Ndebele attacks, had to retreat towards Bulawayo. For many weeks men hoped against hope for survivals. It was not until two months later that the scene of Wilson's last stand was examined, and, with the aid of a captured Ndebele warrior who was an eye-witness, the disaster was reconstructed. The thirty-six men, surrounded by their enemies, fought to the last cartridge and then, so the story goes though there is some uncertainty, sang the National Anthem as they waited to be shot, clubbed or assegaied to death.

A welter of recrimination ensued. The deaths of Borrow's second patrol were deemed especially unnecessary. Forbes's career, despite his earlier success, was wrecked and he was eventually banished to become a Deputy Administrator in the remote north east of Northern Rhodesia. The man who deserved the blame was Jameson, who ought never to have sent Forbes on such an errand in the first place. The fate of Wilson's men moved Rhodes deeply. Their bones, at first interred near Fort Victoria where a memorial commemorates them at Zimbabwe, were later moved at his request to the Matopos and buried beneath a massive granite monument close to the graves of Jameson and Rhodes himself. The episode has come to be a symbol of Rhodesian history, a symbol of courage, heroism and endeavour, a symbol too of the civilized few among the savage multitude. The fact that it was utterly futile and affected the war in no way whatever is irrelevant. The men who died were not to know this and it does not detract from their gallantry.

It is difficult to say quite why a particular episode becomes part of a nation's folklore, legend and inspiration. The stock cliché that 'their loss was not in vain' cannot apply here, for it obviously was. Perhaps Philip Mason is right in suggesting that man is 'deeply suspicious of a free gift, of anything too easily won'. The advance of the Pioneers and the Matabele war had cost scarcely a single life. It was almost too simple. The heroic legend of the Shangani Patrol met the deep human instinct that great gains are not made without some sacrifice. Here was that sacrifice.

Whatever the reasons, no one who has been in Rhodesia for even a few days can doubt the impact of Allan Wilson's last stand. It is by far the most prominent feature in the iconography of Rhodesian history. Paintings galore, sculptures, friezes, tapestries depict it. There is scarcely a public building where one does not see in some medium or other the depiction of a scene which has now become semi-stylized – the troopers firing from behind a rampart of dead horses; Allan Wilson himself, taller than all the rest, shooting a Ndebele warrior with his revolver; the enemy in the background with assegai and gun. There is a flavour of romantic imperialism, the *Boy's Own Paper*, Kipling, Henty and much else which was common coin in the England of the nineties. From there it has long disappeared but in Rhodesia, along with many other pickled pieces of the English past, it still lingers on.

8

Conquest 1893–95

Lobengula perished soon after the Shangani Patrol. It is not certain how. According to one account he died of smallpox, according to another he committed suicide by taking poison. There are many other versions and the truth is not now likely to emerge. His body was never found by any white man but his death was not in doubt. The Ndebele *indunas* surrendered one by one. The war was over.

It is hardly conceivable that Lobengula's monarchy could have survived in its existing form. It might with time have gradually disintegrated, as his subjects became absorbed into the white labour system, but one can doubt whether the Ndebele military aristocracy would have allowed this to happen without a fight. Conceivably a different military outcome might have produced a compromise peace and a new treaty. Whatever happened, an Iron Age monarchy would not for long have coexisted with the Chartered Company.

Yet, if it be the case that Lobengula was blown away by the gale of the world, one can neither withhold sympathy from him nor extend it to Rhodes and his agents. They cheated him over the Moffat Treaty which did not give him the protection he expected. They defrauded him over the Rudd Concession which did not mean what he believed it to mean, and when he found this out Jameson simply threatened him with a white *impi*. They did him down yet again over the Lippert Concession, Rhodes's purchase of which Moffat regarded as 'detestable whether viewed in the light of policy or morality'.[1] Finally they forced a war on him which he could only have avoided at the price, as he saw it, of abandoning half his kingdom. The Ndebele state was cruel and barbarous. Its passing need cause little regret. 'No one knowing their abominable history', wrote Selous to his mother, 'can pity them or lament their downfall. They have been paid back in their own coin.'[2] But in the same letter Selous half in jest observed, 'So you

[1] R. U. Moffat, *John Smith Moffat*, 1921, 258.
[2] NAR SE1/1/1, November 15, 1893. Quoted Ranger, op. cit., 98.

see the campaign is virtually over and the fair-haired descendants of the northern pirates are in possession of the great King's Kraal, and the calf of the black cow has fled into the wilderness'.[3]

This was the reality under all the high sounding verbiage. It was a war of conquest, and conquest henceforth constituted the title deeds of the white man in both Mashonaland and Matabeleland; for the conquest of the latter entailed that of the former. It is true that the Shona paramounts in no way recognized this until after the rebellion. The point, rather, is that the juridical sovereignty of Britain as a country ceased to be a matter of doubt among the British themselves. Within the white world there might be much dispute as to the powers of the Crown, the Company and the settlers; learned lawyers far away in London a quarter of a century later were to argue many subtle points in that connexion. But the land and possessions of the Ndebele and the Shona were as much at the mercy of the white man after 1893 as those of the Saxons were at the mercy of the Normans after the battle of Hastings. The rebellions were later to produce a reaction on the part of the British government against the white excesses of the post-Matabele war period, but this did not alter the basic relationship of conquerors and conquered, nor the ultimate source of authority and power.

There were many other areas of Africa north of the Limpopo where the British title to rule was in the end as much based on *force majeure* as in Southern Rhodesia, but there were important differences. Relations with Chiefs were frequently regulated by treaties. The Colonial Office, the effective power in all of them except the Rhodesias, felt obliged as a matter of common prudence to respect African land and other rights, not necessarily in full but at least in part, if only to avoid provoking a revolt which its meagre military forces would find hard to suppress. In these tropical and semi-tropical areas there were far fewer white men on the ground and, except in Kenya, they were not on the whole there to stay. Economic development was slower. For years the bulk of the African populations merely supplied labour to coastal settlements and were able to continue a mode of life which was challenged so gradually that there was never a drastic confrontation. Lack of money obliged the Colonial Office to adopt a system of indirect rule which preserved many features of the traditional African social system. In these areas Lord Lugard's 'dual mandate' was a reality.

In both Mashonaland and Matabeleland the situation was quite different. Economic development backed by Rhodes's vast resources was very rapid in both countries, by contemporary colonial standards. From the first arrival of the Pioneers white prospectors spread all over Mashonaland and their impact on Shona society was wide and disruptive. The effect of white development was even more sudden and striking in Matabeleland after 1893 when Bulawayo attracted a host of commercial enterprises. The problem of managing 'the natives' bothered Rhodes very little. He did not appoint Native Commissioners in the accepted sense of the term till 1894 and then principally in order to collect taxes and cattle. As

[3] Op. cit., 97.

his speeches to his shareholders show, he took it for granted that the Shona were grateful to the white man for protection against the Ndebele – an assumption widespread among the settlers whose shock when its inaccuracy was demonstrated by the rebellion of June 1896 was all the more traumatic. As for the Ndebele, Rhodes believed, along with Jameson and most white men, that they did not resent their conquest and defeat, and that they were relieved to be rid of witchcraft, superstition and arbitrary tyranny. He could scarcely have been more wrong in both cases.

Rhodes was now at the apogee of his power. Prime Minister of Cape Colony which was the base for the whole Rhodesian expedition, virtually Governor of both Mashonaland and Matabeleland, but a Governor backed by financial resources such as no normal Colonial Governor ever possessed, admired in England if loathed in Portugal, he dominated the whole Southern African scene. His personal foibles and ambitions mattered more than those of a single individual normally do. So far things had gone very much his way. True, he had been foiled over Beira and Katanga, but Nyasaland still seemed about to fall into his lap, and he already had his eye on the Transvaal, the last great impediment to his enormous ambitions. He therefore viewed his newly won domain less as an area in which to build a stable colonial system than as a base for future operations – Cape to Cairo, the overthrow of Kruger. It followed from this and his confidence in the quiescence of the 'native question' that the minimum should be spent on police and administration – the money was needed for more exciting and less humdrum purposes. Government should be left as far as possible with the pros-pectors, traders, farmers, storekeepers who constituted a settler community to which there was no parallel north of the Zambesi. By this decision much of the future course of Rhodesian history was to be shaped.

Rhodes did not intend to be harsh or brutal. He bore no ill will towards those whom he had conquered. It was indifference, negligence, omission, rather than any consciously suppressive purpose, which characterized his policy – together with a deep distaste for the officialdom and the 'red tape' which he associated with civil and military administration and which bored him stiff, just as it did his faithful agent, Jameson. As Rhodes saw it, the important task after the Matabele war was to keep the settlers sweet and carry out his promises to the Victoria volunteers.

Keeping the settlers sweet meant keeping Whitehall out. It was not difficult. The completeness of the Company's victory had already caused the Colonial Office to back-pedal from the Imperial Secretary's declaration that Loch should have sole charge over negotiations with Lobengula. There was now no Lobengula to negotiate with, and the campaign had owed little to the only imperial forces involved, Goold-Adams's Bechuanaland Police. The prestige of the Company stood high in Britain and its shares were booming. Labouchère and his friends cut little ice. Early in 1894 Gladstone, whose conscience about 'oppressed peoples' might have made a difference, resigned and was succeeded by the Liberal imperialist, Lord Rosebery. The Government had to balance the trouble which the radicals could make in the House of Commons against the indignation which any assertion of the imperial factor would provoke in Cape Colony. Lord Ripon, the Colonial Secretary, decided that the latter was more dangerous and he dropped his suggestion that an imperial resident should be sent to Bulawayo. The most that he and Loch were prepared to insist upon was that Ndebele land and cattle should not be expropriated and reallocated until Loch and Rhodes had agreed upon a constitutional settlement of Matabeleland acceptable to the Crown.

Rhodes and Jameson were quite clear what this ought to be. As Jameson put it, Matabeleland should 'be treated as a portion of Mashonaland lately occupied by the Matabele' – a neat inversion of Lobengula's attitude towards Mashonaland. An agreement was executed between the Company and the Crown on May 24, 1894 and confirmed by the Matabeleland Order in Council on July 18. The gist of it was that the two territories were put under the administration of the Company as the grantee of the Crown, now sovereign by right of conquest, though the High Commissioner retained his previous largely theoretical powers. The principal officer of the Company was termed the Administrator and Jameson was to be the first holder of the post. Provision was made for a 'Council' to assist him and for the appointment of a Judge.

The unification of Mashonaland and Matabeleland raised the question of a name to cover the two. Neither 'Zambesia' (Rhodes own preference) nor 'Charterland' (Jameson's suggestion) ever caught on. 'Rhodesia' had become the common journalistic usage by early 1891, and in 1892 the first newspaper in Salisbury called itself the *Rhodesia Herald*. In May 1895 the Company officially adopted the name, but it was not recognized by the British Government till the Southern Rhodesia Order in Council of 1898. It is not clear why the name should have been pronounced with the emphasis on the second rather than the first syllable, but this appears to have been the custom from the beginning and it never changed.

The questions of land and cattle were to be settled by a Commission with power to allocate 'sufficient and suitable' land for the natives in Matabeleland. In Loch's original draft it would have had the same powers in Mashonaland, and there would have been provision for an appeal in both territories by the natives if they thought their allocation inadequate. In the final version this appeal was removed; also a distinction was drawn between the territories. In Mashonaland the Court merely had the right to call on the Surveyor General for periodic reports about native-occupied land and then, if it thought that there was not enough, it could make a further allocation – a difference of emphasis rather than substance, but not unimportant.

There is general agreement among historians that both territories were administered with a deplorable mixture of ignorance, neglect and irresponsibility during the next three years. This verdict is not a matter of applying the moral standards of a later generation. In frequently-quoted words Lord Milner, the High Commissioner and neither a sentimentalist, a do-gooder nor a negrophile, wrote to Asquith on November 18, 1897, 'The blacks have been scandalously used' and to Lord Selborne on December 29, 'A lot of unfit people were allowed to exercise power, or at any rate did exercise it, especially with regard to the natives'.[4] Marshall Hole, who served in the Rhodesian administration for twenty-two years beginning as Jameson's private secretary in 1891 and who was most unwilling to criticize the Company, leaves no doubt about his views on the land settlement and the disposal of cattle in Matabeleland. 'In both respects the decisions of the Commission were unfortunate,' he writes, observing that one of the two reserves was 'quite unsuitable' – in fact both were – and that the cattle question 'became a perpetual source of irritation and probably contributed to the unrest which culminated in the rebellion of 1896'.[5] Hole also refers to the bullying by the newly recruited black police and to 'cases of victimization by a few unscrupulous white men who cheated their labourers of their wages and in other ways made their work hateful to them'.[6]

The least defensible feature of the new regime was its treatment of land. Within a few months of the victory over Lobengula almost all the traditional grazing grounds of the Ndebele had been given away. This was not simply a matter of satisfying the claims of the Victoria volunteers to a farm of 6,350 acres each. There were 948 volunteers and so the total acreage involved cannot have been much over 6m. By 1899 15.7m acres had been alienated to Europeans. This includes grants made in Mashonaland too, but it is reasonable to assume that in the years between 1893 and 1896 not less than half that amount had been disposed of in Matabeleland. Sir John Willoughby alone received 600,000 acres. It would more-over be a mistake to imagine that most or indeed many of the volunteers actually occupied their farms or personally exploited their gold claims. Like the pioneers of 1890 they usually sold them to companies or individual speculators – and not very profitably. Rhodes was indignant at the charge that men were ready to desert their families and fight for a mere £40 or £50. He was technically correct. They did better than that but not startlingly so. A man who sold his land, cattle-loot and gold claims at the end of March 1894 got about £85 to £95. If he held on till October he made about £140. By 1899 more than two-thirds of the original volunteers had sold out.[7]

The trouble did not stem merely from grants to the volunteers. It had always been Rhodes's policy to gain and retain the support of the British governing class for his ventures. Politically the Chartered Company was riding high, but this might not be so always. Jameson faithfully followed what he believed to be Rhodes's wishes by allocating vast tracts to the category described later by Sir William Milton, his successor but one, as 'the Honourable and military elements which are rampant everywhere'. In the same letter Milton continued: 'It is perfectly sickening to see the way in which the country has been run for the sake of

[4] C. Headlam (ed.), *The Milner Papers*, Vol. I, 1931.
[5] Hole, op. cit., 335, 336.
[6] Ibid., 354.
[7] P. Stigger, 'Volunteers and the Profit Motive in the Anglo-Ndebele War', *Rhodesian History*, Vol. 2, 1971, 11–23.

hob-nobbing with Lord this and the Hon. that.'[8] Milton had something of a middle class chip on his shoulder and it does not follow that he was right in regarding all army officers and sons of peers as idle dunderheads. But he was correct about the reckless way in which Jameson alienated land. Lord Grey who was Jameson's immediate successor and who had no dislike of 'hons' and soldiers – indeed he did his best for them himself – was quite clear about the errors that had been made. 'Land is our great difficulty,' he wrote to George Cawston on May 26, 1897. 'It has all been given away. I will not give away another acre until the Native Question has been settled.'[9]

Unfortunately long before Grey wrote these words, there was nothing left worth giving away. The effect upon the Ndebele was calamitous. It is true that the Land Commission could in theory have reversed Jameson's lavish concessions, as the Administrator himself realized for he took care to cover himself by declaring that all his grants were 'provisional'.[10] In practice the Land Commission merely confirmed what he had done and applied itself to finding other land for the displaced Ndebele. Not surprisingly the areas chosen were wholly unsuitable. The Gwai and Shangani Reserves amounting to about 6,500 square miles were remote and waterless. As Grey admitted in a letter to Rhodes in May 1897 'they are regarded by the natives as *cemeteries* not homes'[11] and the natives naturally refused to move.

The result was that the Ndebele stayed where they were as squatters on what had now legally become farms in the private ownership of white individuals or syndicates. For the time being they were not much interfered with, for very few of the immense areas pegged out were actually occupied and worked, but they were well aware of their altered status, subject now to rent in cash or kind, and eviction at short notice. Nor did they even have the advantage which a feudal system might have bestowed, that of continuity under the same master. Farms were constantly being bought and sold, passing from individuals to companies or vice versa. There was no stability, and the Ndebele seldom knew whom he had to deal with. The use of land, which in an African tribal system is so closely tied up with the whole economic, religious and political order or society, became almost overnight a matter of doubt, obscurity and apparent caprice.

Jameson's lavish distribution was not even advantageous to the Company's own financial interests. The white adventurers, whether honourable and military Englishmen or speculators from Cape Colony or the Transvaal, were no asset to the new colony. In theory land was usually granted on the assumption that it would be 'occupied' within a certain time, i.e. that at least a proportion of it should actually be used for crops or pasture, failing which it would be forfeited. In practice the right of forfeiture was seldom enforced. Jameson's policy thus

[8] NAR ML1/1/2, Milton to his wife September 18, 1896. Quoted Ranger, op. cit., 104.
[9] Rhodes House Mss Afr. C1 S77. Quoted Ranger, op. cit., 104.
[10] Colvin, *Jameson*, I, 1922.
[11] Quoted Ranger, op. cit., 105.

resulted in absentee landlordism on an immense scale for many years to come, both in Matabeleland and Mashonaland. As Milner put it in a letter to Joseph Chamberlain, 'They [the Company] feel what a millstone they have tied round their necks with all these syndicates holding thousands of square miles which they are doing nothing to develop'.[12] It became a major problem to find respectable land for bona fide white immigrants.

The question of cattle, the second vital element in Ndebele society, was dealt with no less irresponsibly and insensitively than that of land. Although the 'Bantu cattle complex', as it was called, may have been exaggerated by some observers, for it was by no means unknown for the Ndebele or the Shona to sell cattle to the Whites before 1893,[13] there can be no doubt that their enormous herds were to the Ndebele an asset which had more than a purely economic significance. As Mr Philip Mason puts it, 'the cattle were one of the strands that bound the Matabele people together, the way they were held contributing to the royal dominion, the cult of the ancestors and the stability of marriage'.[14] No one knows quite how many head the Ndebele possessed before the war. Loch put the figure at 200,000, and other estimates are higher.

Jameson had declared when receiving the submission of the *indunas* that the Company would claim the King's cattle by right of conquest and leave the cattle in private hands untouched. This distinction was not in practice an easy one to make. Lord Ripon, alarmed at reports of confiscation on a huge scale and anxious to ensure that enough was left to the Ndebele for subsistence, expressed doubt whether any line could be drawn, 'all cattle being in some sense King's'.[15] It was, he continued, important that enough cattle should be retained on trust for the Ndebele out of those seized, irrespective of their alleged previous ownership. In the end Ripon accepted the distinction on condition that the royal herds could be regarded as a sort of state fund for subsequent allocation if necessary, the Ndebele meanwhile keeping them at their kraals for milking. A final settlement was to be made by the Land Commission.

Long before the Commission reported in October 1894, the situation had drastically changed. In the first place there was the matter of the 'loot'. About 30,000 cattle were delivered to the loot committee and either allocated or sold at auction in satisfaction of claims between July and November. But a far greater amount than that was acquired by white traders, speculators and farmers in various ways which included raiding and other illegal methods. Moreover another 20,000 had been requisitioned by the Company as 'police rations'. When the Commission reported, it decided that, whatever the past situation might have been, there was now no means of distinguishing between royal and private cattle, nor had they any idea of the numbers. They recommended that all cattle in Matabeleland

[12] December 1897, quoted Ranger, op. cit., 104.
[13] See P. Stigger, op. cit.
[14] Mason, op. cit., 188.
[15] Ripon to Loch, December 10, 1893. Quoted Ranger, op. cit., 107.

not in private white possession should be treated as the Company's by right of conquest, and that the Company should undertake to make an adequate allocation to the Ndebele. They advised the appointment of officials with the task of registering every kraal, the number of its inhabitants and cattle, and the duty of ensuring that the cattle were branded with the Company's brand. No cattle were to be slaughtered without permission. The officials thus appointed were to be the origin of the Matabeleland Native Department.

By October a year later this Doomsday Book had been completed, and at the end of November 1895, Judge Vintcent, the Commission's Chairman, announced his award. The Native Department reckoned the number of cattle in Matabeleland still in African possession at 74,500. Of these 40,930 were to go to the Ndebele, the Company retaining the balance to sell to bona fide farmers or to reserve for influential supporters (Sir John Willoughby got 8,850). If we add all these figures together along with those for 'loot' and 'police rations', the total is about 124,000. This leaves at least 76,000 unaccounted for. A large amount almost certainly were taken out of the country and, like the bulk of the loot cattle, probably sold in the well established markets of Kimberley and the Rand. But what mattered was not their destination, rather the effect of the losses upon the Africans. The Ndebele holdings were reduced to 41,000 – only a fifth, and perhaps less than that, of the figure before the war. The whole Ndebele way of life was thus thrown into jeopardy by the manner in which first the question of land and secondly that of cattle was treated by the Company.

These errors were compounded by the harshness of the administrative 'system' – if it can be dignified with that name at all. Until the end of 1894 Matabeleland was under the arbitrary rule of a white police force which regarded one of its functions as the destruction of the Ndebele politico-military order. They behaved oppressively, tyrannically and lawlessly. The creation of a Native Department at the end of the year was a slight improvement, though not much since its main task until the eve of the rebellion was neither administration nor justice nor investigation of native grievances but the distribution of cattle, even as that of its analogue in Mashonaland was the collection of the hut tax. Moreover most of the officers were young men with little experience, who commanded little respect.

In Matabeleland, as in Mashonaland, much reliance was also placed on the recruitment of black police. The usual view, though there is some difference of opinion, is that these were principally chosen from the subordinate tribes and the despised *Amaholi* and that this in itself created intense bitterness among the young *Abezansi* and *Abenhla*.[16] Whatever their exact caste or tribal composition, they behaved in a most oppressive way and seem to have been loathed by the

---

[16] Mason, op. cit., 193; Hole, op. cit., 354. But see Ranger, op. cit., 118, who quotes a report by Colonel Frank Rhodes that the police were 'composed solely of Matabeles' largely from 'the late Lobengula's two crack regiments'. See also E. F. Knight, *Rhodesia of Today*, 1895, 9.

generality of the Ndebele. They were employed in both Matabeleland and Mashonaland largely to secure labour for mining and other purposes. Their reputation was one of cruelty and brutality, and they were unscrupulous in abusing their position with the women of the kraals on which they descended.

Although contemporary observers were reluctant to discuss the matter in that intimate detail which is customary today, there are many hints that the black police were not alone in the matter of sexual exploitation. The white world was for the most part young and male. In Bulawayo in March 1895 there were 1,329 white men and 208 women. There are no statistics for Salisbury at that time, but in November 1897 the corresponding figures were 505 and 134.[17] This imbalance was almost bound to cause trouble and make some Whites seek sexual satisfaction, forced or voluntary, among the indigenous population. 'The conduct of many of the whites towards their black sisters, married or virgin, in Matabeleland certainly contributed to the causes which have led up to this unfortunate rebellion,' wrote F. W. Sykes.[18] It produced the same consequences in Mashonaland, and Olive Schreiner's bitter book, *Trooper Peter Halket of Mashonaland*, published in 1897, though not of course evidence in any sense of the word, certainly reflected widespread beliefs which are unlikely to have been based on nothing at all.

It is easy in retrospect to see that the Europeans in Matabeleland were sitting on a powder keg. Its ingredients consisted not only of the abuses and errors already described. It was made the more explosive because much of the military system of the Ndebele remained intact. So rapid had been the collapse at the centre in 1893 and so half-hearted had been Lobengula's defence that many *impis* were never involved in fighting at all, and had contrived to hold on to most of their weapons. To this military aristocracy – especially its younger members – the new regime was bound to cause intense resentment. Even before 1893 there had been something of a generation gap in Lobengula's kingdom, the older *indunas* preferring peace and a material prosperity in which they had the lion's share, the younger longing for war. The Land Commission had, if anything, enhanced that gap by favouring 'the more deserving *indunas* and headmen' in the distribution of cattle, i.e. the 'collaborators' or 'loyalists' – according to how one looks at them. We can add to this cause of resentment among the young *Abezansi* the impact of the white demand for labour. The essence of this in both territories was to pull the black man into the cash economy voluntarily if possible, involuntarily if necessary. The hated police were much involved in the latter process. To the Ndebele warrior caste work of this sort was a humiliation. To the white prospector and overseer all black labour was the same. As so often in colonial history the fault of the Whites lay not in failing to treat Blacks as

[17] B. A. Cosmin, 'The Pioneer Community of Salisbury in November 1897', *Rhodesian History*, Vol. 2, 1971, 25-37.

[18] *With Plumer in Mashonaland*, 1897, 8-11, quoted Gann, op. cit., 126.

equals but in failing to realize that some Blacks were more equal than others.

The position in Mashonaland was not quite the same as in Matabeleland, but the grievances of the Shona Chiefs were no less bitter. From the very first they had felt the impact of the European invasion. Hundreds of prospectors all over the country, with a seemingly insatiable demand for mining labour and the deepest contempt for and ignorance of Shona religion, economy and history, soon produced a sense of bitter grievance. The juridical position of the Company was so obscure and the need to retrench so acute that Jameson did not attempt to set up a normal colonial system of law and order backed by proper courts and a regular police force. Instead he allowed labour to be conscripted, cattle seized and white security protected by irregular punitive police patrols. Inevitably some of these abused their position commandeering men and not sparing women. According to one of the first Native Commissioners, his hardest task was to overcome the tendency of the Shona to flee from the very sight of a white man. This was especially the case with the women. 'The reason for this appeared afterwards to be on account of some of the police formerly stationed there making a practice of assaulting and raping any native woman they found in the veld alone.'[19] That this was not an isolated case is shown by the complaint of Makoni, later to be one of the most determined of the rebel Shona Chiefs, to the Anglican missionary, Frank Edwards, that white raiders 'had killed some of Mangwende's people [another Shona paramount] and outraged the women'. As Edwards wrote to Jameson, 'You will easily see from this incident how utterly futile any missionary work must be amongst the natives if white men are allowed to kill them and outrage their women with impunity'.[20]

The Order in Council of July 18, 1894 meant nothing to the Shona Chiefs. They had never been conquered. They still had their arms. The defeat of the Ndebele might be a welcome bonus but it did not affect their independence in the least. No treaties had ever been made with them, and their relations with the white man had not altered. The new status of the Company did, however, enable Jameson to set up a Native Department. This ought in theory to have substituted some degree of regularity for the capricious practices of the past. In fact it made little difference. The Chief Commissioner, Brabant, did contrive to collect taxes and labour with more efficiency and less publicity of a disagreeable nature than hitherto. The regular white police were kept out of the business and only summoned for emergencies. Brabant and his eleven commissioners recruited their own native messengers and 'police boys'. Brabant himself, in the words of Commissioner Weale, 'was a rough and ready illiterate young man with an aptitude to learn to speak primitive African languages ... a great believer in corporal punishment ... brave as a lion ... quite honest and with an unquenchable thirst for Kaffir beer'.[21] His methods do indeed seem to have been rough

[19] NAR M. E. Weale's Reminiscences WE3/2/5. Quoted Ranger, op. cit., 67.
[20] NAR, A1/9/1, January 17, 1892. Quoted ibid., 83.
[21] Quoted Ranger, op. cit., 74.

– in the end too rough for the Company, whose Executive Council sacked him in November 1895.

His successor H. M. Taberer endeavoured to put the Department on a more orderly basis and to do some of the things that had been neglected, for example acquire knowledge of native customs and grievances, draw maps and compile statistics. By then it was too late to avert trouble. The hut tax was in itself a source of irreconcilable hostility, and in contrast with other colonial regimes it was imposed far earlier. Professor Ranger points out that the weakness of administrative machinery was not peculiar to Mashonaland. In other African colonies it was just as bad.

> The sharp distinction ... was that in Mashonaland administrative weakness was combined with the presence and pressure of hundreds of settlers, with relatively rapid economic development and with the demands of the over-confident Company itself. Generally speaking other early colonial *regimes* were aware of their weakness and ready to avoid an assault upon the total African society of the territory; moreover they could not even if they wished to do so ignore African economic systems completely and proceed at once to build up a white economy.[22]

The consequence of their self-confidence, their utter lack of intelligence system and the insensitivity of the administration was to give the white population in both Mashonaland and Matabeleland an illusion of security which seems in retrospect scarcely credible. In 1895 there was published a short book by E. F. Knight, *Times* correspondent in the BSA Company's territory. It was partly based on articles which he wrote for his paper, and is a good illustration of the prevailing euphoria:

> Those who were not in the country at the time can scarcely realise the extraordinary rapidity with which this region of turbulent savages, this last stronghold of South African barbarism has been completely pacified. Absolute security to life and property was the immediate result of the successful campaign ... and very great credit indeed is due to the Administrator and other officers of the Chartered Company who have with such admirable tact, discretion and decision brought about this end.... The natives appeared to be unaffectedly pleased to see the white man in their country and there is no doubt that our invasion and occupation have been welcomed by the vast majority of the Matabele nation.[23]

The author goes on to say that the Matabele 'will probably now be far richer in cattle than they ever were before', that 'of magnificent pasture on the High

[22] Op. cit., 86–7.
[23] *Rhodesia of Today*, 6, 8.

Veldt there is practically an unlimited supply', and that 'no conquered people were ever treated with more consideration'.[24]

In this optimistic atmosphere Bulawayo thrived. Immigrants flooded in. Mashonaland including Salisbury became something of a backwater and the main economic activity of the country centred on Matabeleland. A new town was built three miles from the old one, with the immensely wide streets which still survive, designed for the turning of a full span of oxen, and certainly useful for modern traffic. Superficially Rhodesia's course seemed to be set fair. No one expected the whirlwind that was to follow.

[24] Ibid., 14, 20.

9

Rebellion 1896–97

A number of unlucky events sparked off the rebellion in Matabeleland. Ever since the white victory there had been a series of disastrous droughts which suggested that the newcomers, unlike previous conquerors, either did not bother or did not know how 'to make peace with the land'. There were incessant plagues of locusts – another clear sign of white incompetence. Finally the rinderpest or cattle sickness coming down from the north hit the remaining herds of the Ndebele (and the Shona too) with terrible effect. As Lord Grey, Jameson's successor, wrote to his schoolboy son from Bulawayo, 'all the plagues of Egypt have tumbled at once upon this unhappy country – drought – locusts – failure of crops – total annihilation of the cattle by the rinderpest – no milk, no beef in a few days – but lots of lovely smells from dead cattle'.[1] The appalling stench was indeed widely commented on. According to Selous, the disease even affected adversely the vultures which would normally have picked the bones of the dead animals, but 'these useful birds are now as scarce as cows in Matabeleland'.[2] The situation was made worse by the decision to shoot thousands of healthy cattle in order to prevent the infection spreading – an action incomprehensible to the Africans and attributed to malevolence. By 1897 there were less than 14,000 head of cattle in African possession in the whole of Rhodesia. Four years earlier there had been over 200,000 in Matabeleland alone. This is a measure of the catastrophe partly produced by, partly coincidental with the arrival of the Whites.

Then, late in 1895, Rhodes and Jameson launched out on their last great gamble – this time one which did not come off. The Raid, that disastrous short cut towards the elimination of Kruger and the Transvaal, was a clear sign of deteriorating judgement on the part of Rhodes and of *folie de grandeur* on the part of Jameson. Rhodes hoped for a revolution by the unenfranchised foreigners – *Uitlanders* in

[1] NAR GR1/1/1, Earl Grey to Viscount Howick, May 8, 1896.

[2] F. C. Selous, *Sunshine and Storm in Rhodesia*, 1896, 115. This is a vivid account of the Matabele rebellion down to the beginning of Rhodes's famous *indabas*.

Dutch parlance – who had flocked into Johannesburg since the discovery of gold and who felt themselves to be oppressively treated by Kruger and the Boers. The plan was that, as soon as an uprising occurred, the Chartered Company's troops would march in from the west to aid the rebels and overthrow Kruger's regime. The essence of the scheme was that the uprising should be the signal for the Raid, not vice versa. Many volumes have been written about the episode, and there are aspects which remain obscure even today. Of its calamitous consequences on the relations of Boer with Briton and in the long term of both with the Africans, there can be no doubt. What concerns us here is the immediate effect on Rhodesia. Jameson had decided to make the white police the core of his force against Johannesburg. By November 1895 he had quietly moved most of them to Pitsani in Bechuanaland, his chosen jumping off place. On December 29, impetuous and impatient as ever, without orders from Rhodes, he took the plunge and marched his column with Willoughby in command across the Transvaal border. In retrospect he is supposed to have declared 'Clive would have done it'. Disaster followed. The expected *Uitlander* revolution failed to materialize. The Boers proved to be a very different enemy from Lobengula's *impis*. On January 2 Jameson's force surrendered at Doornkop fourteen miles from Johannesburg. By that night Jameson, Willoughby and four hundred men were securely lodged in Pretoria gaol.

Although Rhodes had not – and certainly in the circumstances never would have – authorized this piece of folly, he was up to his neck in the conspiratorial activities which preceded it. He immediately resigned the premiership of Cape Colony, losing as he did overnight the support of the *Bond*. He also resigned, though a good deal later, his directorship of the Company. His life's work seemed in ruins. He would be lucky if he kept the charter. As an earnest of increased imperial vigilance the Colonial Office appointed a regular soldier, Colonel Sir Richard Martin, as Resident Commissioner and Commandant of the armed forces in Rhodesia. The difficulty was that there were scarcely any forces to be Commandant of. The news of Jameson's defeat spread rapidly through black Matabeleland. The Whites were vulnerable as never before. There were only forty-eight European mounted police in the whole country. Now was the moment to strike.

On March 20, 1896 the first sign of trouble appeared when a detachment of African police was attacked at Umgorshwini near the Umzingwani River and two 'boys' were killed. Three days later the murder of the Whites began. According to Selous, whose first hand account is far the best, 'there is reason to believe that by the evening of March 30 not a white man was left alive in the outlying districts of Matabeleland'.[3] During March Marshall Hole reckons that 122 men, five women and three children were killed, and in April another five men, five women and three children.[4] The murders were attended by every circumstance calculated to aggravate their horror. They were committed treacherously, in cold

[3] F. C. Selous, op. cit., 32.
[4] Hole, op. cit., 357, n. 1.

blood, often by Africans who had appeared to be on the friendliest terms with their victims. Men, women and children were shot, clubbed or assegaied to death without scruple or mercy, and their bodies, often horribly 'mutilated', were left to the wild beasts.

Few women or children were killed, as the above figures show, but this was only because in the outlying districts there were very few to kill. The effect of the deaths was to raise a spirit of fury among the Whites unparalleled since the Indian Mutiny. Selous, a man as humane, honourable and chivalrous as anyone who fought in those times, was deeply affected, even though he had a certain understanding for the other side. He had, he tells us, at first no 'very bitter feeling against the Kafirs, for after all looking at it from their point of view ... why shouldn't they try their chance of rebellion?' But the stories he heard in Bulawayo 'not only filled me with indignation but had excited a desire for vengeance which could only be satisfied by a personal and active participation in the killing of the murderers. I don't defend such feelings nor deny that they are vile and brutal when viewed from a high moral standpoint...'[5] Elsewhere he describes the slaughtered remains of the Fourie family, a woman and three children, 'much pulled about by dogs or jackals, but the long fair hair of the young Dutch girls was still intact and it is needless to say that these blood stained tresses awoke the most bitter wrath in the hearts of all who looked at them, Englishman and Dutchman alike vowing a pitiless vengeance against the whole Matabele race.'[6]

And in his preface, he says

I have given descriptions of many barbarous deeds.... I have hidden nothing and related not only how white men, women and children were lately murdered and their senseless bodies barbarously mutilated by black men, but also how black men were shot down pitilessly by the whites, no mercy being shown nor quarter given by the outraged colonists.[7]

These feelings were shared more vehemently by rougher characters. Rhodes's biographers describe the blood lust which seized him as he moved in with the column from Salisbury, how he would return to the scene of action to count the African corpses, how he told a police officer to spare no one even if he threw down his arms and implored mercy. 'You should kill all you can.'[8] A. W. (later Sir Alexander) Jarvis, serving with the Gwelo Volunteers, wished 'to wipe them all out, as far as one can – everything black'.[9] Even such a responsible figure as Sir Frederick Carrington, who became commander of the forces in Rhodesia, advocated at a public dinner the extermination or deportation of the entire Ndebele 'race'.[10]

The nature of the Ndebele rising has been brilliantly analysed by Professor Ranger. It was a loose coalition between two Ndebele groups who had different aims, together with their former subject tribes whose purposes were even more

[5] Selous, op. cit., 30.
[6] Ibid., 209.
[7] Selous, op. cit., xvii.

[8] Lockhart and Woodhouse, op. cit., 349.
[9] NAR JA4/1/1, to his mother, July 30, 1896.
[10] Ranger, op. cit., 182.

divergent. The first of the Ndebele factions was inspired by Umlugulu, the Ndebele high priest who like the Archbishop of Canterbury was responsible for the installation of the King and – unlike the Archbishop – for the Great Dance. His candidate for a revived throne was Umfezela, a brother of Lobengula. His support was based politically on the older Ndebele establishment, geographically on the Essexvale/Filabusi area south east of Bulawayo. A Great Dance to initiate the rebellion had been fixed at the full moon on March 26, but, for whatever reason, the revolt broke out before it could take place.

The second Ndebele group, led by an *induna* called Mpotshwana, had the support of the younger warriors and was based on the area of Inyati north east of Bulawayo. Their candidate was Nyamanda, Lobengula's eldest son. In fact by Matabele law neither he nor Umfezela was in the line of succession, which went only to sons born after Lobengula had become King. These, however, Rhodes had prudently removed to be educated at his own expense in Cape Colony.

The rebellion was surprisingly well supported by the former subjects of the Ndebele. What was little understood at the time was the role played by the priests and officers of 'Mwari', or 'Mlimo' as the Supreme Being came to be called in Matabeleland. This cult of an oracular god was one of two ancient Shona religious systems, the other being that of the spirit mediums or *mhondoro*. The difference was that the priests of Mwari spoke directly on his behalf whereas in the *mhondoro* cult the message came at one remove through spirit mediums, male or female, who when in a trance were supposed to be possessed by the spirits of important ancestral figures and to speak with their voices; the dead being regarded in many African religions as having a special power of communication with the divine creator of all things and protector of the land and its peoples. Professor Ranger considers that the cult of the *mhondoro* had a particular relationship with the Mutapa dynasty and hence with the eastern part of Mashonaland; the cult of 'Mwari' or 'Mlimo' on the other hand was associated with the Rozwi Mambos, and the Great Zimbabwe had been one of its shrines. But the two systems may well have stemmed from a common origin, and far from being antipathetic had many mutual connexions.

The Mwari cult was the one encountered by the victorious Ndebele in the 1830s. They made no attempt to destroy it, but they kept a close eye on its officers. Although it was the religion of conquered peoples, it seems to have fulfilled in some degree a need of the conquerors. They were many hundreds of miles away from the graves of their own ancestors. They too wished 'to be at peace with the land' in which they now lived and to propitiate the god of fertility and good harvests. The cult was not based on the capital of the Ndebele as it had been on that of the Mambos, but it continued to flourish. There were by 1896 four shrines; two in the Matopos, one at Mangwe in the south west, and one in the north east at Taba Zi Ka Mambo, the place where the last of the Rozwi monarchs had hurled himself to his death at the feet of Zwangendaba's *impi* three-quarters of a century earlier.

There is some evidence that the fortunes of the Mwari cult ebbed and flowed in inverse ratio to those of the Ndebele monarchy. For example it flourished in the interregnum after the death of Mzilikazi but became less conspicuous during the heyday of Lobengula. However that may be, the Mwari priesthood did nothing to support Lobengula in 1893. This passivity may partly explain the apathy of the *Amaholi* and the tributary tribes who declined to lift a finger in his support. On the other hand it may have been a symptom rather than a cause, for the subject peoples had good reason to detest the Ndebele aristocracy.

Three years later the situation was very different. Contrary to the complacent beliefs of the Company and the settlers, white rule was almost as bitterly resented by most of the subject peoples as it was by the Ndebele. The Mwari cult rose markedly in prestige, and there is little to confirm the contemporary view that this was because the Ndebele leaders were consciously using it as an instrument to work their will on the superstitious masses. Rather, they were themselves converts. In particular the leading priest stationed at the shrine of Taba Zi Ka Mambo, a former Ndebele slave called Mkwati, acquired great prestige and influence. He was one of the principal inspirers of rebellion and demonstrated by his success that in Africa as in other continents religious superstition can offer a notable *carrière ouverte aux talents*. He had two formidable allies, one his 'wife', who was also credited with magical powers, the other, Siginyamatshe, another wonder-worker and priest of Mwari. The Mwari cult, therefore, was a major factor in cementing an alliance between a number of different groups united only in their hatred of the Whites. By stirring up millenarian dreams and reviving atavistic memories it contributed much to the fanatical zeal which animated the revolt.

It would, however, be wrong to think that the rebellion in Matabeleland any more than the later outbreak in Mashonaland had the universal support of the conquered peoples, still less that it acted as a clarion call to the Africans under white rule elsewhere. The Ndebele had long been loathed by neighbouring Chiefs and tribes. Khama of Bechuanaland sent aid to the British forces. Admittedly it was not very effective but if he had come down on the other side he could have cut part of the life line from the south to Bulawayo – the road between Mafeking and Tati – with fatal consequences. Lewanika of Barotseland was equally hostile and blocked any escape route for the Ndebele to the north after their defeat.

Within Matabeleland itself there was a similar lack of unanimity, among the Ndebele military caste, the priests of Mwari and the tributary peoples. Some important *indunas* with their followings opposed the revolt – Gambo, Mjaan and Faku. The Kalanga and Makalaka of the south west also repudiated it, and the priests at the shrine near Mangwe opposed the rebels too. Their opposition may partly explain one of the most puzzling features of the whole campaign – the fact that no attempt was made to interrupt the main route for reinforcements to Bulawayo, running north from Old Tati through Mangwe and Figtree.

The opposition of the Mwari priests in the south west makes a particular mockery of the famous fraudulent claim on the part of the American Scout, F. R. Burnham who greatly raised white morale in June by declaring that, along with

Native Commissioner Armstrong, he had penetrated the secret shrine of this sinister religion in the Matopos, had 'shot the Mlimo', and had escaped hotly pursued by an *impi*. As some sceptics pointed out at the time, a claim to have 'shot the Mlimo' was strictly meaningless. It was rather like a claim to have shot the Holy Ghost. What Burnham actually seems to have done was to have penetrated a cave, not in the Matopos at all but near Mangwe, and to have killed the leading priest of the only Mwari shrine that was *hostile* to the revolt. By this feat he came as near as a toucher to pushing the most important 'loyalist' group in Matabeleland into the rebel camp – a group moreover which occupied a key strategical position. Luckily, though much upset by what had happened, the Kalanga did not change their policy.

Even if the rebellion in Matabeleland had been fully supported under a unified command and even if the uprising in Mashonaland had occurred simultaneously instead of three months later, it is most unlikely that the British would have been permanently displaced, though they might well have been driven out for the time being. But the Company would certainly not have survived and the future governance of Rhodesia might have developed on very different lines – a crown colony like Kenya perhaps. In the event Company rule continued, though with little margin to spare and in a much modified form.

At first the situation seemed very bad. The settlers were forced into four laagers, Bulawayo, Gwelo, Bellingwe and Mangwe. Bulawayo was of course the key and the principal effort of both attackers and defenders was concentrated there. It soon became clear that the Ndebele had learned the lesson of 1893. They had plenty of ammunition and shot far more accurately, they avoided set-piece battles in the open, they took full advantage of thick bush and hilly or rocky country where their numerical superiority could be used most profitably. The whites were ill prepared for war. The Jameson Raid had depleted the country of white police. The African police were regarded with good reason as unreliable; many of them went over to the other side, the good training which they had received in the use of rifles proving a valuable asset to the rebels; the others were hastily disarmed to avoid risks. There was plenty of small arms ammunition in Bulawayo but there were less than six hundred modern rifles in the whole country. Of the eight assorted machine guns in the town three were out of order. Of the three seven pounders, two needed urgent repairs and the third was usable only *in situ* since its carriage had been eaten by white ants. There were two 2.5 inch 'screw guns' in good order but with only seventeen rounds of ammunition between them. There was a serious shortage of horses, and of course ox transport was greatly hampered by the rinderpest.[11]

The only white force available was the Rhodesia Horse Volunteers, an amateur body raised and equipped the previous year. They were far from being properly trained or ready for action, and the shortage of rifles and horses limited their

[11] Selous, op. cit., 54–6.

scope for the offensive, but some five hundred of them constituted an effective defence of Bulawayo. In general the citizens displayed notable *sang-froid*, though there was an unfortunate panic on the night of March 25 caused by a drunken horseman riding round the town shouting 'The Matabele are here; the Matabele are here'.[12] 'The gallant inhabitants', wrote a regular officer, 'lost their heads and scrambled and fought for what rifles were left in the Government Store. It was a disgraceful scene and the less said about it the better.'[13] At an early stage a formidable laager was constructed to protect the six hundred women and children in the town which was henceforth safe from direct attack, but not from being starved out. By early April Bulawayo was invested on three sides by Ndebele *impis*. The biggest force, led by the Mkwati-Nyanda combination, probably amounted to some 10,000 men on the Umgusa River a few miles north east of Bulawayo. Umlugulu's forces were twenty-five miles to the south east astride the Tuli road, and another *impi* was some fourteen miles south of Bulawayo near Khami. It was a subject of general puzzlement at the time – and has been ever since – that the main road to Tati and the south west remained open. As we saw, the opposition of the Kalanga and the Mwari priests at the Mangwe shrine may be part of the explanation. The other reason often given is that the rebels wished to leave a route for the Whites to get out. Whatever the motive – and we know little about the working of their minds – the insurgents made a grave error of strategy.

Martin had not yet arrived and so the acting Administrator, A. H. F. Duncan, who stood temporarily in Jameson's shoes, took steps to raise as many fighting men as he could. The result was the Bulawayo Field Force which had as its core the Rhodesian Horse Volunteers. It consisted of a number of levies from all over the country and amounted to some 850 men. Although they were able to send out occasional detachments and fend off attacks on Bulawayo, they were not strong enough to suppress the rebellion. At first the Company, alarmed at the expense of bringing in imperial aid, had, to the fury of the settlers, played down the danger of the revolt and issued communiqués of Panglossian idiocy. The settlers were already in an irritable state for they considered with some justice that the Company, which they did not distinguish from Rhodes and Jameson in their personal capacities, had landed them with the whole crisis, thanks to the Raid. It was the beginning of a rift that was to grow much wider over the years.

They felt equal dislike for the Colonial Office. It must be admitted that here too they had good cause. Officialdom fighting, as so often, not the present battle but the last one and ever keen to shut the stable door after the horse had bolted, decided because of the Jameson Raid that arms and ammunition could only be issued with the consent of the High Commissioner. The result was a delay of twenty-four hours followed by instructions that the issue of rifles and cartridges must be limited to not more than a hundred volunteers, lest feeling might be exacerbated among the Boers. The average settler soon convinced himself that

[12] Ibid., 91.
[13] R. Macfarlane, *Some Account of George Grey and His Work in Africa*, 1914.

the rebellion could have been easily suppressed *ab initio* but for the delay thus imposed by the imperial factor. His desire to get rid of both the Company and Whitehall, though quiescent during the crisis, revived when it was over and became a potent factor in subsequent Rhodesian politics.

It was obvious that the existing forces were inadequate, but finance was the great problem which vexed the Company's officials. At this juncture Rhodes appeared unexpectedly on the scene. He had made a flying visit to England in February with the purpose of 'squaring' Joseph Chamberlain. He returned by the eastern sea route and stopped at Beira to visit his domain, less perhaps from solicitude for the Colony than from disinclination to be at the opening of the Cape Town Parliament where there was sure to be a fearful row about his part in Jameson's disastrous exploit. He received the first news of the massacres on reaching Umtali on March 25. He was still Managing Director with the Company's power of attorney – the key figure in Rhodesia to whom everyone deferred. His first instinct was as always to extrude the imperial factor and do things as economically as possible. He promptly organized a column of local volunteers from Salisbury to advance to Bulawayo via Gwelo under the command of Lieutenant Colonel Robert Beal.

But on March 31, just before the rebels cut the telegraph wire to Salisbury, Duncan convinced Rhodes that this was not enough and that at least five hundred more men were needed. Duncan had already been in touch with Rutherfoord Harris and suggested the raising of an irregular force in South Africa based on the Company's police now released from Pretoria and at that moment in transit through Cape Colony to stand trial in London under the Foreign Enlistment Act. This proposal was vetoed by Chamberlain who was no doubt by now sick of the Company and all its works. On April 1 Duncan was told that two hundred regulars were *en route* from England, and that Colonel Plumer, Assistant Military Secretary in Cape Town (later to be one of Haig's Army Commanders, a Field Marshal and a Viscount) would take charge of them and raise in Cape Colony the rest of the force needed. He would move north from Mafeking as soon as possible. The number, originally fixed at five hundred, was later raised to seven hundred and fifty. In the end the Matabele Relief Force, as it came to be known, mustered some eight hundred men.

Plumer's column did not reach Bulawayo in full strength till the middle of May. Long before then the senior and more experienced members of the Company's April offered the new Administrator, Lord Grey, a further contingent of three and Duncan telegraphed to the High Commissioner for further support. These views were echoed in the London press, and the High Commissioner early in April offered the new administrator, Lord Grey, a further contingent of three hundred cavalry, two hundred mounted infantry and an artillery battery. Grey was confronted with what was for him an agonizing decision. One of the most attractive though scarcely one of the strongest figures in early Rhodesian history, this amiable Whig grandee had not been selected by Rhodes to succeed Jameson solely on his merits; perhaps it would be more accurate to say that one of his merits had been carefully weighed, though not in terms of qualification to rule Rhodesia. Grey's sense of honour and honesty made it vital for Rhodes to keep him out of England during the inevitable Parliamentary Committee of Enquiry into the Jameson Raid. For Grey, 'Paladin of Empire', as he was described by H. W. Massingham, knew far more than was good for him or Rhodes about the origins of that episode. Not that he would have dreamed of doing any deliberate harm to Rhodes, whom he regarded with an almost naïve hero worship. The danger was that he also knew too much about Chamberlain's involvement. He would never have been capable of playing the correct part in the subtle manoeuvres by which Rhodes bargained exposure of the Colonial Secretary's role against the preservation of the charter. Under cross-examination he would have given the game away, and it was a game Rhodes could not afford to lose.

Grey had heard the news of the rebellion while on ship to Cape Town where he arrived at the beginning of April. He proceeded at once to Mafeking. He was horrified at the problem of transport created by the rinderpest. Oxen and horses were dying like flies. Mules seemed immune to the disease, but whereas a team of oxen could pull a load of up to four tons, a team of mules could only manage half as much and they tired far more easily. The distance from the railhead at Mafeking to Bulawayo was nearly six hundred miles, and the cost of transporting a ton of goods was £100–£120. Given the problems of transport, it was not clear that further reinforcements were the right answer, and there was the additional worry of the cost of the men's and officers' pay, all of which would fall on the Company. Because of the cut telegraph line Grey could not obtain instructions from Rhodes. He had to decide on his own, and he resolved to accept the offer with the proviso that the troops should not move before Plumer's column had arrived in Bulawayo. He was greatly relieved a couple of days later when communications had been reopened with Salisbury to receive a telegram from Rhodes advising him to do what he had already done.

There was to be much subsequent argument about the quality of the extra forces thus pulled in, but there can be little serious doubt that Hole's verdict – 'providential in the light of after events'[14] – was correct. One immediate consequence, however, was a far greater degree of imperial intervention. Chamberlain was an activist. On April 17 he announced decisions which in theory took the whole conduct of the war and the subsequent settlement out of the Company's hands. All the forces in Rhodesia were to come under the command of General Sir Frederick Carrington, a veteran of native warfare who superseded Sir Richard Martin as far as military operations were concerned. Sir Richard, however, retained his political position as Deputy Commissioner and had sole responsibility with regard to punitive measures, acceptance of submission and the general pacification of the country. These arrangements seemed at first sight a heavy blow to the position of Rhodes and the Company, but events were to show that the Colossus could not be cut down to size easily.

[14] Op. cit., 364.

Grey now proceeded by Zeederburg coach to Bulawayo. His account of one episode on the journey gives a flavour of the times.

We met just north of Palla [Palapye] a coach from Bulawayo crowded with funksticks. One of them, a Mr Mordaunt, an Eton boy and a fine cricketer in Eton and Cambridge elevens, took me aside, warned me most gravely against going up to Bulawayo and told me his coach had been attacked at Tati, that two of his mules had been shot, that there had been a hot fire on the coach and that a lady had had a very narrow escape – a bullet thro' her hat! and that he had seen one Matabele shot within ten yards of the coach.

Well there wasn't a word of truth in it. The poor fellow had lost his nerve and his fellow Passengers had been playing tricks upon him by firing their Revolvers out of the window.

Although Grey makes no criticism, such tricks seem to have been somewhat imprudent, to say the least, for he goes on to say that Mordaunt's 'scare' caused alarm all along the road.

One man ran trouserless for thirty miles because of one of the rumours and some waggons loaded with much wanted Provisions laagered up and prepared for the worst instead of trekking quietly along and so lost valuable time. I hope there are not many Mordaunts for I think he must be really mad poor fellow – but there is every degree of alarmism from Mordaunt downwards .. I don't believe we have many Rotters of that sort in Bulawayo. We have a *splendid* body of men here.[15]

Grey arrived on May 2. By that time the Bulawayo Field Force had fought its first successful pitched battle. This was against the *impis* on the Umguza river not far from what is now Government House. Between April 16 and April 22 no less than four unsuccessful attempts had been made to dislodge them. The promise of the Mwari priests that the white man could not cross the river because his bullets would turn to water seemed partly justified, if not for that particular reason. But on April 28, led by Captain Ronald Macfarlane, an ex-officer of the Ninth Lancers, a detachment of 115 mounted volunteers and seventy 'Colonial Natives' inflicted serious losses on the Ndebele troops and drove them back in confusion. It was a heavy blow to rebel morale, and if the white forces had been able to follow up their success, the revolt might have been crushed there and then. Grey would gladly have pushed ahead but it was not practicable. In any case the High Commissioner's instructions forbade a major offensive before Carrington arrived.

The month of May was therefore one of consolidation on both sides. The only episode of importance was the advance of the column from Salisbury organized

[15] NAR GR1/1/1 ff. 522–6, Grey to Lady, May 2, 1896.

by Rhodes and commanded by Colonel Beal. Rhodes's resignation had been offered to the Company in London on his behalf by his solicitor, Hawksley, on May 3, and published in the press. In spite of a demand by Chamberlain, the Company hesitated whether to accept it and cabled their doubts to Rhodes, who made his famous reply – 'Let resignation wait – we fight Matabele to-morrow'. A strong patrol under Colonel Napier, sent to meet the Salisbury column, routed a Ndebele *impi* at Tabas Induna twelve miles out and effected a junction with Rhodes on the Shangani river on May 21. The combined force returned to Bulawayo on June 1.

The following day General Carrington, with a staff which included Colonel R. S. S. Baden-Powell, later to be the founder of the Boy Scout movement, arrived and took over from Martin who had been in temporary command since May 21. Carrington had at his disposal by now slightly more than 2,000 irregular white troops including the Bulawayo Field Force of 700 under Colonel Napier and the Matabele Relief Force of 800 under Plumer. The residue was mainly accounted for by the Gwelo Field Force of 336 under Captain Gibbs and Beal's Salisbury Column of 150. In addition to these he had at call the 500 regulars which had been offered to Grey and were stationed at Mafeking, and 480 mounted infantry at Cape Town under the command of Lieutenant Colonel E. A. H. Alderson. Carrington resolved to take the initiative at once. It so happened that, inspired by Mkwati, the north-eastern group of the Ndebele forces set out simultaneously with the same purpose. On June 6 a routine patrol encountered a large Ndebele force at the last place expected – the scene of the battle on the Umguza river six weeks earlier. Although their presence was a surprise and although the force appears to have been the cream of the Ndebele warriors, the white column, rapidly reinforced, was able to inflict a decisive defeat on the rebels. Some 300 were killed and the Ndebele *impis* never again tried to take the offensive. One section, that of the *induna* Mpotshwana, retreated to Mkwati's headquarters, the formidable natural stronghold of Taba Zi Ka Mambo. Umlugulu's forces took refuge in the Matopos. There was henceforth little co-ordination between them.

Something of an impasse had been reached. The Ndebele and their allies now had no prospect of winning the war or ejecting the Whites. The most they could hope for was a prolonged defensive campaign. The white forces were faced with less daunting problems, but their position too was far from satisfactory. It was not going to be at all easy to reduce the rebels to submission in the strange desolate terrain to which they had withdrawn, a world of huge granite kopjes, giant boulders, and a maze of caves and crevices which offered limitless opportunities for resistance. In time, no doubt, they could be starved out, but to the Company time was vital.

At this moment something happened which no white man had expected in his worst nightmare. The Shona tribes broke out in revolt during the third week in June. The massacres of Matabeleland were re-enacted in Mashonaland. Once again the outlying settlers were slaughtered with every accompaniment of barbarity and treachery. About 120 Whites, including several women and children, perished in the first few days of the new rebellion. The roads from Umtali to Salisbury and Salisbury to Bulawayo were temporarily blocked. A hasty laager was formed in Salisbury and the settlers made every endeavour to bring back into safety the isolated communities now threatened. One of the most famous of these efforts – almost as much a part of Rhodesian folklore as Allan Wilson's last stand – is the story of the Mazoe Patrol. An isolated group of fourteen including three women was cut off and besieged at Alice Mine, sixteen miles north of Salisbury. Among the party were two telegraphists, T. G. Routledge and J. L. Blakiston. The latter, whose brother later became President of Trinity College, Oxford, was something of an intellectual, quiet, bookish and a student of Macaulay. He was down on his luck and refers sadly in his correspondence to 'my wasted life'. He disliked Rhodesia and his co-settlers. 'Everyone in Mashonaland is either slave to Mammon or to Bacchus,' he despondently wrote to his brother. Yet, in Professor Gann's words, 'Some ironic twist of fortune destined the shy young man . . . to become a martyr for the country's hard-riding, hard-drinking white frontier community'.[16] He and Routledge, at the risk of almost certain death, reached the telegraph office a mile away and sent a message to Salisbury. They were both killed on their way back to the laager, but a couple of patrols rode out to Alice Mine and under heavy fire throughout both journeys brought back the beleaguered garrison. One of the two commanders, Inspector Nesbitt of the company's police, received the VC for his gallantry.

The revolt had begun on June 18 in the Hartley area of west Mashonaland, led by a Shona paramount Chief called Mashiangombi. The first to rise, he was also one of the last to be defeated. He was strongly supported by Chief Mashanganyika in the same area, who also acquired great influence in the later course of the rebellion. Mashanganyika's son-in-law, Gumporeshumba, purported to be the medium of a Shona spirit known as Kagubi. The Kagubi medium played the same revolutionary and charismatic role in the Shona rebellion as Mkwati in Matabeleland. He inspired the same fervour and fanaticism, and he made the same promises to the faithful of invulnerability and immortality. Although his precise role, and that of his principal coadjutor, the woman spirit medium Nehanda who operated in the Mazoe area, have never been fully cleared up by historians, there seems no doubt about its importance. The evidence suggests that in April Mkwati urged Mashiangombi to initiate a slaughter of white men on the lines of the Matabeleland massacres. The Shona Chief sent for the Kagubi medium who set the process of rebellion in motion with sacred injunctions to the paramounts to kill all white men. It may be significant that his link with Mkwati occurred, and plans were made, *before* the decisive defeat of the Ndebele *impis* on June 6. Whatever the exact chain of command and sequence of events, revolt took place simultaneously in western and central Mashonaland. In central Mashonaland the leading rebel chiefs were Kunzi-Nyandoro about thirty miles north-east of Salisbury,

<hr />

[16] Gann, op. cit., 136–7.

Mangwende near Marandellas, and – most formidable of all – Makoni near Rusape. Only the far north, the south and the south west remained immune.

Of course it would be wrong to attribute the rebellion of the Shona paramounts solely to the power of spirit mediums. They had plenty of grievances, and they had the opportunity; the rebellion in Matabeleland had done for Mashonaland what the Jameson Raid had done for Matabeleland – denuded the country of white troops. But if there was no major grievance there was usually no revolt; for example Mtoko's country due east of Salisbury where there had been no forced labour; Melsetter which had escaped the rinderpest; or Fort Victoria where recent experience may well have made the Shona regard a Ndebele *impi* as worse than anything the Whites could do.

Carrington did not allow this new threat to divert him from his main objective. He sent back the Salisbury column together with a detachment of 100 men from the MRF and ordered Alderson with his mounted infantry regulars to proceed to Salisbury via Beira. To supply the gap in Matabeleland he sent for the regulars stationed at Mafeking. Without waiting for their arrival he launched a major assault on the headquarters of Mkwati and the north-eastern group of the Ndebele at Taba Zi Ka Mambo. The column of 750 men was commanded by Plumer. It left Bulawayo on June 30 and arrived at Inyati some twenty miles from the stronghold on July 3. The Tembu scout, John Grootboom, who spoke English and Sindebele reported next day that their presence was known and an attack expected. The defenders intended to dispatch their cattle and other loot northwards on July 5 anticipating an assault some time later that day. They did not however bargain with Plumer's decision to make a night march and attack at dawn. The fortress was formidable and the fighting fierce, but after a battle lasting from six till noon the Ndebele were completely defeated, all their booty falling into the hands of the victors.

Rhodes was prominent in spurring on the assault, riding unarmed with only a switch in his hand. About a hundred Ndebele were killed. White deaths amounted to only nine. But those few casualties and their burial on the spot wrapped in the hides of cattle shot for food moved Rhodes deeply. It was his first experience of hard fighting, and there was something about the deaths of these young men in a wild barbaric country far from home which touched a chord in him that did not often sound. There is no reason to doubt the well known account by Vere Stent, the *Times* correspondent who was present with him, that the battle at Taba Zi Ka Mambo brought home to Rhodes as never before something of the bloodiness and futility of war and turned his mind towards a compromise peace.

The military situation was far from promising, despite this resounding victory. It is true that the north-east group, the largest and most formidable, was now finally broken. Mpotshwana and some of its leaders went north hoping to set up a new Ndebele state across the Zambesi. Others including Siginyamatshe fled south to the Matopos. But Mkwati was not captured. He and his close supporters had departed eastwards a few days before the assault. He had never been at heart committed to the resuscitation of the Ndebele kingdom; Mwari was a Shona not a

Ndebele creed. With a Shona bodyguard he moved gradually into Mashonaland where his presence was to be a potent factor in prolonging the resistance of the rebel paramounts.

Apart from the failure to capture 'the Mlimo', there were other snags. The area of the Matopos was even more difficult to assault and lent itself even better to a prolonged defensive battle than Taba Zi Ka Mambo. Moreover it was defended not merely by demoralized refugees but by the fresh *impis* of Umlugulu and Umfesela, who had so far seen relatively little fighting. A series of inconclusive engagements during the rest of July convinced Carrington that the war could not be ended militarily without a second campaign in the next dry season requiring another 2,500 white troops plus appropriate support. The same experience convinced Rhodes that this was too high a price, in every sense of the word, to pay for military victory. The Company could not survive a second campaign. There was the problem of Mashonaland where the rebellion was still in full swing, and already voices were being raised in favour of imperial rule. Nor could he rely on the settlers who by now both in Bulawayo and Salisbury were in a state of seething discontent.

The tale of how Rhodes negotiated successfully with the Ndebele *indunas* in the Matopos is too famous to need detailed repetition. This period of his life has been called his 'finest hour', and there is no reason to quarrel with the words. The most vivid and reliable published account by a contemporary of a story which later became much overlaid with myth and legend is that of Vere Stent[17] who was actually present at what he described, unlike many other chroniclers. The best modern narrative is by Professor Ranger[18] who co-ordinated early accounts with a source not tapped before – the letters of Lady Grey. These were written at the time to her daughter, and were not written up in retrospect. She was present herself at the third *indaba*, her husband took part in that and others, and she was living in Rhodes's camp in the Matopos for much of the time.

Although some of the later versions exaggerate Rhodes's personal part, almost giving the impression that it was a solo performance, there can be no doubt that, but for him, the campaign in Matabeleland would not have ended when it did. This judgment in no way involves playing down the work done by John Grootboom who made the first contacts, Richardson the Native Commissioner for the Matopos, Colenbrander the Company's ex-envoy at Lobengula's court, and others who ran even greater physical risks than Rhodes. But Rhodes was the only person with the moral courage to initiate peace talks at all, and the eloquence, the personality and the shrewdness to bring them to a successful conclusion. He did it, moreover, against all the odds as far as his own side was concerned. The settlers bitterly opposed the talks as soon as they heard about them, and for once found

---

[17] Vere Stent, *A Personal Record of some Incidents in the Life of Cecil Rhodes*, Cape Town, 1924, 27–62. Other first hand descriptions are by Hans Sauer, *Ex Africa ...*, 309–42; and J. W. Colenbrander in *South Africa*, Vol. 33, 1897.

[18] Op. cit., 237–67.

themselves in alliance with the imperial Government personified by Sir Richard Martin who also strongly objected to the negotiations. Not that the settlers approved of the imperial Government's own efforts to bring the war to an end. A Proclamation issued by General Goodenough, the acting High Commissioner, on July 4 offering a conditional amnesty to the Ndebele rank and file but excluding their leaders had provoked equal wrath – not of course because of the exclusion but because clemency was promised to anyone.

To Rhodes this offer, however much it accorded with 'British justice', was an inversion of the right approach. He believed in 'leadership' and he knew that the only way of bringing the war to an end was to 'square' the *indunas* and not worry about the rest. Theoretically he had no right to take any initiative. Chamberlain had specifically given Martin the task of making the peace settlement and deciding on punitive measures. Moreover Rhodes now held no position in the Company. His resignation had been accepted on June 26. Formally he was just a private person. But his wealth was still vast, his prestige immense in spite of all his late vicissitudes of fortune. He sensed with his strange intuitive power that the Ndebele *indunas* were willing to negotiate. If the state of the Company's finances was parlous and that of the forces under Carrington none too good, the prospects for the rebels were even less inviting. White patrols had for many weeks been systematically burning kraals and destroying crops. Starvation faced the whole nation if the struggle was prolonged through the rainy season, and in fact, despite the conclusion of peace, a great many did starve to death. Lady Grey wrote to her son from Bulawayo after the *indabas* were over.

> We passed several natives cutting the best pieces off the bodies of dead rinderpest oxen which have been lying there decaying for *months*; now that they have no grain left they boil down these hides and eat them. Isn't it too horrible! Mr Colenbrander told Father that he should not be surprised if at least some of the natives were reduced to cannibalism, that the natives would be driven to eat their little ones, but most people seem to think it nonsense; for the Matabele have never been Cannibals and they are *very* fond of their children.[19]

The first successful approach after several abortive efforts was made when Campbell and Grootboom discovered a very old lady in a deserted kraal, who turned out to have been one of Mzilikazi's wives and the mother of an important *induna* called Inyanda. Precisely what followed is not clear, but a good many preliminary moves were made on both sides and Rhodes himself along with Colenbrander contacted some of the rebel leaders on August 14. This led to a further meeting of the *indunas* with Grootboom two days later; the first of the great *indabas*, like all the best diplomatic conferences, had thus been well prepared beforehand. It took place on August 21, Rhodes, Colenbrander, Hans Sauer, Vere Stent, Grootboom and an African interpreter called Makunga being present. It

[19] NAR GR1/1/1, Lady Grey to Viscount Howick, October 23, 1896.

is not true, as is often claimed, that they went unarmed; they had their revolvers with them, but they had no guards. If anything had gone wrong they could easily have been dispatched. Rhodes's party arrived first, and then the *indunas* came down with a white flag. Thousands of Ndebele watched the scene from the neighbouring hills.

Proceedings began with the history of tribal grievances. As recounted by Stent the words of their spokesman, Somabulana, have something of the ring of the heroic literature of long ago – Homer or a Norse saga. He related the story of their wanderings since the day when Mzilikazi fled from the wrath of Shaka. He described their sojourn in Matabeleland, their heyday of prosperity, the fall of Lobengula and the oppression of the Whites; his words made it clear that all sense of solidarity with the Shona had now vanished:

> The Maholi and the Mashona ... what are they? Dogs! Sneaking cattle thieves! Slaves! But we the Amandabili, the sons of Kumalo, the Izulu, Children of the Stars; we are no dogs! You came, you conquered. The strongest takes the land. We accepted your rule. We lived under you. But not as dogs! If we are to be dogs it is better to be dead. You can never make the Amandabili dogs. You may wipe them out ... but the Children of the Stars can never be dogs.

This and other speeches profoundly affected Rhodes. The complaints rang only too true, but Rhodes himself had never consciously intended these abuses. He had merely failed to prevent them. The *indaba* ended at night fall. It was certainly not an unconditional surrender, but the outlook for peace seemed much brighter: Sauer and Stent promptly telegraphed their brokers and bought 'Chartered'.

There were three more *indabas* – on August 28, September 9 and October 13. The meeting of August 28 was the most tempestuous and Rhodes had all his work cut out to keep the peace. The *indunas* proved to be very capable negotiators and displayed a disconcerting knowledge of white politics, including the fact that an inquiry into the Company's administration was on the cards. At the first *indaba* on August 21 Rhodes had in effect promised to disband the black police, to reform the administration, put an end to cattle collecting and guarantee the lives of the senior *indunas*. At the second he felt obliged to go further and he promised to make an adequate land settlement. The *indunas* had demanded that the Queen's representatives should be present at this *indaba* but Sir Richard Martin refused to go without an escort.

Martin had not even been informed in advance about Rhodes's plan to meet the rebels on August 21. Nor did Rhodes see fit to tell him the whole truth about his promise to the *indunas*. After the second *indaba* Martin made a strong protest to the acting High Commissioner who agreed with his proposal to take the negotiations out of Rhodes's hands and proceed himself on the lines of the Proclamation of July 4. Both of them banked on the support of the Colonial Secretary, but Rhodes knew his Chamberlain and he had two cards up his sleeve. One might have been guessed by Martin. An important reason for having an imperial resident at Bulawayo at all was to prevent the Company behaving too harshly. Chamberlain would be very ill-placed if on Martin's advice he found himself advocating a less lenient policy than Rhodes and Grey.

The second card was less obvious. It never had to be played, but the knowledge that it might be shaped the whole future of Rhodesia. Chamberlain, for motives known only to Rhodes and one or two others, was determined not to withdraw the Company's charter and abolish Company rule if he could avoid it. He knew that Rhodes knew things about Chamberlain's own knowledge of the preliminaries to the Jameson raid which would be very damaging if made public; Rhodes knew that Chamberlain was aware of the information which Rhodes possessed. Nothing was ever said directly. No explicit threat or bargain was made. 'Blackmail' though often used is not quite the right word. Chamberlain after all had reputable reasons for preserving the Company subject to a modification of its powers. Rhodes on his side was not the man to reveal at all readily facts which would have given encouragement to enemies of the imperial cause everywhere and forced the resignation of Chamberlain. Nevertheless this tacit unspoken agreement conditioned the whole course of events during the nineteen months between the Raid and the debate on the Report of the Select Committee on July 27, 1897, when Chamberlain, himself a member of that Committee, not only refused to withdraw the charter or deprive Rhodes of his privy councillorship, but declared to an astonished House that Rhodes had done nothing which reflected on his 'personal position as a man of honour'.

Not surprisingly Martin and acting High Commissioner Goodenough got short shrift from the Colonial Office. The Resident Commissioner was told that Rhodes could continue negotiations subject to his 'advice' and that Martin should pay close attention to the views of the Administrator. Since Grey, perhaps unkindly but not incorrectly, was once described by Milton as 'Rhodes's clerk', it was unlikely that Martin would get a different view from that quarter. In this way Martin and the imperial establishment were effectively by-passed and, despite strong support from the indignant settlers, their opinion had only a marginal effect on events. On September 9 the third *indaba* was held. There were present, besides Rhodes and some of the previous participants, Grey, Lady Grey and Martin who lectured the *indunas* in a somewhat tactless style, but confirmed the previous promises, 'even if', as Professor Ranger drily observes, 'Martin had very little idea what those were'.[20]

Everything now depended on whether the Ndebele leaders would literally deliver the goods and give up their arms. At first there was a pause. On September 18 Rhodes delivered an ultimatum – war or surrender – to the minor *indunas* who were the element least willing to give way. His threat was successful and peace became a reality. A factor which may have influenced the senior *indunas* was the knowledge that they would themselves be incorporated as salaried officials into a

[20] Op. cit., 255.

reformed native administration. This idea was apparently Grey's. Lady Grey wrote to her daughter

Albert also naturally wishes it to be thoroughly understood by the English people how Mr Rhodes is *the one man* out here in everyone's estimation and absolutely essential to the country; everyone believes in him and looks to him, and he has done wonderfully good work in bringing this war to an end ... All the same (between ourselves) I daresay it will appear to the world in general that *he* has initiated all this policy about the natives as to paying the chief's a small monthly salary as long as they conduct themselves loyally to the Govt. etc. It is really the initiative of your father who drew up the scheme and inaugurated it.[21]

At the fourth and final *indaba* on October 13 the leading 'loyalists', Gambo, Faku and Mjaan were also present and were rewarded by salaried posts. At the same time the senior rebel *indunas*, among them Umlugulu himself, were promised similar positions on proof of good behaviour. The Ndebele nation had been at last in some measure restored and by the end of the year a large number of them were back on their old lands. At least a promise had been made to meet their principal overt grievances and Rhodes had undertaken to return in due course in order to ensure personally that justice was done. At the same time a great effort was made to meet the impending famine by the large scale import of grain (some five million pounds) and seed. Nothing at this stage could prevent a large number of deaths but the situation would have been far worse if the war had gone on.

It did not entirely end even in Matabeleland with the surrender in the Matopos. Mkwati tried to keep resistance alive in the Somabula and Shangani area, but his control over the Ndebele was waning, and his policy was beginning to be interpreted as pro-Rozwi anti-Ndebele plot. Late in September Baden-Powell captured Mkwati's father-in-law Uwini and had him court-martialled and shot on the spot. Nyamanda, Lobengula's son, now took advantage of the amnesty and so did other members of the royal family in the north-eastern area. Mkwati himself with his Shona adherents escaped to Mashiangombi's kraal in west Mashonaland. As for Mpotshwana's venture to the north, it was equally unsuccessful. Those who crossed the Zambesi were arrested by Lewanika and handed over to the Whites. Mpotshwana himself was not captured till July 1897. He died in gaol before he could be hanged for murder.

The rebellion in Mashonaland proved more difficult to subdue than that of the Ndebele and far more difficult than anyone expected. At first matters went well for the Whites. The Salisbury laager was never threatened as Bulawayo had been. Beal's column cleared the road from Bulawayo via Gwelo and Hartley. Alderson's mounted infantry coming up from Beira soon re-established the vital route

[21] NAR GR1/1/1, to Lady Sybil Grey, Bulawayo, October 23, 1896.

from the sea via Umtali. But the Shona rebel Chiefs who had never been through the Ndebele experience of 1893 seem at first to have thought that the Whites, if they would not go away, would at least leave them alone. Separate and uncoordinated, they adopted a defensive role, and there was no centralized command to deal with. The granite kopjes of Mashonaland and the labyrinthine caves whose ramifications were known only to the denizens were readily converted into formidable strong points almost as difficult for white men to capture as the Matopos.

Why was no attempt made, comparable to Rhodes's in Matabeleland, to secure a compromise peace? Partly this was due to lost opportunity and the fact that even the Colossus could not bestride two places so far apart. The point of no return may have been the treatment of Makoni, one of the most formidable Shona paramounts, whose kraal was at Gwindingwe near Rusape.[22] He was attacked unsuccessfully by Alderson *en route* for Salisbury early on August 3, but his losses were so heavy that on August 18 he offered to surrender in return for an amnesty. Judge Vintcent, acting Administrator at Salisbury, favoured acceptance and so did Rhodes when consulted. But Rhodes had not yet begun his *indabas* with the Ndebele. Goodenough, Martin and the imperial Government were in the ascendancy. Fearing as they did in Matabeleland a deal between the Company and the Chiefs at the expense of their respective subjects white and black, they insisted on unconditional surrender – Makoni to take his trial without any promise. Naturally the Chief refused. A subsequent expedition on August 30–September 3 overcame his defences largely by the terrible technique which was later adopted as the normal form in the reduction of Shona strongholds – dropping sticks of dynamite into the caves where they took refuge; these were seldom completely blocked off from the upper air, and it was usually possible to find some crevice. Makoni was either captured, or surrendered on promise of his life being spared; the facts are not entirely clear. He was, however, at once court-martialled and condemned to death. After some hesitation Major Watts, commanding the patrol, had him shot forthwith at the edge of his own kraal – an action which was illegal even if there had been no promise to spare his life.

Whatever chance there might have been of a series of *indabas* with the Shona paramounts now vanished. Perhaps there was little chance anyway. They were actuated by deeper superstition and greater fanaticism than the Ndebele. Mkwati now joined forces with the Kagubi medium, and even tried in a last despairing throw to revive the Rozwi Mamboship early in 1897. The attempt failed because the 'Jacobite' candidate was – luckily for him – accidentally detained by a Native Commissioner before he could commit himself. The Shona were not so well armed as the Ndebele, but they possessed, thanks to generations of trading with the Arabs and the Portuguese, a great number of old muzzle-loading muskets. With home-made powder and ammunition consisting of nails, glass balls from soda-water bottles, and small bits of telegraph wire, they could inflict at short range hidden in their concealed crannies the most horrible wounds, while the

[22] See Ranger, op. cit., 274 *et sq.*

uselessness of these antique weapons at long distance did not greatly matter.

Rhodes and Grey came to Salisbury late in November. They persuaded Martin to send back the imperial forces under Alderson – Carrington's had already left Matabeleland – although Martin did not share their optimism about finishing the war before the end of the year, and Chamberlain warned Grey that a disaster in the field really would mean the revocation of the Company's charter. Luckily for Rhodes this did not occur. The forces left proved sufficient for the grim but effective dynamiting of the Shona strongholds. The process occupied most of the ensuing year despite some humanitarian protests in England. The later stages in the suppression of the Shona rebellion were little reported and form one of the obscurer pages of Rhodesian history.

Martin himself dealt a heavy blow by capturing the kraal of Mashiangombi near Hartley. He had been one of the main supporters of Mkwati and 'Kagubi'. After a fierce struggle on July 25 and 26 his defences were overcome and he was killed in the battle. This ended the rebellion in western Mashonaland. In the centre the defeat of Kunzi-Nyandoro a month earlier had the same effect. The Shona Chiefs surrendered in increasing numbers. Mkwati, now on the run, vanishes from the scene. He is said to have been chopped up alive into pieces at the order of disillusioned Chiefs who thought he had made enough trouble in his life time and wished to avoid any risk of his bodily reincarnation. His principal followers were caught and executed, though his consort Tenkela, to the astonishment of many Africans, was acquitted for lack of evidence. The Kagubi medium surrendered in October, and Nehanda was captured in December. Both were tried for murder and hanged in Salisbury; 'Kagubi' receiving the last rites of the Catholic Church, having been converted by Father Richartz; Nehanda gibbering, screaming and struggling even on the scaffold. Their bodies were buried in a secret grave.

And so it was all over. No one knows how many Africans perished. The total white death roll including the settlers was 450 with another 189 wounded. For settlers in the country when the rebellion began the figures (including women and children) were 372 dead and 129 wounded – nearly ten per cent of the whole population and, as Professor Gann points out, a far higher proportion than anything experienced by European minorities in modern times, for example in Kenya or Algeria. But the white men of those days never lost confidence. They knew where they stood and they had, apart from a few dissentients, the solid backing of both Cape Colony and the home country. Even the missionaries were 'sound'. There was no nagging guilt about race relations, no uneasy doubt about the white man's civilizing mission. And for those who had not suffered personal bereavement there was something not unattractive – almost exhilarating in a campaign on the high veld, despite its dangers and hardships. There are occasions when a single contemporary letter tells us more than much laborious historical reconstruction. Lady Grey is writing to her daughter about an encounter near Enkledoorn on her way across to Salisbury in the hot dry season of 1896:

Vera and I strolled away from the camp for a little walk towards the sunset

and suddenly saw outlined against a glowing sky a long column of dark horsemen coming from the hills (which were from fifteen to twenty miles off) towards
our road. We recognised them at once as the Patrol of the Seventh Hussars and
Mounted Infantry ... I suppose about 200 men commanded by Colonel Paget
... They had burned a large number of Kraals a day or two before we met
them and killed about thirty natives ... I suppose as white people had been
murdered in that district it was necessary to punish them in this way, but as
far as I could make out they made little or no resistance at all so that it all
sounded rather horrible ... It was a picturesque sight coming upon them (the
Hussars) on the Veldt marching across it on their way from fighting, with a few
waggons carrying their cooking things and forage etc. We had a little chat with
the Officers ... We saw them all march past and file away along the road leading to Gwelo on their way back to Bulawayo 170 miles away. It was an interesting break in our trek and quite excited us. They faded away from sight very
soon in a golden glow of dust through which the setting sun shot its red and
gold rays and we went off to our dinner feeling quite enlivened by the meeting.[23]

Much of the atmosphere of the time and place is there: the romance, the
glamour, the sense of adventure, and also the sadness of that cruel clash between
two alien worlds.

[23] NAR GR1/1/1, to Lady Sybil Grey, November 22, 1896.

10

The Aftermath 1897–1902

The crushing of the rebellions reaffirmed the white man's conquest. Juridically conquest had been his title deeds since 1893, but title deeds are nothing if they cannot be enforced; and at moments during 1896 there must have been some doubt whether they could. That danger vanished with the suppression of the revolt. Although there continued to be occasional scares for many years to come, there was no real chance of a recrudescence in either territory. The Ndebele had now been beaten twice and a settlement had been made which at least conceded something to their traditional institutions. The Shona were potentially a greater threat. They had links with the Shona-speaking peoples in Mozambique where white rule was more precarious than in Mashonaland. The religious creed which inspired the rebellion was essentially theirs and was held by them with far greater tenacity than by the Ndebele. 'The Shona have been rebels at heart ever since,' I was told by one of the most eminent living authorities on their beliefs and customs. But the process of reducing them to submission, which took four times as long as the campaign in Matabeleland, left them correspondingly more exhausted and demoralized for many years to come.

Apart from these considerations, a revolution in communications was imminent, which would make an uprising far more difficult. Grey's correspondence both in Mafeking and Bulawayo is full of his anxiety to speed up the railway. Its construction was indeed one of the original conditions of the charter, and, after a notable effort had been made, the first train steamed into Bulawayo on October 19, 1897, making the long, slow, expensive and dreary haul by ox waggon along the 'missionary road' a thing of the past. The Ndebele rebellion would have been crushed with ease had this occurred a couple of years earlier than it did. In 1898 the line from the Indian Ocean reached Umtali, the old town having been resited by Rhodes to suit the convenience of the railway engineers. Its construction was only achieved at the cost of heavy losses from malaria and blackwater fever.

A year later Umtali was joined with Salisbury, and in 1902 the link with Bulawayo was completed so that Salisbury too was accessible from the south as well as the east by rail. Rhodes had not forgotten his plan of 'Cape to Cairo'. It was never to be achieved, but he drove on to the north. The discovery of coal in the Wankie area made him change the original route which would have crossed the Zambesi near Chirundu. Instead the line went via Victoria Falls. The bridge was built in 1904, but Rhodes did not live to see the reality of his dream that the carriages should cross under the spray.

Railways were to be the greatest single cause of social and economic change in Central Africa during the early years of the twentieth century, even as they had been in England and Europe during the second quarter of the nineteenth. For nearly forty years, until first the tarmac road and then the aeroplane provided alternatives and substitutes, they were the life blood of the Rhodesian economy. They also added something new and conspicuous to the Rhodesian scene. There are comparatively few cuttings and tunnels, and the routes keep to the high veldt with its great vistas, where the long sinuous caterpillar of carriages and trucks, hauled – till very recently – by old-fashioned steam locomotives puffing and mournfully hooting, can be seen miles away, for all the world like children's toys as they chug slowly across the rolling landscape. The effect of the railroad on transport charges and hence on the whole Rhodesian economy need not be spelled out except to observe that it was essentially a mining system and the fact that it ran near to the best European farming areas was more by chance than design. Its strategic importance is less obvious but there can be no doubt that it greatly reduced the chances of a successful revolt.

The Rhodesian railway system was remarkably cheap in relative terms – under £7,000 per mile, compared with over £10,000 in South Africa, over £11,000 in Uganda and over £16,000 in the Gold Coast (Ghana).[1] This was partly due to the favourable terrain and deliberate economy, partly to the ability of the Company, for which it got precious little thanks, to raise cheap loans on the London market. The trouble was that, though cheap by comparison with other African colonies, it was extremely expensive in terms of the tiny European population in Rhodesia. Complaints about high freight rates were endemic till at least the 1930s.

If the repression of the rebellion left the Africans stunned and exhausted, the fact that a rebellion had occurred at all was a profound shock to the Whites. Neither the Colonial Office nor the Company was prepared to act on the simplistic settler view that it all came from being 'too soft to the Kaffirs'. At the top level Rhodes ended his *indabas* with a respect for the Ndebele, whom he believed to have been wronged; and Grey firmly rejected the gloomy view of the Shona held even by the Roman Catholic missionary Father Bieler who considered 'that the only chance for the future of their race is to exterminate the whole people both male and female over the age of fourteen'. Grey went on to say in his letter to his wife who had now gone back to England:

[1] Gann, op. cit., 157, n. 1.

This pessimistic conclusion I find difficult to accept. It must be remembered that the Mashonas have been governed and controlled entirely thro' the influence of fear. They have the habits of a whipped cur and not infrequently bite through terror the hand stretched out to help them. If I were to stay out here longer I sometimes think I might do something to alter this state of things. So long as I remain here my endeavour will be to teach the natives that my Govt. is strong enough both to punish them when they do wrong and to protect them when they do right, and the White Population that the employer who ill treats his native dependents and deprives them of their just rights is a scoundrel who deserves to be treated by his fellows as the I.D.B. [Illicit Diamond Buyer] is treated by White Society in Kimberley.[2]

Although his heart was on the right side, Grey had little chance to put these resolutions into effect. He retired from the Administratorship in June 1897[3] and his hands were full with the rebellion which had by no means ended when he left. Nor is it likely that even in peace time he would have shown the talents needed to put Rhodesia on to a basis of law and order. There is indeed something engaging about him, and one likes to think of him riding to Government House on his red bicycle with solid tyres and a 'G' and a coronet engraved in gold on the rear mudguard. But he was too impulsive, too enthusiastic, too easily distracted. And there was so much to distract him, as the same letter – a typical sample – shows. There was 'my Ball ... in every way a great success ... I believe we drank five cases of claret, five cases of whisky and twenty dozen of mineral waters'. But there were complicated problems of whom to invite and whom to exclude and much time was consumed – as well as drink. Then there was the cost of living. 'This place is ruinous ... My hotel bill at Umtali amounted to £193!!! – a big price to pay for small civilities to people one does not care a damn about.' And other things vexed him:

William is in hospital with fever and the cook has been vomiting blood – and Hubert is running the show! You can imagine what this means ... Pauling is coming to stay with me and is bringing his wife too! I have not recovered [sc. from] the ill temper into which this news has put me.

Besides costing me over £200 a month, for this lady will always have a full dinner table for wh: I as her host will have to pay, I shall have no more peace and quiet. I am too annoyed.

Grey had arrived in Salisbury along with Rhodes in November 1896. Having successfully 'squared' the Ndebele *indunas* Rhodes now directed his attention to

[2] NAR GR1/1/1 Salisbury, January 23, 1897, to Lady Grey.
[3] That is to say he left Rhodesia for London then. He remained formally Administrator for the purpose of negotiating on Rhodes's behalf with the Colonial Office till December when he finally resigned, being replaced by Milton who had been acting Administrator since his departure.

the angry settlers. Salisbury was even more discontented than Bulawayo where, despite initial settler criticism, it was hard to dispute that the rebellion had been successfully ended. This was far from being the case in Mashonaland; the demand for settler representation in the running of the colony was vociferous as a result of a strong feeling that the Company's protection had proved wholly inadequate. There were two reasons why Rhodes was ready to concede a part of the settlers' case. First he had always envisaged that Rhodesia would in the end develop into a self-governing colony, like Natal, and then become, as he hoped Natal would, part of a South African Federation under the British flag. Secondly, although he knew that Joseph Chamberlain would not readily abrogate the charter, he also knew that events might be too much for the Colonial Secretary; it was therefore vital to avoid any general demand for imperial rule; indeed the Company, if it agreed to a certain amount of power-sharing with the settlers, would be much better placed to resist pressure from above for the abrogation of the charter and the substitution of the Colonial Office. It would be harder for Whitehall to bully a representative council than a Chartered Company.

On November 10, though by no means disclosing the whole of his thinking, Rhodes made a speech to an audience of leading settlers in which he told them that he favoured a semi-elective system as a forerunner to self-government. Rhodes had the measure of the settlers. As in Bulawayo, he promised and paid lavish compensation from his own purse to those who claimed that they had been financially damaged by the rebellions. His enormous wealth was an omnipresent element in the politics of the day. The Company paid out £250,000 to the settlers in Matabeleland and £100,000 in Mashonaland.[4] If the numerous private payments are added in and the subsidization of food supplies reckoned too, it can be seen that the settlers were very generously treated. Some idea of the size of the cost of the Jameson Raid and its repercussions emerges from a note in Lord Rosebery's betting book. He records that in May 1898 Rhodes told him that it had cost him and Beit nearly £400,000 each.

Rhodes now departed to England for the great Parliamentary Enquiry – 'the Lying in State at Westminister', as it came to be cynically known. Before he left he had brought into Rhodesian affairs a man who made a more lasting imprint on the country's early history than anyone, apart from Rhodes himself. This was William (later Sir William) Milton who was to govern the country for seventeen years and to create an administrative and judicial system which outlasted Company rule itself. Dr Johnson wrote the *Lives of the Poets*, Lord Campbell the *Lives of the Lord Chancellors*, Samuel Smiles the *Lives of the Engineers*, but no one has ever tried to write the 'Lives of the Civil Servants'. Yet these important functionaries, such as Sir Robert Morant, Sir Warren Fisher, Lord Bridges, have probably done more to shape events than almost any other category of person. The trouble is that their work is to most of us dull, and that a convention of anonymity makes it

[4] *Report on the Native Disturbances in Rhodesia 1896–7*, 21–2.

difficult to discover exactly what they did and how they did it.

Rhodes belatedly realized that what the colony needed was a systematic and orderly mode of government. He may half-consciously have known that he had no talent himself for this sort of thing. He certainly knew that he found it tedious. He had a high respect for Milton who had been his civil service private secretary at Cape Town, and later head of the Prime Minister's Department. In August 1896 Rhodes persuaded him to come up to Rhodesia on temporary secondment as Chief Secretary and Secretary of Native Affairs with a seat on the Advisory Council. We have seen Milton's distaste for the set-up at Bulawayo. At one moment he almost threw in his hand, but he found Salisbury slightly less odious though 'a god-forsaken place to spend one's life in'.

In November Rhodes offered him the succession to Grey. The matter was not entirely simple, for Grey with the consent of the London Board had offered it to one of those 'honourable and military' figures of whom Milton so much disapproved. This was Grey's former private secretary, Captain Arthur Lawley, a son of Lord Wenlock, who had been deputizing for Grey at Bulawayo. A complicated series of misunderstandings, withdrawals, acceptances and general muddles ensued. Rhodes was anxious not to offend Grey who, though back in London from June 1897 onwards, was still Administrator till December and, now that the Enquiry was over, could be safely entrusted to negotiate with the Colonial Office on behalf of the Company, Rhodes himself having returned to the colony. On the other hand he was determined that the real power should go to Milton, not Lawley. The result was one of those curious constitutions which are incomprehensible without knowledge of the personalities involved.

The Southern Rhodesia Order in Council 1898, duly confirmed by Milner and Chamberlain, provided for two Administrators, one at Bulawayo (Lawley), the other at Salisbury (Milton). All communications, however, whether with the London Board or the Secretary of State went through Salisbury as the capital of the senior province. Likewise the Council met there, not at Bulawayo. The Administrator of Matabeleland was a member of the Council whenever he could get to Salisbury – which was not often since there was as yet no railway line – and it was the Council, not the Administrator of Mashonaland, from whom he took his instructions. On constitutional and administrative grounds this arrangement was absurd, but it saved several faces and it did not last long. In 1901 Lawley resigned to become Governor of Western Australia. He was not replaced and Milton became sole Administrator. He had retained his position, throughout, as Chief Secretary and Secretary of the Native Department, and he now held all the strings of power in his hands.

The 1898 Order in Council remained the governing instrument of Southern Rhodesia until Responsible Government a quarter of a century later. It represented a compromise between the imperial and the Company attitude. In many respects the Company lost. But Rhodes and the London Board were in no position to complain. Much could easily have gone wrong. For one thing it was sheer luck that the Select Committee of the House of Commons, having reported on the Jameson

Raid, never took up the second item of its term of reference – the conduct of the Company in the administration of Southern Rhodesia. The verdict on the Jameson Raid had been highly unfavourable but thanks to Chamberlain the charter had not been withdrawn. It could scarcely have survived a serious investigation into the malpractices of the Jameson era. Fortunately for Rhodes, in the mysterious way in which these things happen – the exigencies of the parliamentary time table, loss of public interest, sheer exhaustion of the Committee – the second item just vanished. It was never heard of again; but at the time there could be no certainty that some radical trouble-maker might not resuscitate the whole affair, and so it behoved Rhodes to move cautiously.

Moreover in the new High Commissioner, Lord Milner he had to deal with a man of very different calibre from any of his predecessors. Loch had been unfriendly but only half-heartedly backed by Whitehall. Robinson had been a crony. It was lucky that he, like Grey, did not give evidence either at the Cape Town or the London Enquiry, Chamberlain having skilfully arranged vital engagements for him in England during the former and in Cape Colony during the latter. Milner, who arrived at Cape Town on May 5, 1897, was not only an administrator of proven capacity, he was also a public figure. He had been sent out with a purpose. The attempt to solve the South African problem through the colonial factor had ended in the fiasco of the Jameson raid, but Chamberlain had no intention of abandoning the attempt to solve it. He now resolved to assert the imperial factor, dormant since the days of Lord Carnarvon, and force Kruger into compromise for preference, war if compromise failed.

That part of Milner's career lies outside the scope of this book, but as a byproduct it fell to him to settle the new status of Rhodesia. He admired Rhodes but he knew his limitations: 'a great developer ... but not a good administrator'. We have seen how shocked he was by what he discovered about the Jameson era. It was an important imperial interest in South Africa that the new colony should not cost money and not give trouble. If the Company was to go on ruling – and considerations of expense favoured its continuation – then it must be closely controlled.

Accordingly the new constitution formalized imperial vigilance in the shape of a Resident Commissioner appointed and paid by the Colonial Office and responsible to the High Commissioner. He was an *ex officio* member of both the Executive Council, which was a body of officials, and of the newly created Legislative Council, on both of which he had a voice but not a vote. He had no executive power but he could call for reports through the Administrator, and the information he sent to the High Commissioner at Cape Town helped the latter to decide whether or not to disallow ordinances. These which had been made hitherto by the board of the Company were now made by the Administrator in Council and required the assent of the High Commissioner before they had validity. He had particular instructions to veto any legislation which discriminated against Africans, except in respect of liquor and fire arms. The Administrator also had the power to make regulations under existing legislation. The command of the military and the police came under the High Commissioner through an officer called the Commandant General. This latter post was often held in conjunction with that of Resident Commissioner, and the two posts were formally merged between 1909 and 1913.

The Colonial Office further insisted that there must be some supervision of the Company's internal activities. The South African office under Rutherfoord Harris had been at Kimberley in 1889–91 but was then transferred to Cape Town. With the resignation in 1896 of both Rhodes and Harris it became less important, most of the business now being transacted from London directly to and from Salisbury. The Company's minutes and resolutions under the new order had to be sent to the Colonial Office insofar as they concerned administration and not commerce. The Secretary of State could cancel or amend them. He also had the right to remove the Company's directors or officials.

These imperial powers were not mere window-dressing, but they meant less in practice than in theory. The Resident Commissioner, especially if he was also in command of the police and the army, had little time to deal with more general questions, nor did he possess an executive staff of his own. Much depended on the individual holder of the post, and the examples of vigilance cited in a well known study[5] are largely confined to the period in office of a particular Resident Commissioner, Sir Marshall Clarke who was far from typical. His successors were mediocrities who did little. The High Commissioner was Governor of Cape Colony and after the Boer War of the Transvaal too. He finally became Governor General of the Union of South Africa, and he was too busy to deal with a colony which soon became a back water. As for the provision about the minutes of the London Board, it was easy enough for the directors to avoid it by communicating privately among themselves and with the Administrator.

More significant than the arrangements for imperial control were those for settler representation. The new Legislative Council was to have ten members, the Administrator, five nominated by the Company with the Colonial Secretary's approval, and four elected on a property-cum-literacy qualification by resident British subjects. There was no colour bar but in practice only a handful of Africans qualified.[6] The purpose of the franchise was not so much to exclude Blacks (whom no one thought of seriously in that capacity anyway) as to cut out poor Whites coming up from the Transvaal.

There were conflicting opinions about the wisdom of a partly elected Council. Joseph Chamberlain believed it would serve as a check on Rhodes. Moreover ever since his days in the municipal politics of Birmingham he had had a strong penchant for local government. Rhodes and Milner thought it would have the opposite effect – which was why Rhodes supported it and Milner had misgivings. Milner saw that the elected representatives of the settlers were certain to be illiberal

[5] Claire Palley, *The Constitutional History and Law of Southern Rhodesia 1888–1965*, Oxford, 1966, 173 et sq.
[6] There were fifty-one on the first electoral roll. The number was 500 on the eve of Federation in 1953. No black man became a member of the Legislative Assembly.

on the native question, but he saw too that Chamberlain and Rhodes would have British opinion on their side, and that opposition to a representative element would – ironically as it may seem in the light of later events – appear hostile to the principles of liberty and progress. No great difficulty arose, therefore, in drafting the new constitution.

The system that emerged gave the Administrator much power. He presided over both the Executive and the Legislative Councils. Even when he lost his built-in majority on the latter – parity came in 1903 and an elected majority four years later – his position remained very strong. No financial measure could be introduced except on his initiative, and in practice it was difficult for the elected members to dictate policy since almost any change that they wanted involved extra expenditure. As for the other potential constriction on his freedom of manoeuvre, the High Commissioner, there was little interference except occasionally on native affairs. The Executive Council carefully discussed every ordinance before it went to the Legislative Council, and most of its members also sat on that body too. The advantage which a well briefed and informed group, even if in a minority, possesses in such conditions needs no emphasis.

Milton was both head of the Civil Service and Secretary for Native Affairs. He was therefore responsible for two separate administrative systems which corresponded with the division of the country into 'two nations' – a dichotomy which has remained from that day to this. The Chief Native Commissioners of Matabeleland and Mashonaland[7] reported direct to him, heading in their respective provinces a hierarchy of Native and Assistant Native Commissioners whose task was to collect revenue and administer justice. The Administrator also controlled the magistrates and civil commissioners who were responsible for the white population. Constitutionally his position was in many respects like that of a Colonial Governor but with two important differences; first he was responsible to the Chartered Company and only indirectly to the Crown; secondly he had an indefinite tenure, unlike the customary four years or so of the typical Governor. There were in fact only two Administrators between 1898 and the ending of Company rule twenty-five years later. The result was that he became much more identified with local white sentiment than the Governor of, for example, Kenya.

This tendency was enhanced by the character of the Company's officials. Milton naturally tended to recruit from South Africa, and so the tradition in Salisbury came to be that of Cape Town rather than Whitehall. This was appropriate in a country which was in so many respects – franchise, law, and white population – a northern extension of Cape Colony, but it led to an important contrast with the other non self-governing territories under the Colonial Office. In most of them the officials were based on London; they moved from one colony to another and to Whitehall in the course of a career which usually ended with retirement in Britain. In Southern Rhodesia the official corps like the Administrator was an integrated

---

[7] In 1913 this division was abolished and Sir Herbert Taylor, Chief Commissioner for Matabeleland, became Chief Commissioner for the whole colony.

part of the country's white population and had close ties with it. The situation was perpetuated under Responsible Government, for in practice the Company's officials became the Civil Service of the new self-governing colony which incorporated many of the Company's traditions and procedures. Southern Rhodesian officials tended to be the products of South African – later of Rhodesian – schools and of South African universities. They did not have the English upper middle-class accent or the education at a public school and at Oxford or Cambridge, characteristic of the colonial officials in the territories north of the Zambesi.

This perhaps is the reason for a certain element of 'chip-on-the-shoulder' resentment shown by some of the Southern Rhodesian officials when they had to negotiate with their Colonial Office opposite numbers, and it was not helped by an irritating air of unconscious superiority on the part of the latter. Moreover from the very start the Company had a bad name and few friends in the Colonial Office, especially after the death in 1897 of Edward Fairfield who had been its strongest supporter. If the officials had had their way the charter would probably not have survived at all. What saved it were the links on the top level between the politicians and the directors. The divergent traditions and social differences in the world of officialdom are more important than the historian always appreciates. It is by no means fanciful to see in them one important reason, though not the only one, why the attempt in the 1950s to create a Central African Federation ended in failure.

One cause of Colonial Office dislike for the Company had been a well founded distrust of the quality of its servants. Milton's great success was that he soon removed this cause of criticism. Colquhoun had been a prickly pedant insistent on his 'rights'. Jameson had been an erratic adventurer prepared to gamble on the turn of a card. Grey had been an engaging idealist tilting vaguely at windmills. Milton was the first Administrator whose abilities actually warranted his title. He reorganized the whole system, firmly refused to employ the down and out job-seekers thronging Salisbury during and after the rebellion, and brought in his new men from the south. A criticism levelled at his appointees was that cricket, to which he was devoted, often seemed their principal qualification. However they appear to have been none the worse for that, and they helped to uphold the honour of the colony in its first match with the MCC; a Rhodesia XI against Lord Hawke's XI at Bulawayo in 1899.

Milton was not devoid of defects. He was an engrosser of power and reluctant to delegate. He was criticized with some justice for becoming too much absorbed in detail. He was also criticized for his unwillingness to visit Bulawayo. At this time and long after the capital of Matabeleland was commercially much more important than Salisbury, and after the rail link had been completed in 1902, there was no difficulty about the journey. Probably Milton's reluctance stemmed from his original distaste for the place when he arrived in 1896. These were venial faults. The country's debt to him is great and indisputable.

Just as peace seemed to be settling on the Rhodesian scene hostilities erupted nearby, which were bound to effect the colony. It is unnecessary to discuss the precise responsibility for the South African War. One can, however, safely say that the clash between Afrikaner nationalism and British imperial strategy made war highly probable, and that the likelihood was enhanced both by the Jameson Raid and by the personalities who held the key posts, Kruger, Milner, Chamberlain. (Not, for once, Rhodes, who played no significant part in events in South Africa after 1895.) War broke out on October 11 1899.

Some 1,700 men out of a total white population of about 11,000 volunteered to fight. This is a remarkably high figure, but one has to remember that the Rhodesia of that day contained a large number of young men who knew how to ride and shoot and were familiar with the veld. They also had a great dislike for the Transvaalers and regarded the British cause as entirely righteous. The Rhodesia Regiment under Plumer played an important part in the relief of Mafeking. The British South Africa Police was also active in the war and the Chartered Company did all it could to co-operate in the dispatch of the Rhodesia Field Force which consisted of some 5,000 men from Britain and many parts of the Empire, who were transported via Beira into Rhodesia to attack the Transvaal from the north. Naturally enough some hardship accrued to the settlers. The Boers cut the railway from the south to Bulawayo and the cost of necessities soared. On the other hand Salisbury, which was now the only town of importance with a railway link to the outside world, flourished, enjoying a short boom which soon collapsed after the war.

Before the war was over Rhodes was dead. His malady had been gaining on him during the last few years. His death came as no surprise to Jameson and the few who knew how ill he was, but the outside world did not expect it. He visited England in the summer of 1901 and learned of the seriousness of his condition from an eminent heart specialist. He put the final touches to his will, entertained a large party including Grey and Winston Churchill at his shooting lodge in Scotland, travelled by motor car on the continent with Jameson and Beit, sailed from Brindisi to Egypt where he was able to observe that the Cairo end of his dream railway was advancing southwards, and returned to Cape Town, already a dying man. His remaining weeks were made miserable by the scandal of Princess Radziwill who had forged his name to numerous cheques and against whom he had to give evidence in court. By late February it was clear to all around him that the end was near. Indeed his friends must have wished that it was nearer, as they saw him struggling for breath in the midsummer heat at his seaside cottage at Muizenberg. He died on March 26, some three months short of his forty-ninth birthday. He had packed much into those years.

His body lay in state at Groote Schuur, and then in the Parliament Building in Cape Town. After the service at the Cathedral, the body was conveyed in Rhodes's own private train on the long journey through Kimberley, Vryburg, Mafeking to Bulawayo where a second funeral service was held. On April 10 the coffin was drawn on a gun carriage up into the Matopos to be buried at the place he had chosen – 'The View of the World'. The route was lined by thousands of Ndebele who gave to their dead conqueror the royal salute reserved for Ndebele Kings.

At the side of the grave Rudyard Kipling read the famous lines which he had composed as an epitaph and which are inscribed on Rhodes's memorial at Cape Town.[8] But the granite slab beneath which he is buried bears merely the plain inscription 'Here lie the remains of Cecil John Rhodes'. He had wished his funeral to be 'big and simple, barbaric if you like', and his wish had been granted.

The year of Rhodes's death coincided with a profound change in the purpose and prospects of the country that bore his name. In May the peace of Vereeniging brought the Boer War to an end, and with it an important chapter in the history of Britain's foreign policy. The route to India via the Cape now seemed secure for the foreseeable future. Indeed it was to be secure for as long as it was needed – through two world wars until India achieved independence and the British discovered to their surprise that they could get along quite well without the brightest jewel in the imperial crown.

There had been three principal driving forces behind the creation of Southern Rhodesia. Cecil Rhodes himself regarded it as a base for future extension of British power to the north – 'Cape to Cairo'.

The Pioneers, and the Victoria Volunteers – the men on the ground who worked and who fought when they had to – went in search of gold above all else, with cattle as a consolation prize.

Finally there was the motive which prompted Lord Salisbury to grant the original charter; the need to safeguard British paramountcy in the Cape, its hinterland and shifting frontier, to block the ambitions of the Transvaal, placate the Cape Parliament and create a counterpoise to Kruger.

Yet by 1902 all these motives had vanished. 'Cape to Cairo' had ceased to be a reality, however much Rhodes may have deluded himself, when in 1895 the Foreign Office accepted German objections to a corridor between the Congo and German East Africa. Lord Salisbury had never believed in it. One can see now that he was right. A railway line running from south to north was not the way to open up Africa. The development of sea ports and lateral lines running into the interior on an east–west axis made far better sense and was in fact what happened.

---

[8] The last verse reads:

> There, till the vision he foresaw
> Splendid and whole arise,
> And unimagined Empires draw
> To council 'neath his skies,
> The immense and brooding spirit still
> Shall quicken and control.
> Living he was the land, and dead,
> His soul shall be her soul.

11

The Rule of the Company 1902–18

Whoever were going to determine the way Rhodesia was to go, they would not be black. With remarkable speed after the rebellions the Africans ceased to count politically. This was the penalty of a conquest as complete and apparently conclusive as any in history. Of course the Whites had to take some account of their subject peoples in terms of economics, but politically the Africans became literally a silent majority for more than half a century. As Mr A. J. Wills points out, a commission of 'chartered' directors visiting the country only ten years after a black rebellion which had threatened the very existence of white rule could make a lengthy report in which the only reference to the Africans was in relation to shortage of labour for the mines.[1]

Perhaps this is not too surprising. Even today it is extraordinary how easily in this highly-segregated social system one can forget that Africans exist, save as cooks, servants, gardeners and waiters, although they outnumber the Whites by twenty-five to one and everybody is now aware of their political aspirations. Even jostling in the streets of Salisbury and Bulawayo where the races mingle freely the visitor soon finds himself almost unconsciously noticing only Whites. Seventy years ago when the rebellions had been crushed and before the Africans became articulate, how much easier it must have been to ignore them.

The impact of European conquest on the African way of life, whether that of the Ndebele or the Shona, was far greater than almost any white man of the time appreciated. It was a complete revolution. To say this is not at all to say that their way of life had been idyllic. On the contrary it had been in many respects nasty and brutish, and it certainly tended to be short. But it was to them an ordered and predictable system – even witchcraft, so fiercely denounced by missionaries and officials, had an accepted and recognized place. It was above all

---

[1] A. J. Wills, *An Introduction to the History of Central Africa*, 3rd ed., Oxford, 1973, 225.

freedom – freedom to live in accordance with customs and usages, superstitions and rituals handed down from immemorial antiquity; and freedom not to live in accordance with the overt and tacit rules of a European cash economy.

No belief was more deeply cherished by the white settler than the conviction that the 'Kaffir' male was incurably idle, and that in his pre-conquest state – apart from occasional raiding and slaughtering – his only occupations were drink and sex. As late as the 1970s a research student enquiring about the African policy of the Federation was told by an elderly ex-Federal politician of Scots origin: 'Dinna ye ken, Laddie, that all a native needs is a pot o' beer and a woman'. This view of African society was – and is now recognized to be – quite erroneous. The man had his tasks both of labour and ritual to perform, just as much as the woman. He was certainly not a drone. Even if we set aside the sexual aspect, his removal for months on end to work for a wage made necessary by the imposition of the hut tax for just that purpose was bound to disrupt the whole traditional, time-honoured order of tribal society.

These consequences were little understood at the time. The white man brought up in the Victorian creed of thrift, individualism, self-help and hard work saw nothing immoral – indeed quite the contrary – in compelling the African to enter the labour market. There was, after all, no question of slavery, and the Company now had to watch its step in the matter of forced labour. The Jameson days were over. But Rhodesia had to be developed, and as with all new countries – Australia, Canada, the American west – shortage of labour was the chronic problem. Mining was labour-intensive and very disagreeable – who would ever mine for fun? – and the same need for labour dominated the country's only other industry, agriculture, although this was at any rate more familiar and less unpleasant. The African did not in the least want to work for the white man. He, therefore, had to be compelled indirectly by fiscal pressure. It was hoped that, having thus entered, if unwillingly, the advanced wage economy of his conquerors, he would discover new needs, aspire to new luxuries and so be happy to become, as Wilson Fox, the Company's General Manager put it in an important memorandum, one of 'the privates of the industrial army in every department of work'.

Wilson Fox's *Memorandum on Problems of Development and Policy* (1910) is a clear statement of the official policy of the Company's directors in the Edwardian period. In effect it was the doctrine of assimilation. The Africans' role would be that of a black proletariat and the sooner tribalism, chieftainship and the other ossified institutions of the past vanished altogether, the better it would be for the Africans themselves and their white rulers. The fortunes of both were bound up with the development of the new colony. The same principle applied to the reserves. These were a temporary expedient to shield the natives from the first harsh impact of the white man's economy. They too would wither away with the process of assimilation. As Mr Philip Mason puts it

The Africans of Rhodesia would gradually become a working class, and would grow more and more like the British working class – and perhaps though this was not stated in so many words, there would be men in Rhodesia as in Britain who would rise from the ranks of the working class to positions of wealth and power.

But this latter possibility was precisely where the rub lay. It was one thing for the Administrator, the London Directors and the top officials of the Company to take an Olympian view of the desirable progress of a black working class. It was quite another for the less affluent settlers to accept it. The professional men, doctors, lawyers, accountants could look after themselves in an integrated society. The white artisan, who drew a high wage just because he was white, could not. He saw integration as a threat to his standards, and he and his like constituted the electoral majority which came to control the Legislative Council and to which after 1923 the Rhodesian government was responsible. Even before 1923, when the Company ruled, it had been ill-placed to resist the strongly felt sentiments of the elected members who could rely on radical support at Westminster and on all those vague ideas which since the days of the Durham Report linked the cause of white colonial self-government with that of 'progress'.

The settler majority had a further point on their side. Whatever ideas had actuated the settlement after the rebellion, integration was not one of them. It was a later concept produced by the logic of the economic situation confronting the Company. The original settlement was intended to be one of separation between the two races, with all power in the hands of the victorious one. This did not mean ruthless exploitation of the vanquished. On the contrary, most of the victors genuinely believed that the Blacks would now be happier and more prosperous than they had been under their old rulers. But the settlers could justifiably argue that, although maltreatment of the natives should be deplored and prevented, a policy leading however distantly to racial integration, as in Brazil or the West Indies, was not a part of their bargain. Separation, except in so far as labour on a temporary basis was required for mines, farms and domestic service, was the only safe system if a twentieth century white minority ruling class was to dwell in the same land as a conquered black majority barely emerged from the Iron Age.

This attitude was reinforced by fear and hate – the twin legacies of the rebellion to both sides. White Rhodesians of that era would no doubt have vigorously denied such feelings. Black Rhodesians were still inarticulate. It so happens that in 1912 an intelligent Belgian lawyer, Henri Rolin, visited Rhodesia at some length and wrote an account of the social, legal, and constitutional system of the country.[2] In a minor way his book is like De Tocqueville's *Democratie en Amérique*, a classic work of shrewd observation by an unprejudiced, realistic and far from unsympathetic foreigner. This is what he wrote about racial attitudes:

The white man will not take his meals at the same table as the black; he will

[2] Henri Rolin, *Les Lois et l'Administration de la Rhodesie*, Brussels and Paris, 1913.

not meet him on the footpath of the streets;[3] he travels by rail in separate wagons; he forbids him in principle, though with certain exceptions, access to private property; he relegates him at night to 'locations' outside the urban centres. The farmer sees him as a pilferer [*depredateur*] and cattle-thief and fears his neighbourhood. Those who know the natives add besides that the antipathy of black for white is not less, and that is easily to be understood in view of the brusqueness, the complete lack of consideration with which the European often treats the native.[4]

Rolin noticed too that this contempt for the Africans in or out of their presence was more freely expressed the lower one went down in the white social scale. 'The *petit commerçant* will not hesitate to tell you that the black is a "stupid animal" ... Educated men are naturally more prudent "more discreet" in their language.' This is no less true today. One does not often hear crudities in the Salisbury or Bulawayo Clubs. Spend half an hour at the Long Bar at Meikle's, and it is a different story. Rolin recognized that there were white men with a genuinely different attitude. 'Missionaries, officials of the department of Native Affairs, occasional philanthropists display a sympathy for the blacks which is sometimes very effective.' But his general picture is only slightly modified. '... two castes ... below the whites the blacks ... One has only to see them in their sordid villages, half-naked ... to appreciate the immense difference which divides the victors from the vanquished.'[5]

Nowhere was this difference, this hate and fear more vividly displayed than in regard to that touchstone of race relations – sex. To understand it one has to remember the tradition of Cape Colony whence most of the early settlers came. There had been fleeting and illicit unions between the early Dutch settlers and the Hottentots or with the Malay slaves imported to supply the latter's deficiencies as workers. Such episodes, the result of the imbalance of the sexes within the white population, came to be disapproved of and their offspring stigmatized as time went on and as that imbalance was remedied. The white man under many influences, religion, guilt, remorse, white women, began to regard such intercourse with shame,[6] but above all to consider marriage with the inferior race as an act of much deeper degradation than a casual affair. What, however, seemed the deepest degradation of all was any relationship between a white woman and a black man. For this there could be no excuse whatever and it was taken for granted that it could only occur as a result of *force majeure* by the black man, or criminal immorality on the part of the white woman.

These social and sexual attitudes led to legislation some of which even on paper

---

[3] Plenty of White Rhodesians can still remember – a few with nostalgia – the days when an African had to get off the footpath if he met a white man.

[4] Quoted in *Birth of a Dilemma*, 270.

[5] Quoted, Mason, op. cit., 245.

[6] It is one reason why African servants were and still are almost always men, so as to keep the young white male free from temptation.

– and more of it in practice – discriminated openly against the Blacks. In 1903 two important measures went through the Legislative Council and were duly ratified. One was the Immorality Suppression Ordinance which made extra-marital intercourse between a black man and a white woman illegal, the maximum penalty for the man being five years hard labour, the woman two. There was however no corresponding penalty for a white man engaging in relations with a black woman, and the frequent efforts made by various women's organizations e.g. the Rhodesia Women's League to 'equalize' the law ended in failure.[7] The truth is that Rhodesia was a white male-dominated society. Affairs with black women might be censured – mentioned with 'a shrug of the shoulders or at most a smile of contempt'[8] but there were too many going on for white men to feel inclined to make them illegal; and there was also the awkward problem of the non-discriminatory services tendered by black prostitutes. The reaction of Africans to this differentiation might be expected to be one of resentment and the evidence that we have suggests that it was.

In the same year there was passed an ordinance which imposed the death penalty, at judicial discretion, for attempted rape. Actual rape was already a capital offence. The new measure did not discriminate between black and white, but in practice neither rape nor attempted rape involved the death penalty if the offence was proved against a white man or against a black man assaulting a black woman. It was only where a black man was convicted of raping or trying to rape a white woman that judges felt obliged to impose capital punishment. The arguments used for the 1903 measure are interesting. One was that a white woman who admitted to having been actually raped by a black man would find social life in the white community impossible thereafter, but she could give evidence of an unsuccessful attempt without this stigma, and therefore the attempt ought to merit the death sentence too. Another was that the severity of the law would be a prophylactic against lynching. In fact Rhodesian Whites were not addicted to lynch law, unlike other frontier communities. Only two attempts are recorded – the earlier one in 1893 being stopped by Dr Jameson with the characteristic and effective argument that Mashonaland was expecting a boom which would be wrecked if the world saw that it had no respect for law and order. He then stood drinks all round to the ring leaders.[9]

Whether or not the severity of the law discouraged lynching – and it may have done so – the discrimination involved must have been resented by the Africans; and their feelings cannot have been assuaged by a series of notorious verdicts from white juries. There were some remarkable acquittals of white men accused on the strongest evidence of murdering black men and some equally astonishing con-

[7] See Chapter 21 for the difficulties created by this problem for Garfield Todd in 1957.

[8] Mason, op. cit., 242, quoting the *Rhodesia Herald*, June 20, 1913. It would be wrong to regard the practice as widespread or normal, simply not highly abnormal.

[9] The case was not one of rape but of a particularly brutal quadruple murder of two white men, a white woman and her child. The offender, 'Zulu Jim', was publicly hanged after a proper trial six weeks later.

victions of black men charged on the thinnest evidence with rape or attempted rape of white women. Until 1899 cases involving both races were tried by a judge and assessors. But in 1899 trial by jury was introduced and since the jury was empanelled from the voters, no black man ever served. The change was one of the first fruits of settler representation, but in 1911 even Sir Charles Coghlan, the leader of the elected members and hitherto a staunch supporter of the jury system, changed his mind as a result of a peculiarly perverse verdict and supported the appointment of 'special juries' of five persons selected as suitable for dealing with cases where Africans and Europeans were involved. Since 1927 criminal cases involving an African defendant have been tried by a judge and assessors, just as all criminal cases were before 1899. There can be no doubt that the ordinary white jury could not always be relied upon to play fair in cases where both Africans and Europeans were concerned. Prejudice was too deep, the sense of white solidarity too strong; and how could justice, even if it was done, be *seen* to be done to a member of the conquered race by a jury composed exclusively of his conquerors?

Economic development pointed towards assimilation. The legacy of fear and hate left by the rebellion pointed towards segregation. Other forces were at work sometimes reinforcing one trend, sometimes the other. The influence of the Colonial Office was in practice on the side of segregation though for creditable reasons – the paternalistic tradition of kindly treatment of Africans by Native Commissioners alert to prevent exploitation. The influence of missionaries on the other hand was bound to work at least to some extent on the side of assimilation. It is not easy for the exponents of a religion which preaches that all men are equal in the sight of God to support physical segregation on earth, although some Christian denominations, for example the Dutch Reformed Church, have contrived to do so. Moreover it was an essential part of the inculcation of Christianity that the falsity of the old tribal beliefs should be exposed and the teaching of the Old and New Testaments – Africans like Afrikaners found the Old the easier to understand – should be put in their place. In other words the white man's values would replace the superstitions of the black man. But if he was to become a part of the long heritage of European civilization, how could the black man be expected to remain cut off from white society in a moral and physical enclave of his own?

The attitude of the missionaries to the Blacks and of the settlers to the missionaries was ambivalent. The whole matter became important after 1897, for the defeat of the rebellions brought with it the longed-for Christian breakthrough. The early missionaries had predicted that the gospel could only penetrate these benighted parts if it was preceded by the sword – and they were right. The gods and spirits of the Africans had failed them. The God of the conqueror had prevailed, and as so often in past history, the conquered, hesitantly and with many reservations scarcely recognized by those who had 'converted' them, accepted the creed of the conqueror. The immemorial resistance of the Shona and Ndebele to Christianity began to melt. The success of the missionaries should not be exaggerated. By 1928 it was reckoned that of a population of about a million Africans some 86,000 were Christians. But the missionary influence was greater than this figure suggests. Their approach was via education, and African education – no doubt for the most part of a highly elementary nature – was their exclusive preserve until 1920. It was administered by them and financed too, apart from a few meagre grants made by the Company. Education was the way to modest advancement in the new African society and the missionaries controlled it. They became, as a Native Commissioner observed, the real rulers of large areas of rural Mashonaland.

The missionaries were uneasily placed in relation to both races. To the Blacks they were part of the white establishment. With their substantial grants of land and their control over its use they were like white chiefs, only possessing much more power than any black chief under the new dispensation. It was difficult not to behave in a semi-authoritarian way when operating within the framework of white ascendancy, and at heart most missionaries probably would not have wished it otherwise. To the white settlers, however, they were suspect precisely because of the long-term implications of their work. Individual missionaries might in the early days become, like Native Commissioners, preservers rather than assimilators, anxious to keep their black 'children' from the moral evils of the 'locations', but nothing could alter the ultimate effect of Christianizing the Africans. It was bound to 'Europeanize' them; and this seemed fraught with many perils. The settlers could not overtly object to the conversion of the Africans, whatever they privately said over their whiskies at sun down, but they could and did express doubts about African education as conducted by missionaries. The missionary thus became a faintly suspect figure within the white community, especially if he took any part in politics – witness the prejudices which even a man with the charisma of Mr Garfield Todd did not quite surmount.

There was never a clear-cut distinction in practice between the partisans of assimilation and of segregation. The relations between the races developed as a result of haphazard pressures, ambiguous doctrines, unexpected events. The keenest assimilationists, Wilson Fox or the members of the 1914 Commission on Native Reserves, realized that some land had to be kept as a reserve to cushion the impact of the white economy on black tribal society. The supporters of segregation wanted black labour for their mines and farms, and needed Africans with some smattering of education to do the work. Policy thus proceeded by a series of compromises. Rhodesia did not become, as the logic of one argument entailed, a country divided into great ranches and farms interspersed with mines and a few urban centres – the whole system operated by white landowners and business men supported by a geographically and socially mobile black proletariat. Nor did it become, as the logic of the other entailed, a gigantic native reserve.

These compromises can be seen in many spheres. In 1903 there arose the question of substituting a poll tax for the hut tax. The Chamber of Mines, the Legislative Council and the Administrator wanted to fix it at £2. Father Richartz, a leading spokesman of the missions, thought this excessive. He was backed by the

Resident Commissioner, and the Secretary of State vetoed the ordinance. In the end the figure was fixed at £1. The imperial Government had defeated the assimilationists.

Then there was the problem of land where the reverse occurred. In Mashonaland grants had never been made to Europeans on the lavish scale which prevailed in Matabeleland, and it was not too difficult to allocate what seemed at the time adequate reserves as guaranteed by the 1898 Order in Council. In Matabeleland it was another matter. The original reserves were now recognized to be quite unsuitable. Rhodes had negotiated the surrender of the *indunas* on the basis that they could return to their old grazing grounds, but he had only done this by persuading the white owners, most of whom had not even occupied their farms, to allow the Ndebele undisturbed possession for the next two years. How far this was understood by the *indunas* is not clear. Certainly they made it a cause of complaint that at the end of two years they found themselves liable to pay rent to a white landlord. Grey had hoped to implement Rhodes's promises by large scale purchase, but the Company lacked the money. It did not even have the strength to recover some of the land which the grantees of the Jameson era ought to have forfeited through non-compliance with the conditions of grant. When Milton attempted to do this there was an uproar on the Legislative Council – some of the elected members had connexions with the absentee companies – and little or nothing was done.

The result, in spite of the efforts of the Native Commissioners entrusted with the task of demarcating the reserves, was highly unsatisfactory. There was no land worth having to allocate. In any case it was the policy of the Company as far as possible to keep the Ndebele on European farms, where their labour was badly needed. Since there had been no adequate survey, boundaries were anything but clear, and the Commissioners were further handicapped by lack of any definite criteria to adopt. It has to be remembered however that at this time and for another two decades the reserves were meant to be only temporary expedients – a refuge for Africans who could not cope with the white economy and were not yet able to become individual tenants of land or willing to become landless labourers. The doctrine of assimilation was still in the ascendancy and the reserves were expected to wither away in due course. But when in the early 1920s the rival concept of segregation began to gain the day and the reserves, delimited with a very different purpose, came to be regarded as the permanent African share of the land, their inadequacy ought to have been obvious.

The same conflict of purposes affected the treatment of non-rural land. We have seen how desperate was the white need for labour and how reluctantly the Africans supplied it. Efforts were made to import labour from overseas, but India, one potential source, was vetoed by the Viceroy who made it clear that Indians must not be treated like Africans or for that matter like the Chinese; and China, another possibility, was ruled out after the so-called 'Chinese slavery' scandal on the Rand. The West Indies, Abyssinia, Somaliland and Aden were also considered but without result. It was just as well, for one can only echo Professor Gann that success 'would have turned the country into a sociologist's paradise and a statesman's hell'.[10]

Local labour was the only solution. The logic of the assimilationist case ought to have led to the creation of an African urban and mining proletariat displaced altogether from the rural areas, somewhat as occurred in England in the course of the Industrial Revolution. That process of course was responsible also for great hardship. It is not to the discredit of the early settlers that a system came into being which in the short term mitigated the hardship, although it was a victory for segregationism and has had lasting consequences for race relations. African labourers were put into 'locations' – the urban version of a reserve, where they either rented or built their own huts. The assumption was that they would live there temporarily, apart from wife and family, while they earned enough to pay their hut or poll tax and return to their permanent homes in the rural reserves.

The 'locations' being all male – or at least wifeless-communities – were inevitably places of immorality, drink and rowdiness, for the inhabitants were deprived of most of their rural recreations; they could not hunt, or make the ritual animal sacrifices required by their religion, or even brew 'Kaffir' beer which also had a ritual significance but now had to be sold and drunk under license and must not contain more than three per cent alcohol. When one remembers too that the sanitary habits of people accustomed to living in small communities surrounded by limitless land are not likely to conduce to good health in a semi-urban environment, it is hardly surprising that the 'locations' were kept as far away as possible from European habitation and that Africans were strictly forbidden to live outside them. It may be true that the system at least obviated the terrible urban slums which resulted from the unchecked influx of country dwellers into the cities and towns of England and Europe a century earlier. But it did so at a price – the price of assuming that separation was the norm and that the 'natural' state of affairs was for Africans to lead a primitive life on the land reserved for them by law, with occasional interruptions strictly controlled, when they worked for white employers in the vicinity of towns.

Moreover the system presupposed other checks on freedom. One of the features of Southern Africa which must strike any modern visitor is the elaborate network of regulations about passes and registration certificates which apply to Africans. Even before the rebellion passes had been required for Rhodesian Africans. By 1910 every male African was obliged to carry a registration certificate and produce it when asked. If he went outside his own district he had to have a visiting pass. It lasted twenty-one days and thereafter had to be renewed. If he sought work in an urban area he had to have a special pass for the purpose. There were many arguments in favour of these rules. They helped to prevent urban over-crowding and other evils. The fact remains that in England identity cards were only introduced as a reluctant necessity of total war, were required universally not selectively, and were abolished as soon as possible after war had ended.

[10] Gann, op. cit., 177.

A final illustration of the clash of the two principles comes from the Department of Native Affairs. The Native Commissioner had a more direct control over his district than in most of British Colonial Africa. Rhodes and Grey had never intended the Ndebele Chiefs to be more than relatively minor paid officials with a certain delegated duty of notifying deaths, epidemics and crimes, collecting taxes and catching criminals. The same applied to those Mashona Chiefs who were regarded as trustworthy after 1897. Juridically, authority came downwards through Native Commissioners from the Administrator who could appoint and dismiss Chiefs, as long as the High Commissioner agreed, and even divide or amalgamate tribes. District headmen to assist the Chiefs were appointed by the Secretary for Native Affairs who, throughout Milton's time, was the Administrator under a different hat. It was direct rule on the model of Natal, not indirect rule as in North Western Rhodesia or Nyasaland, where important Chiefs had rights under treaties which could not be disregarded. The Ndebele monarchy had been smashed, the Rozwi Mamboship was only a memory, but in Barotseland, to take an example, Lewanika's kingdom was a reality.

This power in the hands of the Native Department really meant that the Commissioners did not so much guide and rule through as replace the Chiefs in their districts. But if they were in this respect more powerful than their northern counterparts, they were in other respects more restricted. North of the Zambesi the District Officer or Native Commissioner had the backing of authority, ultimately the Colonial Office, behind him and was part of a single official corps, an administrative hierarchy the apex of which was the Governor to whose post he could himself aspire as the summit of a successful career. In Southern Rhodesia he was part of an administrative system which was quite separate from the ordinary Civil Service. Its apex was the Chief Native Commissioner, who was responsible to the Secretary for Native Affairs, i.e. the Administrator. The young official could not go higher than that, and there was little or no interchange with the officials of other departments. The Native Department thus became a sort of *imperium in imperio* with its own traditions, rules and *esprit de corps*, detached from the rest of the Civil Service and never quite trusted by it.

It also inspired the suspicion of non-official opinion, a factor far more powerful than in the northern territories.[11] To European miners and farmers, the Native Commissioner was a brake on their freedom to recruit African workers. He had to steer an awkward line between the disapprobation of the Colonial Office, expressed through the Resident Commissioner, of anything that looked like forced labour, and the pressure of the assimilationists, both the officials of the Company and the settlers who needed African labour in order to develop the country. Wilson Fox expressed the official Company view in its most uncompromising form writing, in the Memorandum already quoted, that the Native Commissioner could not but become 'a retrograde factor in the corporate life of the country' and he

[11] In 1910 there were only 1,500 Europeans in Northern Rhodesia and 700 in Nyasaland. In Southern Rhodesia there were 20,000.

added, perhaps cynically but not untruly, 'he consciously or sub-consciously realises that when there is no native district there will be no Native Commissioner'.

The Native Department might seem to the Company's theoreticians and the labour-hungry settlers an over-fussy, zealous, paternalistic protector of Africans, but it did not follow that it seemed like that to the Africans. On the contrary, in spite of various efforts to set up separate institutions for the recruitment of labour, the Native Commissioner could not avoid being involved in the process. He was after all paid by the Company, not by the Colonial Office, and he had to do something to carry out Company policy. To the Africans he probably appeared no less of an agent for white exploitation than to the settlers he appeared a pre-server of reactionary tribalism.

In fact the influence of the Native Department tended to be in favour of segregation and against assimilation. Its effect on the development of Southern Rhodesia was in one sense preservationist and Wilson Fox was right, but what was being preserved was not as in other colonial territories the old Chiefly powers and the traditional tribal system through the technique of indirect rule which could have helped to ease the transition from the Iron Age to the twentieth century. What was becoming crystallized was a system invented by the Department itself which substituted white Chiefs for black Chiefs and endowed the Commissioner himself with quasi-despotic though benevolent powers in the settling of disputes, allocation of lands, building of huts, location of kraals – in fact almost all the non-religious ordering of tribal society. It is difficult to believe that any of the in-terested parties, the Company, the Colonial Office, the settlers, the Africans or their Chiefs actually wanted this particular solution. It was one of those things that somehow just happen and having happened take on a quality of ineradicable permanence.

The political future of Southern Rhodesia, after twelve years of exploration, war, rebellion and war again, revolved around two main questions, both of which were matters for white not black determination. First there was the system of gov-ernment within the territory. Was it to be by the Chartered Company? Or was Southern Rhodesia to become an orthodox British Colony? And if the latter, was it to be a Crown Colony like Kenya or was it to have responsible government on the lines of Natal and Cape Colony before the formation of the Union of South Africa.

The second great question was whether Southern Rhodesia was viable on its own; not merely in economic terms, though this was important, but in social, moral and political terms too. And here there were two broad possibilities. The country might become a part of the Union of South Africa, its fifth province; the possi-bility of this was deliberately left open under the Act constituting the Union, passed by the British Parliament in 1910 – and there was no requirement of Southern Rhodesian consent. Alternatively Southern Rhodesia might look north-wards and join with its namesake over the Zambesi. The former solution was known at the time and subsequently as 'union', the latter as 'amalgamation', and these expressions will be used hereafter.

Cecil Rhodes had never envisaged the indefinite prolongation of Company rule. The charter gave it twenty-five years in the first instance, subject to renewal. Rhodes saw the future as union, with Cape Colony and Natal as a counterpoise to the Transvaal, but only after Responsible Government had been given to the settlers first. He probably took it for granted that some union would then be their choice. The question must have seemed largely academic while he lived. After his death in 1902, the situation in the country changed for the worse. With his charm and his vast private fortune he had been able to do much to smooth the increasingly prickly sentiments of the settlers. At the same time his prestige with the Ndebele *indunas* blurred, at least in some degree, the acerbities of racial confrontation. It was Matabeleland which in those days mattered; Mashonaland, largely ignored by Rhodes, was a backwater. His death led at once to an intensification of settler feeling against the Company.

Later in 1902 when Jameson, who – such were the strange vicissitudes of Southern African politics – had become 'respectable', toured the country along with Alfred Beit, the two men were assailed with bitter complaints about the remoteness of the London Board and the difficulty of obtaining a hearing. Mining royalties, railway rates and the land question all figured prominently, and there was no longer a Cecil Rhodes to mediate between distant directors and the bored, irritable, struggling, impoverished local white inhabitants. To meet some of the difficulty a new Order-in-Council in 1903 provided for parity between official and elected members on the Legislative Council with the Administrator having a casting vote, and concessions were made over royalties and railway rates, but not on two vital matters; the Company insisted that the colony if and when it became self-governing must accept responsibility for the Company's past administrative (as opposed to any commercial) deficits, and that the unalienated land, i.e. land not granted either to individuals or companies or allocated as native reserves, belonged to the Chartered Company and not to anyone else. There was never to be agreement between the Company and the settlers on either of these issues which were only determined by a judgment from the Judicial Committee of the Privy Council in 1918.

The country remained chronically short of capital. In 1905 the Legislative Council with full support from the Company passed an ordinance which would have allowed the territory to contract its own public debt. The Colonial Office firmly vetoed any such measure as long as the Company remained responsible for the administration of the country and owner of all its assets.

In 1907 the Directors sent out another deputation to enquire into the state of Southern Rhodesia. It recommended some changes. Land titles were to be simplified, the Civil Service reformed, royalties revised. More important, mining should no longer have its previous top-priority in the development programme. European settlement must be accelerated. At 14,000 the white population was far too low. Only a programme of encouraging European farmers could reduce the country's dependence on imports and raise the value of the Company's own assets, in the form of both land and railways. These decisions were to have far-reaching consequences on the land question, which will be considered in a later chapter. They also had a significant demographic effect. Among other things the white population rose by nearly 10,000 between 1907 and 1911 compared with less than 2,000 between 1904 and 1907.

Politically it seemed wise to make further concessions to the pressure for settler representation. There had been requests the previous year, when Lord Selborne, the High Commissioner, toured the country, for the abrogation of the charter and the substitution of representative government under the Crown. He was not prepared to recommend it nor would the imperial Government have agreed, but the Company wished to allay discontent. The Legislative Council was now given a clear majority of elected members by the Company's decision to reduce the 'Officials' from seven to five. Subsequent concessions increased this majority and from 1913 to the end of the Company's rule the balance was twelve to six. The fact remained, however, that the 'Unofficials' could not propose any fiscal measures, nor, under an Order in Council of 1911, could they discuss without the Administrator's leave any 'ordinances interfering with the land and other rights of the Company'. Since finance and the Company's rights were just what the elected members most wanted to discuss, their majority meant a good deal less in practice than it appeared to do on paper.

The increased settler representation, thus informally brought in during 1907, prompted the candidature of a man whose career was to effect the future of the country. Charles (later Sir Charles) Coghlan, a Bulawayo lawyer who had made his career largely in litigation against the Chartered Company, entered the Legislative Council in 1908 and soon became leader of the 'Unofficials'. He was a redoubtable foe of 'chartered' rule and later a strong supporter of Responsible Government as opposed to union with South Africa. The latter question came up very soon after Coghlan's election. A National Convention was held at Durban in October 1908 to consider the unification of the colonies south of the Limpopo. Southern Rhodesia was invited to send delegates to this important assembly with the right to speak but not vote. Coghlan represented the Unofficials, the other delegates being Milton and Sir Lewis Michell. The circumstances were by no means those envisaged by Rhodes. It was union not federation which was going to carry the day, and in the bargaining over seats in the Parliament and their relation to population the Transvaal and Orange Free State gained a disproportionate advantage. Rhodesia, staunchly British, might be inundated by poor Whites from the Transvaal and her native labour interests subordinated to the demands of the Rand. The delegates were all agreed that entry, though not precluded at some future date, was out of the question for the time being.

When therefore the expiry of the charter came up for discussion in 1914, there was little opposition to the grant of a Supplemental Charter for ten years expiring in 1925. This provided that, if the Legislative Council wanted Responsible Government at an earlier date and could show that the country could pay for it, the Crown might set up a new constitution on those lines. Meanwhile, despite the usual grumbles, the Company's rule seemed better than any alternative. As for the vexed question of the land, Whitehall referred it to the Judicial Committee of the Privy Council which took four years to answer. There matters stood when in August from a seemingly cloudless international sky the cataclysm of world war descended.

There is no need to discuss at any length Southern Rhodesia's military role. As in the case of the Boer War the contribution of an intensely patriotic people was remarkable in the light of its slender resources. Some 5,500 white men, out of a population of 27,000, and 2,700 Africans served in the armed forces. Of the Whites 1,720 held commissions, and there can be no question that young Rhodesians were excellent 'officer material'. The First Rhodesia Regiment took part in the early and successful seizure of German South West Africa. It was then disbanded; some of its members left for England to offer their services in the European theatre; others joined the newly formed Second Rhodesia Regiment which embarked at Beira for Mombasa in 1915 to participate in one of the least known campaigns of the war – in German East Africa.

The German commander, General von Lettow-Vorbeck, was a soldier of formidable ability; his instructions were to pin down as many enemy troops as he could, and he proved to be a singularly elusive opponent. After 1915 General Smuts commanded the Allied forces which comprised Indians, Africans, West Indians, British and South Africans as well as Rhodesians. Tsetse fly, fever, dysentery and lack of supplies produced more casualties than shells and bullets. The Second Rhodesia Regiment at one time fell to only 126 men. After experiencing great hardship and discomfort it returned via Beira in April 1917 in a state of depletion and exhaustion to a hero's welcome. There were not enough men in the country for it to be kept going as a unit, and some of the survivors left for Europe where they became absorbed in the South African infantry. Unlike Nyasaland and Mozambique, the Rhodesias, despite a drain on white manpower reminiscent of the Jameson raid, were not threatened by even a sign of an African uprising. Indeed in sharp contrast to South Africa the Rhodesian authorities enlisted African troops, and the First and Second Rhodesian Native Regiments with white officers and a core of white NCOs acquitted themselves well in the German East African campaign. Although von Lettow-Vorbeck's main force was broken late in 1917, he himself at the head of some fifteen hundred men escaped and continued the struggle till the end. Owing to telegraphic difficulties the news of the German surrender in Europe did not reach the area of African hostilities till November 13 and the shots fired that day are supposed to be the last fired in the Great War. The Rhodesian forces were not in on the final scene. The German commander surrendered formally to General Edwards of the King's African Rifles at Abercorn on November 18.

The war did not have a great impact on African society. The number involved in the armed services was only a tiny fraction of the population. That strange disease, 'Spanish' influenza – the last of the great plagues – caused far more deaths than the war itself, especially in Africa where its effects were particularly lethal.

Economically the rising cost of living which a war always brings was counter-balanced by increased income from the agricultural products of the African farmer.

The impact of the war in white society was far greater. Primary producing countries usually do well in war. The demand for munitions caused a world shortage of base metals. The price of Rhodesian ores, such as copper, tungsten, chrome, zinc, antimony and asbestos, shot up. Gold mining also boomed and Wankie coal found a ready market. The Rhodesian economy, stagnant before 1914, received a welcome boost. War gave it an impetus which, in spite of later depressions, never died away; the effect on the development of the country was profound and lasting.

Part 2

A SELF-GOVERNING COLONY

12

Responsible Government 1914–23

No major decision about the country's political future could be made during the war, although the matter was not forgotten and positions began to be taken against the day when Company rule would end. The outbreak of hostilities virtually coincided with the advent of a new administration. Milton had reached the retiring age, and he was succeeded in October 1914 by Sir Drummond Chaplin. With a grandfather who had refused a baronetcy and the background of Harrow, Oxford and the Bar, Chaplin ranked rather higher in the subtle English social hierarchy of the day than Milton, son of a parson and educated at Marlborough. Like Milton he was a protégé of Rhodes. Politically he stood well to the right. He was much influenced by Milner and a close friend of Jameson. He had sat in the Transvaal and Union Assemblies as a 'Progressive', but in Southern Africa as elsewhere these labels need to be translated, and a 'pro-England conservative' is the correct version.

Drummond fully shared his predecessor's orthodox outlook on imperial affairs, but his experience in business, journalism and politics gave him more of a flair for public relations. He quickly spotted the umbrage caused by Milton's neglect of Bulawayo, and made a point of entering his new domain by that route. He revisited it three months later, held an *indaba* in the Matopos and toured the south west which Milton had not visited for many years. He was slightly cynical, rather shy and aloof and far from 'hail fellow well met', but he was devoted to sport and games – always a passport to popularity in Southern Africa – and he and his wife entertained lavishly, although they found Government House somewhat odd:

> This house is most curious – all glass and windows. It is not conveniently planned ... For the money spent they might have had a *vastly* better house, but that can't be helped now.
>
> The worst part of it is that there is no entrance hall at all. You go straight

into the main sitting room off the stoep – nowhere to put hats and coats: a most stupid arrangement. Generally it feels rather as if one were living in the open air and I should be sorry to go through a Johannesburg winter in it.

Anyone who has been to Government House, Salisbury, can see Chaplin's point, but living accommodation was to be the least of his difficulties. Conditions were never 'normal' during his nine years in office. War, its aftermath, and the approaching end of Company rule overshadowed them throughout. Nor was his original appointment devoid of controversy. The Treasurer, Francis Newton, who was an older man, was deemed to have a prior claim by some including himself. Relations were smooth for the time being, but after his retirement in 1919 Sir Francis (as he had now become) was a most effective opponent of the Company's and Chaplin's policy of union with the south.

Then there was the perpetual problem of the Colonial Office. After the end of the Company's rule Chaplin wrote a reply to a courteous letter from Sir John Chancellor, the first Governor. After suitable thanks he went on:

Certainly it was a difficult job: so many people to consider – High Commissioner, Board of Directors, Secretary of State, to say nothing of local politicians with a majority in the Council. Looking back on the last nine years the thing which has perhaps left the clearest impression on my mind is the antagonism, sometimes active, sometimes passive, of the Colonial Office and its officials. The only time we got any sort of assistance was when Milner was Colonial Secretary ... Harcourt was actively hostile; the average Secretary of State, Milner excepted, seemed usually content to leave matters to the officials who seem to have continued this Harcourt tradition.[1]

Harcourt may have inherited something of a family feud from his father, Sir William, one of Rhodes's strongest critics. 'Gott straff Harcourt' was a customary greeting among the Company's executives at London Wall, after the war began. But the antagonism of the Colonial Office ante-dated his tenure. There is no reason to suppose that personalities much affected the matter. The Colonial officials disliked the Company partly because it was an anomaly which did not fit into the established colonial categories – they were to dislike the successor regime for the same reason throughout its existence – and partly because they believed that a commercial company, even one which paid no dividend, was bound to be pulled two ways in its governing role. This was precisely the point so often made by the settlers, and they had the ear of the section of the House of Commons most likely to ask awkward questions. Radicals at that time regarded the Company as 'bad' and the settlers as 'good'. It was not till well after the grant of Responsible

[1] NAR CH8/2/1, Muizenberg, November 1, 1923, Chaplin to Sir John Chancellor. the relevant Colonial Secretaries in Chaplin's time were Lewis Harcourt 1910–15, Bonar Law 1915–16, Walter Long 1916–18, Lord Milner 1918–21, Winston Churchill 1921–22, the Duke of Devonshire 1922–24.

Government that a new syndrome replaced the old; the settlers became 'bad' and the Africans whom few people had hitherto bothered about became 'good'. Wilson Fox, now an MP, wrote to Chaplin on January 3, 1918:

We did our utmost with Walter Long [the Colonial Secretary] but it was no use. He is absolutely under the thumb of Fiddes [Sir George Fiddes, the Permanent Under-Secretary] and although we should now have on form a friendly Colonial Office, so far the running has not been up to our expectations.... Walter Long has the greatest friendship and admiration for you personally ... but he has not the strength to impose his will on his officials. He is frightened to death of questions in the House and gives to our local politicians an importance far beyond their value, mainly because they are able to become vocal through the Radical gang in our deplorable House.[2]

The episode which prompted this outburst is typical of the relationship between the Company, the settlers and the Colonial Office. Jameson and D. O. (later Sir Dougal) Malcolm, a subsequent president of the Company, favoured amalgamation with the north. Chaplin strongly supported them. The case was based partly on economy, partly on a better Civil Service career structure, partly on the wider argument that a single Rhodesia would be better placed to stake its claim at the peace settlement.

An even more important consideration – and it was to colour discussion about the future of the Rhodesia for the next fifty years – was the possibility of creating an English counterpoise to Afrikanerdom. A greater Rhodesia, perhaps incorporating much of East Africa, might play such a part. It was this notion which converted a section of the liberal/left in England to support of Central African Federation in the late 1940s. Chaplin, regarding the Boers as irreconcilable foes, naturally favoured amalgamation. Later, when it was clearly not 'on', he plumped for union partly because Smuts's terms for the expropriation of the Company were much better than the British Government's, but also because Southern Rhodesia as a fifth province of South Africa could do much to stop the advance of the nationalists – the counterpoise argument in a different form.

The settlers in both territories were hostile. In the north they constituted a mere handful, little over 3,000 who believed that they would be swamped, that Livingstone would become a backwater and that their proposed representation on an enlarged Legislative Council would be no compensation. The southern settlers who might have paused, had they even dreamt of the enormous mineral wealth hidden below the surface of what is now called the Copper Belt, feared that the great addition of Africans would make it even harder than it would be anyway to extract Responsible Government from London. In Southern Rhodesia the ratio of black to white was 27 to 1. If the north came in it would be nearly 60 to 1.

Amalgamation was carried in the Legislative Council, but the elected members

[2] NAR CH8/2/1, 2027–31, Fox to Chaplin.

were against it by eight to four. Jameson and Chaplin decided, therefore, to drop it, but they proposed as a compromise a few weeks later that the territories should come under a single Administrator. Although this was a very different proposal from amalgamation Coghlan strongly objected. After the usual delay Long turned it down, to the annoyance of Wilson Fox whose letter has been quoted. Henry Lambert of the Colonial Office wrote a letter to Long which deserves quotation since so much of Rhodesian history is implicit in it:

> Mr Long would not willingly do anything to injure the position of the Administration. At the same time he feels that he must constantly bear in mind the peculiar constitution of Southern Rhodesia. Under this constitution, which was set up with the Company's concurrence while the Executive consists exclusively of the Company's officials, the Legislative contains a large elective majority. This majority, though it does not, as under responsible government, in effect appoint administrations, has in its power to produce administrative deadlock and therefore necessarily possesses an influence over administrations much greater than in the Crown Colony type of administration ...
>
> The elected members for whom Sir Charles Coghlan speaks have protested against the Company's proposal on the ground that the Company is engaged in an endeavour to carry into effect a Constitutional change without any reference to the people or their representatives.[3]

The question of a single Administrator for the two protectorates was not in itself very important. In 1921 Chaplin doubled the two offices and no one minded, but by then Company rule was clearly on its way out. What mattered in 1917 and afterwards was the power of the settlers to block an arrangement they disliked. That power stemmed from the very nature of the original occupation, when Rhodes pulled the imperial Government's chestnuts out of the fire. It might have been lost – indeed it nearly was – after the Jameson Raid and the rebellions. Rhodes recovered it. From then onwards the dictum of a Victorian Chancellor of the Exchequer applies. 'We can never govern from Downing Street any part of [Southern] Africa in which the whites are strong enough to defend themselves.'[4] The colonists in Southern Rhodesia were not strong enough in 1896 and had to be reinforced. Hence the narrowness of the margin by which they retained autonomy. Indeed they would have lost it but for Rhodes's peculiar relationship with Joseph Chamberlain. Thereafter, however, they clearly could defend themselves and they have been able to do so from that day to this, although one can only guess how long the situation will last.

The most important event in Chaplin's Administratorship was the Privy Council's decision on the ownership of the unalienated land. The Legislative

[3] NAR CH8/2/1, 1989–90, to BSA Company (copy) December 17, 1917. The Company's memorandum is in CH8/2/1, 1977–83 n.d.

[4] Quoted Peter Joyce, *Anatomy of a Rebel, Smith of Rhodesia, a Biography*, Salisbury, 1974, 243.

Council's claim that it never belonged to the Company had been referred by Harcourt to the Judicial Committee on July 14, 1914. Jameson who was President assured the Company's shareholders that he was not worried, that the Company was confident about its title and that the action was a friendly one to settle once and for all a technical point which could not seriously be disputed. He hoped that there would not be undue delay.

In all these matters, as so often in his ebullient past, the Doctor was over-optimistic. The issue which had begun as a duel between the Company and the settlers soon became a four-cornered contest. The Colonial Office, after a silence of a quarter of a century during which no hint of its claim had ever been uttered, argued that the ownership vested in the Crown. At the same time yet another claim was put forward. The Aborigines Protection Society, supported by some missionaries and by a group of Ndebele, led by Nyamanda, eldest son of Lobengula, made a case for 'native' ownership. Matters henceforth proceeded at the brisk pace of Jarndyce v. Jarndyce in *Bleak House*. Four elaborate claims had to be made and then had to be met by four no less elaborate rebuttals. The Company's solicitor, Hawksley, inopportunely expired, and his successor had to get up the whole complicated case *de novo*. The original leading counsel for all four parties either died, were made judges or became ministers of the Crown before the statements had been filed, and new counsel had to master the old briefs. Jameson died at the end of 1917 before judgement was given. He would have had a disagreeable shock if he had lived.

The Judicial Committee did not challenge the title of those to whom the Company had granted land, nor did it dispute the Company's right to reimburse itself from the sales of land for proper administrative costs as long as it was running the country. But the Committee dismissed all claims to the ownership of the unalienated land other than that of the Crown. The 'natives' had lost by conquest whatever title they possessed. The Company had no claim independent of the Crown, the Lippert Concession being legally worthless, if historically interesting. The Company had conquered the country as the Crown's agent under its charter and had acted as agent ever since. Nor had it acquired a title by lapse of time. Because the Crown had not annexed the territory at once it did not follow that the Crown had renounced the right to do so at a future date. As for the settlers, their only possible claim was on the basis that ownership vested in the Crown. This was indeed correct, but the corollary argued by their counsel that the Crown was bound to hand the land on to a settler government did not follow at all. The Crown could not be bound in any way whatever.

The Judicial Committee, while feeling obliged to find for the Crown, gave a rap on the knuckles of the Colonial Office:

It may be a matter of regret that on a subject so important, it should have been thought fit to leave the rights of the parties to be ascertained by a legal enquiry... In 1894 a single sentence either in an Order-in-Council or a simple agreement would have resolved the questions which have for so many years given rise to conflicting opinions in Southern Rhodesia ... Matabeleland and Mashonaland were rich in promise; the right to enjoy the fruition might well have been determined before and not after the field was tilled and the harvest began to ripen.

The Privy Council further declared that the Company when it ceased to rule could claim against the Crown for the recovery of its accumulated administrative deficit, (i.e. that incurred in its governmental capacity). The Judges, however, did not regard it as part of their duty to quantify the figure – 'with items or details, with the amounts or the book-keeping of such expenditure, and with the terms of reimbursement, their Lordships have nothing to do'. These 'items and details' were, of course, crucial. However, the Company had no serious cause for complaint at this stage. Its land rights in Northern Rhodesia, its mineral, railway and commercial rights in both territories were unaffected. If anyone ought to have regretted the decision it was the Legislative Council which started the proceedings.

Evidently, there was no point in the Chartered Company continuing to administer the country. The proceeds of sales of land could now never be transferred to the commercial side for the benefit of the shareholders, and the administrative deficit was the Crown's liability. The duty of the board to its shareholders was to pitch this as high as possible. They put in, without undue modesty, a claim for £7,866,000. The Government appointed a high powered Commission to assess the figure. Lord Cave, a Lord of Appeal and later Lord Chancellor, was Chairman. Lord Chalmers, former head of the Treasury and Sir William Peat, a distinguished chartered accountant were the other members. The Commission, appointed in July 1919, did not report till February 1921. The delay was not its fault. The Colonial Office displayed a well proven power of procrastination to the full, and Lord Cave felt obliged to deliver a public snub to the Attorney General when he asked for yet further delay on behalf of the Crown.

The Cave Commission's report was a disappointment to the Company. It not only fixed the Crown's liability for administrative deficits at £4,435,000, with no addition for interest, but it ruled that from this there should be deducted 'the value as at dates of appropriation of areas of Crown land appropriated for the Company's farming and ranching undertakings and in respect of the value of grants of land made to other persons for considerations other than cash' – the last clause being a palpable hit at the shadier transactions of the Jameson era. But it referred the determination of these deductions to an independent valuation and left in the air the whole question of the Company's counterclaim for the value of public buildings and works. A further lengthy vista of negotiation and litigation was thus opened up. The Colonial Officials, hard liners to the end, now pressed their battle on three fronts: first, they pitched the deductions as high as possible; second, they argued that the balance, after the Company's rule ended, should be paid gradually by sales of land rather than at once in cash down; third they claimed, two million pounds in respect of governmental advances to the Company for expenses incurred in the war.

Meanwhile important political developments occurred in Southern Rhodesia. The alternatives when Company rule ended had narrowed down to two: Responsible Government or union with South Africa. In 1917 the Responsible Government Association was founded; it was in part based on the Rhodesia Agricultural Union, an organization of farmers who feared union on grounds of competition for black labour on the Rand. Coghlan joined it in 1919. His prestige as leader of the 'Unofficials', his tenacity, integrity, political skill, and his cogent if ponderous oratory made him a notable accession. He was quickly elected President, to the chagrin of some of those in on the act from the start.

The ideologue of the party was Colquhoun's widow, Mrs Tawse-Jollie. She had remarried a farmer 'of no account', according to Chaplin, and too fond of the bottle according to others. She was good looking, clever and articulate, the first woman to enter a colonial legislature. Her book, *The Real Rhodesia* (1924), contains a vivid, though highly partisan, account of the Responsible Government campaign. Coghlan did not like her.

Smuts succeeded Botha as Prime Minister of South Africa in 1919. His political position was too precarious (and became even worse in 1920) for him to say much, but he was known to favour union. The Rhodesia Unionist Association was founded in the same year. Its chairman, Herbert Longden, was a Bulawayo lawyer like Coghlan. Union had the support of the mining companies, the senior civil servants and the better off professional men, although there were many back eddies in the stream. It was not a straight case of 'haves' against 'have-nots'. Afrikaners, who constituted a fifth of the European population of 33,000 'had not', but were unionists. In general, however, farmers (not a well-heeled group then), artisans, railwaymen, small workers, minor civil servants, and trade unionists favoured Responsible Government, while the 'establishment' was for union.

The Responsible Government cause made all the running in 1919 and 1920. It is true that Milner returned in 1919 a dusty answer to a request from the Legislative Council for the criteria by which he would judge the territory fit for self-government. He replied that he did not think it yet fit and suggested that the temporary continuation of Charter rule might be best. He had been privately in favour of union, but Smuts dwelt on the difficulties in South Africa – surprisingly in view of his preference. Milner was uncertain what to do. He was less hostile to Responsible Government than he seemed. By the end of 1920 he saw no alternative.

Milner was influenced by Earl Buxton, High Commissioner and Governor General of South Africa 1916–20, who early became convinced of the case for Responsible Government. He in his turn was influenced by Sir Herbert Stanley, his Imperial Secretary who had previously been Resident Commissioner in Salisbury. Stanley may have converted Newton, to whom he was related by marriage, although the latter's failure to succeed Milton and an acrimonious dispute with the Company in 1919 about his pension may have made him ready to take up a cause which by 1921 was anathema to his old employers. He was notoriously tight-fisted, which was no doubt why he left a substantial sum when he died. Whatever the reason, he became one of the most effective advocates of a cause which in 1920 he had denounced as 'a wild-cat scheme'. His and Stanley's work behind the scenes was an important element in the success of Responsible Government.

The Legislative Council elections of April 1920 gave it a further push. Twelve out of thirteen elected members were in favour, the odd men out supporting a Crown Colony variant. Of 11,000 electors only 6,765 voted, but the supporters of union (814) and the *status quo* (868) were heavily defeated. In May the Council sent another resolution to Milner and requested Responsible Government. It was many months before he answered – the Colonial Office did not believe in undue haste – but when he did so in October he conceded the basic point. Responsible Government would be granted and put into effect not later than October 1924, provided that the Legislative Council elections of 1923 showed that the settlers still wanted it. This answer did not satisfy Coghlan, and the Council replied with a request for Responsible Government forthwith.

During the 1920 session of the Legislative Council there was an interlude in politics. Dr Jameson had died in 1917. It had been agreed that he should be buried in the Matopos near Rhodes. A multitude of difficulties had hitherto prevented this being done. Now it was at last possible. In the third week in May the Council suspended its sittings and a funeral almost as impressive as Rhodes's own took place at World's View on May 22. Bishop Gaul, a close friend, conducted the service, and Chaplin pronounced the address. And there the impetuous boon companion, the political and medical counsellor of the country's founder was laid to rest. He was, wrote Smuts, who could not attend, to Chaplin, 'a great Doer and one thinks little of the errors that marked the course of his real creative life'. Over half a century later, with the wisdom of hindsight, we may perhaps see these errors looming larger than they did in 1920, but Jameson's career, for good or ill, was scarcely less remarkable than that of Rhodes himself.

In February 1921, shortly after the Cave Commission had reported, Milner resigned. His successor as Colonial Secretary was Winston Churchill. By this time the officials, after a good deal of uncertainty, had come down definitely in favour of Responsible Government. Milner, with reluctance, concurred. Churchill, though little interested in the subject – the Middle East dominated his thoughts – was not wholly convinced. But he came at once under strong pressure from Coghlan. On the verge of departure for Egypt he adopted the time-honoured delaying tactic of setting up a committee to advise him on both Rhodesias. This would postpone an immediate decision, and in any case there were complicated problems to be disentangled, some of them arising from the Cave Report.

Both the personnel of the 'Rhodesia Committee' and its terms of reference, however, show how far the cause of Responsible Government had advanced. The Chairman, Earl Buxton, by whose name the Committee is known to history, was as we saw a strong supporter of Responsible Government. So was Sir Henry Lambert of the Colonial Office, another prominent member. Moreover the terms of reference as regards Southern Rhodesia gave little choice: to recommend when and under what safeguards Responsible Government should be granted; to advise on the procedure for drafting a new constitution; to suggest interim measures for phasing out Company rule. There was no hint of any alternative. Union was not even mentioned.

If Churchill had really hoped for delay he must have been disappointed. The Buxton Committee worked with remarkable speed. Set up on March 7 it sent its recommendations on Southern Rhodesia to the Colonial Secretary on April 12, and on Northern Rhodesia seventeen days later. The latter does not directly concern this story. On Southern Rhodesia the Committee's recommendations were clear enough. The opinion of the electorate should be taken by a referendum as soon as possible. First, however, a draft constitution should be drawn up by the Colonial Office and if possible agreed with a delegation from the elected members of the Legislative Council visiting London for that purpose, so that the electorate would know clearly what it was voting about. The Committee's terms of reference did not include the drafting of the constitution, but it recommended in broad terms the model of Natal before the South Africa Act with similar safeguards for the unrepresented Africans.

So far all had gone swimmingly for Coghlan and his cause, but at this juncture two adverse influences began to operate. The chartered board and the Administrator, though resigned since 1918 to the loss of Company rule, had never been easy about the prospect of settler government. The Cave award turned uneasiness into downright hostility. There had been sporadic correspondence with Smuts ever since he came into power. The day after the award was announced the board telegraphed Chaplin that union would henceforth be the Company's policy. The terms that Smuts would offer could not fail to be better than anything now obtainable from the British Government.

Simultaneously Smuts's own political position was transformed. He had been governing on a shoestring majority since the general election of 1920, but during the ensuing year he did a deal with the 'unionist' (ex-'Progressive') party headed by Sir Thomas Smartt. A combination of the unionists with Smuts's 'South African' party gained a conclusive victory in February 1921 over the 'nationalists' (the party of Afrikanerdom headed by J. B. M. Herzog). The incorporation of Southern, and ultimately Northern Rhodesia had long been the objective of the anti-nationalist forces, for obvious reasons connected with the balance of 'racial' – i.e. Boer versus English – power in the Union. Lord Selborne, High Commissioner at the time of the South Africa Act of 1909, had pressed the case strongly. Botha and Smuts always had their eyes fixed on this possibility. Smuts at last had the majorities in both Houses needed to carry Addresses to the Crown requesting the incorporation of new territory into the Union. Any political offer from him would now have to be taken seriously both by the British Government and the Southern Rhodesian electorate.

The difficulty for the supporters of union was that their opportunity came so late in the day. Smuts, unwell and preoccupied by his own electoral campaign and its aftermath, did not immediately appreciate how damaging the terms of reference of the Buxton Committee were to his policy. As soon as he did he was quick to urge on April 2 that the Committee should be asked to delay its report, and even wait to confer with the Rhodesian representatives before finalizing it. In his new and greatly strengthened political position he meant to use the Imperial Conference due in London that summer both to enlist Churchill's aid, and to over-persuade the Rhodesian delegation which he hoped would be there at the same time. Like all charismatic politicians – Disraeli, Cecil Rhodes, Lloyd George, Churchill himself – Smuts attached great importance to 'the personal'. Coghlan was well aware of the danger. He knew that Churchill's attitude was uncertain and he feared the persuasiveness and the prestige of the South African Prime Minister. He prudently delayed the departure of the Rhodesian delegation till the end of August when Smuts was safely back in Cape Town.

Churchill's attitude was by no means clear. He refused in May to rebuff Smuts and to that extent might be regarded as moving against Coghlan. He requested Coghlan's delegation to call on Smuts while *en route* for London – which again perhaps implied a penchant for the unionist solution. (Smuts when they met offered to reveal his terms, but Coghlan replied that his delegation had no mandate to discuss the matter.) The truth seems to be that Churchill was being pulled two ways by two rival exponents of imperial ideals. He was to be impressed by Coghlan's loyalty to the flag – something particularly welcome from an Irish Catholic when the 'troubles' were at their height. He was also impressed by Smuts's powerful arguments about the future of South Africa. But he knew that, whatever the letter of the law, there could be no question of imposing union on unwilling settlers. The most he could do was to insist to the Rhodesian delegation which was in London for the whole autumn of 1921 that the referendum suggested by the Buxton Committee must contain union as an option and therefore must await Smuts's terms. Coghlan protested that the Legislative Council elections had already settled the matter, but his hand was weakened when a petition got up by the unionists and signed by over 8,000 Rhodesian electors was sent to the Colonial Office asking for postponement of any decision till Smuts's terms were known.

The rest of the delegation's time was spent on the draft constitution which was agreed at the end of the year. It was, as expected, similar to that of Natal but since its details were virtually the same as those in the Letters Patent issued in 1923, it will be discussed in the next chapter. Coghlan and his colleagues returned in January 1922. The next step was to talk with Smuts who arranged to see a Rhodesian delegation at the beginning of April.

Smuts had by this stage become very keen indeed on securing Rhodesia. Party politics played their part. His long-term as opposed to his immediate political position was none too safe. His advances in the 1921 election had been at the cost of the Labour party. His real enemies, the nationalists, actually gained one seat and obtained 6,000 more votes than in 1920. A bloc of Rhodesian seats bound to vote on his side would be a great help, as his opponents naturally pointed out. Yet this was not the only consideration. Sir Keith Hancock in his great biography of Smuts writes:

From the start of the war to its finish they [Botha and Smuts] held constantly in view two paramount objectives: national security, national status.

From Kruger and Rhodes and even from their former British conquerors they had inherited an expansionist concept of security – wide frontiers for the Union and an economic and political hegemony extending beyond those frontiers far into equatorial Africa.[5]

Something of the grand, perhaps grandiose, sweep of Cecil Rhodes's imagination seemed to have descended to the Afrikaner philospher king who ruled in Pretoria and Cape Town. If he could incorporate Southern Rhodesia would he not have a jumping off place for the line of rail to Katanga, and – who knows? – a route to East Africa where he had fought such a hard and hazardous campaign, and thence to Kenya? Might Cape to Cairo become a reality after all? And would not Southern Rhodesia give him that long-coveted hold over Mozambique, in particular Delagoa Bay and Beira.

The fluidity of frontiers which so often follows a war made these dreams by no means absurd. As Smuts wrote in a state paper on the League of Nations, 'The very foundations have been shaken and loosened, and things are again fluid. The tents have been struck, and the great caravan of humanity is once more on the march.' After all even the boundaries of Europe, far more firmly fixed than those of Africa, had been re-drawn during 1919–20 in a scarcely less radical fashion, and Smuts had played a major part in the process. He was never over-sanguine, but he enjoyed what a character in one of Disraeli's novels calls 'real politics', i.e. foreign affairs; and there is a touch of Disraeli in a letter of April 27, 1922 to his friend Arthur Gillett.

I am rushed almost beyond endurance . . . I have just finished with the Rhodesian Delegation who came to see me on the question of incorporation into the Union. I am now busy with the Chartered Company in order to see whether we can arrive at an agreement on the expropriation of their assets. The work really means a financial review of the history of Rhodesia. And over and above all this, the Portuguese Delegation have arrived from Lisbon to negotiate a new Mozambique Treaty. I am now like an Oriental Despot giving audience to suitors from the ends of two continents. All very interesting but very exacting. It does not look like achieving success – either the Rhodesian or the Mozambique business. But I am going to try very hard. It would be a great thing to round off the South African state with borders far flung into the heart of the continent. But I fear I am moving too fast, and patience will be necessary.[6]

Smuts had much going for him. His prestige was immense. He was by far the most famous statesman of the Empire. He had the good will of Lloyd George,

[5] Keith Hancock, *The Fields of Force*, Vol. II of *Smuts*, 1968, 4.
[6] Quoted Hancock, op. cit., 151–2.

Churchill and many other wartime ministers. He was on excellent terms with King George V. He was familiar with Whitehall. He was in a curious way almost a part of the British 'establishment'. But there was one snag; he had to win the votes of the Rhodesians. To do so would mean a remarkable reversal of the verdict of 1920. He tried every trick. He even offered Coghlan, through Sir Abe Bailey and in suitably cautious terms, a post in the South African Cabinet, but Coghlan was not to be bought off.[7]

The truth was that Coghlan really did believe in Responsible Government. It may be true, as Sir Ernest Guest, a unionist and a partner in Coghlan's law firm, told the author, that Coghlan 'said in public on more than one occasion: "As sure as the sun will rise tomorrow Rhodesia's inevitable destiny is amalgamation with the Union – but we must get Responsible Government first and I do not trust the BSA Company to negotiate on our behalf" '. In reality this was only a long-term prediction. J. G. McDonald, deputy leader of the unionists, hit the nail on the head when he wrote to Chaplin, 'Warn him [Smuts] against believing that Coghlan only wants Resp. Govt. to negotiate terms. If he swallows that he'll never cease regretting his error. Coghlan wants Respon. Govt. to the last. Make no mistake about that.'[8] McDonald was right. The terms that Smuts eventually offered hardly could have been more generous, but the offer made not the slightest difference to Coghlan and his campaign.

It is safe to say that Smuts was under no delusions on this score. He never underestimated Coghlan's tenacity and ability. But events moved against him throughout 1922. From within a few months of the general election of the previous year South African affairs were marked by violent episodes which might well have made anyone pause at the prospect of joining such a turbulent country. There was the bloody suppression in May 1921 of some five hundred 'black Israelites' who defied the law at Bulhoek in the Western Cape. The dead numbered 167, and Smuts was christened by his enemies 'the Butcher of Bulhoek'. Early in 1922 there was a strike followed by a rising on the Rand. The strikers, largely Afrikaners, were protesting against the attempt of the mining companies to cut costs by modifying the conventional colour bar and job reservation. On March 10 Smuts declared martial law, took personal command and crushed the rebellion with heavy casualties – 157 dead and 687 wounded. Eighteen ring leaders were condemned to death and four were executed. Then in May and June came the so-called 'massacre of the Bondelzwarts', when 115 out of 600 men from this South West African tribe were killed in a punitive expedition.

Of these episodes the most damaging was the rebellion on the Rand. It aroused the worst apprehensions among organized labour in Rhodesia, and the fury of the nationalists in South Africa. By a stroke of ill fortune the Rhodesian delegation, newly arrived in Cape Town on March 31, was taken to the Strangers Gallery to see how the House of Assembly comported itself. It was the first day of the

[7] J. P. R. Wallis, *One man's hand: the story of Sir Charles Coghlan* ... 1950, 176–8.
[8] NAR CH8/2/2, 913–4, June 30, 1921.

debate on the Rand uprising. Language of the most virulent nature was used, and Herzog declared that Smuts's 'footsteps dripped with blood'. The spectacle of this sort of rancour was not likely to encourage Rhodesians to join the Union.

The delegation, moreover, got nothing out of Smuts. This was not his fault. He could not make a political offer till he had settled financial terms with the Company. Neither he nor the Company trusted each other an inch and Smuts guessed that, if he reversed the process and committed himself politically first, the Company would screw up its terms accordingly. But the negotiations with the Company's embassy proved to be enormously complicated, and were even protracted beyond the end of the session. His opponents in South Africa accused him of by-passing Parliament, though constitutionally he was in the right. More serious, the delay inspired deep suspicion in Rhodesia, for it was an article of faith with the unionists that time was on their side, and the Responsible Government party was correspondingly anxious for speed.

On May 25 Coghlan forced Smuts's hand by carrying, strongly against the will of the Colonial Office and the Company, an ordinance in the Legislative Council fixing June 30 as the latest day for publication of Smuts's terms and October 27 as the date of the referendum. Smuts asked for the publication day to be postponed till July 30. Coghlan agreed since this was tantamount to a promise that there would be no further delay, and the referendum would in any case be held on the appointed day. The terms were generous, ten members of the House of Assembly (the total at the time was 134) and five of the Senate, rising to seventeen and ten respectively with a named rise in population. There was to be a Provincial Council of twenty. There were generous financial provisions for development, and compensation for loss of tariffs. The Civil Services would be amalgamated, but vested rights of Rhodesians would be guaranteed by law. There would be no recruitment of Rhodesian native labour to other parts of the Union. Two other provisos, however inevitable, were bound to be less popular. Dutch must become a co-equal official language, and there would be no restriction on the movement of white men between provinces. Smuts could scarcely ask for less if he was to get the deal through his own Parliament.

His terms for the Company were equally generous – £6,836,500 in cash for the unalienated land, public works and railways, the Company to retain all its other assets, including its mineral, commercial and ranching rights. As a further encouragement the British Government agreed to drop its claim, which was widely regarded as outrageous anyway, to the return of two million pounds advanced for war expenses. To the Company, now more deeply embroiled than ever in its battle with the Colonial Office, the offer came as a godsend. The board, angry at the Cave and Buxton reports, was even more dismayed by the draft constitution for Responsible Government. This denied two of its key claims: that payment should be in cash down, not by a leisurely sale of land; and that interest, if not payable before March 31, 1918, was at least due thereafter. They decided to file a petition for a Declaration of Right, in effect an action against the Crown, if the draft constitution was promulgated. A depressing prospect of protracted litigation lay ahead. The shareholders and board understandably accepted Smuts's offer with alacrity at the end of July.

Everything now depended on the referendum. Although he badly wanted the unionists to win, Chaplin could not as Administrator take an active part in the campaign. The unionists were not very effective. They had the money but they lacked oratory and organization. Coghlan and his friends were more colourful – literally, for they opened the battle with banners of red and green. These were popularly assumed to be based on the initials of the party's name. In fact they were the King's racing colours – Coghlan was a devotee of the turf – and the unionists riposted by renting a window on the corner of Maria Road and Second Street in Salisbury where they displayed a notice: 'The Colours of the Unionist Association are Red, White and Blue', with a Union Jack below.[9] Thus both sides beat the patriotic drum.

It is hard to believe that passions were as violent in this conflict as they seem to be in modern politics. Sir Ernest Guest claims that 'feelings ran very high', but Godfrey Huggins (later Lord Malvern, and at that time a young surgeon), who was also a unionist, says 'there was no deep moral division on grounds of principle'. His wife, who was producing their first baby on the very day of the referendum, supported Coghlan, but could not vote: her husband honourably declined to take advantage of an incapacity for which he had some responsibility and 'paired' with her.

The campaign was fought with vigour. 'Rhodesia for the Rhodesians, Rhodesia for the Empire' was Coghlan's slogan. He seemed to have all the big guns against him, the press, apart from *Umtali Advertiser* (not an organ which counted for much), most of the establishment, the financial resources of the mining companies, and the British Government which, while ostensibly neutral, had given a clear hint by its waiver of war costs in connexion with Smuts's offer to the Chartered Company. Because of these hostile forces historians have expressed surprise at the result. They forget that only two and a half years earlier Responsible Government had won an overwhelming victory in the Legislative Council elections, and that since then almost every development had worked in its favour. The surprise is not that Responsible Government won, rather that the unionists fared as well as they did.

In August Smuts himself made an ostensibly 'non-political' visit to the country to open an agricultural show. No one took the excuse seriously and the visit may have been counter-productive. Smuts was none too sanguine. He wrote to a friend:

I hope they will vote to come into the Union, but I am told that the great current of opinion is still the other way. They are afraid of our bilingualism, our nationalism, my views of the British Empire. In fact they are little Jingoes and the sooner they are assimilated by the Union the better for them and for us.

His fears were justified. Despite an eve of poll message from him, which much

[9] Rex Reynolds, *Discussions with Lord Malvern*, 4, comment by Sir Ernest Lucas Guest.

annoyed Coghlan, the verdict was decisive. Out of a European population of 35,000 some 20,000 were on the register. (The black population was nearly 900,000 with sixty on the register.) The vote for Responsible Government was 8,774, for union 5,989. Nearly 26 per cent of those who were in theory eligible did not vote, but the register was unreliable and contained as Gann puts it 'both dead and dud votes'. Many electors in the more remote areas of the backveld found it difficult to get to the polling booth. In the circumstances the turn-out was high. It is interesting to note that of the thirteen districts into which the country was divided for electoral purposes, twelve voted for Responsible Government. Marandellas was the only one against it, as in 1920; and, again as in 1920, by the narrowest of margins. The thirty months that had elapsed since the Legislative Council elections had seen no real shift at all in Rhodesian attitudes. Coghlan had been fully vindicated by events. The Rhodesians remained staunch patriots or 'little Jingoes', according to taste. The final result, because of the difficulties of the count with such a scattered electorate, was not announced till November 6 at the Bulawayo Court House. Coghlan made a speech ending with the words, 'For King and Empire that is our motto'. But Herbert Longdon declared, 'I have no doubt that Union will in the fullness of time be realized. I feel that Nature intended it.'

Before the announcement, but after the result had become obvious, Chaplin wrote at some length to Smuts analysing the causes of their defeat.[10] Like most unionists he believed that time was on their side and that 'the real mistake was made by Churchill when he appointed the Buxton Committee and altered Milner's plan of leaving the question of Responsible Government to be voted upon at the general election for the Legislative Council, which would have taken place in the ordinary course next year.' As for the victory of the Responsible Government party its main causes were: 'anti-Dutch feeling especially among the women'; 'the belief of the trade union element ... that they will be in a position to dictate to the government'; a feeling in the same quarter that, if 'most of the better-class people ... were for Union, their proper course was to vote the other way'; and finally the satisfactory state of the Administration's finances 'which has blinded people to difficulties in the future'. As for the actual campaign he considered that, although the Unionists had the money, they were ineffective and too defensive. 'If they had hit harder they would have had more success.'

Analysing the vote in rather more detail, he thought that the majority of farmers and nearly all senior civil servants were for union, but that the Public Services Association and the Posts and Telegraphs Association 'were captured by Responsible Government extremists', and pressed all sorts of unreasonable demands to which Coghlan agreed whereas Smuts refused. The Indian and Coloured voters – not that there were many – opposed union. Teachers and clergymen (apart from the Dutch Reformed Church) were also hostile, along with 'most of the Labour people'.

[10] The letter appears in full in Jean van der Poel (ed.), *Selections from the Smuts Papers*, Vol. V, 1973, 144–7.

One can perhaps put one or two glosses on this account. The farmers are supposed by most contemporaries to have been anti-union for reasons given earlier. Then, Chaplin could hardly be expected in writing to Smuts to mention the unfortunate effect of certain recent episodes in South Africa. Nor would he have wished to dwell on the unpopularity of the Company. A good many people were voting for Responsible Government precisely because the Company was against it. But on the whole his assessment seems a reasonable one. The vote was in part an anti-establishment vote, and in part a racialist vote – a vote against the Afrikaners. This hostility was not only an echo of the Boer war, it was also born of fear; fear of poor Whites who nearly all were Afrikaners migrating to the north and undercutting the standards of living of English-speaking artisans, and railway workers. Nor should one underestimate the dislike felt by minor civil servants – and in a newly developed country their numerical proportion tends to be very high – for South African bilingualism.

Finally, there was loyalty to 'the flag – loyalty to a Britain and a British way of life that was already fast vanishing' – in Mr Frank Clements' words, an attachment to 'an ever further receding past till it was completely divorced from the realities of the present'.

It is fully in keeping and in no way inconsistent that very similar social and emotional forces should produce the Declaration of Independence in 1965. Then, too, the Establishment was in the minority. Then, too, there was a revolt against the people who had for so many years been ruling the country. Then, too, there was racialism – dislike of a different race, it is true, for the Afrikaners were in favour of UDI – but the basic ingredient was similar, fear of an alien people whose advancement would in the end threaten the security and standards of the white artisans. The same forces which in 1922 propelled a majority of white Rhodesians to proclaim their loyalty to a Britain still believed to be on the side of the settlers, forty-three years later propelled them into breaking with a Britain which palpably was not.

The Chartered Company thus ceased to rule the Rhodesias. Its board of directors and its officials were often criticized and sometimes abused, but its contribution to the building of the country was a notable one, and Southern Rhodesia owes it a debt too often forgotten. It continued to be by far the most important commercial concern in the area even when its rights over minerals had been bought out in 1933 and over railways after the Second World War. Its resident director was a person of much influence and in the 1950s when Lord Robins held office, June Hill, his official abode in Salisbury, became under Lady Robins a rival social magnet to Government House itself. The Company was eventually taken over on a friendly basis by the giant Anglo-American Corporation of South Africa with which it long had had close relations.

13

The New Order 1923–31

The referendum result was a decisive episode in the history of Southern Africa. It cannot be called a 'turning point'. Responsible Government, given the tradition of the Colonial Office and the character of the settler community, was on the straight line of constitutional development. But a decision not to turn can be just as important. Smuts and his policies received a set-back from which they never recovered. By-elections were already going against him, and the referendum was a heavy blow to his prestige. Now a mirror image of the alliance with which he had dished Herzog in 1921 was created in 1923 by an electoral pact between the nationalists and the Labour party. The new coalition won the general election of 1924 by a majority of twenty-seven, and Smuts not only lost his office, but his seat as well.

The objective of a greater South Africa 'with borders far flung into the heart of the continent' was never to be attained. It all depended on the acquisition of Rhodesia. The referendum finally dispelled the dream of Cape to Cairo. No wonder Smuts could write to a friend a fortnight after the result was announced: 'I get scores of letters from all sorts of people who say that it is indeed a paradox that Rhodes' country should have stood in the way of Rhodes' ideal being accomplished.' Belgium and Portugal, both of which had displayed a not entirely disinterested solicitude for the cause of Responsible Government, could now slumber on in the Congo, Angola and Mozambique until black nationalism blew up in their faces a generation later. It may be that Smuts could not have succeeded in his wider ambitions even if he had acquired Southern Rhodesia. What is certain is that even the possibility vanished after November 6, 1922.

Within Southern Rhodesia the result was equally decisive. Although people might talk about financial difficulties forcing the country to join the Union, there was never any serious question of it. The nationalist victory of 1924 was one reason, and financial difficulties are nearly always exaggerated in these arguments. The same was claimed at various times about Ulster, Palestine and Pakistan but it never proved to be very important. Moreover, once established, Responsible Government created its own set of vested interests. Membership of the Legislative Council of a self-governing colony was grander than being a Provincial Councillor, and to be its premier was a cut above being a minister in a South African cabinet. William Pitt could overcome analogous difficulties with the Irish Parliament in 1801 by the lavish distribution of honours and bribes. Such means were not open to South African Prime Ministers.

In the immediate aftermath, however, Smuts and many unionists believed that the result of the referendum was only a temporary set-back to the unionist cause. By coincidence there had been at the same time a convulsion in British politics. The Lloyd George coalition had fallen on October 19, and on November 15 Bonar Law, leading a purely Conservative administration, won the general election with a majority of eighty-eight over all other parties combined. The Duke of Devonshire, with William Ormsby-Gore as his Parliamentary Under-Secretary, replaced Churchill at the Colonial Office. The new Government was deeply pledged to fiscal retrenchment.

Displaying perhaps more tenacity than tact, Smuts wrote at some length to Bonar Law on November 29 suggesting that he might abandon any promise to Coghlan and revert to Milner's policy of awaiting the Legislative Council elections in 1923 and postponing the grant of Responsible Government till he had seen the results. He cleverly dwelt on the financial questions involved in the Chartered Company's Petition of Right. If, after the Letters Patent for the new constitution had actually been promulgated, the Company subsequently won its case against the Crown, the British taxpayer might be liable for as much as five million pounds. Would it not be wiser to wait for the Privy Council's judgement on a lawsuit which, as Smuts no doubt hoped, was likely to be slow and protracted? He ended by urging Bonar Law to extend no financial favours whatever to Southern Rhodesia, since financial embarrassment was the strongest reason for the country joining the union. He wrote on similar lines to Ormsby-Gore and Churchill.[1]

One may doubt whether these tactics, presupposing as they did the early reversal of a verdict already twice pronounced by the Southern Rhodesian electorate, could ever have worked, but in any case matters had now gone too far. Ormsby-Gore does appear to have hankered somewhat after Smuts's greater South Africa policy, and there was a delay in promulgating the new constitution, which prompted Coghlan to write at one stage to Newton in London 'I have never trusted Ormsby-Gore and I don't do so now'.[2] But the delay was caused rather by the inherent procrastination of the Colonial Office, and even more by the slow financial negotiations with the Chartered Company, than by any attempt to revert to Milner's programme.

[1] For these letters see *Smuts Papers V*, 149–54.
[2] NAR NE1/1/1, May 28, 1923.

On July 10, 1923 the Colonial Office abruptly announced with the minimum notice its terms for the expropriation of the Company. The shareholders had to decide whether to accept within a fortnight so that the necessary supplementary vote could be introduced in the House of Commons on July 25. The Colonial Office, possibly influenced by Ormsby-Gore who was related by marriage to Malcolm, behaved slightly less rigidly and parsimoniously than hitherto. The Company was offered three and three-quarter million pounds in settlement of the balance of its claims and the Crown's counter-claim, which had been left undetermined after the award of the Cave Commission. It would also receive till 1965 a half share of the proceeds of land sales in North-Western Rhodesia. In return it had to surrender the unalienated land, the administrative buildings and other administrative assets in both territories. The Crown would recognize and guarantee the Company's railway and mineral rights and leave its other commercial assets undisturbed. The Crown would drop any claim regarding the liability of the Company for land appropriated for the Company's own commercial undertakings, or granted, for whatever consideration, to other parties. Finally the Crown consented to forgo its claim for two million pounds war costs. As this had been already agreed in the event of the bargain with Smuts going through, it would have been awkward to do otherwise now, although Smuts himself in a letter to Ormsby-Gore argued strongly to the contrary.

As a corollary of this settlement, the Chartered Company would cease to administer either of the Rhodesias. The new government, under Letters Patent, would take over Southern Rhodesia on October 1, 1923, when the territory would be formally annexed to the Crown as a colony. The Crown would take over Northern Rhodesia in April, 1924. Sir John Chancellor, a distinguished soldier and colonial administrator, was appointed as the first Governor of Southern Rhodesia – Chaplin, who was an obvious candidate, being regarded by Coghlan and Newton as too much committed to unionism. Sir Herbert Stanley was appointed as the first Governor of Northern Rhodesia. The settlement, thus achieved after so much litigation, intrigue and acrimony, was finally confirmed on September 29 and is known as the Devonshire Agreement. It was not accepted in any spirit of good will or gratitude by the chartered board or its shareholders. The most that could be said for it, as far as they were concerned, was that it put an end to litigation and uncertainty, and was a rather less adverse financial deal than that contemplated by the previous government. Their general sentiments were probably well expressed by Sir Henry Birchenough (President 1925–37), writing to Chaplin two days after the offer was announced: 'I doubt whether any Government has ever made a shabbier bargain with a great Corporation which has performed undoubted and striking services'.[3]

The Letters Patent promulgating the terms of the Responsible Government constitution were published on September 24, 1923. Since a good deal of subsequent Rhodesian history has revolved either around disputes about its meaning

[3] NAR CH8/2/2, ff. 162–4, July 12, 1923.

or efforts at amendment, it has to be examined in some detail. As with all constitutions one must distinguish between outward form and the inner reality which developed over the years.

Formally the executive and legislative power in Southern Rhodesia was subordinated to that of the United Kingdom. Not only did the imperial Government retain the right to legislate, to appoint the Governor and give him orders, and to remit legal appeals to the Judicial Committee of the Privy Council; but it also imposed substantial limitations on the power of the new Legislative Assembly to make laws. The Assembly could by a simple majority pass measures for 'the peace, order and good government' of the country, but any bill required the assent of the Crown for whom the Governor normally acted, and the amendment of certain clauses in the Letters Patent required a two-thirds majority of the Assembly. Moreover, there were some areas of great importance in Southern Rhodesian affairs in which the Assembly could not legislate at all. In particular, it could not touch the Native Department, whose staffing, salaries and conditions of service were thus in theory safeguarded from local interference. Nor could it deal with native reserves, the rights of Africans to purchase land, or the establishment of native councils. All these matters came under the High Commissioner, who was also Governor General in South Africa.

These were not the only restrictions on the Assembly's legislative power. Although, in the case of most bills, the Governor's assent was a formality, being given on the advice of his Executive Council, which was simply the Cabinet under a different hat, there was a whole category which came under another procedure. Measures requiring a two-thirds majority, bills concerning the Company's mineral or railway rights, bills imposing differential tariffs or affecting the currency, and measures which discriminated against the Africans (except in respect of arms and liquor) could not receive the Governor's assent unless they contained a clause suspending their operation until the King had signified his intention not to disallow them. The King in this context meant the British Government which thus had in certain areas a veto power over and above that of the Governor.

The Letters Patent created a Legislative Assembly of thirty members. The franchise was based on property qualification (real property or mining claims worth £150, or an income of £100 p.a.) together with a literacy test. Electors had to be over twenty-one and British subjects. There was formally no racial discrimination, but in practice the electorate was almost exclusively white, with a few Indian shopkeepers and a handful of prosperous African farmers. The Governor could appoint up to six ministers, each with particular departmental responsibilities. One of them would be designated 'Premier' – a title with a slightly inferior connotation to that of 'Prime Minister' which was not conferred till 1933. The six ministers constituted the Governor's Executive Council. The word 'Cabinet' was not mentioned in the Letters Patent, but it was assumed that they would also sit separately as such under the chairmanship of the Premier. The Premier was to be Minister of Native Affairs, and since he was, like the rest of the Cabinet, 'responsible' to the legislature, there existed to that extent an overlap between the governmental system dealing with Europeans and the one that dealt with Africans.

The system formally was, therefore, not self-government at all, although often so described. The Letters Patent were more accurate when they termed it 'responsible government subject to certain limitations'. In the words of Mr D. J. Murray:

> It provided for self-government for only approximately 19,000 electors in a total population which was reckoned at that time as being approximately 864,000. Self-government covered approximately 2 per cent of the population, and the vast majority of the remainder were supposedly provided with a distinct system such as was expected to safeguard their interests.[4]

In practice, the limitations meant less than they did in theory. From the very beginning the Legislative Assembly behaved, and was treated by the UK Government, as the competent body to pass laws for the whole population, not simply for the minority who had the vote. The Parliament at Westminster never exercised its right to legislate, nor did the British Government use its power to issue orders-in-council or proclamations, even in areas from which the Southern Rhodesian Assembly was excluded from legislating. If it was deemed desirable to encroach on those areas, the procedure was to amend the Letters Patent so that the Legislative Assembly could pass an acceptable local measure. The British Government could, of course, block anything that it did not consider 'acceptable', and the fact that it never used its power to disallow laws enacted in Salisbury did not mean that Salisbury could get away with anything. The power was not used because it became the custom for the Southern Rhodesian Government to submit measures to Whitehall before introducing them in the Assembly and to drop them or amend them if the UK Government objected.

The important point was that the initiative always originated from Southern Rhodesia, and a convention, so strong and so important that it came to be known as 'The Convention', was established, under which the British Parliament never legislated for Southern Rhodesia except by agreement with, or at the request of the Southern Rhodesian Government. The existence of this convention was one of several features which made Southern Rhodesia's status far closer to that of a self-governing Dominion than even a Crown Colony with Representative Government. No British Government would have dreamed of initiating a bill dealing with Australian or Canadian affairs. It was symbolically appropriate that when the Dominions Office was set up in 1925, Southern Rhodesia should have come under it rather than remain in the sphere of the Colonial Office.

Time only hardened 'The Convention'. One of the more ridiculous canards spread by the Rhodesia Front in the run-up to UDI was that Harold Wilson intended to pass an Act of Parliament imposing majority rule on Southern Rhodesia. It was, of course, inconceivable that he or any other British Prime Minister would have done anything of the sort. The credulity of those who believed

---

[4] D. J. Murray, *The Governmental System in Southern Rhodesia*, 1970, 5-6.

the story is only matched by the disingenuousness of those who spread it.

As soon as he took office the new Governor appointed Sir Charles Coghlan as Premier and head of an interim Government pending the elections for the Legislative Assembly. Coghlan's Cabinet consisted of P. D. Fynn, Treasurer; Sir Francis Newton, Colonial Secretary (i.e. Minister of Internal Affairs); Robert Hudson, Attorney General and Minister of Defence; W. M. Leggate, Minister of Agriculture; H. U. Moffat, Minister of Mines and Public Works. The Premier, anything but radical in his views, wished to conciliate the establishment, so many of whom had been unionists, and he had little use for some of his own supporters; in particular, he meant to keep out Mrs Tawse-Jollie, come what might. He changed the party's name to that of Rhodesian Party. The unionists were no less anxious to forget past battles, and their mainstay, the Chartered Company, had every interest in establishing good relations with the new regime. The unionist party was dissolved.

The only other organized party was Labour which had supported the Responsible Government campaign. Coghlan was prepared to concede them five seats, i.e. not to run Rhodesian Party candidates there. Jack Keller, the Labour leader, assuming that there would be single member constituencies, stuck out for eight. The deal, therefore, collapsed. In fact Labour support was concentrated in a number of geographically small areas, and when the Governor used his power under the Letters Patent to divide the country into fifteen two-member constituencies,[5] the Labour vote was effectively swamped. At the 1924 election, the Rhodesian Party won twenty-six seats, and Labour none. The opposition consisted of four Independents.

There was thus set a political pattern destined to last without much change for over thirty years. Of eight general elections down to and including Garfield Todd's victory in 1954 (by exactly the same margin as Coghlan's), the Government party under whatever name won six with a majority of not less than fourteen in the Legislative Assembly i.e. not less than twenty-two seats or 73 per cent of the total. Only once did the opposition actually win. Calling itself at that time the Reform Party it obtained sixteen seats in the 1933 election under the lead of Godfrey Huggins, himself an ex-Rhodesian Party man. But the basic reality was emphasized when he jettisoned the Reform Party, concluded an alliance under the title of United Party with his former friends, dissolved the Legislative Assembly and won the election of 1934 with twenty-four seats. On only one occasion was he seriously challenged thereafter when the 1946 election gave the opposition, now calling itself the Liberal Party, twelve seats; Huggins with only thirteen had to conduct a minority Government for two years, but the election of 1948 restored

---

[5] The Legislative Assembly had the power to change this, and in 1928 split the country into twenty-two single-member constituencies, leaving four two-member constituencies for Bulawayo and Salisbury. In 1938 these were abolished and thirty single-member constituencies became the pattern till the enlargement of the Legislative Assembly in 1961 under the 'Whitehead Constitution'.

the old balance. Rhodesia had in effect throughout these years a one-party system similar in some respects to the British political pattern under the first two Georges; and Huggins was its Walpole.

The politics of Southern Rhodesia were thus profoundly different from those of the contemporary Britain which Southern Rhodesians so nostalgically admired. It was not merely that no single party governed Britain for those thirty years, although the Conservatives came near to doing so. Nor was it because Parliamentary majorities were not as overwhelming in percentage terms, although in 1924, 1935 and 1945 they came little short of the typical Rhodesian figures, and in 1931 far surpassed them. The real difference was not in terms of percentages, but of absolute numbers. The British system depends on parties which, even though they do not literally alternate in power, base their assumptions when in opposition on the likelihood of soon returning. Hence the concept of the 'shadow cabinet' – an alternative government with an alternative programme ready to take office, if the electoral pendulum swings the right way. But this presupposes a reasonable number of persons involved. The Southern Rhodesian Legislature outnumbered less than one-twentieth of the British House of Commons, but the Rhodesian Cabinet of six was nearly a third of the size of its average British counterpart. Since the entire opposition elected in six out of the eight Rhodesian elections during the period consisted of not more than eight members and twice fell as low as four, the notion of a shadow cabinet would have been absurd. The numbers simply did not exist.

Coghlan was anything but a radical. He left the administrative framework much as it was under the Company. The same civil servants did much the same things. True, they soon had grievances. The new political ministers behaved as if they were permanent administrative heads of departments, the Civil Service felt that there was excessive political interference in the management of personnel matters, and the new Government, under pressure for economy and lower taxation, seemed less sympathetic than the Company. Nevertheless there was nothing in the nature of a drastic change, and many of the complaints were rectified by Huggins ten years later. Nor was Coghlan in a position to interfere, had he wished, with one vital part of the administration. The Native Affairs Department remained as it was under the Company, a state within a state. The Chief Native Commissioner was almost as hard to remove as a judge. Appointments and promotions were made by the Governor in Executive Council, but needed the approval of the High Commissioner (who was also the Governor General) in South Africa. The 'reserved powers' in the Letters Patent gave the British Government a veto on any legislation detrimental to the African population, although there was no corresponding power to do anything positive.

Coghlan, relatively liberal in racial matters by the very different standards of that day, far from resenting the reserved powers, regarded them as a necessary safeguard and told the Governor that he would not advise their removal. He was conscious of the risk that a settler legislature would be indifferent to the needs of the voteless majority or worse still, would improperly exploit their helplessness.

He strongly opposed attempts by white farmers in the remoter districts to conscript labour in order to exploit the tobacco boom. He obtained the British Government's assent in 1926 to a Native Juveniles Act which was welcomed by native parents (though possibly not by native juveniles) since it empowered Native Commissioners to send truant children home, to terminate labour contracts which they considered undesirable, and to make contracts for juveniles who had no parents or guardians, the latter provision being enforceable by summary whipping. The measures which in fact did much to remove the worst abuses of child labour provoked, because of the whipping clause, an uproar in England led by the Rev. Arthur Shirley Cripps, an unworldly, left-wing Puseyite priest-cum-poet who spent most of his life on his mission station, 'Maronda Mashanu', near Enkeldoorn, but had a cure of souls in his home country from 1926 to 1930. He was the quintessential figure of the dissentient Englishman prepared to believe almost any evil of his compatriots settled in the far flung empire. These figures are less familiar today now that the empire has vanished – a disappearance to which they made their own by no means negligible contribution.

Cripps himself had been in Southern Rhodesia since 1901, except for an interlude as a wartime chaplain in East Africa. He had formed an idyllic picture of the African past and had been agitating for years about the alleged abuses of Company and settler rule. The significance of the juvenile natives issue was in kindling for the first time a spark which lighted a fairly widespread fire of humanitarian and negrophile indignation among the liberal/left in Britain. In this particular case their opposition was largely misplaced. The coercive part of the Act soon became a dead letter, and the Native Commissioners' powers to disallow certain types of juvenile labour contract proved to be an important safeguard. The episode was, however, symptomatic of a change in the climate of 'enlightened' opinion. The sympathy felt for the settlers when they were fighting the Company was rapidly evaporating. Now that they ruled they were seen as oppressors rather than oppressed, and every measure proposed in the field of native affairs was scrutinized with mounting suspicion and distrust.

There was, however, one measure enacted shortly before Coghlan died which humanitarians should have welcomed. This was the Criminal Trials Act of 1927. Coghlan's earlier perturbation at the perverse verdicts returned by juries in cases of violence between black and white has already been mentioned, but the 'special juries' (i.e. juries selected by the Attorney General) introduced in 1911 did not really meet the problem. These too were all-white, they might be prejudiced and would not necessarily have any understanding of the African mentality. The new Act provided that anyone charged upon indictment before the High Court could opt to be tried before a Judge and two Assessors who must be experienced Native Commissioners of long standing. Given the then social structure of Southern Rhodesia, this was about as far as reform could be expected to go.

The African voice in the country, dumb since the rebellions, began in the early 1920s to become audible, but the sound was faint and far away, the message confusing and obscure. The earliest and most articulate came from Matabeleland, as one would expect, for the Ndebele aristocracy had not been utterly crushed like the Shona Chiefs. Nyamanda and his supporters, defeated in their claim before the Privy Council, pressed for a sort of Ndebele home rule within Matabeleland. They aspired to Protectorate status under the direct supervision of the British Crown. This was what Khama had obtained in Bechuanaland, Lewanika in Barotseland, Mosheshwe in Basutoland. Lobengula might well have settled for it, given the chance. Nyamanda and his movement were realistic enough not to claim all of Matabeleland and they ignored Mashonaland entirely; they were supported by the South African Congress and in Britain by the Aborigines Protection Society. In March 1919 he petitioned the Crown for the return of 'the so-called unalienated land to the family of the late King Lobengula in trust for the tribe according to Bantu custom'. It was, of course, far too late. The question of settler rule had in reality been determined when the settlers secured a majority of elected members on the Legislative Council as long ago as 1907. However, it still remained for formal decision, and, as Professor Ranger points out, Nyamanda's movement, though it achieved none of its objects 'was the only African voice to make itself heard at a key moment in Rhodesian politics – the achievement by the white settlers of political control'.[6]

Nyamanda was protesting against the creation of the new regime. Another quite separate movement tried to operate within it. At Gwelo in January 1923 Abraham Twala, an African from South Africa who had migrated to Southern Rhodesia, formed in conjunction with a handful of educated Shona and Ndebele allies the Rhodesian Bantu Voters Association. It was modelled on the Association operating in the Cape, and the object was to get the Africans on the electoral register to bargain votes for Responsible Government in return for limited concessions to African demands. Nothing came of it. Whereas in the Cape there were sufficient Bantu voters to make a difference in closely fought elections, in Southern Rhodesia there were reckoned to be only sixty on the entire register. The European leaders of Responsible Government showed no interest.

Other bodies came into existence: the Gwelo Native Welfare Association, the Rhodesia Native Association, etc. They had little effect. It was significant that their leadership was largely in the hands of immigrants, Fingos and Sothos from the south, and Nyasas from what is now Malawi – countries where native educational standards were at that time superior to those of Southern Rhodesia. These were not the only collective manifestations of African consciousness. There were various Christian independent churches with millennial dreams of the Whites being blown away in a 'big wind'. In 1927 the South African Industrial and Commercial Workers Union (ICU), headed by a Nyasa, Clemens Kadalie, sent a compatriot, Robert Sambo, to start similar trade union activities in Southern Rhodesia, but it never developed into the mass organization that it was south of the Limpopo. The Shamva mine strike of the same year, the first serious instance of African workers' strike action in Southern Rhodesia, owed nothing to

[6] T. O. Ranger, *Aspects of Central African History*, 1968, 222.

the ICU. Significantly it occurred in a mine where less than five per cent of the Africans employed were Southern Rhodesians.[7]

By far the most important event in Coghlan's premiership was the report in 1925 of the Land Commission over which Sir Morris Carter, an ex-Chief Justice of Uganda and Tanganyika presided. The land question in Southern Rhodesia is so strange (to non-colonial eyes), so complicated and so widely misunderstood that a discussion of the problem may be appropriate here, even at the risk of going both backwards as well as forwards in time.

It is important to distinguish two aspects of what is basically the same issue: the allocation of native reserves and the allocation of native purchase areas. The latter only came into existence as a consequence of the Carter report. The former constituted a part of the original settlement after the conquest of Matabeleland in 1893. We have seen how the inadequacy, remoteness, dryness and infertility of the reserves allocated by Jameson contributed to the Ndebele rebellion in 1896. When it was over Sir Richard Martin, the first Resident Commissioner, condemned the allocation most severely in a devastating report in 1897. As a result some 5.3 million acres were added to the original 4.1 million in Matabeleland, and a further 7 million were allocated in Mashonaland. Subsequent grants made the figure up to 20.5 million in 1914 for the two provinces, out of a total Southern Rhodesian acreage of 96 million.

The Company's policy of European agricultural settlement from 1908 onwards meant that further land was needed, and this entailed an attack on either the European absentee landlords or else on the reserves. An attack on the latter seemed easier, but it was effectively repulsed by the Native Department in Mashonaland where most of the demands were made. The Company accordingly argued for a general settlement of the whole question, Maguire observing: 'Do not consider that in any other way we have any chance of reclaiming areas set apart for native reserves, but not required'.[8] Under this pressure the British Government in 1914 set up a Native Reserves Commission headed by Sir Robert Coryndon, formerly Rhodes's private secretary and Administrator of North Western Rhodesia; the Commission was charged with the task of making a final delimitation of the reserves and reporting to the High Commissioner. Coryndon, as a former Company employee, was not the ideal choice for a post which required detachment from Company interests. The Commission operated in close co-operation with F. W. Inskipp, Acting Director of the Company's Land Settlement Department, who pushed his cause almost beyond the call of duty. The Commission operated, more-over, at a time when, because of war, some vigilant Native Commissioners and missionaries were away and only half aware of what was happening. It recommended

[7] See I. R. Phimister, 'The Shamva Mine Strike of 1927: An Emerging African Pro-letariat', *Rhodesian History* 2, 1971, 65–88, for an interesting analysis of this episode.

[8] Quoted R. H. Palmer, 'Aspects of Rhodesian Land Policy 1890–1936', *Central Africa Historical Association Local Series* 22, Salisbury, 1968, 21.

a net deduction in the reserves of about 1 million acres (5.6 million were added and 6.6 million were deducted).

This was not as bad as some historians have claimed,[9] and at the end of it all Southern Rhodesia could be said to come out better than South Africa, although that standard of comparison is low. The point is not so much the net reduction as the exchange of good land for bad, and it was only the forceful intervention of Herbert Stanley, the Resident Commissioner, which prevented the Africans being even worse treated. The Colonial Office approved the report in February 1917 and it was confirmed with certain amendments by Order-in-Council in November 1920, despite strong protests from the Aborigines Protection Society, Arthur Cripps, and others. The reserves were vested in the High Commissioner and the new allocation was, in the words of the Order-in-Council, to 'be taken to be a final assignment to the natives inhabiting Southern Rhodesia'.

That the Commission was heavily biased in favour of the Company's and settlers' interests which in this matter happened to coincide cannot be seriously doubted. It is perhaps surprising that the Colonial Office agreed, and the explanation may be the impression now shown to be erroneous that the Native Department acquiesced in the recommendations. In fact individual Commissioners were highly critical, but they only saw the detailed proposals after the report had been endorsed by the imperial Government.[10]

The report was, however, supported by rational arguments – or, rather, arguments that seemed rational at the time – and it is in that respect an archetypal warning against all those social and economic investigations which extrapolate alleged present trends into an uncertain future, and base policy recommendations upon these dubious predictions. The Coryndon Commission believed that the rate of increase in the African population would be slow, that tribalism was disappearing, that water supplies would increase the carrying capacity of the reserves, that cattle would soon have only a commercial purpose, that native cultivation would become intensive, and that little future conflict would soon arise between the races.

Almost all these prophesies were belied by events. The African population of 870,000 in 1921 was 1,080,000 in 1931, 1,430,000 in 1941 and had passed the 2 million mark by 1951. The European population did, it is true, increase proportionately at a higher rate, being at the respective dates, 33,800; 50,100; 69,300; and 138,000. But they remained numerically a small white island in a black sea. The carrying capacity of the reserves did not meet the rise in population or stock. Important areas of Matabeleland began to dry up. Cattle retained their traditional role, and attempts at destocking in order to prevent the deterioration of the soil met with silent but effective resistance. Africans continued to practise extensive

---

[9] Colin Leys, *European Politics in Southern Rhodesia*, 1959, 10, puts the deduction at 'over six million acres', and the figure has been repeated elsewhere. Presumably he took the gross deduction figure, and forgot the additions.

[10] Palmer, op. cit., 29.

agriculture, fearing *inter alia* that a change would merely give the Government the excuse to reduce the reserves. Far from becoming detribalized the vast majority clung to their surviving ancestral lands, and, despite the advance of the Christian missions, to a large part of their ancestral beliefs. Far from being a period of relaxation of racial conflict, the next three decades saw its acute intensification.

The Commission was not unaware that an actual reduction in the area of the reserves would be open to criticism. Their reply was logical, given certain pre-suppositions. In their interim report they pointed out that the various increases made since 1894 had been interpreted in some quarters to mean that every individual in a tribe had an 'indefeasible' right to enough land upon which to subsist. If this interpretation was correct and if, as was likely, the prevention of disease led to a gradual increase in the African population, 'there can be no limit to the extension of the native reserves; and if the argument is pursued to its logical conclusion the whole of Southern Rhodesia will, in course of time, be required for this purpose'. The Commission reasonably enough concluded that an 'indefeasible' right could not be conceded to every unborn native 'to live on the soil and by the primitive and wasteful methods of cultivation practised by his forefathers'.

These words are much quoted but, as Mr Rifkind points out, the argument depends on 'two other observations often overlooked by the quoters of the above'.[11] The first was that, tribal subsistence being incompatible with economic progress, it must be assumed that the European economy would obtain its labour force from the African population; an increasing proportion would, therefore, become an urban proletariat permanently uprooted from the land, as had occurred during the Industrial Revolution in England. The prediction that more and more Africans would be employed in the European economy was quite correct, but successive Southern Rhodesian Governments have refused to accept the corollary that the urban African worker should have a permanent home in the cities and towns. On the contrary he was and still is regarded as a migrant whose ultimate destiny was to go back to the reserves. Thus a vital premise to the whole of the Coryndon Commission's argument was in the event disregarded.

The second point is equally important. The Interim Report made it clear that the reserves were intended to provide only for those natives 'who are not ready for the new order' an area where they could 'continue to live under their old conditions'. This presupposed that the Africans who had left or would leave the tribal system in increasing numbers would have the same legal rights as any other Rhodesian citizen. At the time of the publication of the report that was indeed the case. An African had in law – the practice was another matter – as good a right as any European to purchase land in the remaining 75 million acres of the country including the urban areas. When the Responsible Government constitution was promulgated in 1923 this right was specifically spelt out, but within eight years, largely as a result of the Morris Carter Report, the whole situation had changed. The African right of purchase had become highly restricted, and another

[11] Malcolm Rifkind, *The Politics of Land*, University of Edinburgh Thesis, 1968, 29.

vital premise to the Coryndon Commission's recommendations had disappeared.

The Carter Commission originated from an undertaking by the Colonial Office when the draft constitution was published in January 1922. If an impartial enquiry showed that there was a need to amend the law of land tenure, the Colonial Secretary promised to act accordingly. The pressure for amendment which, of course, meant a restriction on African rights came from diverse quarters, but there can be no serious doubt that the principal motive was the deep dislike felt by European farmers at Africans buying land in their midst. From 1908 onwards rural members of the Legislative Council had carried motions for repeal of the existing law. The reason was not solely colour prejudice, although it played a big part. African farmers were in many ways bad neighbours, and they would be competing at cut prices with access to markets which Europeans regarded as their own. The reports of the Chief Native Commissioner in 1919 and 1920 had recommended that land near the reserves should be kept for native purchase only, and commented on the 'inevitable friction' with European neighbours, which would arise if Africans could buy land anywhere. From quite another quarter there was the argument of Cripps and some missionaries that segregation would prevent the Africans being corrupted by European influences. There was also, again from negrophile quarters, the fear that Europeans with their superior wealth would buy up all the land worth having and that Africans would find, as they had in the Eastern Cape, that there was nothing left.

These fears or hopes mainly concerned future events. The Company, aware of the intense unpopularity that it would acquire with the settlers if it sold land to Africans, had in practice refused such offers to purchase, and most private owners had acted similarly. By 1925 only nineteen farms amounting to 47,000 acres had been sold to Africans, whereas some 31,000,000 acres were in European possession. Of the European-owned land only half could be described as 'occupied' and even less as being actually farmed or cultivated – every allowance being made for the areas which could not be expected to produce anything. The danger of either major infiltration by African peasant farmers or at the other extreme of Europeans buying up everything was not imminent. Nonetheless, the problem generated a considerable head of steam.

The Carter Commission took evidence all over Southern Rhodesia from most of the interests concerned. The initiative for change was mainly European. There is little to suggest any African pressure. In spite of subsequent mythology repeated in book after book, there can be no doubt that the idea of land segregation stemmed from the Whites, not the Blacks; the object was to dispel European fears rather than to protect African interests. It is less clear how the Africans reacted to this European initiative. On the whole the evidence suggests a division between urban and rural society, the former being opposed, the latter favourable in principle, as the Carter Commission strongly maintained – and at that time tribalized rural Africans far out-numbered the rest.

It is another matter when one departs from the principle to the actual physical division on the ground. This was bitterly opposed – and with good reason – by articulate Africans of every background. The Carter Commission recommended that out of the 75 million acres outside the native reserves just over 48 million should be purchasable only by Europeans and just under 7 million only by Africans. Of the remainder, 17.8 million acres was unassigned land which could, according to circumstances, be allocated to either race. The rest was forest land and game reserves, including the enormous Wankie Game Reserve, and came under the control of the Government. The European purchase area was not only far larger than the native area, it also included all the urban centres, and all the best agricultural land. Nevertheless, after much discussion and scrutiny the Dominions Office agreed. Although Ramsay MacDonald's Government was in power, there was little opposition in the British Parliament, except in the House of Lords from Lord Olivier. Lord Passfield (Sidney Webb), the Dominions Secretary, raised no objection. After the Land Apportionment Bill had been passed by the Legislative Assembly the lawyers discovered that it was *ultra vires* the Constitution. In accordance with now established usage Parliament amended the Letters Patent. The bill was reintroduced and became law on April 1, 1931. With a few minor changes (the native area went up from 6.8 million to 7.4 million acres and the European to 49 million) the Carter Commission's proposals were enacted.

The Land Apportionment Act has been defended on many grounds – most of them dubious. It is important to remember that it had nothing to do with the native reserves (or, as they are now called, tribal trust lands). These were enshrined in the Constitution. Defence of the Act on the ground that it prevented European encroachment on the reserves is irrelevant. It could have been repealed at any time without affecting them in the least. Nor can it be argued that the Act was needed in order to save the Africans from an Eastern Cape situation. The native purchase area and the reserves could have been kept for them while those who did not feel the need for protection could have been allowed to take their chance in competition with the Europeans for the rest.

Although it is true that 7 million acres was probably a reasonable allocation for the number of Africans likely to seek individual tenure in the then foreseeable future, and although it is also true that the right to purchase land anywhere had never been a practical reality, nevertheless it is hard to justify an apportionment of 28 million acres (including the reserves) to 1 million Blacks and 48 million acres to 50,000 Whites. The white allocation becomes even more remarkable if we remember that of the 31 million acres which white owners had acquired by 1925 half was still unoccupied and that even as late as 1965, by which time there had been a vast extension of European farming, only 36 million acres were occupied, and nearly all the development had occurred on the 31 million acres already in European ownership forty years earlier.

The feature of the Land Apportionment Act which is the least defensible of all was the inclusion of virtually every town and city in the European purchase area. This meant that no African could buy or rent a house in Salisbury, Bulawayo or any urban area. The Carter Commission recognized that African labour had become an integral part of the urban economy and that a category of Africans had or would come into being which no longer wished for rural life; but it assumed that the urban labourer was employed on a 'temporary' basis – although this could mean his whole working life – and that he would on retirement go to exclusively African townships which the Governor-in-Council would be empowered to create in African purchase areas. The native labourer had, of course, to live somewhere while he was working. The Act empowered but did not compel municipalities to create areas for the exclusive occupation by Africans. It was many years before all local authorities took advantage of this power, but even when they did there was no question of the Africans having any right to permanent occupation.

It is probably not conscious hypocrisy which has caused so many Rhodesians to maintain that the purpose of the Land Apportionment Act was to protect the African. Political human nature is such that men cannot easily accept naked self-interest as their own conditioning motive, even though they are quick enough to see it in others. In politics people need the justification of an altruistic purpose, and there were some sections of the Act which could be fairly regarded as beneficial to Africans as well as Europeans. After all, even such an arch-enemy of the settlers as Cripps supported it. Nevertheless, no one who studies the contemporary argument used at the time of the passing of the Act can be left in any serious doubt that the purpose was at least as much to protect Europeans against Africans as vice versa, and to protect, moreover, those were already in an highly advantageous position. In what is one of the most illuminating books ever written about the country, Sir Robert Tredgold comments thus:

It has become a feature of Government propaganda in Rhodesia to claim that the Land Apportionment Acts and other supporting legislation were passed primarily in the interests of the Africans. This is simply untrue, as anyone must bear witness who watched the growth of the ideas behind the legislation and saw its passage through the House. If anyone has doubt on the subject, let him refer to the Hansards of the debates. I would concede that the legislation was intended to be in the interests of all the inhabitants, black or white, of the Colony, but the Europeans had much more to gain from it than the Africans.[12]

Sir Robert goes on to point out that the pressure for repeal has nearly all come from Africans, that the measure has been repeatedly described by its supporters as the 'White Man's Magna Carta' and that pressure for retention is of almost exclusively European origin. He could have added that the only Rhodesian Government which has ever proposed its abolition, Sir Edgar Whitehead's, crashed to disaster at the general election of 1962 largely for that reason.

The Morris Carter Report and the resultant legislation has profoundly affected race relations from that day to this. No doubt a large degree of possessary and social segregation already existed, but, as Mr Rifkind says, 'this had been of a

[12] *The Rhodesia that was my Life*, 1968, 154-5.

pragmatic rather than an ideological nature'; it was 'a social fact rather than a deliberate policy'. There is a great difference between a *de facto* situation which may change with changing economic and moral concepts, and a *de jure* segregation sanctified by the authority of an impartial commission and the sovereignty of Westminster itself. Nor should one forget the hardship and uncertainty entailed for Africans who had been living under rent agreements on what had become the European area and whose tenure was now scheduled to expire by 1937. It is true that practical considerations – among them the inadequacy of the reserves – made this policy impossible to enforce to the letter of the law. The fact remains that under the first Land Apportionment Act, and its successors which tended to be even more rigid and meticulous, many thousands of Africans were compulsorily moved from land which they had occupied for generations. No wonder that the measure became the very symbol and embodiment of everything most resented in European domination.

14

The Decline of Rhodesian Party 1927–33

Although the Land Apportionment Act was a measure with far reaching consequences for Southern Rhodesia's future, it would be wrong to think that 'native affairs' were a part of the European political debate in Coghlan's time or in the earlier years of his successor's premiership. There was a convention that these matters should be treated as technical and 'non-party', and the entrenched position of the Native Department with its responsibility not only to the Premier but also in some degree to the South African High Commissioner emphasized the point. Coghlan was primarily concerned with the economic problems of a poor colony which was badly under-capitalized. Railway rates, the Company's mineral rights, the powers reserved to Whitehall, European land settlement, relations with South Africa and Portugal – these were the stuff of political debate and action.

Coghlan established good relations both with Herzog, who was from his view point a much easier opposite number than Smuts, and with the Portuguese Government. He managed to meet the grievances about railway rates by a Railways Bill in 1927 which set up an inter-territorial Commission representing the two Rhodesias and Bechuanaland, and specified minimum and maximum earnings.[1] He came to a satisfactory customs agreement with South Africa. Newton as High Commissioner in London managed to negotiate satisfactory terms for a loan from the Bank of England.

This was useful because the colony, which operated on a small budget, began life with a debt of £2,300,000 to the British Treasury. Of this sum £300,000 represented advances made in 1921 and 1922, and the obligation could not be disputed. The liability for the rest was more controversial, though Coghlan felt

[1] It also marked a constitutional advance from the Rhodesian standpoint, for railway legislation no longer had to be 'reserved' pending approval from London.

that he had to accept it. When the British Government bought out the Chartered Company for £3,750,000 it regarded £2,000,000 as payment for the unalienated land plus the buildings and public works constructed by the Company in its governmental capacity. The residue was the accumulated administrative deficit. Having forgone what was – no doubt coincidentally – exactly the same sum in respect of wartime advances, the Colonial Office was all the more determined to extract the £2,000,000 for the public works and land rights. The matter can be looked at in two ways. The settlers felt a grievance, repeated in many books about Rhodesia, that they were the only British colony which in effect had to pay for the privilege of Responsible Government. On the other hand it could well be argued that they were liable for the accumulated deficit as well as the land and public works. On that view, the British Government was paying nearly half the colony's equivalent of the national debt – and a much higher proportion if one includes the waiver of war costs.

The case is, therefore, not as clear cut as many of the colonists liked to believe. Nevertheless, £2,000,000 was a lot at that time, and the public finances of the country both then and some years to come were not easy to manage. The administrative system was top heavy, for the Government in order to persuade immigrants had to provide the services expected by an English community without at first being able to use them to capacity. The same was broadly true of railways, banks and businesses. Sir Henry Clay, an eminent economist invited in 1930 to report on the colony, compared it to a firm with heavy overheads and an inadequate turnover.[2] More capital, more immigrants, greater African purchasing power were needed, but world economic conditions from 1931 onwards did not help. Moreover, Southern Rhodesia's was not a diversified economy. Gold, maize, tobacco and cattle were the main products, and there was little else to fall back on if those went wrong.

Grievances about railway rates, insufficient immigration, and the Company's mineral rights had stirred up a certain amount of opposition to the ruling party by 1926–27. It crystallized around the flamboyant personality of Colonel Frank Johnson who after a long interval once again makes a fleeting appearance on the Rhodesian stage. Elected at a by-election for Salisbury South in 1927 he campaigned for a 'whiter Rhodesia', the buying out of the Chartered Company's mineral rights and the acquisition of a western port at Walvis Bay. A new group known as the Progressive Party was formed. This mixture of radicalism and racialism cut substantially into the Labour Party's support and it also secured some defectors from the Rhodesian Party.

In that same year Coghlan died. His health had for some time been deteriorating because of drink and worry about his finances; he had no money and in his will asked for a pension for his wife and daughter.[3] He was buried along with Rhodes and Jameson at World's View – the last person to have received this honour.

[2] Quoted Gann, *Southern Rhodesia*, 283.
[3] Wallis, op. cit., 244.

His death removed the only personality in the ruling party.

He had always looked upon Moffat as his successor and during his recent illness had treated him as his deputy. The Governor, Sir John Chancellor, who found time heavy on his hands as a 'constitutional monarch', had other views.[4] He had been accustomed to being a 'real' Governor and had not appreciated how little latitude he was to have in Southern Rhodesia. There were, however, two discretionary powers which were unquestionably vested in him under the constitution: the right to choose a new premier, and the right to grant or refuse a dissolution. Chancellor decided to exercise the former. He had no very high opinion of Moffat whom he believed to be incapable of holding together an apparently divided Rhodesian Party, nor did he favour any one else in the Cabinet or the Assembly. His candidate was Murray Bisset, the Senior Judge who had, in accordance with the Constitutional rules, deputized as Governor in Chancellor's absence from February to September 1926. Bisset was a distinguished South African lawyer, but he knew little about Southern Rhodesia and had no chance of commanding any general support. Chancellor consulted the Cabinet. With the exception of Moffat who said he would gladly serve under Bisset, they strongly disapproved of the Governor's suggestion. In such circumstances a constitutional monarch has no choice. Chancellor reluctantly appointed Moffat.

Moffat was not a very strong figure, and he perhaps inherited from his missionary forebears rather too tender a conscience for a politician, but Chancellor's misgivings about his ability to hold his party together proved to be quite unfounded. In reality he had been *de facto* Premier for the last four months and had by now acquired the full confidence of his supporters. At the general election of 1928 the Rhodesian Party lost four seats, but the opposition was hopelessly divided between Progressives (four) and Labour (three) with one Independent. In any case twenty-two out of thirty was quite enough, and Moffat was in a strong position. Frank Johnson lost his seat (he returned to England in 1930) and the Progressives soon faded out as a serious political force, if they had even been one.

Before the election there occurred an episode[5] worthy of a play by John Galsworthy or Terence Rattigan, the sort of thing which could only happen in the small closed society of Southern Rhodesia. It was highly embarrassing for all three persons involved in the succession to Coghlan. In September 1927 John Meikle, Moffat's brother-in-law, who in a mood of ill temper had branded one of his African employees on the bottom, pleaded guilty to the charge of assault. The offence would have been considered as a bit much even in the heyday of the Jameson regime, but Bisset's sentence of fifteen months hard labour was regarded by most Europeans as harsh; Bisset told the Governor that he refused to give the option

---

[4] See R. W. Baldock 'Chancellor and the Moffat Succession', *Rhodesian History*, Vol. 3, 1972, 41–52, for a most interesting account on which the following paragraphs are based.

[5] Baldock, op. cit., 48–50.

of a fine because he knew that, though Meikle was a bankrupt, others would pay up. Meikle's brother, Thomas, who owned hotels and stores all over the country, was reputed to be the richest man in the Rhodesias.

The Meikles were of early Rhodesian stock and highly respected. A petition signed by 8,000 residents was submitted to the Governor on December 19 requesting remission of the rest of the sentence on the ground of the prisoner's connexion with the Territory since 1892, his part in the first Matabele war, and his pro-native efforts as a member of the Legislative Council 1903–5 to stop the hut tax being doubled. The Meikle family freely attributed the severity of the sentence to Bisset's alleged mortification at being passed over for the Premiership – a charge which appears to be wholly unfounded. The Governor had the right of pardon, but was obliged to seek, though not necessarily to accept, the advice of the Executive Council. It would clearly be most awkward if Moffat attended. He was now not on speaking terms with Bisset, whose health suffered as a result of the affair, and their wives were also heavily embroiled. Moffat tactfully absented himself from the crucial meeting. Fortunately for Chancellor who was pro-Bisset and regarded the sentence as a salutory example the Executive Council did not advise remission. Even more fortunately for all parties concerned, the medical profession always powerful in Rhodesia came to the rescue. It was alleged that continued imprisonment might be fatal to Meikle's health and, after a report by the Senior Government Medical Officer, Chancellor felt obliged to release him. He did so with reluctance, fearing a row in England from the negrophile organizations, though in the event nothing happened.

The sequel to these strange events was even stranger. Chancellor who cannot, one feels, have been a very sensitive character decided to press for a knighthood for Bisset in March 1928. This was, on any view of the *cursus honorum*, a premature recommendation, for the Senior Judge had only served two years of the conventional five. The Governor's ground was largely recognition of Bisset's courage in sentencing Meikle in the teeth of public opposition. But he disregarded the fact that Southern Rhodesia was not a Crown Colony. The Dominions Office, unlike the Colonial Office, could not submit such a recommendation to Downing Street simply on the advice of the Governor. The approval of the Premier was essential also. Chancellor, therefore, was in the invidious position of having 'to request Moffat to agree that the man responsible, three months previously, for the onerous sentence on his wife's brother, should receive a knighthood, and largely because of that sentence'.[6] Whether one regards it as a sign of weakness, high-mindedness or over-scrupulosity, Moffat endorsed the recommendation, though he made it plain that he would have preferred Bisset to wait 'till he had earned it'.

Sir John Chancellor's term of office came to an end soon afterwards. He replaced Lord Plumer as High Commissioner in Palestine – a post far more congenial for it involved the exercise of real power. As the first Governor of a colony whose constitution had no recent analogue it is perhaps not surprising that he

[6] Baldock, op. cit., 50.

failed at times to appreciate the limitations of his position. His successors recognized that their role, like that of the monarchy, was primarily social, symbolic and advisory, and that the actual powers of the Governor, as opposed to his potential personal influence, though not negligible, were extremely limited, and must be treated as such.

Moffat's premiership lasted for five years. An aura of failure hangs over it in retrospect, but the reason is largely the fiasco of its finish; and even so it is right to remember that the world economic crisis of the 1930s swept many other sitting tenants into political oblivion and it is difficult to argue that a different premier would have achieved much more, or that Moffat made any palpable errors. His most notable 'success' in terms of what was expected of him by the electorate was the Land Apportionment Act. Its significance and defects have already been discussed, but at the time it was not much criticized from a liberal standpoint. Rather, Moffat came under fire for being too kind to the Blacks. One of his important measures, highly praised later by his opponent, Godfrey Huggins, was the creation of a Native Development Department in 1929 – 'They did a fine job on agriculture and conservation services and earned the country a high reputation that has lasted ever since'.[7]

At the end of his time Coghlan, who had been long opposed to amalgamation with Northern Rhodesia, had come round to the opposite view, largely because of the problem of integrating the railway systems. Moffat was a strong advocate of amalgamation. He was sadly disappointed at the outcome of the Hilton Young Commission set up in 1929 to investigate the whole question of Britain's Central and East African possessions. The Commission unanimously recommended that Kenya, Uganda and Tanganyika should be federated and that the federation should not include Northern Rhodesia or Nyasaland. On the future of those two protectorates the Commission was divided. Sir Hilton Young himself favoured the frequently suggested solution of amalgamating the Railway Belt (a central strip including the route to Katanga) with Southern Rhodesia. North Eastern Rhodesia would be joined to Nyasaland as a Crown Colony, while Barotseland would constitute a native reserve and a separate protectorate. A central authority to co-ordinate defence, communications and tariffs would be set up under the presidency of the Governor of Southern Rhodesia as High Commissioner, and the supervisory powers of the Colonial and Dominion offices over African and imperial affairs would be transferred to him.

The rest of the Commission which included Dr J. H. Oldham, Secretary of the International Missionary Society, favoured leaving things alone for the time being. Their reason was partly a hope that, although federation with East Africa was inexpedient for the moment, some sort of link might become feasible in future. There were two other reasons, however, and they were to dominate consideration of the problem for the next twenty years.

First, it was now clear that copper could be profitably mined on a huge scale

[7] RR 13.

in Northern Rhodesia. This was the result of an important technological change which made it possible to exploit the low grade sulphide ores characteristic of the region. The new industrial revolution of the 1920s, involving the electrical, motor car and communications industries, produced a great demand for copper, and Britain was anxious not to depend solely on American supplies. The BSA Company now discovered that the bargain struck under duress with the Colonial Office had not been so bad after all. Northern Rhodesian mineral rights worth £13,000 a year in 1922 reached over £300,000 by 1939. The Company pursued a policy of giving concessions on a big scale to heavily capitalized firms. After a complicated series of kaleidoscopic mergers and separations two vast combines acquired control over the entire Copper Belt. The larger whose key figure was Sir Ernest Oppenheimer was the Rhodesian Anglo-American Corporation. It had links with the British South Africa Company which it was ultimately to absorb, and it was a part of the great South African corporation of the same name which dominated the gold and diamond mines of the Union. The other and smaller combine was the Rhodesian Selection Trust which had substantial American backing. It was founded by the American mining engineer and financial genius, Chester Beatty.

The entire economic prospect for what had been an impoverished and unimportant protectorate was thus transformed. The strategic importance of copper is obvious, and clearly no British Government was lightly going to relinquish its control over the region. That control was much easier to enforce under Crown Colony rule than Responsible Government. The very change which made Southern Rhodesia more anxious to amalgamate with its northern neighbour made the British Government less willing to consent.

The second reason why successive British Governments had misgivings about amalgamation was the whole question of 'native trusteeship'. This was tied to the doctrine of 'paramountcy' laid down in 1923 by the Duke of Devonshire in the Colonial Office's *Memorandum relating to Indians in Kenya*. Kenya was to be regarded as primarily an African territory and, therefore, native interests must be treated as 'paramount' over those of the immigrant races in the event of conflict. The paper, in Gann's words, 'started a long and bitter controversy over the definition of "paramountcy", comparable in intensity with the debates that used to rage over the details of obscure theological doctrines in ancient Byzantium.'[8] Although the occasion for the paper was the status of the Indians, its arguments were equally applicable to Europeans in Kenya, or for that matter in Northern Rhodesia. The white Kenyans fought a battle for the settlers in all the territories north of the Zambesi and eventually in 1927 the Colonial Office in a paper entitled *Future Policy in regard to Eastern Africa* back-pedalled to the extent of conceding that immigrant communities were entitled to share in political and economic development and that settlers should be 'associated' in the imperial trust, whatever that might mean.

The controversy died away for the moment, but it burst into furious flames

[8] L. H. Gann, *A History of Northern Rhodesia*, 1964, 240–1.

when Lord Passfield in 1930 announced the government's *Conclusions . . . as regards Closer Union in East Africa*. The Colonial Secretary reaffirmed the Devonshire doctrine and asserted the need to retain final political control in London for the sake of the native interests, even if local legislatures eventually acquired elected majorities. Settlers all over East and Central Africa were highly indignant. Southern Rhodesia was not directly affected but, if this doctrine was to prevail with the British Government, the chances of amalgamation at once receded. It is true that the Northern Rhodesian Whites for the same reason became more favourable to amalgamation, but they did not control their destinies. The clash between the economic advantages of amalgamation and the political danger, as seen from Whitehall, of putting the Africans north of the Zambesi under a settler government dominated the argument for many years to come. The doctrinal dispute was diplomatically and temporarily shelved by the report of a Joint Select Committee of both Houses of Parliament in 1931 which defined 'paramountcy' as meaning merely that the interests of natives should not be *subordinated* to those of the immigrants, but the basic conflict remained. Gann, writing of Northern Rhodesia, puts it admirably:

> . . . the great majority of white Rhodesians bitterly resented the idea that upper class civil servants with Oxford accents and 'Thirds' from Balliol, or expatriate parsons from Cuddeston, should regard themselves as impartial arbiters between black and white, and [as] the African's chosen champions. The settlers made Rhodesia, they paid the bulk of its revenue, and they should ultimately run their country, self-government in any case constituting an Englishman's birthright.
>
> The officials sharply dissented. They tended to think of themselves as the country's 'guardians' in a way Plato might have approved, and they alone regarded themselves as competent to hold a balance between conflicting interests: their independent income untainted by 'trade' would assure their freedom from local pressure groups. Over and over again official speakers would thus stress the settlers' supposed political immaturity, their lack of numbers and the danger of entrusting power to a tiny white oligarchy.[9]

These contrasting attitudes were to condition much of the later history of Central Africa.

Moffat could have done nothing to prevent this particular defeat. The arbitrament lay in other hands. In any case graver matters of more immediate moment began to weigh upon him soon after Lord Passfield's decision. The world slump hit Rhodesia as everywhere else. Primary producers were the worst affected, and the value of Rhodesian exports declined catastrophically. Gold was an exception. Southern Rhodesia followed Britain off the Gold Standard in 1931, but South Africa, her chief competitor, retained the old parity for another year, and Rhodesian exports received a minor temporary boost.

[9] Op. cit., 240.

Despite this alleviation the fortunes of the Government continued to decline. In 1931 Fynn, the Minister of Finance, felt obliged, like his opposite numbers all over the world, to cut government expenditure, thus adding more deflation to a deflationary situation already quite bad enough. One of his proposed economies was a reduction in the pay of civil servants. Since their emoluments were protected by the reserved clauses of the constitution, a two-thirds majority of the Legislative Council was required. As a result of defections the Rhodesian Party needed the support of all its remaining members. Godfrey Huggins who represented a Salisbury constituency full of civil servants acutely disliked the Public Services Economy Bill, as it was called, and made it the occasion for crossing the floor. Nevertheless he voted for it, 'thereby implying its necessity', as Sir Robert Tredgold writes, adding: 'This on a highly unpopular measure was rather like having his cake and eating it'.[10]

Whatever his precise motives – and general dissatisfaction of a not very definable nature was probably the main one[11] – Huggins's decision was fateful. He offered to resign at a constituency public meeting at the Duthie Hall early in 1932, but his speech gained an ovation, and with the approval of his electors he became first an Independent, then a member of the Reform Party newly created by an alliance between the old Progressive Party, a small group called the Country Party and dissident members of the Rhodesian Party. Its chief was Robert Gilchrist, a Scottish Rhodesian farmer, and its other leading light was Jacob Smit, a Dutch greengrocer who had worked his way up in the world and had won a surprise anti-government victory at the Salisbury South by-election in 1931. But the Reform Party largely consisted of 'wild men', in the jargon of the day. Huggins, essentially an establishment figure, was just the person to give them tone and respectability.

His speech at his readoption meeting was gay, amusing, and hard-hitting. He had already in 1931 argued the case in the Legislative Assembly for a sort of apartheid – later known as the 'two pyramids' policy and he repeated these views to his constituents. 'I suppose my speech was good rabble-raising stuff', he reminisced to Rex Reynolds, 'I went for Moffat's liberalism, taking the popular line that native affairs should be kept out of politics.'[12] There is a curious *non sequitur* here, and one can but echo Sir Robert Tredgold's comment on the relevant passage in Huggins's official biography: 'I find it difficult to understand how it could be possible to attack the government strongly on its Native policy without making Native policy a party issue?' Native affairs were bound to come into European politics sooner or later. The Shamva strike, the Industrial and Commercial Workers Union, the growth of an articulate class of clerks and schoolmasters, the general 'advancement' of Africans – all combined to make it inevitable. The fact remains that Huggins, reputed later to be a liberal at heart, was the first white politician

[10] Op. cit., 115.

[11] He maintained (RR 15) that he did not wish to cause a general election, but this sounds like an *ex post facto* justification.

[12] RR 16.

of any importance to bring racial issues in a big way before the electorate.

Huggins's other target was the Chartered Company, its railway rights and especially its mineral rights which he maintained were not legal. In retrospect he was to admit his error on that point. 'We were a lot of novices really, all thinking with our blood pressure, rather like the present crowd.' Reynolds pointed out that the railway and mineral rights were the Company's 'perks' for having opened up the country. Huggins replied that at the time he differentiated between them. The Company had paid for the railways 'but we reckoned the minerals should belong to the people of the country,' and he added with the engaging candour of someone long out of the political battle, 'Of course if you think about it a bit more that would have been the munts'.[13]

In fact those who agitated about the Company's mineral rights had not a legal leg to stand on, but, under strong pressure of public opinion, Moffat felt obliged to ask the Company whether it would agree to submit the whole matter to the Judicial Committee of the Privy Council. The board, understandably, felt that they had had enough trouble already from that august body; in any case they regarded their position as impregnable; their answer was no. Moffat who was invited to the Imperial Economic Conference at Ottawa in August 1932 tried to raise the matter with J. H. Thomas, the Dominions Secretary. He got nowhere, though on a quite different line he did succeed in elevating the Southern Rhodesian Premier to Prime Minister. This seems to have been regarded as a feather in his cap, though it is hard to see what difference it made.

In November the Permanent Under-Secretary informed J. W. Downie, the Southern Rhodesian High Commissioner in London, that the British Government considered the mineral rights to be indubitably vested in the Company, not only under the Rudd Concession, but also under the much more recent Devonshire Agreement. It was a part of the 1923 settlement and written into the Constitution.

Moffat sensibly decided that he could not go along with the mounting agitation for a legal decision. It would be better to buy out the Company while there was at least some flicker of doubt about its rights. A lawsuit would merely confirm the Company's position and enhance the price. After much haggling the Company, which at the nadir of the slump was, like most concerns, short of liquid resources, sold out on April 1, 1933 for £2,000,000. It was not an obviously bad bargain for the Company on the short view. Southern Rhodesian mineral royalties had from 1924 to 1932 brought in an average of £84,000 a year net, after the agreed annual payment of £5,000 to the Geological Survey Department, and in 1933 the prospect for gold-mining which produced three-quarters of Rhodesia's mineral wealth did not look good. Furthermore, however legally strong the Company's case may have been, extreme political unpopularity was bad for business and worth avoiding. Nevertheless the Company would almost certainly not have sold at this price but for an acute shortage of cash.

[13] RR, loc. cit. 'Munt' is a slightly patronizing but not unfriendly white Rhodesian word for an African.

As events turned out the Southern Rhodesian Government made far the better bargain. Royalties increased beyond all predictions in the years that followed. But at the time Moffat was bitterly criticized for having paid too much for something which, it was claimed, belonged to the Government anyway and therefore ought to have been handed over for nothing. A sinister significance was attached to the absence of litigation. There were charges of collusion and hints that the Cabinet was under the sway of the Company – the sort of rumours which gain credence easily in a small closed society.

Meanwhile the Reform Party held a Congress at Gwelo in 1932 to decide on policy, tactics and leadership. Johnson had by now departed. Max Danziger, a clever Jewish lawyer who strongly supported segregation, was too unpopular. Neither Gilchrist nor Smit had the right talents to head a party. Huggins who did not attend went round to the Salisbury Club for a drink on the evening of the day of the Congress and found a telegram informing him that he had been elected Leader of the Opposition. He decided to take the plunge and accepted.

A general election had to be held in 1933. Moffat was by this time widely regarded as a liability to his party. He had more than once indicated his readiness to retire, but it was not so easy to get rid of him as might have been supposed. Allan Welsh, the Rhodesian Party chairman, and Ernest Guest, his legal partner, on the strength of a party meeting just before the Ottawa Conference were deputed to tell him that he no longer had the party's confidence. He was much distressed, but gave them the impression that he would resign after Ottawa. On his way back through London he saw Downie, the High Commissioner, who persuaded him to fight it out. At a meeting of the Party Executive Guest proposed for the leadership the name of George Mitchell, Minister of Mines since 1930. The man who was to have seconded him, however, nominated Moffat instead. Great confusion ensued, but Moffat solved the problem by withdrawing his name at the ensuing party Congress so that Mitchell could be elected unopposed.

The Ministerial Titles Bill had just become law; Mitchell, therefore, goes down to history as the first Rhodesian 'Prime Minister'.[14] He goes down for little else except the unenviable record of forming the shortest-lived administration in the annals of the colony. An elderly business man and former President of the Chamber of Mines, Mitchell was not the ideal man to defend the establishment in a climate of seething discontent. It is probably fair to add that no other member of the Rhodesian Party would have done any better. There was for the first and only time in the country's history serious white unemployment. Out-of-work Europeans were set on the task of building strip roads at a wage of five shillings a day – a process which was greatly encouraged by the next Government too. Although motoring, hitherto a slow and hazardous mode of transport, was thus much improved, and the isolation of the backveld farmers reduced, such a situation was bound to be unpopular. The white artisan not only blamed the Government for

[14] It also changed the titles of Treasurer to Minister of Finance, Colonial Secretary to Minister of Internal Affairs and Attorney General to Minister of Justice.

unemployment, he also blamed it for permitting black competition for the lower-grade white jobs. There was the perennial grumble about the railways and there was the grievance of the purchase of the Chartered Company's mineral rights. On top of all this came a diffused discontent and a general feeling that the Rhodesian Party was drifting and failing 'to get a move on'. The slump produced political convulsions all over the world, and the tiny colony was no exception.

Huggins was, therefore, on a good wicket during the run up to the August general election. He frankly beat the racialist drum, and, although his own language was moderate, that of some of his supporters was not. The Reform Party made segregation or 'separate development' one of its main planks. The native voter was to be removed from the Common Roll, territorial segregation to be further encouraged, and white artisans to be protected by legislation. The ideology behind all this was the 'twin pyramid' policy of N. H. Wilson, a journalist and member of the Legislative Assembly who saw Rhodesia's future in terms of two pyramidical structures; a white one which, though beginning with a black base at the lowest grade would ultimately, with immigration, become entirely white; and a black one in which all trades and professions would be open to blacks, and which would, with African advancement, become almost wholly black, though not entirely, for of course, ultimate European control was essential.

Huggins observed some thirty-five years later:

> What it boiled down to was plain apartheid, with a lot of fancy bits to show how fair and realistic it was. The black and white pyramids were illustrated as being the same size: what was never defined was how far up the black pyramid went before the little white dot that represented real power came and sat on it.
>
> But even so you must remember that what at this time [i.e. 1970] is an essentially a restrictive policy, trying to limit African influence in politics for all time, was then, in the short term actually a constructive policy. It aimed at giving the Natives some say in matters that affected them and, perhaps more important, some experience in making decisions and carrying them out.[15]

In power Huggins was far too realistic to implement this highly doctrinaire policy. The practical difficulties are proving almost insuperable in South Africa. In Rhodesia with its very different white black ratio it was impossible. How far the argument about the twin pyramid policy contributed to the election results one cannot say – probably not very much, for it was largely a quasi-theological debate about the distant future, and most Europeans must have seen it through a reversed telescope. But the general tone of the Reform Party on the racial question was likely to appeal to the white electorate, and there were numerous additional sticks with which to beat the Government. In many ways the political line-up was like the struggle between Coghlan and the unionists, eleven years

---

[15] RR 60.

earlier. The Reform Party was the party of the non-establishment whites, the less prosperous farmers, small-workers, minor businessmen, shopkeepers, etc. – and it competed with Labour for the artisan vote – whereas the Rhodesian Party was the party of the larger companies and their executives, the wealthier professional men, in fact the majority of those with 'a stake in the country', as the saying then was. It had the support of the Argus Press, and no doubt commanded a majority in both the Salisbury and the Bulawayo Clubs.

Mitchell had become Prime Minister in July. The election took place in September, and resulted in a narrow victory for the Reform Party of two over the other parties combined. The Reform Party won sixteen seats, the Rhodesian Party nine and the Labour Party five. Mitchell, Moffat, and W. M. Leggate, the highly unpopular Minister of Agriculture, all lost their seats. On September 6, 1933 Huggins was sworn in as Prime Minister. He was to hold the post without interruption for twenty years, and only left it to go up higher as Prime Minister of the new Central African Federation in 1953. He did not finally retire from Rhodesian politics until 1956 at the age of seventy-three, after twenty-three years continuous power – a record unsurpassed in any of the countries under the British Crown and only approached by Sir Robert Walpole in England and Mackenzie King in Canada.

15

The Huggins Era 1933–39

The new Prime Minister was to be the symbol and embodiment of Southern Rhodesia for a political generation. He was the first holder of his office to be purely English in birth and education. He was born at Bexley in Kent in 1883, son of a not very successful Wykehamist stockbroker. At the age of ten he suffered from an acute mastoid in his left ear. Despite repeated operations he never recovered proper hearing. This was not an unmixed political liability. When well proven bores were in full flood in the Assembly he would remove his hearing aid in a marked manner which sometimes abbreviated their orations. His education was retarded by illness, and there was no hope of following his father into Winchester. He scraped into Malvern, a school whose academic standards were then not high – unlike today – and even so got the lowest place in the lowest form.

Because of his many operations he acquired as a boy a keen interest in medicine, but examinations were not his forte and he only managed to qualify as a medical student through an obscure backdoor soon afterwards closed. He became registered at St Thomas's and achieved his FRCS in 1908. His father's finances were in a tottering state. Huggins had to earn a living quickly, and he accepted a locumship in the firm of Appleyard and Cheadle in Salisbury in 1911 at the then lavish salary of £50 a month. In spite of the uninviting conditions of life in the colony at that time he decided to accept the offer of a partnership in the firm. It turned out to be lucrative. By the early 1920s he was earning £8,000 a year, though the figure dropped to £5,000 in the year when he decided to specialize thenceforth only in surgery – the first Rhodesian doctor to do so. Meanwhile, he had served two tours of twelve months in the RAMC during the war – the customary engagement at the time – in 1914–15 and again in 1916–17; the interval, and the residue of the war, were spent in his practice in Salisbury. During his first tour he was mostly in Malta where he operated on the casualties shipped from Gallipoli. His views on amputation were published in the *Lancet* in 1917, and the following year in expanded book form under the title, *Amputation Stumps: Their Care and After Treatment.*

Back in Rhodesia Huggins soon became a well known figure. He hunted and shot and played polo. He was amusing, shrewd and sociable, and he was the most distinguished doctor in the country. Politically a mild unionist he had no very strong feelings, and when Coghlan suggested that he should stand with Fynn for Salisbury North in the 1924 election, he saw no reason to refuse. They were elected unopposed, but had a less easy ride in 1928 when Frank Johnson with a Progressive Party stablemate tried to oust them. The public thronged to Johnson's flamboyant meetings and applauded, but they voted for Fynn and Huggins whose audiences rarely exceeded twenty.

In fact Huggins was an excellent speaker, lively and entertaining. But he did not have in any degree an original or far-seeing mind. Few successful Prime Ministers have. He was highly intelligent, but not in the least intellectual, and he possessed the ideal Prime Ministerial temperament. Cheerful, good-humoured, imperturbable, not given to remorse, worry or doubt, he managed affairs with much efficiency and an occasional streak of ruthlessness. Essentially pragmatic, he was the least doctrinaire of men. He was quick to drop policies espoused in opposition when they proved impracticable in office, but consciously or unconsciously he rapidly learnt the lesson that one should never – or hardly ever – admit such reversals in public. Sir Robert Tredgold describes him as 'a consummate politician'. Sir Ernest Guest said that, although Huggins had no ideas of his own, he had a genius for selecting the right idea from others; he was a great conciliator and a master of the art of plastering over cracks in the Cabinet.

Huggins's political outlook was that of an Edwardian English Conservative. Coghlan and Moffat, had they been Englishmen, might have voted Liberal. Huggins would never have done so. He never doubted the civilizing role of the white man in Africa, though he did not deny that selected Africans with the necessary property and educational qualifications might join him in due course. He had no use for busy-body clerics, left-wing agitators, academic do-gooders. He had a limitless confidence in the Empire. He thought of himself as a servant of the Crown, and, though it occurred long after his retirement, did not conceal his profound disapproval of UDI. He remained to the end entirely Anglicized and barely concealed his dislike for Afrikaners. He spoke in the tones of an upper class Englishman and never acquired a trace of a Rhodesian accent. Much to the irritation of some Rhodesians, he usually referred to England as 'home', but his marked Englishness was not a defect in a colony whose population was constantly being reinforced by English immigrants, and it was a positive asset in dealing with English politicians and civil servants of the same social class who did not and could not think of him as a rough 'colonial' with a chip on his shoulder. He was on their wavelength, he knew what they meant, and they knew that he knew. It was to be different when Sir Roy Welensky succeeded him in 1956. Diplomacy cannot, of course, achieve an understanding where there is a fundamental clash of interest, and the Federation, despite appearances, was probably even then beyond salvation, but the bitterness and ill-feeling of the final dissolution might have been softened, if Lord Malvern had been a younger man and still in charge.

On the morrow of the 1933 election Huggins was by no means in a strong position. The Rhodesian Party with 39 per cent of votes cast was slightly ahead of the Reform Party with 38.6. Then there was the Labour and the Independent vote. This did not constitute a very clear mandate, but the opposition was deeply divided and in fact his majority of two in the Assembly proved enough. He chose a cautiously conservative Cabinet. When he presented it to the Governor the latter said, 'I did not know you had such decent men in your party', to which Huggins replied, 'You're just like all the rest of them, you only looked at my left wing and nothing else'.[1] What was most disturbing was the unreliability of some of this group, though 'left wing' is an inappropriate description of them. If they were 'left' economically, they were extremely 'right' racially – particularly the ideologue N. H. Wilson who was a born anti-Government man and helped to organize the opposition party under its various names from 1926 onwards for the next thirty years. This element in the party expected something like a Rhodesian New Deal in terms of pyramid policy and the removal of the Whitehall 'checks' in the Constitution. Huggins's ministry proved from their standpoint disappointingly orthodox. Smit, the new Finance Minister who held the second most important office, proved to be a follower of Montagu Norman rather than Maynard Keynes and set his face firmly against an unbalanced budget.

The Dominions Office dug in its toes against a scheme concocted by Huggins and Colonel Carbutt, the Chief Native Commissioner, an arch-segregationist who wished in effect to 'export' the problem of African advancement. Northern Rhodesia and Nyasaland would become 'black'. Africans would there be trained to reach the highest posts, while in Southern Rhodesia they would be kept on a lower level. This, of course, was what ultimately happened, though for different reasons and in a different way. Nor would the British Government agree to the abolition of the common roll and its replacement by a system of selected European members to represent black interests. Huggins did not press very hard for either of these schemes. Like Coghlan he believed that the imperial Government was in principle entitled to disallow Southern Rhodesian legislation, and he had no ambition for Dominion Status. He was far more concerned that the Dominions Office did not block his most important piece of legislation, the Industrial Conciliation Act.

This measure which followed South African models was designed to protect the white artisan against African competition. It did so by the ingenious and apparently egalitarian method of obliging urban employers to pay the same wage to skilled black men as to skilled white men. This was a successful way of selling the policy to the Dominions Office, but it gave in practice a great advantage to

[1] RR 23-4.

the Whites; employers had no inducement to prefer Blacks unless their wages were lower. Black men were excluded under the bill's definition of 'employees' and, therefore, could not be members of recognized trade unions, coming instead under the Master and Servants Act. The new bill did not cover unskilled Blacks at all or apply to rural areas. No wonder that the measure along with the Land Apportionment Act and the much later Native Registration Act (1946) came to be described as one leg of the tripod supporting white supremacy.

Huggins, however, was not moving far or fast enough for the radical wing of his party. Moreover, they were most indignant when on the sudden death of C. S. Jobling, the Minister of Agriculture, he chose as successor 'Frankie' Harris, who was not even a member of the Assembly and whose only qualification, so his enemies said, was his position as Chairman of the Stewards of the Bulawayo Turf Club.[2] It was symptomatic of the coming shift in politics that the Rhodesian Party decided not to field a candidate against Harris at the ensuing by-election. Perhaps Huggins remembered Sir Charles Coghlan's remark to him after the defection of some members of the Rhodesian Party: 'I can only trust you bloody ex-Unionists'[3] – an observation which taken in its context epitomizes much of party politics in Southern Rhodesia under Responsible Government.

At all events the Prime Minister decided – perhaps he was forced – to have a confrontation with his dissident supporters. The actual issue – a measure to put the now nearly bankrupt railway system back on its legs – is of no historical significance. Huggins had taken care to associate Wilson with the negotiations at Cape Town preceding the bill. Wilson and his supporters subsequently reneged, and Huggins resolved to break them or go. He broke them. On August 21, 1934 he negotiated a deal with Sir Percy Fynn, the leading figure of the Rhodesian Party's survivors in the House. Fynn promised the Party's unconditional support for a National Government under Huggins who now asked for a dissolution, no doubt in order to forestall the Reform Party Congress on September 4. The Acting Governor, who was the Chief Justice, Sir Fraser Russell, refused on the ground that a dissolution before the Assembly's statutory period had expired ought not normally to be granted except after defeat in the House – a doctrine which, if British usage applied, was very questionable.

Huggins now had to face the Congress held at Gwelo. He refused to accept attacks on his right as Prime Minister to act in what he regarded as the country's interest. An ill-tempered meeting ended indecisively, but the Prime Minister made up his mind to go ahead. At the Party's Executive meeting on September 17 he insisted that the Party constitution should be suspended so that a National Government could be formed; his argument was slightly weakened by his admission that he had never read the constitution, but his proposal was carried. He saw Fynn again and they agreed to form a United Party composed of the old Rhodesian Party and the conservative section of the Reform Party. He requested

[2] Gann and Gelfand, op. cit., 102.
[3] Op. cit., 65.

a dissolution for the second time. He had not been, nor was he likely to be, beaten in the House; but he could plausibly argue the need to secure electoral backing for a fresh party alignment. This time Russell agreed. At the ensuing election held in November the coalition won an overwhelming victory with twenty-four seats. The dissident Reformers were routed and had only one survivor. The remaining five were Labour.

Huggins now led from a position of strength. The only Rhodesian Party man whom he invited to serve in the Cabinet was Fynn as Minister without portfolio, though he included others subsequently. Of his twenty-four supporters returned at the election eighteen were sitting members – nine Rhodesian Party, nine Reform Party. Six were new, and only one of them had ever stood before, V. A. Lewis, as an unsuccessful Progressive in 1928. The United Party was both a coalition to meet a crisis and a political party; in theory it was a matter for future decision whether they fought the next election on a joint platform. In fact the Reform Party soon withered away. The anti-Huggins group was in the wilderness, the pro-Huggins group saw no point in keeping it alive and regarded themselves as a part of the United Party.[4]

As for the Rhodesian Party, its organization became more and more shadowy. Before long it was only representing Moffat, Leggate and the members defeated in the 1933 election. Those elected in 1934, like the pro-Huggins members of the Reform Party, considered themselves to be United Party men first. Efforts at fusion were made, but broke down, for Huggins saw no reason to accept a demand for cabinet offices or to bargain over the allotment of seats. When the Rhodesian Party Congress rejected his terms early in 1938, its sitting members in the Assembly, with one exception, resigned from the Rhodesian Party. The United Party became the only Government party, and its coalition aspect disappeared. The Rhodesian Party now went into opposition. At the election of 1939 it fielded sixteen candidates everyone of whom was beaten; thereafter it ceased to exist.[5]

The Rhodesia which Huggins governed during the next few years was not so very different from the colony which Coghlan ruled on the morrow of Responsible Government. The white population had increased. It was just under 35,000 at the time of the Referendum, just over 50,000 eleven years later, and 65,000 in 1940. The African population had risen too. It was about 900,000 in 1922, 1,150,000 in 1933 and 1,390,000 in 1940. The ratio, therefore, had not greatly changed. Then as now Asians and Coloureds were a mere handful.

The composition of the white population had become less male-dominated than in the past. In 1904 there had been only 407 women to every thousand men. By 1921 the figure had risen to 771. Fifteen years later it was 864. Southern Rhodesia was a youthful country with a high birth rate and few grandparents. By the 1930s more than half the Europeans lived in urban areas. Life was dominated

[4] Colin Leys, *European Politics in Southern Rhodesia*, 1959, 138.
[5] Ibid., 139.

by Salisbury and Bulawayo, the latter still being the larger and also the more thrusting and enterprising. Salisbury because of its concentration of civil servants was widely regarded as more stuffy and stand-offish, but numerically it was beginning to overtake its western rival. Today it is nearly double the size of Bulawayo which has become something of a backwater. White Southern Rhodesians were overwhelmingly British, although it has to be remembered that this description then included everyone of Empire origin. Thus the Afrikaans-speaking minority which constituted nearly one-fifth of the total counted as British, although in many respects behaving as a foreign enclave.

From 1933 onwards the Prime Minister was involved in three major issues which constituted the themes of Rhodesian politics till the outbreak of the Second World War (and two of them were to do so long beyond that): recovery from the slump; the 'destiny' of the country; the 'native problem'.

Southern Rhodesia remained a primary producer of gold and other minerals, tobacco, maize, cattle. To the structural problems, outlined by Sir Henry Clay, of heavy overheads and low turnover was added the adverse impact of the slump on the export of commodities throughout the world. There was not a great deal which any government could do. Huggins expanded Moffat's strip road programme to give more white employment, and he contemplated in 1933 a Works Colony Bill which would have treated the unemployed on severe Victorian lines of 'less eligibility', but he dropped it in deference to his radical supporters, saying in retrospect:

It never got as far as Parliament and I didn't really expect it would, but it served as a useful warning to the workshys that even if we were a Reform Party they needn't expect us to look after them while they sat on their backsides and moaned about the slump.[6]

On the other hand he tried to help the poorer European farmers by a measure which allowed the Government to pay some of their debts or give a moratorium. But it is hard to please everybody. ''Uggins, what's all this rot about paying farmers' debts?' a once impoverished but by then prosperous farmer asked him in the Salisbury Club. 'Well, Fred, the idea is to keep these people on the land. We don't want them to go away.' 'Oh is that it? I reckon if a bugger can't earn his own living, let him starve.'[7]

The Southern Rhodesian economy gradually improved. The value of the colony's output trebled between 1931 – admittedly a dismal base year – and 1939. The copper mines in Northern Rhodesia began to make a major impact from 1931 onwards. Demand for coal for smelting gave a boost to the prosperity of Wankie, the biggest coal producing area in Southern Africa, and the railways benefited from freight rates on copper exports through Southern Rhodesia to the

[6] RR 20.
[7] Ibid., 21.

port of Beira. In the later 1930s the colony's then relatively modest production of base metals was helped by the British decision to rearm against the threat of Nazi Germany.

On the agricultural front, tobacco weathered the economic blizzard better than most crops, though it went through a bad period from 1929 to 1931, the yield declining from 25,000,000 pounds in 1928 to 3,500,000 in 1931. By 1934, however, it was up to 26,700,000. The policy of imperial preference agreed at the Ottawa Conference in 1932 was a help, and later Huggins negotiated a little-publicized agreement with the British Government to persuade the principal manufacturers to give up advertising with the words 'Nothing but pure American Virginia is used in our products', thus enabling them to mix in some cheap Rhodesian tobacco without infringing the Trade Descriptions Act.[8] Tobacco grows better in Mashonaland than Matabeleland. The increasing agricultural prosperity of the area had indirect consequences for Salisbury. In the late 1930s its population caught up with that of Bulawayo. This situation was never to be reversed. By 1966 the white population of Salisbury was nearly twice as big as Bulawayo, and its African population larger by over one third.

In the matter of agricultural policy Huggins and his Cabinet did the things which governments faced with the depression were doing all over the world: they introduced tariffs, export bounties, subsidies, cheap loans, control boards, etc. His departure from orthodoxy was to buy out and nationalize the Rhodesian branch of the Cold Storage Company. The Company pressed for £572,000. The Rhodesian Government offered £200,000. After arbitration the figure was fixed at £286,000. Huggins told Rex Reynolds that the bill nationalizing the company in 1937 'was almost the first major action the Reform Party took, that the old Rhodesian Party wouldn't have done'.[9] Fynn's loyalty was sorely strained, but he did not resign.

The second major issue was the future of the colony *vis-à-vis* its neighbours. Obscure, remote and little noticed by England or the world, white Rhodesians – at any rate the more thoughtful among them – continued to worry about their purpose and their destiny. Events, despite Smuts' conviction and Coghlan's alleged long-term prediction, had by the 1930s made union less and less likely. No one can say just when it ceased to be a serious option, but it had disappeared well before Huggins came into power. 'Greater South Africa' had given way to a brand of Southern Rhodesian sub-imperialism with amalgamation as its objective. The Copper Belt was a significant motive and became more important over the years, but it was not the only one; the concept of creating a united central Africa pre-dates the first realization of Northern Rhodesia's mineral wealth. A co-ordinated railway system, a customs union, improved administration, a vague sense of the advantages of the larger scale in every field of commercial and governmental activity – all had been for many years part of the argument.

The defenders of the *status quo* in both territories asked disturbing questions.

[8] RR 26-7.
[9] RR 30.

Europeans in Southern Rhodesia wondered whether a single Rhodesia could remain a white man's country after such a vast change in the racial balance. Blacks in Northern Rhodesia, however, feared that it would, and saw the move as an extension of white settler rule bringing the Land Apportionment Act and other odious features of white ascendancy across the Zambesi. In both countries there were important vested interests potentially threatened, and this was also true of Whitehall where the ultimate decision had to be taken.

The hiving off from the Colonial Office of a new department, the Dominions Office, in 1925 had both advantages and disadvantages for the Southern Rhodesian Whites. On the one hand the new department, dealing as it did for the most part, like a miniature Foreign Office, with countries that were virtually independent, was inclined to regard Southern Rhodesia in a similar light and not to oppose too strongly the removal of 'checks' on the advancement of settler self-government. On the other hand the 'official mind' of the Colonial Office which ruled the African colonies north of the Zambesi tended to see the problem in terms of West Africa, especially Nigeria which had a bigger population than all the rest put together and by far the greatest potential wealth. Here there was no settler difficulty; 'paramountcy' and 'trusteeship' prevailed. At first the overlapping of personnel blurred these differences and until 1930 the departments were under the same Secretary of State, but the creation of a separate Secretary for the Dominions enhanced the divergences. No longer in charge of Southern Rhodesia the Colonial Office was resolved to hold on to the territories which it still ruled and for whose indigenous peoples it felt a special responsibility. The geographical frontier of the Zambesi thus coincided with an administrative frontier in Whitehall; the result was to make it easier for the Whites to secure supremacy within Southern Rhodesia, but harder to extend it outside.

Majority settler opinion in both countries favoured amalgamation from 1933 onwards. Huggins had long been a supporter; the isolationist Labour party cut little ice in Salisbury; the anti-Huggins Reformers were routed in the 1934 election. In Northern Rhodesia Leopold Moore, the Livingstone chemist, newspaper proprietor and 'unofficial' member of the Legislative Council, for years the noisiest and most obstreperous opponent of amalgamation, went over to the other side. His elected colleagues took the same line. Northern Rhodesian settlers feared that the only alternative would be absorption in an East African Association where white interests would be irrevocably subordinated to black.

There were other powerful forces on the amalgamationist side. Although the Northern Rhodesian civil servants and the 'officials' on the Legislative Council were inclined to be against closer union, the new Governor, Sir Hubert Young (1934–38), was much more sympathetic: Sir Herbert Stanley, the first Governor of Northern Rhodesia, whose earlier role in the Responsible Government campaign has already been mentioned, became in 1935, after a spell as High Commissioner in South Africa, Governor of Southern Rhodesia. He was a strong supporter of uniting the two countries. The British South Africa Company, though opposed to amalgamation at the time of the Hilton Young Commission, was now in favour;

Sir Henry Birchenough, its chairman, urged Huggins to look to the north. Sir Ernest Oppenheimer, who controlled the major part of the Copper Belt, was also a supporter of amalgamation; and the South African coalition Government in which Smuts was prominent indicated that there would no longer be any objection on its part.

The opposition stemmed from the Africans in both territories, and from their articulate white supporters among the clergy, the missionaries and the academics in Africa and Britain. Their misgivings influenced the imperial Government to some extent, and reinforced the prevailing attitude of the Colonial Office. It would, however, be wrong to think that all colonial servants were against a closer association. The case for a powerful British influence to counterbalance a South Africa already moving towards apartheid, and – more disturbingly – towards neutrality in the event of war with Germany, could not be ignored; and Southern Rhodesia was regarded with some justice as providing better social services for Africans, whatever the defects of its segregatory policies, than either Northern Rhodesia or Nyasaland. The position of the latter in any political reshuffle was a complicating consideration, adding yet another range of possible permutations. Ought Nyasaland to be united with Northern Rhodesia, or should it form part of an East African Federation, while the two Rhodesias became a separate unitary state? Alternatively it might join the Rhodesias as part of a Central African Federation, but there was more than one possible realignment even here. The two protectorates and the colony might federate as they stood, or there might be new frontier lines, a 'white' Rhodesia in which the line of rail and the Copper Belt were added to the existing Southern Rhodesia leaving two 'black' protectorates; North Western Rhodesia on one side, and on the other a new political unit created by the fusion of North Eastern Rhodesia with Nyasaland.

It would be tedious to recount the various moves that ensued. There were informal conversations in January 1938 between the three Governors (Sir Harold Kittermaster was Governor of Nyasaland) in the train from Salisbury to Bulawayo. In April there was a formal Conference between Stanley, Young, Kittermaster and Huggins which led in the end to the establishment of a Supreme Court of Appeal for the two Rhodesias, and set a precedent for regular consultation, though Young received a firm warning from the Colonial Office against any action to promote amalgamation, or even federation. An 'unofficial' conference at the Victoria Falls in 1936 plumped for a united Rhodesia. These strong pressures from the settlers and other powerful interests induced the two Secretaries of State, after a high level meeting attended by their principal officials, to set up another commission to look into the whole subject, on the prima facie assumption that closer links between the three territories were desirable. The British Government would have liked to exclude amalgamation from the Commission's terms of reference, but Huggins insisted on the matter being left open, though he had no high hopes of amalgamation being actually recommended.

The Commission was headed by Lord Bledisloe, a former Governor General of New Zealand. Its membership, in accordance with a long established tradition of prudent impartiality, was carefully balanced so as to cause the minimum offence to anyone: an expert on finance; an experienced colonial administrator; the obligatory trio of MPs drawn from the three political parties. The Commission took evidence from all over British Central Africa and consulted more people and more organizations than any such body had done before. Much of the evidence is highly significant in the light of later events. The majority of African opinion was everywhere hostile to amalgamation. A note in an appendix to the report warned against discounting African opinion on the ground of backwardness or incomprehension. The African, it said, 'possesses a knowledge and shrewdness, in matters affecting his welfare, with which he is not always credited. It would be wrong to assume that his opposition is based, to a very large extent, on ignorance or prejudice or an instinctive dread of change.' It is an interesting commentary that this should have come as a slight surprise to Huggins. 'I remember it was a point which made quite an impression on me at the time,' he told Rex Reynolds,[10] though it seems obvious enough with hindsight.

The Commission, with numerous reservations and with separate notes by particular members, advised against amalgamation on the ground that the native policies of the three territories were at present too divergent. Unification might be desirable in principle, but not until northern welfare standards had improved and southern segregation had diminished. A 'testing period' was suggested in order to see how far these discrepancies would be reduced. The Commission also ruled against federation for comparable reasons; the constitutional differences between the three countries were too great and their legal status too dissimilar for a federal system to be effective. Later events were to confirm many of these doubts; but, naturally the Commission could be – and was – pilloried as having 'funked the issue', a procedure for which there is a lot to be said in some circumstances, though it is seldom admired at the time. The Commission favoured the unification of Northern Rhodesia and Nyasaland if the problem of the latter's railway finances, still subsidised by the imperial Government, could somehow be solved; but as far as Southern Rhodesia was concerned, the most that it would recommend was an Inter-Territorial Council to co-ordinate administration, economic policy and development.

The Bledisloe Report was debated in both Houses of Parliament. In July 1939 Lord Bledisloe himself argued in suitably moderate terms the case for Southern Rhodesia's native policy. Lord Lugard, the inventor of what was called 'indirect rule', i.e. rule through traditional African institutions, came out against it, and against any sort of political union. He was supported in the university world by leading Africanists and constitutionalists such as Margery Perham, Professors A. B. Keith and E. A. Walker. The academic 'establishment' from that time onwards was firmly anti-settler. Huggins went over to Britain to pursue his cause, but he got nowhere. With the outbreak of war in September the question was shelved indefinitely.

[10] RR 67.

The third theme of politics in these years was the native problem. More than thirty years later Lord Malvern, long since retired from the political scene, said to the author: 'Rhodesia is a black man's country. People used to talk about "the native problem". What they ought to talk about now is "the European problem".' Such things are easier to say when one has ceased to depend upon European votes. Lord Malvern was, of course, right, but that had not been how either he or his white compatriots saw the matter in the 1930s.

The Prime Minister's attitude in the 1930s and beyond was one of cautious conservatism. From his long medical experience he probably knew more than most white politicians about how Africans, rural and urban, actually lived. His biographers compare his attitude to that of the great nineteenth-century medical consultants towards the London poor – 'people who needed help, advice and sympathy, but should not criticize their betters' prescriptions'.[11] Huggins combined benevolence of that sort towards the Africans with a strong disinclination to change their political and social position.

From the white 'political nation' there was no pressure to do so. The Labour Party which constituted the opposition in the Legislative Assembly with only five members did not share the brotherly sentiments professed by its namesakes elsewhere. It was hostile to anything that smacked of racial equality and stood for a rigid white ascendancy in the matter of job reservation. The Native Department, the most powerful element in the Rhodesian bureaucracy, was equally opposed to change. Huggins's own party contained some who were less conservative than others on the racial question, the most conspicuous being Robert Tredgold and Ernest Guest, but in the 1930s enlightened liberalism was not a cause which had much hope of success in the Assembly.

Nor was there any effective pressure from the Africans. The Southern Rhodesian African National Congress founded by Aaron Jacha in 1934 did not achieve much more than the Rhodesian Bantu Voters Association. True, its name was to be used in 1957 when young African radicals initiated a new mass movement. Moreover, Joshua Nkomo, who had held office in the old Congress, became leader of the new. But this was not really a revival, rather the adoption of a convenient historical symbol. The old Congress was essentially an élite confined to educated men, the difference from its predecessor in the 1920s being that the leadership was normally indigenous – Shona or Ndebele, not Fingo, Sotho or Nyasa, as in the past. One of its principal figures was the Rev. Thompson Samkange, a Shona Methodist Minister.

Such mass movements as there were at this time took the form of millenarian independent churches. Matthew Zwimba's Church of the White Bird was an amalgam of atavistic Shona beliefs and Christianity, but it did not last for long and there were others equally transitory. A movement which disturbed the Government and which was not indigenous was the Watch Tower Church. Its spokesmen, largely Nyasa, prophesied that God would overthrow the Whites and give

[11] Gann and Gelfand, *Huggins of Rhodesia*, 113.

their wealth and power to the Africans. The movement caught on in north-western Mashonaland. It was originally propagated by Nyasas who had come to Rhodesia as domestic servants – 'boys' in the local argot. It thus struck home (literally). The Government decided to suppress the movement. Perhaps they recollected Lord Melbourne's remark that things have come to a pretty pass when religion interferes with private life. More probably they were alarmed at the refusal of Watch Tower congregations to obey their Chiefs. An *ad hoc* Sedition Act was passed in 1936 and the Nyasa leaders were deported, despite objections by H. H. Davies, leader of the Labour Party who denounced the suppression of free speech, behaving for once in the way that might be expected from a person of his political colour.

None of these quasi-religious African movements counted for much. Nor did more material discontents. Destocking of cattle, cattle-dipping and other manifestations of the Government's native-cum-agricultural policy produced much indignation, but there was no co-ordinated effort against the regime. Universal suffrage and a black government must have seemed a mere dream even to the politically conscious Africans. The Whites were firmly in the saddle, and they possessed all the confidence of an 'ascendancy class'. Nevertheless they had a problem. The Africans were not going to disappear.

Huggins had campaigned in 1933 on the ticket of complete territorial segregation. This was not feasible, as he soon came to appreciate. It logically entailed the replacement of the African labour force in European areas by white artisans. There was no chance of that. The ensuing upheaval would have disrupted the entire economy. But Huggins had no intention of causing unnecessary alarm to those who had voted him into power on a programme of racial separation. He continued to use the language of segregation or 'parallel development', as it was sometimes called. One of his best known and most often quoted enunciations of that creed was made as late as 1938 to an audience of missionaries:

> The Europeans in this country can be likened to an island of white in a sea of black, with the artisan and the tradesman forming the shores and the professional classes the highlands in the centre. Is the native to be allowed to erode away the shores and gradually attack the highlands? To permit this would mean that the leaven of civilisation would be removed from the country, and the black man would inevitably revert to a barbarism worse than anything before.[12]

In practice the natives were allowed to erode away the shores, even though the highlands remained firmly in white hands. It was impossible to maintain an expanding economy on any other basis. Africans constituted the labour force of Rhodesia's two most flourishing industries, mining and agriculture. Those industries flourished precisely because the low wages paid made them highly competitive on the world market. White labour would have been much more expensive. Nor

[12] *Rhodesia Herald*, March 31, 1938.

was African labour confined to mining and agriculture. By the 1930s much of urban life depended upon Africans performing menial tasks and working in secondary industries.

These considerations did not prevent what Mr Rifkind calls 'a last ditch battle against the creation of an urban African population',[13] though they did prevent Huggins from giving way to it. The attack was led by the Labour party and came to a head with a motion put down on its behalf in March 1935 by Donald Macintyre, a wealthy member of the Legislative Assembly, to the effect that the creation of native village settlements within European areas was 'detrimental to the best interests of this colony'. It was defeated easily. The Government argued that such settlements were essential for European society and for economic progress, and that they conformed with the Land Apportionment Act.

The truth was that African urbanization could not be avoided unless the Government encouraged a huge influx of Europeans prepared to do the same sort of jobs. Possibly in the latter part of the decade refugees from Hitler's Europe might have provided such a flow, but it is hard to believe that they would have been content for long to play that part in a society where the stratification of colour and jobs so closely corresponded. The same 'might-have-been' is floated by Gann and Gelfand apropos of the Federation twenty years later.[14] Huggins, reflecting the sentiments of the Rhodesian establishment in this as in many other matters, had no use for such plans. He dreaded the creation of the class of 'poor Whites' which had caused much trouble in the Union of South Africa and he did not see how any practicable rise in white immigration could change the fundamentals of the racial balance. Much depends on what was practicable. It is hard to say just when changes of quantity become changes of quality, but in terms of power the European world in South Africa with its ratio of one in six or seven is far more securely ensconced than it can ever hope to be in Rhodesia with one in twenty-five. No doubt there are many other reasons for the difference, but numbers probably have something to do with it. On the other hand, one may doubt whether at any time European immigration on the scale needed to achieve a similar balance in Southern Rhodesia or the Federation would have been forthcoming. To be comparable with South Africa, Southern Rhodesia would have needed a population of 200,000 Europeans instead of 54,000 in 1935, and the Federation twenty years later would have had to add over 900,000 to its actual European population of 236,000. What is certain is that such an influx, if practicable at all, would have produced a veritable social revolution, and the intensely traditionalist and conservative English-speaking élite which ruled the colony were not there for social revolutions.

The Government paid lip service to physical segregation, but confined its actual measures to land segregation. The Prime Minister had to concede that the full implementation of the Land Apportionment Act would take longer than at first

[13] *The Politics of Land*, 56.
[14] *Huggins of Rhodesia.*

envisaged. Under the Act all Africans on European farms, apart from farm labourers who had no claim to any possessory title, were due to have departed before 1937 to the reserves, but by 1934 the number was actually larger than it had been when the Act was passed. In 1936 the Government shifted the deadline to 1941. In 1937 a further amending Act was passed substituting, with agreement from Whitehall, the Dominion Secretary for the High Commissioner as the authority for the approval of legislation on native rights. The urban problem was dealt with to some extent by setting up the native townships to which the Labour party was so strongly opposed. Huggins argued that they were a compromise between the principles of humanity – allowing black labourers to set up house with their wives – and occupational segregation, for the inhabitants gained no permanent tenure and when their period of employment came to an end were supposed to move into the reserves.

Huggins was acutely conscious of the deficiencies of the reserves. He was not the only person to see that the Land Apportionment Act could not work at all unless they were improved. Indeed the black urban incursion was not only a product of the expanding urban economy, but also of the inadequate quality and quantity of the reserves and the native purchase areas. The Government made a considerable effort to inculcate efficient methods of husbandry, and it allowed the formation of Native Councils composed of Chiefs, headmen and other nominated Africans with the power to make by-laws. It was hoped that these would take the initiative in agricultural matters too. A further step towards giving Africans an element of self-sufficiency was the Native Courts Act which allowed African tribunals minor jurisdiction in civil disputes between Africans.

By the end of the 1930s it could safely be said that physical segregation was in practice dead, though not yet repudiated in theory. The African and European economies were inextricably mixed. The time for separating them, if there ever had been one, had long since passed. The tribal African, it is true, lived in a subsistence economy which constituted a world of its own divorced from the money economy of the urban and rural European areas, but he depended to a considerable degree on contributions from his urban relatives who in their turn welcomed presents of food from the rural areas. As for the European economy, it could not have existed at all in its current form without the African labour upon which it heavily depended.

Occupational, possessary or land segregation on the other hand were very much in force. The trend was towards renewed and stricter implementation of the Land Apportionment Act which came to be regarded more than ever both by Blacks and Whites as the principal bastion of European ascendancy. The 'native problem' had in no sense been 'solved'. It is difficult to see how it could have been, and perhaps that well used terminology is irrelevant in any case. Pre-war Rhodesia was not a country where rigid doctrines or long term plans played much part. The Whites were there because they liked the climate, hoped to make money, enjoyed a way of life that was a pleasant mixture of the English and the un-English. The Blacks were there ... because they were there.

16

War and Aftermath 1939–48

Hitler's seizure of Prague early in 1939 convinced the Rhodesian Prime Minister along with many others that war was imminent. It would affect the colony in a multitude of ways; there was a strong case for a general election to give renewed authority to a Legislative Assembly which might have to enact drastic emergency laws. The existing Assembly's term did not expire till November. When Huggins decided to ask the Governor for an April election, the Opposition protested, arguing as Sir Fraser Russell had in 1934 that unless the Government was defeated in the House – of which there was no prospect whatever – only the most exceptional circumstances could justify a 'premature' dissolution. What is 'exceptional' must be a matter of judgement. The Governor was not bound to accept the Prime Minister's advice, but he decided to do so.

The ensuing election justified the Opposition's fears. Labour managed to gain two seats, giving them a total of seven. The United Party won all the rest. The popular vote was less overwhelming – 11,161 for the UP and 7,353 for Labour. The Rhodesian Party, which contested 16 seats, lost every one of them and, along with the Reform Party, vanished from the political scene. Two men who were destined to play an important part in post-war politics entered the House for the first time, Edgar Whitehead, destined to be the last United Party Prime Minister, and Hugh Beadle, whose role as Chief Justice after UDI was to be the subject of much controversy.

Huggins reconstructed his Cabinet and invited Tredgold, Minister of Justice, to take on the portfolio of Defence as well. This combination would be odd in any other country, but was quite natural in Southern Rhodesia. There was no regular army. The British South Africa Police with their military training were regarded as the first line of defence, and they came under the Minister of Justice. Tredgold too was convinced that war would soon break out, and he was supported by Ernest Guest, Minister of Mines and Public Works. But he had the greatest difficulty in extracting money from the Treasury over which Jacob Smit presided. He was a Hollander and had sources in Europe which led him to believe that Hitler had passed his apogee and that Germany was on the verge of economic collapse.

These delusions were swept away by the events of September. Huggins was in England when Germany invaded Poland. As a Crown Colony Southern Rhodesia was automatically involved by Britain's declaration of war, unlike South Africa which could have remained neutral and only entered hostilities by the narrowest of parliamentary margins. However, patriotism would certainly have brought the colony in, even if there had been an option to stay out – not only patriotism but self-preservation. Thirty years later Huggins was reminded of a speech he made in the Assembly in March 1940 when he pointed out that if the war was lost the colony was lost too. He commented:

> This is rather interesting in view of the indignant ex-servicemen, and others who write to the papers nowadays [protesting at sanctions, etc.] and say they fought for Britain. If the Nazis had won, Britain probably wouldn't have been occupied, but Rhodesia certainly would. I wrote that in a private letter to Ian Smith very early on [in Smith's premiership]. I should have known what we were fighting for: I was running the show.[1]

He was right about Rhodesia if not Britain. The colony could not have survived if Britain had gone under.

According to Guest,[2] he and Tredgold conceived the idea while Huggins was in London that a small Defence Committee of the Cabinet consisting of themselves and the Prime Minister should be responsible for the day to day decisions in running the Rhodesian war effort. Whatever the origins of the idea, Huggins instituted such a committee early in 1940, having, shortly before, given Guest the newly created Department for Air (now split off from Defence) in addition to Mines and Public Works. Like Tredgold's combination of portfolios, this was not quite as dotty as it sounds. Southern Rhodesia's major contribution to the war was to be its air training scheme, and the massive construction of airfields which this entailed would naturally be carried out by the Public Works Department.

The Defence Committee seems, by general agreement, to have worked admirably, the only serious complaint coming from Smit who resented his own exclusion and grumbled about financial extravagance. All three had had some experience of military matters. Tredgold had the least. He had arrived in England in the early spring of 1918 hoping to see action in France, but by the time he was commissioned after his training in the OTC, the war was over. Huggins had, of course, served in the RAMC. Guest was the war veteran. He had enlisted at sixteen in the South African war, concealing his age. Living as he did into

---

[1] RR 34.
[2] Ibid., 35.

his nineties, he must have been among its last survivors. He also fought in the Kaiser's war. Sir Robert Tredgold wrote:

> He was a soldier born. Mechanisation has ground the meaning out of the phrase 'the joy of battle', yet he had known it. With no illusions to disguise its horrors, he hated modern warfare, but he did not shrink from it as so many do. He believed that there were worse things than war, even at its worst; that if from fear of war, we allowed certain values to perish from the face of the earth, life would not be worth living.[3]

Tragically both his sons were to be killed in action.

Tredgold was clear that the limited Rhodesian manpower should on no account be concentrated into a national force which might be destroyed in a single battle. He had in mind the fate of the Newfoundland Regiment and the South African Brigade in the First World War. On a small country such a disaster could have irrevocable effects. Something near to it had already occurred once before to Rhodesia with the losses incurred by the 2nd Rhodesia Regiment in the East African campaign against General von Lettow-Vorbeck. Fortunately, the enemy had no comparable base in the Second German war. Whatever the threat posed by the Italian army in Abyssinia, it was much further away and was soon extinguished by General Alan Cunningham's campaign in which Rhodesian units and the Rhodesian 237 Squadron of the RAF played their part. Huggins and Guest agreed with the policy of spreading the risks, and so did the British Government.

White Rhodesians, constituting as they did an élite governing class, were accustomed from earliest youth to giving orders – especially the children of farmers who, in the words of Gann and Gelfand, 'were used to "bossing up" African playmates, and, however regrettable this might appear to liberal critics of their society, Rhodesian youngsters learned habits of command from early childhood'.[4] Clearly the best way of employing them was as officer rather than 'other rank' material. The rather bogus egalitarianism which in England obliged the officer class to serve as private soldiers before entering an OCTU and gaining a commission did not apply in Southern Rhodesia, or if it did, applied very differently; the Africans were the 'other ranks'. White Rhodesians were employed to instruct and command in the first place African soldiers from West, Central and East Africa, and later, when, to the horror of South African opinion, the Rhodesian African Rifles were formed, they commanded Africans from Southern Rhodesia itself. As Sir Robert Tredgold observes, 'At least our men had seen a black man outside a Christy Minstrel performance and had a basis on which understanding between officer and man could be built'.[5]

---

[3] *The Rhodesia that was my Life*, 131–2.
[4] *Huggins of Rhodesia*, 148.
[5] *The Rhodesia that was my Life*, 133.

Rhodesians white and black – some twelve small contingents – served in many lands on many fronts. A history of the Rhodesian war effort could easily become shapeless and diffused. In any case it has been fully described elsewhere,[6] and it is too wide a subject for this book. By far the most important contribution was in the air. This consisted not only in the gallantry of leading Rhodesian officers in the RAF such as Hardwicke Holderness, John Plagis, Charles Green, Johnnie Deal, all of whom acquired a host of well-deserved decorations. There was also the air training scheme already mentioned. It was the result of an initiative by Sir Charles Meredith who commanded Southern Rhodesia's small pre-war air force. He persuaded the Air Ministry in London that Southern Rhodesia would be an ideal place for training RAF flying crews on a large scale. It was remote from hostilities, intensely loyal, and had the perfect climate. Planes are scarcely ever grounded because of bad weather. Southern Rhodesia thus became the first country in which the great Empire Training Scheme was launched, beating Canada by a short head when the first air school was opened at Belvedere, Salisbury in 1940.

Altogether, eleven air stations were built, with concomitant runways, quarters, townships for families, and all the ancillary water and electricity supplies, etc. It was a major effort. At the peak of the operation over 15,000 Europeans were involved. Many of them became fond of the country and returned to make their lives there after the war. Relations with the local citizenry were cordial, though dyed-in-the-wool Rhodesians were shocked by the absence of any sexual colour bar among the youthful RAF personnel who took their pleasure when and where they could get it. Any moral disapprobation was compensated by the boom in agriculture and industry created by this temporary immigration which raised the white population by over twenty per cent.

One by-product of the war was a closer relationship with South Africa. Tredgold, after a visit to Nairobi, was responsible for opening Smuts's eyes to the dangerous weakness of the British position *vis-a-vis* the Italians in north-east Africa. South African artillery and technical units from South Africa Command were quickly dispatched and contributed substantially to Cunningham's startling successes. The Rhodesian Government firmly resisted any attempt to put the colony under the East African Command partly on constitutional and partly strategic grounds. Huggins describes a conference with Smuts and Lord Harlech in Pretoria:

Harlech said, 'You know, Huggins, you can't be a command on your own. There's West Africa Command, East Africa, Middle East and South Africa: which would you like to join?' I said: 'Obviously South Africa. All our supplies and communications come from there. We have no communication with the north except a few aeroplanes.'

We gave our people permission to go over from the Imperial to the South

---

[6] J. F. Macdonald, *The War History of Southern Rhodesia*, 2 vols, 1947–50, is the 'official' account.

African Service. So most of them did. The pay was better and the South African government made up the difference. So our armoured car regiment and many of the other troops joined the South African Sixth Division. It suited Smuts who was getting short of manpower and it worked out very well.[7]

This was not Huggins's only motive. To go in with Northern Rhodesia and Nyasaland under the East African Command had constitutional implications which he wished to avoid. Southern Rhodesia's juridical status was unique, but it was much nearer to South Africa's than Northern Rhodesia's and he meant to keep it that way. His relations with Smuts were close and cordial throughout the war.

Compared with that of the major, or even most of the minor combatants, the Southern Rhodesian contribution to the war was minuscule – some 8,500 white men and 1,500 women in the armed services, of whom 693 were killed; the African figures were 14,000 with 126 losses. These statistics serve to remind us how tiny the colony was – as indeed it is. But if we remember that the entire European population was only 65,000 in 1940, they do not look so trivial. No account of Southern Rhodesian history can omit the war. The attitudes engendered by it shaped much that lay ahead, and its memory has been a potent factor in the events of the last thirty years. Nor should one forget the strain on the colony's economic resources. At the end of it all Rhodesians could legitimately look back and feel that they 'had done their bit'.

Historians of the Second World War tend to ignore domestic affairs. Military and foreign policies are more conspicuous and more exciting; but the result is a curious gap. Historians are liable to behave as if party politics had gone into hibernation in 1939, only to re-emerge from a deep sleep in 1945 – an impression enhanced by the party truce and the suspension of general elections in Britain and most of her dependencies. Yet in fact the political world never slumbers, and Southern Rhodesia was no exception to the rule.

When war broke out Huggins invited the Labour leader, H. H. Davies, and one of his close associates, Jack Keller, an old-fashioned railway trade unionist, to join the Government. They accepted, but some of their colleagues dissented, and it proved impossible to secure an inter-party pact about by-elections. The dissidents, though strongly supporting the war, felt free to oppose the Government on details. Huggins was, of course, politically safe enough, and he was quite ready to risk Labour wrath even on an issue which had a potential element of class confrontation.

In 1942 there was trouble on the Copper Belt. Frank Maybank, the General Secretary of the Mine Workers Union, who as an admirer of Stalin was anti-war (though not to the extent of changing his mind when Germany attacked Russia), had formed an alliance of opposites with a group of Afrikaans-speakers who supported the *Ossevabrandwag* – a quasi-Fascist South African Nationalist

[7] RR 38.

organization, bitterly hostile to Britain. Copper was a vital strategic commodity and the threat of a strike was a serious one. There was even fear that it might develop into the sort of armed rebellion which Smuts had been obliged to suppress – with heavy loss of life – on the Rand in 1922. The Northern Rhodesian Government's Defence Force contained too many miners for comfort; and it was considered impossible to use black troops and unwise to employ British troops against Afrikaners because of repercussions in South Africa. The Governor of Northern Rhodesia called on Huggins for aid. He responded by promptly dispatching the Southern Rhodesian Armoured Car Regiment to the Copper Belt. The leading agitators were arrested and deported. More moderate figures came to the fore and no serious trouble occurred for the rest of the war. The Rhodesian Labour party accepted this intervention with equanimity.

The exigencies of war and that intangible, but not the less real phenomenon, a change in the climate of opinion, caused the Government to move to the 'left'. It was a miniature version of the trend in Britain where the Conservative party found itself accepting, even initiating policies which would have been anathema before 1939. In matters of social and economic policy the United Party was by any standard conservative, but war by its very nature necessitates – at any rate for the duration – measures of a 'socialist' character; high taxation, rationing of scarce commodities, controls, direction of labour and investment. Huggins was anything but a socialist. On the other hand he was anything but a doctrinaire, and his approach was highly pragmatic. To some extent he cut the ground from under the feet of Labour. In 1942 he decided to nationalize the Iron and Steel Works at Bulawayo in which ISCOR, the South African government-controlled trust, had a large shareholding. He was afraid that a post-war slump might induce ISCOR to pull out and concentrate within the Union. This decision was embarrassing for Donald Macintyre, who was chairman of the Bulawayo Company as well as being leader of the dissident Labourites. He thus combined a theoretical belief in nationalization with a personal and practical awareness of the case for capitalism. His efforts to explain why nationalization was in principle right, but in this case wrong, caused mirth among his opponents, and did not deter the Government.

In 1943 the two Labour parties reunited. It was made clear to Huggins that they would now function as an 'official' opposition, that those who served in the Cabinet were only there while the war lasted and would, even so, be expected to take orders from the 'caucus'. The Prime Minister jibbed at this and accepted the resignations of Davies and Keller, who now went into opposition under the leadership of Macintyre. In the same year, for wholly different reasons, he lost the services of Tredgold, who had long been uneasy about the Land Apportionment Act and its amendments, though he saw the futility of opposing a measure so strongly supported by every element of the white electorate. A judgeship had become vacant. It provided an escape, and he accepted the offer.

The position of the Prime Minister by the end of 1943 was beginning to look precarious. There had been a number of secessions from the United Party. Labour was now in opposition and appeared to have made up its internal disputes. Moreover a new threat had emerged from the right – a group of conservatives who, in accordance with the Rhodesian tradition of adopting the most misleading political nomenclature possible, called themselves 'Liberals'. Early in 1944 they were joined by Smit who resigned from the Treasury and soon became their leader. The party stood for 'two pyramids', Treasury economy, free enterprise, low taxation and dominion status. It strongly opposed closer ties with the northern territories, and saw 'amalgamation', with some justice, as a bar to 'independence'. There is a direct line of political descent from the Liberals of the 1940s through the Dominion Party of the 1950s to the Rhodesia Front of the 1960s, the party which made the Unilateral Declaration of Independence – and still governs the country today.

Huggins, faced with triple opposition – Labour, Liberals and dissidents in his own party – was now under some pressure to solve matters by a general election. He was determined to avoid this while the war continued, and in 1944 received a welcome boost when the Labour party broke up in disorder. The cause was a decision by Colonel Walker, who had succeeded Macintyre as leader, that there ought to be an element, however modest, of black participation in the party's organization. To the Davies-Keller bloc this was heresy of the worst sort. They broke away and formed a party called the 'Rhodesia Labour Party' as opposed to the 'Southern Rhodesia' Labour Party, thus adding to the general confusion of party names. This split proved in the end fatal. The breach was never repaired, and after the general election of 1948 the two Labour parties disappeared into limbo.

Huggins and his political friends, whether in war or peace, at no stage abandoned the goal of closer union with the north. The Bledisloe Report had been a disappointment, but not a defeat. The necessities of war soon worked in favour of 'amalgamation'. Both Northern Rhodesia and Nyasaland had to look south for supplies. In 1941 an important decision was taken at Whitehall by the creation of a Permanent Inter-Territorial Secretariat in Salisbury to co-ordinate policies. It was headed by K. L. Hall, a Colonial Office official whose current post was Chief Secretary of Nyasaland. The Colonial Office accepted this arrangement with reluctance and, despite the title of 'Permanent', had no intention of continuing it after the war or making it a stepping stone towards amalgamation. Nevertheless, events moved in that direction. The 'unofficials' on the Northern Rhodesia Council led by Roy Welensky (of whom more later) were increasingly favourable. On October 18, 1944 Oliver Stanley, Colonial Secretary, announced that the Government intended to implement the Bledisloe Commission's recommendation to set up a permanent Inter-Territorial Council, soon to be known as the Central African Council.

This proposal fell far short of 'amalgamation'. The body was advisory and consultative with no 'teeth', and the British Government took the opportunity to state officially that amalgamation was not a 'runner' for the time being, prudently giving no indication when 'the time being' would end. Sir Godfrey Huggins (he had been knighted in 1941) regarded the Council as a mere 'sop', but he deemed it wiser to accept than reject and dissuaded Welensky from opposing it on behalf of the Northern Rhodesia 'unofficials'.

The root of the objections made by the Colonial Office and in other quarters was Southern Rhodesia's treatment of its Africans. Partly for that reason, and partly because he was not impervious to the 'liberal' ideas that were in the wind, the Prime Minister began to move away from the ideology of physical segregation, even as he already had, in some degree, from its practice. In June 1941 he had issued a *Statement on Native Affairs* which sharply contrasted with the tenor of his previous pronouncements. He suggested that the lines of parallel development would and should meet earlier than at infinity, that although land segregation and white job reservation must continue for a time, they should not be permanent features of Rhodesian society. He even went so far as to say that white men and black men were blood brothers and that the gap between them, vast though it was, stemmed from history, climate and environment rather than innate genetic differences. Colonel Sir Frank Johnson, who at Huggins's strong request had been knighted at the same time that he was, wrote from England in support. Reminded of this Huggins told Rex Reynolds:

> That certainly was a controversial White Paper. I should think it displeased the majority of white Rhodesians and, of course, it was abhorrent to South Africans. It's funny to think about old Frank Johnson. As I think I told you, he and N. H. Wilson were the people who 'sold' me on the twin pyramid policy.[8]

Huggins's 'liberalism' should not be over-stated. In that same year he passed an entirely new Land Apportionment Act which tightened up the old one. But it did contain provisions which were intended to help local authorities to develop native urban areas. Previous legislation had merely allowed such areas to be set aside, but had done nothing to encourage the building of decent houses on them. The new legislation was, however, like the old, merely permissive, and the municipal authorities did little about it.

In 1945 Huggins passed an amendment to the Act which made it obligatory for local authorities to do what had hitherto been permissive. In 1946 he carried the important Native (Urban Areas) Accommodation and Registration Act. This obliged urban employers of African labour to provide free accommodation for their employees within the municipality's native urban area. At the same time it contained stringent pass laws along with inspection and registration rules designed to control the influx of Africans into the towns. These measures certainly led to an improvement, though from a very low level, of the condition of the urban African, but they did not alter the fact that he was still regarded as a transient visitor, housed there only while he was employed, and liable to

[8] RR 76-7.

be sent to some remote area of which he knew nothing as soon as his employment ended.

Even these mildly 'liberal' measures inspired the wrath of the mis-named Liberal Party. What with that and the other discontents accumulated during war, the prospects of the United Party in the first post-war election did not seem very good. Apart from the native question, the Liberals could make a plausible case against controls, extravagance and waste. Sensing that the threat came from the right rather than the left Huggins concentrated on their inexperience and the contradictions in their programme. They wanted dominion status but their native policy would ensure that they never got it. They agreed to nationalization of coal and railways, but then declared that private enterprise was sacrosanct.

Attack in politics is usually the best defence, but Huggins only just survived the election of April 1946. He obtained thirteen seats on a popular vote of 11,864. The aggregate opposition vote was 15,587. The Liberals won twelve seats, the Rhodesia Labour three, the Southern Rhodesia Labour Party two. The United Party received one slight bonus. After a petition for a recount the High Court decided that the Liberal candidate declared as the winner in Lomagundi had lost, and seated the United Party man in his place. The balance now became UP 14, Liberals 11. This was an improvement, but the fact remained that Huggins was head of a minority government with all the problems that the position involves.

In the event the problems were not as serious as they might have been. As Huggins put it:

> The Opposition Members certainly didn't want to risk their seats at another general election: the one in 1948 proved how wise they had been – up to then. They didn't call for many divisions and when they did, either Labour or the Liberals supported the Government. It isn't difficult to run a minority government unless you want to introduce very controversial legislation.[9]

This situation lasted for two years. Two events of importance occurred before the next election. First the Government bought out the railways from the Chartered Company. Because the system covered Northern Rhodesia and Bechuanaland as well, this required the consent of the British Government. Oddly enough Whitehall was sticky, although there was a Labour Government in office which had only recently nationalized the British railways. Huggins was not a natural believer in state ownership, but his consultations with the Chartered Company suggested that there was no prospect of the Company raising the money for the necessary development of a system which was obsolete and unable to cope with post-war demands. In the event, after elaborate negotiations and some tough bargaining by Sir Edgar Whitehead, who was the new Minister of Finance, the equity was bought for £3,150,000, and a loan of £32,000,000 at 2½ per cent was raised in London to cover the debentures and further development. This was the heyday of the Dalton cheap money period, and the deal proved to be an excellent bargain.

[9] RR 45.

The second episode of importance was on a very different front. The revival of the ICU in Salisbury by Charles Mzingeli, himself an ultra moderate, led to an upsurge of African trade unionism. In Bulawayo the leader was Benjamin Burumbo, and in April 1948 a strike of African municipal workers began, which soon spread to something like a general strike in both Bulawayo and Salisbury, even involving domestic servants. It was disorganized and ill-coordinated, but it constitutes something of a watershed in the history of the colony. Huggins met it with a combination of show of force – mobilization of Territorials and police reserves – together with prudent negotiation. The strike petered out in a few days. The wage increases that were granted, after an enquiry over which a judge, Sir Robert Hudson, presided, disappointed African expectations. Huggins himself thought that the grievances which led Bulawayo's municipal employees to strike were largely justified. The episode was a portent of future African mass action, and its significance was noted by black and white alike; their worlds were not going to be quite the same again. In the Assembly Huggins, opposing the call for drastic action, said 'We are witnessing the emergence of a proletariat and in this country it happens to be black'.[10]

Throughout the two years of minority Government a variety of alliances, fusions, coalitions were mooted. Huggins was against any 'deals'. He reckoned that Labour of both varieties would on the whole support him against the Liberals, and from the beginning of 1948 the two members of the Southern Rhodesia Labour Party (the less illiberal branch) offered formally to do so. He was not prepared to accept overtures from the Liberals. He disliked Smit and he had now come to regard their policy – in effect apartheid – as impracticable. Moreover, by a curious paradox, the Liberal programme of 1947, if carried out to the letter, by dividing Rhodesia into two halves, one exclusively white the other wholly black, would have given Africans far more power in their own sphere than anything contemplated in any part of Rhodesia by the United Party.

Huggins, nevertheless, felt something should be done about African representation. Any approach to parity, let alone one-man-one-vote, was out of the question. Black men were believed by all except a few left-wing intellectuals to be incapable in the foreseeable future of operating a parliamentary democracy on the Westminster pattern. Under the existing franchise, there was no immediate prospect of any African representation at all in the legislature, but this was because only 136 out of a potential 6,000 who were qualified had bothered to register. If all of them did the African voice might be far too loud for the number was rising all the time. What Huggins proposed to do was to adapt the system recently introduced in Northern Rhodesia whereby white members of the Legislative Council were nominated to represent and speak for the millions of voteless Africans. In return for this he planned to freeze African membership of the common voters roll. Those who had got the vote could keep it, but no further additions would be made.

[10] Gann and Gelfand, op. cit., 201.

The proposals involved a constitutional amendment which required a two-thirds majority in the Legislative Assembly. There was no hope of doing this without an inter-party agreement. Labour was as usual divided, but the Liberals who had enough seats on their own to block an amendment refused to contemplate such an arrangement. The idea of white representation of black men could not be squared with their policy on race relations. The scheme, therefore, came to nothing. It would probably have been vetoed at Whitehall anyway.

In July 1948 a chance came to break the deadlock in the Assembly. It has to be remembered that in Southern Rhodesia the Prime Minister's power of dissolution was more restricted than in Britain – even there it is not wholly unlimited – and the Governor's right to refuse unless good reason could be given was something which no Prime Minister could ignore. Huggins was looking for an opportunity. It came when a clause in a bill of no great importance enabling the Inter-Territorial Currency Board to put up buildings at its own expense for its offices and strong-rooms in Salisbury was defeated by an alliance of Liberals and Labour. The defeat, by 14 to 12, reflected the jealousy of the Southern Rhodesian Legislature towards the Central African Council; it was not as if the Government was being asked to find the money.

Huggins decided to make the reinstatement of the clause an issue of confidence on the ground that the bill embodied an inter-territorial pact which must be honoured. He was beaten a second time – by 14 votes to 13. There was a current story to the effect that the Government 'rigged' their own defeat. However this may be – and it is certainly not impossible, given the cosy club-like quality of politics in Salisbury – Huggins could point to an ostensible vote of no confidence which in any parliamentary system based on the Westminster model is a strong reason for dissolution. The Governor, Sir John Kennedy, was nevertheless reluctant. The international scene was stormy. The Berlin blockade was in full swing, and a European war did not seem impossible. Huggins, however, declared that he could carry on all the same. The Governor saw Smit who was against an election and said that he believed he could himself form an administration with help from Labour and waverers in the United Party, but he soon found that he had no support and Kennedy agreed to dissolve.

The election which followed on September 16 gave Huggins a victory as conclusive as that of 1934 and even more crushing than that of 1939. The Southern Rhodesia Labour Party withdrew from the struggle, regarding Huggins and his friends as preferable to the Liberals, and not wishing to split the vote. Macintyre himself joined the United Party. The Rhodesia Labour Party, now little more than a Bulawayo faction, only secured one seat, that of Jack Keller. The Liberals fell from 11 to 5, Smit himself being defeated. Huggins thus won twenty-four seats and was in an impregnable position for the next five years. The popular vote for the United Party was 19,732, for the Liberals 10,714, and for the Rhodesia Labour Party 4,558.

The election of 1948 set the trend in Rhodesian politics for nearly a decade and a half. What came to be called the 'liberal' establishment (though the adjective has only a relative significance) was to be in power in Southern Rhodesia until Sir Edgar Whitehead was defeated by Winston Field in December 1962, and in the Central African Federation throughout its existence till it was dissolved the following year. The supporters of dominion status, apartheid, territorial segregation, twin-pyramidism and isolationism received a defeat from which it took them many years to recover, years which saw vast and unexpected changes on the central African scene. Huggins himself, sprightly, trim, urbane, remained unchallenged till he chose to bow out from the Federal premiership eight years later. As far as Southern Rhodesia was concerned, the election gave a clear go-ahead to the advocates of closer union with the north. There were obstacles to overcome before it could be achieved, but they were in Lusaka, Blantyre and London – no longer in Salisbury.

17

The Origins of Federation 1945–51

There is as yet no fully documented history of the Central African Federation, although one is in the process of being written. It would be foolish to attempt the task in a book of this size. Nevertheless the problems of federation cannot be ignored by the historian of Southern Rhodesia. The colony provided the main impetus behind the federal movement, and it was politically and economically the most powerful of the three constituent 'territories'. The circumstances in which, after ten years of increasingly uneasy existence, the Federation was dissolved profoundly affected the future of Southern Rhodesia.

By the end of the second German war the territories had developed on very different lines in terms of racial balance, economic structure and constitutional status. In 1925 the European population of Southern Rhodesia was 38,200 as against 922,000 Africans. In Northern Rhodesia the figures were 4,000 and 1,000,000, in Nyasaland 1,700 and 1,350,000. All three territories also contained a tiny number of 'Asians' (mostly Indians) and 'Coloureds' (people of mixed racial descent). The figures for Southern Rhodesia, which had the largest number, were 1,400 and 2,100 respectively. Twenty years later the European population of Southern Rhodesia had more than doubled, 80,500, and was just under 5 per cent of that of the Africans, which had risen to 1,640,000. In Northern Rhodesia the white population had expanded relatively far faster. It was five times as big as it had been in 1925 and constituted $1\frac{1}{4}$ per cent of the number of Africans, which was now the same as in the south. In Nyasaland there were 2,300 Europeans, half of them being officials or missionaries. The African population was 2,100,000. The expansion of the European in relation to the African population steadily increased in the two Rhodesias, reaching a peak in 1960. In that year Southern Rhodesian Europeans numbered 223,000, which was just under 8 per cent of the African population. Asians and Coloureds numbered 6,700 and 9,900 respectively. In Northern Rhodesia there were 76,000 Europeans and 2,340,000 Africans. In

Nyasaland the corresponding figures were 8,300 and 2,810,000.

Their economies too were very different. Southern Rhodesia, with a gross domestic product of £54 per head in 1954 (the first year of Federation), was the richest, but Northern Rhodesia with £51 ran it close. Nyasaland at £11 was far the poorest. The Southern Rhodesian economy was the most diversified: various types of mining which included gold, chrome and asbestos; agriculture which constituted the biggest single sector of the economy (25 per cent), and in which tobacco was one of the principal crops; also an increasing element of manufacturing industry in Salisbury and Bulawayo.

The Northern Rhodesian economy, apart from African subsistence agriculture, depended almost exclusively on copper, of which it was among the world's major producers. The growth of its white population was directly connected with the prosperity of the copper market. It had nearly tripled during the boom of the late 1920s. It actually fell with the recession after 1930. Rearmament all over the world before and during the war gave copper a huge boost which was reflected in the white immigration figures. Over half the European population and over half of all African wage earners lived on the Copper Belt which constituted what was in many respects a world of its own. To the Europeans of both Rhodesias a favoured method of redrawing the map of central Africa was to amalgamate the Copper Belt with the South, and join north eastern Rhodesia to Nyasaland, leaving Barotseland as a purely African Protectorate. Not surprisingly, this plan never found favour with the Colonial Office where it was seen as a fatal barrier to Whitehall's cherished ambition of making someone else take over Nyasaland's debts.

For Nyasaland was economically in a much worse condition than the Rhodesias. The basic reason was the far slower development of its railway system. This slowness can be explained by the fact that the country was never a part of Cecil Rhodes's 'empire' and therefore did not benefit from the heavy expenditure which Rhodes's companies poured into railway construction in the other two territories. Rhodes was a fanatical believer in the virtues of the railroad and his impetus long outlived him. Harry Johnston did not have these resources, and his dream of turning the Shiré Highlands into something like the 'White Highlands' of Kenya was never realized. A through-line from Beira to Lake Nyasa was not completed till 1935, and its construction put Nyasaland heavily in debt to the imperial Government which had financed the work. No railway link was ever built between Nyasaland and Northern Rhodesia. Nyasaland remained a poor country with few white settlers. Its economy was wholly agricultural, tea, tobacco and cotton being the principal exports.

These differences in the social and economic systems of the three countries were reflected in their constitutional arrangements. Southern Rhodesia was internally self-governing. The control exercised by the white electorate was not wholly unchecked, but the best that Whitehall could do was negative – the right to veto certain types of discriminatory legislation. The two other territories were 'Protectorates'. Their Governors actually governed – unlike the Governor of

Southern Rhodesia who normally acted on 'advice'. The Governor in Northern Rhodesia or Nyasaland was the apex of the social and administrative hierarchy. He represented the Crown and was appointed by it on the advice of the Colonial Secretary. In the small, closely-knit European society of the Protectorates, Government House was the equivalent of Buckingham Palace and invitations were eagerly sought. The Governor was not only a social figure, he was the Commander-in-Chief and the President of both the Executive Council (the nearest equivalent to a Cabinet) and the Legislative Council. He made appointments, issued pardons and could veto legislation. He also had the right to disregard the advice of his Executive Council, but if he did so, had to give his reasons in writing to the Colonial Secretary.

The powers of the Legislative Council were limited. It was subordinate to Parliament which had final authority on all matters. Subject to the Governor's assent its members could introduce financial measures and pass ordinances, i.e. local laws; but the Governor's powers were frequently exercised. All legislation of importance was made from London by Orders-in-Council and formally promulgated by the Crown on the advice of the Colonial Secretary who kept closely in touch with the Governor. Nevertheless, the composition of the Legislative Council mattered, and there was a significant difference between its status in Nyasaland and in Northern Rhodesia.

In Nyasaland the number of 'officials', i.e. members nominated as representatives of the Government was the same as the number of 'unofficials' representing 'the governed'. But all of them were Europeans nominated by the Governor who also had a casting vote as President of the Council. This was the basic Crown Colony set-up and it ensured control from Whitehall with the minimum of friction. The settlers were too few to stake a serious claim to self-government.

In Northern Rhodesia 'the governed' – or, to be more accurate, a small slice of them – had established from an early stage the right to elect some of the 'unofficials'. After the end of Company rule in 1934, a Legislative Council of fourteen was established, of which there were five 'unofficials'. These were not nominated as in Nyasaland, but all elected on a property qualification. The electors had to be British subjects as in Southern Rhodesia. But Africans in the north were 'British protected persons' and could only convert themselves into British subjects by paying a fee. The question was somewhat academic since the property qualifications, even higher than in Southern Rhodesia, precluded almost all Africans anyway. What mattered was that the settlers had an elected, albeit minority, voice in the Legislative Council from 1924 onwards.

A number of constitutional changes which recognized their powerful economic position increased the strength of the 'unofficials'. In 1948 the Governor was replaced as President of the Legislative Council by an elected Speaker. The Legislative Council now consisted of nine 'officials', ten elected 'unofficials' and four nominated 'unofficials' to represent African interests, two being themselves African. Even more significant was a change in the composition of the Executive Council. Five out of eleven were 'unofficials' and a convention was declared, by which the Governor would treat their unanimous advice as the advice of the whole Council and only reject it if prepared to give his reasons to the Colonial Secretary. The following year two of the elected 'unofficials' received ministerial portfolios. These changes left the Governor's powers theoretically intact, but in practice it was very difficult for him to carry on a consistent policy to which the elected unofficials strongly objected.

Their leader from 1945 was Roy Welensky, one of the most remarkable characters to figure on the Rhodesian scene. His life, compounded of romance and tragedy, triumph and disaster, achievement and failure, might in a less humdrum era have made the stuff of a Shakespearean drama. Born in 1907 he was the thirteenth child of a Lithuanian Jew married to an Afrikaner wife. His father had made and lost money in many countries, Sweden, America, South Africa. In the end he lost – and his arrival in Southern Rhodesia in 1896 did not restore – his fortunes. His wife died in 1918. Roy was only eleven, and he lived alone with his impoverished and aged father for the next three years. It must have been an uneasy existence, although he claimed that he learned a great deal from the old man. A primary education was all that could be afforded. At fourteen Roy Welensky left school to earn his living in various ways – as a storeman, a barman and an auctioneer's assistant, until he joined the railways, that white artisan élite, three years later.

He was a voracious reader and thus made up for his lack of formal education. Politics, biography and history were his favourite subjects. Not that he was a bookworm. He was both tough and self-reliant. He was also a formidable heavyweight boxer. His Afrikaner colleagues on the railways found it wise to restrain their penchant for anti-Semitic jokes in his presence. When he sought to reconstruct the moribund railway union branch at Broken Hill, it was not only his charm and persuasiveness that enabled him to extract money from even the most recalcitrant non-payers of union dues. His 'banishment' to that remote spot may have been the result of his activity in the Wankie strike of 1930. Whatever the cause, it diverted his ambitions from the south, and Northern Rhodesia became his political base. In 1938 he succeeded Sir Stewart Gore-Browne as elected member for Broken Hill, and set out on the path that was to bring him to power and fame.

Like Disraeli he did not have a drop of English blood in his veins. Like Disraeli he fought his way through life and it could perhaps have been said at times of him as Lord Derby said of Disraeli to Queen Victoria, '[He] has had to make his position, and men who make their positions will say and do things which are not necessary to be said or done by those for whom positions are provided'. Like Disraeli, he had a romantic view of the British Empire, and, like him again, he reached 'the top of the greasy pole'. But there the parallel ceases. Roy Welensky was unlucky in the times in which he lived. Disraeli died while Britain was still at the apogee of her grandeur. Welensky was to see the Federation, of which he was a principal architect, collapse in ruins – and collapse, as it seemed to him, because the successors to Disraeli's heritage were either nerveless or indifferent.

If Southern Rhodesia represented one side of the imperial coin in Southern Africa and Nyasaland the other, what was the status of Northern Rhodesia? It can only be described as ambivalent – in fact somewhere between the two.

The European population was in a less powerful position politically, though not less powerful economically, than in the south, but all the signs suggested that the gap was rapidly closing. The quarter century since the creation of the protectorate had seen a steady increase in the strength of the 'unofficials'. The doctrine of 'paramountcy' which was the only serious move the other way had been whittled down into meaninglessness. The demand for Responsible Government became more and more vociferous. Given the climate of Whitehall at that time it seemed unlikely, despite the Labour victory of 1945, that this pressure could be long resisted.

The year 1948 was crucial for the future of the two Rhodesias. The elections held in the north on August 27 under the new Constitution were a decisive endorsement of Welensky who secured a further gain for the settlers, formally announced the following year, when by a skilful combination of bargaining and bluff he achieved a deal with the Chartered Company and the Colonial Office over mineral royalties. This removed one of the settlers' main grievances, viz. that the two million pounds a year to which these now amounted virtually all went either to shareholders or to the UK Inland Revenue. Under the new arrangement the Company agreed to pay twenty per cent to the Northern Rhodesian Government in return for exemption from any special tax (the threat Welensky held over their heads) for thirty-seven years, after which in 1986 all mineral rights would be transferred to the government. In Southern Rhodesia the general election held on September 16 was a clear vote of confidence in Huggins. The way was now clear for the supporters of closer union both in Lusaka and in Salisbury.

Before these two elections there had occurred an even more significant event south of the Limpopo. At the South African general election held on May 28, Dr Malan's Nationalist Party, with a minority of the popular vote but a narrow majority of seats, defeated General Smuts. The British Government was deeply disturbed. The triumph of apartheid was in itself bad enough. The triumph, only three years after the end of the war with Germany, of those who had most bitterly opposed South Africa's entry was even worse. Inevitably the makers of British imperial policy looked with new eyes at the whole scene in Central and Southern Africa. The case for an English dominated and therefore 'liberal' Central African State as a counterpoise to Afrikaner nationalism appealed to a broad political spectrum in Britain. Economic arguments – the dollar-earning capacity of copper and tobacco – and strategic considerations – the danger of South Africa drawing the territories north of the Limpopo into her orbit – alike pointed towards a new departure from traditional policies.

On one point, however, British politicians of all parties were emphatic. If a closer union was to come, it must be by way of federation of the three Territories, not amalgamation of the two Rhodesias. Both Huggins and Welensky were strong supporters of a unitary state and preferably one which would not include Nyasa-land. Both of them were in London early in October 1948 and Welensky saw Arthur Creech Jones, the Colonial Secretary, who told him not only that the Labour Cabinet would refuse even to consider amalgamation, but also that, in his opinion, no Conservative Cabinet would either. If Welensky had any doubts on the point he should talk to Oliver Stanley, Colonial Secretary in the late Government. Welensky lunched with Stanley at the Dorchester that same day. The latter confirmed what Creech Jones had said, and urged him to think in terms of federation. No British government could contemplate putting the four million Africans in Northern Rhodesia and Nyasaland under a Southern Rhodesia type of settler government – which was what amalgamation really meant. Welensky called on Huggins at his hotel that afternoon. The two men regretfully agreed that amalgamation was really now a dead duck, although it was still worth keeping as a bargaining point.

Neither of them accepted the arguments against it. Early in 1949 a conference of representatives of the three Territories, under the chairmanship of Sir Miles Thomas, was held at that familiar *venue*, the Victoria Falls Hotel. The Colonial Office was not told in advance. Huggins, who spoke first after the chairman, made it clear that he would have far preferred amalgamation and that he regarded federa-tion as second best. He supported it only because the British Government believed, erroneously in his view, but obdurately and irrevocably, that the Africans in the north would never accept amalgamation. In fact the actual constitutional proposal which Huggins put forward for the suggested federation gave such negligible powers to the Territories that it virtually amounted to a unitary state. For this very reason other delegates expressed their misgivings.

The conference ended with a unanimous resolution in favour of federation, but no clear decisions about its nature. The minutes were not published; such press reports as were released aroused the worst suspicions among articulate Africans in Northern Rhodesia and Nyasaland already much disturbed that none of them had been asked even as observers. In London a group headed by Dr Hastings Banda of Nyasaland and Harry Nkumbula of Northern Rhodesia set about drafting a strong anti-federation memorandum which was later to have much effect on African opinion. Creech Jones, alarmed at the progress which the federal cause appeared to be making in the European electorates of the Rhodesias, visited all three Territories later in the year. He caused fury by declaring that white settle-ment might have to be controlled in the African interest – an apparent reversion to 'paramountcy' which prompted Welensky, never a man for moderate language when aroused, to declare that the British Government would have to bring in troops to implement such a policy. Partnership was one thing 'and for as long as I can see, in that partnership we will be senior partners – but I will never accept that Northern Rhodesia is to be an African state'.

Creech Jones had a long past connexion with African affairs. He belonged to the Friends of Africa and the Anti-Slavery Society. He was chairman of the Fabian Colonial Bureau from 1940 to 1945. During his ten years as a back-bencher he had been, as one historian puts it, 'the principal voice of the House of Commons' conscience on colonies'.[1] A man with this background was not likely to hit it off with either Huggins or Welensky. They believed that he would never accept federation, but would try to fob them off with a revamped version of the Central African Council, a body which they detested.

The federal 'cause' languished throughout the year 1949. There were moments when Huggins and Welensky felt inclined to abandon the effort. Hugh Beadle, Huggins's Minister of Justice, went to London in November to discuss the legal problems of federation, but he made little headway. While he was there he consulted Professor K. C. (now Sir Kenneth) Wheare, then Gladstone Professor of Government at Oxford, whose book, *Federal Government* published in 1946, was and still is the leading authority on the subject. Sir Kenneth Wheare could not give Beadle much encouragement. There were great difficulties in creating a federation out of territories at very different levels of constitutional development. It would scarcely be conceivable for Nyasaland to be elevated to the status of Southern Rhodesia, but unless something like that was done, Southern Rhodesia would be faced with an unacceptable reduction in its own autonomy. Then there was the problem of the British Government's control over native policy in the north. Constitutionally a unitary state would be a better answer. These misgivings were to be fully justified by later events.

Nevertheless the prospect for federation brightened early in 1950. In Britain the Labour Party received a staggering setback at the election of February and found its lead over the Conservatives reduced from 180 to 17 – its majority over all other parties being only six. One of the casualties was Creech Jones, who lost his seat. His successor, James Griffiths, was a trade unionist of the old school who had not been much concerned hitherto with colonial affairs. From the point of view of Huggins and Welensky he was an easier person to deal with than a man deeply involved in African causes.

More significant was one of those intangible and elusive changes in the British climate of opinion which are so difficult to define yet so potent in effect. The Labour Party's loss of votes was itself symptomatic of a shift which, among many other side effects, made federation appear more reputable to those – and they were of course relatively few in number – who took any interest at all in African affairs. The 'liberal' orthodoxies of the past few years had suddenly become less convincing.

The turning point in a complicated history of conferences, resolutions, proposals and counter-proposals, which it would be as tedious for the author to describe as for his reader to follow, was the decision of the Colonial Secretary announced in November 8, 1950 to allow a conference of officials of the four Governments involved (Britain, the two Rhodesias and Nyasaland) to meet in London in order to examine the feasibility of federation. It was the result of a suggestion made in August by Huggins who argued that the discussions had

[1] David Goldsworthy, *Colonial Issues in British Politics 1945-61*, 1971.

hitherto been on too high a level. Although the British Government emphatically disclaimed any notion of commitment to federation the decision was widely recognized as an important step in that direction. It was unlikely that a conference of officials would assert that federation was not feasible, and their conclusion would give powerful ammunition to those who believed that it was not only feasible, but highly desirable. Creech Jones, who had now become his successor's severest critic, at once saw the danger, but he now cut little ice outside the left wing of the Labour Party.

The conference met in London at the Commonwealth Relations Office on March 5, 1951 under the chairmanship of G. H. Baxter, a senior civil servant in the Commonwealth Relations Office. Its constitutional and legal advisers were Professor K. C. Wheare, and W. L. Dale. The Central African Council was represented by A. E. T. Benson (later Sir Arthur Benson and Governor of Northern Rhodesia 1954–59). The leader of the Southern Rhodesia delegation was Andrew Strachan supported by Athol Evans. Both were to have distinguished careers in the Federal public service and to receive knighthoods. Their brief was to press for amalgamation – perhaps more as a tactic than anything else – and above all to insist on the unification, even under a federal scheme, of as many government departments as possible. The Southern Rhodesians were responsible for nine of the fifteen preliminary memoranda with which the conference was to deal. The Northern Rhodesian delegation took the opposite line on almost every issue. They were members of the British Colonial Service and their position was, of course, quite different from that of the Southern Rhodesian civil servants who were carrying out the policies of a Government elected by white Rhodesian voters. Responsible Government might be on the Northern Rhodesian horizon. It had not yet arrived, and the officials in that delegation were very far from reflecting the views of Welensky and the white electors. They dwelt repeatedly on African opposition to any move towards closer union, on African mistrust of Southern Rhodesia's 'native' policy and on the British Government's duty to safeguard African interests. The Nyasaland delegation took much the same line.

There was, however, at the conference one very important Colonial Office figure who had become converted to the cause of federation. This was Andrew Cohen, the leader of the Colonial Office's own delegation. His conversion was the more significant because he was a known sympathizer with African aspirations and stood well to the left of centre in the political spectrum. Cohen had received striking promotion under Creech Jones, becoming in 1947 Assistant Under-Secretary in charge of African affairs at the age of thirty-eight. If Labour had won the general election of 1951, he would almost certainly have been made Permanent Under-Secretary to the Colonial Office.[2]

Cohen was thus about as 'political' an official as any British civil servant could allow himself to be, and his brand of politics was certainly not the sort which

---

[2] D. Goldsworthy, *Colonial Issues in British Politics 1945–61*, 1971, 52, citing an interview with James Griffiths.

inspired the admiration of Huggins, Welensky and the white electorate in the two Rhodesias. Nevertheless, he was one of the principal architects of the federal compromise which emerged from the conference, and which, with amendments, eventually became the basis of the Central African State. It was indeed largely on his advice that Griffiths made the crucial decision to convene such a conference at all. What was it that moved a man of Cohen's views to promote a constitutional arrangement which was bitterly opposed by the politically articulate Africans in the north, which was anathema to the British Left and which became within a decade, however unjustly, the symbol of entrenched settler colonialism?

There can be no doubt that his principal motive was the fear that the new Nationalist Government in South Africa would pull Southern and possibly Northern Rhodesia too into its economic and ideological orbit. It may be that people of Jewish origin were and are peculiarly susceptible to the fear of racialism and that this was especially true in the aftermath of Hitler's policy of genocide. It was, moreover, a fact that some of those who had risen to power in Pretoria after the Nationalist victory in 1948 had been active Nazi sympathizers. But one did not need to be Jewish or even notably 'liberal' to feel serious anxiety at the growth of apartheid and the effect it might have on European attitudes in the Rhodesias. There was a large amount of Afrikaner immigration into both countries after the war. The trade agreements with South Africa concluded by Huggins seemed to presage closer economic links, and Southern Rhodesia's native policy, balanced uneasily between the northern concept of gradually extending rights to Africans and the rigid policy of separatism in the Union, might plausibly be feared to go the wrong way.

It is a moot point how far these anxieties were warranted. There were certainly elements in Southern Rhodesia which hankered after a South African solution. The victory of the Rhodesia Front in 1962 and the policies pursued by the Smith regime after UDI are evidence of this. As for South Africa herself, it is true that disciples of even the most anachronistic creed can believe in the possibility of making converts. On the very eve of the American Civil War, the southern slave states were still seeking to extend their 'peculiar institution' to new territories. On the other hand, there is little to suggest that in fact Malan and Strijdom were expansionists. Smuts after the First World War had been much more ambitious. His successors after the Second were basically on the defensive. And in Southern Rhodesia the causes which brought about the Unilateral Declaration of Independence and the ascendancy of the racialist hard-liners simply did not exist fifteen years earlier.

History, however, is made as much by fear of turnip ghosts as by reaction to genuine dangers. No one can be quite sure what the realities were. It was still harder at the time. Whatever the truth may be, no one can doubt the potent effect which the new course in South African policy had upon the attitude of a large section of the British liberal/left who might have been expected to oppose federation. This was a far more significant reason for its acceptance in London than the economic arguments which played such an important part in the Rhodesias. Nor should it be regarded as merely negative – an attempt to prevent Southern Rhodesia from being 'South-Africanized'. There was in Britain and in both Rhodesias a genuine streak of idealism among those who worked for and achieved federation.

Whereas Asia had dominated the 'colonial scene' before the war, Africa was now in the forefront of the stage. India and Britain's other Asiatic dependencies had become for good or ill self-governing states, and London no longer had any responsibility for them. But over the continent of Africa there hung a great question mark. That it was Britain's duty to bring self-government at some stage and in some way to her African colonies no one doubted. The problems were when and how. Behind them lay even bigger issues – the advance of communism, the emergence of the Third World, the question of colour, the gulf between the rich and the poor nations, the control of vital raw materials, the implication of all this upon strategy and tactics in the long three-way cold war between Russia, China and the West, which shows no sign of ending yet.

In addition to all the difficulties of decolonization, there was one which was peculiar to Africa, though not confined to the African colonies ruled by Britain. That was the existence of the substantial white populations which had settled there and had become a semi-indigenous ruling class, unlike the Europeans in Asia, who were birds of passage and regarded Europe as their home. If a great Central African state based on genuine multi-racialism and a genuine partnership between black and white could be created with a built-in machinery for constitutional development, might it not become in the end a self-governing dominion which would set a pattern for the archaic colonies of Belgium and Portugal on the one hand and on the other perhaps soften by its example the racialist policies of the Union? Such a state could by its very existence prevent the polarization between black and white Africa which seemed otherwise inevitable and which in the event occurred. This was certainly not an ignoble aim, and the ultimate failure of the Federation is no reason to forget that there were high principles among the motives of its founders as well as more mundane considerations.

The Conference of Officials took place in cold, bleak, wet weather, which was abnormally odious even by the standards of an English March. The Southern Rhodesian delegates, conscious of being outside the Colonial Office 'establishment', worried by the opposition of the 'northern' delegates and depressed by the rigours of the weather, came near to breaking off the discussions which after five days of nit-picking seemed to have got nowhere. They told Benson, who was a personal friend of Cohen. The latter was at his home in Hampstead, out of action through influenza. Benson saw him on the Friday evening (March 9) and Cohen, despite his illness, agreed to have a talk with Strachan next day. Their conversation convinced Cohen that he must do something quickly or the conference would collapse. Accordingly, though far from well, he attended the next plenary session on Monday, March 12. There was at once a new and powerful voice on the side of federation.

Throughout the week the Southern Rhodesians continued to argue the case for amalgamation. Cohen was not prepared to back this. He conceded its advantages and he agreed that both in Britain and the northern protectorates Southern Rhodesia's native policy was too often confused with that of South Africa, but he considered that these prejudices, British or African, were for the time being ineradicable and that the British Parliament would not give up its responsibility for the Africans in the north in return for the right to veto laws passed by the legislative assembly of a unitary Central African State. The tacit assumption that this had not worked satisfactorily with Southern Rhodesia under Responsible Government may not have pleased their delegates, but by the end of the week they accepted that the fight would not be between federation and amalgamation, but between federation and confederation or some even looser bond.

From March 19 onwards the conference directed its collective mind towards the details of a federal scheme, and eventually an agreement was hammered out. The essence of it was that the three Territories retained their own constitutions, their control over African affairs and their relationship with the British Government, but there would henceforth be a federal legislature and cabinet to which certain specific fields of government would be allocated – defence, economic policy, currency, federal taxation and borrowing, custom and excise, European primary and secondary education, all higher education, external trade, railways, aviation, trunk roads, posts and telegraphs, electricity supply and a long list of others – most of them the sort of functions which one would expect any federal government to exercise.

The Territories were to retain nearly everything that pertained to African affairs including all education below the university level. They also kept control over health, labour, mines, local government, Territorial income tax, agriculture, forestry, veterinary services, prisons, Territorial roads and irrigation. One function about which there was much dispute they also retained, and that was law and order which carried with it control of the police.

The new federal government was to consist of a Governor-General (who would not, however, supplant the three Territorial Governors) and a single-chamber legislature of thirty-five members. It was considered desirable to avoid giving an overall majority to any one Territory; accordingly Southern Rhodesia was to have seventeen, Northern Rhodesia eleven, Nyasaland seven. Three members from each Territory would be chosen specially to represent Africans and in the northern Territories two would actually be Africans. There was to be no uniform franchise. The Governor-General would appoint as Prime Minister the member most likely, in his view, to command a majority in the legislature. The Prime Minister would form a cabinet in much the same way as the Prime Minister of Southern Rhodesia had done since the advent of Responsible Government. It was suggested that six would be an appropriate number and that a convention should be established whereby each Territory was represented by at least one minister.

The conference devoted much time to the safeguarding of African interests. Although African policy as such was allocated to the Territorial governments, federal legislation could have an important bearing on it. The conference proposed an African Affairs Board of ten members, a chairman and three from each

Territory, one of the three being the Territory's Secretary for Native Affairs. The other two would be appointed by the Governor. One of them must be an African, the other a member of the Territorial Legislature. The Board would examine all federal legislation before it was published and its opinion would be attached to the bill. If the Board considered that the measure would be damaging or discriminatory as regards African interests, the Government could still introduce it, but the Governor-General had to refer it to the Colonial Secretary before giving assent.

In spite of Southern Rhodesian doubts, the conference agreed that the Chairman (who would be appointed by the Governor-General without reference to the Federal Ministers) should sit *ex officio* in the cabinet as Minister for African Affairs. He was described by opponents of the scheme as the 'cuckoo' Minister. The most that the Southern Rhodesians could secure for the moment was that he must be a member of the Federal Legislature. In the end the provision was one of the few proposals of the Conference of Officials which were not adopted.

The findings of the conference were drafted with great speed and were ready on March 31. They were divided into two parts, one for publication, one for limited circulation to the four Governments. The main report, which could have been published at once, but was held up till June 15, summarized the positive recommendations and stated some of the reasons behind them. The objections of the Africans were not suppressed, but their fears were discounted on the ground that few of them understood the difference between amalgamation – a unitary state in which Southern Rhodesia would predominate – and federation – an elaborate system of checks and balances which would safeguard African interests. The proposed constitution for Central Africa was spelled out, with a clear warning that the conference was exploratory and that its recommendations committed no one. The published report made the case for federation mainly in terms of economic, administrative, logistical and military efficiency; better economic development for all races being the principal argument.

In a 'confidential minute' annexed to the report, but restricted in its circulation to the four Governments, the conference set out further reasons for recommending federation. To publish these would clearly have offended the South African Government. For the historian it is, however, the most significant part of the story. The 'minute' emphasized the danger of South Africa extending its influence northwards through Afrikaner immigration into the Rhodesias and through economic power. The racial implications of this extension could be very serious, and the whole future of southern and central Africa might be jeopardized. In the event of a slump the pulling power of the Union could be overwhelming. Only a strong and viable Central African State could provide a rival magnet.

These arguments were decisive. The Federation could not have come into existence if the Labour Party in Britain had been strongly against it. The danger, real or unreal, of South African expansionism was a threat to which Labour supporters were particularly susceptible. In that sense apartheid can be regarded as the father of federation.

18

Federation Achieved 1951-53

In theory the Officials Conference committed no one. In practice it was decisive. As Huggins said many years later, 'it was the right level to get things done: without it Federation would never have come about'.[1] There were to be further meetings and much negotiation, but the report of the Officials Conference was a turning point. For good or ill it made the creation of a Central African state both plausible and probable.

Griffiths announced the publication of the report in a statement to the House of Commons on June 13, 1951 and commended it on behalf of the Government as 'a constructive approach to the problem which deserves careful consideration of all the peoples and Governments concerned'. He said that he and the Commonwealth Secretary, Patrick Gordon Walker, would visit the Territories later in the year in order to assess public opinion.

The reactions in the three Territories varied. In Northern Rhodesia European opinion was solidly in favour, African opinion against. In Nyasaland also the Africans were hostile. Europeans, themselves on the side of federation, were doubtful how far they could go without African support. In Southern Rhodesia African opinion was rather less clear than in the north, but the predominant view was opposed to federation. European attitudes were mixed. A body known as the United Central Africa Association was set up with the object of gathering money and making propaganda for federation. The cause received support from the great copper companies and other business interests. But some important voices were raised against federation, although not always for the same reasons. Raymond Stockill, leader of the attenuated opposition (the 'Liberal' Party) saw it as a barrier to dominion status. That Huggins missed the opportunity to achieve this in 1950 or 1951 is one of the entrenched legends of Rhodesia Front mythology. No one can say with

[1] RR 27.

complete certainty what the British Government's answer would have been to a question which was never asked, but it seems most unlikely that dominion status would have been conceded at this stage. The last occasion when power had been handed over to a European minority in a British dependancy was in South Africa in 1910. For those who believed in 'partnership' and racial equality it was hardly an encouraging precedent, and a great deal had happened since. Sir Ernest Guest, despite his former role as a member of Huggins's wartime cabinet, opposed federation on the obverse ground to the objections of the northern Africans. He feared that northern 'liberalism' would spread south, whereas they feared that southern 'obscurantism' (as they saw it) would spread north.

Sir Robert Tredgold, Chief Justice of Southern Rhodesia and in that capacity legal adviser to the Governor, objected to federation for a different reason. He regarded 'native policy' as the crucial question of the future, and he could not see how a subject of common interest to all three Territories could be left to each of them to handle separately. In a memorandum to Sir John Kennedy, the Governor, which he subsequently showed to Gordon Walker, he drew the analogy with the question of slavery in the United States.

> It took one of the bitterest civil wars in history to prove what should have been obvious from the beginning, that a problem the concern of the whole union could not be settled in one way in some states and in another in other states.
>
> This, to my mind, is the fatal defect in the proposals in the Report. They seek to avoid an issue which is unavoidable. They endeavour to postpone a decision which can only be made vastly more difficult by delay.[2]

He was highly critical of the extent to which the report depended on a memorandum which he describes as 'Survey of Native Policy'. This document, officially called 'Comparative Study of Native Policy' and drawn up by Benson, Chief Secretary to the Central African Council and the three Territorial Secretaries for Native Affairs, is indeed one of the most interesting of the many papers which the conference considered. It is remarkable in that its conclusion, which was that the native policies of the Territories did not greatly diverge, bears little relationship with its analysis of those policies, which suggests that they differed in one most important respect. Paragraph 4 of the study is actually headed 'The Fundamental Difference'. The authors point out that in the north the assumption had been that the African must from the outset have some political and administrative responsibility for his own affairs or else 'there can be no assurance that any purely material or economic betterment will endure under his own management'; 'his economic, cultural and social advance is a pre-requisite if he is to be enabled to exercise full political rights'.

---

[2] Large extracts of this memorandum are printed in his book *The Rhodesia that was my Life*, 1968, 193–9.

The truth was that the south and the north reflected two very different British traditions. They could be summarized as the 'English Experience' and the 'Irish Experience'. In England during the nineteenth century it really was broadly true that social and economic advance preceded the granting of the franchise which was extended more slowly and cautiously than in the USA or almost any country in Europe. Gladstone was converted to a new Reform Act when a deputation of working men asked him to legislate for the security of their savings. The vote was the symbol and reward of respectability. The English were allowed to govern themselves when they had reached 'civilized standards'.

The history of the Irish, whom the 3rd Marquess of Salisbury in an imprudent impromptu once compared with the Hottentots, was different. What they wanted was to govern themselves, and they wanted this whether they were poor or prosperous, whether they were suffering from misery and famine or enjoying the fruits of Balfour's policy of 'killing Home Rule by kindness'. Ireland was a colony. The Irish got self-government through violence and agitation, not because Westminster thought they were fit for it. Not surprisingly the Irish experience has been the precedent for most of Africa. It is no answer to say that Africans govern themselves badly. Of course they do. Nineteenth-century England was probably better governed than twentieth-century England, but we cannot expect to repeal the Reform Acts of 1867 and 1884. Rhodesia is better governed than Uganda, but it does not follow that Rhodesian Africans prefer being ruled by Europeans. The right to mis-govern oneself is as valid as any other political right and is exercised more often than most.

Sir Robert Tredgold's criticism was well justified by the course of events. It was on the rock of native policy that the Federation would founder. Whether his solution would have worked is less certain. He wanted a unitary state with a second chamber composed as a safeguard for African interests; and reservation of legislation to the UK government in the last resort. It would not have been easy to 'sell' a unitary state to the Africans and there was the problem of composing the second chamber. Nevertheless, the idea had its attractions and he was not the only advocate of a bi-cameral system. At least it would have had the merit of being cheaper and simpler – two legislative bodies, one Governor and one Civil Service instead of four of each.

Tredgold, Guest and Stockill from their different standpoints spoke only for a minority of European opinion in Southern Rhodesia. A story was sedulously spread after UDI that the British Government forced the Federation upon the colony. Nothing could be less true. The majority of white Southern Rhodesians including the whole of the party in power were strongly in favour, as the figures in the subsequent referendum promised by Huggins were to show. It was their pressure combined with that of the Europeans on the Copper Belt which brought the Federation into existence. The Conservatives were more friendly to the idea than Labour, but no British government of whatever party complexion would have taken the initiative. The only element of truth in the myth is that, if there was to be a Federation at all, Britain did insist on the inclusion of Nyasaland. This is a far cry from the notion that the Federation itself stemmed from British pressure.

In the interval between the publication of the report of the Officials Conference and the arrival of the two Secretaries of State in Africa it was agreed that the Territorial Governments could commend the report to their Africans on the Territorial level, but that District Officers should be neutral; they could explain its details, but not tell their hearers that it was a good thing. This decision was apparently made because Griffiths (with the typical vanity of the politician) wished to do the work of persuasion himself. It has been bitterly criticized on the ground that Africans traditionally looked for guidance from District Officers, and neutrality was bound to be interpreted as disapproval. One cannot say how much difference would have been made by a more positive policy. Perhaps an opportunity was missed. Griffiths himself came to regret his decision in retrospect.

Welensky, during July 1951, was in London for the Commonwealth Conference. The possibility of an election and a change of government in the near future was obvious. On an earlier visit in April he had met Alan Lennox-Boyd, Anthony Eden, and Lords Altrincham and Swinton. He renewed these contacts in July and saw many other prominent Conservatives, including Winston Churchill, who however took little interest in the affairs of Central Africa. Welensky persuaded Lord Swinton to launch a debate on federation in the House of Lords. Most of the speakers were favourable, though Lord Hailey, one of the greatest experts on Africa, took the same line as Tredgold about the danger of divergent native policies. Welensky returned to Africa satisfied that he had powerful support within the Conservative Party and that a change of government in London might be no bad thing for the federal cause.

That cause received a further boost after the visit in August of a British delegation under the auspices of the Commonwealth Parliamentary Association. Stanley Evans on the Labour side was leader (he was to become celebrated as one of the few Labour rebels against the party's policy over Suez in 1956) and Julian Amery was the most conspicuous of the others. The delegation saw a large number of European and African witnesses. It recognized the fact of African suspicions, but did not believe them to be justified, and came out clearly in favour of federation on both economic and political grounds.

Griffiths started his tour of the Northern Territories on August 24. Gordon Walker arrived in Salisbury on September 10. The visits were to culminate in a second Victoria Falls Conference on September 18. It was a grander affair than anything held hitherto – the first 'official' conference of representatives of the four Governments. The Governor of Southern Rhodesia, Sir John Kennedy, took the chair. The two Secretaries of State were present with Andrew Cohen in support – and the Territories fielded delegations at the highest level. Moreover there were African as well as European members from the north – three from Nyasaland, two from Northern Rhodesia.

There were no Africans from Southern Rhodesia. It was symbolic of the Africans' status in the colony that they were 'represented' by the Minister for

Native Affairs. The current holder of the portfolio was Patrick Fletcher who had recently observed in reference to Gordon Walker's discussions with African leaders in Salisbury that their opinion did not signify since it was the business of the Governments to settle the question of federation.

The conference was a frustrating affair. From the outset its purpose had been to act as a forum of discussion rather than a means of decision, but the achievement of even that limited objective was hampered by an announcement on the second day of Attlee's decision to hold a general election on October 25. The deliberations of the conference had a certain air of unreality from then onwards. The two British Ministers naturally expressed their confidence in victory. The delegates of the Rhodesias were not so sure; they might soon be dealing with a new government, new men and new ideas.

There were other difficulties. The British Ministers wished to discuss African objections. Huggins, however, wanted to modify some of the 'safeguards' recommended by the Conference of Officials, but did not wish to do so in front of the Africans. He tried to claim that, since they had declared against the whole idea of federation they ought to leave anyway. Griffiths refused, and the conference nearly broke up. In the event Huggins did not submit his amendments and they were not even discussed; this explains some of his anger about the whole affair which he later described, to Griffiths's fury, as 'a Native Benefit Society led by the Secretary of State for the Colonies'.

The conference's final communiqué stated that, apart from the five Africans, the delegates favoured federation, but were against amalgamation unless a majority of the inhabitants of all three Territories supported it. As for the division of powers, the conference endorsed in general terms the report of the Conference of Officials. Griffiths stated that there would be another conference in London in July 1952. He recognized African hostility, but hoped that it would evaporate.

The general election of October 1951 gave the Conservatives a narrow majority in the House, although Labour obtained slightly more popular votes. No one could have guessed that this precarious victory was to inaugurate thirteen years of Conservative rule. The Party was to see the Federation in – and to see it out.

The new Colonial Secretary was Oliver Lyttleton, big, breezy, tough and not over-conciliatory. A late entrant to the House of Commons, he never quite gauged its quirks and oddities. He stemmed from an old political family, but his own career had been in business. He looked at federation from that point of view – a plan to raise the standard of living in all three Territories. On November 21 he made a statement in the House of Commons supporting closer association on the lines of the recommendations of the recent Victoria Falls Conference. Early in 1952 Huggins went to London for informal talks with him and Lord Ismay, the Commonwealth Secretary. The two northern Governors also attended.

Huggins, possibly for bargaining purposes, possibly to reinsure himself with his own party, continued to press for amalgamation or, failing that, for a reasoned statement of the case for rejection. The British Government put down a final stopper by declaring that amalgamation would contravene their long-standing treaties with the Africans in the north, and that in any case they were effectively committed against it by the previous administration. It would only take place if the inhabitants of the three Territories desired it. This had been stated at the Victoria Falls Conference and endorsed by Lyttleton on November 21.

Accepting the federal frame of reference Huggins pressed for amendments to the officials' scheme on three points, the African Affairs Board, the Civil Service and the nine nominated members of the Federal Legislature. He was, of course, particularly hostile to the 'cuckoo' Minister. 'If he comes in we shut down the talks at once,' he jauntily told a press conference. More and more people had come to regard the proposal as a constitutional anomaly which could hardly be defended, and Huggins was assured that it would be dropped at the subsequent conference. On the question of a unified and locally based Civil Service he obtained no change then, or in any subsequent negotiations. The vested interests of the Colonial Office were far too powerful. For the moment the issue was postponed. On nominated members he did rather better. No definite decision was taken, but it was generally accepted that nine were too many and that some special system of electing the Africans must be discovered. His proposal to have no specially elected members at all, however, was flatly turned down. It would never have got through the House.

Although there was nothing in Lyttleton's statement on November 21 from which Griffiths could dissent, there were soon straws in the wind to suggest a subtly changed climate. Whereas Griffiths's principal anxiety was the African objections, Lyttleton showed more worry about the possible recalcitrance of the Southern Rhodesian electorate.[3] A master of tactics and quick to perceive the nuances of political opinion, Huggins skilfully exploited this shift of opinion. He pressed for speed. 'If closer association this year is rejected,' he said, 'it will be gone for all time and the three Territories will be the poorer for it.'[4] Philip Mason cites an interesting example of the swing in 'informed opinion' since the general election. On January 22, *The Times* welcomed the talks as 'the first serious effort to reconcile the British and Southern Rhodesian standpoints. Because of preoccupation with the views and concerns of Africans this was never done at Victoria Falls.' The writer added that it could be the duty of a trustee to act in what he considered the best interests of his ward, even though the ward dissented – a point endorsed by Julian Amery in the House a few weeks later. It followed that one might go ahead with federation despite refusal by the Africans to take part in the negotiations. Three months earlier *The Times* had categorized such a course as 'calamitous'.[5]

Huggins managed to inculcate sufficient sense of urgency to have the date of the next formal conference advanced to late April. Apart from this announcement it was deemed politic to say as little as possible. The negotiators did not wish to give

[3] Philip Mason, *Year of Decision*, 1960, 30–1.
[4] Ibid., 31, quoting *Daily Telegraph*, January 7, 1952.
[5] Mason, op. cit., 31.

the impression that they were fixing up the whole affair behind the backs of both the Europeans and the Africans in the three Territories. The Territorial Governments were asked to submit their proposals by the end of March, and it was agreed that the first plenary meeting should take place at Lancaster House on April 23.

Both in Britain and in the northern Territories opposition gathered apace. In Northern Rhodesia Harry Nkumbula agitated vigorously against any form of closer association and there was no dissent among articulate African opinion. In Nyasaland, too, it was equally clear that such opinion as expressed itself at all was hostile to federation. Of course it could always be said that there was no evidence to show how far the illiterate or semi-literate African masses accepted a handful of educated Africans as their spokesmen. Much play was made by sceptics about the alleged absence of a word in any African language for 'federation'. It may be true that what the masses really feared was the extension of Southern Rhodesian native policy to the north and that there was no more chance of this occurring under a federal system than under the *status quo*. On the other hand, the supporters of federation avowedly had dominion status as a long-term aim, and the experience of South Africa showed how unreal in that event the safeguards for Africans could become.

All these points were made with vigour in Britain. Dr Hastings Banda went on a successful tour of Scotland where he could appeal effectively to the churches, conscious of their great missionary tradition in Nyasaland. Prominent academics expressed their misgivings about federation and Miss Margery Perham wrote a powerful and prophetic letter which appeared in *The Times* on March 4. On that same day Griffiths divided the House sitting in Committee of Supply, on the ground that the Africans were not being properly consulted and that the advancement of the date for the conference made it look as if federation was being 'railroaded' through. Lyttleton tried to preserve bi-partisanship by offering to have a second conference in July 1952. This act of appeasement did not work, for Griffiths pursued the matter to a division in spite of it. But the Central African Governments were landed with extra conference nonetheless – to the annoyance of Welensky and others.

The division on March 4 marks the end of bi-partisanship as far as federation was concerned. Griffiths did not, it is true, divide the House on the next two occasions when the matter was debated (April 29 and July 24), but there were special reasons in each case. On October 1, the Labour Conference pronounced against federation unless the Africans accepted it. On March 29, 1953 and on frequent occasions thereafter till the Order-in-Council setting up the Federation went through on July 27 the Labour Party opposed the proposals and divided the House.

The charge made by the Conservatives that Labour was tacking according to the wind of left-wing pressure does not seem justified. Griffiths was quite consistent, and there was nothing self-contradictory in saying that federation was a good thing, but should not be imposed if the Africans objected. The weakness of the argument lay elsewhere, as the Labour group headed by Creech Jones and centred around the Fabian Colonial Bureau were quick to see. A member of its Advisory Committee writing to Marjorie Nicholson, the Secretary, pointed out:

> To oppose federation exclusively or mainly on the ground that Africans oppose it plays into the Government's hands. HMG has a moral duty to do what it considers to be right in the interests of Africans, and only in exceptional circumstances can a government be justified in following the cowardly line of abandoning what it thinks to be right in deference to mob pressure.[6]

This was basically the same point about trustees and wards made by *The Times* and endorsed by Julian Amery. The Creech Jones group drew the conclusion that federation must be attacked as a bad thing in itself. The Government naturally made the most of the other side of the coin, and claimed that the main body of the Labour Party was indeed abandoning what it thought to be right in deference to mob pressure. And so the dispute rolled on, neither side making the slightest impression on the other.

There was, however, one small group of Labour dissentients. Gordon Walker had always been much keener on federation than Griffiths. He believed that the danger of Afrikaner expansion to the north was grave enough for the British Government to disregard African opinion and if necessary impose federation. It was a matter of saving the Africans despite themselves. He was joined by George Brown and Stanley Evans. Altogether some sixteen silently abstained in the critical divisions of 1953.

Meanwhile the supporters of federation found that they could be embarrassed by their friends as well as their enemies. Colonel David Stirling, DSO, after a most distinguished war record as a commando in the Western Desert, had settled in Salisbury. He was an enthusiastic idealist and founded in 1947 the Capricorn Africa Society – a body devoted to the concept of partnership between the races. He was in favour of closer association, but wished to go far beyond the three Territories. He wanted the Federation to comprise also Kenya, Uganda, Tanganyika, Zanzibar and Northern Bechuanaland. This greater Central African Federation would be a bulwark against the diverse threats of Afrikanerdom, communism, Asian immigration and African nationalism. He wrote to Churchill, Salisbury, Ismay and Lyttleton, and planned a conference of British settlers from all these countries at Salisbury on the lines of the Philadelphia Convention of 1774. Enthusiasts are liable to overestimate the impact of their own enthusiasm. Huggins and Welensky, concerned with the attitudes of right-wing Europeans, were reluctant to alienate a potential ally, but they were determined not to be diverted from their own objective. There was no possibility of realizing Stirling's dream and his letters were politely ignored by the Conservative leaders in London.

The conference promised by Lyttleton met at Lancaster House on April 23

[6] Quoted in David Goldsworthy, *Colonial Issues in British Politics 1945–61*, 1971, 228.

under the joint chairmanship of Lyttleton and Lord Salisbury who had replaced Lord Ismay as Commonwealth Secretary. Huggins led the Southern Rhodesian delegation, Sir Gilbert Rennie and Sir Geoffrey Colby, Governors respectively of Northern Rhodesia and Nyasaland, led the two northern delegations. Welensky was present as leader of the Northern Rhodesian unofficials and Barrow (later Sir Malcolm Barrow) in the same role for Nyasaland. The African representative bodies in the two northern Territories were invited to send delegates to have informal talks with the Colonial Secretary and to take part in the conference. They came to London and had the informal talks, but declined to attend the conference as delegates or even as observers, although they remained in London throughout its duration and, in the words of the official report, 'had discussions with many interested individuals and groups'. Paradoxically the only Africans to participate were members of the delegation from Southern Rhodesia. In view of previous criticisms Huggins thought it wise to bring with him two Africans, Jasper Savanhu and Joshua Nkomo who was destined to play such a conspicuous part in the later history of his country.

The recommendations of the first London conference in the vast majority of cases were to be endorsed by the second and final conference.[7] There was to be a Federal Legislature on the lines proposed by the Officials' Conference consisting of thirty-five members and a Speaker[8] – seventeen for Southern Rhodesia, eleven for Northern Rhodesia and seven for Nyasaland. Of these, twenty-six were known as Elected Members – fourteen for Southern Rhodesia, eight for Northern Rhodesia and four for Nyasaland. In the Rhodesias they were to be elected at the first general election on the existing franchise, and in Nyasaland, where there was no franchise, under regulations made by the Governor-General with the agreement of the Governor and the Colonial Secretary. Thereafter the Federal Legislature could itself at any time settle the franchise and qualifications for election in the Rhodesias, but could not do so in Nyasaland before a date appointed by the Protectorate's Legislative Council. In order to change the franchise the Federal Legislature had to secure an affirmative vote of two-thirds of all its members, and the bill would be reserved by the Governor-General for Royal Assent, i.e. that of the UK government.

In addition to the twenty-six Elected Members, there were to be seven Elected Members for African Interests and two Appointed Members for the same purpose. In Southern Rhodesia there would be three Elected Members in this category, two of whom had to be African and one European; the system of election was to be settled under regulations made by the Governor. In each of the Northern Territories there were to be two Members elected by such body as the Governor would 'designate as a body representative of Africans' and under regulations made

---

[7] Cmd. 8753. See below pp. 267–8 for such changes as were made in the final scheme put to Parliament in 1953.

[8] The Speaker, unlike his British prototype, could be elected from outside, and, if elected from inside the Legislature, had to vacate his seat.

by him. They did not have to be Africans. An Appointed Member would be nominated for each northern Territory by its Governor. The status and election of the nine Members for African Interests could not be varied by the Federal Legislature.

These arrangements were a success for the Southern Rhodesians who had always objected to the idea of nine *nominated* members for African interests. They scored a further victory over the composition of the African Affairs Board. They eliminated the 'cuckoo' Minister. The Chairman was no longer to be a member of the Federal Cabinet. They also managed to reduce the number of members, apart from the Chairman, from nine to six, and to exclude the Secretaries for Native Affairs. Under the new proposals there had to be an African and a European from each Territory nominated by their respective Governors, and no one in the public service or in any legislative body, Federal or Territorial could be appointed. Huggins did not like the latter exclusion, but for the moment he had to bide his time.

As with the American and Australian Constitutions, the 'enumerated powers' were allocated to the Federal Legislature, and the 'residual powers' (i.e. everything else and therefore not specified) went to the regional legislatures. There was also a list of concurrent powers – a field in which both sides could operate, but Federal laws prevailed if there was a conflict. The 'enumerated powers' were much the same as those suggested for the Federal Legislature by the original Conference of Officials.

The Southern Rhodesian delegates lost two critical battles. They failed to secure a unified Civil Service. The Federation was to suffer throughout its brief life from the existence of four sets of officials whose divergent traditions, opportunities and loyalties constituted a perpetual background of uneasiness and uncertainty.

More serious was the question of the enforcement of law and order. Huggins fought hard to make this a Federal responsibility, but E. I. G. Unsworth, QC, the Northern Rhodesian Attorney General, insisted on law and order remaining territorial, and Welensky supported him. Huggins said towards the end of his life:

I maintained there would be nothing but chaos unless there were one police force free of local pressures and so able to stand up to these intimidators and rioters. I told Roy that if the Northern Rhodesian 'elected members' wouldn't support us on things like that we hadn't a hope, and I very nearly closed the proceedings then and there. The next day they offered me Defence as a sop. On that day [*sic*] Federation was born and died, but there's probably not much point in publishing that sort of thing now.[9]

The opinion of an old man looking back cannot be regarded as conclusive. Defence could never have been anything but a Federal power. The 'sop' argument is not convincing. But the conflict over law and order was seen by both sides as crucial.

[9] RR 124.

The determination of the Colonial Office and the northern Territories to ram home their case emerges from the report of the final conference in January 1953 (Cmd. 8753, Chapter II, 20): 'The preservation of law and order will, however, remain entirely the responsibility of the Territorial Governments.'

The other features of the proposed constitution were relatively uncontroversial. The Governor-General was, like the Governor of Southern Rhodesia, a constitutional monarch with certain additional discretionary powers, rather than a ruler. A system of Cabinet government analogous to the Southern Rhodesian was set up. As in most federations there was a Supreme Court which could pronounce on the constitutionality of federal and territorial legislation.

Amendment of the constitution (which was specifically stated to include the setting up of a second chamber if desired) required a two-thirds majority of the whole Legislature. But, if the amendment was disapproved by either the African Affairs Board or by a resolution of any Territorial Legislature within sixty days of being passed by the Federal Assembly, then the Royal Assent could only be given by Order in Council. This meant that it would be laid before each House of the UK parliament and an opportunity given for rejecting it. This was a compromise between the UK Government's view shared by the northern delegations that all amendments should be laid before Parliament and the Southern Rhodesian view that none should be. The colony's own constitution provided for a straightforward two-thirds rule, except in the case of amendments affecting African interests. These required the assent of the Secretary of State, but did not have to go to parliament.

The conference decided that in certain fields it had insufficient expertise to make valid recommendations. It therefore established three commissions of experts to investigate the problems of finance, a supreme court, and a Federal Civil Service. These would report to the second conference, but it was clear that they could not do so by July – the date originally intended. In the end the second conference was postponed to January 1953.

The closing stages of the Lancaster House Conference saw a sharp dispute about the right of secession. Stockill, the leader of the Southern Rhodesian opposition, was on the delegation and pressed for such a clause, arguing that the Southern Rhodesians might wish to opt out, after ten years or so, if they saw their way of life endangered. The general sense of the other delegates was that it would be fatal to include such a provision. It existed in no known federal constitution except, ironically, in that of Soviet Russia, and it would shatter public confidence in the whole idea. Stockill was effectively overruled. He probably never expected to succeed.

On May 5 the conference ended. Among the final speeches Nkomo's was conspicuous for its moderation. He declared that his own suspicions had been allayed and that he would do his best to expound the case to the Africans in the colony though he was by no means sure of success. The following day Lyttleton saw the northern Africans who had boycotted the conference. He explained the safeguards and appealed for partnership, but their only speaker reaffirmed the absolute African antipathy to federation in any form.

The White Paper (Cmd. 8573) setting out the proposals was published on June 18, 1952. The document made it clear that it was not a final version, but a draft for consideration by the Governments concerned. Meanwhile Welensky had been busy in London lobbying for the cause. It was important to counter what he regarded as the misrepresentations of the liberal/left do-gooders. Prince Yurka Galitzine, a White Russian turned public relations officer, was his ally and became chairman of a body called 'The London Committee of the United Africa Association'. It was a highly efficient organization and did much to influence British public opinion.

What really mattered, however, was Southern Rhodesian public opinion. The British Government was committed and unless the Conservatives fell from power – which was unlikely, despite their small majority – they would endorse federation. The two northern protectorates being ultimately ruled from London were also certain to agree. But Huggins had promised a referendum for the colony, and no one can be quite sure of the result of a referendum until it has happened. From June 23 to June 27 the Southern Rhodesia Assembly debated a motion 'to consider Federation especially in the light of the White Paper'.

Huggins made an eloquent case for adopting its proposals. He begged his hearers not to worry about certain remarks made in the UK. The British, he said, 'suffer from a kind of unctuous rectitude and apparent hypocrisy which is disliked by foreigners and their overseas kinsmen ... Macaulay described this unpleasant habit of the people in England in his essay on their behaviour during the O'Shea case.'[10] Macaulay died thirty years before O'Shea cited Parnell in the divorce court, and 'unctuous rectitude' was first used seven years after that by Joseph Chamberlain when retaliating upon the critics of the Jameson raid. But such minor anachronisms would not have worried the Prime Minister, even if they had been pointed out – which was not likely in the Southern Rhodesian Assembly.[11] 'It is', he said, 'up to us to take a lead and (to misquote a familiar saying) save Central Africa by our exertions and Africa by our example.' Winding up for the Government on the last day of the debate he said, 'The Scheme in front of us now is for the emancipation of Northern Rhodesia and Nyasaland and the preservation of Southern Rhodesia'.

The difficulty faced by both Huggins and Welensky, as Philip Mason points out, was that the arguments which reassured the Europeans alarmed the Africans and the arguments which might persuade the Africans disturbed the Europeans. The dilemma reflected a fundamental ambiguity in the motives of the Federationists. It is well illustrated by Huggins's own statements in the debate. In one breath he could defend the safeguards for the Africans:

What I wish to emphasise here ... is that in the face of world opinion the

[10] LAD, Vol. 33, No. 47, June 23, 1952, 2632.
[11] Huggins probably had in mind the passage in Macaulay's *Essay on Byron* beginning, 'We know no spectacle so ridiculous as the British public in one of its periodic fits of morality'.

United Kingdom are trusting the Europeans of Central Africa sufficiently to hand over 6,000,000 primitive Africans to a Parliament dominated by local Europeans.... It is a great testimonial to us ... [But] We are not the plaster Saints as some people think. I think it would be a grave breach of duty in the United Kingdom if they did not provide some protection to this new organism which is being tried out ...[12]

And he went on to say 'We have lost parts of an empire because a coloured man was blackballed at a club'.[13]

Yet in the same debate he could say that it would be mad to believe that the twenty-six Elected Members would ever pass legislation to 'enable the native African to hold all or a majority of seats in the Federal Legislature within any time that we can visualise now' and he described the African Affairs Board as 'a frightful waste of money and man power'. A few months later at Umtali he said it was 'a little piece of Gilbert and Sullivan' which would make no difference. Here was the dilemma ever-present in the Rhodesias. Appealing to a European electorate of which a large section was profoundly anti-African, Huggins – and Welensky too – naturally tended to use language to allay European fears – the more so since an adverse European vote was the one thing that could wreck the scheme; but Huggins was making it all the harder for Africans to accept European bona fides about 'partnership'. He was expediting the advent of the Federation, but diminishing its chances of success when it came.

The reports of the three specialist commissions were published in October, and the final conference met at Number 10, Carlton House Terrace on January 1, 1953. The joint chairmen were Lyttleton and Lord Swinton who had recently become Commonwealth Secretary. Lord Salisbury, now Lord President of the Council, was also there. The principal figures among the Central African delegations were for the most part the same as in the previous conference, but there were no Africans present. The boycott had extended into Southern Rhodesia too.

The conference sat for a month, and the upshot was two White Papers: Cmd. 8753 setting out the background, purpose and principal features of the scheme, and Cmd. 8754 the detailed scheme itself. A few alterations were made to the earlier scheme. The four Members elected for African Interests in the northern Territories had to be African and the two nominated Members had to be European, whereas they could have been either under the previous proposal. Otherwise the composition of the Federal Legislature was the same. The biggest change was in the composition of the African Affairs Board. Here Huggins at last got his way. It was now to be a Standing Committee of six from the Federal Legislature. The idea of an independent body referring 'differentiating' legislation to the UK government had always rankled, though it is hard to see what was gained by the new version for the Board was not going to be elected by the Federal

[12] LAD, Vol. 33, No. 47, June 27, 1952, 2946–54.
[13] Ibid., 2954.

Legislature as a whole. It would consist of the three European Members with special responsibilities for African interests, and three of the Elected Africans chosen by majority vote of the three Europeans and the six Elected Africans acting together. The Governor-General would nominate one Member of the Board as Chairman with an ordinary and a casting vote.

At Southern Rhodesian request, the Federal Government was to control Southern Rhodesian agriculture – a Territorial function elsewhere. The Federal Government was also given the power to raise a Federal police force, but it could only be used in any Territory 'at the request of the Governor of the Territory in addition to, or in substitution for the Territorial Police Force'. There followed the sentence quoted earlier about law and order being exclusively a Territorial matter. In fact the provision for a Federal force became a dead letter and none was ever raised.

The provisions for amending the Constitution remained unchanged except for one important new proviso. In order to ensure a reasonably stable framework for the Federation in its experimental years no amendment was to be introduced until after the expiry of ten years from the date when the Constitution came into force. An exception would be made to this rule only if positive resolutions were passed by all three Territorial Legislatures stating that they had no objection to the Bill being introduced. Not less than seven or more than nine years after the Federation had been set up a conference representing the four Governments and the UK Government would be convened to review the Federal Constitution.

Huggins and Welensky obtained a minor victory in the Preamble to the Constitution. They had already secured a statement that the Territories were 'the rightful home of all lawful inhabitants thereof, whatever their origin' – a hit at those who talked about 'settlers' and 'paramountcy'. They now obtained a clause to the effect that the new association of the Territories would 'enable the Federation, when the inhabitants of the Territories so desire, to go forward with confidence towards the attainment of full membership of the Commonwealth'. These provisions and the changed composition of the African Affairs Board were useful counters in the imminent referendum campaign.

Huggins returned at once to Southern Rhodesia in order to pass the necessary legislation for a referendum – the third in the colony's history, the second having been a not very important affair about state lotteries. Stockill unsuccessfully tried to amend the Bill so as to require a two-thirds majority. The referendum held on April 10, 1953 resulted in a conclusive victory for the Federationists. There voted for the Federation 25,570 against 14,729 – in fact little short of the two-thirds majority demanded by the opposition. The Assembly thereupon passed the necessary legislation. In the northern Territories the Legislative Councils approved Federation, despite the opposition of Africans and Asians.

Meanwhile, the subject was further debated in the House of Commons, and on March 24 a motion to approve 'the proposals on Central African Federation as set out in Command Papers Nos 8753 and 8754' was carried by 304 votes to 260. This was a good deal more than the Government's normal majority, partly because of abstentions by the Gordon Walker group. The Rhodesia and Nyasaland Federation Act received the Royal Assent on July 14. Under the Act the Government was empowered to introduce the federation by Order-in-Council. On August 1 the Order was promulgated. On September 4, 1953 at 10 a.m. the train carrying Lord Llewellin, the first Governor-General, steamed into Salisbury station. It was a rather oppressive day and the sky was somewhat overcast, as the procession after a nineteen gun salute went through the city to Government House. There Lord Llewellin was sworn in by Sir Robert Tredgold, the first Federal Chief Justice. The Federation had been born. Few could have predicted that little over ten years later it would be dead.

Part 3

FEDERATION AND THE WHITE BACKLASH

19

Southern Rhodesian Society 1946–53

The Southern Rhodesian world had greatly changed in the years between the end of the war and the launching of the Federation. It was to change even more during the next decade. The European population was 82,000 in 1946. In the next five years it increased by 53,000 – the fastest rate in the whole history of the colony. This first wave of immigrants was followed by a second. Between 1951 and 1960 the white population rose from 135,000 to 223,000. By 1950 there were more post-war immigrants among white adults than persons born in the country or settled there before the war. They were nearly all English-speaking. There was a strictly limited quota of foreigners. Very few, even from among the Italians imported to build the Kariba dam, were allowed to take up permanent residence.

This massive immigration did not have any immediate political effects. The newcomers could not claim the franchise till they had resided for three years, and even then did not vote as a block. Indeed they tended to take little interest at first in politics. They were more concerned to earn their living and adapt themselves to an unfamiliar way of life. It would be idle to pretend that the Britons who came to Southern Rhodesia in the aftermath of the war were actuated by religious and political motives or by the sense of challenge or by the poverty and desperation which had influenced waves of settlers at earlier times in Rhodesia itself and in other lands and which had given them the determination to create a new society. The post-war immigrants tended to be people of some modest means – Rhodesian regulations required the guarantee of a certain amount of capital – and to be stimulated less by a desire for adventure than for escape from the drabness of a socialist society. (It is not surprising that there is a similar rise in emigration from Britain today – though naturally not to Rhodesia.) They were people who did not see a clear way ahead in their own country. To quote Frank Clements:

They were the misfits of British society; that is, of course, not the same thing as the failures and the rejects, though indeed they themselves had decided that they were not equipped to succeed at home. In no field of activity, from accountancy to welding, from journalism to selling, did Rhodesia offer inducements to the successful or the conspicuously talented.[1]

Not all the immigrants came from the discontented ranks of the British *petite bourgeoisie*, although enough did to lend plausibility to the comment that if Kenya was the Officers', Rhodesia was the Sergeant's Mess. Officers, however, were not unrepresented in Rhodesia, especially those from Indian regiments, who had left the great sub-continent after the ending of the British Raj, in search of a country where men of colour knew their place. Umtali was their favourite haunt, hallowed by the presence of Dornford Yates who had departed from the England of reality to seek an England of his dreams. These immigrants came to be known unkindly as 'the Bengal Chancers' and Umtali was nicknamed 'Poonafontein'.

A large number of immigrants came from South Africa, but, as the statistical returns only show the country of immediate origin, many of them were probably transients from the UK who had spent a few months in the Union to try their luck before moving on. Others were 'real' South Africans, but they were by no means of a uniform category. There were Afrikaners coming north to get better jobs. There were English speakers escaping from Afrikanerdom, and there were a few dissident liberal Afrikaners leaving for the same reason. The escapers were among the most politically active of the immigrants and their influence was strongly pro-Federation.

The net increase in European population conceals the amount of emigration which also took place, indeed always had. For example, between 1926 and 1936 there had been in round figures 29,000 immigrants and 20,000 emigrants. In the post-war decade 1946–56 125,000 Europeans came into the country and 53,500 left it.[2] The Rhodesian population was much more shifting and less static than is sometimes believed. By 1951 only 32 per cent of all Europeans had actually been born in Rhodesia. The white population thus differed markedly – and still does – from that of South Africa. The Afrikaners and a high proportion of the English-speaking South Africans are indigenous; they can claim in one sense of the word to be 'African', and they can fairly ask the question 'Where are we to go if we are forced out from here?' This was true only of a minority of Europeans in Southern Rhodesia. As Frank Clements writes:

> For all that has been made of the claim it is not and never was true for the majority of white Rhodesians that they have 'no other home'. The high ratio of emigration to immigration has always given it more in common with the transient white communities of, for example, India and West Africa, with which it so strenuously contrasts itself in support of its claim for true nationhood.[3]

[1] Frank Clements, *Rhodesia, The Course to Collision*, 1969, 80.
[2] Figures taken from Colin Leys, *European Politics in Southern Rhodesia*, 1958.
[3] Op. cit., 93.

Conceding that the number who have stayed for more than one generation is proportionately higher in Rhodesia, he nevertheless ends in a sentence highly unpalatable to his fellow-countrymen (one can see why Ian Smith engineered his departure after UDI): 'But white Rhodesians in the final analysis more closely resemble expatriates than patriots.'

What sort of a country were these expatriates coming to? The climate, geography and scenery have already been described. The first feature which would strike a visitor brought up on the traditional stereotypes was the overwhelmingly urban nature of the society he had entered. The notion of the typical Rhodesian as a keen-eyed man on a horse, riding round his ranch with a gun slung over his shoulder and a broad-brimmed Pioneer Column style hat on his head would soon have vanished. In 1951 15 per cent (6,500) of economically active white men were farmers. This was certainly much higher than the corresponding proportion (2 per cent)[4] in England and Wales, but it was a long way from a majority, and it was diminishing. Five years later there were 5,000 registered farmers in Southern Rhodesia, 3,000 of them in Mashonaland where the tobacco boom was making fortunes for some of them.

It is, however, true that farming was and is a prestige occupation. Rather like the English nineteenth-century entrepreneurs who set the seal on their social success by purchasing land often at highly uneconomic prices, almost everyone who was anyone owned a farm. There has never yet been a Southern Rhodesian Prime Minister who did not. The word 'farmer' in Britain has – or had till recently – overtones of a slight inferiority, a carry-over from the 'tenant farmer' who would not expect to be asked to dinner at the great house. It never had this connotation in Southern Rhodesia. Mr Harold Macmillan, with his unfailing touch for subtle social distinctions, describes Winston Field, the rich tobacco farmer who was Prime Minister before Ian Smith, as 'a plantation owner', and Southern Rhodesia as a country 'governed by 200,000 whites among whom the planter interest predominates'.[5] The expression, with its echo of the southern states before the American Civil War, admirably catches the flavour of this element in Southern Rhodesian society. Winston Field and his like did indeed lead the life, as nearly as it could be led a century later, of the planter aristocracy in Virginia or Kentucky.

Although ownership of land may have set much of the tone of the élite within an élite which constituted the governing class in Southern Rhodesia, the fact remains that most Rhodesians lived in towns and always had. The figure for urban dwellers was 59 per cent in 1936. It had risen to just under 70 per cent by 1951 and was to go on rising. By 1958 it was 77 per cent. Nine out of ten immigrants took up urban employments and one in every two established himself in Salisbury.

Yet even these figures understate the effective urbanization of life. A dweller in

---

[4] If agricultural workers are added in, the figure becomes over 7 per cent. There were, of course, scarcely any white agricultural workers in Rhodesia.

[5] Harold Macmillan, *The End of the Day*, 1973, 327.

pre-war Salisbury, described by Professor Gann as 'a dusty dorp', would have no doubt that he was in Africa. The bush was omnipresent and the dangers of the veld could be sensed even if one could not actually see it – likewise the space, the romance, the adventure. All this was changing. The new suburbs were inward looking. Flowering shrubs, neat hedges, cultivated trees, rather than the endless blue horizons of the veld, made the background for the Salisbury citizen. A by-product of this development was an even wider gulf between the races. The European no longer had the experience, which he had once had in common with the African, of struggling with a harsh and hostile environment which neither could control. The environment created by the post-war white Rhodesians for themselves with their new found wealth was 'as different from that outside its narrow boundaries as islands in a sea or oases in a desert'.[6]

The Salisbury and Bulawayo that we know today were only beginning to emerge in 1953. It could not yet be said of Salisbury that it is 'one of the most beautiful smaller cities in the world',[7] but the shabby houses with their corrugated iron roofs were being replaced by trim villas of the bungalow type set in an acre of garden, embellished by a well watered green lawn and by jacaranda, bougainvillaea, and poinsettia. As prosperity rose a private swimming pool came to be an essential feature for the richer inhabitants. It was a glorified version of an English 'garden city'. The area covered was always large in proportion to population. Salisbury, with less than 100,000 Europeans and not much more than 300,000 of all races, covers today an area as large as that of the old London County Council. The city may have been, as someone once said, 'Surbiton in the bush', but it was Surbiton writ large, more attractive, more spacious. In the centre of both cities towering hotels and office blocks divided by wide streets – Bulawayo must have the widest streets in the world – have a less oppressively claustrophobic effect than in London. The two cities today have a freshness and cleanliness which any Londoner would envy.

At the time of inauguration of the Federation, these developments were only just beginning. They were notably assisted in the case of Salisbury by the decision of both the great copper combines – Rhodesian Anglo-American and Rhodesian Selection Trust – to transfer their headquarters from London to the Southern Rhodesian capital, the former in 1950, the latter in 1952. Together with the British South Africa Company the two corporations constituted the dominant financial and commercial interests in the Rhodesias to such a degree that a shrewd analyst could write in 1957: 'It is not too much to say that the meetings of their boards of directors can be as important for the inhabitants of the Federation as those of the Federal Cabinet.'[8]

Our symbolic immigrant would not at first have been aware of all this. What he would at once have seen – and it was the lure that brought him out – was

[6] Clements, op. cit., 91.
[7] Lord Caradon writing in *The Times*, August 13, 1976.
[8] Colin Leys, op. cit., 112.

the high standard of living enjoyed by his fellow white men. This was a startling contrast to the pre-war Southern Rhodesia. The average family income according to a sample survey made in 1950–51 was £925 p.a. For the modern reader inflation has made nonsense of all past figures, British and Rhodesian; it is enough to point out that this was not only a great deal more than the British average, but that pound for pound a Rhodesian could buy more for his money. He paid very little income tax and there were no heating bills. One of the cheapest commodities was domestic service. It was reckoned in 1950–51 that there was an average of two African servants to every European household. It was in this or some other menial role that the urban immigrant had his first personal experience of the African.

The experience did not improve race relations. Domestic servants were fast becoming extinct in Britain, and the class in society to which most immigrants belonged had never employed them anyway. At this time few Africans could speak English and a newly arrived housewife naturally enough could not speak Bantu, or even 'Kitchen Kaffir' – the amalgam of Bantu, Afrikaans, Portuguese and English which, for the settled white Rhodesian, served as a means of communication with her servants. Africans are not the best servants in the world, but, even if they had been, the scope for muddle and misunderstanding was limitless when neither side could understand a word the other said. Immigrants on their first arrival were probably more disposed than the established Europeans to treat Africans as equals. Disillusionment soon set in. On the immigrant mind there was imprinted an image of the African as stupid, idle, feckless, incompetent, dishonest and disloyal. Racial hatred replaced vague good will, and the newcomer became even more intolerant than the 'indigenous' White whose attitude, though severe, paternalistic and repressive, was not devoid of a certain fundamental humanity.[9]

The Southern Rhodesian government did nothing, until much later, to prepare immigrants for African customs and terms of service. Before the war it had not been necessary. The numbers were small enough for example and precept to do the job. It was a different matter when 10,000 were arriving every year – one eighth of the entire European population in 1946.

The society which immigrants entered was intensely, almost overpoweringly, British in sentiment, apart from the Afrikaners, nominally 'British' for census purposes, but regarded as outsiders. But its way of life was more American than British – competitive, conformist, mobile, ostentatious, socially (at first sight), though not economically, egalitarian. In 1952 there was one motor car to every four Europeans – a figure almost equal to that of contemporary America, and not solely explicable by suburban sprawl and poor public transport. The quality of housing and the extent of home ownership was far more American than British. Education was for most Europeans better than in either country. It was universal, compulsory and free of charge from seven to fifteen. For whatever reason, it produced better results than in Britain. A survey conducted in 1952 showed that whereas

---

[9] Clements, op. cit., 88–90.

30 per cent of Rhodesian school leavers had passed the Cambridge Overseas Certificate and some 7 per cent the Higher Certificate too, the number achieving the same standard in Britain was 12 to 15 per cent. In 1954 17 per cent of Rhodesian school leavers were going on either to universities or into some other sort of training which would qualify them for the top professional and managerial posts – Social Class I in the British and Rhodesian Census forms.[10] In general Southern Rhodesia was a prosperous thrusting country with one of the highest living standards in the world.

In two respects there was a contrast with America. The prosperity of Southern Rhodesia never threw up as a by-product any sign of intellectual, literary or artistic life. The European population was perhaps too small and too much concerned with earning its living. The fact remains that Southern Rhodesia was a cultural desert; neither literature, music, nor the visual arts flourished in its arid soil.

The other contrast was that, although white Rhodesians were rich, they did not, in general, feel rich; rather they felt economically insecure, and vaguely uneasy. Of course there were plenty of exceptions, but they tended to overspend even when, as happened far more often than in contemporary Britain, their wives went out to work and they were very conscious of income and the status going with it. This insecurity did not stem merely from the absence of the welfare state. That was equally true in America, and Rhodesians like Americans had to devote a substantial part of their incomes to insurance against medical expenses and old age. The uneasiness was probably the result in part of the strain of 'keeping up with the Joneses', in part of the alien and slightly frightening habitat. To quote Frank Clements again, referring to the women rather than the men, but it applies to both: 'The scale of Africa, even within a small town, the extremes of weather, the ever present black faces, unreadable, exotic and separate, the high chattering incomprehensible voices filled them with a sense of being menaced.'[11]

Here is the contrast with America. The American standard of living was based on the application to industry of the most advanced technology in the world. It depended on machines; and machines, except in a Wellsian fantasy, cannot rebel. The white Rhodesian standard depended on men, and they were men of an alien race. For nothing could conceal the fact, however much white men blurred it in their own minds, that the European lived as he did because all unskilled and nearly all partly skilled occupations (Social Classes IV and V in the Census) were filled by Africans whose wages were about a tenth of his own. In Britain in 1951 Social Classes IV and V accounted for just under 30 per cent of men employed. Among Whites in Southern Rhodesia it was 3 per cent.

A similar situation prevailed in South Africa, and Southern Rhodesian 'culture' was in many ways neither British nor American, but English-speaking South African. The Southern Rhodesian who went to a university had to go south until a multi-racial university came into being with the Federation. Many continued

[10] Leys, op. cit., 90–1.
[11] Op. cit., 94.

to do so partly just because University College, Salisbury was multi-racial. For purposes of sport – that fetish worshipped more ardently in southern Africa than anywhere else in the world – Southern Rhodesia was a province of South Africa. Its legal system, Roman–Dutch, unlike that of the northern protectorates, was derived from South Africa. People went to the Union for holidays, they married South African spouses, they thought in South African terms, drank South African wine. Nearly everyone who came to the colony came via South Africa. There were strong business connexions and the ultimate control over Rhodesian Anglo-American lay with the Oppenheimer family in Johannesburg. In the end the British South Africa Company was itself to become a part of that huge commercial empire.

The effects of this relationship were not all of them anti-'liberal'. The Oppenheimers' influence was, and has been ever since strongly exercised in favour of liberalism, and they were not alone. Many liberal South Africans came north and reinforced that element in Southern Rhodesia. Nevertheless, the sight of a much larger country in a not dissimilar situation adopting with theological rigour and apparent success a policy of racial separatism was bound to have its repercussions north of the Limpopo. There were plenty of back eddies, and, like Canada vis-à-vis the USA, Southern Rhodesia had many people and interests hostile to the drawing power of an over-mighty neighbour. But the pull of the only major dissentient minority, the Afrikaners, unlike that of the French Canadians, was in the direction of absorption rather than independence.

The Afrikaners of Rhodesia tend to be forgotten. They did not count socially. Among them were to be found some of the least skilled European labour. But they constituted in 1951 13.5 per cent of the European population, and, more significantly, nearly one quarter of the white rural population. Since the electoral boundaries, thanks to the power of the agricultural interests, were drawn in a way which over-weighted the rural vote, Afrikaners mattered more in an election than their numbers might suggest. The constituencies where they held the balance did not return Afrikaners – an Afrikaans name was as rare on the roll of the Assembly in 1951 as on the list of the Salisbury or Bulawayo Clubs – but these seats were fortresses of the anti-establishment party. Fifteen years later with the decline and severance of the British connexion the Afrikaners came into their own.

Two other features of Rhodesian society should be mentioned. An immigrant would at once have become aware that the most rigid aspect of the colour bar concerned sex. In South Africa intercourse between the races, whether marital or extra-marital, was, or came to be, actually forbidden by law. Southern Rhodesia (see Chapter 11) never went to that length. Mixed marriages were not illegal, and although the law vetoed intercourse outside marriage between black men and white women, there was no reciprocal barrier. White men could have liaisons with black women. Nevertheless such behaviour was regarded as unspeakably discreditable. The few Europeans who engaged in it were eccentrics unreceived in society and living beyond the pale in the shoddiest areas of Salisbury and Bulawayo, or more likely in some broken-down farmhouse in the bush.

There was pressure from time to time to forbid such relationships by law – at any rate if they were non-marital. The difficulty was prostitution. In 1957 Garfield Todd (see Chapter 21) called for a report on the whole problem from the police. He was told:

The traffic is mainly confined to coloured women and an increasing number of natives. The Europeans are few ... Of the former type ... a number are married or being kept, but continue to operate as a side line. No brothels ... A number of better type Europeans are operating from bars or hotels, but not on the street. The charges are on a sliding scale from £1 to £5 usually (short/ long time basis). If in the nude (even in a taxi or car) apparently minimum is £5. Takings are as much as £140 per month in some cases.

Police and others regard all this from but one point of view only, as a terrific safety valve as it is in any big city. They feel denial would inevitably lead to an increase in rapes ...

The police recommended strongly against a change in the law:

If such legislation is enacted it would be easy to enforce against the comparatively small number of European males who cohabit more or less openly with particular native females, but it would be extremely difficult to detect the more numerous clandestine casual associations which take place between European males and African prostitutes in the larger urban areas.

Legislation might deter many potential offenders as well as remove the grounds for complaint against discriminatory legislation, but the difficulties of detection and the opportunities of blackmailing activities by prostitutes and their protectors should not be overlooked.[12]

No change was made in the law, but Salisbury and Bulawayo are small cities in which everyone soon seems to know everything about everyone else, and social pressures are very strong. The few European males who sought variety of this kind found it on holiday in Beira or Lourenzo Marques where a multitude of colours and pleasures was available until Dr Machel put an end to all that.

The other feature was the somewhat delusory nature of Rhodesian egalitarianism. Before the war the difference of income among Europeans had not been very great, and most of them were struggling to survive. Even so there were social distinctions. After the war, the boom in tobacco and copper caused fortunes to be made and lost. Economically society became highly inegalitarian. Socially it seemed less so. There was not the distinction by accent which still prevailed in

[12] Todd Papers, Commissioner of Police to Secretary, Dept of Justice, April 30, 1957.

England. One could and can walk into the Salisbury Club and hear a wide variety of voices ranging from flat indigenous vowels to clipped Etonian syllables. Yet a newcomer who tried to become a member would soon find that some people were more equal than others. Southern Rhodesian society may have been more egalitarian than English but it was not as egalitarian as all that.

What would the average immigrant in the late nineteen-forties or early fifties know about that vast majority of his fellow countrymen who happened to be black. The category about whom he would know least was the most important, the few thousand educated Africans – black schoolmasters, clergymen, clerks, hospital dispensers, etc. who were the core of the African nationalist movement. They made little impact on the average settled White, still less on the immigrant. As we saw, his direct experience was largely with servants or perhaps with labour gangs engaged in relatively humble work.

He would know, though he would probably never see, that some one and a half out of two million lived in remote, dusty, arid reserves eking out their existence on subsistence agriculture. He would be aware that the half million wage earners were paid at a rate which was only a fraction of his own. Most of them were engaged in agriculture or mining. Those in urban employment lived away, often several miles, from the city centres in native urban locations, areas, settlements or townships – few people understood the difference – and occupied their neat, but hot and tiny houses only for so long as they held their jobs. Legally they were transients there on sufferance, and their 'home' was in the reserves which, like a vast sponge (if that simile is permissible for the least well watered area of the country), absorbed the old, the unemployed, the incapable, and thus obviated the need for social security. Whether the reserves could sustain indefinitely a fast multiplying population was scarcely a matter to concern the newcomer.

He would notice more immediately other aspects of African life. Africans were only served in shops after every White had been served. Shop assistants were themselves always white. There were separate entrances and counters for Blacks and Whites in post offices. There was rigid separatism in state schools, hospitals, hotels, restaurants, transport, swimming baths and lavatories. Our immigrant would observe, but soon find it natural, that an African was called 'boy' whether he was six, sixteen or sixty. Nor would he long be surprised that Africans could not touch European alcoholic drinks, beer, wine or spirits, but only 'Kaffir beer'.

He would also discover that Africans were governed by a rigid system of certificates and passes. An African had to have a *Certificate of Registration* which allocated him to some area that was African under the Land Apportionment Act even if he had been born in an urban location. Armed with this he could travel, but as soon as he entered an urban area he had to secure another document, either a *Current Visiting Pass* or a *Town Pass to Seek Work*. If and when he had got some sort of job he had to procure either a *Certificate of Service* or a *Certificate of Self-Employment*. The head of a family had to have a *Certificate of Occupation*. A woman, unless employed, was required to have a *Certificate of Recognition of*

An Approved Wife.[13] These documents had to be produced on demand from the police and other officials. It was fear of extension of this system to the north, which, more than anything else, made the Africans of the protectorates dig in their toes against federation.

Of the other non-white groups our new arrival would have taken little notice. The Indians were mostly storekeepers catering for Africans. The Coloureds, treated as pariahs, were a depressed class constituting a standing reminder of the evils of miscegenation. Both groups lived in a sort of limbo. Under the Land Apportionment Act they counted as European, but in almost all other respects their status was inferior, though above that of the Africans.

Immigrants might have been puzzled by these features of a strange society, but they soon accepted them as normal. They were not personally affected nor were they a gaggle of Mrs Jellabys. They had come out to do good for themselves, not for anyone else. Beginning at the bottom of the European ladder they were from the first conscious of their precarious situation. There was no fall-back of the sort provided by social security in Britain. Admittedly a white man would not be allowed to sink below a certain level, but this was because of the colour bar. Most Europeans of the artisan class must have known that Africans either could do, or could be trained to do, their jobs as well as they could.

It has sometimes been suggested that immigrants from 'liberal' Britain had a liberalizing effect on Southern Rhodesian native policy. This was certainly not the case with the first wave of post-war immigrants largely belonging to the artisan class. But it is true that many of the more offensive forms of discrimination were removed in the later 1950s, and the second wave of immigrants in the earlier years of the decade did contain a higher proportion of professional men, managers and administrators who may have been more 'liberal' in the Rhodesian sense of the word than the artisan class. But they were never more than a minority even among the later immigrants. The measures taken against discrimination by the Todd and Whitehead Governments sprang from other causes. Settled Rhodesians of the pre-war vintage probably contributed more than post-war immigrants.

This, then, was the world into which some nine or ten thousand Europeans entered every year from 1946 to 1958. Many of them left, but more stayed. The description given of race relations should not be taken to imply that the Europeans were peculiarly harsh or heartless. The system had grown up over the years and there were reasons to justify it. As in all countries where the majority is governed by a minority of different race, religion or nationality, it was a caste system, but it was no harsher than the British Raj in India and less harsh than Afrikaner rule in South Africa. White leaders defended it sincerely and with good cause on the ground that European capital, skills, enterprise and technology were lifting primitive peoples out of tribal barbarism into prosperity, with the co-operation

[13] Philip Mason, op. cit., 183.

of those peoples themselves. On such grounds they regarded it as quite natural that the state should provide free education for Whites, but not for Blacks, although the average African income was a mere fraction of the European.

'Partnership' to the Europeans meant economic progress and a rising standard of living achieved by the efforts of both races guided for the foreseeable future by the Whites. To the educated black man it meant something else – and, whatever the scepticism of the Whites, it was his lead that the Africans in all three territories were to follow. The partnership he looked for meant civility, equality and above all a say in his own destiny. The two concepts need not necessarily have conflicted, but in the event they did, and the conflict was fatal to the Federation.

20

The Heyday of Federation 1953–57

The Federation of Rhodesia and Nyasaland was one of the most elaborately governed countries in the world. Few Europeans – and fewer Africans – could have understood it accurately. This defect, in the words of Professor Gann, 'turned out to be a serious, though a rarely recognized weakness for an instrument designed to ensure parliamentary government through an instructed electorate'.[1]

Five governments had interlocking responsibilities for the Federation's affairs. Ultimate authority lay with the United Kingdom Parliament and Cabinet. In Whitehall two departments with distinct traditions and policies were involved. The Commonwealth Relations Office dealt with both Southern Rhodesia and the Federation through separate sets of High Commissioners in Salisbury and London. The Colonial Office dealt with the northern Territories which retained their status as protectorates. There the link was the Governor who, despite a measure of self-government in each Territory, still had great powers and communicated confidentially with the Colonial Secretary. The Federal government dealt directly with the three Territorial governments on matters of common concern, but its relationship with Northern Rhodesia and Nyasaland was subject to supervision by the Colonial Office. There was, however, no corresponding supervision by the Commonwealth Office in the case of Southern Rhodesia. In addition to all this there was local and municipal administration, together with the complex system of safeguards, checks and balances within the Federation itself. The new arrangement was anything but simple.

But Federal systems always are complicated. There was no easy way of simplifying this one, given the assumptions on which the original legislation was founded. These were first that the Territories should be solely responsible for all matters closely affecting Africans and that their own Constitutions could not be altered

[1] L. H. Gann, *A History of Northern Rhodesia*, 1964, 436.

284

by Federal action; secondly that in those areas where the Federal government could legislate with consequences for Africans – and there were bound to be some – safeguards must be established to prevent the abuse of power. If these requirements were to be fulfilled, the Constitution could not fail to be a complicated document.

There were probably only two matters of any importance which might have been simplified. The Civil Service could have been unified, or at least it could have been Territorially based in the northern protectorates instead of being a mere section of a much wider Colonial Service. Huggins and Welensky repeatedly pressed for this change, but it was anathema to the Colonial Office and, though promises were made, nothing happened. The other matter was law and order. Huggins attached great importance to this being Federal, and there was no inherent reason why it should not have been. A Federal police might have handled more effectively some of the riots and disturbances which took place later in the north.

Both these defects, however, sprang from a third which could not have been eliminated at that time. The divergent traditions of the Colonial and Commonwealth Offices have already been noticed. The rivalry – at times jealousy – of these two great departments of State was certain to cause friction. Welensky, less than four months after succeeding Huggins as Federal Prime Minister, wrote on 15th February, 1957 to Lord Home, the Commonwealth Secretary, suggesting the creation of a Central African Department in order to avoid 'the anomaly of two departments, with two outlooks and two policies, controlling our relations with the United Kingdom Government'.[2] Nothing came of the proposal. A Central African Department was in the end set up, but not till five years later and its task was to dissolve, not preserve, the Federation. The Commonwealth and Colonial Offices were put under the same Minister in July 1962, and both were ultimately merged with the Foreign Office, but these changes came too late to make any difference.

It is doubtful whether the Federation could have been saved by any politically feasible alterations in the original Constitution. It fell partly because the Europeans did too little to make 'partnership' a reality and too much to create the belief that their motive force was a sort of Southern Rhodesian sub-imperialism. Even more damaging was the creation of black self-governing states all over Africa. The Africans of the northern Territories inevitably saw the Federation as the main barrier to the attainment of that objective for themselves, and it was one which they far preferred to a multi-racial partnership where, as white spokesman after spokesman emphasized, they would remain junior partners indefinitely.

All this lay ahead when Huggins on September 7, resigning as Prime Minister of Southern Rhodesia, accepted Lord Llewellin's commission to form an interim Federal Cabinet, pending a general election to be held on December 15. He and Welensky, who became Minister of Transport, had been busy organizing a new

[2] Sir Roy Welensky, *Welensky's 4,000 Days*, 1964, 75.

political party, the United Federal Party, to contest the Federal seats. It was a development of the United Central Africa Association which now dissolved itself. The Party was opposed by another new group, the Confederate Party led by Dendy Young, QC, a former United Party Member of the Southern Rhodesian Legislative Assembly. He was the only candidate to win a seat, although the Confederates polled almost half as many votes (15,234) as the UFP (32,582) – a striking example of the eccentricity of the first-past-the-post system. A Liberal won a seat in Lusaka. Otherwise the UFP made a clean sweep with twenty-four out of twenty-six Elected Members. Huggins, now in clear control of the Federation Legislature, re-formed his administration.

Meanwhile his long expected decision to become Federal Prime Minister had created a vacancy in the Southern Rhodesia premiership and in the leadership of the United Party. A contest took place in August 1953 at the Party Congress held in Bulawayo between Julian Greenfield, the cautious, clear-headed, capable Minister of Justice in the Southern Rhodesian Cabinet, and Garfield Todd, a New Zealand born missionary with good looks and spellbinding oratory, who had sat for the last seven years as a back-bencher. New Zealanders were popular, but missionaries were not. The average European elector feared that missionary belief in the equality of all men in the sight of God was too liable to extend into the secular sphere; and he was certainly not prepared to regard Africans as his equal in the sight of man. Although Todd had entered the Assembly with the help and encouragement of Huggins, that veteran politician had no intention of giving him office. Todd recalls that the very candour with which the Southern Rhodesian Prime Minister used to talk to him about his Cabinet colleagues was a clear sign that Todd was not intended to be one of them.

Although Huggins preferred Greenfield, he did not wish to interfere. A body based on Bulawayo known as 'the Action Group', which included some of the younger and more impatient members of the United Party, and Greenfield himself, decided to go for Todd, despite the stigma of his being a missionary. Greenfield was a reluctant candidate. He told Todd, with whom he was then on very friendly terms, that he was by nature a lieutenant, not a captain, and would rather be a Federal Minister than the Territorial Prime Minister. When the vote was taken the candidates tied with fifty each. The chairman was Humphrey Gibbs. Todd recalled what followed:

> Humphrey looked at us from under his eyebrows as he does, and he said, 'Well, I have to give my casting vote and as Mr Greenfield is obviously the one with the experience, I will give him my vote. Everything is over and finished. Mr Greenfield is going to be Prime Minister.' There was pandemonium in the audience – people jumping up, utterly refusing to accept it and so on and so on. Greenfield was very reluctant, but not actually refusing – this is his indecisiveness all the way through you see.

Rhodesian politics are not conducted as formally as in Britain. Someone had the bright idea of adjourning for lunch and resuming discussion afterwards. Todd, his wife and Greenfield lunched amicably together and in the afternoon a fresh vote was taken in their absence. Todd was elected easily. Presumably Greenfield's palpable reluctance brought some of his supporters over to the other side. Todd, like Huggins, thus had the distinction of becoming Prime Minister without holding any previous office – a record rivalled in Britain only by Ramsay MacDonald.

The choice was not quite as strange as it seems. The majority of Southern Rhodesian politicians saw their future in Federal politics. There was a shortage of candidates in the Territorial field. Todd may have been a missionary, but he was also a rancher on a big scale, owning at one time some 90,000 acres near Shabani, and he had never publicly committed himself much, if at all, beyond the general attitude expected from a liberal – but not excessively liberal – adherent of the United Party. In his first speech on native affairs on March 12, 1946, he had endorsed the Party's abortive plan to stop more Africans being added to the electoral roll and to compensate by a system of nominated European Members representing their interests.[3] This was hardly the action of an advanced liberal. Six years later in the Legislative Assembly's debate on Federation he was sceptical about the usefulness of the African Affairs Board, dubious about special representation of Africans on the Federal Legislature – he far preferred a common roll – and emphatic against universal suffrage 'which could and would, I believe, lead to universal chaos'.[4] These were reasonable sentiments and were largely shared by liberal European politicians. If Todd had proclaimed anything which went much beyond them, he would never have been elected. To say this is not to say that his views remained the same nor to accept the claim of his opponents that his eventual ejection from office was the result of unchanged political arrogance rather than changed political opinions. The truth is that Todd was a liberal of his times, and his times were to change greatly during the next decade.

I asked him once whether he had any particular aim or purpose when he accepted office. Our conversation was more than fifteen years later, but his answer is borne out by contemporary records and speeches. He said that it had always been his ideal as a Christian that no one should be at a disadvantage because he was black or coloured. Every position should be attainable on grounds of merit and ability. This certainly did not mean universal suffrage. The right to vote had itself to be attained on grounds of merit and ability. Where he differed from even the liberal element in his own party – and came to differ more and more over the years – was in his belief that a considerably greater number of Africans had reached the standard required to exercise the franchise than his colleagues would concede. This belief was quite compatible with a firm conviction that the law must be enforced whatever the motives of the law breakers.

I asked him about federation. He said that if he had been ambitious he would have gone into Federal politics, but he was not. He did indeed support federation,

[3] See above p. 240.
[4] SLA Debates, Vol. 33, No. 43, June 23, 1952, 2670–7.

but he supported it as a second best. He would have preferred a unitary state for precisely the opposite reason to that of most amalgamationists. He did not see how even a Central African Federation, let alone a Central African unitary state, could resist African advancement indefinitely when the ratio of black to white was 66 to 1, whereas in Southern Rhodesia it was 16 to 1. He thought in terms of the greater liberalism of the north extending south, not in terms of Southern Rhodesian native policy being extended north. He was convinced that federation was only a stepping stone on the way to amalgamation. He considered that his function as Prime Minister was 'to work myself out of a job. And I believe I said so at the time.'

Meanwhile he had more urgent matters to consider. Nine United Party Members of the Assembly had moved into Federal politics. It seemed advisable to reconstruct the Government Party. Negotiations took place with elements of the Labour Party and of the Liberals who now called themselves the Rhodesia Party. Under Todd's leadership a new party calling itself the United Rhodesia Party (URP) came into being. It was the old Government Party under a new name, with a few additions. The ensuing election early in 1954 gave Todd a victory as conclusive as that of Coghlan thirty years earlier after the referendum on Responsible Government. In fact the figures were almost identical. The URP with 56.6 per cent of the popular vote won twenty-six seats, its only opponents being four Independents. Coghlan on 58.3 per cent of the vote had achieved exactly the same result. Indeed the parallel goes further. In 1954 the official opposition, the Confederate Party, with 22.6 per cent of the vote, won no seats at all. In 1924, the Labour Party also lost every ·seat, and its share of the popular vote was even lower – 13.7 per cent.

In Northern Rhodesia the pro-Federationists won ten out of the twelve elected unofficial seats, and in Nyasaland too the unofficials were similarly committed to the Federation which began in an atmosphere of European good will – almost euphoria – but sullen African resentment.

The economy of the Federation was booming in its early years. Its gross domestic product was £350.6 million in 1954 and in absolute figures had risen to £448.7 million by 1956. It fell during the next two years to £430.9 million because of a temporary collapse in copper prices. These revived in 1959, but never reached their previous peak during the remaining lifetime of the Federation. Measured in constant prices, with 1954 as a base, output rose by 25 per cent from 1954 to 1958 and by 54 per cent from 1954 to 1963. Oddly enough – and contrary to received wisdom – this rate of increase was considerably less than that enjoyed by the area during the five years before Federation. If 1949 is taken as a base, output rose by 62 per cent between then and 1954[5] – an average annual increase of 12.4 per cent. The corresponding figure for the Federation was 5.4 per cent. It does not follow that this deceleration was caused by the new constitu-

[5] Arthur Hazlewood, 'The Economics of Federation and Dissolution in Central Africa' reprinted from *African Integration and Disintegration*, 1967, 206.

tional set-up – it might have been worse if there had been no Federation, or better – but the statistics must cast doubt on the repeated claim that federation led to an increase in the rate of economic growth in Central Africa. The one Territory of which this was true – though only marginally – was Southern Rhodesia. The others certainly grew, but at a slower speed than before 1954.

But prosperity and expansion are also a matter of how people feel. Nobody notices figures of the national income at the time. It is only long afterwards that they are analysed by economists, trends are observed and conclusions drawn. There were far more outward and visible signs of wealth than earlier. The changing skylines of Salisbury and Bulawayo, especially Salisbury, the spread of the suburban garden city, the boom in property, and the arrival of the great copper companies with a host of subsidiaries were mentioned in the last chapter. In addition there began a revolution in transport. Wide, fully tarmacked highways replaced the old strip roads and gravel tracks, and motoring became quicker, less dusty and more comfortable. The first railway extension was built since Company rule – a line linking the Midlands of Southern Rhodesia with Lourenzo Marques. It was destined to prove invaluable after UDI for the conveyance of sanctions-breaking oil tankers, until the advent of Frelimo in Mozambique put an end to the traffic. Air transport became a regular means of travel, and by 1961, the *Year Book* of the Rhodesias and Nyasaland could plausibly describe Salisbury as 'the aerial Clapham Junction of the continent of Africa'.

Salisbury became a far more cosmopolitan capital than hitherto and, however much the inhabitants of Bulawayo or other cities might protest, it was Salisbury, with over one in four of the whole European population, which set the 'tone' of the Federation. Visitors flocked in. One of the great sights was the holding of the tobacco auctions in what was at the time the biggest individual tobacco market in the world. Tourists could easily fly to the Victoria Falls to see one of the wonders of the world or to Bulawayo to see Rhodes's grave, or to Fort Victoria to see the mysterious ruins of Zimbabwe.

Moreover Salisbury was becoming cosmopolitan in respect of residents as well as visitors. There was not only a much wider business community. There were also far more diplomats. In pre-Federation Southern Rhodesia the only countries apart from Britain to maintain diplomatic representation were South Africa and Portugal. The Federation, with its widely trumpeted economic prospects and a constitutional status nearer to that of a dominion than anything and apparently soon likely to achieve it, was a different proposition. By 1961 the principal European powers west of the Iron Curtain, together with the USA, Canada, Australia, Turkey and India had legations, consulates or some sort of regular representation in Salisbury. There were actually parties outside Government House where the men wore white tie and decorations. All this vanished soon enough. A long-established Rhodesian sadly told me in 1969 that he had not worn a tail coat since UDI. Frank Clements commenting on the rise in diplomatic activity writes:

As they never before had been able to do, Rhodesians met men of ideas and achievement from beyond their limited southern African parish. Also it was at diplomatic receptions and, even more importantly, at private lunches and dinners that many Rhodesians made their first social contacts with Africans and other non-whites.[6]

In a Federation whose preamble committed itself and its Territories to 'foster partnership and co-operation between their inhabitants', there had to be – and there was – a considerable relaxation in the colour bar. Africans now sat in the Federal Assembly, and before its demise there was to be an African, J. Z. Savanhu, as a Parliamentary Secretary, and others in the top levels of the Civil Service, including one who represented his country abroad. In 1954 the Southern Rhodesian Assembly amended the Land Apportionment Act to make it possible for hotels, clubs and restaurants to become, if they wished, multi-racial – though very few did – and to enable African professional men to occupy offices and premises for the conduct of their business, but not to live in European areas. In August 1956 Welensky as Minister of Transport announced that dining cars were open to all races. The University College was multi-racial from the start, and still is. Its premises were exempted from the provisions of the Land Apportionment Act.

In November 1956 Todd's Government decided that Africans should be called 'Mr'. This seems trivial enough, but it was a startling change for those accustomed to the old ways. Hitherto the title had been 'Native' or 'AM' (meaning 'African Male', but ruefully interpreted by some sufferers as 'Ape Man').[7] In the same month the Anglican Church conducted its first mixed confirmation service. In March 1957 Todd's Cabinet agreed that the word 'African' should be substituted for 'Native' in all its legislation. In May a Liquor Amendment Bill was passed to allow Africans to drink European beer and wine, but not spirits. Though hailed by Africans as a great step forward, most of them soon reverted to 'Kaffir beer' for reasons of expense, but there was African protest on egalitarian grounds when it was announced in November that in future spirits could be sold to Africans as long as they were Members of the Legislature or university graduates. When an African delegate to the United Federal Party urged the case for all drinks being available to all races he was told by Sir Roy Welensky that such a measure would lose the next election.[8]

Incredible though all this may seem, one has to remember the long-held belief based on the early years of the occupation that Africans were more susceptible to drink than white men and more excitable and dangerous under its effects. A not dissimilar belief in class distinction over the use of alcohol existed in Britain as late as the First World War. It was widely held in 1914–15 that drink inhibited the making of munitions. The King's pledge, however, was all that came of it.

[6] Op. cit., 112.
[7] Mason, op. cit., 180.
[8] Ibid., 185.

The Prime Minister did not intend to give up whisky and champagne for anyone, and there was, despite Curzon's alleged belief, no distinction of skin to render feasible a law restricting alcohol to the use of the upper classes.

There was a marked effort on the part of some Whites to diminish social barriers. The Capricorn Society continued its activities. A body called the Interracial Society tried to bring science and scepticism to bear on the more ridiculous prejudices against Africans. White women encouraged Africans of their sex to form women's organizations. Devoted persons worked hard for African welfare in the reserves. Much charity and benevolence was exercised by the churches which, apart from the Dutch Reformed, used their influence towards reconciliation between the races. A few liberal hostesses invited the occasional educated African to drinks or even a meal. The experiment had only limited success. Inevitably there was an element of patronage. In such an unequal society it could not be otherwise. Nor were Africans blameless. They tended not to answer invitations and, with that curious timeless sense, a sort of *mañana*, to turn up hours late if they came at all. More than one liberal couple, after several episodes of waiting while dinner either congealed on the plates or dried up in the oven, vowed never to ask an African again. There was also, even with educated Africans, the problem of their wives, who seldom moved in society and were rarely what the French call *sortable*. Still, an effort was made and during the first few years of the Federation it had some impact.

Race relations were relatively harmonious to begin with for another reason. African wages, having been static in real terms for fifty years, at last began to rise, and to do so faster than European incomes. In the first five years in the Federation as a whole average African earnings per man rose from £58 to £79, average European earnings from £905 to £1,060. It was not a great relative change that the average European should earn rather over thirteen times, instead of nearly sixteen times as much as the average African, but the absolute increase in the African wage did mean something. The rises broken down by Territories were in Southern Rhodesia for Europeans £841 to £995, Africans £57 to £80; in Northern Rhodesia £1,098 to £1,273, £74 to £99; in Nyasaland £734 to £889, £33 to £46. It must be remembered that in the Federation as a whole African wage earners constituted less than one-fifth of the total earning African population[9] and that their proportion was slightly diminishing. The rest were engaged in subsistence agriculture which was reckoned, though figures must be very uncertain, to earn them £13 a head in 1954 and £15 in 1958. In Southern Rhodesia African wage earners numbered over half a million at the beginning of Federation, considerably more than the combined figure for the other Territories. It was of course in the wage earning – especially urban – sector that nationalist passions were most likely to erupt. Therefore its relative prosperity tended to have a calming effect for the time being on African sentiment generally in Southern Rhodesia. The

[9] It was 5.22 million in 1954 and 5.8 million in 1958. The total African population was 7.5 million in 1958.

depressing fact remains, however, that in 1957–58 somewhere between one- and two-fifths of urban Africans were 'not earning enough to keep their families' and, of those with two children or more, the majority had insufficient food and clothes.[10]

Todd tried to tackle some of the major obstacles to African advancement. It is often said that more progress was made by Whitehead who succeeded him. This is true, but only in the sense that a ship moves more rapidly in an arctic sea than the ice-breaker that goes ahead of her. Whitehead's achievement was to build on Todd's foundations, but he would have accomplished little had they not been laid. In the fields of urban housing, education, labour relations and agriculture notable advances were made. It was only in the matter of land apportionment that there was a standstill, and even here by setting up the Plewman Committee on urban land, Todd started a process which led to the Quinton Report and the courageous but unsuccessful attempt by Whitehead to do away with land apportionment altogether.

The great hindrance to any change in native policy was the Department of Native Affairs. This severe, paternalistic, highly conservative *imperium in imperio* now came in for a degree of public attention which it had hitherto escaped. African affairs were only one of many other matters dealt with by the old Southern Rhodesian administration. With the arrival of Federation they became by far the most important function of the new Territorial Government. Todd was convinced that 'partnership' would only become a reality if the Native Department was broken up. Its functions could then be hived off and either put under the department which dealt with the corresponding European function or under a separate department if, as was often the case (e.g. education), the European function came under the Federal Government. This latter difficulty was an additional reason in Todd's mind for preferring amalgamation. Todd was, of course, quite right to aim at breaking up the Native Department. In a racially integrated country it would not exist at all. One does not, for example, have a department for the lower income groups in Britain. But although he was right, he soon encountered powerful opposition. In the end he managed to extract African agriculture, education and labour relations from the Native Department, but he was ousted before he could hive off justice which he regarded as symbolically of great importance.

Todd may have regarded it as his task to work himself out of a job, but he was fully prepared to press the Territory's claims within the existing constitutional framework. The northern Territories from the outset were suspicious of Southern Rhodesian ambitions. There was a considerable debate about the location of the capital of the Federation which, under the Order in Council, was to be Salisbury unless and until the Federal Legislature determined otherwise. People argued for Bulawayo, for Gwelo, for a new capital out in the bush, or for one in Lusaka or elsewhere north of the Zambesi in order to avoid association with the Southern Rhodesian Territorial Government. All these plans involved trouble and expense and many genuine disadvantages. No move was made. On grounds of administra-

[10] Mason, op. cit., 150, based on the Plewman Report.

tive and economic convenience it was the right decision, but it looked like a score for Southern Rhodesia.

Even more controversial – for here there was no *status quo* to disturb – was the question of siting the new giant hydro-electric plant which by general consent was essential for the expanding needs of industry. The Wankie coal reserves were vast, but they could not last for ever, and transport of coal placed an excessive burden on the railways. Discussions had been going on since 1941. Eventually the choices were narrowed to two alternatives, an installation either on the Kafue River which was entirely in Northern Rhodesia or at Kariba on the Zambesi. The Kafue project would require two stages and would produce power sooner, but the first would not give enough for the predicted long-term increase in demand. The second stage would meet the demand, but its feasibility was not certain. The Kariba project would do all that the two stages of Kafue would do, but it would be more expensive than Kafue's first stage. There would be a longer delay before any power at all was produced, and there were problems about the siting of the dam wall.

Huggins and the Federal Cabinet opted for the Kafue scheme and in 1954 he introduced a bill to start it off. Todd, however, fought with great tenacity for Kariba. He was helped by technical advice that a satisfactory site for the dam wall did exist. A major political battle now loomed up, and the Federal Government sought to evade controversy by withdrawing the Bill and calling for a neutral opinion from a firm of French consultants. Their advice was emphatically in favour of Kariba, and Huggins in February 1955 announced a U-turn; but he did not escape controversy. A furious row broke out in the north. There was wild talk of secession. The copper companies themselves could not agree. Sir Ernest Oppenheimer supported Kariba, but the Executive Vice-President of the Rhodesian Selection Trust resigned from the Federal Hydro-Electric Power Board in protest. Kariba went ahead, and the whole operation which raised the dry river level by 340 feet and created what was then the largest man-made lake in the world, 180 miles long, is an extraordinary feat of engineering. For technical and economic reasons the generating station was placed on the south bank of the Zambesi. The project in the end cost £78 million of which £46 million was raised by external loans largely from the International Bank.

Kariba was undoubtedly the most spectacular achievement of the Federation. Yet, like the siting of the capital, it seemed to suspicious northerners another example of Southern Rhodesian ascendancy. It brought no benefit to Nyasaland, while Northern Rhodesians would obviously have preferred Kafue. In fact the Federal Government could justify the choice of Kariba by the clear recommendation of neutral consultants; it is only in the light of hindsight that the placing of the generating station on the south bank looks like anticipation of the break up of the Federation or of UDI. No one thought in those terms at the time, and there was an overwhelming technical case for bringing up the heavy engineering equipment from the south.

Although Huggins had decided in favour of the course pressed by Todd, he did not necessarily enjoy the pressure. Nor did he welcome speeches from the Territorial Prime Minister, which seemed to impinge on the Federal field or even on the British Government's relations with the protectorates. That Todd took a tough line on law and order within Southern Rhodesia was his own concern, though his decision to proclaim a State of Emergency and call in Territorial troops early in 1954 over the illegal strike of African coal miners at Wankie seemed somewhat 'trigger-happy'. It was another matter when he alleged Federal or Territorial softness towards 'trouble-makers' in the north. The possibility of a clash between the Southern Rhodesian assembly with its thirty years' tradition of almost unfettered authority and the new Federal Assembly which had been given so many of the powers of the older body was built into the Federal Constitution. Huggins would have retired a year earlier if he had not thought it wise to stay long enough to calm down the ebullience of Todd and do his best to oil the wheels.

The Federal Prime Minister was also anxious to see in a further move towards dominion status. He made little progress. The Preamble to the Constitution declared that the new association between the colony of Southern Rhodesia and the northern Territories would advance the welfare, etc. of their inhabitants 'and enable the Federation *when those inhabitants so desire*, to go forward with confidence towards the attainment of full membership of the Commonwealth'. Huggins, according to his biographers, argued strongly in London during the summer of 1956 that this proviso was not intended to give the Africans a veto. What was meant, he said, was that dominion status should not be given to an amalgamated Central African state unless its inhabitants had agreed to the amalgamation.

He was on very weak ground. The Preamble was quite specific, and the report of the London Conference of January 1953, Cmd. 8753, refers to the question of amalgamation as a separate issue. In paragraph 7 it confirms the decision of the Victoria Falls Conference that amalgamation was not to be considered 'unless a majority of the inhabitants of all three Territories desired it'. Paragraph 17 comments on the Preamble and does not link it in any way with amalgamation. True, the wording is not identical, for it refers to 'a majority of the inhabitants', but it is difficult to see any significance in this. One can hardly suppose that the Preamble envisaged consent of a minority.

The British Government was not prepared, as Huggins suggested, to concede independence to the Federal Government leaving the territories as they were. A shadowy analogy with the Australian states did not carry conviction, nor was the Cabinet willing to conclude a treaty containing safeguards for the Territories – another suggestion of Huggins. They argued that this would prejudge the review conference. Huggins, created Viscount Malvern, returned to Salisbury. He now resolved to quit the political stage. At the UFP's annual congress in September he announced that he did not seek renomination as leader, and at the end of October he resigned from office.

Lord Malvern had served as Prime Minister for a longer continuous period than anyone else under the British Crown. For twenty-three years he had dominated first Southern Rhodesian and then Federal politics. As Lord Salisbury said of Disraeli, he was both near-sighted and clear-sighted. He did not look much ahead, and met problems as they turned up, with the jauntiness of a Palmerston rather than the heart-searching of a Gladstone. He was a master of the art of cautious reform clad in conservative clothes and he both understood and got on with Whitehall better than any other Rhodesian politician. It is, however, true that almost until the close of his active career the attitude of the British establishment did not greatly differ from his own. To the end his mental framework remained that of an enlightened pre-1914 Tory imperialist who moved, not with the times, but seldom very far behind them. This attitude was tenable – if only just – till the mid-nineteen-fifties. Thereafter the times changed with devastating rapidity. Before he died he saw the Federation, his greatest achievement, dissolve into its component parts and the colony launch itself on the fatal road of rebellion – an action he publicly condemned at the time, and never condoned. It was a sad twilight to a great career.

Malvern's inevitable successor was Sir Roy Welensky, co-architect of the Federation and, next to Malvern, the best known figure in Federal politics. He was elected leader of the UFP in September and became Prime Minister on November 1. His accession coincided with the Suez expedition which split the Commonwealth from top to bottom. Among many other consequences, it was to have a highly adverse effect on the Federation. This was not predicted at the time. Sir Roy Welensky at once declared that his Government fully supported the British action, and for the moment many white Rhodesians drew more significance from the British decision to assert imperial power than from the resounding defeat that followed it.

On January 24, 1957 the Governor-General died. Lord Llewellin had had a long experience of British politics and politicians. Formally a constitutional monarch he was much consulted both by Malvern and, for the brief period of life left to him, by Welensky too. His successor, Simon Ramsay, sixteenth Earl of Dalhousie was an entirely estimable figure, but he had never held high office and could not be expected to carry the same weight. Welensky greatly missed Lord Llewellin's advice. A further difficulty was Lady Welensky's serious illness. 'A Prime Minister like a general has to have luck. I say it without complaint and as objectively as I can: my share of luck was on the thin side.'[11]

[11] *4,000 Days*, 68.

21

A Turning Point 1957

In retrospect the year 1957 and the first few months of 1958 can be seen as a turning point in the history of the Federation and the colony. When it began there was a chance – a slender one no doubt – that the educated African would try to realize his aspirations with the framework of the Constitution. By the end that chance had slipped away for ever.

The question on which everything turned was the franchise. The qualifications and system of voting are matters of importance in any democratic state, but in countries where a racial minority holds effective power and yet is morally committed to share that power sooner or later, the question is not merely important; it is crucial. By the end of 1956 it could no longer be shelved; something had to be done about the Federal and the Territorial franchises.

Under the Federal Constitution the franchise for the first election to the Federal Assembly was the same as that prevailing in each Territory. Thereafter it could be changed by a two-thirds majority in the Federal Legislature, subject to the Royal Assent which in the event of objection by the African Affairs Board could only be given by Order-in-Council. The franchise did not have to be uniform, but there were obvious advantages if it was. In 1953 the Southern Rhodesian electoral law was based on literacy plus a minimum income of £240 p.a. or property worth £500. This was a recent change made in 1951 after very little discussion. From 1914 to 1951 the figures were £100 and £150. The 1951 franchise was formally non-racial. In practice it qualified about 1,000 Africans to vote, of whom 429 were on the register in 1953. In Northern Rhodesia, where nearly all Africans were British protected persons who could not claim the vote, only ten Africans were registered. In Nyasaland there were none. If the Federation was to go forward to independence within the Commonwealth based on 'partnership' and act as a counterpoise to South Africa, it would have to convince the UK government by a major step towards African enfranchisement.

Consultations took place between the heads of the Federal and Territorial Governments in mid-December concerning the size of the Federal Legislature, resulting in an agreement to enlarge it. Failing such a consensus this could not have been done under the Constitution. No agreement was achieved about the Federal franchise, but on this the Territorial Legislatures had no veto. Todd made clear his strong preference for a common roll of electors. Welensky, following the views of Malvern, favoured a system of separate rolls which would elect particular categories of Members. On December 28, 1956 Todd announced the appointment of a Commission under the chairmanship of Sir Robert Tredgold to consider the Southern Rhodesian franchise. Although its recommendations could bind nobody and only applied to the colony, they were certain to have implications for the Federation.

The Federal Prime Minister held his hand and pursued negotiations on other aspects of the Federal Constitution. These were on different lines from Lord Malvern's unsuccessful proposals in London in the summer of 1956. On January 8, Welensky had lengthy discussions in Salisbury with the new Colonial Secretary, Alan Lennox Boyd (now Viscount Boyd of Merton). On February 8 he sent a long letter to Lord Home, the Commonwealth Secretary. He followed this up by a visit to London in April, which resulted in agreement on some important changes in the Constitution, but nothing was publicly said about the Federal franchise.

Before Welensky left for London the Tredgold Report had been published on March 14. The report would certainly not be considered as a particularly liberal measure by European standards now, or even then. Its arguments sound strange in the context of mid-twentieth century democracy. But if we cast our minds back to the considerations discussed at the time of the Reform Acts of 1832 and 1867, or to the various abortive Bills which were debated in between, we are at once in the same world of discourse as the Tredgold Report. As so often occurs, Rhodesia seems to be preserving in pickle pieces of the British past, sometimes that of only a generation earlier, sometimes a century or more. John Bright, in reference to Disraeli's more eccentric proposals for electoral qualification, used the phrase 'fancy franchises'. He would have had a field day had he been alive to deal with the history of the Rhodesian voting system between 1951 and 1961.

The Commission did not depart from the principle of the common roll, which was a vital point for Todd. The essence of its recommendations was a compensatory sliding scale between property and educational qualifications, the broad principle being that the more property a voter had, the less education he needed in order to qualify, and vice versa. The most controversial features of the Tredgold proposals were the 'special qualifications' which were designed to increase the number of African voters. The Commission recommended that, in addition to the ordinary voters qualified by literacy and various combinations of means and education (ranging between £300 p.a. with education up to Form IV and £720 p.a. with no education at all), there should be special voters qualified by an income of £180 p.a. plus literacy.

In order to allay white fears the Commission recommended that in any constituency the special votes cast should never count for more than half the general votes, i.e. not more than a third of the total. For example, if 1,500 votes were cast and the special votes amounted to 500 or less, they would be counted in exactly the same way as the ordinary votes, but if they amounted to 600 they would be scaled down to 450 (half the 900 general votes cast and one-third of the total which now amounted to 1,350). Thus each special vote would count as three-quarters of a vote. If there were 750 special voters, the figure would be scaled down to 500 and each special vote would become two-thirds of a vote – and so on. Thus, although special voters could never become a majority in any constituency, they would as a substantial minority exercise an influence which could not be ignored. European candidates would have to pay continuing attention to the African voice.

Commenting on his own proposals Sir Robert Tredgold wrote in his autobiography:

> We ourselves did not believe (and at the time we were obviously in a special position to judge) that this limitation on the special vote would ever come into operation. We believed that the number of ordinary voters both black and white would grow steadily and prevent this happening. At the same time the limitation would give the white electorate reassurance against swamping.[1]

Unhappily the white electorate turned out to be very far from reassured and a set of proposals which might – just conceivably – have led to a genuine multiracial state were soon amended into something superficially similar, but in practice far less effective.

On April 27, three days before the Tredgold Report was due to be debated in the Southern Rhodesian Assembly, Sir Roy Welensky issued a joint communiqué with the British Government as a result of his talks in London. It can be regarded as the high water mark of Federal constitutional 'advancement' and it was very relevant to developments in the colony. He had secured agreement on six important points: the enlargement of the Federal Assembly from 36 to 60;[2] greater Federal responsibility for external affairs; a British undertaking only to legislate in Federal matters at the request of the Federal Government; a categorical declaration against secession; a promise (never implemented) that the northern Territorial Civil Services should be locally based; the holding of the review conference in 1960, the earliest date permitted by the Federation Order in Council, together with a statement that the conference would 'consider a programme for the attainment of such a status as would enable the Federation to become eligible for full membership of the Commonwealth'.[3]

---

[1] *The Rhodesia that was my life*, 218.
[2] Including the Speaker.
[3] Quoted *4,000 Days*, 77.

All these were concessions by the British Government to the Federal Government and diminished to some degree the power of the Colonial Office to protect the Africans in the northern Territories. The only one that need not have had this effect was the first, but in the event, for reasons set out below, effective though not nominal African representation was reduced as a result of the enlargement of the Assembly. To balance these gains the Federal Government made two minor concessions. One was recognition that amalgamation was just as far out of the question as secession, and would not even be considered by the review conference. The other was agreement that the Federal franchise would allow 'a reasonable number' of British protected persons to vote without having to become British subjects.

Before considering the detailed events in Southern Rhodesia during 1957–58 it is necessary to look ahead and outline briefly the changes soon to occur in the Federal Constitution. The Act amending it to enlarge the legislature was carried in the Federal Legislature on July 31. Its significance cannot be appreciated without reference to the Federal Electoral Bill whose broad provisions were announced in London by Welensky in June and whose details were set out by Julian Greenfield, Federal Minister of Justice on July 18.

Like the Tredgold Report the Federal Franchise White Paper (C.Fed. 72) which was published on September 19 established two categories of voters – ordinary and special. The qualifications were also very similar, but there was one vital difference which distinguished the Federal franchise not only from the Tredgold Report but from the watered-down version of it eventually enacted by the Southern Rhodesian Assembly. There were to be two rolls – the General Roll which elected 44 (theoretically from any race) out of the 59 Members (apart from the Speaker) and on which ordinary voters, in practice almost all Europeans, could alone vote, and the Special Roll, in practice predominantly Africans subject to property and educational qualifications; these, along with the electors on the General Roll who far outnumbered them, voted for eight Special African Members (four from Southern Rhodesia, and two from each Protectorate) and one European Member from Southern Rhodesia, who had responsibility for African interests. There remained as before two Specially Elected African Members from each Protectorate elected indirectly by African Representative Councils and one European nominated by each Governor. The net effect was that Africans elected by Africans remained the same – four. But their proportion had fallen from one-ninth (four out of thirty-six) to one-fifteenth (four out of sixty).

The Federal Electoral Bill had its second reading on December 18, and was carried on January 8, 1958. Not surprisingly both the Constitutional Amendment and the Electoral Bill were referred in turn to the British Government by the African Affairs Board as 'differentiating' measures – on July 30, 1957 and January 6, 1958 respectively. Equally unsurprisingly, the British Government advised Royal Assent, the Labour Party opposed the necessary Order-in-Council and the Conservative majority carried the day in Parliament. Whether or not Sir Roy Welensky had 'squared' the relevant ministers on his London visit in April 1957 is not known. Perhaps nothing was said, but those who negotiated with him must have done so on the basis of general agreement about the proposed changes and have known that, if the UK Government subsequently accepted adverse reports from the African Affairs Board, its decision would be bitterly denounced as a belated double cross.

African opinion was deeply disappointed. Confidence in the African Affairs Board, never very great, fell to nothing. It looked as if a bargain had been struck in advance between the British and Federal Governments, and no one believed that the submissions made by the Board had been considered on their merits. The disillusionment fostered by these events was greatly enhanced by developments in Southern Rhodesia.

Garfield Todd by early 1957 had acquired a unique position. He had held his own party together, and the new Dominion Party founded in February 1956 on the ruins of the old Confederates and led in the Federal sphere by Winston Field appeared to offer no serious threat, consisting as it did of a diverse collection of anti-governmental critics with little in common. Todd had displayed firmness – some said that he over-reacted – in dealing both with black labour trouble in Wankie and white labour trouble on the railways. He had criticized the Federal Government for lack of vigour – which had not endeared him to Malvern and Welensky, but did him no harm with the European electorate. He had shown considerable toughness in dealing with offences against law and order, and he had not hesitated to criticize the protectorate Governments for weakness in this respect. He had himself threatened to suppress the African National Congress. At the same time he had managed to inspire the Africans with a confidence in his leadership which they had never showed and never would again show towards any other European politician.

The roots of this confidence stemmed not only from his achievements in the direction of African advancement, although these were substantial and greater than his later critics allow. They stemmed above all from the way he spoke and the genuine impression which he gave of having African interests at heart. It was his oratory, his manner, his general political 'style' which, in the disapproving words of some of his colleagues 'give rise to a feeling in the country [and they meant the Africans] that he is a sort of "Saviour"'.

Here lay the old trouble. How could a European politician hope for long to retain the confidence of both white men and black men in a society of this sort? Todd's Government had lasted for three and a half years without overt dissension and with legislative success, but from April 1957 onwards this harmony was punctuated by notes of ever louder discord. The trouble came to a head at the beginning of the next year. It resulted in a major conflict within the United Party, the deposition of Todd from the premiership, his replacement by Sir Edgar Whitehead and a general election in which the Party survived by the narrowest of margins.

The course of events which led up to this crisis have been the subject of much controversy. No less controversial has been its significance in terms of Rhodesian history. Did it represent a turning point – a decision by the European electorate to reverse the trend towards moderate liberalism which appeared to have dominated political sentiment since the formation of the Federation? Or was it merely a personal question – the rebellion of a long-suffering Cabinet against a Prime Minister who was behaving indiscreetly, dictatorially, and with mounting disregard for the opinions of his colleagues and his party? There is no agreement on these questions, but perhaps a tentative answer can be given after examining the successive stages of the revolt against Todd

The speeches made at the caucus meeting on January 14, 1958 when the rebel ministers made their case, show the principal matters on which they were prepared to complain in front of Todd himself. There may have been other grievances of a more confidential nature which they hesitated to mention. It seems clear that the first major issue on which members of the Cabinet felt uneasy was the attitude of the Prime Minister towards a proposal to amend the Immorality Act. As we saw, the law from 1903 onwards forbade sexual intercourse outside marriage between black men and white women, this situation being confirmed by further legislation in 1916. But in 1916, and on many subsequent occasions, efforts were made to extend the prohibition to sexual relations outside marriage between white men and black women. In April 1957, Max Buchan, Member for Gatooma, announced that he intended to put forward a motion in the Assembly calling on the Government to legislate in this sense.

The subject was a hardy perennial often raised by such bodies as the Rhodesia Women's League, the Women's Branch of the Reform Party and the Loyal Women's Guild. The spark that set off this particular flare was the news that an African, Patrick Matimba, was coming with his Dutch wife to live at St Faith's Mission near Rusape where a by-election was pending, and it was believed that the Dominion Party would exploit the situation to the full. Todd asked the CID, Bulawayo, to produce a report on the whole question. The document, which contains an interesting and detailed account of 'miscegenation' and prostitution in Rhodesia, ends:

> From the police point of view it must be said that any such legislation, although it might serve as a nominal deterrent, could only be enforced by continued clandestine observation and intrusion of a type which would probably not be tolerated by our public.

Todd, whose instinct was to abolish the old law about black men rather than introduce a new one about white men, made it clear – or at any rate thought he had made it clear – to his colleagues that he would vote against Buchan's resolution. The other four ministers all voted in favour of it. Stumbles was particularly emphatic, ostensibly on the grounds of making the law 'fair'. Todd suggested that one way of being 'fair' would be to forbid all sexual intercourse of any sort outside marriage, but his colleagues were not amused.

The resolution was carried on May 3 by a comfortable majority (17–8), Todd voting with the minority. It did not bind the government to take any action, but it obviously created an embarrassing situation; the problem of a new version of the Immorality Act was to vex the party for many months to come.

The four ministers convinced themselves that Todd in voting as he did had gone back on his word. He himself was equally convinced that he had made his position entirely clear. The Dominion Party did not, in the event, try to exploit the Matimba affair. Winston Field, whatever his deficiencies as a statesman, was never a racialist and he declared the matter to be a 'nine day wonder' – with considerably more accuracy than Ian Smith on sanctions. He advised the electorate to get on with their work and keep things in perspective.

There was an even odder sequel. A year or so later Sir Edgar Whitehead, Todd's successor, seems to have had no difficulty in making the law 'fair' by the obvious means of repealing the old legislation against black men having sexual relations with white women. True, there was a specific reason. He was engaged in his well-intended but abortive campaign to bridge the gap between black and white and 'build a nation'. Unfortunately, a Rhodesian African of high intellectual calibre and good general repute – in fact, just the sort of person whose aid was being sought for the campaign – had the bad luck to be discovered at night building a nation in a parked car in Salisbury with a white girl in what the police considered to be a prosecutable posture. The Government could – and naturally did – refrain from prosecuting. But a law capable of thus hampering the campaign to secure African participation on the United Party side in the coming election had to be repealed. The very electoral exigencies which had prompted ministers and members of the party to vote for Buchan's restrictive resolution in 1957 induced many of the same ministers and members to support the opposite policy a few years later; there has been no attempt since to put the Immorality Act on the Statute Book.

The repercussions of the Immorality Resolution were still reverberating when an even more contentious issue came up. The Tredgold Report was debated on April 30, 1957 and on four occasions during May. Although no vote was taken it became clear that a number of Todd's supporters believed the recommendations to be too 'liberal'. The Government now had to consider what proposals to put forward. Much argument followed in Cabinet, and some drastic modifications were made.

First, the relationship between special votes and general votes was changed from a third to a sixth. Second, whereas Tredgold would have applied his figure to each constituency separately and only to votes actually cast, the new plan applied to the electorate as a whole and to all registered voters whether or not they voted. Third, the amended version closed the Special Roll for ever as soon as the figure reached a fifth of the General Roll, i.e. a sixth of the combined total of the two. Under Tredgold's plan no special voter would have lost his vote, although it would have been devalued if the number of special votes cast in his constituency exceeded a third of the total.

These changes, the first in particular, were far less favourable to Africans than the Tredgold Report. It is true that in theory an African might now be elected by special voters (i.e. by Africans) in a constituency where they were sufficiently concentrated to outnumber the general voters. Under the Tredgold plan this could not happen until enough Africans qualified as general voters, because his one-third rule applied to each constituency separately. But it would be a dubious gain; the possibility that one or two black faces might appear in the Assembly was a poor exchange for the probability that in a large number of seats the African vote would have an important influence on which of the white candidates would win and so upon the policy of European parties generally.

The Cabinet also decided to change the qualifications of special voters. The Tredgold Report had recommended a means test of not less than £180 p.a. The conservatives in the Cabinet pushed it up to £240. At this stage Todd, who had accepted the previous modifications with reluctance, insisted on adding a further special qualification. This was the attainment of Standard VIII (which meant ten years schooling) with no other test apart from continuous employment for the last two years. It was reckoned that some 6,000 Africans of educated type would thus be enfranchised. The proposal met such strong opposition in the Cabinet that Todd resolved to make a public threat of resignation if it did not go through. This was in itself an action bound to excite the wrath of his ministerial colleagues. Even more controversial was the occasion he chose – the Annual General Meeting of the Inter-racial Association on June 15 – a body whose very existence was regarded with misgiving by the more conservative members of the United Rhodesia Party. At the end of a longish speech, he said:

> To the north of us and to the south of us, racial politics are the fashion ... Southern Rhodesia finds itself the custodian of Rhodes' liberal dictum of equal rights for civilised men regardless of colour. If legislation further to im-plement that policy, when introduced to our House in July, were so changed as to continue to keep off the rolls our 6,000 Africans who have had ten years education and who work as teachers, agricultural demonstrators, medical order-lies and so on, we would be so betraying the spirit of Rhodes that I would not continue to lead my Party. However, I am confident that our legislators will meet the challenge of the spirit of the Tredgold Report, whatever may be the eventual letter of the law.

The matter, time and place of this oration greatly annoyed Todd's colleagues in the Cabinet. It also disturbed many back-benchers, and gave offence to some of those constituency party stalwarts who play an even bigger part in Rhodesian than they do in English politics. On the other hand, liberal supporters of Todd, such as Hardwicke Holderness – one of the *bêtes noires* of the conservative wing of the party – believed that without a threat of this sort he would never have got his way.

For the time being the Governmental ranks were closed. The Cabinet accepted the special qualifications, albeit with misgiving. In the Assembly, Stumbles, who was in charge of the Bill, made a point of emphasizing that it was not 'Todd's

Bill', but a Government measure supported by all ministers. The Party as a whole also presented a façade of unity with one exception, an Australian Member called Wightwick (pronounced Wittick) who was by trade a jute manufacturer and who had a long standing feud with the Prime Minister. He called for Todd's resignation and circularized all ministers and members of the caucus to that effect, but he received no support. Indeed he was nearly drummed out of the Party himself.

The Franchise Bill went through without any serious hitches. Todd accepted an amendment in committee requiring his Standard VIII electors to have a minimum income of £120 p.a.; he reckoned that nearly all of them had it anyway. The Act was duly promulgated on October 18, 1957. Apart from the special qualifications, the most contentious issue was a clause introducing the alternative vote. The object of this, which is a not uncommon feature of other Commonwealth Constitutions, was to ensure that where three or more candidates are contesting a single member seat, it should not be won on a split vote by a candidate with only minority support. If no candidate secures more than half the first preference votes, the bottom candidate drops out and his second preferences are distributed among the top two to determine the winner. A trial of this system was recommended in the Tredgold Report. So it cannot fairly be condemned as a piece of gerrymandering by the Government. Nevertheless, it was a measure clearly bound to benefit the United Rhodesia Party rather than any other.[4] For if candidates of a party to the left of the URP and appealing to African votes came forward, they were most unlikely to win a clear majority, and their second preferences would obviously go to the URP rather than the Dominion Party. Likewise, the DP's second preference would certainly not go to any candidate left of the URP.

The exiguous DP opposition protested vigorously, but vainly against the clause. Their fears were to be fully justified. When the general election took place a year later, it was largely a three-cornered contest between Whitehead's United Federal Party in the centre. Todd's Rhodesia Party on the left and the Dominion Party on the right. Had it not been for the alternative vote, the Dominion Party would have won.

The next event of significance in this eventful year was the annual conference of the URP on September 20. It was one of unusual importance. For some time past the idea of fusion between the United Federal Party and the URP had been canvassed. Todd seems to have had misgivings about this, although he did not press them. There were obvious advantages in amalgamating the two parties; they stood for similar ideas; both stemmed from the same governing party which had ruled Southern Rhodesia under Lord Malvern for twenty years till 1953; there was already much co-operation between them; a formal fusion would reduce overlapping, increase efficiency, and streamline the organizational side of Party politics;

[4] Just as it would clearly benefit the Liberal Party if it were to be introduced in Britain.

moreover, the opposition Dominion Party was already organized on the basis of a single party for both sets of elections.

Nevertheless, these were not the only considerations in the minds of some members in both the Federal and the United Rhodesia parties. If Todd sensed that fusion was in part a hit at him, he was right. The fact that the vociferous Wightwick voted for it, having in the past been a strong opponent, was a straw in the wind. Four months later, Sir Patrick Fletcher, when giving his reasons to the caucus for resigning from Todd's Cabinet, said he thought that fusion would bring the Prime Minister 'under other influences and that this would make the situation all right'.[5] There was a move, sponsored by Wightwick and Straw, another dissident back-bencher, to challenge Todd's leadership at the conference, and Fletcher's own name was put forward for election. He refused, however, to stand, declaring, with more tact than truthfulness, that the Cabinet was a happy team and that no change in leadership would improve it.

Under pressure from Fletcher and Ellman-Brown Wightwick and his friends did not press their challenge for the leadership. The proposals for fusion went through. The URP conference ended in apparent harmony. The ball was now in the court of the Federal Party, whose conference was due to take place at Ndola in November. Sir Roy Welensky's support was assured and fusion was certain to be carried. A final URP conference would take place in March 1958, to ratify the arrangements in the light of any changes proposed at Ndola.

The peaceful ending of the URP conference had been a delusion. During November while the Prime Minister was away in the Eastern Highlands, three of the four Ministers, Stumbles, Ellman-Brown and Hatty, came to the conclusion that the chances of the URP winning the next election under Todd were negligible. They were especially uneasy about the security problems which were being caused in the reserves by militant manifestations of the recently formed African National Congress, which had been defiantly inaugurated at Harare on September 12 – Pioneers' Day. Ellman-Brown, who had already once tendered his resignation (in August that year), but had been persuaded to withdraw it, was particularly disturbed at information which he had about Todd engaging in talks with Nkomo, Sithole and Clutton-Brock.[6] Todd, in the view of all three ministers, seemed in his public speeches to be more concerned with African advancement than general economic development and even if this was not a fair picture of his actual position, as they conceded it might not be, the public image was what mattered.[7] Sir Patrick Fletcher, who had been away at Kariba, was not involved in these discussions, but when the others told him, he agreed. Meanwhile, the Federal Party Congress had duly met at Ndola and endorsed the plans for fusion. Sir Roy Welensky returned to Salisbury well satisfied, only to be greeted with the news that the

[5] Todd Papers, File 87, 'Memo for private file of H.H.C.H.' (Hardwicke Holderness) on caucus meeting held on 14 January, 1.

[6] Information from Mr Ellman-Brown.

[7] Todd Papers, File 86, 'Notes (by Todd) on recent happenings in the Political Situation in Southern Rhodesia, Jan 14, 1958', 1.

Cabinet appeared to be in full revolt and that a major crisis was imminent.

The time was now late November – a period of the year when Rhodesians are seldom at their best. It is very hot and the climate does not conduce to clarity of mind. Todd returned from Inyanga unaware of the discontent among his colleagues. On Sunday, November 24, Fletcher called on him at his house in the evening with the news that the Cabinet were going to resign. Fletcher did not himself, he said, approve of this way of proceeding without any advance warning. He spoke in high praise of Todd's personal leadership, but felt bound to say that he thought his colleagues to be right on the substantial point, viz. that Todd could not win the next election.

The news came as a disagreeable surprise to the Prime Minister, who had no inkling of trouble. Naturally he was anxious to hear direct from the other ministers what their views were. He expected them next morning, but owing to some muddle, none of them appeared; alone came Hatty in the afternoon, and added to the confusion by saying that Fletcher acted without his authority and 'I myself have never thought that the political situation was irretrievable'.[8] The following morning the full Cabinet met. There was no longer any talk of resignation. Todd agreed to accept some of the suggestions made by the others with a view to the next election. He undertook to make strong speeches about the behaviour of the ANC, and he even agreed to bring forward an amendment to the Immorality Act on the lines favoured by Buchan earlier in the year, observing that he hoped to be in the UK when it came up and so would not have to speak himself.[9]

The Cabinet revolt had so far gone unnoticed in the press, but two days later the *Rand Daily Mail* announced that there was a serious split in the Southern Rhodesian Government, and that Garfield Todd was about to resign. The Prime Minister and his colleagues had to issue a categorical denial. Todd in the notes referred to above, says that 'in the new unity which we had now achieved ... as far as I was concerned, I believed that my denial was the truth'.[10]

---

[8] Todd Papers, File 87, 'Notes for Congress, February 8, 1971' (by Todd) 10.
[9] Todd Papers, File 86, 'Notes on recent happenings', 2.
[10] Ibid.

22

The Fall of Todd 1957–58

Todd had been over-optimistic. He ought to have been warned by a suggestion from Ellman-Brown that the leadership should be reconsidered in three or four months' time when the first congress of the new 'fused' party met – a clear sign that all was not harmonious.[1] In the circumstances, he was unwise to depart again from Salisbury. There is a proverb about cats and mice which applies in politics as in other things – and with particular force in Africa. But Mrs Todd had not been well and the Prime Minister himself badly needed a holiday. His colleagues reassured him. On December 16, 1957 he left for a month's stay in South Africa.

No sooner had he gone than a new storm blew up. Regulations, published on the very day of his departure, gave a big rise in wages for the lower grades of African employees. Todd's old enemy, Wightwick, whose jute factory operating on the margin of profitability employed a large number of Africans, was particularly incensed, and he resigned from the party in a rage. Todd telegraphed that he could, if necessary, return by January 5. He was relieved to receive a message saying that there was no need. In fact, his colleagues seized on this question as a *casus belli*. They persuaded themselves that Todd had not consulted the Cabinet properly about the regulations, and had failed to secure the agreement of the Federal Government.

The documents show that neither charge has any substance. The regulations were discussed at length in the Cabinet; the member who pressed the complaint was not present at the meeting where the subject was most fully dealt with, though he could presumably have read the minutes. As for the Federal Government, labour regulations were not in its province. The relevant ministers had been informally consulted, and had approved, but they asked not to be quoted publicly on an issue which was purely Territorial.

[1] Todd Papers, File 86, 'Notes on recent happenings ...' 2.

Todd had not meant to return until January 16, but hearing that some American friends were visiting Southern Rhodesia, he decided to come back on the ninth. There was to be a Cabinet meeting on the tenth, and once again rumours were rife. He was greeted at Johannesburg Airport by reporters with the information, new to him, that he was about to see Sir Roy Welensky and would then hand in his resignation to the Governor. He pooh-poohed these stories as a carry-over of the November crisis, but when he reached Salisbury, he realized that this was far from being the case. Sir Patrick Fletcher, once again the bearer of woe, met him as he stepped out of his plane and told him that the four ministers who made up the Cabinet intended to offer their resignation *en masse* the following morning.

Todd spent the evening bringing himself up to date and reading the Cabinet papers. Next morning he confronted his colleagues. They began by attacking his minimum wage regulations, but it became clear after about an hour that their charges would not stick. The discussion then turned to the question of leadership. Ellman-Brown and the other ministers once again asserted their doubts about Todd's chances of victory at the next election. Finally, Todd asked them in turn whether they intended to withdraw their support, and each said yes.

> One then said, perhaps you would like time to consider the matter. Stumbles said it must not be drawn out. I asked for 24 hours to consider it and they agreed I could have it. I asked if they were handing in their resignations, and they said they would if they were required. I then asked if they were quite sure that they had made up their minds on this, and each said he had. I then pointed out that they had made their decisions and therefore could hand in their resignations ... I had 24 hours now to make up my mind, and while I might not need their resignations, if they handed them in, I would then have a clear field to make my decision.[2]

After discussing the problem with some of his friends, Todd resolved to fight it out. However, the resignations did not come that afternoon, as expected, nor had they arrived by the following morning. The ministers had assumed that Todd would have to resign after a vote of no confidence from all his colleagues. Indeed they had gone so far as to meet that afternoon without the Prime Minister, and authorize an important contract as if they were still the Government – an action with which Todd made much play in the later debate. But they were in for a disagreeable shock. Todd waited till 10.15 a.m. and then telephoned Hatty, probably the least unsympathetic member of the Cabinet, about the resignations. 'Oh, do you require them?' he said.[3] Todd said he did – and promptly.[4] At noon he held a press conference and declared his intention to form a new Cabinet. Its composition was announced three days later, on January 14. It consisted of the

---

[2] Todd Papers, File 87, 'Notes by Todd for Congress, February 8, 1968', 21.
[3] Ibid., 22.
[4] J. G. Quinton – Fletcher's Parliamentary Secretary – also resigned.

following: Sir George Davenport (Mines), A. E. Abrahamson (Finance), A. D. H. Lloyd (Justice), E. D. Palmer (Native Affairs), R. D. Palmer (Native Education and Agriculture).

The struggle was now fully joined, but where was the field of battle to be? Sir Patrick Fletcher who had assumed the lead among the dissidents argued for the Assembly which was not sitting, but could be summoned if necessary – though only with the joint consent of the Speaker and the Prime Minister. He reckoned that he had fifteen votes and as the Speaker had to be neutral, this gave him a majority. Another possibility was the caucus. A third was the electorate if the Governor would agree to a dissolution. Yet a fourth was a party congress.

It soon became clear that the caucus would not support Todd. A meeting was held on January 14 and the late ministers stated their reasons for resignation.[5] These were not all the same and a familiar variety of charges came up; wages, the miscegenation vote, dictatorship, the franchise dispute, etc.; but common ground to each was Todd's attitude towards African advancement. Fletcher 'had got worried over the Prime Minister talking at every street corner on racial matters', and about a television talk in which he referred to 'the Africans catching up in twenty years'. Stumbles and Ellman-Brown 'felt that the PM's conduct had been such as to give rise to a feeling in the country that he was a sort of "Saviour" '. They considered that he should not have talked to Nkomo and Clutton-Brock. Quinton thought that this meeting with the former 'had put a halo round Nkomo's head'. Todd defended himself with vigour, but the voting, according to press reports, was 13 to 7 against him.

He saw no reason to accept this as final. The question now was whether to ask for a dissolution or appeal to a party congress. He consulted Sir Robert Tredgold, who advised him to take the matter to a party congress; if the vote went against him there, he would have to resign. If, on the other hand, he won, he should continue the business of the country until he was defeated in the House. After that he could legitimately ask the Governor for a dissolution. If he asked for one straight away, the Governor might well refuse, acting on the precedent of Chief Justice Russell's refusal of a request made in somewhat similar circumstances by Huggins in 1948.

There was strong pressure from the Fletcher party to reconvene the Assembly, but Todd had no intention of complying. After some delay, a meeting of the party congress was fixed for February 8. Here too, there was a problem. The merger of the Federal Party with the URP had not yet been formally ratified. Was the sovereign body to be a meeting of the congress of the URP or of the Southern Rhodesian Division of the United Federal Party? This was not a mere question of semantics. The Territorial Division of the UFP was, as we saw, likely to be less favourable to Todd than the old URP congress. But Todd and his advisers felt that fusion was too far advanced for them to exploit a technicality. It was agreed to accept the decision of the Territorial Division, with Julian Greenfield, the Federal

[5] See Todd Papers, File 87, 'Memo for private file of Hardwicke Holderness . . .' *passim.*

Minister of Justice, as chairman. Even this did not conclude the matter. There was a brisk argument about the credentials of some of the branch delegations, conducted rather like the disputes which have often vexed American nominating conventions. The anti-Todd party accused him of putting in his own supporters and vice versa. The chairman had an unenviable task in sorting it all out.

The meeting took place in an atmosphere of ill-temper and recrimination. The first question was whether to admit the press. The Todd-ites were in favour, but were heavily defeated. A prolonged debate on the leadership ensued, keenly followed by a large collection of journalists listening at windows which had to be kept open lest the Hall became a sort of white hole of Calcutta. At one stage in proceedings Sir Patrick Fletcher brought the house down. He had been accusing the Prime Minister of misleading his colleagues and was challenged to substantiate the charge: 'The Prime Minister said ... he said ... he said ... Well, I can't remember just what he said, but I know it wasn't true.'[6] All day the battle raged. Todd defended himself in a speech of an hour and three-quarters. His eloquence, humour and wit gained the applause of his audience, but not their votes. Late in the day a new development occurred. It was announced that Sir Edgar Whitehead, the High Commissioner in Washington, would allow his name to go forward as a compromise candidate.[7]

By this time the delegates were exhausted and they decided to retire for food and drink. The Chairman ruled against further debate after dinner. The vote was then taken. On the first ballot, Todd won. The figures were Todd 129, Whitehead 122, Fletcher 73. Fletcher was then eliminated. On the second ballot, Todd held all his votes, but the supporters of Fletcher transferred *en masse* to Whitehead. The final figures were: Whitehead 193, Todd 129.

Whitehead returned to Salisbury from Washington four days later, on Wednesday, February 12. He took a suite in Meikle's Hotel and entered into strenuous negotiations. By Friday, he came to the conclusion that he must give up; the gap seemed unbridgeable, and he issued a statement of his position that evening. The following day, Todd, who was still – on a caretaker basis – Prime Minister, called a meeting of his former colleagues and told them that the choice was up to them. Who was it to be? There was silence. No one replied, but three pairs of eyes swivelled slowly round and fixed on Sir Patrick Fletcher. Todd accepted the unspoken verdict. Walking out of the room he met two of Sir Roy Welensky's closest associates – Sidney Sawyer and Alf Adams, the Secretary of the Federal Party. They asked him who was to be his successor. When he told them their faces 'fell a mile', as Todd put it, and one of them said: 'Roy will never agree to this.'[8]

Renewed pressure was now put on Whitehead. Late on Saturday night he

---

[6] Information from various people present.

[7] Nominated by the Umtali branch. Mr Ellman-Brown informed the author that the branch offered to nominate him but he refused.

[8] Information from Mr Garfield Todd.

composed a Cabinet which he submitted to a meeting of the caucus on Sunday (February 16) at 11 a.m. It was a compromise. Todd generously agreed to serve. His short-lived second administration was represented by himself and Sir George Davenport, his old one by Ellman-Brown and Hatty. R. J. Knight, a newcomer, completed the list. The caucus ratified this arrangement and Whitehead was now in a position to meet the Assembly, but for one slight snag; he was not a member of it.

Whitehead could have had the pick of several safe United Party seats. Instead, with one of those curious bursts of self-confidence and misjudgement which from time to time punctuated his career, he persuaded the party managers to arrange a vacancy at the Hillside constituency in Bulawayo. True it had been uncontested at the last election, but this was only because of the total disarray of the anti-Government forces. At the previous three elections there had been an opposition majority. Hillside was anything but safe. The by-election was fixed for April 16. Todd spoke and loyally supported Whitehead, but – such had been the change in European sentiment – this turned out to be the kiss of death. Whitehead lost by 691 to 604. Both he and the successful Dominion Party candidate agreed that the votes were really being cast for or against Todd.[9]

Whitehead decided, after this rebuff, that he must appeal to the country as soon as possible in order to confirm his position. The Governor agreed to dissolve, and the election was fixed for June 5, 1958. It now seemed clear to some that Todd's mere presence in the Cabinet was as much of an electoral liability as his headship of the Government. On April 23 at a meeting of the UFP Southern Rhodesian Members of the Assembly – the 'caucus' – eight out of twenty-two present made Todd's exclusion a condition of support for Whitehead who agreed that there was no chance of winning if Todd remained. Todd at once resigned and with six other Members resolved to revive the old United Rhodesia Party and fight the election independently.[10]

Somebody unknown attempted a last minute hoax to discredit the Dominion Party by exploiting the electorate's anti-Afrikaner sentiment.[11] A letter purporting to be signed by one W. K. van Tonder, who gave his address as 'PO Kopje (Salisbury)' appeared in the *Rhodesia Herald* on May 29. The author noted with pleasure that there were three Afrikaans-speaking Dominion Party candidates – 'It is not enough, but it is a start' – and went on to hope that a Dominion Party victory would bring the Afrikaners into their own at last. 'We have a chance of getting a say in the Government so that there will be jobs in the Government for our children and we can tell the British Liberals there is no place for them in South Africa or Rhodesia.' And the author ended: 'Keep courage! Stand firm! The long struggle is nearly over.' The *Herald* wrote a grave leader asking the Dominion Party where it stood on this important question.

[9] Mason, op. cit., 196; Leys, op. cit., 144 and n. 1.
[10] Leys, op. cit., Appendix IV, 307.
[11] Leys, op. cit., 308–9.

The Party replied with a request for authentication of the letter, but no one ever answered to the name of van Tonder, and the address of 'the Kopje' – a celebrated but uninhabited landmark in Salisbury – was about as convincing as 'PO Marble Arch (London)'. How far this latter-day Looking Glass version of the Zinoviev Letter affected the election results no one can say.

In the event, the UFP was victorious, but only because of the alternative vote to which the DP had so strongly objected. In four constituencies where DP candidates won on first preferences, but failed to get an absolute majority, the distribution of the second preferences of Todd's URP supporters put UFP candidates in.[12] The result was a victory by 17 seats to 13, which would have been exactly reversed, but for the new electoral system. Even on the final count the DP scored more popular votes than the UFP, 18,314 to 17,516. But this only proves what students of electoral arithmetic have long known – that the alternative vote can no more guarantee a proportionate result than the first-past-the-post system; all it does is to ensure that no one gets in on less than half the votes cast in his constituency – a very different matter.

The URP failed to win a single seat. Todd himself was defeated in Shabani, and his leading supporter, Hardwicke Holderness, lost his Salisbury constituency to Whitehead. Some 4,600 electors voted for the URP on the first round. About 1,700 were Africans who, if contemporary estimates are right, did not exercise their second preference at all – a significant sign of 'alienation' from the major parties. The remainder nearly all gave their second preference to the UFP. In terms of 'European ascendancy' versus 'liberalism', it is reasonable, as Colin Leys suggests, to add the final vote for the UFP and the URP together. On that assumption the 'Government Party' won 52.8 per cent of the vote against the opposition's 47 per cent – not exactly an overwhelming victory, but enough.

Todd's fall dealt a heavy blow to the incipient *rapprochement* between African nationalism and white liberalism. 'Todd is the Moses of our age', wrote the *African Weekly*. Lobengula's grandson issued a statement deploring his defeat. Nathan Shamuyarira, whose *Crisis in Rhodesia* (1965) is one of the best recent books on the subject by an African, wrote:

> The years of hope for peaceful co-operation and swift progress towards racial equality – or better, a non-racial state – were over. Whitehead might prove to be as liberal as Todd, who knew? But he had come to power on a wave of reaction, and Africans had lost faith in partnership. A sad but perhaps treasured compliment was paid to Todd at that time when an African composed a song which became a best selling record.

[12] There were ten seats which required a second count. Beside the four mentioned, there were four where the UFP candidate led and had his position confirmed by URP preferences. There were two including Todd's at Shabani where the UFP candidate came last. In neither case did the second preferences put in the URP candidate.

'Todd wasichya,
Hamba Kahle mudale ...'
(Todd has left us
Go well, old man).
There was little more that we could say.[13]

Todd's defeat marks a turning point in Rhodesian history. This is not because his successor's policy was less liberal; it was in some ways more. The chance lost was one which, given the intensely personal nature of Rhodesian politics, only Todd could at that moment have taken, to bring the educated, politically-conscious African into the political system. African nationalism only began to emerge as a powerful force in 1955 after nearly sixty years of comparative quiescence. For a fleeting period it seemed just possible that its leaders would accept partnership and try to become part of 'the political nation'. The franchise question was vital. There was a world of difference between a Common Roll, even with special qualifications, and the system of separate rolls which the Federal Government enacted and which Whitehead was to copy in the 1961 constitution. The latter might produce more black faces in the legislature, but at the cost of creating a sense of second class citizenship; and the effective influence of the African voter was probably less than with a Common Roll.

Todd's policy presupposed contacts with African nationalists. It meant that the Prime Minister actually talked to people like Nkomo, Sithole and Clutton-Brock (a white member of the ANC who had helped to draft its constitution). But to the majority of his party, and *a fortiori* to the opposition, such contacts were anathema. The leaders of the ANC, like nationalist leaders all through history, used extreme language and their conduct seldom seemed far from sedition and violence. To talk to such people was, for most members of the Government Party, almost to condone crime. One can compare the outcry in England when Gladstone actually negotiated with Parnell, the prototype of the innumerable nationalist leaders who were to undermine English ascendancy down the years that followed.

It was this above all which brought Todd down. Of course there were a host of other complaints, as is often the case on such occasions: moral 'smears', none of which when analysed has any substance; accusations of impulsiveness, lack of consultation, dictatorship and by-passing the Cabinet. It strains credulity to suppose that these charges would have been pursued if the content of Todd's policy had been acceptable to his colleagues. Some of them said that they objected because it would cause the loss of the next election, others because they believed it wrong on its merits. The two motives were probably so tangled together that the objectors themselves could hardly distinguish. The point was that, on the great question of the division between the 'The Two Nations', Todd wished to move faster and further towards closing the gap than his Cabinet and his party. What is more he wanted to do this in a particular way, by bringing educated, politically-conscious

[13] p. 25.

Africans into the élite which governed the country and making them feel that they were part of the very process of decision-making.

How then do we explain a seeming paradox? If this view is correct, Todd fell because he was too 'liberal'. Yet his successor was in one sense just as 'liberal'. Indeed he passed measures which went well beyond Todd's. Moreover Todd's Cabinet and party protested quite sincerely again and again that they were no less 'liberal' than he. It became almost an article of faith in the circles of the old establishment, the survivors of the party that governed Southern Rhodesia for thirty years and the Federation for its brief life, to believe that Todd was not really very liberal and that his liberalism was not the cause of his fall.

Sir Roy Welensky wrote on January 17, 1958 in a letter to a close friend, Mr Don Taylor, editor of the *New Commonwealth*,

> Don't swallow the story that this is an issue based on liberalism versus anti-liberal elements. That is bunk ... There may have been differences in the Cabinet in regard to the speed, in regard to the emphasis, but there has been no member of that Cabinet who has attempted to retard the development of the African. I don't really know the facts. I have heard versions given first, second and third hand, all making up rather a grim story, but all I ask you is not to make any hasty decisions. You can take it from me that five men don't resign lightly, particularly a man like Fletcher, who has served the country well for twenty years ...[14]

The letter is significant for two reasons. First it is one of the many pieces of evidence in the Welensky papers which count against the allegation made by Frank Clements and Sir Robert Tredgold that Sir Roy in some way engineered Todd's removal. He certainly had his misgivings on account of Todd's political inexperience and disliked the attacks made on Lord Malvern and the Federal Government in November 1955 and June 1956. But there is nothing to suggest that he played any part in the intrigues which brought the Territorial Prime Minister down, and much to suggest that he found the whole episode highly inconvenient. Todd himself has never believed that the Federal Prime Minister was involved at all closely in the affair.

Clements says that the dissident Southern Rhodesian ministers 'were no strangers to Sir Roy's home or his ideas' and that 'at any time during the leadership crisis a few words from Sir Roy would have preserved Garfield Todd's position, but Sir Roy never spoke them'.[15] Sir Roy probably took the view that interference on his part would cause resentment rather than otherwise. He may well have decided that the only hope of preserving party unity was to secure a compromise. This fits with Todd's story about the reaction of Welensky's *aides* when Whitehead appeared to have thrown in the sponge and the premiership

[14] Welensky papers.
[15] Op. cit., 129–30.

seemed about to go to Fletcher who could not possibly be called a compromise candidate. It is another matter to assume that Welensky was actively endeavouring to undermine Todd.

The second point that emerges from Sir Roy's letter concerns Todd's 'liberalism'. The more one looks at the conflict of opinion here, the more apparent it becomes that the two sides mean by 'liberalism' two quite different things. The dissident Southern Rhodesian Cabinet ministers were right to repudiate the charge that any of them had 'attempted to retard the development of the African'. On the contrary they genuinely wished to advance it, but to do so gradually and cautiously following the tradition of Lord Malvern that one should not talk much about it lest one frightened the white electorate which possessed the effective monopoly of political power. This was broadly the attitude of Welensky and his Federal colleagues, and it was the attitude that most people anticipated of Whitehead, though we shall see that as Prime Minister he did not turn out to be quite what was expected.

'Liberalism' in this sense consisted in the conferment upon the Africans of a series of boons granted by Europeans from a position of authority – special qualifications for the franchise; extension of education; amendment, perhaps abolition, of the Land Apportionment Act; the removal of racial discrimination in public places, etc. It was estimable in itself. It was the opposite to the legislative trend in the Union of South Africa; and it was the reverse of the policies which were to be pursued by the Rhodesian Front after UDI. But it was not what Todd and his friends meant by 'liberalism' – or rather it was only a part, and not the most important part, of what they meant.

The difference is summed up admirably in a document[16] written for Todd by Hardwicke Holderness, one of his most intelligent and loyal supporters. Holderness, a successful lawyer from an old Rhodesian family, was a Rhodes Scholar at Oxford (Magdalen) before the war and later served with great distinction in the RAF. He is said to be the most decorated of all Rhodesian pilots. He wrote:

> The fundamental reason why the former Ministers have revolted . . . is a fundamental difference in conception as between them and the PM . . . The former Ministers consider that, as far as the African population is concerned, everything in the garden will be lovely as long as economic development is maintained, any manifestations of activities hostile to the established government are dealt with 'firmly' and European leaders remain apart and in a position of authority.

He went on to contrast the attitude of the Prime Minister:

[16] Todd Papers, File 87, 'Notes setting out certain conclusions arrived at by H.H.C.H. on a Review of the Evidence at the Caucus Meeting', n.d. but presumably soon after January 14, 1958.

Mr Todd's approach is based on the assumption that the leadership of the country must carry with it the confidence of at any rate a substantial part of the African population, and this necessarily involves making statements which command such confidence from them. In this situation statements made by the Prime Minister in pursuance of his conception of our problem are regarded, quite sincerely, by the former Ministers as being dangerous . . . 'putting ideas into the minds of the Natives', and they regard this as being almost criminally irresponsible.

And he ironically commented on their fear of antagonizing white voters and letting in the Dominion Party 'which incidentally they say they regard as most undesirable because that would prevent them pursuing the "liberal" policy in which they believed'. He then referred to a speech of Todd's at Bulawayo on St Andrew's Night 1957. The Prime Minister had invited the African National Congress to eradicate undemocratic behaviour or else the Government would have to pass further security measures. His colleagues approved this line, but not its implications:

> . . . implicit in that appeal was the prospect of the African National Congress leaders coming to the Government and saying that they would conform. And implicit in that was the possibility of the Prime Minister having a direct interview with them. But it is quite clear now . . . from the sort of approach which the former Ministers have adopted in the House that a personal interview between a member of the Government and any of the 'naughty boys' on the African side of the fence is quite abhorrent . . .
>
> It is clear now, therefore, that from early in the second half of 1957 the former Ministers had resolved to get rid of Todd at some stage.

He ended with an analysis of the situation as he saw it, particularly in relation to the problem of 'security'. In the peculiar circumstances of the colony – a vast gap between the enfranchised minority and the voteless millions – a movement like the ANC was inevitable. Would it operate within the Constitution rather than become purely destructive? He believed that in Southern Rhodesia, unlike the north, there was a chance, but only 'if the present leaders, who as a result of Todd's speech are fully prepared to commit themselves to follow the proper line, are contacted directly by the Government'. If the approach failed 'there is no lack of evidence that Todd would not hesitate to apply the toughest measures. The former Ministers, however, want to apply the tougher measures without making any direct contact at all.' And he ended:

> The result of that approach, and indeed the result of Todd's defeat if this occurs will almost certainly be to compel the African National Congress Move-ment to become precisely what we do not want it to be; to make it virtually impossible for Africans to join the United Federal Party and participate properly

316

in the Party System, and to leave the now militant and destructive African Congress Movement as virtually the only vehicle for the expression of their views. Not that that need lead to revolt or rebellion. It is possible by modern methods to prevent revolt and rebellion, as is being done in the Union of South Africa, almost indefinitely. But it would lead to a Police State. And who wants to live in a Police State?

This was the authentic voice of one of the last 'Whigs', and in the strange circumstances of Southern Rhodesian politics it could still be heard, though not for much longer. Whether the African leaders would have responded to Todd's appeal cannot be known for certain. And as for the Europeans, alas events were to show that most of them did not in the least mind living in a police state if this was the only means of preserving their 'way of life' – no doubt a very mild sort of police state at first, but a system which has abrogated in the course of time almost every one of the traditional British freedoms.

Perhaps the last word should be with Garfield Todd himself, still deeply concerned with current affairs, but long repudiated by the electorate. I stayed with him for the first time in September 1970, though I had met him at a dinner party before, and had worked on his papers in his absence on a previous occasion. I was enchanted by his intelligence, kindness and humour, and by his intriguing combination of other-worldliness and realism.

He still lived, as he did before he became Prime Minister, at the mission station at Dadaya near Shabani. His ranch was not as large as it had been for he sold the greater part a few years earlier, but it remained substantial and profitable. His house is new. Built on a bluff high above a bend of the Ngesi River which is dammed and so is never short of water, it commands an unforgettable view. If one is there at the right time one can see hippopotami basking on the muddy bank below. At high noon during the long rainless season the bush is brown, parched and arid; the almost vertical sun dazzles the eye and shrivels up the mind; one wonders how cattle can possibly be pastured in this desolate landscape. About a mile away through his property runs the railway line from Lourenzo Marques to Bulawayo. Twice a day, as if in mockery of all that he stood for, a locomotive chugged slowly across the scene hauling a long string of sanction-busting oil tankers – the then life blood of the 'illegal regime'.

As the sun went down, during that brief period just before the starlit tropical night descends, we sat out on the lawn. I asked Garfield Todd what he thought about the 1958 crisis in retrospect. He did not at first answer directly. 'It has been my ideal in politics all my life', he said, 'to see that no one should be handicapped by the colour of his skin and that advancement should be possible on merit to any position irrespective of race ...' He paused and then went on: 'But how can one expect the Europeans to give up all this when they haven't got to. Living as we do, all of us here are guilty; but I sometimes think it is asking for a generation of white saints to hope that they will voluntarily abandon what they hold.'

The shadows were already longer, and he was silent for a bit. 'You asked about the crisis of 1958. Well, I was very angry at the time and I do not believe in giving up – I never understood why poor Winston Field gave up as he did – but I can see the point of view of Ellman-Brown and Co. They were convinced that I would lose them the next election, and they were probably right, you know. I expect we would have lost. As it was, those fellows got another four years, and it might have been more if Whitehead had not made a mess of things ... But it didn't do old Ben Fletcher any good, did it?' And he laughed. The sun had almost vanished. 'Let's go and have a drink,' he said.

23

The Decline of the Federation 1956–60

The new Prime Minister was a very different character from his predecessor. Where Todd was passionate, emotional, and out-going, Whitehead was cool, intellectual and withdrawn. He was probably the cleverest man to hold his office in the history of the country, but he lacked the common touch and he had no one to keep him down to earth. Like all Southern Rhodesian Prime Ministers before Ian Smith, he was born out of the country – in fact at the British embassy in Berlin in 1905, son of the head of chancery, Sir James Whitehead, and Lady Marian Whitehead, daughter of the Earl of Middleton. He was educated at Shrewsbury and University College, Oxford. In 1928, his doctor advised him to go to Rhodesia for his health. He became a civil servant for two years and then bought a farm at Vumba in the eastern highlands. He entered the Legislative Assembly in 1939 as a supporter of Malvern, but gave up his seat in 1940 to serve in the British Army. For a short time at the end of the war he acted as High Commissioner in London.

In the 1946 election he was re-elected to the Assembly and at once was appointed by Malvern as Minister of Finance. He played an important part in the negotiations for federation. Many Rhodesians felt themselves at a disadvantage in dealing with their English opposite numbers. A certain 'colonial' inferiority complex tended to make them awkward and ill at ease. Not so Sir Edgar Whitehead. With his roots deep in the English 'establishment' and with a knife-like brain he had no difficulty in coping with Wykehamist officials and Etonian ministers. His problem was health. Like Lord Malvern, he was very deaf, and he also suffered from eyesight so bad as to render him nearly blind. These defects enhanced his isolation from the ordinary run of men – and women, with whom he was particularly uncomfortable. He was a confirmed bachelor with no gift for small talk, shy, a bad 'mixer', and quite unlike the sort of person one would expect to flourish in Rhodesian politics. Nevertheless, he would certainly have been in the Federal Cabinet, but for another breakdown in health in 1953. On medical advice he retired from politics. Four years later, however, he was sufficiently recovered to accept Sir Roy Welensky's offer to become Federal High Commissioner in Washington. Then the convulsions of early 1958 brought him back to Rhodesia.

He was an eccentric figure with few intimates. His house on the farm was celebrated for its untidiness and confusion. He was a great beer drinker, though without apparent ill-effects. He liked to show his will power by giving up alcohol for one month in the year – choosing February because it was the shortest. No one could have been more informal. On occasions while Prime Minister he actually delivered the milk personally from his farm to the well known Leopard Rock Hotel at Vumba. He was a very clear incisive speaker when he had some theme to expound. His deficiency in sight and hearing was compensated by an excellent memory. He could manage with the minimum of notes, or none at all. But he wholly lacked Todd's magnetism. He was more effective in the Assembly than on the public platform. Very much the intellectual in politics, he possessed a certain arrogance which caused him to ignore advice. It was typical of him that he chose a risky Bulawayo seat as his route back into the House – and lost it.

One can compare Lord Malvern's remark to Rex Reynolds, who had quoted to him an historian's description of Whitehead as 'this unassuming man'. Lord Malvern said: 'I would never have called Edgar "unassuming". He was one of those people who are quiet, but basically very conceited.'

He was undoubtedly liberal – more liberal probably than most of his supporters at the UFP congress bargained for. But he was unable to obtain any *rapport* with the African nationalist leaders. This was partly because of his personality: also because of the circumstances of his elevation. Nothing could alter the fact that, however liberal he might be, he owed his position to the less liberal elements in the party, and that he had replaced Todd, whom the African nationalists regarded as their friend and ally.

It would, however, be wrong to assume that Todd's replacement by Whitehead was the only reason for the alienation of African nationalists from the European electorate, which gathered momentum after 1958. The world was rapidly changing. No one can be sure that Todd would have managed any better than his successor. The most that can be said is that he would have faced the new situation with some advantages which Whitehead did not possess. He would have needed them, for the next few years were to see developments both inside and outside Central Africa which were in almost every respect deleterious to the hopes of racial partnership on which the Federation had been founded and which the mildly liberal Southern Rhodesian Government had been seeking to realize since 1953.

To follow the fortunes of Whitehead's Government it is necessary to remember some of these developments. The first had occurred while Todd was still in office and at just the moment when Sir Roy Welensky succeeded Lord Malvern as Federal Prime Minister. The Suez crisis of November 1956 might appear to have little connection with Central Africa. It occurred several thousand miles away and involved issues which had nothing to do with the problems of the Rhodesias. But its bearing on events there, though indirect, was important. Sir Roy himself at once saw its significance. The British withdrawal made a deep impression on his mind. One of his closest allies, Julian Greenfield, Federal Minister of Justice, told the author that in retrospect he saw the graph of the Federation's fortunes ascending steadily and steeply till Suez. Then it wavered on an uncertain plateau for a short while, soon to turn downwards. Within five years the Federation was doomed. Within six it was dead.

To know precisely what happened and when it would be necessary to have access to the documents which, if they exist, record reasons for the major conclusions of the British Cabinet. These will not be available, under the 'thirty years 'rule', until the late 1980s. It is unlikely that they will uncover startling secrets. Suez was indeed a traumatic episode, a 'moment of truth' which showed that Britain was no longer a great power. Some members of the establishment may have drawn the inference that Britain could no longer hold on to her colonial empire, and in their minds they may well have replaced 'could' by 'should'. It is always nicer to believe that one is voluntarily doing the right thing than involuntarily doing what till yesterday one thought to be the wrong thing. Yet it is an error to think that the process of 'decolonization' was merely the result of military weakness. Britain could not have governed her African colonies indefi-nitely, but she could certainly have done so for much longer than she did. The colonial empire had been acquired in a haphazard higgledy-piggledy fashion for many reasons and over many years, but the moral justification for hanging on – or rather for hanging on after strategic and economic reasons ceased to apply – had always been preparation for self-government. The rapidly changing climate of world and national opinion in the second half of the 1950s made self-government suddenly appear more urgent and more practicable than it had been ever before.

Whatever the mixture of motives may have been, a profound change took place in the attitude of the governing elements of the Conservative Party to-wards the process of 'decolonization'. Speed replaced gradualism. In the words of David Goldsworthy:

> Such criteria as harmony among ethnic groups, economical viability, a developed infrastructure of voluntary organisations and demonstrably stable political institutions, so often stressed by politicans and Colonial Officers in the past, were now scarcely heard of. All that mattered was that an indigenous political élite, with some degree of local support, should exist and be willing to take over.[1]

This change was advantageous to the politically aspiring African everywhere

[1] David Goldsworthy, *Colonial Issues in British Politics 1945–61*, 1971, 361.

except in Southern Rhodesia. There it led first to the disappearance of the Federation, then to a white backlash which swept away the European liberals, and finally to UDI.

The consequences of the new outlook were seen earliest in the treatment of those Crown Colonies which were clearly destined to have ultimate self-government by the indigenous population. The classic example of the gradual devolution of power had been the Gold Coast (Ghana) which secured 'independence' early in 1957. The last country to undergo this leisurely process was Nigeria which received its long prepared autonomy in 1960. But elsewhere the speed greatly increased. In 1959 most people who thought about such matters at all would have considered Tanganyika and Uganda as needing a good ten or fifteen years before they were fit for self-government. In fact their independence was granted in 1961 and 1962 respectively, and this was to be the pattern everywhere.

Self-determination for the colonies with settled white populations raised greater problems. Kenya was the easiest to deal with. It was a Crown Colony with representative, not responsible, government. The Civil Service, police and armed forces looked to London, not Nairobi. There might be a 'settlers' lobby, but a determined Government could over-ride that, and treat the occupants of the White Highlands as de Gaulle treated the 'pieds noirs' of Algiers. This was just what happened. The Lancaster House Conference of January 1960 marked the moment of decision. Kenya was independent by the end of 1963.

The problem of the Rhodesias and Nyasaland was less easy. Their status could only be changed by repealing a major Act which had recently been passed, after careful preparation and lengthy discussion. To treat the northern Territories like Kenya, and hand over to an indigenous élite meant the dissolution of the Federation, for the African nationalist movements in the two countries were determined to break away from Southern Rhodesia. It would be a drastic step to terminate so soon after its inception an experiment which seemed to have begun so promisingly. Of course the British Parliament had the power to repeal one of its own Acts, but the Federal Government would have every reason to complain of promises broken and pledges betrayed.

On the other hand the preservation of the Federation against the bitter hostility of the African nationalist parties in the northern Territories was not going to be easy even if it was thought to be morally justifiable. In the last resort it meant the use of armed force to suppress them and no British government could view with equanimity the prospect of a series of Irelands in Africa. The Cabinet was thus the victim of strong conflicting pressures; the great majority of the European populations of the Territories – particularly Southern Rhodesia – were determined, if they could, to keep the Federation in existence, arguing that time would bring even greater economic prosperity and thus draw the sting from African nationalism; the African nationalists clamoured for extension of the franchise, political autonomy and the destruction of the Federation. Each side had their allies in London. There was a vociferous Rhodesia lobby with strong

322

support from the right wing of the Conservative Party. The African nationalists had close links with Labour. A general election was due at the very latest in May 1960. It is hardly surprising that these eddying currents and changing breezes caused the British Government to veer uncertainly.

African nationalists in the north opposed the Federation from the beginning. The nearer the date of the review conference, the more determined they were to demonstrate to London their irreconcilable hostility to Salisbury. In Southern Rhodesia the question was at first less clear. If Federation really meant what it said, there were advantages in being part of a Central African State with an African/European ratio as high as 66 to 1. Nkomo and Standlake Samkange, another leading figure among Southern Rhodesian African nationalists, stood as independents in 1953 – though unsuccessfully – for the Federal Legislature. Other Africans tried to influence the establishment from within and joined the UFP which now had delegations from African townships at its congresses.

Some African leaders took a different line, fighting their cause on narrower fronts. Benjamin Burumbo conducted a vigorous battle against the Land Husbandry Act of 1951 – a measure designed to convert communal tenure in the reserves into individual ownership. There was, on grounds of efficiency, much in its favour, but it made no sense without drastic change in the Land Apportionment Act, which never occurred. It deprived the urban African of his prospective stake in the reserves without giving him the compensation of secure tenure in the townships where he continued to be treated as a transient migrant.

Resentment built up in the townships for other reasons too. Segregation meant long distances of travel to work. In 1956 a body called the City Youth League founded by James Chikerema, Edson Sithole (no relation of Rev. Ndabaningi Sithole, the founder of ZANU) and George Nyandoro made the first concerted African effort of protest since the strikes of 1948. When an increase in bus fares was announced later in the year, the League organized a boycott in Harare, the African township in Salisbury. Solidarity was broken by African prostitutes whose earnings at a pound a go not only put them beyond the reach of most black clients, but enabled them to afford the fare for the job. Riot and rape ensued. When the commotion had died away the Government prudently stabilized fares by a subsidy. The Youth League did not die away. It developed into the Southern Rhodesian African Congress with Joshua Nkomo as President and Chikerema and Nyandoro as Vice-President and Secretary-General respectively.

Nkomo, a large, genial, well-educated man, fond of life's pleasures, was anything but an extremist. His formal and defiant inauguration of the Congress at the recreation hall in Harare on Pioneers' Day (September 12) 1957 was a significant sign of the alienation of the African élite. Congress was a movement ultimately intended to remove white rule entirely and substitute a black state based on majority rule. Not that its supporters wanted to expel the settlers. On the contrary Whites were urged to join the Congress Party and one or two liberal eccentrics did. European skills and capital were regarded as assets, but not European rule.

Spokesmen of such a movement were certain to use inflammatory language. Liberal Whites saw their own policies thus being damaged by a white backlash. Even Todd early in 1958 threatened to ban the African National Congress. Events throughout that year contributed to the racial polarization of Federal and Territorial politics, culminating in the crisis of February/March 1959. The changes in the Federal Constitution, the eviction of Todd, the return of Dr Banda to Nyasaland in July, the breakaway, led by Kenneth Kaunda, from Nkumbula's Northern Rhodesian ANC all contributed to this darkening prospect.

At the same time relations between Whitehall and the Federal Government abruptly deteriorated, never to recover. A new franchise of remarkable complexity was designed – or at any rate endorsed – by the Governor, Sir Arthur Benson. He was not the most popular of figures in Salisbury. In June 1956 he had sent to Lennox-Boyd under strict secrecy a devastating indictment of the Federal Government, a copy of which, by means never disclosed, came into Lord Malvern's hands. It described, so Sir Roy Welensky says, 'our "attacks" on Territorial jurisdiction as ambitious and sinister, subtle and insidious'.[2] A constitution with such an author was likely to be ill-received. Welensky had the right to be consulted, but the British Government had the last word.

Harold Macmillan, who had not hitherto been closely involved in African affairs, now began to take notice. 'A great row is brewing in Rhodesia,' he noted in his diary on October 25, 1958, 'partly because of Welensky's character, partly because the Colonial Office and Commonwealth Office are at daggers drawn.'[3] Even so, the British Prime Minister did not know the full strength of Sir Roy Welensky's feelings. On October 14 he had made enquiries from the Federal Attorney-General and the Federal Minister of Commerce about the consequences of 'a Boston Tea Party'. The reply from the former was that 'we would be isolated in a cold hard world', from the latter that 'if we want an all-in wrestling match with the UK, we must not be surprised if she proves that her favourite grip is an economic strangle-hold cum back-breaker'.[4] Whether because of this advice or other considerations, Welensky did not pursue the matter. He managed to secure delay and some minor changes in a Constitution which was finally confirmed by Lennox-Boyd on December 19.

Before the end of the year Whitehead and his Cabinet came to the conclusion that unrest in the reserves and troubles in the townships could only be allayed by the arrest and detention of the leading figures of the ANC. This required proclamation of a state of emergency. The decision to do so was taken before Christmas, but the timing was to be settled later. Early in 1959 disorder broke out in Nyasaland, economically the poorest, politically the most advanced and numerically the least Europeanized of the three Territories. A secret conclave of ANC delegates took place in the bush near Blantyre on January 25. Reports

[2] *4,000 Days*, 70.
[3] *Pointing the Way*, 134.
[4] Welensky papers.

of its proceedings reached the Governor, Sir Robert Armitage and the Federal Prime Minister early in February. These could be interpreted as plans for a sort of St Bartholomew's Day massacre of Whites and 'quisling' Blacks.

On February 20, a meeting of the two northern Governors and the Federal and Southern Rhodesian Prime Ministers was held under the chairmanship of Lord Dalhousie. The meeting as such had no power to act, law and order being a Territorial responsibility, but it is inconceivable that there was no co-ordination of plans. The situation in Nyasaland seemed about to explode. On February 21 Welensky announced that Federal troops were being flown to Blantyre. On February 26 Whitehead declared a state of emergency in Southern Rhodesia, and as a result of a dawn swoop the police arrested nearly 500 Congress leaders, though not Nkomo, who was absent. The timing of this action was later admitted by the Prime Minister to be connected with the Nyasaland crisis and more Federal troops were flown there the same day.

On March 3 at 7 a.m. Sir Robert Armitage, with the assent of the Colonial Secretary, proclaimed a state of emergency in Nyasaland. Four hours earlier Dr Banda and his principal lieutenants had been arrested and flown to Federal prisons in Southern Rhodesia. Twelve days of rioting ensued and order was restored not without casualties; but the total number of deaths was under fifty. On March 10 in Northern Rhodesia, on the eve of Territorial elections, Benson felt obliged to ban Kaunda's breakaway Zambian African National Congress and to arrest him along with his principal colleagues.

These events caused a major uproar in the Labour Party in Britain, backed by the Liberals, the Scottish Church (because of Nyasaland) and even by elements left of centre among the Conservatives. Labour rage had been augmented by the Southern Rhodesian Government's decision to expel Mr John Stonehouse, MP, just before the declaration of emergency in Nyasaland. Much of this wrath was directed at the Federal Government, although the task of enforcing order was a purely Territorial function and Sir Robert Armitage, in his dispatch published as a White Paper on March 23, could not have been more clear and categorical in assuming full personal responsibility.

The Colonial Secretary felt obliged on March 24 to announce the appointment of a Commission to investigate the Nyasaland affair. Its chairman was Sir Patrick Devlin, a judge of the High Court (later Lord Devlin). The report, one of the most controversial official documents of modern times, appeared on July 23. It was sceptical about the 'murder plot' and said that Nyasaland 'is – no doubt temporarily – a police state where it is not safe for anyone to express approval of the policies of the Congress party'. But the Report agreed that 'in the situation that existed on March 3 the Nyasaland Government had either to act or to abdicate'. The phrase 'a police state' reverberated; the offence that it caused diminished the report's effectiveness as far as the Conservative Party was concerned, but added fuel to Labour flames.

As a result of the emergency, the whole question of the Federation became drawn into British politics. Harold Macmillan wished to preserve it if possible, but he began to doubt whether it could survive. He wrote on March 5: 'It looks as if the Federation plan, although economically correct (since Nyasaland is not "viable") is regarded with such great suspicion by "advanced" native opinion as to be politically unacceptable.'[5] He feared that the Labour Party, sorely in need of an election 'cry', might in default of other themes find it 'tempting to concentrate on Africa and Tory reaction', and even pledge themselves to dissolve the Federation. It seems odd today that such a question should appear to either side as being capable of swinging an election. Bloody and brutal occurrences all over the world, not least within the United Kingdom itself, have hardened our hearts and blunted our susceptibilities. The consequences of independence in many black African states have sadly tarnished the nationalist cause. In those days the 'liberal' outlook was more idealistic and the 'liberal' conscience was more tender.

Macmillan resolved to dampen the flames by appointing a wide-ranging Royal Commission to 'advise upon the future of the Federation' and prepare the way for the review conference of the five Governments due to meet in 1960. He hoped that the opposition, Labour and Liberal, would agree to be represented and that the whole matter could thus be lifted – anyway for the time being – out of British party politics. The assent of both the Federal and the Southern Rhodesian Governments was necessary. Sir Roy Welensky was anything but enthusiastic. Prolonged and complicated negotiations followed between him and Lord Home, the Commonwealth Secretary. Eventually a measure of agreement was achieved, but Hugh Gaitskell was not willing to associate the Labour Party with the Commission. The matter had to be reopened with Welensky who came to London in July. There was also a lengthy quasi-theological dispute about terms of reference. Gaitskell had wanted these to include the possibility of secession by one of the Territories. Welensky was adamant against this, and Macmillan agreed, but he did, when pressed by questioners in the House, say that, although the Commission's task was to try to make the Federation work, 'if the Commission thinks it could not fulfil its task to its satisfaction within the terms of reference no doubt it would say so'.

In September Walter Monckton, a distinguished lawyer, an able politician, a skilled conciliator and an old friend of Macmillan, agreed to become chairman. In the general election of October 8, Conservatives increased their overall majority from 58 to 100. Noting that the Liberals, though remaining with only six seats, had doubled their popular vote and for the first time seemed to have taken more from Labour than from Conservatives, Macmillan wrote: 'This may prove important. The great thing is to keep the Tory party on *modern* and *progressive* lines.'

At the end of October Welensky, in the light of a hostile Labour amendment to the Address in reply to the Queen's Speech and of the continued refusal of Labour to take part in the Commission, suggested that the whole thing should

[5] *Pointing the Way*, 135.

be dropped. He only gave way for fear that the UK Government might do what it had the power to do without his consent – set up a Parliamentary Committee to investigate the affairs of the two protectorates. He and Whitehead would have had no say in its composition or procedure and the consequences might be even worse. On November 24, 1959, Macmillan announced the personnel and the terms of reference of the Monckton Commission. The Commission arrived in Salisbury in February 1960 to take evidence and left early in April. Its report was published early in October.

During this gestatory period important events occurred. Early in the New Year Harold Macmillan made his long-heralded journey to Africa. He left London on January 5 and returned on February 15, having visited Ghana, Nigeria, the Federation and finally South Africa where he addressed Parliament in Cape Town and made the speech immortalized by his famous reference to 'the wind of change ... blowing through this continent'. In the Federation he not only held talks in Salisbury with both Welensky and Whitehead, but he also visited Northern Rhodesia and Nyasaland. His first impression of the Federation was 'the sense of uncertainty whether among Europeans or Africans'. He quickly observed a difference of emphasis between Welensky and Whitehead whom he saw first alone and then in the presence of the Southern Rhodesian Cabinet. Welensky was ardent for the Federation. Whitehead was also a committed supporter, but he was concerned with white demand for Southern Rhodesian independence and foresaw grave trouble if the existence of the Federation appeared to be an obstacle. Macmillan also met the leaders of the white opposition who 'proposed immediate independence for Southern Rhodesia to whose territory they wished to add Kariba and the copper belt'.[6]

Macmillan received his most worrying impression of affairs on his two day visit to Nyasaland, and he left feeling that 'the cause of Federation was almost desperate because of the strength of African opinion against it'.[7] This raised the question of the release of Dr Banda. The Federal Government supported by the Commonwealth Office was bitterly against it – particularly while the Monckton Commission was still in Salisbury. Welensky felt confirmed in this view by conversations between Banda and his legal adviser, Sir Dingle Foot, in Banda's prison cell which was secretly wired for sound. The Colonial Secretary, Iain Macleod, was equally convinced that he ought to be released before the departure of the Monckton Commission so that he could give any evidence he wished to give as a free man, not a detainee. The ensuing altercation was so vehement that Macmillan at one time feared that either Home or Macleod would resign, and according to the latter's biographer, Mr Nigel Fisher, the Colonial Secretary would have resigned if he had failed to get his way.[8] In the end he managed to persuade Macmillan. Banda was released on April 1, and had a

[6] *Pointing the Way*, 144.
[7] Ibid., 148.
[8] Nigel Fisher, *Iain Macleod*, 1973, 157.

long talk with Macleod who was in Zomba at the time. The anticipated riots did not occur and it was now possible to treat with the man who, whatever his failings, was the undoubted and sole leader of nearly three million Africans.

Iain Macleod had become Colonial Secretary in October 1959 when Macmillan reconstructed his Cabinet after the general election. The Prime Minister had strongly pressed Lennox-Boyd to stay. It was only the urgency of business and family reasons which decided him to leave – a decision announced in March several months earlier. Although Macleod came to symbolize the process of African decolonization – the white hope of the Blacks and the *bête noire* of the Whites – his appointment was not the result of a deliberate change of policy or a conscious alteration of course. He had never set foot in a British colony and he had expressed no particular opinions on colonial affairs. It is true that he stood in a general way to the left of centre and could fairly be described as a Tory radical, but he himself said in an article in the *Weekend Telegraph* on March 12, 1965,[9]

Those who now study and write about British colonial policy after the 1959 General Election assume that some dramatic Cabinet decision was taken to speed up the granting of independence in Africa and that Macmillan's 'Wind of Change' speech was designed to announce this to the continent and to the world. This is not true. What did happen was that the tempo accelerated as a result of a score of different and deliberate decisions. For myself, some months before the election and before of course I had any idea that I would become Secretary of State, I had convinced myself that for all the manifest dangers of moving quickly in Africa, the dangers of being too slow were greater.

To the Europeans of the Federation all this seemed 'betrayal', duplicity, appeasement, cowardice, loss of nerve and of the will to rule. Sir Roy Welensky's book is full of such complaints, and he regarded Macleod 'this strangely complex man ... probably the most powerful holder of his office since Joseph Chamberlain'[10] with profound mistrust. 'I doubt if we ever talked the same language ... He was subtle and secretive ... To me his mixture of cold calculation, sudden gushes of undisciplined emotion, and ignorance of Africa was perplexing and discouraging.'[11]

Macleod did play his cards close to his chest, and he did indeed have some of the brilliance, charm, deviousness, ruthlessness, eloquence, and emotion which are, rightly or wrongly, attributed to the Celtic temperament. But both he and Macmillan thought it neither right nor possible to withhold black self-determination in Africa simply because white settler communities had become estab-

---

[9] Quoted Goldsworthy, op. cit., 35.
[10] *4,000 Days*, 162.
[11] Ibid., 187.

lished in certain dependencies. The British Government was in a position when it came to a showdown to grant majority rule everywhere except in Southern Rhodesia, and there, as Macmillan writes in his memoirs, 'it was "unthinkable" that power should be handed to the Europeans as it had been in 1910 to the Boers in South Africa'.

There was thus a fundamental difference of outlook which did not stem merely from clash of temperament. The first few pages of Chapter VI of Mr Macmillan's fifth volume of memoirs[12] are a classic statement of the British attitude. He wrote:

It is a vulgar but false jibe that the British people by a series of gestures unique in history abandoned their Empire in a fit of frivolity or impatience. They had not lost the will or even the power to rule. But they did not conceive of themselves as having the right to govern in perpetuity. It was rather their duty to spread to other nations those advantages which through the long course of centuries they had won for themselves.

He cited the history of British rule in India whose independence was 'the culmination of a set purpose of nearly four generations'. And appropriately as the last Whig statesman before the hard dichotomy appeared between left and right, which has characterized British politics since 1964, he quotes Macaulay's *Essay on Milton:*

Many politicians of our time are in the habit of laying down as a self-evident proposition that no people ought to be free till they are fit to use their freedom. The maxim is worthy of the fool in the old story, who resolved not to go into the water till he had learnt to swim. If men are to wait for liberty till they become wise and good in slavery, they may indeed wait for ever.

Would it have been better if British Ministers had been more outspoken, and had spelt out these fundamental divergencies more clearly? Certainly they might have avoided some of the charges of duplicity, dishonesty and false dealing which became plausible, if not entirely justified. It is not enough to cover oneself by perpetual reference to the small print. On the other hand, honourable frankness might have led to a Federal UDI and the consequences could have been even more disastrous than these recriminations.

Events now moved rapidly. Between 1958 and 1960 De Gaulle granted independence to the whole French Empire in Africa. His treatment of Algeria was a particularly ominous precedent for white settlers elsewhere. In the second half of 1960 chaos broke out in the Congo as a result of an abdication of Belgian power as sudden as it was irresponsible. Whites who had been encouraged to stay in order to see in the new regime fled from scenes of

[12] *Pointing the Way,* 116–19.

murder, rape, arson and pillage which lost nothing in the telling when the refugees came through the Rhodesias. A series of shifting and confused campaigns and secessions ensued, reminiscent of the Wars of the Roses. Welensky supported an independent state in copper-rich Katanga bordering on Northern Rhodesia and led by Moise Tshombe whose name to African nationalists later became synonymous with that of Quisling – all the more so when, early in 1961, Patrice Lumumba, the Marxist hero of the left, was murdered after being sent in custody by the Congolese President Kasawubu to Elizabethville, Tshombe's capital. Macmillan and President Kennedy believed that Katangan separatism would leave the rest of the Congo in economic ruins and thus a prey to communist subversion. They preferred to work for a single state through the United Nations Organization – a body for which Welensky had unlimited contempt.

This was another source of Anglo-Federal tension. Welensky now seemed a symbol of reaction to African nationalists everywhere. In September 1961 the United Nations General Secretary, Dag Hammerskjöld, agreed to meet Tshombe at Ndola in Northern Rhodesia, along with Lord Alport, the British High Commissioner, and Lord Lansdowne, Under-Secretary for Foreign Affairs. Hammerskjöld's plane crashed a few miles away and he and all the crew perished. Welensky was freely charged with murder throughout the Communist and the Afro-Asian world, though there is not the slightest doubt that it was an accident. The question of Katanga continued to vex relations between London and Salisbury for the remaining lifetime of the Federation.

Meanwhile Whitehead's troubles had only temporarily disappeared with his declaration of emergency. On January 1, 1960 a moderate African Michael Mawema, who, like Nkomo, had been away during the arrests of February 1959, formed the National Democratic Party – in reality Congress under a new name. In July 1960 a mass demonstration in Salisbury was followed by riots in the townships accompanied with pillage, looting and stoning. Unrest broke out in Bulawayo too. A white territorial battalion was called up, and eleven Africans were killed in Bulawayo, three wounded in Salisbury before order was enforced – the first bloodshed resulting from such operations within the colony since the rebellion of 1896. Early in October there were riots in Gwelo and Salisbury. Whitehead decided to meet the situation by adding yet further repressive legislation to the formidable armoury that he already possessed.

The Law and Order Maintenance Act, and the Emergency Powers Act of 1960 taken in conjunction with earlier measures converted Southern Rhodesia into a police state. Sir Robert Tredgold resigned in protest from the office of Federal Chief Justice. Under the constitution he would have had to adjudicate on appeals arising from the new laws. In his autobiography he writes of the Law and Order Maintenance Act: 'It almost appeared as though someone had sat down with the Declaration of Human Rights and deliberately scrubbed out each in turn.'[13] It is an irony of Rhodesian history that a government

[13] *The Rhodesia that was my Life*, 229.

claiming to be 'liberal' should have enacted legislation so drastic as to need very little amendment by a successor government committed to repression and never even claiming to be liberal. No doubt Ian Smith has added various refinements, but Winston Field and he inherited from Whitehead most of what they required to suppress African political activity.

Of course Whitehead regarded all this as an unfortunate necessity; it is one of the first duties of a government to preserve law and order, and that was naturally the argument used by him and his colleagues to justify ' ie measures. Law and order were restored, though not quickly, and the legislation was accompanied by a notable increase in the strength of the police, which, Sir Robert Tredgold suggests, may well have been more efficacious than changes in the law.

The disturbances and the Southern Rhodesian Government's reaction made an unpromising background to the Monckton Report published a day or two later on October 11, 1960. Copies had already been sent to the principal parties concerned early in September. The report produced apoplectic symptoms in Salisbury. True, all but two of its twenty-five members were strongly favourable to the Federation on economic grounds (which they took for granted after very little enquiry). The problem was African hostility, and, to meet it, they made some sweeping recommendations about the franchise, the distribution of functions, the Southern Rhodesian colour bar, and the venue of the Federal Legislature. These, though far from agreeable to the Federal Cabinet, were not the principal causes of the fury. What enraged Welensky and his colleagues was the suggestion that the British Government should declare its intention to permit secession of any of the Territories if asked after a stated time or at a particular stage of constitutional development. This, the Commission believed, 'would have a very favourable effect and might be decisive in securing a fair trial for the new association'.

Welensky complained bitterly that the commission had exceeded its terms of reference, that a categorical promise had been broken, that the Federal side had given its evidence on the assumption that secession was not in question, and that the proposal to permit it sounded the death knell of the Federation. Any detached historian of the negotiations which led to the establishment of the commission must agree with Welensky on the first three counts in his indictment. There can be no doubt that the commission did exceed the terms of reference which Welensky had agreed as a condition of it being established at all. But the recommendation about secession was not the 'death knell of the Federation'. Whatever Monckton said would have made little difference at this stage.

Already in July 1960 a new constitution had been agreed for Nyasaland. It gave an African majority on the Legislative Council. The European members of the constitutional conference signed the agreement – including those from the UFP. Since Banda was committed to leaving the Federation as soon as Nyasaland became independent, and since the UFP members would scarcely have acquiesced if Welensky had objected, one can reasonably assume that he was privately reconciled to letting Nyasaland go. The country had always been an economic liability wished on the Rhodesias by Whitehall. The trouble was the precedent. If Nyasaland went, why not Northern Rhodesia? It was to be the Northern Rhodesian Constitution over which the decisive and the fiercest battle was to be fought.

The Federal Review Conference to which the Monckton Commission was in theory an advisory curtain-raiser opened in London on December 5. Macmillan was surprised to find that Welensky was meeting Banda and Kaunda for the first time. Duncan Sandys, one of the hardest, most persistent and most obstinate politicians of our day, had replaced Lord Home on July 27 at the Commonwealth Office. Although his relations with Macleod were distant – described by Hugh Fraser 'as being as cold and bleak and silent as between the Matterhorn and Mont Blanc'[14] – this did not make him any the more congenial to Welensky who recognized him as very different from Macleod 'but no easier for me to understand: tenacious of his own point of view, slow to see that of others, dogged and ruthless'. The Review Conference adjourned after twelve days having got nowhere. It agreed to reconvene when the Territorial conferences, which were meeting at the same time to deal with the constitutions of the two Rhodesias, had done their work. To any thoughtful observer of the Federation the writing on the wall could clearly be seen.

[14] Nigel Fisher, op. cit., 164.

24

The Eclipse of Whitehead 1960–62

The Territorial conference on the Southern Rhodesian Constitution moved to Salisbury. All the principal political parties were represented, including the NDP led by Nkomo, back since November 1960 from self-imposed exile in London, and by the Reverend Ndabaningi Sithole of whom much more was to be heard later. Surprisingly, agreement was achieved without too much difficulty and was announced in February 1961. It was recognized in London that there could be no practical possibility of African political advancement at the speed which now seemed feasible in the protectorates.

Sandys acquiesced in a constitution which eliminated most, though not all of the reserve powers of the UK Government in return for a number of safeguards and an extension of the franchise. The Assembly was increased from thirty to sixty-five. Of these, fifty were to be elected from 'constituencies', fifteen from 'electoral districts', the Territory being thus divided into two different sets of overlapping voting areas covering the entire country. There were two separate voters' rolls – the 'A' Roll and the 'B' Roll. The qualifications were similar to those for general and special voters on the existing franchise. Each voter had two votes, one for his 'constituency', one for his 'district'. A system of reciprocal devaluation operated. In 'constituencies', if 'B' Roll votes exceeded a quarter of the 'A' Roll votes cast, they were devalued so as to be only worth 25 per cent in the final count – and vice versa in the 'districts'. In theory there was no racial division. In practice members for the fifty 'constituency' seats would be returned by an overwhelmingly European electorate, and for the 'districts' by an electorate predominantly African, though the Africans thus qualified would amount to only 4 per cent of the adult African population.

The safeguards replacing most of the reserve powers of the UK Government included a Declaration of Rights, ultimately justiciable by the Judicial Committee of the Privy Council, and a Constitutional Council which could 'report' discriminatory bills. Its report could, however, be overriden by a two-thirds majority of the Assembly or, if six months were allowed to elapse, by a simple majority. Neither the Declaration of Rights nor the Constitutional Council could be invoked against laws existing when the Constitution came into effect, e.g. the Land Apportionment Act. In general a two-thirds majority of the whole Assembly was all that was needed for a constitutional amendment, but there were certain entrenched provisions, including the Declaration of Rights and the franchise, which required in addition either a majority vote by a referendum taken separately in all of the four racial groups – African, European, Asian and Coloured – or alternatively, the approval of the British Government.

The precise degree of 'independence' thus secured caused much esoteric dispute. Whitehead insisted on 'the Convention' being put into writing and formally endorsed by the Commonwealth Secretary, but the ultimate sovereignty of the British Parliament could not be abrogated. The White Papers submitted for the referendum on the Constitution did not pretend to cover every aspect and specifically stated that some powers would be reserved. Much play was made by Whitehead's enemies over the subsequent insertion into the Act of Section 111 which reserved full powers for the Crown to amend, add or revoke certain sections by Order-in-Council. This was claimed to go beyond the 'trifling' powers which Sandys said Britain would retain. A British double-cross was later alleged and even cited as an excuse for UDI. Formally Section 111 did contain more than might have been expected from Sandys's description, but the Convention was a guarantee that Britain would not legislate unasked in the colony's internal affairs – a guarantee frequently reaffirmed. The most that the Section amounted to was that Southern Rhodesia could not legally break off her connexion with Britain unless Britain agreed.[1]

Perhaps surprisingly the NPD delegates agreed, if unenthusiastically, to endorse the new Constitution. There was, however, vigorous opposition from their colleagues who had not attended the conference. Kaunda and Banda also expressed misgivings and the London representative of the party, Leopold Takawira, used language of strongest hostility. Nkomo was at first inclined to fight and flew to London to deal with Takawira, but when he returned his attitude had completely changed. There has been much speculation about the reason, and a threat by independent African states to cut off his funds is often suggested. Whatever the truth may be about this, Nkomo now opposed the new constitution with vigour, and insisted that his party should boycott elections held under it.

Sir Edgar Whitehead had promised that the new constitution would be submitted to the electorate for acceptance or rejection. From February till the referendum on July 26 the constitutional question dominated the Southern Rhodesian political scene. The Territorial Dominion Party opposed it strongly as giving away too much to the Africans. Elaborate – and futile – calculations were

[1] James Barber, *Rhodesia: Road to Rebellion*, 1967, 79.

made about the time needed for them to gain a Parliamentary majority. There was no way of predicting it, for enfranchisement depended on African educational and economic advance, which in its turn depended on the policies of a European-controlled government. The reality was that the Europeans could retain their majority for a very long time without setting the franchise clock back by a single minute.

White politicians opposed for a variety of reasons. Ian Smith resigned from the UFP and from his post as Welensky's Chief Whip on the ground that the Constitution was 'racialist' – or so he said. He did not join the DP, but gave support to a bizarre alliance between Winston Field and Sir Robert Tredgold who opposed the Constitution from entirely different points of view, the former because it was too liberal, the latter because it was not liberal enough. Todd's multi-racial Central African Party also came out against the new franchise, and the NDP, now fully united behind Nkomo, bitterly attacked it declaring their intention to hold a private African referendum of their own.

Meanwhile the early months of 1961 – indeed the whole year – were featured by increasingly ferocious in-fighting over the Northern Rhodesia constitution. Strictly speaking it lay outside the purview of Welensky and certainly of Whitehead, but the two Prime Ministers argued that the success of the Southern Rhodesian referendum depended on the electorate's belief in the continuation of the Federation; and that this belief would be shattered if the proposed Constitution would obviously result in an African majority on the Legislative Council.

Central African affairs now became a serious bone of contention within the Conservative Party. Welensky was in close alliance with Lord Salisbury who felt that the Monckton Report had been a betrayal of the understandings on which the Federation was founded. There was a formidable settlers' lobby, and there were the important business interests in Katanga represented by Tanganyika Concessions with its large share holding in the Belgian giant, Union Minière. These powerful elements could not be ignored by Macmillan. They did not in the end save either the Federation or Katanga, but they inflicted lasting harm on Macleod. Matters came to a head in February with the issue of a White Paper which produced a constitution likely to give an African majority on the Legislative Council. Macmillan feared a *coup d'état* in Northern Rhodesia and took some precautionary measures.[2] Welensky claims that these amounted to plans for a pre-emptive air strike from Nairobi, that he was apprised of the danger and that he took corresponding defensive steps.[3] Nothing happened, but a concerted right-wing attack was launched on the Colonial Secretary.

Macleod had a cool reception on February 21 when he announced his plan to the House of Commons, but it was in the House of Lords that the damage was done. Lord Salisbury, who had resigned from the Cabinet over the return to Cyprus of Archbishop Makarios in 1957, was now the leading figure on the

[2] Harold Macmillan, *At the End of the Day*, 1973, 311.
[3] *4,000 Days*, 296-7.

right wing of the party. He was also greatly respected. His carefully calculated description of the Colonial Secretary as 'too clever by half', tying this up with Macleod's skill at bridge which he characterized as a game where two players try to outwit two others, just as the Colonial Secretary was trying to outwit the Whites in East and Central Africa, caused a sensation. There is a strong tradition of courtesy in the House of Lords and it is unusual to make a personal attack on a member of the House of Commons. Macleod did not lack defenders, but the famous epithet was never forgotten because, as his biographer says, 'many people thought there was an element of truth in it'.[4] The Conservative right cannot normally push their own man into the leadership, but they can stop someone they dislike. Macleod lost his chance. Neither in 1963 when Macmillan was stricken down nor in 1965 when Sir Alec Douglas-Home bowed himself out was he a serious contender. Asked in 1970 about his African policy and its effect on his own career he replied: 'I could not have done anything else and stayed in politics. You must just take the consequences of the actions you believe to be right.'

It may be that Macleod allowed himself to be over-committed personally and emotionally to the cause of African advancement. He and Sandys, each backed by the officials of two mutually hostile departments, engaged in a series of wrangles which became something of a bore to the Prime Minister and it was Macleod who seemed the more tiresome of the two. His biographer vividly records the moment when this was first apparent to one of Macleod's closest allies. Macmillan had been accustomed to greet the Colonial Secretary in the lobby with special signs of friendship and enter the House with his arm on his shoulder. One evening early in 1961 Macleod came into the lobby. Macmillan was sitting opposite. 'He caught Iain's gaze and his eyes flickered away.'[5]

The dispute seemed interminable. Mr Macmillan writes:

The niceties and complexities of the various plans would be tedious to describe in detail and seem almost incomprehensible today. In a style worthy of the Abbé Sieyès one formula followed another in the attempt to reach agreement .... It was upon such refinements that at one time even the stability of the British Government seemed to depend. Yet they were to prove but transient phantoms in an unreal dream.[6]

In June a formula was found which appeared to be rather more favourable to the Europeans. It provoked something near to an African rebellion in Northern Rhodesia, but it may have helped the UFP in their campaign in the south. At all events the referendum on July 26 resulted in a conclusive victory for Whitehead who handled the NDP and its private poll with tact and firmness. The votes for the new Constitution were 41,919 and against it 21,846. The NDP's

---

[4] Fisher, op. cit., 171.
[5] Fisher, op. cit., 169.
[6] *At the End of the Day*, 1973, 319.

'referendum' was said to have produced a vote of 372,546 to 471 in the opposite sense. A few weeks later Banda and his Malawi Congress Party won 22 out of 28 elected seats in the Nyasaland Legislative Council.

The subsequent history of the Northern Rhodesian Constitution can be briefly summarized. The dispute lasted until February 1962. By then Macleod had been moved up to the post of Leader of the House in October 1961 and replaced by Reginald Maudling. The final version of the Constitution roughly split the difference between the Macleod plan and the June White Paper, and did in the event produce an African majority on the Legislative Council when the election took place on October 30, 1962. Welensky protested that the change was a fraud on the Southern Rhodesian electorate which had voted under the impression that the June plan was final. Not for the first time he toyed with the idea of a Federal UDI. Just before he left for London late in February 1962 he expressed his feelings to a former British Cabinet minister with whom he was on intimate terms. He was so weary of what seemed to him to be the limitless procrastination and evasiveness of Whitehall that he wondered whether the time had arrived for him to break with Britain entirely and to suggest that the Federation should henceforth go it alone. He reflected on some of the military, constitutional and juridical problems involved, especially the question of the position of the Governor-General. It is hard to know quite how serious he was. The recipient of his letter would certainly have discouraged such a move. Sir Roy himself must have seen the immense difficulties of a UDI for the Federation – Southern Rhodesia was a different matter – and he may have been merely thinking aloud. Despite his genuine anger, he was, is and always has been a loyal subject of the Queen; although he sometimes talked rebelliously he could never have been a rebel.

Whitehead's policy was threefold: 'independence', African advancement; law and order. They were closely intertwined. African advancement was a pre-condition of Britain's consent to 'independence'. Law and order along with 'independence' were preconditions of white acquiescence in African advancement. Apart from these complications, Whitehead was confronted by a white opposition party which demanded European independence with little regard to African advancement, and by a black opposition party which demanded African independence with little regard either to white interests or to law and order.

The referendum result gave the Southern Rhodesian Whites as much independence as they could hope to get within the Federation. Whitehead now concentrated on African advancement, partly because it would contribute, so he hoped, to Federal or Southern Rhodesian independence, but even more because he genuinely believed in it. He pursued his objective with courage, vigour, determination – and tactlessness. He had the clarity and impatience of mind which make their possessor bad at suffering fools gladly, bad at dissimulation, ambiguity and double talk. He was a Chamberlain rather than a Baldwin, an Attlee rather than a Wilson. He left the electorate in no doubt of the direction where he was heading and they increasingly disliked it. He lacked Lord Malvern's gift of covering even liberal measures with a conservative veneer – 'acting left and talking right' as it was once described. Up to a point his policy was accepted. A new Education Act promised elementary education for every African child by 1964. An Industrial Conciliation Act in 1959 removed racial distinction in wage negotiations and made possible the creation of multi-racial trade unions. The higher grades of the Civil Service were opened to Africans, though Whitehead emphasized that it would be a long while before any of them actually got there. Separate counters in post offices were abolished. Discrimination in the laws about betting and the sale of drink was removed. The archaic Immorality Act was repealed. Swimming baths became multi-racial.

More important perhaps than any of these measures was an attempt to deal with land apportionment. In 1957 Todd had set up a commission under the chairmanship of Robert Plewman to investigate the situation in the urban areas. The report is of great importance in Rhodesian history – the first serious effort to deal realistically with the plight of the urban African; but it came out in February 1958 at the height of the political crisis. It was not debated till July and Whitehead made it clear that the Government could not accept all its recommendations. The Legislative Assembly was only invited to 'consider' the report. This is understandable for it was a radical document, proposing freehold tenure for Africans in towns; the removal of all native urban areas into the control of the dominant local authority; African representation on certain key municipal committees; non-racial industrial areas; and the abolition of the pass system.

Whitehead took no immediate action, but later in the year he set up a select committee on the resettlement of natives. Its chairman was Jack Quinton, the Parliamentary Secretary to the Minister of Native Affairs. The Committee produced two reports. The first, appearing in October 1959, dealt exclusively with urban areas and did little more than reaffirm the Plewman Report.

The second appearing in August of the following year was far more sensational. If the Plewman Report was, by Rhodesian standards, radical, the Second Quinton Report was revolutionary. It advocated the total repeal of the Land Apportionment Act. 'Land in general whether urban or agricultural, should be purchasable by anyone, anywhere, irrespective of race or colour.' To achieve this object they went even further than recommending the repeal of the Land Apportionment Act. They proposed that the native reserves (which were protected not by the Act, but by the 1923 Constitution) should also be opened up, on the ground that, if the rest of the country was open to purchasers of all races, areas reserved only for Africans would be doomed to economic stagnation.

These conclusions were the more striking because they came unanimously from a committee consisting of three UFP members by no means predisposed towards repeal and two Dominion Party members who began by being strongly against it. One of them, Stewart Aitken-Cade, had been for a short while leader of his party. He and his colleague, Peter Grey, now resigned from the DP. Harper, the current leader and a hard line reactionary, described the report as 'a sledge hammer blow at European settlement' and declared in the Legislative Assembly that the consequences of implementing it would be such as to make 'Little Rock – look like a tea party at the Vicar's'. The Quinton Report was an unusual example of conversion by weight of evidence; even the UFP members had begun with the assumption that, though the Land Apportionment Act might need amendment, it could not be dispensed with altogether. From now onwards the old argument that the Act was there to protect the Africans lost all semblance of plausibility. Whatever the original motives behind it – and we have seen that they were mixed – no one could convincingly argue in the 1960s that it was anything but the White Man's Magna Carta. This, however, in no way diminished the fervour with which it was defended. The consequences of the Second Quinton Report were to be among the most potent causes of Whitehead's defeat and the demise of the UFP. At the Party's Congress in October 1961 there was unanimous agreement that the Land Apportionment Act should be repealed, and Whitehead made this one of the main planks of his platform for the general election to be held late in the following year.

In retrospect the result of the referendum can be seen as ambiguous; people were voting as much for 'independence' as for African advancement, and the two causes, if not incompatible, by no means automatically went together. But Whitehead and his colleagues interpreted the verdict as the go-ahead for partnership. For the first time in Rhodesian history a European political party made a direct appeal to Africans, and the Prime Minister campaigned for the next election on two slogans – 'Build a Nation' and 'Claim a Vote'. The underlying assumption was the existence of an African 'middle class' willing to find its future in terms of co-operation with the 'liberal' Whites rather than leadership of the militant Blacks. The assumption was not irrational, but it was wrong, and it exemplifies the profound European ignorance of the African outlook, the lack of communication which has always bedevilled the relations between the races in this divided society.

No one can say when, if it ever existed, the chance of assimilating the African middle class disappeared. Todd might perhaps have achieved it, but there is much to suggest that even he was too late. Certainly there was little likelihood of success after the Congress Party had got off the ground. Yet this was not self-evident at the time. There were always some Africans who supported partnership, and their failure to convert others could always be ascribed to nationalist bullying, intimidation and terrorism. It does not follow that fear was the only reason why the African middle class as a whole was unwilling to accept Whitehead's offer either to build a nation or to claim a vote, but the riots and brutalities which occurred both in the townships and the reserves were a potent element in the white backlash soon to transform the entire political scene.

The African nationalist leaders failed to appreciate this danger. They were in a mood of excited euphoria. The 'progress' of the Africans in the northern Territories seemed an example and pattern for their own future. They behaved as if they did not understand the deep constitutional gulf between Southern Rhodesia and the rest of the Federation, and they seemed to assume that the British Government would somehow bring them through to the same destination now in sight for Northern Rhodesia and Nyasaland. This was a profound error of judgement for which they were to pay dearly. The re-assertion of 'the Convention' ought to have been a warning; the British Government could stop things getting worse for the African cause in the colony, but it could not make them get better. Legally, no doubt, Parliament was entitled to do anything. Practically, after the bitter rows over the protectorates, it was certain that no government, Conservative or Labour, would try to legislate for Southern Rhodesia unless asked to do so by the Southern Rhodesian Government.

Whatever the disclaimers of Nkomo and his entourage, there can be no question that violence was a part of the authorized nationalist technique. It is said that the African leader was influenced by a talk with the Duke of Devonshire, then Commonwealth Under-Secretary, in London in July 1961 when the Duke allegedly told him that Britain would never hand over power to the Africans in a country where there was such heavy capital investment, for fear of the political instability which would ensue. Nkomo is supposed to have drawn the conclusion that Britain might take the opposite view if it was demonstrated that even greater instability would result from a refusal to make concessions to the Africans.[7] However this may be – and the emergent militancy of the party's Youth Wing was probably an even more important factor – intimidation, assault, stoning and arson (the most frightening of all crimes in the rural areas with their grass-thatched habitations) multiplied during late 1961 both in the townships and the reserves. These actions were very much an inter-African affair – attacks by the NDP upon African supporters of the UFP or other parties, upon Chiefs and even upon people who were merely apathetic or uninterested. Europeans were in general left alone, but they naturally felt something of the anger inspired among their forebears by the raids of Lobengula's *impis* after the occupation of Mashonaland in 1890.

On Pioneer Day 1961 Nkomo called for a fast to mark an occasion for mourning. At the NDP Congress in Bulawayo in October it was agreed to boycott the forthcoming general election to attack the industrial basis of the 'settler economy' and to use violence at the appropriate moment. There were widespread riots in the Bulawayo townships. When early in December Terence Ranger, the distinguished historian of Central Africa and a supporter of the NDP, addressed a party meeting and urged the case for peaceful methods, the chairman of the Harare Youth Council on the same platform replied that violence paid.[8] Something near to anarchy now prevailed in the rural and many urban areas. On December 9 the Government banned the NDP and took possession of its funds. Troops and police were moved into disaffected areas. The leading figures of the NDP were put into restriction, apart from Nkomo who had a remarkable knack,

[7] James Barber, *Rhodesia: the Road to Rebellion*, 1967, 134.
[8] Barber, op. cit., 135.

not unnoticed by his enemies, of being out of the country on such occasions. Ten days later a new party called the Zimbabwe African Peoples Union (ZAPU) was founded with Nkomo as President (in absence) and Sithole as Chairman. It was really the ANC and the NDP under a new name. Whitehead was strongly pressed to ban it too, but he hoped that it would be less militant and violent; for some months his hope seemed justified, and his harder line over law and order contributed to a state of relative calm.

During the first half of 1962 Nkomo concentrated his efforts on the international aspect of his movement. The United Nations gave him a sympathetic hearing – particularly the Afro-Asian block. He behaved as if he believed that majority rule and 'one man one vote' were just round the corner. In the middle of April after visits to New York, London and Accra where he declared that the people would act for themselves if Britain failed and that he would 'not celebrate another birthday as a slave', he announced that ZAPU would shortly take over the country; it was just a matter of 'straightening up the papers'. In June he contrived to force a debate on Southern Rhodesia in the UN Assembly to the great annoyance of both the British and the Southern Rhodesian Governments which regarded Russian denunciations of slavery as the last straw in the load of hypocrisy – which indeed it was. The Assembly passed a resolution demanding a new constitution to be drafted after discussions between all races.

Nkomo returned in triumph to Salisbury in July asserting that the British Government would be bound to implement the resolution. A new wave of militancy and intimidation now began. Whitehead's reaction was to add even further weapons to the armoury of repressive legislation which the Government already possessed. On September 20 ZAPU in its turn was banned and its leaders were restricted for the next three months to particular rural areas. As usual Nkomo was out of the country, but on this occasion he reluctantly gave way to very strong pressure and returned in October to go into restriction with his colleagues.

A general election was now imminent. It had been intended for October, but problems of defining the constituencies and districts caused postponement till December. It was already clear, however, that the UFP's campaign to claim a vote had been a failure. The nationalist boycott was far more effective, and although there was no doubt an element of intimidation, the boycott basically succeeded because the African 'middle class' simply did not believe that the Europeans meant what they said or that they would ever give up their own position as a ruling caste. It is this profound distrust which has long been a feature of race relations in the colony. It was to be seen again ten years later when the Pearce Commission received a resounding 'no' to the constitutional proposals negotiated by Lord Goodman, Sir Alec Douglas-Home and Ian Smith. By September 1962 out of an estimated 5,500 Africans eligible for the 'A' Roll and 60,000 for the 'B' Roll, the respective registrations amounted to just under 2,000 and just under 10,000. There were indeed African members of the UFP. At the Congress held in November a third of the delegates were black, and

Sir Edgar Whitehead persuaded himself that a genuine break-through for multi-racialism was about to occur. In reality the Africans in the UFP represented little except themselves and, although the Prime Minister was confident of winning at least half the fifty 'A' Roll seats – which, with fifteen 'B' Roll seats virtually in the bag, would give him a comfortable majority – the white delegates too had ceased to represent the majority opinion of their race.

Whitehead was misled by his success over the referendum – it seemed inconceivable that a near two-thirds majority could be converted into a minority within eighteen months – and by the palpable disarray of the Dominion Party which constituted his only parliamentary opposition. Early in 1962 Ian Smith formed a party which during its short life called itself the Rhodesia Reform Party. In March he and a wealthy farmer, D. C. Lilford, known as 'Boss' Lilford – a boyhood nickname quite unconnected with the political use of the word – entered into negotiations with Winston Field and other members of the moribund Dominion Party whose Territorial leader, William Harper, a man with inconveniently out-spoken racialist views, now resigned. The result was the creation of the Rhodesian Front under the leadership of Winston Field. He was elected because he was well-known, good-looking, personable and wealthy (with a large tobacco estate near Marandellas) – in every sense an 'establishment' figure. Smith and Lilford were as landowners also qualified to belong, but they were far less in the public eye. Privately they and some others who voted for Field regarded him as expendable. They had every intention of ousting him if he did not achieve their objective which was independence, to be achieved legally and by negotiation if possible, illegally and unilaterally if not. The new leader was unaware of what was in the minds of some of his colleagues. Unilateral independence was not spelt out at this time as a plank of the party platform, while independence in one sense or another of the word was the slogan of nearly all white politicians. Field was a 'gentleman', honourable, straightforward, not very clever, but equally, not stupid. He had a good war record, he was liked by most people, disliked by very few. He was a sound and competent speaker. On all personal grounds he was a much more attractive leader than Whitehead.

The platform on which he campaigned was preservation of the Land Apportionment Act (though he did not exclude amendment), rejection of 'forced integration' and opposition to 'dominance by the African of the European before he has acquired adequate knowledge and experience of democratic government'. The more extreme statements of Nkomo and other nationalist leaders, the apparently endemic violence in the townships and the reserves, the events in the Congo, the Mau Mau atrocities in Kenya, all contributed to make this seem a reasonable programme. It did not deny for ever the possibility of African political control. That extreme position was to come later. Winston Field encouraged Africans to join the Rhodesian Front, and a few actually did. All that he argued for was a slowing down of political advancement which Whitehead was alleged to be pushing too far and too fast. A great many Europeans agreed, and many of Whitehead's own supporters thought that he was too 'soft' over law and order. There was as yet no suggestion of a unilateral declaration of independence. People could vote for the Rhodesian Front without committing themselves even hypothetically to rebellion.

Whitehead, who had moved well to the left of centre within his own party spectrum, was confident of victory and refused to trim his sails to a reactionary wind which would, he believed, soon die away. But his position was fatally impaired by the attitude of the African nationalists. Their determination to boycott the elections and their ill-concealed commitment to violence seemed to make a mockery of white liberalism. It has been reckoned that after the Second World War about a third of the European electorate was 'progressive' and a third including the Afrikaners was 'reactionary' – the hard core which voted against the Federation in 1953 and against the Whitehead Constitution eight years later. The remaining third on this assessment were 'floaters'. In 1953 and in 1961 it seemed safe to float on the tide of progress. In 1962 that tide had suddenly begun to ebb. There was a new current of opinion setting in a different direction. People were afraid of the consequences of Whitehead's policy.

The Rhodesian Front was a new phenomenon in the colony's politics. Hitherto Rhodesian parties had operated from the top downwards. Their country-wide organizations were extensions of the party in the legislature and only functioned seriously during a general election, although annual congresses were held to preserve continuity and morale. The Front operated from the bottom upwards. The initiative over policy came from small local meetings and opinions were conveyed to the leadership which took care to listen to them. The Front thus made something of the impact that the Labour Party made on British politics in the first quarter of the twentieth century. Moreover, unlike other Rhodesian parties it did not depend for its funds on a few rich individual or corporate subscribers. Most of its money came from a multitude of small donations, and the very process of raising these made for a strong local machine and assisted the Front to win over the 'small man', the clerks, shop assistants, artisans to whom African advancement presented the greatest threat.

All the evidence suggests that the general election was taken with unusual seriousness. Politics had been treated fairly lightly hitherto by most voters. On this occasion the contest was seen – and rightly – as a decisive event which would shape the country's future for many years to come. The campaign was fought with acerbity and venom. Whitehead was ill-advised to use the argument that a RF victory would break up the Federation. Most voters knew that it was already on its way out. The RF had not even bothered to fight the last Federal general election in April, which gave a numerically overwhelming but politically meaningless victory to Sir Roy Welensky. Privately Sir Edgar knew that the British Government had agreed to allow Nyasaland to secede, but he pressed successfully if irrelevantly for silence until after polling day.

The result of the election held on December 14 was unexpected. The Rhodesian Front won thirty-five seats against the United Federal Party's twenty-nine of which fourteen were won by African UFP candidates in 'districts'. The registered Africans were only a small proportion of those who could have claimed a vote, but even among them there was massive abstention on polling day. It was later estimated that if 5,000 more 'B' Roll voters had turned out for the UFP, Whitehead would have won. The boycott was decisive. In that sense Joshua Nkomo was the true architect of the victory of the Rhodesian Front.

25

The Rhodesian Front 1962–63

By the end of 1962 all three Territorial Governments had ceased to support the continuation of the Federation. Secession had already been in principle conceded to Nyasaland, and it was only a matter of time before the coalition Government of Northern Rhodesia under Kaunda and Nkumbula would follow the same course. The Rhodesian Front was less hostile to Federation than the northern nationalists, but they regarded it without enthusiasm. The United Federal Party had been defeated everywhere except in the unopposed elections to the Federal legislature.

In March 1962 policy towards Central Africa had at last been put under a single authority. Weary of the constant bickering between the Commonwealth and Colonial Offices, Macmillan had on the 19th appointed the most important member of his Cabinet, R. A. Butler, as Minister in charge of Central African affairs with a small department of his own independent of the two older departments, but containing some of its ablest officials. In July 1962, the 'day of the long knives', as his drastic reconstruction of his Cabinet came to be known, resulted in Sandys becoming Secretary of State for the Colonies as well as the Commonwealth. Butler became 'First Secretary of State' – a curious and short-lived invention by the Prime Minister, but African affairs remained his field until the Federation was finally dissolved in July, 1963.

Butler wished to preserve as much of the Federation as he could. In his memoirs he tells us that he never supported the appointment of the Monckton Commission, for which the arguments 'were largely couched in terms of our own domestic politics ... In fact a comprehensive enquiry followed by maximum publicity was bound to highlight without solving the Federation's central political dilemma.'[1] As far as Nyasaland was concerned he had no option. On his first

[1] Lord Butler, *The Art of the Possible*, 1971, 209.

visit there in May 1962 he discovered from the Governor, Sir Glyn Jones (known as 'Malawi' Jones because of his deep devotion to the nationalist cause), that in February Sandys, although at that time possessing no jurisdiction over colonial affairs, had promised Banda the right of secession.[2] Butler told Welensky that he found no document in Whitehall to confirm this, nor is there anything in Macmillan's memoirs to suggest that an undertaking had been made at such an early stage. But the truth was that the Nyasaland elections of summer 1961 made secession inevitable if Banda insisted upon it. The most that Butler could do was to hold up the announcement until after the Southern Rhodesian election in December so that Whitehead's prospects would not be unnecessarily damaged.

Bitter exchanges followed between the Federal and the British Governments. Welensky adduced chapter and verse to show that secession from the Federation could only occur with the consent of all the Governments involved, including his own, and he cited pledges by Lords Swinton and Chandos. There was a fierce debate in the House of Lords and Lord Malvern added his voice to those who alleged betrayal. The Lord Chancellor declared that nothing could abrogate the right of the British Parliament to legislate for the Federation. He and Butler caused a White Paper to be prepared, showing 'that no pledge in the literal form expressed by Sir Roy Welensky could be established'.[3] And Article 29(7) of the Federal Constitution specifically reserved the power of the United Kingdom Parliament. If the letter of the law was on Butler's side, the spirit was probably on Welensky's; but the juridical argument had ceased to have much relevance. The political reality was that no British Government could preserve the Federation if two of its three components wished to quit and if the third did not care whether it continued or not.

Nyasaland did not really matter. The crunch came over Northern Rhodesia. Late in March 1963 delegations from that Territory and from the Federal Government went to London. Field was also there on his first visit as Prime Minister to stake a claim for Southern Rhodesian independence. Macmillan noted of Field: 'He seems a sensible man, tough, but not conceited. His other Minister, Dupont (Minister for Justice) is an English solicitor – clever but not impressive.'[4] Macmillan told him that independence could not be settled until the now inevitable steps had been taken for the dissolution of the Federation.

On March 28 the Cabinet decided that Northern Rhodesia must be allowed to secede and that the Federation would have to be dissolved. The disagreeable task of imparting this information on the following morning to the Federal delegation fell to Butler. It hardly seems conceivable that Welensky and his colleagues at this stage could have expected the Federation to go on, but one should never underestimate human capacity for wishful thinking. The scene

---

[2] See *4,000 Days*, 318 and 362, and Butler, op. cit., 211.

[3] Butler, op. cit., 213.

[4] *At the End of the Day*, 325. Dupont became after UDI 'Officer Administering the Government' and later 'President' of the illegal regime.

which followed is described by both the principal participants in their memoirs. Sir Roy describes Butler as looking 'wan and grey', and Butler referring to the description says, 'I certainly felt it'. The delegation was due to lunch that day at Number Ten with the Prime Minister. When Butler had read out his proposed press statement Welensky at once requested him to send a message cancelling their acceptance of lunch. 'I don't want to be discourteous, but I cannot accept the hospitality of a man who has betrayed me and my country.' According to Butler he added that he refused because 'the food would choke them'.

Thus the Central African Federation came to an end. There was to be a conference in June–July at that familiar *venue*, the Victoria Falls Hotel, to apportion its assets, and the formal dissolution did not occur until January 1, 1964. But March 29, 1963 is the day when the wind of change finally blew down the edifice which had been constructed with much care and patience ten years earlier.

The Rhodesian Front Cabinet was unique in that not a single member had ever held office before, and Winston Field, who had hitherto sat only in the Federal Legislature, must have achieved a record by making his maiden speech as Prime Minister. The virtues of experience tend to be exaggerated by those who possess it, and the Southern Rhodesian Civil Service is highly efficient. No doubt errors and gaffes were made which caused mirth among the old stagers, but it soon became clear that the new Government, with one or two exceptions, could make a reasonable showing – the more so since the UFP was badly demoralized and half its members were Africans, often with an imperfect command of English, who had never sat in a legislative assembly before and found its procedure bewildering.

Winston Field's first objective was to secure independence for Southern Rhodesia as soon as the Federation was dissolved. It is clear from the memoirs of Mr Macmillan and Lord Home that the possibility of conceding this was seriously considered in London and that the British policy of refusing independence unless Southern Rhodesia liberalized her franchise was not adopted unthinkingly or without consideration of alternatives. Lord Home writes:

Ought the British Government to have faced the Governments of Northern Rhodesia and Nyasaland with the independence of all three parts [of the Federation] or none.

It would have been possible and perhaps in terms of real politics we could have done so with a reasonably clear conscience, but hitherto when handing over power to another government, we had always done so to a majority; and if there was to be an exception, and we were to pass authority to a minority, we felt that we must take scrupulous care to ensure that the majority would be helped along the road of shared political authority and eventually of majority rule.[5]

[5] Lord Home, *The Way the Wind Blows*, 1976, 133.

347

In his diary on March 28, 1963 Harold Macmillan recorded his impression of the Cabinet discussions which settled the fate of the Federation.

> Southern Rhodesia demands (with a certain show of reason) that if the Federation is to break up S. Rhodesia must also be independent and Welensky will support this claim. Actually H.M.G. have no *physical* power to take any part in the affair. But we have a *legal* position and some *moral* influence. S. Rhodesia is a Government of several million Africans by 200,000 whites. Are we to give this country with this constitution and now under Field formal independence ... ?[6]

He went on to reflect that if Britain did 'we shall be blamed by all progressive and even moderate opinion'. On the other hand, refusal would 'do *no* benefit to the Africans and we shall force S.R. into the hands of S. Africa'. And he ended the passage: 'This will mean a bloc of White power from the Cape to the Zambesi. Is this a good thing or not? These are the questions that pose themselves now.'

Field at this juncture formally notified Butler on March 29 that the promise of independence was a condition of the Southern Rhodesian Government attending the Victoria Falls Conference on dissolution. Macmillan was well aware that a good many Conservatives would sympathize if only because it was unrealistic to refuse something that Britain could not prevent. Thus even at this early stage it seems that the British Government had written off any possibility of using force to hold the colony to its allegiance. Other Conservatives took the line that, even if Britain was impotent, it would be dishonourable to grant independence without a built-in guarantee of African advancement; and no doubt there was always the consideration that, however much the Southern Rhodesians might huff and puff, they might not in the end take the plunge. On April 9 Butler sent a carefully worded reply in which he stated what would have to be done before independence could be granted – dissolution of the Federation, discussion of the period of transition and of future relations between Territories, and the convening of a conference 'to discuss financial, defence, constitutional and other matters which always have to be settled before self-governing dependencies are granted independence'.

The sting was in the word 'constitutional' and in their reply of April 20 the Southern Rhodesian Government, while agreeing that discussions about dissolution might be necessary, pointed out that a promise of independence was logically a quite unconnected matter, and that a new Constitution which provided ample safeguards for all the races had been agreed by the British Government as recently as 1961. The letter ended by saying that, unless Field received 'unqualified recognition' of Southern Rhodesia's right to full independence on the first day that either Northern Rhodesia or Nyasaland obtained theirs, he would not attend the dissolution conference.

[6] Harold Macmillan, *At the End of the Day*, 1973, 327.

In taking this line Field was throughout strongly backed by Welensky. The Federal Cabinet agreed that they would only attend the conference if the Southern Rhodesian Government also did, and Welensky repeatedly pointed out to Field, with whom he got on much more easily than he did with Whitehead, that refusal to attend the conference was almost the only card in Field's hand. The Southern Rhodesian Government was constitutionally one of the two contracting parties to the original Federation, HMG being the other, and it followed that the dissolution conference could not be conducted if Southern Rhodesia was not represented. This argument was not in itself conclusive. It was open to Butler to deal with the matter even if Field did not attend, and his absence from the carve-up of Federal assets could have been damaging to Southern Rhodesia's longer-term interests. On the other hand from the British Government's point of view Field's absence could lead to endless delay, protracted legalistic argument and much trouble all round.

In the end and very late in the day Field, with full backing by his Cabinet, decided on June 13 to go to Victoria Falls, although he had not secured the categorical promise of independence for which he had stipulated earlier. Welensky naturally felt that the Federal Government had to follow suit. On June 24 he wrote to Lord Salisbury:

I think that Field has to a large extent knocked the ground from out under his own feet. I don't know what the real reasons were for it, but on his return from the United Kingdom, it was quite clear to me that he had made up his mind to attend the Falls Conference and there was little I could do about it. I thought at one stage I had convinced him that the only weapon he really had in regard to his own independence was the fact that Butler had committed himself to this Conference and had to have Field and his Government there. I backed him one hundred per cent and made it conditional on the Federal Government attending that Field should be satisfied, but he has faltered, and I think he will pay bitterly in the days that lie ahead.[7]

It is clear that Field's decision was entirely his and that of his Cabinet. The idea that he was pushed into it by Welensky, though often alleged, is false. He told Welensky and the Federal ministers, 'I have played this card of non-attendance at the Conference until the pips are worn off. We are now going.' It is impossible to be sure whether, from his own point of view, he was right or wrong. Sir Albert Robinson, the Federal High Commissioner in London, recalls the relief and glee with which Butler received the news of Field's agreement to go to Victoria Falls.[8] It evidently lifted a weight off his mind, but one cannot for that reason assume that Field could have obtained independence by sticking out. The evidence suggests that the British Government's attitude, after much doubt and discussion, had

[7] Welensky papers.
[8] Private information.

crystallized; it would probably not have changed merely because of procedural troubles however embarrassing.

The Southern Rhodesians duly went to the conference which began on June 28 and ended on July 5. At the last moment it looked as if it might break down. On June 27 Field and Smith had talks with Butler about independence and were dismayed at the terms presented, which included a legislature in which one third plus one were Africans, widening of the 'B' Roll franchise and the gradual repeal of the Land Apportionment Act. Field now began to wonder whether he had been right to come at all, and told Butler that he contemplated withdrawing even at this late hour. Meanwhile Kaunda and Nkumbula were also threatening to withdraw if Southern Rhodesia got her independence on any terms other than 'one man one vote'. Butler could not make that concession, for Field and Welensky would have left at once. On the other hand, he could not or would not grant independence on the existing franchise. In the circumstances he had a tricky task in preventing the conference from breaking up before it even began.

Both Field and Smith subsequently claimed that Butler conned them into staying by promising independence as soon as the other Territories obtained theirs. Smith in 1966 told Kenneth Young, who reports his words in the book he wrote about UDI:

It is a fact ... that we were inveigled into going to the Falls Conference on promises of independence made by the British Government and in particular a definite promise made by Butler. I am prepared to state quite categorically that I heard him say to Winston Field that if we were prepared to co-operate in the dissolution of the Federation ... he would give an undertaking that as soon as the Conference was successfully concluded the British Government would attend to our wishes for independence and that we would be given our independence at a date not later than the date of granting independence to the other two members of the Federation.[9]

Smith admitted that he had nothing in writing, but claimed the support of Field. The latter left no memoirs, but when I saw him in 1968 a year before his death he certainly confirmed the story.

Despite these allegations, it is most unlikely – indeed hardly conceivable – that Butler made a promise of this kind. Neither Welensky, nor the Rhodesian civil servants involved, recall any such pledge. On May 20, 1964 Sir Alec Douglas-Home categorically denied in reply to a message from Smith that any promise of independence had been given. Butler, referring to that reply in a debate in the House of Lords on November 15, 1965, confirmed this denial in the most emphatic terms and he repeats it in his memoirs.[10]

None of this is absolutely conclusive. There were occasions when Butler, Field and Smith were alone, and there can be no doubt that the two Rhodesians

[9] *Rhodesia and Independence*, 2nd edition, 1969, 89–90.
[10] Butler, op. cit., 226.

genuinely believed their story, but, in view of Butler's emphatic disclaimer, the most probable explanation is a misunderstanding. The First Secretary was liable to make Delphic statements, and the two Rhodesian ministers were in a state of high excitement. People say things and believe things over cocktails and after dinner which need to be confirmed if they are to be treated as a considered declaration of intent. If the two Rhodesians were convinced that Butler had decided to make this startling reversal of previous policy, they should have secured it in writing as soon as possible – and in the presence of officials of both sides. It was a point on which Rhodesian ministers had been repeatedly warned by their own civil servants and their failure to do so casts doubt on their version.

Although Sir Roy Welensky had made it a rule, on the grounds of not choking on his food, to avoid lunching or dining publicly with the British delegates, he was less severe in private, and the arrangements for dissolution went smoothly. The details have been described at length elsewhere.[11] The most important feature of the division of Federal assets was that Southern Rhodesia obtained virtually the whole of the Federal armed forces. Welensky had made this a condition of his attendance. All the planes, apart from a few transport machines, went to Southern Rhodesia, also most of the army. As a result Southern Rhodesia had the strongest forces of any country south of the Sahara, other than South Africa. This fact together with the colony's control over the Kariba power stations was to be a crucial element in the decision for UDI.

The Federation was formally and legally dissoved at midnight on December 31, 1963. Lord Malvern, who was asked earlier that day what he thought about it all and whether he was worried, replied, 'No, I shall have my usual whisky with dinner. Then I shall go to bed and allow the Federation to pass away in my sleep.'[12]

There were no discussions about independence between the end of the Falls Conference and the end of the year. The reason was partly the Southern Rhodesian Government's preoccupation with the problems of transition. But, apart from this, the convulsions of British politics, beginning with the Profumo affair in the summer, the trial of Stephen Ward and the Denning Report, and culminating in Harold Macmillan's illness and resignation in October 1963, would have made the resumption of talks almost impossible. In the reconstructed Cabinet under Sir Alec Douglas-Home, R. A. Butler became Foreign Secretary. There was no longer a Central African Department, and Duncan Sandys, who retained his position as Secretary of State both for Colonies and Commonwealth, was now the minister with whom Field had to deal.

The year saw some important developments in African nationalist politics – a split followed by a division between contending factions, which has lasted ever since. It might be thought that a movement as precariously based as African nationalism was in Southern Rhodesia could ill afford a contest of this sort, but one

[11] Kenneth Young, op. cit., ch. 5.
[12] Kenneth Young, op. cit., 94, quoting *The Times*, January 1, 1964.

must remember that the election result of 1962 was regarded by most African nationalists as a clear victory. By abstention they had brought down Whitehead and eliminated his confusing appeal for partnership. There was now a straight fight with white extremism, and surely, so they argued, it was one which the Whites could not win in the long run. But it is unlikely that any of the African leaders foresaw how long the run would be, or predicted the dreary years that many of them were themselves to spend in the timeless ennui of prison or detention in the hottest, most desolate and most remote regions of the country.

When Field came into office ZAPU was banned and most of the African nationalist leaders were in restriction. The Government continued the ban, but lifted the restrictions and declared that it would in future operate through the courts. Nkomo did not accept this olive branch, but his movement lost its steam during the first part of the year, and in April, anticipating either a negotiated or an illegal declaration of white independence far sooner than actually occurred, he removed his executive to Tanzania to avoid the full weight of a government unhampered by Britain. In June, however, needled perhaps by charges of 'funk' he returned to Rhodesia and a new wave of agitation began.

Meanwhile rumours were rife of the imminent formation of an anti-Nkomo break-away group. The rebels hoped to operate within the executive in Tanzania and to depose Nkomo while he was in Rhodesia, but the African leader intercepted some letters which revealed what was being planned, and at a mass rally in Salisbury he denounced four members of the executive-in-exile as the ring leaders of the revolt, including Robert Mugabe and the Rev. Ndabaningi Sithole. He followed this up with a telegram to Dar es Salaam dismissing the rebels.[13] Whatever hope the latter had of ousting Nkomo quietly now vanished and open battle was joined.

On July 15 at Salisbury Airport an African crowd awaiting the return of Sithole, who in the event failed to appear, dissolved into violent strife between the rival factions. This was the beginning of a period of arson, assault, brutality and intimidation comparable to the fearful feuds in Northern Ireland since 1969, though lacking the additional menace of bombs and guns. As in that unhappy land political violence soon became inextricably entangled with personal vendettas and gang warfare. Appalling atrocities were committed, and for over a year life in the African townships was rendered insufferable for ordinary citizens.

On August 9, 1963 Sithole and his associates formed the Zimbabwe African National Union (ZANU). Nkomo for prudential reasons did not attempt to refound ZAPU as a formally organized political party. Instead he set up the People's Caretaker Council (PCC) to guide the political forces which he represented. The split in the African nationalist movement was now institutionalized and the feud between ZAPU/PCC and ZANU, under whatever names, has not been healed to this day.

[13] The other two were Leopold Takawira and Moton Malianga. Three members of the executive remained loyal to Nkomo – J. Z. Moyo, Joseph Msika and Clement Muchache.

The reasons for the conflict are by no means clear. White Rhodesians like to dwell on the tribal aspect. It is true that Sithole is Shona-speaking, and that Nkomo, though not actually a Ndebele but a member of a Karanga tribe, speaks Ndebele and draws a good deal of support from that area. Yet it is now clear that the division between ZANU and ZAPU has never followed tribal lines with any precision. Nor was there any deep ideological difference. Sithole's programme laid slightly more emphasis on socialism, but not so much as to warrant a contest of such bitterness.

The cause is more likely to be personal. Nkomo, amiable, easy-going, fond of pleasure and therefore not fond of detention, was a sharp contrast to Sithole, who was austere, puritanical and very much the stuff of which martyrs are made. Something of the same contrast existed in Zambia between Harry Nkumbula and Kenneth Kaunda. In the struggle to be free Africans, though not all puritanical by nature, are nevertheless inclined to listen to those who are. This was Sithole's strength; against him was Nkomo's power to draw mass audiences, and his established position as leader.

The ensuing battle did nothing but harm to the nationalist cause. The two factions, confident of early African victory, behaved as if the white regime was about to vanish. The Government, which controlled all the levers of power, had no intention of vanishing, and its security forces gained much gratuitous information about African personalities and purposes from the now open and reckless fight between the rival parties. Early in 1964 Field carried legislation which empowered the Government to take the most drastic steps to suppress this disorder. On August 26, 1964 Ian Smith, who was now Prime Minister,[14] banned ZAPU and ZANU. By the end of the year most of the African nationalist leaders were in gaol or restriction. School teachers, the category from whom their potential successors would be likely to come, were forbidden to take part in any political activities. Relative peace descended upon the townships.

Political activists are never more than a minority, usually a small one, in any community. There can be little doubt that the restoration of law and order came as a profound relief to the great majority of urban Africans, but it does not follow, as supporters of the Rhodesian Front argued, that this sentiment was associated with willing acceptance of white hegemony. Many Africans may have resented – with good cause – the incompetence and selfishness of individual nationalist leaders and the violence which resulted from their feuds, but there is no evidence to suggest that they preferred for that reason the rule of Winston Field and Ian Smith, or indeed of any alternative government which might have been formed by the European ascendancy caste.

In fact there was little likelihood of such an alternative emerging. The UFP, which re-christened itself the Rhodesia National Party (RNP), was in no condition to provide it. Whitehead, who had been in government all his life, was an ineffective leader of the opposition. The party was divided between those, mainly

[14] See below, p. 359–61.

European, who thought that it had lost by being too liberal and those, principally African, who blamed it for not being liberal enough. By far the most effective opposition came from Dr Ahrn Palley, an independent member and the only white winner of a 'B' Roll seat (the Highfield electoral district). He was a lawyer of sharp intellect and much courage. He continued as a lone voice harassing the Government long after UDI, and playing something of the role in Rhodesia that Mrs Helen Suzman played in South Africa when she was for many years the only member of the Progressive Party with a seat in Parliament.

The Rhodesian Front gained ground as the months went by. This was shown at a by-election in May 1963 for the Matobo constituency, which had been won by the RF candidate with a margin of only 34 votes in the general election. The 'B' Roll voters, it is true, turned out in much greater numbers for the RNP candidate, who got 192 out of 194 votes, but their support was heavily outweighed by a marked swing to the right among the 'A' Roll voters. At the general election the 'A' Roll voters had given a majority of only 77 to the RF candidate. At the by-election the RF candidate won by 463 out of a total poll that was slightly less.

In September there occurred the first Party Congress of the RF since its victory. There were many signs of the white backlash – attacks on the Argus Press, which had and has a monopoly of white Rhodesian readership and has always been critical of the RF, protests at television and radio reporting, attacks on the University College, regarded as a centre of subversion. In the end the Government was to seize total control over broadcasting, and during the heyday of the illegal regime the quality of the Rhodesian Broadcasting Corporation's programmes was of a degree of mediocrity that needed to be seen to be believed. Curiously enough, however, the Government, after a short period of censorship in the immediate aftermath of UDI, did not expropriate the Argus Press – although no doubt there were many pressures which in practice softened its hostility – nor did it close down, or even withdraw its grant to the University College. Despite a series of convulsive disturbances, despite the hostility of the illegal regime and its minor toadies, the College, later to become the University of Southern Rhodesia, has remained to this day the only important multi-racial institution of higher education in southern Africa.

The Congress was nonetheless symptomatic of much that was to come. The delegates displayed an intense resentment of criticism which they equated with treachery to the country, and much determination to reverse the steps towards African advancement taken, however haltingly, by the Whitehead Government. There was strong pressure for independence, and there were hints that if it could not soon be negotiated it must be taken, whatever the British attitude might be. There was, however, no overt criticism of Winston Field and he appeared to emerge from the Congress unscathed and strengthened.

This was to prove an illusion. The leading figures of the Rhodesian Front were, as we can now see, determined upon independence and they were not prepared to wait for long. Soon after the end of the Congress Field reopened discussions with the British Government, sending Ian Smith, his deputy as Prime Minister and the 'hard-liner' of the Cabinet, to London to see for himself how the land lay. Ostensibly Smith, as Minister of the Treasury, was on a mission to negotiate certain development loans, but he was expected to raise the whole question of independence. He was in London from October 27 to November 7. He saw Sir Alec Douglas-Home for an hour and Duncan Sandys for much longer. He got nowhere. The Prime Minister and the Commonwealth Secretary made it clear that they could not accept the argument that the 1961 Constitution was ever intended as the basis for independence if the Federation came to an end. On this point the British ministers were undoubtedly right. No document to the contrary has ever been produced and at no stage in the public debate about the referendum had Whitehead ever claimed that independence would be granted on the franchise laid down in the 1961 Constitution.

Smith returned empty-handed. On December 7, 1963 Sandys reiterated in a letter to Field the reasons why the British Government would not grant independence: 'The present difficulty arises from your desire to secure independence on a franchise which is incomparably more restrictive than that of any other British territory to which independence has hitherto been granted.' This was a line from which neither he nor Home were willing to deviate any more than Harold Wilson was when he became Prime Minister in October 1964.

There were many reasons for the British attitude, although to most Rhodesians seeing independence go to black countries in their view far less 'civilized' than their own it appeared wholly unjust. The constant attacks in UNO on colonialism was one. Britain in September 1963 had been forced to use her veto for the first time since Suez, in order to stop the passage of a resolution which would have forbidden the transfer of the Federal armed forces to Southern Rhodesia. In October of the previous year the British representative at UNO, Sir Hugh Foot (now Lord Caradon), had resigned because he could no longer support his country's Rhodesian policy. British ministers felt that they were doing their best for an ungrateful colony, but that they could not go further without concession from the settlers.

Then there was the fear that the Commonwealth might 'break up' if Southern Rhodesia got her independence on the 1961 franchise. It was not only a matter of the African and Asian members of the Commonwealth, who would certainly be furious. Even the older white members viewed Southern Rhodesian aspirations with little sympathy.

Twelve years later all this seems slightly unreal. UNO is regarded with sceptical contempt and the Commonwealth is disappearing as rapidly as the Cheshire Cat. But in those days a Conservative Government about to face an election, still believing that victory would go to those who could capture the 'middle ground', and lacking Iain Macleod, the symbol of its 'progressive' wing, who had refused to serve under Sir Alec Douglas-Home, could ill-afford to make concessions to white Rhodesia.

26

The Fall of Field 1964

Early in the new year Winston Field decided to try his own hand at negotiation for independence. On January 24, 1964 he and his wife arrived in London on what was announced as a private visit. He spent a long evening with Duncan Sandys and the Duke of Devonshire who was Minister of State. In notes for the draft of a letter to Ian Smith, he wrote:

> It soon became obvious that their attitude had changed a little and that what was wanted was a face-saver in regard to the Commonwealth ... Sandys' only objection appeared to be that the Commonwealth would object. I pointed out that it was nothing to do with them and that any idea of them attending a meeting to discuss our affairs was out. I think this is accepted now.
>
> We tried to explore what the effect would be if we took unilateral action and declared independence. He said this would make things difficult and that it would not be possible for HMG to recognise us and we would be on our own and so on and so on . . .[1]

The next day Field, accompanied by Sir Athol Evans, till recently one of the top civil servants of the Federation, went to Chequers for talks with the Prime Minister.

> Home very understanding and sympathetic. Admitted their policies had failed in Africa because all too quick. Again brought in Commonwealth reaction. I suggested we should become an independent Dominion and that the Commonwealth was finished anyway and that perhaps a new relationship could be started with the older members.

[1] Field papers, Field to Smith, n.d.

356

As usual this appeared to shock. However I pressed the point that we must have our independence and again Home said they must have a formula which would help to meet the *older* Commonwealth.

I asked if the British Government was going to recognize Zanzibar and how could the Commonwealth continue with Communist countries in it.[2]

The Commonwealth argument came up again and again. In a Rhodesian Cabinet document among Field's papers, dated February 3, 1964, the official who wrote it said:

There was no doubt that Sir Alec was much more sincere in his approach than Mr Sandys ... Sir Alec made it very clear that he wanted a façade as it was a question of presentation to the world. He was quite cynical about this. He felt that, by (a) widening the 'B' Roll (b) making discrimination illegal (c) a gradual fade out of the Land Apportionment Act (d) an alteration of the property/earning qualification of the 'A' roll, he might be able to sell independence to the Commonwealth and the world. The Prime Minister [Field] made it absolutely clear that, whilst he would examine everything suggested, he would not at any time alter the wage and educational qualifications for the 'A' roll.[3]

While he was on his abortive visit Field and Evan Campbell, the Rhodesian High Commissioner, had talks with Harold Wilson and Arthur Bottomley, the Labour 'shadow' minister for Commonwealth affairs. The minute of the discussion certainly does not suggest that Wilson was the rabid proponent of immediate majority rule who was to figure so prominently later in the demonology of the Rhodesia Front.

Mr Wilson's chief interest appeared to be the relative positions of Nkomo and Sithole. He was obviously interested to know whether either of them had a viable political machine ... He accepted the Prime Minister's [Field's] contention that there should be no 'handover' of power and that the acceptance by the [British] Government of the 1961 Constitution really meant a slow evolution of political power. It seems that Mr Bottomley is convinced that the whole problem is one of timing and would be amenable to the Prime Minister's belief that a natural and evolutionary system is better than one of speed.[4]

Field returned to Salisbury with nothing to show for his visit. At 9 p.m. on February 11 Campbell handed to Sandys the Rhodesian Government's reiterated request for independence, subsequently published in Cmnd. 2807 of 1966. Sandys had already seen the contents. 'My reception was to say the least of it cool,'

[2] Ibid.
[3] Ibid., 'Summary of Discussions with British Cabinet Ministers'.
[4] Field papers, n.d.

wrote Campbell. 'I certainly was not offered any whisky nor was I shown to the door as is the usual custom.'[5] Two days later Campbell reported, on the strength of talks with 'old friends like Colyton, Patrick Wall, Lord Hobson, Freddie Bennett and Harwood Harrison,' that Sandys did not want to solve the Rhodesian problem before the general election, believed at that time to be likely in May or June. 'If they lose it will be on Labour's plate. If by some miracle they win, they would then do something knowing that there was a reasonable time ahead of them.'[6]

UDI was very much in the air after Britain rejected Field's plea. Sandys felt obliged to put in writing to the Rhodesian Prime Minister some of the consequences of such action. He also persuaded the Prime Ministers of the three 'old' Commonwealth countries, Canada, Australia and New Zealand to write in a similar vein, and in mid-February Field received letters to this effect from Pearson, Menzies and Holyoake. Field replied defending the case for Rhodesian independence, and at the opening of the Assembly on February 25 he put into the speech from the throne, read by the Governor, language of so strong a nature that both Salisbury and London were full of talk of an imminent breach.

Field's papers show that detailed plans were being made at this time for a declaration of independence and that the economic and legal consequences were being closely examined by the relevant government departments. The economic predictions were not optimistic. 'Unless it can maintain exports at the present level as a minimum Southern Rhodesia can expect to achieve nothing better than economic stagnation,' was the advice in one document; and in another, 'The economy is not at present in a condition to stand *any* additional strains for anything like a long period'. The Ministry of Justice warned that UDI would unquestionably be illegal: 'There would have to be a break in legal continuity with the past.' The paper went on to say that it was vital to prevent the legality of a new constitution being challenged in the courts. 'To this end provision should be made for judges to declare to uphold the constitution and laws of Southern Rhodesia on pain of forfeiture of office.' There should be a fresh oath of allegiance for police, armed forces, officials, etc.

Field, whether or not influenced by these memoranda and by the letters from the old Commonwealth, evidently decided that the time for UDI was not ripe. I asked him whether, if he had still been Prime Minister, he would have declared independence when Smith did. He said that he certainly would not have done so at that particular moment. He might have had to do it in the end, but he would have tried to whittle away the powers – such as they were – of Whitehall until he could have said, 'Now look. What after all have you really got left? Why not concede independence within the Commonwealth?'[7]

Field took no immediate action after his visit to London, and stated on

[5] Ibid., Campbell to Field, February 11, 1964.
[6] Ibid., Campbell to Field, February 13, 1964.
[7] Interview with Mr Winston Field, March 20, 1968.

February 26 that although he was bitterly disappointed he intended 'to pursue any course within the framework of the Southern Rhodesian Constitution'. This taken with a similar statement a month later seemed a clear indication that he was against UDI. On March 27 he said 'I do not envisage any immediate unilateral action by ourselves unless the British Government gives us cause to take such action'.[8]

What followed is still obscure in detail, though the outline is clear enough. Already Field was aware of discontent in the RF ranks. He had received notice of a back-bench resolution to be submitted on March 11 to the caucus meeting. Among other things it asked the caucus, 'to ascertain from the PM to what extent appreciations and plans have been made to decide whether UDI is indeed possible, and to ascertain whether the PM is prepared to lead the country in a UDI should the appreciations show this is possible at a suitable time'. Winston Field wrote at the bottom of the paper 'Leadership is in doubt by myself'.

Events now moved to a crisis. The RF Parliamentary Party – 'the caucus' – decided that Field must go, and on April 3, Ian Dillon, the Chief Whip, wrote, after expressing thanks for his services:

In the light of events, it is with regret, therefore that I have to inform you that the Caucus no longer has confidence in your leadership and has withdrawn its support of you as PM.

I have as a consequence the duty of giving you formal intimation of this decision which was rendered at a meeting of the Caucus held on Thursday, 2nd April 1964, and to request you to make way for a successor.

I am, Sir

Your obedient servant,
Ian Dillon
Chief Whip[9]

Field did not resist this dismissal which was confirmed by the Cabinet, although he could have done so had he wished. Indeed, there was an argument for fighting the matter out in the Legislative Assembly, and it is by no means certain that he would have been defeated on a vote of confidence. But his health was none too good, and there were already signs of the heart condition from which he was to die five years later. He accepted the Party's verdict, merely asking to postpone the date of resignation till Monday, April 13, and he informed the Governor who vainly urged him to meet the House. The delay caused leakages, and on the weekend of April 11/12, George Rudland, Minister of Trade, at a political meeting in Bulawayo actually announced that a secret meeting of the Cabinet had, with one

[8] Both quotations are from Barber, op. cit., 192.
[9] Field papers.

dissentient, decided that Field must resign; this announcement made while Field was still Prime Minister naturally caused a sensation.

Precisely what manoeuvres and meetings took place it is impossible to say on current information. The Rhodesian Front caucus has preserved a clam-like silence – anyway to outsiders – and the matter, unlike the Todd affair, never went to a Party Congress where publicity could hardly have been avoided. Field's announcement to the press was brief and uninformative. He merely said that 'serious disagreements' had arisen between him and his 'party in the House', and that he had been asked 'to retire in order to make way for someone else'. He ended: 'I have therefore tendered my resignation to H.E. the Governor and have advised him to call on Mr I. D. Smith to form a new Government.' Only one member of the Cabinet, J. D. Howman, the Minister for the Interior, resigned in sympathy.

No public statement was ever made about the nature of the 'serious disagreements'. Field said to me on two occasions, 'I never knew why I was deposed'. Evidently the plans for the revolt were well concealed, and it seems that the Prime Minister had no inkling of the blow until it hit him. Writing to Lord Salisbury, Sir Roy Welensky said:

> There isn't a great deal one can add to the Field fiasco. He was a decent enough fellow in himself, but the facts were that he wasn't of the right kidney to be a Prime Minister; basically decent, but short-tempered and not always tolerating fools gladly. In addition, he was leading a party that contained almost every political malcontent in Southern Rhodesia.
>
> The way they dealt with him was despicable. Everybody bar him knew that the revolution was going on and the strange thing is that Smith was so close to him and he was so loyal to Smith that it does savour very much of a night of the long knives the way it was handled. I've just seen Field and he is very bitter. I just don't understand why he didn't fight, but that's his business, not mine.[10]

Although there was the usual talk, as with Todd, about the personal deficiencies of the deposed Prime Minister, it would be foolish to regard these as the reason. No doubt Field was quick tempered, and he had never been liked by a section of the Rhodesian Front who regarded him as an expendable asset after they had won the election. He had also incurred criticism for bestowing patronage on people (like Evan Campbell) who had been on the other side in politics, and for being less of a hard liner on racial issues than most of his supporters. But the real cause of his removal is obvious. He was not prepared to commit himself to UDI, whereas the inner ring of the Front were determined upon it. In Ian Smith they had a leader who shared their views to the full.

The late Lord Malvern, in the carrying tones of the very deaf, once described

[10] Welensky papers, April 24, 1964.

Ian Smith to me at lunch in the Salisbury Club as 'a farm boy from Selukwe [a small town regarded by most Rhodesians as 'the back of beyond'], devious, parochial and suspicious'. Much has been written of the new Rhodesian Prime Minister, both adulatory and condemnatory. He was and is, as Lord Malvern said, a devious character. He has been a master of ambiguity and is skilled in the art of double-talk. He has, of course, had his own hesitations and doubts. But if he has vacillated from time to time, this has been only in terms of tactics. The strategy has always been consistent. Ian Smith is the epitome and symbol of the white Rhodesian ascendancy caste. His objective has never ceased to be the preservation, as long as it is possible, of their dominant position. He has echoed their thoughts and reflected their opinions.

For a long while he was believed by many people both in Britain and Rhodesia to be a front for abler and more ruthless people – if not a puppet, at best a broker or a middle man. There is little to support this notion and much to refute it. The evidence suggests that his own attitude on the racial question – the only one which has mattered in Rhodesia for the last quarter of a century – has never deviated from that of his followers. Indeed, who follows and who leads? Whenever there has been an issue to be decided Smith has always and predictably come down on the side of the most obdurate and intransigent elements in white Rhodesia. This is not because they find him easy to overawe, bully or persuade, but because he is himself as obdurate and intransigent on this subject as any of them – or at any rate he was until, in September 1976, *force majeure* compelled him to alter course.

Ian Smith is a somewhat disconcerting person to meet. One side of his face is rigid and immobile owing to the plastic surgery necessitated by his injuries after a crash when he served in the RAF in the Second World War. His appearance enhances in this accidental way the inflexibility of his attitude. He talks with a slow Southern African drawl which is very marked even by Rhodesian standards. This, too, seems to emphasize his unyielding attitude and apparently immovable determination. He is a capable speaker and an effective broadcaster. People who by no means sympathize with his opinions have been impressed by his appearances on television and his air of reasonableness. Yet, whatever he may say in public, he has always been an implacable opponent of African claims to equality. A contemporary of his at the University of Grahamstown just after the war vividly recalls the passion with which, at a meeting of the Students Representative Council of which he was chairman, he opposed a 'liberal' motion in favour of mixed racial admissions. This outlook has not been softened by his marriage. Mrs Smith, who was the widow of a South African Rugby player, is, if anything, even more of a hard-liner than her husband. No one can say how much influence she has, but it is certainly not exercised in the direction of moderation.

Lord Malvern was right too in describing Smith as 'parochial'. He is the only Prime Minister of Rhodesia to have been born in the country. That does not in itself make him parochial. No one would apply the adjective to Sir Robert Tredgold who was the third generation of his family to be Rhodesian born. But Smith has seldom been outside southern Africa for long, and he has a deep devotion to the country of his birth and to the way of life enjoyed by his white compatriots. This parochialism was almost an asset in dealing with Britain, for which he cared little, on behalf of Rhodesia which he loved. He understood his followers (80 per cent of the white electorate), their fears, emotions and prejudices, largely because he shared those very feelings. He has much more of a *rapport* with white Rhodesians than Todd or Whitehead ever had. But the same quality is a defect in dealing with the outside world. He has frequently failed to foresee foreign reactions and has made bad miscalculations about the consequences of some of his own decisions – for example the closure of the Zambian frontier in 1973 and the 'hot pursuit' into Mozambique in 1976, which was probably the last straw for Vorster and determined him to put pressure on Rhodesia's tottering economy. On a more fundamental issue too his parochialism betrayed him. No one who understood the world of 1965 would have expected UDI to be, as Smith prophesied, a 'nine day wonder'.

It is perhaps this intense 'Rhodesian patriotism' which makes him almost unnaturally sensitive to criticism, although, to be fair, such sensitivity seems to be a characteristic of most Rhodesian Front politicians. I can remember the surprise with which in 1973 I heard him after a dinner party denouncing at great length and in extraordinarily bitter language a RF member of the Assembly, Alan Savory, who had just renounced the party whip and proclaimed himself to be independent. There was something obsessional about the way he spoke. Savory's personal 'UDI' was obviously not appreciated. Yet the RF's strength in a House of 66 was only reduced from 50 to 49, and it seems odd that a Prime Minister, who previously held all the European seats, should have been disturbed to find himself instead holding all but one.

There is as yet no documentary evidence to show why Field was ousted or when Smith decided upon UDI. Perhaps it does not exist. If it does it could well be soon destroyed. One can perhaps hope that at some future date one or two of the principal participants will tell their stories, but the exact details may never be known. It is, however, reasonable to surmise that Smith was installed in Field's place because he was known to be ready to make the decisive break – if it had to be made. This did not mean that he was committed to instant action. He was to be in office for nineteen months before he declared independence. If he could have obtained it legally he would certainly have done so, and he was prepared to negotiate for a long time in the hope of getting agreement from the British Government; for a long time but not indefinitely – and one always has to remember that for Ian Smith negotiation was not a matter of compromise, but of wearing down one's opponent till he concedes all the points at issue that matter.

27

Smith 1964–65

Smith's first step[1] was to clamp down as hard as he could on the African nationalists. The terrorism and lawlessness rife in the townships warranted drastic action and Whitehead did not oppose it. Smith and his successive Ministers of Justice, Clifford Dupont and D. W. Lardner-Burke, exploited to the full the formidable powers which had been conferred on the executive branch of government by the Legislative Assembly during the past few years. The principal nationalists were either gaoled, or put into restriction in places like Gona Kudzingwa, situated in the hot, dreary, remote area of the low veld. Many of them were to be there for over ten years. The most important pro-nationalist newspaper, the *Daily News*, was banned – the opposition did protest at this – and the two rival nationalist parties were declared to be illegal organizations.

Having dealt with African dissidents, Smith now turned to the task of consolidating white opinion behind him. His political position was not on paper strong. The RF had a majority of only five, and if the resigning ministers, Field and Howman, voted consistently against him, it would fall to one. However, the Assembly was not sitting and Smith saw no reason to recall it. He embarked on a speaking tour of the country to revive morale and to put his own personality across to the party faithful. He was highly successful, but he was careful at this stage not to promise immediate independence, dwelling rather on his hope of negotiating a satisfactory settlement with the British Government. As soon as his tour was over he took up the correspondence with Sir Alec Douglas-Home which had been begun by Winston Field. He reiterated the claim that the 1961 Constitution had been negotiated in the belief that if the Federation broke up, Southern Rhodesia would receive independence. On May 20 Sir Alec and his officials pointed out, not for the first or last time, that no such undertaking had

[1] See above, p. 353.

ever been given. The British Government could not grant independence on the 1961 franchise. On the other hand, they would not break the convention and legislate for Southern Rhodesia. The only way to get through the impasse was for the Southern Rhodesian Government to make proposals for a more liberal franchise which Britain might be able to accept.

Smith was naturally dissatisfied with this answer, and he was even more dissatisfied a few days later when he learned that as a result of African pressure he was not going to be asked to attend the Commonwealth Prime Ministers' Conference in July. He announced this rebuff on June 7 in a particularly acid speech. This, taken in conjunction with other strong ministerial statements, caused some expectation of an immediate UDI. Duncan Sandys issued a strong warning in a broadcast, and privately in London allowed it to be known that Britain would treat such action as rebellion and adopt severe measures to crush it. There was serious alarm among the European opposition. Whitehead was strongly opposed to UDI, and there can be little doubt that at this stage he would have had powerful support. He and his party saw the possibility of using the threat of UDI as a springboard for recovery. During this same month of June the RNP Congress passed a resolution assuring the Governor, Sir Humphrey Gibbs, that they were loyal to the 1961 Constitution and would give him their support if he felt he had to take steps 'to prevent unconstitutional action by the Government in power'. The Congress re-elected Whitehead as leader, but at the same time declared itself anxious to broaden its base in the European electorate – which meant a move away from some of the liberal policies that were believed to have contributed to the loss of the 1962 election. Whitehead said that he would be happy to stand down if a more popular leader could be found.

Behind these declarations lay a move to bring Sir Roy Welensky back into politics. On August 6 he announced that he would be willing to aid in the formation of a new party. It came into being a week later, christened in the usual confusing way as the Rhodesia Party. The old RNP was merged in it. Sir Edgar Whitehead stepped down to become deputy leader, but he agreed to continue leading the party in the Assembly until Sir Roy could find a seat. The opportunity came at once. The election of A. R. W. Stumbles as Speaker and the resignation of another Whitehead supporter for business reasons caused by-elections in two of the wealthiest suburbs of northern Salisbury, Arundel and Avondale. Welensky decided to stand for the former and Sidney Sawyer who had been a junior minister in the Federation, for the latter. In Rhodesia as in South Africa the white liberals tend to be rich rather than poor. Mrs Helen Suzman was returned by the most affluent constituency in Johannesburg for many years as the sole Progressive in the South African Parliament. Welensky's chances looked excellent, and the Government took the matter seriously enough to put up against him Clifford Dupont, the Deputy Prime Minister who resigned his own safe seat at Charter. The date of the elections was October 1, and a vigorous campaign with few holds barred began almost at once.

Meanwhile on July 31 Sir Alec Douglas-Home, disturbed by the deteriorating relations between London and Salisbury, invited Smith to go over the ground again in personal discussion. Smith hesitated, but on August 8 decided to accept. He flew to London on September 2. Smith and Evan Campbell represented Rhodesia. The British participants were the Prime Minister and Duncan Sandys, together with Lord Dilhorne to give legal advice and Sir Burke Trend as Secretary of the Cabinet. Smith arrived with the threat of UDI in his pocket. The talks at first proceeded on the old unprofitable lines, but at an unexpected moment Smith suddenly withdrew the threat of UDI. The ostensible reason was Sir Alec's reply to his question whether Rhodesia would be granted independence on the 1961 Constitution if it could be demonstrated that the majority of the population was in favour. The British Prime Minister said that a referendum or some such procedure would be needed. Sandys, Sir Burke Trend and Campbell were then left to draw up the appropriate document for Smith to see. He was mysteriously unavailable. When discovered he indicated doubts, reservations and misgivings – a familiar feature of his conduct of business ever since. The subsequent negotiations, complicated and tedious, resulted in a communiqué in which it was agreed that the British Government would only grant independence if satisfied that the proposed franchise was acceptable to the country as a whole. The British Prime Minister took note of the Rhodesian Prime Minister's conviction that the majority of the population favoured independence on the existing franchise; but he required evidence that this was really true. He would 'take account of any views which might be freely expressed by the population on the issue involved; but he must make it plain that the British Government reserved their position'.[2]

The obvious problem was how to discover these 'freely expressed' views. Smith maintained that it could be done through an *indaba* of Chiefs and Headmen together with a referendum of those entitled to vote. The British Government was not prepared to agree. A referendum would in practice be confined to an overwhelmingly white electorate. An *indaba* was dubiously representative of African opinion. Chiefs as a class had been deliberately depressed for most of Rhodesian history, although in recent times there had been an effort by the Government to revive their powers. A Chief has been described as combining the functions of a parson, a tax collector, and a justice of the peace. These are respectable offices, but one would not regard an electoral college taken from the names on the Commission of the Peace, the list of Inland Revenue Inspectors and in *Crockford* as the ideal body to determine – say – Britain's attitude to the EEC. The Chiefs, moreover, were and are paid by – and removable by – the Government. Another defect was their extreme antiquity. Under the Mashona rules of inheritance Chiefs seldom succeeded to their position until late in life. They tended, therefore, to be both elderly and reluctant to quarrel with the Government on which they depended for income and status.

It is not clear how far Smith appreciated the strength of the British Govern-

[2] Kenneth Young, *Rhodesia and Independence*, 2nd ed., 1969, 155.

ment's determination not to accept the verdict of an *indaba* and to insist on some additional method of ascertaining public opinion. Possibly there was a genuine misunderstanding, but it is also possible that he saw the advantage of claiming a greater measure of agreement than really existed in order to make a plausible temporary renunciation of UDI and cut the ground from under the feet of Welensky and the RP. Speaking in London he made the much publicized statement that Rhodesia had thrown a unilateral declaration of independence 'out of the window for the time being', and on his return to Salisbury he expressed confidence in an agreed all-party solution negotiated with Britain by Christmas. Any careful reading of the documents would have shown that the two Governments were still poles apart. The British had not committed themselves to granting independence on the 1961 Constitution even if Smith could demonstrate that this was acceptable to the people as a whole, though no doubt his hand would have been greatly strengthened; but in any case the British ministers and officials were extremely sceptical as to how such a demonstration could be made, and there was an agreement that Smith would privately put his proposals for testing public opinion to Whitehall before taking any action.

However, in the febrile atmosphere of Rhodesian politics these reservations were disregarded. Welensky's whole campaign was based on the threat of UDI which now seemed a mere turnip ghost. The fight against him was conducted in the most discreditable manner. At public meetings cries of 'bloody Jew', 'Communist', 'traitor', 'coward', attested to the mentality of some of the riff-raff that supported the Rhodesian Front.[3] The two by-elections were won easily by the Government candidates. Ian Smith triumphantly declared: 'This day a New Rhodesia is formed.' In a sense he was right. The by-elections were indicators of what would happen when he held a general election seven months later and won all fifty 'A' Roll seats.

The by-elections marked the beginning of the end for the old 'liberal establishment'. The impetus behind the Rhodesia Party died away in an aura of despondency and despair. In December Sir Roy Welensky, humiliated and rebuffed, resigned the leadership. His successor after a contest with Whitehead was David Butler, a wealthy young Olympic yachtsman who had little political experience. The party still had a substantial representation in the Assembly, but its morale was low and the next general election was contemplated with dread.

Smith had been preparing for the possibility of a UDI ever since he entered office and his announcement about throwing it out of the window had no effect whatever on his plans. It was important to be sure of support – or at least the absence of strong opposition – in three vital areas of public life: the media; the Civil Service; the armed forces.

P. K. van der Byl, who was the scion of an old and wealthy South African family and one of the hardest liners in the party, was made Parliamentary Secretary for Information. Arguing that, because of the alleged hostility of the

---

[3] James Barber, *Rhodesia, The Road to Rebellion*, 1967, 260.

Argus Press, the Government possessed a special claim on broadcasting, van der Byl had before the end of 1964 established effective monopoly control over both radio and television. His principal adviser was an eccentric right-wing ideologue, Ivor Benson, a South African who was genuinely obsessed by the conspiracy theories dear to the Rhodesian Front mentality. He preached the doctrine that an alliance of Moscow, Peking, Wall Street, the BBC and the World Council of Churches was plotting to overthrow the Smith regime. Television and radio may well be more powerful than the press in forming public opinion even in a society where there is freedom for all the media. In Rhodesia, as far as political comment was concerned, broadcasting put out little except Rhodesian Front propaganda, but the Argus Press did not provide a consistent counterbalance; it was not pro-Smith but, under a host of pressures, it was equivocal.

The Civil Service was and is one of the most important supports of the structure of the Rhodesian government. Its top echelon was small, but highly able, and its members seldom missed a trick in the interminable exchange of memoranda, communiqués and statements which constituted so much of the documentary battle between London and Salisbury. One has only to meet Rhodesian ministers to realize what they must owe to the efficiency and clarity of their advisers. But in 1964-65, a question of loyalty also had to be considered. Cautious enquiries were made. Some officials were unobtrusively excluded from certain discussions. Departmental business was conducted on two levels – the ordinary affairs of state and, for an inner ring, the implications of UDI. It was rightly reckoned that most of the Civil Service would accept orders from an 'illegal regime', if only through sheer habituation to the chain of command which stemmed *de jure* from the Crown via the Governor, but *de facto* from the Prime Minister of Rhodesia.

The attitude of the armed forces was even more important. Their Commander-in-Chief was legally the Governor. Sir Robert Tredgold in a speech to the National Affairs Association in July 1964 said that if the Rhodesia Government declared independence, it would be treason and 'it would be the plain duty of every soldier, policeman or civilian to do everything in his power to defeat these actions even by the use of force'. What would happen if the Governor in the event of an illegal declaration of independence ordered the armed forces to arrest the usurpers? The General Officer Commanding in Rhodesia was Major-General Anderson, a loyalist well known to be hostile to UDI. On October 23 on bogus grounds of age – he was only fifty-one – he was retired in favour of a more pliable figure, Brigadier Putterill.

Emboldened perhaps by the by-elections and knowing that a British general election was due on October 15, Smith now proceeded to force the pace. Without any of the prior consultation which he had promised, he informed Sir Alec Douglas-Home on the afternoon of October 14 that he intended to ascertain African opinion by holding an *indaba* a week later. He invited the British Government to send observers, and apologized for the short notice. At the same time he announced that on November 5 a referendum would be held on the existing electoral rolls.

Sir Alec did not wait for the election before he answered. With his authority Duncan Sandys sent a telegram to Smith from the Commonwealth Office on polling day itself. He referred to the London conversations and reaffirmed that an *indaba* would not be regarded as a valid expression of African opinion; for that reason the Government would not send observers since their mere presence might imply that the British Government regarded it as valid.

The general election gave Labour a majority of three. The new Commonwealth Secretary was Arthur Bottomley, a trade unionist politician of the old school who had been Under-Secretary for the Dominions in 1945–47 and had later been on numerous delegations to British overseas dependencies. He was likeable, well-meaning and non-doctrinaire. It is true that he was inclined to be impulsive and had a tendency to drop bricks when he made public speeches. But his approach to colonial problems was empirical and he could learn from experience. Smith might have had much more difficult people to deal with. Bottomley promptly confirmed Sir Alec's reply. Smith had been ill-advised to provoke it. He would, of course, have got the same answer from a Labour Government, but the Conservatives would not have been committed, and in opposition might just possibly have softened their views on an *indaba* or accepted it in some modified form. As it was Labour could justly claim to be implementing a bi-partisan policy on one of the most crucial issues in the whole argument – the test of acceptability to the Rhodesian people as a whole.

Bottomley was due to attend the Zambian independence celebrations on October 26 and proposed to visit Salisbury for conversations with Smith, but he insisted on also seeing Nkomo and Sithole. Smith refused on the ground that both were in gaol for criminal offences; Bottomley declined to go. Wilson then asked Smith to come to London. He in his turn declined on the ground that the referendum campaign was in full swing, but said that he would 'be very pleased' to do so when it was over. At this juncture a spate of rumours of an imminent UDI again swept Rhodesia. The High Commission in Salisbury apparently believed them and the Commonwealth Relations Office felt obliged to take the matter seriously. It was said that the Zambian independence day would be chosen or else the day after the referendum. Wilson asked Smith to make a categorical denial and gave him a draft of the warning which he (Wilson) would feel obliged to publish if the denial was not made. Smith did not reply, and on October 27 the British Prime Minister issued to the world the strongest statement about the consequences of UDI which had so far been made.

Wilson's warning corresponded very closely to what did happen a year later. He said that all financial and economic relations with Britain would be broken off. No Commonwealth country would recognize an act of rebellion which it would be treasonable to assist. Southern Rhodesians would cease to be British subjects. The country's economy would be gravely injured.

In short an illegal declaration of independence in Southern Rhodesia would bring to an end relationships between her and Britain, would cut Rhodesia off from the rest of the Commonwealth, from most foreign Governments and international organisations, would inflict disastrous economic damage upon her and would leave her isolated and virtually friendless in a largely hostile continent.[4]

This was blunt language. It was described in the House of Commons by Sir Alec Douglas-Home as 'rough but right'. In his book *The Road to Rebellion* Professor Barber surmises that it may have delayed UDI by a year.[5] In fact it is very unlikely that Smith contemplated declaring independence at that juncture, despite the plausibility given to the rumours by the dismissal of Major-General Anderson. He had made a particular point of stating that an affirmative answer to the question posed in the referendum – 'Do you want independence under the 1961 Constitution?' – was not a vote for UDI. The Rhodesian Front slogan was 'Yes means Unity, not UDI'. He could hardly, after that, have declared independence on the day after the vote had been taken. Nor is it likely that he would have offered to visit London for further discussion if he was on the verge of making such a move.

Mr Kenneth Young considers that this communication from Wilson, coupled with Bottomley's imprudent appeal to the Rhodesian electorate to 'rally round Garfield Todd, Whitehead and Welensky' and his statement that there was no intention to use troops *'at the moment'*, rendered 'almost impossible a happy outcome by negotiation to Rhodesia's agreed right to independence'.[6] He goes on to say that whereas Smith felt that Sir Alec Douglas-Home was basically friendly to the Rhodesian Government and was only concerned with 'selling' a solution to the Afro-Asian bloc, Harold Wilson and his Cabinet were fundamentally hostile to the whole Rhodesian system. Mr Young's book is a source of unique value as far as Smith's attitude is concerned, for he had many talks with him in the immediate aftermath of UDI. Smith's reaction no doubt was what Mr Young describes.

It does not, however, follow that the Rhodesian Prime Minister's assessment was correct. It may be that Labour politicians were more deeply convinced than Conservatives of the inherent merits of majority rule. On the other hand it may have suited Conservative ministers to dwell on the problem of the Commonwealth if only to avoid endless harangues from Rhodesian leaders about 'civilized standards'. Motives were not the main question. What mattered was the deep division between the terms of independence which any British Government could accept and those which the Rhodesians could offer. No amount of courtesy and polite language could bridge that gap, and it is hard to see what the difference would have been if Sir Alec had won, as he nearly did, the October general election. Perhaps there would have been less acrimony and recrimination, but the discussions would almost certainly have broken down in the end, and the illegal

[4] Quoted, Harold Wilson, *The Labour Government 1964-70*, 1971, 25.
[5] Op. cit., 265.
[6] Young, op. cit., 170.

declaration of independence would almost certainly have been made at about the same time that it actually was. One cannot easily point to any move in the tortuous negotiations of the next twelve months which a Conservative Prime Minister would obviously not have made, nor to any omission which he would obviously have rectified.

Before Harold Wilson dispatched his warning, the result of the *indaba* had been announced. It was held at Domboshawa some twenty miles away from Salisbury and was attended by 622 Chiefs and Headmen. The verdict was unanimously in favour of independence on the 1961 Constitution, but its significance was open to question. Many of the Chiefs did not even purport to be representing their tribes; they were avowedly stating what they thought tribal opinion ought to be, not what it was. Moreover they were palpably in no position to speak for the urbanized Africans, although the Rhodesian Government would have replied that it did not matter since these constituted a minority anyway.

The referendum too gave a clear affirmative to independence on the 1961 Constitution. There was a good deal of apathy. Little over 60 per cent of the electorate voted, compared with 76 per cent in 1961, but out of more than 100,000 voters, 58,000 said yes and only 6,000 no. Smith now maintained to Wilson, though not of course in exactly these words, that the opinions of 622 aged African placemen and the affirmative vote of an electorate numbering less than one-sixteenth of the adult population conclusively proved that independence on the 1961 Constitution 'was acceptable to the people of Rhodesia as a whole'. That Smith did not have his tongue in his cheek and was indeed entirely serious merely shows how remote, unreal and parochial the political world of Salisbury had become. It was most unlikely that any British Prime Minister would accept such a claim.

Smith now suggested that Bottomley should visit Salisbury. Bottomley insisted once again that he must be free to see anyone he wished, and, since Smith again refused to let him do so, he declined to come. Wilson then invited Smith to London, but the Rhodesian Prime Minister said that he saw no useful purpose in a visit unless there was common ground for discussion, and he adverted to a letter which Wilson had written to a Rhodesian African, Dr E. C. Mutasa, a fortnight before the British general election and which had received wide publicity in Rhodesia. It contained the sentence: 'The Labour party is totally opposed to granting independence to Southern Rhodesia so long as the Government of that country remains under the control of the white minority.' Smith, who was to refer again and again to this letter, like a terrier worrying a bone, said he would only come if he had an assurance that this was no longer Labour party policy. The course of subsequent negotiations shows that in fact Wilson did not feel bound by this pre-prime ministerial statement, and in practice before UDI he never pressed for anything more than 'unimpeded progress to majority rule' as a precondition for independence; but it would no doubt have been awkward formally to disavow what he had written. He took refuge in the well-known device of saying nothing. He suggested that, if Smith would not go to London, an all-party mission of senior Privy Councillors who were members of the British Parliament might go to Salisbury. Smith did not reply till after the New Year. On January 12 he refused point blank and a day or so later again rejected an invitation to see Wilson in London.

The deadlock was broken by the death of Sir Winston Churchill. Smith flew out to attend his funeral on January 30, 1965. Harold Wilson tells us[7] that he recommended the Queen to ask him to the reception in Buckingham Palace held after the funeral for heads and other representatives of governments. Just before 2 o'clock, after the reception had been going for over an hour, the Queen commented on Smith's absence. An equerry was sent to find him, and ran him to earth at the Hyde Park Hotel eating a steak. He was brought to the Palace and 'stammered out his excuses to the Queen – I thought unconvincingly'. His excuse was that he never got the invitation, but Evan Campbell told Wilson that it was in his pocket all the time.

Wilson persuaded him to go on afterwards to 10 Downing Street. He insisted on coming in secretly by a back entrance, but he stayed for an hour and a half. 'He was extremely difficult, extremely sour, and not a little offensive about his obsessional aversions.' These included the present and previous British Governments, UNO, the Commonwealth and the independent African states. He did, however, agree to receive a visit from Bottomley and Lord Gardiner, the Lord Chancellor, and to allow them to see whom they wanted. An hour or so later Lester Pearson, the Canadian Prime Minister, called on Wilson and remarking that he had just met Smith observed that it was a pity that Smith and Wilson could not meet. Smith had told him that they had not met and it was politically impossible to do so. Pearson was astonished when Wilson informed him of what had happened. Smith also told Sir Robert Menzies that there had been no meeting, this time claiming that Wilson had refused to see him. 'The whole episode', writes Wilson, 'did cause some little doubt in my mind about the involved character of the man with whom I was to be dealing.'

The Bottomley–Gardiner mission which lasted from February 22 to March 6 produced little result, other than Bottomley's loss of temper on one occasion with van der Byl.[8] Anyone who has met van der Byl will sympathize with Bottomley. Smith did, however, throw out a private, off-the-cuff suggestion about 'entrenched' clauses. He had always opposed the idea of 'a blocking third', i.e. a system in which one third of the legislature could block constitutional amendments and in which at least a third were African or African-elected. He wondered whether 'a blocking quarter' might be better. Wilson in a message of March 29 did not reject this, though he observed that 'we would, of course, have to carry our cabinets and parliaments with us on any solution which might eventually emerge'.[9] At the same time he reaffirmed the general British position

[7] Op. cit., 73–5.
[8] Young, op. cit., 190.
[9] Cmnd. 2807, Wilson to Smith, March 29.

– no intention to impose changes by force or to break the convention, the hope for peaceful transition to majority rule, the unacceptability of the *indaba* as a test of African opinion.

Two days later Smith announced that there would be a general election on May 7. He called for a two-thirds majority for the RF. This was what was needed to amend all except the entrenched clauses of the 1961 Constitution, and it would be necessary if he was to carry the 'blocking quarter'. He was also alleged by the opposition to have other changes in mind – some of them highly reactionary such as the elimination of cross-voting, a legislative role for Chiefs and restrictive amendments of the Declaration of Rights.

One cannot but wonder whether both the Governor and the opposition leader missed a chance here. The Governor's right to refuse a dissolution had always been preserved and it was used by his predecessors more freely than the Crown had ever used it in Britain. The Assembly had another two and a half years to run and, whatever Smith said, the only conceivable reason for dissolving it was to strengthen his hand for UDI. It is true that his party majority was well short of the two-thirds needed to amend the Constitution, but he had never even presented these amendments to the House.

Sir Humphrey Gibbs consulted the Chief Justice, Sir Hugh Beadle who, while not categorical, thought the request probably could not be refused. He then sent for David Butler to ask him if he could form an administration in the event of Smith resigning. Butler told Gibbs that he could not. Curiously enough, however, the interview took place in the presence of both Beadle and Smith.[10] At the very least, one would have thought, it might have been wiser to see Butler on his own and insist on his taking a day or so to make soundings before finally refusing. Butler did not have a majority, but he might have rallied Field, Howman and Welensky, formed a government and put down a motion of confidence calling for independence and categorically repudiating UDI. If he lost he could have appealed to the country on a clear issue instead of the one fudged up by Smith. Of course he might well have lost, but the warning would have been clear for all to see.

Throughout the run up to the election Smith continued to deny that he was asking for a mandate for UDI. The Rhodesia Party naturally alleged that he was being less than honest and that UDI, if not specifically intended now, would be the inevitable result of his policies. On April 26 the Prime Minister's Office, while maintaining the official line on UDI, issued a White Paper with the object of allaying public anxiety about its consequences. The document was extremely disingenuous. Although little has been published of the advice which the Rhodesian Government had been collecting for many months from a large number of commercial and other sources about the economic implications of UDI, enough is known to make it clear that the verdict was highly adverse. Naturally these opinions were given on the assumption – quite correct – that the British Govern-

[10] Private information.

ment meant what it said. The most that the authors of the White Paper could do was to suppress as much adverse advice as they could, to argue that the British Government did not mean what it said, and to dwell on the reasons why that might be so. Their predictions were wrong in almost every respect.

The election resulted in a crushing victory for the Rhodesian Front. It won all fifty 'A' roll seats. Only half were even contested by the Rhodesian Party. Among the losers were its leader, David Butler, and Sir Edgar Whitehead. In the contested seats the RF secured 28,165 votes to the RP's 6,377. The opposition won ten of the fifteen 'B' Roll seats, in each case with African candidates. Five independents were elected, of whom only one, Dr Ahrn Palley, was a European. He now had to fight an even lonelier battle than before. At the end of May the Rhodesia Party suspended its activities *sine die* and divided into two groups. The African members of the Legislature became the United Peoples Party (UPP) led by J. M. Gondo. The defeated Whites formed the Rhodesian Constitutional Association (RCA) which can be regarded as the last feeble flicker of the flame which Huggins, Todd, Welensky and Whitehead in their day and in their way had kept alive and burning. It was perhaps sad and symbolic that even at this last hour 'liberal' Europeans felt obliged to keep themselves separate from a party whose leader and parliamentary membership had become wholly African. Yet, although the 'old establishment' had many shortcomings, it stood for some values which were now fast vanishing from the Rhodesian scene – enough to make it not wholly extravagant to recall the lines:

> Men are we, and must grieve when even the shade
> Of that which once was great is passed away.

28
UDI 1965

The election greatly strengthened Smith's hand. He now had his two-thirds majority in the Assembly. His overwhelming victory demonstrated that the European population was solidly behind him. The opposition was feeble both in and out of the House. Smith could claim a degree of authority which had never been his while he had a majority of only five and owed his premiership to the subterranean intrigues of the Rhodesian Front caucus.

The electoral triumph also had another effect – not perhaps quite so welcome to those concerned with the external impression made by the Front. It released into public discourse all that strange world of fantasy inhabited by such figures as Ivor Benson, Harvey Ward (the Director of News Broadcasts on the Rhodesian Radio), P. K. van der Byl and many others.[1] Theories were propounded about the hopeless and inherent inferiority of Africans and the danger of a world-wide conspiracy against Rhodesia consisting not only of Communists, independent African states and international financiers, but also comprising the Fabian Society, the London School of Economics, the BBC, the American Peace Corps, the State Department, the World Council of Churches, the World Bank, UNESCO and other 'offshoots of the greatest communistic and devilish institution in the world known as the United Nations' – to quote J. R. Ryan, the RF Member for Salisbury Central. it was against this unholy – and, one might think, somewhat improbable – alliance that the Rhodesian Front was doing battle on behalf of 'civilized, responsible, Christian standards'.

Multi-racialism in any form merely sapped the strength of those in the forefront of the struggle. When the Bishop of Mashonaland suggested that a white skin could not in future be regarded as an automatic passport to authority a

[1] See James Barber, op. cit., 281–94, for an excellent account of the RF ideology, on which this and the next paragraph are based.

374

Lieutenant-Colonel Ichabod Allen wrote: 'If the European is ousted from his pride of place, it could only be done by an intelligent race – a requirement that precludes the African.' 'Every Christian knows . . .', wrote a columnist in another context, 'that Christianity itself could not survive without white supremacy.' Even nearer the knuckle was the debate on multi-racial hospitals in the Rhodesian Front Congress held in August 1965 after the election. A Mr Dominion of the RF executive said in despair: 'We will end up being presented with the alternative of going to a multi-racial hospital or dying.' Professor Barber drily observes that 'it was not reported whether Mr Dominion indicated which of these terrifying alternatives he would choose in a crisis'. Many supporters of the Rhodesian Front would not have gone along with the more extreme aspects of the conspiracy theory, but most of them were emphatic opponents of multi-racialism and of African political advancement in the foreseeable future. Such public ebullitions as those just quoted were not calculated to encourage any British Government which was being asked to grant independence on the 1961 Constitution.

Smith was not deterred. If the British Government would not agree, he would not offer any concessions; he would opt for what he had now persuaded himself was the only alternative. Exactly when he and his Cabinet decided on UDI is not known. Even Mr Kenneth Young was unable to extract the date from him, other than the fact that it was long before September 2, 1965 – which Mr Young had suggested as a possibility. On the other hand, Smith emphatically denied that he had intended to declare independence at any time in 1964. In a significant speech on August 13 he said:

If we had decided to take matters into our own hands twelve months ago, it would have proved disastrous. It would have failed miserably and would have been the end of this Government and the Rhodesia we know. Even six months ago, while we had strengthened our case, it would still have been doubtful.

I am pleased to tell you today, if we are forced to resort to such action, not only can we carry this out with complete safety inside Rhodesia, but as far as the external position is concerned we have far more sympathy and support.[2]

The probability is that the crucial decision was taken very soon after the May election. There were two pointers. At the end of May Smith removed Evan Campbell, a known opponent of UDI, from his post as High Commissioner in London. As early as January Campbell had written to Winston Field: 'There is not the slightest liaison between me and Smith; in fact I get nothing from him at all.' In another letter he observed that he was confident that Labour would carry out their October 1974 ultimatum to the letter. Neither the advice nor the political attitude of the High Commissioner suited Smith. He replaced

[2] Quoted in Young, op. cit., 212.

him on May 31 by Brigadier Andrew Skeen, a former regular British army officer, now an orthodox Rhodesian Fronter, who in his own words had emigrated in 1947 to avoid 'the frustrations and discomforts of life in England'. He was fully aware of what was impending and accepted the post in that knowledge.

If the British did implement the October ultimatum – and even Smith must have reckoned that they might – the consequences in Mozambique and South Africa were crucial. If either of them closed their frontiers his position would be most precarious. If both did, Rhodesia would be ruined. South Africa he probably reckoned to be safe. The Government, it is true, would certainly not welcome UDI – on the contrary. But it had to respect white opinion in the republic and a substantial element there would see the white Rhodesians as fellow combatants in a common cause. Portugal too was unlikely to make difficulties, but the country was a member of NATO, there would be pressure from Britain and other allies, and the Portuguese in Mozambique itself, however sympathetic, did not control affairs in one of the few remaining colonies governed from a European capital. Smith resolved to send an envoy to Lisbon. Since Rhodesia was not a sovereign country in external affairs, he had to ask permission from Whitehall. The British Government strongly objected, but he found ways nonetheless to have his representative, Harry Reedman, an ex-minister, accepted in Portugal.

Apart from these two diplomatic moves, there is another reason to believe that by the end of May an early UDI had become settled as the alternative choice for Smith, if he could not shift the British Government on the question of the 1961 Constitution. The fact was that he could at this stage gain nothing by delay, and might well lose by it. His preparations had been made as far as they could be. Now that the right wing was triumphant, he must have been aware of the danger of appearing as another Welensky, a Prime Minister with overwhelming internal support uttering bluster and threats which he nevertheless failed again and again to implement.

There is little point in describing in detail the exchanges which occurred between London and Salisbury during the six months following the election. After the Commonwealth Conference in June, where Wilson with much difficulty fended off extreme demands for no independence before majority rule (not to mention the use of armed force), and after a great deal of correspondence, together with a visit to Salisbury by the Minister of State at the CRO, Cledwyn Hughes, Bottomley on September 21 sent a communication laying down the five principles which would have to be satisfied before independence could be granted. These were:

1. The principle and intention of unimpeded progress to majority rule, already enshrined in the 1961–62 Constitution, would have to be maintained and guaranteed.
2. There would also have to be guarantees against retrogressive amendment of the Constitution.

3. There would have to be immediate improvement in the political status of the African population.

4. There would have to be progress towards ending racial discrimination.

5. The British Government would need to be satisfied that any basis proposed for independence was acceptable to the people of Rhodesia as a whole.[3]

In his letter Bottomley maintained that the Rhodesian proposals so far had not met the requirements of any of these principles. That is perhaps debatable, but it is certainly true that Smith had not met 2, 3, 4 or 5. It could perhaps be argued that he had met 1, since it was true that the 1961 Constitution if not amended would eventually lead to majority rule.

Smith resolved to have a final fling at obtaining what he wanted by agreement – by which, of course, he meant the British Government agreeing with him. He told Wilson he would arrive in London on October 4. The British Prime Minister was not over-anxious to see him. The advice from the High Commission in Salisbury was that UDI was unlikely because of the opposition of the business community;[4] and Wilson saw little prospect of talks getting anywhere. He was right. They were as fruitless as ever. The old questions were again the old stumbling blocks. In the first place Smith would not agree to any device which resulted in a 'blocking' third or quarter of elected Africans who could thus prevent retrogressive amendments to the Constitution. He would agree to a chamber of Twelve Chiefs, but no British Government could accept this. Secondly, he refused to consider any sort of referendum among Africans as a test of acceptability. It is true that such a referendum would have run into genuine difficulties, but the real, if concealed, objection was that any fair assessment of African opinion would almost certainly have resulted in the rejection of the 1961 Constitution – and this Smith well knew.

Before his departure Smith made a very successful broadcast on Independent Television on the evening of October 7. Wilson did not intend to let this happen again. The BBC invited Smith to appear the following night, but late that afternoon Rhodesia House was informed that the plan had been cancelled. It was in fact cancelled as a result of representations from the Prime Minister's Office. Later, in reply to a question in the house, Wilson said he had drawn the BBC's attention to what would happen if Smith announced UDI while he was still in London – about as unlikely a contingency as one could imagine. Before Smith departed on October 12 a communiqué was agreed which said, 'Despite intensive discussion no means has been found of reconciling the opposing views. No further meeting has been arranged.'

[3] A sixth principle was added in February 1966: Regardless of race, no oppression of the majority by the minority or of the minority by the majority.

[4] Young, op. cit., 219. He does not give his source and naturally none of these dispatches have been published, but it is common knowledge that the High Commission was in closer touch with 'liberal' and business opposition circles than with the RF which was secretive and hard to penetrate.

It is a little odd that Harold Wilson should have consented to this statement since it played into Smith's hands in terms of internal Rhodesian politics. He may well have realized this for he seems to have been trying to undo the possible consequences when he broadcast to the nation after Smith's departure. He paid tribute to Smith's sincerity 'even though I disagree with him and even though I feel we are living in different worlds, almost different centuries'. But he went on to assert that differences were not irreconcilable. 'We are not giving up. Too much is at stake.' He announced that he had invited Smith to receive a mission of senior Commonwealth Prime Ministers. 'I know I speak for everyone in these islands, all parties, all our people when I say to Mr Smith "Prime Minister, think again".' Mr Smith had done enough thinking. He turned the proposal down flat. He probably would have declared UDI in the last week of October if Wilson had not insisted on coming personally to Salisbury in a last moment attempt to save the situation.

Wilson flew in on October 25 with a powerful delegation and set himself up at Government House. He saw the leaders of almost every opinion group, the UPP, the Independent MPs, the RCA, the Coloured Community, the Christian Council of Churches, the Council of Chiefs (whom he found remarkably ignorant of the most elementary constitutional matters) and the two African Nationalist leaders. He had talks with Lord Malvern, Garfield Todd (who had just been placed in restriction), Sir Roy Welensky and Winston Field – Sir Edgar Whitehead, the only other living ex-Prime Minister, had returned to England. Wilson also met Evan Campbell, Sir Robert Tredgold and Sir Victor Robinson, Chairman of the Constitutional Council.

By nature equable and good humoured, Wilson was infuriated by the treatment of Nkomo and Sithole, each of whom was flown from detention, kept in a police van in boiling heat till required for interview, and would have had no lunch if the matter had been left to the Rhodesian authorities. Wilson insisted on a square meal for Nkomo. He saw Sithole later and when he discovered that the same treatment had been applied, he lost his temper. His rage was effective and Sithole and his companions were soon sitting down to a three course meal. But even if limited gastronomic progress was made, politically there was a complete impasse. Nkomo and Sithole were adamantly agreed that they would never consent to independence before majority rule – which Wilson knew to be politically impossible. They were no less adamantly agreed that they disagreed with each other on everything else.

Social relations with the Rhodesian ministers were cool. Wilson does not – indeed cannot – conceal a quick mind, a ready wit and the intellectual background of an Oxonian who became a Fellow in Economics at the age of twenty-two. Smith is a farmer, slow of speech, suspicious of clever men. Farmers and dons are not naturally very compatible. As a Scottish agriculturalist Smith got on personally better with a Scottish grandee like Sir Alec Douglas-Home who, though also very quick, can hide the fact if he wants to. Smith probably found it difficult and exhausting to conduct a dialogue with Wilson. One can guess that most members of the Rhodesian Cabinet felt the same. This may be why a dinner given by Smith for his Cabinet and the British visitors, which had been expected by Wilson to provide a chance for serious discussion, was turned by the Rhodesians into an occasion for post-prandial anecdotage. After a very 'blue' piece of mimicry by Lord Graham (the Duke of Montrose), who sat next to Wilson and whose political views were and are extreme, the British Prime Minister made it clear that he was not amused. 'I now understand', he said, 'what qualifications you have to become the Regent of Rhodesia' (a post for which Lord Graham had been tipped by some commentators in the event of UDI).

Wilson formed the impression during his visit that Smith was being 'pushed around by the right-wing, almost fascist element in his Cabinet'. He urged him to ditch them and move to the centre; Smith's prestige, he said, was such that he could easily give a successful lead for a liberal constitution. Smith's reply was equivocal. Wilson came to believe later that Smith was 'to some extent a prisoner of some of the extreme right'. Rhodesian politics are so convoluted and obscure that no one can be sure of the truth. Many of those who have met Smith would take a different view. They would argue that, far from being a prisoner of the extreme right, he has always shared the same general views, even if as a practical man of affairs he rejected its more absurd manifestations and felt obliged to talk in a different and more reasonable tone to a British Prime Minister.

The talks were abortive. Smith continued to refuse a referendum of all adult tax-payers as the test of acceptability. The only new idea was an alternative suggestion by Wilson that a Royal Commission might be set up to recommend the constitutional arrangements by which Rhodesia could move to independence on a basis acceptable to the people as a whole. He thought it might be chaired by Sir Hugh Beadle and have three other members: a Rhodesian (possibly Sir Victor Robinson, the Chairman of the Constitutional Commission); a distinguished Englishman like Lord Butler, Lord Amory or Sir Jocelyn Simon; and a leading Australian jurist to be nominated by Sir Robert Menzies. Although the Commonwealth Secretary and Sir Elwyn Jones, the Attorney General, were left behind to discuss this proposal after Wilson's departure, nothing in the end came of it except an abortive dispute over its terms of reference and authority.

Throughout the whole of the long wrangle since Smith first came to power successive British Governments had eschewed the possibility of armed intervention, even in the event of UDI. The reason was partly the logistic difficulties in mounting the operation, but also the possibility that a repetition of the Curragh Incident might occur and the services would decline to fight against their 'kith and kin'. Yet on October 27 the Archbishop of Canterbury, Dr Michael Ramsey, sent a remarkable message to Wilson in Salisbury on behalf of the British Council of Churches then meeting in Aberdeen. It expressed suitable hopes for a settlement, but ended by saying that if negotiations broke down and 'if you and your Government should judge it necessary to use force to sustain our country's obligations, I am sure a great body of Christian opinion would support you'. This was not a wise communication to send at that particular moment, but it provoked an even less wise reaction in Rhodesia. Over two hundred Salisbury citizens declared that they would burn their Bibles and send the ashes to the Archbishop – not perhaps the most convincing demonstration of the Christian values which white Rhodesia claimed to be defending.

Wilson and most of his entourage flew back on October 30. The last poster which he saw, so he tells us, as he was driven through the suburbs to Salisbury airport said 'Home Rule for Scotland'. UDI was now a certainty. In Britain the officials of various departments were planning the appropriate legal measures. In Rhodesia their opposite numbers had long been preparing the appropriate illegal measures. On November 5 the Governor, punctiliously observing constitutional usage to the last, signed the proclamation of a state of emergency throughout Rhodesia. Sir Hugh Beadle indefatigably whizzed over to London to try to salvage the Royal Commission. It was in vain. On November 8 Smith sent his final message to Wilson before UDI, asserting that their differences were irreconcilable. On November 10 Wilson received incontrovertible evidence that UDI would take place the next day. He tried to telephone the Rhodesian Prime Minister at once, but could not get through till early the next morning, by which time the Rhodesian Cabinet was in session.

The conversation, tape-recorded at the London end, is worth reading.[5] Wilson confirmed that if the Royal Commission, after it had tested African opinion, was unanimous in saying that independence on the 1961 Constitution was acceptable to the Rhodesian people as a whole, then Her Majesty's Government would recommend such an arrangement to Parliament. As a quid pro quo, he said he expected the Rhodesian Government to drop its claim to independence on the 1961 Constitution if the Commission was unanimous in the opposite sense. In that event he proposed that the Royal Commission should be reconstituted with wider terms of reference, but he added words which are of some significance in view of the repeated post-UDI assertions by spokesmen of the Rhodesian Front that Wilson was planning to enforce amendments to the 1961 Constitution, and therefore that UDI was the only option left. After suggesting what might happen if the Commissioners were against the acceptability of the 1961 Constitution, he said: 'This does not rule out, of course, if you want to press this, that the 1961 Constitution continues, but it would not be a basis for independence. That is what we mean by dropping your claim.'

Wilson reiterated the point at least four times. After he had discussed what would occur in the event of an interim report, a majority report and various other complicated possibilities, his final word on this subject was this:

We have never ruled out the *status quo* ... What we are saying is that if

[5] It is printed in the Blue Book laid before Parliament, but is most easily available as Appendix 3 in Young, op. cit.

there were a unanimous report against independence on these terms [i.e. the 1961 Constitution], then if you are still demanding independence we should have to get something that *was* acceptable – we suggested a Royal Commission for that. If, of course, you say you are prepared in those circumstances, having lost the unanimous report, to maintain the *status quo*, without independence, we have never said we would not agree to that.

Wilson said that Beadle would clear up any ambiguities. He was also prepared to send a senior Cabinet Minister to Salisbury for further discussions that very day. He again urged Smith, whom he credited with good faith, to throw over even at this eleventh hour the group of allegedly reactionary colleagues whom Wilson believed to be his evil counsellors. Smith, whose side of the conversation was, like Napoleon's definition of the ideal Constitution, 'short and obscure', largely because he had a heavy cold, gave no ground for hope. A characteristic excerpt went thus:

> Well now, as I said, we are in the midst of discussing this and I take it that it would not be right of me if I do not tell you that the feeling seems to be that it looks as though this thing has gone too far. I would be wrong to say the feeling was optimistic.

In fact an irrevocable decision had been taken, and nothing now could have stopped UDI except total British capitulation. Moving at 10 a.m. from the Cabinet Room to what was called the Phoenix Room, Ian Smith and his ministers signed their Proclamation of Independence, a document embellished with red, green and gold scrolls, and couched in slightly absurd archaic language intended to echo the American Declaration of 1776. It ended, however, with the words 'God Save The Queen' – a futile attempt to dissociate Her Majesty from Her Majesty's Government. The time of its issue was 11 a.m., the eleventh hour of the eleventh day of the eleventh month – another historical allusion, though less obviously relevant.

But, reckless and disastrous as their action was, the Rhodesian Cabinet can be forgiven for making something of it. The occasion will always figure in the annals of history – the first rebellion by a British dependency since the eighteenth century. Whether it will be recorded as a crime, a folly or a misfortune, is a matter for posterity. It will certainly not be recorded in terms of virtue, wisdom or success.

What was it in the end that drove the white Rhodesians into an act which was on any view fraught with great risks and whose consequences were unpredictable? In spite of all that was said and written at the time and since, the answer is by no means clear. There was undoubtedly a deep sense of grievance that Southern Rhodesia was not treated after the end of the Federation on the same basis as the colonies which became Zambia and Malawi. A great many

Rhodesians persuaded themselves quite genuinely that a promise of independence on the 1961 Constitution had been made and subsequently withdrawn, although there is no substance at all in the claim and no one has ever been able to produce any evidence of its validity.

Whether Britain ought to have conceded independence is another matter. Morally it would not have been easy, but governments are – and have to be – actuated by expediency as often as by morality. We have seen that neither Harold Macmillan nor Sir Alec Douglas-Home ruled out the idea altogether. If either of them had believed that refusal would involve the certainty or even high probability of UDI, their decisions might perhaps have been different. One could certainly make a strong case for avoiding at almost any price the humiliating situation of responsibility without power in which Britain has found herself ever since 1965. It has been alleged that the Commonwealth Relations Office in briefing the Cabinet under-estimated the danger of UDI and over-estimated later the easiness of bringing it to an end. One cannot know without seeing the documents and these will not become available to historians until 1995. Whatever the truth may be about the advice received, the British Government, having taken a clear decision early in 1963, would have had great difficulty in going back on it thereafter.

The Rhodesians naturally did not see the matter in that light, but even so what had they to gain by declaring independence illegally? They had governed themselves internally for all practical purposes since 1923. Although it may have suited some politicians to pretend otherwise, no Rhodesian who understood the Constitution could have imagined that the British Government would break the Convention and pass an Act extending the franchise, unless asked to do so by the Rhodesian Government. Harold Wilson made it clear again and again. There was nothing to stop Rhodesia continuing on the basis of the 1961 Constitution; according to Lord Malvern and the 'Old Hands' this was what Smith ought to have done. If Britain ever did try to enforce a major change in the franchise – and it is true that there was constant Afro-Asian pressure at UN and elsewhere upon her to do so – that would be the moment for a declaration of independence which would unite the whole of white Rhodesia.

On the Malvern view, UDI becomes a piece of madness, a sort of collective rush of blood to the head, which cannot be explained by rational means at all. One should not reject this explanation out of hand. Countries can behave like this. There was a feverish atmosphere in the colony at the time, a deep sense of frustration and a feeling of injustice. The mere existence of a Labour Government exacerbated the situation even though it is unlikely that a Conservative Prime Minister would have played his hand very differently. Among the Labour Party were some of the strongest supporters in Britain of African rights and some of the strongest opponents of the white regime. This should not be forgotten by anyone trying to analyse the reasons for UDI. The Labour Party was deeply distrusted by white Rhodesians and there was no lack of extreme statements which could be pulled out of files of press cuttings to substantiate this distrust. And it is true that the middle-class left-wing intellectuals who at that time formed much of Labour opinion on colonial matters felt a particular lack of sympathy with the rich, philistine, sport-addicted, war-experienced 'hearties' who, as it seemed to them, set the tone of white Rhodesian life – a sentiment that was vigorously reciprocated. To use a schoolboy analogy appropriately archaic, there was an element of 'swots' against 'bloods' and vice versa, translated into adult politics.

My first visit to Rhodesia was in 1968. By then attitudes had hardened, and all sorts of *ex post facto* explanations were rife. I found it almost impossible to extract any logical reasons for UDI from the many members of the Rhodesian Front or its sympathizers who were kind enough to listen to my questions. I was told again and again that there was 'no alternative'. From politeness I forebore to say that there was a perfectly simple one, viz. to do nothing. Dark hints were uttered about Wilson's ulterior intentions. I was told in hushed confidential tones by a minister that the Cabinet had reason to believe that the Labour Government intended to legislate for majority rule. 'Why not wait till they began?' I asked. 'Ah, but by then it would be too late,' was the reply.

There is something to be said for examining what people do as well as what they say, and one can begin by looking at the new (1965) Constitution promulgated on the same day as the Declaration of Independence. At first glance it looks like the 1961 Constitution with the obvious amendments involved in severing ties with Britain (though not the British monarchy) – an Officer Administering the Government instead of a Governor, removal of appeal to the Judicial Committee of the Privy Council, the substitution of 'Parliament' for 'Legislative Assembly', 'Rhodesia' for 'Southern Rhodesia', etc. Such vital features as the composition of the Legislature, the franchise, the Declaration of Rights, the Constitutional Council were left much as they were.

A closer examination reveals, however, a fundamental change which could never have been achieved under the *status quo*. The provisions of the 1961 Constitution were in general amendable by a two-thirds majority of the Legislative Assembly, but there were certain entrenched clauses which in addition required either Her Majesty's assent (i.e. that of the British Government) or concurrent majority votes in a referendum taken separately among each of the four racial communities – African, European, Asian and Coloured. In the case of the last three groups those qualified to vote were the same as those qualified to vote on the 'A' and 'B' Rolls in elections for the Legislative Assembly, but there was a significant difference in regard to Africans. The Constitution laid it down that, until the number of Africans registered on the 'A' and 'B' Rolls reached 50,000, all Africans over twenty-one and able to show that they had completed a course of primary education of a prescribed standard would be entitled to vote in a referendum. The number of Africans registered on the 'A' and 'B' Rolls combined was just over 13,000 in 1965 ('A' Roll 2,330, 'B' Roll 10,689). Since the British Government was entitled to decline to give a decision on a proposed amendment if they thought a referendum more appropriate, the effect of these provisions was to give primary-educated adult Africans an effective veto on any proposals which restricted the franchise or affected the Declaration of Rights, appeals to the Privy Council, the Constitutional Council, the Judiciary and the provisions governing the amendment of the Constitution itself.

This feature of the 1961 Constitution had always been disliked by the Rhodesian Front. It was removed by the new Constitution which abolished the whole concept of specially entrenched clauses and provided that any amendment could be made to the Constitution as long as it received an affirmative vote of two-thirds of the members of 'Parliament'. Since the Rhodesian Front had a majority of over three-quarters, they were in a position to make all the changes they wished. As Sir Robert Tredgold observes, 'this is equivalent to drawing up a long, elaborate, and solemn agreement and then inserting at the end a clause giving one of the parties the right to alter it at will.'[6] Smith's critics from among the old establishment were quite right to say that the Declaration of Independence was madness if it was being made in order to prevent Britain forcing the pace of African advancement. They did not sufficiently appreciate that there might be method in the madness if the real object of the Front was not just to preserve the *status quo*, but actually to put the clock back. That indeed was what Smith did four years later. The avowedly racialist Constitution of 1969 which in his own words sounded 'the death-knell of majority rule' could not have been legally enacted under the provisions of the 1961 Constitution. If all along the unavowed purpose of the Rhodesian Front had been to introduce a form of apartheid, insofar as this was practical in Rhodesian circumstances, then UDI was an essential preliminary. Events during the next few years were to suggest more and more strongly that this was indeed the basic objective of Smith and the forces behind him.

[6] Op. cit., 243.

Epilogue 1965-77

At the time of writing (June 1977) over eleven years have gone by since UDI. The prospect for Rhodesians of all races has never been darker and more dangerous. Although this book was designed as a history of 'Southern' Rhodesia and to end with the events of November 11, 1965, it may be worth tracing what has happened since – always with the reservation that much is clouded in the secrecy of a cold war, and that it may be many years before the full truth emerges, if indeed it ever does.

There is no need to spend much time on the immediate legal and constitutional measures taken by each side. The moment UDI was declared Sir Humphrey Gibbs dismissed Smith and his Cabinet in accordance with long-standing instructions from London. Legally he was now the Southern Rhodesian Government and his position was confirmed by an Enabling Act of the UK Parliament. Ought the Governor's powers to have been invoked earlier? The question of refusing a dissolution to Smith earlier in the year was discussed in a previous chapter. The possibility of dismissing Smith at some stage between then and November must have been considered. In Australia in 1975 the Governor-General, rightly not consulting anyone in London, dismissed the Prime Minister – whether wisely or unwisely will be long debated. He acted entirely on his own initiative and there could have been no question of instructions or even advice from the British Cabinet. The Governor of Southern Rhodesia was not in the same position as the Governor-General of a Commonwealth Monarchy;[1] and such action could scarcely have been undertaken unless he had received specific orders from the Crown, i.e. in effect the British Government. They were not given – probably because of a fear that they would provide a

[1] See Claire Palley, *Constitutional History and Law of Southern Rhodesia 1888–1965*, 1966, 719–24, for the position and powers of the Governor.

plausible excuse for UDI – which was just what Wilson wished to avoid.

The Rhodesian Government's riposte to its dismissal was to proclaim the new Constitution, substituting an Officer Administering the Government (OAG) upon whom were conferred all and more than all the powers of the Governor. An impudent attempt was made to approach the Queen direct and ask her to appoint the OAG, but the letter was at once forwarded to the Commonwealth Office. The person appointed was Clifford Dupont, previously Deputy Prime Minister. Under the 1969 Constitution he was to become Rhodesia's first President. A clever London Solicitor, who emigrated to Southern Rhodesia in the late 1940s, Dupont was the archetypal refugee from the bleakness and restrictions of post-war Britain. He and many others who did the same thing developed more and more of an anti-British chip on their shoulders as the Empire began to crumble and the sunny world to which they had escaped to make their fortunes began to be menaced by alien shadows and incomprehensible forces. He was one of the prime architects of the Rhodesian Front and only those in the know can tell whether he or Smith played the greater part in its construction.

Sir Humphrey Gibbs was asked to resign and to vacate Government House. He would gladly have done both, but he refused, in accordance with instructions from London where it was felt that he could still be a link in restoring legality. His salary, car, and telephone were cut off, but no further action was taken. Funds privately subscribed enabled him to keep up something of the style of the old days. It was a moving experience to dine at Government House – black tie, ADCs, etc. – and to drink the toast to the Queen with a sense of its significance which does not always impinge at banquets in Britain. For the Governor, living in a sort of ghostly world, it was not a happy life. He was virtually confined to his house and grounds, not because of any restrictions by the Rhodesian authorities, but for fear of the action that might be taken in his absence. He had no power and little to do, although he must have been cheered by the number of loyalists who 'signed the book' at Government House. Sir Hugh Beadle, still at that time on the side of legality, deemed it his duty to take up residence there too, though he continued to deal with his normal judicial business in the High Court. The relations between two people without much in common obliged to see each other every day for months on end usually become slightly strained, and the situation in Government House was no exception. Sir Hugh was and is an irrepressible, bouncy extrovert, who does not always perceive the reaction which he causes in others. Sir Humphrey Gibbs remained loyally at his post. At the end of November he was made a Knight Commander of the Royal Victorian Order (KCVO), one of the few honours within the Queen's personal gift. It was a clear rebuff to the Rhodesian Government's effort to divide the Queen from the Queen's Government.

There can be no doubt that the leaders of the illegal regime saw the Governor as one of the few threats to their continuance in power, which in other respects seemed surprisingly secure. They spared nothing in the way of innuendo and abuse against him. A particularly absurd canard was a story put about on the Rhodesian Radio that he had close links with the Labour Party in England. To anyone who knew the Gibbs family background this was not very likely; Sir Humphrey is a younger son of the 3rd Lord Aldenham, and uncle of the present peer. His brother, the late Sir Geoffrey Gibbs, was a leading figure in the City. Anthony Gibbs and Company is a famous merchant banking firm with a long history behind it. Establishment families do sometimes produce mavericks, but it was about as obvious as it could be that Sir Humphrey was not one.

Why did the Rhodesian Government not simply expel him from Government House? The answer probably is that Smith was anxious in the early stages of the rebellion to preserve as much of a semblance of legality as he could. All regimes which come to power after a *coup*, bloodless or otherwise, try to do this; the instinct for law and order is very deep-seated. He remained ostensibly loyal to the Queen. Perhaps he genuinely was. Wilson on the occasion of his last visit before UDI had given him a personal letter from the Queen in her own hand, which Smith read out at a luncheon given by the Mayor of Salisbury and which moved him to recite the monarch's speech about St Crispin's Day from *Henry V*. The episode prompted some cynics to describe the luncheon as Smith's Crispins.[2] The National Anthem continued to be sung, and the Union Jack continued to fly. Both were dropped later. A rather drab green and white Rhodesian national flag was devised in place of the Union Jack, but all efforts to produce a plausible national anthem have foundered so far.

As time went by there was a further reason for not interfering with the Governor. The British Government used him as a bridge for the inception of negotiations. Smith was not against this, and there is no evidence that he entered upon either the *Tiger* or *Fearless* talks in bad faith, i.e. as mere window-dressing with no serious intention to seek agreement. On the contrary, it is more likely to have been the old story that negotiation to him meant seeking an agreement on his own terms and wearing the British Government down till they were accepted. As long as Smith saw any chance of doing this – and the last hope did not evaporate till late in 1968 – there was nothing to be gained by a move against Sir Humphrey Gibbs. After that both sides gave up; Smith declared a republic and Wilson saw no point in pursuing matters any further. The question was not to be reopened during his premiership.

Smith was careful to avoid as far as he could the delicate question of oaths of allegiance. He could not be completely sure just how much loyalist opposition there would be or how far it would go. In fact there was to be very little, but he did not know this for certain, although he had satisfied himself that there would be no serious trouble among the Civil Service or the armed forces. The opposition to UDI was vociferous, but not at all solidly based. It included Garfield Todd and his supporters, who had moved well to the 'left' in Rhodesian terms.

[2] Young, op. cit., 258-9. For the benefit of American readers, Smith's Crisps are one of the favourite brands of potato chips.

It also comprised most of the old establishment – Lord Malvern, Sir Roy Welensky, Sir Robert Tredgold, Sir Edgar Whitehead, David Butler and the survivors of his party. The financial and business elements in the community were in principle against UDI, but had little option save to co-operate with it. Mr Harry Oppenheimer, Chairman of the giant Anglo-American Corporation which, having absorbed the British South Africa Company, had ramifications all over Rhodesia, as well as the Republic, was a strong opponent of UDI, just as he was a strong opponent of apartheid in the south. But it is a vulgar error of left-wing polemicists to argue that in 'capitalist' countries businessmen always determine the power of government. The converse is far more often true.

Two features of the situation greatly helped the illegal regime. The first was that nothing looked obviously different after UDI – or indeed looked different at all, apart from the blanks in censored newspapers. For as long as most people could remember Rhodesians had made their own laws in their own 'Parliament', had interpreted them in their own courts, had executed them through their own civil servants and enforced them through their own police. Rhodesians had for many years enjoyed the protection of their own army and air force. They had for years also travelled on their own passports; and here one of the few palpable changes did occur. It soon became impossible to travel anywhere except to South Africa, Portugal and one or two other countries on a Rhodesian passport, but, since so many Rhodesians were also entitled to a British passport, travel was not too serious a problem, except for those openly involved in membership or active support of the illegal regime, who were liable to have their British passports invalidated or removed. A vindictive and petty-fogging instance of this was the deprivation of the passport of Sir Frederick Crawford (who had been Governor of Uganda and was the Resident Director in Salisbury of the Anglo-American Company) largely because Lady Crawford was a friend of Mrs Ian Smith. The matter was rectified by Sir Alec Douglas-Home after 1970.

In general, life in Salisbury and Bulawayo appeared very much a case of business as usual, and the result was that with every day that passed it seemed more and more absurd for people to think of themselves as having passed through a constitutional revolution and being members of a rebel colony. Sundowner parties were just the same. Sport was as much a fetish as ever. The people who had always put on dinner jackets for evening parties continued to put them on. The food they ate was as plentiful – and as indifferent – as ever. The drink they consumed was, however, another matter. At first there was no great change, but shortage of foreign currency, caused by sanctions, did in the course of time have an adverse effect. Gin which is distilled locally and tastes much like any other gin has always been in good supply, likewise beer. But by the time I went out there in 1968, French wine was rare, although there seemed ample quantities of Cape wine which, whether red or white, can be excellent when drunk in the southern hemisphere. By 1973, however, it too had largely vanished, and little remained except some Portuguese wines and some peculiarly vile indigenous products (the climate is wholly unsuited to viniculture). Whisky by then was no less scarce. In Britain if you are offered brandy or whisky and happen to want to save your host money you accept whisky. In Rhodesia the opposite was true, with the proviso, however, that Rhodesian 'brandy' had nothing to do with the grape, but was a form of local cane spirit. In the course of time Scotch whisky began to vanish, and, since Rhodesian 'whisky' was also made of cane spirit, the tactful guest could take his choice with a clear conscience.

The second feature of the post-UDI situation which helped to consolidate the regime was Harold Wilson's statement in Parliament, the day after UDI, that it was the duty of public servants in Rhodesia to remain at their posts so that they could preserve law and order and maintain essential services. Neither the Civil Service, police, nor armed forces, he added, should take any oath of loyàlty to the illegal Government, nor should they do anything to further its purposes. The former condition raised no problem since Smith still maintained that he was loyal to the Crown and had no intention of substituting a new oath. The latter was impossible to fulfil. How could one distinguish between preserving order and essential services, and furthering the purposes of the regime? In one sense, to do the first was to do the second. In any case, who was to give guidance and draw the line? The practical effect was to 'legitimize' the action of public servants, who decided to continue to function just as they always had before November 11, 1965.

Harold Wilson's advice to the Rhodesian public service disposes of one charge made by the extreme right in Britain as well as Rhodesia, viz. that the economic sanctions which followed were intended to produce some sort of black Spartacist rebellion. If he had had any such purpose he would not have invited the enforcers of law and order to remain at their posts. In fact there was no likelihood of an African revolt. Rhodesia's African population has been likened to a 'sleeping giant', and it is remarkable how docile five or six million Blacks have been under the rule of only a quarter of a million Whites.

One can only surmise the reasons. Certainly they do not include, as some white Rhodesians like to believe, any widespread acceptance of UDI or of Ian Smith. The profound African distrust of him and his colleagues was to be shown in the findings of the Pearce Commission in 1972. Among the reasons no doubt was the incarceration of all the African leaders and the effective steps taken to prevent the emergence of new ones. Another was the success of the Government in dividing and ruling. There are black troops in the army, there are black policemen in the British South Africa Police Force and there is a host of black informers. A further element in this relative quiescence may have been the sense of relief that violence in the townships had come to an end.

Perhaps two more reasons could be added. First, the Rhodesian Africans, even more than the Rhodesian Europeans, are deeply conscious of inherited folklore. The total crushing of the rebellions in Matabeleland and Mashonaland was never forgotten; the Africans of Southern Rhodesia, to a far greater degree than those north of the Zambesi, were conscious of being a conquered race; they did not like it, but their whole way of life had been so utterly convulsed that they lacked any social structure on which to found an effective resistance. This was true of South Africa too, but there was greater bitterness and resentment there for causes which bring one to the second reason for relative Rhodesian quiescence. The white rulers of Rhodesia have never been as rigid, uncompromising and doctrinaire as their counterparts in the south. During the Smith regime they have moved in that direction, but they still have a long way to go. Personal relations between black and white in Rhodesia are – or still were till very recently – far less hostile than in the Republic. One only has to move across the frontier to sense the difference immediately. Apartheid south of the Limpopo is a religion, north of it a dubious and impracticable expedient.

Harold Wilson's advice to the Rhodesian public service signified another decision – no use of force. He had already disclaimed it, but the illegal regime could not till the eleventh hour feel quite certain. What would have happened if, on the news of UDI, the Governor had called upon the police and the army to arrest Smith as a rebel? One cannot be sure. In retrospect it may be thought that nothing would have been lost by the attempt. But Sir Humphrey himself was – or is said to have been – strongly opposed to it, and in the end it made no sense if Britain was not willing to back it by armed intervention. At the time of UDI Wilson was clearly not willing.

There were formidable difficulties involved in the use of force, even apart from the sentiments of 'kith and kin' likely to be felt by both officers and men in the British units concerned. Mr Kenneth Young[3] quotes an article in *The World Today* of December 1965 written by William Gutteridge pointing out the problems which would arise if, as was suggested in Parliament, armed intervention became necessary in the event of a collapse of law and order in Rhodesia or a threat to Zambia's power supplies. If, as Mr Young claims, he was writing with the support of the Ministry of Defence it is clear that the Government would have received the minimum of encouragement for such a venture. There was only one brigade group of 3,000 to 3,500 men on immediate call, and it would take a week for Transport Command to move them to a base in Zambia, the only country from which operations could be mounted. The author reckoned that three brigade groups were needed and that the Rhodesian Air Force with forty to fifty Vampire, Hunter and Canberra aircraft, as well as transports, helicopters and light planes would be a formidable force in relative terms.

Harold Wilson was under continuous pressure from the new Commonwealth countries, from the Afro-Asian members of UNO and from a minority of the Labour Party to use force. But he had a majority of only one in the House until the election of March 31, 1966, which gave him an easy victory. Even if he had believed in the viability of such a policy he could not have afforded to risk the ensuing political storm. It is safe to say that he did not at any stage contemplate military intervention unless Rhodesia collapsed into complete anarchy. There was no doubt in his mind about the electoral risk involved. Re-

[3] Op. cit., 329–32.

ferring to Heath and the Conservative divisions over the oil embargo he wrote: 'It is true, of course, that, had we decided to intervene by force of arms he would have led a united party and almost certainly won majority support in the country. But this was never on.'[4]

His principal problem was to avoid giving offence to President Kaunda. The cutting off of copper supplies would, he says, have meant two million unemployed in Britain. Kaunda was strongly against UDI, but he depended on Wankie coal and Kariba hydro-electric power for the production of Zambian copper and on the railway through Rhodesia to Beira for its export. Kaunda wanted the British to send troops to seize the installations at Kariba. This Harold Wilson refused to do. As he points out in his memoirs 'one civilian in a white coat could have pulled the switches before the power station could be occupied'. On the other hand he had to take account of the Zambian President's fear of a preemptive strike by the Rhodesians and he was anxious not to offend a Government which, albeit at the cost of a Samson-like treatment of its own economy, had the power to inflict so much damage on Britain.

Matters were complicated further by oil sanctions. The issue of the illegal regime had been taken to the Security Council which on November 20 demanded sanctions on a formidable scale including the stoppage of oil supplies. Britain agreed in mid-December to apply oil sanctions, but it was obvious that Rhodesia would in that case cut off the supplies which went through to Zambia, and it was feared that the resultant tension might produce a military crisis.

In fact Smith had no intention of taking any sort of military action. Indeed, it would have been the height of folly. However, Wilson offered to send troops to man the north bank of the Zambesi and Britannia transport planes to fly supplies of oil from Dar es Salaam to Lusaka. He also offered to send some RAF Javelin fighters. Kaunda accepted the Javelins and the Britannias, but he insisted that he would only accept troops if they had orders to occupy Kariba at once. No troops were sent. The Javelins duly arrived in Lusaka. The spirit in which the Rhodesian Government took their arrival is shown by the fact that they were guided in the closing stages of the flight by Air Traffic Control at Salisbury.

The whole affair was a somewhat nonsensical piece of sabre-rattling. Smith's health was reputed to have been drunk in the RAF Officers' Mess in Lusaka on New Year's Eve. A touch of comedy was provided by the Minister of State from the CRO who wished the RAF personnel a 'happy white Christmas', and by Arthur Bottomley, also in Lusaka, who found it difficult to avoid substituting Gambia for Zambia in his speeches. Eventually Kaunda, who must have realized by then that he was in no military danger, asked for the Javelins to be withdrawn. What he wanted was planes for an air strike, but the British Government was no more willing to provide these than to occupy Kariba.

Oil sanctions broke the hitherto uneasy truce between Labour and Conser-

[4] Wilson, op. cit., 181.

vatives in Britain. Edward Heath had been leader of his party for only a few months and Southern African affairs were not his speciality. After UDI the Conservative line was at first one of guarded support for the Government. The oil question showed up the concealed fissures in the Party's front. Some argued that the sanctions were too harsh, some believed that they were justifiable and might be effective, some maintained -- rightly as it turned out -- that whatever their justice they would not work, since they presupposed a blockade of the whole of southern Africa. This proved to be the case. The Naval patrol off Beira effectively prevented oil being landed and piped thence to Umtali, but no one from that day to this has been prepared to cut off supplies from the Republic and, since Rhodesia's needs were but a tiny proportion of South African oil imports, no problem arose. Thirty Conservatives voted with the Government -- some of them former office holders in the Commonwealth Relations Office. Fifty voted against, some because they thought sanctions futile, others because they were at heart pro-settler, even if they disapproved of UDI. The rest including the Leader abstained. In the circumstances there was little else that Heath could do without causing even greater dissension among his own ranks; but this three-way split in the party shattered its credibility as far as Rhodesia was concerned, and Wilson, despite his miniscule majority, could afford to disregard Conservative criticism from then onwards.

By the end of the year the British Government had implemented all the threats made before UDI, and had indeed gone well beyond them. On the other hand, the Rhodesian Government could now feel quite safe from military action. In the course of debating a Conservative motion deploring the use of force, Wilson on December 21 categorically declared that he had no intention of restoring legality by armed intervention. There was nothing new in this declaration, but such a reaffirmation, however necessary for internal consumption in view of the continuing risk of an enforced general election, was bound to help the illegal regime. He also stated that it would be unnecessary to blockade Beira, though he did not rule this out as a future move.

Harold Wilson has always been by nature optimistic. There is no doubt that by the beginning of 1966 he had become convinced that sanctions and other measures would very soon bring the Rhodesian economy to a halt and oblige Smith to come to the negotiating table. At the Commonwealth Conference which began in Lagos on January 10 and which produced the usual demands for armed intervention, Wilson used his famous phrase about the collapse of the Rhodesian economy being a matter of 'weeks not months'. Since it has not yet collapsed, eleven years later, the prophecy was about as wide of the mark as Ian Smith's 'nine day wonder'.

What prompted this euphoria? In his memoirs Harold Wilson says that he had been advised that the closure of the Beira pipeline would be effective and that 'Portugal would not challenge the determination of the UN nor seek to encourage sanction-breaking. We were misled but what I said to my colleagues appeared at the time to be a safe prophecy.' It would be interesting to know who gave this advice. No doubt Dr Salazar, like the South African Prime Minister, Dr Verwoerd, disapproved of UDI, which focused world attention to an embarrassing extent upon the racial problems of southern Africa. On the other hand, presented with a *fait accompli*, they were unlikely to make any effort to restore legality. From their point of view it was important that sanctions should *not* work, for there had been constant rumblings from outside against their own regimes and unsuccessful attempts at boycotts and other measures including sanctions.

Even if the Portuguese had supported the UN call for sanctions – and Salazar being a dictator had the power to do so – the South African Government which had its own public opinion to consider was almost certain to refuse. Here, according to one story,[5] lay the source of another misconception under which the British Government at first laboured. The advice said to have been received from Pretoria via the Commonwealth Relations Office was that South Africa would treat Rhodesia on the basis of 'business as usual'. This was interpreted as meaning that there would be no change in the current volume of trade between the two countries. Had that happened, and had the Portuguese applied sanctions, Rhodesia certainly would have been wrecked; it was in effect the threat of South African pressure along with the closing of the Mozambique frontier which made Smith do his deal with Dr Kissinger in September 1976. But what the South Africans meant in 1966, if the story is true, was merely that the Government did not intend to interfere with trade which would find its own level – a very different proposition for, of course, it at once greatly expanded.

Whatever the exact nature of the technical advice received by Harold Wilson at this juncture, it was evidently misleading, and it may well have contributed, as Kenneth Young suggests, to the decision to merge the Commonwealth Relations Office into the Foreign Office two years later; the CRO's record over Rhodesia had not been good, and the general quality of the officials in the Foreign Office was higher. In the event South Africa gave tacit support to the illegal regime, later even reinforcing the Zambesi frontier with detachments from its own security forces. As for Mozambique, there were other oil routes besides the Beira pipeline. The point about Beira was that oil landed there could only be intended for Rhodesia. This did not apply to Lourenzo Marques. Oil landed there might be destined for Johannesburg and other places in South Africa linked by rail with the port or it might be destined for Rhodesia via the line running north west through Mozambique to Shabani and subsequently bifurcating west to Bulawayo and north to Salisbury. Oil could also find its way to Rhodesia from South African ports. Britain with huge investments in the Republic simply could not afford a major economic war.

The Rhodesian Government showed considerable skill in its management of economic and fiscal matters. The Finance Minister, John Wrathall, one of the less ideologically committed members of the Front, was an able man. He held his office for over ten years until he was rewarded with the presidency in succession

[5] Private information.

to Clifford Dupont. He had efficient advisers in the Civil Service, and he was greatly helped by the Governor of the Reserve Bank, a highly capable Afrikaner, surprisingly named Bruce, who was reputed to be a member of the *Broederbond*, the secret society formed between the wars to preserve Afrikaner domination in southern Africa. At least three recent South African Prime Ministers are supposed to have belonged to it. That a member (if Bruce really was one) should be holding such a key position in Rhodesia is a significant pointer to the direction in which Afrikaners saw their interest to lie at that time.

In March the Rhodesia–Mozambique Oil Pipeline Company announced that it intended to continue pumping oil to the Rhodesian refinery at Umtali. The British Government now resolved to reverse its decision and blocked the port, but a test case brought by the owners of two tankers chartered to a South African company and flying a Greek flag made it clear that Britain had no legal power to do this unless she had the authority of the Security Council. On April 10 the Security Council, with singular lack of plausibility, asserted that the supply of oil to Rhodesia was a threat to peace. Britain was enjoined to enforce the blockade on Beira and all countries asked to refuse supplies. Wilson's action marked a final parting of the ways as far as the Conservatives were concerned. They opposed both force and the reference to the Security Council.

The Beira Patrol established in order to enforce the blockade was effective as far as the pipeline was concerned, but the supply of oil to Rhodesia continued through other channels. By the middle of the year it was clear that, although the Rhodesian economy had ceased to expand at its pre-UDI rate, if indeed it was now expanding at all, the situation was by no means disastrous. Imports were expensive, the process of exporting, especially in the case of tobacco, was difficult, clandestine and only feasible at cut prices; but a great many countries ignored the UN; the imposition of selective mandatory sanctions by the Security Council at the end of the year made no great difference, nor did a similar resolution in favour of comprehensive mandatory sanctions passed in May 1968. American, French, Italian, Swiss, West German and Japanese businessmen were constantly in Salisbury. At times it looked as if Britain and the Scandinavian countries were the only nations to take sanctions seriously.

Certainly there were some changes. Rhodesia had been essentially a primary producer. She now diversified into secondary industries. This was probably less economic than exchanging tobacco for manufactured goods, but, again, it cannot be called disastrous, though it had the unintended side-effect of creating a class of managers and owners with a vested interest in avoiding a settlement. Rhodesian tobacco is easily identifiable and therefore difficult to market. This was not true of the country's ores. In 1968 important new deposits of nickel and chrome were discovered. In January 1972 the United States Senate, against the advice of the Administration, actually amended the Strategic Materials Act so as to legalize the purchase of Rhodesian chrome, which the Russians had already been buying for some time past. The amendment was, however, reversed early in 1977 under strong pressure from the new President, Jimmy Carter.

Sanctions on specific items were probably less injurious than the decline in foreign exchange earnings which was the generalized consequence of Rhodesia's partial economic outlawry. To judge from personal impressions is dangerous, but it is impossible to believe any figures put out by the Rhodesian Government and so there is little else to go on. The impression on a regular visitor between April 1968 and October 1973 was of a decline in the European standard of life, but not a marked one. Moreover, it was a decline from what had been a very high standard materially. Wine and spirits have been mentioned, but there were also more shortages of other goods in the shops in 1973 than there had been five years earlier. One heard more complaints about the difficulty of replacing spare parts and more grumbles about the problem of buying new cars, new equipment, new machinery. Nevertheless, as far as the European world was concerned Rhodesia seemed to be a prosperous, stable, well ordered republic.

It is far more difficult to gain any impression of the condition of the Africans. In 1964 59 per cent of them lived in the tribal trust areas, 23 per cent in European farming areas and only 18 per cent in urban areas. The problem is, therefore, essentially a rural one. Visitors are not encouraged to wander round the tribal trust areas, nor indeed are Rhodesian citizens. It is a closed and largely unknown world. There can, however, be little doubt that sanctions have aggravated what has all along been the great problem for Africans – rural unemployment. The African population is increasing annually by a figure as large as that of the entire European population. Unless there is a rapid growth in both the African and European rural economy, unemployment (though it is statistically concealed) must rise. Growth of the rural economy pre-supposes a reopening of export markets and a massive capital investment in the form of dams, irrigation, new roads, etc. Neither of these things are going to happen until sanctions are lifted. There is every reason to believe that the conditions in which the vast majority of Africans live have deteriorated since UDI, though no reliable figures are available or ever will be under the present regime.

Rhodesia since 1965 has been like a man suffering from a slow haemorrhage or a gradual wasting disease. If it goes on, it will be fatal in the end. But the end seems a long way off, and there is always the chance of some new drug or some fresh technique which will arrest the process or even produce a cure. This is the background to the successive attempts by British Governments to achieve a settlement. In September 1966 a second Commonwealth Conference took place. Like the previous one it was dominated by the question of Rhodesia. The British Prime Minister was once again under great pressure to apply force, but in the end – and only after he had spoken his mind to the Conference in the strongest words – the agreed communiqué stated that if Smith had not returned to legality within three months the British Government would make no subsequent proposals unless they included the principle of 'NIBMAR' (no independence before majority rule) and it would at once sponsor in the Security Council a resolution calling for 'selective and effective mandatory sanctions' against Rhodesia.

After a good deal of to-ing and fro-ing and much exchange of enigmatic correspondence Smith agreed to the suggestion that he and his Foreign Minister, Jack Howman, should meet Wilson at Gibraltar in the cruiser HMS *Tiger* and try to reach an agreement. According to Wilson's memoirs, the official who saw Smith in Salisbury, Sir Morrice James, was instructed to make the offer on the strict condition that Smith had full power to settle on the spot. He carefully spelt this out and Smith having consulted his Cabinet obtained their authority to do so.

The details of the discussion are too complicated and tedious to describe at any length. The broad principle behind the British proposals both in *Tiger* and in *Fearless* two years later was the continuance of the 1961 Constitution, modified in order to give Africans more seats immediately and to bring about eventually and more speedily an African majority as education and income improved. There was to be a double safeguard over retrograde amendments to the vital entrenched clauses. They required a three-quarters majority of the two houses voting together (the plan involved the creation of a senate, always envisaged as a possibility in the 1961 Constitution), and there was also an appeal to the Judicial Committee of the Privy Council on specific grounds of racial discrimination or infringement of the Declaration of Rights. The Legislature, i.e. Legislative Assembly plus Senate, was to be composed so as to ensure that African elected members constituted over a quarter of the total number.

There was also to be a built in 'blocking quarter' of elected Europeans in order to meet Harold Wilson's sixth principle which he had advanced as a sweetener for Ian Smith, viz.: 'to ensure that, regardless of race, there was no oppression of majority by minority or minority by majority'. The final version of the proposed Legislature was an Assembly of 33 'A' Roll seats, 17 'B' Roll seats and 17 Reserved European seats; and a Senate consisting of 12 European Seats (elected by Europeans on the 'A' Roll), 8 African seats (elected by Africans on the 'A' and 'B' Rolls voting together) and 6 Chiefs (elected by the Chief's Council). Cross-voting was to continue as under the 1961 Constitution, but the 'B' Roll franchise would be widened to all Africans over thirty satisfying the necessary residential and citizenship qualifications. The 'A' Roll qualifications remained the same and were of course 'entrenched'.[6]

The acceptability of such a constitution to the Rhodesian people as a whole was to be tested by a Royal Commission. Pending its report the country would be governed under the 1961 Constitution, but Smith would have to form a 'broad-based' cabinet in agreement with the British Government. The return to legality would be made under its auspices. There would also be a bilateral treaty incorporating the necessary guarantees and registrable with the United Nations. When and if the Royal Commission found the new constitution acceptable to the Rhodesian people, its provisions would be put to Parliament and the process of removing sanctions could begin.

[6] See Cmnd. 317, 87–90, Appendix B.

The 'broad-based' cabinet would be chosen formally by the Governor. It would have five additional ministers not of the Rhodesian Front including two 'constitutionalist' Africans; the Front would still have a majority, but two or three individuals from the existing Cabinet would have to go. The only one named in the published documents was Dupont who by purporting to represent the Crown had ruled himself out for any Crown appointment. One might surmise that others may have been; Lord Graham and Mr Lardner-Burke, the Minister of Justice, a lawyer who, strange as it may seem, had at one time been Garfield Todd's solicitor. He was an extreme hard-liner closely associated with the illiberal exercise of emergency powers.

The Governor during this interim period of 'return to legality' would have full legislative powers, the existing Assembly having been dissoved. He would, however, exercise them in internal matters of administration on the advice of ministers (except in areas where he already had discretion). As soon as the Constitution had been pronounced by the Royal Commission as acceptable, there would be elections held under its provisions. As far as law and order and protection of human rights were concerned during the interim period, the Governor in his capacity as Commander-in-Chief would be advised by a Defence and Security Council comprising the responsible ministers, the heads of the defence forces, the Chief of Police and a representative of the British Government. The point here which is spelt out more fully in the British Government's Statement of October 15, para. 17,[7] was that the Governor, while normally acting on ministers' advice, must have the discretionary power to act against fresh unconstitutional action and to call for British military assistance. There were a number of other points in the proposed settlement which do not require detailed discussion – establishment of an impartial tribunal to consider the illegally detained prisoners, the removal of censorship, the establishment of a Royal Commission to investigate racial discrimination. The crunch came on other issues.

At about 10 p.m. on the night of December 1 the Prime Minister arrived on *Tiger* with his party which included Herbert Bowden, Commonwealth Secretary, Sir Elwyn Jones, Attorney-General, and the Secretary of the Cabinet, Sir Burke Trend. It was vile weather and getting from a sea rescue launch to the cruiser was none too easy. In the small hours of the morning they were followed by Sir Humphrey Gibbs and Sir Hugh Beadle who had to be hoisted aboard because of a back injury. Finally at 2 a.m. on Friday December 2 Ian Smith, Jack Howman and supporting civil servants arrived. The choice of a cruiser for these talks may have been a solution to the problems of secrecy and security, but in all other respects the arrangement was anything but convenient.

Discussions began next morning and were to continue till 1 a.m. on Sunday, December 4. At first the prospect of agreement seemed promising. Smith appeared to accept in principle nearly all the provisions of the revised constitution. There was the usual haggle over Chiefs and electoral arithmetic, but he did not

[7] Cmnd. 3171, 23.

resist British insistence that any 'blocking quarter' must consist of elected Africans, whatever additional representation might be provided for Chiefs. Nor did he object to an appeal to the Judicial Committee of the Privy Council if amendments to the entrenched clauses were challenged. He was more sceptical about the proposals for the return to legality, but even in this area he was, according to both the official record and Sir Harold Wilson's memoirs, surprisingly conciliatory to begin with. When the Prime Minister suggested an additional five members for the broadly based cabinet and observed that if two or three existing members of a cabinet of thirteen had to go, the numbers in the new cabinet would need to rise to fifteen or sixteen, Smith replied that he would probably take the opportunity to reduce his cabinet to twelve. The Prime Minister, who had not pressed for this, observed that it would imply the dismissal of five or six (not two or three) of the existing Cabinet. The official record does not expatiate, but Sir Harold Wilson says in his memoirs that when he asked Smith whether some of his right-wing ministers would resign in the event of an agreement on these lines, Smith replied that it would not be a matter of resignation; he would get rid of them. It may have been at this stage that plans were made for a champagne celebration of agreement.

Just what Smith really meant remains, as so often both before and since, obscure; but it soon became clear that the return to legality was to be the issue on which he or his advisers were likely to break off negotiations. On the evening of Friday, December 2 Smith declared that he would have to refer the proposals by telegram back to his colleagues in Salisbury. Wilson accepted with reluctance, but worse was to follow. On Saturday morning (December 3) Smith said that he must return in person to consult the Rhodesian Cabinet. The Prime Minister protested strongly on the ground that Smith had avowedly come to *Tiger*, as he (Wilson) had, with plenary powers to make a settlement. There can be no doubt that Sir Morrice James was given this impression when he originally sounded Smith with a view to the talks.

The ensuing recriminations went beyond the language of diplomacy. In the end Wilson had no option but to agree, though he had the satisfaction of observing, when Sir Hugh Beadle had departed from the Admiral's Day Cabin after proposing some sort of compromise, that he 'could not understand how any man could have a slipped disc whom Providence had failed to provide with a backbone'.[8]

Smith and his party flew back on Sunday, with a deadline for their answer by 12 noon on Monday, December 5. The Rhodesian Cabinet met early, but had not reached a conclusion by the end of the morning – it would have been very hot and steamy by that time of the year – and asked for a further few hours which were granted. At 6 p.m. the British Government received the news that the proposals had been rejected. The reports which reached the British Government suggested that by noon the Rhodesian Cabinet had been in favour of acceptance and that when Lord Graham threatened to resign Smith invited him to do so.

[8] Wilson, op. cit., 315.

Smith then, according to Wilson, 'weakly agreed to an adjournment, during which interval the extremist party bosses exerted their pressure and invoked all the grass roots threats of which they were capable'.[9] A slightly cynical but not inexperienced observer of the Rhodesian scene explained the events to me rather differently. 'You must remember,' he said, 'Salisbury is not like London. Here, people go home for lunch and come back in the afternoon. The Cabinet talked to their wives and of course received storm signals. The women are the real hard-liners.'[10]

Whatever the truth about the lunch interval, the final answer was to shut the door.[11] The ostensible issue on which the break was made concerned the return to legality, but it was almost certainly not the only one. Could the *Tiger* talks have been handled more successfully? Lord Home in his memoirs, conceding that it is easy to be wise after the event, suggests that 'having agreed the terms, Mr Wilson and Mr Smith ought to have summoned the press of the world and have been photographed toasting in champagne a remarkable achievement'. He believed that 'the small men of Salisbury' could not in such circumstances have defied Smith. An alternative would have been for Wilson himself to fly to Salisbury with Smith. 'Their combined authority would certainly have carried the day.'[12]

Lord Home's argument presupposes that Smith and Wilson were in basic agreement and that the problem was to 'sell' a settlement to the Cabinet in Salisbury. Wilson's own account, though more cautious and qualified, also implies that Smith was personally in favour of the revised constitution. He ascribes his inability to carry the day to weakness, though he states, 'Looking back on it I feel that I underrated the fears that he always had that, even while he was in the air, his colleagues would "do a Winston Field on him".'[13] It would be wrong to give a confident answer to these questions. Smith may have been uneasy. 'Had Zimri peace who slew his master?' He may have been a 'moderate' who surrendered to extremists. But there is an alternative possibility, and this is that he, like many politicians, speaks one language to one set of people, another to another; that he has always been at heart a hard-line supporter of white ascendancy; that, whatever the obscure and unpredictable promises and denials which he makes from time to time, he has only one purpose – the preservation till the last hour possible of the Rhodesia he knows and loves; and that it is he who controls his

[9] Loc. cit., 321.

[10] Private information.

[11] According to 'Insight' in the *Sunday Times* of February 13, 1977 the voting was 8 to 5 against acceptance. Ian Smith, Wrathall, Arthur Smith, Howman and Dunlop voted for the settlement. Harper, Lardner-Burke, Lord Graham, Musset, Partridge, Rudland, Van Heerden and Lance Smith voted against. The source is said to be a report to Harold Wilson by the late Henry Kerby, a Tory MP, who paid a secret visit to Rhodesia in May 1967 under the auspices of Lord Graham. 'Insight' does not say how this report was obtained.

[12] *The Way the Wind Blows*, 224-5.

[13] Wilson, op. cit., 316.

Cabinet, not they him. Certainly those who have met him on private occasions in congenial company would have grave doubts about any wishful picture of him as a 'moderate'. Whatever moderation he was to display would be the result of *force majeure*, not conviction.

For the next few years the force was not major enough. Harold Wilson at once declared for 'NIBMAR' and invited the United Nations to impose mandatory sanctions. These had no obvious effect on the Rhodesian economy. During 1967 and early 1968 there occurred a complicated series of lawsuits involving the whole question of the status of the Rhodesian judiciary and the validity of appeals to the Privy Council. Sir Hugh Beadle and the majority of the Appellate Division declared that the Rhodesian Government was a *de facto* government. The appeals of three Africans condemned to death for murder before UDI were dismissed and the Privy Council's judgement ignored. As a result two Rhodesian Judges, first Mr Justice Fieldsend and later Mr Justice Young resigned. The Governor sent Sir Hugh packing (literally) from Government House, but the Africans were duly hanged for crimes which, it is fair to say, were peculiary horrible and in no way connected with a political purpose.

These events naturally made Rhodesia's relations with Britain and the world at large worse than ever, but talks about talks continued nevertheless. In 1967 Lord Alport, former High Commissioner to the Federation, paid a visit to Salisbury, as did Sir Alec Douglas-Home early in 1968. In June that year Harold Wislon decided that there was the possibility – faint perhaps, but not wholly invisible – of a settlement. He invited Sir Max Aitken, who had a connection with Ian Smith in their RAF days, and Lord Goodman, who happened to be Sir Max's solicitor as well as Wilson's, to go on a secret mission to Rhodesia. Any negotiation meant dropping NIBMAR, for Smith would never agree to that, but his replies over the blocking quarter and the appeal to the Privy Council seemed satisfactory. On the question of return to legality he reserved his position till he heard what new proposals would be made by the Prime Minister.

As a result of these discussions Wilson resolved to make a further attempt, and from October 9 to 13 he and Smith once again held talks, this time on HMS *Fearless* moored to the quay at Gibralter. The talks were more amicable than before. The Rhodesian delegation was not treated in the petty pin-pricking way which had been a feature of the proceedings on board *Tiger*, and Ian Smith had his own accommodation in *Kent* which was moored alongside *Fearless*. On this occasion, moreover, there was no specific deadline, and it was accepted that neither side had plenary powers. Smith returned on October 13. A certain amount of headway had been made, but the British party noted with some concern the intransigent attitude of one of the Rhodesian officials, the Secretary for African Affairs, Hostes Nicolle, who played a surprisingly prominent and wholly non-cooperative part in the proceedings. He subsequently circulated to his district officers a document denying all possibility of a settlement, although Smith had not yet formally closed the door, and indeed had invited George Thompson for talks in Salisbury. Thompson had been Commonwealth Secretary and was now Minister without

Portfolio having special responsibility for Rhodesian affairs. His discussions, held from November 2 to 16, with an interval to avoid UDI celebrations on November 11, got nowhere.

The details of the proposals and counter-proposals do not matter. This time – at any rate ostensibly – it was not the return to legality which seemed to be Smith's sticking point, but the appeal to the Privy Council, although that had also been a part of the *Tiger* proposals and no objections had then been made. It was the end of serious negotiations as far as Wilson was concerned; there were some unfruitful exchanges early in 1969, but the Rhodesian question was in effect shelved till after the next general election.

How far Smith was serious in these negotiations remains a puzzle. We do not know what is in the relevant Rhodesian documents, if indeed there is anything at all to throw light on the matter. We do not know the exact relations between Smith and his ministers or between the Cabinet as a whole and the Rhodesian Front – its caucus, committees and Congress. The illegal regime has displayed a degree of secrecy and security only paralleled in Britain during war; and of course the Rhodesians felt themselves to be at war. We do not know what sort of advice the Rhodesian Government was receiving on the economic front and how far this made Smith veer towards a settlement in 1966 and 1968 – or again in 1971. It seems reasonable to suppose that economic conditions had some connexion with the second of these moves. Mandatory sanctions appear to have been biting in the early part of 1968 and new loopholes had not yet been found. Matters were made worse by a severe drought which dried up the pasture and killed thousands of cattle. Smith came under attack both from moderates who wanted a settlement and from hard-liners who wanted a clean break and an overtly racialist constitution.

By the time the *Fearless* talks were finished the economic situation was looking better. Discoveries of chrome and nickel were important elements in renewed Rhodesian intransigence. Smith now decided to move to the right – always his natural inclination. For some time past a commission on the Constitution had been sitting under the chairmanship of W. R. Whaley, an able Salisbury lawyer. The report published on April 5, 1968 recommended a constitutional and electoral system which would ultimately produce 'racial parity', but never anything more – and even then that would take a very long time. In the words of Chapter 2, para. 44, 'Europeans must surrender any belief in permanent European domination and Africans must surrender any belief in ultimate African domination'. But in practice European domination would continue for many years to come.

The Rhodesian Front caucus produced in July their own gloss on these proposals with the ultimate objective of a system of quasi-Bantustans. The extreme right found even this inadequate. On July 4 William Harper resigned. He was followed on September 12 by Lord Graham. Smith was probably pleased to see the last of them, not so much on ideological as personal grounds – rivalry in the one case, ineptitude in the other. Whatever threat they posed vanished with the failure of the *Fearless* talks. Smith proceeded to put forward his own revamped constitution. It was a major and illiberal departure from those of 1961 and 1965 which now disappeared into the documentary limbo where so many colonial constitutions gather dust and oblivion.

The new. Constitution was published on May 21, 1969. It abolished cross-voting, created a lower House of 66 (50 members returned by European, Asian and Coloured voters, 16 Africans, of whom 8 were elected on an African Roll and 8 chosen by Chiefs, Headmen and Councillors). There was also a Senate of 23 (10 Chiefs, 10 Europeans elected by the lower House and 3 – 2 Europeans and 1 Coloured – nominated by the Head of State). There were entrenched provisions, but they could be amended by two-thirds majorities of each House sitting separately. There was a non-justiciable – i.e. meaningless – Declaration of Rights. The number of African seats in the lower House could in theory increase to fifty per cent, though never more, and only when African contribution to income tax equalled that of Europeans – a provision which effectively postponed even parity to the 'Greek Kalends'. On June 20, 1969 this palpably white supremacist document was approved in a European referendum by some 55,000 to 20,000 and at the same time the electorate voted in favour of a republic. Sir Humphrey Gibbs was at last released from his dismal thraldom. Clifford Dupont duly took over Government House. On March 2, 1970 Rhodesia was proclaimed a republic and Dupont was officially elected as its first President. Ten days later a general election resulted in the Rhodesian Front winning all fifty European seats.

The Rhodesian results were not surprising, but in June 1970, contrary to the predictions of the soothsayers and the opinion pollsters, the British general election was won by the Conservatives with a majority of some forty seats. Edward Heath, the new Prime Minister, was anxious for a settlement, but personally was more interested in Europe than Africa. His Foreign Secretary, Sir Alec Douglas-Home, who had been so deeply involved in Rhodesian affairs in the past when he was Prime Minister, believed that there might be a chance to do a deal with Smith. Heath left the matter in his hands. Sir Alec, as we saw, thought the *Tiger* negotiations might have succeeded if Wilson had flown to Salisbury with Smith and backed the settlement in person with their combined authority. Of the *Fearless* talks he says that 'failure derived from the rigidity of the counsel given by Mr Wilson's principal legal advisors'.[14] He clearly had in mind the insistence on the appeal to the Privy Council, 'the second safeguard'.

The Foreign Secretary, who bore both these 'mistakes' (if such they were) in mind, was as well placed as anyone to achieve a settlement which would get the British Government off the hook and at the same time avoid a palpable sell-out. He was on all personal grounds far more acceptable in Rhodesia than Wilson, and the Conservative Party was, from the point of view of the Rhodesian Front, at least preferable to Labour. He proceeded warily. Once again, the aid of Sir Max Aitken and Lord Goodman was invoked. Once again they went to Salisbury on a private visit and returned with a not unhopeful message. Lord Goodman, with great generosity and at much personal expense, undertook the preliminary

[14] *The Way the Wind Blows*, 225.

negotiations in strict secrecy. 'He was scarcely inconspicuous,' as Sir Alec observes, 'but with luck that was uncanny he completed his exploration without attracting attention, and by the time he was detected on the job, it was clear that yet another attempt to settle ought to be made.'[15] At this stage Lord Goodman, backed by a team of officials, openly got down to the job of negotiation at which he is supremely adept. It was only when Smith had committed himself beyond even his capacity for evasion that Sir Alec agreed to fly to Salisbury, accompanied by Sir Peter Rawlinson, the Attorney-General, and Sir Denis (now Lord) Greenhill, the Permanent Under-Secretary at the FCO, and to enter into personal negotiations and discussions. After several days of talks and interviews with a wide variety of Rhodesians of all races and after reference back to the Cabinet, he signed a provisional agreement with Ian Smith on November 21, 1971.

The agreement went far towards meeting Smith's demands. There was no longer any question of a 'broad-based' interim government; Smith and his existing Cabinet remained in charge. There was no longer a 'second safeguard'; the appeal to the Privy Council was dropped. The document to be amended was no longer the 1961 or even the 1965 Constitution, but the newly-promulgated republican Constitution of 1969. The electoral provisions would, it is true, be amended so that Africans would in the long run have a majority instead of being halted for ever at parity in the Assembly. But the run still seemed likely to be a very long one indeed.

Separate rolls as in the 1969 Constitution were preserved for Africans and Europeans (including Asians and Coloureds). The Europeans would continue to elect 50 members. Of the 16 Africans in the existing Assembly of 66, 8 would continue to be elected on the existing African roll. To begin with there would also be, as before, 8 chosen by Chiefs, Headmen and Councillors. The important change would be an African Higher Roll with certain educational and property qualifications. When those registered on it reached 6 per cent of the European roll an extra two African seats would be created, followed by another two for the next 6 per cent and so on until parity was reached with European representation. At the next election after the attainment of this somewhat millennarian objective ten extra seats would be created and elected by a common roll consisting of European and Higher Roll Africans voting together. Since the Africans on this roll would ultimately out-number the Europeans, they would eventually have a majority in the Assembly.

The franchise, the composition of the Legislature and the process of transition were to be 'entrenched', and so was a justiciable Declaration of Rights which, however, as in the 1961 Constitution, would not affect existing laws. Amendment required a two-thirds majority in each House (there was a Senate composed on the same lines as in the 1969 Constitution). But, since the Europeans could at first easily secure this in the Lower House by sheer numbers and in the Upper House through influence on the Chiefs, there was a further provision that, until parity

---

[15] Lord Home, op. cit., 252. (Lord Goodman is, of course, a man of generous proportions.)

had been achieved in the Assembly, amendments would also require a majority in each House of Europeans and Africans voting separately. This gave the elected Africans in the Assembly a veto on retrogressive amendments, as long as they voted solidly together. It was a marginal and somewhat precarious veto, but it was just enough and it was the most that Smith would concede.

The provisional agreement also included clauses about racial discrimination, state of emergency, detainees, fairer dealing over land, and an offer from Britain of five million pounds a year for ten years to improve the tribal trust lands and African purchase areas and to promote educational and employment opportunities for Africans.

The provisional settlement was within the Five Principles – if only just within. It provoked the inevitable wrath of the Labour Party and the Liberals in Britain. In Rhodesia it was at first welcomed, but later repudiated by Garfield Todd. The African Nationalists predictably denounced it. The Rhodesian Front supported it with reservations, and most European organizations seemed favourable. But what was the view of the inarticulate African masses? Who really spoke for them? The fifth principle required that the British Government would need to be satisfied that the basis of the settlement was acceptable to 'the people of Rhodesia as a whole', before going ahead and conceding recognition to an independent Rhodesian republic.

As with the previous abortive efforts at a settlement, the task was to be given to a commission. The difference was that on this occasion the commission was actually set up and went out to Rhodesia. It was headed by Lord Pearce, a distinguished Law Lord. His appointment was announced on November 25. Lord Harlech, Sir Maurice Dorman and Sir Glyn Jones were the deputy chairmen of the commission. There were some twenty others who assisted in the task of ascertaining opinion all over Rhodesia. The advance guard went to Salisbury on January 4, 1972. Lord Pearce and his colleagues arrived a week later.

There can be no doubt that Smith expected the answer Yes. Sir Alec Douglas-Home and his officials, partly because of Smith's confidence, also believed that the proposals would be accepted. The commissioners were probably of the same mind, though they were not going to allow the thought to influence their assessment of the facts. The result was a major shock to European opinion in Rhodesia and a deep disappointment to those in Britain who hoped to get rid of this tiresome albatross. The commission spent two months on its task. It concluded that most Europeans were in favour of the proposals, but

> We are equally satisfied, after considering all our evidence including that on intimidation, that the majority of Africans rejected the Proposals. In our opinion the people of Rhodesia as a whole do not regard the Proposals as a basis for independence.[16]

In an earlier passage in the Report the commission spelt the matter out in

[16] Cmnd. 4964, May 1972, para. 420.

404

more specific terms in the section headed 'Reasons for African Rejection', para. 311
– 'The wider issues'.

> Mistrust of the intentions of the Government transcended all other considera-
> tions. Apprehension for the future stemmed from resentment at what they felt
> to be the humiliations of the past and at the limitations of policy on land,
> education and personal advancement. One summed it up in saying 'We do not
> reject the Proposals, we reject the Government'. This was the dominant motiv-
> ation of African rejection at all levels and in all areas.

The Pearce Report is one of the most interesting documents to have appeared
on Rhodesia in the last decade. The commission never exceeds its terms of
reference and the report is couched in cool language. But it is well written even
by the standards of official reports (which are in general much better written
than most people appreciate). Moreover it throws a great deal of light on
Rhodesian society and politics. Nor can there be any serious doubt about the
validity of its main conclusion. The Africans, after years of silent observation of
the Rhodesian Front's attitude towards them, its hatred of their political
aspirations, its determination to repress them, at last had a chance to get their
own back. No one could henceforth believe that Smith governed with African
support, or on any other basis than *force majeure*.

The verdict of the Pearce Commission put a stopper on further negotiations.
In Britain Rhodesia became a non-subject; people yawned at its mention. In
Rhodesia Britain seemed more remote and alien than ever. Sanctions continued to
be largely evaded or ignored; they were not wholly ineffective, but the economy
still limped along, and life for the ruling minority remained much as it was –
slightly less comfortable, rather more parochial perhaps; not fundamentally different. There was, however, one new and disagreeable feature. Guerrilla activity,
endemic since UDI, was markedly stepped up in 1972 and 1973. It was not
yet a serious threat, but it had a considerable nuisance value. The call-up of young
white Rhodesians became more and more frequent and was beginning to have a
considerable disruptive effect on business and the professions. There were signs
that the younger generation were not enjoying this aspect of the Rhodesian way
of life. Outwardly conformist and respectful to their elders, more and more of them
were voting with their feet and looking elsewhere for a career. Boredom probably
played as big a part as military service in this silent exodus. By the beginning
of 1974 the European ruling class had become an ageing and diminishing, or at
best static, group, under five per cent of the whole population; but there seemed
no obvious reason why they should not remain for many years in control of the
levers of power in their strange, anachronistic little white republic.

In April of that year, however, there occurred an event with far reaching
consequences, of which we have yet to see the full implications. The authoritarian
regime in Lisbon was overthrown by a *coup d'état* staged by a group of younger
officers who regarded the drain upon wealth and manpower involved in preserving

the Portuguese colonies as no longer worth the effort. For years past both in Mozambique and Angola there had been a guerrilla war between the Portuguese army and African nationalist forces. It was a stalemate in that neither side looked like obtaining a military victory. If either of the colonies had been self-governing and had controlled their own armies, the nationalists might have encountered a tougher resistance, for the settlers would have been fighting for their whole way of life. But the colonies were governed from Lisbon and were in no way geared for a UDI. In Portugal it became less and less obvious what advantage there was for one of the poorest and smallest countries in Europe to hang on to these legacies of a great, but remote imperial past. The victors of the *coup* pledged themselves to cede independence in both Angola and Mozambique as soon as possible.

The frontier of Angola does not march anywhere with that of Rhodesia being separated by Zambia and the Caprivi Strip. Mozambique and Rhodesia on the other hand are contiguous for hundreds of miles, and the colony under a friendly government at Lisbon was one of Rhodesia's mainstays in the battle against sanctions. This situation was rapidly transformed. The left-wing, Marxist-dominated FRELIMO, which under President Machel became by the end of 1975 the ruling party in Mozambique, cut off supplies to Rhodesia and gave open encouragement to guerrilla incursions.

Events in Angola, though more remote, were also of crucial significance. Unlike the nationalist movement in Mozambique, the Angolan equivalent was split into contesting factions, and in 1975, with the departure of the Portuguese, civil war broke out between the MPLA, led by Agostinho Neto and supported by Russia, and the non-Marxist UNITA, surreptitiously backed by South Africa, allegedly with American encouragement. The Russians, however, stole a march on the west by convoying and supplying with arms Cuban troops to support the MPLA which, not surprisingly, ended up victorious, although at the time of writing UNITA is still conducting a campaign of resistance in the bush.

The ever-orbiting Henry Kissinger, who had hitherto taken little interest in African affairs, now became alarmed. Southern Africa is the repository of immense known mineral wealth, and probably much that is as yet unknown. Two vast areas had now fallen, for the time being at least, into the Russian sphere of influence. What would happen in Rhodesia? The South African Government was evidently going through a similar reappraisal. In terms of *realpolitik* as opposed to ideology, the best hope was a 'moderate' black regime – ideally a Kenya or a Malawi, but if necessary a Zambia or a Zaïre. What had to be avoided at all costs was the equivalent of a Machel or a Neto in power in Salisbury.

The revolution in Portugal meant that Rhodesia now depended on South Africa for survival. Exactly what happened behind the scenes during the summer of 1976 can only be inferred from events. We have as yet no authentic information. All we do know is that, after intensive negotiations and discussions with Kissinger and Vorster in Pretoria, Ian Smith on September 24 made an astonishing *volte-face*. The man who had declared that black majority rule would not occur within a thousand years announced that he was prepared to accept it two years after the establishment of an interim government, subject to the conditions agreed with Kissinger.

Precisely what those conditions were has never been revealed, but one crucial point is clear; the control of the armed forces and the police was to be in white hands during the period of transition. The rest is obscure. There was apparently to be a two-tier government: a 'Council of State', half white and half black, which would function as a sort of Collective Governor; and a 'Council of Ministers' which would have a majority of Africans. But it was not to be a two-thirds majority, although a two-thirds majority would be required for any decisions by either body, and the Council of Ministers would be appointed by the Council of State. Since the two Councils had the task of drawing up the new constitution the prospect of rapid progress in that crucial field did not look good.

In his broadcast Smith referred to the substantial economic support to be provided by a trust fund financed internationally. Among other things it would guarantee pension rights and 'the investment of the individual in his own home and/or farm'. The plan apparently was not, as in Ireland at the turn of the century or Kenya in the 1960s, principally concerned with buying out the landowners. 'I made it clear', Smith said, 'that Rhodesians were not enamoured of schemes to buy them out', though those who wished to go ought to be compensated. 'Accordingly whatever plan is produced to assist those who decide to leave, the incentive should be aimed at making it worthwhile for Rhodesians to stay.' Presumably this meant a sort of sliding scale by which the first people to go would get less than those who took the risk of staying on for five years, ten years or some other period. No details were ever announced, but the plan sounded on the face of it a sensible solution to one of the most difficult problems attending the transfer of power in a society like Rhodesia's.

Smith's broadcast was both moving and dignified, but it contained provisos which ought to have warned the optimists that the process of transition to majority rule was not going to be easy. The Rhodesian Prime Minister emphasized the 'package' nature of the deal. The proposals all stood or fell together, and he dwelt on the 'categorical assurance' that Kissinger had given him about the 'cessation of terrorism', after 'the necessary preliminaries have been carried out' – an expression not entirely clear, but presumably meaning the formation of an interim government. He went on to emphasize that the British as well as the United States Government was convinced that this condition could be implemented, though he agreed that 'if we are realistic we must accept that terrorism cannot be halted at the drop of a hat', and he therefore urged the security forces not to diminish their vigilance. Smith also expressed his views on majority rule. He supported it, he said, 'provided that it is responsible rule'. He did not say by whom or how responsibility was to be judged.

It soon became clear that the package was not going to be accepted either by the so-called 'front-line' Presidents (of Botswana, Angola, Zambia, Tanzania and Mozambique) or by the various African groups in exile. Kissinger had cut his corners in this respect and had not secured the acceptance of these important elements – important because they alone had the power to call off the guerrilla campaign. At the ensuing Geneva Conference (October/December 1976) chaired by Ivor Richard (British ambassador to the UN) and convened to try to settle the process of transition, Smith stuck rigidly to what he believed – or said he believed – to be the Kissinger package. The African delegations refused to be bound by a contract to which they had never been parties, and, after the formation of the frankly left-wing 'Patriotic Front', headed by Nkomo and Robert Mugabe, it must have looked more and more doubtful to Vorster whether any bargain with them could result in a 'moderate' black regime. The change of Administration in America added a further element of confusion.

Smith left Geneva at an early stage. The latest evidence in the form of secret documents, extracts of which were published in the *Observer* of June 19, 1977, suggests that, with good reason from his point of view, he never intended to reach a settlement with the Patriotic Front. The documents were sent in October 1976 to leading figures in the Rhodesian political and military world. If they are authentic – and there is no reason to doubt the fact – it is clear that the Rhodesian Prime Minister was determined to keep European control over all the levers of power during the two year interim period. He was 'selling' the Kissinger deal to his supporters on the ground that it would buy time at a moment when the military and economic situation was deteriorating. One of the documents dwells on the promises that Smith said he had extracted from the 'Western World'. These included the lifting of sanctions, the cessation of 'terrorism' (i.e. guerrilla warfare) and the promise of financial aid. The documents emphasize that the interim government would be so constituted that the Europeans could prevent any major changes. The Council of State controlled the Council of Ministers and since it could only act with a two-thirds majority there was in effect a European fifty per cent blocking vote. Moreover, although the Rhodesian Parliament would be temporarily suspended, it would have to be recalled to ratify any sort of majority rule constitution proposed by the interim government, and ratification would also need a two-thirds majority. In effect Smith was saying in confidence that the interim government might or might not in the course of two years produce an acceptable majority rule constitution, but the mere establishment of such an interim government (which would be firmly placed in white hands) would mean the removal of sanctions, the discouragement by the West of guerrilla activity and, even if the war continued, valuable breathing space to deal with it more effectively.

None of this precluded an internal bargain with nationalist elements inside Rhodesia, leading to some form of majority rule modified by built-in safeguards for the Europeans, but it did preclude any deal with the Patriotic Front. The internal leader who seemed most promising was the Methodist Bishop Muzorewa, who had made his name during the course of the Pearce Commission's investigations as the foremost opponent of the Douglas-Home/Smith agreement. He is said by most people to be a 'moderate'; by some to be of a mild, but firm disposition, by others to be weak and ineffective. He is, or has been till very recently, by far the best known African leader within Rhodesia, for it has to be remembered that a decade of detention has made Nkomo, Sithole and Mugabe virtually non-persons to a whole generation of African youth.

The Patriotic Front is by no means in a strong position. Few people believe that it represents more than a plastering over of the old split between Nkomo's ZAPU and Sithole's ZANU which now appears to be under the control of Mugabe, a younger man than Sithole who is fading out. Mugabe is said to be a devout Roman Catholic, but also a Marxist. His power base is Mozambique and the guerrilla forces operating from there are under his control insofar as they are under anyone's. They probably represent the most serious threat to Rhodesian security. Hence the recent hot pursuit forays (June 1977) by Rhodesian forces. If they were ever to be reinforced by Cuban troops supplied with Russian weapons, as in Angola during 1975–6, the situation for Smith would be very bad indeed, but there is no evidence of this at the time of writing and much to suggest that Mozambique on its own is not in a condition to do anything very effective. The threat, therefore, can be regarded as serious only by comparison with others.

Nkomo's power base is the guerrilla forces operating from Zambia. No doubt he will try to build these up as fast as he can, but he was for a long while a genuine 'moderate' and it is only late in the day that he has committed himself to a solution by force – and not necessarily irrevocably. A deal between him and the Bishop is not inconceivable. Meanwhile he has every reason to strengthen his own armed forces as a counterpoise to those of Mugabe whom he certainly sees as a rival, not an ally. The wide open question remains, and can be fairly asked by Smith or any European successor, what claim can either Nkomo or Mugabe or any other African in exile make to 'legitimacy' in terms of representing the Rhodesian majority and hence to power in the future 'Zimbabwe'?

The conference was adjourned before Christmas, the only point agreed being that majority rule should be brought in by March 1978. The Chairman decided to tour the relevant southern African capitals and late in January 1977 he brought new proposals to Salisbury. These involved a resident British Commissioner at the head of a multi-racial Security Council and in effect almost immediate black majority government under the control of the 'Patriotic Front'. It was inconceivable that Smith would accept the notion of someone like Mugabe in charge, or even partly in charge of security; equally inconceivable that he would acquiesce in a semi-Marxist government. Nor was Vorster likely to press him to do so. Smith flatly rejected the Richard proposals and announced that he would proceed with his own internal plans for transition to majority rule. He added, without being very specific, that he intended to take immediate steps to remove racial discrimination. At about the same time Vorster declared that a settlement was a matter for Rhodesians and that he had no intention of putting pressure on their Government.

The Kissinger initiative failed partly because it was made by an Administration with a very uncertain tenure and by a Secretary of State who was unlikely to remain long in office even if the Republicans won the election. President Carter made it clear, however, that he was as keenly interested as his predecessor in securing a peaceful solution in Rhodesia. In April Dr Owen, the British Foreign Secretary, decided in conjunction with the new American Administration to make a fresh effort at persuading the Rhodesian Government to accept majority rule in 1978. Dr Owen paid a round of visits to the principal capitals concerned, and an Anglo-American team of officials began to operate from Lusaka in May. Nkomo and Mugabe objected to the American role, insisting that Rhodesia was a British colony and that the responsibility lay solely with the British Government, but this view was not accepted by Whitehall. At the time of writing no clear results have emerged or look like emerging at all soon.

It is impossible to say what will happen next. Vorster agreed in May to try to persuade Smith to move to majority rule, but just what this will amount to in practice is anyone's guess. That he has the power to force Smith's hand is undeniable, and one can only assume that it was his threat to do so which induced the Rhodesian Prime Minister to make his apparent *volte-face* in September 1976. It does not follow that he is prepared to lean so heavily on Smith again. A great deal depends on what sort of Black politicians he thinks are likely to control 'Zimbabwe'. Bishop Muzorewa or even Nkomo might be all right. Mugabe based on Marxist Mozambique would not.

We are in the realm of speculation. The historian should in general stick to the past and avoid the future, but there are some tentative predictions which can be justified by a knowledge of the past. The rule of the Europeans in Rhodesia is unlikely to last much longer. The whole tide of events is against it. South Africa is in a different position. The proportion of Whites to non-Whites is far higher than in Rhodesia and the non-Whites are more divided. To a much greater extent than is true of Rhodesia the Europeans in South Africa 'have nowhere to go'. Their determination to retain power is thus even stronger. Moreover, South Africa possesses strategic materials and a strategic location which are still of great importance to the West. Rhodesia has none of these assets, and the days of European monopoly are numbered – which is not to say that it will necessarily end next year or the year after. The most that anyone who wishes well to the white Rhodesians can hope is that the inevitable transition will be accomplished peacefully and not by blood and iron.

At the moment the chances do not seem good. It may be that Smith will produce – or be forced to produce – a genuine internal settlement leading to majority rule, but it does not seem likely. Nor should one be too censorious about the white Rhodesians whom he represents. They are not, after all, behaving oddly or out-rageously. What ruling class has ever voluntarily given up its position in the certain knowledge that its power would vanish overnight? Analogies with the British in India or with the English aristocracy in the nineteenth century are misleading. The British in India obeyed a government in London. The nineteenth century landowners when they accepted Reform Acts did not expect their power to vanish overnight, and they were quite right. But the white Rhodesians know that under majority rule theirs would, and they too are quite right. What they have they hold and it is all too likely that they will hold it either till it is prised from their grasp by force, or till the threat of revolution and civil war causes capitulation.

If so, it will be a sorry ending to a regime which, for all its failings and errors, has achieved during its 87 years great things for the country. It was not an unworthy ideal which inspired Cecil Rhodes, and he and his successors managed against all the odds to build up a flourishing colony in which the standard of living for Africans as well as Europeans improved out of all recognition. It is sad that the multi-racialism which genuinely inspired some of the makers of Rhodesia should have ended in a bleak and seemingly irreconcilable confrontation between black and white – sad but not perhaps wholly surprising.

Yet one should not conclude on too cynical a note. Within the European world there has been all along a minority which did not accept this harsh dichotomy between 'them' and 'us'. Although Ian Smith has regularly won every European seat, a solid core of 20 to 25 per cent of the electorate has consistently voted against him. There are many Europeans who have a conscience and a sense of their obligation to improve the lot of the African population among whom they so incongruously dwell. Their hope of a multi-racial society is not likely to be realized, but their aim was neither foolish nor ignoble and their contribution to African welfare was substantial and honourable. The historian of 'Zimbabwe' in the year 2000 will probably forget their existence or, if he remembers it, sneer at their political ineffectiveness. The obvious winners and losers are the natural objects of historical interest. It would be a pity, however, to disregard those who neither won nor lost, but tried to soften the acerbity of conflict and to provide some bridge between the polarized extremes towards which race relations have been moving in the second half of the twentieth century. This is an aspect of the rather melancholy twilight of white rule which deserves to be remembered amidst the increasing stridency of conflict.

APPENDIX
SELECT
BIBLIOGRAPHY
INDEX

Appendix: The Beit Trust

No history of Rhodesia should fail to mention the remarkable generosity of Sir Alfred Beit, Rhodes's silent and self-effacing partner. He died in 1906 and left a part of his fortune, £1,200,000, to set up what was called 'the Railway Trust' with the object of benefiting the colony which he had played his part in creating. The Trust was allowed to accumulate till 1927, which is the maximum period allowed by law, and the Trustees took advantage of this provision, although they did make large payments out of income during the 'dormant' period. The Trust contained the odd proviso, given the source of Beit's wealth, that it could be invested in anything except mining shares, but, as the authors of *The Will and The Way* (p. 53) put it, 'none knew better than Beit the speculative character of an investment of this kind'.

The primary purpose of the Trust, which was valued in 1927 at over £2,700,000, was to finance the construction of railways and so to break the vicious circle constricting the development of a poor and struggling colony. Unless it could export and import goods cheaply and quickly its taxable capacity would be low and the government would be unable to raise the money to build the railways which alone could solve the problem. If and when the problem no longer existed the Trustees had the power to use the fund for such educational, public or other charitable purposes in the two Rhodesias as they saw fit. The Trust made important contributions to the railways and objects closely connected with them, e.g. it financed the building of the Victoria Falls Hotel. By 1927 there had ceased to be such need for this sort of help and the Trustees concentrated on other forms of communication and transport, causeways and low-level bridges across the smaller rivers, and later the major all-weather bridges across the great rivers. The Alfred Beit Bridge across the Limpopo, which was opened in 1929, is the most famous. Others are the Birchenough Bridge over the Sabi River and the Otto Beit Bridge across the Zambesi at Chirundu. These were notable contributions to the prosperity of the country.

As time went on the Trustees tended to concentrate on education, both European and African. 'Beit Halls' are a feature of many schools. In the first fifty years of the Trust's existence it contributed over £750,000 towards education in Rhodesia. It also contributed generously in the field of health and social service. After the Federation had come into being, an Act of Parliament in 1954 enlarged the scope of the Trust to include Nyasaland, and it continues to this day to distribute sums of money in all three countries.

Select Bibliography

A. Manuscript Collections

The Papers of Lord Malvern
The Papers of Sir Roy Welensky
The Papers of Garfield Todd
The Papers of Winston Field
The National Archives of Rhodesia

B. Printed Works

Axelson E., *South East Africa 1488–1530* (1940)
Axelson, E., *The Portuguese in South-East Africa, 1600–1700* (1960)
Baldock, R. W., 'Chancellor and the Moffat Succession', *Rhodesian History* (Vol. 3, 1973)
Barber, James, *Rhodesia: The Road to Rebellion* (1967)
Beit, Sir A. and Lockhart, J. G., *The Will and the Way* (1957)
Bent, Theodor, *The Ruined Cities of Mashonaland* (1892)
Boxer, C. R., *Race Relations in the Portuguese Colonial Empire 1415–1825* (1963)
Butler, Lord, *The Art of the Possible* (1971)
Cary, Robert, *A Time to Die* (1969)
Cary, Robert, *Charter Royal* (1970)
Cecil, Lady Gwendolen, *The Life of Robert, Marquis of Salisbury* (Vol. iv, 1932)
Churchill, Lord Randolph, *Men, Mines and Animals in South Africa* (1892)
Clements, F. and Harben, E., *Leaf of Gold: the Story of Rhodesian Tobacco*
Clements, F., *Rhodesia, The Course to Collision* (1969)
Colquhoun, A. R., *Dan to Beersheba* (1908)
Colvin, Ian, *Life of Jameson* (2 vols, 1922)
Cosmin, B. A., 'The Pioneer Community of Salisbury in November 1897', *Rhodesian History* (Vol. 2, 1971)
Cripps, A. S., *An Africa for Africans* (1927)
Dachs, J. A. (ed.), *Christianity South of the Zambezi* (1973)

D'Erlanger, E. B., *The History of the Construction and Finance of the Rhodesian Transport System* (privately printed 1939)

Dorey, A., 'The Victoria Incident and Matabele War', *Central Africa Historical Association* (Local Series 16, 1966)

Fage, J. D., *An Atlas of African History* (1963)

Ferris, Colonel A. D., *Draft History of the British South Africa Company* (unpublished but completed in 1963)

Fisher, Sir Nigel, *Iain Macleod* (1973)

Fitzpatrick, Sir Percy, *Through Mashonaland with Pick and Pen* (1892)

Fort, G. S., *Dr. Jameson* (1908)

Fort, G. S., *Alfred Beit* (1932)

Gann, L. H., *A History of Northern Rhodesia, Early Days to 1953* (1964)

Gann, L. H., *A History of Southern Rhodesia, Early Days to 1933* (1965)

Gann, L. H. and Gelfand, M., *Huggins of Rhodesia* (1964)

Gelfand, M. and Ritchken, J. (ed.), *Godfrey Martin Huggins, Viscount Malvern 1883–1971* (1972)

Gelfand, M., *Tropical Victory: an Account of the Influence of Medicine on the History of Southern Rhodesia 1890–1923* (1953)

Gelfand, M., *Shona Religion with special reference to the Makorekore* (1962)

Glass, S., *The Matabele War* (1968)

Goldsworthy, D., *Colonial Issues in British Politics 1945–1961* (1971)

Gray, R., *The Two Nations* (1960)

Hailey, Lord, *An African Survey* (1956)

Hammond, R. J., *Portugal and Africa 1815–1910* (1966)

Hancock, Sir Keith, *Smuts, Volume 2: The Fields of Force 1919–1950* (1968)

Hanna, A. J., *The Story of the Rhodesias and Nyasaland* (1960)

Hazlewood, Arthur, 'The Economics of Federation and Dissolution in Central Africa' in *African Integration and Disintegration* (1967)

Headlam, C. (ed.), *The Milner Papers* (1931)

Hickman, Colonel A. S., *Men who made Rhodesia* (1960)

Hillier, V. W. (ed.), *Gold and Gospel in Mashonaland 1888* (1949 Oppenheimer Series, No. 4)

Hole, H. Marshall, *The Making of Rhodesia* (1926)

Hole, H. Marshall, *Lobengula* (1929)

Home, Lord, *The Way the Wind Blows: an Autobiography* (1976)

Johnson, Frank, *Great Days: The Autobiography of an Empire Pioneer* (1940)

Johnston, Alex, *The Life and Letters of Sir Harry Johnston* (1929)

Johnston, Sir Harry, *The Story of My Life* (1923)

Joyce, Peter, *Anatomy of a Rebel: Smith of Rhodesia* (1974)

Katzellenborgen, S. E., *Railways and the Copper Mines of Katanga* (1973)

Keatley, P., *The Politics of Partnership* (1962)

Knight, E. F., *Rhodesia of Today* (1895)

Leonard, Arthur, *How We Made Rhodesia* (1896)

Leys, Colin, *European Politics in Southern Rhodesia* (1959)

Lockhart, J. G. and Woodhouse, C. M., *Rhodes* (1963)

Long, B. K., *Drummond Chaplin: His Life and Times in Africa* (1941)

Lovell, R. I., *The Struggle for South Africa 1875–1899* (1934)

Macdonald, J. F., *The War History of Southern Rhodesia* (2 vols, 1947–50)

MacDonald, J. G., *Rhodes: a Life* (1927)

Macfarlane, R., *Some Account of George Grey and his Work in Africa* (1914)

Macmillan, Harold, *Pointing the Way* (1972)
Macmillan, Harold, *The End of the Day* (1973)
Mason, Philip, *Birth of a Dilemma* (1958)
Mason, Philip, *Year of Decision* (1960)
Michel, Sir L., *The Life of the Rt. Hon. Cecil John Rhodes 1853–1902* (2 vols, 1910)
Millais, J. G. M., *The Life of F. C. Selous* (1918)
Millin, S. G., *Rhodes* (1933)
Moffat, R. V., *John Smith Moffat* (1921)
Mulford, D. C., *Zambia: The Politics of Independence 1957–1964* (1967)
Murray, D. J., *The Governmental System in Southern Rhodesia* (1970)
Oliver, Rowland, *Sir Harry Johnston and the Scramble for Africa* (1957)
Palley, Claire, *The Constitutional History and Law of Southern Rhodesia 1888–1965* (1966)
Palmer, R. H., 'Aspects of Rhodesian Land Policy 1890–1936', *Central Africa Historical Association* (Local Series 22, 1968)
Paton, Alan, *Hofmeyr* (1964)
Perham, Margery, *Lugard, The Years of Adventure 1858–1895* (1956)
Plomer, William, *Cecil Rhodes* (1933)
Ranger, Terence, *Revolt in Southern Rhodesia* (1967)
Ranger, Terence (ed.), *Aspects of Central African History* (1968)
Reynolds, Rex, *Discussions with Lord Malvern with comments by Sir Ernest Guest* (1969–71 unpublished, see Acknowledgements). Cited as RR
Rifkind, Malcolm, *The Politics of Land* (unpublished MS thesis Edinburgh University 1968)
Robinson, R. and Gallagher, J., with Denny, A., *Africa and the Victorians* (1961)
Rolin, Henri, *Les Lois et l'Administration de la Rhodésie* (1913)
Samkange, S., *The Origins of Rhodesia* (1968)
Schreiner, Olive, *Trooper Peter Halket of Mashonaland* (1897)
Schrender, Derek, *Gladstone and Kruger* (1969)
Selous, F. C., *Sunshine and Storm in Rhodesia* (1896)
Shee, Charles, 'The Ill Health and Mortal Sickness of Cecil John Rhodes', *Central Africa Journal of Medicine* (April 1965)
Shamuyarira, Nathan, *Crisis in Rhodesia* (1965)
Skeen, Andrew, *Prelude to Independence* (1966)
Stent, Vere, *A Personal Record of some Incidents in the Life of Cecil Rhodes* (1924)
Stigger, P., 'Volunteers and the Profit Motive in the Anglo-Ndebele War', *Rhodesian History* (Vol. 2, 1971)
Summers, R., *Zimbabwe: A Rhodesian Mystery* (1964)
Sykes, F. W., *With Plumer in Mashonaland* (1897)
Tanser, G. H., *A Scantling of Time, The Story of Salisbury, Rhodesia 1890–1900* (1965)
Tawse-Jollie, E. M., *The Real Rhodesia* (1924)
Taylor, A. J. P., *Germany's First Bid for Colonies 1884–5* (1938)
Tredgold, Sir Robert, *The Rhodesia that was my Life* (1968)
Van der Poel, J. (ed), *Selections from the Smuts Papers* (6 vols, 1973)
Wallis, J. P. R., *One Man's Hand: the Story of Sir Charles Coghlan* (1950)
Welensky, Sir Roy, *Welensky's 4,000 Days* (1964)
Williams, Basil, *Cecil Rhodes* (1921)
Wills, A. J., *An Introduction to the History of Central Africa* (3rd edition 1973)
Willson, F. M. G. (ed.), *Source Book of Parliamentary Elections and Referenda in Southern Rhodesia 1898–1962* (1963)

Willson, F. M. G. and Passmore, G. C., *Catalogue of Parliamentary Papers of Southern Rhodesia 1899–1953* (1965)

Willson, F. M. G. and Passmore, G. C., *Southern Rhodesia: Holders of Office and Members of the Legislature 1894–1964* (1966)

Wilson, Harold, *The Labour Government 1964–70* (1971)

Wilson, Monica and Thompson, Leonard (ed.), *The Oxford History of South Africa* (Vol. 2, 1971)

Young, Kenneth, *Rhodesia and Independence* (2nd edition 1969)

C. Official Publications

UK Government Publications

Cmd. 7284 (1894) South Africa: correspondence respecting death at Tati of two *indunas* in October 1893.

Cmd. 7555 (1894) Matabeleland: report by F. J. Newton upon circumstances connected with collision of Matabele with forces of BSA Company at Fort Victoria July 1893.

Cmd. 8547 (1897) BSA Company report by Sir E. R. Martin on native administration ...

Cmd. 9318 (1898) BSA Company: Southern Rhodesia Order in Council.

Cmd. 7970 (1914) BSA Company's Supplemental Charter.

Cmd. 8674 (1917) Southern Rhodesia: papers relating to the native reserves commission, 1915 (Coryndon Report).

Judicial Committee of Privy Council: Ownership of unalienated land in Southern Rhodesia ... 1918.

Cmd. 1129 (1921) Southern Rhodesia: papers concerning Cave Commission.

Cmd. 1573 (1922) Southern Rhodesia: draft letters patent ... for responsible government.

Cmd. 1984 (1923) Southern Rhodesia: agreement between Secretary of State for colonies and BSA Company.

Cmd. 1922 (1923) Memorandum concerning Indians in Kenya (Devonshire Memorandum).

Cmd. 3234 (1929) Report on Closer Union in East and Central Africa (Hilton Young Commission).

Cmd. 3573 (1930) Memorandum on Native Policy in East Africa (Passfield memorandum).

Cmd. 5929 (1939) Report of the Rhodesia and Nyasaland Royal Commission (Bledisloe Report).

Cmd. 8233 (1951) Report of Conference of Officials on Closer Association in Central Africa (First London Conference).

Cmd. 8234 (1951) The Central African Territories: Historical, Geographical and Economic Survey.

Cmd. 8235 (1951) Comparative Survey of Central African Native Policies.

Cmd. 8573 (1952) Draft Federal Scheme.

Cmd. 8753 (1952) Report of Conference on Federation (Second London Conference).

Cmnd. 815 (1959) Report of Nyasaland Committee of Enquiry (Devlin Report).

Cmnd. 1148–51 (1960) Report of the Advisory Commission on Review of the Federal Constitution (Monckton Report).

Cmnd. 1291 (1961) Report of Southern Rhodesia Consititutional Conference in Salisbury.

Cmnd. 1399–1400 (1961) Southern Rhodesia Constitution Parts I and II.

Cmnd. 2807 (1965) Southern Rhodesia: documents relating to the negotiations between the UK and Southern Rhodesian Governments, November 1963–November 1965.

Cmnd. 3171 (1966) Rhodesia: documents relating to proposals for a settlement 1966 (HMS *Tiger*).

Cmnd. 3793 (1968) Rhodesia: documents relating to proposals for a settlement 1968 (HMS *Fearless*).

Cmnd. 4065 (1969) Rhodesia: report on exchanges with the regime since the talks held in Salisbury in November 1968.

Cmnd. 4835 (1971) Rhodesia: proposals for a settlement agreed on November 21 1971 between the British and Rhodesian governments.

Cmnd. 4964 (1972) Rhodesia: report of the commission on Rhodesian opinion (Pearce Commission).

Southern Rhodesian and Rhodesian Publications

CSR. 3 (1926) Report of the Land Commission for Southern Rhodesia (Morris Carter Report).

CSR. 3 (1930) Report on Industrial Relations in Southern Rhodesia (Henry Clay Report).

L.A.S.C. (1959) First Report of the Select Committee on Resettlement of Natives (first Quinton Report).

L.A.S.C. (1960) Second Report of the Select Committee on the Resettlement of Natives (second Quinton Report).

The Constitution of Rhodesia (1965).

CSR. 49 (1966) Relations between the Rhodesian Government and the UK Government November 1965–December 1966.

Report of the Constitutional Commission (Whaley Report 1968).

CSR. 32 (1969) Proposals for a new Constitution for Rhodesia.

CSR. 36 (1969) Statement on Anglo-Rhodesian Relations December 1966 to May 1969.

The Pearce Commission Report: a Statement by the Rhodesian Government May 23, 1972.

Index

Abenhla, 20, 118

Abercorn, James Hamilton, 2nd Duke of, 52, 53*n*, 73

Abezansi, 20, 118, 119

Aborigines Protection Society, 50, 51, 58, 177, 197, 199

Abrahamson, A. E., 309

'activism', 30

Adendorff *trek*, 69, 90, 94, 98

Administrator, post of, 152, 153, 166

African Affairs Board, 253–4, 260, 264, 265, 267–8, 287, 296, 299, 300

African Lakes Company, 77, 79, 91

African National Congress, 227, 300, 305, 306, 313, 316, 323–5

Africans:
   franchise, 150, 240, 263, 267, 287, 290, 296, 297, 299, 302–3, 313, 333, 342, 344, 383, 396; impact of white rule on, 155–60; as labour force, 156–7, 161, 162–3, 164, 196, 200, 202–3, 228, 277, 281; assimilation and integration, 156–7, 160, 161–5; segregation, 157–8, 160, 161–5, 215, 228, 229–30, 281; sexual discrimination, 158–60, 279–80, 301–302; missionaries' attitude to, 160–1; land problem, 162–3, 197, 198–204; 'locations', 163; passes and registration certificates, 163, 281; increasing voice of, 196–7; strike action, 197, 240, 294; population, 199, 221, 223, 243; urbanization, 203, 229–30, 238, 281, 338; opposed to amalgamation, 225, 226; quasi-religious movements, 227–8; in armed forces, 233, 235; trade unionism, 240; opposed to federation, 255, 258–9, 261–2,

265, 266, 268, 322–3, 327, 331, 343; in domestic service, 277; immigrants' view of, 281; in Federal Assembly, 290; lessening social barriers, 290–1, 338; earnings, 291, 307; alienation of nationalists, 320, 323; extension of self-government, 322, 326, 329–330; nationalist misjudgements, 340, 342; nationalist divisions, 351–3; docility under UDI, 389–90; deteriorating living conditions, 395; rejection of Home/Smith agreement, 404–5

Afrikaner Bond, 30, 31, 90, 124

Afrikaners, 17–18; sympathy with Boers, 29–30; nationalism of, and Boer War, 153; and union, 179; immigrants, 274, 277, 279

agriculture, 223, 275

Aitken, Sir Max, 400, 402

Aitken-Cade, Stewart, 338

Alderson, Lieut.-Colonel E. A. H., 133, 135, 140–1, 142

Algeria, 329

Alice Mine, 134

Allen, Lieut.-Colonel Ichabod, 375

Alport, Lord, 400

Altrincham, Lord, 258

Amaholi, 20, 118

amalgamation, 165, 175, 209, 210–11, 224–6, 237, 247–8, 252–3, 259, 294

Amery, Julian, 258, 260, 262

Amory, Lord, 379

Anderson, Sir Percy, 91

Anderson, Major-General (GOC Rhodesia), 367, 369

Anglo-Portuguese Treaty: (1890) 82–3, 84, 87,

90; (1891) 89
Angola, 30, 76, 89, 90, 91, 189, 406, 409
Angra Pequena, 31
apartheid, 212, 240, 247, 251, 254
Appointed Members, 263–4, 267
Argus Press, 354, 367
Armitage, Sir Robert, 325
Arnold-Forster, Hugh, 51
assimilation, 156–7, 160, 161–5
Austral Company, 55

Babyan (*induna*), 50
Baden-Powell, Colonel R. S. S. (later Lord), 133, 140
Bailey, Sir Abe, 184
Bailie, Alexander, 26
Baines, Thomas, 25
Bamangwato tribe, 25
Banda, Dr Hastings, 248, 261, 324, 325, 327, 331, 332, 334, 337
Bantu, 6, 8–12, 14–16, 197
Banyailand, 90
Barkly, Sir Henry, 26
Barnato, Barney, 36, 44
Barotseland, 62, 81, 83, 90, 91, 164, 197, 209, 244
Barreto, Francisco, 12
Barrow, Sir Malcolm, 263
Basutoland, 197
Beadle, Sir Hugh, 231, 249, 372, 379, 380, 386, 397, 398, 400
Beal, Lieut.-Colonel Robert, 130, 133, 140
Beatty, Chester, 210
Bechuanaland, 26, 31, 49, 53, 197; railway, 40, 41
Bechuanaland Border Police, 107, 113
Bechuanaland Exploration Company, 42, 62
Beira, 11, 85–7, 89, 183, 223, 391
Beira Patrol, 392, 393, 394
Beit, Alfred, 35, 44, 51, 53*n*, 55, 58, 97, 153, 166, 415–16
Belgium, 31, 189
Bellingwe, 128
Belvedere (Salisbury), 234
Benson, Sir Arthur, 250, 252, 256, 324
Benson, Ivor, 367
Bent, Theodore, 96
Bere, Shona Chief, 103
Bieler, Father, 145
Birchenough, Sir Henry, 191, 225
Biscoe, Lieutenant Tyndal, 75
Bismarck, Otto von, Prince, 31, 36, 37
Bisset, Sir Murray, 207–8
blacks – *see* Africans
Blakiston, John L., 134

Blantyre, 77, 324–5
Bledisloe Commission (1938), 225–6, 237
Blood River, 15
Boers, 17–22, 25–7, 29–30, 38, 59, 90–1, 124
Boer Wars:
   first (1880–1) 26–7, 30; second (1899–1902) 30, 153, 154
Boggie, Alexander, 44
Bondelzwarts massacre, 184
Borrow, Henry, 62, 63, 65, 67, 109
Botha, Louis, 179, 183
Botswana, 23, 25, 31
Bottomley, Arthur, 357, 368, 369, 370, 371, 376–377, 391
Bowden, Herbert, 397
Bower, Graham, 108
Boyle, Frank, 44
Bright, John, 297
British Bechuanaland Police, 62, 68*n*
British Council of Churches, 379
British South Africa Company – *see* Chartered Company
British South Africa Company Police, 67, 68*n*, 69, 71, 73, 102, 107, 153, 231
Broederbond, 394
Brown, George (now Lord George-Brown), 262
Buchan, Max, 301, 306
Buchanan, John, 79, 80
Bulawayo, 19, 26, 38, 52, 63, 112, 119, 122, 147, 152, 173, 276, 340; missions to Lobengula at, 42, 43–8, 55, 56; Jameson in, 57–8, 59–61, 70; *coup* against, 105, 107, 108; and Matabele rebellion, 128–9, 130, 131, 132–3; railway, 144, 145; Administrator at, 148; secondary to Salisbury, 222, 223; Iron and Steel Works, 236; industrial unrest, 240
Bulawayo Field Force, 129, 132, 133
Bulhoek, 184
Burnett, Ted, 62, 74
Burnham, F. R., 127–8
Burumbo, Benjamin, 240, 323
Bushmen, 6
Butler, David, 366, 372, 373, 388
Butler, R. A. (now Lord), 345, 346–7, 348–50, 351, 379
Buxton, Sir Fowell, 50
Buxton Committee (1921), 179, 180–1, 182, 187

Caborabassa dam, 89
Campbell, Evan, 357, 360, 365, 371, 375, 378
'Cape to Cairo' plan, 37, 38, 78, 113, 145, 154, 183, 189
Cape Colony, 25–6, 68, 106, 151, 165, 197; early Dutch settlers, 16, 158; British policy in, 16–19,

Cape Colony —*cont.*
  29–32, 40–1; self-government, 29; 'colonialism', 29–31; Transvaal challenge, 31, 32, 38, 166; Rhodes as Premier, 72, 113, 124
Capricorn Africa Society, 262, 291
Caradon, Lord, 276, 355
Carbutt, Colonel, 219
Carnarvon, Henry Herbert, 4th Earl of, 26, 30
Carnarvon Commission (1881), 17
Carrington, Sir Frederick, 65 and *n*, 125, 131, 133, 135, 136, 142
Carter, President Jimmy, 394, 410
Carter Commission (1925), 198, 200–3
Cary, Robert, 64, 66*n*
cattle, 117–18, 119, 120, 123
Cave Commission (1919), 178, 180
Cawston, George, 42, 49, 50, 53*n*, 55, 58, 62, 66
Central African Council, 237, 241, 250
Central African Federation, 152, 175, 216, 225, 242; origins of, 243–54; achievement of, 255–269; Constitution, 263–8, 284–5, 296–9, 324; heyday of, 284–95; economy, 288–9; race relations, 291–2; siting of capital, 292; and dominion status, 294, 298; franchise, 296–8, 299–300, 302–4, 313, 333; Cabinet revolts, 306, 307–9; decline of, 319–32; African nationalist opposition, 322–4; secession from, 331–2, 345–346; 1961 Constitution, 333–5, 355; dissolution inevitable, 346–7; dissolution (1963), 351
Central African Party, 335
Central Search Association, 55
Cetewayo, 26
Chalmers, Lord, 178
Chamberlain, Joseph, 22, 36, 133, 137, 148, 150, 176; and 'imperial factor', 30, 149; and South Africa Committee, 51; distrust of Rhodes, 52; and Jameson Raid, 130, 131, 139; anxiety to preserve Chartered Company, 138–9, 142, 147, 149
Chancellor, Sir John, 174, 191, 208–9
Changa, King of the Karanga, 9
Changamire kingdom, 9, 11, 12, 14, 20
Chaplin, Sir Drummond, 173–4, 175, 176, 180, 181, 186, 188, 191
Chartered Company, 51, 57, 115, 121, 174–5, 185, 198, 276, 279; granting of charter, 52–5; powers of, 53–4; share capital, 55, 98; first mining operation, 60, 61; *coup* against Bulawayo, 62, 63–7; Johnson's contract with, 65–7; Pioneer march into Mashonaland, 67–75, 76, 82, 93; failure to take Katanga, 82; alarm at Adendorff *trek*, 90; and Nyasaland, 91–2; and title to allocate land, 94; and settler discontents, 97–8, 166; tottering fortunes, 98–9; juridical position,

100–2; and Matabele war, 102–10, 111–13; unification of Matabeleland and Mashonaland as Rhodesia, 114; and rebellions, 129–33, 138–139, 142; closer control of, 148–50; character of officials, 151–2; its rule from 1902–18, 155–169; doctrine of assimilation, 156–7; Supplemental Charter (1914), 167; expropriation of, 183, 190–1, 206, 210, 239; mineral rights, 210, 213–14
Chelmsford, Lord, 26
Chiefs and Headmen, 164; *indabas* on independence, 365, 367, 370; in 1966 proposed Constitution, 396, 397–8; in 1969 Constitution, 402, 403
Chikerema, James, 323
Chitako, 8
Chocko, Monomatapa, 14
Choua Hill, 89
Church of the White Bird, 227
Churchill, Lord Randolph, 40, 96–7
Churchill, Winston, 153, 174*n*, 180–1, 182, 190, 258, 371
City Youth League, 323
Civil Service, 151–2, 260, 264, 285, 290, 338, 361, 367, 387, 389
Clarke, Sir Marshall, 150
Clay, Sir Henry, 206, 222
Clements, Frank, 37, 188, 273–4, 278, 289, 314
climate, 5, 94–5
Clutton-Brock, Guy, 305, 309, 313
coal, 222, 293
Coghlan, Sir Charles, 160, 190, 191, 205, 209, 215, 218, 220, 288; tomb of, 7, 206; leader of 'Unofficials', 167, 179; and Responsible Government, 179, 180, 184, 190; contest with Smuts, 181–2, 184–7; Premier, 194–6; death, 206
Cohen, Sir Andrew, 250–1, 252, 258
Coillard, Francis, 81
Colby, Sir Geoffrey, 263
Cold Storage Company, 223
Colenbrander, John, 49, 61, 73, 106, 136, 137
Colonial Office, 29, 30, 38, 101, 129, 139, 148, 199, 201, 237, 284; and charter, 41, 42, 52; and indirect rule, 112; dislike and distrust of Chartered Company, 150, 152, 166, 174–5, 185; favours segregation, 160; and ownership of unalienated land, 177; and expropriation of Company, 190–1, 206, 210; discourages amalgamation, 224, 225; merged with Foreign Office, 285
'colonialism', 29–30, 31, 37
Colquhoun, Alexander, 72, 76, 81, 83–7, 95–6, 97–8, 100, 152

Commandant General, 150
Commonwealth Parliamentary Association, 258
Commonwealth Relations Office, 284, 285, 382, 393
Confederate Party, 286, 288, 300
Congo, 76, 77, 80, 82, 154, 189, 329–30
Conservative Party, 249; changed attitude to 'decolonization' after Suez, 321–2; and federation, 257, 258, 259, 262, 335–6; and UDI, 393, 402
Consolidated Goldfields of South Africa, 44, 51
Constitution:
  (1898) 148–51
  (1923) 182, 185, 191–5, 200, 202, 213
  (1953) 263–8, 284–4, 296–300; changes in 299–300, 324
  (1961) 333–5, 355, 363, 364, 376–7, 383–4; referendum on, 334, 336; independence based on, 365, 366, 370, 380; revised proposals, 396–9
  (1965) 372, 383, 384, 386, 403
  (1969) 386, 401–4
  (1971) proposals, 403–4; rejected by Africans, 404–5
Constitutional Council, 333–4
'Convention, The', 193
Cooper-Chadwick, J., 44, 57
copper, 222, 236, 244, 391
Copper Belt, 210, 223, 225, 235–6, 244, 257
Coryndon, Sir Robert, 81, 198
Coryndon Commission (1914), 198–200
Country Party, 212
Crawford, Sir Frederick, 388
Creech Jones, Arthur, 248–9, 250, 262
Criminal Trials Act (1927), 196
Cripps, Rev. Shirley, 196
Cunningham, General Alan, 233, 234

Dale, W. L., 250
Dalhousie, Simon Ramsay, 16th Earl of, 295, 325
D'Almeida, Francisco, 11
Dambarare, 12
Danziger, Max, 214
Davenport, Sir George, 309, 311
Davies, H. H., 228, 235, 236
De Beers, 43, 44, 55, 99
De Gaulle, General Charles, 329
De la Penouse, Vicomte, 96
Deal, Johnnie, 234
Declaration of Rights, 333–4, 396, 402, 403
Defence Committee, 232
Delagoa Bay, 15, 183
Derby, Edward Stanley, 14th Earl of, 22, 31, 57, 246
Devlin Report, 327

Devonshire, Victor Cavendish, 9th Duke of, 174n, 190, 340, 356
Devonshire Agreement (1923), 191, 210, 211, 213
diamonds, 25–6, 32, 35
Dias, Bartolomeo, 11
Dilhorne, Lord, 365
Dilke, Sir Charles, 17
Dillon, Ian, 359
'Dingaan's Day', 15
Dingiswayo, Chief of Mthethwa, 14–15
Disraeli, Benjamin, 26, 57, 246, 297
District Officers, 258
Dombo, Changamire, 12
Domboshawa: indaba on independence (1964), 370
Dominion Party, 237, 300, 301, 302, 304, 311–12, 316, 334, 338, 342
Dominions Office, 193, 219, 224
Doornkop, 124
Dorman, Sir Maurice, 404
Douglas-Home, Sir Alec – see Home, Lord
Downie, J. W., 213, 214
Doyle, Denis, 59, 61, 70, 87
Dreyer, C. D., 43, 46, 48
Duncan, A. H. F., 129, 130
Dupont, Clifford, 363, 364, 386, 394, 397, 402
Dutch, 16–18
Dutch Reformed Church, 160, 187, 291

economy, 168–9, 210, 211, 222–3, 244, 288–9, 393–5, 401
Eden, Anthony (later Lord Avon), 258
education, 161, 277–8
Edwards, Frank, 120
Edwards, S. M., 43
Elebe, 62
Elected African Members, 263, 267, 268, 299
Elected Members, 263–4, 267, 268, 299
Ellman-Brown (MP), 305, 307, 308, 309, 311
Empire Training Scheme, 234
Evans, Sir Athol, 250, 356
Evans, Stanley, 258, 262
Executive Council, 149, 151, 192, 195, 245
Exploring Company, 42, 49, 50

Fabian Colonial Bureau, 262
Fairbairn, James, 44, 49, 53
Fairfield, Edward, 154
Fearless talks (1968), 400–1, 402
Federal Assembly, 296, 298, 299
Federal Electoral Act (1958), 299
Federal Franchise Act (1957), 299, 303–4

Federal Legislature, 253–4, 263–4, 267, 287, 296, 297, 299
Federal Review Conference (1960), 332
Federation – *see* Central African Federation
Fernandes, Antonio, 11
Ferriera, Colonel, 69, 88–9
Ferriera, Commandant Ignatius, 90, 105
Fiddes, Sir George, 175
Field, Winston, 242, 275, 318, 331, 372, 378; leads Dominion Party, 300, 302; opposes 1961 Constitution, 335; leads Rhodesian Front, 342, 343; seeks independence, 346, 347, 348–50, 354–5, 356–9; boycotts Victoria Falls Conference, 348–9; restrictions on African Nationalists, 352, 353; disappointing London talks, 358–9; dismissed, 359–60, 362
Fife, William Duff, 6th Earl of, 51, 52, 53*n*
First Rhodesia Regiment, 165
First World War, 168–9
Fitzpatrick, Percy, 97
Fletcher, Sir Patrick, 259, 305–6, 308–9, 310, 314, 318
Foot, Sir Dingle, 327
Forbes, Major, 85–7, 96, 107, 108–9
Fort Tuli, 95, 97, 107
Fort Victoria, 74, 103, 104, 105, 106, 107, 109, 135
Fox, Wilson, 156, 164, 165, 175
franchise:
  qualifications, 150, 192, 263, 296, 303, 304, 333; Tredgold Report on, 297–8; common roll, 297, 313, 403; separate rolls, 297, 313, 403; 'special votes', 297–8, 302–3; General Roll, 299, 302; Special Roll, 299, 302; 'A' and 'B' Rolls, 333, 341, 350, 354, 373, 383, 396; reciprocal devaluation, 333
FRELIMO, 406
Frere, Sir Bartle, 26
Fynn, Sir Percy, 194, 211, 218, 220, 221

Gaitskell, Hugh, 326
Galitzine, Prince Yurka, 266
Gallagher, John, 17*n*
Gama, Vasco da., 11
Gann, L. M., 104, 134, 142, 162, 210, 211, 276, 284
Gardiner, Lord, 371
Gazaland, 81, 84, 87, 89
General Elections:
  (1924), 194, 218; (1928), 207, 218; (1933), 194, 214–16, 219; (1934), 194, 221, 224; (1939), 221, 231; (1946), 194, 239; (1948), 194, 237, 241–2, 247; (1953): Federal, 285–6; (1954), 288; (1958), 311–12; (1962), 341–4; (1965),

372–3, 374
General Elections (British):
  (1950), 249; (1959), 326; (1964), 368; (1970), 402
Geneva Conference (1976), 408–9
German East Africa, 76, 80, 154, 168
German South West Africa, 31, 168
Germany, 31–2, 63
Gibbs, Sir Humphrey, 364, 372, 385, 386–7, 390, 397, 402
Gibbs, Captain: and Gwelo Field Force, 133
Gifford, Lord, 42, 46, 49, 50, 53*n*, 55, 58, 62, 66
Gilchrist, Robert, 212, 214
Gladstone, W. E., 26, 27, 29, 57, 113
gold, 24, 25, 29, 32, 35, 67, 93–4, 99, 211
Gold Coast (Ghana), 322
Goldsworthy, David, 321
Gomalla, headman, 103
Gona Kudzingwa, 363
Gondo, J. M., 373
Goodenough, General, 137, 139, 141
Goodman, Lord, 341, 400, 402–3
Goold-Adams, Colonel, 107–8, 113
Gordon Walker, Patrick, 255, 256, 259, 262
Gorongoza, 84, 86
Graham, Lord (Duke of Montrose), 379, 397, 398, 399*n*, 401
Grant, J. A., 81, 82
Great Fish River, 16
Great Northern Trade and Gold Exploration Company, 62
Great Trek, 15, 16, 17, 18–19
Green, Charles, 234
Greenfield, Julian, 286–7, 309, 321
Greenhill, Lord, 403
Grey, Albert, 4th Earl, 51, 73, 123, 148, 152, 153; and Chartered Company, 52, 53*n*; as Administrator, 116, 130; and rebellions, 130–2, 139, 140, 142, 145–6
Grey, Lady, 136, 137, 139, 140, 142–3
Grey, Peter, 338
Griffiths, James, 249, 251, 258–9, 260, 261
Griqualand West, 25–6
Grobler Treaty (1887), 35, 39
Grobler's Drift, 70
Grootboom, John, 135, 136, 137
Groote Schuur, 97, 153
Guest, Sir Ernest, 184, 186, 214, 218, 227, 231, 232–3, 256, 257
Gumporeshumba, 134
Gungunhana, Chief of Gazaland, 81, 84, 87
Gutteridge, William, 390
Gwai Reserve, 116
Gwelo, 128, 197, 214, 220

Gwelo Field Force, 133
Gwelo Native Welfare Association, 197

Haggard, Alfred, 56
Hailey, Lord, 258
Hall, K. L., 237
Hammerskjöld, Dag, 330
Hammond, R. J., 80
Hancock, Sir Keith, 183
Harare, 323
Harcourt, Lewis, 174 and n
Harcourt, Sir William, 174
Harlech, Lord, 234, 404
Harper, William, 338, 342, 399n, 401
Harris, Frank, 79
Harris, 'Frankie', 220
Harris, Dr Rutherfoord, 56, 57, 63, 82, 84, 87,
    92, 98, 104, 105, 106, 130, 150
Hartley, Henry, 25
Hatty (MP), 305, 306, 308n, 311
Heany, Maurice, 62, 63, 65, 67, 74
Heath, Edward, 392, 402
Helm, Rev. C. D., 39, 44, 46, 47, 49, 58
Hepburn, Rev. E. D., 64
Herzog, J. B. M., 181, 185, 205
Heyman, Captain, 71, 88–9
High Commissioner, 149–50, 151
Hillside (Bulawayo), 311
Hilton Young Commission (1929), 209
Hofmeyr, Jan, 31, 90
Holderness, Hardwicke, 234, 303, 312, 315–17
Hole, Marshall, 38, 48, 66n, 67, 94, 99, 103, 115,
    124, 131
Home, Lord (also as Sir Alec Douglas-Home),
    257, 326, 327, 336, 347, 350, 369, 378, 382, 388,
    400; negotiations with Smith and Field, 341,
    355, 356–7, 363, 364–5, 367–8; agreement,
    402–3, 404
Homer, Fernandes, 12
Hoste, 'Skipper', 71, 72, 74, 75, 94n
Howman, J. D., 360, 372, 396, 397, 399n
Hudson, Sir Robert, 194, 240
Huggins, Sir Godfrey (later Lord Malvern), 63,
    186, 194–5, 209, 255, 297, 309, 320, 346, 378,
    382; leaves Rhodesia Party and later joins
    Reform Party, 212; and native problem and
    racialism, 212, 215, 219, 227, 228, 238; attacks
    Company, 213; leader of Opposition, 214;
    Prime Minister after 1933 election, 216, 219;
    character and views, 217–19, 295; his Industrial
    Conciliation Act, 219–20; heads coalition after
    political upheaval, 220–1; economic policy,
    222–3; and amalgamation, 224, 225, 226, 237,
    259–60; and 'parallel development', 228, 238;
and African urbanization, 229–30, 238; 1939
election success, 231; forms Defence Committee, 232; closer relations with South Africa,
234–5; and Labour, 235, 236; precarious
position, 236–7; 'liberalism', 238–9, 241–2;
narrow 1946 victory, 239; buys out railways,
239; and African strike, 240; rejects political
'deals', 240; engineers dissolution, 241; sweeping 1948 victory, 241; supports federation, 242,
247–9, 257, 260, 263, 266–8; at Lancaster
House Conference, 263–4; difficulty over safeguards for Africans, 266–7; wins referendum,
268; Federal Prime Minister, 285–6, 293–5;
seeks dominion status, 294; resigns, 294; on
dissolution of Federation, 351; on Smith,
360–1; opposes UDI, 388
Hughes, Cledwyn, 376
hut tax, 156, 161
hydro-electricity, 293, 391

immigration, 273–4, 282
Immorality Suppression Act (1903), 159, 301,
    302, 306, 338
'imperial factor', 30, 31, 35, 37
Industrial and Commercial Workers Union
    (ICU), 197, 212, 240
Industrial Conciliation Act (1934), 219–20;
    (1964), 338
Inskipp, F. W., 198
Inter-racial Association, 291, 303
Inter-Territorial Secretariat, 237
Inyati Mission, 21–3
Iron Age peoples, 8
Isandhlwana, 26
ivory trade, 23

Jacha, Aaron, 227
James, Sir Morrice, 396, 398
Jameson, Dr (later Sir) Leander Starr, 33, 52,
    64, 69, 81, 86, 90, 99, 113, 152, 153, 159,
    166, 177; tomb of 7, 57, 180; and Lobengula,
    22, 56–7, 59–61, 63, 70, 73, 102, 105, 106, 108,
    111; career, 56–7; and Pioneer Column, 72, 73,
    76; reconnoitres route from Manicaland to sea,
    84–5; Managing Director in Mashonaland,
    97–8, 100; and Matabelé war, 102–8; Adminis-
    trator, 114, 115–17; and land and cattle allo-
    cation, 115–17; his raid, 123–4, 131, 147, 148–
    149; favours amalgamation, 175, 176; death, 180
Jarvis, Sir Alexander, 125
Johnson, Sir Frank, 42, 52, 57, 97, 98, 214, 238;
    career, 62–3; and Lobengula, 62, 63; and
    Selous, 63, 64–5, 66; plans to occupy Mashona-
    land, 63–4, 65–7; alleged contract, 63–4; con-
    tract with Chartered Company, 65–7; and

Johnson —*cont.*
  Pioneer Column, 67–9, 71, 93; and route from Manicaland to sea, 84–5; and Progressive Party, 206, 207, 218
Johnston, Sir Harry, 36, 38, 78–9, 80, 83, 91–2, 244
Jones, Sir Elwyn, (now Lord Elwyn-Jones) 379, 397
Jones, Sir Glyn, 404
June Hill, 188

Kadalie, Clemens, 197
Kafue River, 293
Kagubi medium, 134, 141, 142
Kalanga, 127, 128, 129
Kaparavidze, King of the Karanga, 12
Karanga tribe, 8–12
Kariba, 293, 391
Katanga, 62, 77, 81–2, 330, 335
Kaunda, Kenneth, 324, 325, 332, 334, 350, 353, 391
Keith, A. B., 226
Keller, Jack, 194, 235, 236, 241
Kennedy, Sir John, 241, 256, 258
Kenya, 209, 210, 322, 407
Kerby, Henry, 399*n*
Khama, Chief of Bamangwato, 45, 46, 62
Khama of Bechuanaland, 127, 197
Khoikhoi (Hottentots), 16, 18
Kimberley, Lord, 17
Kimberley, 34, 35
Kipling, Rudyard, 27, 68, 154
Kissinger, Dr Henry, 293, 406–8, 409–10
Kittermaster, Sir Harold, 225
Knight, E. F., 121
Knight, R. J., 311
Knight-Bruce, Dr, Bishop of Bloemfontein, 44, 89
Knutsford, Lord, 39, 42, 50, 51, 52, 55, 58–9, 60, 94, 101, 106
Kruger, Paul, 123, 149; and London Convention, 31; rivalry with Rhodes, 38, 40, 123; and Grobler Treaty, 38, 39; discourages Adendorff *trek*, 69, 90
Kulumana, son of Mzilikazi, 24, 26
Kunzi-Nyandoro, 134, 142
Kuruman Mission, 20, 23

Labouchère, Henry, 51, 67, 103, 113
Labour Party (British), and federation, 248, 249, 254, 257, 261, 262, 326; and independence, 368–73, 375, 382–3, 390, 392, and 1971 provisional settlement, 404
Labour Party (Rhodesia), 206, 221, 224, 240, 288;

electoral defeats, 194, 207, 216, 219; opposes racial equality, 227, 229; 1939 election, 231; and Huggins, 235–7; split and eventual extinction, 237, 239, 241
Lambert, Sir Henry, 176, 180
Lancaster House Conferences: (1952), 261, 262–265; (1960), 322
land:
  alienation by Chartered Company, 115–17, 162; Ndebele grievances over, 162–3; Privy Council's decision on, 176–8; problem of, 198–204
Land Apportionment Act (1931), 202–4, 205, 209, 220, 224, 229–30, 236, 342, 350, 357; Amendment (1941), 238, 281, 282, 290; (1961), 338–9
Land Commission: (1894), 114–15, 116, 117–18, 119; (1925), 198, 200–3
Land Husbandry Act (1951), 323
Lardner-Burke, D. W., 363, 397, 399*n*
Law and Order Maintenance Act (1960), 330
Lawley, Arthur, 36, 148
Leask, Thomas, 44
Leggate, W. M., 194, 216, 221
Legislative Assembly, 192–3, 194, 241, 333–4, 383, 396
Legislative Council, 149, 150–1, 157, 166–8, 175–178, 180, 185, 186, 187, 190, 197, 245, 335, 337
Lendy, Captain, 101–2, 103–5
Lennox-Boyd, Alan (now Viscount Boyd), 258, 297, 324, 328
Leonard, Major Arthur, 68, 71
Leopold II of the Belgians, 31
Lesseps, Ferdinand de, 78
Lettow-Vorbeck, General von, 168, 233
Lewanika, Barotse Chief, 81, 127, 140, 197
Lewis, V. A., 221
Leys, Colin, 199*n*, 276
Liberal Party (British), 326
Liberal Party (Rhodesia), 194, 237, 239, 240, 241, 286, 288, 404
Lilford, D. C., 342
Limpopo River, 4, 5, 15, 19, 90, 412
Lippert, E. A., 44, 49, 94
Lippert Concession, 94, 111, 177
Liquor Amendment Act (1957), 290
living standards, 277–9, 291, 388–9, 395
Livingstone, David, 5, 21, 77
Livingstone, 175
Llewellin, Lord, 269, 285, 295
Lloyd George, David, 183, 190
Lobengula, King of Matabele:
  concessions to Chartered Company and others, 19, 25, 43–53, 55–61, 69–70, 94; and Jameson, 22, 56–7, 63, 70, 73, 102, 105, 106,

108, 111; and Moffat, 23; problem of succession, 23, 24, 26; his rule, 24–5, 27, 45–6; murder of British emissary, 26; and Grobler Treaty, 38–9; and Moffat Treaty, 39, 42; territorial claims in Mashonaland, 49, 50, 52, 65, 73, 100; slaughter of opponents, 59; and Johnson, 62; and route of Pioneer Column, 69–70, 73; and Matabele war, 100–9, 111, 127; death, 111

'locations', 163

Loch, Sir Henry, 50, 64, 69, 71, 101, 106–7, 113–114, 117, 149

Lochner, F. E., 81

Lockhart, J. G., 67, 97n

Lomagundi, Shona Chief, 100

London Chamber of Commerce, 51

London Convention (1884), 31, 38

London and Limpopo Mining Company, 25

London Missionary Society, 23

Long, Walter, 174n, 175, 176

Longden, Herbert, 179, 187

Lotje, induna, 46, 59, 70

Lourenzo Marques, 11, 289, 393

Lugard, Lord, 36, 52, 112, 226

Lumumba, Patrice, 330

Lyttelton, Oliver (later Viscount Chandos), 259, 260, 261, 262, 263, 265, 267, 346

Macaulay, Lord, 266, 329

McDonald, J. G., 184

MacDonald, Ramsay, 287

Macequece, 89

Macfarlane, Captain Ronald, 132

Machel, Samora, 406

McIntyre, Donald, 229, 236, 237

McIver, Randall, 96

Macleod, Iain, 327–8, 332, 335–7

Macloutsie River, 65, 70

Macmillan, Harold, 275, 324, 325–9, 332, 335, 345, 346, 348, 382

Mafeking, 130, 131, 133, 153

Maguire, J. Rochfort, 43, 46, 48, 55–6, 57, 81

Main Drift, 90

Majuba, 26, 30

Makalanga tribes, 19

Makoni, Shona Chief, 120, 141

Malan, Dr Daniel, 247, 251

Malawi, 40; Congress Party, 337

Malcolm, Sir Dougal, 175, 191

Malianga, Moton, 352n

Malvern, Lord – see Huggins, Sir Godfrey

Mangwe, 126, 127, 128, 129

Manicaland, 12, 62, 76, 83–5, 89

Manyau, induna, 104, 105

Marandellas, 187

Marico valley, 16

Martin, Colonel Sir Richard, 124, 129, 131, 137–139, 141, 142, 198

Mashanyika, Shona Chief, 134

Mashiangombi, Shona Chief, 134, 140, 142

Mashonaland, 10, 12, 83; concessions, 19, 49, 57–8; Portuguese claims, 49, 50; Lobengula's claims, 49, 50, 52, 65, 73, 100, 102; Rhodes's plan to occupy, 52, 60, 62, 63–4, 65–70, 76; Pioneer Column march to, 63–75; occupation of, 94–110; economic depression, 99; British assertion of sovereignty over, 101–2, 112; steps to war, 103–7; war, 107–10, 111; union with Matabeleland as Rhodesia, 114; absentee landlordism, 117; Shona Chiefs' grievances, 120; administrative weakness, 121; rebellion, 128, 133–5, 140–3, 147; demand for settler representation, 147; land allocation, 162, 198; native reserves, 198; farmers in, 275

Mashonaland Horse, 98

Mason, Philip, 101, 109, 117, 260, 266

Massi Kessi, 88, 89

Matabele Relief Force, 130, 133, 135

Matabeleland, 27, 83; Ndebele rule, 20–3; missionaries, 20, 21–3; and Transvaal, 21; concessions, 47, 49; war and occupation, 51, 102–110, 111; economic development, 112; union with Mashonaland as Rhodesia, 114; land and cattle question, 114–15, 117, 162, 198–9; police force tyranny and sexual exploitation, 118–19; explosive situation, 119–21; rinderpest catastrophe, 123; rebellion, 123–33, 135–40, 147; surrender of indunas, 136–40, 162; movement for 'home rule', 197

Matimba, Patrick, 301

Matlokotloke, 19

Matobo by-election (1963), 354

Matope, King of the Karanga, 9

Matopo hills, 6, 7, 128, 133, 135; Rhodes's meeting with indunas in, 136–40

Mauch, Karl, 6–7, 25

Maudling, Reginald, 337

Maund, A. O., 55

Maund, Lieutenant E. A., 42, 46, 49–51, 55, 58, 59

Mawema, Michael, 330

Maybank, Frank, 235

Mazoe Patrol, 134

Meikle, John, 207–8

Melsetter, 89, 135

Menzies, Sir Robert, 371

Meredith, Sir Charles, 234

Methuen, Lord, 70–1

mfecane (the crushing), 15, 19
mhondoro cult, 126
Michell, Sir Lewis, 167
Millais, J. G. M., 64
Milner, Lord, 30, 114, 117, 149, 150, 174 and *n*, 179–80
Milton, Sir William, 115–16, 146*n*, 147–8, 151, 152, 162, 167, 173, 179
Ministerial Titles Act (1933), 214
missionaries, 18, 20, 21–3, 40, 44, 160–1
Mitchell, George, first 'Prime Minister', 214, 216
Mkwati (Mwari priest): and Matabele rebellion, 127, 133, 134, 140; and Shona rebellion, 134, 135, 140
'Modus Vivendi' agreement (1890), 85, 86, 87, 88
Moffat, H. U., 194, 207, 209, 211–14, 216, 221
Moffat, John, 22, 23, 44, 106; envoy to Lobengula, 39, 58, 59, 60, 61
Moffat, Dr Robert, 20, 21–2
Moffat Treaty (1888), 39, 42, 44, 49, 111
Moir, J. W., 81
Mombasa, 11, 12
Monckton Commission (1960), 326–7, 331, 335, 345
Monclaro, Father, 12
Monomatapa kingdom, 8–13, 14, 20
Moodie, Dunbar, 87
Moore, Leopold, 224
Morier, Victor, 67
Mount Hampden, 65, 67, 71, 74
Moyo, J. Z., 352*n*
Mozambique, 11, 14, 30, 62, 76, 77, 78, 88, 183, 189, 289, 362, 393, 406, 409, 410
MPLA, 406
Mpotshwana (*induna*), 126, 133, 135, 140
Mshete (*induna*), 50
Msika, Joseph, 352*n*
Msiri, Katanga Chief, 81–2
Mthethwa tribe, 14–15
Muchache, Clement, 352*n*
Mugabe, Robert, 352, 408, 409, 410
Murray, D. J., 193
Mutasa, Dr E. C., 370
Mutota, King of the Karanga, 8
Muzorewa, Bishop, 408
Mwari cult, 6, 10, 14, 19; and Matabele rebellion, 126–8, 129, 132
Mzilikazi, 16, 19, 20–3, 24
Mzingeli, Charles, 240

Napier, Colonel, 133
Natal, 11, 14–15, 38, 147, 164, 165, 166, 181
National Democratic Party (NDP), 330, 333, 335, 336, 340–1

Native Affairs Department, 195
Native Commissioners, 151, 160, 164, 195, 196
Native Courts Act, 230
Native Department, 118, 120–1, 164–5, 198, 227, 292
Native Development Department, 209
Native Juveniles Act (1926), 196
Native Purchase Areas, 198, 200–1, 202
Native Registration Act (1946), 220
Native Reserves, 156, 163, 198, 199–200, 202, 230, 281, 323, 324; Commission on (1914), 161, 198–200
Native Townships, 230, 323, 324, 367
'native trusteeship', 210
Native (Urban Areas) Accommodation and Registration Act (1946), 238
Ndebele, 4, 7, 16–28, 45–6, 59, 73, 76, 98, 101–110, 111–13, 115, 116–20, 123, 125–8, 132–3, 134–8, 139–40, 144, 145, 162, 196–7
Nehanda medium, 134, 142
Nesbitt, Inspector, 134
Neto, Agostinho, 406
Newton, Sir Francis, 104, 174, 179, 191, 194
Ngoni people, 14, 15–16
Ngomo, Chief, 101
Nicolle, Hostes, 400
'NIBMAR', 395, 400
Nigeria, 224, 322
Nkomo, Joshua, 227, 263, 265, 305, 309, 313, 323, 325, 333, 334, 335, 340–1, 344, 352–3, 357, 368, 378, 408, 409, 410
Nkumbula, Harry, 248, 261, 350, 353
Nogomo, King of the Karanga, 12
Norseman (ship), 88
Northern Rhodesia:
    Buxton Committee and, 181; question of union with South Africa, 181; becomes protectorate, 191; question of amalgamation with Southern Rhodesia, 209–11, 224, 237, 247; copper mines, 210, 222, 244; mineral rights, 210, 214; Huggins's scheme to make 'black', 219; and union with Nyasaland, 225, 226; industrial trouble, 236; and Second World War, 236, 237; African representation, 240; racial balance, 243; economy, 244; constitutional status, 244–5, 250; 1948 election, 247; amalgamation rejected, 247, 248; move to federation, 247–54; reaction to Officials' Conference, 255; African and Asian opposition to federation, 261, 268, 322, 323; and Lancaster House Conference, 262–5; proposed Constitution, 263–5, 267, 284; 1954 election, 288; African earnings, 291; franchise, 296; ANC banned, 325;

battles over Constitution, 332, 335–7; fears
of *coup d'état*, 335; secession, 345, 346–7
Nyamanda, son of Lobengula, 126, 140, 177, 197
Nyandoro, George, 323
Nyasaland, 40, 62, 113, 164, 209; acquisition of,
77–80; becomes protectorate, 91–2; and federation, 225, 226, 248, 253, 255, 257, 263, 288,
296; racial balance, 243, 244; economy, 244,
324; constitutional status, 245, 249, 263, 296;
African opposition to federation, 255, 261, 288,
327; disorder in, 324–5; new Constitution, 331;
secession, 332, 345–6

Officials' Conference (1950), 249–54, 255, 258,
259, 264
oil sanctions, 391–3, 394
Oldham, Dr J. H., 209
Ophir, 7, 8, 12
Oppenheimer, Sir Ernest, 210, 225
Oppenheimer, Harry, 380
Orange Free State, 25, 38, 167
Orange River Sovereignty, 21
Ormsby-Gore, William, 190, 191
Ossevabrandwag, 235
Owen, Dr David, 410

Palley, Dr Ahrn, 345, 373
Palmer, E. D., 309
Palmer, R. D., 309
'parallel development', 228, 238
'paramountcy', 210–11, 247
Passfield, Sidney Webb, Lord, 202, 210
Pater, Walter, 79
'Patriotic Front', 408, 409
Patterson, Captain R. R., 26
Pearce Commission (1972), 389, 404–5, 408
Pearson, Lester, 371
Peat, Sir William, 178
Pennefather, Lieut.-Colonel E. G., 69, 70, 71, 73,
74, 75, 95, 100
People's Caretaker Council (PCC), 352
Perham, Dame Margery, 226, 261
Phillips, L. C., 44
Pickering, Neville, 36, 56
Pinto, Serpa, 77, 79–80
Pioneer Column, 61, 64–75, 76, 93–4
Pitsani, 124
Plagis, John, 234
Plewman Commission (1957), 292, 338
Plumer, Colonel (later Field-Marshal Lord), 130,
131, 133, 135, 153, 208
poll tax, 161
population:
African, 199, 221, 223, 243; European 166–7,

199, 221, 223, 235, 243, 273, 274
Portugal, 7, 8, 15, 63; arrival and expulsion of,
10–13, 14; British dilemma over, 39, 40, 53;
territorial claims, 49, 50, 77; surrender over
Nyasaland, 79–80; Convention and later Treaty
with Britain, 82–3, 84, 87–9; 'Modus Vivendi',
85, 86, 87, 88; and UDI, 376, 392–3; 1974
revolution, 405–6
Potgieter, Hendrick, 19, 21
Pretoria Convention (1881), 31, 38
Progressive Party, 206, 207, 212
Providential Pass, 74
Public Services Economy Bill (1931), 212
Putterill, Brigadier (GOC), 367

Quinton, J. G., 309, 338
Quinton Report (1960), 338–9

racialism, 156–65, 282; integration of Africans,
156–7, 160, 161–5; segregation, 157–8, 160,
161–5, 215, 228, 229–30, 281; sexual attitude,
158–60, 279–80, 301–2; and vote against union
(1922), 188; apartheid, 212, 240, 247, 251, 254;
'twin pyramid' policy, 212, 215; 'parallel
development', 228, 238; Federal relaxation of,
290–2
railways, 40, 41, 54, 90, 99, 144–5, 209, 213, 215,
239, 244, 289
Railways Bill (1927), 205
Ramsey, Dr Michael, Archbishop of Canterbury,
379
Rand – *see* Witwatersrand
Ranger, T. O., 121, 125, 136, 139, 197, 340
Ransford, Oliver, 23
Rawlinson, Sir Peter, 403
Reedman, Harry, 376
Reform Party, 194, 212, 214–16, 219, 220–1,
223, 224, 231
religion, 9–10, 126–8
Renders, Adam, 7
Rennie, Sir Gilbert, 263
Renny-Tailyour, E. A., 44, 49, 58, 94
Resident Commissioner, 149–50, 164
Responsible Government, 166–8, 175, 179–88;
referendum, 185, 186–8, 189, 190; grant of
190–1; Constitution, 191–5, 200
Responsible Government Association, 179
Reynolds, Rex, 212, 213, 223, 226, 235, 238, 239,
264, 320
Rhodes, Cecil, 4, 6, 30, 31, 77, 97–9, 116, 145, 162,
176, 244; tomb of, 7, 154; early life, 32; septal
defect and general ill-health, 32–3; at Kimber-
ley, 34; partnership with Rudd, 34; at Oxford,

Rhodes, Cecil —*cont.*
34–5; influenced by Ruskin's 'racial hierarchy', 35, 37; wealth, 35; personality, 35–7; as 'colonialist', 37–8; option on Matabeleland, 38–9; and Chartered Company, 41, 42, 43, 47–60; plan to occupy Mashonaland, 62, 63–4, 65–70, 76; and Johnson's idea of military *coup*, 63–4; Premier of Cape Colony, 72, 113; and Johnston, 78, 79, 83, 91–2; failure to take Katanga, 81–2; attempts to obtain route to Indian Ocean, 87–9; buys Lippert Concession, 94, 111; expects Matabele war, 102, 106, 108; at apogee of power, 113–14; and Jameson Raid, 123–4, 130, 131, 149; resigns premiership, 124; and rebellions, 130–1, 135–40, 142; negotiations, with *indunas* in Matopos, 136–40, 146; and settlers' discontents, 146–7; and new Constitution, 148, 150; death, 153; foresees union, 166
Rhodes, Rev. Francis William, 32
Rhodes, Frank, 32, 118*n*
Rhodes, Herbert, 32, 33, 34
'Rhodesia': choice of name, 114
Rhodesia Agricultural Union, 179
Rhodesia Field Force, 153
Rhodesia Horse Volunteers, 128, 129
Rhodesia–Mozambique Oil Pipeline Company, 394
Rhodesia National Party (RNP), 353, 354, 364
Rhodesia Native Association, 197
Rhodesia and Nyasaland Federation Act (1953), 269
Rhodesia Party, 194, 220, 288; decline of, 206, 207, 211–12, 214–16, 219; extinction, 221, 231
Rhodesia Party (new), 364, 366, 372, 373
Rhodesia Reform Party, 342
Rhodesia Regiment, 153
Rhodesia Unionist Association, 179, 184, 185, 186, 194
Rhodesia Women's League, 159
Rhodesian African Rifles, 235
Rhodesian Anglo-American Corporation, 210, 276
Rhodesian Bantu Voters Association, 197
Rhodesian Constitutional Association, 373
Rhodesian Front Party, 237, 251, 315, 363, 397; creation of, 342; 1962 election victory, 342–4; Field's Cabinet, 347; and claim for independence, 349–50, 354–5, 357, 358–62, 364, 366–373, 376–83; fall of Field, 358–60; Smith as leader, 360; 1965 election victory, 372–3, 374; ideology of, 374–5; and apartheid, 384; and 1968 proposals, 401; 1970 election success, 402; and provisional settlement, 404

Rhodesian Selection Trust, 210, 276, 293
Richard, Ivor, 407–8
Richartz, Father, 142, 161
Riebeeck, Jan van, 16
Rifkind, Malcolm, 200, 203, 229
rinderpest, 123, 128, 131
Ripon, Lord, 55, 116, 117
Robinson, Sir Albert, 349
Robinson, Sir Hercules, 39, 43, 48, 50, 149
Robinson, Ronald, 17*n*
Robinson, Sir Victor, 378, 379
rock paintings, 6
Rolin, Henri, 157–8
Rosebery, Lord, 92, 113, 147
Routledge, T. C., 134
Royal Air Force, 234
Rozwi Mambo, 9, 14–16, 19, 126, 141
Rudd, Charles, 34, 39, 42–3, 44–5, 55, 57
Rudd, Frank, 43, 48
Rudd, Thomas, 55
Rudd Concession, 46–61, 67, 94, 99, 100, 106, 111, 213
Rudland, George, 359
Ruo River, 79–80
Ruskin, John, 35
Russell, Sir Fraser, 220, 221, 231
Ryan, J. F., 374

Salazar, Dr Antonio, 393
Salisbury, Robert Gascoyne Cecil, 3rd Marquis of, 30, 36, 39, 40–1, 53–4, 68, 77–80, 82, 83, 87, 88, 89, 154
Salisbury, Robert Gascoyne Cecil, 5th Marquis of, 263, 267, 335–6
Salisbury:
settlement of, 74–5, 93–9; racial imbalance, 119; rail links, 145, 289; compared with Bulawayo, 222, 223; population growth, 223; development and character, 276, 289; as Federal capital, 292; riots, 330, 352
Sambo, Robert, 197
Samkange, Standlake, 323
Samkange, Rev. Thompson, 227
Sand River Convention (1852), 21
Sandys, Duncan (now Lord Duncan-Sandys), 332, 333, 334, 345, 351, 355, 356–8, 364, 365, 368
Sauer, Hans, 137, 138
Savanhu, Jasper, 263, 290
Savory, Alan, 362
Schreiner, Olive, 119
Schreuder, Derek, 17
Schulz, Aurel, 81, 84, 87
Sebastian, King of Portugal, 12

Second Rhodesia Regiment, 168, 233
Second World War, 231–8
Sedition Act (1936), 228
segregation, 157–8, 160, 161–5, 215, 228, 229–30, 281
Selborne, Lord, 167, 181
Selous, Frederick C., 23, 52, 81, 111, 123, 124, 125, 128, 129; and Pioneer Column, 61, 67, 71, 72, 73–4, 76; and Johnson, 63, 64–5, 66; concessions in Mashonaland, 63; plans to occupy Mashonaland, 63–6, 67; and Lobengula, 70
Selous Exploration Syndicate, 63, 65
Setoutsie, Maholi Chief, 103
Shabani, 312
sexual attitudes, 158–60, 279–80, 301–2
Shaka, Mthethwa Chief, 15, 16
Shamuyarira, Nathan, 312
Shamva mine strike (1927), 197, 212
Shangani patrol, 7, 104, 108–10
Shangani Reserve, 116
Sharpe, Alfred, 79, 82
Shaw, Flora, 52, 57
Shee, Dr Charles, 33, 36
Shepstone, Sir Theophilus, 26
Shepstone, Captain, 75
Shiloh Mission, 23
Shippard, Sir Sidney, 27, 39, 46, 60, 64
Shiré River, 77, 79
Shona tribes and Chiefs, 7, 19, 100–1, 102–4, 106–7, 112, 120, 123, 133–6, 140–2, 144, 145–6
Siginyamatshe (Mwari priest), 127, 135
Silveira, Goncala da, 11–12
Sithole, Edson, 323
Sithole, Rev. Ndabaningi, 305, 309, 313, 333, 341, 352–3, 357, 368, 378
Skeen, Brigadier Andrew, 376
Smartt, Sir Thomas, 181
Smit, Jacob, 212, 214, 219, 232, 240, 241
Smith, Arthur, 399n
Smith, Ian:
    resigns from UFP, 335; forms Rhodesian Front, 342; claim to have been promised independence by Butler, 350, 363; Prime Minister, 353, 360, 363; clamps down on nationalists, 353, 363; fruitless London talks (1963), 354–5; character, 361–2; 'parochialism', 361–2; determined on UDI, 362; consolidates white opinion, 363; renewed London talks (1964), 365; withdraws UDI threat, 365; asks for indaba of chiefs and referendum, 365–6, 367; prepares for UDI, 366–7, 369, 376; encouraged by indaba and referendum, 370; tortuous negotiations, 370–2;
376–84; crushing 1965 election victory, 372–373, 374; committed to UDI, 375–84; sends envoy to Portugal, 376; last visit to London, 377; deadlock, 377, 379; final message to Wilson, 380; declares UDI, 381; dismissed by Governor, 385; anxiety to preserve image of legality, 387; Tiger and Fearless talks, 396–401; new Constitution, 401–2; declares republic, 402; agreement with Home, 403; negotiates with Kissinger and Vorster, 406; volte-face over black majority rule, 406–8, 410; rejects Richard proposals, 409
Smuts, Jan Christiaan, 168, 179, 180, 181–8, 189, 190, 191, 234–5, 247, 251
Sousa, Manuel Antonio de ('Gouveia'), 84, 85
South Africa:
    independence recognized, 21; 'colonialism' and 'imperial factor' in achieving union of, 29–30, 149; railway system, 145; possibility of Southern Rhodesia's union with, 165, 167, 175, 179, 180, 181–3, 185–8, 189–90, 223, 247; violent episodes, 184; end of 'greater South Africa', 189, 223; and Second World War, 234; 1948 election, 247; racialism, 247, 251, 254; expansionism danger, 254; immigration to Southern Rhodesia, 274, 279; relations with Southern Rhodesia, 279; and UDI, 393, 406, 407–9; pressure on Smith, 407–10
South Africa Committee, 51, 52
South African Goldfields Exploration Company, 25
Southern Rhodesia Order in Council (1898), 148
Stairs, Captain, 82
Stanley, Sir Herbert, 179, 191, 199, 224
Stanley, Oliver, 248
Stead, W. T., 52
Stent, Vere, 135, 136, 137, 138
Stevenson, Sir Edward, 36
Stirling, Colonel David, 262
Stockhill, Raymond, 255, 257, 265
Stonehouse, John, 325
Strachan, Sir Andrew, 250, 252
Strijdom, J. G., 251
Stumbler, A. R. W., 301, 303, 305, 309, 364
Suez Canal, 17; 1956 crisis, 295, 321
Suzman, Helen, 354, 364
Swinburne, Sir John, 43
Swinton, Lord, 258, 267, 346
Sykes, F. W., 119
Sykes, Rev. William, 22, 23

Taba Zi Ka Mambo, 126, 127, 133, 135, 136
Tabas Induna, 133

Taberer, H. M., 121
Tainton, W. S., 44
Takawira, Leopold, 334, 352n
Tanganyika, 209, 322
Tanganyika Concessions, 335
Tanzania, 352
Tati gold discovery, 25
Tati Concession, 25, 43, 47
Tawse-Jollie, E. M., 83, 179, 194
Taylor, Sir Herbert, 151n
Territorial Legislatures, 253, 254, 264, 265, 268, 297
Tete, 12, 13, 14, 23, 69, 70
Thomas, J. H., 213
Thomas, Sir Miles, 248
Thomas, Rev. Morgan, 22, 23
Thompson, George (now Lord Thompson), 400
Thompson, Joseph, 81
Thompson, Leonard, 29
Thompson, 'Matabele', 43, 46, 48, 57, 59–61, 73
Tiger talks (1966), 396–9, 402
tobacco, 223, 275
Todd, Garfield, 161, 194, 280, 320, 324, 335, 339; Prime Minister, 286–8; his aim of African advancement, 287, 290, 300, 305, 317; leads United Rhodesia Party (URP), 288; wins 1954 election, 288; liberal measures, 290, 292–4; attempt to break up Native Department, 292; tough line on law and order, 294; ascendancy, 300–1; African confidence in, 300; White misgivings over, 301–5; Cabinet rebellion, 305–306; new rebellion, 307–8; forms new Cabinet, 308–9; repudiated by caucus and Congress, 309–10; succeeded as Prime Minister by Whitehead, 310–11; revives URP, 311; loses every seat in 1958 election, 312; his defeat as turning-point, 313; reasons for fall, 313–18; his 'liberalism', 315–16; his view of crisis, 317–18; opposes UDI, 387; opposes provisional agreement, 404
Transvaal, 16, 21, 23, 25–8, 29–32, 38, 39, 90–1, 113, 123–4, 153, 166, 167
Tredgold, Sir Robert, 203, 212, 218, 227, 233, 236, 269, 298, 309, 314, 361, 378, 384; Minister of Justice and Defence, 231–3; objects to federation, 256, 257, 258; urges unitary state, 257; resigns as Chief Justice, 330; alliance with Field, 335; opposes UDI, 367, 388
Tredgold Report, 297–9, 302–3
Trend, Sir Burke (now Lord Trend), 365, 397
Tshombe, Moise, 330
Twala, Abraham, 197
'two pyramids' policy, 212, 215

UDI (Unilateral Declaration of Independence), 188, 237, 334; contingency plans for, 358; Rhodesian Front's determination on, 359, 360, 362, 364, 366, 369–73; Smith withdraws threat of, 365; his growing pressure for, 366–73; attitude of media, Civil Service and armed forces, 366–7, 387, 389; Smith committed to, 375–6; talks on, 376–81; declaration of, 381; reasons behind, 381–4; legal and constitutional measures, 385–6; opposition to, 387–8, 391; relative quiescence, 389–90; force not to be used against, 390, 392; sanctions against, 391–392, 393, 394, 395, 400; economic and fiscal matters, 394–5; judicial battles, 400; Republic proclaimed, 402
Uganda, 209, 322
Ulundi, 26
Umfezela, brother of Lobengula, 126
Umfuli River, 25
Umgandan (*induna*), 104, 105
Umguza River, 132, 133
Umgorshwini, 124
Umlugulu, Ndebele high priest, 126, 133, 140
Umtali, 89, 90, 144–5, 146, 274, 394
Umtasa, Manicaland Chief, 84–5
union, 165, 175, 179, 180, 181–3, 185–8, 194, 247. *See also* Central African Federation
Union Minière, 335
UNITA, 406
United Central Africa Association, 255, 286
United Concessions Company, 55, 99
United Federal Party (UFP), 286, 294, 295, 304, 305, 309–11, 312, 323, 331, 335, 336, 339, 341–344, 345, 347, 353
United Nations, 330, 341, 355; and UDI, 390, 392–3, 394, 395, 400
United Party, 220–1, 231, 236–7, 239, 240–1, 286–7, 288
United Peoples Party (UPP), 373
United Rhodesia Party (URP), 288, 300–1, 303, 304–6, 309, 311, 312
University College, Salisbury, 279, 290, 354
Unsworth, E. I. G., 264
urbanization, 275–6
Usher, William, 44

Van der Byl, P. K., 366, 371, 407
Victoria, Queen, 49, 50, 58, 61
Victoria Falls, 5–6, 21
Victoria Falls Conferences: (1951), 258–9, 260; (1963), 347, 348–51
Vintcent, Judge, 141
Voortrekkers, 21, 27
Vorster, B. J., 406, 408, 410

Walker, E. A., 226
Walker, Colonel (Labour leader), 237
Wankie, 19, 145, 222, 293, 294, 391
Wankie Game Reserve, 202
Ware Concession, 81
Warren, Sir Charles, 31
Watch Tower Church, 227–8
Weale, M. E., 120
Welensky, Sir Roy, 218, 246, 297, 325, 350–1, 372, 378; leads 'Unofficials', 237, 238, 246, 263; career and character, 246; and federation, 247–9, 258, 268; lobbies London, 258, 266; at Lancaster House Conference, 263, 264; Federal Minister of Transport, 285, 290; forms UFP, 285, 295; becomes Prime Minister, 295; and Constitution, 298–9; and UFP/URP fusion, 305; and Todd's defeat, 314–15; and Suez, 321; bad relations with Whitehall, 324, 326–8, 331–2, 335; symbol of reaction, 330; objects to Monckton Report, 331; conflict on Northern Rhodesia Constitution, 335, 337; contemplates UDI, 337; 1962 election victory, 344; and end of Federation, 346–7, 349; and fall of Field, 360; tries to return to politics, 364; by-election defeat, 366; opposes UDI, 388
Welsh, Allan, 214
Whaley, W. R., 401
Wheare, Sir Kenneth, 249, 250
Whitehead, Sir Edgar, 203, 231, 242, 300, 302, 318, 327, 352, 364, 373, 378; Minister of Finance, 239; compared with Todd, 292; succeeds Todd as Prime Minister, 310–12, 314; career and character, 319–20; declares state of emergency, 330–1, 341, 363; and new Constitution, 334, 336; repressive measures, 330–1, 341, 363; concern with African advancement, 337–9; defeat in 1962 election, 342–4; ineffective opposition leader, 353; opposes UDI, 388
Wightwick (MP), 304, 305, 307
Willoughby, Captain Sir John, 69, 74, 75, 88, 115, 118, 124
Wills, A. J., 155
Wilson, Major Allan, 109, 110
Wilson, Benjamin, 44
Wilson, Harold, 193; talks with Smith, 357, 368–371, 377–81, 382, 389, 390–1, 392–3, 396–402
Wilson, N. H., 215, 219, 220
Witwatersrand ('the Rand'): gold discovery, 28, 29, 32; rebellion (1922), 184
World's View, 7, 57, 153, 180, 206
Wrathall, John, 393–4, 399n

Yates, Dornford, 274
Young, Dendy, 286
Young, Sir Hilton, 209
Young, Sir Hubert, 224, 225
Young, Kenneth, 350, 369, 375, 390

Zambesi River, 4, 5–6, 12, 16, 77, 79, 412
Zambesia, 21, 38, 39–41, 52, 100
Zambia, 91, 362, 368, 390–1, 409
Zimbabwe, 6–7, 8, 9, 12, 14, 15, 74, 96, 109, 126, 409; ZANU, 352–3, 409; ZAPU, 341, 352–3, 409
Zwangendaba, 15–16
Zwimba, Matthew, 227

A NOTE ABOUT THE AUTHOR

Robert Blake, who has been Provost of The Queen's College, Oxford, since 1968, was Student and Tutor in Politics at Christ Church, Oxford, from 1947. Educated at the King Edward VI School, Norwich, and at Magdalen College, Oxford, where he took a First in Modern Greats, he served in the Royal Artillery during the war, became a prisoner of war in Italy from 1942–4, escaped and was mentioned in despatches. He was Senior Proctor, 1959–60, and a Conservative member of the Oxford City Council, 1957–65. In 1967 he was elected a Fellow of the British Academy. Best known for his magnificent biography of Disraeli (1966); he has also written The Unknown Prime Minister: The Life and Times of Andrew Bonar Law 1858–1923 *(1955),* The Conservative Party from Peel to Churchill *(1970) and* The Office of Prime Minister *(1975). He was made a life peer in 1971.*

A NOTE ON THE TYPE

The text of this book was set in a film version of Ehrhardt, a typeface receiving its name from the Ehrhardt foundry in Frankfurt. The original design of the face was the work of Nicholas Kis, a Hungarian punchcutter known to have worked in Amsterdam from 1680 to 1689. The modern version of Ehrhardt was cut by The Monotype Corporation of London in 1937.

Composed by Northumberland Press Ltd, Gateshead, Tyre and Wear, Great Britain

Printed and bound by R.R. Donnelley & Sons Company, Crawfordsville, Indiana